Encyclopedia of Plant Care

Meredith® Books
Des Moines, Iowa

CONTENTS

HOW TO
USE THIS BOOK

Most gardening encyclopedias focus on plant characteristics and plant selection. Miracle-Gro's *Encyclopedia of Plant Care* is different. While the book provides you with an overview of plant characteristics and siting information on where to place plants for best effect, the emphasis is on how to care for the plants once they are in your garden, yard, or home. Customized care details on planting, pruning, feeding, watering, grooming, and propagating for more than 900 trees, shrubs, flowers, grasses, fruits, vegetables, herbs, and houseplants ensure you success in growing and enjoying a wide variety of plants. Including descriptions of related cultivars and species you'll find advice on more than 3,300 plants. An outstanding team of university horticulture specialists and professional garden writers has collaborated to develop this extensive and authoritative yet accessible gardening reference book.

The Miracle-Gro *Encyclopedia of Plant Care* begins with the basics. Introductory chapters on soils, watering, feeding, pruning, propagation, and plant problems guide you through the fundamentals of plant care. If you are new to gardening, start with these introductory chapters to familiarize yourself with the building blocks of successful gardening. No matter which plants you choose to grow in and around your home, the techniques and tools described in these introductory chapters will apply. You'll learn how to amend soils to improve plant growth. You'll discover how planting techniques differ between container-grown plants and bare-root plants. You'll find advice on how to water plants efficiently with drip or sprinkler irrigation systems. Plant foods and feeding techniques are explained. The how, when, and why of pruning is demystified in the chapter on training and pruning. You'll learn how to start new plants from seed or cuttings in the propagation chapter. And in the section on plant problems, discover how to diagnose common maladies that arise in the yard and garden. (For details on diagnosis and control of specific environmental, disease, and insect pest problems on particular plants, consult Ortho's *Home Gardener's Problem Solver*.)

As a seasoned gardener you will also find valuable tips in these introductory chapters to enhance your gardening experience. In "Soil Preparation and Planting" (see pages 6–37) you'll find trouble-shooting tips for soil problems and composting problems as well as guidelines for replacing overgrown foundation plantings. In "Watering and Irrigation" (see pages 38–45) you'll learn what you need to know about backflow prevention devices for irrigation systems to keep your potable water supply safe. The chapter on feeding (see pages 46–51) provides specifics on amending soil for pH management of either acid or alkaline soils. The pruning chapter (see pages 52–87) details techniques for pruning everything from shade and fruit trees

'Armada' rose is a hardy shrub rose that reblooms throughout the summer.

to grapes, roses, and bonsai. The same chapter offers techniques to keep your equipment in top condition, from sharpening and adjusting hand shears to maintaining your lawn mower. In the chapter on propagation (pages 88–107), techniques described include seed stratification and scarification and the vegetative techniques of layering, budding and grafting. In "Problems with Plants" (pages 108–123) you'll learn how to set up plant health care for your yard, scout for potential problems, and diagnose the problems that occur.

'Rustic Dwarfs' gloriosa daisy adds rich color to the sunny, summer landscape.

The majority of the book consists of encyclopedias of plant-care organized by plant type—houseplants, grasses, flowers, trees and shrubs, and vegetables, fruits, and herbs. If you're looking for care guidelines for a specific plant, go directly to the encyclopedia section for the type of plant of interest. For example, you'll find several listings for pines in the encyclopedia of trees and shrubs. Encyclopedia listings are alphabetized by botanical name because many plants have multiple common names, and deciding which common name to use for alphabetization becomes confusing. Latin names are unfamiliar to many gardeners, so a cross-reference of common names with the botanical names is provided at the beginning of each encyclopedia. For example, you may know *Pinus mugo* as mugo pine, while others know it as Swiss mountain pine or dwarf mountain pine. All three common names are listed in the tree and shrub cross-reference guide beginning on page 367, and all direct you to page 434 for the encyclopedia entry for *Pinus mugo*.

Another useful feature of the Miracle-Gro *Encyclopedia of Plant Care* is the listing of plants for specific sites and purposes in chapter 12 (see pages 570–589). Here you'll find lists of plants best adapted to certain environmental conditions such as tolerant of heavy clay soil or of heavy shade. You'll also find lists of plants resistant to feeding by deer, rabbits and other pests such as Japanese beetles. In the

Ural false spirea forms large clusters of white blooms from early summer through fall.

section on landscape use and special interests, you'll find listings for such things as trees or shrubs by size, by foliage color, or by special use such as to attract birds or butterflies. Each list provides you with the botanical name, a common name and the plant's hardiness rating.

Resource pages at the back of the book list some sources for plants, seeds, and supplies. In addition you'll find the USDA Hardiness Zone map so you can determine whether a particular plant will grow in your area. First and last frost date maps are also included to assist you in planning proper planting dates for tender plants.

An identification photograph begins each encyclopedia entry. Alternate common names are given in the caption.

Solid-bar heads identify major subtopics within each chapter. Tips and problem-solving ideas are highlighted in colored text boxes.

Step-by-step how-to photographs show general techniques in the introductory chapters and specific processes for individual plants in the encyclopedias.

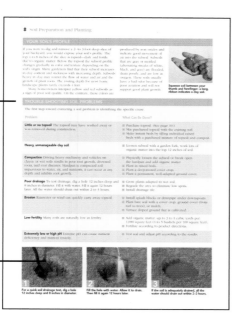

Encyclopedia heads list plants by common name and botanical name, including a pronunciation guide for the Latin name. Entries are alphabetized by botanical name.

Encyclopedia text provides siting, care, propagation, and pest and disease information for each plant. Related cultivars and species are included.

Profile abstracts provide key plant characteristics such as size, hardiness, environmental preferences, and garden uses at a glance. Flower color and fall foliage color are identified by blocks of color.

A botanic name index cross-reference list begins each encyclopedia to help you find plant listings no matter what common name is familiar to you.

Common and botanical names are listed for all plants within the encyclopedia.

Colorful photographs identify some of the plants you'll find featured in the encyclopedia.

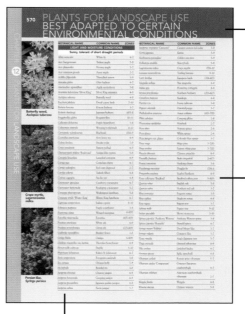

Plant lists of plants best adapted to specific environmental conditions or with certain landscape features provide a quick selection guide.

USDA Hardiness Zones are listed for each entry in the plant lists, which include even more plants than those discussed in the encyclopedias.

Page numbers for each plant are listed so that you can quickly find the plant of interest to you.

Botanical and common plant names are included for each entry in the plant lists for easy identification.

SOIL PREPARATION AND PLANTING

Digging in organic matter is the most important step in soil improvement.

GETTING TO KNOW YOUR SOILS

Many astute gardeners attribute their green thumb to good soil. They know that garden success starts in the ground. This chapter explains the basic parts and properties of soils and describes the qualities of a good soil. You'll learn how to improve the soils around your home—the essential first step in creating a beautiful landscape.

Soil is the dynamic living ecosystem that supports all life on the planet. Soils do such a wonderful job of producing our food, forests, and ornamental plants that gardeners may take them for granted. They forget that poor soil can cause plant problems. Digging into and assessing your particular soil can help you prevent common plant problems and pave the way for years of gardening pleasure.

Soils are as valuable and essential to life as water and air. Yet every year, tons of topsoil are lost from farm fields, public grounds, and private landscapes through wind and water erosion. The plant nutrients contained in soil that washes away often contribute to water pollution. In urban and suburban areas, soils are often disturbed, removed and compacted, causing problems for new or established plants. Conserving, protecting, and improving the soils around you are good for your home landscape and the environment.

WHAT'S IN A TYPICAL SOIL?

Soil has three major components. An average handful of garden soil contains:

Clay, silt, and sand in various proportions make up 45–50 percent of soil by volume. These minerals come from rocks that have broken down over millennia through the action of wind, rain, ice, and vegetation. The rocks, or parent material, that many mineral soils are derived from are sometimes inadvertently struck or unearthed by homeowners. Sand is the largest of the particles; you can see individual particles without a magnifying glass. Silt is next smallest in size. Individual clay particles are so small that you'd need a microscope to view them.

Pore space makes up another 45–50 percent of soil. The large (macropore) and small (micropore) spaces between individual soil particles are filled with a combination of air, water, roots, microorganisms, mites, earthworms, and beetles. During ideal growing conditions, 50 percent of these pore spaces are filled by air and 50 percent by water.

Soil organic matter makes up 1–5 percent by weight. This is the biologically active portion that drives the soil ecosystem and releases nutrients necessary for plant growth.

TEXTURE AND STRUCTURE

Soil texture is the term used to describe how a soil feels. It's simply a measure of the relative proportion of sand, silt, and clay in a soil. For example, a soil with a mineral portion that is 60 percent sand, 15 percent clay, and 25 percent silt is classified as sandy loam. Sandy soils feel gritty; silty soils have a powdery texture when dry; and soils high in clay feel sticky when wet. Texture also determines how quickly the soil warms up in spring and how easy it is to till. Sandy loam feels gritty, warms up relatively quickly, and is easy to till. Soil texture is not easily changed. Although soil structure can be improved with amendments, soil texture is more a function of the parent soil material and more difficult to alter. For example, adding sand to a heavy clay soil can produce a hard, cloddy, and inhospitable soil.

There are dozens or perhaps hundreds of soil types classified according to texture, slope, drainage, and parent material. It's not uncommon to encounter several soil types in a single home landscape. Contact the Natural Resource and Soil Conservation Service (an agency of the United States Department of Agriculture). They may have a copy of your county's soil map. You'll be able to find out what specific type of soil covers your property.

Soil texture has a huge effect on the establishment and growth of plants. For example, coarse-textured sandy soils contain many large pore spaces, which allow for rapid water drainage. That's good during a wet spring but a potential problem during hot, dry weather. Rapid drainage also leads to the quick leaching of some nutrients out of the root zone. With sandy soils,

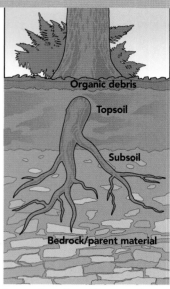

Layers in soil profiles vary in characteristics and thickness depending on soil type.

you'll find yourself fertilizing plants more frequently during wet weather and watering more often during hot, dry weather. Fine-textured soils with a high percentage of clay have many tiny pore spaces that hold water and drain slowly. Roots need air and water to grow. During wet weather clayey soils may become oxygen-deficient, causing root death and plant wilting.

Soil structure is a measure of how individual soil particles are arranged. In soils with good structure, soil particles are connected into larger crumbs or aggregates, creating many large and small pores that encourage air and water flow and root growth. The structure of poor mineral soils can be improved through the regular addition of organic matter—compost, aged farm manure, shredded leaves, grass clippings, and bark mulch.

The three types of particles that make up the mineral fraction of soil are sand, silt, and clay.

DEALING WITH CLAY

Clay gets a bad rap from gardeners. But clay provides some positive benefits when present. Unlike sand and silt particles, clay particles carry a negative charge which enables them to attract and hold positively charged ions of important nutrients such as potassium, ammonium, calcium, and magnesium. Almost all soils have some clay in them. When a high percentage of clay makes gardening difficult, it's best to avoid that area or add organic matter to improve soil structure.

SOIL ORGANIC MATTER AND HUMUS

Soil organic matter makes up a small percentage of the total volume of soils but has a big impact on soil structure and fertility. It is made up of dead and decaying plants and soil creatures—from bacteria to earthworms. More than 90 percent of soil organic matter is found in the top 8 inches of soil, where the majority of plant roots are located. It gives topsoils their dark brown color and earthy aroma and supports diverse populations of soil microorganisms and invertebrates (centipedes, beetles, mites, earthworms). This vast world of creatures produces the "glue" that improves soil structure by binding tiny clay particles and large sand particles into stable aggregates.

There may be up to 1 billion microorganisms in a gram of topsoil. These bacteria and fungi digest organic matter, releasing nutrients available for uptake by plant roots. The end product of the decomposition process is humus, a stable, prized material that holds water like a sponge. As with clay particles, humus is negatively charged and attracts and holds positively charged nutrient ions, reducing their

being leached by rainfall. Gardeners depend heavily on this storehouse of recycled, organically held nutrients to produce healthy plants.

This sandy soil has a low percentage of organic matter.

Soils high in organic matter have a crumblike structure.

YOUR SOIL'S PROFILE

If you were to dig and remove a 2- to 3-foot deep slice of your backyard, you would expose your soil's profile. The top 4 to 8 inches of the slice is topsoil—dark and fertile due to organic matter. Below the topsoil the subsoil profile changes gradually in color and texture depending on the soil's origin. Many gardeners find that their subsoil increases in clay content and stickiness with increasing depth. Subsoils heavy in clay may restrict the flow of water and air and the growth of plant roots. The rooting depth for most home landscape plants rarely exceeds 4 feet.

Many homeowners interpret yellow and red subsoils as a sign of poor soil quality. On the contrary, these colors are produced by iron oxides and indicate good movement of air into the subsoil. Subsoils that are gray or mottled (alternating streaks of white, black, and gray) are flooded, drain poorly, and are low in oxygen. These soils usually have a bad odor because of poor aeration and will not support good plant growth.

Squeeze soil between your thumb and forefinger: a long, ribbon indicates a clay soil.

TROUBLE-SHOOTING SOIL PROBLEMS

The first step toward correcting a soil problem is identifying the specific cause.

Problem	What Can Be Done?
Little or no topsoil The topsoil may have washed away or was removed during construction.	▪ Purchase topsoil. (See page 10.) ▪ Mix purchased topsoil with the existing soil. ▪ Make instant beds by filling individual raised beds with a purchased mixture of topsoil and compost.
Heavy, unmanageable clay soil	▪ Loosen subsoil with a garden fork; work lots of organic matter into the top 12 inches of soil.
Compaction Driving heavy machinery and vehicles on clayey or wet soils results in poor root growth, drowned roots, and root diseases. Hardpan is compacted soil impervious to water, air, and nutrients; it can occur at any depth and inhibits root growth.	▪ Physically loosen the subsoil or break open the hardpan and add organic matter. ▪ Plant in raised beds. ▪ Plant a deep-rooted cover crop. ▪ Plant a permanent, well-adapted ground cover.
Poor drainage To test drainage, dig a hole 12 inches deep and 8 inches in diameter. Fill it with water. Fill it again 12 hours later. All the water should drain out within 2 to 3 hours.	▪ Grow plants adapted to wet soil. ▪ Regrade the area to eliminate low spots. ▪ Install drainage tile.
Erosion Rainwater or wind can quickly carry away topsoil.	▪ Install splash blocks or drainpipe under downspouts. ▪ Plant bare soil with a cover crop, ground cover (from turf to trees), or mulch. ▪ Terrace sloped ground that is cultivated.
Low fertility Many soils are naturally low in fertility.	▪ Add organic matter: up to 3 to 4 cubic yards per 1,000 square feet (4 to 5 bushels per 100 square feet). ▪ Fertilize according to product directions.
Extremely low or high pH Extreme pH can cause nutrient deficiency and nutrient toxicity.	▪ Test soil and adjust pH according to the results.

1

For a quick soil drainage test, dig a hole 12 inches deep and 8 inches in diameter.

2

Fill the hole with water. Allow it to drain. Then fill it again 12 hours later.

3

If the soil is adequately drained, all the water should drain out within 2–3 hours.

After moving into a home in a new or established neighborhood, gardeners are frequently disappointed to discover that the soil is causing landscape plants to struggle for survival. The soil may be full of clay or stones, too acid or shallow, compacted, or lacking in organic matter.

With a little knowledge and a good bit of determination, you can use soil amendments to improve poor soil and make your landscape flourish. Soil amendments are materials that are mixed into the topsoil to promote healthy plant growth. Plant food is not usually classified as a soil amendment because its primary function is to supply nutrients. Soil amendments such as lime change the soil pH; but others, such as compost, supply nutrients that are most important as soil conditioners—bulky organic materials that improve soil structure. Better soil structure results in an increase in pores in the soil leading to better air and water movement and root growth.

Most garden and landscape plants perform best in soils high in organic matter (3 percent organic matter, by weight, in the topsoil). These soils are loose, easy to dig and plant in, and contain a large number of earthworms. You won't see a dramatic change the first year when you add soil amendments to a difficult soil. But over three to five years of regular incorporation, you will witness significant improvement in soil conditions and plant growth. Because organic matter is "used up" through oxidation (especially in warm climates and where soils are frequently tilled) and downward movement, organic matter should be added to the soil every year.

AVOID NITROGEN TIE-UP

All organic materials contain varying proportions of carbon and nitrogen. Soil microorganisms digest the carbon compounds for energy and use the nitrogen to make proteins. Soil amendments with a high carbon to nitrogen ratio (wood chips, sawdust, straw, newspaper) can cause a tie-up of nitrogen in the soil if they are tilled in prior to spring planting. The expanding population of microorganisms required to digest the amendment will use up available nitrogen in the soil. The problem can be avoided by adding nitrogen after tilling in high-carbon materials.

TYPES OF SOIL AMENDMENTS

Coir is made from coconut fibers. It is used in commercial soil mixes to help prevent overwatering and underwatering. Coir improves the water-holding capacity of soil mixes and reduces shrinkage that causes the soil to pull away from the sides of the container. Reduced shrinkage results in easier watering because water will soak in to the root ball rather than run down the gap between the root ball and the pot.
Compost is made from decayed organic materials such as straw, grass clippings, newspaper, leaves, fruit and vegetable food wastes, spent plants, hay, chipped brush and trees, and farm manures. Compost holds 225 percent of its weight in water and, unlike peat moss, does not repel water when dry. Compost is not nutrient dense—it may contain only 1 percent nitrogen by weight—but it slowly releases a wide range of nutrients essential for plant growth. The pH of most compost is in the 6.6 to 7.2 range. Compost is the most important and frequently used soil amendment. It is easy to make at home and provides long-lasting benefits. Incorporate it into soils prior to planting, spread it over turf and beds of perennials and annuals (top-dressing), and use it to grow plants in containers.
Gypsum is calcium sulfate. Apply gypsum to heavy, clay soils that are high in sodium to improve soil structure and add calcium and sulfur without raising the soil pH. It also ties up excess magnesium. Gypsum can help leach out sodium when mixed into the top few inches of soil with a high salt concentration. This can help prevent the burning of plant roots from excess salts.
Humus is produced slowly from the decomposition of organic matter in soil. Adding compost and other organic materials to soil will increase the humus content. Humus holds water and nutrients, aids soil aggregation, and contains huge microbial populations. It can be purchased in bags; the quality will vary.

Tilling in high-quality organic amendments will loosen and enrich your garden soil.

1 Add at least one inch of compost each year to beds.

2 Mix the compost into the top 4–8 inches of soil.

Manure (check with nearby farms) helps build good soil. Ask for manure that has been mixed with bedding material and allowed to compost for at least two months. Farm manures usually contain 3 percent or less of each of the three main nutrients found in plant fertilizers—nitrogen, phosphorous, and potassium.

Organic mulches such as straw, newspaper, and grass clippings can be tilled into the soil at the end of the growing season. Others, such as shredded pine bark and hardwood chips, are not incorporated, but they act as soil amendments by slowly decomposing in place.

Sand can be used in small areas to improve clay soils and create better growing conditions for certain types of plants, such as Mediterranean herbs and cacti. Only sharp builder's sand should be used; add enough so that the soil is 50 percent sand. Smaller amounts of fine sand can cause clay to set up like concrete.

Sawdust that is well aged and decayed can be added to soil. Fresh sawdust can tie up nitrogen as it decomposes.

Peat moss is partially decomposed sphagnum moss mined from bogs. It absorbs 10 to 20 times its weight in water, but it repels water when it's dry. Peat moss contains little nutritive value but has a high nutrient-holding capacity. It is very acidic and is often mixed into beds prepared for plants in the blueberry, azalea, and rhododendron family.

Topsoil can be purchased by the bag or in bulk. Quality can vary widely. Inspect topsoil prior to purchase and delivery, and ask about the soil's history. Where did it come from? Have tests been performed for pH and nutrient levels and for heavy metals such as lead and cadmium? Blended topsoil and leaf compost mixes are excellent for an instant raised-bed garden. You can purchase them by the cubic yard in many areas.

Water-absorbing polymers are sold as granules that can absorb 300 to 400 times their weight in water. As soil dries, stored water is released slowly back into it. Polymers' cost-effectiveness has not been demonstrated for outdoor garden use, but they are useful in containers.

COMPOSTING: MAKING AND USING "BLACK GOLD"

THE BREAKDOWN PROCESS

Composting is the controlled biological and chemical decomposition of organic matter. The goal is to manage the materials and environmental conditions to ensure rapid and complete breakdown of organic matter. It can be done in open piles, bins, barrels, or other enclosures. There are six important, interrelated factors in composting:

■ Microorganisms and other animals that digest organic matter.
■ Organic materials (their food)
■ Air
■ Water
■ Size of the particles
■ Volume of the pile

The Digesters

Fungi, bacteria, and hundreds of species of soil animals are the real compost makers. These organisms feed on and break down organic matter, producing heat in the process. Microorganisms are active in small numbers at temperatures just above freezing but are most efficient at 110 to 140°F. They are assisted by larger organisms such as earthworms, slugs, snails, millipedes, and sow bugs.

Ingredients: Carbon/Nitrogen Ratio

All plant parts contain carbon and nitrogen in varying proportions. The digesters use carbon for energy and nitrogen for making amino acids and proteins. When you mix different types of organic material in your compost bin, it is important to achieve a proper balance of carbon (C - brown) to nitrogen (N - green). Blending green and brown materials by weight or volume to create a C/N ratio of about 30:1 results in an ideal diet for these digesters.

Green materials consist of fresh grass clippings, flower and vegetable plants, weeds, fruit and vegetable peels, and manure. They are low in carbon and high in nitrogen and moisture.

Brown materials may be fallen leaves, straw, newspaper, or sawdust. They are high in carbon, low in moisture, and slow to break down.

Things to avoid:
■ diseased plants
■ weeds with seed heads or that spread easily by stolons or rhizomes
■ branches and wood chips, which take a long time to break down
■ cat and dog droppings, which may spread certain human diseases
■ cooked foods, grease, and meat
■ glossy, coated, or treated paper products
■ lime, because finished compost has a neutral pH. Lime can drive off nitrogen as ammonia gas.
■ soil, which is dense and in large quantity may smother a pile. Instead, inoculate piles with finished compost.
■ commercial bioactivators or compost starters are unnecessary.

Apply compost around trees and shrubs. To avoid root damage, don't dig it in.

Water and Oxygen

The digesters need air and water to grow and reproduce. Microorganisms function best when composting materials are about as damp as a wrung-out sponge. Dry a wet compost pile by mixing the pile or incorporating coarse materials such as leaves, straw, or sawdust. To wet a dry pile, turn the ingredients while gradually adding water.

Particle Size

Shred or chop organic materials into smaller pieces. Although not essential, it speeds up the process.

Pile Volume

A compost pile should be at least 3 feet wide by 3 feet long by 3 feet high (1 cubic yard). A smaller pile may not have sufficient critical mass to heat up and stay hot. A pile higher or wider than 5 feet is difficult to manage and may not allow sufficient aeration in the center.

GETTING STARTED

When locating your composting system, select a spot that is
- Level and near your main sources of organic materials.
- Near a source of water.
- Screened from your property and neighbors' property.
- Away from wooden buildings to avoid attracting termites.
- Away from trees and shrubs, which will send their roots into the compost.
- Large enough to stockpile ingredients, turn the pile, and store finished compost.

COMPOSTING METHODS

There is no correct composting technique that all gardeners should follow. Select your particular methods based on your own circumstances.

Slow method: It works well if you have plenty of room and time.
- Add chopped and shredded organic materials when they become available.
- Piles should not exceed 5 feet wide or high.
- Turning the pile is not necessary.
- Remove finished compost from the bottom of the pile or wait 12 to 18 months for the entire pile to break down.

Fast method: It's best for those who use lots of compost and don't mind turning piles. You need one or more bins that are each 1 to 1½ cubic yards in volume.
- Fill one bin with an even mixture of shredded "greens" and "browns." Sprinkle in a 5-gallon bucket of finished compost or add a pint of 10-10-10 fertilizer.
- Add water until the pile is thoroughly moist.
- Cover the pile to prevent excess moisture loss and to aid decomposition in dry periods. Covering also protects the pile from becoming too wet during heavy rainfall and prevents nutrient leaching.
- The pile will heat up rapidly and should reach 150 to 180°F. It will cool when most of the sugars and starches are digested by the growing population of microorganisms. The digesters will also deplete oxygen and nitrogen. Turn the entire pile with a garden fork into an adjacent bin. Add another 5-gallon bucket of finished compost or compost tea, and the pile will heat up again. Two or three turnings are needed to produce a finished pile of compost.

For fast compost load your bin with an equal mix of green and brown ingredients.

Add water so that all ingredients are moist as a wrung-out sponge.

Mix all ingredients with a fork. Mix again when pile cools down two to three weeks later.

SMALL-SPACE COMPOSTING

Tumbler or barrel composters work best where space is limited, appearance is important, and kitchen scraps are the primary ingredients. They usually hold about 6 to 8 cubic feet of material and are rotated every few days, allowing the material inside to be mixed and aerated. To use tumblers effectively, it is important to
- Load the barrel to capacity with a mixture of "greens" and "browns."
- Avoid excess moisture.
- Keep the ingredients aerated. You can also dig 1-foot-deep trenches in your beds and bury appropriate chopped kitchen scraps. This on-site composting method will increase the soil fertility and can be done anytime of the year as long as the ground is not frozen.

Barrel composters are ideal for small spaces.

Place kitchen scraps into holes to improve garden soil.

USING COMPOST

Compost is ready to use when its temperature has decreased to slightly above air temperature. Finished compost is dark and fairly homogeneous, although pieces of the original ingredients are visible. Screen out coarse particles by passing the material through a 1-inch mesh and returning them to the compost pile for further decomposition.

Application Rates

How much compost do you need to cover a 200-square-foot flower bed with 2 inches of compost?
200 sq. ft. × ⅙ ft. =
      33.33 cu. ft.
33.33 cu. ft. = 1.2 cu. yd. =
41.66 bushels = 83.33 five-gallon buckets

CONVERSIONS

3 cubic feet of organic matter will cover 36 square feet to a depth of 1 inch.

7.5 gallons = 1 cu. ft.
1 bushel = 1.25 cu. ft.
27 cu. ft. = 1 cu. yd.

TIPS FOR USING COMPOST

- Mix it into the top 6 to 8 inches of garden soil.
- Spread a 1-inch layer on top of the ground around perennial plants.
- Spread a ¼-inch layer of screened compost over turf.
- Apply coarse-textured compost as an organic mulch on the soil surface.
- Use it as an ingredient (not more than 50 percent by volume) in growing medium for house plants and outdoor container plants and for starting seeds.

GRASSCYCLING

Contrary to common wisdom, grass clippings neither add to thatch nor increase chances for disease. As long as you mow your lawn at the right height and at proper intervals, clippings quickly break down without a trace because they're mostly water. As they break down, they contribute nitrogen and other nutrients to the soil and supply it with organic matter.

The clippings from a 1,000-square-foot lawn contribute ½ to 2 pounds of nitrogen, depending on how much you fertilize. The more you fertilize, the more nitrogen the clippings return to the soil.

Regardless, you may have reasons for collecting clippings, such as wanting the lawn to be extra neat for an event or a concern that the layer of clippings is so thick it might smother the grass. If you pick up clippings, the best place to use them is in the garden as mulch or add them to your compost pile.

Mulching mowers chop clippings into small pieces that decompose rapidly and improve your lawn.

TROUBLE-SHOOTING COMPOSTING PROBLEMS

PROBLEM	POSSIBLE CAUSES	POSSIBLE SOLUTIONS
Rotten odor	- Excess moisture (anaerobic conditions) - Compaction (anaerobic conditions)	- Turn pile and add dry, porous material, such as sawdust, wood chips, or straw. - Cover pile with tarp. - Make pile smaller.
Ammonia odor	- Too much nitrogen (lack of carbon)	- Add high-carbon material, such as sawdust, wood chips, or straw.
Low pile temperature	- Pile too small - Insufficient moisture - Poor aeration - Lack of nitrogen - Cold weather	- Make pile bigger or insulate sides with an extra layer of material such as straw. - Add water while turning pile. - Turn pile. - Mix in nitrogen sources such as grass clippings or manure.
High pile temperature (greater than 140°F)	- Pile too large - Insufficient ventilation	- Reduce pile size. - Turn pile.
Animal pests	- Presence of meat scraps or fatty food waste	- Remove meat and fatty foods from pile. - Build an animal-proof compost bin or turn pile to increase temperature.

n nature, plants thrive in natural areas without anyone turning a single spade of soil. Gardens and landscapes are quite another matter; active management is required for success. Tilling, digging, or amending is necessary to create a hospitable environment for root establishment and plant growth. But digging too much, with the wrong tools, at the wrong time can damage soil and plants. Work thoughtfully with your soil to conserve and improve it and create optimal conditions for planting.

CHOOSE THE RIGHT TOOL

Hand Tools

A wide range of hand tools is available to home gardeners through local retail outlets and mail-order garden supply catalogs. Here are three of the most versatile and essential tools.

Garden spade. It usually has a D-shaped grip, a short handle, and a rectangular blade 10 to 12 inches long, made from carbon steel or stainless steel. It is used to dig new beds, remove sod, edge existing beds, turn and amend soil, and remove large weeds.

Garden fork or digging fork. It also has a D-shaped grip on a short handle. This tool has three or four straight, pointed tines. Use a garden fork for loosening, turning, fluffing, and amending soil.

Steel rake. It's the perfect tool for removing stones and debris when preparing soil. It also removes weeds and creates a smooth soil surface for planting seeds and transplants.

Other Useful Tools

■ A long-handled, round pointed shovel is good for digging holes and moving organic materials and soil.

■ Many styles of hoes are available for cutting weeds.

Scuffle or stirrup hoes quickly remove young weeds at the soil surface and work nimbly between plants.

■ Trowels are indispensable for digging small holes for setting out flower and vegetable transplants.

It's worthwhile to pay a little extra for high-quality tools that appear well constructed and feel balanced in your hands. Good tools usually have ash, hickory, or plastic resin handles. Remove soil and debris from tools after each use, and file edges to remove nicks and keep them sharp. At the end of the season, rub down wood handles with linseed oil, remove rust with steel wool or sandpaper, and rub down metal parts with an oily rag. Store tools inside a shed, garage, or basement.

Tillers

Gas-powered tillers enable gardeners to turn soil much more quickly than is possible with hand tools. Rear-tine models are more expensive but are more effective at tilling the top 6 to 8 inches of soil than front-tine tillers. Tillers can also be used to cultivate— lightly turning soil to destroy growing weeds. Lightweight tillers till or cultivate an 8 to 10 inch width. These tillers work well to prepare beds for planting and cultivate between plants. They bounce around and work poorly on heavy clay soils. When used in loose soil, they can dig to a depth of 8 inches.

It should take only one or two passes with a power tiller to prepare soil for planting or till under compost and dead plants. Turning the soil more frequently can damage the soil structure by pulverizing individual soil aggregates.

This electric minicultivator tills soil in small spaces.

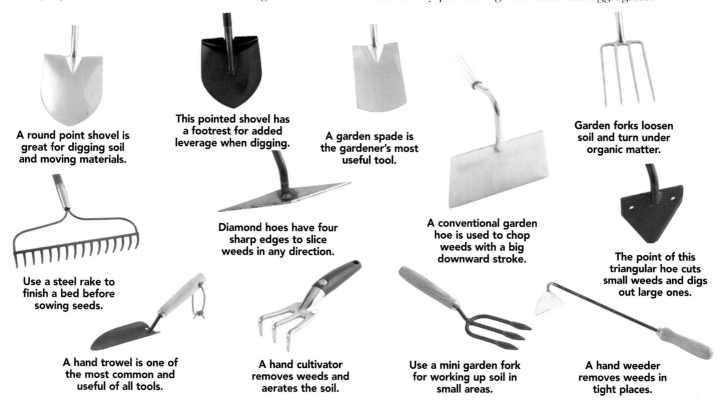

A round point shovel is great for digging soil and moving materials.

This pointed shovel has a footrest for added leverage when digging.

A garden spade is the gardener's most useful tool.

Garden forks loosen soil and turn under organic matter.

Use a steel rake to finish a bed before sowing seeds.

Diamond hoes have four sharp edges to slice weeds in any direction.

A conventional garden hoe is used to chop weeds with a big downward stroke.

The point of this triangular hoe cuts small weeds and digs out large ones.

A hand trowel is one of the most common and useful of all tools.

A hand cultivator removes weeds and aerates the soil.

Use a mini garden fork for working up soil in small areas.

A hand weeder removes weeds in tight places.

CHOOSE THE RIGHT TIME

Most soil preparation is done during spring and fall because most planting takes place at that time. Balmy spring days stir gardeners to go outside and "play in the dirt." Too often they work the soil when it is too wet. This can force sticky clay particles together, damaging soil structure. The soil then dries into hard, unmanageable clods. Avoid this by performing a simple field test: shape a handful of garden soil into a ball and bounce it a few times in your hand. If it breaks apart, the soil is dry enough to dig. If the ball stays intact, you should wait. On the other hand, tilling during hot, dry weather can turn certain soil into a dusty powder.

How Much Is Enough?

The degree of soil preparation depends on soil conditions and what's being planted. Deep, well-drained soils high in organic matter require less effort to prepare for planting than compacted soils low in organic matter. Flower and vegetable beds are usually turned or tilled in spring to create a fine seedbed. High-quality soil may need only spring fluffing with a garden fork, then a surface raking to remove rocks, debris, and early spring weeds. Areas to be planted in turfgrass should be lightly tilled and raked smooth. Grass seed needs to be rolled, pressed, or raked into contact with soil to ensure good germination and establishment. To thicken a lawn (overseeding), break up the top one to two inches of soil prior to sowing seed. Planting containerized herbaceous perennials or woody plants may require only a shovel and rake, although a tiller may be justified for large group or island bed plantings.

Tilling wet soil can damage its structure and produce persistent large clods.

CREATING NEW PLANTING AREAS IN TURF

Cover the ground with cardboard or black plastic and leaves to kill grass and weeds.

Double dig soil to a depth of 16–20 inches to loosen soil and increase root growth.

turfgrass, or simply incorporate it into the soil.

Smother the sod. Lay cardboard or black plastic on top of turf in fall and secure it to the ground with rocks or boards. The sod beneath it will die and begin decomposing by spring. Remove or till under the dead sod. Or cover the area in fall with multiple sections of newspaper. Pile 8 to 12 inches of compost on top of the newspaper. Plant directly into the compost or till the organic matter into the top 6 to 8 inches of soil in spring.

Some type of turfgrass covers the land around most American homes. The challenge is to find the easiest way to kill or remove turfgrass so you can create a new garden bed or planting site for trees and shrubs. Turfgrass will compete with new landscape plants for nutrients and water, and allowing turfgrass to grow too close to ornamental plants can invite lawn mower or string trimmer injury. Here are several techniques for eliminating sod to make room for flowers, vegetables, trees, and shrubs.

Strip sod: Cut through sod with a garden spade along the outline for the bed. Then use your spade to strip off the sod, leaving the soil in place. Incorporate organic matter into the top 6 to 8 inches of soil.

Till sod under: A powerful walk-behind rototiller is required to cut through and till under thick sod. A tractor-powered tiller can perform the job easily.

Apply herbicides: Apply a nonselective herbicide (Roundup, for example) to the area that you have clearly outlined with string and short stakes. Some formulations of the popular herbicide Roundup also contain the herbicide diquat, so read the product label carefully. It will let you know when the treated area can be planted. You can use a garden spade to slice through and remove the dead mat of

EFFECT OF DIGGING

A good garden spade and a strong back may enable you to turn over a new planting bed and literally replace the topsoil with subsoil. This inversion of soil may move soil organisms that break down organic matter and release nutrients out of reach of young plants, forcing plants to grow in inhospitable subsoil. If this is the case, soil amendments may be necessary to promote healthy plant growth. In cases where the topsoil is deeper than the depth of your spade, turning over the soil will not result in such problems.

Raised Beds

Raised beds are planting areas that are higher than the existing soil grade. They can be any shape or size and may be enclosed by boards, stones, or other materials or left open. Raised beds for flower and vegetable gardens are usually no more than 4 feet wide, so the middle of the bed can be reached from either side. The beds are elevated by adding soil such as Miracle-Gro Garden Soil to the bed. The result is deep, rich topsoil that extends rooting depth and enhances plant growth. An excellent soil structure can be maintained when you minimize tilling and don't walk on the beds. Raising the soil can help compensate for poor drainage and prevent root and crown rots during wet spring weather. The soil will also warm up more quickly in spring, helping to get your garden off to a quick start.

Double-Digging

Digging soil to twice the depth of the blade on your garden spade can double the effective rooting depth of your soil and increase garden productivity. It is done mostly in flower and vegetable gardens and is especially useful for growing root crops such as beets, carrots, turnips, and potatoes.

NO-TILL GARDENING

Frequent turning and tilling of soil causes compaction, erosion, and the oxidation of organic matter. No-till row crop farming has been widely adopted in many parts of the United States as a means of conserving and improving soils. No-till practitioners plant their crop seeds directly into the remains or stubble of the previous crop without turning the soil. More vegetable gardeners are experimenting with this technique as a way of saving time and eliminating the need for tilling. One technique is to sow a fall cover crop (for example, oats or hairy vetch) that can be cut down at soil level in spring. Seeds and transplants can then be planted directly into the decaying cover crop.

Last fall's cover crop turns into a decomposing mulch for vegetable plants.

WORKING WITH DIFFICULT SITES

Certain sites require extensive modification to ensure favorable growing conditions for plants.

Neglected areas: Much work is required to rid an area of weeds, brambles, and small woody plants. It may take a combination of cutting, digging, and herbicide applications before the soil can be prepared.

Compacted soils and lack of topsoil: "Instant" raised beds are a good option for gardeners with problem soil. Loosen the existing soil in the proposed bed with a garden fork and surround it with an enclosure 6 to 12 inches high. Purchase good-quality topsoil that has been mixed with compost and fill the enclosed area.

Slopes: Create a flat, terraced area for flower and vegetable beds that require soil preparation each year.

Poor drainage: Underground streams, high water tables, and impervious soil layers can create drainage problems. Sometimes it's best to simply grow plants adapted to wet conditions. To correct poor drainage, cut an 18- to 24-inch-deep trench from a point above the poor drainage area to a point below the area. Shovel 2 inches of coarse gravel into the bottom of the trench and lay 4- to 6-inch-diameter perforated plastic drainage pipe on top. The pipe should slope slightly to allow gravity to carry water through it. Cover the pipe with 2 inches of coarse gravel and backfill with soil. The pipe should end near a storm drain or dry well. Consult a landscape architect, landscaper, or building contractor for difficult situations.

Improve a tight clay soil by inserting a garden fork and rocking it back and forth.

Compacted, poorly drained soils with little topsoil contribute to tree decline.

A gardening challenge: new home sites usually have little topsoil.

SELECTING AND BUYING QUALITY PLANTS

It's easy to attribute a neighbor's lush and beautiful yard to a proverbial green thumb. It actually takes a lot more than a magic touch to create a landscape that will turn heads. Selecting and purchasing high-quality plants and being sure that they are the right plants for particular locations are essential prerequisites for an attractive and productive landscape. This is the case for annuals such as zinnias and tomatoes as well as for herbaceous perennials, trees, and shrubs. As with most things in life, you get what you pay for when you go plant shopping. Vigorous, high-quality plants may be more expensive, but they will establish quickly and reach their genetic potential for size, appearance, and productivity. You can produce a pleasing design and select the correct species and varieties of plants only to have the endeavor fail if poor plant material is used.

Books, websites, cooperative extension publications, and local nurseries are good sources of information on plants adapted to your locale. You might also consult with neighbors, friends, and coworkers who have gardening experience before selecting and purchasing plants.

WHERE TO BUY PLANTS

These high-quality bedding plants will take off once they are transplanted.

It is best to patronize reputable garden centers and nurseries in your area. These businesses usually offer a good variety of high-quality plants and personalized service. You may find that certain local businesses specialize in bedding plants and vegetable transplants whereas others excel at growing trees and shrubs. Carefully inspect plants prior to making a purchase and determine the company's guarantee and return policy. Select plants that are free of diseases and insect pests. Look for healthy, vigorous plants that have been well cared for. Shop at garden centers and nurseries that offer some provision for returning plants, especially trees and shrubs, that fail to become established. Expand the scope of your search by selecting a high-quality mail-order nursery. Many have excellent and informative online catalogs.

Neighbors and friends can be a good source of herbaceous perennials that need dividing, such as purple coneflower, tiger lily, or iris. Politely decline plants that look diseased or unhealthy.

Many garden plants are grown from seed. Some examples are annual flowers such as cosmos, cleome, and zinnias, and vegetables such as lettuce, beans, and beets. Many herbs and herbaceous perennials can also be grown from seed. Check the seed packet to be sure you are buying a suitable variety for your area. Seed companies often include growing instructions on the back of the packet. You can assume that the seeds you buy have met minimum federal standards for germination.

Many bare-root plants are shipped by mail. This healthy root system was wrapped in moist sphagnum moss to prevent drying.

WHICH PLANTS TO CHOOSE

Resist the impulse to buy plants you don't need just because they are inexpensive or appealing. Your plant selection should follow the design that you created for your yard. There will always be opportunities to move, divide, and add plants. Squeezing in extra plants leads to overcrowding and frustration. Consider the eventual, mature size of each plant. Trees and shrubs will decline and die prematurely if spaced too closely together or planted too close to the street or structures. Crowding causes stressful growing conditions that may contribute to insect and disease problems. Buy dwarf forms of desired plants when they are appropriate and available. Carefully measure and mark the area that each plant will occupy. It's relatively easy to divide and move herbaceous perennials; trees and shrubs are another matter.

Always select plants adapted to your specific landscape and general region. Consult with local nurseries, gardening experts, and cooperative extension publications to determine a plant's pest susceptibility and invasiveness. If you live in an urban area, choose plants that can tolerate challenging site conditions such as compacted soil and air pollution.

Planting trees and shrubs too closely together is a common, yet avoidable landscaping mistake.

Select well-adapted native plants for an attractive, ecologically rich landscape.

Busy people often look for trouble-free plants to stock their landscape. Native plants are widely promoted as the key to a beautiful, low-maintenance garden. It makes good sense to select plants that are indigenous to your region. It's also true that many nonnative plants have become invasive and undesirable. It's a good idea to use native plants where appropriate, but don't exclude all nonnatives on principle. Native plants also need to be pruned, mulched, and watered to grow well.

WHAT SIZE PLANT IS BEST?

Shrubs and trees that have been actively growing in a nursery for more than four years are more expensive, difficult to transplant, and slower to establish than younger woody plants. And large, older plants suffer greater transplant shock when dug up, transported, and planted than younger plants, making the greater investment in labor and money more risky. However, the greater investment in larger plants may be worthwhile if your objective is to fill a bare space as quickly as possible.

There are no such size and age guidelines for annuals and herbaceous perennials. Certain plants, such as cucumber and melon, grow well in the garden after being grown in a greenhouse in small plastic cells for only three weeks. Large tomato transplants with thick stems will produce tomatoes more quickly than smaller plants, but only if they are grown in large containers and don't experience stressful conditions outdoors. Large plants that outgrow their containers or lack nutrients or water make poor garden plants.

A one-gallon herbaceous perennial grass will quickly grow into a full-size clump.

WHAT TO LOOK FOR

Take your time when selecting plants for your garden. Bring a checklist to help remind you what species and cultivars will best fit into your plan. Look for these characteristics of high-quality plants.

■ Plants are true to type; they have the correct leaf color, size, and shape. They also have the correct tag. (Mislabeling is not uncommon, especially with bedding plants and vegetable transplants.)

■ The root system is white to light beige in color, and roots are growing throughout the container or root ball.

■ Top growth and root mass of container plants is balanced. Bedding plants and vegetable transplants are generally as wide as they are tall.

■ Tall tree species have a single trunk or leader that is thickest at the base. The trunk is strong enough to stay vertical without stakes or supports.

■ Some smaller tree species, such as crape myrtle, have multiple trunks.

■ On older trees, branches are spaced along the trunk.

Before buying a plant, gently remove it from its container to examine the root system. Healthy roots are white or light brown.

When purchasing a tree, look for one that has a gradual taper to the trunk and well-spaced branches.

The large number of healthy young roots will enable this container-grown tree to become quickly established.

Large roots growing out of the drainage holes or circling in the pot suggest a stressed, undesirable plant.

WHAT TO AVOID

Stressed vegetable plants will bloom prematurely. Remove the blooms after transplanting to encourage root growth.

Most trees grow best with a single trunk. Trees with double leaders often split later in life. Avoid purchasing them.

Sometimes plants in greenhouses and nurseries appear healthy at first glance but have problems that are revealed upon closer scrutiny. Look carefully at the crown, bark, leaf undersides, and root system (it's OK to remove plants from containers to examine roots). Watch out for the following:

■ Foliage that is off-color and undersize indicates stressful conditions, such as lack of water or nutrients, or root damage.

■ Dead or dying twigs at the ends of branches indicate poor growing conditions, root injury, or even insect or disease problems.

■ Scraped, dented, or missing bark reveals physical injury from support wires, tools, and so forth, which can retard plant growth.

■ Plants that are wilted, have weeds growing around the main stem, or are waterlogged indicate poor care.

■ Dead (brown), overgrown, or circling roots indicate a plant that has been in a container too long. Roots that grow around the crown of the tree can girdle and kill the plant.

■ Plants with obvious signs or symptoms of pests or diseases indicate poor care. Spongy black bark at the base of the plant indicates crown and root rots. Small raised bumps on tree and shrub bark may be scale insects, which suck sap and debilitate plants.

■ Bedding plants and vegetable transplants without blooms are more desirable than plants with blooms. Plants that bloom prematurely may be stressed and may not perform as well in the garden.

TRANSPORTING PLANTS

Care and forethought are necessary to ensure that your plants arrive home in good condition. Lift woody plants by the root ball or container, not the trunk. Be careful not to drop plants, which causes roots to separate from the soil and reduce water uptake. Protect the interior of your vehicle with plastic or paper and keep plants steady during the ride home. If using an open-bed truck, water the plants prior to loading and group them tightly at the front of the bed next to the cab. Drive slowly to minimize wind-burned foliage. If possible, secure a tarp over or around the plants.

This tree is cushioned and wrapped to prevent injury to the bark and dessication by wind.

BARE-ROOT PLANTS

Deciduous trees, shrubs, grapevines, brambles, roses, and fruit trees are sometimes sold as bare-root plants. Bare-root plants are less expensive than container-grown plants and are available through garden centers and mail-order companies. They are grown in rows in nurseries, dug up during the dormant season at a relatively young age (two to five years), and made available for planting from late winter through early spring. The soil clinging to the roots is washed or shaken off prior to packaging and shipment. Roots are then wrapped in moistened shredded newspaper, sphagnum moss, or other organic materials that can hold water. The roots should not be allowed to dry out.

The major disadvantage of bare-root plants is that you must be able to plant during unpredictable weather that may be cold, wet, and windy. You can minimize this problem by digging and amending the planting area the previous fall. If you cannot plant when your order arrives, bury the entire plant (or at least the root system, depending on the plant) horizontally in a shallow trench of moist garden soil. This heeling-in technique will keep plants dormant until conditions are more favorable for planting. Some gardeners soak the roots of large bare-root trees and shrubs in a container of water for up to 24 hours prior to planting to hydrate the root system. Soak the roots of smaller plants for at least four hours for best results. Avoid soaking roots for longer periods to prevent roots dying from lack of oxygen.

Quick to Establish

Novice gardeners may mistakenly believe that bare-root plants are less desirable than container or balled-and-burlapped (B&B) plants because they appear to lack substance. They are sold in a dormant state without a mass of soil and with no leaves or flowers. But a healthy, well-grown bare-root plant is easy to plant and may establish a root system faster than container or B&B plants. The roots of the latter types must grow out of a soil or growing medium to which they are accustomed into a soil with a different texture and structure. This often retards root development and can lead to decline and death if the new soil is of poor quality. Bare-root plants, on the other hand, can quickly exploit their new soil environment to grow roots.

Qualities to Look For

Here are some characteristics of a healthy bare-root plant:
- Buds are tight and dormant, not leafing out or blooming.
- Trunk and stems are free of cankers (dark or sunken areas).
- Crown (juncture of shoots and roots) is firm and solid to the touch.
- Roots are white or light brown and firm, not black or slimy.
- Identification tag and growing information are attached to the plant.

1 Moist shredded newspaper kept these bare-root raspberry plants from drying out during shipment.

2 The roots of healthy bare-root plants should be firm and fleshy; not dry and brittle or soft and slimy.

BALLED-AND-BURLAPPED TREES AND SHRUBS

Soil balls of B&B trees are heavy. Move them with care to avoid breaking roots.

Prior to planting cut the twine or wire cage holding the burlap in place.

Support the B&B root ball from below when moving the ball. Cut and remove the burlap covering the top of the rootball.

Balled-and-burlapped (B&B) trees and shrubs are grown in rows in nurseries and are periodically root pruned. Root pruning keeps the root systems fibrous and compact; it promotes new root growth; and it makes eventual digging and transporting more efficient. The plants are dug out with machinery that creates a spherical root ball. This shape is the most stable and helps the plant retain a large number of roots with a small amount of soil. Even so, the vast majority of the root system is left behind in the nursery. The root ball is dug when the soil is wet; otherwise, the root ball may break apart and severely damage the root system. The largest percentage of B&B plants sold by nurseries and garden centers are large deciduous trees and large evergreen trees and shrubs.

The root ball is wrapped in burlap to hold it together after it is dug. A wire cage is often used to hold the root ball and burlap in place. B&B trees and shrubs establish relatively quickly and can be planted successfully in spring and fall. Summer plantings are also feasible as long as the plants are watered deeply and regularly.

Weighing the Pluses
■ B&B stock can be planted anytime the ground isn't frozen.
■ B&B plants are usually large and will fill the allotted area more quickly than bare root or container plants.

Weighing the Minuses
■ B&B trees and shrubs are relatively expensive.
■ Because they have drastically reduced root systems, they have difficulty taking up enough water to support the top growth. They must be watered frequently, especially during extended hot, dry weather.
■ The root ball is heavy; a cubic foot of soil and roots can weigh more than 100 pounds.

B&B Tips

■ Always pick up B&B planting stock from underneath the root ball. Otherwise, the weight of the soil may cause it to pull away from the roots and trunk, damaging the plant.
■ The root system should feel solid; a loose root ball indicates broken roots and careless handling. Check the root system by gently moving the trunk back and forth. The whole root ball should move with the trunk.
■ Keep the root ball uniformly moist prior to planting. Maintain uniform moisture for at least the first two growing seasons after planting, until roots reestablish.

CONTAINER-GROWN PLANTS

This well-grown clump of daisies easily slides out of its container. It will make an instant impact of color in the landscape.

Containers are a convenient way to purchase, transport, and plant nursery stock and herbaceous perennials. All flowering annuals, vegetables, and herbs are grown and sold in some type of plastic or fiber container. Container plants can be purchased and planted anytime the soil is not frozen.

Watch for Root Problems

One drawback to container plants is that they can become root-bound. The root system may outgrow the container if the plant remains in the same size container too long. Gently remove the container to examine the root system. A healthy root system will have white growing tips. Roots should be visible throughout the planting mix but should not be matted at the edges or the bottom of the root ball. Overgrown roots growing tightly around the crown and trunk of woody ornamental plants can cause injury and eventual death. These strangling or girdling roots may be obvious. If they are not observable, look for them by gently scraping aside the top few inches of growing medium.

Before planting container-grown plants, tease apart the roots and spread them horizontally in the planting hole. This action will break some of the roots and stimulate new root growth. Snipping off long root ends has the same effect. Container-grown trees, shrubs, and herbaceous perennials often perform well in the landscape even if they are slightly root-bound, whereas annual flowers and vegetable plants are easily stressed when root-bound and may not meet your expectations in the garden.

Avoid purchasing container-grown plants if the root mass has an off-odor, is dark brown, or if roots are circling the bottom of the container. Container plants may become waterlogged if they sit in puddles or poorly drained areas in the nursery or garden center. This can lead to root rots and poor growth when they are planted in a landscape.

Keep Plants Well Watered

Container-grown plants may require more frequent watering after planting than bare-root plants or B&B plants. Container plants are grown in a loose medium that drains well but dries out more quickly than garden soil. Even healthy-looking container plants typically undergo significant water stress. The plants tend to develop a compact root system with a large number of fine roots. After planting, they may require water every other day if rainfall is lacking to keep the concentrated roots alive and to encourage new roots to grow into the native soil.

A large container plant can be coaxed out of its pot by tilting the container and pulling on the trunk. Loosen the large circling roots from the root ball before planting it into the ground or into a new container.

GETTING READY TO PLANT

You've carefully selected plants that are adapted to your area and fit into your overall landscape plan. Now it's time to select specific planting sites and create the best conditions for rapid root establishment. The thoughtful planning and preparation you put into these steps will pay off handsomely in the long run.

SITE SELECTION

The success of a particular plant in a particular site will be determined by a host of factors such as soil conditions, sun and wind exposure, availability of water, and proximity to roads, buildings, and other trees.

Soil Type, Drainage, and Slope

As a general rule, landscape and garden plants grow best in soils that drain well, contain some organic matter, and are loose and friable. Know each of your plant's specific requirements. You may want to create a privacy screen in a poorly drained area using evergreen trees, only to find that they cannot tolerate wet feet. Certain desirable shade trees and shrubs that are adapted to your area grow fine in heavy, clay soils; others do best in light, sandy soils.

Ensure success when growing perennials on a slope by covering the planting area around these plants with a mulch or ground cover to prevent soil erosion. Avoid growing annual flowers and vegetables on a slope because the soil can easily wash away after the area is tilled or cultivated. In addition, vegetable plants are watered and fertilized more frequently than most other plants. Sloped ground makes watering difficult and causes nutrients to run off into groundwater or surface water. The best approach is to create level terraces.

Aspect and Microclimates

Aspect is the compass direction that a garden bed or particular landscape plant faces. A vegetable or flower bed located on the south side of a dwelling has a southern aspect or exposure. Plants that require a lot of sun to grow well do best with a southern or western aspect. For perennial or annual borders or a vegetable garden, locate the tallest plants on the north side, so they don't block the sun for lower-growing plants. Aspect, buildings, fences, privacy screens, and vegetation create microclimates in landscapes. Tender perennial plants, for example, are more likely to thrive on the south side of a structure than if grown in an open bed away from a structure.

It is helpful to track the sun and shade patterns across your landscape through spring, summer, and fall prior to creating garden beds and planting trees and shrubs. Full sun means five to six hours of direct sun per day; partial shade means shade for two to three hours per day. There are degrees of sun and shade. For example, some plants grow well in dappled or filtered sun but can not tolerate deep shade. A sun-loving plant such as chile pepper will yield more fruits if it receives late-afternoon shade. Plants with a northern aspect may have full exposure to the open sky but receive no direct sunlight.

Mesoclimates are created by topography, bodies of water, and human intervention. For example, urban areas create and hold more heat than comparable rural areas, and gardens near large bodies of water are least likely to suffer late frosts.

Match the plant to the growing site. If planted in a microclimate to which it is unadapted, the plant will be stressed and subject to disease and insect problems.

The temperature difference between the north and the south sides of a building can be 10–15°F, creating varied microclimates.

If you can't plant your new shrub right away, heel it in to a mound of wood chips to keep temperatures around the roots moderate.

Obstacles and Challenges

Street plantings in areas with winter snow and ice are easily injured by salt applied to roadways. It is best to locate valuable landscape plants at least 20 feet from the road. Trees planted too close to driveways, sidewalks, and homes often damage these structures as a result of root growth. Planting trees and shrubs within the rooting area of established woody plants can cause the latter to decline.

You may be surprised to find large roots from trees long ago removed, pieces of concrete, drain tile, and other hidden debris when you begin to dig. Contact your local utilities for information on buried cables. Overhead wires should also be considered when locating and planting tall trees.

Keep the root mass of bare-root plants cool and moist at all times until they are planted.

BEST TIMES TO PLANT

1 Early fall is a good time to plant trees and shrubs. Roots will have time to reestablish before winter freezes occur.

2 Backfill the hole with existing soil. Avoid using compost, peat moss, or other materials of differing textures from the existing soil.

The best times to plant are when soil and environmental conditions are favorable for rapid root growth. Annuals, herbaceous perennials, vegetables, and fruits are typically planted in spring when all danger of frost has passed. Fall and early spring are the best times for planting ornamental trees and shrubs and herbaceous perennials. Spring-flowering bulbs are typically planted in fall before the ground freezes.

If you need to hold plants that are ready to go into the ground because you don't have the time to plant them or the site is not yet prepared, keep the root systems moist and cool. Surround the roots of bare-root plants with moistened burlap, shredded newspaper, sphagnum moss, or another material that will hold water. Store plants in the shade until they can be planted. Bare-root and container plants can also be temporarily planted in garden soil, in the shade. This is known as heeling in and can help acclimate plants to their eventual planting site.

Leaf burn of tomatoes can be caused by light frosts in early spring.

PLANTING BASICS

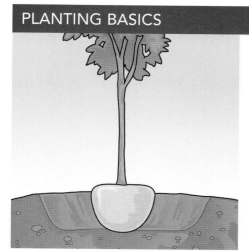

A wide, shallow planting hole is best for most woody plants and perennials.

1 Mark the planting area with string, a garden hose, or a thin stream of flour or lime.

2 Insert a spade along the outline to begin excavating the planting area.

Planting—whether a tomato seedling or a shade tree—is one of the most satisfying acts of gardening. Proper planting techniques have a profound impact on the beauty and productivity of the home landscape.

Digging the Hole
Dig a hole suited to the plant. The holes for trees and shrubs should be no deeper than the depth of the root ball or root mass. Planting too deep results in slow establishment and poor growth of woody ornamentals. The roots at the top of the root ball should be level with the soil surface. Avoid adding extra soil on top of the root ball after planting, but do add a 2- to 3-inch layer of mulch to cover the root ball.

The diameter of the hole should be at least twice the diameter and preferably three to four times the diameter of the root ball. Trees and shrubs will establish more quickly if a large area of soil is loosened and improved.

When planting in poorly drained soil, dig the hole 2 to 4 inches shallower than the root ball so that the top of the root ball is above ground level. This will prevent the roots from drowning in wet soil. An alternative method is to create a raised bed that contains 8 to 12 inches of loose, well-drained soil above grade level.

Amending the Soil
Flowering annuals, herbaceous perennials, and vegetable plants will grow best in beds where all the soil has been loosened to a depth of 12 inches and amended with organic matter. When amending soil prior to planting, incorporate the amendment throughout the entire eventual root zone of the plant. Avoid amending only the soil in a small hole. If the surrounding soil is high in clay, for example, the new roots will grow only in the amended soil. Rainwater will be held by the amended matter in the hole and will not easily drain through the tight clay soil lining the hole. Work soil amendments into the top 8 inches of soil in a 2-foot radius from the center of each new plant. If a soil-testing laboratory recommends plant food, an acidifying agent, or lime based on a soil sample, add them to the planting area as described above.

1 Remove exposed burlap when planting B&B stock to prevent it from wicking water away from roots.

2 Place the plant in the hole no deeper than the surrounding soil level. This yew has been properly situated in the planting hole.

Preparing the Plants

Balled and burlapped: Remove the burlap from balled-and-burlapped trees and shrubs if the material is synthetic burlap (it melts rather than burns when touched with a lit match). For real burlap, cut and remove the fabric on top of the ball, and peel the burlap down the sides so it stays below soil level. Real burlap will eventually decompose in the soil, whereas synthetic burlap will retard root growth. Avoid damaging the root ball when removing any burlap. Leave the wire basket that surrounds the root ball and burlap or, at most, clip off enough to keep the wire from showing above the ground. Set the plant in the hole so it is about an inch higher than it was planted in the nursery (where the bark is darker near the top of the root ball). This will compensate for minor settling caused by the weight of the root ball.

Bare root: The roots of bare-root plants grow down at an angle, so mound some soil in the bottom of the hole and place the bare-root plant on top of the mound. Arrange the roots around the mound and angle down and out toward the sides of the planting hole. Trim any roots that may circle the bottom of the planting hole.

Container: Gently tap plants out of their containers. Use your fingers to tease apart the roots along the sides and bottom of the root mass. If the plants are severely pot-bound, use a large knife or trowel to cut into the root mass, slicing through circling or girdling roots in three or four places. Spread the roots horizontally in the planting hole, and snip off long roots that don't fit.

Planting and Backfilling

After setting your plant in the hole, shovel in the loosened soil that was piled next to the hole. Break up any clods before adding this backfill soil to the hole. Tamp down the backfill soil with your foot when the hole is half filled. Fill the rest of the hole with loose soil and tamp again with your foot. This will force out any large air pockets and ensure good contact between roots and soil.

Soak the planting area with water to settle the soil and moisten the root zone. Create a 2- to 3-inch-high basin, or "doughnut", around the plant for catching rainfall and irrigation water. Omit this step if the soil does not drain well. Mulch to conserve moisture and control weeds.

Use a sharp knife to slice through an overgrown root mass. Spread the roots out to hasten their growth into the surrounding soil.

Tamp down soil when backfilling to remove air pockets that can dry out roots.

Use a rake or hands to create a shallow basin or depression around the trunk.

Always water newly planted nursery stock to soak the root ball and surrounding soil.

SUPPORTING A YOUNG TREE

Provide physical support for newly planted trees to hasten root establishment and keep lawn mowers and string trimmers from injuring tender young trunks and crowns. Supports can also prevent upheaval of root systems during winter freeze and thaw cycles and blow-over during windy weather. If the new planting is in a protected site, out of line from strong winds, avoid staking. Trunks grow sturdier when they are free to gently move back and forth naturally. If staking is necessary, remove the supports after a season or two.

WHICH TREES NEED SUPPORT?

Bare-root trees more than 8 feet tall or greater than 6 inches in diameter are most likely to need stakes or guy wires. Bare-root trees are more top-heavy than B&B or container-grown plants because they don't have a significant mass of roots and attached soil to counterbalance the force of wind on their crown. Temporary support to prevent wind damage also benefits container-grown or B&B trees in a shallow planting hole on a windy site or those that are very large. Only very large shrubs need staking.

Tall trees may require support for the first year after planting while their root system becomes established. Remove stakes or guy wires after a year of establishment to avoid injury on the trunk and branches from the supports.

METHODS AND MATERIALS

The single-stake method is the simplest and works well for most small bare-root trees. It requires a single stake of untreated wood at least 1-inch square and the same height as the tree to be supported. After digging the planting hole, drive the stake into the ground about 6 inches from the center of the hole. Tie the tree to the stake after planting is complete. Slide a short piece of old rubber hose over a length of heavy wire. Tie the wire to the stake with a loop (figure eight), then tie it loosely to the tree, making sure that the tree bark is protected by the rubber hose. Avoid driving a wooden stake through the root mass of a B&B or container-grown plant.

The two-stake system provides more support. After planting, drive two stakes into the ground on either side of the tree 18 to 24 inches from the trunk. The stakes should be 18 to 24 inches deep. Loop a thick piece of wire surrounded by a piece of rubber hose loosely around the trunk and secure the ends to the two stakes.

STAKING TIP

Avoid pulling the wire and rubber hose tight against the tree bark. It will rub the bark and damage the thin layer of tissue under the bark that carries water and nutrients up and down the tree. Moisture and organic debris can also collect around the rubber hose and contribute to disease problems. With the wire affixed, the trunk should be able to move in any direction when you push against it. Tightly supported trees develop a weaker root system than trees that can sway in the wind.

Very large or heavy trees can be supported with three guy wires, each attached to an individual wooden stake. Notch the stakes at the top and drive them 18 to 24 inches into the ground at an angle away from the tree. Use the same method as described above for the two-stake system to support the tree with heavy wire and pieces of old rubber hose (or other suitable material).

REMOVE SUPPORTS

After a year, the tree's root system will have had ample time to become established. Continued support can cause the wire to girdle the trunk as the tree expands in diameter. Remove staking or guying supports before this can happen.

Supports were left on this tree for too long, causing damage to the trunk.

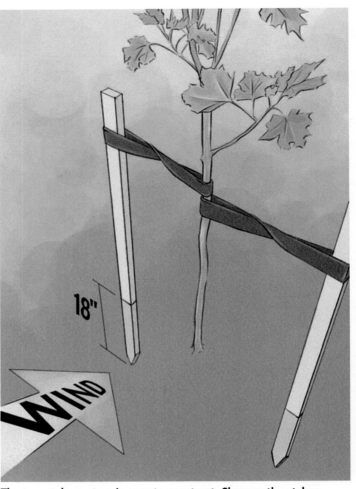

The two-stake system is easy to construct. Sharpen the stakes before driving them into the soil with a hammer or post driver.

These fabric strips are wrapped loosely around the trunk and will not dig into the bark.

Altering or completely renovating foundation beds is one of the most common landscape projects. Makeovers can solve a number of problems, including poor plant selection, plants that have overgrown their allotted space, and plants that are too close to buildings, power lines, entry doors, driveways, and walkways. It may be that foundation plants on one side of the house became increasingly shaded by mature trees and began to decline as a result. Or perhaps you've grown tired of individual plants or the overall design and want to make a change. Well-designed and well-maintained landscape plants can add significant value to a home. Changing foundation plants can have a big impact on a home's appearance at a reasonable expense. Front beds are usually the focus of these makeovers.

Foundation plants usually include shrubs, small trees, and herbaceous perennials and ornamental grasses. Popular woody foundation plants of the past 50 years in many parts of the United States are junipers, yews, hollies, privet, boxwood, photinia, euonymus, nandina, dwarf conifers, azaleas, and rhododendrons. Consider the amount of work that will be required to dig up and remove foundation shrubs before you reach for the bow saw. For example, mature upright junipers and yews have large and woody root systems and require considerable effort to remove. Trees that were allowed to grow against the house may require the services of a professional tree removal company.

These foundation plants have overgrown their location, detracting from their value.

Remove as much of the root system as possible when replacing foundation plants.

STEPS TO FOLLOW

Mix abundant organic matter into the soil before planting new foundation plants.

1. Develop a plan for your renovated foundation beds. Determine which plants will work better for your site and situation.

2. Mark the plants you wish to remove and cut them down near ground level with a handsaw.

3. Cut through major roots and remove the crown using an ax, mattock, or shovel. Remove as many roots as possible; don't worry about fine feeder roots that get left behind. Avoid underground utilities.

4. Grade the existing soil so it drains away from the house.

5. Take a soil sample of the area. Follow the soil test recommendations for fertilizer and lime prior to setting in new plants. Improve the soil by working in lots of compost.

6. Replant the area with your new plant selections.

PLANTING IN CONTAINERS AND RAISED BEDS

Over the past 15 years, interest in all forms of container and raised-bed gardening has exploded. This has been related to the aging of the baby-boom generation and the quest for lower-maintenance gardens. The demand has been matched by the introduction of innovative containers and new dwarf cultivars of all types of plants. Even gardeners with large yards and extensive gardening areas enjoy the beauty and intimacy of flowers in window boxes or the freshness of basil and lettuce grown in a container on the deck.

DESIGN CONSIDERATIONS

Having a minilandscape plan for your container plantings will help make them successful. Decide what you'd like to grow and what size, type, and shape of containers will be needed. Will you need to move the containers once they are planted? If so, the containers should be light enough for one person to lift easily or have casters on the bottom for greater mobility. If you are placing containers directly on a wood, brick, or concrete surface, be aware that the containers may leave stains by season's end. The stains are from fertilizers and organic compounds in the planting media that leach out of the drainage holes. Move containers indoors for the winter. The freezing and thawing of water and planting medium can damage containers left outdoors.

Fan flower and purple fountain grass make a pleasant team in this container garden.

Enhance outdoor living areas with an array of container gardens. A mix of upright, mounding, and trailing plants soften harsh architectural lines.

Container plants add dramatic accents to outdoor spaces. This combination of cascading ornamental sweet potato vine, silvery helichrysum, magenta petunias, and yellow daisies adds season-long color to the deck.

TYPES OF CONTAINERS AND PLANTING MEDIA

Suitable containers range from elegant galvanized flower buckets and glazed terra-cotta to used wooden vegetable crates and recycled olive oil containers. Inexpensive plastic troughs may not add beauty to your balcony, but they are durable and inexpensive and can produce excellent results. Select from a wide array of sizes, shapes, and materials or construct your own container to fit any unique space and aesthetic look.

Large, heavy containers become weightier still when filled with potting mix, water, and plants and can be difficult to move. Conversely, lightweight containers with large plants may tip over in strong winds.

A variety of containers are suitable for container gardening. As long as the vessel holds several inches of growing media and drains water, it is suitable for container gardening.

Soilless growing mixes work nicely in indoor and outdoor containers.

Add planting media to pots, leaving enough headroom for watering.

Pots in full sun may need to be watered every day to keep plants healthy.

DESIRABLE QUALITIES OF PLANTING MEDIA

Garden soil is too variable, heavy, and weed-infested to be of practical use for container plants. Most gardeners choose from among dozens of different types and brands of growing medium sold in retail garden centers. Some gardeners create their own container medium using a combination of store-bought and locally available ingredients. Here's a list of some important qualities of container growing medium:

- Holds water and nutrients.
- pH 6.0–7.0; low in soluble salts.
- Good porosity, drains well, and allows strong root growth.
- Lightweight.
- Free of weeds, diseases, insects, and contaminants.

Commercially available soilless potting mixes meet most of these requirements and are suitable for all types of containers and plants. These mixes contain three principal ingredients: peat moss, vermiculite (a mined mineral that holds water), and perlite (expanded volcanic rock that improves drainage). Manufacturers add lime (because peat moss is acidic) and plant nutrients (because the main ingredients lack them).

Potting soil is a generic term for a wide range of products that differ greatly in content and quality. If you find one you like, stick with it. But you're likely to be more successful using commercial soilless mixes. They can be enhanced by mixing them with high-quality compost in a ratio of two-thirds soilless mix to one-third compost. Used growing media from disease- and pest-free plants may be bagged and reused the following year. However, nutrients will be depleted and feeding will be especially important for plants grown in the recycled mix.

WATERING AND FERTILIZING TIPS

Container plants have smaller root systems and less room to grow than garden plants, so they require frequent watering and fertilization. Plants grown in full sun often need daily watering in hot summer months. Exposed, windy locations and reflected heat from buildings and hard surfaces increase the need for frequent watering. Soluble plant nutrients quickly leach out of containers and must be replaced.

■ Buy or make self-watering containers that have a reservoir of water at the bottom that plant roots can grow into. Some containers have a capillary mat that wicks water up into the root zone. The drainage holes are on the side of the container, not the bottom. You can leave plants in these containers for a few days without watering.

■ Plastic containers hold water better than porous containers such as wood or terra-cotta.

■ Use a water breaker on the end of your hose to deliver a soft, steady stream of water that won't damage or dislodge plants and medium.

■ Build a simple drip irrigation system for your containers to reduce water use and improve efficiency.

■ Water containers until you see or hear water draining out the bottom.

■ Group containers together to reduce the heat gain around plants, increase humidity levels, and make watering more efficient.

■ Use a special soil mix specifically designed for container use. An example is Miracle-Gro Moisture Control Potting Mix. This soil is enriched with plant food and helps protect against overwatering and underwatering.

ANNUALS AND VEGETABLES IN CONTAINERS

Container gardening is the easiest way for beginners to achieve gardening success. For an attractive yet practical container, plant it with tomato, basil, and lettuce plants surrounded by dwarf marigolds or trailing petunias. These plants are easy to purchase, plant, and maintain through the growing season. You can even rotate several types of annual plants through a single container from spring through fall. Start with cool-season pansies, for example. Replace with warm-season petunias in summer then flowering kale in autumn.

Grow lettuce in spring or fall at the base of a Confederate jasmine in a container.

Feed the lettuce regularly with diluted all-purpose plant food to extend harvests.

PERENNIAL PLANTS FOR CONTAINERS

It is common to see beautiful evergreen trees and shrubs growing in large containers on concrete in front of apartment buildings, stores, and town houses. Perennials that are well adapted to your area will probably also grow well in containers. Winter protection and avoiding water stress are the two greatest challenges to growing woody ornamentals in containers. Check water needs frequently to prevent moisture stress. Some plants are finicky and may need special consideration when grown in containers. In temperate regions, cut back tender perennials in early fall and store them in a protected area, such as a garage, porch, or basement. Cut back hardier perennials and leave them outside in their containers, but surround the container with insulating material such as weed-free hay. Bury smaller containers in a protected area of the garden.

Trees, shrubs, and herbaceous perennials planted in containers need protection through the winter to prevent injury to roots. Insulate with mulch or bury the pot in the ground.

RAISED BEDS

You can build a raised bed in an afternoon. Here rot-resistant cedar lumber contains the growing media planted with flowering kale, chrysanthemums, pansies, and ornamental grass.

Cedar planks painted in cheery colors add to the attractiveness of these raised-bed vegetable gardens planted with cabbage, onions, eggplant, basil, tomatoes, and Brussels sprouts.

Raised beds are a well-established gardening tradition. People have been growing plants in improved soil mounded above grade for thousands of years. Raised beds help plants overcome poor soil and improve growing conditions in small, defined areas. Raised beds are larger in size than containers and sit on the ground, although not necessarily on soil. Build up the soil with Miracle-Gro Garden Soil.

If your garden soil is heavy or drains poorly, a raised berm may be the answer for growing lush plantings.

Design, Function, and Types

Raised beds can be designed to fit any size or type of outdoor space—on patios and lawns, in gardens, or under trees. They are easy to construct, fill, and disassemble if necessary. Raised beds are typically 2 to 4 feet wide and 6 to 12 inches high. One of the principles in creating raised beds is to improve soil fertility and structure by mixing up to 8 inches of compost or bark into the raised-bed soil. The soil remains loose and fluffy because people and equipment don't move across the beds. Raised beds typically are enclosed by stones, bricks, or wooden or recycled-plastic boards. It is also possible to create them without any physical border. Berms are a type of raised bed for ornamental plantings. They serve the dual purpose of creating visual interest in a landscape while getting plants above poorly drained soil.

Advantages of Raised Beds

◼ Create instant planting sites where soil is poor. Fill them with a purchased mixture of topsoil and compost.
◼ Avoid drainage problems by raising plants above excessively wet soils.
◼ Warm soils more quickly in spring.
◼ Create improved root and plant growth due to improved soil conditions.
◼ Allow you to work with plants when the ground is wet.

One disadvantage of raised beds is that they dry out more quickly than level garden beds during periods of drought. This drawback is easily overcome by installing drip irrigation to keep plants in the beds moist with little extra effort. Drying of raised beds can be minimized by mulching the soil surface with an organic mulch.

CARING FOR NEW PLANTS

Your vegetable seeds have sprouted in the garden, your newly planted shrubs are taking root, and you've just filled in your foundation beds with bedding plants. Take a moment to enjoy a sense of accomplishment. Then remember—your job has just begun. Watering, weeding, and mulching are some of the tasks that lie ahead. This section gives you pointers on taking care of new plants in your garden and landscape.

WATERING NEW PLANTS

Supplying water to developing root systems is the single most important thing you can do for new plants. Vegetable and flowering annual plants have relatively shallow root systems, as do many herbaceous perennials, woody shrubs, and small fruits. Natural rainfall alone will probably not give your new plants adequate water at the right time. New plants require frequent watering to promote root growth. Here are some guidelines to follow to determine when and how much to water.

■ Water all plants after planting. The amount will depend on the type of soil, the size of the planting area, and the weather conditions at planting time.

■ Water plants growing in sandy soils more frequently. Soils high in clay absorb, release, and drain water slowly. Adding lots of organic matter to soils helps them hold more water for plant growth and drain away excess water.

■ Water before you notice wilting foliage. New plants may require watering two to three times per week in spring if rainfall is lacking.

■ Water plants deeply and thoroughly. Dig down 4 to 6 inches with a screwdriver or finger to test for moisture.

■ Water in the morning if possible. Avoid wetting foliage if watering late in the day. Plants need time to dry off before nightfall to avoid disease.

Drip irrigation is an efficient method for watering the root zone of perennials.

■ Water spring-planted shrubs and trees throughout the growing season and into the fall. Roots actively grow in fall even though leaf growth has ceased.

■ Once garden and landscape plants are established, water them deeply and less frequently to encourage a more extensive root system and improved plant growth.

■ Avoid applying excessive water where soil drainage is inadequate. Roots die off when the soil's pore spaces are filled with water instead of air for more than 24 hours.

MULCHING

1 Place mulch no more than 2–4 inches deep. Keep it away from the trunks of trees.

2 An attractive pine straw mulch works well in annual and perennial flower beds.

3 Hardwood and softwood bark mulches are widely used in foundation plantings.

4 Cedar mulch breaks down more slowly than hardwood mulches.

5 Gravel and crushed-stone mulches can be useful and appealing in the landscape.

6 Black landscape fabric should be covered with decorative mulch.

The key to good weed management is to prevent their growth or remove them when young. Weed control methods range from mulching to hand weeding, hoeing, rototilling, and herbicides such as Miracle-Gro Garden Weed Preventer.

Types of Mulch

Newspaper: All pages except glossy paper can be used. Most newspaper inks are soy based and contain no dangerous heavy metals. Overlap the newspaper sections, and cover them with straw or grass clippings.

Shredded bark or woodchip mulches: These are used extensively around foundation plants; shredded pine bark lasts the longest. You can freshen these mulches with a new thin layer each year. Avoid buying bulk mulch that is unseasoned, smells of alcohol, or is steaming and hot to the touch.

Straw, grass clippings, shredded leaves: These organic mulches are used in vegetable and flowerbeds.

Black plastic: This type of mulch is laid down on top of the soil and secured to the ground two or more weeks prior to planting. It hastens growth and increases yields of warm-season crops such as pepper, tomato, melon, and eggplant. The soil under black plastic warms appreciably, spurring rapid root growth. Plastic restricts air movement into soil.

Woven landscape fabrics: Lay these materials over a defined bed and secure the edges to the ground with landscape staples or soil. Cut holes into the fabric, then plant through them. Cover with an organic or natural mulch.

WINTER PROTECTION

Make certain that woody plants are watered well going into the winter.

Antitranspirants must be reapplied several times to maintain the protective coating.

Use straw to protect the crowns of tender perennials such as chrysanthemums.

Young perennial plants are especially susceptible to winter injury caused by ice-melting salts, extended freezing temperatures, alternating freezes and thaws, and browsing animals. Plants that are only marginally hardy in your area are more prone to these problems. Frost cracks may occur on the southwest side of thin-bark trees, such as apple and peach, caused by wide temperature swings through the day. Prevent the problem by painting the trunk of these trees with white latex paint or wrapping them.

You can minimize these potential problems by taking good care of your new plants. Avoid pruning or fertilizing in late summer; both practices stimulate late growth at a time when perennial plants are naturally becoming dormant. Water woody ornamentals throughout the fall and winter months if rainfall is inadequate. Evergreen plants in particular can dry out and suffer winter burn when the soil freezes—preventing water uptake—while leaves continue to lose moisture during windy, cold weather. Antitranspirants are available to coat evergreen leaves and reduce water lost by the foliage. These products degrade rapidly and must be reapplied often throughout the winter to be effective.

PROTECTING NEW PLANTS FROM WILDLIFE AND PEOPLE

Many animals feed on and damage new plants during the growing season and through the winter. Surround trees and shrubs with hardware cloth, a tree guard, or fencing to prevent deer and rodent feeding. Apply repellents to dissuade deer and use snap traps to reduce the rodent population.

Mulch the area around new plants to prevent unintentional run-ins with lawn mowers, string trimmers, footballs, bicycles, and so forth. Or tie a brightly colored ribbon to new plants if there is a lot of people activity in your landscape.

Cut and shape hardware cloth into cylinders to prevent deer and rodent feeding.

Trees grown in turf are easily damaged by lawn mowers and string trimmers.

WATERING AND IRRIGATION

Beautiful gardens depend on the proper amount of water to keep them in top shape. Either too much or too little water can have detrimental effects on plant growth.

LANDSCAPE IRRIGATION

In many regions it is possible to garden with only the water provided by natural precipitation. However, gardeners understand that plants sometimes need additional water to supplement rainfall. Even areas with sufficient total moisture may not have proper seasonal distribution for optimal plant growth. Landscapes adapted to frequent precipitation suffer in seasons when natural rainfall fails to arrive in sufficient quantities. Irrigation is needed to establish new plants in most landscapes. In arid regions the need for irrigation is obvious, but even in arid regions gardeners often fail to understand the complexity and diversity of irrigation systems.

Why do plants need water? Water is used by plants to inflate their cells, which are complex, living, water balloons. They also need water to convert sunlight into food for themselves through photosynthesis (making oxygen for humans to breathe in the process). Water is necessary for the absorption of dissolved minerals from the soil and it carries nutrients from the roots to the leaves. Food for plants produced in leaves and hormones to regulate plant growth are carried in water to the roots and all other parts of the plant. Finally, the plant must cool itself by transpiring water into the atmosphere.

How do plants obtain water? Most plants absorb water through their roots. Only the very small root hairs absorb water. Larger roots serve as support for the plants to hold them upright and as pipes to conduct water from the small roots to the other parts of the plant. The absorbing roots are found at the end of the larger woody roots of trees, but in herbaceous plants and grasses they are close to the base of the plant. This distribution of absorptive roots must be considered when irrigation water is supplied to plants.

WATER SOURCE CONSIDERATIONS

The source of water for irrigation ranges from municipal or community water systems, to private wells, to irrigation ditches. The degree of filtration to remove particles of silt and clay varies among sources and must be considered when installing irrigation systems. Breaks in water lines allow entrance of sand, silt, and clay into the water pipes. These can clog sprinkler and drip irrigation systems.

Another factor to consider is the quantity of dissolved solids in the water and their likelihood to precipitate from solution in the irrigation system. Hard water minerals may form a scale inside pipes then break loose to clog small orifices in irrigation systems. These particles must be filtered from the water before entering sprinkler and drip irrigation systems.

Water from water softeners is damaging to plants. Water softeners replace the "hard water salts" calcium and magnesium with the "soft salts" sodium or potassium. This is good for maintenance of pipes and for laundry uses of water, but not for plants. The replacement minerals are harmful to plants. Sodium is toxic to plants in relatively small quantities and can destroy soil structure. And although potassium is a necessary plant nutrient, it can cause salt burn when present in high concentrations.

SPRINKLER IRRIGATION

Sprinkler irrigation is the most common method of landscape irrigation. For many years it was considered the only effective way to uniformly apply water over large areas such as athletic fields and lawns. But sprinkler irrigation can be extremely inefficient. Large quantities of water may be lost to evaporation as small water droplets fly through dry air. These droplets may be blown away from the intended application area by the wind, causing misapplication of water. Water blown onto streets, sidewalks, and other unintended locations provides no benefit to the landscape.

In spite of these efficiency issues, sprinkler irrigation remains the most common method of irrigating landscapes, perhaps because it is quick, easy, and convenient. Changes in sprinkler head design combined with proper system design, installation, management, and maintenance improve the water use efficiency for sprinkler systems.

The simplest system requires a portable sprinkler attached to the end of a garden hose and an outside water tap. This is adequate for small areas to be irrigated and in regions where irrigation is needed infrequently. In arid regions and increasingly in humid regions, more complex inground systems with automatic controllers are being installed. Inground systems are more expensive to install, but provide advantages over the hose and portable sprinkler. With an inground system, you need not drag a hose to the site to be watered. And you avoid getting wet from placing the sprinkler in just the right spot.

Oscillating sprinklers water large rectangular areas of the yard and deliver more water to the middle of their sweeping cycle.

Impact sprinklers rotate in a circular motion and deliver a lot of water to a small area in a short period of time.

Purchase a heavy-duty hose for greater durability and fewer problems with kinking.

Adjustable watering nozzles allow you to select the forcefulness of the water spray applied to plants.

Fan-shaped water breakers spread the force of the water stream over a broader area.

This traveling tractor sprinkler creeps along a hose to water large areas of the yard.

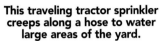

Quick-connect couplers save time when changing hoses or watering accessories.

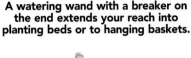

A watering wand with a breaker on the end extends your reach into planting beds or to hanging baskets.

Wall-mounted reels keep hoses out of the way.

This sprinkler with multiple flexible heads allows you to direct the water where it is needed.

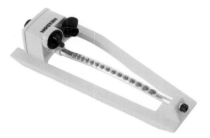

This whirling sprinkler sprays water from three nozzles.

Pulsating sprinklers are driven by water pressure and make a sweeping circular pattern.

Oscillating sprinklers water large areas quickly and conveniently, but water distribution is uneven.

Spot water individual plants or containers with a watering can.

SPRINKLER SYSTEM COMPONENTS

Shutoff valve: The first component of an inground sprinkler system, beginning at the water source, is a main shutoff valve, allowing repairs to any portion of the system.

Filter: The next element in the line should be a filter, to remove any particulate matter in the water. Particulates may be hard water scale from upstream pipes, material not previously filtered from the water, or soil that entered pipes following breaks in water lines or construction that replaces or adds pipes. A filter allowing back-flushing is a good investment but must be properly installed to work correctly.

Pressure regulator: After the filter a pressure regulator is often included, especially for low-volume irrigation systems. In sprinkler systems this maintains a consistent water pressure, allowing uniform water applications with consistent droplet size.

Irrigation filters trap dirt and debris that might otherwise clog drip or sprinkler irrigation systems.

Pressure regulators prevent fluctuations in water pressure that could damage irrigation systems or result in uneven water coverage.

Valves enable you to install multiple irrigation zones in the landscape. Each valve controls a single zone, allowing different plants to be irrigated according to their needs. Trees and shrubs can be irrigated less often but more deeply than plants in the flower border or the lawn. Each of these plant types can be on a different zone to allow proper irrigation. Independent irrigation zones allow irrigating the zones at different times to prevent excessive reduction in water pressure, which results in inefficient irrigation. Before installing the valves, run water through the system to flush sediment from the lines. Sediment that remains in the lines can cause failure of automatic valves.

Valve boxes, set into the ground, allow easy access for testing, maintenance, or replacement of valves installed in the boxes. (When installing the boxes, be sure to allow room for valve repair or replacement.) These boxes may be insulated during the winter to protect the valves from freezing. The boxes are inviting habitat for snails, spiders, wasps, and bees (be especially careful when opening or working near valve boxes in regions where Africanized bees may have colonized the boxes).

A manual-on, automatic-off valve uses a timer, so it shuts off after a preset interval. This allows you to switch on the system any time, safe in the knowledge that it will shut itself down.

A backflow prevention device is installed next to protect the home potable water supply from reverse flow. This antisiphon device prevents contaminated water from entering the home water supply when water pressure in the main lines is decreased. Several forms of this device are available and mandated by municipal ordinances. Even when ordinances do not require their use, backflow preventers are a good investment for the safety of home and neighborhood water supplies. There are several types, but not all types are allowed in all municipalities. Check city ordinances to determine which you may use. Some must be installed after the valves; others may be installed before the valves. Some must be installed so that they are higher than any downstream element in the system. Some must be installed by a state certified installer. Check with your local water utility or irrigation professional.

A backflow preventer ensures that irrigation water isn't siphoned back into the potable water supply.

In cold-weather regions drain water from inground pipes at the end of the growing season to prevent damage from freezing. Use compressed air to blow out the remaining water.

Piping to the sprinkler heads comes next. These pipes should be buried deep enough to avoid freezing or they must be drained each winter to prevent bursting. Pipe size must be large enough to carry water to all sprinkler heads, maintaining sufficient pressure and flow volume for the last sprinkler to operate properly. Consult with a certified irrigation expert. Many irrigation supply companies provide free or inexpensive system designs for their customers purchasing the components.

Sprinkler heads are a good choice for large flat areas with no water runoff problems. These provide high application rates, so water is applied quickly. Sloping areas or areas where water runs off before wetting the soil benefit from rotor-type heads. Proper placement of sprinkler heads is extremely important to maximize system efficiency. In general space them so that water from one head overlaps the pattern from the adjacent head (head-to-head spacing). Match the water delivery rates from each head in an irrigation zone. For example, quarter-circle heads deliver one-fourth the amount of water in a given time as full-circle heads. This prevents uneven application of water. The sprinkler heads must be high enough above grass and other vegetation so that their water is not blocked or deflected. Risers and pop-up heads allow for proper clearance. Plan their placement to accommodate the growth of plants and grass.

The force of water shooting against the impact sprinkler head rotates the head in a circular direction.

Installing pop-up sprinkler heads in lawns helps avoid damage to the head from mowers.

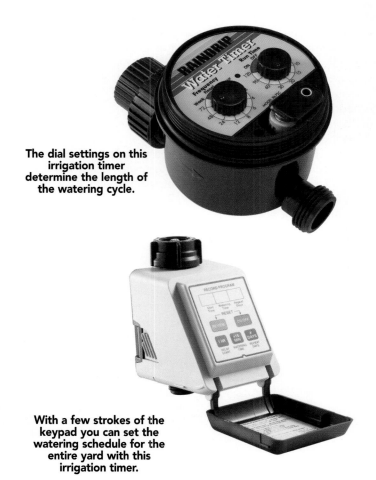

The dial settings on this irrigation timer determine the length of the watering cycle.

With a few strokes of the keypad you can set the watering schedule for the entire yard with this irrigation timer.

Timers or irrigation controllers are optional elements for the irrigation system. They allow you to program and automate the beginning and ending irrigation time for each zone in the system. Early morning irrigation results in less wind dispersal of droplets and less evaporative water loss because this is the time of least wind and coolest temperatures. Inspect the system frequently for broken or clogged spray heads and for even distribution of water by running the system manually to observe its operation. Although the system is automated, adjustments to it will be needed during the irrigation season. Compensate for natural precipitation, and make adjustments to the amount of water applied as plant water needs change with changing temperature and humidity. There are also rain sensors and soil moisture measurement devices to allow irrigation cycles to be skipped when it is raining or adequate moisture is available. Make this adjustment to ensure that water is not wasted.

DRIP IRRIGATION

Drip irrigation is a newer, more efficient form of irrigation. While sprinkler systems are high flow rate/high application rate systems, drip is a low volume/low application rate system of supplying water to the landscape. The basic components are similar to those for a sprinkler system: main shutoff valve, filter (important), pressure regulator (important), valves, and a pipe system to distribute water to the drip emitters.

Create a homemade drip irrigation system by poking small holes in the bottom of a five-gallon bucket. Place it near a tree or shrub, fill with water, and allow it to drain out.

Zip this drip irrigation bag around newly planted trees, fill it with water, and let the moisture slowly soak in.

This hose functions as a sprinkler when the openings are placed upright or as a drip system when placed facing down.

Water oozes through the small pores of this soaker hose.

Valves for low volume systems are different from those for sprinklers; they are designed to operate with lower pressure and flow rates. Using valves designed for sprinklers in low volume systems will often result in system failure because valves do not close at the end of an irrigation cycle. This wastes water and results in poor application of water in other parts of the system.

The distribution pipes may be of simpler materials because the pressure is lower, but proper installation is still important to prevent freeze damage and leaking at locations where pipes are joined together. A greater variety of methods of joining pipes exists. Some joints are glued joints, other use barbed compression fittings, and in others the spaghetti tubing is just pressed into a hole in a soft plastic (polyethylene) pipe.

Flexible polyethylene tubing, sometimes called funny pipe, allows sprinkler heads to bend, rather than break when accidentally bumped.

Schedule-40 PVC pipe is used for inground irrigation systems.

A shutoff valve inserted between the water supply and the distribution pipes allows you to easily repair your drip system.

1

To set up a drip irrigation system, begin by staking the distribution lines to the ground.

2

Punch holes in distribution pipe into which emitters will be set.

3

Insert an emitter coupling into the hole.

4

Pinch off the end of the distribution line. Open the end of the line to flush out the system if necessary.

5

Place individual emitters next to the plants you want to water. Here an emitter is being placed into a container of pansies.

The emitters through which the water is applied to the soil are extremely variable, with different types of emitters adapted to different uses. Simple soaker hoses may be used, but they rarely apply water uniformly. In-line drip hose have built-in drip emitters to regulate the amount of water at each orifice. The spacing of orifices must be appropriate for the plants being irrigated.

Other emitter systems use old spray system risers that are adapted by the addition of appropriate valves and upstream components and a distribution head attached to the top of the riser. This distribution head contains several drip emitters that may deliver different flow rates so that plants with differing water requirements may be irrigated by this system. This only varies the quantity of water, not frequency of irrigation, and does not replace the need for separate zones in the irrigation system.

Still another system uses lateral distribution lines into which smaller diameter (spaghetti) tubing is inserted with an emitter to regulate the rate of water delivery at the delivery end of the spaghetti tubing. The emitters may deliver the water drop by drop, or may be a small spray head that wets a larger area. This area is smaller than that wetted by a sprinkler spray head.

Before installing the emitters, flush any sediment from the lines. Sediment can quickly clog emitters. Most systems are designed to allow periodic flushing to help prevent future problems. Some emitters have a flow-through feature to allow flushing of sediment. It is also wise to place removable caps on the end of the distribution pipes to allow flushing the distribution lines as well.

In each of the drip irrigation systems the water is delivered only to the soil in the area of the absorbing roots of the plants being irrigated. Because drip are low flow rate systems, only small areas of soil surface are wetted, so spacing of emitters according to plant needs is important. Use of multiple emitters for shrubs and trees is important to ensure that water is available to the plant if one emitter becomes clogged.

A common error is to combine drip (low flow rate) and sprinkler (high flow rate) systems in the same zone, being controlled by a single valve. This usually results in under-irrigation of drip-irrigated plants in which water is delivered at a gallons-per-hour rate compared to the sprinkler system's gallons-per-minute rate.

XERISCAPE PRINCIPLES

Wise gardeners also apply the concepts of Xeriscaping to their landscapes. The concept of Xeriscape was developed to conserve water in times of drought and regions of limited availability of water by applying seven principles of good gardening practices to the landscape.

Planning and design that incorporates proper irrigation zones into the landscape creates zones for high water use that must be watered frequently, moderate water use that may be watered infrequently, and low water use that are irrigated only in times of drought. Irrigation zones for each system are included in the landscape. Limit high water zones and place them where they provide the maximum benefit to the landscape. Trees and shrubs are among the plants in a moderate water-use zone. Native plants and plants adapted to natural precipitation occupy the low water-use zone.

Use of mulch conserves water and benefits plants in the landscape in a number of ways.

Proper preparation of soil allows better root growth as well as better absorption of water. Addition of organic matter where needed improves the soil's water-holding capacity and provides nutrients to plants.

Use of appropriate turf areas reduces labor and chemical applications while allowing for turfgrasses appropriate to use and water availability in the landscape.

Efficient irrigation maximizes water-use efficiency and provides the best conditions for plant growth in the landscape.

Selection of appropriate plants requires that plants be sited in the appropriate water-use zone and that they be climatically adapted.

Appropriate maintenance of plants assures that plants are maintained in a manner that maximizes their health, reducing the need for applications of water to compensate for poor plant care.

Group plants of similar water needs for best plant performance and to avoid wasted water.

A soaker hose placed around hostas is an efficient way to keep these moisture-loving plants watered.

WATER HARVEST

A final consideration in landscape irrigation is maximizing efficiency of natural precipitation for the benefit of plants in the landscape. Water-harvesting technology collects water falling on structures and paved areas and directs that water to the appropriate parts of the landscape or into cisterns to hold the water for later use. Water falling on hard surfaces usually runs off your property and is unavailable for your plants to use. Water from rainfall is often of much higher quality, with lower mineral content, than water from wells. An additional benefit is that harvested water is "free" water and not purchased or obtained at the cost of drilling wells and pumping water from the depths. The cost for harvested water is the installation of the system to collect and direct water within the landscape. Water collected in cisterns can easily be distributed to the landscape through drip systems.

Collect rainwater and direct it to planting beds to make use of all the moisture that falls on your property.

FEEDING

Plants need nutrients to flourish and thrive. Plant food provides a steady supply of minerals for healthy growth and prolific flowering and fruiting.

DETERMINING PLANT FOOD NEEDS

Plants use the nutrients released from plant foods and organic matter to produce the carbohydrates, proteins, and other compounds that fuel all growth processes. Often your existing landscape soil doesn't provide enough of the nutrients plants need to thrive. Simply planting and watering your garden without feeding the plants leaves them lacking in what they need for best growth. Applying plant food to flowers, vegetables, fruits, trees and shrubs can make a tremendous difference in overall beauty, amount of bloom, and harvest. The important factors in determining which plant food is right for you and your garden are as follows:

■ the amount of nutrients needed by a specific plant (broccoli is a heavy feeder, for example).
■ the type of nutrients needed most by the plant (azaleas require plant food for acid-loving plants).
■ the measured levels of nutrients in your soil.
■ your level of involvement or time spent in the garden.

WHAT DO PLANTS NEED FOR OPTIMAL GROWTH?

Plants need oxygen, hydrogen, and carbon in large amounts. These are three nutrients gardeners don't need to provide to their plants as plant food because water and air supply these elements to plants. Plant nutrients are further divided into three groups:

Primary nutrients: Nitrogen (for leaf growth and dark green leaf color), phosphorous (for root growth and seed formation), and potassium (for vigor, disease and stress resistance, flavor and color) are the major nutrients needed by plants. After oxygen, hydrogen, and carbon, these are the nutrients that plants need in the greatest amounts. They are the nutrients most commonly included in plant foods.

Secondary nutrients: Calcium, magnesium, and sulfur are also needed in relatively large amounts by plants. Calcium and magnesium may be found in lime which raises soil pH, and sulfur is available as a component of many plant foods or as elemental sulfur or sulfate which lower soil pH.

Micronutrients: Boron, copper, chlorine, iron, manganese, zinc, and molybdenum are required by plants in very small quantities. They may be found in some plant foods.

HOW DO PLANTS GET WHAT THEY NEED?

The minerals in soil supply all of the 13 essential nutrients listed, except nitrogen and sulfur. Organic matter supplies all including nitrogen and sulfur. Plants take up nutrients from through their roots. The nutrients are attached to clay and organic matter particles and dissolved in the soil water as charged ions. A series of complex processes allows these nutrients to enter plant roots, where they are used as building blocks to drive and regulate plant growth.

Leaves can also directly absorb nutrients. This occurs mostly on the lower leaf surface where breathing pores, called stomata, are located. Nutrient uptake by this means is very efficient and is a good method for fertilizing seedlings in the spring or correcting a short-term nutrient deficiency. But it is impractical for delivering adequate levels of all nutrients to plants over a growing season.

IMPORTANCE OF SOIL TESTING

1

2

3

To get an accurate soil test, pull cores of soil 6–12 inches deep. Take random samples from throughout the growing area.

Mix the core samples in a clean container such as a bucket. Break up any clods and remove debris.

Label the sample with the name of the lawn or garden area from which the soil was taken.

Soil testing gives you an idea of your soil's nutrient status. More importantly, it tells you the pH. If soil is overly acid or alkaline, plants will not grow well. Soil tests are available at a relatively low cost. In many regions, the cooperative extension service offers the tests. If not they can provide you with names of private laboratories that will do the tests. Test the various sections of your landscape every 3–4 years. Problem areas may need to be tested more frequently.

SELECTING AND USING A SOIL-TESTING LABORATORY

Home soil test kits are available to gardeners, but they are not as accurate or complete as the analysis performed by land grant university and private soil-testing laboratories. Contact your local cooperative extension office for a list of approved soil-testing laboratories in your state.

A basic soil test is relatively inexpensive and measures levels of potassium, phosphorous, sulfur, magnesium, and calcium, as well as the soil pH. Some basic tests may include organic matter, cation exchange, and other nutrients. The lab will also issue a set of recommendations for feeding and liming.

You'll notice that nitrogen may not be included in soil test analyses. Nitrogen is a very mobile element in the soil and levels fluctuate based on soil temperature and moisture. Laboratories assume that all plants need a certain level of nitrogen each year and that it must come from

Home soil-testing kits provide rough estimates of soil pH and fertility needs.

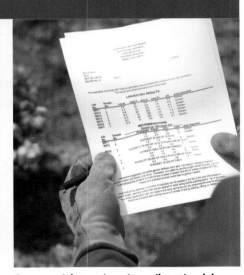

Commercial or university soil-testing labs send a detailed report of soil test results.

decomposing organic matter or supplemental plant foods. Nitrogen recommendations may be based on a combination of the organic matter level of the soil and the type of plant you plan to grow in the soil.

SOIL PH AND PLANT GROWTH

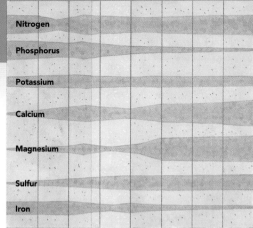

Most nutrients are readily available to plants in the pH range of 6.0–7.0.

Soil pH is a measurement of the hydrogen concentration in the soil solution. The pH scale ranges from 1 to 14. Soil with a pH of 7 is neutral; anything below 7 is considered acid and numbers above 7 mean that the soil is alkaline. The pH scale is logarithmic, which means that a soil with a pH of 5.0 is 10 times more acidic than a pH of 6.0.

Soil pH is important because it determines the availability of nutrients for plant uptake. The illustration at right shows most nutrients have greatest availability at a pH of 6.0–7.0. Of course, there are exceptions. Certain plants grow better in low pH soil (azaleas, blueberries) or high pH soil (alfalfa, beets). The microbial populations in the soil also are most active and abundant when the soil pH is 6.0–7.0. Plants may show symptoms of nutrient deficiency or toxicity at very high or low soil pH levels. For example, azaleas grown in high pH soil may show symptoms of iron deficiency (yellowing between leaf veins) in young leaves because iron is less available at the high pH.

Soil pH is determined by many factors, including the parent material from which the soil is derived, acid rain, additions of organic matter, and use of acidifying plant foods. In eastern North America, soils tend to become more acidic with time. In the West, soils are more likely to be alkaline.

RAISING SOIL PH WITH LIME

Excessively high soil pH puts plants under stress by limiting the availability of certain nutrients. You can easily correct low pH by adding lime to the soil. Lime is high in calcium and neutralizes acid soils. The calcium ions in lime replace hydrogen ions held by clay and organic matter particles. The hydrogen ions combine with hydroxyl ions (OH^-) to form water, resulting in an increase in soil pH. The process takes several months, so lime is best added in the fall.

Fine-textured soils high in clay require more limestone than coarse sandy soils to effect the same rise in soil pH. This is because clay soils have a much larger number of exchange sites that hold more of hydrogen ions. Till under or fork in liming materials applied to flower and vegetable garden beds. Spread or broadcast lime on tree and shrub beds at the recommended rate anytime the ground is not frozen. Rainfall will carry the lime down to the root zone.

Types of lime

Lime: There are two kinds of naturally occurring mined limestone: calcite (calcium carbonate) and dolomite (calcium carbonate and magnesium carbonate). Dolomitic is recommended when magnesium levels are low.

Agricultural limestone: A finely granulated calcitic limestone. The finer the grind or mesh size, the more readily it will act to raise soil pH. Powdered forms of lime are faster acting.

Hydrated lime: Also known as calcium hydroxide, produced by adding water to burnt lime. Quick acting. Need apply only 75 percent of calcitic recommendation.

Burnt lime: Calcium oxide, caustic. Produced by heating limestone to an extremely high temperature. Apply only 50 percent of calcitic recommendation. Will burn plant roots upon direct contact.

Pelletized lime: Similar to ground agricultural lime but easier to apply—also more expensive.

LOWERING SOIL PH WITH SULFUR

Excessively high soil pH can be just as harmful to plant growth as is low soil pH. Lower pH benefits plant growth in rhododendrons and other acid-loving plants (see page 573) and when soil pH creeps up over time in garden beds that receive large amounts of organic matter each year. Use elemental sulfur, sold as "flowers of sulfur" or microfine sulfur, to lower soil pH. At a pH above 6.0, iron sulfate lowers pH more quickly than elemental sulfur. Follow label directions or contact your local cooperative extension office for specific recommendations.

Aluminum sulfate is also available as an acidifying agent but should be avoided because aluminum can be toxic once the pH is lowered.

Use sulfur to lower the pH for acid-loving plants such as rhododendrons.

If your soil pH is too low, correct it by broadcasting lime to raise the pH.

TYPES
OF PLANT FOODS

There is a wide range of plant food products available to the home gardener. Products sold as plant foods are regulated by state departments of agriculture and must contain the advertised amounts of nutrients. Most plant foods are balanced; they supply nitrogen, phosphorous, and potassium (the element symbols are N-P-K, respectively). These nutrients are represented by the three numbers on the product label, and are always listed in the order of N-P-K. The numbers indicate the percentage by weight of each nutrient. For example, a 50-pound bag of a 5-10-10 plant food contains 2.5 pounds of nitrogen, 5 pounds of phosphorous, and 5 pounds of potassium. The other 37.5 pounds is a carrier or filler usually made from clay (similar to cat litter).

Plant foods come in a variety of forms—granules, powder, liquid, coated, and pelletized. Granular plant foods are easy to apply and popular with home gardeners. Water soluble powders are used to produce fast results.

CHEMICAL VS. ORGANIC

Organic plant foods differ from manufactured plant foods in their chemical makeup, nutrient content, release rate of nutrients, and affect on soil structure and biology. However, the nutrient elements released from both types of plant foods and taken up by plant roots are identical. A nitrate molecule (form of nitrogen) from an application of compost is identical to a nitrate molecule from a container of 24-8-16 plant food.

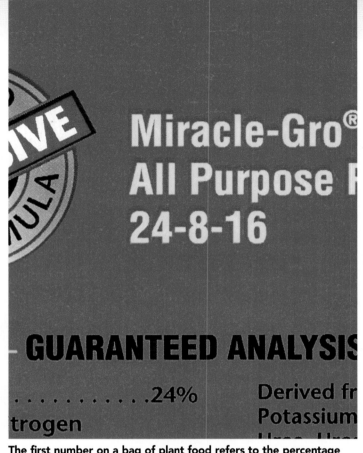

The first number on a bag of plant food refers to the percentage of nitrogen, the second to phosphorus, and the third to potassium.

COMPARISON OF ORGANIC AND MANUFACTURED PLANT FOODS

	Advantages	Disadvantages
Organic	Can produce compost at home and find local sources of farm manure, leaves, etc.	Manures and compost may contain difficult-to-control weed seeds
	Contains many different nutrients and other plant stimulants	Are more expensive to purchase per pound of nutrient than manufactured plant food
	Improve soil structure; feed microorganisms	Are bulky to transport and store
	Slow release of nutrients over extended period	Nutrient content is more variable; cannot easily determine release rate of nutrients
Manufactured	Less expensive per pound of nutrient	Usually contains no more than 3–4 nutrients
	Easy to store and use	May acidify the soil
	Can provide nutrients quickly to plants	
	Enable you to determine how much nutrient is being applied	
	Can buy plant foods with predictable release rates over various time frames	

Some examples of commercially available organic or natural fertilizers include rock phosphate (phosphorous), greensand (potassium), bone meal, fish emulsion, and seaweed extract. Blood meal, cottonseed meal, alfalfa meal, and composted chicken manure are examples of organic nitrogen sources. Compost and well-rotted manure are soil amendments and fertilizers. They improve soil structure and release many different nutrients. It's important to consider that only 5 percent or so of the nitrogen in compost will be available to plant roots in a given year. This may increase for aged farm manure, but the rest is locked up in organic form and will be slowly released in subsequent years.

Specialty plant foods: Starter plant foods formulated for seedlings and transplants are high in phosphorus to foster root establishment. Some are ready to use; others should be mixed with water. Follow label directions and apply the solution in the row at the base of each plant or spray it directly on foliage. Acidifying plant foods are sold for acid-loving plants and special plant food formulations are available for roses, bulbs, tomatoes, and many other specific types of plants.

Continuous feeding or instant feeding: Some plant foods can be absorbed immediately upon application. These are known as instant-feeding or highly soluble plant foods. They are useful when rapid results are desired. They come in liquid, powder, or crystal form and are applied to root zones or sprayed directly on foliage.

To reduce maintenance and cut down on the need for reapplications of plant food, inorganic continuous-feeding plant foods, such as Osmocote and sulfur-coated urea, make nutrients available in small amounts over an extended period. Either continuous-feeding or instant-feeding plant foods produce great results. The form to use depends on the amount of time you wish to spend caring for the garden.

CONTINUOUS-FEED PLANT FOODS

Continuous-feed plant foods have become increasingly popular with gardeners. By selecting plant foods with a continuous release over two, three or four months, you can match the feeding you provide your plants with the length of your growing season. Once-per-season feeding is a convenient way to save time yet provide the nutrients plants need.

Pelletized plant foods release their nutrients over several weeks or months.

Water soluble plant foods are easy to apply and are immediately available to plants.

Spread granular plant foods from shaker dispensers for easy, mess-free application.

Specialized formulations of plant food are available for plants such as African violets.

Acid-loving plants such as azaleas and camellias respond best to acid plant foods.

STORING PLANT FOOD

Store plant foods in containers or jars with tight-fitting lids to prevent caking. Plant foods absorb excess moisture in the air causing the plant food to harden.

FEEDING METHODS AND EQUIPMENT

Good health in plants depends on a continuous supply of available nutrients from the soil or, in the case of container plants, the growing media. Regular feeding with either instant water-soluble or continuous-release plant foods replaces nutrients leached by watering or taken up by plants, and will make a big difference in how well your plants grow and appear.

Once you've selected a plant food, calculate how much to apply, and determine when and how to apply it. Plant foods can be applied to the root zone, the soil surface, or to plant foliage. Use the method most convenient for you.

The best time to apply nutrients varies from plant to plant. Vegetables benefit from 2–3 plant food applications beginning at transplanting. Annual flowers need a constant supply of food all season long to keep them blooming profusely. Root system structure also varies between plants and has an affect on feeding techniques. Blackberry and raspberry plants have shallow root systems. Mixing granular plant food into the soil around the plants may physically damage the roots. Instead, use a water-soluble product.

FEEDING TIPS

■ Read and follow label directions on plant food products. Manufacturers provide recommendations for use that will give the best results for their product.

■ Use products with low risk of injury to plants. High-quality plant foods are unlikely to injure plants even if applied at rates greater than recommended levels.

■ When applying plant foods during hot, dry weather, water in the plant food, and keep plants actively growing by continuing to water regularly afterwards.

■ Mix granular plant foods into the top 4–6 inches of soil and apply water afterward if rain is not forecasted.

■ Brush plant food granules off foliage when broadcasting granular plant foods.

■ Feed trees and shrubs in the fall after leaf drop or during spring and summer when they are actively growing. In cold climates avoid feeding woody plants in late summer or early fall to prevent succulent late-season growth that doesn't harden off properly before winter.

SEE THE DIFFERENCE

Avoid making the mistake of starving your plants of needed nutrients. When plants receive the right amount of food, they will reward you with lush growth. Leaves will be larger and darker green; flowers will be more numerous and more colorful; and fruit and vegetable harvests will be more abundant. Use the proper amount of plant food for vigorous, healthy plants. Simply follow the label directions to know how much to apply.

Unfed petunias may grow and bloom, but plants will be smaller and flowers less prolific.

The same petunias fed regularly with a water-soluble plant food put on a spectacular display.

APPLICATION TECHNIQUES

The method of plant food application to use depends on the product you select and the type of growing situation plants are in. Use a hose-end feeder or watering can for instant feeding. Spread continuous feeding granules on the soil surface. For containers use a soil that contains nutrients to get plants going, then begin feeding with an instant feeding plant food every two weeks, or a continuous feeding plant food according to label directions. For individual plants sprinkle plant food around the plant according to label directions. For beds broadcast plant food throughout the bed prior to planting according to label directions.

Broadcast: Granular plant food can be applied with a drop spreader, rotary spreader, or by hand with a sprinkler applicator. Broadcasting is a good way to distribute plant food over a large area where it can either be left on the surface or tilled in. Lightly tilling in the plant food will make it more quickly available to plant roots.

Side-dress: Side-dressing means applying plant food alongside plants at critical times after planting, when additional nutrients are needed. An example is when the first tomato fruits develop.

Foliar: Soluble plant foods can be mixed with water and sprinkled on foliage from watering cans. There are also siphon devices that draw up liquid plant food from a container and mix it with the stream of water coming out of a hose. You can also spray liquid plant foods on plants with a small sprayer dedicated for that purpose. Many indoor gardeners use this technique.

Fertilizer stakes or tablets: Place these continuous-feeding formulations directly within the soil in the root zone. The stakes or tablets dissolve as you water the plant, and release their plant food over time directly where the roots are growing. Follow product directions for amount and frequency of application.

PRUNING AND TRAINING

Pruning can mean anything from removing buds or new growth with your fingertips to using a chain saw for removing large branches or trunks. When done properly, pruning is almost always beneficial to the plant.

PRUNING TOOLS

In the average landscape, it helps to have a variety of pruning tools. The right size tool makes the job easier. Large loppers are fine for large branches but can't get into the fine, dense growth of many plants where only one or two small twigs need removing. Instead use a hand pruning shears for tight work.

A landscape pruning set should contain, at a minimum, a sharp, small-bladed knife, pruning shears, a long-handled lopper, a pruning saw, a pair of gloves, and safety glasses.

SMALL-BLADE KNIVES

A folding knife, such as a pocketknife or a small, straight-blade knife with a sheath will work. The blade should be sharp. A dull knife will tear or crush plant tissue. Use a knife to remove small shoots or smooth frayed tissue around pruning cuts or areas of natural damage to the plant's stem.

PRUNING SHEARS

Pruning shears come in two basic styles: bypass or anvil. Either style of shears may have ratchet action for greater cutting force.

Bypass pruners, also called hook-and-blade pruners, or scissor-cut pruners, act like scissors. One handle has a slightly curved hook on the far end; the other handle has a blade. When the handles are squeezed together, the sharp blade passes close to the hook and makes a smooth scissor-like cut. Pruning shears are used to cut twigs or small branches less than ¼" in diameter. Make a close cut by placing the blade, not the hook, where the cut will be.

Anvil-cut pruners have a soft-metal plate, such as brass, at the far end of one handle. The other handle has a sharp blade. When the handles are squeezed together, the sharp blade passes through the twig and presses against the soft plate. This type of pruner crushes and bruises the tissue. An advantage of anvil-cut pruners is that they generally weigh less than other pruners of the same size.

Ratchet and compound, or mechanically enhanced, pruners come in both the bypass and anvil-cut styles. The mechanically enhanced mechanism enables a great amount of force to be exerted on the cutting area, with minimal force on the handles. Enhanced pruners increase cutting action with only a slight increase in weight. Manufacturers have made other ergonomic modifications to improve cutting ability and relieve stress on hands and joints. Ergonomic features of pruners include:

- handles attached at an angle to the blades
- soft, molded handle grips
- right- and left-hand models
- shock-absorber pads between the handles
- rotating handles, which spread effort over all five fingers
- smaller handles to accommodate smaller hands

Most pruning shears have replaceable parts. When purchasing pruning tools, save information found on the package, including make and model number as well as the manufacturer's address and telephone number. Handles and blades vary from one make and model to another. Correct information makes it easy to order replacement parts.

Specialty pruning shears, for removing difficult-to-reach twigs, have an overall length of four to six inches. A cut-and-hold feature allows you to retrieve the cut twig.

Pruning tools with nonstick coated blades cut through twigs easier than do uncoated blades and are less apt to collect sticky sap. Some blades have a built-in wire-cutting notch. Cutting wire with a regular blade can ruin the blade. The wire-cutting notch saves the blade for pruning tasks when working with wire in the landscape.

Pruners can spread disease to plant tissues. To eliminate this problem, at least one company has developed pruning shears that automatically spray disinfectant on the blades of the pruners and the surface being cut.

LONG-HANDLED LOPPERS

This lopping shears features telescoping handles (*right*) and a ratchet action on the head (*left*) for greater leverage.

Hardwood handles and a bypass head make quality lopping shears.

Composite handles with handgrips ease cutting action.

Loppers are larger than pruning shears and are used to cut through branches 1½" or less in diameter. Loppers are made in the same configurations as pruning shears: bypass, anvil, and mechanically enhanced. Handles are usually 16 to 36 inches long. Wooden handles are common, but metal and composite materials are also frequently used.

The manufacturer's maximum recommended branch size should not be exceeded when cutting a branch. Although larger branches will usually fit in the open jaws, trying to cut them may damage the loppers. Instead, use a pruning saw to remove such branches.

HEDGE SHEARS

Hedge shears have long handles and long blades; they resemble overgrown scissors. The cutting action of the blades is the same as scissors and is similar to a barber cutting hair. Because they cut multiple branches at the same time, hedge shears give a sculpted look to the shrub.

Powered hedge trimmers have an electric motor or a gasoline engine that forces a serrated blade to slide over a fixed, notched blade. Powered hedge trimmers are fast and easy to use. Electric trimmers are available in either corded or cordless models. Gas-powered shears are heavier and are usually justified only for trimming a large expanse of hedge. String trimmers often come with an attachment that converts them for trimming hedges.

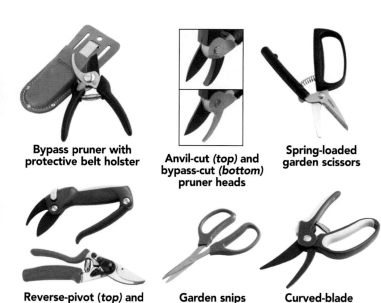

Bypass pruner with protective belt holster

Anvil-cut (*top*) and bypass-cut (*bottom*) pruner heads

Spring-loaded garden scissors

Reverse-pivot (*top*) and rotating-handle (*bottom*) ergonomic pruners

Garden snips

Curved-blade garden shears

PRUNING SAWS

Pruning saws come in a variety of shapes and sizes. When selecting a pruning saw, pick it up to make sure it is not too heavy and it fits your hands. Most pruning saws have teeth that point back toward the handle and cut only on the pull stroke, unlike carpentry saws that cut on the push stroke.

Small saws with a curved blade and a solid or folding handle are used on smaller limbs. The folding handle covers the teeth when the saw is not is use, protecting clothing and skin from accidental cuts.

Bow saws have an arched handle and a thin blade. They are lightweight and convenient to use except where branches are crowded tightly together.

Use large saws with coarse teeth on large limbs. Most large pruning saws have a D-shaped handle for easier gripping and are 15 inches long.

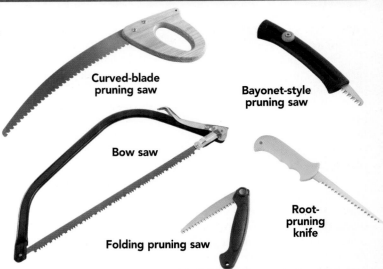

Curved-blade pruning saw

Bayonet-style pruning saw

Bow saw

Root-pruning knife

Folding pruning saw

POLE PRUNERS

Pole pruners have a metal hook and blade attached to a long pole. Place the hook around the branch you are removing. For most models, pulling a long rope attached to the blade cuts the branch. With a pole pruner you can prune high in a small tree while standing on the ground, or prune dense areas of a tree where a ladder would not fit. Pole pruners sometimes have a saw blade mounted on the pruning head. This blade cuts branches that are too large for

the hook and blade head. The handle on a pole pruner is usually made from fiberglass or wood rather than metal. This reduces the chance of electrocution if the pole pruner comes in contact with electrical wires.

Ropeless pole pruners are now available that eliminate ropes tangling in branches. The compound action of the pruning head, similar to that of other pruners, reduces the force required during cutting.

Lopping head on pole pruner

Pole pruner with saw attachment

CHAIN SAWS

Chain saws have a gasoline engine or an electric motor that powers a cutting chain. They are used to cut large limbs or tree trunks and are faster and less physically tiring than hand-pruning saws. However, they are heavier and pose more danger to the operator. A chain saw consists of a power unit, a chain bar, and a toothed cutting chain. An oiler is built into the unit to supply lubrication for the chain as it slides in a groove along the bar.

Battery-powered chain saw

Chain bars come in various lengths. The bar should be longer than the diameter of the material being cut. A 16-inch bar will easily cut a branch or tree trunk that is 15 inches or less in diameter. A 14- to 16-inch bar length is best for most home landscapes.

Follow the manufacturer's instruction book to minimize the danger involved in using a chain saw. Keep children and pets away from the area while sawing. Wear safety

glasses and hearing protection when using a gasoline-powered chain saw. When buying a saw select one with an automatic brake. The brake quickly stops the cutting action in an emergency.

Chain saws require adjustment to be safe and perform properly. Periodically check the cutting chain for proper adjustment. A loose chain can come off the bar, causing injury to the operator and damage to the saw. The operator's manual describes the steps needed for proper adjustment.

After using a chain saw, let it cool down, then wipe off accumulated sawdust and dirt. Avoid using soapy water. For gasoline-powered chain saws, periodically check the air filter and clean it if it is dirty. If the saw will be stored for several months or more, remove all fuel from the system. Fuel left in a stored engine turns gummy and can plug the carburetor.

TOOL MAINTENANCE

1 Disassemble shears.

2 Clean parts with soapy water.

3 Rinse parts with water, dry, and apply oil.

4 Reassemble parts and adjust for proper action.

When finished pruning for the day, clean the tools before putting them away. Sap, disinfectants, moisture, and plant debris cause rust to form on tools. Wash tools with a soapy water solution, rinse, and dry thoroughly. Wipe a thin film of lightweight lubricating oil on exposed metal parts to form a protective coating.

Sharpen the cutting blade with a file or whetstone.

Sharp blades on cutting tools make cuts easier and neater. Sharpen knife blades with a whetstone or knife-sharpening kit. Sharpen blades on pruning shears and loppers with a flat file. File with long strokes at the same angle as the blade was originally sharpened. Sharpen only the cutting blade, because neither the hook nor the anvil has any cutting ability. Take pruning saw blades to a professional sharpening service because the exact angle of the sharp teeth is critical. Chain saws require a round file to sharpen the cutting teeth. During equipment sharpening, always wear gloves and safety glasses.

Pruning tools work better when properly adjusted. If pruners tear plant tissue instead of cutting cleanly, the problem may involve a loose connecting bolt, dull or improperly sharpened blades, or a bent blade.

Over time the bolt holding together the two halves of pruners and loppers can loosen. This prevents bypass-type pruning shears and loppers from making a clean cut. Using a wrench, tighten the bolt slightly, until the hook and blade make good contact. If pruner handles are difficult to move, loosen the bolt a little. If the pruners still don't cut correctly, make sure the blade is sharp. After tightening and sharpening blades, check to be certain that the hook and blade make contact during the entire cutting action. If a gap exists, the hook or blade is probably bent. Straightening the hook and blade is difficult; it's time to buy a new set of pruners.

TIME OF PRUNING

Time of pruning is critical for flowering trees and shrubs. Pruning at the wrong time of year can result in little flowering that year.

Many trees and shrubs bloom in spring and develop flower buds on summer growth for the following spring. Heavily pruning these plants in late winter removes most of the flower buds, resulting in little or no flowering. Prune just after bloom in spring for the best flower display the following spring.

For trees or shrubs that bloom during late summer

SPRING-FLOWERING SHRUBS

1. Late winter: Leaf and flower buds are ready to grow.

2. Early spring: Flowers open and leaves begin to grow.

3. Late spring: Prune once flowers have faded.

4. Summer: Next year's flowers develop on new stems.

SUMMER-FLOWERING SHRUBS

1. Late winter: Leaf buds are ready to grow, but flower buds are not yet developed.

2. Early spring: Prune just before peak growth begins.

3. Late spring: Each cut yields new stems, each producing flower buds.

4. Summer: Flower clusters develop on new stems.

or early fall from buds formed on current season's growth, the best time to prune is late winter or spring.

Pruning in fall or midwinter leaves open wounds that lose moisture. Pruning cuts made during these times commonly cause dieback, resulting in more pruning in spring to remove the dead stubs. Pruning cuts made in spring, just before or during active growth, seal over quickly forming a callus, preventing moisture loss and dieback.

Always cut young shoots and branches just above a bud or a twig. Make the cut ¼ inch past the bud or twig. Cutting closer can damage the remaining bud; cutting farther out will leave a dead stub. Before cutting, observe the direction the bud is pointing. The bud produces a shoot that will turn into a branch; the bud points in the direction of the future branch. If the resulting branch will interfere with other branches, choose another bud for the location of the cut. If a shrub needs to fill a wide space, prune to buds or branches pointing outward. For shrubs that need to be narrower, prune to buds pointing toward the center of the plant.

PRUNING
SHADE TREES

Training young shade trees properly helps develop strong, healthy older trees. When you select a tree at the nursery, look for a straight trunk with well-placed branches. Avoid any tree with one-sided growth or sporadic branch placement. On young trees in the landscape, remove branches that are weak, dead, or rubbing, or have narrow crotches. Strong older branches develop from young branches with at least a 45-degree angle between the trunk and branch.

Prune older shade trees to remove dead, diseased, dying, or dangerous branches first. Next remove branches rubbing against other branches or structures. Finally, thin and shape. While pruning, occasionally step back and look to ensure the tree isn't becoming lopsided.

Avoid pruning any part of a tree within 10 feet of electrical lines, and avoid using a metal ladder or metal pole pruner near electrical lines.

Proper branch removal is critical to the health of the tree. A flush cut to the base of the branch used to be the accepted method of branch removal. More recent research shows that a flush cut causes damage and decay in the trunk. A better method of branch removal is called a collar cut. Most trees develop a collar, or swollen area, where the branch attaches to the trunk.

Make a smooth cut through the branch at the edge of the collar. Cut parallel to the outer edge of the collar. With a proper cut, a callus covers the wound in a short time. A callus is the way a plant repairs a damaged area and keeps disease and decay organisms from invading the exposed cut surface.

Some branches don't show a definite collar, and inexperienced gardeners may cut several inches farther out on the branch than they should. To avoid a dead branch stub, make a cut from the top of the branch where it attaches to the main stem or trunk, angling outward to the bottom of the branch. The proper angle is usually half that of the angle of branch attachment to the main stem.

Collar cuts callus over quickly and cause no trunk damage.

Flush cuts promote disease and decay in the trunk.

A 45-degree branch angle is much stronger than a narrower angle.

Shade trees with two leaders split easily in storms because of a weak crotch. Remove the weaker leader.

Remove lower branches for easy access to the areas under the tree.

REMOVING A LARGE BRANCH

1 To remove a large limb, cut upward about one-third of the way through the branch approximately six inches from the trunk.

2 Make the second cut downward, a few inches beyond the first cut, until the branch breaks back to the first cut.

3 Remove the remaining stub at the collar.

To avoid damaging the trunk when cutting a large branch from a tree, use a three-cut removal process. With just a single cut from above, the heavy weight of the branch can cause the trunk tissue below the branch to tear.

Make the first cut about six inches out from the collar. Cut upward approximately one-third of the way through the branch. Make a second cut from the top of the branch about six inches beyond the first cut. Cut downward until the weight of the branch causes the branch to break back to the first cut. Remove the remaining stub at the branch collar.

Exercise extreme caution while standing on a ladder to remove large branches. When a large branch falls the flexible small twigs at the tip of the branch usually hit the ground first. This can cause the branch to spring back into the air and knock the ladder out from under you. To prevent this, remove the large branch in short pieces rather than all at once. As an added safety measure, tie the top of the ladder to the tree trunk.

A topped tree develops bushy growth and weak branch attachment.

PRUNING
FRUIT TREES

The point where a young shoot arises from the trunk is where the older branch will be located many years later. As the tree grows in height, the location of the branches on the trunk stays the same. A branch four feet above the ground today will be the same height above the ground 10 years from now.

Train fruit trees grown in the landscape to an upright growth structure or central leader system to make mowing underneath them easier. In an orchard or in landscape beds a more open, spreading growth pattern will produce a greater quantity of fruit yet not interfere with maintenance.

Heavy fruit crops require thinning (removing immature fruit) to keep branches from splitting and sagging. Although propping up a fruit-laden branch will help keep it from permanently sagging, thinning the fruit is the preferred option. An average apple weighs half a pound. Twenty-five pounds or more of apples may develop on a branch during a good year. The heavy fruit load during the summer causes the branch to droop. The branch will only partially return to its original position after the harvest. Several years of heavy crops cause the branch to permanently droop and interfere with work under the tree. Once the branch has reached this point, it's best to remove it.

1 High branch attachment causes crowding of future growth.

2 Cut back the young trunk to force lower branching development.

3 Cut back the remaining side shoots, leaving two dormant buds on each.

TRAINING YOUNG FRUIT TREES

Apple: Apple trees come in several sizes. Dwarf trees are suitable for small yards; they grow 5 to 6 feet tall and have about a 6-foot spread. Dwarf apple trees remain small because of the dwarfing root system they are grafted onto, but the leaves and fruit are standard size. Their root systems may be weak, so the trunk may require extra support. Use stakes or fasten the tree to a trellis.

Columnar dwarf apple trees grow straight up with a single trunk and a few short, upright branches. These upright trees reach a height of 7 to 9 feet and work well on a patio. Fruit is produced on short, stubby twigs called spurs; no large branches form. Pruning the top of the tree forces more branching and a bushier tree. Plant columnar trees individually in large containers, such as halved whiskey barrels. If you decide to plant the trees in the ground, space them 2 feet apart.

Semidwarf trees are between one-half and three-quarters the size of a standard tree. Dwarf and semidwarf trees are usually trained to a pyramid shape with a central leader. These trees can also be trained to form a hedgerow: Plant several trees close together and allow them to grow with a central leader. When the trees reach the desired size, remove the leader in each tree. Staking or a trellis might be necessary for support when the trees are young.

Prune standard-size apple trees upright with the central leader left in place if the landscape is crowded. If space is not an issue, remove the central leader and use a scaffold branch structure. When the tree is young, select four or five well-placed branches for the tree's framework. Scaffold branches arise from the trunk several feet above the ground.

A scaffold branch structure makes tree maintenance and fruit harvest easier.

These branches should have a spiral arrangement evenly spaced around the trunk. As the tree matures, the scaffold branches form a wine-glass shape. Branches attached at a 45-degree angle have good strength and good fruit production. A strongly upright growing branch with a narrow angle of attachment bears less fruit than a more horizontal branch. Increase the angle of branch growth by placing a branch spreader between the trunk and branch.

Narrow branch angles produce weak attachments and less fruit than wider angles.

Gently spread the branch and insert the spreader to maintain the desired angle.

Make a branch spreader from a 6-inch-long piece of 1×2-inch wood. Cut a notch into each end. Where the branch attaches to the trunk, gently spread the crotch. When the crotch angle is slightly greater than 45 degrees, insert the spreader, with one notch into the trunk and the other into the branch. Leave the spreader in place during the growing season. An option is to make a spreader from plastic foam cups filled with concrete. When the concrete is still wet, embed the end of a clothes-hanger-size wire in the concrete. Once the concrete has hardened, remove the cup and bend the exposed end of the wire into a hook. The concrete forms a weight that is then hung on the branch to widen the crotch angle. Move the weight farther out on the branch if the crotch angle is too narrow. Place the weight closer to the trunk if less change in angle is desired.

When scaffold branches are established, remove the leader. The resulting tree has a more open structure. Sunlight reaches into the center of the tree producing more uniform fruit distribution and making harvest easier. Apples ripening in sunlight have a more intense color than those in shade. Pruning and other maintenance on the tree is easier because climbing a tall ladder isn't necessary.

Cherry: Little pruning is needed on tart cherry trees, only enough to maintain structure and shape. Sweet cherries grow into larger trees than tart cherries and require early shaping to develop a strong structure. Top the trees by removing the central leader after planting. Allow four scaffold branches to grow. The open center that results makes a shorter tree that is easier to care for. Birds eat cherries just before the fruit is ready for picking; bird netting to protect the fruit is easier to place over shorter trees.

Citrus: About two dozen citrus varieties are available in dwarf form. Prune standard trees to fit your needs. More fruit is produced on the lower two-thirds of the tree, so leave lower branches if fruit production is your goal. If you want to maintain a lawn under the tree, remove the lower branches. But use caution: Exposing the lower trunk to direct sunlight may cause sunburn, which can kill the bark and tree. Exposed trunks may be temporarily protected by wrapping with crepe tree wrap.

Peach: Genetic dwarf peach trees are suitable for planting in pots and growing on patios. They require little pruning and develop a bushlike growth. Standard trees are usually grown on a scaffold branch system similar to apples. Cut the trunk of a young tree back to 2–3 feet above the ground. Select four or five new shoots developing from the trunk as scaffold branches. Eliminate all other shoots sprouting from the trunk.

Pear: Asian pears and European pears are two types suitable for home gardens. Most pear varieties have strong vertical growth. Allow branches to grow naturally, but remove some of the branches to allow sun to penetrate into the tree and air to circulate among the branches. Depending on growth habit, prune the trees to either a central leader system or a scaffold branch arrangement. For the central leader system, keep the main leader and remove a few side branches to open up the space between branches. For a scaffold branch system, select four to six strong branches as main branches and remove other branches, including the leader. These main branches will grow upright, but the tree structure will not be as dense as it would be if all of the branches had been allowed to grow. Upright-growing pear trees resist attempts to make them more spreading even when they are young.

Plum: An open center system with three or four main scaffold branches is the preferred training system for plums. Japanese varieties are more vigorous and scaffold branches require pruning back more often than European varieties do.

PRUNING OLDER FRUIT TREES

On all fruit trees, remove dead, dying, or diseased wood, suckers, and water sprouts (vigorously growing upright shoots that produce little if any fruit). Next thin crowded growth and eliminate crossing and rubbing branches. Crossing branches usually develop into rubbing branches over time. Rubbing branches wear away bark at the point of contact, forming an open wound where insects and disease can enter the tree.

Apples, pears, and cherries produce short, stubby shoots (spurs) on their branches. Spurs contain the flower buds for

[Tree diagram with labels: Leader, Narrow crotch, Laterals, Scaffold, Watersprouts, Wide crotch, Sucker, Trunk]

next year's crop of fruit. Avoid removing spurs when pruning. Because these are small, twiggy-looking growths, many people remove them when pruning, then wonder why their trees don't flower the following spring.

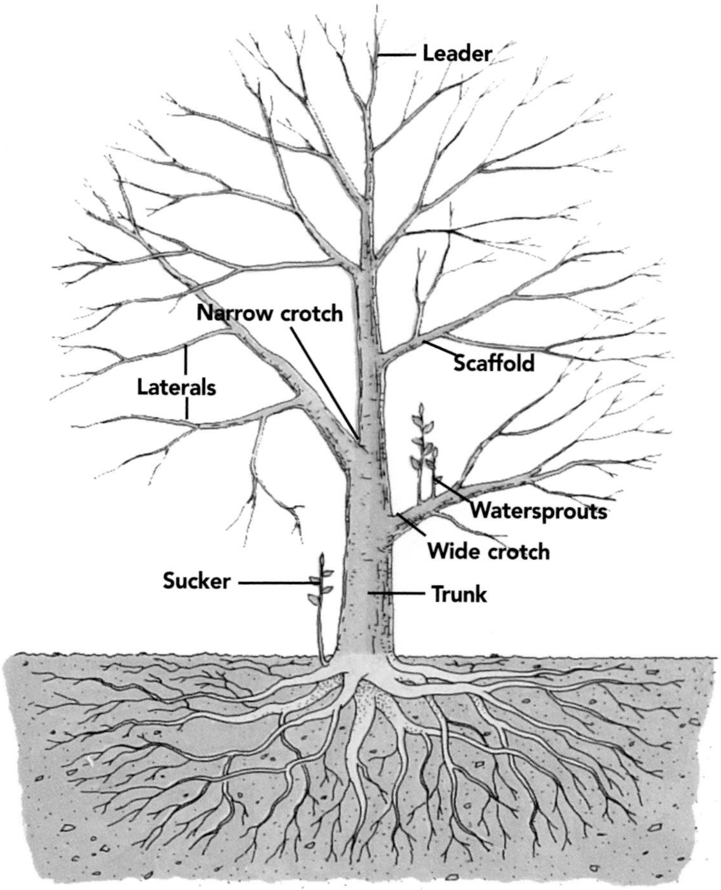

Late winter or early spring, just before growth starts, is one of the best times to prune deciduous fruit trees. The branch structure is easily seen because there are no leaves, and pruning cuts cover over with a callus when new growth begins. Twigs and branches pruned earlier in winter lose moisture from the cut surface, resulting in dieback. Dormant pruning removes some of the flower buds growing on twigs and branches. Fewer flowers in spring reduce the need for fruit thinning during the summer. At the same time it opens up the tree structure so sunlight penetration and air circulation is improved for the remaining flowers. During thinning, always remove branches where they join another branch and prune back twigs or shoots to a bud or to the place where they originate from the branch.

Apple: Mature standard apple trees reach 30 to 40 feet without pruning. The method of pruning to use depends on the form of the tree.

Prune an open-center tree, the most common style, to maintain a low, open shape. Remove any water sprouts arising from the top of the scaffold branches. Water sprouts fill in the center of the tree structure and add to tree height, both of which are undesirable. Remove hangers (downward-drooping branches) to leave about a 3-foot open vertical space between major limbs.

Upright-growing shoots are called water sprouts.

Remove water sprouts because they produce few fruits and interfere with normal branches.

Prune central-leader trees to remove competition for the main leader. Water sprouts and other upright-growing branches compete with the main leader. Most of the branches in a central-leader tree grow outward, but upward-growing water sprouts intersect with and interfere with the normal growth of the outward-growing shoots.

For either the open-center or central-leader tree, the object is to keep the total tree height less than 12 to 14 feet. A taller tree is difficult to maintain and harvest. If it is difficult to reach the top of the tree while standing close to the top of a ladder, the tree is too tall.

Remove suckers, which develop from the rootstock.

Prune back the tips of major branches on vigorously growing trees to promote side branching. Remove about half of the previous year's growth. Thin out interior growth to maintain good sunlight penetration for large size and good color of fruit.

Cherry: Prune mature sweet cherries only enough to maintain the desired height and to eliminate crowding in the center of the tree. Tart cherries require only occasional thinning to maintain shape and to keep them productive.

PRUNING MATURE FRUIT TREES

Citrus: Little pruning is necessary on mature citrus trees. Remove dead growth and prune the tree to a desired shape. Because most citrus are evergreen, pruning can take place at any time, but the best time is just after fruit production. Remove suckers anytime you notice them developing.

Properly pruned open-center peach trees are structurally sound and produce abundant fruit that is easy to harvest.

Peach: Prune peach trees more heavily than most fruit trees. Remove up to 50 percent of the previous season's growth each year. Remove weak growth first, then thin twigs and branches for uniform placement to avoid crowding.

Pear: Maintain ladder openings with regular pruning so it's easy to pick fruit. Remove half of the length on slow-growing shoots to induce vigor. Trees pruned to an open-center system will produce water sprouts that must be removed. Many varieties of pear are upright growing. Most of the fruit is produced toward the end of the branch. Long, closely spaced upright branches whip around in strong winds, knocking fruit off. Treetops can easily grow taller than a ladder can reach, and pruning to shorten top growth is an annual event. Use spreaders to train some upright branches to grow outward. Spreading the branches is a

difficult process, but it, along with removing many of the upright branches, enhances fruit production.

Plum: Prune mature European plum varieties only enough to maintain the desired height and spread of the tree. Thin the tops of plums every few years. Remove dead growth anytime you see it. Japanese plums are more vigorous than European varieties and require more pruning to maintain a desired shape. Head back the vigorous top growth of Japanese plums yearly.

Sanitation when pruning: Pruning tools can spread several plant diseases. Fire blight in apples and pears are two examples of diseases transmitted through pruning cuts. When pruning diseased trees, sterilize your pruning tools between cuts.

One of several products may be used for sterilizing tools. Rubbing alcohol placed in a spray bottle is one of the easiest to use. After making a cut, spray the blade with alcohol, then allow it to dry before making the next cut. If you drop the plastic bottle, it won't spill or break. Bleach solution (9 parts water to 1 part bleach) in an open container may also be used. Dip the pruner blade in the solution, then make the next cut. When bleach is used, tools must be rinsed with water at the end of the pruning day, dried thoroughly, and oiled to prevent corrosion.

Disinfect pruning tools between pruning each plant to prevent the spread of plant diseases.

PRUNING AND TRAINING FRUITING BUSHES

Brambles include raspberry, blackberry, and trailing dewberry. Cane growth is a two-year process. The first year, a nonfruiting vegetative cane (primocane) emerges from a root or plant crown. The second year the cane is called a floricane. A floricane flowers and produces fruit; the cane dies a short time later. To prevent crowding, which causes a lack of light and weak growth, and to reduce disease, prune canes at ground level after fruiting.

Raspberry and blackberry: There are many types of raspberries: summer-bearing red raspberries, summer-bearing yellow raspberries, fall-bearing red raspberries, fall-bearing yellow raspberries, summer-bearing black raspberries, and summer-bearing purple raspberries. The type of raspberry determines the way it is trained and pruned.

Summer-bearing raspberries produce a primocane the first year, followed by flowers and fruits in early summer of the second year. Fall-bearing raspberries produce flowers and fruits on the top part of the primocane in late summer of the first year, followed by flowering and fruiting on the lower part of the floricane in early summer of the second year of growth.

Raspberries and blackberries have vigorously growing primocanes. Support the canes with a trellis system, either temporary or permanent, to keep the tips from bending over and letting the fruit come in contact with the soil. Many forms of trellising are used; one of the simplest employs 8-foot-long posts set 2 feet in the ground every 15 to 20 feet along the plant row. Attach a set of heavy-gauge wires to the posts, placing one wire 3 feet above the ground and the other 2 feet higher. When the canes reach the wires, tie them loosely in place to maintain upright growth.

Remove fruited canes from raspberries soon after they have finished producing.

Prune summer-bearing red and yellow raspberries in the second spring, only removing any winterkilled cane tips and thinning dense growth. Remove old canes at ground level after fruiting. Take care to remove only the floricanes at that time and not the primocanes.

Remove fruited tips of fall-bearing raspberry canes after they have finished bearing.

Fall-bearing red raspberries produce a crop in late summer. To simplify pruning, cut off all shoots at ground level after the fruit is picked the first year. A simple method is to mow down the plants with a sharp-bladed lawn mower. The following growing season, new canes emerge and produce fruit at the end of summer. With this method, no pruning is necessary until fall. At that time, remove all the aboveground stems. If first-year shoots are allowed to grow for two years, a crop will be produced on the tips of canes the first year and a second crop on the lower part of the canes the second year. In this method, prune shoot tips following fall fruiting, and remove the entire cane the following summer after fruiting.

Cut or head back primocanes of erect-growing blackberries to 4 or 5 feet in midsummer. Heading develops a stout cane and promotes lateral branching with more fruit the following year. Less vigorous varieties will not reach the top wire and should be headed at 3 or 4 feet. In early spring, shorten the lateral branches to about 16 inches. After the floricanes have fruited, remove them.

Pinch cane tips of black and purple raspberries to develop stout canes and laterals.

Prune back excessively long purple or black raspberry canes in winter.

Grapes: Because grapevines naturally climb, train them to an arbor or a trellis. A fence also works as long as you can easily reach the vine for pruning and picking. A simple trellis called the Kniffen system is one method of support.

Erect the Kniffen system by placing stout posts at each end of the row where the grapevines are growing. Place the end posts deep enough in the ground (3 feet) so tension on the attached wires from the weight of vines and fruit won't move the posts. Fasten two 10-gauge wires to the end posts, one at 2½ feet and the other at 5 feet above the ground. Place line posts between the end posts at 8-foot intervals as needed.

After planting, select a vigorous shoot (cane) as the main trunk. Train the cane upward until it reaches the bottom wire or support. Select two vigorous shoots at the height of the lowest wire and remove all other shoots. Loosely tie the resulting canes to the wires to maintain horizontal growth. In late winter of the second year, prune the canes back to three or four buds at the bottom wire; if a cane has reached the top wire, do the same at that location. Early in the third spring, select two of the most vigorous canes at each wire and prune them back, leaving three or four buds on each. Remove all other canes on the plant. Spring pruning causes bleeding of sap from pruning cuts, but the bleeding causes no damage to the plant.

Through the third year, remove all flower buds or developing fruit clusters to keep energy directed into plant growth. Leave two main canes pointed in opposite directions on each wire in the fourth year of growth. Prune back these canes, leaving a dozen buds on each cane. Abundant fruit should be produced during the fourth growing season. Prune the plants in future years the same as in year four.

Gooseberries and currants: Gooseberries and red currants produce fruit on spurs of two- and three-year-old canes; black currants produce fruit on one-year-old shoots. Prune all currants and gooseberries in late winter or early spring before growth begins.

Remove canes of gooseberries and red currants four years old and older, because these canes are past fruit-bearing age. Leave ten to twelve main canes ranging in age from one to three years. For good sunlight penetration prune so the center of the plant is left open.

On black currants, maintain about a dozen canes with good one-year-old shoots, because this is where the fruit is produced. If a fruit crop of black currants is desired only every other year, a simple method of pruning is to cut the plants to ground level every other spring. New growth developing from the plant crown produces shoots the first year but no fruit. The second year, the shoots produced the previous season will be loaded with fruit. The following spring the canes may again be cut back to the ground.

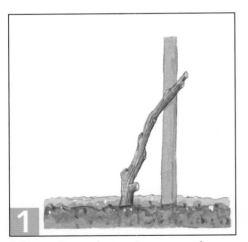

Select a vigorously growing cane as the main trunk.

Tie the trunk to a support to maintain upright growth.

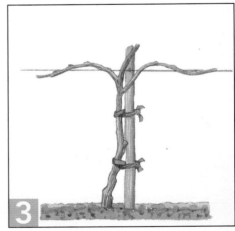

Select two main laterals for fruit production.

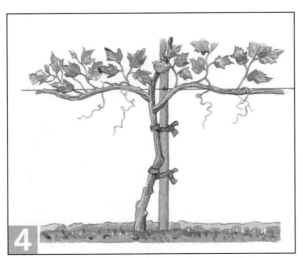

Laterals produce vigorous growth from each bud. Fruit is borne on these lateral shoots.

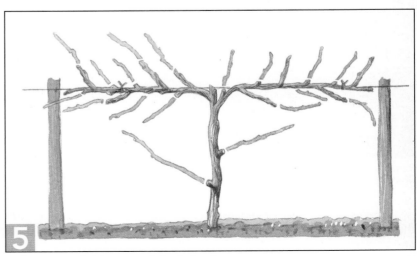

Each year, cut fruiting growth back, leaving replacement spurs for each spur removed.

PRUNING SHRUBS AND HEDGES

Start training shrubs and hedges when the plants are very young. If allowed to grow without pruning, the plants usually have sparse growth at the bottom.

Pruning back the top growth on young, multistemmed plants causes more branching closer to the plant base. Remove some top growth or entire branches each year to allow more light penetration into the plant, resulting in dense, spreading foliage at the bottom. An exception is a shrub grown in the shade of a large tree or building where the entire shrub doesn't get enough light and has weak, sparse growth. In that case, not much can be done to help the shrub become more dense.

Prune spring-flowering shrubs after blooming. If the shrub produces fruit valued by wildlife or the fruit has showy characteristics, prune after fruiting. Prune all other shrubs before active growth starts. Remove dead growth or storm-damaged growth whenever you see it.

Hedges: Train hedges to a broad base and narrower top. In areas of the country where snow falls, heavy snow accumulation on top of an improperly pruned hedge may cause stems to bend and break. A properly pruned hedge stands up well to a heavy snow load. A narrow-top hedge allows more light for bottom branches, resulting in more foliage lower on the plant.

Uniform shearing results in a formal look often seen in elegant gardens. Removing individual branches with pruning shears and loppers gives a more informal look. Trim a hedge several times during the growing season to maintain proper growth. As a general rule, remove half the length of new growth at each trimming on informal hedges.

Plants that can be developed into hedges range from citrus trees to Siberian elms (*Ulmus*). Select plants that naturally grow about as tall as the desired height of the finished hedge to keep pruning and shearing to a minimum.

Deciduous hedges grow quickly and require reshaping at least twice a season. Privet (*Ligustrum*) hedges often

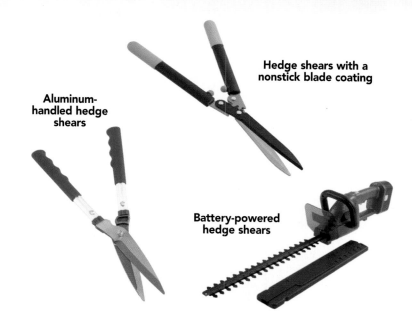

Aluminum-handled hedge shears

Hedge shears with a nonstick blade coating

Battery-powered hedge shears

need pruning several times a season depending on growing conditions. When pruning established hedges, look for the location of the previous cut, and prune back within about an inch of that cut.

Junipers can be pruned into a hedge if training starts while they are young. Many varieties of junipers grow dense foliage, causing the interior to die from lack of light. Pruning older untrained junipers into a hedge form exposes the dead areas. Unlike many deciduous shrubs, junipers and other coniferous evergreens won't send out new foliage in older areas of the plant where foliage isn't present, so they will not tolerate severe cutting back.

Older deciduous hedges and shrubs can be rejuvenated if they are larger than desired; see "Shrub Renewal and Rejuvenation Pruning" (page 68).

Improperly shaped hedges have sparse lower foliage and are prone to snow breakage.

Properly shaped hedges have a narrow, tapered top and a broad base with dense foliage.

PRUNING EVERGREENS

Remove select branches on yew to allow more light and air to penetrate the plant and to maintain a natural form.

Evergreens refer to woody or semiwoody plants that retain green foliage all year long. Evergreens can be divided into narrow-leaved and broadleaved categories. Narrow-leaved types include junipers, arborvitaes, pines, yews, firs, and spruces. Broadleaved types include evergreen magnolias, rhododendrons, mountain laurels, hollies, and leucothoe.

Cut back the new candle on pines by half to develop denser branching. Pruning or pinching on pines must be done before the new growth hardens. Otherwise new buds will not form.

Prune junipers and arborvitaes from spring to late summer. Pruning just before or during active growth is preferred because new foliage will hide the cut. Use hedge shears for formal pruning and a pruning shears or a sharp knife for informal pruning.

Prune spreading junipers in layers to allow more light to enter. Remove entire branches where they attach to the trunk. To keep spreading junipers from sprawling too much, trim back branches. Start pruning on these shrubs when they are very young to maintain shape and size; shaping an overgrown, out-of-control spreader is difficult.

Remove long juniper branches completely back to a main shoot to limit their spread.

Prune pines in late spring when the new shoots (candles) have elongated and the new needles are starting to elongate. Use fingers, a knife, or pruning shears to break out (pinch) part of the candle. Sticky sap in the new candles makes pinching a messy job. To remove sap from hands use alcohol or a commercial hand cleaner. Removing half of the length of a candle will make a more compact tree or shrub with a natural shape and dense foliage. If the pine is lopsided, pinch out the entire candle on the full side and none or only a little on the other side. Once symmetry has been restored in a few years, pinch all of the candles by the same amount.

Prune back branch tips of spruces to within ½ inch of a side bud. The side bud will produce a new lateral shoot.

Prune spruce trees for symmetry or to keep them in the desired growing space. Use pruning shears to prune back one-year-old growth. Prune the shoots to a lateral growth junction, where a side shoot connects to the shoot being pruned or to a bud on the main shoot. If pruning farther back on the branch, always make the cut to a lateral shoot.

Avoid cutting off the main leader of a spruce tree. Doing so disfigures the pyramidal shape of the tree. If the main leader breaks off in a wind storm, to return the tree to its normal shape, replace the upright leader. Take a piece of broomstick, dowel, or similar object and tie it to the stub at the top of the tree. Tie the stick so that half is below the cut and half extends above the cut. Select a vigorously growing shoot near the cut, gently bend it upright, and loosely tie it to the stick. After one growing season remove the stick. If left to nature, depending on the species of tree, multiple leaders may form or no leaders at all. Overcome these problems by selecting a lateral and training it to be the new leader.

Broadleaved evergreens require little if any pruning. Holly, pyracantha, and similar shrubs occasionally require some thinning of branches or heading back of shoots to maintain the desired shape and density. Remove dead, dying, or diseased wood. Thin crowded growth and eliminate crossing and rubbing branches. Removing old flowers on rhododendrons and similar flowering evergreen shrubs is about all the maintenance that is required. Use your fingers to remove the old flowers. Avoid using pruners because they damage new shoots emerging at the base of the old flowers.

Southern magnolias are large trees that need little pruning. Removing storm-damaged growth is about all the pruning they require.

1 Damaged leaders occur frequently on pines and spruces. Remove the damaged leader.

2 Train a side shoot to replace the leader. Multiple leaders develop if a single shoot is not selected as a replacement.

SHRUB RENEWAL AND REJUVENATION PRUNING

Regular pruning is necessary to keep many shrubs vigorous and to maintain a natural shape. Without regular pruning, most shrubs become overgrown with a canopy of foliage at the top and bare stems below. Flowering and fruiting are also reduced on old growth. Renewal pruning is a term used for removing several older stems from a shrub to induce new growth. Between one-quarter and one-third of the older stems are removed each year for three to four years.

Red-osier dogwood and yellow-twig dogwood respond well to renewal pruning. The brightly colored younger stems turn a dull gray as the bark ages. Renewal pruning stimulates new stem production and the attractive color is maintained.

Lilacs produce better blooms on young wood. Lilacs become tall and leggy if not regularly pruned. In areas with heavy winter snow, these shrubs are more prone to breakage than those with short young growth.

An old, overgrown shrub with bare branches at its base can be pruned to promote new growth to fill in the base and to encourage more profuse flowering. This lilac could be pruned back severely to stimulate development of vigorous new shoots that would bloom more profusely than the old wood.

1 Older, overgrown shrubs have limited new growth and poor bark color.

2 Remove ⅓ of the shoots to the ground to stimulate new growth.

3 After old shoots are removed, vigorous new ones will replace them.

Some shrubs such as butterfly bush become overgrown unless pruned severely each year.

Rejuvenation pruning is best done in late winter when plants are still dormant. Cut all shoots within six inches of ground level.

Within a few weeks rejuvenation pruning, vigorous new shoots will start to grow from the pruned stems.

Rejuvenation pruning is a term for removing all of the stems on overgrown shrubs. Many shrubs, including Japanese barberry and potentilla, respond well to this severe cutback. However, rejuvenation pruning can kill some types of shrubs. When in doubt use renewal pruning (removing only older stems) to determine whether the shrubs produce new shoots.

Use saws or loppers to remove older stems. Cut stems to within 6 inches of the ground. It is important to prune early in spring so new growth can mature during the summer. An exception is shrubs such as forsythia that bloom early in spring. Allow them to bloom, then cut them back when the blooms have withered. The time from cutting back the stems to the production of new shoots can last several weeks or months depending on the plant and the age of old stems.

Some shrubs that benefit from rejuvenation pruning are beautybush (*Kolkwitzia*), butterfly bush (*Buddleia*), bluebeard (*Caryopteris*), red-osier dogwood (*Cornus*), southern bush-honeysuckle (*Diervilla*), forsythia, hibiscus, honeysuckle (*Lonicera*), Annabelle hydrangea, coralberry (*Symphoricarpos*), lilac, mallow, potentilla, privet, St. Johnswort (*Hypericum*), spirea (except bridalwreath and other white-flowered types), and sumac (*Rhus*).

In warmer areas less severe pruning works for several shrubs. Cut back the following plants to 6 to 12 inches above the ground: abelia, azalea (*Rhododendron*), Burford holly (*Ilex*), camellia, crape myrtle (*Lagerstroemia*), privet (*Ligustrum*), and heavenly bamboo (*Nandina*).

Topping or heading back is not the same as renewal or rejuvenation pruning. If the tops of shrubs are pruned back, a flush of new growth results just below the cuts, but new shoots seldom develop at the bottom of the stems.

PRUNING ROSE PLANTS

There are many different types of rose plants. Even though roses are usually referred to as bushes, growth habits of these plants vary from shrubs to climbers. Pruning also varies depending on where the plants are grown. Roses grown in Florida, where freezing weather is rare, are pruned much differently than the same rose variety grown in areas with long, severe winters.

Different types of roses require specific pruning styles to produce good flowers. Rose types include shrub roses, polyanthas, miniatures, ramblers, large-flowered climbers, standard tree roses, and weeping tree roses. In addition the

Prune rose plants to maintain shape, vigor, and proper flowering. Make pruning cuts just above the point of leaf attachment to the stem.

American Rose Society lists 56 classes of rose, including China, damask, rambler, shrub, and species.

Most of the United States has winter temperatures that cause roses to go dormant. The southern part of the country has various degrees of winter dormancy ranging from none to slight.

Older rose stems are referred to as canes. On all rose varieties, remove dead, diseased, and damaged canes whenever you see them. With the exception of varieties where the hips (fleshy fruits) are left for their showy bright red appearance, remove all flower stems after the petals fall, a technique called deadheading. Below the flower there are three-leaflet, five-leaflet, and sometimes seven-leaflet leaves. Cut back flower stems to the second five-leaflet leaf below the flower.

The graft union is a swollen area from which the main canes arise. In grafted roses it is where the hybrid top (scion) is connected to the hardy rootstock. Remove suckers arising from below the graft union on the main trunk or arising from the soil, because these suckers grow from the rootstock rather than the hybrid top. Suckers usually produce inferior flowers. Exceptions are own-root roses, which are grown on their own rootstock rather than grafted to a different type of rootstock.

Cutting flowers for enjoyment indoors stimulates regrowth from the cut stem.

1 **Prune just above a 5-leaflet leaf with the angle of the cut sloping away from the leaf.**

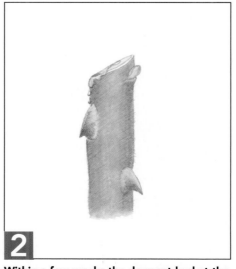

2 **Within a few weeks the dormant bud at the base of the old leaf will begin to swell.**

3 **A new shoot emerges from the bud and grows into a flower-producing stem.**

Prune back rose stems as described in the paragraph on pruning young stems and branches earlier in this chapter (page 55). Bypass pruning shears are the best style for pruning younger growth. Loppers and even a pruning saw may be necessary on older canes. Prune the canes back to outward-pointing buds so future growth will be directed outward, allowing more sunlight and air to reach the interior of the plant. Many rose diseases thrive in areas of the plant with low light and stagnant air.

Prune roses in late winter or early spring, just before active growth starts. In many parts of the country, this coincides with forsythia bushes flowering. Harsh winter conditions may cause cane ends to die back. As spring approaches, younger live canes will have a greenish color. Dead areas at the ends of the canes will be gray or straw colored. Prune back dead canes to just above a plump bud in a section of live growth.

Disbudding refers to removal of a flower bud or buds. Many species of roses look best if a single flower is produced on a long, strong stem. The plant usually produces several flower buds on each stem. To produce one large flower per stem, leave the largest flower bud and pinch out the young flower bud stems with your fingers. Pruning shears may be used, but in dense clusters of buds, exercise care so the main bud is not snipped accidently.

In colder areas of the country, apply heavy mulch over the lower part of the plant to protect the graft and the lower part of the canes. In spring, remove the mulch and inspect the canes. In some cases winter damage kills the canes down to the mulch cover. Remove dead areas of the canes.

Deadhead spent flowers to stimulate new growth and more flowering.

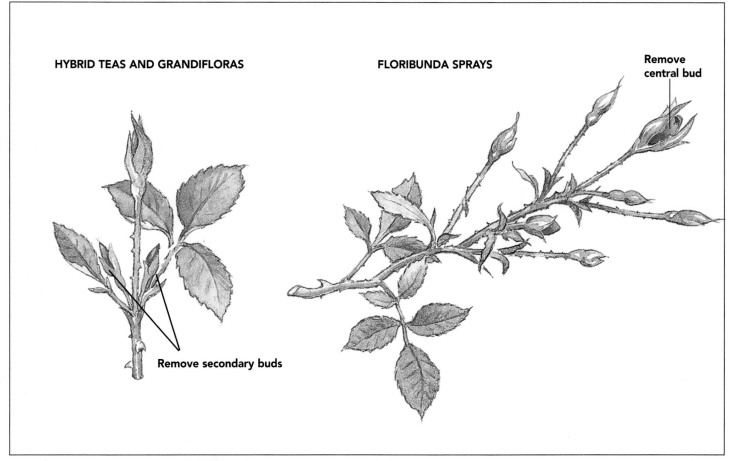

HYBRID TEAS AND GRANDIFLORAS

Remove secondary buds

FLORIBUNDA SPRAYS

Remove central bud

Disbudding techniques for roses vary depending on the type of rose. Remove the secondary buds of hybrid teas and grandifloras (left) to allow the main flower to develop. For floribundas (right), remove the central flower bud so that the secondary buds develop uniformly.

Hybrid teas and grandifloras: Flowers produced on hybrid tea plants are the same types that are carried in florist shops—one large flower on a long, disbudded stem. Grandifloras have flowers similar to the hybrid teas, but there are many flowers per stem.

To prune these types of roses, select three to six strong canes arising from the main stem. In colder areas of the

After pruning, a hybrid tea rose will have several strong, well-spaced canes that emerge from the bud union.

When pruning hybrid teas, remove suckers, pencil-thin stems, old, nonflowering wood, and dead stem tips. Prune to outward-pointing buds.

country, prune these back to 15 to 18 inches above the graft. Prune back dead canes to live tissue, or 3 feet high, in milder areas. Remove any small, twiggy growth.

In southern Florida, the winter months are when hybrid teas and grandifloras produce their best flowers. No severe pruning is necessary, but you may remove one-third of the top of hybrid tea roses to control height if they are getting too tall.

During the summer in the cooler parts of the country, pinch side flower buds from hybrid tea roses, leaving only terminal flowers. Pinch the terminal flower bud from grandifloras to make a more uniform cluster of flowers. In southern Florida, prune roses minimally during the summer months.

Ramblers and climbers: These roses bloom on canes that are one year or older. The easiest way to prune them is to remove dead canes, then remove the oldest canes, leaving five to seven canes on the plant. This type of pruning makes room for new canes but leaves adequate older growth for good flowering. Climbers flower best on horizontally growing canes, so prune and train to promote growth in that direction.

Miniatures: No special pruning is needed. Just remove old flowers and dead canes.

China roses: Because these roses produce thin growth, only a light pruning is necessary

wherever they are grown. Heavy pruning will shock the plant and reduce the amount of new growth.

Standard or tree roses: These roses are produced by budding a hybrid tea, grandiflora, or floribunda on the top of a tall rootstock. To produce a compact, rounded top with a good display of flowers, prune the canes back to 8 to 12 inches.

For specific pruning practices on other types of roses in your area, contact your local cooperative extension office.

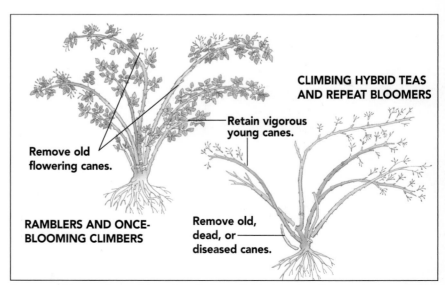

Prune ramblers and once-blooming climbers (*left*) after they flower. Remove old flowering canes, retaining four or five vigorous new canes. Prune climbing hybrid teas and repeat bloomers (*right*) while they are dormant. Remove old, weak, and dead canes, retaining three or four vigorous young shoots.

SPECIAL FORMS OF PRUNING

ESPALIER

Espaliered fruit trees soften stark walls and provide fruit production in otherwise unused space.

Privacy fences are good support for fruit trees. Avoid exposures that have bitter winter winds and intense winter sun.

For a limited growing space, the espaliered fruit tree offers an artistic way to break up a bleak wall or fence as well as produce edible fruit. The two-dimensional configuration allows the fruit to receive maximum sun, resulting in good color and size.

Apples and pears are the preferred espaliered fruit trees, but plums and cherries are also used. Ornamental plants such as camellia, crape myrtle, flowering plum, flowering quince, magnolia, and pyracantha work well. The main criteria for selection are plants that produce long, flexible shoots.

The plants must be trained from a very young age. Locate the espalier where direct sun won't shine on it in winter. This can break dormancy and cause freeze damage to the plant at night.

If wire is used to form the framework on a wall or fence, fasten eyebolts to the structure and string heavy-gauge wire between them. Loosely tie the shoots to the framework using twine, string, or strips of rubber. Check the ties for tightness every few weeks during the growing season. If the ties become too tight as the shoots grow in diameter, they can girdle and kill the shoots.

Do most structural pruning during the dormant period. During the growing season, bend and tie new shoots to follow the framework.

TOPIARY

Topiaries are suitable for areas from formal gardens to theme parks and zoos. Shapes range from a single elongated stem with a round top that looks like a lollipop to swans, elephants, and even cartoon characters.

Make a form from wire and bend it into the general shape you desire. Place the wire form over the young shrub and allow the shrub to grow around and through. Pinch back or shear shoots that reach too far beyond the form.

Maintain topiary shapes using metal frames and frequent pruning.

COPPICING AND POLLARDING

Coppicing is a pruning practice in which the tree is cut off a few inches above the ground. The resulting new shoots arising from the stump are vigorous and straight with few side branches. After several years, when they have reached the desired size, cut the pliable stems to make baskets or other woven wooden items.

Use pollarding for the same purpose as coppicing, but allow the main trunk of the tree to grow. Cut back the major branches so new shoots will develop from them.

Numerous shoots develop from a coppiced tree or shrub.

Pollarding is useful for the flexible branches produced as well as its artistic value.

PLEACHING

Pleaching involves intertwining and grafting branches to form fences, archways, benches, and other objects.

Pleaching can be used to form covered walkways. Two fencerows of trees are planted parallel about 6 feet apart. To form the canopy top, long, flexible shoots are arched between the two fencerows. Pruning is necessary to keep the walkway from becoming overgrown and bushy.

Pleached trees make an inviting covered walkway.

BONSAI

Training a bonsai takes many years; if properly cared for a bonsai will live for generations. Most small-leaved trees or shrubs such as fir, spruce, pine, yew, cotoneaster, and azalea make good subjects for bonsai.

Bonsai can be started from seeds, cuttings, young plants, or sometimes even older plants. Strangely shaped nursery-grown plants that are left over at the end of the season can make good bonsai. Nursery plants might already have some of the dead branch stubs, skinned places on the trunk, and other characteristics desirable in bonsai.

Careful root pruning and branch and foliage pruning keep normally full-size trees less than 3 feet tall. Over the centuries, many specialized tools have been developed for bonsai pruning. These tools have strange names compared to more familiar landscape pruners. The following are specialized bonsai pruning tools: concave branch cutter, utility bonsai shears, trimming scissors, bud and detail shears, knob cutter, bonsai cut paste, jinning pliers, branch bender, and graver.

Many bonsai resemble ancient seaside trees shaped by strong storms, or timberline trees battered by ice and blowing snow. To achieve these characteristics, special pruning techniques have been developed. Small-leaved trees are used so the leaf size appears in proportion to the small size of the tree. Narrow-leaved evergreens are also a favorite for training because the small-scale foliage appears in proportion to the tiny tree.

Creating a bonsai is much like painting a picture. A plan of action must be developed and many decisions must be made. The eventual size of the bonsai is one of the first decisions. Size categories have Japanese names. *Mame* are plants less than 6 inches in height. *Ko* range in size from 7 to 11 inches. *Chui* is considered a medium size and is 12 to 24 inches tall. The largest is *Dai*, with a range of 24 inches to more than 36 inches. In choosing a size, consider that the plant must be large enough to give the impression of old age yet small enough to be easily moved and worked with.

During the initial potting of the bonsai, remove soil from the roots and spread out the root system. Determine the position of the tree in the pot and prune back roots so they will not touch the sides of the container. Place the tree in the container, then add soil and firm it over the root system. If some of the roots will be exposed where they attach to the trunk to give a feeling of old age, gradually start the process by removing some soil at the first potting. If the tree is top-heavy and tends to fall over, place some rocks on the surface of the soil for stability. Sometimes the tree must be wired in place for stability.

Repot and root-prune as needed. Only when the roots touch the edge of the container is repotting necessary. For a young deciduous tree, this may be every two to three years, for older trees every five to six years. Conifers require less frequent repotting— every three to four years for young trees.

Remove the tree from the container and gently take away some of the outer soil from the root mass. Specialized root cutters work well for larger roots and pruning in soil; gritty soil dulls regular pruners. Prune back the roots so there will be a few inches of room between the root mass and the edge of the container. Replace the tree in the container and add fresh soil. Prune the top growth to keep in proportion to the smaller root mass.

Training a bonsai is an art form. The goal is to produce a mature-looking tree at a fraction of its normal size.

Pruning bonsai is micromanagement. Fingertips are the first tool to use in pruning. Carefully look at where new growth is developing; if it is not in a desired location, pinch it out. The more twigs and foliage a branch contains, the more diameter it produces. Allowing large amounts of foliage to grow on a thin branch increases the diameter. Once the branch reaches the desired diameter, reduce the foliage to match the rest of the tree.

If removing a larger branch, use concave branch cutters. They leave a small indented cut that reduces scar tissue. Coat the cut with bonsai cut paste; it contains a fungicide and an insecticide to enhance wound closure.

Prune larger bonsai using knob cutters to remove unsightly knobs from trunks and branches. You may find it helpful to place a piece of newspaper over a branch to block it from view before removing it. This gives a view of the tree as if the branch wasn't there. The best bonsai result from a clear vision of how the tree should look as it is trained. The vision of a shoreline tree that has been battered by storms usually includes some dead branches. In bonsai these dead branches are called Jin. Use a dull knife to scrape away bark and foliage on branches where Jin are desired. A dull knife will scrape off only the bark and won't cut the wood.

Training branches and shoots to a desired shape involves wiring as well as pruning. Copper or anodized aluminum wires are readily available and easy to bend into the desired shape. If the wire is too stiff or too shiny, annealing will make it more pliable and dull the bright finish. To anneal wire, heat it with a propane torch or flame from a gas stove.

Several sizes of wire are necessary to train different size branches and young shoots. Having wire from 6 gauge through 20 gauge is helpful. Use wire cutters to cut wire;

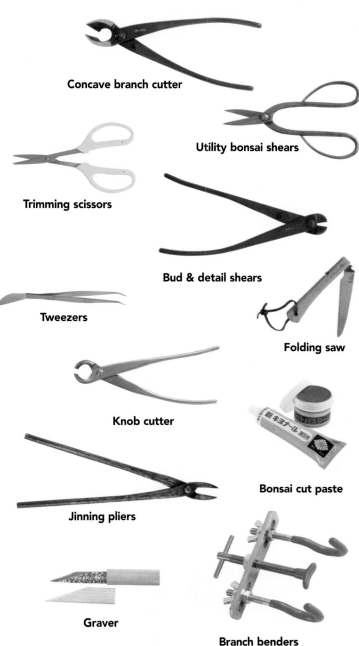

Concave branch cutter

Utility bonsai shears

Trimming scissors

Bud & detail shears

Tweezers

Folding saw

Knob cutter

Bonsai cut paste

Jinning pliers

Graver

Branch benders

Plants grown in the home as bonsai must be tropical or subtropical in origin. Ones from temperate zones require winter dormancy.

cutting it with pruning shears will ruin the shears. Larger branches require larger-size wire (smaller gauge number). Start by wrapping the wire around the trunk, then out onto the branch; wrapping just the branch is difficult. Without wrapping around the trunk to start, the angle of the branch to the trunk cannot be changed. Avoid crushing buds or small shoots under the wire. Gently bend the wire and branch to the desired shape. Leave the wire on during the growing season, or for at least three to four months. Train large, difficult-to-bend branches using a special branch-bending tool. Use tweezers for delicate work, such as removing evergreen needles or small buds.

Wrapping the wire around branches and trunks is not always necessary. If a branch needs only a gentle bend, bend a hook in each end of a wire, then hook one end around the branch and the other end to the pot or some other object. Or wrap a wire around a rock and bend a hook into the other end of the wire; place the hook around the branch and use the weight of the rock to bend the branch downward.

TRELLISING

Trellising is a form of training in which a plant is fastened to a structure to give support or shape. A trellis can be as simple as a wooden stake or as intricate as interwoven latticework.

A plant may be trained on a trellis to conserve space, increase light penetration in the plant, display the plant and flowers in an interesting way, improve air circulation, reduce disease, ease harvesting, or give support to a weak trunk.

Tomato plants are usually trained to grow in tomato cages rather than flat against a traditional trellis. These wire mesh cages keep the foliage and fruit from coming in contact with the soil, thus avoiding soil rots.

Because a trellised plant is trained to conform to the trellis, it is usually two dimensional, having only height and width. In crowded gardens, a trellis can be mounted on a wall or in a place where a normally bushy plant will not work.

Espaliered plants (see page 73) can be trained on a set of wires, a wooden latticework on a wall, a privacy fence, or a freestanding structure. Grapevines can be trained on an arbor, a fence, a pergola, or a wire trellis. A trellis or an arbor is a perfect way to display a climbing rose.

The construction of a trellis can be conventional or left to the imagination. Even an old swing set can be used as a trellis.

Trellises come in a variety of shapes and sizes. Here a bamboo trellis with vines trained on it provides screening and enhances privacy on this porch.

Wires or fencing can be attached to the ground and then, in the same A-frame style as the swing set, pulled over the top of the frame and attached to the ground on the other side. Plants can grow at the base of the wire on both sides of the A-frame structure. When climbing vining vegetables such as peas or beans are trained on such a trellis, the fruit or pods can be picked from the inside of the A-frame as well as the outside. Because most vines have tendrils that cling to objects, they don't need to be tied to the structure. Direct any vine that grows in the wrong direction to a wire where it will cling and grow.

Clematises cling to a trellis by twining around its support structure. They can also weave themselves through shrubs and other vines for support.

Vines on a trellis can be used to frame a destination. Here sweet autumn clematis complements 'Annabelle' hydrangea.

Vines that cling by tendrils may need some assistance at first to clasp their supporting trellis.

This grape is fastened to keep the cane in one spot and to prevent wind from whipping it.

For plants that have no clasping tendrils or twining shoots, attach the plants to the trellis with fasteners—simple strips of cloth tied around the plant and trellis, or plastic or metal clips especially designed to hold the plant to the trellis. The fastener must not be attached so tightly on the plant that it crushes, bruises, or strangles the growth. Fasteners that are loose when applied might be too tight within a few weeks as the stem grows in diameter. Material that stretches is preferred to rigid fasteners, but even stretchy materials can become too tight.

Many materials may be used as fasteners—twine, metal clips, or pieces of cloth. The fastener should cradle the stem gently to avoid damage to the plant.

Make sure the trellis is sturdy enough to hold up the plant and long-lasting enough that it doesn't rot or collapse while the plant is still growing. If the trellis will be anchored in the soil, the bottom of the trellis should be made from a rot-resistant material such as treated wood.

The usual approach is to plant a young plant at the base of the trellis, but some older plants such as silver lace vine can be transplanted to a trellis after they have been cut back severely to 6 to 8 inches above the ground and dug from their existing sites.

As trees or long-lasting perennials grow, train the stronger branches to the trellis and prune out the weaker ones. This forms a good, strong structure for the plant in future years.

STAKING

There are several reasons for staking plants. Those with weak trunks need staking to keep the trunks from bending and breaking. Some perennials need staking to keep the foliage and flowers upright. Tomatoes need staking to keep the foliage and fruit from coming in contact with the soil. Newly transplanted trees in windy areas need staking to keep the trees from being blown over.

Use a wood or metal stake placed near the trunk of a tree rose to provide the support it needs.

Staking offers support, keeping newly planted trees from blowing over in strong winds.

Tree roses usually need a stake to help support the crown of flowers and foliage. Tree roses grow for many years and need support the entire time. Tree roses usually come with a wooden stake fastened to the trunk. Over time the wooden stake rots at the soil line and the trunk can snap in the wind. Before the wooden stake rots, replace it with a metal stake.

Newly transplanted trees are often staked to keep strong winds from blowing them over. Once the roots have grown into the surrounding soil, staking is no longer necessary. Over the years many methods of staking trees have been touted, including fastening the tree so securely that little movement of the trunk can take place. Research shows that movement of the trunk is necessary to develop a strong trunk.

One method of staking involves placing three or more stakes, similar to tent stakes, a few feet out from the trunk. Evenly space the stakes in a circle with the tree trunk in the center of the circle. Fasten a cord or wire to each stake, then to the trunk where a branch attaches. The cord should be at about a 45-degree angle to the trunk. The problems with this method are that the diagonal cords are tripping hazards and cords fastened too tightly prevent movement of the trunk.

Another method of staking trees is to place two posts 6 to 8 feet tall about 2 feet out on opposite sides of the trunk. Place one post on the side from which the strongest winds blow. Place the second post directly opposite the first. Tightly fasten a cord or wire to each post about 4 feet above the ground. Loosely fasten a web strap, 2-inch-wide strip of fabric, or similar wide, soft material as a loop

Fasten guy wires to the trunk so the trunk can still move a few inches in any direction.

around the trunk at the same height as the wires or cords. Attach each cord or wire to a loop of material around the trunk. Use one loop for each wire. Once fastened, the trunk should be able to move several inches in any direction. This method of staking allows the trunk to move and develop strong trunk tissue but limits the movement so the tree is not uprooted in a storm.

Some perennials also need staking. When grown in ideal conditions, with plenty of water, fertilizer, and sunlight, perennials develop lush growth that is often soft rather than woody and contains a lot of moisture, which adds weight to the foliage. Staking bolsters the soft stems and helps support the lush foliage and flowers.

Cut off the tops of staking material below the expected mature height of the plant.

Crisscross twine between the stakes to form a support maze the plant will grow through.

Staking perennials can be as simple as inserting a piece of bamboo in the soil next to a weak stem and tying the stem to the stake. On plants with flower spikes, push the stakes into the soil, then cut the stakes so the top is below the bottom of the flowers. This supports the individual stems, yet the foliage hides the stakes. You can also surround the plant with several stakes and string twine or other material between them. Green bamboo stakes and green or beige twine are less noticeable than more brightly colored materials.

Place the stakes and string the twine before the plants get too large. As the plants grow up through the stake and twine maze, tuck stems and foliage inside. The support system is not visible if done correctly, and the plant growth looks natural.

Place a wire support cage over false indigo. As the plant grows through the cage, it will be held upright.

Small branches can be cut and used as staking material. Push the base of the branches into the soil next to the weak-stemmed plant. As long as the twiggy branches are shorter than the mature height of the plant, the foliage will hide the twigs.

When growing perennial flowers, it is best to stake the plant the first year if there is any doubt about the growth habit. If the plant is not staked and then flops over when it gets tall, it is too late to salvage the original look of the plant. The flattened plant stem may resemble a bent or collapsed soda straw.

Stake dahlias at planting. Staking later risks piercing a tuber as the stake is placed.

A wire tomato cage is effective for many bushy perennials, such as peonies, whose flower stems sprawl and can end up on the ground. Placing tomato cages over the young plant and tucking the foliage into the cage as the plant grows keeps the plant upright. During flowering, the tomato cage should not show above the flowers. If the plant needs support but does not grow as tall as a tomato cage, cut off some of the cage with wire or bolt cutters before inserting it in the ground.

When tying a stem to a stake, secure the string to the stake first, then make a loose loop around the stem. Avoid tying the stake and stem all in one loop. If the loop is too loose, it will slide down the stake and be of little use. If the loop is tight enough to stay up, it can easily crush the stem.

Tall varieties of dahlias need stakes put in place when the tubers are planted. A stake pushed into the soil after the dahlias are planted can pierce a tuber and damage it.

Tall, spiked plants such as delphinium often need staking to prevent wind and rain from knocking them down.

Place twigs used to support lilies or other tall plants so that the branches are hidden by foliage.

DEADHEADING

After blooming, the petals on flowers fade and wilt or fall off. In the natural process this happens after pollination. Seeds form and energy that otherwise would go into producing more flowers or plant growth is directed into the seeds. By removing the flowers after the petals fade but before seeds form, you can encourage some plants to produce more flowers. The term for removing the old flowers is deadheading.

Not all plants respond by continuing to bloom, and in some cases seed and fruit formation is desirable. Several rose varieties produce large, showy fruits called hips. Rose hips remain after the plants go dormant for the winter, adding color to the otherwise bare branches. Many annuals self-seed in the flower beds where they grow. Allowing some flowers to go to seed will produce a new crop of plants the following spring.

Deadheading makes flower beds more attractive. Old flower stalks projecting above healthy plants give an unkempt appearance to the garden. With a pair of sharp

Pinks and many other blooming plants will produce more flowers if the old ones are removed after they fade.

pruning shears, cut the old flower stalks back below the foliage canopy.

Roses are particular about deadheading. When you make a cut you're not only removing the old flower, but also determining the quality of the next flower the plant will produce on that cane. On the stem below the flower there are one or two three-leaflet leaves, and several five-leaflet leaves below those. When a newly planted rose starts to bloom, deadhead to build a vigorous plant. Foliage produces the energy used by the plant to increase growth. Cut the flower stem just below the flower and just above the first three-leaflet leaf, leaving as much foliage as possible on the plant. On an older rose plant, the object is to force the plant to produce a strong stem that will quickly rebloom. In this case cut the flower stem just above the second five-leaflet leaf.

When deadheading daffodils in spring after they bloom, remove the flower stalks to keep seeds from forming and to allow the foliage to produce food. Food reserves are stored in the bulb until the following spring. Cut the old flower stalk carefully so none of the leaves are removed. If the foliage is removed before it naturally withers, the bulb may not have enough stored food to produce flowers or foliage the following year.

Use a diagonal cut to deadhead rose stems at the second five- leaflet leaf.

Daylilies, irises, and many other plants produce flowers on tall stems. After flowering, the dead stems remain above the foliage. Deadheading gets rid of the brown stems so the foliage looks attractive.

Generalizing about deadheading plants is risky. Most bigleaf hydrangeas bloom on woody growth produced the previous year, whereas peegee hydrangeas produce flowers on new growth. Deadhead bigleaf varieties as soon as the flowers fade. Peegee varieties can be pruned almost to the ground in early spring and still produce large flower heads on new shoots. If most bigleaf varieties are pruned to the ground, they will not produce any flowers that year because one-year-old growth is necessary for flowering.

1

Removing old flowers diverts energy from seed production into new growth.

2

Pruning shears are necessary to deadhead woody flower stalks of hydrangea.

REASONS FOR MOWING AND TYPES OF MOWERS

A well-maintained lawn and landscape add value to a home.

In most developed areas of the world, groomed lawns are common. In the United States alone, about 63 million households have lawns. Lawns have many benefits. There is a large psychological benefit in having a green lawn in comparison to packed dirt or pavement in an area for relaxing. Just 25 square feet of green grass provides the oxygen requirements for one person for a day as grass plants convert carbon dioxide into oxygen. Gravel, asphalt paving, and concrete increase the amount of heat around a home, whereas grass provides natural cooling. The grassy lawn areas in front of eight average suburban houses is equivalent to the cooling capacity of approximately 70 tons of air-conditioning.

The practice of grooming grass areas has been around for centuries. Starting in Europe, then gradually coming to the United States, lawns were considered a sign of wealth.

Many theories have arisen about the start of manicured lawns. One theory concerns the keeping of livestock close to houses where the cows would be handy for milking and horses could easily be caught for work. Sheep grazed plants to within a fraction of an inch above the soil and were raised for mutton and wool. Wealthy landowners with many animals usually had well-grazed grassy areas. Later, large estates used sheep and deer to graze broad expanses of grass. Closer to the house, the landowners had workers walk in lines and use scythes to cut the grass.

In the United States, lawns did not become practical until the Industrial Revolution, and then they were still primarily grown by the wealthy. Homeowners with lawns had to be wealthy enough to hire workers to cut the grass with hand tools.

The first lawn mower was invented in England in 1830. Two people were required to operate the mower, one pushing and one pulling. Various companies produced mowers, including one that was pulled by a horse. In the 1890s gasoline-powered reel-type mowers as well as steam-powered mowers were developed. In 1902, a 42-inch-wide steam-powered mower weighing 1½ tons was marketed.

This rotary mower is self-propelled. It adjusts the pace of forward motion according to the pace of the operator.

This electric push mower comes with a bagger attachment for collecting clippings. Electric mowers are quiet in operation.

After World War I, innovations in technology made large-scale production of gasoline-powered mowers possible. In the 1920s and 1930s, millions of mowers were produced and sold to the public. The first electric-powered mower was produced in 1926.

Mower design has come a long way with the use of plastics, lightweight metals, and newer

A reel mower is an ecologically-friendly option for a small lawn.

Riding lawn mowers are a convenience for larger properties. This gasoline-powered model discharges clippings out the side of mowing deck.

engines. Lightweight mowers without wheels that hover on a cushion of air were developed in the 1960s. Recently mower designs have evolved still further. Some mowers do not need human operators to control them. They feature sensors that allow the mower to stay within a defined area yet avoid trees and other objects.

Modern mowers cut grass with one of two basic designs: a reel, or rotary blades. Reel mowers have several blades mounted in a cylindrical arrangement. The blades

rotate with the cylinder; as they pass the bed knife, a scissor-type action cuts the grass blades. Reel mowers are available in five-, seven-, or ten-blade models. Five-blade models are used on upright-growing-grass areas. Seven-blade models are usually used on warm-climate grasses such as zoysiagrass and Bermudagrass. Ten-bladed models work well on home putting greens, where they cut bentgrass at less than ⁵⁄₁₆ inch.

Rotary mowers have a horizontally spinning blade or, in some cases, a heavy-duty cord. The mower blade cuts the lawn when the sharp, fast-spinning blade impacts the grass. Heavy-duty string trimmers on wheels have cords mounted to a head where the rotary blade would usually be. These mowers work best in weedy areas and where a blade might be damaged. Brush-cutting blades are available for some models for cutting sapling trees and other material that is too heavy for the cord to cut.

Lawn mowers range from hand-propelled, push-type reel mowers (used on small lawns) to large riding mowers. The size of the lawn area dictates the type of mower to use. Large lawn areas may be mowed using a garden tractor or larger tractor pulling a group of reel mowers (gang mowers) behind. Unless the lawn area consists of many acres, a riding mower with rotary blades mounted underneath works well. Gasoline or electric-powered reel or rotary mowers are best for intermediate-size lawns.

Some riding mowers are designed for turning in tight spaces. This model has a zero-turn radius.

Mower accessories and options vary depending on the manufacturer. Some reel-type mowers have grass catchers mounted in the front, others in the back. Some riding mowers have grass-bagging attachments; some even have indicators to show when the bagger is full. Rotary mowers are available with side discharge, back discharge, bagging, and mulching options. Mulching mowers have specially designed blades or a mower deck that finely cuts the grass clippings and forces them into the turf.

Trimming grass around trees, shrubs, walkways, and other objects requires different equipment. A simple pair of grass shears will usually take care of the trimming, but they can be hard on hands and require stooping or getting on hands and knees. New tools have been designed to relieve the physical stress. Even modifications of the basic grass shears make trimming easier. Grass trimmers with an

extended handle allow the operator to stand while working the trimmer blades. Battery-operated grass trimmers relieve stress on fingers and hands, because only a trigger needs to be squeezed to operate the cutting action.

String trimmers use a material similar to monofilament fishing line to cut grass and weeds. The trimmers are powered by either gasoline or electricity and have a long tube with a rotating driveshaft connecting the power unit to the trimmer head. String trimmers can be used while standing upright; the flexible cord used to cut plant material

Rotary edger   **Edger**

Pivoting grass shears   **Grass shears**

allows trimming close to fence posts and other objects. Care is necessary in trimming around plant stems or tree trunks, the fast-spinning cord has enough force to bruise or remove tree bark. The string-trimmer head can be detached from the power unit on some brands of string trimmers and replaced with other attachments such as a tiller or brush cutter.

Power edgers are available to trim grass that creeps onto sidewalks, driveways, curbs, patios, and other growing areas. Gasoline- or electric-powered units have a vertically mounted metal blade, similar to a small rotary mower blade, that spins and cuts the grass at the edge of the paving. Some models have an adjustable cutting head, allowing the blade to be rotated to a horizontal position to trim close to retaining walls or other upright objects.

Manually propelled edgers have a rubber drive wheel that turns a cutting disk. More muscle power is needed to operate these, because there is no motor involved and downward pressure is exerted to give good contact between the drive wheel and the sidewalk. Another edging tool consists of a blade on a long handle. The blade is forced into the area where the walkway meets the turf, cutting the grass that is growing over the boundary.

CARE OF MOWING EQUIPMENT

1 Remove the spark-plug wire to prevent accidental starting.

2 Block the blade with wood and a C-clamp to keep the blade from turning.

3 Remove the blade with a wrench.

4 Scrape dried clippings from the underside of the mower deck after removing the blade.

Proper maintenance of mowing equipment is important for safety as well as prolonging life of the equipment. Dull mower blades take a long time to mow an area because the dull blades tear the grass instead of cutting it. Shredded ends on grass blades turn brown. After mowing with a dull blade, the lawn has a brownish cast instead of a vibrant green color. The damaged tissue is also an open pathway for disease organisms to enter the grass plants.

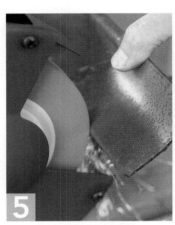

5 Use a hand file or power grinder to sharpen the blade.

6 Check the blade balance by placing a screwdriver through the center hole in the blade.

Sharpening a rotary mower blade is a simple job requiring only a few tools: an adjustable wrench or a box-end wrench, a wire brush, a putty knife, a 6-inch-long piece of 2×4 lumber, a C-clamp, and a flat file.

The mower can be turned on its side if it has a two-stroke-cycle engine (oil is mixed with the gasoline) or an electric motor. If the mower has an engine with oil in the crankcase, it is better to place the mower on two sawhorses so the blade can be removed from below without turning the mower on its side. Be careful if the mower is up on sawhorses that it doesn't slip and fall. Oil in lawn mower engines should be changed after 20 hours of operation. If it is time to change the oil as well as sharpen the blade, drain the oil from the engine before sharpening the blade. Rotary mower blades should be sharpened after about every 10 hours of use, although operating conditions may require more frequent sharpening. Mowing sparse turf growing in sandy soil causes the blade to dull quickly.

Pull the spark-plug wire off the spark plug on gasoline engines. This prevents accidentally starting the engine if the blade is turned. On electric mowers, be sure the power cord is unplugged. Periodically clean and gap the spark plug for best performance. Remove the spark plug from the engine. This might require a socket and socket wrench or a spark-plug wrench. Look at the part of the spark plug that was inside the engine. A whitish coating on this part of the plug is normal. If there is a dark, oily coating, have a professional examine the mower. Check the opening or gap between the side electrode (piece of metal extending to the center from the side of the plug) and the center electrode, in the middle of the plug. The owner's manual for the mower should list the correct gap between the two electrodes. Clean any ash deposit from the plug, set the gap to the specified opening, and place the plug back in the engine after the blade is sharpened.

To prevent the blade from turning while removing the bolt from the engine crankshaft, secure a 6-inch piece of 2×4 lumber inside the mower deck using a C-clamp.

Once the blade is removed, use a putty knife to scrape the underside of the deck to remove caked-on dirt and dead grass. Use a wire brush to remove debris from the blade. Closely inspect the blade to see whether there are cracks in the metal or the blade is bent. In either case, replace the blade.

To sharpen the blade, clamp the center of the blade securely in a vise with the blade ends exposed. Wearing gloves, use long strokes of a file to sharpen the cutting edge at the same angle as it was before. If that angle can not be determined, sharpen it to a 45-degree angle. Remove the same amount of metal from each end of the blade. Removing more metal from one end than the other results in an unbalanced blade that can damage the engine. Avoid sharpening the blade any farther toward the center than it was originally sharpened. At the speed the blade is turning when the mower is operating, only about an inch on each end of the blade actually cuts the grass.

A bench grinder, portable drill with a grinding wheel, or other grinding device can also be used to sharpen rotary mower blades.

Before replacing the blade on a mower, check it for balance. For an accurate check, use an inexpensive cone-style blade balance. Set the blade on the cone. If one end tilts downward, it is heavier than the other and needs to have more metal removed. Remove metal until the blade sits level on the balance. A simple but less accurate balance can be made with a screwdriver or metal washer and a piece of string. Tie the string through the hole in the washer and thread the string through the hole in the blade. Hold the string and position the washer perpendicular to the direction of the blade. With the washer on edge in the center of the hole in the blade, observe whether one end is heavier than the other. Once the blade is balanced, reattach the blade to the mower.

Reel mowers are more difficult to sharpen than rotary blades and usually need to be sharpened by a professional. Reel mower blades stay sharp longer than rotary blades because of the metal-to-metal contact of the reel blades with the bed knife. This close contact is also the reason why precision sharpening is necessary.

String trimmers with a gasoline engine require periodic maintenance. Clean and gap the spark plug as on a mower. Lubricate the flexible driveshaft following the manufacturer's directions. Use a wire brush to remove debris that becomes caked on the trimmer shield.

Clean air is important to any gasoline engine. Mowers and string trimmers operate in dirty environments, and the air filters—either paper or foam—frequently become clogged with dirt and debris. Paper filters should be held up to a strong light source. If light is seen through the filter, it is

probably okay to use; if you see no light or if you observe any holes, replace the filter. Some paper air filters have a foam prefilter that fits over the paper element. Remove the foam from the paper element and wash in soapy water. Rinse the foam in clean water and let it dry. Replace the foam over the paper element when dry. Clean foam air filter elements when they become dirty. Remove the filter and wash it in warm, soapy water to remove oil, dirt, and other debris. Inspect the filter for deterioration or holes, and replace the filter if any are seen. Dry the foam element, then add about a teaspoon of engine oil to the element. Squeeze out any excess oil, then reattach the filter on the engine. The oil film traps debris particles that are small enough to pass through the pores in the filter and could damage the engine. Avoid running the engine without an air filter because any material that enters the engine with the air can cause the engine to wear out prematurely.

Avoid storing gasoline engines with fuel in the system for long periods. Gasoline degrades over time and causes carburetor parts to plug and stick. Costly repairs are usually necessary to correct the damage. Either drain all the fuel from the system or add a gasoline stabilizer to the fuel in the tank to prevent this problem.

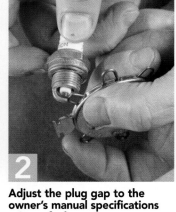

1 Use a socket or spark plug wrench to remove the spark plug.

2 Adjust the plug gap to the owner's manual specifications using a feeler gauge.

3 Place a few drops of oil in the cylinder before replacing the spark plug.

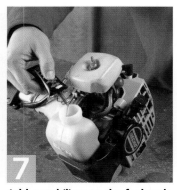

4 Clean foam or paper air cleaner elements as directed in the owner's manual.

5 Clean the air cleaner cover before installing the cleaning element.

6 Remove dead, caked-on grass and dirt from the cutting shield with a stiff brush.

7 Add a stabilizer to the fuel tank if the trimmer will be stored.

HEIGHT OF MOWING

Turn off the mower before adjusting wheel height. Adjust all wheels equally to ensure an even cut.

Become familiar with the mower adjustments. Always follow the owner's manual instructions.

levers on each wheel that are adjusted, or a handle that adjusts all four wheels at the same time.

Adjusting the mowing height on reel-type mowers involves raising or lowering the roller behind the blades. Some mowers have nuts and bolts that must be loosened, then retightened; others have fast adjustment levers. Follow the manufacturer's instructions for the best adjustment.

Proper adjustment of the cutting height helps prevent scalping the lawn. Scalping occurs when the mower on a low height setting runs over an uneven place in the lawn. The blades cut low enough to remove most or all of the grass and may even dig into the soil. Scalping damages the grass and dulls the mower blades.

Change the direction of mowing every few times the lawn is mowed. Mowing in the same direction every time causes the grass to bend and grow in that direction. Altering the mowing direction causes the grass blades to grow more upright and give a more even appearance to the lawn.

No more than one-third of the grass blade should be removed at each mowing. If the grass has grown extremely tall, mow off one-third of the existing blade, then go back a few days later and remove more of the blade. Some grass varieties may require mowing several times a week, whereas others might grow for more than a week with no need for mowing.

Uneven soil or low mower height can cause scalping.

A properly mowed lawn is healthy and visually appealing. Uncut grass can mat and become unattractive.

Cutting the lawn at a specific height is important for the health of the grass plants as well as the appearance of the lawn. In most areas of the country, mow the lawn at a higher level in the hotter summer period and lower in cooler seasons.

Most grass plants respond to a long leaf length by growing a longer, deeper root system. In hot weather the longer leaf blades help shade the crowns, or growing points, of the plants from sun damage. Longer roots bring in more moisture. In cooler seasons the grass blades can be cut shorter, because the sun is less intense, and the plants do not require as much moisture.

Adjust the mower during the mowing season to provide the best plant growth. Some rotary-type mowers have a bolt and nut attaching the wheel to the mower deck in a series of holes. Adjusting these involves removing the nut and placing the bolt in the proper hole for the desired cutting height. Replace the nut and tighten securely. Doing this the same amount on all four wheels keeps the blade level and results in an attractive cut. Some rotary mowers have simple

WHEN TO MOW

Wet grass clippings clump together, making discharge from the mower difficult. Wet clippings plaster against the underside of the deck on rotary mowers and unless they are removed after mowing they accumulate, harden and prevent proper mower operation. Wet grass clippings can cause rust on the underside of the deck and until dry, they are a breeding ground for small gnats.

Clumps of wet clippings on the lawn shade and suffocate living grass plants. Light raking with a leaf rake will distribute and dry the clippings. If large clumps of clippings are present, you may want to entirely remove them from the lawn.

Using heavyweight riding mowers in wet areas can cause compaction of clay-based soils. Compacted soils may kill grass roots and limit water infiltration and air spaces in the soil.

Avoid mowing grass when conditions are wet. Saturated soil compacts easily, and wet grass blades mat and clump together.

GRASS GROWTH CHART

Maintaining the proper mowing heights for your turf is essential to the health of your lawn. Each variety has a recommended minimum and maximum height. Set your mower at the maximum height during the dry summer months and minimum height during the cooler off-season or leave it at the higher setting all year.

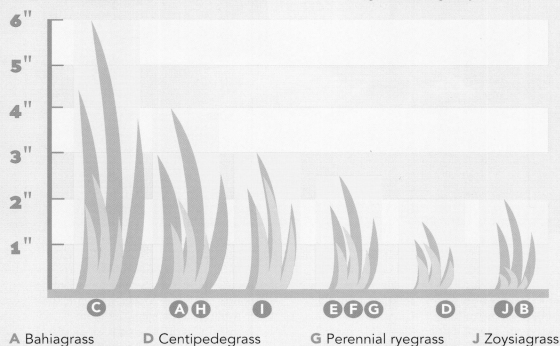

A Bahiagrass
B Bermudagrass
C Buffalograss

D Centipedegrass
E Fine fescue
F Kentucky bluegrass

G Perennial ryegrass
H St. Augustinegrass
I Tall fescue

J Zoysiagrass

PROPAGATION

Propagation is one of the most rewarding aspects of gardening. Start new plants either by seed or vegetatively using plant parts, such as cuttings of roots or shoots, grafting, layering, or division to increase your plant collection.

STARTING FROM SEED

Hybrid seed produced by a seed company and purchased from a catalog or a local store is reliable. Plants from hybrid seed are uniform in height, color, and other characteristics.

Seed collected from a local garden can yield unusual and interesting results. Insects carry pollen from one flower to another of the same species. Because of the genetic mix that results from this cross-pollination, the plants, flowers, and seeds might not look like the parent. If uniform results are necessary, buying seeds from a reliable source is best.

A seed consists of two basic parts. Stored food available for use by the newly germinated seedling forms the major portion of the seed. A seed also contains a small embryonic plant waiting for proper conditions to start growing.

Seed storage is important to successful germination. To preserve the stored food in the seed and to prevent the embryo from dying, cool, dry storage is best for most seeds. Place the seed packets or collected seed in a sealed jar in a refrigerator to preserve the viability of the seed.

GERMINATION REQUIREMENTS

To initiate growth, the seed must have the correct moisture, temperature, and light. The newly emerging roots and shoots must have proper growing conditions. If the soil is too hard, the tiny new roots cannot penetrate, nor can the new shoot break through to the light.

You can find useful information by looking at the label on a seed packet. Usually the germination year the seed was packaged for—for example, packed for 2005—is stamped on the label. If the seed is outdated, it might not have good germination depending on how it was stored. When in doubt, take a few seeds and place them on a moistened paper towel. Place the paper towel in a plastic bag at room temperature and check the seeds every few days. If the seeds have not germinated within the germination time listed on the packet, purchase new seeds.

Seed packet labels contain information on culture, including germination. A seed packet for oregano might read as follows: Plant in full sun to part shade in well-drained garden soil. Good for kitchen window. Sow anytime in mild climates, or late spring for cold areas. Scatter tiny seeds on soil surface and lightly cover with fine soil. Keep evenly moist until germination in 8 to 10 days. Thin to 12 inches apart.

Some seed packets contain little information, whereas others have information printed on the outside and inside of the packet.

Most vegetable seed should be sown where the plants will grow to maturity. The diverse soil types throughout the country, from sand to heavy clay, require some preparation to give good germination. Add organic matter such as Miracle-Gro Garden Soil to sandy soil to hold moisture and to heavy clay to open up pore spaces.

Most vegetable gardens are planted in rows, unless the gardener is using block or intensive growing practices. Using row planting as an example, make a depression for the row in the garden soil. Place a seed-starting mix such as Miracle-Gro Seed Starting Potting Mix in the row depression

Seed packets give information on germination requirements, days to germinate, seed spacing, and other helpful hints.

to give germinating seeds, roots, and shoots the best conditions for growth. Sow seeds in the starting mix. If seeds are placed directly in clay soil, cover the seed row with a light layer of seed starting mix to allow new shoots to easily poke through. Clay can crust over and kill shoots. Carrots often fail to grow in clay soil as a result.

Once seeds are sown, provide moisture to start the germination process. Use drip irrigation or a water breaker device on the end of a hose to slowly moisten the soil. A strong stream of water from a garden hose can wash seed from its desired location.

Some plants take a long time to reach maturity and flower or produce fruit. In cooler climates plants such as tomatoes are usually transplanted to the garden when 6 inches or taller. Plastic cones with sectioned walls filled with water can be placed around the plants to conserve warmth and prevent frost damage. Old tires, placed flat on the ground around the plant, have been used in a similar way for protection.

1 Sprinkle seed-starting mix over the area to be planted.

2 Evenly sow seeds to minimize clumping and the need for thinning.

3 Water the seeded area with a gentle shower.

4 Before seedlings crowd one another, thin by hand or scissors.

SEED-STARTING EQUIPMENT

Pinch seeds between your thumb and forefinger and allow them to gently fall into place as you rub your fingers back and forth. Small seeds can be difficult to sow because they clump together, resulting in dense groups of seedlings: Seeds from kalanchoes and begonias resemble dust, making individual seeds difficult to distinguish. Mix small seeds with fine sand or other fine, inert material before sowing to lessen the chance of clumping.

Sowing individual seeds can be difficult. A device designed to pick up individual seeds has a rubber bulb connected to a tube. Squeeze the rubber bulb, place the end of the tube in a group of seeds, and release the bulb. The vacuum produced in the tube picks up a seed on the end of the tube. Place the tube where the seed is to be sown, then squeeze the bulb to release the seed from the end of the tube. Various-size ends are available for the tube to accommodate different seed sizes and prevent the seed from being sucked inside the tube.

One specialized seeder is battery operated and has a handle attached to a shallow, vibrating trough. Place seeds in the trough. The vibration causes the seeds to line up down the center of the trough. Tipping the trough at a steeper angle results in higher seeding rates; holding the device almost horizontal results in lower rates.

Some companies make biodegradable tape with seeds spaced evenly along the tape. Place the tape in the row and cover with soil. When the seeds germinate, they produce evenly spaced seedlings in the row.

A thermometer is a valuable tool when germinating seeds indoors. Water evaporating from the germination soil mix causes cooling. Placing the germinating seeds close to a window in late winter or early spring will cool the soil mix. Even though the room temperature feels comfortable, the temperature of the seed germination area may be much cooler. A thermometer will indicate the true temperature.

Specialized watering devices are available for watering the seeds. A stream of water poured on the germination soil mix disturbs the seed location. A gentle, fine spray or shower of water is important. A plastic bottle with a squeeze trigger-operated pump gives a fine spray or mist of water. (Avoid spray bottles that have previously contained cleaning products or other chemicals). A rubber bulb attached to a small showerhead full of holes provides a gentle syringing. Place the head in a source of water; squeeze the bulb, then release it. The bulb will fill with water. Gently squeeze the bulb above the seeds, and water will shower down.

Properly label the seeds when you sow them. Many seedlings look similar. Cabbage, cauliflower, Brussels sprouts, kohlrabi, broccoli, and turnip seedlings look nearly identical when they are young. A good label with lettering that will not wash off or fade in the sun is ideal for distinguishing seedlings. Plastic labels marked with indelible ink, wooden labels marked with a dark pencil, or aluminum labels will help prevent confusion.

Plastic cell packs are perfect for growing individual plants. Cell packs contain multiple small plastic growing pots, or cells, connected together as a unit. These are available in six, eight, twelve, or other numbers of cells. Cell construction allows water to flow from one cell to the next, so applying water to the pack waters all of the cells without having to water each one individually.

Rolling seeder/sower

Mister

Metering seeder

Vacuum seeder

Seeding counter

Indoor thermometer

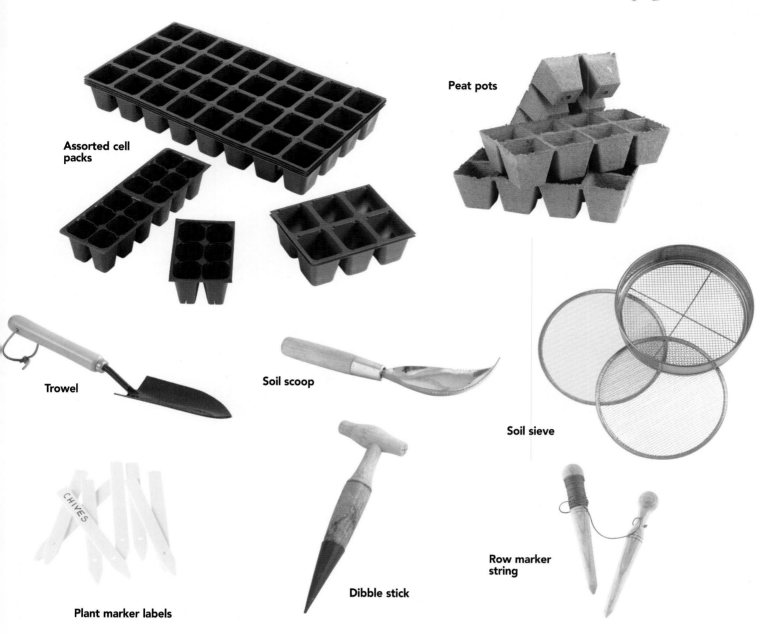

Assorted cell packs

Peat pots

Trowel

Soil scoop

Soil sieve

Plant marker labels

CHIVES

Dibble stick

Row marker string

Peat pots are available in two basic types: a pot-shaped container that looks like a regular flowerpot but is made from compressed peat, and a compressed peat pellet covered with nylon netting. The peat pot is designed to be filled with growing mix. As the plant grows, the roots grow through the wall of the peat pot. You can plant the peat pot and seedling in the garden without disturbing the roots of the plant. Place the compressed peat pellet in water. As it absorbs water, it expands to approximately seven times its compressed height. Plant seeds or seedlings directly in the peat without adding any other growing mix. Roots grow through the nylon mesh surrounding the peat. Plant the undisturbed peat and roots directly in the garden.

When sowing seeds directly outdoors, use good-quality garden soil for starting seeds and covering rows of seeds. To eliminate small sticks or dirt clods that can interfere with seed germination, use a soil sieve, a small wire mesh held tightly across the bottom of a metal or plastic ring. Gently shake or rub the soil across the screen to separate the large particles from the smaller ones.

A garden trowel is one of the most important tools in the garden. Trowels are used for many garden activities, from planting to transplanting, so comfort is important.

Before purchasing a trowel, pick it up and make sure it fits the grip of your hand. An improperly fitting grip will cause blisters and hand fatigue.

Soil scoops are handy because they are larger than a trowel and have a shorter handle than a shovel. Soil scoops make filling pots or flats fast and easy.

A handy tool with a strange name is the dibble stick, known in North America as a dibble and in England as a dibber. It is simply a sharpened stick used to make a hole in the ground to plant seeds or seedlings. A broken shaft on a D-handle shovel makes an excellent dibble. Make a point on the broken shaft about a foot below the D-shaped end. Cut small notches in the wood at 1-inch intervals to gauge the depth of the hole. Dibble sticks made of plastic are available commercially. Or make a simple dibble with a wooden pencil to poke holes; sharpen it to lift seedlings.

Many devices have been invented to mark straight rows in a garden. For overall convenience, a row-marking string still works best. Place a stake at each end of the garden and attach string between the two stakes. Pull the string taut so the wind does not blow it around. Make a furrow of the proper depth in the soil below the string, sow the seed, then move the string over where the next row will go.

Good seeds may germinate poorly in a low-quality soil mix. Germinating seeds in a commercial soil mix specially blended for this operation will give the best results. The mix will not have weed seeds, insects, disease spores, or other germination-inhibiting elements. Commercial mixes may also contain a wetting agent that promotes water absorption by peat (a component of the soil mix) as well as a dilute fertilizer that gives newly germinated seeds a boost in growth. If a bag of seed-germinating soil mix has been open for some time, it might be dry and powdery. Lightly moisten the soil mix with water until it almost holds its shape when squeezed into a ball.

Commercial seed-starting mixes are specially blended for optimum germination.

Assemble necessary materials on a comfortable work area where spilled soil mix can be easily cleaned up.

Containers for growing plants should have drainage holes. Cell packs are good containers for growing young plants from seed until they are ready to set in the garden. Plastic flats or other containers where many seeds can be sown and later transplanted to individual pots also work well. Scoop seed-germinating soil mix into the cell pack or flat, scrape off any excess, and gently firm the soil mix.

Check the seed packet label to determine whether special germination requirements are necessary. Some seeds, such as yarrow, hollyhock, and alyssum, require light to germinate; once the seeds are sown, they are not covered with soil mix so they receive the required light. When the seed packet provides no specific light recommendation, cover the seeds to the recommended depth.

When planting a cell pack, use a small dibble or wooden pencil to poke a hole in the soil mix. Make the hole no deeper than the sowing depth specified on the seed packet. Place one or two seeds in the hole in each cell.

When using a flat or other large container, sow the seeds in rows. Mark shallow rows in the soil mix by pressing a pencil horizontally into the surface. For accurate seeding, place the seeds in a vibrating seeder and follow label directions for use of the seeder. After germination, transplant seedlings into individual containers or directly into the garden.

As soon as seeds are planted in packs or flats, place a label on the container. Include the date the seed was sown and the plant name. Gently water the seeds and soil mix with a trigger-type spray bottle or a bulb with a syringe

Use a seeding device for accurate seed placement.

2

Fill germination containers with seed-starting mix. Scrape off excess material with a trowel. Moisten the seed-starting mix.

3

A pencil serves as a dibble to poke shallow holes in the seed-starting mix for seed placement.

5

Label seeded containers with waterproof tags as you sow each variety to avoid mistaken identity.

6

Water the seeded trays with a gentle shower to soak the soil mix and speed germination.

head, or by soaking the containers in a shallow basin, letting the soil mix absorb water through the drain holes.

Expandable peat pellets are easy to store and ready to use after soaking in water. Place the peat pellets in a container of water making sure that the opening in the thin netting covering the pellet is facing up. Once the pellet has fully expanded, it is ready for planting. A dibble makes a suitable hole in the pellet for sowing seed or placing a transplant.

Once seeds are sown in the cell pack, flat, or peat pellet, maintain uniform moisture in the soil mix. To prevent evaporation, some commercial flats have a clear plastic top designed to fit perfectly over the flat, similar to a miniature greenhouse. Or make a cover from a bent coat hanger and a painter's lightweight plastic drop cloth. Check the moisture content of the seed germination mix at least daily. If it dries out as the seeds begin to germinate, the tender seedlings may die because their roots extend only a short distance into the germination mix.

Provide supplemental lighting for emerged seedlings to prevent them from elongating excessively in low light. Either fluorescent lights or special grow lights will provide the light needed by the developing plants. Keep the light source approximately 6" above the soil or tops of the seedlings. Place seedlings on adjustable shelves to maintain the proper distance from the light source, or move the light up or down as necessary.

1 A dry peat pellet (*left*) will expand to several times its size when fully moistened.

2 Place seed in a seed sower.

3 Place one or two seeds in each expanded peat pellet.

4 Cover the seeded peat pellets with a clear plastic cover to maintain high humidity.

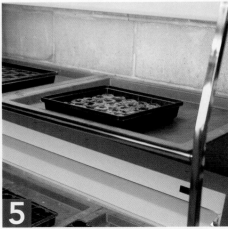

5 Supply supplemental light as soon as germination begins to prevent weak, leggy seedlings.

TEMPERATURE AND MOISTURE REQUIREMENTS

Germination can be delayed or completely inhibited if the temperature of the soil mix is too low. In a home where the temperature is maintained at 68°F, the temperature of the germination soil mix may be 5 to 10 degrees lower than the surrounding air. Evaporation of moisture from the soil mix can lower the temperature below the optimum for seed germination.

Germination soil mix placed in a sunny window will warm enough during the day so that another heat source is usually not needed. Fluorescent lights do not provide enough warmth, so bottom heat is necessary for seeds started under lights.

Waterproof propagation heat mats or heat cables are two types of bottom-heating devices. Place the germinating seed containers on top of them. To provide the optimum temperature for germination and to keep the mats or cables from overheating the soil mix, a special thermostat is attached to the heating device. Place the temperature-sensing probe attached to the thermostat into the germination soil mix.

Once the seeds have started to germinate, they require constant moisture to survive. With most seeds, the roots start to grow before the new shoots. If the soil mix is allowed to

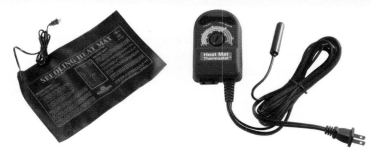

A heat mat provides additional warmth for seed germination.

A thermostat keeps the mat from overheating.

dry out, the seedlings are killed. Bottom heat accelerates the drying of the soil mix, and within a few hours a moist soil mix can become too dry. Simply touching the surface of the soil mix with your finger will indicate the moisture level. A moist soil mix feels damp like a moist sponge.

Watering the soil mix on the surface works well, but provide some way to catch excess moisture that flows from the drain holes. To water a large number of containers, attach a fog-producing nozzle to a hose. The dense fog moistens the soil mix yet is gentle enough that the seeds or seedlings are not disturbed.

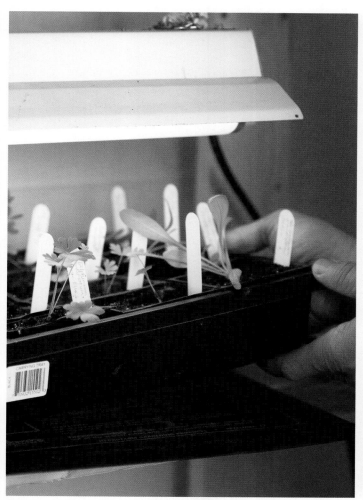

Many seeds require a warm germination soil mix to sprout. Place the seed germination containers on a waterproof heat mat for optimum germination.

Water seedlings with a misting nozzle to moisten the soil mix but not wash it away.

Plants may be divided into two basic groups depending on the way their seeds form. Monocotyledons, or monocots, are commonly represented by corn and grassy types of plants. Dicotyledons, or dicots, such as beans, have two halves to the seeds.

The cotyledon is a part of the seed used to store food, such as starch, sugar, oil, and protein. These are necessary for growth until the seedling can produce its own food from sunlight through photosynthesis.

When a dicot germinates, the two cotyledons stay attached to the newly elongating stem of the seedling. They turn green and look like leaves for a short time; they are called cotyledonous or seed leaves. When true leaves form, the two cotyledonous leaves shrivel and drop off. This distinction between cotyledonous leaves and true leaves is important when considering time to transplant.

Monocots do not have easily recognizable cotyledonous leaves. Leaves produced by monocots are considered true leaves. Once a monocot seedling produces two or three visible leaves, it is ready to transplant.

The halves of a dicot seed form leaflike structures. True leaves develop above the cotyledons.

Monocots produce no noticeable cotyledons. All the foliage that develops from a monocot seedling consists of true leaves.

1 Avoid pulling seedlings from the soil mix by their leaves. Pry the plant from below with a pencil or wooden label.

2 Once seedlings are removed from the soil mix, hold them gently by the leaves to prevent damage to the tender stem.

3 Place seedling roots in holes large enough to accommodate the roots. Gently firm soil around the seedling and water in.

Proper transplant timing is important to the survival and growth of seedlings. The best time for transplanting is just after the first set of true leaves forms. There is little transplant shock at this stage of development. If you transplant seedlings too soon, you risk seedling damage and death of the young plants. Transplanting too late may break roots entangled with others growing close together, resulting in transplant shock as the roots regrow.

Start the seeds in a large container or flat to conserve room and allow more precise bottom heating and watering. After the first set of true leaves forms, transplant the seedlings to individual containers to develop healthy root systems and provide more room for top growth. From the individual containers, transplant directly into the garden or into larger containers in the case of houseplants.

Proper transplanting produces the least amount of damage to the seedling. First prepare the containers and growing soil mix. Use a soil mix similar to that used for seed germination. Moisten the soil mix before placing it in the containers; moist soil mix is easier to firm around the root system than dry soil mix. Using a dibble, poke a hole in the soil mix of each container. Make sure the hole is large enough for the root system to fit without bunching or coiling.

Even though the seedlings seem as though they could be easily pulled out of the soft germination soil mix, avoid pulling on the top of the seedling to remove it from the soil mix. Most of the roots may break off or the stem may break, killing the seedling. Many of the important roots on a seedling are no larger than a human hair.

The easiest way to avoid damaging the seedling when transplanting is to insert a pencil, tongue depressor, row label, or similar tool at a 45-degree angle into the soil mix under the seedling. Gently lift upward on the tool, steadying the seedling by gently holding onto the leaves. Carefully lower the root system into the prepared hole in the transplant pot to the same depth it was growing in the germination container. Gently firm the soil mix around the roots to prevent the seedling from falling over the first time it is watered.

Transplant containers are available in assorted sizes and with various carrying trays.

Collected seeds do not always produce the same type of plant, flower, or fruit as the seed parent because of cross-pollination with the pollen parent. However, collecting seeds is fun, and a plant similar to the parent may result.

Proper timing is important for seed harvesting. If the seeds are harvested before they are ripe, they will not germinate. If harvest is delayed too long, the seeds may scatter and be difficult to collect. In most cases, seeds turn brown or tan at maturity. To be sure the seeds are ripe and do not scatter, tie a small cloth bag over the seed head before the seeds mature. Check periodically; when the seeds have fallen from the stem, they are ripe and contained in the bag.

Collect seeds formed in pods just as the pods begin to split open. Peas, beans, catalpas, redbuds, and many other plants produce pods. Siberian peashrub (*Caragana*) produces a pod that violently splits and twists when ripe, shooting the seeds several feet from the plant. Collect these pods just as they start to turn brown and store them in a closed paper bag. When the pods ripen, the seeds will be expelled from the pods but contained in the bag.

Pinks (*Dianthus*) and columbine (*Aquilegia*) produce many small seeds in a capsule that forms after the flower petals drop. When the capsule turns brown, pick it from the stem and gently crush it between your fingers to release the seeds. Pieces of pulverized seed capsule (chaff) mix with the small seeds. Gently blow on the seeds and chaff to separate them.

Flower and vegetable seeds collected at the end of one growing season will germinate in the next growing cycle if given the proper moisture, temperature, and light. Most annuals, such as zinnia, produce seeds in their dried flower heads. Collect the dried seeds and store them in a cool, dry place; the following spring, plant the seeds. Unless the seeds are extremely large, place them in a film canister. Label the canister and store it in the refrigerator. Large numbers of seeds can be stored in a sealed canning jar.

1 Harvest hollyhock seeds when the seed capsules turn brown.

2 Remove the hollyhock seeds from seed heads and separate them from chaff and debris.

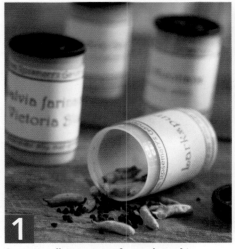

1 Store small amounts of saved seed in recycled film canisters.

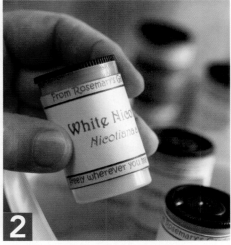

2 Label the canister with the type of seed it contains. Seal it with the canister lid to keep seeds dry.

3 Place the seed storage containers in the refrigerator to maintain seed viability.

Some seeds, such as walnut, require stratification to germinate.

One method of stratification is to place walnut seeds in moist sand and peat in a bag in the refrigerator.

Stratify walnuts naturally by burying them in the soil in the fall. Place them on a bed of sand and cover with peat.

The seeds of many landscape plants have a built-in natural dormancy. Dormancy prevents the seeds of plants growing in cold areas from germinating before warm conditions arrive the following spring. If the seeds germinated in fall, the young seedlings would be killed by frost. Buffalograss, a native of the dry western plains states, has a three-year dormancy. The first growing season, only a few of the seeds germinate. More germinate the second season, and some remain dormant until the third season. This ensures survival of the plants in the harsh climate where it is native. When buffalograss is planted from seed as a lawn, the seed is treated with a chemical to reduce the dormancy, so the first year germination increases to 80 percent.

Removing dormancy from seeds occurs naturally with cold temperatures or microorganisms attacking the seed coats. Stratification is a process in which seeds are placed in a soil mix in cool, moist storage to break down natural chemicals in the seeds that inhibit germination. A few of the many seeds that benefit from stratification are grape, hickory, persimmon, birch, clematis, and honeysuckle. The seeds are removed from their fleshy fruit coatings before stratification.

The seeds can be stratified in almost any soil mix that holds moisture, provides aeration, and is nontoxic. Peat moss and sand, sphagnum moss, vermiculite, perlite, or seed-starting mix may be used. Place a handful of moist (not soggy) mixture in a sealable plastic bag. Mix the seeds with the soil mix and seal the bag. Using an indelible marker, write the plant name, date collected, and date that stratification started on the bag. Place the bag in the refrigerator where the temperature ranges between 35 and 50°F. Keep the bag refrigerated for at least 90 days. At the end of the stratification period, remove them from the bag and plant the seeds as you normally would. If the seeds are small and difficult to separate from the soil mix, include the soil mix when you plant.

Some seeds have complex dormancy requirements that are difficult for the average gardener to overcome. An example is elder (*Sambucus* spp.). Elderberry seeds have both seed-coat dormancy and embryo dormancy and must be stratified at 70 to 85°F for two months, followed by 40°F for three to five months.

A process called scarification is necessary for seeds with a hard, impermeable seed coat. Some seeds benefiting from scarification are lead plant (*Amorpha canescens*), cotoneaster, sumac (*Rhus*), rose (*Rosa*), American elder (*Sambucus*), snowberry (*Symphoricarpos*), honey locust (*Gleditsia*), wisteria, silk tree (*Albizia*), linden (*Tilia*), and lupine (*Lupinus*). With these seeds, use mechanical methods to make the seed coat thinner or to cut a small opening in the seed coat. In nature the seed coat breaks down from passing through the digestive tract of birds or other animals or from the action of soil microorganisms when seeds contact the ground. Once water and oxygen pass through the seed coat, germination can start.

In commercial operations, seeds requiring scarification are placed in rotating drums lined with sandpaper. After various amounts of time, the seed coat wears thin enough to allow germination. Home gardeners can scarify their own seeds by carefully rubbing larger seeds on sandpaper or carefully nicking the seed coat with a file or knife.

Nick the seed coat of hard-coated seeds such as lupine or Kentucky coffeetree with a knife before sowing.

Rub hard-coated seeds on sandpaper to scarify before sowing them.

VEGETATIVE PROPAGATION TOOLS AND EQUIPMENT

Vegetative propagation includes, but is not limited to, cutting, layering, division, grafting, budding, and tissue culture. Many of the tools used to germinate seeds can also be used for vegetative propagation. Germination soil mix, containers, and lights are all used in starting cuttings. One important tool not used in seed germination is a sharp knife or other sharp-bladed tool,

suspended from a framework that keeps the plastic from coming in contact with the cuttings. This cover lets light through to the cuttings and keeps the humidity high around them.

Cuttings taken further down the plant, below the tip or terminal, are called stem cuttings. They are treated the same as terminal cuttings. Remove the lower leaves from the

Bypass or scissor-cut pruners give a clean cut when making cuttings.

Rooting hormone promotes rooting on most cuttings.

Coleus cuttings root easily in water or potting mix. One plant produces many cuttings.

such as a box cutter or single-edge razor blade. The blade must be sharp to avoid damaging plant tissue. Bypass pruners are effective for cutting tough stems.

You can take softwood cuttings from new shoots of many types of plants during the growing season. Coleus can have softwood cuttings taken from new shoots while it is growing in the home or in the outdoor flower bed.

Use a clean, sharp knife to take cuttings from coleus, geraniums, and other herbaceous plants. If the plant stem easily breaks without crushing or tearing, you may snap the cutting from the plant instead of using a knife. Snapping the cutting avoids spreading disease with an unclean knife.

New shoots on roses, geraniums, coleus, and many other plants make good terminal cuttings. Cut approximately 4 to 6 inches from the tip of the shoot. Remove the lower leaves from the cutting so they will not be buried in the rooting soil mix and rot. Dip the lower inch of the cutting in rooting hormone, then place the cutting upright in a rooting or germination soil mix, such as Miracle-Gro Seed Starting Potting Mix, with the lower inch inserted into the moist mix. Cover the propagation area with clear plastic sheeting

Take chrysanthemum cuttings in early summer before flower buds form.

Cut a scented geranium stem and remove its lower leaves.

Dip the lower inch of the cutting in rooting hormone.

Stick the cut end of the geranium in rooting soil mix.

Cover the propagation tray with clear polyethylene sheeting to maintain high humidity around the cuttings.

cuttings, dip the cuttings in rooting hormone such as Miracle-Gro Fast Root™ Rooting Hormone, and place them in rooting soil mix. Be sure to place at least one bud and the basal part of the cutting (the part that was nearer the base of the plant) in the rooting soil mix. If the cutting is placed in the soil mix upside down, roots will fail to form.

When taking cuttings from vining plants, such as pothos, philodendron, Virginia creeper, or grape, place the stem cuttings on the surface of the soil mix. Make cuttings at least 6 inches long. Exert slight pressure to press the stem into contact with the soil mix. Rooting hormone speeds root development on most species. It is unnecessary to remove leaves unless they prevent the stem from touching the soil mix. Roots form at nodes, areas where leaves attach to the stem.

Take semihardwood cuttings from woody, broad-leaved evergreen trees and shrubs. Semihardwood cutting is the term that applies to leafy summer and early fall cuttings taken from partially matured wood of deciduous plants. Take semihardwood cuttings from wood that is partially matured but still easy to snap. Take the cuttings early in the morning when the foliage is full of moisture. Wrap the

cuttings in moist paper towels until they can be placed in the rooting soil mix. On large-leaved plants such as rhododendron, remove the outer half of the leaves. This practice reduces moisture loss from the cutting. The remaining part of the leaf will be enough to sustain the cutting.

Hardwood cuttings can be made from many trees and shrubs. Take hardwood cuttings with bypass pruners in late winter or early spring when the plant is dormant. Treat the cuttings the same as softwood coleus or geranium cuttings. Because hardwood cuttings are taken during the dormant season, there are no leaves to remove from deciduous plants. For evergreens such as arborvitae or juniper, simply remove the lower few inches of foliage from the cutting before inserting it into the rooting soil mix.

On all cuttings, the new roots are fragile and easily damaged. When checking the cuttings to see whether roots have formed, gently tug on the cutting. If the cutting resists being pulled from the soil mix, roots have probably formed. Use fingers or a pencil to gently dig under the cutting and lift it from the rooting soil mix to avoid damaging the new roots.

Make an English ivy cutting just below a leaf. New roots develop best at the node (point of leaf attachment).

Root boxwood from semihardwood cuttings taken in late summer. The cuttings should snap from the plant if bent sharply.

LEAF CUTTINGS AND LAYERING

Cut an African violet leaf from the parent plant to start a new plant.

Dip the leaf petiole in rooting hormone to stimulate rooting.

To start a new rose plant by layering, bend the stem down to the soil, make a wound in the stem, apply rooting hormone, and cover it with soil. Roots will form in several weeks or months.

Most plants cannot be started from leaf cuttings, but a few can, such as African violet, peperomia, Rex begonia, and gloxinia. African violet and peperomia leaves, with their petiole (stemlike structure that attaches the leaf to the crown of the plant), root easily to start new plants. Cut or snap the petiole and attached leaf from the crown of the plant. Dip the base of the petiole in rooting hormone and insert the lower 1 to 2 inches in propagation soil mix. Place the soil mix and cutting in a bright location out of direct sunlight. Within a few months, the petiole will form roots and new leaves at its base. A short time later, the new leaves push up through the soil mix.

An alternative method is to place the petiole in a container of water, with the attached leaf above the water. In a clear container, the formation of roots and leaves can be easily observed. To keep the leaf above the water, place a piece of waxed paper over the top of the container and partway down the sides. Use a rubber band around the container to hold the waxed paper in place. Cut an X in

To propagate begonia from leaf cuttings, slice through the major veins on the back of the leaf.

Place the leaf on moist soil mix with the cut veins in contact with the soil mix.

the middle of the paper and insert the petiole through the cut and into the water.

Leaf cuttings are used to start new plants of gloxinia and Rex begonia. Remove a leaf from the plant and turn it over, exposing the veins on the underside of the leaf. Use a knife or sharp blade to slice through major veins, then apply rooting hormone to each cut. Place the leaf flat on the propagation soil mix with the sliced veins facing down

and in contact with the soil mix. New plantlets form at the sliced veins as well as at the end of the petiole. Once the plantlets are approximately an inch tall, separate them from the leaf and pot them individually.

In many cases where cuttings will not work, layering is used to produce new plants. This method of propagation works best on plants or shrubs with a bushy or spreading form. In spring or summer, bend a lower branch on the parent plant downward so it contacts loose soil. Using a knife, scrape away a small area of bark in the contact area. The wound should extend about halfway around the stem. Apply rooting hormone to the wound and press the wounded area into the soil. Set a brick or other heavy object on the stem to hold it in position and keep it from moving. Periodically check the wounded area for root formation. When the new plant is well rooted, cut it from the parent and pot it or transplant it to a new location.

To easily propagate a spreading juniper by layering, dig a shallow trench near a low branch. Wound the bottom of the branch where rooting is wanted and bury that part of the branch in the trench. Bend heavy-gauge wire to form a large U-shaped pin and insert it over the branch and into the soil to hold the branch in place. Leave the growing tip of the branch exposed aboveground. Roots will form at the wound in a few months. Dig up the rooted branch, slice through the stem between the new roots and the parent plant, and transplant the new juniper to a different location.

When houseplants such as rubber tree, croton, or split-leaf philodendron grow too tall, it is time for air layering. Air layering produces a new plant and reduces the height of the existing plant.

Select a place on the stem and remove all of the bark around the stem for a distance of 1 inch. An alternative

1 To layer a spreading juniper, dig a trench under a low-growing shoot.

2 Make a small wound on the underside of the shoot, apply rooting hormone, and pin the shoot onto the soil with a wire loop.

3 When roots form, dig the rooted shoot and cut it from the parent plant.

method is to make a 1½-inch slanting cut upward extending halfway through the stem. Use a toothpick or sliver of wood to wedge in the cut so it will not close and grow back together. Apply rooting hormone to the wounded area.

Moisten long-fibered sphagnum moss and form it into a ball (about the size of a baseball) around the wound. Wrap clear plastic or aluminum foil over the moss and fasten it with twist ties, tape, or string above and below the moss. Check every few weeks to make sure the moss is still moist. When you see roots within the clear plastic, remove it. Use pruners to cut the stem below the root mass, and pot the new plant. The old plant will produce new shoots below the cut, resulting in a shorter, bushier parent plant.

1 To air layer, remove a small section of bark or knick the stem where roots will form.

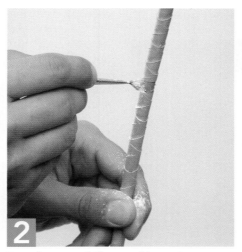

2 Dust the wounded area with rooting hormone.

3 Place moist sphagnum moss around the wound and cover with polyethylene.

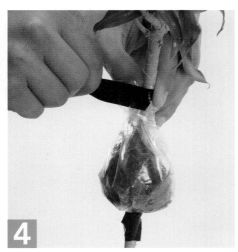

4 Tape or tie the polyethylene above and below the moss.

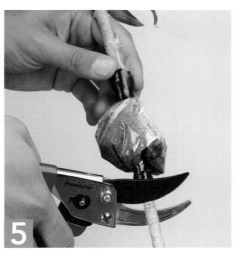

5 Cut the rooted top from the parent plant.

6 Place the rooted top in a new pot.

DIVISION

Many garden perennial flowers and houseplants may be divided as a means of propagation. Division is simple and reliable, giving exact duplicates of the parent plant. Plants with multiple stems or shoots emerging from the soil are the best candidates for division.

Houseplants such as Boston fern, peace lily, snake plant, cast-iron plant, prayer plant, and spider plant are easily divided. Make divisions when the plant gets too large for its pot or location and repotting to a larger container is not feasible. You may also divide plants when new plants are desired.

Divide a peace lily with a large knife, cutting the root mass into sections.

Repot each section into a separate pot.

Remove the plant from the pot and place it on a solid surface. Using a large, sharp knife, cut down through the plant and soil. Depending on the size of transplants desired, cut the parent plant in half, quarters, or smaller divisions.

When planting divisions into new containers, you may need to remove the bottom few inches of soil and roots for a proper fit. Divisions usually suffer some transplant shock;

new growth may not appear for several weeks. Once new roots start growing, new top growth soon follows.

Many garden perennials require division every few years to rejuvenate the plants or keep them in bounds. Herbs such as mint, sage, and thyme are easily divided. Flower garden perennials commonly propagated by division include aster, bleeding heart (*Dicentra*), chrysanthemum (*Dendranthema*), coreopsis, daylily (*Hemerocallis*), hosta, iris, liriope, lily-of-the-valley (*Convallaria*), peony (*Paeonia*), and yarrow (*Achillea*). Without division, perennials such as bearded iris develop dead central areas with a ring of living plants around the outside. In the process of division, remove the central dead areas of the plant and replant only the healthy, live parts.

Avoid dividing perennials when they are flowering. Divide spring-flowering plants in early fall, and divide late-summer- or fall-flowering plants in early spring.

Daylilies are an example of a perennial that grows in a dense clump with many leaves emerging from the ground. First, carefully dig the clump from the ground. Then remove some of the soil from the root system with a strong stream of water or by hand. This allows the clump to separate easier. The plant can either be cut into sections with a large knife or pulled apart. Very dense older clumps may require two spading or turning forks to tease apart the clump. Insert the forks back-to-back into the clump. Pull the handles in opposite directions forcing the clump to divide. After separating the larger plant into smaller units, trim each division to remove dead plant parts. Division techniques for peonies and dahlias are similar. In late summer or after the foliage has first been frosted in fall, carefully dig the plant and its large roots from the soil, taking care to avoid damage to the tuberous roots. Gently

To divide a daylily, dig the entire clump.

Wash soil from the roots to allow easier separation and to see the root system.

Cut the root system into sections using a large knife, or simply pull the roots apart.

Space divisions in holes 18 inches apart.

Backfill around the plants with soil and water in.

shake the soil from the roots, or use a gentle spray of water to remove the soil. A strong stream of water may damage dahlia tubers. Only with clean roots and crowns can the plant structure be observed for division.

Dahlia tubers are connected to a stem, and small, light-colored buds are attached around the stem. Use a large, sharp knife to divide the stem into sections. Each section must have a tuber (swollen rootlike structure containing stored food) and an eye (the bud from which new top growth arises) for the new plant to grow. Remove any roots attached to the tuber, including the root on the end of the tuber. Reduce the length of extremely long tubers by up to one-third to facilitate storage and planting. In cold climates, pack tubers in peat moss (to keep them from shriveling) and store in a nonfreezing but cool location.

Peonies have thick roots attached to a crown. Divide the cleaned crown and root system into sections using a large, sharp knife. Plan the cuts so each section has several good roots and at least three buds attached. Remove any dead or damaged plant material. Plant peony divisions where they will not be disturbed for five to ten years.

As a precautionary measure, use a fungicide to treat cut areas on divisions to prevent invasion of rot-causing fungi. Dip the divisions in a liquid fungicide solution or dust them with a powdered formulation.

1 Carefully dig the clump of peonies.

2 Each division of peony must have healthy pink buds (eyes) from which new shoots will grow.

3 Place a section of the division with good roots and at least three eyes in a prepared hole.

4 Cover the eyes with only an inch or two of soil, mulch the surface, and water well.

1

To divide bleeding heart, first cut back the foliage.

2

Carefully cut completely around the root system.

3

Gently separate the brittle, ropelike roots.

4

Replant each division in a prepared hole.

Bleeding heart is another perennial that becomes overgrown and needs division periodically. After the foliage begins to decline in late summer, cut it back, dig the plant and separate the crown into several sections. This plant is not as sturdy as many other perennials and should be handled carefully. The large, ropelike roots may be cut into sections as root cuttings, with each cutting producing a new plant. Elongated buds and attached roots on the outer portion of the crown may be gently pulled from the plant and started as new plants.

Lily-of-the-valley requires division when the shoots become crowded and blooming decreases. Dig the plants from the soil and divide the individual crowns and root systems by pulling them apart. Make sure the crowns, also known as "pips," have a healthy root system. Replant the crowns 3 to 4 inches apart and 1 inch deep.

Bearded iris have a growing point at the end of a stout rhizome. Over many years plants become crowded with dense masses of rhizomes. New growth forms at the outside of the clump, and old, dead rhizomes fill the center. Dig clumps of rhizomes from the ground and rinse with a stream of water. Use pruning shears or a sharp knife to cut the rhizomes apart. Cut healthy rhizomes with fans of leaves attached from the clump. Discard old rhizomes or dead portions of the plant. Replant healthy rhizomes horizontally, with the top half of the rhizomes visible above the soil surface.

1

To divide iris, dig the clump.

2

Wash soil from the roots and rhizomes so you can see their structure.

3

Using a sharp knife separate the leaves and rhizomes from dead plant parts.

4

Replant healthy iris divisions in a triangular pattern.

BUDDING AND GRAFTING

Plant parts may be spliced onto other plant parts for a variety of reasons, such as creating a dwarf plant, producing a hardier tree or shrub, increasing resistance to disease and insect pests, or creating a novelty form of the plant.

Grafting kits contain grafting wax, a knife, budding strips and budding tape.

Splicing a standard variety of apple onto a root system that keeps the tree small produces a dwarf apple tree. As long as the plants are closely related and the cambium tissue (green tissue between bark and wood) of the parts align in the splice, the cells will grow together. Almond, apricot, European plum, and Japanese plum may be grafted onto a peach root system.

Budding and grafting are two types of tissue splices. Budding uses a bud from the desired variety and unites it with a compatible rootstock. Grafting unites a section of twig from the desired variety with a rootstock. Both budding and grafting require much practice to be successful. Budding and grafting should be done when the air is still, the humidity is high, and temperatures are cool to prevent drying and killing the cambium tissue.

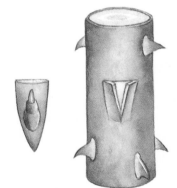

T-budding must be done when the plant is actively growing. Peel back the bark of the understock and slip a shield-shaped piece of stem with a bud eye into place. Hold the bud in place with electrical tape or a budding strip.

Chip budding may be used on grapes, fruit trees, or woody ornamentals such as roses. Remove a chip of wood a few inches above the soil from the plant that will function as the root system. Remove a chip exactly the same size from another plant that will form the plant top. Place the bud chip in the chip void on the rootstock. Be sure the green cambium on each part lines up. Cover the cut surfaces with budding tape or budding strips of rubber to prevent tissue drying. Avoid covering the bud by carefully wrapping above and below it and leaving the bud protruding. Once the bud starts growing into a new shoot, remove the old stem above the bud to allow the new shoot to become the new plant top.

In whip-and-tongue grafting, a 3- to 4-inch-long piece of twig (scion) with one or two buds is spliced onto the root system of another plant. Make the graft in late winter on a dormant, bare-root plant using a dormant scion. Make a 2-inch sloping diagonal cut through the stem of the root system about 6 inches above the soil line. Next make a ½-inch-long vertical cut down the stem starting one-third of the way down the slope from the tip. Prepare the scion with cuts of the same shape. Force the two cut surfaces to slide together. A tonguelike projection from each will fit into the other. Make sure the cambium tissues line up as much as possible between the two parts. Wrap the joined area with twine to hold it together and cover with grafting wax or pruning paint to prevent tissue drying.

A whip and tongue graft is one of the easiest grafts to make on young trees.

To chip bud place a bud chip of the desired variety into a chip opening cut into the rootstock.

Use cleft grafting in spring on large diameter trunks or limbs before growth begins.

Use cleft grafts on large rootstocks. Cut off the top of the plant selected for the rootstock. Using a hatchet or cleft-grafting tool, make about a 4-inch-long split (cleft) down the center of the rootstock trunk. Cut wedge-shaped ends on two scions ½ inch in diameter. Force a cleft-grafting tool into the cleft to spread it open. Place the wedges of the scions in the cleft with the cambium of the rootstock and scions contacting one another. Remove the spreading device to leave the scions firmly held in place. Cover all of the exposed cut areas with grafting wax or pruning paint.

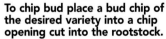

PROBLEMS WITH PLANTS

The health of plants is in the hands of home gardeners. They plot the garden or landscape, choose plants that are compatible with the conditions that exist there, and tend to the plants' needs. Plant health care (PHC) focuses on providing plants with the proper care. It emphasizes preventing conditions that foster insect pests and diseases. Good gardeners educate themselves on ways to make their plants thrive.

PLANT HEALTH CARE VS. INTEGRATED PEST MANAGEMENT

Plant health care (PHC) is a holistic approach to gardening. It considers the garden as part of the whole landscape. A homeowner with a lawn, trees, shrubs, perennials, annuals, and a vegetable garden needs an effective garden plan that takes them all into consideration. A plan that focuses on only one or two problem plants (which is the approach of integrated pest management or IPM) does not address the best interests of the entire yard and garden.

Planning and record-keeping are the first steps in plant health care. A garden plan is a calendar of activities designed to prevent problems. It helps you set and achieve goals, such as incorporating new plants, new gardens, and even new hardscapes. A garden plan should focus on fixing problems from previous years and preventing problems in the future. Keep in mind that your garden plan is just that—a plan. It should be adaptable to weather conditions. Success in gardens, just as in life, requires a certain degree of flexibility and the recognition that the best-laid plans may require tweaking.

Begin your record-keeping by listing the plants you are growing, including notes about performance. Many computer programs include templates to get you started. Identify, or at least note, any problems that you've had to date and investigate potential causes and what control strategies you can use to minimize problems for next year. When setting up your garden calendar, be sure to refer to your records. Using them in conjunction with your calendar creates a personalized plant health care strategy for your yard and garden.

This xeric garden in New Mexico features plants adapted to the sunny, dry climate.

Plants in tropical gardens are adapted to hot, humid conditions. They suffer when it becomes cold or dry.

Growing plants with widely different requirements together results in environmental stress to nonadapted plants.

BEGINNING A PLANT HEALTH CARE PROGRAM

There are six simple things you can do to maintain healthy plants during the growing season.

1. Make certain the plant is appropriate for the site.

2. Maintain appropriate levels of nutrients.

3. Supply plants with adequate moisture, especially during droughts.

4. Mulch to conserve moisture and prevent the growth of weeds.

5. Harvest fruits, vegetables, and flowers at timely intervals. Overripe produce attracts insects and is susceptible to disease. Unremoved flowers result in seed formation instead of new flower production; they also serve as a potential site of infection.

6. Clean up each fall. Remove dead plants as soon as you have finished harvesting a particular fruit or vegetable and remove any rotting leftovers.

Healthy gardens consist not only of plants but bacteria, fungi, insects, and nematodes. Most of these organisms are benign and merely coexist with plants. Some of these organisms, such as fungi that form mycorrhizae, or nitrogen-fixing bacteria, are beneficial and are necessary for healthy plant growth. Other fungi and bacteria are essential for breaking down dead plant material into humus in the compost pile. Beneficial insects and nematodes prey upon and parasitize pests in addition to playing important roles in pollination. Although it may not seem like it to an embattled gardener, only a small percentage of insects actually cause damage, and only a few microorganisms are capable of causing disease.

When confronted with a plant problem, most gardeners assume that an insect or a disease is involved, then wonder what pesticide to spray. Most plant problems, however, are not due to disease-causing agents (pathogens) or insects but to environmental conditions and stresses. More often than not, these problems are caused by or due to actions taken—or not taken—by gardeners.

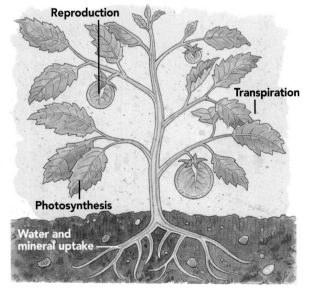

Reproduction

Transpiration

Photosynthesis

Water and mineral uptake

Keep your garden lush and healthy by inspecting it regularly for normal healthy plant functions.

HOW PLANTS PROTECT THEMSELVES

There are advantages and disadvantages to being rooted in one spot. First, plants can't "run away" and must contend with whatever they encounter. Actually, plants are able to escape or avoid insect, animal, or disease damage, but not in the way we usually think of escape. Escape for a plant means it avoids development of a problem even though the insect or disease is present. Second, plants do not have an immune system. They have developed elaborate structural and chemical defenses, but they do not produce antibodies or white blood cells to fight disease. Finally, plants can survive most destructive conditions. Loss of roots, leaves, branches, or even stem tissue does not necessarily result in death of the plant.

At this point, you may wonder how any plant survives, let alone produces flowers and fruits, when the potential for animal damage, insect infestation, and disease problems is everywhere.

Structural Defense

Plants have numerous features that prevent pathogens from attacking and invading. The most obvious plant defense mechanism—needles and thorns—prevent or discourage all but the hungriest herbivores from eating some plants. Thick hairs may keep insects or pathogens from ever coming in contact with the leaf surface.

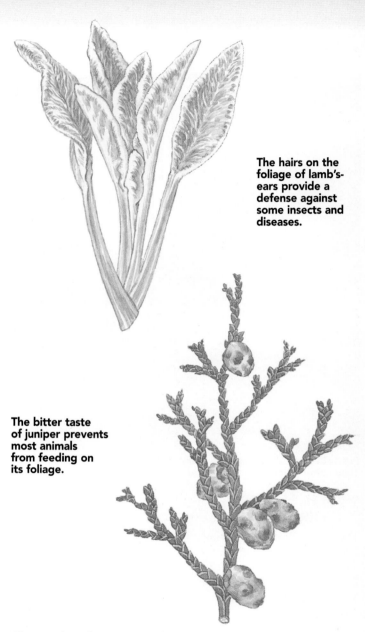

The hairs on the foliage of lamb's-ears provide a defense against some insects and diseases.

The bitter taste of juniper prevents most animals from feeding on its foliage.

Spines on cactus keep grazing animals at bay.

Chemical Defense

Plants are veritable chemical factories. We use plant chemicals all the time: Aspirin, originally derived from willow, is used to treat headaches. Many people keep aloe plants and rub the sap from leaves on burns. The plant-derived drug taxol is used to treat cancer and coumarin is used a blood thinner. Some plants, such as sugar beets and sugarcane, produce sweet-tasting chemicals. Some plants produce bitter and unpalatable chemicals that prevent disease or stop animals from feeding on them. Few animals or fungi attack young sorghum because of the high levels of cyanide the seedlings produce soon after germination. Plants contain thousands of chemicals that can slow or stop the growth of animals, insects, and disease-causing agents. Some of these are being produced all the time, like the chemicals that cause most people to develop a rash when they touch poison ivy or poison oak. Other chemicals are "turned on" by the plant when it is injured or infected.

Combination Defense

Some plants produce structural barriers in response to infection. When injured cells die, tannins, lignins, and resins (to name a few) are produced and form a barrier. Resin that exudes often traps the insect that caused the damage. Most of the time, these barriers prevent damage or disease-causing pathogens from spreading.

Most plants are immune to most diseases and are ignored by most insects. An elm cannot be a host to tomato hornworm. A tomato plant cannot become infected with Dutch elm disease or oak wilt. Although most American

elms died during the initial epidemic of Dutch elm disease, a few individual trees did not. Such trees have been carefully evaluated and found able to resist the pathogen that causes Dutch elm disease. Plant breeders screen thousands of plants to identify resistant cultivars and make them available for the nursery trade.

Disease resistance is one factor that protects plants from specific diseases, but no plant is protected from all diseases. A fire blight-resistant flowering crabapple may still be susceptible to apple scab or cedar-apple rust. Knowing what diseases a plant is susceptible to or resistant to can

Although powdery mildew on lilac has an unappealing appearance, the disease does little harm to the shrub.

aid in the diagnostic process. When evaluating a tree for your garden, it is important to know what problems exist in neighboring gardens so you can choose a plant that will stand up to infection or resist disease. Lists of resistant plants can be found on many cooperative extension websites and in books and seed catalogs. One of the simplest methods of avoiding plant problems is to incorporate resistant plants, and plants known to have few problems, in your yard and garden.

Some plants are bred to be tolerant of disease instead of resistant to it. This means that the plant can be infected by a disease and still perform well. Many older lilacs succumb to severe powdery mildew infection in late summer but produce beautiful blooms the following spring.

Many cucumbers, squash, and melons tolerate powdery mildew. This means that they can produce a good crop of fruit despite severe infection.

Plants can also escape infection. Starting seeds when the weather is too cold and wet can result in damping-off, which kills seeds and seedlings. Heat-loving plants, such as pepper, tomato, and zinnia, that develop under cold, wet conditions are delayed and don't perform as well as transplants set out several weeks later. By waiting until the soil is warm seeds and transplants escape diseases such as *Pythium* and *Phytophthora* root rots and benefit from the optimal conditions for germination so they get off to a strong start.

Crabapples are beautiful in bloom. Select varieties with resistance to apple scab and fire blight to prevent disfigurement later in the season.

Zinnia seedlings started in a pot indoors will get the flowers off to a faster start than those sown directly in cold soil outdoors.

Only a few resistant elms have survived the ravages of Dutch elm disease.

SCOUTING FOR PROBLEMS

Diagnosing a problem is easiest if you catch the perpetrator in the act. The first nearby insect or fungal growth you see may not be the cause of the problem. The process of evaluating an area for weed, insect, and disease problems is called scouting. Before you determine and diagnose a problem, you need to find it first; this is where scouting comes in.

Weeds

Scouting for weeds is the easiest aspect of the scouting process. Unlike insects that can fly or crawl away, "catching" a weed is relatively simple. You don't need a microscope to identify a weed. Most people weed without thinking about the reasons. Weeds compete with plants for limited resources and may also serve as alternate hosts for insects and disease. Weeding is scouting in the purest sense. Once weeds are identified, they are usually removed without much thought. However, identifying the weed and determining why it has invaded is the first step in managing weeds in lawns and gardens.

Horsetail spreads quickly on wet sites.

Creeping Charlie often out-competes turfgrass in the shade.

Weeds as Indicators of Other Problems

Although weeds are nuisances, they can serve as indicators of underlying problems. Horsetail thrives on wet sites and serves as an indicator of excessive soil moisture. One of the most reviled weeds in the home lawn provides another excellent example: Creeping Charlie thrives in cool, moist shade. Because most lawns do not perform well under these conditions, creeping Charlie has a competitive advantage: It can outgrow the grass in shade.

Some lawns support a variety of weeds. This usually indicates poor overall health of the lawn or poor management practices. The best way to prevent weeds in your lawn is to keep your lawn healthy. There is simply no place for weeds to grow in a healthy well-established lawn.

Traditional weed control consists primarily of hand pulling and mulching. When properly timed, this two-pronged approach is usually effective. Weeds are easiest to control when their seeds are germinating. To prevent them from becoming established, they are most easily removed when soil is moist, although not excessively wet. Once weeds are established, control often requires hard work, herbicides, or both. For this reason, prevent weeds from going to seed in or near the garden. If you need to use an herbicide, be sure to apply it only to actively growing weeds. Before using any herbicide, read the label. Many herbicides are specific to grass or to broad-leaved weeds. "Weed-and-feed" formulations should not be applied near flower or vegetable gardens. The "weed" portion of "weed-and-feed" is specific to broad-leaved plants and includes most vegetables and flowers grown in the garden.

After identifying the weeds, review your garden and lawn-care practices. Carefully consider what adjustments are needed to maintain a healthy lawn or weed-free garden. One of the most important practices in preventing weed establishment is selecting the proper grass. Different grasses thrive under different specific conditions, so be sure to match the seed or sod to your conditions. After a lawn is established, consider what type and how much feeding, watering, mowing, thatch management, and related practices you wish to do. Following the annual lawn program found on lawn product packages will help keep the lawn weed-free from proper nutrition and timing of weed control treatments.

Hand pull weeds such as tree seedlings before they become well established.

Apply weed preventer to flower beds before weeds germinate.

Broad-leaved weeds in a lawn may be controlled by spraying a selective herbicide.

Use a sharp hoe to slice off weeds in the vegetable garden.

SCOUTING FOR INSECTS

1

If insect populations are low, pick them off affected plants by hand. If you are squeamish about handling bugs, use rubber gloves.

1

Roses are a favorite plant of Japanese beetles. Inspect your rose plants regularly to observe when the beetles begin to feed.

2

After removing the insects from the plant, drop them into soapy water to kill them.

2

Insecticidal sprays may be necessary to manage Japanese beetles.

Scouting for insects is much more challenging than scouting for weeds. In a matter of days, insects can arrive, damage your plants, then seemingly disappear. Monitoring your plants routinely will help you keep on top of the insect population and prevent infestations. Biweekly scouting of plants enables you to make some control choices before the damage reaches destructive levels. You can remove some pests physically from the plants by handpicking them, by using a water hose to wash them from the plants, or by spraying them with insecticidal soap or horticultural oil. These approaches are the least toxic way to control insect problems. For them to be effective, you must be vigilant to make sure the problem insect doesn't become established.

When scouting your yard or garden, include all plant groups (lawn, trees, shrubs, fruits, vegetables, annuals, and perennials) and inspect several plants within each group. Be sure to choose them at random. Inspect the tops and undersides of multiple leaves or leaflets per plant. Determine how much damage is acceptable to you. If damage is minimal, you may choose to hand-pick pests, avoiding the need for chemical control. If the infestation is severe, you may need to spray to prevent the problem from increasing or to reduce insect populations to a "pickable" level.

Inspect undersides of leaves and tender new foliage of plants for insects.

Small holes in the leaf are evidence that this eggplant has been attacked by flea beetles.

Irregular holes chewed in leaves (*above*) are evidence of grasshopper feeding. Also check nearby plants to find the insects (*left*).

Dig up a square of sod (*above*) to check for presence of grubs. If they are present, you will see white larvae (*left*).

Aphids are a favorite food of ladybugs. Here an adult ladybug is feasting on rose aphids.

Scouting home lawns poses different issues due to the speed at which grass problems develop. Always be on the lookout for damage. Scout as you pick up branches and other debris before you mow. Branch removal will also extend the life of your mower blade. Carefully examine any discoloration—not only the pattern, but individual areas of grass. Use a hand trowel to excavate roots if necessary. Digging sod may reveal feeding injury from grubs.

Anyone who gardens will inevitably confront an infestation of something. Before reaching for a pesticide to spray, carefully examine the problem. Sometimes it will take care of itself. Insects are susceptible to disease and predation too. Large populations of aphids are a food source for adult and immature ladybugs. These beetles are voracious. One can eat several hundred aphids. Praying mantis prey upon smaller insects, as do spiders. Remember your garden and yard are part of the larger environment. When spraying to control an insect pest problem, consider that you may unintentionally kill beneficial insects as well.

SCOUTING FOR DISEASE

While scouting plants for the presence of insects, carefully examine leaves for evidence of disease. Leaf spots, discoloration, and wilting are indications of plant distress. When found early, diseases such as canker or leaf spot can be easily removed through careful pruning or pinching.

Early detection, accurate diagnosis, and understanding how pesticides work are essential for plant disease management. Why is early detection important? Just like human disease, plant disease can quickly reach epidemic proportions. If your scouting reveals early evidence of powdery mildew, spraying the foliage with the appropriate fungicide allows you to protect the remaining growth. Spraying after the mildew is widespread is ineffective because fungicides help prevent mildew; they don't "cure" it. They act like a vaccine (that you have to apply every few weeks) to protect the plant. By scouting regularly, you can quickly discover problems, correctly diagnose them, and prevent further spread of the pathogen.

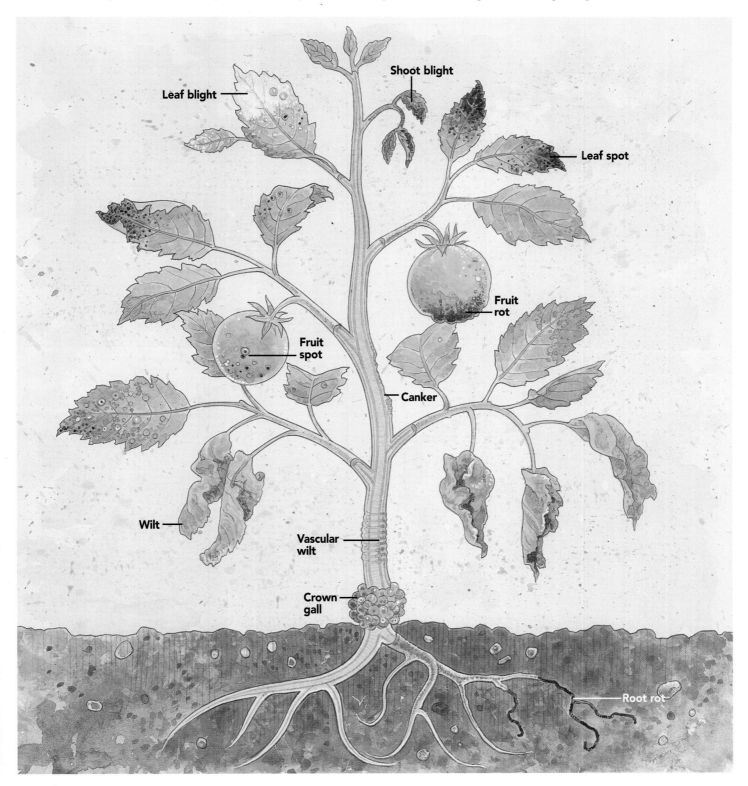

After finding evidence of a disease, the next step is accurately identifying it. The fungi that cause plant disease are very different from one another—so different that many fungicides are labeled for use on specific fungi. Fungicides labeled for control of downy mildews and other "water molds" won't work against powdery mildew. It is important to accurately diagnose the problem, so your plans for managing it will succeed!

Because most disease diagnoses are not easily made in the field, it is important to harvest a good representative sample for your own diagnostic purposes, or for referral to your cooperative extension service or local garden center. Collect a sample that characterizes the problem. Include an unaffected portion if possible. The disease-causing agent is often found at the interface between healthy and dead tissue. Wrap plant samples in newspaper or paper towels—plastic causes samples to rot. If you suspect an insect as well as a disease, include the intact insect in a small container such as a pill bottle or film cannister. Even experts have a difficult time identifying squished "suspects."

1 Leaf spots and fungal blights are common problems on tomatoes grown in humid sections of North America.

2 If the infection is not severe, you may be able to keep it under control by removing infected leaves.

3 When disease pressure is high, use protective fungicide sprays. Begin sprays before leaves show symptoms.

4 To reduce overwintering disease spores, remove tomato vines and supports at the end of the growing season.

5 As an added precaution, clean tomato cages with a dilute bleach solution (nine parts water to one part bleach). The bleach will kill disease spores clinging to the wire supports.

DIAGNOSING PLANT DAMAGE

Cedar (Cedrus) is one type of tree commonly known as cedar.

Eastern red cedar (Juniperus) is a different tree, but also known as cedar.

Western red cedar (Thuja) is yet another tree known as cedar.

Diagnosing plant problems takes an investigative approach, like a criminologist working on a case. The key difference is that neither your victim nor the "witnesses" can talk. You need to reconstruct the event and the factors that contributed to the problem. There can be numerous causes for any given symptom, not all of them related to insects or diseases. Soil nutrition and texture, weather conditions, quantity of light, and other environmental and cultural conditions influence the health of a plant. An accurate diagnosis helps ensure the success of your management strategy.

STEP ONE: KNOW YOUR HOST

Correctly identifying the affected plant is the first step to successful diagnosis. Using the plant's botanical (Latin) name is more helpful than using its common name. Cedars are planted throughout the United States. There are many types of cedar: True cedar (Cedrus), eastern red cedar (Juniperus), western red cedar (Thuja), false cedar (Chamaecyparis), and incense cedar (Calocedrus). Even though all of these trees are called cedar, they are all very different and they suffer from distinctly different pests and diseases.

STEP TWO: DETERMINING IF A PROBLEM EXISTS

Plants go through established life cycles. Many conifers lose their needles in fall; certain hollies and rhododendrons drop their leaves in spring. Knowing what is normal and when it occurs allows you to recognize abnormalities. Keep in mind that many ornamentals have variegated leaves, brightly colored new growth, or double flowers. Hosta 'Sun Power' is a cultivar prized for its bright yellow leaves. To the unknowing, it may appear to be suffering from severe nitrogen deficiency. Familiarity with your plants allows you to decide whether or not there is a problem.

The chartreuse foliage of 'Sun Power' hosta could be mistaken for a nutrient deficiency, but it is normal coloration for this cultivar.

STEP THREE: DECREASE THE SUSPECT LIST

Consider your favorite detective show: The first act of business is identifying the victim, then listing the characters who interacted with the victim. Plant identification does the same thing. The insects and diseases that affect plants are usually host-specific. Remember that an elm cannot be a host to tomato hornworm, or a tomato plant cannot become infected with Dutch elm disease or oak wilt. By accurately identifying the host plant, you've reduced many possible suspects down to a few dozen.

Use a reliable reference book such as Ortho's *Home Gardener's Problem Solver* to correctly identify the problem and determine possible control measures.

After identifying the host, look in books or log onto a website to research which insects and diseases affect that plant. Many beginning gardeners confronted with their first garden problem look at pictures of problems in gardening books and attempt to match the problem with the picture. Outstanding books such as Ortho's *Home Gardener's Problem Solver* have useful photos to aid you in your diagnosis. However, it is easy to make a simple, but incorrect diagnosis instead of determining the cause of more complex problems. Like any skill, diagnosing plant problems requires practice. The more you garden, the more practice you will get.

STEP FOUR: DEVELOP AN INVESTIGATIVE APPROACH

Diagnosing plant problems is easier if you know which questions to ask. There are two terms you need to learn: symptoms and signs.
Symptoms describe how a plant responds to damage. Symptoms can be vague—wilting, leaf spotting, or discoloration—and are often so similar for different

Wilting is a symptom with many possible underlying causes.

Webs of fall webworm are a sign that the pest is present.

problems that diagnoses should not be made based upon symptoms alone. Conclusive diagnosis requires the presence of one or more signs.
Signs are direct evidence of an organism causing the damage that creates characteristic symptoms. A sign could be a mushroom, a tiny pustule caused by a fungus, ooze from bacteria, living insects, webbing, frass (insect excrement), or insect exoskeletons. The presence of signs confirms involvement of a particular pest in causing the symptoms you observed. But lack of signs doesn't exclude the pest of possible involvement.

STEP FIVE: DETERMINING CAUSE OF THE PROBLEM

Plants require appropriate light, temperature, humidity, nutrients, and water. Plants undergo stress when they receive too much or too little of these basic necessities. Stress predisposes plants to insect and disease attack.

Nonliving (Abiotic)
Plant disorders due to injury don't "spread" to other plants, although other plants may be affected. A good example of this is misuse of chemical spray affecting several plants—the intended target and nearby innocent victims.
Environmental damage: Despite hail, flooding, drought, sunscald, and ice storms, most plants persist and some even thrive under the extremes of weather. However, environmental damage is more than just weather. Plants that are grown in the wrong conditions, such as a blue flag iris on dry sand or a cactus in a water garden, also suffer environmental damage. It is important to know what conditions a plant prefers for optimal growth.
Mechanical damage: Dead branches in a tree can be caused by rough play by active children, severe winds, or ice damage. All result in broken branches. Other causes of mechanical damage include injury to the base of a tree by string trimmers, lawn mower damage to aboveground roots, or even impact by a car or other vehicle.
Chemical damage: Chemical damage may result from the spills of fertilizers or pesticides that burn the foliage or even cause plant death. Chemical damage can also result when acid-loving plants, such as azalea or blueberry, are grown in alkaline soils. In this instance the damage mimics nutritional deficiency. Damage from road salt spray or dog urine spots on lawns are other examples of chemical injury to plants.

Living (Biotic)

Living organisms multiply over time. The spread of insects and disease-causing agents can be exponential and cause increasing levels of damage.

Animal damage: Small rodents and other animals can cause significant mechanical damage to plants while feeding. Small mammals commonly chew the bark and cambium tissue on small trees and shrubs. This damage is often found above the snow line during the winter. Larger mammals, such as deer, browse on the lowest branches. Damage ends at the highest point they can reach.

Insect damage: As the smallest animals, insects are capable of causing damage in a big way. In evaluating insect damage, it is important to identify the location and type of damage. It can be due to feeding and egg-laying.

Pathogen damage: Because most pathogens are microscopic for the majority of their lives, disease problems are probably the most difficult to diagnose. Distinguishing between fungal, bacterial, viral, and nematode damage often requires a microscope or professional consultation.

STEP SIX: DEFINE THE PROBLEM

Closely examine the entire plant and others around it. Are you sure you've correctly identified the plant genus, species, and even cultivar? What do you know about the plant in question? The indentations in the leaves of sassafras or water oak may look like insect damage to the unobservant gardener. 'Pandora's Box' miniature hosta may appear stunted and suffering a nutrient deficiency because of its small size. 'Razzmatazz' purple coneflower, with its numerous petals, may be incorrectly diagnosed with aster yellows. The brown pustules on the underside of a fern frond may be mistaken for rust instead of being recognized as the

'Razzmatazz' purple coneflower has unusual petals that look similar to aster yellows, but are normal for this cultivar.

Raised spore clusters on fern look similar to rust pustules but they are normal for healthy plants.

spore-producing organ of the fern. Know what "normal" looks like so you can define what is abnormal about the plant. In describing the abnormality, distinguish between the symptoms—how the plant responded to the damage— and the signs, which are the cause of the damage you are observing. Remember that symptoms are not definitive. Spots on leaves can be due to insect damage, disease, or chemical factors.

In defining the problem, determine exactly what is going on. If the plant's leaves have insects, examine the leaves with insects on them. Can you observe the insects actually causing the damage, or are they "innocent bystanders"? When evaluating foliar symptoms such as wilt, examine the affected branch, making sure that mechanical damage or a developing canker isn't the problem. Evaluate from the crown to the roots to make sure that the problem isn't at the base of the plant or that the roots aren't rotted.

Note the plant's overall health and whenever possible, its history. Plants that have undergone environmental stress, such as flooding or drought, or plants that are growing in poor sites (compacted soil, near roads, or surrounded by asphalt) are often predisposed to attack by opportunistic insects or pathogens. An accurate assessment of the overall situation helps you manage the pest or pathogen.

STEP SEVEN: LOOK FOR PATTERNS

To find patterns, examine nearby plants to see whether they have the same problem. Consider whether the problem is seasonal. Evergreens do lose their needles in fall and throughout the winter. Check to see whether the affected plant(s) are all the same type. Pathogens are host specific; insects are less so. Are the affected plants in the same place or in different locations? Damage to a few species of plants or only to plants of the same species may indicate the presence of living factors.

Damage to different types of plants in a single location often indicates nonliving factors. Damage caused by misapplied herbicide will affect only the leaves of a specific age or leaves facing a specific direction and will affect all the plants that were sprayed (including any nearby weeds). Sunscald on the bark of thin-barked trees such as maple or apple commonly occurs on the southern or western side of the tree.

STEP EIGHT: EXAMINE THE PROBLEM'S DEVELOPMENT

Living factors tend to multiply over time, resulting in a problem that spreads from one plant to the next. Note whether the problem is increasing on a single plant or multiple plants within a planting. This can indicate living factors. Many people mistakenly believe that a problem "suddenly

Yellowed leaves with green veins are symptomatic of plants affected by iron chlorosis.

developed" overnight. In most instances problems were present at very low levels, and environmental conditions changed to favor the growth of the living factor.

Symptoms that develop suddenly (within three days) or remain in a particular spot or on a particular plant are usually due to nonliving factors. They progress or get worse if they are not corrected. An excellent example of this is iron chlorosis in pin oak. For the first 10 years, no noticeable symptoms appear. As the tree matures and requires more iron than is available in the soil, the foliage begins to fade while the veins remain dark. This pattern is characteristic of iron chlorosis. Under severe conditions, the foliage can be a pale lemon yellow and is more susceptible to scorch. Trees begin to die back and decline. Death is the usual prognosis and eventual outcome.

STEP NINE: IDENTIFY THE SPECIFIC CAUSE

Decide whether the problem is caused by nonliving factors or living factors.

Nonliving Factors

Uniform, unusual, distinct, or repeated patterns indicate damage caused by nonliving factors. Determining what the factor may be requires additional examination of the problem. Take into account construction that may have damaged roots or changed water flow, unusual weather conditions, and chemical use by you or your neighbors.

Chemical factors: Inappropriate use of weed-and-feed products, drift from a neighbor's yard, and inappropriate rates of pesticides can cause symptoms such as bleaching, leaf burn, distortion, yellowing, or even death. Follow product label directions to avoid injury to plants.

Nutrient disorders: Although nutrient deficiencies develop slowly, they aren't usually recognized until the symptoms become severe. On the other extreme, excessive nutrients can compete with other required nutrients and give the appearance of a deficiency that doesn't exist, such as stunting, yellowing, or reddening of foliage. Excessive fertilizer can produce overly succulent growth which becomes susceptible to disease and insect damage. Excessive fertilizer can also burn leaves and roots and even result in plant death. In the lawn, symptoms of excessive fertilizer use often follow distinct patterns of application.

Mechanical damage: Check for broken or girdled stems or roots. Check the base of trees and shrubs to rule out lawn mower or string trimmer damage. Most leaf damage is corrected the following year, whereas damage to the stem or crown can result in long-term problems or even death of the affected plant.

Environmental factors: Damage caused by cold, heat, light, and moisture extremes can physically harm the plant.

■ **Cold damage:** Plants vary in their hardiness or cold tolerance. Damage appears on plants that are not zone appropriate. After particularly severe winters, nonhardy deciduous trees damaged by cold may leaf out, then die. Some plants fail to leaf out at all. Plants that flower on old wood may fail to flower year after year. Conifers suffering from cold damage will have all needles of the same age affected. Frost cracks and sunscald from the warming of tissue exposed to sun and the subsequent "quick freeze" that develops when temperatures plunge at night, commonly occur on the southern and western sides of trees. In instances of late frost, damage will appear on new growth of both evergreens and hardwoods. Plants that are overwintered in aboveground containers are especially susceptible to cold damage to the root system.

■ **Heat damage:** The early afternoon sun during the warmest days of summer can cause significant damage to broad-leaved plants. Symptoms develop on unshaded leaves and often have significant patterns if other leaves have shaded the plant. Variegated plants are more susceptible to this type of damage than their nonvariegated counterparts. Excess heat causes scorch symptoms on leaf tips and interveinal areas. Care must be taken in diagnosing this as heat injury because infection by vascular pathogens can cause this symptom as well.

■ **Moisture extremes:** Drought and flooding produce similar symptoms that include yellowing and leaf drop. Eventually the plant will wilt. If the situation becomes severe in either instance, death can result.

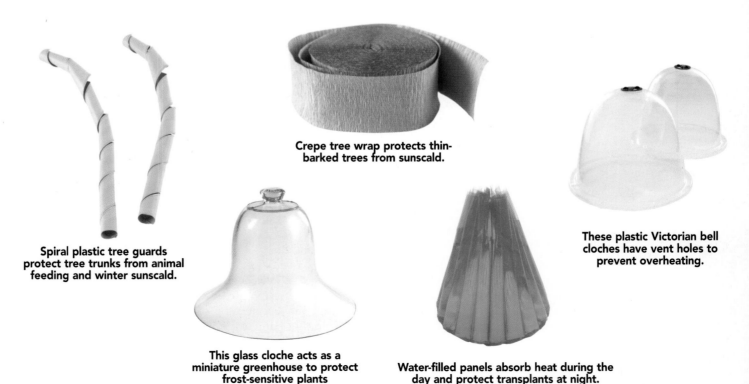

Crepe tree wrap protects thin-barked trees from sunscald.

Spiral plastic tree guards protect tree trunks from animal feeding and winter sunscald.

These plastic Victorian bell cloches have vent holes to prevent overheating.

This glass cloche acts as a miniature greenhouse to protect frost-sensitive plants

Water-filled panels absorb heat during the day and protect transplants at night.

■ **Irregular watering:** Because irregular watering results in plant stress, affected plants are then predisposed to attack by insect and disease. On tomatoes, moisture fluctuations can cause blossom drop, cat-facing (puckered, misshapen fruit) and blossom-end rot. It can also cause flower drop, reduced flowering, or shortened flowering time.

■ **Transplant shock:** Most plants respond poorly to rapid changes in their environment. A rapid change from low light to high light can cause yellowing of leaves, sunburn, reduced growth (particularly in leaf size), leaf drop, or even death. Too little light weakens plants, predisposes them to disease and insect problems, and can reduce flowering. Too much light applied too suddenly can result in scorch.

Living Factors

Animal damage extends only as far as the animal can reach. Browse lines usually stop at specific heights or when a preferred food source runs out. Insect damage is usually specific: The leaves are mined, chewed, or skeletonized. Plant diseases form patterns too. Root rots usually occur in discrete areas and start with a center and radiate outward from the initial site of infection. Root rots and foliar diseases due to "water molds" often follow the drainage patterns or sprinkler lines in lawns and gardens.

Animal Damage

Small mammals: Small rodents and rabbits commonly chew the bark and living tissue directly beneath the bark. Mice, voles, and rabbits can cause tree death if their feeding circles the entire stem and results in "girdling" the stems of young trees. The underground feeding of voles and pocket gophers can sever roots from the crown of the plant and lead to plant death. In their hunt for grubs, moles cause considerable damage to lawns or gardens.

Larger mammals: Deer browse larger branches and can completely rip off smaller branches from trees and shrubs.

Birds: Woodpeckers and sapsuckers cause considerable damage to trees, houses, and decks as the birds attempt to extract grubs and other larvae. Sapsuckers drill uniform rows of holes in the branches and trunks of declining trees.

Use a live trap to remove unwanted animal pests.

A cylinder of hardware cloth placed around the tree trunk prevents vole and rabbit feeding over winter.

Rabbits can tunnel under a fence. Staple chicken wire to a fence and bury it in the ground to keep rabbits out of the garden.

1 Make a planting basket from chicken wire.

2 To prevent squirrels from digging your tulip bulbs, plant them in the wire basket.

3 Cover the bulbs with gravel and more wire.

Insects

Insect damage is caused by chewing, piercing-sucking, and rasping. The presence of an insect is additional evidence that may support your diagnosis. Make sure that the damage you find is the type caused by the insect you suspect.

This swallowtail butterfly caterpillar is feeding on a fennel plant.

Chewing damage:

Insects with chewing mouthparts feed on all parts of the plant.

■ **Entire leaf:** If the entire leaf except for the midvein is eaten, examine leaves for the presence of caterpillars, sawflies, or webworms.

■ **Holes in flowers** can indicate the presence of insects. Rose flowers are regularly damaged by rose chafers, false Japanese beetles, and Japanese beetles.

■ **Pattern feeding:** Distinct notches on the leaf margin are often due to black vine weevils. Circular holes cut into the edge of the leaf are probably due to leaf-cutter bees.

■ **Random damage** found throughout the leaf is often due to feeding by beetles, grasshoppers, or weevils.

■ **Skeletonized leaves** result when the inner green portion of the leaf is consumed, leaving the upper and lower membranes of the leaf.

■ **Leaf miners**

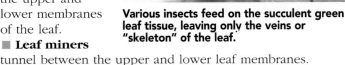

Various insects feed on the succulent green leaf tissue, leaving only the veins or "skeleton" of the leaf.

tunnel between the upper and lower leaf membranes. Common hosts of leaf miners include columbine, hollyhock, aspen, birch, and elm.

■ **Webbing:** Fall webworm is an example of an insect that encloses plant tips in webbing and feeds on blossoms, leaves, and buds.

■ **Petiole borers** burrow into the petiole, the stem that attaches a leaf to the branch. Maple petiole borer is common where maples are planted.

■ **Borers** include several types of insects. Eggs laid at the base of the affected plant hatch, and larvae (grubs or caterpillars) chew their way into the plant. Wilting and dieback are common symptoms. Squash vine borer and iris borer develop into moths at maturity.

■ **Bark borers** feed on living tissue under the bark and form beetle galleries. Damage is recognized by a general decline of the plant or a specific branch. Close examination reveals holes in the bark, insect frass, or sawdust. Conifers, such as pine or spruce, may produce large amounts of resin in response to the borer. Examples of bark borers include pine bark beetles, elm bark beetles, and emerald ash borer.

■ **Root feeding** can be done by grubs and caterpillars, which are the larval stages of beetles, weevils, and moths. This damage results in loss of vigor and decline. Common root feeders include Japanese beetles and sod webworms.

Piercing-sucking: Unlike chewing insects, insects with piercing-sucking mouthparts pierce plant tissue and suck liquid, such as sap and water, into their stomach. While piercing and sucking, they inject saliva into the plant to aid in feeding. The saliva can be toxic to the plants and transmit viruses and other diseases to healthy plants. Piercing-sucking damage can cause various symptoms, such as small flecks, deformed plant or flower growth, wilting, or discrete leaf damage.

■ **Spittlebugs** pierce the stems of plants and feed on the juice. The presence of frothy spittle allows for easy diagnosis of this insect.

■ **Leaf spotting and stippling:** Toxic saliva can also cause lesions. Aphids, scale, mealy bugs, plant bugs, and spider mites may cause spotting or stippling.

■ **Galls** are irregular plant growths that result when insects inject plant hormones and other growth regulating chemicals. Galls may occur on leaves, bark, flowers, buds, acorns, or roots. Oaks are particularly susceptible to leaf and twig attack.

Spider mites cause stippling of leaves. This anthurium shows typical damage.

■ **Leaf distortion:** Many insects inject toxins that result in curling or puckering of leaves or other deformities that mimic disease symptoms. Examples include honeysuckle witches' broom aphids, eriophyid mites, and cyclamen mites.

Rasping damage: The mouthparts of rasping insects scrape plant tissue then feed on moist inner tissue.

■ **Slugs and snails** rasp at plant tissue with their mouths. Slugs are easily identified by the shiny slime trails they leave in surrounding mulch and on affected foliage. Slugs are more common during periods of wet weather.

■ **Thrips** feeding results in silvering from the scrape-and-suck combination when they feed. Depending on the host species, feeding injuries occur on fruit, flowers, flower buds, leaves, and leaf buds. Thrips often carry tomato spotted wilt virus, a serious disease for many plants.

Pathogens

Pathogens include fungi, bacteria, viruses, nematodes, and even parasitic plants such as dodder or mistletoe. Use a hand lens to locate and identify the signs and symptoms of these causal agents of plant disease.

Leaves, flowers, and fruits

■ **Powdery mildew:** This white dusty covering of fungus can be easily rubbed off. Powdery tissue is the sign of the disease.

■ **Rust:** This fungal disease is characterized by orange pustules that appear on the leaves. It may produce chlorotic symptoms in areas surrounding the pustule.

■ **Leaf spot:** Circular lesions, with or without concentric rings, may appear and grow through leaf veins. Pimplelike fruiting bodies may appear on the diseased tissue. Most leaf spots are due to fungi.

Cedar apple rust on crabapple shows up as circular orange spots with yellow edges.

■ **Angular, water-soaked leaf spot:** Bacterial leaf spot is usually angular because the lesion is stopped by the leaf veins. Spots often appear water-soaked.

■ **Scattered, dry, angular leaf spot:** Foliar nematodes cause angular leaf spot delimited by the leaf veins.

■ **Anthracnose:** This fungal leaf spot progresses through the leaf vein and into the

Irregular black blotches on yellowed rose foliage is symptomatic of black spot.

woody stem of the plant. It can produce blightlike symptoms.

■ **Leaf distortion:** Infected leaves vary from their normal shape and size. This symptom is associated with plant diseases such as viruses and fungi or is due to infestations of insects and mites.

■ **Mottling, mosaic:** Viruses cause varying shades of green or yellow that produce an irregular, variegated appearance.

■ **Ringspot:** Round, target-shaped spots are symptoms of viral disease. Tomato spotted wilt virus infects hundreds of annuals and perennials and often causes ringspot on infected plants.

Roots

■ **Rot:** Roots appear darkened and soft. Plants may be easily pulled from soil. Few root hairs are present. Earliest symptoms usually include wilting or stunting. Fungus may be present. Root rots often develop due to overly wet or overly dry conditions.

■ **Gall, knot:** Roots attacked by nematodes often have galls or knots. Nematodes are microscopic roundworms that cause diseaselike symptoms. Symptoms of nematode

damage are wilting and stunting. Some bacteria can cause galls or unusual root proliferation. Avoid mistaking it for the nitrogen-fixing nodules on clover, lupine, peas, and beans.

Stem, trunk, and branches

■ **Canker:** These sunken or swollen dead areas in the stem may be target-shaped in woody perennials. They are usually associated with wounds, which served as an entrance for infection. Small pustules (fungal fruiting bodies) may be present, or bacterial ooze may be observed during wet weather. Wilting may occur outward from the canker.

■ **Gall:** This round or elongated swelling in the main trunk or branches can be small or large and like cankers, they prevent nutrient flow. Galls can be fungal or bacterial.

■ **Wilt:** Wilt disease affects the water-conducting vascular tissue of the plant. Discoloration of the vascular tissue is usually present. The problem may lie below ground. Common wilt diseases include Dutch elm disease, oak wilt, verticillium wilt, and fusarium wilt.

Fungus plugs water-conducting tissues, causing wilting in vascular wilt diseases.

■ **Rot:** Stem- and branch-rotting organisms are usually secondary and invade previously damaged tissue.

■ **Rust:** Rust fungi affect leaves and branches. The fungal signs are usually visible for only a few weeks in spring.

■ **Blight:** Shoot blights result in death of new growth, usually with shoots blackening, curling, and dying. Young shoots are more susceptible than older shoots.

■ **Witches' broom:** Proliferation of new growth from a single site may be due to parasitic plants such as mistletoe or certain rust fungi. Phytoplasmas are wall-less bacteria that cause aster, ash, and elm yellows. These diseases also produce witches' brooms, but the signs are not visible.

Fire blight on pear is caused by a bacterium. Leaves appear scorched.

STEP TEN: BE PATIENT

Experience with plant problem diagnosis is born of practice. There is no better teacher than to diagnose the plant problems outside your own door. Know the host and learn its interactions with the factors that cause plant damage, both living and nonliving. Keep a balanced approach in managing problems rather than relying on any one strategy. Seek professional help when in doubt.

A–Z ENCYCLOPEDIA OF
HOUSEPLANT CARE

Gardening indoors removes plants from their natural environments. You control the amount of light, moisture, and warmth they receive through the care that you provide. The rewards of lush foliage and blooms in your living space is well worth the effort.

COMMON NAME	BOTANIC NAME	SEE PAGE
African mask	Alocasia ×amazonica	137
African milk tree	Euphorbia trigona	175
African tree grape	Cissus antarctica	154
African violet	Saintpaulia ionantha	220
Agave	Agave americana	136
Airplane plant	Chlorophytum comosum	153
Air plant	Kalanchoe daigremontiana	192
Algerian ivy	Hedera canariensis	185
Alii fig	Ficus maclellandii	179
Aloe	Aloe vera	138
Aluminum plant	Pilea cadierei	211
Amaryllis	Hippeastrum spp.	187
Angel wing begonia	Begonia coccinea	145
Anthurium	Anthurium andraeanum	139
Arboricola	Schefflera arboricola	222
Areca palm	Chrysalidocarpus lutescens	153
Arrowhead vine	Syngonium podophyllum	228
Artillery plant	Pilea microphylla	212
Asparagus fern	Asparagus densiflorus	142
Azalea	Rhododendron spp.	219
Baby rubber plant	Peperomia obtusifolia	207
Baby's tears	Soleirolia soleirolii	226
Balfour aralia	Polyscias scutellaria	216
Bamboo palm	Chamaedorea erumpens	152
Banana leaf fig	Ficus maclellandii	179
Barroom plant	Aspidistra elatior	143
Bay tree	Laurus nobilis	193
Beautiful hoya	Hoya lanceolata ssp. bella	190
Bird's nest fern	Asplenium nidus	143
Bishop's cap cactus	Astrophytum spp.	144
Bishop's hat cactus	Astrophytum spp.	144
Bloodleaf	Iresine herbstii	191
Blushing bromeliad	Neoregelia carolinae	198
Boat lily	Tradescantia spathacea	231
Boston fern	Nephrolepis exaltata	199
Bottle palm	Beaucarnea recurvata	145
Brake fern	Pteris cretica	217
Buddhist pine	Podocarpus macrophyllus	215
Bunny ear cactus	Opuntia microdasys	199
Burn plant	Aloe vera	138
Burro's tail	Sedum morganianum	224
Butterfly palm	Chrysalidocarpus lutescens	153
Button fern	Pellaea rotundifolia	204
Calamondin orange	×Citrofortunella microcarpa	155
Calla lily	Zantedeschia aethiopica	233
Candelabra plant	Euphorbia trigona	175
Cape primrose	Streptocarpus ×hybridus	228
Cast-iron plant	Aspidistra elatior	143

COMMON NAME	BOTANIC NAME	SEE PAGE
Cathedral windows	Calathea picturata	148
Cattleya orchid	Cattleya hybrids	149
Century plant	Agave americana	136
Ceylon creeper	Epipremnum aureum	172
Chenille plant	Acalypha hispida	133
Chicken gizzard	Iresine herbstii	191
China doll	Radermachera sinica	218
Chinese evergreen	Aglaonema commutatum	137
Chinese fan palm	Livistona chinensis	194
Chinese lantern	Abutilon ×hybridum	133
Chinese rose	Hibiscus rosa-sinensis	187
Chirita	Chirita sinensis	152
Christmas cactus	Schlumbergera ×buckleyi	224
Cineraria	Senecio ×hybridus	225
Clivia	Clivia miniata	157
Coffee	Coffea arabica	158
Coleus	Solenostemon scutellarioides	227
Compact wax plant	Hoya compacta	189
Copperleaf	Acalypha wilkesiana	134
Coralberry	Ardisia crenata	141
Corn plant	Dracaena fragrans	168
Cow tongue	Gasteria spp.	183
Creeping fig	Ficus pumila	181
Cretan brake	Pteris cretica	217
Croton	Codiaeum variegatum var. pictum	157
Crown-of-thorns	Euphorbia milii	174
Crystal anthurium	Anthurium crystallinum	139
Cuban oregano	Plectranthus amboinicus	213
Cut-leaf philodendron	Philodendron bipinnatifidum	208
Cyclamen	Cyclamen persicum	162
Cymbidium orchid	Cymbidium spp.	163
Dendrobium orchid	Dendrobium hybrids	165
Devil's backbone	Pedilanthus tithymaloides	202
Devil's ivy	Epipremnum aureum	172
Donkey's tail	Sedum morganianum	224
Drop tongue	Homalomena rubescens	188
Dumb cane	Dieffenbachia amoena	165
Dumb cane	Dieffenbachia picta	166
Dumb cane	Dieffenbachia seguine	167
Dwarf papyrus	Cyperus alternifolius	163
Earth star	Cryptanthus bivittatus	160
Easter cactus	Rhipsalidopsis spp.	219
Elephant ear	Alocasia ×amazonica	137
Elephant foot	Beaucarnea recurvata	145
Emerald feather	Asparagus setaceus	142
Emerald ripple peperomia	Peperomia caperata	206
English ivy	Hedera helix	186

Boston fern, *Nephrolepis exaltata*

Cyclamen, *Cyclamen persicum*

Dieffenbachia picta

English ivy, *Hedera helix*

Flame violet, *Episcia reptans*

Mosiac plant, *Fittonia verschaffeltii*

Polka dot plant, *Hypoestes phyllostachya*

Regier begonia, *Begonia*

COMMON NAME INDEX HOUSEPLANTS *continued*

COMMON NAME	BOTANIC NAME	SEE PAGE
False African violet	*Streptocarpus ×hybridus*	228
False aralia	*Schefflera elegantissima*	223
False heather	*Cuphea hyssopifolia*	161
False holly	*Osmanthus heterophyllus*	200
Fat-headed Lizzy	*×Fatshedera lizei*	176
Fiddleleaf fig	*Ficus lyrata*	179
Fiji fire plant	*Acalypha wilkesiana*	134
Finger aralia	*Schefflera elegantissima*	223
Firecracker flower	*Crossandra infundibuliformis*	160
Fishtail palm	*Caryota mitis*	149
Flame violet	*Episcia* spp.	173
Flamingo flower	*Anthurium andraeanum*	139
Flaming sword	*Vriesea splendens*	232
Florist's cyclamen	*Cyclamen persicum*	162
Flowering maple	*Abutilon ×hybridum*	133
Freckle face	*Hypoestes phyllostachya*	190
Friendship plant	*Pilea involucrata*	211
Fuchsia	*Fuchsia triphylla* 'Gartenmeister Bonstedt'	182
Gardenia	*Gardenia augusta*	182
Glorybower	*Clerodendrum thomsoniae*	156
Gloxinia	*Sinningia speciosa*	226
Gold dust dracaena	*Dracaena surculosa*	170
Golden barrel cactus	*Echinocactus grusonii*	172
Golden pothos	*Epipremnum aureum*	172
Goldfish plant	*Columnea* spp.	158
Good luck plant	*Cordyline fruticosa*	159
Grape ivy	*Cissus rhombifolia*	154
Green dracaena	*Dracaena deremensis*	168
Guppy plant	*Nematanthus* spp.	198
Guzmania	*Guzmania lingulata*	184
Hare's foot fern	*Davallia fejeensis*	164
Hawaiian ti plant	*Cordyline fruticosa*	159
Haworthia	*Haworthia fasciata*	185
Heart-leaf philodendron	*Philodendron scandens*	210
Hearts entangled	*Ceropegia linearis* ssp. *woodii*	150
Hearts-on-a-vine	*Ceropegia linearis* ssp. *woodii*	150
Hen-and-chicks	*Echeveria* spp.	171
Hibiscus	*Hibiscus rosa-sinensis*	187
Holly fern	*Cyrtomium falcatum*	164
Indian laurel fig	*Ficus microcarpa*	180
Iron cross begonia	*Begonia masoniana*	145
Jacob's coat	*Acalypha wilkesiana*	134
Jade plant	*Crassula ovata*	159
Japanese aralia	*Fatsia japonica*	177
Japanese aucuba	*Aucuba japonica*	144
Japanese euonymus	*Euonymus japonicus*	174
Japanese holly fern	*Cyrtomium falcatum*	164
Japanese pittosporum	*Pittosporum tobira*	212
Jasmine	*Jasminum polyanthum*	191

COMMON NAME	BOTANIC NAME	SEE PAGE
Jewel orchid	*Ludisia discolor*	195
Kafir lily	*Clivia miniata*	157
Kalanchoe	*Kalanchoe blossfeldiana*	192
Kangaroo vine	*Cissus antarctica*	154
Kentia palm	*Howea forsteriana*	188
Lace fern	*Asparagus setaceus*	142
Lace-flower vine	*Alsobia dianthiflora*	138
Lady of the night orchid	*Brassavola nodosa*	147
Lady palm	*Rhapsis excelsa*	218
Lady's eardrops	*Fuchsia triphylla* 'Gartenmeister Bonstedt'	182
Lawyer's tongue	*Gasteria* spp.	183
Lemon	*Citrus limon*	155
Lemon-scented geranium	*Pelargonium crispum*	203
Lipstick plant	*Aeschynanthus radicus*	135
Living stones	*Lithops* spp.	194
Lollipop plant	*Pachystachys lutea*	201
Lucky bamboo	*Dracaena sanderiana*	170
Madagascar dragon tree	*Dracaena marginata*	169
Maidenhair fern	*Adiantum pedatum*	134
Medicine plant	*Aloe vera*	138
Mexican heather	*Cuphea hyssopifolia*	161
Mexican mint	*Plectranthus amboinicus*	213
Ming aralia	*Polyscias fruticosa*	216
Miniature wax plant	*Hoya lanceolata* ssp. *bella*	190
Mistletoe fig	*Ficus deltoidea* var. *diversifolia*	178
Monkey plant	*Ruellia makoyana*	220
Monstera	*Monstera deliciosa*	197
Moon valley friendship plant	*Pilea involucrata*	211
Mosaic plant	*Fittonia albivenis verschaffeltii*	181
Moses-in-the-cradle	*Tradescantia spathacea*	231
Mother-in-law's tongue	*Sansevieria trifasciata*	221
Mother of thousands	*Kalanchoe daigremontiana*	192
Mother-of-thousands	*Tolmiea menziesii*	229
Moth orchid	*Phalaenopsis* hybrids	208
Myrtle	*Myrtus communis*	197
Neanthe bella palm	*Chamaedorea elegans*	151
Nerve plant	*Fittonia albivenis verschaffeltii*	181
Norfolk Island pine	*Araucaria heterophylla*	141
Northern maidenhair fern	*Adiantum pedatum*	134
Oakleaf fig	*Ficus montana*	180
Oakleaf ivy	*Cissus rhombifolia*	154
Old man cactus	*Cephalocereus senilis*	150
Orange	*Citrus sinensis*	156
Oxalis	*Oxalis regnellii*	201
Ox tongue	*Gasteria* spp.	183
Oyster plant	*Tradescantia spathacea*	231
Painted century plant	*Agave victoria-reginae*	136
Painted feather	*Vriesea splendens*	232

COMMON NAME	BOTANIC NAME	SEE PAGE
Painted leaf begonia	Begonia Rex cultorum hybrids	146
Panama hat palm	Carludovica palmata	148
Panda plant	Kalanchoe tomentosa	193
Parlor maple	Abutilon ×hybridum	133
Parlor palm	Chamaedorea elegans	151
Peace lily	Spathiphyllum wallisii	227
Peacock plant	Calathea makoyana	147
Peanut cactus	Chamaecereus sylvestri	151
Peppermint-scented geranium	Pelargonium tomentosum	204
Persian violet	Exacum affine	176
Piggyback plant	Tolmiea menziesii	229
Pineapple dyckia	Dyckia brevifolia	171
Pink quill	Tillandsia cyanea	229
Pleomele	Dracaena reflexa	169
Plumose fern	Asparagus setaceus	142
Poinsettia	Euphorbia pulcherrima	175
Polka dot plant	Hypoestes phyllostachya	190
Ponytail palm	Beaucarnea recurvata	145
Pothos	Epipremnum aureum	172
Prayer plant	Maranta leuconeura	196
Primrose	Primula spp.	217
Princess Astrid peperomia	Peperomia orba	207
Purple heart	Tradescantia pallida	230
Purple-leaved Swedish ivy	Plectranthus purpuratus	215
Purple passion	Gynura aurantiaca	184
Purple shamrock	Oxalis regnellii	201
Purple velvet plant	Gynura aurantiaca	184
Pussy ears	Kalanchoe tomentosa	193
Pygmy date palm	Phoenix roebelenii	210
Queen Victoria agave	Agave victoria-reginae	136
Rabbit's foot fern	Davallia fejeensis	164
Rattail cactus	Aporocactus flagelliformis	140
Red dracaena	Cordyline terminalis	159
Red flame ivy	Hemigraphis alternata	186
Red-leaf philodendron	Philodendron erubescens	209
Reed palm	Chamaedorea erumpens	152
Rex begonia	Begonia Rex cultorum hybrids	146
Ribbon plant	Chlorophytum comosum	153
Ribbon plant	Dracaena sanderiana	170
Roman laurel	Laurus nobilis	193
Rosary vine	Ceropegia linearis ssp. woodii	150
Rose mallow	Hibiscus rosa-sinensis	187
Rose-scented geranium	Pelargonium graveolens	203
Rubber tree	Ficus elastica	178
Sago palm	Cycas revoluta	162
Satin pothos	Epipremnum pictum	173
Schefflera	Schefflera actinophylla	222
Schefflera	Schefflera arboricola	222
Screw pine	Pandanus veitchii	202

COMMON NAME	BOTANIC NAME	SEE PAGE
Sensitive plant	Mimosa pudica	196
Silverleaf peperomia	Peperomia griseoargentea	206
Silver vase plant	Aechmea fasciata	135
Snake plant	Sansevieria trifasciata	221
Snowball cactus	Mammillaria bocasana	195
Song of India	Dracaena reflexa	169
Spider plant	Chlorophytum comosum	153
Spineless yucca	Yucca elephantipes	232
Split-leaf philodendron	Monstera deliciosa	197
Spotted dumb cane	Dieffenbachia maculata	166
Sprengeri fern	Asparagus densiflorus	142
Spurflower	Plectranthus forsteri	214
Staghorn fern	Platycerium bifurcatum	213
Strawberry begonia	Saxifraga stolonifera	221
Strawberry geranium	Saxifraga stolonifera	221
String-of-beads	Senecio rowleyanus	225
String of hearts	Ceropegia linearis spp. woodii	150
Striped inch plant	Tradescantia fluminensis	230
Swedish ivy	Plectranthus australis	214
Sweet bay	Laurus nobilis	193
Sweet myrtle	Myrtus communis	197
Sweet olive	Osmanthus fragrans	200
Sweetheart plant	Philodendron scandens	210
Swiss-cheese plant	Monstera deliciosa	197
Sword fern	Nephrolepis exaltata	199
Table fern	Pteris cretica	217
Tahitian bridal veil	Gibasis geniculata	183
Tail flower	Anthurium andraeanum	139
Teddy bear vine	Cyanotis kewensis	161
Thanksgiving cactus	Schlumbergera truncata	223
Touch-me-not	Mimosa pudica	196
Trailing velvet plant	Ruellia makoyana	220
Tree ivy	×Fatshedera lizei	176
Tree philodendron	Philodendron bipinnatifidum	208
Umbrella plant	Cyperus alternifolius	163
Umbrella tree	Schefflera actinophylla	222
Urn plant	Aechmea fasciata	135
Velvet plant	Gynura aurantiaca	184
Velvet leaf philodendron	Philodendron scandens f. micans	210
Venus flytrap	Dionaea muscipula	167
Wandering Jew	Tradescantia zebrina	231
Watermelon begonia	Peperomia argyreia	205
Watermelon pellionia	Pellionia repens	205
Watermelon peperomia	Peperomia argyreia	205
Wax plant	Hoya carnosa	189
Weeping fig	Ficus benjamina	177
Yucca	Yucca elephantipes	232
Zebra haworthia	Haworthia fasciata	185
Zebra plant	Aphelandra squarrosa	140
Zeezee plant	Zamioculcas zamiifolia	233

Sago palm, Cycas revoluta

Hawaiian ti plant, Cordyline terminalis

Weeping fig, Ficus benjamina

Silverleaf peperomia, Peperomia griseoargentea

SELECTING PLANTS

The best-looking houseplants result from choosing plants that are suited to your growing conditions. Available light is an important variable for houseplants. If you have south-facing windows, houseplants that need a sunny location will do well. If you have only north-facing windows, success will come from choosing plants that thrive in shade. Plants sited in other than their preferred growing conditions will be stressed and prone to diseases and insects. If you can prevent problems by proper siting, you will have better-looking plants and a happier caretaker—you!

If you decide on a particular plant with characteristics you like, make sure you can provide what it needs for ideal growth. Do some research to understand the ideal conditions for the plant and make sure you have the right location at home. Or choose your site first, then select a suitable plant for it.

Most houseplants originate in tropical or desert climates and become favorites because they are adaptable enough to grow in a wide range of home conditions. Tropical plants come from climates where temperatures rarely drop below freezing. Plants from temperate climates, where temperatures drop well below freezing, often need a cold period for survival. They also spend part of their life cycle in a dormant state, usually without leaves. For these reasons plants from temperate climates seldom perform well as houseplants.

In addition, houseplants vary in their needs for high to low light, high to low humidity, and moist to dry soil. As you map out the sites in your home for plants, keep in mind that the conditions may change from season to season. Home heating and cooling, drafts from open windows and doors, and the angle of the sun's rays through a window must all be considered. You may find that the perfect spot for a plant in winter is not appropriate for the same plant through the summer.

DECOR

Houseplants can complement your decorating style with an almost endless array of choices. If you have a southwestern scheme in your home, complement it with cactus, succulents, and arid-climate plants. A Victorian parlor will look luscious filled with flowering plants, ferns, and a terrarium or two. An array of palms lends a tropical Caribbean flair.

If you have an open floor plan, large architectural plants will provide excellent focal points. For intimate spaces, small blooming plants and fine-textured specimens will enhance the coziness of the room.

SELECTING HEALTHY PLANTS

Check the backs of leaves carefully for pests before bringing the plant home. If a plant has pests, choose another so you don't bring pests home.

Once you've decided on the perfect species of plant, it's time to select one at the garden center. Although mail-order plants are acceptable, particularly for something unusual that your local garden center doesn't carry, mailed plants may be damaged during shipping, and weight limitations may mean that you must start with smaller plants.

Whether you order by mail or visit the garden center, inspect the plant with a critical eye before introducing it into your houseplant display. Pests and diseases of any kind are not acceptable; if you see evidence of either, choose another plant.

Pull your new plant away from the other plants in the garden center and look at it carefully in the light. Check the undersides of the leaves, the leaf axils, the base of the plant, and even the soil. Anything that isn't quite right, such as webbing, browning leaf tips, fertilizer buildup on the soil, or a sour smell can indicate a problem. Find another plant or another garden center to protect your investment.

BRINGING PLANTS HOME

If you are purchasing your plant in summer, avoid leaving it in a hot car. Be sure to open the windows and

Take special care to control temperature when transporting plants in a car in winter and summer.

provide plenty of air circulation. A few minutes at hot temperatures can literally cook a plant.

When transporting a plant in winter, take care to avoid temperature stress. Some plants can be harmed by only a few minutes below 40°F. A plant sleeve helps, but it is intended for only a short distance. Warm your car before putting a plant in it; have the garden center put the plant and pot in a large plastic bag. Tie the top securely, keeping a bubble of warm air around the plant. Avoid leaving it in the car for any length of time.

ACCLIMATING PLANTS

Once you have your plant home, isolate it for a few days to make sure it has no insects or diseases you may have missed. Remember that the plant was most likely grown and displayed in the perfect conditions of a greenhouse—high light and humidity—so give it a gradual adjustment to its permanent home. Watch it carefully for several weeks for any signs that the spot you've selected for it is not ideal.

DESIGN

DESIGN BASICS

Giving some consideration to the basics of design can make your collection of houseplants a lovely addition to your decor. As in an outdoor landscape, large plants form the "bones" of the display while smaller plants complement them. You will achieve the most effective presentation if you vary height, form, texture, and color.

An effective way to avoid dealing with the large pot and weight of an immense specimen is to stage a plant. This simply means putting a smaller plant on a pedestal or an overturned pot to raise it in the display. This gives the appearance of a larger plant yet allows the use of a smaller amount of space.

Texture—the appearance and feel of a plant—adds energy and movement to a room. Large smooth leaves have a calming effect and make a room feel bigger. Fine-textured plants with small leaves generate excitement and activity, yet can also make a space feel intimate. An effective contrasting of textures makes a plant display interesting and diverse; combining similar textures gives a display simplicity and elegance.

Choosing color is perhaps the most fun aspect of designing a plant display.

Group upright and trailing plants, blooming and foliage plants to provide interest and variety in your houseplant display.

Bright colors such as scarlet and yellow are usually best used as focal points, surrounded by more subtle shades of green, white, and silver. Blues and pinks are easier to combine with other colors in the same palette. They may be beautifully set off with bits of silver- and white-variegated foliage or flowers.

Silver and white containers provide a neutral background to show off your houseplants in their full beauty.

SITUATING PLANTS

SUPPLEMENTAL LIGHT

Light exposure is the most critical element in siting a plant. When a plant has the light it requires for the best growth, it will look its best.

The classifications low, medium, and high light are general guidelines for siting plants. Low light comes from a north-, east-, or northeast-facing window, where plants get some light but nothing direct. Low light may keep a plant looking good but not be enough to make it bloom. High light generally means several hours of direct or indirect sun, usually a southern or western exposure. Medium light means several hours of bright but not necessarily direct light, such as an eastern or western exposure.

You can measure light intensity with a light meter, but a simpler method is to follow the light guidelines in this encyclopedia, place your plants, and then observe them over several weeks. Remember that light intensity changes with the season. You can easily vary the amount of light a plant receives by changing its distance from the light source or by adding supplemental light.

The best supplemental light source for the average home is fluorescent lighting. Standard fluorescent bulbs come in warm white and cool white, each with different enhanced parts of the spectrum. Using a combination of the two types gives you a fairly wide spectrum in which plants will thrive. Another type of fluorescent bulb is the "grow light," which has almost 90 percent of the sun's spectrum. The drawback is that a grow light is much more expensive than a standard fluorescent bulb.

Many plants thrive when grown on a light cart under artificial lights as a supplement for natural light.

A gauze curtain will reduce light in a bright window and keep a plant from sunburning.

1 The sun in summer is intense, but it extends only a short distance into the room.

2 Winter sun extends far into the room but is less intense than in the summer.

TEMPERATURE

Most plants perform well if the house is kept between 60 and 75°F. Many plants do better with a 5- to 10-degree drop at night, mimicking nature. A few plants require colder temperatures in winter for a resting period; you can take advantage of cool spots near windows and doors to provide this. Keep an eye out for evidence of chilling injuries such as downward-curled leaves, water-soaked spots, or blackened leaves.

Isolate new plants initially to make sure there are no pests or diseases you might have missed.

HUMIDITY

A plant that comes from a naturally humid climate will need a source of extra humidity that isn't naturally present in your home. The most efficient (but most expensive) way to raise humidity is with a humidifier installed directly on the furnace. This will raise the humidity throughout the house. Or you can use a room humidifier placed near plants that need extra humidity. A simple way to increase humidity is to group plants.

Grouping plants closely raises the ambient humidity for the entire group and reduces moisture loss.

To increase humidity, place one pot inside another with moist sphagnum moss between the pots.

This reduces some of the air circulation around them and keeps the ambient humidity higher than if each plant were on its own.

Another simple yet effective way to increase humidity is to place the plant pot on a tray of moist pebbles. Avoid sinking the pot into the pebbles, which would keep the soil soggy.

An alternative is the pot-in-pot method. Simply place the potted plant in another decorative pot a couple of inches larger in diameter and fill the cavity between them with sphagnum or Spanish moss that you keep damp. Be sure to elevate the interior pot so it does not sit in water.

CULTURE

WATERING

Giving plants the proper amount of water is simply a matter of getting to know your plants and the habitat from which they come. Push your finger an inch or two into the soil. If a plant needs constantly moist soil, the surface should be damp but not soggy. If a plant needs to dry somewhat between

Fill the inch of space between the soil and the top of the pot with water and let it drain well.

waterings, the soil should be dry to a depth of about an inch or two below the surface.

For most plants, the simplest watering method works fine. Pour water onto the soil surface, filling the space between the top of the soil and the top of the pot. If water runs off the top and down the sides of the pot without wetting the soil, place the entire pot in a sink with tepid water for about 20 minutes, then let the pot drain well.

FEEDING

Plants need 16 basic nutritional elements to grow, with nitrogen, phosphorus, and potassium in the greatest quantities. Nitrogen is used in making leaves, phosphorus stimulates roots and flowers, and potassium helps in overall health as well as fruit development. Blooming plants will thrive on plant food high in

phosphorus. Foliage plants and most others do well on a balanced food with equal amounts of nitrogen, phosphorus, and potassium.

When feeding plants, always follow the directions on the label for amount and frequency of application.

Diluted fertilizer can be easily applied during regular watering time. Water as you normally would, letting the pot drain well.

GROOMING, PRUNING, STAKING

Plants look much better when they are groomed and pruned. The most time-consuming grooming task is removing faded leaves. If a leaf has begun to yellow, remove it. Assess whether yellowing leaves are part of the plant's natural leaf shed or whether there is a cultural problem you need to attend to. Give a plant a quarter turn every time you water it to keep it symmetrical. Every couple of weeks, dust plants to remove particles that can clog the pores and prevent light from reaching the leaf surface. Wipe large-leaved plants with a soft, dry cloth.

Once every month or two give the plant a shower. In summer this can be done outdoors; in winter you can use a tub or deep sink. Be sure to use tepid water to avoid shocking the plant.

Many plants look better if pinched back or pruned regularly to keep them shrubby and full. This can help correct structural problems, and rejuvenates some plants. It may be necessary to produce new flowering wood.

Some plants benefit from staking, although stakes should be used only when necessary because they can detract from the look of a plant.

Start staking when plants are young and have pliable stems. The stems can be bent as needed, and new growth will camouflage the stakes. Choose stakes or trellises that are at least as thick as the stem you are supporting. Tie the plant loosely to the stake in a figure-eight form with a naturally colored material such as twine, raffia, grape tendrils, or green twist ties.

Dust plant leaves to control pests and to improve the plant's appearance.

Pinch out the stem tips to make plants branch and stay shrubby and attractive.

Pin vining plants to a stake with U-shape wire clips to help them climb.

REPOTTING, CONTAINERS

A plant needs repotting if it outgrows its container or if the soil is depleted. Repotting is best done in spring just before active growth begins.

Resist the urge to step up into a much bigger pot. One or two inches bigger is best. Or prune the roots and put the plant back in the same pot to keep the plant at a particular size.

Plant roots need adequate air and moisture. The potting mix must be loose enough to allow air in but contain enough organic materials to retain moisture and plant nutrients. Look for a mix that is enriched with plant food such as Miracle-Gro Potting Mix. Some potting mixes also have natural moisture control ingredients

such as coconut fibers and sphagnum peat moss.

When choosing a container for your plant, consider its size in relation to the plant's roots. Choose a pot with a drainage hole. Make sure the pot is large enough to accommodate the roots. Leave room on top of the soil to allow water to collect until it soaks into the mix when watering.

1 **Grasp a pot-bound plant gently by the crown and tap it out of its pot.**

2 **Gently tease the roots apart and remove some of the existing soil.**

3 **Set the plant in its new pot at the same level and fill with soil, tamping gently.**

MOVING PLANTS OUTDOORS FOR THE SUMMER

Houseplants benefit from being moved outdoors for the summer. Rain removes the dust of being indoors in winter, and natural predators can deter pests.

Allow plants to slowly acclimate to being outdoors so they can toughen and adapt to different conditions. Put them in a place where they are protected from wind, sun, and cold for the first couple of weeks. After this adjustment time, move them to a spot where you can enjoy them as part of your patio or outdoor landscape.

Keep in mind that few plants grown as houseplants can tolerate direct outdoor sun, regardless of their usual light requirements. Tuck them under high-canopy trees where they might receive a couple of hours of morning sun. Place low-light plants under shrubs or eaves where they receive no direct light. Monitor moisture levels carefully. These plants may need daily watering.

Place houseplants in a shaded location outdoors to prevent scorching their leaves.

PROBLEMS

An integrated pest management system is a practical and responsible method for trouble-shooting problems and improving plant health. Start with clean, healthy plants. Make sure that your plants receive proper culture. Understand your plants' requirements and give them what they need to reduce stress and prevent problems. Monitor your plants carefully. Be especially attentive to changes in the way they look. When you discover a problem, isolate the plant. Then correctly identify the pest or disease.

After determining what the problem is, decide on a method of control. These steps will take you through a logical progression of methods to use.

■ Correct cultural problems that may be stressing the plant.
■ Prune out the infested parts if this can be done without harming the plant or destroying its pleasing form.
■ Wash the foliage with a strong spray of water to dislodge insects.
■ If weather permits, move the plant outdoors to let natural predators handle the pests.
■ Remove pests physically with a fingernail, tweezers, or cotton swabs dipped in rubbing alcohol or horticultural oil. Wipe the leaves with a soft, clean cloth.
■ Wash all parts of the plant with warm, soapy water.
■ Apply insecticidal soap.
■ Repot if you have root pests or disease.
■ Spray with an appropriate houseplant insect control.
■ Discard the plant.

INSECTS

Scale insects are some of the hardest pests to control. The damage shows as leaf yellowing and eventual leaf drop. Sticky residue may coat the plant leaves. The most effective way to control scale is with horticultural oil, which smothers the adult insect.

Aphids are soft-bodied, slow-moving insects that are easily controlled with a strong spray of water, hand-picking, insecticidal soap, or horticultural oil. Aphid damage shows as distorted new leaves, stem tips, and buds. Aphids also excrete sticky honeydew.

Mealybugs appear as cottony masses in the leaf axils. They secrete a waxy coating over themselves, so they are impervious to insecticides. Control mealybugs by dipping a cotton swab in alcohol or horticultural oil and rubbing it on the insects.

Spider mites are troublesome pests that thrive in heat and low humidity. Correcting these cultural problems will often take care of many of the mites. Spider mite damage shows as yellow stippling of the leaves; once the populations are high, you will see webbing on the undersides of leaves. Washing off the leaves regularly takes care of most mites; the remaining populations can be controlled with horticultural oil or insecticidal soap.

Scale insects on houseplants will leave sticky residue and can usually be controlled with horticultural oil.

Mealybugs congregate in the leaf axils and cover themselves with a waxy coating.

DISEASES

Diseases are uncommon on well-tended plants. The most common disease problems are fungal leaf spots. These can usually be controlled or contained by pruning out the damaged leaf or plant parts. Changing the cultural conditions may help prevent the return of the spots.

Other leaf problems include viral and bacterial diseases, neither of which is easily controlled. It is often more cost effective to discard the plant.

Most leaf spots are caused by fungal diseases and can be controlled by removing the affected leaf.

Plants that sit in soggy soil or standing water often develop root or crown rots, which are fungal in nature. They can often be cured by drying out the plant. It may help to repot the plant, pruning off damaged and diseased roots at the same time.

CULTURAL PROBLEMS

The most common cultural problem that occurs on plants is over- or underwatering. Both of these practices produce the same symptoms. If a plant is overwatered repeatedly, the saturated soil kills the root hairs, which take up water. The plant loses color, wilts, and eventually dies if the soil is not dried out somewhat to allow new root hairs to grow. Underwatering is easily corrected by providing water. However, if a plant wilts completely from lack of water, it may not recover; if it does, it may never look the same.

Another common cultural problem is brown leaf tips or edges. This is most often caused by lack of humidity, but it can also appear on plants that do not receive enough moisture or are sensitive to chemicals found in water. Plants that are pot-bound and have little soil with which to hold water are susceptible.

Plants drop leaves for many reasons. In most cases it is natural leaf shed. If a plant's leaves turn crisp and fall or if a substantial number of leaves yellow and fall, you need to check the plant's cultural conditions.

Placing a plant in direct sun may cause leaf bleaching or actual sunburn, in which the leaf tissue bleaches to white and then shrivels.

Leaf spots not attributable to disease can be caused by splashing cold water on the leaves. African violets are particularly sensitive to cold-water leaf spot development. Use warm water when watering them.

FLOWERING MAPLE
Abutilon ×hybridum *a-BEW-tih-lahn HY-brih-dum*

Flowering maple is also know as Chinese lantern or parlor maple.

SIZE: 5'h × 3'w
TYPE: Woody shrub
FORM: Treelike or weeping
TEXTURE: Medium
GROWTH: Fast
LIGHT: Medium

MOISTURE: Moist
SOIL: Potting soil mix
FEATURES: Maple-shaped green or variegated leaves
USES: Focal point
FLOWERS: ■■■■□

SITING: Flowering maple performs well in medium light but also tolerates full sun. Provide temperatures of 60–75°F while it blooms, but move it into a cooler situation in winter. Flowering maple performs well with 30 percent or greater humidity.
CARE: Water to keep the soil moist while it is blooming, but in winter allow the top

2" of soil to dry between waterings. The plant may drop leaves when it receives too little water. Feed weekly with a dilute solution of plant food for flowering plants or once monthly with a full-strength solution during the blooming season. Feed every 2 months with acid food. Flowering maple blooms best when pot-bound, but if growth is active, it may need repotting annually. Give plants a shower once a month to remove dust. Deadhead the spent flowers regularly. As the plant

begins spring growth, pinch out branch tips to encourage bloom. Cut the entire plant back by half after blooming to make it shrubby and full.
PROPAGATION: Root semihardwood stem cuttings from the annual pruning in fall. Take softwood tip cuttings at any time or start plants from seed immediately after the pods have dried on the plant. Use bottom heat for germination.
PESTS AND DISEASES: Treat mealybugs and aphids with horticultural oil.

1 Training a plant to grow as a standard will take initial pruning and shaping and occasional pruning.

2 Begin by pruning off the lower branches and heading back some of the upper shoots to side buds.

3 A finished plant grown as a standard gives an indoor landscape a formal touch.

CHENILLE PLANT
Acalypha hispida *ak-uh-LIE-fuh HISS-pih-duh*

Chenille plant offers not only attractive flowers, but also striking foliage even when it is not blooming.

SIZE: 3–6'h × 3'w
TYPE: Woody shrub
FORM: Upright
TEXTURE: Coarse
GROWTH: Fast
LIGHT: High

MOISTURE: Evenly moist
SOIL: Potting soil
FEATURES: Large, fuzzy leaves
USES: Focal point
FLOWERS: ■■

SITING: Chenille plant blooms best when given full sun in winter and bright, indirect light in summer. Direct sun in summer will cause the leaves to fade and will reduce flowering. The plant tolerates lower light

but won't bloom well. Provide warm temperatures (70–75°F) and higher than average humidity. The pot-in-pot method works well to increase humidity.
CARE: Keep evenly moist but not soggy during active growth in spring and summer. Allow the soil to dry slightly between waterings in winter. Feed only three times in summer during active growth with a formula for blooming plants. Repot annually when the plant is small; when it gets too large to repot, remove the top couple inches of soil and replace with fresh potting mix. Cut the plant back by about one-third in early spring to keep it shrubby and attractive when blooming.
PROPAGATION: Chenille plant tends to get leggy, so take semihardwood stem cuttings every 2 years or so to start new plants. Dust cuttings with rooting hormone and provide bottom heat for root development.

PESTS AND DISEASES: Deter spider mites by raising the humidity and giving the plant a shower once a month.
RELATED SPECIES: *Acalypha hispida* var. *alba* has creamy white flowers. *Acalypha repens* is a trailing form with the same flowers as *A. hispida*.

Chenille plant, is a favorite with children because of its soft pink and red "tails."

COPPERLEAF

Acalypha wilkesiana ak-uh-LIE-fuh wilk-see-AY-nuh

Copperleaf, also known as Jacob's coat or Fiji fire plant, has uniquely variegated leaves to use as a colorful focal point.

SIZE: 4'h × 3'w
TYPE: Woody shrub
FORM: Upright
TEXTURE: Coarse
GROWTH: Fast
LIGHT: High
MOISTURE: Evenly moist

SOIL: Potting soil mix
FEATURES: Variegated bronze-green leaves
USES: Foliage display, focal point

SITING: Provide copperleaf with bright light but keep it out of direct sun. The plant will tolerate lower light, but the bright crimson, purple, lime, green, gold, pink, or cream variegation of the leaves will fade somewhat. Warm temperatures (70–75°F) are essential. The plant performs best when the nighttime temperature doesn't drop much, so avoid leaving it near a window where the temperature drops considerably at night. Provide high humidity or the plant will drop leaves. Place on a saucer of moist pebbles or near a humidifier.

CARE: Keep the soil evenly moist but not soggy during the growing season. Let it dry out slightly between waterings in winter. Feed only three times in summer during active growth with a formula for foliage plants. Repot annually when the plant is small. When it gets too large to repot, remove the top 2" of soil and replace with fresh potting mix. Cut plants back in spring to keep them shrubby. Pull off faded leaves regularly and give the plant a monthly shower.

PROPAGATION: Plants tend to become leggy, so propagate new plants every couple of years. Take semihardwood stem cuttings in midsummer to early fall. Dust cuttings with rooting hormone and provide bottom heat for root development.

PESTS AND DISEASES: Copperleaf may have spider mites and drop leaves when the humidity is low.

RELATED SPECIES: Cultivars are available with all types of variegation, including curled leaves and miniatures that are popular for bonsai.

MAIDENHAIR FERN

Adiantum pedatum ah-de-AN-tum peh-DATE-um

Maidenhair fern, also known as Northern maidenhair fern, offers soft, arching fronds that lend a touch of elegance to any room.

SIZE: 18"h × 18"w
TYPE: Fern
FORM: Arching, mounded
TEXTURE: Fine
GROWTH: Slow
LIGHT: Medium to high, filtered

MOISTURE: Moist
SOIL: Potting soil
FEATURES: Bright green leaflets on shiny stems
USES: Terrarium, textural accent

SITING: Maidenhair fern, with its shiny black or maroon stems and bright chartreuse to deep green fronds arranged in a half-circle, performs best in medium to bright, indirect light. It is quite tolerant of lower light, but will tend to be more open and airy. This fern thrives in average to warm temperatures (60–80°F) and needs high humidity. A pebble tray is an excellent method to keep the humidity high around the plant.

CARE: Keep moist but not soggy in spring, summer, and fall; let soil dry out only slightly during the winter. Feed every month during active growth with general houseplant food, and every 2 months during its resting phase in winter. Remove the occasional faded frond or fronds browned from lack of humidity.

PROPAGATION: Maidenhair fern is difficult for the novice to propagate. The most successful methods are spreading spores on soil mix with bottom heat and constant moisture, or carefully dividing the root clump.

PESTS AND DISEASES: Treat scale with horticultural oil.

RELATED SPECIES: There are no readily available cultivars of maidenhair fern. There are many related species (all similar

Setting a pot on a tray of wet pebbles will raise the humidity surrounding the fern.

to *Adiantum pedatum* in appearance), among them *A. formosum, A. aleuticum, A. raddianum,* and *A. pubescens.*

SILVER VASE PLANT
Aechmea fasciata *AYK-mee-a fas-see-AH-tah*

Silver vase plant, also known as urn plant, is a unique trouble-free plant that provides a room with long-lasting color.

SIZE: 12–18"h × 18–24"w
TYPE: Bromeliad
FORM: Vase-shaped
TEXTURE: Coarse
GROWTH: Slow
LIGHT: High
MOISTURE: Dry between waterings
SOIL: Epiphyte mix
FEATURES: Blue-gray leaves streaked with white
USES: Focal point
FLOWERS: ■■ ■

SITING: Vase plants require high light to bloom, but they don't do well in direct sun. The plants thrive at 60–85°F and 10–60 percent humidity.

CARE: Let the soil dry out almost completely between waterings, but keep the "vase" full of water. Every couple of months, empty and refill the vase to keep the water fresh. Feed by applying blooming plant formula to the potting soil three times in summer or by adding half-strength formula to the vase every month. Repot only when the potting mix begins to break down and no longer has recognizable chunks of bark. When the main flower spike has faded, the plant begins to develop side shoots. When these

Silver vase plant's leaves form a cup at their bases, which should be kept filled with water.

are about 6" tall, remove the main vase and leave the side shoots to grow.
PROPAGATION: Propagate by removing the offsets or side shoots when they are about one-third the size of the parent plant. Pot up the offsets and keep them in a warm, bright spot until they establish themselves.
PESTS AND DISEASES: Treat scale with horticultural oil.
RELATED SPECIES: The cultivar 'Morgana' has dusty gray-green leaves with silvery cross bands. Its flower spike is bright fuchsia with small lavender-blue flowers.

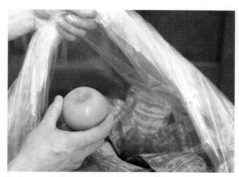

Induce a silver vase plant to flower by putting it in a plastic bag with an apple for a couple of weeks.

LIPSTICK PLANT
Aeschynanthus radicans (lobbianus) *Ess-cuh-NAN-thus RAD-ih-kanz (lob-ee-AY-nus)*

Lipstick plant blooms with bright tubular flowers nestled into rich green foliage on softly vining stems.

SIZE: 1'h × 3'w
TYPE: Gesneriad
FORM: Mounded, vining
TEXTURE: Medium
GROWTH: Medium
LIGHT: High
MOISTURE: Medium
SOIL: Epiphyte mix
FEATURES: Glossy green foliage on vines
USES: Hanging basket
FLOWERS: ■

SITING: Provide lipstick plant with bright light but not direct sun. It prefers average to warm temperatures (60–80°F) and high humidity (65 percent or higher). The pot-in-pot method is the most practical for

raising humidity when this plant is grown in a hanging basket.
CARE: Allow the soil to dry slightly between waterings, but let it dry considerably during the winter rest. Feed every 2 weeks when blooming with a formula for blooming plants, and every 2 months in fall and winter. Lipstick plant blooms best when pot bound, so repot only when watering becomes difficult

Cut the vines back to rejuvenate the plant and keep it blossoming.

because of a large root mass. Plants must be mature to bloom well. The blossoms look like tubes of lipstick (hence its common name) and fall cleanly from the plant. Although lipstick plant usually has draping vines that can reach 2–3' long, it becomes scraggly if not rejuvenated occasionally. Pinch back the tips to make it look better while blooming; after it has finished flowering, cut the plant stems back to 6 inches. Lipstick plant may shed leaves when it's too cold; the leaves may brown and dry when the humidity is too low.
PROPAGATION: Propagate by taking softwood stem or tip cuttings in spring before blooming.
PESTS AND DISEASES: Spider mites may take hold in low humidity. The plant may also develop botrytis, a fungal disease that shows as black leaf spots. Pull off the affected leaves or cut back the stems and let the potting soil dry out somewhat.
RELATED SPECIES: 'Black Pagoda' has mottled red and green foliage and brown-specked yellow and green flowers. *A. micranthus* is smaller than *A. radicans*; *A. speciosus* has orange-yellow flowers.

CENTURY PLANT

Agave americana *uh-GAH-vee a-mer-ih-CAHN-a*

Century plant, also known as agave, gives a room a dramatic southwestern flair with its architectural form.

SIZE: 3'h × 3'w
TYPE: Succulent
FORM: Upright rosette
TEXTURE: Coarse
GROWTH: Slow
LIGHT: High
MOISTURE: Dry between waterings

SOIL: Cactus mix
FEATURES: Blue-white leaves with sharp spines
USES: Architectural accent
FLOWERS: □

SITING: Provide the brightest, most direct sun possible. Agaves do well in any common indoor temperature or humidity, although they benefit from a 10-degree temperature drop at night. Be sure to locate plants away from traffic. The sharp spines can injure animals and people.
CARE: Allow to dry out substantially between waterings. Water only once a month in winter while the plant is resting.

Overwatering rots the roots. Root-rotting is indicated by a sour smell and the plant eventually falling over. Feed once every 3–4 months during active growth with a

Place agaves out of traffic areas because they have very sharp spines on each leaf that can inflict injury.

general plant food. Repot only when the bottom leaves make it difficult to reach the soil with a watering spout. A small pot restricts the plant's size. Agaves can reach up to 6' tall if not pot-bound. Remove damaged leaves and give the plant a shower occasionally to remove dust.
PROPAGATION: If your plant blooms indoors, which can take up to 10 years, quickly start new plants from the offsets; as soon as the flower spike fades, the parent plant dies. Simply cut away the offsets including a few roots and pot them up.
PESTS AND DISEASES: Agaves have few pests or diseases.
RELATED SPECIES: The cultivar 'Marginata' has a yellow leaf margin. 'Mediopicta' has a yellow center stripe. Threadleaf agave (*A. filifera*) has broad leaves with white margins and threads peeling off them. Little princess agave (*A. parviflora*) has the same leaves as *A. filifera* only in miniature.

QUEEN VICTORIA CENTURY PLANT

Agave victoria-reginae *uh-GAH-vee vick-TOR-ee-uh reh-GEEN-aye*

Queen Victoria century plant has elegant, striking foliage for an extraordinary flair. It is also known as painted century plant.

SIZE: 6"h × 12"w
TYPE: Succulent
FORM: Upright rosette
TEXTURE: Coarse
GROWTH: Slow
LIGHT: High

MOISTURE: Dry between waterings
SOIL: Cactus mix
FEATURES: Triangular leaves edged in white
USES: Focal point

SITING: Provide the brightest, most direct sun possible. These are perfect plants for a sunny, southwestern-style decor. Agaves do well in any common indoor temperature or humidity, although they benefit from a 10-degree temperature drop at night.
CARE: Allow to dry out substantially between waterings, and water only once a month in winter while the plant is resting. Feed every 3–4 months during active growth with a general plant food. Feeding more often will cause the plant to outgrow its pot and may contribute to root rot. Repot only when the bottom leaves make it hard to reach the soil with a watering spout. A small pot restricts the plant's size, keeps the plant looking its best, and prevents it from rotting. As it gets bigger, it loses the attractive attributes for which it is grown. Keeping the plant pot-bound also

makes it produce offsets. Remove damaged leaves and shower off the plant foliage occasionally to remove dust.
PROPAGATION: If your plant blooms indoors, which can take many years, quickly start new plants from the offsets; as soon as the flower spike fades, the parent plant dies. Simply cut away the offsets, including a few roots, and pot them up. Agaves can also be started from seed (available from suppliers), and the plants take a long time to mature.
PESTS AND DISEASES: Agaves have few pests or diseases.
RELATED SPECIES: *A. victoria-reginae variegata* is a spectacular cultivar with delicately dipped edges of cream.

CHINESE EVERGREEN
Aglaonema commutatum ag-lay-oh-NEE-ma kom-yew-TAH-tum

Chinese evergreen is a carefree charming foliage plant that is especially nice in low light areas.

SIZE: 3'h × 2'w
TYPE: Herbaceous
FORM: Vase-shaped
TEXTURE: Medium
GROWTH: Medium to fast
LIGHT: Low to medium

MOISTURE: Dry between waterings
SOIL: Potting soil
FEATURES: Lance-shaped, variegated leaves
USES: Low light
FLOWERS: □

SITING: Chinese evergreen is best suited to medium light to show off its leaf variegations, but the plant also performs well in low light. Provide average temperature (60–75°F) and high humidity.

Leaf tips may brown if the humidity is too low. These plants do not tolerate drying winds or cold drafts, so put them in a spot that is sheltered from doors, windows, and heat registers.

CARE: Allow the soil to dry slightly between waterings. Avoid letting the plant stand in water or it will rot. If growing in low light, feed only a couple of times a year with a general plant food. In higher light, feed three times in summer and not at all in winter. In higher light, repot every 3 years or so. Shower the plants

Rejuvenate Chinese evergreen by division.

Cut the root ball in half and pot up the two divisions.

occasionally to keep the glossy leaves clean. Remove spent flowers and damaged or faded leaves.

PROPAGATION: Propagate by dividing the root ball, by removing basal shoots when the plant is young, or by taking stem cuttings anytime. Stem and tip cuttings can be rooted in water, but they get a faster, sturdier start if rooted directly in potting soil. As plants mature and form woody stems, they can also be air layered.

PESTS AND DISEASES: Control mealybugs and spider mites with horticultural oil.

RELATED SPECIES: Cultivars with differing leaf variegation include 'Silver Queen', which is probably the most well known with its beautiful silvery striping and flecking, 'Emerald Beauty', with its dark green leaves splashed with chartreuse patches, and 'Silver King', with almost completely white leaves and green flecks. *A. crispum, A. modestum,* and *A. costatum* are close cousins to Chinese evergreen but are not as readily available.

AFRICAN MASK
Alocasia ×amazonica al-oh-CAY-see-uh am-uh-ZONE-ih-cuh

African mask will bring comments of awe with its rich tropical appearance. It is also known as elephant ear.

SIZE: 2'h × 3'w
TYPE: Herbaceous
FORM: Shrubby
TEXTURE: Coarse
GROWTH: Fast
LIGHT: Medium
MOISTURE: Moist

SOIL: Potting soil
FEATURES: Variegated dark green and white leaves
USES: Focal point, texture

SITING: African mask looks best when given bright to medium light in winter and indirect, medium light in summer. It should not receive direct sun at any time. It thrives in average home temperatures of 60–75°F, but requires high humidity (above

65 percent). A pebble tray is effective in raising the humidity around the plant. If the plant is chilled or dries out, it immediately drops its leaves and goes dormant. If you correct the problem, it will send out new leaves.

CARE: Keep the soil moist at all times during the active growing season; allow it to dry somewhat in winter. The top 2" of soil should dry out before watering again. Feed once a month during the growing

The substantial velvety leaves of African mask are quite unlike any other houseplant.

season with standard foliage plant food; do not feed in winter. Repot annually; divide at this time if needed. Wipe the velvety dark green leaves occasionally to clear them of dust and keep them looking pristine.

PROPAGATION: Propagate by carefully dividing the root ball, making sure to have several pieces of the fleshy rhizome on each division. You can also propagate by removing suckers from the sides of the shoot with roots attached, or by lifting the plant from the pot, removing a rhizome, and cutting it into pieces for rooting.

PESTS AND DISEASES: African mask is generally pestfree, but you may see spider mites and scale on plants that are stressed. Treat infestations with horticultural oil.

RELATED SPECIES: The cultivar 'Polly' has bright silvery-white veins on almost black leaves with purple undersides, and 'Hilo Beauty' has ivory mottling on bright green leaves. Dwarf elephant ears (*A. corozon*) has pewtery leaves with a waxy surface. Hooded dwarf elephant plant (*A. cucullata*) has heart-shaped dark green leaves with a twisted tip and upturned margins.

MEDICINE PLANT

Aloe vera (barbadensis) *AH-low VEH-rah (bar-buh-DEN-sis)*

The sap from medicine plant leaves has long been used to soothe burns and insect bites. It is also called burn plant or aloe.

SIZE: 3'h × 3'w
TYPE: Succulent
FORM: Vase-shaped
TEXTURE: Medium
GROWTH: Fast
LIGHT: High
MOISTURE: Dry between waterings
SOIL: Cactus mix
FEATURES: Spiky leaves with white marks
USES: Dish garden, southwestern theme
FLOWERS: ☐

SITING: Provide aloe with bright light. In lower light it becomes leggy. A bright kitchen window where the soothing sap in its leaves is handy for burns is perfect. Aloe thrives in average to hot temperatures (60–85°F) and low humidity (below 30 percent).

CARE: Allow to dry out fairly well between waterings, then thoroughly soak. Make sure the pot drains well; the plant will quickly rot if it sits in water. Repot only if the plant becomes top heavy. It performs best in a terra-cotta pot, which allows the soil to dry out easily. Feed three times in summer with a foliage formula. Remove damaged leaves.

PROPAGATION: Divide when the plant has a substantial root system or separate the offsets that form around the base.
PESTS AND DISEASES: Treat the occasional mealybug infestation with horticultural oil.
RELATED SPECIES: Tree aloe (*A. arborescens*) has a stalk and bears its leaves at the top. *A. zanzibarica* has stubby, thick leaves and remains small. Spider aloe (*A. humilis*) looks like a spider with incurved blue-green leaves.

Aloe plants produce small plantlets at the base that can be easily separated from the mother plant.

Once potted into well-drained potting mix, small plants will grow quickly into sturdy plants.

LACE-FLOWER VINE

Alsobia dianthiflora *al-SO-bee-a dye-an-thi-FLOR-a*

Lace-flower vine makes a handsome display as a ground cover beneath a larger plant.

SIZE: 6"h × 12"w
TYPE: Gesneriad
FORM: Semitrailing
TEXTURE: Fine
GROWTH: Fast
LIGHT: High, indirect
MOISTURE: Evenly moist
SOIL: African violet mix
FEATURES: Dark green leaves, drooping stems
USES: Hanging basket, floral display
FLOWERS: ☐

SITING: Lace-flower vine shows the best color on its velvety leaves in bright, indirect light. The graceful hanging stems will be covered with lacy-edged flowers in optimum growing conditions. Provide average temperatures (60–75°F), but avoid cold drafts. *Alsobia* needs medium to high humidity (30–65 percent).

CARE: Keep the soil evenly moist but not soggy. Feed with African violet food at half strength at every watering. Once a month, water with clear water to flush out salt buildup. Like other gesneriads, *Alsobia* blooms best when pot-bound, so repotting is seldom necessary. Prune the long stems back occasionally to keep the plant fresh; if training on a topiary frame, simply tuck the stems in around the frame.

PROPAGATION: Propagate by dividing the crown when the plant is mature or take stem cuttings, which are easy and fast rooting.
PESTS AND DISEASES: Spot-treat mealybugs with horticultural oil. Avoid spraying the entire plant with oil; it will cause severe leaf spotting.
RELATED SPECIES: The cultivar 'Cygnet' has larger flowers and is more floriferous than the species. 'San Miguel' has large blooms with maroon dots. 'Costa Rica' has scalloped leaves.

The fringed edges of its white flowers with purple spots give lace-flower vine its common name.

Lace-flower vine has tiny leaves and wiry stems that are easily trained and pruned into a topiary.

FLAMINGO FLOWER
Anthurium andraeanum *an–THUR–ee–um an–dree–AN–um*

Flamingo flower makes a room feel like a tropical paradise with its striking foliage and bold flowers.

SIZE: 3'h × 2'w
TYPE: Herbaceous, blooming
FORM: Rounded
TEXTURE: Medium
GROWTH: Medium
LIGHT: Low to medium
MOISTURE: Dry between waterings

SOIL: Half average, half epiphyte mix
FEATURES: Heart-shaped leaves on slender petioles
USES: Focal point, blooming plant
FLOWERS: ■ ■ □

SITING: Provide low to medium light and no direct sun to keep the striking, long-lasting flowers coming. Anthurium does well in average to high temperatures (60–80°F) and high humidity (up to 65 percent). If stressed by low humidity, it stops blooming. If given the right conditions, the plant will produce enough flowers for cutting.

CARE: Allow the soil to dry out only slightly between waterings. Feed every other month with blooming plant food; repot only when stems crowd the pot and watering is difficult. Pinch out faded leaves and flowers. Staking is generally not necessary, although you may need to support the flowers on some large cultivars. Thin bamboo skewers are excellent for this. Simply insert the skewer into the soil and gently tie the flower stem to it with soft thread.

PROPAGATION: Divide the root ball or separate side shoots when they form roots. Growing from seed is difficult.

PESTS AND DISEASES: Spider mites can be a problem. Give the plant an occasional shower to keep spider mites from developing high populations. Use insecticidal soap, horticultural oil, or a miticide if necessary. You may see physical damage to leaves and flowers if the plant is placed in a high-traffic area. Flamingo flower is not an easy plant to keep in the average home, so be prepared to give it extra care.

RELATED SPECIES: Pigtail flower (*A. scherzerianum*) has large, leathery leaves, a curved spadix, and large, bright red flowers.

Anthurium flowers may be red or pink. They are sometimes known as tail flower.

Remove faded blossoms regularly to keep flamingo flower in constant bloom and looking its best.

Flamingo flower blossoms are long-lasting and thus make superb cut flowers.

CRYSTAL ANTHURIUM
Anthurium crystallinum *an–THUR–ee–um cris-tahl-INE-um*

Crystal anthurium makes a shining statement with its velvety green foliage striped in silver.

SIZE: 3'h × 2'w
TYPE: Herbaceous, blooming
FORM: Rounded
TEXTURE: Medium
GROWTH: Medium
LIGHT: High
MOISTURE: Moist

SOIL: Half average, half epiphyte mix
FEATURES: Vertical deep green leaves with silver marks
USES: Foliage, focal point
FLOWERS: □

SITING: Crystal anthurium needs bright, indirect light. Full sun will fade and eventually kill the bronze-purple leaves, which turn velvety deep green with silver markings. Provide warm temperatures (above 60°F) to keep this plant healthy and attractive. Cold drafts will harm the leaves. Humidity above 65 percent is a must. Provide it by grouping the plants, setting pots on pebble trays, or using the pot-in-pot method. It would help to use more than one method. Yellowing leaves that eventually drop are indicators of dry soil and humidity that is too low.

CARE: Keep the soil moist but not soaking wet. Drying out at any time may mean loss of leaves. Feed monthly with a general foliage food. Repot only when the plant becomes leggy. Place the root ball high in the pot; as the plant grows, it will develop new roots above the soil line. Pack sphagnum moss around the plant; the new roots will penetrate it. Once new roots have formed in the sphagnum moss, cut off the plant below the new roots and repot it. Wipe the leaves gently once a month to keep clean and reduce spider mite populations.

PROPAGATION: Propagate by dividing the root ball in spring or grow from seed.

PESTS AND DISEASES: Watch the leaves for mites, scale, and mealybugs. Give the plant an occasional shower to keep spider mites at bay. Use horticultural oil to manage outbreaks of scale or mealybugs.

RELATED SPECIES: Queen anthurium (*A. warocqueanum*) has large, tapered dark leaves with blond veins, and king anthurium (*A. veitscheii*) has puckered emerald green leaves.

ZEBRA PLANT
Aphelandra squarrosa *a-fuh-LAN-dra square-OH-sa*

A warm humid room is the perfect place to display the striking zebra plant.

SIZE: 3'h × 2'w
TYPE: Herbaceous
FORM: Upright stems, horizontal leaves
TEXTURE: Medium to coarse
GROWTH: Medium
LIGHT: High to medium

MOISTURE: Evenly moist
SOIL: Potting soil
FEATURES: Large dark leaves with silver veins
USES: Focal point, blooming
FLOWERS: ■

SITING: Zebra plant grows best in medium light; it tolerates low light but won't bloom. Give the plant direct sun in winter. Constant warmth is necessary to keep the leaves looking their best; any exposure to cold will cause the plant to drop its leaves. High humidity (65 percent or more) is essential.

CARE: Keep moist but not soggy. Reduce the watering during winter dormancy. The leaves will likely drop from dry soil, so cut the plant back hard to rejuvenate it for spring growth. Feed three times in summer or at half the rate at each watering during its active growth period. Zebra plant seldom needs repotting and blossoms best when pot-bound. Remove the flower spike after the plant blooms to force it to develop side shoots.

PROPAGATION: Remove side shoots complete with roots and pot them up. Stem cuttings are also successful.

PESTS AND DISEASES: Few pests bother zebra plant.

RELATED SPECIES: 'Dania' has silvery veins and yellow-orange flowers and is more compact than the species. *A. squarrosa louisae* has creamy white veins and red-tipped bracts. *A. aurantica* has orange-scarlet blooms and gray-veined leaves.

The unique blossom of zebra plant emerges from the leaves like a glowing flame.

Even a very brief exposure to cold will cause a zebra plant to quickly drop its leaves.

RATTAIL CACTUS
Aporocactus flagelliformis *a-POUR-o-cac-tuss fla-jel-li-FOUR-miss*

Rattail cactus is a unique hanging cactus with magnificent blossoms, just right in a hanging basket.

SIZE: 6' long × 1'w
TYPE: Cactus
FORM: Trailing
TEXTURE: Medium
GROWTH: Fast
LIGHT: High
MOISTURE: Dry between waterings

SOIL: Cactus mix
FEATURES: Long stems covered with spines
USES: Hanging basket, focal point
FLOWERS: ■

SITING: Full sun will make rattail cactus produce exquisite 3" fuschia-pink blossoms along the 6' stems in spring. The flowers will last up to 2 months. Rattail cactus needs 60–80°F in summer and 55°F in winter. If given the same temperatures year-round, it will not flower. Low humidity prevents stem scarring and leaf spots.

CARE: Keep well watered in summer but allow it to dry slightly between waterings. Provide little water in winter. Feed only once in spring. This plant seldom needs repotting. Clip out any browning stems to keep the plant looking pristine.

PROPAGATION: Propagate by stem cuttings. The long stems will form roots along the entire length, so small pieces are all that are needed for a cutting. Allow the cuttings to dry a few days to form a callus before potting them up.

PESTS AND DISEASES: Watch for mites and mealybugs. Wash mites off the plant with a forceful spray of water. Swab rubbing alcohol on mealybugs to control them.

RELATED SPECIES: *A. martianus* has thicker stems and larger flowers than rattail cactus. *A. flagriformis* has fewer spines, more slender stems, and carmine-pink flowers.

The growing tips of rattail cactus have an attractive pink cast to them.

Remove shriveled brown shoots regularly to keep the rattail cactus looking its best.

NORFOLK ISLAND PINE
Araucaria heterophylla *ar-aw-CARE-ee-uh het-er-oh-PHIL-luh*

Norfolk Island pine lends stature and an architectural statement to any room.

SIZE: 5'h × 4'w
TYPE: Woody, evergreen
FORM: Upright, pyramidal
TEXTURE: Fine
GROWTH: Slow
LIGHT: Medium to high

MOISTURE: Moist in summer, dry in winter
SOIL: Average
FEATURES: Bright green needles, drooping branches
USES: Architectural accent

SITING: Provide indirect, bright light to keep this tree, with its gracefully drooping branches, healthy. It tolerates temperatures of 50–80°F in summer but should be kept around 55°F in winter. It needs average to high humidity (50–75 percent) and often suffers in dry, warm homes. Low humidity causes branch loss and tip browning.

CARE: Keep the soil evenly moist in summer; allow it to dry between waterings in winter. Feed only once a year to restrict growth; use a food for acid-loving plants. Lower branches periodically die; remove them with a clean cut at their point of attachment. Turn the plant frequently to keep it symmetrical. Move outdoors to a protected spot in summer.

When using as a Christmas tree, use only lightweight ornaments and avoid Christmas lights that can injure the plant.

PROPAGATION: This plant requires greenhouse conditions to propagate successfully. Try air layering the top if the plant becomes too spindly.

PESTS AND DISEASES: Pests include spider mites and mealybugs. Use rubbing alcohol or horticultural oil to control mealybugs, and insecticidal soap or horticultural oil for spider mite outbreaks.

RELATED SPECIES: New Caledonian pine (*A. columnaris*) is similar in appearance but seldom available as a houseplant.

Because Norfolk Island pines naturally lose their lower branches, group small plants at the base for an attractive display.

CORALBERRY
Ardisia crenata (A. crispa) *ar-DEE-zee-uh kreh-NAY-tuh (KRISP-uh)*

Coralberry thrives in a cool spot and will produce attractive blossoms and fruit almost year-round.

SIZE: 24"h × 18"w
TYPE: Woody shrub
FORM: Single stem, rounded crown
TEXTURE: Medium
GROWTH: Slow
LIGHT: High, indirect
MOISTURE: Evenly moist, dry in winter

SOIL: Potting soil
FEATURES: Glossy green leaves, bright red berries
USES: Focal point, holiday decor
FLOWERS: ☐

SITING: Provide bright, indirect light year-round to keep the plant producing glossy red berries. They remain for several months. Ripe and green berries often occur simultaneously, making a more attractive display. The plant performs well in cool to average temperatures (55–70°F) and requires high humidity (above 65 percent).

CARE: Keep moist but not soggy. Allow to dry out between waterings in winter. Feed with a blooming plant food three times in summer. Repot only when the roots fill the container. Lightly prune back after the berries drop and put it outside for the summer. This will cause the plant to produce berries for the following winter holiday season.

PROPAGATION: Propagate by semihardwood stem cuttings in summer or by seed when the berries shrivel.

PESTS AND DISEASES: Spider mites can be a problem if the plant is grown in low humidity. Spray the plant with a forceful water spray to dislodge them, or use insecticidal soap, horticultural oil, or a commercial miticide to control large populations of mites.

RELATED SPECIES: Japanese marlberry (*A. japonica*) is smaller and has leathery leaves. Some cultivars develop yellow to cream markings on the foliage.

Coralberry fruits make a striking display, especially because there are often green and red fruits on the plant at the same time.

ASPARAGUS FERN
Asparagus densiflorus uh-SPARE-uh-guss den-sih-FLOR-us

Asparagus fern, also known as Sprengeri fern, is a longtime favorite for hanging baskets and as a foil for other blooming plants.

SIZE: 1'h × 2'w
TYPE: Herbaceous
FORM: Arching, mounding
TEXTURE: Fine
GROWTH: Medium
LIGHT: High to medium

MOISTURE: Moist in summer, dry in winter
SOIL: Potting soil
FEATURES: Needlelike leaves on arching stems
USES: Hanging basket, filler
FLOWERS: ☐

SITING: Asparagus fern thrives in bright to medium light and tolerates lower light although it will be less full. Provide average temperatures (60–75°F) and average humidity (30–65 percent).
CARE: Keep evenly moist in summer; allow the soil to dry slightly during the winter. Feed with a dilute solution of foliage plant food every time the plant is watered. Repot annually; otherwise, the thick tuberous roots will push out of the soil and break the pot. It is time to repot when the plant must be watered daily. Prune only when needed for aesthetics; be mindful of small thorns at the leaf nodes. Too much sun or dry soil will yellow the foliage, and the plant may drop its leaves when the light is too low. This is common when plants come in from a summer outdoors. Plants often receive enough light outdoors to produce small red berries. Be aware when bringing in the plants that these berries may drop and are poisonous to animals and children.

PROPAGATION: Propagate by seed if your plant produces fruits. Otherwise, divide the root ball. Slip the plant from its pot and use a sharp knife to cut the root ball into two or more pieces. It may be necessary to remove some of the potato-like tubers to fit the plants into new pots. This will not harm the plant.
PESTS AND DISEASES: Asparagus fern often has spider mites when the humidity is low; aphids may be attracted to the asparagus-looking shoots as they emerge from the soil.
RELATED SPECIES: The foxtail fern *A.d.* 'Meyersii' has compact, cattail-like fronds that are upright.

1 Asparagus fern fills its pot quickly with fleshy roots and will need division every year.

2 Slip the plant out of its pot and slice cleanly through the root ball with a sharp knife.

3 Repot the pieces in clean potting soil, making sure they are at the same soil level as before.

PLUMOSE FERN
Asparagus setaceus (plumosus) uh-SPARE-uh-guss seh-TAY-see-us (ploo-MOH-sus)

Plumose ferns are also known as emerald feather and lace fern. They give an airy feel to terrariums and tabletop groupings.

SIZE: 3'h × 1'w
TYPE: Herbaceous
FORM: Upright, horizontal fronds
TEXTURE: Extremely fine
GROWTH: Medium
LIGHT: High

MOISTURE: Moist
SOIL: Average
FEATURES: Spreading branches, fernlike leaves
USES: Terrarium, foliage
FLOWERS: ☐

SITING: Provide bright, indirect light to keep the plant full. Average temperatures (60–75°F) and average humidity (30–60 percent) will keep the plant producing healthy fronds, which make beautiful additions to cut bouquets. As a young plant, it works well in a hanging basket. The ferny foliage is held at right angles to the upright stems, but arches gracefully out of a pot. With age, the plant becomes more erect, with nearly a climbing growth habit. The long fronds may be trained up a trellis or you can trim them back to keep the plant more compact. At intermediate stages, the layered needles foliage resembles an aged pine tree, providing an appearance of bonsai.
CARE: Plumose fern will drop its leaves if it dries out. Feed with a dilute solution of foliage plant food every time the plant is watered. Repot only when roots fill the pot. This plant can become spindly with age, so prune out old stems to allow new growth to appear. Plants can be cut back completely to the ground, and will resprout with vigorous new growth.
PROPAGATION: Propagate by dividing the root ball into several pieces, or by seed if your plant produces blue-black berries. This usually happens only when the plant is taken outdoors for the summer.
PESTS AND DISEASES: Watch for spider mites in low humidity. Keep them at bay by giving the plant an occasional shower of water.
RELATED SPECIES: The cultivar 'Nanus' is 3–6" tall. 'Pyramidalis' is up to 2' tall with erect instead of horizontal fronds. Asparagus fern (*A. densiflorus*) is a coarser plant but requires similar care. 'Sprengeri' is the most widely available cultivar. Foxtail fern (*A. d.* 'Meyersii') has compact, cattail-like fronds that are upright.

CAST-IRON PLANT
Aspidistra elatior *as-pih-DIS-tra ee-LAY-tee-or*

Cast-iron or barroom plant is aptly named because it tolerates any light conditions as well as the occasional missed watering.

SIZE: 2'h × 2'w
TYPE: Herbaceous
FORM: Upright, vase-shaped
TEXTURE: Medium
GROWTH: Slow
LIGHT: Low to medium

MOISTURE: Dry between waterings
SOIL: Average
FEATURES: Lance-shaped dark green leaves
USES: Very low light

SITING: Cast-iron plant is best situated in medium light; direct sun causes the leaves to fade. This plant does well in all house temperatures and amounts of humidity, making it one of the most tolerant houseplants. It grows and looks good in very low light, and its attractive dark green leaves are striking in any situation.

CARE: Allow the soil to dry somewhat between waterings. Cast-iron plant is tolerant of the occasional missed watering, but it will not tolerate overwatering. Feed every 3–4 months when growing in low light with half-strength plant food for foliage plants. If growing in higher light, feed monthly with a full-strength solution. Repot only every couple of years, when the plant begins to push out of its container. Wash the dust off the leaves occasionally and remove damaged leaves.

PROPAGATION: Divide the root ball every couple of years if needed, or simply pull a leaf with a crown portion attached off the root ball and pot it up.

PESTS AND DISEASES: Control spider mites with horticultural oil. The plant also gets fungal leaf spots. Prune out damaged leaves and cut back on watering.

RELATED SPECIES: 'Milky Way' has white spots; 'Variegata' has yellow stripes. *A. caespitosa*, *A. linearifolia*, *A. longiloba*, *A. lurida*, and *A. saxicola* are available as outdoor plants for southern climates.

1 Black plastic nursery pots are usually unattractive in a display, so use your imagination to find an attractive container.

2 Remove the plant from its pot, settle it into the decorative container, and fill in around the edges with clean potting soil.

3 Water the plant in well after potting to settle out any air pockets in the soil and give the roots a boost.

BIRD'S NEST FERN
Asplenium nidus *as-PLEE-nee-um NYE-duss*

Bird's nest fern unfurls its unique wavy light green fronds toward the ceiling as if presenting them to the viewer.

SIZE: 15"h × 12"w
TYPE: Fern
FORM: Upright, vase-shaped
TEXTURE: Medium
GROWTH: Slow
LIGHT: Medium to high

MOISTURE: Moist
SOIL: Epiphyte mix or potting soil
FEATURES: Wavy, glossy green fronds
USES: Foliage, focal point

SITING: Bright to medium, indirect light is best for bird's nest fern. In high light the glossy fronds bleach out. Provide average to warm temperatures (60–80°F) with no drafts. High humidity (65 percent or more) is essential. This is an excellent plant for use in a terrarium or a tropical grouping.

CARE: Keep moist at all times. Water somewhat less in winter but don't allow

Bird's nest fern must have a well-drained potting mix and seldom needs repotting because of a very small root system.

it to dry out. Keep moisture out of the cup that is formed by the fronds—the "bird's nest." Feed only twice a year, once in spring and once in summer, with a foliage plant food. It seldom needs repotting because it has a miniscule root system; it can even be grown on a slab as long as you provide extremely high humidity. Remove older leaves as they fade. These plants can have fungal leaf spots, but the most common leaf problems are frond-tip dieback, from lack of humidity; frond death from the potting mix drying out; and severely curled leaf tips, from being too cold.

PROPAGATION: Propagate by dividing the root ball or by starting from spores.

PESTS AND DISEASES: Bird's nest fern can have scale, aphids, and mealybugs. Learn what the fern spores look like (they will be in regular lines) to distinguish them from scales (irregularly scattered).

RELATED SPECIES: The cultivar 'Fimbriatum' has notched leaves. *A. crispifolium* is similar to *A. nidus* except that it has crinkled edges.

BISHOP'S CAP CACTUS

Astrophytum spp. *a-stro-PHY-tum*

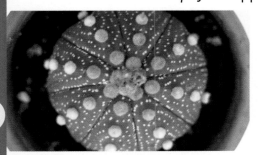

Bishop's cap or bishop's hat cactus get their names from their unique shapes, quite unlike any other cactus or houseplant.

SIZE: 24–48"h × 6"w
TYPE: Cactus
FORM: Ball-shaped
TEXTURE: Medium to coarse
GROWTH: Slow
LIGHT: High

MOISTURE: Dry
SOIL: Cactus mix
FEATURES: Spiraling ribs, grooves
USES: Dish garden, focal point
FLOWERS: ☐

SITING: Being a true cactus, *Astrophytum* needs full sun to keeps its striking, unique look. Keep the plants warm (65–85°F) when in active growth; allow them cooler temperatures (55–60°F) during the winter dormant period. Low humidity (20–30 percent) keeps them looking their best.

CARE: Let it dry out considerably between waterings. Overwatering causes root rot. Feed with half-strength plant food only after flower buds form. A small root system makes repotting seldom necessary.

PROPAGATION: Propagate by seed, or graft to speed growth.

Monk's hood, another type of Astrophytum, is covered with spines and may be adorned with delicate yellow flowers.

PESTS AND DISEASES: Mealybugs and scale can mimic the plant's natural flecks and spots. Examine plants closely for presence of these insect pests.

RELATED SPECIES: Available species include Sea urchin cactus (*A. asterias*), Monk's hood (*A. ornatum*), and Bishop's cap (*A. myriostigma*).

The true Bishop's cap looks quite like a mitre and may also be topped with soft golden flowers.

JAPANESE AUCUBA

Aucuba japonica *AW-cube-a juh-PAN-nih-kuh*

Japanese aucuba lends itself to most any conditions and provides deep green foliage, often with yellow flecks.

SIZE: 4'h × 4'w
TYPE: Woody shrub
FORM: Rounded
TEXTURE: Medium
GROWTH: Fast
LIGHT: Medium to low

MOISTURE: Moist to dry
SOIL: Potting soil
FEATURES: Small green leaves or spotted with yellow
USES: Foliage

SITING: Medium light is best for Japanese aucuba, although it tolerates high and low light. Avoid full sun in summer; it will bleach the leaves. This plant tolerates cool temperatures (to 50°F), although it does best in medium temperatures (60–75°F). Provide high humidity (65 percent or higher) to keep the plant looking its best.

CARE: Keep moist at all times in high light; let it dry out between waterings in medium and low light. Feed three times in summer only, or it will quickly outgrow its pot. Repot annually to keep up with growth. Pruning keeps it within bounds and looking shrubby and full. It can be pruned into a hedge shape as an attractive backdrop to focal-point houseplants. Put it outdoors for the summer. In ideal conditions cultivars that have a male shoot grafted onto a female plant will produce attractive red berries.

PROPAGATION: Propagate by semihardwood stem cuttings taken in late summer.

PESTS AND DISEASES: Mealybugs and spider mites may be pests in dry situations.

RELATED SPECIES: The cultivar 'Variegata' has gold flecks, 'Crotonifolia' has gold and white variegation, and 'Rozannie' is self-fruitful. *A. chinensis* has narrower leaves but is the same in all other aspects. *A. japonica* f. *longifolia* leaves are much longer than wide.

Japanese aucuba will reach four feet high and wide but can be easily pruned to keep it smaller. It can even be pruned in a hedge shape.

PONYTAIL PALM

Beaucarnea recurvata (Nolina) bob-CAR-nee-ub ree-cur-VAH-tub (no-LEE-nub)

Ponytail palms are also known as bottle palm and elephant foot. They are carefree plants that provide elegant architectural drama to any room.

SIZE: 3'h × 2'w
TYPE: Succulent
FORM: Treelike
TEXTURE: Medium
GROWTH: Medium
LIGHT: High to low
MOISTURE: Dry between waterings

SOIL: Half average, half cactus mix
FEATURES: Curved leaves, large-footed base
USES: Architectural accent
FLOWERS: □

SITING: Bright light with some direct sun keeps this plant looking its best, although it tolerates medium and even low light. Ponytail palm performs best in average to high temperatures (60–80°F) when it is actively growing, and cool temperatures (50–55°F) when in winter dormancy. Low humidity keeps the plant healthy.

CARE: Ponytail palm generally needs dry conditions, because it is susceptible to root rots. It stores water in its large base; water the potting mix thoroughly, then let it dry between waterings. You may need to water only once a month. Hold back water in winter; if in doubt, don't water. You have overwatered if the new growth is a light color. Underwatering is indicated by shriveling of the stem. Feed only once a year in spring with general foliage plant food. Ponytail palm rarely needs repotting. Wash the leaves occasionally and remove dead leaves. The plant will naturally shed its long, curly, straplike leaves as it grows.

PROPAGATION: Ponytail palm is usually propagated commercially by seed. Because the plants rarely flower in the home, you will have to rely on purchasing new plants rather than trying to grow your own.

PESTS AND DISEASES: Overwatering causes stem rots and bacterial soft rot. Control mealybugs, spider mites, and scale with horticultural oil.

RELATED SPECIES: Oaxacan ponytail palm (*B. longifolia*) has straplike leaves up to 7' long.

The "foot" of the Ponytail palm is a water-storage organ, indicating that the plant needs infrequent watering.

ANGEL WING BEGONIA

Begonia coccinea beb-GON-yuh cabk-SIN-ee-uh

Angle wing begonias have graceful wing-shaped speckled and spotted leaves on long canes.

SIZE: 3'h × 4'w
TYPE: Herbaceous
FORM: Upright
TEXTURE: Medium to coarse
GROWTH: Fast
LIGHT: High, indirect
MOISTURE: Moist

SOIL: Average
FEATURES: Elongated leaves, long canes
USES: Foliage, blooming
FLOWERS: ■ ■

SITING: Bright, indirect light provides the most attractive plants, although they tolerate medium light as well. Provide average to warm temperatures (60–80°F) and high humidity.

CARE: If growing angel wing begonia in high light, keep the soil somewhat moist. In medium light, allow it to dry slightly between waterings. Feed the plant monthly with a foliage plant food when active, then every 2 months when resting. This begonia can be repotted every spring, but because they decline quickly, you will have more attractive plants if you start new ones annually. The canes on angel wing begonia will get large quickly and can outgrow the pot. Clip out any leaves that show tattering or browning. Trim faded flowers and flower stems. Prune long canes back to the base to encourage new growth from the bottom of the plant.

PROPAGATION: Propagate by tip, stem, or leaf cuttings or by seed. Leaf cuttings are particularly successful.

PESTS AND DISEASES: Angel wing begonia can have leaf spots, root and stem rots, and powdery mildew if grown in stressful conditions.

RELATED SPECIES: *B.* ×*corallina* 'Lucerna' has silver-dotted leaves with salmon-rose flowers, and *B. radicans* is a trailing variety with red flowers.

1 Cut a stem tip about 3–5" long and remove all but one or a partial leaf.

2 Dip the stem in rooting hormone, and insert it into the potting soil mix.

3 Cover the cuttings with a plastic bag to keep the humidity high.

IRON CROSS BEGONIA
Begonia masoniana *beh-GON-yuh may-soh-nee-AH-uh*

Iron cross begonias are unique with their crinkled leaves and distinct black to brown markings.

SIZE: 18"h × 12"w
TYPE: Herbaceous
FORM: Mounded
TEXTURE: Medium
GROWTH: Medium
LIGHT: High to medium
MOISTURE: Dry between waterings

SOIL: Potting soil
FEATURES: Black pattern on hairy leaves
USES: Hanging basket, blooming
FLOWERS: □ ▪

SITING: Iron cross begonia keeps its attractive color best in bright, indirect light. It tolerates medium light and benefits from some direct sun in winter. Average temperatures (60–75°F) are fine, but avoid windows where it might become chilled. It requires high humidity. A pebble tray works well.

CARE: If growing iron cross begonia in high light, keep the soil somewhat moist. In medium light, allow it to dry slightly between waterings. Feed monthly with a foliage plant food when active, then every 2 months when resting. This begonia can be repotted every spring (pot-bound plants lose their leaf color), but because begonias notoriously decline quickly, you will have more attractive plants if you start new ones annually. Clip out any leaves that show tattering or browning. Iron cross begonia may randomly go dormant and shed its leaves, but the surface rhizomes will soon produce new ones.

PROPAGATION: Propagate by dividing the rhizomes or taking leaf cuttings.

PESTS AND DISEASES: These plants may occasionally have mealybugs, but a more prominent problem is powdery mildew. To avoid, keep leaves dry. A plant with mildew can be treated, but you might have better luck starting a new plant from shoots or leaves without any mildew.

RELATED SPECIES: There are hundreds of begonia species available, with all shapes of leaves, and sizes and colors of flowers.

Iron cross begonias can be easily propagated by dividing the creeping rhizomes that meander across the soil.

REX BEGONIA
Begonia Rex Cultorum hybrids *beh-GON-yuh*

Rex begonias are fairly easy to grow and come in a phenomenal variety of leaf colors. It is also known as painted leaf begonia.

SIZE: 1'h × 2'w
TYPE: Herbaceous
FORM: Mounding
TEXTURE: Medium
GROWTH: Medium
LIGHT: Medium to indirect

MOISTURE: Moist
SOIL: Potting soil
FEATURES: Variegated leaves
USES: Foliage
FLOWERS: □

SITING: Bright light makes the cream, pink, and chartreuse leaf variegations brighter on some varieties; lower light enhances the metallic sheen on others. Provide high humidity and temperatures of 60–80°F.

CARE: If growing rex begonia in high light, keep the soil somewhat moist. In medium light, allow it to dry slightly between waterings. Feed monthly with a foliage plant food when active, then every 2 months when resting. Repot every spring; because begonias decline quickly, you will have more attractive plants if you start new ones annually. Clip out any leaves that show tattering or browning. Because the flowers are not attractive and can detract from the foliage display, remove them unless you want the seed.

PROPAGATION: Propagate by tip, stem, or leaf cuttings or by seed. Sprinkle the seeds on top of the soil and press in lightly.

PESTS AND DISEASES: Rex begonia can have numerous problems including leaf spots, root and stem rots, and powdery mildew if grown in stressful conditions.

RELATED SPECIES: Rex begonia comes in three basic classes: brilliant leaves, spiral (wavy) leaves, or miniature (less than 8"). Beyond these classifications there are hundreds of cultivars available, each with different characteristics.

1

To propagate begonias by leaf cuttings, simply remove a leaf with part of the petiole attached.

2

Lay the leaf on sterile potting soil and pin it to the soil with a hairpin. Make slits across the veins to induce plantlets to form.

LADY OF THE NIGHT ORCHID

Brassavola nodosa bra-SAH-voh-luh no-DOSE-uh

The mysterious lady of the night orchid has a magnificent blossom that sends out an intoxicating fragrance at night.

SIZE: 15"h × 6"w
TYPE: Orchid
FORM: Upright
TEXTURE: Medium
GROWTH: Medium
LIGHT: Medium to high

MOISTURE: Moist
SOIL: Orchid, slab
FEATURES: Fragrant flowers
USES: Focal point
FLOWERS: ☐ ▨

SITING: Medium light is best, but this orchid can tolerate higher light if kept moist. This may mean watering every 2–3 days, but the extra care is worth it when you experience the spidery white to pale yellow blossoms with red or purple specks in the throat. *Brassavola* thrives in temperatures of 75–90°F during active growth and 65–75°F during winter rest. If it is cooler than this during rest, reduce watering even more. Provide with 80 percent humidity if possible.

CARE: Keep moist throughout the growing season, watering every few days if needed. *Brassavola* needs at least a 2-week rest period in winter to produce flowers.

Lady of the night orchid is a parent of hybrids such as this hybrid of Brassavola × Laelia 'Richard Mueller' × Brassavola × Cattleya 'Walanae Leopard'.

During this time, allow it to dry out somewhat, and water only once every 2–3 weeks. Feed with a balanced plant food at half-strength weekly while it is actively growing. A plant food with high phosphate (the middle number in the analysis) in fall will improve blooming for the next season. Leach the pot once a month. Do this by watering with plain water until excess water flows out the bottom of the pot. Repot as soon as new growth begins or immediately after flowering. Plants grown on a tree-fern slab should be watered daily.

PROPAGATION: Propagate by seed or dividing the rhizome. Be sure to have at least three healthy pseudobulbs in old and new plants for survival and faster blooming.

PESTS AND DISEASES: Control scale with horticultural oil.

RELATED SPECIES: *B. digbyana* (*Rhyncholaelia*) has green flowers with ruffled edges. It is used in hybridization.

PEACOCK PLANT

Calathea makoyana cuh-LAY-thee-uh mak-o-YAH-na

Peacock plants offer a wide array of beautifully variegated foliage with all shades of purples, greens, pinks, and silvers.

SIZE: 12–15"h × 12–15"w
TYPE: Herbaceous
FORM: Mounded
TEXTURE: Medium
GROWTH: Medium
LIGHT: Medium to low

MOISTURE: Moist
SOIL: Potting soil
FEATURES: Variegated foliage
USES: Foliage, architectural accent

SITING: Provide medium to low light, keeping in mind that the beautiful purples and silvers of this plant develop better in medium light. Provide average to warm temperatures (71–85°F) and high humidity (60 percent or more). This is an ideal terrarium plant.

CARE: Keep constantly moist through spring, summer, and fall. In winter the plant usually goes into a rest and needs much less water. Feed only three times in summer with a foliage plant food. Repot before plants become potbound—usually every 2 years. Plant growth slows down as winter approaches. Plants begin to look ragged, indicating that it's time to tuck the plant out of the way for a while. Reduce watering. When new sprouts appear, prune out old leaves and water the plant well.

PROPAGATION: Propagate by dividing the root ball.

PESTS AND DISEASES: Watch for mealybugs and spider mites.

RELATED SPECIES: *C. warscewiczii* has leaves in many hues of green with purple undersides, and *C. vittata* has bright yellow stripes on rich green leaves.

1 Peacock plants will need dividing every 2 years. Lift the rootball out of the pot and cleanly slice it in half.

2 Set the divided plants into pots with clean potting soil, fill with more soil, tamp gently, and water in well.

CATHEDRAL WINDOWS
Calathea picturata *cuh-LAY-thee-uh pik-chur-AH-tuh*

Cathedral windows gets its name from the beautifully picturesque veining and striping on the leaves that resembles stained glass.

SIZE: 12–15"h × 12–15"w
TYPE: Herbaceous
FORM: Mounded
TEXTURE: Medium
GROWTH: Medium
LIGHT: Medium to low

MOISTURE: Average
SOIL: Moist
FEATURES: Variegated foliage
USES: Foliage, architectural accent

SITING: Cathedral windows may need a little extra care in siting, but the beautiful foliage is worth the effort. Provide medium to low light, keeping in mind that the purples and silvers of the foliage develop better in higher light. Provide average to warm temperatures (71–85°F) and high humidity (60 percent or more). This is an excellent terrarium plant.

CARE: Keep constantly moist through spring, summer, and fall. It needs much less water during the winter. Feed only three times in summer with a foliage plant food. Repot before it becomes so pot-bound that it no longer takes up water—usually every 2 years. The plant begins to look ragged, indicating that it's time to tuck it out of the way for a while. Continue to keep the humidity high. As soon as new sprouts appear, prune out the old leaves and water the plant well.

PROPAGATION: Propagate by dividing the root ball.

PESTS AND DISEASES: Pests include mealybugs and spider mites.

RELATED SPECIES: 'Argentea' has a central silver stripe with a green border and wine undersides. 'Vandenheckei' has elliptical dark green leaves with feathery white central and marginal bands.

To keep the plant looking its best, trim out any damaged or shriveled leaves, especially if watering has been neglected.

PANAMA HAT PALM
Carludovica palmata *kar-loo-DOH-vih-kuh pal-MATE-uh*

Panama hat palm adds a classic tropical appearance anywhere. Give it plenty of space.

SIZE: 5–8'h × 4–5'w
TYPE: Palmlike
FORM: Tree
TEXTURE: Coarse
GROWTH: Medium
LIGHT: Medium
MOISTURE: Dry between waterings

SOIL: Potting soil
FEATURES: Fan-shaped leaves
USES: Architectural accent

SITING: Panama hat palm is not a true palm. It thrives in average home conditions. Provide medium light; the leaves bleach out in high light. It tolerates minimal direct sun. It prefers average home temperatures (60–75°F) but will tolerate 85–90°F. It performs best in high humidity (above 65 percent) although it tolerates 30–65 percent. Frond tips may become brown in low humidity. Keep out of drying winds to prevent damaging the wide fronds.

CARE: Allow to dry only slightly between waterings, then soak the soil (it should be well-drained). Keep it fairly dry during its winter rest. Feed only three times in summer with a foliage plant food. Feeding more often will cause it to outgrow its site quickly. Repot annually in March. For large plants that are hard to maneuver, remove the top inch of soil and replace it with fresh soil. Wash the leaves monthly to remove dust. Prune only to remove damaged leaves.

PROPAGATION: Propagate by dividing the rhizome in spring.

PESTS: AND DISEASES Control spider mites and mealybugs with monthly washing of the leaves.

RELATED SPECIES: This is the only species used in the home, although there are several used in landscaping in southern climates.

The immense stiff fronds add an architectural flair not easily obtained with plants of lesser stature.

FISHTAIL PALM

Caryota mitis *kar-ee-OH-tuh MITE-is*

SIZE: 6–8'h × 3'w
TYPE: Palm
FORM: Upright
TEXTURE: Coarse
GROWTH: Medium
LIGHT: High to medium
MOISTURE: Moist
SOIL: Potting soil
FEATURES: Leaflets like fishtails
USES: Architectural accent

A fishtail palm will brighten a dull corner with its crinkled gray-green leaves on upright stiff stalks.

SITING: Fishtail palm thrives in bright, filtered light but performs well in medium light. It prefers average to warm temperatures (65–85°F) and average to high humidity (30 percent or above).

CARE: Keep evenly moist except during its winter rest when it should be a bit drier. Stem rot results from too much water. Feed once a month in the growing season with foliage plant food. Repot in spring if the plant is outgrowing its pot, but keep in mind that it does best when pot-bound. Remove damaged fronds. Shower off the plant once a month to keep dust down and control mites.

PROPAGATION: Although it can be grown from seed, it rarely blooms in the home, so you must acquire seed from a supplier. Or separate the plantlets found at the base of the parent plant, pot them up, and keep them warm until roots are established.

PESTS AND DISEASES: Spider mites can become bothersome in low humidity.

RELATED SPECIES: *C. urens* and *C. obtusa* are both called giant fishtail palm and may be available through specialty suppliers. Both grow to 12' or more.

Asymmetrical leaflets called pinnae have an almost whimsical appearance with ragged edges that make them look like a fish tail.

CATTLEYA ORCHID

Cattleya hybrids *kat-LAY-uh*

Cattleya orchids are some of the easiest of all the orchids to grow, as long as they receive bright indirect light.

SIZE: Varies
TYPE: Orchid
FORM: Upright
TEXTURE: Medium
GROWTH: Slow
LIGHT: High
MOISTURE: Dry between waterings

SOIL: Orchid mix
FEATURES: Exquisite blossoms
USES: Blooming accent
FLOWERS: □ ▪ ▪ ▪ ▪ ▪

SITING: Cattleya orchid needs bright light, but avoid direct sun in the middle of the day. It prefers 75–80°F but will tolerate higher temperatures if the light is decreased and the humidity is increased. It needs humidity levels of 50–80 percent, which can be provided with a pebble tray or a pot-in-pot system.

CARE: Mature cattleya orchid should dry out fairly well between waterings, but younger plants and seedlings must be kept moist. Use unsoftened water above 50°F. Because cattleyas are grown for their flowers, feed with a blossom-boosting food every 4–6 weeks. Feed with foliage food every 2 weeks or at half strength at every watering. When the plant is resting, feed only once a month. Flush out fertilizer salts once a month. Repot when the rhizomes creep over the edge of the pot or when the potting mix breaks down and doesn't drain thoroughly. Repot before new roots appear—after blooming or in spring. When the flower stem appears, place an orchid stake close to the center of the plant, making sure not to pierce the pseudobulbs when doing so. Gently tie the flower spike to the stake.

PROPAGATION: Propagate by dividing the root ball. The plant must be mature enough to provide 3 to 5 pseudobulbs for each division. After dividing the plant, cut off any damaged or diseased roots, and spread the remaining roots on a small mound of soil in the bottom of the new pot. Fill with orchid mix, pack down firmly, and place a stake in the pot if necessary. Keep in a cool spot with lower light and dry roots until established.

PESTS AND DISEASES: Cattleya orchid is prone to leaf spots when the air is still and cool. Provide air circulation and keep the plants warm.

RELATED SPECIES: There are hundreds of cattleya orchids available as well as many crosses with other species.

'Nacouchee' has delicate lavender flowers.

'Landate' features variegated petals surrounding a pink center.

OLD MAN CACTUS

Cephalocereus senilis seh-ful-oh-SEER-ee-us seh-NILL-us

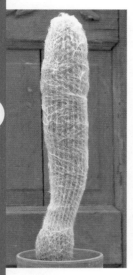

SIZE: 1'h × 4"w
TYPE: Cactus
FORM: Upright
TEXTURE: Coarse
GROWTH: Slow
LIGHT: High
MOISTURE: Dry
SOIL: Cactus mix
FEATURES: Wavy white hairs
USES: Dry garden, accent

Old man cactus is aptly named with its tall stature and covering of whitish hairs over spines.

The hairs of old man cactus look soft, but actually cover spines that can inflict a painful wound.

SITING: Old man cactus needs full sun to keep its unique form. Keep the plants warm (65–85°F) when in active growth, and provide cooler temperatures (55–60°F) during their dormant period in winter. Low humidity levels (20–30 percent) will keep them looking their best.

CARE: Let soil dry out considerably between waterings during active growth, and even more during the dormant stage. Feed with half-strength plant food only after flower buds form. Old man cactus has a small root system so repotting is seldom necessary. Root rot is caused by overwatering. Occasionally a plant will die from overwatering yet remain standing until someone knocks it over and finds it is hollow inside.

PROPAGATION: Because of the form of this cactus, the only way to propagate is by seed. It seldom flowers in the home, so you will need to acquire seed from a supplier.

PESTS AND DISEASES: Pests include mealybugs and scale, which may be hidden under the long, wavy white hairs.

RELATED SPECIES: Several species are appropriate for growing only outdoors.

ROSARY VINE

Ceropegia linearis ssp. *woodii* seer-oh-PEE-jee-a lin-ee-AIR-is WOOD-ee-eye

Rosary vine is also known as hearts entangled, hearts-on-a-vine, and string of hearts.

SIZE: 2–4' long
TYPE: Herbaceous
FORM: Vining
TEXTURE: Fine
GROWTH: Fast
LIGHT: High to medium
MOISTURE: Dry between waterings

SOIL: Potting soil
FEATURES: Heart-shaped leaves on long vines
USES: Hanging basket, focal point
FLOWERS: □

SITING: Give rosary vine bright light for the best form. It will tolerate medium light but will not be as full. It performs best in warm temperatures (70–75°F) during the summer and cooler temperatures (60–65°F) in winter. This plant tolerates low to average humidity. If you see signs of stress such as browning leaves, provide more moisture by placing it on a tray of moist pebbles.

CARE: Allow to dry considerably between waterings, then soak the soil well. When it is resting in winter, water sparingly. Feed monthly with half-strength foliage plant food during active growth; do not fertilize in winter. It performs best when pot-bound. If necessary repot in April before new growth begins. A summer outdoors in dappled light will benefit the plant.

PROPAGATION: Propagate with stem cuttings, by seed, or by planting the small tubers that form at the leaf bases. Press a tuber into potting soil while it is attached to the parent plant; keep moist, then sever it from the parent plant when rooted.

PESTS AND DISEASES: Occasional pests are mealybugs and spider mites, but generally the plant is tolerant of neglect.

RELATED SPECIES: *C. ampliata* has white flowers and twining stems. *C. gemmifera* has succulent stems and leaves.

"Beads" form along the stem and can be used to propagate new plants by resting them on soil and keeping them moist.

PEANUT CACTUS

Chamaecereus sylvestri (Echinopsis chamaecereus) *kam-eh-SEER-ee-us sil-VEST-rye*

Peanut cactus is a diminutive cactus in gray-green covered with white hairs. It is tolerant of neglect.

SIZE: 6"h × 2"w
TYPE: Cactus
FORM: Upright
TEXTURE: Medium
GROWTH: Slow
LIGHT: High

MOISTURE: Dry
SOIL: Cactus mix
FEATURES: Peanut-like knobs on main stem
USES: Dish garden

SITING: Peanut cactus needs full sun to thrive. Keep the plants warm (65–85°F) when in active growth; provide cooler temperatures (55–60°F) during their dormant period in winter. Low humidity levels (20–30 percent) will keep them looking their best.

CARE: Let soil dry out considerably between waterings during active growth, and even more during the dormant stage. Feed with half-strength plant food only after flower buds form. Peanut cactus has a small root system, like other cactuses, so repotting is seldom necessary.
PROPAGATION: Propagate peanut cactus by separating the peanuts from the parent plant. They root easily when they touch moist soil.
PESTS AND DISEASES: Root rot results from overwatering.
RELATED SPECIES: There are hundreds of other species, few of which are suitable for home culture. Some cultivars are available, but they are mostly for outdoor use.

1 Propagate by removing the offsets that form at the base of the plant.

2 Set offsets at the same soil level and keep the soil moist until they take root.

PARLOR PALM

Chamaedorea elegans (Neanthe bella) *cam-ee-DOH-ree-ah EL-e-ganz (nee-AN-thuh BELL-uh)*

Parlor palms have graced homes for centuries because of their ability to adapt to almost any cultural situation.

SIZE: 3–6'h × 1–2'w
TYPE: Palm
FORM: Upright
TEXTURE: Medium
GROWTH: Fast
LIGHT: High to low
MOISTURE: Dry between waterings

SOIL: Potting soil
FEATURES: Elegant fronds
USES: Architectural accent, foliage
FLOWERS: ☐

SITING: A worthy feature of the parlor palm is its adaptability. Although it performs best in bright light, it will adapt to medium and even low light. The fronds will be somewhat lighter in bright light and dark green in low light. Parlor palm does well in warm temperatures (75°F and above), but adapts to average temperatures. It is adaptable to low humidity; very low humidity causes the frond tips to turn brown. Keep the plant out of drafts, which may also brown the tips. Plants suffering from under- or overwatering have yellowing fronds and dropping leaves.
CARE: Allow to dry slightly between waterings while in active growth; let dry more during winter rest. Feed monthly with a foliage plant food during spring and summer only. Repotting is seldom necessary; parlor palm does well when pot-bound. Shower off the plant monthly to keep it looking pristine and to deter spider mites. Remove faded fronds occasionally. When you remove a frond, wait to remove the leaf sheath until it is brown and dry and pulls away easily.
PROPAGATION: Propagate by seeds, which take 1–6 months to germinate.
PESTS AND DISEASES: Spider mites, mealybugs, and scale can be problems in dry conditions.
RELATED SPECIES: The cultivar 'Bella' is a compact form.

Keep a close eye out for mites and scale insects. If you find them, treat the plant with horticultural oil or a good shower.

BAMBOO PALM

Chamaedorea erumpens cam-ee-DOH-ree-ah ee-RUM-penz

Bamboo palm, also known as reed palm, offers an attractive architectural statement because of its size.

SIZE: 7–12'h × 3–4'w
TYPE: Palm
FORM: Upright, open
TEXTURE: Medium
GROWTH: Medium
LIGHT: High, medium

MOISTURE: Dry between waterings
SOIL: Average
FEATURES: Clustered stems, bamboolike
USES: Foliage, architectural accent

SITING: Bamboo palm is used extensively in indoor culture because it is extremely adaptable. It prefers bright, indirect light, although it adapts to medium and even low light. Direct sun will bleach the fronds. Bamboo palm prefers warm temperatures (75°F and above), but adapts to the average temperatures of most homes and offices. It tolerates lower temperatures better than parlor palm. High humidity (65 percent or more) is best; low humidity causes the frond tips to turn brown. Keep the plant out of drafts, which may brown the tips.

CARE: Allow to dry slightly between waterings while in active growth; let dry out more during winter rest. Under- or overwatering causes browning leaf tips, yellowing fronds, and dropping leaves. Feed monthly with a foliage plant food during spring and summer only. Repotting is seldom necessary; bamboo palm does well when pot-bound. Shower the plant off monthly to keep it looking pristine and deter spider mites. Remove faded fronds. Trimming brown tips off the leaves often makes the leaf brown farther down, so removing the entire frond is preferable (but do not remove the leaf sheath until it is brown and dry and pulls away easily).

Rotate the pot every time you water to keep the plant symmetrical.
PROPAGATION: Seeds take 1–6 months to germinate but then grow fairly quickly. Bamboo palm is easily propagated by dividing the root ball.
PESTS AND DISEASES: Spider mites, mealybugs, and scale can be problems, especially in dry conditions.
RELATED SPECIES: *C. glaucifolia* has bluish-green foliage with glaucous stems and frond ribs. *C. microspadix* has wide blue-green leaflets.

To divide bamboo palm you may first need to saw through its tough roots.

Bamboo palm benefits from monthly showers to remove dust and mites.

CHIRITA

Chirita sinensis kee-REE-tuh sih-NEN-sis

Chirita is grown for its striking quilted leaves with silver patterns. In the right light conditions the plants will produce clusters of lavender tubular blossoms.

SIZE: 6–10"h × 6–10"w
TYPE: Gesneriad
FORM: Mounded
TEXTURE: Medium
GROWTH: Medium
LIGHT: High
MOISTURE: Evenly moist

SOIL: Organic
FEATURES: Thick quilted leaves in rosette with silver pattern
USES: Blooming accent
FLOWERS: ■

SITING: Chirita thrives in the same conditions as African violets, with bright, indirect light or even artificial light if desired. Full sun bleaches or scorches the attractively quilted and patterned leaves, so early morning and late afternoon sun is appropriate but not midday sun. Chiritas do well in temperatures of 65–85°F and average to high humidity (greater than 30 percent).

CARE: Keep chirita evenly moist, but the soil must be porous and free-draining to prevent rotting. It can be bottom-watered although it loses some of its compact shape. Chirita goes semidormant during the winter, so reduce watering and let it rest. Feed chirita by using half-strength blooming plant food at every other watering. Pruning is not necessary, and the only grooming needed is occasionally removing a faded leaf or spent flowers.

PROPAGATION: Propagate chirita from leaf cuttings. Simply remove a leaf with the petiole attached, dip it in rooting hormone and stick in sterile potting soil. Soon a cluster of tiny plants will form at the soil level and can be lifted, separated, and potted up as individual plants.

PESTS AND DISEASES: Cyclamen mites may be a problem and are quite difficult to get rid of. It may be necessary to discard the plant if an infestation persists. Otherwise chirita has few problems. Bronzed leaves indicate too much light or possible over-fertilization.

RELATED SPECIES: 'Hisako', with bright silvery markings on the leaves and lavender flowers, is one of the most popular cultivars. *C. s. angustifolia* has lavender flowers with yellow throats and thin dark leaves veined with silver.

SPIDER PLANT
Chlorophytum comosum clor-oh-FIE-tum co-MOE-sum

Spider plant is also known as airplane plant or ribbon plant. This cultivar is 'Vittatum'.

SIZE: 1'h × 2'w
TYPE: Herbaceous
FORM: Mounded
TEXTURE: Medium
GROWTH: Medium
LIGHT: Medium
MOISTURE: Evenly moist

SOIL: Average
FEATURES: Variegated or solid green leaves
USES: Hanging basket
FLOWERS: ☐

SITING: Spider plant prefers bright, indirect light; it will sunburn or fade in direct sunlight. In lower light it will not produce plantlets unless you supplement the light to mimic outside light in fall. Spider plant thrives in a cool home (55°F) but tolerates average temperatures. It is superb at cleaning toxins from the air.

CARE: Keep the soil moist but not soggy. Allow to dry slightly in winter. Feed once a month with a foliage plant food. Spider plant fills the pot with water-storing thickened roots, so it needs to be repotted regularly—as soon as watering becomes difficult. Wash off the plants regularly to keep them healthy and mite-free. Spider plant almost always gets brown tips, so trim them regularly. Eventually the leaf will become ragged looking and should be removed. When brown tips become rampant—a sign of water stress—repot or divide the plant. Brown tips may also indicate excess salts in the soil.

PROPAGATION: Propagate by dividing the root ball or planting offsets. To propagate by offsets, place a small pot next to the parent plant, set the plantlet (still attached to the parent plant) on moist soil and pin it down with a hairpin. When the plant has extended its roots in the soil, sever it from the parent plant. You can also root the plantlet in the same pot as the parent plant. When it has rooted, dig it carefully and move it to its own pot.

PESTS AND DISEASES: Spider plant may develop scale and spider mites when it is water stressed.

RELATED SPECIES: 'Picturatum' has a central creamy stripe. 'Variegatum', has a creamy white margin. 'Vittatum' has a central white stripe on each leaf.

To start new spider plants, place plantlets into a pot of soil mix. They root quickly.

Water stress causes brown tips which are easily trimmed from the leaves.

ARECA PALM
Chrysalidocarpus lutescens (Dypsis lutescens) kris-al-ih-doh-CAR-puss loo-TES-ens

Areca palm, also known as butterfly palm, has majestic long fronds that extend upward and then arch gracefully.

SIZE: 10–12'h × 4–5'w
TYPE: Palm
FORM: Upright, vase-shaped
TEXTURE: Coarse
GROWTH: Slow
LIGHT: Medium, indirect

MOISTURE: Evenly moist
SOIL: Average
FEATURES: Long, tropical fronds
USES: Architectural accent

SITING: Areca palm maintains its attractive, upright shape in bright, indirect light. It will not tolerate full sun. Give it average temperatures (60–75°F) and high humidity (65 percent or more) to prevent browning tips. It will not tolerate cool temperatures or drying winds.

CARE: Areca palm takes a good bit of care to keep it looking good in the home. Water with distilled or rainwater to keep the plant from getting spots on the leaves. Keep the soil evenly moist. Do not let the plant sit in water or it will rot. Feed with foliage plant food only once or twice a year. Overfertilization causes tip burn. Repot only when it becomes difficult to water; it prefers being pot-bound. Remove fronds as they yellow and trim out brown tips. Give plants a shower at least once a month to deter spider mites.

PROPAGATION: Propagate by dividing the root ball or by seed.

PESTS AND DISEASES: The only pests are spider mites.

RELATED SPECIES: *C. lastelliana* has a red trunk. Triangle palm (*C. decaryi*) is another unusual specimen houseplant.

Areca palms are a lovely architectural feature in a site with bright, indirect light.

These palms benefit greatly from monthly showers to keep them clean and mite-free.

KANGAROO VINE

Cissus antarctica SIS-us ant-AHR-ti-kuh

Kangaroo vine, also known as African tree grape, is an adaptable plant that can hang elegantly or be trained to climb.

SIZE: 4' long
TYPE: Climbing vine
FORM: Mounded, ground cover
TEXTURE: Medium
GROWTH: Fast
LIGHT: High to low

MOISTURE: Dry between waterings
SOIL: Potting soil
FEATURES: Long vines
USES: Foliage, ground cover

SITING: Kangaroo vine is adaptable to most home situations. It grows best in bright to medium light but will tolerate lower light if the soil is kept somewhat dry. It prefers 60°F or below and moderate to high humidity (30–70 percent), although it tolerates drier air.

CARE: Keep the soil slightly moist in active growth; allow it to dry somewhat during resting phase. Feed with a foliage plant food three times in summer only. It seldom needs repotting. Pinch back the tips to keep it shrubby. The plant climbs by tendrils and will cover a frame to make a delightful room divider or living curtain.

PROPAGATION: Propagate by stem cuttings. Take cuttings anywhere along the stem, remove all but one leaf at the tip of the cutting, dip the base into rooting hormone, and insert it in sterile potting mix. The plants can also be propagated by layering. Simply bend a vine so a leaf node comes in contact with moist soil. Hold in place with a hairpin. When roots have formed in the soil, sever the vine from the parent plant and pot it up.

PESTS AND DISEASES: Spider mites are usually the only pest. Wash off in the shower occasionally and treat with horticultural oil if necessary.

RELATED SPECIES: The cultivar 'Minima' is a small-leaved, spreading type that works well in a hanging basket.

To train a kangaroo vine to climb, start by wrapping the vines around a frame. The plant will eventually climb on its own.

GRAPE IVY

Cissus rhombifolia SIS-us rom-bih-FOLE-ee-uh

Grape ivy, also known as oakleaf ivy, tolerates bright to low light, making it one of the most versatile houseplants.

SIZE: 4' long
TYPE: Climbing vine
FORM: Mounded, ground cover
TEXTURE: Medium
GROWTH: Medium
LIGHT: High to low

MOISTURE: Dry between waterings
SOIL: Potting soil
FEATURES: Bronze leaves, tendrils
USES: Hanging basket, foliage

SITING: Grow grape ivy in high to low light but not full sun. In lower light, pinch it frequently to keep it shrubby. It prefers 60–80°F but tolerates lower temperatures. Average humidity is best. Ensure good air circulation to prevent powdery mildew.

CARE: Keep it somewhat dry between waterings, because it is prone to root rot. Feed with half-strength foliage plant food. More fertilizer can cause leaf burn. Grape ivy seldom needs repotting. Pinch back the tips to keep it shrubby. To rejuvenate a lanky plant, cut back about one-third of the vines in early spring to about 6" long. As new growth appears, cut back the other vines, never removing more than one-third of the plant at a time. To encourage grape

Grape ivy makes an excellent soft ground cover when planted in a pot with a larger plant.

ivy to climb, insert a stake or bamboo frame into the root ball. Tie the vines to the stake with soft twine and let the ends gently drape.

PROPAGATION: Propagate by stem cuttings. Take cuttings anywhere along the stem. Remove all but one leaf at the tip of the cutting, dip the base into rooting hormone, and insert in sterile potting mix. The plant can also be propagated by layering. Simply bend a vine so a leaf node comes in contact with moist soil. Hold it in place with a hairpin. When roots have formed in the soil, sever the vine from the parent plant and pot it up.

PESTS AND DISEASES: Occasional bouts with spider mites are inevitable. Shower off the plant periodically, and use horticultural oil to control them. Control powdery mildew by pruning out the affected parts.

RELATED SPECIES: 'Ellen Danica' was the first improved cultivar on the market. 'Manda Supreme' has larger, more succulent leaves. Miniature grape ivy (*C. striata*) has bronze-green leaves. Rex begonia vine (*C. discolor*) has dark green and silver leaves with maroon undersides.

CALAMONDIN ORANGE

×*Citrofortunella microcarpa* *sih-troh-for-toon-ELL-uh my-kroh-KAR-puh*

Calamondin orange fills a room with the fragrance of orange blossoms.

SIZE: 3'h × 2'w
TYPE: Woody shrub
FORM: Upright
TEXTURE: Medium
GROWTH: Slow
LIGHT: High
MOISTURE: Moist
SOIL: Potting soil
FEATURES: Glossy foliage, fragrant flowers, edible fruit
USES: Blooming, fruiting accent
FLOWERS: ☐

SITING: With more than a half-day of direct sun, Calamondin orange will bloom at least twice a year and almost continuously provide attractive, pungent tiny oranges. The plant performs best around 55–68°F and average humidity (30–60 percent). It tolerates higher temperatures but may not fruit.

CARE: Keep the soil moist but not soggy. Feed every 2–3 months with an acid plant food. Repot every 3 years but avoid too large a container. The plant has a shallow root system, so a wide pot is better than a deep one. To keep it looking good and producing well, thin to three sturdy stems. Although the plant may bloom periodically during the year, it may not produce fruit unless helped with pollination. Dust a small, soft paintbrush over the stamens of each flower; fruit should begin developing

Calamondin orange may be filled with blossoms, green fruit, and ripe fruit all at the same time.

in a few weeks. Shower the plants often to reduce pest problems. Plants benefit from spending the summer outdoors, especially for pollination. Gradually introduce them to a protected spot or they will drop leaves and abort fruits. Reverse the process when bringing them back indoors in fall (when outdoor temperatures drop below 50°F).

PROPAGATION: Seeds take a long time to make a sizable plant. The best way to ensure a fruiting specimen is to propagate by stem cuttings. Take the cuttings of semihardwood in early summer; root in sterile potting mix with rooting hormone and bottom heat.

PESTS AND DISEASES: Pests include aphids, mealybugs, spider mites, and scale, particularly if the humidity is low. Control insect populations with horticultural oil and frequent showers of water.

RELATED SPECIES: There are many citrus species and hybrid crosses with a flavor and size to suit every gardener. *Fortunella margarita* (kumquat) is related to Calamondin orange and is easy to grow indoors.

LEMON

Citrus limon *SIH-trus LYE-mun*

Lemon is an ideal plant for a bright spot, providing an architectural element as well as tasty fruit.

SIZE: 3'h × 2'w
TYPE: Woody shrub
FORM: Upright
TEXTURE: Medium
GROWTH: Slow
LIGHT: Bright
MOISTURE: Moist
SOIL: Potting soil
FEATURES: Glossy foliage, fragrant flowers, edible fruit
USES: Blooming, fruiting accent
FLOWERS: ☐

SITING: With at least a half-day of direct sun, lemon blooms at least twice a year and almost continuously provides fruit. It performs best at 55–68°F and average humidity (30–60 percent). Use a room humidifier, a pot-in-pot system, or a pebble tray to increase humidity.

CARE: Keep the soil moist but not soggy. Feed every 2–3 months with an acid plant food. Repot every 3 years but avoid too large a container. Being pot-bound is what keeps dwarf citrus dwarf. To keep it looking good and producing well, thin the plant to three sturdy stems. Although it may bloom periodically during the year, it may not produce fruit unless helped with pollination. Dust a small, soft paintbrush

Lemon blossoms are waxy white and intensely fragrant.

Thin all but one fruit per node to help develop large fruits.

over the stamens of each flower; fruit should begin developing in a few weeks. Shower the plants often to reduce pest problems. Plants benefit from spending the summer outdoors, especially for pollination. Gradually introduce them to a protected spot or they will drop leaves and abort fruits. Reverse the process when bringing them back indoors in fall (when outdoor temperatures drop below 50°F).

PROPAGATION: Seed-grown plants seldom produce fruit. The best way to ensure a fruiting specimen is to propagate by stem cuttings. Take the cuttings of semihardwood in early summer; root in sterile potting mix with rooting hormone and bottom heat. Provide a clear plastic tent for plenty of humidity while rooting.

PESTS: Pests include aphids, mealybugs, spider mites, and scale, particularly if the humidity is low. Control populations with horticultural oil and frequent showers.

RELATED SPECIES: Meyer lemon (*C.* ×*meyeri*) is one of the most commonly grown lemons for the home. *C. limon* 'Dwarf Ponderosa' has grapefruit-sized lemons, yet the plant is small enough to be easily grown indoors.

ORANGE
Citrus sinensis SIH-trus sib-NEN-sis

Orange not only is a beautiful addition to the indoor garden but also provides you with tasty fruit.

SIZE: 3'h × 2'w
TYPE: Woody shrub
FORM: Upright
TEXTURE: Medium
GROWTH: Slow
LIGHT: High
MOISTURE: Evenly moist

SOIL: Potting soil
FEATURES: Glossy foliage, fragrant flowers, edible fruit
USES: Blooming, fruiting accent
FLOWERS: □

SITING: With at least a half-day of direct sun, orange plant will bloom at least twice a year and almost continuously provide attractive, tasty fruit. It performs best at 55–68°F. It tolerates higher temperatures but may not fruit. Keep the humidity at an average level (30–60 percent) with a room humidifier, pot-in-pot system, or pebble tray.

CARE: Keep the soil moist but not soggy. Feed every 2–3 months with an acid plant food. Repot every 3 years but avoid too large a container. To keep it looking good and producing well, thin the plant to three sturdy stems. Although it may bloom periodically during the year, it may not

Fertilize oranges and other citrus with a fertilizer designed for plants that need acid soil.

produce fruit unless helped with pollination. Dust a small, soft paintbrush over the stamens of each flower; fruit should begin developing in a few weeks. Shower the plants often to reduce pest problems. Plants benefit from spending the summer outdoors, especially for pollination. Gradually introduce them to a protected spot or they will drop leaves and abort fruits. Reverse the process when bringing them back indoors in fall (when outdoor temperatures drop below 50°F).

PROPAGATION: Seed-grown plants seldom produce fruit. The best way to ensure a fruiting specimen is to propagate by stem cuttings. Take the cuttings of semihardwood in early summer and root in sterile potting mix with rooting hormone and bottom heat. Provide a tent for plenty of humidity while rooting.

PESTS AND DISEASES: Pests include aphids, mealybugs, spider mites, and scale. Control populations with horticultural oil and frequent showers.

RELATED SPECIES: The cultivar 'Valencia' is seedless and bears fruit up to 4" in diameter. 'Dwarf Washington' is easily peeled and delicious.

GLORYBOWER
Clerodendrum thomsoniae kler-ob-DEN-drum tom-SOHN-ee-eye

Glorybower can give you a striking hanging basket or even a wall of color when trained onto a trellis.

SIZE: 8'h × 5'w
TYPE: Woody vine
FORM: Trailing, upright
TEXTURE: Medium
GROWTH: Medium
LIGHT: High

MOISTURE: Moist
SOIL: Potting soil
FEATURES: Blossoms
USES: Hanging basket, trellis
FLOWERS: □ ■

SITING: Glory bower is a beautiful accent when in bloom from July through October. It needs bright, indirect light to develop flowers. Provide average (70–75°F) temperatures, not dropping below 55°F. It needs high humidity (above 60 percent).

CARE: Provide plenty of water during its active growing period, but hold back on watering and let dry somewhat during the winter. Repot every spring into a slightly larger container. Feed every 2 weeks with

When glorybower has finished its summer blooming, prune out the faded bracts to keep the plant attractive.

half-strength blooming plant food until its winter rest in November. Pinch regularly to avoid unkempt-looking growth. Although its natural inclination is to climb and you can train it to a trellis, it can be maintained in shrubby form by pruning. Prune back after flowering in fall (it blooms on new wood).

PROPAGATION: Take stem cuttings in spring and give plenty of humidity and bottom heat. Plants can also be started from seed.

PESTS AND DISEASES: Control mealybugs and spider mites by keeping the humidity high. Use horticultural oil if the populations get out of hand.

RELATED SPECIES: The cultivar 'Variegatum' has creamy white and pale green mottled leaves. Most species are more suited to the conservatory or growing outdoors in the South because of their large size. Butterfly flower, *C. ugandense* has blue flowers that hang down like butterflies.

CLIVIA
Clivia miniata *KLI-vee-uh (KLY-vee-uh) min-ee-AH-tuh*

Clivia, also known as Kafir lily, provides you with spectacular orange to red blossoms if kept pot-bound and somewhat dry.

SIZE: 1–2'h × 1–2'w
TYPE: Herbaceous
FORM: Vase-shaped
TEXTURE: Medium to coarse
GROWTH: Medium
LIGHT: High

MOISTURE: Dry
SOIL: Well-drained
FEATURES: Blossoms
USES: Blooming accent
FLOWERS: ■ ■ ■

SITING: Clivia prefers morning sun or bright, indirect light all day. It will not tolerate direct afternoon sun. Provide daytime temperatures of 70°F or higher, and nighttime temperatures not lower than 50°F. Drop the temperature during the rest period to just above 40°F.

CARE: Clivia roots are fleshy and store water, so they easily rot if overwatered. It's better to neglect a clivia than to overwater it. Feed monthly with a blooming plant food during active growth. In late fall give the plant a rest by withholding plant food and watering only enough to keep the leaves from wilting. Repot in spring just

As a clivia grows, the bottom leaves may turn yellow. Simply prune these off by hand to keep the plant attractive.

as it begins active growth. Well-drained potting soil is essential. Some gardeners pot clivia in orchid mix. Keep the same size pot; clivia needs to be pot-bound in order to bloom. The plants are top heavy, so use a terra-cotta pot. Move clivia outdoors into light, dappled shade for the summer.

PROPAGATION: Propagate by separating the offsets from the parent plant. After flowering, remove the plant from the pot and gently tease the roots apart to separate the offsets. Pot them up and give them plenty of water and light as they establish themselves. Clivia grown from seed takes a long time to reach blooming size. Sow seeds on sterile soil mix; press lightly into it, leaving the tops exposed. Keep warm and light. Pot up the new plants about 8 months after sowing.

PESTS AND DISEASES: Remove scale and mealybugs by hand or with a cotton swab dipped in alcohol or horticultural oil.

RELATED SPECIES: *C. nobilis* has pendulous flowers. *C. miniata* var. *citrina* has clear yellow flowers; there are several cultivars of this variety. *C. gardenii* has pendulous flowers that are orange tipped in green.

CROTON
Codiaeum variegatum var. *pictum* *Koh-dee-AY-um vair-eh-GAH-tum PIK-tum*

Croton is perhaps one of the most colorful of all the houseplants. It will thrive if kept warm and humid.

SIZE: 2–6'h × 1–3'w
TYPE: Woody shrub
FORM: Rounded
TEXTURE: Coarse
GROWTH: Medium
LIGHT: High

MOISTURE: Evenly moist
SOIL: Potting soil
FEATURES: Variegated leaves
USES: Focal point, foliage

SITING: Croton needs bright light to keep its remarkable leaf coloration. In lower light the leaves fade and the plant will be stressed. Keep croton above 60°F at all times. It needs high humidity (65 percent or above) to keep its attractive form and to deter spider mites. Grouping plants with croton as the focal point displays this plant well and keeps the humidity high.

CARE: Keep the soil evenly moist but not soggy. In winter, water when the soil begins to dry out; never let the soil completely dry. Feed every 2 months during the growing season with foliage plant food; do not fertilize in winter. Repot in spring if pot-bound (every few years). Remove yellow leaves and shower the plant off at least monthly for aesthetics and insect control.

PROPAGATION: Propagate by softwood cuttings. Take cuttings in early summer. Stop the stem from bleeding by dusting it with charcoal. Remove all the leaves but one. If you are propagating a large-leaved variety, cut the leaf in half. Dust the cutting with rooting hormone and insert it in sterile potting soil. Cover it with a plastic bag to keep high humidity. Croton can also be air-layered.

PESTS AND DISEASES: Pests include spider mites, mealybugs, and scale. Treat mealybugs and scale with horticultural oil. Use a forceful water spray to remove spider mites.

RELATED SPECIES: The cultivar 'Lauren's Rainbow' has ribbonlike emerald green leaves with a golden midrib. 'Goldfinger' has thin gold-hued leaves.

Corkscrew croton has interesting twisted leaves with plenty of colorful variegation.

Unless given quite bright light, croton leaves will tend to lose their beautiful colors.

COFFEE
Coffea arabica KAW-fee-uh uh-RAB-ih-kuh

Coffee seldom blooms or produces berries indoors, but the glossy green foliage is reason enough to grow the plant.

SIZE: 12'h × 3'w
TYPE: Woody shrub
FORM: Rounded
TEXTURE: Medium
GROWTH: Slow
LIGHT: High, indirect
MOISTURE: Evenly moist

SOIL: Potting soil
FEATURES: Glossy leaves, berries
USES: Focal point, blooming
FLOWERS: □

SITING: Coffee plant needs bright, indirect light (not direct sun) to produce its attractive, glossy red berries. It grows best at medium temperatures (60–75°F) and high humidity (65 percent or above).

CARE: Keep evenly moist but not soggy. Feed every 2 weeks during the active growing season with half-strength foliage plant food. Feed monthly in winter. Feed every 2 months with acid fertilizer. Pinch out the growing tips periodically to keep the plant shrubby and attractive or prune more thoroughly once a year. Move outdoors in summer.

PROPAGATION: Propagate from cuttings or seed. Pick the ripe red berries, remove the pulp, and plant the seeds in sterile soil mix. Keep moist and humid until germination.

PESTS AND DISEASES: Wash spider mites from affected leaves with a spray of water.

Pinching out the growing tips of coffee will help the plant maintain an attractive shrubby shape.

GOLDFISH PLANT
Columnea spp. kah-LUM-nee-ah

Goldfish plants have bright red and yellow uniquely shaped flowers on deep shiny green foliage.

SIZE: 1'h × 3'w
TYPE: Gesneriad
FORM: Trailing
TEXTURE: Fine
GROWTH: Moderate
LIGHT: High to medium

MOISTURE: Evenly moist
SOIL: Potting soil
FEATURES: Hanging stems, glossy leaves
USES: Hanging basket
FLOWERS: ■ ■

SITING: Bright to medium light, away from direct sun, will keep goldfish plant looking its best. If the plant won't flower, move it into brighter but filtered light. Average to warm temperatures (60°F or more) and high humidity are needed for the plant to blossom. A pebble tray works well.

CARE: Keep evenly moist but not soggy. When the plant is not actively growing, avoid wetting the foliage or it may develop water scarring. Reducing watering for 6–8 weeks may induce flowering. Feed every 2 weeks with half-strength plant food for blooming plants. Goldfish plant will drop leaves when it gets too cold or too dry or is overfertilized. Every month flush the soil with clear water to wash away fertilizer salts. Repotting is seldom necessary; goldfish plant blooms best when pot-bound. Prune back long, wayward stems regularly to keep the plant full and appealing.

PROPAGATION: Propagate by stem or tip cuttings. Simply insert the cuttings into rooting hormone, then into sterile potting soil. Cover it with plastic to boost humidity. Cuttings will root in a few weeks.

PESTS AND DISEASES: Pests include aphids, spider mites, and whiteflies. The plant is generally problem-free if cultural details are attended to.

RELATED SPECIES: *C. gloriosa* has purplish leaves covered with hairs and bright red flowers with a yellow throat. The cultivar 'Bonfire' has orange-yellow flowers. *C. microphylla* 'Variegata' has grayish leaves with creamy margins and scarlet flowers.

Goldfish plant tends to have long trailing stems that should be pruned back periodically to keep the plant shrubby and attractive.

HAWAIIAN TI PLANT

Cordyline fruticosa (terminalis) *KORE-dih-li-nee fru-tih-KOH-suh (ter-mih-NAHL-iss)*

Hawaiian ti plant has been sold for many years as a symbol of good luck. It is also known as good luck plant or red dracaena.

SIZE: 4'h × 3'w
TYPE: Herbaceous
FORM: Upright
TEXTURE: Coarse
GROWTH: Slow
LIGHT: High, indirect

MOISTURE: Evenly moist
SOIL: Potting soil
FEATURES: Variegated leaves
USES: Architectural accent

SITING: Bright light will keep the ti plant healthy. Direct sun can cause the red and cream variegation in the leaves to fade. It prefers average temperatures (60–75°F), not below 55°F, and average humidity (30–65 percent).

CARE: Keep evenly moist but not soggy. Reduce watering in winter but do not let it dry out. Feed only three times in summer. Repot infrequently; pot-bound plants produce shoots at the base. Remove yellowed leaves and shower monthly to reduce pest problems. Brown tips on the leaves indicate too little humidity. Brown spotting on the leaves may indicate a cold draft or underwatering.

PROPAGATION: Pieces of the cane or crown can be used for propagation. Cut out the crown, dust the base with rooting hormone, and set it in moist, sterile potting soil. For cane cuttings, take pieces 2–3" long, lay them on moist potting soil, and cover them with plastic to raise humidity. They should root in a few weeks.

PESTS AND DISEASES: Usually ti plant is pest free. However occasional pests include mealybugs, mites, and scale.

RELATED SPECIES: The cultivar 'Kiwi' has bright leaves with stripes of pink-red, yellow, and light green. 'White Baby Doll' has slender leaves with streaks of ivory and pink.

A stem cutting, called a ti log, quickly roots when placed on moist potting soil and covered with plastic.

Once the leaves sprout, remove the plastic and bring the plant into good light.

JADE PLANT

Crassula ovata (argentea) *KRASS-yew-luh o-VAH-tuh (ar-JEN-tee-uh)*

The succulent leaves and thick stems of jade plants are easily recognizable and give the home a southwestern flair.

SIZE: 2'h × 2'w
TYPE: Succulent
FORM: Rounded
TEXTURE: Medium
GROWTH: Slow
LIGHT: High
MOISTURE: Low

SOIL: Cactus
FEATURES: Thick leaves on thick stems
USES: Succulent garden, focal point
FLOWERS: ☐

SITING: Jade plant grows splendidly in high light. It grows in all temperatures but does best with low humidity (below 30 percent).

CARE: Let the potting mix dry out before watering, then soak thoroughly. Jade plant does well if not watered until the leaves begin to lose their shine, although it may drop its leaves if it dries out too much. Feed only three times in summer. It seldom needs repotting. But as the plant matures and gets top heavy, it may be necessary to repot into a heavier soil mix and a heavier pot to keep it from falling over. As the plant gets top heavy, prune it to prevent it from falling over and snapping off the succulent stems.

PROPAGATION: Propagate by stem cuttings, leaf cuttings, or seed.

PESTS AND DISEASES: Jade may have scale, but mealybugs are the most common problem. Overwatering causes stem rot.

RELATED SPECIES: 'Tricolor' has creamy white-and-rose-striped leaves. 'Sunset' has leaves tipped in gold. 'California Red Tip' has purple-edged reddish leaves. Silver jade plant (*C. argentea*) has grayish leaves with red margins.

To propagate a jade plant, cut off a leaf with the leaf bud at the base intact.

Dip the leaf-bud end of the leaf in rooting hormone and tap off the excess.

Insert the lower tip of the leaf cutting into sterile potting soil.

FIRECRACKER FLOWER

Crossandra infundibuliformis *kros-AN-druh in-fun-dib-bew-li-FOR-mis*

Firecracker flower explodes into bright impressive blossoms of yellow, red, or salmon.

SIZE: 2'h × 2'w
TYPE: Woody shrub
FORM: Rounded
TEXTURE: Medium
GROWTH: Medium
LIGHT: Medium to high

MOISTURE: Evenly moist
SOIL: Potting soil
FEATURES: Glossy leaves, bright flowers
USES: Focal point
FLOWERS: ■ ■ ■

SITING: Firecracker flower looks its best in bright, indirect light. It tolerates medium light but not direct sun. It prefers medium temperatures (60–75°F), not below 55°F in winter. Provide high humidity by placing the plant on a pebble tray or grouping it with other plants.

CARE: Keep moist but not soggy. Feed weekly with half-strength foliage plant food from spring to early fall. Do not fertilize during the winter resting phase. Repot every 2–3 years as the plant outgrows its pot. Prune regularly to maintain shape. Remove spent flowers to keep the plant blooming from spring to fall.

PROPAGATION: Propagate by softwood cuttings or seed. Take stem cuttings in spring, dip in rooting hormone, and insert into sterile potting soil. Apply bottom heat.

PESTS AND DISEASES: Firecracker flower has few pests or diseases.

RELATED SPECIES: None are readily available.

As soon as the flower spikes fade, trim them off to keep the plant attractive and producing new blooms.

EARTH STAR

Cryptanthus bivittatus *krip-TAN-thus bih-vih-TAH-tus*

Earth star, a bromeliad, will keep its beautiful leaf color when provided bright light and warm temperatures.

SIZE: 6"h × 6–12"w
TYPE: Bromeliad
FORM: Mound
TEXTURE: Medium
GROWTH: Slow
LIGHT: High to medium

MOISTURE: Dry between waterings
SOIL: Epiphyte mix
FEATURES: Stiff, variegated leaves
USES: Focal point, dish garden, terrarium

SITING: Earth star shows its best leaf color in bright, filtered light. Provide warm to average temperatures (60°F and above) to keep the plant from rotting. This bromeliad looks best when grown in medium humidity (30–65 percent).

CARE: Let earth star dry out almost completely between waterings. Earth star may develop leaf spots in low humidity and root rot if it is overwatered. Feed with blooming plant formula three times in summer. Earth star has a miniscule root system that seldom outgrows a pot. If the plant flowers, remove the flower shoots as soon as they have faded and propagate new plants. The old plant will begin to deteriorate.

PROPAGATION: Propagate by removing the offsets that develop between the leaves and pot them up. They will readily develop a root system merely by being in contact with moist soil.

PESTS AND DISEASES: Treat scale with horticultural oil.

RELATED SPECIES: The cultivar 'Pink Starlight' has bright pink, white, and green variegated leaves. *C. zonatus* 'Zebrinus' has reddish-brown leaves with silvery bands.

1 Offsets develop between the leaves of earth star, and these can be removed for propagating the plant.

2 After potting the offsets into sterile coarse potting mix, water them well. They will quickly develop roots.

FALSE HEATHER

Cuphea hyssopifolia *KU-fee-uh hih-sop-ih-FOH-lee-uh*

False heather, also known as Mexican heather, is adorned with soft lavender, white, or pink flowers.

SIZE: 8–14"h × 10"w
TYPE: Woody shrub
FORM: Upright
TEXTURE: Fine
GROWTH: Fast
LIGHT: High
MOISTURE: Evenly moist

SOIL: Potting soil
FEATURES: Tiny leaves, attractive flowers
USES: Blooming plant, focal point
FLOWERS: ■■□

SITING: False heather thrives in bright light but tolerates full sun. Lower light reduces blooming. Provide average to cool temperatures (55–75°F) and average humidity (30 to 65 percent).
CARE: Keep the soil evenly moist. False heather will drop its leaves if the soil dries out. Feed with half-strength foliage plant food at every watering. Repot annually in spring before the blooming season. As soon as the plant has finished blooming, cut back by almost half to rejuvenate it.

PROPAGATION: Propagate by stem cuttings or from seed.
PESTS AND DISEASES: Pests include mealybugs, thrips, and whiteflies. If infestations are severe, discard the plant.
RELATED SPECIES: The cultivar 'Compacta' is a dwarf form. 'Rosea' has pink flowers, and 'Alba' has white flowers. All may be used as annual landscape plants in northern areas, or as shrubs in the South. Cigar flower, *C. ignea*, is a soft-stemmed shrubby plant 1–2' tall with a spread of 1–3'. It develops 1-inch-long tubular red flowers with a white rim.

When false heather has finished blooming, cut the plant back by about half to rejuvenate it and promote new blossoms.

TEDDY BEAR VINE

Cyanotis kewensis *sigh-a-NOTE-is cue-EN-sis*

Teddy bear vine, a vining succulent plant covered with chocolate-colored hairs, is a favorite with children.

SIZE: 12" long
TYPE: Herbaceous
FORM: Trailing
TEXTURE: Fine
GROWTH: Fast
LIGHT: Medium

MOISTURE: Evenly moist
SOIL: Potting soil
FEATURES: Leaves with chocolate hairs
USES: Hanging basket

SITING: Give teddy bear vine medium light and average temperatures (60–75°F). This plant is easy to care for and tolerates medium to high humidity (30 percent or greater). Be sure to place it out of the way of traffic; the stems break easily. Velvety brown hairs on the leaves make the plant soft to the touch, giving rise to its common name.
CARE: Keep the plant evenly moist for optimum growth, but it will tolerate dry conditions fairly well. Feed three times in summer with foliage plant food. Teddy bear vine is so succulent that the fragile stems do not fare well during repotting, and the roots do not grow quickly. It's best to leave the plant in its original pot. Although teddy bear vine can be pinched regularly to keep it shrubby, it doesn't branch well. It will eventually deteriorate, so new plants should be started regularly.
PROPAGATION: Start from stem cuttings. Simply take ends you pinch out during regular pruning, dip them in rooting hormone, and insert them in sterile potting soil. Extra humidity will speed rooting.
PESTS AND DISEASES: Mealybugs can be a problem. Control them with a labelled insecticide or by swabbing with them with rubbing alcohol.
RELATED SPECIES: More succulent pussy ears (*C. somaliensis*) has larger leaves that clasp the plant's stem and are covered with silvery-gray hairs. It grows to 6" tall with a spread of 16". Teddy bear vine is distantly related to *Tradescantia* (see pages 230 and 231), but its hairs help it tolerate dry conditions better.

SAGO PALM

Cycas revoluta *SIGH-kas rev-oh-LUTE-uh*

Sago palms are easy to care for and although they are quite slow growing, they are extremely long-lived.

SIZE: 5'h × 4'w
TYPE: Cycad
FORM: Palmlike
TEXTURE: Coarse
GROWTH: Slow
LIGHT: High to medium

MOISTURE: Dry between waterings
SOIL: Cactus
FEATURES: Stiff, architectural fronds
USES: Architectural accent

SITING: Sago palm (not a true palm) thrives in bright light, even full sun. It also tolerates medium light. Any temperature and any humidity are fine. It grows extremely slowly but is very long-lived.

CARE: Let the soil dry out between waterings. The plant does not indicate when it is dry, so keep track of when it was watered. It tolerates drought but not overwatering. (Old leaves may turn yellow from overwatering.) Feed only once in spring and once in summer. If growing in low light, give it only half-strength plant food. (New leaves will turn yellow from

Sago palm lends a distinct, cleanly formal appearance to an interior landscape.

overfeeding.) Because it is so slow growing, it seldom needs repotting and actually looks best if pot-bound. Remove old fronds when necessary.

PROPAGATION: Propagate by separating the offsets, or "pups," that grow at the base or along the sides of mature plants. Remove them in early spring, late fall, or winter. Use a trowel to take small ones off the trunk or to separate larger ones from the base of the plant. Remove all the leaves and roots from each offset and set it aside to dry for a week. Then plant it in a cactus type soil with half the offset below the soil level. Water it well and move it to a shady area. Allow the soil to dry before watering again. New leaves will appear in several months.

PESTS AND DISEASES: Treat scale with horticultural oil.

RELATED SPECIES: Queen sago palm (*C. circinalis*) has longer, softer fronds than *C. revoluta* and can reach 15' or more under ideal conditions.

CYCLAMEN

Cyclamen persicum *SIGH-cla-men PER-sih-cum*

Cyclamen, also known as florist's cyclamen, brightens up a room with its reflexed blossoms and variegated foliage.

SIZE: 6–10"h × 6–12"w
TYPE: Corm
FORM: Mounded
TEXTURE: Medium
GROWTH: Medium
LIGHT: Medium
MOISTURE: Dry between waterings

SOIL: Potting soil
FEATURES: Variegated, heart-shaped leaves
USES: Blooming accent
FLOWERS: ■ ■ ■ □

SITING: Bright to medium indirect light will make the plant looks its best. Cool temperatures (50–60°F) will prolong

cyclamen's blooming cycle. Provide average humidity (30–65 percent).

CARE: Allow the soil to dry only slightly before watering. Feed with half-strength food for blooming plants at every watering from fall until bud set. Repot in fall, keeping half the corm above the soil line.

Removing spent flowers and yellowed leaves regularly will keep cyclamen looking its best.

Remove faded flowers immediately to prevent seed formation, which shortens the blooming time. Also remove any faded leaves. Gently twist stems of leaves and flowers to remove. Yellow leaves indicate too warm a room or that the plant wilted severely at one time or was overwatered. Cyclamen is often treated as a throwaway plant because it is difficult to bring back into bloom. For the best success, set it under a shrub outdoors for the summer with the pot on its side. Water infrequently and expect the foliage to fade completely. Bring the pot back indoors as soon as temperatures cool in the fall. Repot and begin watering. Keep in a cool, bright spot and water as the soil dries slightly. Begin feeding as directed above.

PROPAGATION: Propagate from seed. The plant sets seed easily.

PESTS AND DISEASES: Cyclamen mites are a perennial problem. Spray with a miticide labeled for indoor use or discard severly infested plants.

RELATED SPECIES: There are hundreds of cultivars with flowers of every color and size. Many related species are grown outdoors and are not appropriate for indoor culture.

CYMBIDIUM ORCHID

Cymbidium spp. sim-BID-ee-um

There is nothing quite as breathtaking as a cymbidium orchid in bloom. This is 'Lavender Falls'.

SIZE: 1–3'h × 1'w
TYPE: Orchid
FORM: Upright
TEXTURE: Medium
GROWTH: Slow
LIGHT: High to medium

MOISTURE: Even
SOIL: Epiphyte
FEATURES: Flowers
USES: Focal point
FLOWERS: ☐■■■
■■

SITING: Cymbidium orchid needs at least medium light to bloom and performs better in brighter, filtered light. Keep at 45–50°F most of the time. It can handle hot temperatures for short periods, but cold is essential to induce flowering.

Reduce the temperature to just above freezing in fall—a cool porch is ideal. Provide medium humidity (30–65 percent), and keep it away from drying winds to preserve the fragrant blossoms.

CARE: Cymbidium orchid is not hard to care for when grown in cool conditions. Keep evenly moist except in winter, when water should be reduced as the growth slows. If you see tip burn, switch to distilled water. Feed with a dilute solution of standard plant food at every watering during active growth. When it comes

'Banff' produces sprays of delicate pink blooms.

'Mary Pinchess Del Rey' has gold blooms.

indoors in fall, feed with a blossom booster at every watering until the plant goes into its resting phase in winter. Repot when the plant begins to outgrow its pot and becomes unwieldy, or when the potting mix begins to break down and you can no longer recognize individual pieces of bark. Tap the plant out of its pot and remove any withered roots. Let any broken roots air-dry for a few hours before potting. Remove faded leaves and flowers. Place outdoors in summer in a bright spot that is well protected from wind and direct sun.

PROPAGATION: Propagate by separating the pseudobulbs from one another; the new plants will bloom 2–3 years after propagation. The preferred method when the plant gets too large is to repot into a larger pot rather than dividing.

PESTS AND DISEASES: Scale and spider mites may be problems in poor cultural conditions.

RELATED SPECIES: There are hundreds of cymbidium cultivars. Newer miniature versions are popular for home use because of their smaller size and tolerance for more heat.

DWARF PAPYRUS

Cyperus alternifolius SIGH-pur-us al-tur-nih-FOHL-ee-us

Dwarf papyrus, also known as umbrella plant, will win you over with its dancing leaflets that sit atop long, elegant stems.

SIZE: 3'h × 3'w
TYPE: Herbaceous
FORM: Vase-shaped
TEXTURE: Fine
GROWTH: Medium
LIGHT: High
MOISTURE: Wet

SOIL: Potting soil
FEATURES: Long stems, starry flowers
USES: Accent, aquatic
FLOWERS: ■

SITING: Provide dwarf papyrus with the highest indirect light possible. A south or west window is perfect as long as the light is slightly filtered, perhaps through a gauzy curtain. Because of its need for water, it is an ideal accent plant for an indoor water

feature. This plant tolerates cool to hot temperatures (50–85°F) and prefers medium (30–65 percent) humidity.

CARE: This unique-looking plant needs constantly wet soil. Use a pot with no drainage and keep the soil soaked, or stand the plant in a container of water. Be sure to use tepid water; cold water will rot the plant. Feed infrequently—about twice a year—with a general foliage houseplant

Dwarf papyrus performs well outdoors as a focal point in a water feature.

To propagate this plant invert a leaf in a container of water until new plants form.

food. Repot with average potting soil when the plant begins to creep out of its pot. Soil with too much organic matter will become sour and rot the roots. Remove any faded fronds. Wipe the leaves regularly with a dry, soft cloth.

PROPAGATION: Propagate by dividing the rhizome, but it's more interesting to take leaf cuttings. Cut one leaf with a small piece of stem attached and cut back the bracts by two-thirds. Invert the leaf in a container of water. New plants will form where the leaf meets the stem. Clip the new plants and pot them up. Another easy way to propagate is to simply bend a stem over and pin the bracts down on wet sand in a new pot. Clip the new plant from the parent plant when rooted.

PESTS AND DISEASES: None.

RELATED SPECIES: The cultivar 'Gracilis' is a stiff-leaved dwarf form. Papyrus (*Cyperus papyrus*) grow to 7' tall.

JAPANESE HOLLY FERN

Cyrtomium falcatum sir-TOHM-ee-um fall-KAH-tum

Japanese holly ferns are handsome foliage plants that require medium light and cool to average temperatures.

SIZE: 1'h × 4'w
TYPE: Fern
FORM: Arching
TEXTURE: Medium
GROWTH: Medium to fast

LIGHT: Medium
MOISTURE: Even
SOIL: Potting soil
FEATURES: Glossy leaves
USES: Foliage

SITING: Japanese holly fern grows well in medium light, making it an excellent companion to many other plants. Its glossy leaves set off a blooming plant such as gardenia, columnea, or even a cattleya orchid. Provide cool to average temperatures (50–75°F) and keep the humidity high (above 65 percent). It will tolerate somewhat lower humidity but will look best when set on a moist pebble tray. Grouping it with other plants will also raise the humidity.

CARE: Keep evenly moist but not soggy. Feed three times in summer with a general foliage plant food. Repot every year into sterile organic potting mix. Remove dead fronds.

PROPAGATION: Propagate by dividing the rhizome. This plant is also propagated fairly easily by spores, but it takes a while to grow into sizable plants.

PESTS AND DISEASES: Thrips are so difficult to control that it may be necessary to discard the plant. Treat mealybugs and scale with horticultural oil.

RELATED SPECIES: The cultivar 'Rochfordianum' (fringed holly fern) has closely fringed margins. *C. fortunei* is smaller than holly fern and more tolerant of cold.

1 Ferns reproduce by spores, borne in small cases on the backs of fronds.

2 Tap ripe spores out onto paper and then sprinkle them on moist soil mix.

3 Cover with glass or plastic to keep the interior moist until small plants form.

RABBIT'S FOOT FERN

Davallia fejeensis (Polypodium aureum) duh-VAHL-ya fee-jee-EN-sis (pahl-ee-POH-dee-um AW-ree-um)

Rabbit's foot fern, also known as hare's foot fern, makes a beautiful hanging basket.

SIZE: 8–12"h × 1–3'w
TYPE: Fern
FORM: Mounded
TEXTURE: Fine
GROWTH: Medium
LIGHT: High to medium

MOISTURE: Even
SOIL: Epiphyte mix
FEATURES: Fronds, creeping rhizomes
USES: Hanging basket

SITING: Rabbit's foot fern makes its best growth in bright, filtered light. It performs well in home temperatures from about 55°F at night to as high as 85°F during the day. It needs high humidity.

CARE: This epiphytic fern grows on the sides of trees in the wild, so keep it moderately moist. It has a resting period from October to February when it needs little water. Feed with a foliage plant food at half the recommended dose from April through September. Tip burn results from being fed too much. The fern's "rabbit's foot" rhizomes creep over the ground and hang over the sides of the pot. It's important not to cover the rhizomes with potting soil but rather let them creep where they want. The rhizomes are succulent and can break, so instead of repotting the entire plant, push new potting mix between the rhizomes when the old potting mix breaks down. Rabbit's foot fern seldom needs pruning but may need yellowed fronds removed occasionally.

PROPAGATION: Propagate by rhizome division. Simply cut pieces of a rhizome and pin them to moist soil. This fern can also be propagated by spores.

PESTS AND DISEASES: Spider mites may be a problem, if the humidity is low. Control them by showering off the plant regularly and keeping humidity high. Browning fronds may result from low humidity.

RELATED SPECIES: Deer's foot fern (*D. canariensis*) has narrow, triangular fronds. Polynesian foot fern (*D. solida*) has more leathery fronds. Squirrel's foot fern (*D. trichomanoides*) has diamond-shaped fronds.

1 This fern gets its name from the fuzzy rhizomes that creep over the edge of the pot.

2 Propagate this fern by placing a rhizome on moist sterile potting soil.

DENDROBIUM ORCHID

Dendrobium hybrids *den-DROH-bee-um*

Dendrobiums will bloom beautifully for you with bright light, warm temperatures, and regular fertilization.

SIZE: 2–6'h × 8–16"w
TYPE: Orchid
FORM: Upright
TEXTURE: Medium
GROWTH: Slow
LIGHT: High

MOISTURE: Even
SOIL: Epiphyte mix
FEATURES: Flowers
USES: Focal point
FLOWERS: ☐ ◼ ◼ ◼ ◼

SITING: Give this orchid bright light with up to 50 percent sun, but shade it from direct sun. It requires a 15–20 degrees difference between day- and nighttime temperature. Maintain a night temperature of 60–65°F and a day temperature of 80–90°F. Low temperatures may cause leaf drop. Dendrobium orchid needs 50–60 percent humidity.

CARE: Keep evenly moist while in active growth. During the resting phase, allow to dry slightly between waterings. This plant thrives when grown outdoors in summer. Dendrobium needs regular fertilization to produce the magnificent blossoms. Feed weekly during the growing period. It blooms best when pot-bound. When the plant outgrows its pot, select a new one of a size that will allow only 1–2 years of growth. When the root ball is out of the pot, trim away any dead roots or shriveled pseudobulbs. Repot only when the plant is in active growth. Remove the occasional yellow leaf or the papery sheath, which detract from the overall beauty of the plant. Dendrobium flower spikes may need support. Before the buds open, anchor a sturdy stake securely beside the root ball. Tie the flower stem gently to the stake with soft twine using a loose figure eight.

PROPAGATION: Propagate by removing offsets when the plant is actively growing. Divided plants may take several years before they bloom. Some species can be propagated by simply laying the offsets on damp moss.

PESTS AND DISEASES: Control orchid scale with horticultural oil.

RELATED SPECIES: Choose the evergreen types for beauty year-round. These are grouped into the "cane," Farmeri, and Formosum groups.

Dendrobium chrysotoxum has fragrant yellow blooms

To support the blossom spike, tie it gently to an orchid stake with soft twine.

DUMB CANE

Dieffenbachia amoena *dee-fin-BAH-kee-uh uh-MEE-nuh*

Dumb canes are absolutely carefree plants when given medium light, average temperatures, and occasional fertilization.

SIZE: 3–6'h × 1–3'w
TYPE: Herbaceous
FORM: Upright
TEXTURE: Coarse
GROWTH: Medium
LIGHT: Medium

MOISTURE: Dry
SOIL: Potting soil
FEATURES: Foliage
USES: Architectural accent, foliage

SITING: Dumb cane takes average conditions and easily tolerates some neglect. Provide medium light and average temperatures (60–75°F). Keep it out of drafts and drying winds. It tolerates medium humidity (30–65 percent) but looks much better in higher humidity.

CARE: Allow to dry out slightly before watering; it tolerates an occasional missed watering. Wilting causes severe leaf loss. Feed mature plants three times in summer with a foliage plant food. Feeding more often may cause succulent growth that is not sturdy enough to tolerate dryness; it also makes the plant top heavy and causes it to outgrow its pot. Repot annually in spring when the plant is young. As the plant ages, it begins to look sloppy, so take cuttings or air-layer to produce new plants. In summer, remove old canes to force new ones at the cut. Wipe the leaves frequently to keep them looking fresh and pest free. Be aware when pruning that the sap is toxic if ingested and may be irritating to the skin.

PROPAGATION: Dieffenbachia naturally loses its bottom leaves, which gives ample opportunity for air-layering. It can also be propagated easily by stem cuttings.

PESTS AND DISEASES: Watch for spider mites, mealybugs, and scale if grown in low humidity.

RELATED SPECIES: 'Hilo' looks much like a canna with large, dark green leaves and a thick white midrib.

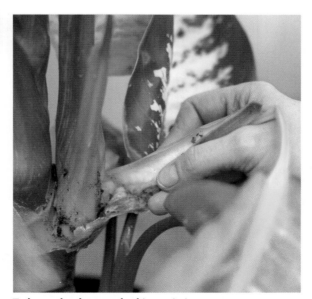

To keep dumb canes looking pristine, remove any yellowing or browning leaves and leaf sheaths.

SPOTTED DUMB CANE
Dieffenbachia maculata dee-fin-BAH-kee-uh mak-yew-LAH-ta

The striking spotted dumb cane is a simple plant to maintain as long as you keep it out of drafts and provide medium light.

SIZE: 5'h × 3'w
TYPE: Herbaceous
FORM: Upright
TEXTURE: Coarse
GROWTH: Medium
LIGHT: Medium

MOISTURE: Dry
SOIL: Average
FEATURES: Foliage
USES: Architectural accent, foliage

SITING: Provide medium light and average temperatures (60–75°F) for spotted dumb cane. Keep it out of drafts. It tolerates medium humidity (30–65 percent) but looks much better in higher humidity.
CARE: Allow to dry out slightly before watering. Feed three times in summer with a foliage plant food once it is mature. Repot annually in spring when it is young. In summer remove old canes to force new ones at the cut. Wipe the leaves frequently to keep them looking fresh and pest free. Be aware when pruning that the sap is toxic if ingested and may be irritating to the skin.

PROPAGATION: Propagate by stem cuttings or air-layering.
PESTS AND DISEASES: Watch for spider mites, mealybugs, and scale when grown in low humidity.
RELATED SPECIES: The cultivar 'Tropic Snow' has beautiful splotches through the center of the leaf. Almost half the leaf of 'Camille' is colored ivory.

1 To air-layer a dumb cane, cut a notch in the cane near the top tuft of leaves.

2 Dust the notch with rooting hormone and prop the cut edges apart.

3 Wrap with damp sphagnum moss and enclose in plastic until roots form.

DUMB CANE
Dieffenbachia picta dee-fin-BAH-kee-uh PIK-tuh

This dumb cane shows another of the myriad of leaf variegations and shapes available for the home interior.

SIZE: 2–3'h × 1–2'w
TYPE: Herbaceous
FORM: Upright
TEXTURE: Coarse
GROWTH: Medium
LIGHT: Medium

MOISTURE: Dry
SOIL: Potting soil
FEATURES: Variegated leaves
USES: Architectural accent, foliage

SITING: Dumb cane takes average conditions and tolerates some neglect. Provide medium light and average temperatures (60–75°F). Keep it out of drafts and drying winds. It tolerates medium humidity (30–65 percent) but looks much better in higher humidity.

CARE: Allow to dry out slightly before watering. Avoid wilting, which causes severe leaf loss. Feed three times in summer with a foliage plant food once it is mature. Repot annually in spring when it is young. In summer remove old canes to force new ones at the cut. Wipe leaves frequently to keep them pest free and looking fresh. Be aware when pruning that the sap is toxic if ingested and may be irritating to the skin.
PROPAGATION: Propagate by stem cuttings.
PESTS AND DISEASES: Spider mites, mealy bugs, and scale can be problems when grown in low humidity.
RELATED SPECIES: There are hundreds of cultivars to suit every taste.

1 Dumb canes elongate and lose their lower leaves. Cut them back occasionally to make them more attractive.

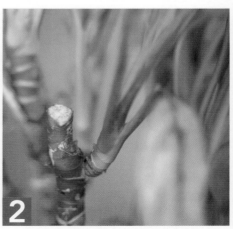

2 Once a plant has been cut back, new growth will emerge from dormant buds alongside the cut stem.

DUMB CANE
Dieffenbachia seguine *dee-fin-BAH-kee-uh sub-GEEN*

Dumb canes make a beautiful statement in the home because of their brightly variegated leaves and large size.

SIZE: 3–6'h × 1–3'w
TYPE: Herbaceous
FORM: Upright
TEXTURE: Coarse
GROWTH: Medium
LIGHT: Medium

MOISTURE: Dry
SOIL: Potting soil
FEATURES: Foliage
USES: Architectural accent, foliage

SITING: Dumb cane is fairly carefree, which is the main reason it is such a staple in the interior plant industry. It takes average conditions and easily tolerates some neglect. It gives a dynamic tropical look to any interior space. Provide medium light and average temperatures (60–75°F). Keep it out of drafts and drying winds. It tolerates medium humidity (30–65 percent) but looks much better with higher humidity. It looks attractive when the pot-in-pot method is used to increase humidity; the two-pot combination helps weight the plant, which tends to be top heavy.

CARE: Allow to dry out slightly before watering. It will tolerate an occasional missed watering, but wilting will cause severe leaf loss. Feed only three times in summer with a foliage plant food once it is mature. Feeding more often may cause succulent growth that is not sturdy enough to tolerate dryness. It also makes the plant become top heavy and outgrow its pot. Repot annually in spring when the plant is young. As it ages, it begins to look sloppy, so take cuttings or air-layer to produce new plants. In summer, remove old canes to force new ones at the cut. Wipe the leaves frequently to keep them pest free and looking fresh. Be aware when pruning that the sap is toxic if ingested and may be irritating to the skin. Dumb cane is not a plant to have in a home with young children and chewing pets.

PROPAGATION: Dieffenbachia naturally loses its bottom leaves, which gives ample opportunity for air-layering. It can also be propagated fairly easily by stem cuttings.

PESTS AND DISEASES: Spider mites, mealy bugs, and scale can be problems in low humidity.

RELATED SPECIES: *Dieffenbachia* 'Hilo' looks much like a canna with dark green leaves and a white midrib.

VENUS FLYTRAP
Dionaea muscipula *dye-oh-NEE-uh myew-SIP-yew-luh*

Venus flytraps are must-haves for the plant collector because they certainly will stimulate conversation.

SIZE: 6–8"h × 6–8"w
TYPE: Herbaceous
FORM: Rounded
TEXTURE: Medium
GROWTH: Medium
LIGHT: High to medium

MOISTURE: Even
SOIL: Mossy
FEATURES: Insect traps
USES: Terrarium, conversation piece

SITING: Venus flytrap does well in medium to high light but not direct sunlight. A healthy plant grown with enough light will have reddish to pink traps. The plant is a challenge to grow. It thrives in average to cool temperatures (55–75°F) but needs a dormant period from November to March in which the temperature is reduced to 38–45°F. The easiest way to accomplish this is to put it in a perforated plastic bagin a refrigerator and reduce watering, but don't let it dry out. It does not need light at this time. Venus flytrap needs high humidity; a terrarium is ideal.

CARE: Venus flytrap needs plenty of moisture to help it thrive. It grows best when planted in long-fibered sphagnum moss mixed with sand. Use distilled or rainwater only and change the water often. Venus flytrap does not need to be fed (it feeds itself!). A spider, pillbug, or fly every month or so is enough. Traps that close empty will reopen in a day or two. Venus flytrap sends up a flower stalk in spring with tiny white flowers and black seeds. Most growers pinch out this stalk as soon as it appears, to enhance formation of traps and to keep the plant vigorous. Older leaves regularly blacken and die. Remove them and new ones will be produced quickly.

PROPAGATION: Remove a leaf at the base of the rhizome and set it in a mix of half sand and half peat moss. Keep watered and humidified until tiny plants form at the base, usually in 6 weeks or more. Separate the plants and discard any that have rotted. Pot them up individually.

PESTS AND DISEASES: If new leaves appear distorted, look for aphids. Wash off with a strong spray of water or handpick.

RELATED SPECIES: The cultivar 'Akai Ryu' has much redder traps than the species.

These plants are naturally found in bogs, so simulate these conditions by repotting them into pure sphagnum moss mixed with sand.

GREEN DRACAENA

Dracaena deremensis *druh-SEEN-uh dair-uh-MEN-sis*

Green dracaena is a stunning architectural plant for use in either medium or low light.

SIZE: 4–10'h × 3'w
TYPE: Herbaceous
FORM: Upright
TEXTURE: Coarse
GROWTH: Medium
LIGHT: Low to medium

MOISTURE: Low to medium
SOIL: Potting soil
FEATURES: Tall stems, variegated leaves
USES: Architectural accent

SITING: Green dracaena grows beautifully in low to medium light and average home temperatures (60–75°F). It benefits from a drop of about 10 degrees at night. It tolerates drying out but not low humidity.

CARE: Allow to dry out slightly between waterings, especially when grown in low light. It will rot easily if the soil remains soggy. Low humidity may cause the tips to brown. Brown tips may also develop from fluoride in the water or excess plant food. Leaves curl downward when temperatures

Leaf tips may brown when the humidity is low, so change the cultural situation and trim the brown off the leaves.

are too low. This can eventually kill the plant. Feed only every couple of months. It has a smallish root system and does well in a small pot. Repot into a heavy container when it becomes top heavy. Remove yellowed leaves. Cut back stems to produce new tufts of leaves along the stems and give a more lush look.

PROPAGATION: Propagate from 2–3" stem cuttings or by air-layering. Make a simple cut and force in a toothpick or skewer to separate the two sides.

PESTS AND DISEASES: Spider mites can be a problem in low humidity. Frequent showers or wiping the leaves will prevent their getting out of hand. Mealybugs may appear in leaf axils. A sour smell in the soil indicates root rot, especially in low light; dry the plant out somewhat and repot to correct the situation.

RELATED SPECIES: The cultivar 'Janet Craig' is the foliage plant industry standard. The leaves are very dark green, and the plant may reach 10' high. 'Warneckei' (striped dracaena) is 4' high with white-striped narrow leaves. It doesn't suffer tip burn as readily as 'Janet Craig'.

CORN PLANT

Dracaena fragrans *druh-SEEN-uh FRAY-gruns*

Variegated corn plant is the most widely grown form. It has a central yellow band on each leaf.

SIZE: 4–10'h × 2'w
TYPE: Herbaceous
FORM: Upright
TEXTURE: Coarse
GROWTH: Medium
LIGHT: Low to medium

MOISTURE: Dry
SOIL: Potting soil
FEATURES: Tall stems, variegated leaves
USES: Architectural

SITING: Corn plant is ideal in a darker corner of the home. It grows best in average home temperatures (60–75°F) and benefits from a drop of about 10 degrees at night. It can tolerate drying out but not low humidity or drying winds.

CARE: Allow it to dry out between waterings. Feed only every couple of months. It has a smallish root system and does well in a small pot. Repot into a heavy container when it becomes top heavy. Very low humidity may cause tip burn. Brown tips may also develop if fluoride is present in the water or when excess plant food is provided. Leaves curl downward when temperatures are too

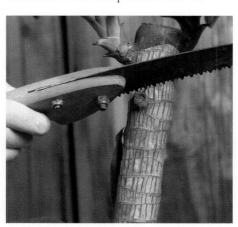

To produce new tufts of leaves, make a cut in the stem and force the cut edges apart with a toothpick.

low. This can eventually kill the plant. Remove yellowed leaves. Cut stems to produce new tufts of leaves along the stems and give them a more lush look.

PROPAGATION: Propagate from 2–3" stem cuttings, or air-layer.

PESTS AND DISEASES: Spider mites can be a problem in low humidity, although frequent showers or wiping the leaves will prevent their getting out of hand. Mealybugs may infest corn plant. A sour smell in the soil indicates root rot, especially in low light. Dry the plant out somewhat and repot to correct the situation.

RELATED SPECIES: The cultivar 'Massangeana' (variegated corn plant) has yellow bands along the leaves. A former species, *D. deremensis,* grows wider and has more stems than corn plant. The glossy dark leaves meet the stem in graceful arches. *D. deremensis* 'Janet Craig' is the foliage plant industry standard. The leaves are very dark green, and the plant may reach 10' high. 'Warneckei' (striped dracaena) is 4' high with white-striped narrow leaves. It doesn't suffer tip burn as readily as 'Janet Craig'.

MADAGASCAR DRAGON TREE

Dracaena marginata *druh-SEEN-uh mar-jin-AH-tuh*

Madagascar dragon tree tolerates the low humidity of most homes.

SIZE: 2–6'h × 2–4'w
TYPE: Herbaceous
FORM: Upright
TEXTURE: Coarse
GROWTH: Slow to medium
LIGHT: Low to medium

MOISTURE: Dry
SOIL: Potting soil
FEATURES: Variegated foliage
USES: Architectural accent

SITING: Madagascar dragon tree grows best in average home temperatures (60–75°F). It tolerates lower humidity than other dracaenas. Its attractive foliage, large size, and interesting stems make an ideal backdrop for smaller plants.
CARE: Allow to dry out about an inch below the soil level between waterings. Growing it with more moisture can cause rotting roots and leaf drop. Reducing water makes the stems stronger, although if you intend to induce bends in the stems, they need to be pliable. Feed only every couple of months. Repot only when it becomes top heavy or the roots begin to creep out of the drainage holes. It's natural for this

Spruce up the soil in a pot of Madagascar dragon tree by covering the soil with decorative mulch such as stones or shredded bark.

dracaena to periodically shed leaves, but extremely low humidity or drying out too much will cause many lower leaves to drop. To produce quirky, meandering stems, start with a young plant and suspend weights from the stems at different places. Produce the same effect by tipping the pot on its side, forcing a stem to change direction, then tipping the pot a different way for several weeks. Because Madagascar dragon tree has such long, bare stems, it is a perfect candidate for attractive mulch in the pot.
PROPAGATION: Propagate from 2–3" stem cuttings, or air-layer.
PESTS AND DISEASES: Spider mites can be a problem in low humidity, although frequent showers or wiping the leaves will prevent population explosions. A sour smell in the soil indicates root rot. Dry the plant out somewhat and repot to correct the situation.
RELATED SPECIES: The cultivar 'Tricolor' has pink, green, and white leaves. It is the most commonly seen dragon tree in commercial settings.

SONG OF INDIA

Dracaena reflexa (Pleomele reflexa) *druh-SEEN-uh ree-FLEX-uh (PLEE-oh-meel ree-FLEX-uh)*

Song of India, also known as pleomele, makes a dramatic statement with its attractively variegated leaves.

SIZE: 7–8'h × 3–4'w
TYPE: Herbaceous
FORM: Upright
TEXTURE: Medium
GROWTH: Medium
LIGHT: High, indirect

MOISTURE: Even
SOIL: Potting soil
FEATURES: Erect stems, clasping leaves
USES: Architectural

SITING: This dracaena grows better in bright, indirect light than the low to medium light preferred by other dracaenas. Because of its large size, it makes a dramatic statement as an architectural feature in the home or office setting. Provide average home temperatures (60–75°F) with a drop of about 10 degrees at night. This plant can tolerate drying out somewhat, but it will not tolerate low humidity or drying winds. Although it is often used as a single plant in commercial settings, it needs average humidity (around 30–65 percent), so group it with other plants. Its attractive foliage and large size make it an ideal backdrop for smaller plants.
CARE: Keep more evenly moist than other dracaenas, but if growing in lower than ideal light, make sure the soil does not become soggy. Reducing water somewhat makes the stems even sturdier and stronger. Winter water reduction helps keep the roots from rotting. Feed with a foliage plant food once a month. If growing in less than ideal light, reduce feeding to once every couple of months. Because of its smallish root system, it does well in a small pot. Repot into a heavy container when it becomes top heavy. Leaves curl downward when temperatures are too low. This can eventually kill the plant. Very low humidity may cause tip burn. Trimmed tips will eventually turn brown again, so remove affected leaves when necessary.
PROPAGATION: Propagate from 2–3" stem cuttings, or air-layer. If the plant blooms, new plants can be started from seed. Root cuttings are sometimes successful as well.
PESTS AND DISEASES: Spider mites can be a problem in low humidity, although frequent showers or wiping the leaves will prevent their getting out of hand. Mealybugs may attack plants. A sour smell in the soil indicates root rot, especially in low light. Dry the plant out somewhat and repot to correct the situation.
RELATED SPECIES: The cultivar 'Variegata' has yellow-edged leaves. 'Song of Jamaica' has buff to yellow stripes. 'Song of India' has bright yellow stripes

LUCKY BAMBOO

Dracaena sanderiana druh-SEEN-uh san-dur-ee-AHN-uh

Lucky bamboo, also known as ribbon plant, can be grown in water or soil and takes little care except for regular fertilizing.

SIZE: 4–12"h × 2–6"w
TYPE: Herbaceous
FORM: Upright
TEXTURE: Medium
GROWTH: Fast
LIGHT: Medium
MOISTURE: Wet
SOIL: Potting soil
FEATURES: Twisted stems, variegated leaves
USES: Focal point

SITING: Lucky bamboo needs bright light to thrive, but it will not tolerate any sun. Browning leaves indicate too much direct light. It can be grown in lower light but it may become leggy. It needs average temperatures (60–75°F) and average humidity (30–65 percent).
CARE: Lucky bamboo is often grown as a hydroponic plant, with the stems set in water and held upright with decorative stones. When grown this way, it is critical to use water that has no minerals, especially fluoride, and to change the water every 3–5 days. The plant can also be grown in soil as long as the soil remains wet at all times. Start the canes in water; as soon as they develop a mass of roots, pot them up in rich soil. Lucky bamboo must be fertilized, especially when grown in water. Use a half-strength foliage plant food every 2 weeks whether grown

Lucky bamboo can be formed into unique shapes by manipulating the light source or wiring stems.

in water or soil. Some gardeners grow the plant in water with a Siamese fighting fish in the same bowl; the fish provides the fertilizer. It is important not to add plant food, or the fish might be harmed. The canes are often grouped together or twisted and shaped to give the plant an unusual appearance. You can twist and shape your own stems simply by manipulating light. Put a young plant in a darkened spot with a single light source directed at the stem. The plant will respond by growing toward the light.
PROPAGATION: These plants are traditionally propagated as 2–3" cane cuttings. A piece of cane is cut, waxed to keep out fungus, and sold. You can propagate your own plants by simply breaking a cane into pieces and putting them in water.
PESTS AND DISEASES: Lucky bamboo plants that are shipped in water from Southeast Asian countries may have tiger mosquito larvae in the water. If your plant came in water, dump the water on dry ground and replenish with fresh water.

GOLD DUST DRACAENA

Dracaena surculosa druh-SEEN-uh sir-kyew-LOH-suh

Gold dust dracaena is carefree like other dracaenas and has the added attraction of gold-spattered foliage.

SIZE: 2–3'h × 2–3'w
TYPE: Herbaceous
FORM: Mound
TEXTURE: Medium
GROWTH: Medium
LIGHT: Medium
MOISTURE: Dry
SOIL: Potting soil
FEATURES: Flecked leaves
USES: Focal point

SITING: Gold dust dracaena needs more light than most dracaenas to keep its beautiful variegation. It grows best in average home temperatures (60–75°F) and benefits from a drop of about 10 degrees at night. It can tolerate drying out somewhat but will not tolerate low humidity or drying drafts. It needs average humidity (around 30–65 percent), so group it with other plants. Its attractive foliage and large size make it an ideal backdrop for smaller plants. This variegated type, in particular, is an attractive backdrop for smaller-leaved plants.
CARE: Allow to dry out slightly between waterings, especially when grown in low light. It will rot easily if the soil remains soggy. Reducing water somewhat makes the stems even sturdier and stronger. Winter water reduction helps keep the roots from rotting. Feed once a month with a foliage plant food. It does well in a small pot. Repot into a heavy container when it becomes top heavy. Leaves curl downward when temperatures are too low. This can eventually kill the plant. Very low humidity may cause tip burn. Trimmed tips will eventually turn brown again, so remove affected leaves when necessary.
PROPAGATION: Propagate from 2–3" stem cuttings, or air-layer. If the plant blooms, new plants can be started from seed. Root cuttings are sometimes successful as well.
PESTS AND DISEASES: Spider mites can be a problem in low humidity, although frequent showers or wiping the leaves will control them. If the plant flowers, mealybugs may appear. A sour smell in the soil indicates root rot, especially in low light. Dry the plant out somewhat and repot to correct the situation.
RELATED SPECIES: The cultivar 'Florida Beauty' has leaves that are flecked with yellow and white, with little green visible.

PINEAPPLE DYCKIA
Dyckia brevifolia DIK-ee-uh brev-ih-FOH-lee-uh

Pineapple dyckia, like other bromeliads, needs high light, average temperatures, and low humidity.

SIZE: 1'h × 2'w
TYPE: Bromeliad
FORM: Horizontal
TEXTURE: Coarse
GROWTH: Slow
LIGHT: High
MOISTURE: Low

SOIL: Cactus mix
FEATURES: Colorful leaves
USES: Focal point, cactus garden
FLOWERS: ■

SITING: Although pineapple dyckia is a bromeliad, it acts more like a cactus. It is found on rocky, dry soils, which hints at its tolerance of neglect. It needs high light and does beautifully in direct sun—the perfect plant for a western or southern windowsill. High light shows off the striking coloration of the leaves, particularly the undersides. Pineapple dyckia is not fussy and does best with nighttime temperatures of 50–55°F and daytime temperatures above 68°F. Being a succulent, pineapple dyckia performs best with low humidity. Be sure to place this plant out of the way of traffic, because the spines can cause a painful stab.
CARE: This plant is ideal for a situation in which the plant might be neglected or plant care is performed only every 2 weeks or so. Allow to dry fairly well between waterings. Root rot might occur if the plant is grown in low light and kept too moist.

Feed only once a year with an all-purpose plant food. Repotting is seldom necessary because of the small root system. Grow it in a heavy terra-cotta pot to keep it well anchored. Remove any yellow leaves. Shower the plant occasionally, because it is prone to collect dust. Move it outdoors for the summer. If grown well, it may produce a bloom spike with bright orange flowers.
PROPAGATION: Dyckia produces multiple crowns, so it is easy to divide to produce more plants. If your plant blooms, you can collect seed for propagating. Sprinkle ripe seed on moist soil mix and tent with glass or plastic until germinated.
PESTS AND DISEASES: Even when neglected, dyckia has no pest problems.
RELATED SPECIES: *D. fosteriana* grows to only 5' wide and has beautiful spines and silvery leaves. *D. cinerea* has broad, succulent leaves and yellow flowers.

HEN-AND-CHICKS
Echeveria spp. ay-shuh-VER-ee-uh

Carefree hen-and-chicks plants have been favorites in indoor and outdoor gardens for many years.

SIZE: 6-36"h × 12"w
TYPE: Succulent
FORM: Mounded
TEXTURE: Medium
GROWTH: Medium
LIGHT: High

MOISTURE: Low
SOIL: Cactus mix
FEATURES: Succulent leaves
USES: Dish garden, cactus garden

SITING: Hen-and-chicks is the perfect houseplant for someone who travels. It withstands neglect and continues to thrive. The only requirement is good light. In summer when it is growing actively, half a day of direct sun is best, with some shading from afternoon sun. In winter all-day sun is preferred. Provide average to hot temperatures (60°F and above) and low to average humidity (60 percent and below).
CARE: Provide plenty of water in spring and summer and little in fall and winter.

Overwatering will cause root rot. If the plant fills the pot, water from the bottom to avoid scarring the leaves. Feed only once a year with a general houseplant food. This succulent plant has a very small root system and will seldom need repotting. If varieties that have a rosette top get too tall, simply cut off the top with a couple of inches still attached, set it aside to callus for a few days, then set it in some cactus mix. It will root in 2–3 weeks. Discard the original plant.
PROPAGATION: Most species of *Echeveria* readily produce offsets. Detach from the parent plant, set on a pot of cactus mix, and water. They will send out roots quickly. For types that produce stolons, cut the stolon and pot up.
PESTS AND DISEASES: Wipe away mealybugs with a cotton swab dipped in alcohol.
RELATED SPECIES: 'Chocolate' has apple green leaves that mature to dark bronze tones from autumn to spring. 'Wavy Curls' has silver leaves with frilled edges.

Use leaf cuttings to start new echeveria plants.

After several weeks new roots will form at the base of the leaf, and later a new shoot will sprout.

GOLDEN BARREL CACTUS

Echinocactus grusonii *ee-KINE-oh-kak-tus gruh-SONE-ee-aye*

Golden barrel cactus is the perfect complement to a decor with a southwestern flavor.

SIZE: 1'h × 1'w
TYPE: Cactus
FORM: Round
TEXTURE: Coarse
GROWTH: Slow
LIGHT: High
MOISTURE: Low

SOIL: Cactus mix
FEATURES: Golden spines
USES: Cactus garden, accent
FLOWERS: ■

SITING: Golden barrel cactus is an appealing design element for southwestern decor. As with all cacti, golden barrel cactus needs high light. If the light is perfect, small, attractive yellow flowers will arise from the woolly center. The preferred temperature is from 50–85°F or higher. It prefers low humidity. This is a plant to grow on a dry, exposed windowsill. Keep the plant out of traffic where its spines can inflict painful wounds.

The plant likes it dry and hot, and mulching the soil with small stones mimics the desert from which it comes.

CARE: Golden barrel cactus needs little water most of the time. Let it dry out completely between waterings, then soak it just as a desert rain would do. It must have perfect drainage. Root rot may occur in overly wet soil and low light. In winter give it a cooler, drier resting time. Feed three times in summer with a general-purpose plant food. Repot only when the plant creeps beyond the edge of the pot, making it difficult to get water to the soil. The spines might make you think twice about repotting, but it can be done without injury. Prepare a larger terra-cotta pot ready with soil to receive the cactus. Take an old piece of carpet or something thick enough to avoid puncture and wrap it around the cactus. Lift it gently out of its pot and lower it into the new pot.

PROPAGATION: Propagate by seed. Because the plant seldom produces flowers indoors, obtain seed from a supplier.

PESTS AND DISEASES: Mealybugs may appear at the base of the spines. They are hard to physically remove, so dab them with horticultural oil on a cotton swab.

RELATED SPECIES: *E. g.* var. *alba* has white spines.

GOLDEN POTHOS

Epipremnum aureum (Scindapsus aureus) *eh-pih-PREM-num AWR-ee-um (sin-DAP-sus AWR-ee-us)*

Golden pothos is also known as devil's ivy or Ceylon creeper. It grows well even in dark corners.

SIZE: 3–10'h × 1–3'w
TYPE: Herbaceous
FORM: Vine
TEXTURE: Medium
GROWTH: Medium
LIGHT: Low to medium

MOISTURE: Dry
SOIL: Potting soil
FEATURES: Variegated leaves
USES: Hanging basket, upright accent

SITING: This plant grows equally well in low and medium light. It prefers average temperatures (60–75°F) but will tolerate cooler periods. It needs high humidity (60–70 percent). When grown on a bark pole or slab, watering the slab helps the aerial roots hold on and provides more ambient humidity for the plant.

CARE: Allow to dry after being thoroughly soaked. Feed once or twice a year with a general foliage plant food. Repot only every 2–3 years as the roots fill the pot. Prune as needed to keep the plant symmetrical. Pinch the tips out frequently to keep the plant shrubby. Pull off the occasional brown or yellow leaf. To train this plant onto a bark pole or slab, insert the pole next to the root ball and drape the vines on it. Use hairpins or plant pins to bring the vine in contact with the pole. Keeping the pole moist will encourage aerial roots to form and attach themselves to the pole.

PROPAGATION: Propagate from stem cuttings rooted in water or soil. Cut the vines you prune off into 3–5" pieces with one leaf attached. Little knobs along the stem will produce roots when in contact with soil or water. You can also layer golden pothos by pinning the vines down to soil; once the roots form, cut the plant from the parent plant.

PESTS AND DISEASES: Treat scale with horticultural oil.

1 Propagate from stem cuttings taken at any time during the year.

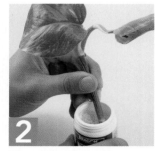

2 Dip cuttings in rooting hormone for faster rooting.

3 Insert cuttings in sterile potting soil and cover with plastic until roots form.

SATIN POTHOS

Epipremnum pictum (Scindapsus pictus) eb-pib-PREM-num PIK-tum (sin-DAP-sus PIK-tus)

Satin pothos makes a stunning trailing plant on a mantel.

SIZE: 3–6'h × 1–2'w
TYPE: Herbaceous
FORM: Vine
TEXTURE: Medium
GROWTH: Medium
LIGHT: Low to medium

MOISTURE: Dry
SOIL: Potting soil
FEATURES: Satiny leaves
USES: Hanging basket, upright accent

SITING: Satin pothos is a stunning ground cover when used with large specimens such as weeping fig. It grows equally well in low and medium light. It prefers average temperatures (60–75°F) but will tolerate brief cooler periods. It requires high humidity (60–70 percent).

CARE: Allow to dry after being thoroughly soaked. Feed once or twice a year with a general foliage plant food. Repot every

Bright light highlights the silvery variegation of satin pothos.

2–3 years. In low light the plant will grow much more slowly and can be left in the same pot for several years. If the vines are allowed to grow long, they may begin to shed leaves and become bare with only a few leaves at the ends. In this case cut off the stems close to the crown and allow the plant to rejuvenate itself. Pull off the occasional brown or yellow leaf and give the plant a shower periodically. To train this plant onto a bark pole or slab, insert the pole next to the root ball and drape the vines on it. You may need to occasionally pinch and reattach vines, but once the aerial roots form, the plant will keep itself upright.

PROPAGATION: Root stem cuttings in water or soil. Simply cut the vines you prune off into 3–5" pieces with one leaf attached. Little knobs along the stem will produce roots when in contact with soil or water. You can also layer satin pothos by pinning the vines down to soil; once the roots form, cut the plant from the parent plant.

PESTS AND DISEASES: Treat scale with horticultural oil.

RELATED SPECIES: The cultivar 'Argyraeus' has more silvery markings than the species.

FLAME VIOLET

Episcia spp. ee-PIS-ee-ah

Flame violets are related to African violets and have many of the same requirements.

SIZE: 4–6"h × 2'+w
TYPE: Gesneriad
FORM: Vine
TEXTURE: Fine
GROWTH: Medium
LIGHT: High to medium

MOISTURE: Medium
SOIL: Potting soil
FEATURES: Foliage, blossoms
USES: Hanging basket
FLOWERS: ■□■

SITING: Flame violet needs bright, indirect to medium light; it will scorch in full sun. This gesneriad requires average to warm temperatures (65°F and up). Avoid hot or cold drafts to prevent leaf damage. Humidity levels of 50 percent or above will

keep the plant from being stressed. It benefits from a pot-in-pot system.

CARE: Water when the soil surface feels dry. Keep moist but not soggy. Feed with half-strength foliage plant food at every watering. Once a month flush out fertilizer salts with several applications of clear water. Remove yellowed leaves and pinch out stolons as needed to keep the plant

Flame violets may develop splotches on their leaves if watered with cold water.

neat. Leaf margins turn brown if humidity is low or soil moisture level is low. Plants will die back severely if overwatered or if they get too cold. Check the plant's root system periodically by removing it from the pot. Flame violet likes to be somewhat pot-bound, but if it is extremely pot-bound, repot into a container about an inch bigger. Use organic African violet mix if possible.

PROPAGATION: Root from stolon cuttings. Plantlets are produced at the tips of the plant, so simply pinch out a stem and place the plantlet on sterile soil mix. Keep it moist and covered until the plant roots. You may need to pin the plantlet to keep it in contact with the soil mix.

PESTS AND DISEASES: Flame violet may have aphids or mealybugs when stressed. Control them by hand-picking or dabbing with alcohol.

RELATED SPECIES: There are many cultivars with all colors of leaves and types of variegation. *E. cupreata* 'Acajou' produces orange-red flowers on plants with dark tan leaves netted in silvery green. *E. lilacina* 'Pink Panther' has rosey flowers on lime green foliage.

JAPANESE EUONYMUS

Euonymus japonicus *yew-AH-nih-mus juh-PAH-nih-kus*

Japanese euonymus is a low-maintenance plant with glossy green foliage that provides beautiful foil to blooming plants.

SIZE: 6'h × 4'w
TYPE: Shrub
FORM: Round
TEXTURE: Medium
GROWTH: Medium
LIGHT: High to medium

MOISTURE: Even
SOIL: Potting soil
FEATURES: Glossy leaves
USES: Backdrop, topiary, bonsai

SITING: Japanese euonymus is a carefree plant if given enough moisture. Site it in a spot with medium to high but indirect light. Give it average to cool temperatures (55–75°F) to keep the growth slowed and prevent it from getting too large to handle.

Average humidity (30–65 percent) will keep it looking its best.
CARE: Give it evenly moist soil, although the soil surface can dry out slightly. Feed only three times in summer. If the plant is being used as a bonsai specimen, give it more regular feeding, because the root system and soil base are minimal. It tolerates and is stimulated by pruning,

These plants tolerate drastic pruning and thus make great topiaries, bonsais, or miniature hedges.

so it can be sheared into topiary shapes or used for bonsai. The variegated leaf forms make a pleasing backdrop for a large flowering plant such as hibiscus or parlor maple. The tiny-leaved varieties are often trimmed as hedges and small topiary for dollhouse or miniature train displays. Regular spraying with water keeps dust at a minimum and prevents spider mite population explosions.
PROPAGATION: Propagate by semihardwood stem cuttings. Take cuttings in late spring to early summer; remove all but one or two leaves, dip in rooting hormone, and insert in moist potting soil. Cover with plastic to keep the humidity high while rooting. The plants may take 6 weeks to develop roots.
PESTS AND DISEASES: Control scale with horticultural oil. Aphids will occasionally occur on new growth and can be easily handpicked.
RELATED SPECIES: Cultivars may be standard size or miniature. The cultivar 'Aureo-variegata' has large leaves with yellow blotches and green edges. *E. j. microphyllus* 'Albovariegatus' has tiny leaves splashed with white.

CROWN-OF-THORNS

Euphorbia milii *yew-FOR-bee-uh MIL-ee-ye*

Crown-of-thorns will reward you with year-round pink, salmon, red, or white blossoms if given high light and low humidity.

SIZE: 1–3'h × 2–3'w
TYPE: Succulent
FORM: Rounded
TEXTURE: Medium
GROWTH: Medium
LIGHT: High

MOISTURE: Low
SOIL: Cactus mix
FEATURES: Bracts
USES: Dry garden, focal point
FLOWERS: ■ ■ □ ■

SITING: Crown-of-thorns needs full sun for continuous bloom. It will tolerate part shade for vegetative growth only. It grows in cool to hot temperatures (50°F and up) and needs low humidity, usually easy to achieve in warmer temperatures.

CARE: Crown-of-thorns will not tolerate wet soil, so let it dry considerably between waterings. Then soak it well, let drain, and empty the plant saucer. Feed only three times in summer. It needs a rest period in winter, so water less and give it no plant food. It seldom needs repotting because of its small root system. If you do repot, use a cactus-type soil mix and a terra-cotta pot to allow the soil to drain well and breathe. To maintain a shrubby form or to contain the size, prune off the plant tips periodically.

Propagate by taking stem tip cuttings that are 3-4 inches long. Wash the milky sap off the cutting and let it air dry for a day or two before potting it in cactus potting mix.

Be aware that the sap from all *Euphorbias* is an irritant and can be toxic, so be sure to wash your hands immediately after pruning. It's also a good idea to wash off the cut ends of the plant after pruning to remove excess sap.
PROPAGATION: Propagate by stem tip cuttings. Simply snip off a stem tip, rinse off the sap, and let it sit for a day or two to form a callus. Then insert it in cactus mix and water in. Keep the soil slightly moist but not soggy or the plant will rot without producing roots. Plants can also be propagated by division and seed but not as easily as with stem-tip cuttings.
PESTS AND DISEASES: Crown-of-thorns may attract aphids and mealybugs; handpick or dab with alcohol. Overwatering causes root rots, stem rots, and perhaps leaf yellowing. Leaf drop may occur.
RELATED SPECIES: 'Koeninger's Aalbaumle' is a dwarf.

POINSETTIA
Euphorbia pulcherrima *yew-FOR-bee-uh pul-KER-ih-muh*

Poinsettia is a traditional holiday plant that can be brought back into bloom the following year with a great deal of effort.

SIZE: 6–12"h × 12"w
TYPE: Herbaceous
FORM: Mounded
TEXTURE: Medium to coarse
GROWTH: Medium

LIGHT: High
MOISTURE: Dry
SOIL: Potting soil
FEATURES: Bracts
USES: Focal point
FLOWERS: ■ ■ □

SITING: Keep poinsettia away from warm or cold drafts from radiators, air registers, or open doors and windows. Give it 60–70°F temperatures during the day and nighttime temperatures around 55°F. Average home humidity (30–60 percent) is fine.

CARE: Water when the soil is slightly dry to the touch. If the plant pot is wrapped in foil, punch holes in the bottom and put the pot in a saucer. There is no need to fertilize while the bracts remain red through the holiday season. If you plan to keep the poinsettia as a houseplant and get it to rebloom, begin feeding in February once a month with a foliage houseplant food. Cut the stems back to about 4–6" high in March to force new growth. In April repot into a slightly larger container. Move it outdoors after nighttime temperatures are above 60°F. Pinch out the growing shoots once or twice to keep the plant compact. Water regularly and feed

When selecting a poinsettia to purchase, make sure the true flowers in the center of the plant look healthy and fresh.

every 2 weeks while outdoors with a foliage plant food. Before nighttime temperatures fall below 55°F, bring indoors to a sunny window. Starting in September, give the plant more than 12 hours of darkness nightly to initiate flower buds.
PROPAGATION: Propagate by stem tip cuttings. Prepare the best stems by pinching them back in early June. The shoots that are produced will be ready to cut in mid-July to early August. Cut 2½–3" tips with one or two leaves. Dip in rooting hormone and insert no more than an inch deep in sterile soil mix.
PESTS AND DISEASES: Whitefly is the worst pest. Check your plant carefully for the tiny larvae that look like small, transparent, oblong bubbles on the undersides of the leaves. If you find them, isolate the plant and treat with horticultural oil.
RELATED SPECIES: The cultivar 'Amazone Peppermint' has pink and white marbled bracts. 'Freedom Marble' has white bracts with soft pink highlights. 'Hollypoint' has green and gold variegated foliage with bright red bracts.

AFRICAN MILK TREE
Euphorbia trigona *yew-FOR-bee-uh try-GOHN-uh*

African milk tree, also known as candelabra plant, requires the same culture as most cacti. But keep it out of direct sun.

SIZE: 4–6'h × 2'w
TYPE: Succulent
FORM: Upright
TEXTURE: Coarse
GROWTH: Fast
LIGHT: High

MOISTURE: Low
SOIL: Cactus mix
FEATURES: Spiny stems
USES: Desert theme, architectural accent

SITING: African milk tree resembles a cactus in every way except that it is not a cactus! It needs bright light but does not handle full sun as well as a cactus would. It tolerates 55–90°F temperatures, but below 50°F there may be some leaf scarring. Low humidity (below 30 percent) is best.

Although African milk tree looks like a cactus, the succulent leaves borne along the stem indicate that it is not a true cactus.

CARE: Water when the soil is dry to the touch; keep drier in winter during its resting phase. Water stress can cause the plant to drop its tender leaves. This doesn't harm the plant, and as soon as it is watered, it will produce leaves again. Feed only three times in summer with foliage plant food. Repot whenever it starts to get top heavy into a terra-cotta pot an inch larger in diameter. African milk tree scars easily, so prune lightly. Occasionally pinch out stem tips to make the stems branch. Remember that African milk tree sap is an irritant and can be toxic, so use gloves and wash the cut ends after pruning.
PROPAGATION: Propagate by stem cuttings. Pinch off the slender stems and set aside to dry and callus for a day or so. Insert the cuttings into moist cactus mix for rooting.
PESTS AND DISEASES: African milk tree has no serious pests.
RELATED SPECIES: The cultivar 'Red' has pink to red stems in high light. *E. tetragona* has four-angled stems.

PERSIAN VIOLET

Exacum affine ECK-sub-cum uh-FIN-ee

Persian violets provide beautiful color indoors. They can be cut back and planted in the outdoor garden as an annual.

SIZE: 10"h × 10"w
TYPE: Herbaceous
FORM: Round
TEXTURE: Fine
GROWTH: Medium
LIGHT: Medium

MOISTURE: Even
SOIL: Potting soil
FEATURES: Flowers
USES: Focal point
FLOWERS: ■■□

SITING: Persian violet thrives in medium light. For the longest display of its starry pastel flowers, purchase a plant that is in tight bud and keep it in a cool room (55–65°F). Average humidity (30–65 percent) will keep the plant looking good, so place it on a pebble tray in dry situations. Place plants where you can enjoy their perfumey fragrance.

CARE: Keep the plant's soil evenly moist but not soggy, especially when grown in cool temperatures. Feed with half-strength plant food for blooming plants at every watering. Remove the spent blossoms regularly to prolong bloom. It is almost impossible to bring Persian violet back into bloom in the home because in its native Middle Eastern range it is an annual flower or short-lived perennial. When it is finished blooming, the foliage deteriorates. Most gardeners discard the plant, although it can be cut back, planted in the garden in full sun, and treated as an annual. It may develop new buds and bloom for the rest of the summer outdoors.

PROPAGATION: Propagate Persian violet from seed. Seeds will germinate in 2–3 weeks at 65°F.

PESTS AND DISEASES: Pests include mealybugs, aphids, and spider mites. They can be handled easily by handpicking or dabbing with horticultural oil. Botrytis blight and root rot may be problems when moisture is excessive.

RELATED SPECIES: Many cultivars are available with lavender, pink, and white flowers. There are also some double-flowered cultivars.

TREE IVY

×*Fatshedera lizei* fats-HED-ur-uh LIZ-ee-eye

Tree ivy, also known as fat-headed Lizzy, is an unusual plant specimen with large glossy leaves.

SIZE: 3–6'h × 3'w
TYPE: Vine
FORM: Upright
TEXTURE: Medium
GROWTH: Medium
LIGHT: Medium to low

MOISTURE: Dry
SOIL: Potting soil
FEATURES: Glossy leaves
USES: Focal point, backdrop

SITING: Although tree ivy will produce its stunning glossy bright green leaves in low light, medium light will keep it looking its best. Keep it somewhat cool (55–65°F) and use the pot-in-pot method for maintaining average humidity (30–60 percent).

CARE: Water when the soil just begins to dry out, making sure to soak it well and drain it well. If it gets too dry, it will go dormant and drop its leaves. The original plant will not recover completely after drying out, so cut off the stem tips and root them. Keeping the plant too moist, especially in lower light, may cause root

Although tree ivy doesn't naturally climb, you can train it onto an upright support by tying the vines to the support with soft twine or twist tie.

rot. Feed only three times in summer with a foliage houseplant food at regular strength. Repot annually to keep it thriving, although you can skip a year if the plant is grown in lower light where the growth is slowed. Pot in average potting mix and go up only an inch in pot size. Although tree ivy will clump or mound if pinched regularly, training it onto a stake makes a much better-looking plant. Tie plant to a stake. Pinch the tips regularly to force it to branch into an attractive, upright plant.

PROPAGATION: Propagate by stem cuttings. Take 3–5" cuttings, dip into rooting hormone, and insert into sterile potting soil. They will root in a few weeks. Or pin a vine to the soil at a node with a hairpin; when roots form at the node, clip it from the parent plant.

PESTS AND DISEASES: Spider mites can be serious pests. Watch for mealybugs in the axils of the large leaves. Swab with alcohol or horticultural oil.

RELATED SPECIES: The cultivar 'Annemieke' has wavy edges. 'Aurea' has light green leaves with white splotches. 'Variegata' has variegated leaves.

JAPANESE ARALIA

Fatsia japonica *FAT-see-uh juh-PON-ih-kuh*

Japanese aralias are perfect plants for dark corners where some tropical interest would be appreciated.

SIZE: 6'h × 6'w
TYPE: Shrub
FORM: Round
TEXTURE: Coarse
GROWTH: Slow
LIGHT: Low

MOISTURE: Dry
SOIL: Potting soil
FEATURES: Leaves
USES: Foliage, backdrop

SITING: Japanese aralia is ideal for low-light situations. It can be grown in medium light but will grow more quickly and outgrow its pot. It tolerates temperature extremes and will thrive in drafty spots, such as in front of a sliding glass door. It needs only low to average humidity.

CARE: Allow to dry out between waterings in low light, but keep the soil more evenly moist when grown in medium light. Feed only three times in summer with a foliage houseplant food to keep it in bounds. Repot annually while it is growing to reach intended size. Once it has achieved the

These naturally large plants can be kept within bounds by regular pruning of long shoots that develop.

desired size, repot only every 2–3 years. Train it to a stake or leave it shrubby. To maintain it as a shrubby, mounded plant, pinch out the tips regularly to promote branching. Keep it shorter than its normal 6' height by selective pruning. If leaves turn yellow and fall, the plant is either overwatered or is receiving too much heat. Put it in a cooler spot and let it dry out and the plant will most likely recover. If the leaves are pale and the leaf edges are brown, the plant is not receiving enough water. Large plants in particular need plenty of water to keep them healthy.
PROPAGATION: Propagate by taking stem cuttings in midsummer. They will root faster if rooting hormone is used. Provide a plastic tent to increase humidity while rooting. This plant can also be propagated by seed or by air-layering.
PESTS AND DISEASES: Pests include scale, mites, and mealybugs. Give the plant a regular shower to keep the large, attractive leaves looking their best and to reduce mite populations.
RELATED SPECIES: The cultivar 'Moseri' is much more compact than the species. 'Variegata' has white-edged leaves.

WEEPING FIG

Ficus benjamina *FYE-kus ben-ja-MYE-nuh*

SIZE: 6–18'h × 2–10'w
TYPE: Tree
FORM: Vase-shaped
TEXTURE: Medium
GROWTH: Medium
LIGHT: Medium to high
MOISTURE: Dry
SOIL: Potting soil
FEATURES: Specimen
USES: Architectural accent

Weeping fig may be grown with braided multiple trunks.

SITING: Weeping fig needs medium to high light and average home temperatures (60–75°F). It tolerates lower light, but growth will be open and sparse. Give the plants average humidity (30–60 percent).
CARE: Allow to dry out slightly between soakings. Feed up to three times in summer with a foliage houseplant food. If the plant is at the maximum size that your space can handle, reduce fertilizing

to once a year. To maintain the attractive weeping shape, prune major branches instead of just branch tips. Be aware that the milky sap exuded from cuts can be irritating and will stain clothes. To train

Weeping figs are sensitive to climate changes, which make their leaves yellow. Remove these yellowed leaves regularly.

stems into unusual shapes such as braids, start with very young saplings and plant three or more to a pot. Repot every third year or so. Prune the roots and crown back by about a third at the same time and put the plant back into its original pot. Weeping fig is well known for dropping its leaves whenever climatic conditions change. If you move your plant outdoors for the summer, place it in shade and gradually move it to a sunnier location. Reverse the process in autumn. This plant also drops leaves whenever the season changes, but will soon put out plenty of new leaves.
PROPAGATION: Propagate by stem cuttings just like any other woody plant. Take cuttings in summer and provide rooting hormone and humidity.
PESTS AND DISEASES: The most common pest is scale, which is easily handled by a routine spraying of horticultural oil.
RELATED SPECIES: The cultivar 'Exotica' has twisted leaf tips. 'Golden King' has gray-green leaves with ivory and light green margins. 'Starlight' has creamy margins on gray-green leaves. 'Citation' is a bush form with curled leaves.

MISTLETOE FIG

Ficus deltoidea var. *diversifolia* FYE-kus del-TOY-dee-uh dih-vur-sih-FOLE-ee-uh

Mistletoe fig has diminutive foliage that makes it a tidy, attractive plant for the home interior.

SIZE: 3'h × 2'w
TYPE: Shrub
FORM: Rounded
TEXTURE: Coarse
GROWTH: Slow
LIGHT: Medium to high

MOISTURE: Dry
SOIL: Potting soil
FEATURES: Leaves
USES: Accent, backdrop

SITING: Provide medium to high light and average home temperatures (60–75°F). Mistletoe fig tolerates lower light, but growth will be open and sparse. Give the plants average humidity (30–60 percent), accomplished most easily on large plants with a pot-in-pot system.
CARE: Allow to dry out slightly between soakings. In lower light, reduce watering somewhat. Feed three times in summer with foliage houseplant food if you want the plant to put on growth. If it is at the maximum size that your space can handle, reduce fertilizing to once a year, particularly if you repot it. Mistletoe fig can reach 6' or more when trained as a standard. Always prune at a node, where you can see which direction the remaining bud is facing. This plant tolerates pruning so well that it is a good candidate for topiary and is often used for bonsai as well. Be aware that the milky sap exuded from cuts can be irritating and will stain clothes. Pick up the small yellow-green fruits and remove yellow leaves. Turn the pot a quarter turn at every watering to keep the plant symmetrical. About every third year or so, repot the plant. Prune the roots and crown back by about a third at the same time and put the plant back into its original pot. This will keep the plant at a reasonable size for the home.
PROPAGATION: Propagate by stem cuttings. Take cuttings in summer and provide rooting hormone and humidity. This plant can also be air-layered.
PESTS AND DISEASES: Treat scale by routinely spraying the plant with horticultural oil. Use a drop cloth because this quantity of oil can make a mess on the floor.

RUBBER TREE

Ficus elastica FYE-kus ee-LAS-tih-kuh

Rubber trees have long been used to add a tropical flair to the home, with their large glossy leaves and sturdy stems.

SIZE: 4–6'h × 3–4'w
TYPE: Shrub
FORM: Upright
TEXTURE: Coarse
GROWTH: Medium
LIGHT: High to medium

MOISTURE: Even
SOIL: Potting soil
FEATURES: Foliage
USES: Architectural accent

SITING: Provide medium to high light and average home temperatures (60–75°F). Rubber tree tolerates lower light, but growth will be open and sparse. Give it average humidity (30–60 percent).
CARE: Keep slightly more moist than other figs when in active growth. Allow to dry out slightly between soakings in winter. In lower light, reduce watering somewhat. Feed three times in summer with a foliage houseplant food if you want the plant to put on growth. If it is at the maximum size that your space can handle, reduce fertilizing to once a year. Although rubber tree can get large, it can be pruned substantially to keep it smaller and in bounds. Always prune at a node where you can see which direction the remaining bud is facing. This allows you to effectively shape the plant. Rubber tree naturally loses its lower leaves but may send out new leaves at the nodes of the old leaves. Giving the plant a slight nick above a node will force new leaves faster. Be aware that the milky sap exuded from cuts can be irritating and will stain clothes. Repot every third year or so. Prune the roots and crown back by about a third at the same time and put the plant back into its original pot. This will keep the plant at a reasonable size for the home. Wipe off the large leaves to keep them looking attractive and to discourage spider mites.
PROPAGATION: Propagate by stem cuttings. Take cuttings in summer and provide rooting hormone and humidity. Rubber tree can be effectively air-layered when the stem gets bare at the bottom. When you cut off the newly rooted top portion, the old stem will produce new shoots from its base.
PESTS AND DISEASES: Treat scale by routinely spraying the plant with horticultural oil.
RELATED SPECIES: The cultivar 'Doescheri' has creamy white variegated leaves; 'Robusta' is much more compact. 'Burgundy' has reddish leaves.

Rubber tree leaves are large and few, so dusting is easy. Dusting enhances the beauty of the plant and prevents a myriad of problems.

FIDDLELEAF FIG
Ficus lyrata *FYE-kus lye-RAH-tuh*

Fiddleleaf fig has uniquely shaped large leaves and can grow to a large size.

SIZE: 20–30'h × 10'w
TYPE: Tree
FORM: Upright
TEXTURE: Coarse
GROWTH: Slow
LIGHT: High to medium

MOISTURE: Even
SOIL: Potting soil
FEATURES: Leaves, bark
USES: Accent

SITING: Provide medium to high light and average home temperatures (60–75°F). Fiddleleaf fig tolerates lower light, but growth will be open and sparse. Give it average humidity (30–60 percent).

CARE: Keep evenly moist when in active growth; allow to dry out slightly between soakings in winter. In lower light, reduce watering. Fiddleleaf fig will drop its leaves if it is overwatered. Feed three times in summer with a foliage houseplant food. If the plant is at the maximum size that your space can handle, reduce fertilizing to once a year. The plant has a tendency

Fiddleleaf figs are easily air-layered when the plant gets leggy with sparse leaves at the bottom.

to grow unbranched, so pinch out the tips of the stems of young plants to force side buds to develop. Be aware that the milky sap exuded from cuts can be irritating and will stain clothes. To increase its size, every third year or so repot into a slightly larger container. Once the plant has reached the maximum size for your space, prune the roots and crown back by about a third when you repot it and put the plant back into its original pot.

PROPAGATION: Propagate by stem cuttings. Take cuttings in summer and provide rooting hormone and humidity. Fiddleleaf fig can also be air-layered.

PESTS AND DISEASES: Treat scale, mealybugs, and spider mites by routinely spraying the plant with horticultural oil. Use a drop cloth because this quantity of oil can make a mess on the floor.

RELATED SPECIES: The cultivar 'Compacta' is a dwarf form with closely spaced leaves and short petioles, giving it a much less coarse appearance.

ALII FIG
Ficus maclellandii (binnendykii) 'Alii' *FYE-kus mack-luh-LAN-dee-eye (bin-en-DYE-kee-eye)*

Alii fig leaves resemble willow leaves, gracefully hanging from the upright stems. It is also known as banana leaf fig.

SIZE: 9'h × 6'w
TYPE: Tree
FORM: Upright
TEXTURE: Medium
GROWTH: Medium
LIGHT: High to medium

MOISTURE: Even
SOIL: Potting soil
FEATURES: Willowlike leaves
USES: Architectural accent

SITING: Provide medium to high light and average home temperatures (60–75°F). Alii fig tolerates lower light, but growth will be open and sparse. Give the plant average humidity (30–60 percent).

CARE: Keep evenly moist when in active growth; allow to dry out slightly between soakings in winter. In lower light, reduce watering somewhat. Alii fig will drop its leaves if overwatered. Feed three times in summer with a foliage houseplant food if you want the plant to put on growth. If it

Alii figs grow quickly enough that it may be necessary to prune back long, wayward stems occasionally.

is at the maximum size that your space can handle, reduce fertilizing to once a year, particularly if you repot it. Although Alii fig can get large, it can be pruned substantially to keep it smaller and in bounds. To maintain the attractive, rounded crown, prune at a node where you can see which direction the remaining bud is facing. This allows you to make the plant symmetrical instead of sending out wayward branches toward the ceiling. Be aware that the milky sap exuded from cuts can be irritating and will stain clothes. Repot every third year or so. Prune the roots and crown back by about a third at the same time, then put the plant back into its original pot. This will keep the plant at a reasonable size for the home.

PROPAGATION: Propagate by stem cuttings. Take cuttings in summer and provide rooting hormone and humidity.

PESTS AND DISEASES: Treat scale, mealybugs, and spider mites by routinely spraying the plant with horticultural oil.

RELATED SPECIES: The cultivar 'Amstel Gold' has wide golden margins. 'Amstel Queen' has larger leaves that are matte green.

INDIAN LAUREL FIG

Ficus microcarpa (retusa nitida) FYE-kus my-kroh-KAR-puh (reh-TOO-suh NIH-tih-duh)

Indian laurel fig has a more upright shape than weeping fig and is more tolerant of lower light. This is a variegated form.

SIZE: 4–12'h × 6'w
TYPE: Tree
FORM: Rounded
TEXTURE: Medium
GROWTH: Medium
LIGHT: High to medium

MOISTURE: Dry
SOIL: Average
FEATURES: Foliage
USES: Architectural accent

SITING: Provide medium to high light and average home temperatures (60–75°F). Indian laurel fig tolerates lower light, but growth will be open and sparse. Give the plants average humidity, accomplished on large plants with a pot-in-pot system.
CARE: Allow to dry out slightly between soakings. In lower light, reduce watering somewhat. Feed three times in summer with a foliage houseplant food if you want the plant to put on growth. If it is at the maximum size that your space can handle, reduce fertilizing to once a year, particularly if you repot it. Although Indian laurel fig can get large, it can be pruned substantially to keep it smaller and in bounds. Although its form isn't weeping as is *Ficus benjamina,* you prune it in the same way. Prune major branches instead of just branch tips and prune at a node where you can see which direction the remaining bud is facing. This allows you to keep the plant rounded instead of sending out wayward branches toward the ceiling. Be aware that the milky sap exuded from cuts can be irritating and will stain clothes. To train stems into unusual shapes such as braids, loops, and twists, start with very

Indian laurel fig has a naturally rounded top, and occasional pruning is necessary to head back shoots to keep this form.

young saplings and plant three or more to a pot. Repot every third year or so. Prune the roots and crown back by about a third at the same time, and put the plant back into its original pot. This will keep the plant at a reasonable size for the home. Plants grown in ideal conditions may produce small hard figs. These will not detract from the plant but can cause a litter problem if not picked up. Indian laurel fig will drop its leaves whenever climatic conditions change. If you move your plant outdoors for the summer, place it in shade and gradually move to brighter light. Reverse the process in fall when you bring the plant back indoors. This plant also drops its leaves whenever the season changes but will soon put out plenty of new leaves.
PROPAGATION: Take stem cuttings in summer and provide rooting hormone and humidity.
PESTS AND DISEASES: Treat scale by routinely spraying the plant with horticultural oil. Use a drop cloth, because this quantity of oil can make a mess on the floor.
RELATED SPECIES: 'Green Gem' has darker, coarser leaves than the species. 'Hawaii' has a dense crown and light gray to white margined leaves. 'Variegata' has a yellow midrib on dark green leaves.

OAKLEAF FIG

Ficus montana (quercifolia) FYE-kus mahn-TAN-uh (kwair-sih-FOH-lee-uh)

Oakleaf fig is a great plant to use as a ground cover in a container with a larger plant.

SIZE: 6"h × 18"w
TYPE: Woody ground cover
FORM: Ground cover
TEXTURE: Coarse
GROWTH: Slow
LIGHT: Low

MOISTURE: Even
SOIL: Average
FEATURES: Oaklike leaves
USES: Planter, ground cover, hanging basket

SITING: Oakleaf fig thrives in low light and average home temperatures (60–75°F). Give this unique plant average humidity, and keep it out of cold or warm drafts. It is perfectly suited to use as a ground cover in a large potted fig, where it will be shaded by a large crown.
CARE: Keep evenly moist but not soggy. In winter reduce watering somewhat. Feed three times in summer with a foliage houseplant food. Pinch to make it branch; otherwise no pruning is needed unless you want to change the form of the plant. Be aware that the milky sap exuded from cuts can be irritating and will stain clothes.

Repot every 2–3 years, going up only an inch in pot size each time. Once the plant reaches its mature size, prune the roots and crown back by about a third at repotting time, then put the plant back into its original pot. This will keep the plant at a reasonable size for the home. Wipe off the leaves periodically to keep them looking shiny and attractive and keep pests controlled. Plants in ideal conditions may produce small, hard figs. These will not detract from the plant but can cause a litter problem if not picked up.
PROPAGATION: Take stem cuttings in summer and provide rooting hormone and humidity.
PESTS AND DISEASES: A well-grown oakleaf fig will have few insect problems.

CREEPING FIG
Ficus pumila *FYE-kus PEW-mill-uh*

Tiny-leaved creeping fig grows long, trailing stems that make it a perfect candidate for a hanging basket or as ground cover.

SIZE: 3"h × 24"w
TYPE: Herbaceous
FORM: Vine
TEXTURE: Fine
GROWTH: Medium
LIGHT: Medium to low

MOISTURE: Even
SOIL: Organic
FEATURES: Trailing stems
USES: Hanging basket, ground cover, topiary

SITING: Provide medium to low light and average home temperatures (60–75°F). Give the plant higher humidity than other figs by placing pots on moist pebbles or using the pot-in-pot method for hanging baskets. Creeping fig lends a soft texture when used as a ground cover under large, bold-leaved plants.

CARE: Keep evenly moist to prevent shedding of leaves. Choose a companion that likes the same conditions when using the fig as a ground cover. Feed three times in summer with a foliage houseplant food or at every other watering with half-strength plant food. Pinch it regularly to keep the long, trailing vines looking good. Be aware that the milky sap exuded from cuts can be irritating and will stain clothes. Repot every third year or so. Prune the

Select a vine and pin it to moist soil at a node where it will take root. Once rooted, sever it from the main plant.

roots and crown back by about a third at the same time, then put the plant back into its original pot. Because creeping fig tolerates pruning so well, it is commonly used for topiary. The slender stems bend easily, and the small leaves make a perfect soft covering for a topiary frame. Fill the frame with sphagnum moss and keep it damp. The vines root and hold themselves to the frame.

PROPAGATION: Propagate by stem cuttings. Take cuttings in summer and provide rooting hormone and humidity. Creeping fig is also easily propagated by layering. Pin a vine to moist soil at a leaf node. Within a few weeks the plant should be well rooted and can be severed from the parent plant.

PESTS AND DISEASES: Creeping fig may have scale, mealybugs, or spider mites. Start new plants annually to prevent these problems from getting out of hand.

RELATED SPECIES: The cultivar 'Curly' has oakleaf-shaped chartreuse leaves. 'Minima' has very fine textured dark green leaves and is often the choice for topiary. Creeping fig is used to climb walls in conservatories, because the vines cling to rough surfaces. 'Snowflake' makes a dense mat with bright green leaves and white margins.

MOSAIC PLANT
Fittonia albivenis verschaffeltii *fit-TOH-nee-uh all-bih-VEN-is ver-schaf-FELT-tee-eye*

Mosaic plant, also known as nerve plant for the netted veins on its leaves, thrives in the humid conditions of a terrarium.

SIZE: 3–6"h × 12–18"w
TYPE: Herbaceous
FORM: Mounded
TEXTURE: Fine
GROWTH: Medium
LIGHT: High to medium

MOISTURE: Even
SOIL: Organic
FEATURES: Prominently veined leaves
USES: Terrarium, hanging basket, ground cover

SITING: Mosaic plant thrives in medium or bright but well-filtered light. It will not

tolerate sun or drying winds. Moderate to warm temperatures (65°F and above) are best; the plant may suffer if temperatures fall below this. Provide at least 60 percent humidity, whether with a pebble tray or

Place mosaic plant on damp pebbles to increase the humidity surrounding the plant.

pot-in-pot. The plant's small size makes it superb for a terrarium or for grouping with other plants to raise the humidity. If tempted to put it on the windowsill because of its diminutive size, be sure it receives no direct sun.

CARE: Keep evenly moist but not soggy. Wet soil can cause rot. Pinch out the growing tips regularly to keep the plant shrubby and pleasing in appearance. If the plant is in ideal conditions, it may produce small yellow flowers. They don't add to the beauty and may even detract from its appearance, so some gardeners pinch them out.

PROPAGATION: Propagate by division, seed, or stem cuttings. Take tip cuttings in spring or layer stems in midsummer. Provide plenty of humidity with both methods.

PESTS AND DISEASES: Treat mealybugs with a cotton swab and alcohol.

RELATED SPECIES: Nerve plant (*F. a.* Argyroneura Group) has silver veins. 'Nana' ('Minima') has smaller leaves. The variety *pearcei* has carmine veins.

FUCHSIA

Fuchsia triphylla 'Gartenmeister Bonstedt'   *FEW-shuh try-FILL-uh*

Gartenmeister Bonstedt fuchsia offers coppery leaves and soft salmon blossoms. It is also known as lady's eardrops.

SIZE: 2–3'h × 2–3'w
TYPE: Shrub
FORM: Draping
TEXTURE: Medium
GROWTH: Medium
LIGHT: High
MOISTURE: Dry

SOIL: Potting soil
FEATURES: Colored foliage
USES: Hanging basket
FLOWERS: ■

SITING: This plant benefits from bright, indirect sunlight to keep its maroon foliage at full color. In lower light it turns greenish bronze and doesn't blossom as well. Keep it somewhat warm (60–70°F) and provide average humidity (30–65 percent).

CARE: Although fuchsia seems fussy and in need of much moisture, it actually needs to dry out slightly between waterings. To prepare for its winter rest, extend the time between waterings starting in fall. Feed every 2–4 weeks with a foliage plant food. Reduce feeding about 2 weeks before the plant will come in for the winter. Hot, dry conditions will cause flower buds to drop. This plant benefits from being outdoors during the summer and can even be grown in the ground outdoors as a butterfly magnet. To bring indoors for winter, cut the plant back severely and keep it in a

Pinch out faded flowers to keep the plant blossoming for a longer time.

cool (45–55°F) location for the duration of the winter. A cool porch that doesn't freeze is ideal. Water only enough to keep the potting soil from becoming completely dry. In spring move the plant into a warmer location and begin watering. As soon as new growth appears, repot the plant using new potting soil. Put it back into the same pot. Pinch each branch tip after it has produced two sets of leaves. This will keep the plant shrubby and attractive. Pinch periodically throughout the summer, but stop pinching a month before first frost.
PROPAGATION: Propagate by softwood cuttings in spring. Take 4–5" cuttings, dip in rooting hormone, and insert in sterile potting mix. Cover with a plastic tent to keep the humidity high.
PESTS AND DISEASES: Whiteflies are common on fuchsia, usually coming to roost on plants outdoors for the summer. Before bringing the plant in for winter, treat the entire plant with horticultural oil, even if you don't see signs of the small white flies.
RELATED SPECIES: 'Firecracker' has cream and green foliage and salmon-orange flowers. 'Mary' has scarlet blossoms.

GARDENIA

Gardenia augusta   *gar-DEEN-yuh aw-GUST-uh*

Gardenias are prized for their intensely fragrant waxy white blossoms set off by deep glossy green foliage.

SIZE: 18–24"h × 18"w
TYPE: Shrub
FORM: Round
TEXTURE: Medium
GROWTH: Medium
LIGHT: Medium

MOISTURE: Even
SOIL: Potting soil
FEATURES: Foliage, blossoms
USES: Focal point, fragrance
FLOWERS: □

SITING: Gardenias need medium light, average home temperatures (65–75°F), and high humidity. For best results, place a small humidifier next to the plant.
CARE: Keep evenly moist. Feed every 2 weeks during spring and summer with

half-strength acid plant food. The plant benefits from spending the summer outdoors, where it is best placed in partial shade. When the plant comes indoors in fall, reduce feeding to once a month. Be prepared for the plant to lose leaves when it comes back indoors. If you provide good conditions, the plant will leaf out again. Gardenia may drop its flower buds before opening when the plant is in low humidity, too-low light, is overwatered or underwatered, or is moved. No flower buds may mean the plant is too warm. Repot annually into organic soil to help retain moisture, and use a plastic pot to stop evaporation through its walls. Prune in late winter or early spring after blooming.
PROPAGATION: Propagate by stem cuttings taken in summer when semihardened. Use rooting hormone and very high humidity to root the cuttings.

PESTS AND DISEASES: Gardenias are prone to several insects, particularly when the humidity is not high enough. Watch for scale, mealybugs, aphids, and spider mites.
RELATED SPECIES: The cultivar 'Shooting Star' has smaller, single blossoms. 'Grif's Select' is more compact than the species. 'Prostrata' grows more horizontally and is often used for bonsai.

Gardenias must be fed with an acid fertilizer to keep the leaves healthy and the blossoms continuous.

OX TONGUE
Gasteria spp. *gas-TARE-ee-uh*

Lawyer's tongue is an unlikely name for this beautifully marked succulent. Another common name is cow tongue.

SIZE: 3–12" × 6–18"
TYPE: Succulent
FORM: Upright
TEXTURE: Coarse
GROWTH: Slow
LIGHT: High

MOISTURE: Dry
SOIL: Cactus mix
FEATURES: Unique leaves
USES: Dish garden, focal point

SITING: Ox tongue tolerates adverse conditions as long as it is in high light. It thrives in temperatures of 50–85°F and requires low humidity (below 30 percent). The succulent leaves are easily scarred, so place *Gasteria* out of the way of traffic.

CARE: *Gasteria* requires many of the same conditions as cactus and other succulents. Allow to dry between soakings during active growth and dry out a bit more during winter rest. Fertilize only once a year in summer with foliage plant food. Wipe off the leaves occasionally to keep them looking pristine and to keep dust to a minimum. Remove the occasional scarred

Ox tongue plants have striking flecked leaves with several shades of green spots.

leaf or faded flower spike. Clump-forming species need to be divided and repotted when the pot fills with many small plants. Use fast-draining cactus mix. Smaller species may need some soil added occasionally, but their small root system will seldom fill a pot. If you choose to move *Gasteria* outdoors for the summer, place it where it will get morning and late afternoon sun but not direct midday sun.

PROPAGATION: Depending on the species, *Gasteria* can be propagated by division, offsets, or seed.

PESTS AND DISEASES: The plant is virtually pest free. But check it periodically for mealybugs, and treat with a cotton swab dipped in alcohol or horticultural oil.

RELATED SPECIES: *G. armstrongii* is a small plant that is perfect for the windowsill. Its pleated leaves have downward-pointing tips. *G. excelsa* resembles an aloe or yucca. Lawyer's tongue (*G. liliputana*) has flat, overlapping leaves with white spots.

TAHITIAN BRIDAL VEIL
Gibasis geniculata (**pellucida**) *jib-BAY-sis jen-ik-yoo-LAH-tuh (pel-LOO-sih-duh)*

Tahitian bridal veil is a stunning vining plant that engulfs its container with tiny leaves and delicate white blossoms.

SIZE: 6"h × 2'w
TYPE: Herbaceous
FORM: Trailing
TEXTURE: Fine
GROWTH: Fast
LIGHT: High
MOISTURE: Dry

SOIL: Potting soil
FEATURES: Leaves, blossoms
USES: Hanging basket, terrarium
FLOWERS: ☐

SITING: Tahitian bridal veil is a striking plant when grown well. It needs high light to keep it compact and shrubby. Average to warm temperatures (65–85°F) will keep the plant looking good. Cooler temperatures slow its growth and make

the leaves hang limply. Provide average humidity (30–65 percent).

CARE: Let dry out slightly between waterings. If given too much water or allowed to sit in water, the stem will rot. Feed once a month with foliage plant food to keep it from becoming too succulent and prone to fungal rots. It grows fairly quickly, so repot annually. To keep the plant in the same-size pot, divide when you repot, and pot up the divisions as separate plants. Pinch out the growing tips every few weeks to keep the plant compact and shrubby. Pinch on the undersides as well as the top or the stems that are blocked from light will begin to die. If the stems do become bare and leggy, cut back all the stems to a few inches and start the plant over. Remove faded and dried leaves and flower stalks by giving the plant a solid shake to dislodge them.

PROPAGATION: Propagate from stem cuttings or by layering. The plant stems root readily at

the leaf nodes, so start new plants in soil or water. Tahitian bridal veil is also easily divided. The root ball is unusually dense, so remove the plant from the pot and use a serrated knife to cut the root ball in half or thirds. Cut back the stems at this time to help the plant recover.

PESTS AND DISEASES: Aphids can be somewhat hard to control in the mass of foliage. Dislodge with a periodic strong spray of water.

The stems of Tahitian bridal veil will become leggy and bare, so pinch them regularly and cut them back to a few inches to completely rejuvenate the plant.

GUZMANIA
Guzmania lingulata *gooz-MANE-yuh lin-gyu-LAH-tuh*

Guzmania is an easy-to-care-for bromeliad that requires only high humidity to keep it looking good.

SIZE: 1–2'h × 1–2'w
TYPE: Bromeliad
FORM: Vase-shaped
TEXTURE: Medium
GROWTH: Slow
LIGHT: High to medium
MOISTURE: Dry

SOIL: Epiphyte mix
FEATURES: Striped leaves, colorful bracts
USES: Focal point, blooming
FLOWERS: ■□ ▨

SITING: Guzmania shows its best leaf color in bright, filtered light. Provide average to hot temperatures (60°F and above) to prevent rotting. High humidity (above 65 percent) is crucial to keep this bromeliad looking good.
CARE: Let the soil dry out almost completely between waterings and keep the "vase" full of water. Every couple of months, empty and refill the vase to keep the water fresh. Feed with blooming plant formula three times in summer. Repot only when the potting mix begins to break down and no longer has recognizable chunks of bark. Guzmania can be grown on a slab but high humidity is essential.
PROPAGATION: Propagate by removing the offsets or side shoots when they are about one-third the size of the parent plant. Take the plant out of the pot and gently pull off each offset, making sure it has some roots. You can also propagate guzmania by seed in spring. Collect the seeds as they ripen and place them on moist paper towels in a covered plastic container until they germinate.
PESTS AND DISEASES: Treat scale and spider mites with horticultural oil. The plant may develop leaf spots in low humidity and root rot if overwatered.
RELATED SPECIES: The cultivar 'Variegata' has white-striped leaves. 'Empire' has bright green leaves and scarlet flowers. 'Marjan' has yellow flowers. *G. lingulata* var. *minor* has a smaller overall stature and smaller leaves.

1 Guzmanias produce "pups," small plants at the base of the mother plant, which can be separated to form new plants.

2 After pulling off a pup with some roots, pot it into damp, sterile potting soil and place it in a protected spot for several days.

PURPLE PASSION
Gynura aurantiaca *guy-NOOR-uh aw-ran-tee-AH-kuh*

Purple passion is also known as purple velvet plant, an apt name considering the fuzzy purple hairs covering its foliage.

SIZE: 6"h × 2'w
TYPE: Herbaceous
FORM: Trailing
TEXTURE: Medium
GROWTH: Medium
LIGHT: High to medium

MOISTURE: Evenly moist
SOIL: Potting soil
FEATURES: Leaves with purple hairs
USES: Hanging basket
FLOWERS: ■

SITING: Purple passion needs bright to medium light to keep its intense purple color and dense form. When grown in the proper light, it remains stocky and thick. If grown in too little light, the plant becomes leggy. Adaptable to a cool window, purple passion tolerates cool to average temperatures (55–65°F) and average humidity (30–60 percent). A pot-in-pot system helps maintain adequate humidity around the plant.
CARE: Keep evenly moist during active growth; reduce watering and allow the soil to dry slightly in winter. Feed three times in summer with foliage plant food. You can repot the plant annually, but it isn't necessary. After a couple of years, the plant may get ragged, so start a new plant every year to keep an attractive specimen. Pinch it regularly to keep it stocky.
PROPAGATION: Propagate by stem cuttings in water or soil. You will get an attractive plant faster if you root several cuttings in a single pot. Use rooting hormone and keep the humidity higher than usual while the plant is developing roots.
PESTS AND DISEASES: Treat mealybugs with a cotton swab dipped in alcohol or horticultural oil. Avoid spraying the entire plant with oil so the hairs don't mat.
RELATED SPECIES: The cultivar 'Purple Passion' is the standard plant. The species is seldom available.

Pinch out the stem tips regularly to keep the plant looking shrubby and attractive. Also pinch out flower buds because they have an unpleasant odor.

ZEBRA HAWORTHIA

Haworthia fasciata buh-WAR-thee-yuh fas-kee-AH-tuh

Zebra haworthia's striking foliage will remain attractive with the same conditions given to cactus.

SIZE: 5–6"h × 5–6"w
TYPE: Succulent
FORM: Mounded
TEXTURE: Medium
GROWTH: Slow
LIGHT: High
MOISTURE: Dry

SOIL: Cactus mix
FEATURES: Foliage with white bands
USES: Dish garden, focal point
FLOWERS: ☐ ▦

SITING: This plant is perfect for the windowsill that receives no direct sun. It prefers filtered bright light. Direct sun will cause the leaf tips to brown. It performs best in average to high temperatures (65°F and above). It needs low humidity (below 30 percent).

CARE: Allow the soil to dry slightly between waterings when the plant is in active growth and dry to an inch below the soil surface during rest times. More water than this will rot the roots. Zebra haworthia grows actively from March through May, then goes into a summer rest until August. In September it begins active growth again. Feed only three times during the active growth periods with a general foliage plant food. Repotting is seldom necessary unless the offsets spill out of the pot or crowd one another in the pot. Use a fast-draining cactus mix for repotting the plant or potting up divisions. Occasionally hose off the leaves to keep them looking clean and healthy.

PROPAGATION: Propagate zebra haworthia by separating the offsets that appear frequently. Use a knife to separate the offsets from the parent plant and pot them up in cactus mix. Roots should appear fairly quickly.

PESTS AND DISEASES: Treat mealybugs and scale with horticultural oil.

RELATED SPECIES: *H. attenuata* looks quite similar to zebra haworthia and is sometimes considered synonymous with it. *H. ×cuspidata* has fat, clumping leaves that form 4" rosettes. Window plant (*H. cymbiformis*) has pale green succulent leaves with translucent tips resembling windows into the plant. *H. reinwardtii* has dense, upright, tightly clasped leaves.

ALGERIAN IVY

Hedera canariensis HEH-der-uh kuh-nar-ee-EN-sis

Algerian ivy, one of the sturdiest of the ivies, will thrive in cool conditions and medium light.

SIZE: 10"h × 5'w
TYPE: Vine
FORM: Trailing
TEXTURE: Medium
GROWTH: Medium
LIGHT: Medium

MOISTURE: Evenly moist
SOIL: Potting soil
FEATURES: Glossy leaves
USES: Hanging basket, ground cover

SITING: Algerian ivy is a vigorous plant that grows thickly enough and long enough to make a living curtain. Provide medium light and cool temperatures (55–65°F) for the best growth. Cooler temperatures make the reddish petioles redder still, an attractive accent. Provide medium to high humidity (60 percent and above) to deter spider mites.

CARE: Keep evenly moist. In winter allow to dry out a bit, but not too much or the plant will begin to brown. Feed with foliage plant food according to label directions. Algerian ivy does not branch well, so pinching may keep the plant within bounds but will not produce a thick, shrubby specimen. Algerian ivy doesn't require frequent repotting; plants can be grown in the same pot for years. If you want to rejuvenate it somewhat, repot into a larger container every 2–3 years. Old plants become woody and leggy, so start new plants from cuttings every few years. If the vines lose their leaves at the base, simply cut the vines off short. They will produce more leaves fairly quickly. If the leaf tips turn brown, raise the humidity and check for spider mites.

PROPAGATION: Propagate from stem cuttings or by layering. The vines will produce roots at the leaf nodes, so pin a vine with the node touching the soil. When the plant roots in a couple of weeks, sever it from the parent plant and pot up.

PESTS AND DISEASES: Ivies have an inherent problem with spider mites, especially if grown in low humidity. Wash off the plant often, raise the humidity, and treat the mites with horticultural oil. Ivies may also have scale, which can also be treated with horticultural oil. If leaves of variegated ivies lose their variegation, give them more light (but not direct sun).

RELATED SPECIES: The cultivar 'Gloire de Marengo' is a standard variegated ivy with golden yellow and light gray variegation. Other cultivars are not widely available.

Algerian ivy makes an attractive accent when planted as ground cover in the container of a large plant.

ENGLISH IVY

Hedera helix *HEH-der-uh HEE-licks*

English ivy comes in many leaf shapes, sizes, and colors, with something to please every gardener.

SIZE: 6–8"h × 2'w
TYPE: Vine
FORM: Trailing
TEXTURE: Medium
GROWTH: Medium
LIGHT: High

MOISTURE: Evenly moist
SOIL: Organic
FEATURES: Leaves
USES: Hanging basket, ground cover, topiary

SITING: English ivy is vigorous when given bright, indirect light during the summer and some direct sun during the winter. It thrives in cool temperatures (55–65°F), which bring out the best color and keep the plant stocky and attractive. Provide medium to high humidity (60 percent and above) to deter spider mites.

CARE: Keep evenly moist. Avoid letting the plant dry out too much or it will begin to brown. Feed with foliage plant food according to label directions. Frequent pinching produces a thick, shrubby plant. Repot about every 2 years. As older stems

English ivy can be trained onto a trellis or topiary frame with a little assistance and gentle ties.

become woody and leggy and lose their bottom leaves, prune them back hard. If the leaf tips turn brown, raise the humidity and check for spider mites. English ivy is an excellent candidate for topiary, because it branches well. If leaves of variegated ivies lose their variegation, give them more light (but not direct sun).

PROPAGATION: Propagate from stem cuttings or by layering. The vines produce roots at the leaf nodes, so pin a vine with the node touching the soil and wait a couple of weeks for the plant to root, then sever it from the parent plant and pot up.

PESTS AND DISEASES: Ivies have inherent problems with spider mites, especially if grown in low humidity. Wash off the plant often, raise the humidity, and treat the mites with horticultural oil. Ivies may also have scale, which can also be treated with horticultural oil.

RELATED SPECIES: The American Ivy Society classifies cultivars according to leaf shape and leaf type. 'Needlepoint' has tiny green leaves and makes an attractive topiary, 'Romanze' has gold-variegated leaves and wavy margins. 'Harrison' has large triangular leaves with white veins.

RED FLAME IVY

Hemigraphis alternata *hem-uh-GRAF-iss al-ter-NAH-tuh*

Red flame ivy will keep its lovely red leaves when given medium light and kept away from drying winds and cold drafts.

SIZE: 6"h × 18"w
TYPE: Herbaceous
FORM: Mounded
TEXTURE: Medium
GROWTH: Medium
LIGHT: Medium
MOISTURE: Evenly moist

SOIL: Potting soil
FEATURES: Maroon leaves
USES: Hanging basket
FLOWERS: ☐

SITING: Red flame ivy needs medium light; high or low light will cause the plant to decline. It will tolerate average to high temperatures (60°F and above) but must be kept away from drying winds and cold

drafts. Medium to high humidity (30 percent and higher) will keep the foliage in peak condition. A pot-in-pot system works well in a hanging basket.

CARE: Keep evenly moist. Allowing it to dry out may cause the leaf edges to brown. Feed only three times in summer with foliage plant food. Repot annually; the plant has a vigorous root system. Red flame ivy branches well when pruned, so pinch out the growing tips regularly to keep the plant shrubby and thick. If the

Pinch out the stem tips regularly to keep the plant shrubby and attractive. The tips can be easily rooted to make new plants.

stems become leggy and bare, cut the plant back severely to rejuvenate it. Occasionally pull off browned leaves and give the plant a shower once a month.

PROPAGATION: Root by stem cuttings or by layering. Stem cuttings will root in water or soil, but you will get the fastest, healthiest plant if you start them in soil. Use rooting hormone and provide warmth and high humidity. These plants root well, so take cuttings to grow in a well-protected spot in the outdoor garden.

PESTS AND DISEASES: Mealybugs and spider mites may be problems on red flame ivy when the plant is grown in low humidity.

RELATED SPECIES: Purple waffle plant (*H. a.* 'Exotica') has puckered purple leaves. *H. repanda* is a prostrate plant with small leaves and tiny white flowers. 'Red Equator' has small metallic green leaves with red underneath and a more compact habit.

ROSE MALLOW

Hibiscus rosa-sinensis hib-BIS-kus ROZE-uh sih-NEN-sis

Rose mallow is also known as Chinese rose or hibiscus. It makes an intensely tropical statement with its magnificent flowers.

SIZE: 6'h × 4'w
TYPE: Woody shrub
FORM: Upright
TEXTURE: Coarse
GROWTH: Medium
LIGHT: High
MOISTURE: Evenly moist
SOIL: Potting soil
FEATURES: Flowers
USES: Focal point
FLOWERS: ■ ■ ■
　　　　　□ ■

SITING: Rose mallow needs bright light to produce flowers. It grows well in cool to average temperatures (55–70°F) and must have high humidity to keep the buds from dropping and to keep spider mites at bay. Avoid drying winds and cold drafts.

CARE: Keep evenly moist. Feed twice a month from April through September with foliage plant food. Repot annually in spring. If you want rose mallow to increase in size, pot into an inch larger container after loosening any wrapping roots. Otherwise, root-prune and put the plant back into the same pot. Establish three or four main branches and remove all others at the base. Cut back these main branches by one-third. The plant blooms on new wood, so pruning in this way will produce

Cut back rose mallow substantially to keep an attractive shape, stimulate new growth, and promote profuse bloom.

plenty of new shoots for blooming. Pinch out the growing tips in early spring to force more flowers along the stems. Leaves yellow when they are old or if the plant is under stress. Conditions that are too dry, too moist, or too cold will cause leaf drop. Usually the leaves return quickly when the conditions are corrected. This plant benefits from spending the summer outdoors in bright, indirect light.

PROPAGATION: Propagate by taking semihardwood cuttings in summer. Use rooting hormone, bottom heat, and high humidity for rooting. The plants can also be layered by pinning a nicked stem to moist potting soil.

PESTS AND DISEASES: Spider mite populations can explode when the plant is grown in dry conditions. Regular rinsing will help deter them.

RELATED SPECIES: Cultivars come with single and double flowers, bicolored flowers, small and large leaves, and variegated foliage. When choosing a plant, keep in mind that coarse texture and large flowers can dominate your houseplant display.

AMARYLLIS

Hippeastrum spp. hip-ee-AS-trum

Amaryllis, treasured for its holiday blooms, produces a magnificent stalk of massive tubular flowers in many different shades.

SIZE: 18"h × 12"w
TYPE: Bulb
FORM: Upright, vase-shaped
TEXTURE: Coarse
GROWTH: Medium
LIGHT: High
MOISTURE: Dry
SOIL: Potting soil
FEATURES: Funnel-shaped flowers
USES: Focal point, holiday accent
FLOWERS: ■ □ ■
　　　　　■ ■

SITING: While the plant is developing new leaves and sending up its flower stalk, give it bright light. It grows well in average temperatures (60–75°F), although cooler temperatures will prolong the bloom.

CARE: Plant bulbs with ⅓ to ½ of the bulb above the soil line. Allow the top inch of soil to dry between waterings. Feed weekly during the growing season. Remove faded flowers then pull the stalk once it softens and yellows. When all danger of frost has passed, sink the pot in a sunny spot the garden. In early September, pull the pot out of the ground. Stop watering and bring the pot indoors to a dry, dark, cool spot for at least 2 months. When you are ready to force it into bloom, bring the plant into warmth, replace the top inch of soil, and water. As soon as foliage appears, move the plant into the preferred light conditions and begin fertilizing. Within 6–8 weeks,

flower stalks should emerge. Stake the stalk if your plant needs it.

PROPAGATION: Amaryllis produces bulblets as it ages; these can be separated and potted up separately. Offsets bloom sooner when left attached to the original bulb. You can also divide bulbs, but be sure that each division has part of the basal plate.

PESTS: Amaryllis bulbs and leaves can be bothered by fungal disease, which is difficult to treat. If you see signs of disease, it's best to discard the bulb.

RELATED SPECIES: Butterfly amaryllis (*H. papilio*) has an elegant lime green flower with maroon markings.

Amaryllis bulbs are often sold dry, ready to be potted and forced into bloom.

Place the bulb with the top one-third above the soil.

Water in well and place in a warm location until shoot growth begins.

DROP TONGUE

Homalomena rubescens *home-uh-lo-MANE-uh roo-BES-sens*

Drop tongue has an unusual name for a very attractive foliage plant that is a wonderful choice in low-light situations.

SIZE: 18"h × 12"w
TYPE: Herbaceous
FORM: Mounded
TEXTURE: Medium
GROWTH: Slow
LIGHT: Medium to low

MOISTURE: Evenly moist
SOIL: Potting soil
FEATURES: Heart-shaped leaves
USES: Foliage, low light

SITING: Drop tongue is a popular plant for use in foliage displays because of its attractive, glossy leaves. Its tolerance of low light makes it useful in darker areas of the home; however if given medium light, the plant looks better. Drop tongue thrives in medium to high temperatures (65°F and above) and requires high humidity (above 65 percent). Avoid drying winds and cold drafts.

CARE: Keep evenly moist. Drying out only slightly can cause the plant to decline. If growing in low light, make sure the soil doesn't become soggy. Feed only three times in summer with foliage plant food. Repot annually; the roots quickly fill the pot and the plant loses its ability to take up water. The flowers are insignificant; pinching them out makes the foliage more lush. Wash the leaves monthly to keep the plant looking its best.

PROPAGATION: Propagate by dividing the root ball. Simply split the root mass down the middle or pull off sections with roots attached.

PESTS AND DISEASES: Treat mealybugs and spider mites with horticultural oil. Neither should get out of hand in high humidity.

RELATED SPECIES: 'Emerald Gem' is an industry standard with compact growth and glossy leaves. Silver shield (*H. wallisii*) has variegated large leaves. *H. picturata* has broad leaves with silvery-green markings.

When drop tongue fills its pot with roots, remove the root ball from the old pot and loosen the roots gently.

Place the plant in a larger pot or root prune it and return it to the same pot to keep it the same size.

Water in the repotted plant to moisten the soil and remove air pockets.

KENTIA PALM

Howea forsteriana *HOW-ee-yuh for-stare-ee-AH-nuh*

Kentia palm is the largest of the interior palms, making an extraordinary statement in a vast room.

SIZE: 10'h × 10'w
TYPE: Palm
FORM: Upright, arching
TEXTURE: Coarse
GROWTH: Slow
LIGHT: Medium to low

MOISTURE: Evenly moist
SOIL: Potting soil
FEATURES: Fronds
USES: Architectural accent

SITING: Kentia palm is majestic in stature and tolerant of a wide range of conditions. It grows as wide as it is tall, so make sure you have a suitable site. Provide medium to low light (it grows slowly in low light and will be somewhat open). It does well in cool temperatures (50–60°F) but also tolerates average temperatures (65–75°F). Provide average humidity (30–60 percent) to deter spider mites.

CARE: Provide evenly moist soil; the plant should not sit in water. In winter it goes through a rest period, so reduce water somewhat. Feed only three times in summer with foliage plant food. Repot when the plant becomes difficult to water, but go up only an inch or two in pot size to avoid a lot of soil and few roots to fill it. Remove the occasional dead frond. Avoid tying the fronds together as the plant widens. Selectively remove fronds if necessary. Brown tips usually indicate dry soil, low humidity, or soluble salt build-up in the soil. Because this palm does not grow many fronds, trim the brown tips rather than removing the entire frond. If the fronds have spots, the plant may be in light that is too bright, or there may be a problem with chemicals in the water.

PROPAGATION: Propagate by seed, which must be attained from a seed supplier.

PESTS AND DISEASES: Spider mites can be a problem, but washing the leaves regularly will help prevent infestations. The leaves are few, so this is not a daunting task. Watch also for mealybugs. Treat with rubbing alcohol.

RELATED SPECIES: Sentry palm (*H. balmoreana*) is slower growing and more susceptible to pests, so it is seldom available for houseplant use.

WAX PLANT

Hoya carnosa HOY-yuh kar-NOH-suh

Wax plant comes with several different types of leaves and flower colors. It is also known as hoya.

SIZE: 3–4"h × 4'w
TYPE: Vine
FORM: Trailing
TEXTURE: Medium
GROWTH: Fast
LIGHT: High
MOISTURE: Dry

SOIL: Potting soil
FEATURES: Waxy leaves
USES: Hanging basket, topiary
FLOWERS: ☐ ▨ ■

SITING: Hoya is an attractive vining plant that, if grown in adequate light, has waxy flowers with a sweet scent at night. it is slow to begin blooming, but flowers annually once it starts to bloom. Plants will tolerate some morning sun but not midday sun. Cool to medium temperatures (55–75°F) will keep the plants stocky; avoid cold drafts.

CARE: Water wax plant only after the top half inch of soil has dried. Feed three times in summer with foliage plant food.

Repot as infrequently as possible. It has a smallish root system and does not take repotting well. Use an average soil that is very well drained. Overwatering will cause leaves to drop. It is possible to pinch out growing tips to make the plant branch, but be aware that it is difficult to recognize the flowering spikes and you may delay flowering. After the plant blooms, allow faded flowers to fall off, but don't remove the flower stalk; the plant will rebloom on the same stalk. Hoya can be trained to grow upright but will need trellising, because its only means of support is vines twining among themselves.

PROPAGATION: Propagate by stem cuttings. Take 3–5" cuttings anytime during active growth; strip all but one leaf, dip in rooting hormone powder, and insert in

sterile soil. Bottom heat and high humidity will ensure rooting. Wax plant can also be propagated by layering. Simply pin a stem to the soil at a leaf node and keep the soil mix moist until the plant forms roots. When rooted, sever from the parent plant.

PESTS AND DISEASES: Mealybugs are frequently a problem, especially on the curly-leaved varieties. Treat by dabbing with a cotton swab dipped in alcohol or horticultural oil.

RELATED SPECIES: The cultivar 'Krinkle Kurl' (Hindu rope) has oddly curved leaves clustered along the stems. 'Exotica' has pink and light green variegated foliage. String bean plant (*H. longifolia*) has long, narrow leaves and an elegant appearance. Imperial wax plant (*H. imperialis*) has huge leaves and large red-brown flowers.

The vining nature of wax plant makes it a good candidate for training onto a topiary form as well as use in a hanging basket.

The flowers of wax plant are uniquely shaped, waxy, and delightfully fragrant, somewhat reminiscent of honey.

COMPACT WAX PLANT

Hoya compacta HOY-yuh kar-NOH-suh kom-PAK-tuh

Compact wax plant is a diminutive variety that is perfect for a windowsill or small hanging basket.

SIZE: 3–4"h × 1'w
TYPE: Vine
FORM: Trailing
TEXTURE: Medium
GROWTH: Fast
LIGHT: High
MOISTURE: Dry

SOIL: Potting soil
FEATURES: Waxy leaves
USES: Hanging basket, topiary
FLOWERS: ☐ ▨ ■

SITING: Hoya is an attractive vining foliage plant, but in adequate light it has waxy flowers with reflexed petals and a sweet scent at night. Compact wax plant is smaller all around than the species, making it perfect for small baskets and windowsills. Provide bright light. Hoya will tolerate some morning sun but not midday sun. Cool to medium temperatures (55–75°F) will keep the plant stocky; avoid cold drafts.

CARE: Water wax plant only after the top half inch of soil has dried. Feed three times in summer with foliage plant food. Repot as infrequently as possible. *Hoya* has a smallish root system and does not take repotting well. Use an average soil that is very well drained. Overwatering will cause leaves to drop. It is possible to pinch out growing tips to make the plant branch, but be aware that it is difficult to recognize the flowering spikes, and you may delay

flowering. After the plant blooms, allow faded flowers to fall off, but leave the flower stalk alone; the plant will rebloom on the same stalk. *Hoya* can be trained to grow upright but will need trellising, because its only means of support is vines that twine among themselves.

PROPAGATION: Propagate by stem cuttings. Take 3–5" cuttings anytime during active growth; strip all but one leaf, dip in rooting hormone powder, and insert in sterile soil. Bottom heat and high humidity will ensure rooting. Hoya can also be propagated by layering. Simply pin a stem to the soil at a leaf node and keep the soil mix moist until the plant forms roots. When rooted, sever from the parent plant.

PESTS AND DISEASES: Mealybugs are frequently a problem, especially on the curly-leaved varieties. Treat by dabbing with a cotton swab dipped in alcohol or horticultural oil.

BEAUTIFUL HOYA

Hoya lanceolata ssp. *bella*   HOY-yuh lan-see-oh-LATE-uh BELL-uh

Beautiful hoya is adorned with diamond-shaped leaves and soft pink and white blossoms. It is also known as miniature wax plant.

SIZE: 3–4"h × 4'w
TYPE: Vine
FORM: Trailing
TEXTURE: Medium
GROWTH: Fast
LIGHT: High
MOISTURE: Dry

SOIL: Potting soil
FEATURES: Waxy leaves
USES: Hanging basket, topiary
FLOWERS: □ ■

SITING: Hoya is an attractive vining foliage plant, but in adequate light it has waxy flowers with reflexed petals and a sweet scent at night. Beautiful hoya is diminutive in stature with diamond-shaped leaves and bicolored white and pink flowers. Provide bright light. Hoya will tolerate some morning sun but not midday sun. Cool to medium temperatures (55–75°F) will keep the plant stocky; avoid cold drafts.
CARE: Water only after the top half inch of soil has dried. Feed three times in summer with foliage plant food. Repot as infrequently as possible. Hoya has a smallish root system and does not take repotting well. Use an average soil that is very well drained. Overwatering will cause leaves to drop. It is possible to pinch out growing tips to make the plant branch, but be aware that it is difficult to recognize the flowering spikes, and you may delay flowering. After the plant blooms, allow spent flowers to fall, but do not remove the flower stalk; the plant will rebloom on the same stalk. Hoya can be trained to grow upright but will need support, because the only means of support is vines that twine among themselves.
PROPAGATION: Propagate by stem cuttings. Take 3–5" cuttings anytime during active growth; strip all but one leaf, dip in rooting hormone powder, and insert in sterile soil. Bottom heat and high humidity will ensure rooting. Hoya can also be propagated by layering. Simply pin a stem to the soil at a leaf node and keep the soil mix moist until the plant forms roots. When rooted, sever from the parent plant.
PESTS AND DISEASES: Mealybugs are frequently a problem, especially on the curly-leaved varieties. Treat by dabbing with a cotton swab dipped in alcohol or horticultural oil.
RELATED SPECIES: The cultivar 'Variegata' has lime green variegation.

POLKA DOT PLANT

Hypoestes phyllostachya   hi-poh-ES-teez fill-oh-STAK-yuh

Polka dot plant, also known as freckle face, is a favorite for its uniquely colored foliage that adds a bright splash of color.

SIZE: 24"h × 9"w
TYPE: Herbaceous
FORM: Mounded
TEXTURE: Fine
GROWTH: Fast
LIGHT: High
MOISTURE: Evenly moist

SOIL: Potting soil
FEATURES: Variegated leaves
USES: Accent, dish garden
FLOWERS: ■

SITING: Polka dot plant has green leaves with pink markings that are made more pronounced when the plant is grown in bright light. It will not tolerate direct sun but does well in a protected bright window. Provide average temperatures (60–75°F) and high humidity (60 percent and above).
CARE: Provide evenly moist soil so the edges of the leaves don't brown. Feed only three times in summer with foliage plant food and repot annually. Trim back regularly so the plant does not become leggy and floppy. Pinch out the growing tips every few weeks to keep the plant shrubby and full. If the stems do become leggy, prune the plant back hard, and new growth at the soil level will come back strong fairly quickly. The flower stalks arise from the base of the plant. Some gardeners feel that they detract from the plant and pinch them out at the base. However, if you want to start new plants from seed, let them grow and ripen their seeds.

PROPAGATION: Propagate by cuttings at any time. The plants can be started fresh from seeds as well. When the stalks begin to dry and the seeds are ripe, collect the seeds and sow immediately on fresh, sterile potting mix. Keep the soil slightly moist but not soggy and cover with glass or plastic to increase the humidity until the seeds germinate. When the seedlings are several inches tall, transplant into pots.
PESTS AND DISEASES: Treat mealybugs and whiteflies with horticultural oil.
RELATED SPECIES: 'Wine Red' has dark red spots. Splash Select Series has bright red, rose, white or pink speckles.

1

To grow polka dot plants from seed, sow the seed on the top of fresh potting mix, sprinkle with soil, and water gently.

2

After watering, cover the seeds with glass or plastic to keep the seeds moist. Remove the cover once seeds germinate.

BLOODLEAF

Iresine herbstii *eye-REH-see-nee HERB-stee-eye*

Bloodleaf provides an intense focal point with its bright maroon and pink leaves. It is also known as chicken gizzard.

SIZE: 2'h × 1'w
TYPE: Herbaceous
FORM: Upright
TEXTURE: Medium
GROWTH: Medium
LIGHT: High, indirect
MOISTURE: Evenly moist
SOIL: Potting soil
FEATURES: Brightly variegated leaves
USES: Foliage, accent

SITING: Given the right light conditions, bloodleaf is a spectacular foliage accent with bright maroon leaves and stems. If this plant is not in the brightest light, the leaves tend to fade and become dull. The light needs to be filtered or the leaves will bleach out and the edges will brown.

Provide average warmth (60–75°F) during the growing season and slightly cooler conditions in winter (not below 55°F however). It prefers average to high humidity (above 30 percent). Provide extra humidity by setting the pot on a tray of moist pebbles.

Bloodleaf branches well, so periodically pinch out the stem tips to keep the plant shrubby and full.

CARE: Keep evenly moist during the active growing season; reduce watering somewhat in winter and allow the soil surface to dry slightly to prevent rot. Feed three times in summer with foliage plant food. Repot annually and pinch the plant frequently to keep it shrubby and full.

PROPAGATION: Propagate in winter and spring by herbaceous stem cuttings. Take 3–5" cuttings; remove all but one leaf, dip in rooting hormone, and insert in sterile potting soil. Cover with plastic to keep in humidity and check daily for rotting. When plants are rooted, remove the plastic cover, pinch back the growing tip, and transplant into pots. Bloodleaf can also be propagated by dividing the root ball.

PESTS AND DISEASES: Bloodleaf may have spider mites in low humidity and aphids as new growth begins. Treat both with insecticidal soap.

RELATED SPECIES: 'Aureoreticulata' has green leaves with yellow veins and red stems. 'Brilliantissima' has bright crimson foliage with pink-red veins. *I. lindenii* has black-red foliage shaped like willow leaves. 'Purple Lady' is a dark purple ground cover that grows to 6" high.

JASMINE

Jasminum polyanthum *JAZ-mi-num pah-lee-ANTH-um*

Jasmine intoxicates you with its fragrance, so put it in a sunny window where the warmth will intensify the perfume.

SIZE: 4"h × 4–6'w
TYPE: Vine
FORM: Trailing
TEXTURE: Fine
GROWTH: Medium
LIGHT: High
MOISTURE: Evenly moist
SOIL: Potting soil
FEATURES: Fragrant blooms
USES: Hanging basket, topiary
FLOWERS: ☐

SITING: It's a must to site this plant in a spot where you can enjoy the intensely fragrant blossoms. Giving it a sunny window will help it bloom, and the warm

sun will release the intoxicating scent. Jasmine grows in average temperatures (60–75°F) but sets flower buds only if grown for a time in fall between 40 and 60°F. Give this plant average to high humidity (above 30 percent). A humidifier helps provide moisture as well as air circulation, which keeps the plant leaves fungus free.

Jasmine requires bright light to develop its highly fragrant white blooms.

CARE: Keep evenly moist during active growth; water sparingly in winter. Feed once a month during active growth and not at all in winter. Move outdoors in bright light during the summer. Leaving it outdoors until temperatures reach about 40°F will set the flower buds. After it has bloomed in late winter, repot the plant and prune it back hard to avoid tangling. It will need some support such as a trellis or topiary frame, or it can be grown in a hanging basket. Prune it often to keep it looking good.

PROPAGATION: Propagate by taking stem cuttings in spring or by layering anytime. To layer, pin a stem to moist soil at a leaf node. When roots have formed, separate the plant from the parent plant.

PESTS AND DISEASES: Spider mites are a frequent pest, so wash the plant often to keep populations low.

RELATED SPECIES: Arabian jasmine (*J. sambac*) has large flowers and is used to flavor jasmine tea. Common jasmine (*J. officinale*) has white flowers and does not vine quite as much.

KALANCHOE

Kalanchoe blossfeldiana *kuh-LAN-cho (kal-an-KO-ee) bloss-fell-dee-AH-nah*

Kalanchoe takes little care and will bloom continuously for months with all shades of pink, red, yellow, or white blossoms.

SIZE: 6–12"h × 6–12"w
TYPE: Succulent
FORM: Upright
TEXTURE: Medium
GROWTH: Slow

LIGHT: High
MOISTURE: Dry
SOIL: Cactus mix
FEATURES: Flowers
USES: Accent plant
FLOWERS: ■ ■ ■ □

SITING: Grow kalanchoe in full morning or afternoon sun, avoiding midday sun. It performs best in average home temperatures (60–75°F) but will tolerate cold and heat for short periods. It needs only low to average humidity (30–60 percent).

CARE: Kalanchoe takes little care; it blooms for a long time with little attention. Water when the soil feels dry. Plants that are underwatered will turn reddish and shrivel, and the flowers and leaves will drop prematurely. Overwatering fosters rot and falling leaves. Feed only when new growth begins. Use a foliage plant food at half strength every 2 weeks. Remove faded leaves and flowers and wash the leaves occasionally. It is difficult to bring kalanchoe back into blossom in the

As flowers fade, pinch out the old blossoms and stalks to force the plant to produce more flower buds.

home. New plants grown from cuttings will bloom better than old plants that have already blossomed.

PROPAGATION: Propagate by stem cuttings. Cut a 3" section of stem, remove all but one leaf, and set aside to callus for 2–3 days. Then dip in rooting hormone and insert in sterile potting mix.

PESTS AND DISEASES: Few pests bother kalanchoe. Mealybugs are easily taken care of with a cotton swab dipped in alcohol or horticultural oil.

To force a kalanchoe into bloom again once it has finished will require an elaborate routine of light and darkness.

MOTHER OF THOUSANDS

Kalanchoe daigremontiana *kuh-LAN-cho (kal-an-KO-ee) deh-gre-mon-tee-ANN-uh*

Mother of thousands derives its name from the tiny plantlets all along each leaf. It is also known as air plant.

SIZE: 3'h × 3'w
TYPE: Succulent
FORM: Upright
TEXTURE: Medium
GROWTH: Medium
LIGHT: High

MOISTURE: Dry
SOIL: Cactus mix
FEATURES: Plantlets along margins
USES: Architectural accent

SITING: Grow mother of thousands in full morning or afternoon sun, avoiding midday sun. High light will cause leaf edges to turn red, an attractive feature. Lower light will cause the plants to be leggy and spindly. It performs best in average home temperatures (60–75°F)

but will tolerate cold and heat for short periods. It needs only low to average humidity (30–60 percent).

CARE: Mother of thousands takes little care. It is a succulent so it doesn't need a lot of water, but it should be watered when the soil is dry to the touch. This may take 1–2 weeks, depending on the type of pot and the temperature in which the plant

The plantlets along the leaves will fall by themselves, but you can remove them, and set them on moist soil to start new plants.

is grown. Plants that are underwatered will turn reddish and shrivel, and the flowers and leaves will drop prematurely. Overwatering or letting the plant sit in water will foster rot and falling leaves. Feed three times in summer with half-strength foliage plant food. Repot when the roots fill the pot. Remove faded leaves and flowers and wash the leaves occasionally.

PROPAGATION: This kalanchoe is called mother of thousands because small plantlets form along the margins of every leaf. These tiny plantlets give the plant a unique look; as they mature, they fall off and start new plants automatically. To produce new plants, place a pot with moist soil beneath a leaf, or remove an entire leaf and place it on the surface of the soil. The plantlets will send out new roots fairly quickly.

PESTS AND DISEASES: Few pests bother kalanchoe. Mealybugs are easily taken care of with a cotton swab dipped in alcohol or horticultural oil.

RELATED SPECIES: Chandelier plant (*K. delagoensis*) has rounded, succulent leaves with bulbils on the edges.

PANDA PLANT

Kalanchoe tomentosa *kuh-LAN-cho (kal-an-KO-ee) toh-men-TOH-suh*

Panda plant's soft, fuzzy leaves thrive in warm, dry conditions. It is also known as pussy ears.

SIZE: 20"h × 20"w
TYPE: Succulent
FORM: Mounded
TEXTURE: Medium
GROWTH: Medium
LIGHT: High

MOISTURE: Dry
SOIL: Cactus mix
FEATURES: Fuzzy leaves
USES: Dish garden, focal point

SITING: Panda plant has a unique texture that contrasts nicely with spiky cactus. Grow panda plant in full morning or afternoon sun, avoiding midday sun. High light will cause the leaf edges to turn red, an attractive feature. Lower light will cause it to beome leggy and spindly. Panda plant performs best in average home temperatures (60–75°F) but will tolerate cold and heat for short periods. It needs only low to average humidity (30–60 percent).

CARE: Panda plant, like the other kalanchoes, takes little care. Kalanchoes are succulent and don't need a lot of water, but they should be watered when the soil feels dry. This may take 1–2 weeks, depending on the type of pot and the temperature in which the plant is grown. Plants that are underwatered will turn reddish and shrivel and the flowers and leaves will drop prematurely. Overwatering or letting the plant sit in water will foster rot and falling leaves. Feed three times in summer with half-strength foliage plant food. Repot when the roots fill the pot. Remove faded leaves and flowers and wash the leaves occasionally.

PROPAGATION: Propagate by stem cuttings. Cut a 3" section of stem, remove all but one leaf, and set aside to callus for 2–3 days. Then dip in rooting hormone and insert in sterile potting mix. Do not cover and water sparingly until the cuttings root. When new growth starts, feed as directed above. The plants can also be propagated by leaf cuttings.

PESTS AND DISEASES: Few pests bother kalanchoes. Mealybugs are easily taken care of with a cotton swab dipped in alcohol or horticultural oil.

RELATED SPECIES: Felt bush (*K. beharensis*) 'Maltese Cross' has cupped, curly leaves covered with brown felt on their upper surface with silver undersides.

SWEET BAY

Laurus nobilis *LOR-us no-BILL-us*

Sweet bay is also known as Roman laurel or bay tree. It makes a magnificent houseplant with its glossy green foliage.

SIZE: 4'h × 3'w
TYPE: Woody shrub
FORM: Upright
TEXTURE: Medium
GROWTH: Slow
LIGHT: Medium to high

MOISTURE: Evenly moist
SOIL: Potting soil
FEATURES: Fragrant foliage
USES: Foliage backdrop, culinary

SITING: Sweet bay is a plant worth having for its culinary value and for its fragrant foliage. Bay performs best in medium to high light and thrives in cool to average temperatures (50–75°F) and low to average humidity (30–60 percent). It is an excellent choice for an architectural plant in a cool foyer or porch.

CARE: Keep evenly moist when the plant is in active growth and somewhat dry during its winter rest. Soil that is too wet in winter will cause leaf yellowing and leaf drop. Feed infrequently to keep the foliage oils strong for flavoring and to control the size (it can grow to 40' in the wild). Repot when roots fill the pot; prune the roots to put the plant back in the same pot. Prune out some of the crown to reduce the stress of root pruning. Sweet bay can be sheared into hedges and topiary shapes. It benefits from spending the summer outdoors in a bright but indirectly lit spot.

PROPAGATION: Propagate by taking 4–6" cuttings in early summer after the new growth has hardened somewhat. Remove all but one or two leaves, dip in rooting hormone, and insert in sterile potting soil. Cover with a plastic tent for extra humidity. Be aware that sweet bay is difficult to root.

PESTS AND DISEASES: Control scale with horticultural oil. Moving the plant outdoors in summer allows natural predators to keep scale in check. Be sure to wash carefully any leaves you use for cooking.

RELATED SPECIES: The cultivar 'Aurea' has yellowish young foliage. 'Angustifolia' has willow-shaped leaves. 'Undulata' has leaves with wavy margins.

The leaves of sweet bay can be used straight from the plant for seasoning food and will surprise you with much more flavor than the dried ones from the grocery.

LIVING STONES

Lithops spp. *LITH-ups*

Living stones' succulent leaves resemble small stones or rocks.

SIZE: 2"h × 4"w
TYPE: Succulent
FORM: Round
TEXTURE: Medium
GROWTH: Slow
LIGHT: High
MOISTURE: Low

SOIL: Cactus mix
FEATURES: Leaves like stones
USES: Dish garden, cactus garden
FLOWERS: ■□

SITING: These oddities of the plant world have evolved to have only one pair of leaves that are plump water storage organs. They resemble stones in their natural habitat, so are left alone by grazing animals. When grown in high light, they produce a daisylike flower from between the two leaves. In lower light, they stretch, lose their stonelike appearance, and can die. Give living stones direct sun, cool to hot temperatures, and low humidity (below 30 percent), and they will live a long time. Keep the plant at 50–55°F in winter. It will not tolerate stagnant air, so keep it well-ventilated, using a fan if necessary.

CARE: Living stones needs very little water. Even more than cactus, it will quickly rot if overwatered. Water only when the soil feels dry. At the end of October, cease watering and let the plant dry completely. For the next few months, it will produce a new set of leaves, consuming the moisture from the old pair which will shrivel. Avoid watering the plants during this time. When new leaves appear in early spring, begin watering again. Soak the soil well, allow it

Living stones grow best in the same conditions as cactus— hot and dry—and benefit from an attractive stone mulch.

to drain completely, then let it dry out a bit before watering again. The general rule is when in doubt about watering, don't. Feed the plants with foliage plant food once a year when the new leaves are fully formed. Living stones has a miniscule root system, so it doesn't need repotting. Once the old leaves and flower stalk have shriveled, use tweezers to remove them. Occasionally wipe off the leaves.

PROPAGATION: Living stones is traditionally propagated from seed. If your plant produces a flower, you can harvest your own seed. Otherwise, order from a supplier. Sprinkle the seeds on moist potting mix and provide bottom heat. Germination can take from 2 days to 2 weeks. When the seedlings are about 6 months old, they are sturdy enough to handle and pot up.

PESTS AND DISEASES: Mice can be troublesome for plants that spend the summer outdoors.

RELATED SPECIES: Species and cultivars vary widely in their leaf markings.

CHINESE FAN PALM

Livistona chinensis *liv-ih-STONE-uh chih-NEN-sis*

Chinese fan palms have a magnificent stature, useful in a vast room where an architectural accent is needed.

SIZE: 12'h × 12'w
TYPE: Palm
FORM: Vase
TEXTURE: Coarse
GROWTH: Medium
LIGHT: High

MOISTURE: Dry
SOIL: Potting soil
FEATURES: Fan-shaped fronds
USES: Architectural accent

SITING: Chinese fan palm looks its best when given bright light and some direct sun. In lower light its magnificent fronds fade to lime green and generally look unhealthy. It thrives in average temperatures (60–75°F) and average humidity (30–60 percent). Make sure you have plenty of room for these large plants. They are not easily kept to smaller proportions, and the fronds will appear ragged if they brush against walls, windows or furniture.

CARE: Allow the soil to dry about an inch deep before watering. Soak the plant well and discard the runoff. The plant should not sit in water. Yellow leaves may result from underwatering; brown spots on the leaves can come from overwatering or chemicals in the water. Feed with foliage plant food every month to keep the color.

Palms of all types perform best when somewhat pot-bound, so you will seldom have to repot a Chinese fan palm. Occasionally remove browned leaves at the bottom and snip the brown tips off the fronds.

PROPAGATION: Propagate by seed, available from suppliers.

PESTS AND DISEASES: Spider mites may appear if the plant is grown in low humidity. Wash the leaves frequently to control these pests. Scale insects can be easily taken care of with a cotton swab dipped in horticultural oil.

RELATED SPECIES: Other species in the genus are grown as outdoor landscape plants. *L. chinensis* is the only one that is grown as a houseplant.

JEWEL ORCHID
Ludisia discolor lew-DEE-see-uh dis-CUH-ler

Jewel orchid has rich velvety maroon foliage that is wonderful even without the stalks of dainty white miniature orchids.

SIZE: 6"h × 12"w
TYPE: Orchid
FORM: Trailing
TEXTURE: Medium
GROWTH: Slow
LIGHT: Medium to low
MOISTURE: Evenly moist

SOIL: Potting soil
FEATURES: Velvety maroon leaves
USES: Focal point, hanging basket, terrarium
FLOWERS: □

SITING: This terrestrial orchid is a lovely addition to a dish garden or as a display piece for the foliage alone. It is easy to grow. The tall spikes hold tiny, perfectly formed white and yellow blossoms. Jewel orchid grows well in medium light and tolerates low light. It needs warmth (70°F or above) and high humidity (above 60 percent) to look its best.

CARE: Keep evenly moist year round. Feed once a month with foliage plant food diluted to half strength. Seldom does jewel orchid need repotting, because it has a fairly small root system. If you choose to

The white flower spikes are set off by the darker striped foliage.

move the plant outdoors in summer, keep it in low light under a tree or shrub where it will receive rain and air movement but no direct sun. Remove the occasional dead leaf and old leaf sheaths to avoid giving scale insects a place to hide.

PROPAGATION: Stem cuttings root readily; the plant can also be layered. The creeping stems automatically root at the nodes, so find a rooted one and sever it from the main plant. Or pin one and wait for it to root. The plant can also be divided.

PESTS AND DISEASES: Scrape off scale insects with your finger and gently wash the leaves frequently. Horticultural oil may harm the plant.

RELATED SPECIES: The *Ludisia discolor* called "type form" has almost black leaves and silvery veins.

SNOWBALL CACTUS
Mammillaria bocasana mam-mil-AIR-ee-uh bok-uh-SAHN-uh

Snowball cactus is easy to grow, and although it looks soft and lush, the hairs hide spines that can prick.

SIZE: 4–6"h × 6–12"w
TYPE: Cactus
FORM: Mounded
TEXTURE: Coarse
GROWTH: Slow
LIGHT: High

MOISTURE: Low
SOIL: Cactus mix
FEATURES: Fuzzy, interlocking hairs
USES: Cactus garden, focal point
FLOWERS: ■

SITING: Snowball cactus is easy for the beginner to grow. Its soft, cuddly look is deceiving; the interlocking hairs that give the fuzzy appearance actually cover hooked central spines that can catch a finger easily. As with all cacti, snowball cactus needs high light. If light in the home is perfect, it produces rings of flowers, followed by red fruits. Provide average to hot (65°F and above) temperatures in spring and summer and cool (50–60°F) temperatures in winter. It prefers low humidity. This is a plant to grow on a dry, exposed windowsill. this location will keep the plant out of traffic, where its spines can inflict painful wounds.

CARE: Snowball cactus needs little water most of the time. Let it dry out completely between waterings, then soak it just as a desert rain would do. It must have perfect drainage, however, or it will rot. Low light may also cause it to rot. In winter give this cactus a cooler, drier resting time. Feed three times in summer with a general-purpose plant food. Repot annually.

PROPAGATION: Propagate by seed and division of the crown as it splits.

PESTS AND DISEASES: Mealybugs may appear beneath the hairs. Dab them with horticultural oil on a cotton swab.

RELATED SPECIES: *M. b.* ssp. *eschauzieri* has longer hairs and pale yellow flowers. *M. densispina* remains as a single ball.

1 The crown of snowball cactus splits into many "snowballs." These offsets can be separated to form new plants.

2 Pot the offsets in a fast-draining cactus mix and set them in a protected place until they form roots.

PRAYER PLANT
Maranta leuconeura *muh-RAN-tuh lew-co-NEW-ruh*

Prayer plant is well recognized by its beautifully variegated foliage in shades of green and maroon.

SIZE: 12"h × 12"w
TYPE: Herbaceous
FORM: Mounded
TEXTURE: Coarse
GROWTH: Slow
LIGHT: Low to medium
MOISTURE: Evenly moist
SOIL: Potting soil
FEATURES: Striped leaves
USES: Foliage, dish garden
FLOWERS: ☐

SITING: Prayer plant is a must-have in a foliage plant collection because of its unique coloration and interesting habit of folding up vertically in the evening. In perfect conditions the plant produces small white flowers with purple spots. This slow-growing plant takes little care if given low to medium light. It thrives in average home temperatures (60–75°F) and tolerates hot temperatures as well. Provide average humidity (30–60 percent); if the leaves begin to brown on the edges, increase the humidity with a pebble tray or humidifier.

CARE: Keep evenly moist. Feed three times a year in summer with all-purpose foliage plant food. Repot only when it is difficult to water the plant, usually once every couple of years. Remove any dead leaves. Wash the leaves monthly to keep spider mites at bay and to clean the leaves so the attractive colors will be at their brightest. The plant may suffer from root rot if overwatered. Leaves will turn pale in too much light and will curl and brown if the plant is too cool or in a draft.

PROPAGATION: Propagate by dividing the root ball, by cutting off rhizomes and potting them, or by stem cuttings.

PESTS AND DISEASES: Spider mites and mealybugs may become pests on prayer plant, but usually only in low humidity.

RELATED SPECIES: 'Massangeana' has dark olive leaves with a silver midrib and veins. Herringbone plant (*M. l.* var. *erythroneura*) has olive to black leaves with bright red markings.

Prayer plant has a habit of folding its leaves upright at night, resembling praying hands.

SENSITIVE PLANT
Mimosa pudica *mim-OH-suh PEW-di-kuh*

Sensitive plants are perfect conversations pieces with their soft gray-green leaflets and pink plumy blossoms.

SIZE: 18"h × 18"w
TYPE: Woody shrub
FORM: Mounded
TEXTURE: Fine
GROWTH: Fast
LIGHT: Medium to high
MOISTURE: Evenly moist
SOIL: Potting soil
FEATURES: Leaflets fold up when touched
USES: Conversation piece
FLOWERS: ▦

SITING: Sensitive plant is a wonderful plant for a child to enjoy. It is softly textured and has the delightful habit of folding its leaves up tightly when stroked. It does have small spines, so it's wise to be cautious. If grown in high light, it may produce pink puffball flowers, a delight to children. The plants thrive at temperatures of 65–80°F. If temperatures fall below this level, the leaves will yellow and drop.

The plant's leaves fold when it is softly touched or brushed, giving rise to its alternate common name, touch-me-not.

CARE: To keep sensitive plant from dropping its leaves, keep moist except during the winter rest period, when watering should be reduced somewhat. This plant can draw nitrogen from the air and fix it in its roots. It needs infrequent feeding—only once or twice a year with a foliage plant food. Sensitive plant will grow woody with age. Repot annually until it becomes unattractive, then discard the plant. Remove faded leaves.

PROPAGATION: Sensitive plant is easily started from the seeds that are prolifically produced when the plant blooms. When the pods ripen, remove the seeds and soak them for 24 hours in hot water. After the seeds have swelled, plant them in sterile potting soil and keep the humidity high until the seeds germinate. Plants can also be propagated by semihardwood stem cuttings, although the success rate for this method is limited.

PESTS AND DISEASES: Spider mites can be a problem, especially in low humidity, so keep the humidity up and give the plant a monthly shower to keep populations low.

RELATED SPECIES: No other *Mimosa* species is grown indoors.

SPLIT-LEAF PHILODENDRON
Monstera deliciosa *mon-STAIR-uh deh-lih-see-OH-suh*

Split-leaf philodendron is also known as Swiss-cheese plant or monstera.

SIZE: 10'h × 10'w
TYPE: Vine
FORM: Upright
TEXTURE: Coarse
GROWTH: Slow
LIGHT: Low to medium

MOISTURE: Dry
SOIL: Potting soil
FEATURES: Cut leaves
USES: Architectural accent
FLOWERS: ■□

SITING: Monstera is a large plant that needs the proper site to look good. If it is grown upright, the leaf shapes will change from juvenile to mature. Monstera has heavy stems with long pinkish aerial roots. If grown in the right conditions, it may produce greenish-white flowers followed by edible fruits that taste somewhat like custard when ripe. (All other parts of the plant are toxic to ingest, and the fruits may be irritating to some people.) Grow monstera in low to medium light, average home temperatures (60–75°F), and low humidity (below 30 percent).

CARE: Allow it to dry somewhat between waterings during active growth, then let it dry out a bit more during the winter rest. Feed three times in summer with foliage

The thick aerial roots can be attached to a moss or bark pole to train the philodendron to have a more upright appearance.

plant food at regular strength and repot infrequently. Prune regularly to maintain a particular size, although trying to make much smaller is seldom successful. Give the plant monthly showers to keep the glossy leaves clean and reduce the incidence of spider mites. Small leaves or leaves with no splits may indicate that the light is too low. Browning leaves indicate too much water. Do not cut off the aerial roots. Direct them back into the potting soil or into a moss pole to give the plant some support. Otherwise it will lean and become unwieldy in the home. Moss poles are a simple way to train the plant, and the damp moss gives the plant some moisture and nutrients.

PROPAGATION: Propagate by stem cuttings and layering. Simply cut off a stem tip with an aerial root and pot it up. If a stem has an aerial root already in the soil, sever the new plant and pot it up.

PESTS AND DISEASES: Spider mites, scale, and whiteflies can be deterred by frequently wiping and washing the leaves.

RELATED SPECIES: The cultivar 'Variegata' has creamy yellow patches that revert to green. 'Albovariegata' has white patches.

SWEET MYRTLE
Myrtus communis *MUR-tiss kuh-MUNE-iss*

Sweet myrtle is a lovely fine-textured plant with glossy dark leaves and attractive diminutive blossoms.

SIZE: 6'h × 3'w
TYPE: Woody shrub
FORM: Upright
TEXTURE: Fine
GROWTH: Slow
LIGHT: Medium to high
MOISTURE: Evenly moist

SOIL: Potting soil
FEATURES: Glossy leaves, attractive flowers
USES: Topiary, bonsai
FLOWERS: □■

SITING: Sweet myrtle is a popular plant for topiary and bonsai because of its adaptation to shearing. The glossy leaves are attractive enough by themselves when the plant is grown in medium light; if the plant is grown in bright, indirect light, it will often produce voluminous small, starry pink or white blossoms. The plants tolerate cool to average home temperatures (55–75°F) and high humidity (above 60 percent). Use a pebble tray or pot-in-pot system to boost the humidity.

Myrtle accepts pruning quite well and is an excellent candidate for training as a bonsai or topiary accent.

CARE: Keep evenly moist. It may lose its leaves if allowed to dry out and it may show some tip chlorosis if the soil is not well drained. When grown in high light, myrtle will suffer if even one watering is missed. Feed with foliage plant food according to label directions. Repot annually or at least every 2 years. It may be worth root-pruning when you repot to keep the plant within bounds. Sweet myrtle naturally gets large but can be kept small by regular pruning. It will tolerate pruning all the way back to stubs and will leaf out again quickly, which is why it is popular for topiary.

PROPAGATION: Propagate by semihardwood cuttings in early summer. Cuttings must be rooted in high humidity. The plants can be propagated by seed as well.

PESTS AND DISEASES: Sweet myrtle can have a myriad of problems, especially when grown in lower light and lower humidity. Watch for spider mites, scale, mealybugs, and whiteflies. All can be controlled with horticultural oil.

RELATED SPECIES: The cultivar 'Variegata' has creamy white margins. 'Microphylla' has tiny leaves and grows to only 2' high.

GUPPY PLANT

Nematanthus spp. *nee-muh-TAN-thuss*

Guppy plants offer striking glossy foliage and unusually shaped brightly colored blossoms on vining stems.

SIZE: 2–4'h × 2–4'w
TYPE: Gesneriad
FORM: Trailing
TEXTURE: Fine
GROWTH: Moderate
LIGHT: Bright to medium

MOISTURE: Dry
SOIL: Potting soil
FEATURES: Glossy leaves, flowers
USES: Hanging basket
FLOWERS: ■ ■ ■

SITING: Bright to medium light, away from direct sun, will keep guppy plant looking its best. If the plant won't flower, move it into higher filtered light. Provide temperatures of 65–80°F for the plant to blossom. In winter, reduce temperatures to 50–55°F and reduce watering. High humidity is a necessity, as with most gesneriads. A pebble tray works well to achieve this.

CARE: Guppy plant is somewhat epiphytic, so allow the soil to dry slightly between waterings. When the plant is not actively growing, avoid wetting the foliage or it may develop fungal leaf spots. Reducing watering for 6–8 weeks may induce flowering. Feed every 2 weeks with half-strength plant food for blooming plants during active growth. Every month flush the soil with clear water to wash away fertilizer salts. Repotting is seldom needed; guppy plant blooms best when pot-bound.

Prune back wayward stems regularly to keep the plant full and appealing. Guppy plant will drop its leaves when it gets too cold or too dry, or is overfertilized.

PROPAGATION: Propagate by stem or tip cuttings. When you prune back long stems to keep the plant looking good, simply insert the cuttings in rooting hormone, then into sterile potting soil. Cover with plastic to keep the humidity up, and in a few weeks the cuttings will be rooted.

PESTS AND DISEASES: Watch for aphids, spider mites, and whiteflies. The plant will generally not have a problem unless cultural details are not attended to.

RELATED SPECIES: *N. crassifolius* has dangling orange-red blossoms. *N. corticola* has orange flowers that dangle on 3–4"-long pedicels (flower stalks). *N. gregarius* 'Golden West' has variegated foliage. 'Christmas Holly' has intensely glossy foliage and bright red flowers.

BLUSHING BROMELIAD

Neoregelia carolinae *nee-oh-reg-EEL-ee-uh kair-oh-LIN-ay*

Blushing bromeliads have attractive variegated foliage that turns bright pink at the base as the plant begins to blossom.

SIZE: 1–2'h × 1–2'w
TYPE: Bromeliad
FORM: Vase-shaped
TEXTURE: Medium
GROWTH: Slow
LIGHT: High to medium

MOISTURE: Dry
SOIL: Epiphyte mix
FEATURES: Striped leaves, colorful vase
USES: Focal point, blooming
FLOWERS: ■ □

SITING: Blushing bromeliad shows its best leaf color in bright, filtered light. The "vase" turns from pinkish to bright crimson when the plant begins to flower. It will not tolerate direct sun. It does well in medium light although it will not be as symmetrical and tight, and the leaves may fade somewhat. Provide average to hot temperatures (60°F and above) to prevent rotting. High humidity (above 65 percent) will keep this bromeliad looking good.

CARE: Let the soil dry out almost completely between waterings, and keep the vase full of water. Every couple of months, empty and refill the vase to keep the water somewhat fresh. Feed with blooming plant food three times in summer, or add half-strength formula to

These epiphytes are best kept moist by keeping the vase formed by the leaf bases filled with water.

the vase every month. Blushing bromeliad has a miniscule root system that will seldom outgrow a pot. Repot only when the potting mix begins to break down and no longer has recognizable chunks of bark. This bromeliad can be grown on a slab, but high humidity is essential. The plant may develop leaf spots in low humidity and root rot if overwatered.

PROPAGATION: Propagate by removing the offsets or side shoots when they are about one-third the size of the parent plant (they will not root if taken when too young). Take the plant out of the pot and gently pull off each offset, making sure it has some roots. Pot up the offsets and keep them in a warm, bright spot until they establish themselves. Water daily. A plant started this way should bloom in 1–2 years. You can also propagate blushing bromeliad by seed in spring. Collect the seeds as they ripen, and place them on moist paper towels in a covered plastic container. Check daily for mold, and leave the lid off briefly for air exchange. When the plant has five leaves, it is ready to pot up. Expect a blooming plant in 6–8 years.

PESTS AND DISEASES: Treat scale and spider mites with insecticidal soap.

RELATED SPECIES: The cultivar 'Tricolor' is most commonly grown. Its leaves have a chartreuse center, dark green margins, and blushing pink in the center of the vase, which turns carmine red when it blossoms.

BOSTON FERN

Nephrolepis exaltata *neh-froh-LEP-iss ex-all-TAH-tuh*

Boston fern, also known as sword fern, has been a favorite for centuries with its arching fronds and delicate foliage.

SIZE: 2'h × 4'w
TYPE: Fern
FORM: Arching
TEXTURE: Fine
GROWTH: Fast
LIGHT: Medium

MOISTURE: Evenly moist
SOIL: Potting soil
FEATURES: Arching fronds
USES: Hanging basket, focal point

SITING: Boston fern has a lush, rich appearance in medium to bright, indirect light and average home temperatures (60–75°F). It needs high humidity (above 60 percent). A common site for these moisture lovers is in a bathroom, where the humidity is naturally high. Keep Boston fern out of the way of high traffic, and where the dropping leaflets will not be noticeable.

CARE: Keep moist but well drained. Feed three times in summer, or with foliage plant food according to label directions. Boston fern fills a pot quickly and should

Most ferns need plenty of humidity. Insert one pot inside another filled with moist sphagnum moss to raise moisture levels.

be repotted annually. Regular root pruning will also keep the plant vigorous. It drops brown leaflets constantly, especially in drafts, so give the plant a good shaking to dislodge the dead leaflets. Any change in a cultural condition will cause leaf drop. Prune out any brown fronds at the base of the plant. Wash the leaves often to keep pests at bay and to keep the plant looking its best.

PROPAGATION: Propagate by dividing the crown. Pull the plant from its pot, cut the crown apart at its obvious joints, and repot the portions. To propagate from spores, wait until the spore cases on the back of the fronds ripen, then tap the spores onto a piece of paper. Scatter the spores on moist, sterile potting mix and cover the container with glass or plastic.

PESTS AND DISEASES: Boston fern is susceptible to scale and mealybugs. Treat both pests with horticultural oil.

RELATED SPECIES: Erect sword fern (*N. cordifolia*) has more fronds that stand more upright than Boston fern. 'Fluffy Ruffles' has curly fronds. 'Dallas' is more compact and does better in low light. 'Golden Boston' has golden-yellow fronds.

BUNNY EAR CACTUS

Opuntia microdasys *o-PUN-tee-uh my-crow-DAY-siss*

SIZE: 18–24"h × 18–24"w
TYPE: Cactus
FORM: Upright
TEXTURE: Coarse
GROWTH: Slow
LIGHT: High
MOISTURE: Low
SOIL: Cactus mix
FEATURES: Flattened "ears" with yellow spines
USES: Cactus garden, southwest theme
FLOWERS: ■ ■ ■

Bunny ear cactus can give you a carefree southwestern focal point provided that it gets high light and low humidity.

SITING: Bunny ear cactus needs full sun to bloom. The yellow or sometimes pink or red flowers are often followed by edible fruits. Keep the plant warm (65–85°F) when in active growth and provide cooler temperatures (55–60°F) during its dormant period in winter. Low humidity (20–30 percent) will keep it looking its

best. High humidity often causes leaf scarring. Be sure to site this plant away from traffic. The large spines are troublesome to passersby, but the smaller glochids (barbed hairs) that are formed in each tubercle (nodule of spines) are just as irritating, because they stick easily into skin and clothing.

CARE: Let dry out considerably between waterings during active growth, and even

These cactus tolerate pruning for propagating new plants or for shaping.

more so during the dormant stage. Feed with half-strength plant food only after flower buds form. Bunny ear cactus has a very small root system, like other cactus, so repotting is seldom necessary. This is one of the few cactuses that can be pruned. Do so by removing a pad. If pruned in summer, new growth will start forming at the cut. When pruning or handling bunny ear cactus, grasp the ears with gloves or several layers of newspaper to avoid the glochids becoming imbedded in your skin. The most common problem with bunny ear cactus is root rot from overwatering. Occasionally a plant will die from overwatering yet remain standing until someone knocks it over and finds that it is hollow inside.

PROPAGATION: Propagate by stem cuttings. Remove a pad and let it sit for several days to callus. Then set it in potting mix.

PESTS AND DISEASES: Mealybugs and scale may be hidden under the spines. Aphids may appear on the flowers.

RELATED SPECIES: *O. m.* var. *albospinna* has white glochids. *O. m.* var. *rufida* has reddish-brown glochids.

SWEET OLIVE
Osmanthus fragrans oz-MAN-thus FRAY-grans

Sweet olives are a must-have for fragrance year-round even though the plant itself is a subtle addition to a foliage plant collection.

SIZE: 1–2'h × 1'w
TYPE: Woody shrub
FORM: Rounded
TEXTURE: Medium
GROWTH: Slow
LIGHT: High to medium
MOISTURE: Dry
SOIL: Potting soil
FEATURES: Glossy leaves, fragrant blossoms
USES: Fragrance, foliage
FLOWERS: ☐

SITING: This unassuming plant will knock you over with its citrusy, jasminelike scent. It tolerates full sun, indirect bright light and even medium light, average to high temperatures (60°F and above), and average to low humidity (60 percent and below).
CARE: Water once a week and feed with foliage plant food once or twice a year. Repot only every 2–3 years. Move outdoors

The tiny white or cream blossoms of sweet olive are intensely fragrant, with hints of citrus and jasmine.

to a protected spot in summer. Pruning is unnecessary, because even the branches that have few leaves will bear flowers. In fact pruning out what looks like dead wood will prune off the flowering wood. So it's best left alone. Sweet olive does benefit from periodic washing of the leaves. If you forget to water for a long while, it will still have green leaves. However, one shake and they will all fall.
PROPAGATION: Propagate from semihardwood cuttings, although the success rate is not high. In early summer after the new growth has hardened somewhat, take 3–4" cuttings, remove all but one leaf, dip in rooting hormone, and insert in sterile potting soil. Tent with plastic until the cuttings have rooted.
PESTS AND DISEASES: Spider mites may be a problem in very dry locations but can be controlled with regular hosing off. Scale may also appear. Treat with horticultural oil.
RELATED SPECIES: The cultivar 'Aurantiacus' has orange flowers. *O. ×fortunei,* a hybrid cross between *O. fragrans* and *O. hererophyllus,* has the same leaves as *O. fragrans* but larger flowers.

FALSE HOLLY
Osmanthus heterophyllus oz-MAN-thus het-ur-oh-FILL-us

False holly has striking hollylike leaves that make an delightful statement in a foliage plant collection.

SIZE: 1–2'h × 1'w
TYPE: Woody shrub
FORM: Rounded
TEXTURE: Medium
GROWTH: Slow
LIGHT: High to medium
MOISTURE: Dry
SOIL: Potting soil
FEATURES: Hollylike leaves
USES: Foliage, focal point
FLOWERS: ☐

SITING: False holly tolerates full sun, indirect, bright light and even medium light, average to high temperatures (60°F and above), and average to low humidity (60 percent and below).

CARE: Water once a week, and feed with foliage plant food once or twice a year. Repot every 2–3 years. Move outdoors to a protected spot in summer. Pruning only to shape the plant. False holly does benefit from periodic washing of the leaves. The plant remains green even when dried out, so don't rely on leaf changes to remind you to water. It's possible to forget to water for a long while and the plant will still have green leaves. However one shake and they will all fall.
PROPAGATION: Propagate from semi-hardwood cuttings, although the success rate is not high. In early summer take 3–5" cuttings; remove all but one leaf, dip in rooting hormone, and insert in sterile potting soil. Tent with plastic until the cuttings have rooted.
PESTS AND DISEASES: Spider mites may be a problem in very dry locations but can be controlled with regular hosing off, particularly the undersides of the leaves, and horticultural oil. Scale may also appear.
RELATED SPECIES: The cultivar 'Variegatus' has variegated foliage. 'Goshiki' (freckle face holly) has gold-flecked leaves.

1 Propagate by taking 3–5" semihardwood cuttings in early summer.

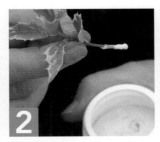

2 Dip the cuttings in rooting hormone, tapping off the excess powder.

3 Stick cuttings in holes, tamp gently, water, and cover with plastic.

OXALIS
Oxalis regnellii *ocks-AL-iss reg-NEL-ee-eye*

Oxalis, also known as purple shamrock, is grown for its clover-shaped leaves as well as its soft pink and white flowers.

SIZE: 12"h × 12"w
TYPE: Bulb
FORM: Mounded
TEXTURE: Fine
GROWTH: Medium
LIGHT: High, indirect
MOISTURE: Evenly moist
SOIL: Potting soil
FEATURES: Velvety leaves
USES: Focal point
FLOWERS: □ ▨

SITING: Provide oxalis with bright, indirect light during most of the year. It tolerates full sun in winter if it is actively growing. Daytime temperatures should be 65–75°F and nighttime temperatures around 55–60°F. More warmth than this will cause the plant to go into dormancy faster. Keep oxalis away from drafts and provide average humidity (30–60 percent).
CARE: Keep evenly moist when the plant is actively growing; the soil must be well-drained to prevent waterlogging. The plant may develop brown spots on the leaves if it is overwatered and yellow leaves if underwatered. Feed with half-strength foliage plant food weekly while growing. Remove spent flowers and leaves. If your plant does not bloom, it may be too young; in an older plant, it may need dormancy. Give the plant a shower occasionally to rinse the dust off the leaves. After oxalis finishes blooming, it begins to go into a dormant phase. Gradually reduce water and gently pull off the spent leaves. Once the foliage is gone, store the bulbs in soil in a cool, dark spot for 1–3 months. When green shoots appear, bring the pot back into a sunny window and begin watering and feeding.
PROPAGATION: Small bulbs can be separated when you repot the plant. Simply sever or pull them off and pot them up, making sure that they are about ½" below the soil line.
PESTS AND DISEASES: When grown in dry conditions, oxalis may have spider mites. Leaves go off-color long before you see any webbing. Control with frequent showers.
RELATED SPECIES: Lucky plant (*O. tetraphylla*) has triangular leaves and reddish-purple flowers. *O. purpurea* is only 4" tall with dark green leaves and pink flowers. Wood sorrel (*O. acetosella*) is dark green with rosy-pink blossoms.

1 To propagate an oxalis plant, simply lift the plant out of its pot and gently separate the tubers.

2 Repot the tubers in clean potting soil, making sure they are about ½" below the soil line.

LOLLIPOP PLANT
Pachystachys lutea *pak-ee-STAK-iss LOOT-ee-uh*

Lollipop plant has long-lasting yellow bracts that reveal sparkling white blossoms.

SIZE: 18"h × 18"w
TYPE: Woody shrub
FORM: Rounded
TEXTURE: Coarse
GROWTH: Medium
LIGHT: High, indirect
MOISTURE: Evenly moist
SOIL: Potting soil
FEATURES: Rich green rugose leaves
USES: Accent
FLOWERS: ▨ □

SITING: The most striking feature of lollipop plant is its yellow "candles," flower stalks that rise high above the leaves. These stalks are adorned with golden-yellow bracts from which white flowers arise. This plant effectively blooms from spring until fall if given bright, indirect light in summer and full sun in winter. It thrives in temperatures of 60–75°F and not below 55°F at night. It needs high humidity (60 percent and above).
CARE: Keep evenly moist during active growth, with watering reduced somewhat during the plant's winter rest. Feed with foliage plant food according to label directions. Repot only when the plant seems to be too packed in the pot to take up water effectively. Prune back the stem tips before blooming to keep the plant compact. Shower off occasionally and move the plant outdoors in summer to stimulate growth. Low humidity may cause browning leaf edges and even leaf drop.
PROPAGATION: Propagate by taking stem cuttings in spring or summer. Take 3–5" stem tips, dip in rooting hormone, and insert into sterile potting soil. Provide bottom heat for the best success in rooting.
PESTS AND DISEASES: Treat mealybugs with horticultural oil.
RELATED SPECIES: *P. coccinea* has bright red flowers in green bracts.

Before the plant begins to bloom, pinch back the stem tips to keep the plant shrubby and compact.

Propagate new plants by dipping the stem tips in rooting hormone and sticking them in sterile potting mix.

SCREW PINE
Pandanus veitchii *pan-DAN-us VET-chih-eye*

Screw pine is a unique architectural accent for a spot that is hot and in direct sun. It can spend the summer outdoors.

SIZE: 4'h × 4'w
TYPE: Palmlike
FORM: Upright
TEXTURE: Coarse
GROWTH: Medium
LIGHT: High

MOISTURE: Dry
SOIL: Cactus mix
FEATURES: Sword-shaped foliage
USES: Architectural accent

SITING: Screw pine has 2–3' long leaves that are variegated with creamy bands. They are arranged in 3 spiralling ranks, forming a terminal rosette of foliage.

The leaves are slightly serrated and can hurt a passerby, so site the plant away from traffic. A well-grown plant will be tall with an arching crown on an attractive trunk, with many aerial roots alongside it. In its native Polynesia, these aerial rootlets act as prop roots when they come into contact with the soil. It withstands high light, including direct sun during the winter and tolerates high temperatures, so it is an excellent choice for a hot, sunny site. Provide low humidity (below 30 percent).

CARE: Allow the soil to dry slightly between waterings and reduce watering somewhat during the winter rest time. Feed monthly with a balanced foliage plant food. Repot every 2–3 years. Screw pine sends aerial roots toward the soil as it ages. The roots should not be removed but encouraged to root near the trunk so they can provide support for the increasingly heavy crown. Wash the foliage carefully once a month and remove any damaged or unsightly leaves. Move the plant outdoors for the summer.

PROPAGATION: Propagate by removing basal suckers when they are about 6" long and pot them up. Use rooting hormone and bottom heat until they root. Screw pine can also be propagated by seed from a supplier. Soak the seeds for 24 hours before sowing. Screw pine plants are either male or female, and only the female produces fruits and seeds when pollinated by a nearby male. Because the plant is unlikely to bloom indoors, you will likely have to purchase seed from a nursery that specializes in unusual houseplants if you wish to grow plants from seed.

PESTS AND DISEASES: Control scale and spider mites with horticultural oil. Keeping the foliage clean will help eliminate spider mites. You can also keep spider mites at bay by washing the foliage occasionally with a forceful spray of water. If screw pine receives excess humidity and moisture basal stem rot, anthracnose, and leaf spot can occur.

RELATED SPECIES: *P. utilis* is a green-leaved form with red spines that is similar in all other aspects to *P. veitchii*.

DEVIL'S BACKBONE
Pedilanthus tithymaloides *ped-ill-AN-thus tith-ee-mal-OY-deez*

Devil's backbone resembles a euphorbia with interesting zigzagged succulent stems. This cultivar is 'Variegatus'.

SIZE: 3'h × 1'w
TYPE: Succulent
FORM: Upright
TEXTURE: Medium
GROWTH: Medium
LIGHT: High
MOISTURE: Low

SOIL: Cactus
FEATURES: Zigzag stems
USES: Succulent garden, accent
FLOWERS: ■

SITING: Devil's backbone gets its name from the habit of leaves growing along the stem in zigzag fashion. It will retain the best color with bright, indirect light, although it will tolerate some winter sun. Daytime temperatures are best kept at 70–85°F; nighttime temperatures should be 50–70°F. Provide low humidity (below 30 percent).

CARE: Keep the soil moderately dry, allowing it to dry slightly between soakings. Watch for root rot if the plant is overwatered. If kept very dry, it will have attractive stems and blossoms but no leaves. But if given the right amount of water, it will produce attractive leaves. The plant must have a near-dormant winter rest to initiate its red flowers, which are borne in terminal clusters. Feed only three times in summer with foliage plant food. The plant has a small root system, so repot infrequently. Prune as needed to shape the plant, but beware that the sap is somewhat caustic.

PROPAGATION: Propagate by stem cuttings. Take 3–5" cuttings from the tips or middle of the stems, let sit to dry for 2–3 days, then pot up in sterile potting soil. Devil's backbone can also be propagated by seed.

PESTS AND DISEASES: This plant has almost no pests. Powdery mildew and leaf spots are occasional problems.

RELATED SPECIES: The cultivar 'Variegatus' has creamy variegation and pink to red leaf edges. It is the form most commonly available commercially.

Because devil's backbone prefers low humidity, clean leaves by wiping them with a soft cloth rather than washing the foliage.

LEMON-SCENTED GERANIUM
Pelargonium crispum *pel-ar-GOHN-ee-um KRIS-pum*

Lemon-scented geraniums will be graced with soft pink blossoms when grown in a south or west window.

SIZE: 12"h × 12"w
TYPE: Herbaceous
FORM: Mounded
TEXTURE: Medium
GROWTH: Medium
LIGHT: High
MOISTURE: Dry

SOIL: Potting soil
FEATURES: Fuzzy, scented foliage
USES: Focal point, foliage
FLOWERS: ■

SITING: Scented geraniums are renowned for the delicious scent of the leaves when brushed or crushed. These plants also have attractive enough foliage to stand as a foil for other plants or as a unique potted plant on their own. Scented geraniums are best grown in a south or west window to give them high light to promote blooming. Give them lower light in winter if you want to overwinter them without blooming. Provide cooler temperatures in low light or they will fail. Provide average warmth (60–75°F) when growing them on a windowsill. Reddening of the leaves indicates that conditions are too cool.

CARE: Water thoroughly, then allow the soil to dry between waterings. Overwatering is one of the most common problems with scented geraniums. Feed with foliage plant food according to label directions. It is seldom necessary to repot plants. Pinch stem tips often to encourage shrubbiness and remove yellow or brown leaves as they appear.

PROPAGATION: Propagate by stem cuttings. Snip stem tips and middle sections about 3" long, leaving only one leaf. Allow the cuttings to dry for a day, then insert them in sterile potting mix with a plastic tent. Cuttings should be rooted in 2–3 weeks.

PESTS AND DISEASES: Whiteflies and aphids may be troublesome, particularly when the plant is initially brought indoors in fall. Control both with horticultural oil. You may see blackening of stems during the winter, indicating fungal disease. This is difficult to control, so take cuttings of healthy stems to root and discard the original plant.

RELATED SPECIES: 'Peach Cream' has pink flowers and peach-scented leaves. 'Minor' has tiny leaves. 'Variegatum' is variegated.

1 Propagate by taking stem cuttings any time the plants are in full growth.

2 Snip off all but one or two small leaves on the 3" cuttings.

3 Dip the cuttings in rooting hormone, tapping off the excess powder.

4 Stick cuttings into holes in rooting media, firm in place, and water.

ROSE-SCENTED GERANIUM
Pelargonium graveolens *pel-ar-GOHN-ee-um gray-vee-OH-lenz*

Rose-scented geraniums will fill a room with lovely aroma when given the full sun they love.

SIZE: 3'h × 3'w
TYPE: Herbaceous
FORM: Mounded
TEXTURE: Medium
GROWTH: Medium
LIGHT: High
MOISTURE: Dry

SOIL: Potting soil
FEATURES: Fuzzy, scented foliage
USES: Focal point, foliage
FLOWERS: ■

SITING: Scented geraniums are renowned for the delicious scent of their leaves when brushed or crushed. These plants also have attractive enough foliage to stand as a foil for other plants or as a unique pot plant on their own. The leaves and blossoms are edible. Scented geraniums are best grown in a south or west window to give them high light to promote blooming. Give them lower light in winter to overwinter them without blooming. Provide cooler temperatures in low light or they will fail. Provide average warmth (60–75°F) when growing them on a windowsill.

CARE: Water thoroughly, then allow the soil to dry considerably between waterings. Overwatering is one of the most common problems with scented geraniums. Feed with foliage plant food according to label directions. It is seldom necessary to repot plants. Pinch stem tips often to encourage shrubbiness and remove yellow or brown leaves as they develop.

PROPAGATION: Scented geraniums are so easily propagated by stem cuttings that it's possible to give plants to your friends and to use them as bedding plants outdoors in summer. Snip stem tips and middle sections about 3" long, leaving only one leaf. Allow the cuttings to dry for a day, then insert them in sterile potting mix with a plastic tent. Cuttings should be rooted in 2–3 weeks.

PESTS AND DISEASES: Whiteflies and aphids may be troublesome, particularly when the plant is initially brought indoors in fall. Control both with horticultural oil. You may see blackening of stems during the winter, indicating fungal disease. This is difficult to control, so take cuttings of healthy stems to root and discard the original plant. Reddening of the leaves indicates that conditions are too cool.

RELATED SPECIES: The cultivar 'Variegatum' has lightly cream-tinged leaves.

PEPPERMINT-SCENTED GERANIUM
Pelargonium tomentosum *pel-ar-GOHN-ee-um toh-men-TOH-sum*

Peppermint-scented geraniums have fuzzy gray-green hairs that release the bright cleansing scent of peppermint when something brushes against the plant.

SIZE: 2'h × 2'w
TYPE: Herbaceous
FORM: Mounded
TEXTURE: Medium
GROWTH: Medium
LIGHT: High
MOISTURE: Dry

SOIL: Potting soil
FEATURES: Fuzzy, scented foliage
USES: Focal point, foliage
FLOWERS: ▩

SITING: Scented geraniums are renowned for the delicious scents of the leaves when brushed or crushed. These plants also have attractive enough foliage to stand as a foil for other plants or as a unique pot plant on their own. The leaves and blossoms are edible. Scented geraniums are best grown in a south or west window to give them high light to promote blooming. Give them lower light in winter if you want to overwinter them without blooming. Provide cooler temperatures in low light or they will fail. Provide average warmth (60–75°F) when growing them on a windowsill. Reddening of the leaves indicates that conditions are too cool.

CARE: Water thoroughly, then allow the soil to dry considerably between waterings. Overwatering is one of the most common problems with scented geraniums. Feed with foliage plant food according to label directions. It is seldom necessary to repot plants. Pinch stem tips often to encourage shrubbiness, and remove yellow or brown leaves that may appear.

PROPAGATION: Scented geraniums are so easily propagated by stem cuttings that it's possible to give plants to your friends and to use them as bedding plants outdoors in summer. Snip stem tips and middle sections about 3" long, leaving only one leaf. Allow the cuttings to dry for a day, then insert them in sterile potting mix with a plastic tent. Cuttings should be rooted in 2–3 weeks.

PESTS AND DISEASES: Whiteflies and aphids may be troublesome, particularly when the plant is initially brought indoors in fall. Control both with horticultural oil. You may see blackening of stems during the winter, indicating fungal disease. This is difficult to control, so take cuttings of healthy stems to root and discard the original plant.

RELATED SPECIES: The cultivar 'Chocolate Peppermint' has a chocolate-mint scent.

BUTTON FERN
Pellaea rotundifolia *pell-EE-uh roh-tun-dih-FOLE-ee-uh*

Button fern's unique round leaves are borne along glossy brown stems, lending great color to this fine-textured foliage plant.

SIZE: 6"h × 2'w
TYPE: Fern
FORM: Mounded
TEXTURE: Fine
GROWTH: Slow
LIGHT: Medium

MOISTURE: Evenly moist
SOIL: Potting soil
FEATURES: Glossy foliage on black stems
USES: Foliage

SITING: Button fern produces its buttonlike, round leaflets best in medium light. Grow in average to cool temperatures (55–75°F) and give at least average humidity (30–60 percent). Avoid placing the plant where it receives drying winds or drafts.

CARE: The fronds are somewhat leathery but they are not tolerant of drying out. Keep them moist all the time, because drying out even once can cause considerable leaf drop, from which the plant usually doesn't recover. Feed only three times in summer with foliage plant food. Repot annually into a moisture-retentive potting mix; as the pot fills with roots, the plant has a hard time getting adequate moisture. Remove brown fronds, which should be few if the plant is grown well. Shower off regularly to keep spider mites at bay.

PROPAGATION: Propagate by dividing the rhizomes or by growing from spores. Spores are borne on the underside edges of the leaflets. When ripe, they turn dark and can be tapped onto a piece of paper. Sprinkle on moist soil mix and cover the container with glass or plastic. Keep moist until small ferns begin to form.

PESTS AND DISEASES: Scale can be a serious pest but can be controlled with horticultural oil.

RELATED SPECIES: Purple-stemmed cliff brake (*P. atropurpurea*) has purple stems. Sickle fern (*P. falcata*) has upright fronds.

Button ferns require average to high humidity, easily obtained when the plant is grown in a terrarium.

WATERMELON PELLIONIA

Pellionia repens *pell-ee-OHN-ee-uh REP-enz*

Watermelon pellionia will keep its olive-colored foliage in pristine condition with medium light and temperatures.

SIZE: 4"h × 3'w
TYPE: Herbaceous
FORM: Trailing
TEXTURE: Medium
GROWTH: Medium
LIGHT: Medium
MOISTURE: Evenly moist

SOIL: Potting soil
FEATURES: Scalloped, variegated leaves
USES: Hanging basket, terrarium

SITING: The olive and chartreuse leaves look like watermelon rind. The plant is not fussy but must not chill. It thrives in medium light and temperatures of 60–85°F. Provide high humidity; a pot-in-pot system works well in a hanging basket. A

Add humidity to watermelon pellionia by using a pot-in-pot system where one pot is placed in another filled with moist sphagnum moss.

terrarium keeps the humidity high, as well as keeping the plants out of drafts, to which they are unusually sensitive.
CARE: Keep the soil evenly moist but not soggy. For the plant to take in enough moisture, it should be repotted every 2 years. Feed only three times in summer with a general foliage plant food. Remove faded leaves and give the plant regular showers. Pinch the plant occasionally to keep it shrubby.
PROPAGATION: Stem tip cuttings root easily in 2–3 weeks. Snip off the tips, remove all but one or two leaves, dip in rooting hormone, and insert in sterile potting soil. Tent with plastic to keep the humidity high. Watermelon pellionia can also be propagated by division.
PESTS AND DISEASES: Watch for mealybugs and spider mites, especially when the plant is grown in lower humidity. Control them with horticultural oil.
RELATED SPECIES: Satin pellionia (*P. pulchra*) has dark leaf veins and purple undersides.

WATERMELON PEPEROMIA

Peperomia argyreia (sandersii) *pep-per-OH-mee-uh ar-GEYE-ree-uh (san-DER-zee-eye)*

Watermelon peperomia, also known as watermelon begonia, is popular for its succulent silver and green foliage.

SIZE: 1'h × 1'w
TYPE: Herbaceous
FORM: Mounded
TEXTURE: Medium
GROWTH: Potting soil
LIGHT: Medium to low

MOISTURE: Dry
SOIL: Potting soil
FEATURES: Succulent foliage
USES: Foliage, accent
FLOWERS: ■

SITING: Peperomias are used for their striking variegated or highly colored foliage, even in low light. They come in enough leaf shapes and sizes that an entire textural garden could be put together with only peperomias. Provide average temperatures (60–75°F) and be sure to avoid cold drafts and high-traffic areas; the succulent leaves are easily knocked off or scarred.
CARE: Peperomias are fairly tolerant of drought but perform better if watered as soon as the soil surface begins to dry.

Peperomias are easily propagated by stem tip cuttings. Take a 3-5" cutting and remove all but one or two leaves.

Overwatering can cause rotting, especially if the plants are grown in a cool setting. Feed three times in summer only and repot as needed when the roots fill the pot. Peperomias tolerate pruning well, so it is easy to keep plants looking attractive and lush. Occasional showers will keep the leaves pristine.
PROPAGATION: Propagate by dividing the root ball or by removing offsets that form at the outside of the plant. Most peperomias can also be propagated fairly easily from stem tip cuttings.
PESTS AND DISEASES: Peperomias are so pest free that they seem almost artificial. They may have occasional mealybugs, which can be controlled with a cotton swab dipped in horticultural oil.
RELATED SPECIES: Numerous species of peperomia are available for home culture.

EMERALD RIPPLE PEPEROMIA

Peperomia caperata pep-per-OH-mee-uh cab-per-AH-tuh

Emerald ripple peperomia has dark green puckered foliage and unique flower spikes that stand above the soft mound of leaves.

SIZE: 8–12"h ×
8–12"w
TYPE: Herbaceous
FORM: Mounded
TEXTURE: Medium
GROWTH: Average
LIGHT: Medium
to low

MOISTURE: Dry
SOIL: Potting soil
FEATURES:
Succulent foliage
USES: Foliage,
accent
FLOWERS: ■

SITING: Peperomias are used for their striking variegated or highly colored foliage, even in low light. They come in enough leaf shapes and sizes that an entire textural garden could be put together with only peperomias. Provide average temperatures (60–75°F) and be sure to avoid cold drafts and high-traffic areas; the succulent leaves are easily knocked off or scarred.

CARE: Peperomias are fairly tolerant of drought but perform better if watered as soon as the soil surface begins to dry. Overwatering can cause rotting, especially if the plants are grown in a cool setting. Feed three times in summer only and repot as needed when the roots fill the pot. Peperomias tolerate pruning well, so it is easy to keep plants looking attractive and lush. Occasional showers will keep the leaves pristine.

PROPAGATION: Propagate by dividing the root ball or by removing offsets that form at the outside of the plants. Emerald Ripple pepperomia can be propagated from stem-tip or leaf-petiole cuttings.

PESTS AND DISEASES: Peperomias are so pest free that they seem almost artificial. They may have occasional mealybugs, which can be controlled with a cotton swab dipped in horticultural oil.

RELATED SPECIES: The cultivar 'Little Fantasy' has small, heart-shaped leaves and rattail flowers.

The succulent leaves of emerald ripple peperomia can be easily damaged, so simply pinch them out at the base to keep the plant attractive.

SILVERLEAF PEPEROMIA

Peperomia griseoargentea pep-per-OH-mee-uh grih-zee-oh-are-JEN-tee-uh

Silverleaf peperomia is another striking foliage plant with silver-green round leaves on long petioles.

SIZE: 1–2'h × 1–2'w
TYPE: Herbaceous
FORM: Mounded
TEXTURE: Medium
GROWTH: Average
LIGHT: Medium
to low

MOISTURE: Dry
SOIL: Potting soil
FEATURES:
Succulent foliage
USES: Foliage,
accent
FLOWERS: ■

SITING: Peperomias are used for their striking variegated or highly colored foliage, even in low light. They come in enough leaf shapes and sizes that an entire textural garden could be put together with only peperomias. Provide average temperatures (60–75°F) and be sure to avoid cold drafts and high-traffic areas; the succulent leaves are easily knocked off or scarred.

CARE: Peperomias are fairly tolerant of drought but perform better if watered as soon as the soil surface begins to dry. Overwatering can cause rotting, especially if the plants are grown in cool conditions. Feed three times in summer only and repot as needed when the roots fill the pot. Peperomias tolerate pruning well, so it is easy to keep the plants looking attractive and lush. Occasional showers will keep the leaves clean and fresh.

PROPAGATION: Propagate by dividing the root ball or by removing offsets that form at the outside of the plants. Silverleaf peperomia can also be propagated from stem-tip or leaf-petiole cuttings.

PESTS AND DISEASES: Peperomias are so pest free that they seem almost artificial. They may have occasional mealybugs, which can be controlled with a cotton swab dipped in horticultural oil.

RELATED SPECIES: There are thousands of peperomia species, with many widely available for home culture.

BABY RUBBER PLANT

Peperomia obtusifolia pep-per-OH-mee-uh ob-too-sih-FOHL-ee-uh

Baby rubber plant has cupped leaves in dark glossy green, or variegated in shades of cream and olive.

SIZE: 6–8"h × 6–8"w
TYPE: Herbaceous
FORM: Mounded
TEXTURE: Medium
GROWTH: Average
LIGHT: Medium to low

MOISTURE: Dry
SOIL: Potting soil
FEATURES: Succulent foliage
USES: Foliage, accent
FLOWERS: ■

SITING: Peperomias are used for their striking variegated or highly colored foliage, even in low light. There are a myriad of leaf shapes and sizes, enough so that an entire textural garden could be put together with only peperomias. Provide average temperatures (60–75°F) and be sure to avoid cold drafts and high-traffic areas; the succulent leaves are easily knocked off or scarred.

CARE: Peperomias are fairly tolerant of drought but perform better if watered as soon as the soil surface begins to dry. Overwatering can cause rotting, especially if the plants are grown in cool conditions. Feed three times in summer only and repot as needed when the roots fill the pot. Peperomias tolerate pruning well, so it is easy to keep plants looking attractive and lush. Occasional showers will keep the leaves pristine.

PROPAGATION: Propagate by dividing the root ball or by removing offsets that form at the outside of the plants. Most peperomias can also be propagated fairly easily from stem tip cuttings.

PESTS AND DISEASES: Peperomias are so pest free that they seem almost artificial. They may have occasional mealybugs, which can be controlled with a cotton swab dipped in horticultural oil.

RELATED SPECIES: 'Tricolor' has cream, green, and pink variegation on the leaves; 'Golden Gate' has olive foliage with extensive cream variegation. There are thousands of peperomia species, with many widely available for home culture.

Baby rubber plant leaves are smooth and succulent and can be cleaned easily with a soft cloth.

PRINCESS ASTRID PEPEROMIA

Peperomia orba pep-per-OH-mee-uh OR-bu

Princess Astrid peperomia has tiny glossy spoon-shaped leaves that form small soft mounds.

SIZE: 6–12"h × 6–12"w
TYPE: Herbaceous
FORM: Mounded
TEXTURE: Medium
GROWTH: Average
LIGHT: Medium to low

MOISTURE: Dry
SOIL: Potting soil
FEATURES: Succulent foliage
USES: Foliage, accent
FLOWERS: ■

SITING: Peperomias are used for their striking variegated or highly colored foliage, even in low light. There are a myriad of leaf shapes and sizes, enough so that an entire textural garden could be put together with only peperomias. Provide average temperatures (60–75°F) and be sure to avoid cold drafts and high-traffic areas; the succulent leaves are easily knocked off or scarred.

CARE: Peperomias are fairly tolerant of drought but perform better if watered as soon as the surface of the soil begins to dry. Overwatering can cause rotting, especially if the plants are grown in cool conditions. Feed three times in summer only and repot as needed when the roots fill the pot. Peperomias tolerate pruning, so it is easy to keep the plants looking attractive and lush. Occasional showers will keep the leaves pristine.

PROPAGATION: Propagate by dividing the root ball or by removing offsets that form at the outside of the plants. Most peperomias can also be propagated fairly easily from stem tip cuttings.

PESTS AND DISEASES: Peperomias are so pest free that they seem almost artificial. They may have occasional mealybugs, which can be controlled with a cotton swab dipped in horticultural oil.

RELATED SPECIES: 'Pixie' is a dwarf form of the species. There are thousands of peperomia species, with many widely available for home culture.

Princess Astrid's diminutive size makes it the perfect companion for other small plants in a terrarium.

MOTH ORCHID
Phalaenopsis hybrids *fal-in-OP-sis*

Moth orchids are perhaps the easiest of the orchids to grow, highly rewarding for the home gardener.

SIZE: 2'h × 2'w
TYPE: Orchid
FORM: Upright
TEXTURE: Medium
GROWTH: Slow
LIGHT: High

MOISTURE: Moist
SOIL: Epiphyte mix
FEATURES: Long blooming
USES: Accent
FLOWERS: □ ■ ■ ■

SITING: Moth orchid produces successive, rounded blossoms for up to 18 months if given the right conditions. It thrives in bright, filtered to medium light with daytime temperatures of 75–85°F. Nighttime temperatures should drop to about 60°F for 3 weeks in autumn to initiate flower bud development. Provide 50–80 percent humidity by using a pebble tray or humidifier. Low humidity can cause the flower buds to drop prematurely. Air movement is essential to prevent fungal leaf diseases.

CARE: Moth orchid is an epiphyte so it needs evenly moist potting mix. It should not get too moist or sit in water. Rotting from overwatering can kill the plant. Avoid splashing the crown of the plant when watering. Feed with foliage plant food once a month all year. Repot young moth orchids every year with a fine fir bark, and mature plants every 2–3 years after

Moth orchids may need to have their flower spikes supported by bamboo plant stakes or specialized stakes.

blooming. Use a coarse orchid potting mix. Remove the plant from the pot, trim any dead roots, and repot, making sure the roots are surrounded with planting mix. Set the plants in a shady spot for 2–3 days while they recover. Occasionally wipe off the leaves and remove flower spikes just above a node (swollen area where leaves attach to the stem) when blossoming is finished. This will often cause the orchid to produce another flower spike above the node and extend the blooming period.

PROPAGATION: Plantlets, called keikis, sometimes form at the nodes on the flower spike after the plant blossoms. Leave the keikis on the stem until they produce at least two leaves and several roots. Then they can be removed and potted. Cut the keikis from the parent plant, leaving a 2" part of each end of the flower spike. These can be used to anchor the plant in its new pot.

PESTS AND DISEASES: Moth orchid may occasionally have mealybugs, which can be removed with a cotton swab dipped in alcohol.

RELATED SPECIES: Thousands of species and cultivars of moth orchids available.

TREE PHILODENDRON
Philodendron bipinnatifidum (selloum) *fill-oh-DEN-drun bye-pin-ah-TIF-ib-dum (sub-LOH-ubm)*

Tree philodendron, also known as cut-leaf philodendron is a striking architectural feature with glossy, lobed leaves.

SIZE: 4'h × 4'w
TYPE: Vine
FORM: Vine, upright
TEXTURE: Coarse
GROWTH: Fast
LIGHT: Medium to low

MOISTURE: Dry
SOIL: Average
FEATURES: Leaves
USES: Architectural accent

SITING: Philodendrons are coveted in the home because they take such little care yet have shiny, attractive leaves. If given medium to low light, they will thrive. In very high light it will bleach out. Provide average home temperatures (60–75°F) and average to low humidity (65 percent or lower).

CARE: Allow the soil to dry somewhat between waterings, especially in low light. Cold, wet soil can cause rotting. Feed only

Give these plants plenty of room to spread to their maximum size and beauty and clean the leaves periodically to keep them looking their best.

three times in summer with standard foliage plant food and repot when the thick roots fill the container or the plant begins to creep out of the pot. To keep the plant smaller, reduce feeding. In nature all types of philodendron are vining and tend to climb. Lacy tree philodendron can grow fairly upright in a container. Wash the leaves regularly to keep spider mites at bay. Remove the occasional faded leaf.

PROPAGATION: Propagate by taking stem cuttings with at least two nodes and inserting them in potting soil. Keep them moist and cover with plastic to keep the humidity high until they root. This philodendron can also be started from seed obtained from a supplier.

PESTS AND DISEASES: Control mealybugs and mites with horticultural oil.

RELATED SPECIES: The cultivar 'Hope' has a dwarf, more compact habit than the species.

RED-LEAF PHILODENDRON
Philodendron erubescens *fill-oh-DEN-drun air-oo-BES-sens*

Red-leaf philodendron will keep its beautiful coppery leaves with medium light and average temperatures.

SIZE: 5'h × 5'w
TYPE: Vine
FORM: Upright
TEXTURE: Coarse
GROWTH: Fast
LIGHT: Medium

MOISTURE: Dry
SOIL: Average
FEATURES: Coppery leaves
USES: Accent, foliage

SITING: Philodendrons are coveted in the home because they take such little care yet have shiny, attractive leaves. The leaves of this philodendron have coppery undersides and edges, making it a striking foliage accent. As long as philodendrons are provided medium light, they will thrive and maintain their bright leaves. If grown in very high light, the leaves will bleach out; in lower light they will be greener. Provide average home temperatures (60–75°F) and average to low humidity (65 percent or lower).

CARE: Allow the soil to dry somewhat between waterings, especially when the

Philodendrons climb in their natural settings, so they can be trained onto a moss or bark pole by tying the vining stems.

plant is grown in low light. Cold, wet soil can cause rotting. Feed only three times in summer with standard foliage plant food and repot when the thick roots fill the pot or the plant begins to creep out of the pot. To keep the plant smaller, reduce the feeding. In the home this philodendron can grow fairly upright when trained to a moss pole in a container. Remove the occasional faded leaf.

PROPAGATION: Propagate by taking stem cuttings with at least two nodes and inserting them in potting soil. Keep them moist and cover with plastic to keep the humidity high until they root. These philodendrons can also be started from seed obtained from a supplier.

PESTS AND DISEASES: Control mealybugs and mites with horticultural oil. Wash the leaves regularly to keep spider mites at bay.

RELATED SPECIES: Although the species tends to be vining, several cultivars are shrubby. 'Black Cardinal' has red leaves that mature to almost black. 'Red Empress' has lobed burgundy leaves and is shrubby. 'Burgundy' has glossy reddish leaves, red veins, and stems.

VELVET-LEAF PHILODENDRON
Philodendron scandens f. *micans* *fill-oh-DEN-drun SKAN-dins MY-kanz*

Velvet-leaf philodendron has velvety heart-shaped leaves that drape gracefully out of a container.

SIZE: 8"h × 6'w
TYPE: Vine
FORM: Trailing
TEXTURE: Medium
GROWTH: Slow
LIGHT: Medium

MOISTURE: Moist
SOIL: Average
FEATURES: Velvety, heart-shaped leaves
USES: Hanging basket, foliage

SITING: Philodendrons are coveted in the home because they take such little care yet have attractive foliage. Velvet-leaf philodendron has soft, velvety dark green to coppery leaves that are arranged along trailing stems. If provided medium light, it will thrive and maintain dense, attractive foliage. In lower light the plant will survive but may lose some of the velvety appearance. Provide average home temperatures (60–75°F) and average to low humidity (65 percent or lower).

To propagate new plants of velvet-leaf philodendron, pin a stem to damp soil at a leaf node. When rooted, sever from the mother plant and pot up.

CARE: Keep the soil evenly moist but not soggy. Cold, wet soil can cause rotting, and cold drafts can cause leaf drop. Feed only three times in summer with a standard foliage plant food and repot when the thick roots fill the pot or the plant begins to creep out of the pot. Velvet leaf philodendron is easily trained to a moss pole to give it an upright form. If the plant begins to get leggy, prune back the stems at different lengths to rejuvenate it.

PROPAGATION: Propagate by taking stem cuttings and inserting them in potting soil or water. Keep them moist and cover with plastic to keep the humidity high until they root. This plant can also be propagated by layering the stems or by starting from seed obtained from a supplier.

PESTS AND DISEASES: Control mealybugs and mites with horticultural oil. Shower the plant regularly to keep spider mites at bay.

HEART-LEAF PHILODENDRON
Philodendron scandens (oxycardium cordatum)

*fill-oh-DEN-drun SKAN-dins
(ahx-ee-KAR-dee-uhm kor-DAH-tum)*

Heart-leaf philodendron, also known as sweetheart plant, looks great in a hanging basket, sitting on a windowsill, or in a dish garden with other plants.

SIZE: 8"h × 6'w
TYPE: Vine
FORM: Trailing
TEXTURE: Medium
GROWTH: Fast
LIGHT: Low to medium

MOISTURE: Dry
SOIL: Potting soil
FEATURES: Heart-shaped leaves
USES: Hanging basket, ground cover, dish garden

SITING: Philodendrons are coveted in the home because they take such little care yet have attractive foliage. Heart-leaf philodendron has glossy dark green to coppery leaves that are arranged along trailing stems. The plant thrives if provided medium to low light, making it a superb choice for spots in the home where other plants won't grow well. Provide average home temperatures (60–75°F) and average to low humidity (65 percent or lower). **CARE:** Allow the soil to dry slightly between waterings. In low light, reduce

Heart-leaf philodendron has the appeal of growing in very low light. It can be grown on a moss pole for a more upright accent.

watering even more. Cold, wet soil can cause rotting, and cold drafts can cause leaf drop. Feed only three times in summer with a standard foliage plant food and repot when the thick roots fill the pot or the plant begins to creep out of the pot. Heartleaf philodendron is easily trained to a moss pole to give it an upright form. If the plant begins to get leggy, prune back the stems at different lengths to rejuvenate it. Remove the occasional faded leaf to keep the plant tidy. **PROPAGATION:** Propagate by taking stem cuttings and inserting them in potting soil or water. Keep them moist and cover with plastic to keep the humidity high until they root. The plant can also be propagated by layering the stems or by starting from seed obtained from a supplier. **PESTS AND DISEASES:** Control mealybugs and mites with horticultural oil. Shower the plant regularly to keep spider mites at bay.

PYGMY DATE PALM
Phoenix roebelenii FEE-nix roh-buh-LEEN-ee-eye

Pygmy date palms are ideal houseplants because of their tolerance of varying conditions and even some neglect.

SIZE: 6'h × 6'w
TYPE: Palm
FORM: Vase-shaped
TEXTURE: Medium
GROWTH: Slow
LIGHT: High

MOISTURE: Dry
SOIL: Potting soil
FEATURES: Airy fronds
USES: Architectural accent

SITING: Pygmy date palm is an ideal houseplant because it will tolerate some abuse. It performs best in bright, indirect light but tolerates some sun as well as lower light. It does best in a somewhat cool (60–65°F) spot with good air movement. It will tolerate low humidity, but spider mites can be a problem in these conditions. When placing this plant, give it plenty of room so its arching fronds can be appreciated. Be aware that the lower

Place pygmy date palms where you can appreciate the arching regal fronds that make a superb architectural statement.

fronds contain spines that can prick, so place the plant out of traffic areas. **CARE:** Pygmy date palm is fairly tolerant of a wide range of moisture, but chronic overwatering will cause the tips to blacken. Chronic underwatering will make the fronds droop and become lighter in color. Let the top 1–2" of soil dry out between waterings. Feed monthly during the summer with foliage plant food and not at all in winter. Repot only when the roots fill the pot and the plant is hard to water. The root system is minimal, so repotting will not be frequent. As the lower fronds fade, remove them to reveal the striking trunk. **PROPAGATION:** Propagate by seed, usually obtained from a supplier. With plants that have multiple crowns, divide the crown and pot up the two parts. **PESTS AND DISEASES:** Spider mites occur in low humidity. Treat with monthly showers and horticultural oil. **RELATED SPECIES:** Canary Island date palm (*P. canariensis*) is a larger, coarser palm with a spiky appearance and attractive, diamond-shaped markings on its trunk.

ALUMINUM PLANT

Pilea cadierei pye-LEE-uh kad-ee-AIR-eye

Aluminum plants have beautifully variegated leaves in shades of silver and deep green. These plants are also appealing because they are so easy to grow.

SIZE: 12"h × 12"w
TYPE: Herbaceous
FORM: Mounded
TEXTURE: Medium
GROWTH: Medium
LIGHT: Medium

MOISTURE: Dry
SOIL: Potting soil
FEATURES: Colorful, textured leaves
USES: Foliage, dish garden, terrarium

SITING: Aluminum plant is generally easy to grow. Provide medium light; higher light will burn the leaves. The plant will thrive in a temperature range of 60–70°F; it will tolerate higher temperatures if the humidity is high (60 percent and above). It will not do well when exposed to low humidity.

CARE: Let the soil dry out slightly between waterings, but don't let the soil get so dry that the plant begins to droop. With a small root system, aluminum plant seldom needs to be repotted. Feed with foliage plant food according to label directions during the active growing season. Don't feed at all in winter. Pinch regularly to keep the plant shrubby. When the plant begins to get leggy, start a new plant to replace the old one. Frequent showering will help keep pests at bay. The plant may exhibit brown leaves from low humidity and yellow leaves from too much water.
PROPAGATION: Propagate by stem cuttings or by division.
PESTS AND DISEASES: Spider mites can be a problem in low humidity and will cause the leaf edges to brown. Mealybugs and scale may also appear.

RELATED SPECIES: *P. c. minima* 'Patti's Gold' has yellow flecking that turns cream with maturity. Chinese money plant (*P. peperomioides*) has waxy, round leaves on upright stems.

When an aluminum plant starts to stretch and become unappealing, simply cut back the leggy stems to rejuvenate the plant, or take cuttings to start a new plant.

MOON VALLEY FRIENDSHIP PLANT

Pilea involucrata pye-LEE-uh in-vol-yew-KRAYT-uh

Moon Valley friendship plant gets its interesting name from the craters in the deeply crinkled green and black leaves.

SIZE: 12"h × 12"w
TYPE: Herbaceous
FORM: Mounded
TEXTURE: Medium
GROWTH: Medium
LIGHT: Medium

MOISTURE: Dry
SOIL: Potting soil
FEATURES: Colorful textured leaves
USES: Foliage, dish garden, terrarium

SITING: Moon Valley friendship plant is generally easy to grow. Its highly textured leaves are reminiscent of the craters and valleys of a moonscape. Provide medium light; higher light will burn the leaves. The plant will thrive in a temperature range of 60–70°F; it will tolerate higher temperatures as long as the humidity is high (60 percent and above). It will not thrive when exposed to drying winds and low humidity.

Friendship plant is easy to share with friends since it is so easily propagated from stem-tip cuttings.

CARE: Let the soil dry out slightly between waterings, but don't let the soil get so dry that the plant begins to droop. With a small root system, *Pileas* seldom need to be repotted. Feed with foliage plant food according to label directions during the active growing season. Don't feed at all in winter. Pinch regularly to keep the plant shrubby. When it begins to get leggy, start a new plant to replace the old one. The plant may exhibit brown leaves from low humidity and yellow leaves from too much water.
PROPAGATION: Propagate by stem cuttings or by dividing plants.
PESTS AND DISEASES: Spider mites can be a problem in low humidity and will cause the leaf edges to brown. Mealybugs and scale may also appear. Frequent showering will help keep pests at bay.
RELATED SPECIES: *Pilea repens* grows 4-6" tall with almost black leaves and small white flowers.

ARTILLERY PLANT

Pilea microphylla pye-LEE-uh mye-kroh-FILL-uh

Artillery plants are ferny plants that pack a punch by shooting ripe seeds, sometimes across the room.

SIZE: 12"h × 12"w
TYPE: Herbaceous
FORM: Mounded
TEXTURE: Medium
GROWTH: Medium
LIGHT: Medium

MOISTURE: Dry
SOIL: Potting soil
FEATURES: Colorful, textured leaves
USES: Foliage, dish garden, terrarium

SITING: Artillery plant is unique in that it shoots its seeds when they ripen, sometimes several feet. This plant often becomes a nuisance in a greenhouse, and in the home you may have small plants appear in other plant pots. Provide medium light; higher light will burn the leaves. The plant will thrive in a temperature range of 60–70°F; it will tolerate higher temperatures as long as the humidity is high (60 percent and above). It doesn't thrive when exposed to drying winds and low humidity.

CARE: Let the soil dry out slightly between waterings, but don't let it get so dry that the plant begins to droop. With a small root system, artillery plant seldom needs to be repotted. Feed with foliage plant food according to label directions during the active growing season. Don't feed at all in winter. Pinch regularly to keep the plant shrubby. When it begins to get leggy, start a new plant to replace the old one. The plant may exhibit brown leaves from low humidity and yellow leaves from too much water.

PROPAGATION: Propagate by stem cuttings or by dividing plants. Artillery plant produces many seeds, so if you can catch them, you can easily start new plants. Otherwise you will find seedlings starting themselves in the pot.

PESTS AND DISEASES: Spider mites can be a problem in low humidity and will cause the leaf edges to brown. Mealybugs and scale may also appear. Frequent showering will help keep pests at bay.

RELATED SPECIES: The cultivar 'Variegata' has white new leaves. *Pilea depressa* is a small-leaved creeping form.

Keep artillery plants shrubby and attractive by pinching out the stem tips periodically.

Start new plants by dipping the pinched tips in rooting hormone and sticking into sterile potting soil.

JAPANESE PITTOSPORUM

Pittosporum tobira pit-oh-SPOR-um toh-BYE-ruh

Japanese pittosporums are beautiful backdrops for other blooming plants. The plants will occasionally produce orange-scented flowers.

SIZE: 3'h × 3'w
TYPE: Woody shrub
FORM: Rounded
TEXTURE: Medium
GROWTH: Slow
LIGHT: High

MOISTURE: Dry
SOIL: Potting soil
FEATURES: Glossy foliage
USES: Foliage accent, fragrance

SITING: Japanese pittosporum is fairly carefree in the home environment as long as it is given bright light. In the right light conditions, its glossy foliage is a foil for other blooming plants. In bright light it will occasionally bloom with orange blossom-scented flowers, a characteristic that leads to an alternate common name, Japanese mock orange. Provide it with temperatures of 50–70°F and average humidity (30–65 percent).

CARE: Allow the plant to dry slightly between waterings. Feed once a month with foliage plant food during the active growing season; cease feeding during the winter when it is semidormant. Repot only when the plant outgrows its container. Using a small pot will help keep the plant in bounds (it can grow to 10'). Prune Japanese pittosporum regularly to shape it. This plant is often used for bonsai.

PROPAGATION: Propagate by taking softwood cuttings in spring and inserting them in sterile potting mix. Cover cuttings with a plastic tent to keep in humidity. Provide bottom heat to speed rooting.

PESTS AND DISEASES: Spider mites may be a problem in low humidity, and scale can be a frequent visitor on Japanese pittosporum. Treat either with horticultural oil. A monthly shower keeps pests at bay.

RELATED SPECIES: The cultivar 'Variegata' has white leaf margins. It is more commonly available than the green-leaved species. Pittosporums are used for outdoor plants in southern climates, so you may find the greatest selection from a southern nursery source. 'Compactum' is a dwarf variety and may be preferable for the home environment because is will not grow as quickly as other varieties.

STAGHORN FERN
Platycerium bifurcatum *plat-ee-SEER-ee-um bye-fur-KAY-tum*

Staghorn ferns offer a unique look in the interior landscape. Give plants bright light and good air circulation.

SIZE: 3'h × 3'w
TYPE: Fern
FORM: Abstract
TEXTURE: Coarse
GROWTH: Slow
LIGHT: High
MOISTURE: Dry
SOIL: Moss
FEATURES: Fronds
USES: Focal point

SITING: Whether grown on a slab or in a hanging basket, staghorn fern should be located high up where the drooping fronds will not be in the way of passersby. Although the sterile frond that is attached to the slab lies flat, the fertile fronds, from which the plant gets its name, hang down. Provide bright but indirect light and average home temperatures (60–80°F). The plant will tolerate average (30–60 percent) humidity but must have good air circulation. A humidifier is a good way to provide both.

CARE: Staghorn fern is an epiphyte, so it can take moisture from the air. However, in the home this is seldom possible, so when growing this plant on a slab in high light, soak the slab in the sink for about 15 minutes every couple of days. During

A favorite way to display staghorn ferns is to fix them to a wooden slab which is then hung on the wall.

winter rest, give the plant only enough water to keep it from drying out completely. To grow in a hanging basket, pot the fern in equal parts peat moss and sphagnum moss. Or mount young plants on a slab, to which they will eventually root. Place the same potting mix for a hanging basket between the flat frond and the slab, cover the fern and potting mix with chicken wire, and staple it to the slab. Replace the potting mix once a year. Feed newly potted staghorn ferns weekly with half-strength foliage plant food. Once the fern is established, feed it once a month with full-strength food. Dust the fronds occasionally.

PROPAGATION: Staghorn fern produces plantlets on its roots. Propagate by separating these plantlets and potting them up. A healthy mature fern can be divided. Make sure to get adequate roots with each part of the division; seldom should you divide the fern into more than two pieces.

PESTS AND DISEASES: Scale insects are common. Treat by dabbing them with horticultural oil.

RELATED SPECIES: *Platycerium grande* has wedge-shaped 4–6'-long fertile fronds.

CUBAN OREGANO
Plectranthus amboinicus *plek-TRAN-thus am-boh-IN-ih-kus*

Cuban oregano, with gray-green leaves, is a carefree plant that thrives outdoors in summer as well as indoors. It is also known as Mexican mint.

SIZE: 12–18"h × 3'w
TYPE: Herbaceous
FORM: Trailing
TEXTURE: Medium
GROWTH: Fast
LIGHT: Medium
MOISTURE: Moist
SOIL: Potting soil
FEATURES: Fuzzy foliage
USES: Hanging basket, culinary
FLOWERS: ☐

SITING: This easy-to-grow plant is favored by gardeners because it looks good even when neglected. It has velvety gray-green leaves edged in white. Given the right conditions, it will produce starry white flowers on stalks held above the foliage. The leaves are used in Cuban and Indonesian foods to flavor meats. It thrives in medium light and average temperatures (60–75°F) but will tolerate cooler temperatures. Provide average humidity (30–60 percent). This plant can easily be grown outdoors, and many gardeners use

Cuban oregano is at its best in a hanging basket where the tips should be periodically pinched to keep it shrubby and attractive.

cuttings from their indoor plant to provide outdoor vining plants for hanging baskets.

CARE: Keep the soil evenly moist but not soggy. Feed only three times in summer. Repot occasionally. Once the plants start looking drab and leggy, take cuttings to start new plants. Pinch out stem tips to keep the plant shrubby and full, but be aware that the sap will turn your fingers orange.

PROPAGATION: Propagate from stem cuttings rooted in water or soil. The crown can also be divided easily. Cut the plant back when you divide it in order to rejuvenate it as well as making it easier to separate shorter vines.

PESTS AND DISEASES: Treat mealybug and whiteflies with horticultural oil or insecticidal soap or labelled insecticide.

RELATED SPECIES: The cultivar 'Varietgatus' has thin white margins. 'Ochre Flame' has varying shades of green and cream.

SWEDISH IVY

Plectranthus australis plek-TRAN-thus aus-TRALL-iss

Swedish ivy, with glossy foliage and scalloped edges, is an easy-to-grow plant that will tolerate most temperatures and light levels. This is a variegated form.

SIZE: 12–18"h × 3'w
TYPE: Herbaceous
FORM: Trailing
TEXTURE: Medium
GROWTH: Fast
LIGHT: Medium
MOISTURE: Moist
SOIL: Potting soil
FEATURES: Foliage
USES: Hanging basket
FLOWERS: ☐

SITING: This easy-to-grow plant is favored by gardeners because it looks good even when neglected. The species has medium green scalloped leaves. Given the right conditions, it will produce starry white flowers on stalks held above the foliage. It thrives in medium light and average temperatures (60–75°F) but will also tolerate cooler temperatures. Provide average humidity (30–60 percent). This plant can easily be grown outdoors, and many gardeners use cuttings from their indoor plant to provide outdoor vining plants for hanging baskets.

CARE: Keep the soil evenly moist but not soggy. Feed only three times in summer. Repot occasionally. Once the plant starts looking drab and leggy, take cuttings to start new plants. Pinch out stem tips to keep the plant shrubby and full, but be aware that the sap may turn your fingers orange.

PROPAGATION: Propagate from stem cuttings rooted in water or soil. The crown can also be divided easily. Cut the plant back when you divide it in order to rejuvenate it as well as to make it easier to separate shorter vines.

PESTS AND DISEASES: Treat mealybug and whiteflies with horticultural oil or insecticidal soap.

RELATED SPECIES: The cultivar 'Variegata' has white marked leaves. Other selections are variegated with green centers and gold leaf margins. *P. prostratus* has tiny green leaves and forms a solid mat.

Regularly pinching out the tips of Swedish ivy keeps the plant shrubby and attractive.

SPURFLOWER

Plectranthus forsteri (coleoides) 'Marginatus' plek-TRAN-thus FOR-stir-eye (koh-lee-OY-deez)

Spurflower has deep green foliage edged in white and makes a beautiful hanging basket. In medium light it will occasionally bloom with white, starry blossoms.

SIZE: 18"h × 10"w
TYPE: Herbaceous
FORM: Trailing
TEXTURE: Medium
GROWTH: Fast
LIGHT: Medium
MOISTURE: Moist
SOIL: Potting soil
FEATURES: Foliage
USES: Hanging basket
FLOWERS: ☐

SITING: This easy-to-grow plant is favored by gardeners because it looks good even when neglected. Its large, succulent leaves are fuzzy and variegated white and green with occasional pink streaks. It thrives in medium light and average temperatures (60–75°F) but tolerates cooler ones. Provide average humidity (30–60 percent). This plant can easily be grown outdoors, and many gardeners use cuttings from their indoor plant to provide outdoor vining plants for hanging baskets.

CARE: Keep the soil evenly moist but not soggy. This *Plectranthus* is more drought tolerant than the other species. Feed only three times in summer. Repot more often than its relatives because everything about it is larger, including the roots. Once a year cut the plant back and repot into clean soil. If the plant starts looking drab and leggy, take cuttings to start new plants. Pinch out stem tips to keep the plant shrubby and full, but be aware that the sap may turn your fingers orange.

PROPAGATION: Propagate from stem cuttings rooted in water or soil. The crown can also be divided easily. Cut the plant back when you divide it in order to rejuvenate it as well as to make it easier to separate shorter vines.

PESTS AND DISEASES: Treat mealybug and whiteflies with horticultural oil or insecticidal soap.

RELATED SPECIES: The cultivar 'Green on Green' has gray-green leaves edged with chartreuse. Silver spurflower, *P. argentatus*, grows upright with strong stems and large gray leaves.

PURPLE-LEAVED SWEDISH IVY
Plectranthus purpuratus *plek-TRAN-thus pur-pur-AY-tus*

Purple-leaved Swedish ivy has velvety dark purple-green leaves with dark purple undersides and purple stems.

SIZE: 12–18"h × 3'w
TYPE: Herbaceous
FORM: Trailing
TEXTURE: Medium
GROWTH: Fast
LIGHT: Medium
MOISTURE: Moist

SOIL: Potting soil
FEATURES: Purple foliage
USES: Hanging basket
FLOWERS: ■■

SITING: This easy-to-grow plant is favored by gardeners because it looks good even when neglected. It has velvety dark purple-green leaves with dark purple undersides and purple stems. Given the right conditions, it will produce lavender flowers on stalks held above the foliage. The plant thrives in medium light and average temperatures (60–75°F) but tolerates cooler temperatures. Provide average humidity (30–60 percent). This plant can easily be grown outdoors, and many gardeners use cuttings from their indoor plant to provide outdoor vining plants for hanging baskets.

CARE: Keep the soil evenly moist but not soggy. Feed only three times in summer. Repot occasionally. Once the plants look leggy, take cuttings to start new plants. Pinch out stem tips to keep the plant shrubby and full.

PROPAGATION: Propagate from stem cuttings rooted in water or soil. The crown can also be divided easily. Cut the plant back when you divide it in order to rejuvenate it as well as to make it easier to separate shorter vines.

PESTS AND DISEASES: Treat mealybug and whiteflies with horticultural oil or insecticidal soap.

RELATED SPECIES: *Plectranthus* 'Mona Lavender' has magenta flowers and glossy deep purple leaves on purple stems.

You can easily start new plants of purple-leaved Swedish ivy by rooting cuttings in water.

BUDDHIST PINE
Podocarpus macrophyllus *poh-doh-KAR-pus mak-roh-FILL-us*

Buddhist pines, dark green to almost black in color, are beautiful architectural accents in cool spots such as entryways and foyers.

SIZE: 8'h × 3'w
TYPE: Woody evergreen
FORM: Upright
TEXTURE: Fine
GROWTH: Slow
LIGHT: Medium to high

MOISTURE: Moist
SOIL: Potting soil
FEATURES: Foliage, tree form
USES: Architectural accent

SITING: Buddhist pine is an excellent candidate for a cool space with bright light, such as a foyer. The dark green, almost black foliage contrasts well with the cinnamon-colored bark. This plant is fairly carefree and will maintain its attractive foliage if given medium to high light and average to cool temperatures (50–75°F).

It tolerates low humidity (below 30 percent) but may be prone to spider mites.

CARE: Keep evenly moist during the growing season and allow to dry between waterings during dormancy in winter. Feed three times in summer with foliage plant food, or only once a year if the plant is as large as you want it. Repot only when the plant would look better in a larger pot. It grows so slowly that roots will seldom overtake the pot. This plant seldom needs pruning except to shape it gently. It has a natural tendency to lose its inner leaves regularly, so remove them as part of regular grooming. It may need the support of a stake as it gets tall. Find a stake that looks as natural as possible and insert it close to the trunk. Tie the trunk to the stake with soft dark brown jute. Give the plant monthly showers.

PROPAGATION: Buddhist pine can be propagated by stem cuttings, but not easily. Take semihardwood cuttings in late spring; use rooting powder and bottom heat.

PESTS AND DISEASES: Control scale, mealybugs, and spider mites with horticultural oil.

RELATED SPECIES: The cultivar 'Maki' has white new foliage.

These plants respond well to pruning and can be kept attractive by attending to this task when necessary.

CHAPTER **7** A–Z ENCYCLOPEDIA OF HOUSEPLANT CARE

MING ARALIA

Polyscias fruticosa pah-lih-SKEE-us froo-tih-KOH-suh

Ming aralias with their ferny graceful foliage can be grown in the home as long as the right conditions are provided.

SIZE: 5'h × 2'w
TYPE: Woody tree
FORM: Upright
TEXTURE: Fine
GROWTH: Slow
LIGHT: Medium

MOISTURE: Dry
SOIL: Potting soil
FEATURES: Foliage
USES: Architectural accent, Oriental theme

SITING: Ming aralia has a reputation for being difficult to grow in the average home. This delicate, Asian-looking plant can be successful once the right environmental conditions have been provided, but this plant is not one to neglect. It responds by dropping all its leaves. Provide medium to bright light, average to high temperatures (60–85°F), and most importantly, high humidity (above 65 percent). Putting the plant on a bed of moist pebbles works well, as does a humidifier as long as the air does not circulate too much. Cool drafts are deadly for Ming aralia.

CARE: Even though Ming aralia needs high humidity, it does not need constantly moist

Since Ming aralias need high humidity to keep them healthy, place pots on trays of moist pebbles to raise the ambient humidity around the plant.

soil. It can be prone to root rot from overwatering. Allow it to dry slightly between soakings. Feed three times in summer with foliage plant food, or according to label directions during active growth. This plant grows so slowly that it needs repotting infrequently, only when the plant is no longer able to take up water. Ming aralia can be pruned to keep it looking good but it seldom needs drastic pruning.

PROPAGATION: Propagating Ming aralia is difficult at best, but stem cuttings taken in late spring and rooted with hormone powder and bottom heat may be successful. The plant can be air-layered with some success as well.

PESTS AND DISEASES: Scale and spider mites can be controlled with high humidity, regular showering, and horticultural oil.

RELATED SPECIES: The cultivar 'Elegans' has contorted, curled leaves. Parsley-leaf aralia (*P. filicifolia*) has slightly larger leaves and denser foliage. *P. guilfoylei* 'Victoriae' has small, deeply cut leaves edged with white teeth.

BALFOUR ARALIA

Polyscias scutellaria (balfouriana) pah-lih-SEE-us skoo-tuh-LAR-ee-uh (bal-foor-ee-AY-nuh)

Balfour aralias are unique Asian-looking plants that need average temperature, medium light, and high humidity to thrive.

SIZE: 6'h × 3'w
TYPE: Woody tree
FORM: Upright
TEXTURE: Fine
GROWTH: Slow
LIGHT: Medium

MOISTURE: Dry
SOIL: Potting soil
FEATURES: Foliage, tan bark
USES: Architectural accent, Asian theme

SITING: Balfour aralia has a reputation for being hard to grow in the average home.

This Asian-looking plant can be quite successful once the right environmental conditions have been provided, but it is not a plant to neglect. It responds by dropping all its leaves. Provide medium light, average to high temperatures (60–85°F), and most importantly, high humidity (above 65 percent). Putting the plant on a bed of moist pebbles works well, as does a humidifier as long as the air does not circulate too much. Cool drafts are deadly for Balfour aralia.

CARE: Even though Balfour aralia needs high humidity, it does not need constantly moist soil. It is more prone to root rot from overwatering than the other species. Overwatering will show up first as shiny, dark spots on the backs of leaves, which will then yellow and fall. Allow the plant to dry slightly between soakings. Feed three times in summer with foliage plant food, or according to label directions during active growth. This plant grows so

slowly that it needs repotting only when it isn't able to take up water any longer. Balfour aralia can be pruned to keep it looking good, but it seldom needs drastic pruning.

PROPAGATION: Propagating Balfour aralia is difficult at best, but stem cuttings taken in late spring and rooted with hormone powder and bottom heat may be successful. The plants can be air-layered with some success as well.

PESTS AND DISEASES: Balfour aralia may have scale and spider mites, although both can be controlled with high humidity, regular showering off, and horticultural oil.

RELATED SPECIES: The cultivar 'Pennockii' has vertically held leaves that are mottled gray and green. (This cultivar is reputed to be hard to grow.) 'Marginata' leaves are delicately and irregularly edged in white. Chicken gizzard aralia 'Ruffles' (*P. crispata*) has lime green foliage and is more compact than other aralias.

PRIMROSE

Primula spp. *PRIM-yoo-luh*

In cool regions primroses can be planted into the outdoor garden as perennials after you have enjoyed their bloom indoors.

SIZE: 4–6"h × 6–8"w
TYPE: Herbaceous
FORM: Mounded
TEXTURE: Medium
GROWTH: Medium
LIGHT: Medium to high
MOISTURE: Evenly moist

SOIL: Potting soil
FEATURES: Fragrant blossoms
USES: Blooming accent
FLOWERS: ■ ■ ■
■ □

SITING: Indoors, primroses need only medium light to keep them attractive while blooming, although they will tolerate bright, indirect light as long as they are kept cool. They tolerate medium temperatures (65–75°F), but cool temperatures (55–65°F) will keep them blooming much longer. Average humidity (30–60 percent), easily achieved with a pebble tray, keeps the leaves looking their best.

CARE: Keep primroses evenly moist for their entire blooming time or the buds may shrivel. However, do not let the plants sit in water. Feed with half-strength plant food at every watering while in bud and in flower. Repotting is seldom needed; put

Primrose flowers come in a broad array of cheery spring colors.

the plants outdoors into the garden after the blossoms fade. Regularly remove faded blossoms to keep the buds coming.

PROPAGATION: Propagate by crown division or by seed. Start seeds indoors and move the plants outdoors as seedlings. The plants are perennials and usually need 2 years to come into bloom outdoors.

PESTS AND DISEASES: Primroses may have occasional problems with mealybugs and spider mites. Control mealybugs with a cotton swab dipped in alcohol, and spider mites with a strong spray of water on the undersides of the leaves.

RELATED SPECIES: Common primrose (*P. vulgaris*) is most often sold as a blooming houseplant. The dark, crinkly leaves surround bouquets of flowers held close to the center of the plant. The blossoms are usually sweetly scented. Fairy primrose (*P. malacoides*) has tall flower spikes of white, pink, red, and lavender. These plants are not hardy outdoors so are best treated as annuals and discarded after blooming. *P. obconica* is also sold as a blooming plant with large, showy flowers. Be aware that leaf contact can cause dermatitis in some people.

TABLE FERN

Pteris cretica *TAIR-iss KREH-tih-kuh*

'Albo-linata' table fern brightens the home with its white-banded fronds that look best viewed from above.

SIZE: 12–24"h × 12–24"w
TYPE: Fern
FORM: Mounded
TEXTURE: Medium
GROWTH: Medium
LIGHT: Medium to high

MOISTURE: Evenly moist
SOIL: Potting soil
FEATURES: Fronds
USES: Foliage, accent, terrarium

SITING: Table fern does not drape like other ferns, so it is more suited to a table than a hanging basket. Provide medium to bright, indirect light for the best growth. It prefers cool to medium temperatures (55–75°F). It needs high humidity, as do most ferns, but will survive at even 40 percent humidity.

CARE: Keep evenly moist but not soggy. It requires more water than it would seem for its size, so work to find the right balance. It may take twice-a-week watering. Leaves will brown on the edges and then curl if the plant is in low humidity or gets too little water. Feed three times in summer with foliage plant food. Because of its vigorous nature, it needs to

Table fern is also known as brake fern or Cretan brake. The species has solid green branching fronds.

be repotted annually. Use a rich, moisture-retentive planting mix and move up one pot size larger each time.

PROPAGATION: Table fern can be propagated carefully by division. It is easier to propagate by spores. Spores form in lines along the edges of the frond leaflets and, when ripe, can be tapped out of the spore cases and scattered on fresh potting soil.

PESTS AND DISEASES: Table fern may have occasional scale and mealybugs; both are controlled with a cotton swab dipped in horticultural oil or alcohol. Do not spray the entire plant with oil, however, or the fronds will be damaged. The plant benefits from monthly showering to keep the fronds clean and free of spider mites.

RELATED SPECIES: The cultivar 'Albo-linata' has a broad white central band on the fronds. Other cultivars have various types of cresting and lobing on the fronds. Silver brake (*P. argyraea*) has dark green fronds with a broad silver stripe in the center. Australian brake (*P. tremula*) is a vigorous fern with ferny fronds. Painted brake (*P. tricolor*) has reddish fronds when young.

CHINA DOLL
Radermachera sinica ray-der-MAK-er-uh SIN-ih-kuh

China doll, as its name implies, is a delicately elegant plant with glossy leaves and an attractive upright shape.

SIZE: 3–4'h × 2'w
TYPE: Herbaceous
FORM: Upright
TEXTURE: Medium
GROWTH: Medium
LIGHT: High
MOISTURE: Moist
SOIL: Potting soil
FEATURES: Glossy leaves
USES: Foliage

SITING: China doll has been around for many years as a beautiful foliage plant, but it didn't become popular in the United States until the 1980s. Its lovely glossy compound leaves make an appealing statement in a foliage plant collection or as a backdrop for a blooming plant.

When China doll is grown in bright, indirect light, it will grow quickly but remain attractive. In lower light it becomes leggy. A south or east window with a gauze curtain is ideal. This plant is tolerant of average temperatures (60–75°F) and low humidity (below 30 percent). It performs

China dolls grow best in bright indirect light, achieved easily in a west or south window that is draped with a gauzy curtain to block direct sunlight.

well in a heated home in winter, unlike many other foliage plants.

CARE: Keep the soil evenly moist. Leaves will yellow if the plant is too dry or turn brown on the edges and fall if the plant is too wet. Reduce watering somewhat in winter. Repot annually in spring into a pot the next size larger. When the desired size is reached, continue repotting annually, but root prune to put it back in the same pot. Feed three times in summer with foliage plant food. Let the plant rest in winter. To keep the plant shrubby and compact, pinch the stem tips often. Remove faded leaflets and give it a shower once a month.

PROPAGATION: Propagate by stem tip cuttings taken in summer. Use rooting hormone and bottom heat as well as a plastic tent. Do not expect a high rate of success.

PESTS AND DISEASES: Spider mites can become a problem when the plant is grown in low humidity. Monthly showering should help keep them in check. Mealybugs may also appear but are easily controlled with horticultural oil.

RELATED SPECIES: The cultivar 'Crystal Doll' has golden-edged leaves.

LADY PALM
Rhapis excelsa RAY-pis ek-SELL-suh

SIZE: 5–6'h × 4–5'w
TYPE: Palm
FORM: Upright
TEXTURE: Coarse
GROWTH: Slow
LIGHT: Low to medium
MOISTURE: Moist
SOIL: Potting soil
FEATURES: Glossy leaves
USES: Architectural accent

Lady palm, one of the most elegant of the palms, has short leaflets on stiff fronds and thrives in low light.

SITING: Lady palm performs best in low to medium light. It thrives in average temperatures (60–75°F) but will tolerate low temperatures (below 60°F) for short periods. Lady palm needs high humidity (60 percent or higher), which can be accomplished by the pot-in-pot method, a tray of wet pebbles, or a room humidifier.

CARE: Keep the soil evenly moist, but allow it to dry somewhat between waterings in winter. Feed only three times

Give lady palm plenty of room to enjoy its full size and shape as an architectural accent.

in summer with a foliage plant food. Repot when considerable new growth forms around the edge of the pot. Remove the occasional faded leaf. If leaf edges and tips brown from low humidity, trim them or remove the leaflet.

PROPAGATION: Propagate by dividing the rhizomes or by sowing seeds obtained from a supplier.

PESTS AND DISEASES: This plant is fairly carefree but may have occasional bouts with spider mites, scales, and mealybugs. All can be controlled fairly easily with horticultural oil. Shower the plant regularly to keep spider mite populations under control and retain the glossy, clean look of the foliage.

RELATED SPECIES: The cultivar 'Zuikonishiki' is variegated. 'Tenzan' has curling leaves. Several dwarf varieties are popular for bonsai.

EASTER CACTUS
Rhipsalidopsis spp. (Hatiora gaertneri) *rip-sal-ib-DOP-sis (bah-tee-OR-uh GART-nur-eye)*

Easter cactus blooms with its exquisite pink, red, or white flowers in April and May after being given a cool resting period from September through March.

SIZE: 12–18"h × 12–18"w
TYPE: Forest cactus
FORM: Upright, trailing
TEXTURE: Medium
GROWTH: Slow
LIGHT: High

MOISTURE: Dry
SOIL: Potting soil
FEATURES: Scalloped leaves, showy flowers
USES: Blooming accent
FLOWERS: ■ ■ □

SITING: Easter cactus does best in medium light during active growth and bright, indirect light in winter. Ideal temperatures during active growth and blooming are 70–80°F, no less than 60°F during bloom time. It is tolerant of low humidity (less than 30 percent).

CARE: Easter cactus is magnificent in bloom, but it takes a specific regimen to get it to bloom. If it does not get a cool resting time with short daylength, it will not form flower buds. It may drop flower buds if the growing conditions are changed once buds are set. The plant blooms in spring, during which time it should be watered regularly, allowing

Easter cactus performs best if taken outdoors to spend the summer months and then brought back indoors in mid-September.

the potting soil to dry slightly between waterings. In summer move it outdoors to a shady spot. Around mid-September, bring it indoors into a cool spot (around 55°F) and reduce watering for its resting phase. Keep the soil only slightly moist. Continue to keep it somewhat dry and cool as it forms flower buds. At the end of March, bring it into warmth and begin watering. It should begin flowering again in April.

PROPAGATION: Propagate from leaf cuttings. Pinch off leaf segments and allow them to dry for a couple of days before inserting into sterile soil mix. When propagating by seed, allow the fruits to ripen, then extract the seeds. Clean the seeds and dry them for a few days, then sow on sterile soil mix.

PESTS AND DISEASES: Spider mites, scale, and aphids may affect Easter cactus. Dab scale with alcohol and wash off spider mites and aphids. The plant may develop root rot if overwatered.

RELATED SPECIES: *R. gaertneri* is the standard Easter cactus, with fuchsia to dark red flowers. *R. sirius* is white flowered, and *R. rosea* has tiny pink flowers and is smaller overall.

AZALEA
Rhododendron spp. *rob-dob-DEN-drun*

Azaleas are favorite plants to share for all occasions, and with a little perseverance, can be brought back into bloom.

SIZE: 30"h × 30"w
TYPE: Woody shrub
FORM: Rounded
TEXTURE: Medium
GROWTH: Slow
LIGHT: Medium to high

MOISTURE: Evenly moist
SOIL: Potting soil
FEATURES: Blossoms
USES: Blooming focal point, foliage
FLOWERS: ■ ■ □ □ ■

SITING: During blooming time, medium light is the best for azaleas. When blossoming is over, move the plant into bright light to bring it back into bloom. The key to bud set is a distinct difference between summer and fall/winter temperatures. In summer it will tolerate warm temperatures (75–90°F). In fall and winter, the temperature needs to drop to 40–50°F and be held there until buds set. Average humidity (30–60 percent) is preferred, although the plant will tolerate lower humidity.

CARE: Drying out at all will damage the plant and cause the flower buds to abort. Feed with acid plant food according to label directions during active growth. Stop

Azaleas must be kept evenly moist throughout their blooming time, and drying out even one time may cause the flower buds to abort.

feeding in fall and don't resume until after flower buds are set in February or March. If you intend to keep your azalea, repot it into a larger pot after blooming. Prune immediately after blooming to rejuvenate and shape the plant. Azalea benefits from spending the summer outdoors, but be sure to place it in shade. Bring it indoors before danger of frost and keep it in a cool spot with low humidity until flower buds are set. In late February or March, bring it into warmth and raise the humidity. Azalea can have chlorosis from soil that is not acidic enough. Remedy with acid fertilizer.

PROPAGATION: Propagate by stem cuttings soon after blooming. Take semihardwood cuttings in late spring, dip in rooting hormone, and insert in sterile potting mix. Cover with a tent, and provide bottom heat.

PESTS AND DISEASES: Watch for spider mites in dry conditions. Wash them off with a forceful spray of water.

RELATED SPECIES: There are literally thousands of species and cultivars of *Rhododendron*. The most commonly grown houseplants are *R. indica* and *R. simsii*.

MONKEY PLANT

Ruellia makoyana roo-EL-ee-uh mak-oy-AH-nuh

Monkey plant, also known as trailing velvet plant, has attractive foliage and bright pink blossoms that resemble petunias.

SIZE: 6–12"h × 12–18"w
TYPE: Herbaceous
FORM: Trailing
TEXTURE: Medium
GROWTH: Medium
LIGHT: High
MOISTURE: Moist
SOIL: Potting soil
FEATURES: Olive-colored leaves with silver veins
USES: Hanging basket, blooming focal point
FLOWERS: ▪

SITING: Monkey plant will keep its velvety, attractive foliage and will bear attractive petunia-like pink flowers during almost all of its growing season if given bright, indirect light in summer and some direct sun in winter. Provide average home temperatures (65–75°F), not below 55°F. High humidity (above 60 percent) is best and easily accomplished by using a pebble tray or room humidifier.

CARE: Although monkey plant is fairly tolerant of neglect, it's best to keep it evenly moist when blooming, then reduce the water somewhat in winter, allowing the plant to dry slightly between waterings. Feed three times in summer with blooming plant food at full strength. Repot as necessary, usually every couple of years. Pinch out the growing tips regularly to keep the plant shrubby. Remove faded blossoms to keep the plant attractive.

PROPAGATION: Propagate by stem tip cuttings taken in summer. Provide rooting hormone and bottom heat for the best success. Monkey plant is also easily started from seed. When the green pods open, extract the black seeds and sow on sterile potting mix. Keep moist until the seeds germinate.

PESTS AND DISEASES: Spider mites can be a problem if the humidity is not kept high. Shower the plant with a forceful spray of water to control them. Also, poor air circulation can encourage mildew to grow on the leaves.

RELATED SPECIES: *R. macrantha* is a larger plant with darker flowers and solid green leaves. *R. brittoniana* 'Katie' is a dwarf form with lance-shaped solid green leaves and blue flowers. 'Strawberries and Cream' has purple flowers and speckled foliage.

AFRICAN VIOLET

Saintpaulia ionantha saynt-PAWL-ee-uh eye-oh-NAN-thuh

African violets have long been favorites because of the multitude of colors and forms available and their ability to thrive under artificial lights.

SIZE: 2–6"h × 4–8"w
TYPE: Herbaceous
FORM: Mounded
TEXTURE: Medium
GROWTH: Medium
LIGHT: Bright
MOISTURE: Moist
SOIL: Potting soil
FEATURES: Attractive foliage, constant bloom
USES: Blooming focal point
FLOWERS: ▪ ▪ ▫ ▪

SITING: African violets do well in bright, indirect light, or under artificial lights about 12 inches from the plant and left on for 13 hours a day. The plants will be injured if kept too cool; 60°F at night and 75–80°F during the day are adequate. African violets perform better in low humidity (below 30 percent).

CARE: Keep evenly moist. Avoid getting cold water on the leaves; it may cause spotting. Many gardeners water from the bottom instead of the top. Feed with blooming plant food according to label directions. Repot annually or when the leafless portion of the stem is about 1½" long. Remove faded blossoms and leaves. To remove dust, use a soft feather duster or pressurized air. Avoid washing or rubbing the leaves.

PROPAGATION: Propagate by leaf cuttings. Cut off a leaf and insert the petiole and bottom half of the leaf into sterile potting mix or vermiculite. In 2–6 months, small plants will form at the soil level.

PESTS AND DISEASES: African violets are generally carefree but may become infested with cyclamen mites, thrips, mealybugs, or aphids.

RELATED SPECIES: Cultivars have single or double flowers in many colors and many bicolors. There are varieties with crinkly, scalloped, or variegated leaves, and trailing, upright, or miniature forms.

African violet leaves can be harmed if they get wet, but watering from the bottom can prevent this.

1 Propagate African violet by snipping off a leaf and its petiole.

2 Dip the petiole into rooting hormone and insert it in potting soil.

SNAKE PLANT
Sansevieria trifasciata *san-seh-VEER-ee-uh trye-fas-ee-AH-tuh*

Snake plant, also known as mother-in-law's tongue, makes a beautiful upright accent plant and thrives on neglect.

SIZE: 6–48"h × 10–36"w
TYPE: Succulent
FORM: Upright
TEXTURE: Coarse
GROWTH: Slow
LIGHT: Low to medium

MOISTURE: Dry
SOIL: Potting soil
FEATURES: Variegated foliage
USES: Low light, foliage accent
FLOWERS: ☐

SITING: Snake plant grows well in medium light but tolerates extremely low light. It thrives in average home temperatures but tolerates hot conditions as well. It does best in average humidity (30–60 percent); and tolerates dry, but not high humidity.

CARE: Let it dry out between waterings; it will quickly rot if overwatered. When planted in low-light situations where it takes up little water, allowing it to stand in a saucer of water can be deadly. The leaves will fall over at the soil line, accompanied by a foul-smelling ooze. Feed only once a year with foliage plant food and repot only when the plant fills the pot. It has a minimal root system, so the leaves will fill the pot before the roots do. Remove damaged leaves. Wipe the leaves regularly to keep them looking good.

PROPAGATION: Propagate by leaf cuttings or by separating the rhizomes. Leaf cuttings with yellow bands at the margins produce solid green-leaved plants. Cut leaves into 3" sections and place in sterile potting mix or vermiculite. New plants will arise at the soil level and can be potted up.

PESTS AND DISEASES: Few insects bother snake plant.

RELATED SPECIES: Bird's nest snake plant (*S. t.* 'Hahnii') is small and has dark green rosettes striped with lighter green. 'Golden Hahnii' has gold and olive green striped leaves and grows to about 6" high. 'Laurentii' (pictured at left) is a tall cultivar with light and dark green variegation and wide yellow leaf margins.

Propagate from leaf cuttings several inches long. Notch the top side so you don't insert a cutting upside down.

Dip the bottom end in rooting hormone and insert in sterile potting soil. Cover with plastic until the cuttings take root.

STRAWBERRY BEGONIA
Saxifraga stolonifera *saks-ih-FRAY-guh stoh-luh-NIH-fer-uh*

Strawberry begonia, also known as strawberry geranium, makes a superb accent with its scalloped leaves and multitudes of plantlets.

SIZE: 3"h × 12"w
TYPE: Herbaceous
FORM: Mounded, trailing
TEXTURE: Fine
GROWTH: Medium
LIGHT: Medium

MOISTURE: Moist
SOIL: Potting soil
FEATURES: Leaves with silver veins
USES: Hanging basket, ground cover
FLOWERS: ☐

SITING: Strawberry begonia is irresistible with its delicate foliage in shades of reds and maroons with silver veins and the tiny plantlets that seem to leap over the sides of the plant like spiders on silk. This plant thrives in medium light and average home temperatures (60–75°F). It needs average

To start new plants, simply peg the plantlets down on moist soil with hairpins. They will root quickly and can then be cut from the main plant.

humidity (30–60 percent), easily provided with a pebble tray or pot-in-pot system.

CARE: Keep soil evenly moist during active growth, but water less in winter when it is resting. Too much water will quickly rot the plant. Feed three times in summer with foliage plant food and repot annually, or when the pot fills with small plants and the stolons hanging over the sides become a thick mat. Remove faded leaves. Remove the stolons if you don't care for that look. Give an occasional shower. Move the plant outdoors in summer.

PROPAGATION: Strawberry begonia almost propagates itself with its tiny plants hung on delicate pink stolons. Give these plants moist soil on which to rest and they will readily root. You can also propagate the plants by dividing the root ball.

PESTS AND DISEASES: Treat mealybugs and aphids with a strong spray of water or alcohol-dipped cotton swabs.

RELATED SPECIES: 'Cuscutiformis' is a dwarf form with tiny leaves and plantlets. 'Tricolor' is variegated green, white, and rose. 'Rubra' has dark reddish leaves.

UMBRELLA TREE
Schefflera actinophylla (Brassaia) *schef-LAIR-uh ak-tin-oh-FYE-luh (brass-AY-ee-uh)*

Umbrella tree, also known as schefflera, is a carefree houseplant that gives a tropical impression to the indoor landscape.

SIZE: 8'h × 4'w
TYPE: Herbaceous
FORM: Upright
TEXTURE: Coarse
GROWTH: Fast
LIGHT: Medium

MOISTURE: Moist
SOIL: Potting soil
FEATURES: Glossy foliage
USES: Architectural accent

SITING: Umbrella tree has been the standard for large houseplants for many years, appreciated for its ease of maintenance and its tropical, glossy foliage. It does well in medium light and average home temperatures (60–75°F), although it tolerates high light and high temperatures.

It drops leaves if it gets too cold. Umbrella tree needs only average humidity (30–60 percent). When siting it, place it out of the way of drying winds and cold drafts. Keep umbrella tree out of high-traffic areas because it takes up so much room.

Occasionally wipe the leaves of schefflera with a soft cloth to avoid pest problems.

CARE: Keep evenly moist during active growth; reduce moisture in winter. These plants will rot if overwatered, so make sure the potting mix is well drained. Feed three times in summer with foliage plant food, and repot when the rootball completely fills the pot. These plants are fast growing, so if you fertilize regularly, you may need to repot annually. Scheffleras tolerate pruning well, so you can shape them to a smaller size. A plant that gets top heavy should be pruned back to a better shape. Remove any wayward branches or faded leaves. If the stems become spindly, move the plant into higher light and cut it back to 12" to produce new growth at ground level. Scheffleras benefit from spending the summer outdoors if they are hardened off before being exposed to the elements.
PROPAGATION: Propagate by stem cuttings or air layering.
PESTS AND DISEASES: Control mealybugs, scale, and spider mites with horticultural oil. Shower off the plant occasionally to deter spider mites.
RELATED SPECIES: The cultivar 'Amate' stays compact even in lower light.

SCHEFFLERA
Schefflera arboricola (Heptapleurum, Brassaia) *schef-LAIR-uh ar-bor-ih-KOH-luh (hep-tuh-PLUR-um, brass-AY-ee-uh)*

Arboricola, a miniature version of the standard schefflera, has more diminutive umbrella foliage in medium and dark green.

SIZE: 2–3'h × 2–3'w
TYPE: Herbaceous
FORM: Upright
TEXTURE: Coarse
GROWTH: Fast
LIGHT: Medium

MOISTURE: Moist
SOIL: Potting soil
FEATURES: Foliage
USES: Architectural accent

SITING: Scheffleras do well in medium light and average home temperatures (60–75°F), although they are tolerant of high temperatures. They will drop leaves if they get too cold. They need only average humidity (30-60 percent). Place them out of the way of drying winds and cold drafts.

Keep them out of high-traffic areas because they take up so much room.
CARE: Keep the soil evenly moist while the plant is actively growing; reduce moisture somewhat in winter. These plants will rot if overwatered, so make sure the potting mix is well drained. Feed only three times in summer with foliage plant food and repot

Scheffleras may get leggy, but are easy to contain by cutting back. They will take severe pruning if necessary to get them back to an attractive shape.

when the rootball completely fills the pot. These plants are fast growing, so if you feed regularly, you may need to repot annually. Scheffleras tolerate pruning well, so you can shape them to a smaller size. A plant that gets top heavy should be pruned back to a better shape. Remove any wayward branches or faded leaves.

If the stems become spindly, move the plant into higher light and cut it back to 12" to produce new growth at ground level. Scheffleras can spend the summer outdoors if they are hardened off before being exposed to the elements.
PROPAGATION: Propagate by stem cuttings and air layering.
PESTS AND DISEASES: Control mealybugs, scale, and spider mites with horticultural oil. Shower off the plant occasionally to deter spider mites.
RELATED SPECIES: The cultivar 'Green Gold' has golden-flecked leaves. 'Pittman's Pride' is a compact form.

FALSE ARALIA
Schefflera elegantissima (Dizygotheca elegantissima)

schef-LAIR-uh el-uh-gan-TISS-ih-muh
(diz-ih-GOTH-eh-kuh el-uh-gan-TISS-ih-muh)

SIZE: 3–5'h × 1–2'w
TYPE: Herbaceous
FORM: Upright
TEXTURE: Fine
GROWTH: Fast
LIGHT: Medium
MOISTURE: Moist
SOIL: Potting soil
FEATURES: Linear leaves
USES: Architectural accent, foliage

False aralia, also known as finger aralia, has deep green linear foliage that looks almost black. The foliage stands at a 90-degree angle from the black stems.

SITING: False aralias do well in medium light and average home temperatures (60–75°F), although they are tolerant of high temperatures. They will drop leaves if they get too cold. They need only average humidity (30–60 percent), easily provided with a pebble tray or pot-in-pot system. False aralia is a bit more difficult to grow in the home than other scheffleras because it suffers in low humidity. Place it out of the way of drying winds and cold drafts. Keep it out of high-traffic areas, because it takes up so much room.

False aralias need average humidity, and in a dry home, this can be accomplished by placing the plant pot on a tray of moist pebbles.

CARE: Keep the soil evenly moist while the plant is actively growing, but reduce moisture in winter. The plant will rot if overwatered, so make sure the potting mix is well-drained. Feed only three times in summer with foliage plant food, and repot when the rootball completely fills the pot. This plant is fast growing, so if you feed it regularly, you may need to repot annually. False aralias tolerate pruning well, so you can shape them to a smaller size. Remove any wayward branches or faded leaves. If the stems get spindly, move the plant into higher light and cut it back to 12" to produce new growth at ground level. False aralias can spend the summer outdoors as long as they are hardened off before being exposed to the elements.

PROPAGATION: Propagate from stem cuttings or by air layering.

PESTS AND DISEASES: Control mealybugs, scale, and spider mites with horticultural oil. Shower off the plant occasionally to deter spider mites.

RELATED SPECIES: 'Pink Rim' has pink-edged leaves.

CHRISTMAS CACTUS
Schlumbergera xbuckleyi *shlum-BER-ger-uh BUK-lee-eye*

Christmas cactus blooms in shades of red, pink, and white. It needs slightly moist soil, medium light, and warm temperatures when blooming.

SIZE: 8–12"h × 12–18"w
TYPE: Forest cactus
FORM: Upright, trailing
TEXTURE: Medium
GROWTH: Slow
LIGHT: High
MOISTURE: Dry
SOIL: Potting soil
FEATURES: Scalloped leaves, showy flowers
USES: Blooming accent
FLOWERS: ■ ■ □

SITING: Christmas cactus does best in medium light during active growth and bright, indirect light in winter. Ideal temperatures during active growth and blooming are 70–80°F. Give it no less than 60°F during bloom time. It is tolerant of low humidity (less than 30 percent).

CARE: Christmas cactus is magnificent in bloom, but it takes a specific regimen to get it to bloom. It needs a cool resting time with short daylengths to form flower buds. In summer put it outdoors in a shady spot. Around mid-September or after the outdoor temperatures have fallen to

Place Christmas cactus outdoors in summer where they will receive good light. Leave outdoors until temperatures fall to 45°F in order to set flower buds.

45°F at night, bring it indoors into a cool spot (around 55°F) and reduce watering for its resting phase. Keep the soil only slightly moist. The plant may develop root rot if overwatered. Continue to keep the plant somewhat dry and cool as it forms flower buds. It may drop flower buds if the growing conditions are changed once buds are set. Fertilize monthly with half-strength blooming plant food starting in April and continuing until the plant comes indoors in fall. Repot only every 3 years, since it does better if somewhat pot-bound. The potting mix must be well drained but not as coarse as regular cactus mix.

PROPAGATION: Propagate from leaf cuttings. Pinch off leaf segments and allow them to dry for a couple of days before inserting into sterile soil mix. When propagating by seed, allow the fruits to ripen, then extract the seeds. Clean the seeds and dry them for a few days, then sow on sterile soil mix.

PESTS AND DISEASES: Treat scale with a cotton swab dipped in alcohol. Wash off spider mites and aphids.

RELATED SPECIES: There are hundreds of cultivars of Christmas cactus, with all colors of flowers, bicolors, and doubles.

THANKSGIVING CACTUS

Schlumbergera truncata *shlum-BER-ger-uh trun-KAY-tuh*

Thanksgiving cactus is a magnificent fall bloomer with blossoms in shades of red, salmon, and white. Give it a cool period outdoors in fall to set flower buds.

SIZE: 8–12"h × 12–18"w
TYPE: Forest cactus
FORM: Upright, trailing
TEXTURE: Medium
GROWTH: Slow
LIGHT: High

MOISTURE: Dry
SOIL: Potting soil
FEATURES: Scalloped leaves, showy flowers
USES: Blooming accent
FLOWERS: ■■□

SITING:. When siting Thanksgiving cactus, consider a spot that is not visible when it is resting, then bring it onto center stage when in bloom. It does best in medium light during active growth and bright, indirect light in winter. Ideal temperatures during active growth and blooming are 70–80°F. Give it no less than 60°F during bloom time. It is tolerant of low humidity (less than 30 percent).

CARE: Thanksgiving cactus is magnificent in bloom, but it needs a cool resting time and long nights to form flower buds. This plant usually blooms in November, during which time it should be watered regularly, allowing it to dry slightly between waterings. The plant may develop root rot if overwatered. In June, July, and August, put it outdoors in a shady spot protected from pests. Around mid-September, or after outdoor temperatures have fallen to 45°F at night, bring it indoors into a cool spot (around 55°F) and reduce watering for its resting phase. Keep the soil only slightly moist. Continue to keep the plant somewhat dry and cool as it forms flower buds. It may drop its buds if the growing conditions are changed once buds are set. Around the beginning of November, bring into warmth and begin watering.

Commercial growers give Thanksgiving cactus 20–25 days of short days to ensure bud set and bloom in time for Thanksgiving. Fertilize monthly with half-strength blooming plant food starting in April and continuing until the plant comes indoors in fall. Repot only every 3 years; the plant does better if pot-bound. Potting mix must be well drained but not as coarse as regular cactus mix; this cactus grows in moist conditions in the wild.

PROPAGATION: Propagate from leaf cuttings. Pinch off leaf segments and allow them to dry for a couple of days before inserting into sterile soil mix. When propagating by seed, allow the fruits to ripen, then extract the seeds. Clean the seeds and dry them for a few days, then sow on sterile soil mix.

PESTS AND DISEASES: Treat scale with a cotton swab dipped in alcohol; wash off spider mites and aphids.

RELATED SPECIES: There are hundreds of cultivars of Thanksgiving cactus, with all colors of flowers, bicolors, and doubles.

BURRO'S TAIL

Sedum morganianum *SEE-dum mor-gan-ee-AY-num*

Place burro's tail, also known as donkey's tail, out of traffic because the succulent leaves break off easily when touched.

SIZE: 4–6"h × 3'w
TYPE: Succulent
FORM: Trailing
TEXTURE: Medium
GROWTH: Medium
LIGHT: High
MOISTURE: Dry

SOIL: Cactus mix
FEATURES: Silvery-blue foliage
USES: Hanging basket, succulent garden

SITING: Burro's tail is a delightful, unique plant. Provide it with bright light, either filtered or direct sun, for the best growth. It will tolerate medium light but tends to become leggy. Burro's tail thrives in average to hot temperatures (60–85°F) and low humidity (below 30 percent). Be sure to site the plant away from traffic because the "tails" are easily damaged and will drop leaves.

CARE: Let it dry out fairly well between waterings, then soak. Make sure the pot drains well; overwatering will cause crown rot. In winter allow the plant to dry out completely between waterings, giving only enough water to keep the leaves from shriveling. A plant that is underwatered will experience leaf drop. Repot only if the plant becomes top heavy. It performs best in a terra-cotta pot, which allows the soil to dry out easily. Be sure the rim of the pot is rounded or it will cut the stems and leaves of the heavy tails. Feed only once a year, in summer, with foliage plant food. Remove any damaged leaves and shorten the tails if they become too heavy.

PROPAGATION: Propagate by leaf or stem cuttings. Pinch off a leaf or a stem tip, let it dry for a couple of days, and then set it on moist soil.

PESTS AND DISEASES: Burro's tail has no pest problems except for occasional mealybugs.

RELATED SPECIES: *S. sieboldii* 'Mediovariegatum' has flat leaves with a creamy center and blue-green edges.

Even though the leaves break off easily, you can take advantage of the situation by sticking the leaves in potting soil to start new plants.

CINERARIA
Senecio xhybridus (Pericallis xhybrida) *seh-NEE-shee-oh HYE-brid-us (pair-ih-KAL-iss HI-brid-uh)*

Cineraria, lovely blooming plants in all shades of purples, pinks, and blues, are showy additions to a blooming display.

SIZE: 6–8"h × 8–12"w
TYPE: Herbaceous
FORM: Rounded
TEXTURE: Medium
GROWTH: Medium
LIGHT: Medium

MOISTURE: Moist
SOIL: Potting soil
FEATURES: Flowers
USES: Blooming accent
FLOWERS: ■ ■ ■ ■
■ □

SITING: Provide cineraria with medium or indirect, bright light. This plant is enjoyed for its intense blossoms, so site it in a cool spot to prolong the display. Temperatures above 65°F will make the flowers open and fade quickly, so provide temperatures of 55–65°F during the day. If kept cool, cineraria will bloom for 4–6 weeks. It is not particular about humidity.

CARE: The key to keeping cineraria blooming as long as possible is to keep the soil evenly moist throughout its bloom cycle. The plant wilts easily if not provided plenty of moisture, and once it wilts, cineraria seldom recovers. At time of purchase, the plant is usually pot-bound so it will take up little water and may need watering every other day. Discard these plants after blooming rather than attempting to grow them for rebloom. Cineraria is forced into bloom by a rigorous schedule in the greenhouse. After blooming, plants begin to look ragged and unkempt in spite of the ideal care.

PROPAGATION: Propagate by seed, but greenhouse conditions are needed to get the plants to bloom unless raised outdoors as a bedding plant.

PESTS AND DISEASES: Shower the plant regularly to remove aphids. Other pests include spider mites and whiteflies. Check the undersides of the leaves for pests before you purchase a plant. If you start with a blooming pest-free plant, control measures will likely be unnecessary.

Pay close attention to watering of cinerarias. Once they wilt, they seldom recover.

STRING-OF-BEADS
Senecio rowleyanus *seh-NEE-shee-oh roh-lee-ANN-us*

String-of-beads is an unusual-looking plant with gray-green foliage that forms small balls of leaves strung on green thread. High light and average temperatures are best.

SIZE: 2"h × 2'w
TYPE: Herbaceous
FORM: Trailing
TEXTURE: Fine
GROWTH: Medium
LIGHT: High

MOISTURE: Dry
SOIL: Potting soil
FEATURES: Ball-like foliage
USES: Hanging basket, focal point

SITING: String-of-beads seems to catch everyone's fancy, especially that of children. This plant will keep its unique shape and form a dense mat of "beads" on the surface of the soil when given high light protected by a gauzy curtain during active growth. In winter the plant can tolerate a couple of hours of direct sun every day. Average home temperatures (60–75°F) are fine during the growing season, but reduce the temperature to 50–55°F in winter.

CARE: Allow the soil to dry between waterings during active growth. In winter when the plant is semidormant, provide only enough water to keep the beads from shriveling. Feed string-of-beads every 2 weeks with half-strength foliage plant food when it is actively growing. Repot about every 2 years or when the plant begins to look ragged. Cut it back severely to keep the plant compact. Use trimmings as cuttings to start new, fresh plants.

PROPAGATION: String-of-beads propagates easily by stem cuttings or leaf cuttings. Simply place some of the beads on the soil, where they will root. Or pin the stem to moist soil at a leaf node; roots will quickly form.

PESTS AND DISEASES: Keep aphids at bay by washing the plant periodically. Remove mealybugs with a cotton swab dipped in alcohol or horticultural oil. Keep the plant somewhat dry to prevent root rot.

RELATED SPECIES: The genus Senecio includes a large array of species, but few others adapt well to indoor environments. German ivy (*S. mikanioides*) is a succulent vine sometimes grown as a houseplant. Dusty miller (*S. cineraria*) is well known in the flower garden for its velvety, deeply-lobed silver foliage.

GLOXINIA

Sinningia speciosa *sin-NIN-gee-uh spee-see-OH-sah*

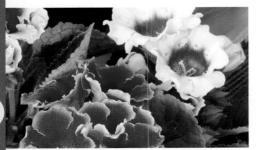

Gloxinias are lovely velvet-flowered plants with coarse, deep green foliage that is reddish on the undersides. Keep the plants cool while blooming.

SIZE: 12"h × 12"w
TYPE: Herbaceous, tuberous
FORM: Mounded
TEXTURE: Coarse
GROWTH: Medium
LIGHT: High
MOISTURE: Moist

SOIL: Potting soil
FEATURES: Velvety leaves, large blossoms
USES: Blooming accent
FLOWERS: ▨ ☐ ▪
▪ ▪

SITING: Gloxinia's large, tubular flowers are set off by velvety foliage that is reddish on the undersides. It needs bright, filtered light to keep it blooming for a long period.

It thrives in average home temperatures (60–75°F) but needs high humidity.
CARE: Keep evenly moist but not soggy while in active growth. Avoid getting water on the leaves, because they will spot. The leaves will curl when the air is too dry, and the plant may rot if kept too cool and moist. Direct sun will scorch the leaves. Gloxinia doesn't need fertilization when blooming. After blooming reduce the watering and fertilize every 2 weeks. To bring into bloom, stop watering when

When the foliage turns yellow, stop watering to let the leaves dry. Remove the foliage and store the tuber in a cool, dry spot. Repot in spring and begin watering.

the foliage turns yellow. Remove the foliage and store the tuber in a cool, dry spot in its pot until spring. Then repot the tuber, keeping it at soil level to prevent rotting. Bring it into a warm spot and begin watering sparingly. When foliage appears, keep the soil evenly moist and provide high humidity.
PROPAGATION: Propagate by leaf cuttings or stem cuttings. Use bottom heat and insert the cuttings in vermiculite or sand for rooting. This plant can also be grown fairly easily from seed.
PESTS AND DISEASES: Mealybugs, spider mites, and whiteflies may cause problems. Check the undersides of the leaves carefully for pests before bringing a plant home. Use a strong spray of water to dislodge spider mites and whiteflies. Treat mealybugs with a cotton swab dipped in alcohol.
RELATED SPECIES: Cultivars are classified into two groups: The Fyfiana group has upright flowers, and the Maxima group has nodding flowers. *S. canescens* has dull green leaves and pink flowers. *S. cardinalis* has scalloped leaves with upright red blossoms.

BABY'S TEARS

Soleirolia soleirolii *sol-eh-ROH-lee-uh sol-eh-ROH-lee-eye*

Baby's tears has the look of a delicate mossy cascading plant, but it is a tenacious plant that thrives in bright or medium light and cool to medium temperature.

SIZE: 2"h × 9–12"w
TYPE: Herbaceous
FORM: Trailing
TEXTURE: Fine
GROWTH: Fast
LIGHT: Medium
MOISTURE: Moist

SOIL: Potting soil
FEATURES: Tiny leaves
USES: Hanging basket, terrarium, ground cover

SITING: Baby's tears is a delicate, sweet plant that makes a lovely hanging basket, or a soft ground cover for larger plants. Site it carefully because it grows quickly and can overwhelm other plants. It does

best in bright, indirect light but will tolerate medium light. Provide cool to medium temperatures (55–75°F) and average humidity (30–60 percent).
CARE: Baby's tears should not dry out or the succulent stems and leaves will collapse and die. The plant can rot fairly easily if kept soggy. Feed every second

Baby's tears makes a superb groundcover plant in the container of a larger plant. Be careful not to use it with a small plant as it will quickly overcome the other plant.

or third week with half-strength foliage plant food. Stop fertilizing when the plant stops active growth in winter. It can be repotted annually, but older plants look ragged after a while. Start new plants every year from cuttings; they grow quickly. Remove faded leaves occasionally.
PROPAGATION: Propagate by stem cuttings, which root readily at the leaf nodes. Because the stems are so fine, remove a chunk of the plant and lay it on moist potting soil. It will soon take root. You can also divide the root ball when repotting.
PESTS AND DISEASES: Baby's tears may have occasional whiteflies and aphids. The plant is very hard to treat because of the tiny leaves and succulent, breakable stems, so cut it back severely or simply discard an affected plant.
RELATED SPECIES: The cultivar 'Aurea' has bright green foliage with a golden cast. 'Variegata' has silver-edged leaves.

COLEUS
Solenostemon scutellarioides   *soh-len-AH-steh-mun skoo-tuh-lair-ee-OY-deez*

Coleus's variegated foliage makes a great indoor plant. Bright light and high humidity indoors keeps it colorful.

SIZE: 6–12"h ×
6–12"w
TYPE: Herbaceous
FORM: Mounded
TEXTURE: Medium
GROWTH: Fast
LIGHT: High

MOISTURE: Moist
SOIL: Potting soil
FEATURES: Colored foliage
USES: Foliage accent
FLOWERS: ■

SITING: Because coleus is grown for its bright foliage, give it ideal conditions. A poorly grown coleus is not appealing. Coleus provides wonderful colors as long as it receives bright, filtered light and fairly high humidity (above 60 percent). In low light the plant will get leggy and the leaf colors will fade. Full sun will also fade the leaves. Average home temperatures (60–75°F) are fine.

CARE: Keep evenly moist during the growing season. Leaves will drop if the plant dries out. Keep it barely moist in winter when the plant is resting. Feed every 2 weeks with half-strength foliage plant food during active growth. Repot annually by cutting the plant back substantially and repotting into new organic soil. This plant will flower in the house, although some gardeners feel that the flowers detract from the foliage. Simply pinch out the flower stems if you don't like the look. Pinch the leaf tips regularly to keep it shrubby and full. It will send out new shoots quickly at leaf nodes.

PROPAGATION: Grow from seed and from stem cuttings. Start stem cuttings in water or soil; they will produce roots in a week or so.

PESTS AND DISEASES: Spider mites may be a problem if the humidity is low and temperatures are warm.

RELATED SPECIES: There are hundreds of cultivars with all types of wildly variegated leaves that are ruffled, deeply incised, and scalloped.

1 Coleus readily roots from cuttings of any size and from anywhere along the stem.

2 Coleus roots as well in water as it does in soil. Roots form quickly.

PEACE LILY
Spathiphyllum wallisii   *spath-ih-FYE-lum wall-EE-see-eye*

Peace lily is a superb foliage plant that tolerates neglect. Its foliage looks good when grown in low light, and it will thrive in low humidity.

SIZE: 18–24"h ×
12–18"w
TYPE: Herbaceous
FORM: Vase
TEXTURE: Coarse
GROWTH: Medium
LIGHT: High to low

MOISTURE: Dry
SOIL: Potting soil
FEATURES: Glossy foliage, attractive blossoms
USES: Foliage, low light
FLOWERS: □

SITING: Peace lily tolerates neglect and is the plant of choice for offices, because the glossy foliage and attractive white spadix and spathe flowers do well in bright, filtered light as well as medium, and even artificial light. Light that is too intense will yellow the leaves. The plant performs well in average to warm temperatures (60–85°F) and will thrive even in low humidity (below 30 percent). It may suffer chilling injury if the temperature drops below 60°F.

CARE: If growing peace lily in high light, keep the soil somewhat moist. The lower the light, the drier the soil should be kept. If the plant is allowed to dry to the point of wilting, the leaf edges will turn yellow, then brown. It does well in a self-watering container. Feed only three times in summer with foliage plant food. Overfeeding will prevent flowering and cause brown spots on the leaves. Repot only when shoots begin to crowd the original plant. Dust or shower the leaves once a month. Plants begin blooming when they are more than a year old.

PROPAGATION: Propagate by dividing the root ball. Lift the plant from its pot, cut through the root ball, and pot up the divisions separately.

PESTS AND DISEASES: Control mealybugs with horticultural oil.

RELATED SPECIES: The cultivar 'Mauna Loa' is larger and more robust. 'Lynise' has matte-finish leaves and is one of the most floriferous peace lilies available.

1 To repot the plant, pull it from its pot and slice cleanly through the root ball.

2 Replant the two portions of the root ball in clean potting soil in separate pots.

CAPE PRIMROSE

Streptocarpus ×hybridus strep-toh-KAR-pus HYE-brid-us

Cape primrose is a favorite blooming houseplant with its attractive foliage and pink, white, purple, or blue flowers.

SIZE: 6–12"h × 6–12"w
TYPE: Herbaceous
FORM: Mounded
TEXTURE: Medium
GROWTH: Medium
LIGHT: High
MOISTURE: Moist

SOIL: Potting soil
FEATURES: Blossoms, fuzzy foliage
USES: Blooming accent
FLOWERS: ■■□■

SITING: Cape primrose will continuously bloom if given the right conditions and not moved around. It does best in bright, indirect light and temperatures of 60°F at night and 75–85°F during the day. Higher temperatures may cause plants to rot; cool temperatures cause leaf injury. Cape primrose performs best in medium to high humidity (30 percent and higher).

CARE: Keep evenly moist. Avoid wetting the leaves; it may cause spotting. Many gardeners water from the bottom instead of the top. Feed with blooming plant food according to label directions. Repot only when the plant seems to be languishing. Remove faded leaves; remove faded

False African violet has fuzzy gray-green leaves and blue-purple flowers that seem to dance on long wiry petioles.

False African violets perform best in medium to high humidity. Place the pots on trays of moist pebbles.

flowers quickly unless you want seeds for propagation. Preventing seed production will promote longer blooming.

PROPAGATION: Propagate by leaf cuttings. Break off a leaf and insert the petiole and bottom half of the leaf into sterile potting mix or vermiculite. In 2–6 months, small plants will form at the soil level.

PESTS AND DISEASES: Cape primrose is generally carefree but may become infested with mites, thrips, mealybugs, or aphids. Wash off most insects with a strong spray of lukewarm water. Heavy infestations may call for a pesticide; choose appropriately so the plant will not be harmed or discard the plant.

RELATED SPECIES: False African violet (*S. saxorum*) has gray-green leaves and abundant light lilac blossoms.

ARROWHEAD VINE

Syngonium podophyllum (Nephthytis) sin-GOH-nee-um poh-doh-FIL-lum (nef-THIGH-tiss)

Arrowhead vines are well loved for their variegated silvery-green arrowhead-shaped leaves. These plants thrive in average to low light and average temperatures.

SIZE: 1–3'h × 6'w
TYPE: Herbaceous
FORM: Trailing, upright
TEXTURE: Medium
GROWTH: Fast
LIGHT: Medium to low

MOISTURE: Dry
SOIL: Potting soil
FEATURES: Arrow-shaped foliage
USES: Hanging basket, foliage accent

SITING: Arrowhead vine is a lush foliage plant that is an old favorite because of its fairly carefree nature. Leaves retain their variegation in medium and low light. It does well in the artificial light of an office but is more compact and shrubby in higher light. Low light makes the plant leggy. It performs well in average home temperatures (60–75°F) and humidity above 30 percent, easily provided with a pebble tray or room humidifier.

Arrowhead vine can be trained to an upright form by pinning the vining stems onto a moss pole.

CARE: In low light allow the soil to dry slightly between waterings; in medium light keep the soil somewhat moist. Avoid soggy soil or the plant will rot. Repotting is seldom needed. Feed with foliage plant food three times in summer. Because the plant is naturally vining, pinching it often will help keep it compact and shrubby. To train it to a moss pole, pin the aerial roots to the pole and keep the pole moist. Remove the occasional faded leaf.

PROPAGATION: Propagate easily by stem tip cuttings or by division.

PESTS AND DISEASES: Arrowhead vine may have scale, mealybugs, and spider mites. Give monthly showers to control spider mites.

RELATED SPECIES: Arrowhead vine has many cultivars with gold, light green, cream, and white markings. Several cultivars have pinkish variegation on the leaves, which lose their blush in lower light. New cultivars are less vining and more compact.

PINK QUILL

Tillandsia cyanea till-AND-zee-uh sye-ANN-ee-uh

Pink quill is an easy-care bromeliad with stunning pink bracts from which emerge bright blue flowers.

SIZE: 1–2'h × 1'w
TYPE: Bromeliad
FORM: Upright, vase-shaped
TEXTURE: Coarse
GROWTH: Medium
LIGHT: High

MOISTURE: Moist
SOIL: Epiphyte mix
FEATURES: Flower spike, grassy foliage
USES: Blooming accent
FLOWERS: ▨ ■

SITING: Pink quill's rewarding flowers begin with a bright, fan-shaped flower head that emerges from the grassy foliage, then brilliant blue flowers emerge one or two at a time from between the pink bracts. To get this plant to produce its flower, provide bright, indirect light, such as a south window with a gauzy curtain. It performs best in daytime temperatures of 68°F and above and nighttime temperatures of 50–65°F.

CARE: Although this plant is an "air" plant that can be grown on a slab, it performs better and blooms better when grown in an epiphyte potting mix. Keep the mix evenly moist. Feed with a foliage plant food according to label directions. Avoid handling the plant, which will rub off the small scales on the leaves that help absorb moisture. Repot when the potting mix breaks down. Occasionally wash off the leaves and remove spent flowers.

PROPAGATION: Propagate by dividing the root ball, starting from seed, or removing offsets. "Pups" will form at the base of the parent plant and can be removed and rooted.

RELATED SPECIES: *T. c.* var. *tricolor* has blue flowers with a white throat. *T. caput-medusae* has silvery curled leaves and a red flower stalk. *T. utriculata* var. *pringleyi* has a branched orange or red flower stalk.

Propagate pink quill by carefully removing offsets produced at the base of the plant.

Plant the "pups" in loose potting mix and place in a protected spot until roots form.

PIGGYBACK PLANT

Tolmiea menziesii TOLL-mee-uh men-ZEE-see-eye

Piggyback plant, also known as mother-of-thousands, has the unique feature of producing plantlets right on the leaves.

SIZE: 6–12"h × 12–18"w
TYPE: Herbaceous
FORM: Mounded, trailing
TEXTURE: Medium
GROWTH: Fast
LIGHT: High to medium, indirect

MOISTURE: Dry
SOIL: Potting soil
FEATURES: Scalloped foliage with plantlets
USES: Hanging basket, unique focal point

SITING: Piggyback plant thrives in average home conditions. The plantlets that grow on top of the leaves are abundant and fun to see. Give piggyback plant indirect bright to medium light. It will be more compact in higher light but will not tolerate direct sun. Provide cool to average temperatures (55–75°F) and average humidity (30–60 percent). Low humidity will cause the leaf margins to brown.

CARE: Allow to dry out between waterings when grown in medium light; keep more moist in higher light. Letting the plant dry out to the point of wilting will cause the leaf margins to brown. Repot only when roots fill the container. This plant looks best when several are planted in one pot. Feed with foliage plant food three times in summer only. Pinch frequently to keep it shrubby and compact.

PROPAGATION: Start from seed or take leaf cuttings. Remove a leaf with a plantlet and a short piece of the petiole attached. Insert the petiole into the soil so the leaf lies on the soil surface. Pin the leaf to the soil with a hairpin to keep it in contact with moisture. The plantlet will soon produce roots, and the old leaf can be cut away.

PESTS AND DISEASES: Treat spider mites, aphids, and mealybugs with horticultural oil, and raise the humidity somewhat.

RELATED SPECIES: The cultivar 'Taff's Gold' has golden-variegated leaves. 'Aurea' has leaves with a golden tinge.

To quickly produce a new plant, clip off a leaf with a sturdy plantlet intact.

Set the leaf and plantlet on moist potting mix and pin it to the soil to keep it in place.

STRIPED INCH PLANT

Tradescantia fluminensis *trad-es-KANT-ee-uh floo-min-EN-sis*

Striped inch plant is a carefree vining plant that makes a stunning hanging basket with brightly variegated foliage.

SIZE: 4–6"h ×
12–18"w
TYPE: Herbaceous
FORM: Trailing
TEXTURE: Medium
GROWTH: Fast
LIGHT: High

MOISTURE: Dry
SOIL: Potting soil
FEATURES:
Variegated foliage
USES: Hanging
basket
FLOWERS: ■

SITING: Striped inch plant is a rewarding foliage plant that offers bright variegation with little care. Its foliage brightens up a foliage display almost as effectively as flowers. Provide bright, indirect light to keep the variegation strong, although it tolerates medium light. It bleaches out in full sun. Cool to average home temperatures (55–75°F) keep it compact; give it 30 percent or higher humidity to keep the leaf edges from browning.

When striped inch plant begin to get leggy, prune it back substantially to produce compact new growth.

CARE: Allow the soil to dry between waterings; give a bit more water in bright light. Feed only three times in summer with foliage plant food. Repot as soon as roots fill the container. Pinch regularly to keep them shrubby. If they get leggy, prune them back severely to promote new, compact growth. Shower them occasionally, because it is impossible to wipe off the leaves. Start new plants regularly; older ones may begin to look ragged.

PROPAGATION: Propagate by stem cuttings in soil or water.

PESTS AND DISEASES: Control mealybugs with horticultural oil.

RELATED SPECIES: The cultivar 'Albovitatta' has light green leaves with white stripes. 'Aurea' has golden stripes. 'Variegata' has white, purple, and cream leaves.

PURPLE HEART

Tradescantia pallida (Setcreasea purpurea) *trad-es-KANT-ee-uh PAL-id-uh*
(set-KREE-zee-uh pur-pur-EE-uh)

Purple heart has deep purple leaves that add a rich element to any display. In bright, indirect light it will bloom with delicate three-petaled blossoms.

SIZE: 4–6"h ×
12–18"w
TYPE: Herbaceous
FORM: Trailing
TEXTURE: Medium
GROWTH: Fast
LIGHT: High, indirect

MOISTURE: Dry
SOIL: Potting soil
FEATURES: Purplish
foliage
USES: Hanging
basket, ground cover
FLOWERS: ■

SITING: Purple heart offers bright foliage with little care. Its foliage brightens a display almost as effectively as flowers. Provide bright, indirect light to keep the color strong, although it tolerates medium light. Cool to average home temperatures (55–75°F) will keep it compact. Give it 30 percent or higher humidity to keep the leaf edges from browning.

CARE: Allow the soil to dry between waterings; give a bit more water in bright light. Feed only three times in summer with foliage plant food. Repot as soon as roots fill the container. Pinch regularly to keep plants shrubby. If stems become leggy, prune back severely to promote new, compact growth. Shower them occasionally, because it is impossible to wipe off the individual leaves.

PROPAGATION: Propagate by stem cuttings in soil or water.

PESTS AND DISEASES: Control mealybugs with horticultural oil.

RELATED SPECIES: The cultivar 'Purpurea' has dark purple foliage and pink flowers.

1 Tip cuttings of purple heart root easily to produce new plants.

2 Dip tip cuttings in rooting hormone and stick in sterile potting soil mix. Keep away from high light until the cuttings take root.

BOAT LILY
Tradescantia spathacea *trad-es-KANT-ee-uh spath-ay-SEE-uh*

Boat lily is also known as Moses-in-the-cradle or oyster plant. Bracts and flowers are cradled in leaf axils, giving rise to the common names.

SIZE: 6–12"h × 12–18"w
TYPE: Herbaceous
FORM: Trailing
TEXTURE: Medium
GROWTH: Fast
LIGHT: High, indirect

MOISTURE: Dry
SOIL: Potting soil
FEATURES: Deep purple foliage
USES: Hanging basket
FLOWERS: ☐

SITING: Boat lily is a rewarding foliage plants that offers bright color with little care. Its foliage brightens up a display almost as flowers would. Provide bright, indirect light to keep the color strong.

It bleaches out in full sun. Cool to average home temperatures (55–75°F) will keep it

Boat lily spreads enough that it makes an effective ground cover when planted in a container with a larger plant.

compact. Give them 30 percent or higher humidity to keep the leaf edges from browning.

CARE: Allow the soil to dry between waterings; give a bit more water in bright light. Feed only three times in summer with foliage plant food. Repot as soon as roots fill the container. Pinch regularly to keep them shrubby. If they become leggy, prune back severely to promote new, compact growth. Shower them occasionally, because it is impossible to wipe off the leaves. Start new plants regularly; the older ones begin to look ragged.

PROPAGATION: Propagate by stem cuttings in soil or water.

PESTS AND DISEASES: Control mealybugs with rbbing alcohol or horticultural oil.

RELATED SPECIES: The cultivar 'Variegata' has red and yellow-green striped leaves. 'Vitatta' has longitudinal yellow stripes.

WANDERING JEW
Tradescantia zebrina (Zebrina pendula) *trad-es-KANT-ee-uh zeb-REE-nuh (zeb-BRIGH-nuh PEN-dyew-luh)*

Wandering Jew is a traditional easy-care favorite with variegated olive and cream foliage with purple undersides.

SIZE: 4–6"h × 12–18"w
TYPE: Herbaceous
FORM: Trailing
TEXTURE: Medium
GROWTH: Fast
LIGHT: High

MOISTURE: Dry
SOIL: Potting soil
FEATURES: Variegated foliage
USES: Hanging basket
FLOWERS: ☐

SITING: Provide bright, indirect light to keep the variegation strong, although these plants tolerate medium light. They bleach out in full sun. Cool to average home temperatures (55–75°F) will keep them compact. Give them 30 percent or higher

humidity to prevent the leaf edges from browning.

CARE: Allow the soil to dry between waterings; give a bit more water in bright light. Feed only three times in summer with foliage plant food. Repot as soon as roots fill the container. Pinch regularly to keep them shrubby. If they become leggy, prune back severely to promote new, compact growth. Shower wandering Jew occasionally, because it is impossible to

effectively wipe off the surface of all the leaves. Start new plants regularly; the older ones begin to look ragged.

PROPAGATION: Propagate by stem cuttings in soil or water.

PESTS AND DISEASES: Control mealybugs with horticultural oil.

RELATED SPECIES: The cultivar 'Quadricolor' has more intense variegation. 'Purpusii' has bronze-green leaves.

Wandering Jew gets leggy over time if not pinched regularly. The tips that are pruned out can be easily used to start new plants.

Dip tip cuttings in rooting powder, tap off the excess, and stick in sterile potting soil. These tips can also be rooted in water.

FLAMING SWORD
Vriesea splendens VREE-see-uh SPLEN-dens

Flaming sword, also known as painted feather, is often grown for its striking foliage, but it also sends up a tall flower spike with bright red bracts.

SIZE: 1–3'h × 1–3'w
TYPE: Bromeliad
FORM: Vase-shaped
TEXTURE: Medium
GROWTH: Slow
LIGHT: High to medium
MOISTURE: Dry

SOIL: Epiphyte mix
FEATURES: Variegated leaves, colorful blooms
USES: Focal point, blooming
FLOWERS: ■■

SITING: Flaming sword shows its best leaf color in bright, filtered light. In the right conditions, it will send up a tall red flower spike, but often the plants are grown only for their attractive foliage. They will not tolerate direct sun but do well in medium light. Provide average to hot temperatures (60°F and above) to keep the plant from rotting. High humidity (above 65 percent) is crucial to prevent leaf spots.

CARE: Let the soil dry out almost completely between waterings and keep the "vase" full of water. Every couple of months, empty and refill the vase to keep the water somewhat fresh. Feed with

Flaming sword is a bromeliad, so the soil should be kept somewhat dry and the plant watered by filling the cup, formed by the leaves, with water.

blooming plant food applied to the potting soil three times in summer or add half-strength formula to the vase every month. Flaming sword has a miniscule root system that seldom outgrows a pot. Repot only when the potting mix begins to break down and no longer has recognizable chunks of bark. This bromeliad can be grown on a slab if high humidity is provided.

PROPAGATION: Propagate by removing the offsets or side shoots when the parent plant has died. Take the plant out of the pot and gently pull off each offset, making sure it has some roots. Pot up the offsets and keep them in a warm, bright spot until they establish themselves. Water daily. A plant started this way should bloom in 1–2 years.

PESTS AND DISEASES: Treat scale and spider mites with insecticidal soap.

RELATED SPECIES: 'Vulcana' has an all-red flower head. *V. hieroglyphica* is grown for its light and dark green mottled foliage. *V. carinata* has a yellow and red flower head. *Vriesea* 'Red Chestnut' has white flecks and bands on the leaves and a yellow flower head.

SPINELESS YUCCA
Yucca elephantipes YUK-uh ell-uh-fan-TYP-eez

Spineless yucca is a coarse-textured architectural plant for a spot out of the way of traffic. Although called spineless, the tips are sharp and pointed.

SIZE: 3–5'h × 2–3'w
TYPE: Woody tree
FORM: Upright
TEXTURE: Coarse
GROWTH: Slow
LIGHT: High

MOISTURE: Dry
SOIL: Potting soil
FEATURES: Spiky foliage
USES: Architectural accent

SITING: Spineless yucca is an ideal plant for a neglectful situation as long as its light requirements are met. When grown in full sun, it stays compact and sturdy. If grown in lower light, it stretches and loses its attractive shape. It tolerates low humidity (below 30 percent) and all temperatures except freezing. Choose a site carefully, because the leaf edges and spines on the tips are sharp.

CARE: In the active growing season, water the plant when the top couple inches of soil dry out. During winter rest, water only enough to keep the foliage from wilting. Overwatering will result in brown tips; underwatering shows as shrunken trunks and solidly brown or yellow lower leaves. Feed with foliage plant food twice a year. Repot every 2 years in spring. Cut back severely if the plant becomes too tall; new heads will grow. Spineless yucca benefits from a summer outdoors and a cool, bright spot in winter.

PROPAGATION: Propagate by separating and potting up the offsets that form at the base of the plant. Propagating by root cuttings is more difficult.

PESTS AND DISEASES: None are serious.

RELATED SPECIES: The cultivar 'Variegata' has cream-edged leaves.

Spineless yucca looks its best when grown in full sun, so move it outdoors in summer if possible to give it a good dose of sunlight.

ZEEZEE PLANT
Zamioculcas zamiifolia *zam-ee-oh-KULL-kus zam-ee-ih-FOH-lee-uh*

Zeezee plant is a glossy foliage plant that will tolerate neglect and low light, yet continue to look attractive.

SIZE: 3'h × 3'w
TYPE: Herbaceous
FORM: Upright
TEXTURE: Medium
GROWTH: Slow
LIGHT: High to low

MOISTURE: Dry
SOIL: Potting soil
FEATURES: Glossy attractive leaves
USES: Foliage accent

SITING: Zeezee plant is popular because it tolerates neglect yet keeps its attractive foliage. Choose a site where the plant can make its natural spread and not be crowded. Zeezee plant can take very low light but also does well in bright, filtered light. Direct sun may burn the leaves.

This plant prefers temperatures above 40°F and low humidity (below 30 percent). Colder temperatures will cause rotting.
CARE: Keep the plant slightly more moist in high light; let it dry between waterings in lower light. Overwatering will result in yellow leaves. Repot when suckers fill the container. Feed three times in summer. Remove faded leaves. Give occasional showers to keep the foliage shiny and clean. Move it outdoors in summer to a shaded site.
PROPAGATION: Propagate from leaf cuttings. Remove a leaf and insert it in sterile potting mix. Water lightly and provide a tent for humidity. Rooting takes a long time.
PESTS AND DISEASES: None are serious.

1 Propagate zeezee plant from leaf cuttings. Simply remove a leaf, dip in rooting hormone, and insert it in potting soil.

2 It may take several months to form roots, but the plant will send up new shoots from the soil at the base of the leaf.

CALLA LILY
Zantedeschia aethiopica *zan-teh-DES-kee-uh ee-thee-OH-pik-uh*

Calla lily has long been a favorite for its striking spadix and spathe blossoms in shades of pink, white, and yellow.

SIZE: 1–3'h × 1'w
TYPE: Bulb
FORM: Upright
TEXTURE: Coarse
GROWTH: Medium
LIGHT: High, indirect
MOISTURE: Moist

SOIL: Potting soil
FEATURES: Glossy foliage, flowers
USES: Blooming accent
FLOWERS: □ ■ ■ ■

SITING: Calla lily is a striking plant that needs perfect conditions to grow indoors. It needs bright, indirect light to produce blossoms. It tolerates average home temperatures (60–75°F) but needs high humidity (above 60 percent) to thrive.

CARE: Keep evenly moist while in active growth. Feed with half-strength foliage plant food from February to November. Stop watering in November and allow the foliage to die. Remove the tubers and store them in vermiculite or peat moss at around 40°F. In February, repot, bring into warmth and light, and begin watering. Foliage should appear quickly. Remove faded flowers. Give an occasional shower.
PROPAGATION: Divide the rhizomes before potting up in February. The small offsets that form take 18 months to bloom.
RELATED SPECIES: The cultivar 'Red Desire' has a pink spadix. 'White Giant' has white-speckled leaves and 7'-tall flower stalks. 'Pink Mist' has soft pink-blushed spathes.

1 To coax calla lily back into bloom, stop watering it in November and allow the foliage to die.

2 Trim off dead foliage and remove the tubers from their soil, brushing off as much soil as possible.

3 Store tubers until midwinter. Then pot up, water, and bring into warmth to renew growth.

A–Z ENCYCLOPEDIA OF
ORNAMENTAL AND
LAWN GRASS CARE

Grasses complement other landscape
plants. Here feather reed grass and
pampas grass dominate a fall border
that also includes 'Autumn Joy' sedum
and Russian sage.

The seed heads of *Miscanthus* 'Purpurascens' dazzle in the autumn sun.

Miscanthus sinensis 'Strictus' has yellow horizontal banding on its leaves.

Pennisetum setaceum 'Rubrum' has deep ruby foliage.

GOLDEN JAPANESE SWEET FLAG
Acorus gramineus *ah-KOR-uhs gra-MIN-ee-us*

Golden Japanese sweet flag prefers moist soil. It is deer resistant.

ZONES: 6–10
SIZE: 6–12"h × 18"w
TYPE: Rhizomatous, evergreen perennial
FORM: Tuft
TEXTURE: Medium
GROWTH: Moderate
LIGHT: Sun to part shade

MOISTURE: High
SOIL: Fertile
FEATURES: Golden leaves, cinnamon scent
USES: Pond edge, ground cover, lawn substitute
FALL COLOR: ◻

SITING: Golden Japanese sweet flag grows in water or in boggy conditions. The fan-shaped foliage serves as an excellent companion to golden-colored hostas, moss, camassias, and yellow-flowered shrubs.

CARE: Plant 18–24" apart in spring or fall. Feed with slow-release granular plant food in spring. Maintain a 3" layer of mulch to conserve moisture. In dry soil, the leaf tips may turn brown and wither. This plant spreads quickly by rhizomes.
PROPAGATION: Divide and pot up the rhizomes in spring.
PESTS AND DISEASES: Few pests affect it. Deer generally avoid it.
RELATED SPECIES: 'Ogon' has cream and chartreuse stripes. 'Variegatus' has green and white striped leaves. 'Licorice' smells like anise. 'Pusillus' has smaller, stiff, dark green leaves. Yellow 'Minimus', and 'Minimus Aureus' grow only about 3" tall.

TURKEYFOOT
Andropogon gerardii *an-droh-POH-gon jer-ARD-ee-eye*

Turkeyfoot is named for its turkey foot flowers. It is also known as big bluestem.

ZONES: 3–10
SIZE: 5–10'h × 2–3'w
TYPE: Warm-season clumping grass
FORM: Upright
TEXTURE: Fine
GROWTH: Variable
LIGHT: Full sun

MOISTURE: Low to medium
SOIL: Any
FEATURES: Fall color, winter interest
USES: Specimen, prairie, meadow
FLOWERS: ■
FALL COLOR: ■ ■

SITING: Site turkeyfoot in full sun. It tolerates clay. It tolerates poor, dry places but grows more slowly and remains shorter. Combine it with perennial sunflowers or Joe-Pye weed.

CARE: Space clumps 3–4' apart in spring. Use a slow-release granular plant food at time of planting. Stop feeding when clumps reach the desired size. Mulch between clumps to discourage weeds. Cut back to about 6" tall in early spring.
PROPAGATION: Start from seed or divide in spring. Slice through the clumps with a sharp knife or a pruning saw.
PESTS AND DISEASES: Few pests or diseases affect turkeyfoot. It is a good winter food source for birds.
RELATED SPECIES: Stiffly upright growing broomsedge, *A. virginicus,* is remarkable for its attractive orange winter color. It can become weedy even though it's native.

BULBOUS OAT GRASS
Arrhenatherum elatius ssp. *bulbosum* 'Variegatum' *ah-ren-uh-THEE-rum el-LAT-ee-us bul-BO-sum*

Bulbous oat grass, also known as tuber oat grass or false-oat, is a cool white, striped grass that looks best in cool weather.

ZONES: 4–9
SIZE: 1–2'h × 18–24"w
TYPE: Cool-season clumping perennial grass
FORM: Spiky tuft
TEXTURE: Fine
GROWTH: Fast
LIGHT: Part sun to full shade

MOISTURE: Medium
SOIL: Acid, fertile, well drained
FEATURES: Green-and-white-striped foliage
USES: Rock garden, front of border
FLOWERS: ■
FALL COLOR: ◼

SITING: Bulbous oat grass needs a cool site. It may be up early in the season, disappear and go dormant in the heat of a hot-summer climate, and return when the weather cools. Avoid placing it in a hot spot. Give it afternoon shade and cool,

moist, fertile soil. The cool green-and-white variegation is excellent with pastel-colored flowers such as pink or blue creeping phlox (*Phlox stolonifera*).
CARE: Plant 18" apart. Feed when it is actively growing in spring and again in fall. Cut back foliage that browns during the heat of the summer.
PROPAGATION: Propagate by seed, or divide for additional plants and to keep the clumps looking trim.
PESTS AND DISEASES: Hot weather may bring on rust diseases.
RELATED SPECIES: The green-leaved species, *A. elatius* ssp. *bulbosum,* may become invasive. 'Variegatum' is well behaved.

BLUE GRAMA GRASS
Bouteloua gracilis *boo-tell-LOO-uh grah-SILL-iss*

Blue grama grass produces mosquito-like flowers, giving rise to its alternate common name, mosquito grass.

ZONES: 3–9
SIZE: 8–15"h × 12–15"w
TYPE: Warm-season sod-forming perennial grass
FORM: Vase
TEXTURE: Fine
GROWTH: Moderate
LIGHT: Full sun
MOISTURE: Dry to medium

SOIL: Average to fertile
FEATURES: Drought, cold, and alkaline soil tolerant
USES: Native dryland lawn grass, rock garden, container
FLOWERS: ■
FALL COLOR: ■

SITING: Blue grama is often the dominant native grass on dry prairies. Place it in full sun and average to fertile soil that is dry and well drained. Cut back to 2–3" for a lawn that will survive without irrigation. Uncut, the grass produces attractive flowers that are useful in arrangements.

CARE: For use as a lawn grass, seed it in early summer at the rate of 1½–2 pounds per 1,000 square feet. Keep moist until germination is complete. Then withhold water to encourage deep rooting. Feed monthly during active growth with a low-nitrogen food, but hold back during drought.

PROPAGATION: Start plants from seed or use plugs for lawn establishment.

PESTS AND DISEASES: None are serious.

RELATED SPECIES: 'Hachita' is a vigorous cultivar suitable for lawns. It requires mowing only about once a month.

QUAKING GRASS
Briza media *BREYE-zuh MEE-dee-uh*

Quaking grass is grown for its beadlike flower panicles that dance in the breeze.

ZONES: 4–10
SIZE: 12–24"h × 12–18" w
TYPE: Cool-season, clumping, evergreen perennial
FORM: Clump
TEXTURE: Fine
GROWTH: Medium

LIGHT: Full sun
MOISTURE: Medium
SOIL: Fertile
FEATURES: Soft texture, heart-shaped flowers
USES: Perennial border
FLOWERS: ■

SITING: Grow quaking grass in full sun and moist soil as an edging, in front of the border, or as a delicate accent in the perennial border. It is also known as cow quakes, pearl grass, rattler grass, or trembling grass.

CARE: Provide full sun and consistent moisture to enable quaking grass to bloom well. Cut off the flowers when they become ragged. At the same time cut back the clump to promote fresh, new growth.

PROPAGATION: Divide clumps in spring.

PESTS AND DISEASES: Quaking grass is generally free of pests.

RELATED SPECIES: Little quaking grass (*B. minor*), smaller in clump and flower, is an annual species.

BUFFALO GRASS
Buchloe dactyloides *boo-KLOH-ee dak-til-LOY-deez*

Buffalo grass forms a low-maintenance, dry-climate lawn that needs little mowing.

ZONES: 3–9
SIZE: 2–8"h × 6–12"w
TYPE: Warm-season perennial grass
FORM: Tuft
TEXTURE: Fine
GROWTH: Variable
LIGHT: Sun

MOISTURE: Dry to medium
SOIL: Clay, sandy loam, alkaline
FEATURES: Soft texture, drought and heat tolerant
USES: Drought-tolerant lawn
FALL COLOR: ■

SITING: Buffalo grass thrives in average to dry soil in full sun. It is exceptionally tolerant of heat, humidity, and drought and adapts to alkaline soil. It forms a fine-textured lawn that is soft to walk upon.

CARE: Buffalo grass grows only 4–8" tall and may or may not be mowed to 2–3", depending upon personal preference. It needs only about 2" of water per month to stay green during the heat of summer— 50–75 percent less water than bluegrass.

PROPAGATION: Start from seed or use plugs for lawn establishment.

PESTS AND DISEASES: Chinch bugs may infest buffalo grass; 'Cody' and 'Tatanka' are forms resistant to chinch bugs.

RELATED SPECIES: 'Sharp's Improved', a vigorous turf, can be established by sod or plugs. It grows 4–6" tall. Legacy®, a 4–6" turf variety was developed to duplicate the lush green look of a bluegrass lawn.

FEATHER REED GRASS
Calamagrostis ×acutiflora kal-uh-muh-GRAHS-tiss uh-kyew-tih-FLOR-uh

Feather reed grass is extremely upright, creating a vertical backdrop in the perennial border or an outstanding focal point.

ZONES: 3–9
SIZE: 4–6'h × 12–18"w
TYPE: Cool-season clumping perennial grass
FORM: Upright
TEXTURE: Fine
GROWTH: Medium to fast
LIGHT: Sun to light shade

MOISTURE: Medium
SOIL: Average to rich
FEATURES: Vertical habit, early flowers, sterile
USES: Specimen, ground cover, border
FLOWERS: □ ■ ■
FALL COLOR: ■ ■

SITING: Place feather reed grass in a moist, sunny area. It tolerates clay soils.
CARE: It does best in slightly acid soil that does not dry out in summer. Mulch to conserve moisture and discourage weeds. Feed with water-soluble plant food once a month until seed heads form. Cut back to 3–4" in late winter or early spring.
PROPAGATION: Divide in late winter to early spring using a pruning saw or sharp spade. Reset the divisions, water deeply, and mulch.
PESTS AND DISEASES: No pests or diseases are problems on feather reed grass.
RELATED SPECIES: 'Karl Foerster' is the only cultivar widely found in the nursery trade. *C. ×acutiflora* 'Overdam' grows to 3' with variegated white-and-green foliage. Feather reed grass (*C. arundinacea*) is a strongly rhizomatous European native that is one of the parents of 'Karl Foerster'.

KOREAN FEATHER REED GRASS
Calamagrostis brachytricha kal-uh-muh-GRAHS-tiss bray-key-TRIK-uh

Korean feather reed grass, also known as foxtail grass, bears foxtail plumes in fall.

ZONES: 4–9
SIZE: 4'h × 2'w
TYPE: Warm-season clumping perennial grass
FORM: Vase
TEXTURE: Medium
GROWTH: Medium
LIGHT: Sun to part shade

MOISTURE: Medium
SOIL: Fertile, moist
FEATURES: Cut flowers
USES: Container, massing, specimen
FLOWERS: ■ □
FALL COLOR: ■ ■

SITING: Korean feather reed grass needs even more moisture than feather reed grass and will thrive in a sunny spot if this need is met. Otherwise light shade with morning sun is ideal. The early fall flowers dazzle in the sunlight. The feathery rose-white "foxtails" can be dried. Compact asters such as aster 'October Skies' make attractive, fall-blooming companions.
CARE: Grow this grass in moist soil in sun to part shade. Mulch to preserve moisture. Feed monthly with water-soluble plant food until flowers are fully formed. Cut back in late winter before the new growth emerges in spring.
PROPAGATION: Sow, seed, or divide clumps in spring.
PESTS AND DISEASES: Korean feather reed grass is generally free of pests and diseases.
RELATED SPECIES: Feather reed grass (*C. ×acutiflora* 'Karl Foerster') is more upright and blooms earlier.

MENDOCINO REED GRASS
Calamagrostis foliosa kal-uh-muh-GRAHS-tiss foh-lee-OH-suh

Mendocino reed grass, also known as leafy reed grass, is a striking California native.

ZONES: 8–10
SIZE: 18–24"h × 24–30"w
TYPE: Clumping semievergreen perennial grass
FORM: Broad-spreading clump
TEXTURE: Fine
GROWTH: Medium
LIGHT: Light shade

MOISTURE: Medium
SOIL: Average, moist, well drained
FEATURES: Cascading tan flowers, semievergreen
USES: Ground cover, slope, accent
FLOWERS: ■

SITING: Mendocino reed grass is especially attractive on a rocky slope, where its fuzzy flowers will cascade attractively. Avoid very dry sites. In California where it is native, it thrives in light shade.
CARE: Mendocino reed grass grows well with little care where it is native. Frugal irrigation and judicious pruning will keep it evergreen and looking its best.
PROPAGATION: Start from seed or division.
PESTS AND DISEASES: Mendocino reed grass is generally free of pests.
RELATED SPECIES: Feather reed grass *C. ×acutiflora* 'Karl Foerster,' is an upright, cool-season grass. Korean feather reed grass (*C. brachytricha*) is a warm-season late bloomer.

LEATHERLEAF SEDGE
Carex buchananii KAIR-eks byew-KAN-en-ee-eye

Leatherleaf sedge has copper-brown foliage all season long.

ZONES: 7–9
SIZE: 18–24"h × 24"w
TYPE: Clumping perennial sedge
FORM: Vase
TEXTURE: Fine
GROWTH: Moderate
LIGHT: Sun

MOISTURE: Medium
SOIL: Well drained, average
FEATURES: Bronze foliage
USES: Ground cover, specimen, accent

SITING: Leatherleaf sedge, from New Zealand, thrives in a sunny place in any soil that is moist but well drained. Its unique foliage color invites comment. Yellow-flowered perennials such as 'Moonbeam' threadleaf tickseed (*Coreopsis verticillata*) or goldenstar (*Chrysogonum virginianum*) make excellent companions. The bright green of low-growing mazus (*Mazus reptens*) will highlight the unusual coloring of leatherleaf sedge.

CARE: Trimming tattered, old-looking foliage in spring will rejuvenate the clump. Feed with a slow-release plant food in early spring.

PROPAGATION: Divide in spring or start new plants from seed.

PESTS AND DISEASES: Leatherleaf sedge is generally free of pests.

RELATED SPECIES: Dwarf brown New Zealand sedge (*C. petriei*) grows only 8" tall, resembling a tiny leatherleaf sedge.

BIRDFOOT SEDGE
Carex conica KAIR-eks KON-ih-kuh

Birdfoot sedge, also known as hime kan suge, has fine green and white foliage.

ZONES: 5–9
SIZE: 8–15"h × 12–18"w
TYPE: Clumping, perennial sedge
FORM: Mounded
TEXTURE: Fine
GROWTH: Slow
LIGHT: Light to full shade

MOISTURE: Medium
SOIL: Rich, well drained
FEATURES: Dark green blades are edged white, long-lived
USES: Edging, ground cover, accent, rock garden

SITING: Place birdfoot sedge in light shade in rich, moist soil at the edge of a border where it will not be overwhelmed by taller plants. It is superb in combination with Japanese painted fern (*Athyrium nipponicum* 'Pictum') which shares its coloring.

CARE: Enrich the soil around this plant with compost. Mulch to retain moisture. Trim away winter-damaged foliage in early spring before new growth emerges.

PROPAGATION: Divide in spring.

PESTS AND DISEASES: Birdfoot sedge is generally free of pests.

RELATED SPECIES: 'Snowline' and 'Variegata' are synonyms for *C. conica* 'Marginata'.

BOWLES' GOLDEN SEDGE
Carex elata KAIR-eks eh-LAH-tuh

Bowles' Golden sedge brings a spot of gold into the garden. It is also known as tufted sedge or European tussock sedge.

ZONES: 5–9
SIZE: 2'h × 2–3'w
TYPE: Cool-season clumping, semievergreen sedge
FORM: Vase
TEXTURE: Medium
GROWTH: Medium
LIGHT: Sun to light shade

MOISTURE: Medium to wet
SOIL: Moist, acid
FEATURES: Bright yellow foliage
USES: Waterside, water garden, ground cover

SITING: Place Bowles' Golden sedge in at least a half day of sun for the best color. This sedge will survive in standing water. It is striking when massed in the saturated soil of a river or pond edge.

CARE: Provide acid soil and constant moisture. Protect it from hot, drying winds. Cut back unsightly foliage to promote fresh new growth.

PROPAGATION: Divide in spring.

PESTS AND DISEASES: No known pests affect Bowles' Golden sedge.

RELATED SPECIES: Golden-edged sedge (*C. elegantissima* 'Variegata') is a clumping, evergreen sedge with green leaves edged in gold. Thrives in Zones 8 and 9 in moist, fertile, well-drained soil.

CARNATION SEDGE

Carex flacca (glauca) KAIR-eks FLAH-kuh (GLAU-kuh)

Carnation sedge, also known as glaucous sedge or carnation grass, spreads rapidly.

ZONES: 4–9
SIZE: 12"h × spreading
TYPE: Semievergreen rhizomatous sedge
FORM: Upright, tousled spreading clumps
TEXTURE: Medium
GROWTH: Fast

LIGHT: Sun to light shade
MOISTURE: Medium
SOIL: Loam
FEATURES: Blue-green "carnation" foliage
USES: Ground cover for sun to light shade, erosion control

SITING: Carnation sedge grows best in sun and rich soil with adequate moisure. Its glaucous foliage blends well with hostas of similar color.

CARE: Once established, carnation sedge will survive drought, but grow more slowly and remain shorter. It can become invasive if conditions are right.
PROPAGATION: Start new plants by seed or division in spring.
PESTS AND DISEASES: Carnation sedge is generally free of pests.
RELATED SPECIES: *C. flacca* 'Bias' has leaves that are striped along a single margin.

VARIEGATED SILVER SEDGE

Carex morrowii KAIR-eks MOR-oh-ee-eye

Variegated silver sedge, also known as kan suge, thrives in moist shade.

ZONES: 5–9
SIZE: 18–24"h × 24–30"w
TYPE: Clumping evergreen sedge
FORM: Mounded
TEXTURE: Leathery
GROWTH: Medium
LIGHT: Sun to shade
MOISTURE: Medium

SOIL: Rich, moist, slightly acid loam
FEATURES: Silver margins on evergreen foliage, long-lived
USES: Shady border, accent, ground cover

SITING: With adequate moisture, variegated silver sedge will tolerate full sun but may bleach to an unbecoming yellow. In hot climates, rich, moist, acid loam in partial shade is a must. Hellebores and coral bells (*Heuchera*) make good companions under trees or on the edge of a woodland.

CARE: Enrich the bed with compost before planting. Mulch to conserve moisture. Trim back winter-damaged foliage in spring.
PROPAGATION: Divide in spring.
PESTS AND DISEASES: No known pests affect variegated silver sedge.
RELATED SPECIES: Golden variegated sedge (*C. m.* 'Goldband'), with gold leaf margins, is smaller, growing only about 1' tall; 'Gilt' has creamy white leaf margins and is rhizomatous; 'Ice Dance' has distinct cream-white variegation and is carpet forming; *C. m.* var. *temnolepis* 'Silk Tassel' has fine, threadlike leaves. Formerly called *C. m. aureo-variegata* 'Old Gold' and *C. m. aureo-variegata* 'Everbrite' these sedges are now listed as *C. hachijoensis*.

PALM SEDGE

Carex muskingumensis KAIR-eks moos-kin-goo-MEN-siss

Palm sedge provides rich texture in moist sites in sun or shade.

ZONES: 4–9
SIZE: 18–24"h × spreading
TYPE: Cool-season rhizomatous perennial sedge
FORM: Mounded
TEXTURE: Fine
GROWTH: Medium
LIGHT: Sun to shade

MOISTURE: Medium to wet
SOIL: Moist, fertile
FEATURES: Radiating foliage
USES: Ground cover, water garden, pond edge , container
FALL COLOR: ▆▆

SITING: Palm sedge thrives in light shade and moist, rich soil, where it will form wonderfully textured colonies. Ligularia makes a good companion.

CARE: Provide sun or bright shade to make it stand tall. In too much shade it flops. Although it colors beautifully with frost, this sedge is too fragile to hold up over the winter. Cut it back after frost.
PROPAGATION: Start from seed or divisions in spring or fall.
PESTS AND DISEASES: No known pests affect palm sedge.
RELATED SPECIES: Variegated green and cream *C. phyllocephala* 'Sparkler' has similarly radiating leaves. Is more vibrant, but is less hardy to Zone 8.

DROOPING SEDGE
Carex pendula *KAIR-eks PEN-dyoo-luh*

Drooping sedge, also known as pendulous sedge or weeping sedge, blooms with dramatic, pendulous flowers.

ZONES: 7–9
SIZE: 2–6'h × 3–5'w
TYPE: Cool-season clumping, evergreen sedge
FORM: Cascading mound
TEXTURE: Coarse
GROWTH: Slow
LIGHT: Part shade to shade

MOISTURE: Medium
SOIL: Rich, moist, slightly acid loam
FEATURES: Lustrous evergreen leaves, showy flower spikes
USES: Ground cover, accent, wild garden
FLOWERS: ■

SITING: Drooping sedge grows slowly into an imposing clump in rich, moist soil out of the sun and wind. Place it where the pendulous flower stalks in midsummer can be seen.
CARE: Enrich the soil with well-rotted compost. Very cold winters will brown the leaves; cut back in early spring before new growth emerges. It is long-lived and self-sows where its needs are met.
PROPAGATION: Start from seed or division in early spring.
PESTS AND DISEASES: No known pests affect drooping sedge.
RELATED SPECIES: *C. pendula* 'Moonraker' has attractive, creamy yellow variegated leaves but may be less hardy to Zone 8.

PENNSYLVANIA SEDGE
Carex pensylvanica *KAIR-eks pen-sil-VAN-ih-kuh*

Pennsylvania sedge forms an excellent shady lawn substitute.

ZONES: 4–8
SIZE: 6–8"h × 3–4"w
TYPE: Clumping, semievergreen sedge
FORM: Upright
TEXTURE: Fine
GROWTH: Moderate
LIGHT: Part shade to shade

MOISTURE: Medium to dry
SOIL: Average to sandy
FEATURES: Lawn alternative
USES: Lawn in dry woodland and in shade

SITING: Plant Pennsylvania sedge thickly in a dry, shady woodland or where lawn struggles or is impossible to mow. This sedge will grow into a uniform, fine green lawn where other grasses fail.
CARE: Leave uncut to maintain the appearance of a naturalized meadow, or mow to 2–3" tall for a more highly manicured look. Place plants 8–12" on center and irrigate until established, after which they thrive with little care.
PROPAGATION: Sow seeds or divide clumps in spring.
PESTS AND DISEASES: Pennsylvania sedge is generally free of pests.
RELATED SPECIES: Broad-leaf sedge (*C. plantaginea*) grows taller with broader leaves but will form a grassy green ground cover in shady woodland.

BROAD-LEAF SEDGE
Carex plantaginea *KAIR-eks plant-tuh-jin-AYE-uh*

Broad-leaf sedge, also known as plantain-leaf sedge, is an accent for shade.

ZONES: 4–9
SIZE: 12–18"h × 12–18"w
TYPE: Clumping, evergreen sedge
FORM: Broad spreading
TEXTURE: Coarse
GROWTH: Medium
LIGHT: Light shade to shade

MOISTURE: Medium
SOIL: Rich, well drained
FEATURES: Medium green leaves
USES: Wild garden, shady ground cover, pondside
FLOWERS: ■

SITING: Native to woodlands of eastern North America, broad-leaf sedge thrives in the rich, moist soil of a shady garden or woodland. Its black-tipped spikes in spring are the perfect accompaniment to wildflowers such as Virginia bluebells (*Mertensia virginica*) and foamy Dutchman's breeches (*Dicentra cucullaria*). After the ephemerals fade, broad-leaf sedge will fill in and keep the garden green.
CARE: Plant in light to medium shade in moist, fertile soil. It may tolerate periods of drought. In hot, dry climates, irrigate in dry weather.
PROPAGATION: Grow from seed or divisions in spring.
PESTS AND DISEASES: Broad-leaf sedge has no known pest problems.
RELATED SPECIES: California black-flowering sedge (*C. nudata*), with similar flowers, grows about 2' tall. It is not evergreen.

CREEPING BROAD LEAF SEDGE

Carex siderosticha 'Variegata'   *KAIR-eks sih-der-OH-stih-kuh*

Creeping broad leaf sedge, also known as tagane so, excels in the shade.

ZONES: 4–9
SIZE: 8"h × spreading
TYPE: Cool-season rhizomatous perennial grass
FORM: Spreading
TEXTURE: Coarse
GROWTH: Medium
LIGHT: Part to full shade

MOISTURE: Medium
SOIL: Fertile, well drained
FEATURES: Green leaves with white margins
USES: Ground cover, accent, woodland
FLOWERS: ■
FALL COLOR: ■

SITING: Native to the forests of Asia, creeping broad leaf sedge excels in the woodland garden or at the edge of a shady border. Fresh new growth, sometimes tinged with pink, appears early in spring along with daffodils and woodland wildflowers. Site this sedge in rich, moist, well-drained soil and light shade for best results.

CARE: Enrich the planting bed with well-rotted leafy humus. Keep well mulched to conserve moisture. Frost turns the leaves golden yellow. When they cease to be attractive, cut them back.

PROPAGATION: Divide rhizomes in spring.

PESTS AND DISEASES: Creeping braod leaf sedge is generally free of pests.

RELATED SPECIES: The species (*C. siderosticha*) is solid green. It looks and acts the same, forming dense masses of broad green leaves.

TUSSOCK SEDGE

Carex stricta   *KAIR-eks STRIK-tuh*

Tussock sedge graces wet, boggy soils in sunny sites.

ZONES: 4–8
SIZE: 2–3'h × 2–3'w
TYPE: Cool-season rhizomatous clumping sedge
FORM: Tuft
TEXTURE: Fine
GROWTH: Medium
LIGHT: Sun

MOISTURE: Wet
SOIL: Fertile
FEATURES: Grows in standing water, spreads
USES: Bog garden, low, wet areas
FLOWERS: ■
FALL COLOR: ■

SITING: In low-lying wet areas and bogs, tussock sedge, a native of northeastern North America, forms fine green clumps that rise above the water. Superb companions include cinnamon fern (*Osmunda cinnamomea*) and royal fern (*Osmunda regalis*).

CARE: It needs constant moisture and sunlight to thrive and send out its runners to form new clumps. It is most often seen with the new growth rising above last year's dried leaves. Cutting back the old growth is not practical and not necessary; this is a plant for the wild garden.

PROPAGATION: Slice off emerging shoots and roots from the edge of the clump.

PESTS AND DISEASES: None are serious.

RELATED SPECIES: California black-flowering sedge (*C. nudata*), a native of wet streambeds, grows to 2' tall in sun and abundant moisture.

NORTHERN SEA OATS

Chasmanthium latifolium   *kas-MAN-thee-um lat-ih-FOL-ee-um*

Northern sea oats seed heads dangle gracefully from upright stems. It is also known as wild-oats or wood-oats.

ZONES: 5–9
SIZE: 3–4'h × 2'w
TYPE: Warm-season clumping perennial grass
FORM: Upright
TEXTURE: Medium
GROWTH: Fast
LIGHT: Sun to shade
MOISTURE: Medium to wet
SOIL: Tolerant of a wide range of soil types

FEATURES: Bamboo-like foliage, attractive seed heads, survives occasional flooding
USES: Massing, specimen
FLOWERS: ■ Dangling spikelets form in midsummer.
FALL COLOR: ■ ■

SITING: Give northern sea oats a difficult site; it will take over if conditions are too good. Clawlike roots enable it to survive occasional flooding. It is especially attractive as a ground cover, planted 18" on center around fall-coloring shrubs and trees such as sumac (*Rhus* spp.). Their vivid reds contrast beautifully with the grass's golden wheat color.

CARE: Provide rich, moist soil. In less favorable places, irrigate until it establishes. Mulch to cut down on self-sowing. Cut back in late winter or early spring before new growth emerges.

PROPAGATION: Sow seeds or divide clumps in spring.

PESTS AND DISEASES: No known pests affect Northern sea oats.

RELATED SPECIES: Sea oats (*Uniola paniculata*), a dune-stabilizing native grass, is a relative.

PAMPAS GRASS
Cortaderia selloana *kor-tah-DEER-ee-uh sell-oh-AN-uh*

Pampas grass forms an imposing clump of plumes in warm climates.

ZONES: 7–10
SIZE: 8–10'h × 6–8'w
TYPE: Warm-season clumping perennial grass
FORM: Upright
TEXTURE: Coarse
GROWTH: Fast
LIGHT: Sun

MOISTURE: Dry to medium
SOIL: Any
FEATURES: Blue-green foliage, showy plumes, evergreen
USES: Specimen, massing, windbreak
FLOWERS: □

SITING: Pampas grass needs full sun and plenty of room to grow. The late-summer white plumes are spectacular when backlit. The plumes are good in fresh or dried floral arrangements.

CARE: Pampas grass tolerates a wide range of conditions but grows best in fertile, well-drained soil. It tolerates drought once established. In cooler climates mulch in winter and cut back in spring—wear gloves and long sleeves and use a sharp ax, pruners, or a chain saw. The foliage has razor-sharp edges.
PROPAGATION: Divide overgrown clumps in spring or start new plants from seed.
PESTS AND DISEASES: None are serious.
RELATED SPECIES: *C. selloana* 'Pumila' is compact, growing only about 5' tall; it is hardy in Zone 7. *C. selloana* 'Aureolineata' has golden-yellow variegated foliage and is hardy in Zone 8.

LEMONGRASS
Cymbopogon citratus *sim-boh-POH-gon sib-TRAY-tuss*

Lemon grass is used as an herb to flavor Asian foods.

ZONES: 9 and 10
SIZE: 3–4'h × 3–4'w
TYPE: Clumping, tender evergreen grass
FORM: Mounded
TEXTURE: Coarse
GROWTH: Fast

LIGHT: Sun
MOISTURE: Medium
SOIL: Any
FEATURES: Fragrant, graceful foliage
USES: Flavoring, specimen, container

SITING: Grow lemongrass in the herb garden or, in cold climates, in a container near the kitchen. In addition to providing flavoring for food from its culms—the base of each blade—and a tea from its leaves, lemongrass is a handsome ornamental.

CARE: In cold climates grow lemongrass in a greenhouse or sunny window over the winter. Bring it back into the garden after all danger of frost is past and begin feeding once a month with foliar plant food. Trim off any weather-damaged foliage when it occurs.
PROPAGATION: The culms that are sold in the produce department of supermarkets will often root in water. Lemongrass may also be propagated by seed or divisions.
PESTS AND DISEASES: No known pests affect lemongrass.
RELATED SPECIES: Citronella (*C. nardus*), another subtropical grass, is a relative.

PAPYRUS
Cyperus papyrus *sy-PAIR-us puh-PY-russ*

Papyrus, also known as Egyptian paper reed, can come indoors over the winter.

ZONES: 9–11
SIZE: 6–8'h × 6'w
TYPE: Subtropical rhizomatous sedge
FORM: Upright
TEXTURE: Smooth stems
GROWTH: Fast

LIGHT: Sun
MOISTURE: Wet
SOIL: Fertile
FEATURES: Mop-head flowers
USES: Water garden, container
FLOWERS: ■ ■

SITING: Site papyrus in sun at pondside or in standing water in a pond or pool. It grows dense and tall in rich fertile soil and abundant moisture. It is a good companion to water lilies. One-foot diameter balls of threadlike stems bearing tiny flowers are produced throughout the growing season.
CARE: Grow in a container of clay soil that can be lowered into a pool or pond. Cover the surface of the soil with pebbles to hold the plant in the container. In cold climates bring the container inside over the winter. Divide yearly. In Zone 9 freezing temperatures will kill the top part of the plant, but the roots will produce new growth in spring if mulched heavily or kept underwater. If the center of the papyrus clump dies out, divide and replant the divisions.
PROPAGATION: Propagate it by division in spring.
PESTS AND DISEASES: None are serious.
RELATED SPECIES: Umbrella plant (*C. alternifolius*), often cultivated as a houseplant, may be grown in water. Broad-leaved umbrella plant (*C. albostriatus*), is a miniature for small containers.

HAIRGRASS
Deschampsia caespitosa deb-SHAMP-see-ub sess-pib-TOH-sub

Hairgrass, also known as tufted hairgrass or tussock grass, produces clouds of bloom.

ZONES: 4–9
SIZE: 1–3'h × 2'w
TYPE: Cool-season, clumping grass
FORM: Pincushion
TEXTURE: Medium
GROWTH: Medium
LIGHT: Part sun to shade
MOISTURE: Medium

SOIL: Cool, damp, heavy clay
FEATURES: Evergreen, clouds of flowers
USES: Ground cover, accent, tall lawn substitute
FLOWERS: ■ ■
FALL COLOR: ■

SITING: A native in damp woods and bogs and on streamsides, hairgrass needs a cool place in part sun to shade. Fine, hairlike flowers, emerging green and turning shades of gold, form clouds above the plant in summer. Team it with ligularia or primrose.

CARE: Avoid planting hairgrass in hot, dry places where the foliage will discolor. Feed with a foliar spray once each month during the growing season. Mulch to conserve moisture. Trim back weather-worn foliage in spring. Hairgrass blooms best with some sun and may not bloom in deep shade.
PROPAGATION: When grown from seed (start in spring), flowers are variable. For uniformity, take divisions in spring or fall.
PESTS AND DISEASES: Hairgrass is generally free of pests.
RELATED SPECIES: Flowers of *D. caespitosa* 'Bronzeschleier' resemble a bronze veil; 'Goldstaub' flowers open a golden yellow; 'Tardiflora' blooms in late summer.

WEEPING LOVE GRASS
Eragrostis curvula air-ub-GROSS-tis KURV-yew-lub

Weeping love grass thrives in hot, dry soils, forming a lovely cascading mound.

ZONES: 7–10
SIZE: 2–3'h × 3–4'w
TYPE: Mild-climate clumping, evergreen perennial grass
FORM: Cascading mound
TEXTURE: Very fine
GROWTH: Medium
LIGHT: Sun
MOISTURE: Medium to dry

SOIL: Sandy, well drained
FEATURES: Fine texture, weeping flowers
USES: Accent, ground cover, container
FLOWERS: ■
FALL COLOR: ■

SITING: Weeping love grass, from southern Africa, thrives in sun and well-drained soil.

It can be interplanted with poppies and makes a fine companion to blanket flower.
CARE: Weeping love grass needs plenty of sun and perfect drainage. It will thrive in almost any soil, including serpentine. Once established, it is extremely drought tolerant. It is intolerant of wet, heavy clay soils in winter, when the clumps may rot.
PROPAGATION: Start from seed or divisions in spring.
PESTS AND DISEASES: No known pests affect weeping love grass.
RELATED SPECIES: Sand love grass (*E. trichodes*), a native of the western United States, grows 4' tall and is extremely drought tolerant.

PURPLE LOVE GRASS
Eragrostis spectabilis air-ub-GROSS-tis spek-TAH-bih-lis

Purple love grass, also known as tumble grass, has frothy purple flowers.

ZONES: 5–9
SIZE: 15–18"h × 15–24"w
TYPE: Warm-season clumping perennial grass
FORM: Clump
TEXTURE: Coarse
GROWTH: Fast
LIGHT: Sun

MOISTURE: Medium to wet
SOIL: Any
FEATURES: Reddish-purple flowers, extremely drought-tolerant
USES: Meadow, accent, ground cover
FLOWERS: ■
FALL COLOR: ■

SITING: Purple love grass thrives in full sun and any soil. In very moist soils it can be teamed with cardinal flower (*Lobelia cardinalis*). On drier sites asters, evening primrose (*Oenethera* spp.), and threadleaf coreopsis (*Coreopsis verticillata*) would be good companions.
CARE: Purple love grass self-sows. Where this may be a problem, cut back the flowers after bloom to prevent seeds from maturing.
PROPAGATION: Sow seeds directly in the garden.
PESTS AND DISEASES: No known pests affect purple love grass.
RELATED SPECIES: Sand love grass (*Eragrostis trichodes*), a native of lean, dry soils, grows 4' tall. 'Bend' is a lax, arching form.

FOUNTAIN BAMBOO

Fargesia nitida (Sinarundin nitida) *far-JEEZ-ee-uh NIH-tih-duh (sin-uh-RUN-din NIH-tih-duh)*

Dense clumps of fountain bamboo make an excellent large evergreen screen.

ZONES: 5–8
SIZE: 8–10'h × 8–10'w
TYPE: Clumping, evergreen bamboo
FORM: Cascading
TEXTURE: Medium
GROWTH: Fast
LIGHT: Light shade

MOISTURE: Medium
SOIL: Rich, fertile soil
FEATURES: Evergreen, purple cane, does not run
USES: Specimen, screening, container

SITING: Fountain bamboo forms broad, dense clumps in light shade and fertile soil. It grows best when sited out of wind and intense afternoon sun. In a favorable situation, it will grow quickly and provide dense, attractive screening. After flowering, which occurs approximately every 100 years, fountain bamboo dies back to the roots, but it emerges again in several years.

CARE: Plant in fertile soil, enriched with compost. It does not require feeding when grown in rich soil. Avoid cutting back any tall, leafless canes that appear. This can retard growth or kill the plant. Mulch well.

PROPAGATION: Propagate by seeds or divisions in midspring.

PESTS AND DISEASES: Fountain bamboo is generally free of pests.

RELATED SPECIES: Umbrella bamboo (*F. murielae; Thamnocalamus spathaceus*), bloomed in the late 1990s and will not bloom for another 100 years. New seedlings are now available.

BLUE SHEEP FESCUE

Festuca amethystina *fes-TOO-kuh am-eh-thiss-TEE-nuh*

Blue sheep fescue forms a stiff architectural clump with bluish-green foliage.

ZONES: 4–9
SIZE: 8–18"h × 12–18"w
TYPE: Cool-season clumping, evergreen grass
FORM: Tuft
TEXTURE: Fine
GROWTH: Medium

LIGHT: Sun to light shade
MOISTURE: Medium
SOIL: Average, well drained
FEATURES: Gray-blue foliage
USES: Ground cover, accent, container, trough garden

SITING: Blue sheep fescue favors well-drained soils and cool climates. In a hot, humid summer, it is often short-lived, even with excellent drainage and light shade. Small flowers are held above the plants on fine, arching stems in early summer. It is a superb companion to Missouri evening primrose (*Oenethera missouriensis*).

CARE: Space 18" apart in well-drained soil in sun in a place with good air circulation. Mulch to conserve moisture. Cut plants back from fall to early spring before new growth emerges. Divide and replant every 3 years, discarding any center die back.

PROPAGATION: Start from seed or divide in spring or fall.

PESTS AND DISEASES: Blue sheep fescue is generally free of pests.

RELATED SPECIES: *F. amethystina* 'Aprilgruen' has bright green leaves.

CALIFORNIA FESCUE

Festuca californica *fes-TOO-kuh kal-ih-FOR-nih-kuh*

Evergreen California fescue makes a good companion for low-growing flowers in the mixed border.

ZONES: 7–9
SIZE: 2–3'h × 3–4'w
TYPE: Cool-season clumping, evergreen grass
FORM: Cascading mound
TEXTURE: Medium
GROWTH: Medium
LIGHT: Sun to part shade

MOISTURE: Medium
SOIL: Any
FEATURES: Blue-green color, evergreen foliage, airy flowers, drought tolerant
USES: Meadow, hillside, massing, accent

SITING: Place California fescue 3–4' apart on center when massing. Airy flower spikes are held high over the clumps in late spring to early summer. It is stunning as an accent and pairs beautifully with heuchera or rising out of a ground cover of flowering annuals such as meadowfoam (*Limnanthes douglasii*).

CARE: California fescue blooms and performs best in moist, well-drained, fertile soil in sun, but it will tolerate some shade. Mulch to conserve moisture. In coastal climates, it is drought tolerant.

PROPAGATION: Plants do not come true from seed. To preserve a special characteristic, divide plants with desirable traits.

PESTS AND DISEASES: Californina fescue is generally free of pests.

RELATED SPECIES: Atlas fescue (*F. mairei*), a cool-season grass from the Atlas mountains of Morocco, grows 2–3' tall and is hardy in Zones 5–10.

BLUE FESCUE

Festuca glauca *fes-TOO-kuh GLAW-kuh*

Blue fescue is a ground cover for well-drained, sunny places.

ZONES: 4–8
SIZE: 6–10"h × 12–14"w
TYPE: Cool-season clumping, evergreen grass
FORM: Tuft
TEXTURE: Very fine
GROWTH: Medium

LIGHT: Sun to light shade
MOISTURE: Medium
SOIL: Average, well drained
FEATURES: Blue-silver foliage, wispy flowers
USES: Ground cover, accent, container

SITING: Grow blue fescue in sun to very light shade in a place that is well drained and has good air circulation. It is especially attractive as a ground cover or among rocks. The flowers are showy when massed, but inconspicuous in ones and twos. Pair it with Missouri evening primrose (*Oenothera missouriensis*).

CARE: Space 12" apart. Mulch to preserve moisture. Cut back from fall to early spring to encourage new growth. Blue fescue may be short-lived.

PROPAGATION: Start from seed or divide and replant every 3 years, discarding any center die back.

PESTS AND DISEASES: Blue fescue is generally free of pests.

RELATED SPECIES: *F. glauca* 'Elijah Blue', with beautiful silver-blue foliage, grows 8" tall and is somewhat longer lived than the species; 'Tom Thumb' is a miniature growing only about 5" tall.

CREEPING RED FESCUE

Festuca rubra *fes-TOO-kuh ROO-bruh*

Turf-type tall fescue forms an attractive lawn in midlatitudes of the United States.

ZONES: 3–6
SIZE: 4–20"h × 4–6"w
TYPE: Cool-season clumping or running, evergreen perennial grass
FORM: Upright
TEXTURE: Fine

GROWTH: Medium
LIGHT: Full sun to light shade
MOISTURE: Medium
SOIL: Average to rich
FEATURES: Lawn use
USES: Turf
FLOWERS: ■

SITING: Although red fescue is one of the most shade-tolerant lawn grasses, it performs best in sun when it has adequate moisture. It is native to North America, Europe, and Asia. As a result of its broad adaptability, horticulturists have been able to breed many different strains to suit particular areas.

CARE: Cool-season grasses are suitable for the upper South and Midwest and into northern areas. Turf experts recommend early fall as the best time to plant them, because this allows for more growing time under ideal conditions—cool weather with plenty of rainfall from fall into the following spring's new growing season. Spring is the second-best time to plant red fescue. In problem areas, planting in both fall and spring increases the chances for successful cover. Cool-season grasses grow best when the soil temperature is between 50 and 65°F—usually when the daytime air temperature is between 60°F and 75°F. Once established in an area of year-round rainfall, red fescue is drought tolerant. Extremely high summer temperatures may cause it to go dormant. Avoid feeding in the heat of summer. Some people use the following dates to remember when to fertilize lawns: April 15, a slow-release product; Memorial Day, in cool climates where no hot weather is expected for the next several weeks, a quick-release product; Labor Day and Halloween, a slow-release product.

PROPAGATION: Start from seed or sod.

PESTS AND DISEASES: Turf grasses are plagued by a number of diseases, including brown patch, powdery mildew, and leaf spot.

RELATED SPECIES: Among tall fescues, 'Confederate Plus' is a blend of different types with 'Midnight' Kentucky blue grass. It is resistant to brown patch. 'Shademaster II' is a dwarf dark green red fescue that tolerates shade and heat and is resistant to leaf spot and powdery mildew.

Creeping red fescue is a turf-type grass that tolerates some shade.

HAKONE GRASS
Hakonechloa macra *hah-koh-neh-KLOH-ah MAK-ruh*

Hakone grass is an aristocratic subject for shade. 'Aureola' is pictured above.

ZONES: 4–8
SIZE: 1–3'h × 2–4'w
TYPE: Warm-season perennial grass
FORM: Cascading
TEXTURE: Coarse
GROWTH: Slow
LIGHT: Sun to full shade

MOISTURE: Medium
SOIL: Fertile, acid
FEATURES: Cascading foliage, winter color
USES: Ground cover, accent, woodland
FALL COLOR: ▪▪

SITING: Hakone grass requires a cool spot in rich, well-drained soil with plenty of moisture. Its foliage mimics falling water. Grow it around the bare stems of native azaleas or mountain laurel (*Kalmia latifolia*).

CARE: In cool, moist climates hakone grass may be grown in sun. In hot climates shade is a must. Plant in early spring and mulch to preserve moisture. Keep moist until well established. Feed with a slow-release plant food in spring.
PROPAGATION: Divide rhizomes in spring.
PESTS AND DISEASES: Hakone grass is generally free of pests.
RELATED SPECIES: *H. m.* 'Aureola' is a creamy-yellow form variegated with bright green stripes. It is slower growing and shorter than *H. macra* and seems to be generally fussier. *H. m.* 'Albovariegata' is a white-and-green variegated hakone grass and reputed to be more heat tolerant.

BLUE OAT GRASS
Helictrotrichon sempervirens *hel-ik-toh-TREE-kon sem-per-VIE-renz*

Blue oat grass requires excellent drainage to maintain its foliage in best condition.

ZONES: 4–9
SIZE: 12–18"h × 12–18"w
TYPE: Cool-season clumping, semievergreen to evergreen perennial grass
FORM: Tufted mound
TEXTURE: Fine

GROWTH: Medium
LIGHT: Sun
MOISTURE: Dry to medium
SOIL: Loose, fertile, well drained
FEATURES: Striking silvery-blue foliage, arching flower stalks
USES: Ground cover, accent, rock garden

SITING: Blue oat grass needs sun, excellent air circulation and drainage, and fertile soil. It is evergreen in mild climates and semievergreen where winters are very cold.

The delicate flowers, held 2–3' above the clump on fine stems in May, dance in the lightest breeze. Blue oat grass teams brilliantly with lavender.
CARE: Plant in early spring and leave plenty of room between plants. This grass requires moisture to establish. Mulch to conserve moisture and keep down weeds.
PROPAGATION: Start from seed or division in spring or fall.
PESTS AND DISEASES: In hot, humid climates it is susceptible to rust diseases.
RELATED SPECIES: *H. s.* 'Robust' is a rust-resistant cultivar.

JAPANESE BLOOD GRASS
Imperata cylindrica 'Red Baron' *IM-per-ah-tuh sih-LIN-drih-kuh*

The red-tipped foliage of 'Red Baron' Japanese blood grass is striking when backlit by sunlight.

ZONES: 6–8
SIZE: 15–18"h × 10–12"w
TYPE: Warm-season, slowly rhizomatous perennial grass
FORM: Upright
TEXTURE: Coarse
GROWTH: Medium

LIGHT: Sun
MOISTURE: Medium
SOIL: Fertile
FEATURES: Red leaves
USES: Superb container plant, accent
FALL COLOR: ▪

SITING: Japanese blood grass grows best in full sun and abundant moisture. Because it is relatively small, it displays its color best when situated away from taller plants. It is sensational rising out of low-growing dwarf mondo grass (*Ophiopogon* 'Kyoto'). It is also an excellent container plant.

CARE: Keep well watered until it is established. Mulch to conserve moisture. Feed with a slow-release plant food in spring when growth begins. Remove any parts of the plant that have reverted to green. After frost, remove the dormant foliage.
PROPAGATION: Divide in spring.
PESTS AND DISEASES: Japanese blood grass is generally free of pests.
RELATED SPECIES: The species (*I. cylindrica*), is a serious pest in subtropical and tropical climates. The cultivar 'Red Baron' is not invasive. To avoid problems from self-seeded plants, cut off any flowers that may appear.

COMMON RUSH

Juncus effusus JUN-kuss eh-FYOO-suss

Common rush thrives in standing water.

ZONES: 4–9
SIZE: 3–4'h × 2'w
TYPE: Clumping perennial rush
FORM: Upright, vase
TEXTURE: Medium
GROWTH: Medium
LIGHT: Medium

MOISTURE: Medium to wet
SOIL: Rich, peaty
FEATURES: Architectural, upright form, round stems
USES: Pond, bog, container

SITING: Common rush, native to moist and wet soils of Europe and North America, is a striking feature in a small pond or container of water. It will also grow in moist garden soil. Flowers form at stem tips in early summer.

CARE: Keep moist or grow in standing water. After the stems become dormant in fall, cut them back when they are no longer attractive.
PROPAGATION: Start from seed or by dividing existing clumps in spring.
PESTS AND DISEASES: Common rush is generally free of pests.
RELATED SPECIES: *J. e.* 'Spiralis' is a dark green smaller plant with oddly contorted stems.

HAIRY WOOD RUSH

Luzula acuminata loo-ZOO-lah ah-koo-me-NAH-tuh

Snowy wood rush graces the woodland garden with its medium green foliage and white flowers.

ZONES: 4–8
SIZE: 6–10"h × 15–18"w
TYPE: Evergreen rush
FORM: Spreading clump
TEXTURE: Coarse
GROWTH: Slow
LIGHT: Part shade

MOISTURE: Medium
SOIL: Any
FEATURES: Twisted blades, evergreen
USES: Woodland, ground cover
FLOWERS: ■

SITING: Hairy wood rush is a handsome, low-growing, gently spreading ground cover for bright or part shade. It is lovely along a woodland path or under deciduous trees, where it adapts to drought.

CARE: Keep irrigated, weeded, and mulched when establishing. Thereafter it is maintenance free and very long lived.
PROPAGATION: Divide in spring or start from seed.
PESTS AND DISEASES: Hairy wood rush is generally free of pests.
RELATED SPECIES: Snowy wood rush (*L. nivea*), a European native, grows about 15" tall with narrower leaves than common wood rush and white flowers; greater wood rush (*L. sylvatica, L. maxima*), grows to 2' tall and is evergreen in mild climates.

BOWLES' GOLDEN GRASS

Milium effusum 'Aureum' MIL-ee-um eh-FYOO-zum

Bowles' golden grass brightens the shade with its chartreuse foliage.

ZONES: 6–9
SIZE: 8–18"h × 6–12"w
TYPE: Cool-season clumping, evergreen grass
FORM: Upright
TEXTURE: Coarse
GROWTH: Medium

LIGHT: Part to full shade
MOISTURE: Moist
SOIL: Fertile
FEATURES: Chartreuse foliage
USES: Ground cover, accent
FLOWERS: ■

SITING: A denizen of moist meadows in Europe, Eurasia, and North America, Bowles' golden grass is the perfect choice for a dark area that needs brightening. The brilliant yellow foliage and charming flowers can bring interest to a shady spot from early spring through summer, when the dangling flowers bloom. It is

splendid with bright yellow hostas such as 'Solar Flare'.
CARE: Site Bowles' golden grass in moist shade and fertile, well-drained soil. Keep it irrigated until it establishes. Mulch to conserve moisture.
PROPAGATION: Plants come generally true from seed, but divide those with the best color to ensure retention of the same foliage coloration.
PESTS AND DISEASES: No known pests affect Bowles' golden grass.
RELATED SPECIES: Wood millet (*M. effusum*), a solid green, is common in moist meadows and woods in northeastern North America.

GIANT MISCANTHUS
Miscanthus 'Giganteus' *mis-KAN-thus jeye-GAN-tee-us*

Giant miscanthus is a dramatic fall bloomer that towers above low-growing perennials.

ZONES: 4–9
SIZE: 10–14'h × 4–6'w
TYPE: Warm-season, clumping perennial grass
FORM: Upright
TEXTURE: Coarse
GROWTH: Fast
LIGHT: Sun to light shade
MOISTURE: Medium to wet
SOIL: Average to rich
FEATURES: Tall, upright canes; salt tolerant
USES: Accent, screening
FLOWERS: □
FALL COLOR: ▧

SITING: Giant miscanthus needs enough sun to grow upright and dense. When properly sited, it develops lustrous white plumes in fall. It is a great screen backdrop to tall plants such as perennial sunflowers.

CARE: Giant miscanthus grows best in sun and moderately fertile, moist, well-drained soil. After frost it drops the blades that cascade from its bamboolike canes. A thorough clean up will keep the frost-blanched almond-colored leaves from blowing around the garden. In late winter cut back the canes with hand pruners or a chain saw. Cinch the stems together with twine, cut, and carry off the bundle.
PROPAGATION: Propagate by seed or division in spring
PESTS AND DISEASES: Giant miscanthus has no known pest problems.
RELATED SPECIES: *M. floridulus,* is a coarse, summer-blooming running grass from Asia.

EULALIA GRASS
Miscanthus sinensis *mis-KAN-thus sin-EN-sis*

Eulalia grass is also known as maiden grass. 'Strictus' is a cultivar with horizontal yellow banding on its foliage.

ZONES: 5–9
SIZE: 4–6'h × 3–4'w
TYPE: Warm-season, clumping perennial grass
FORM: Upright, fanning
TEXTURE: Medium to coarse
GROWTH: Fast
LIGHT: Sun to light shade
MOISTURE: Medium
SOIL: Average
FEATURES: Large clump, autumn flowers
USES: Specimen, screening
FLOWERS: ■ ▨
FALL COLOR: ▧

SITING: Eulalia grass and cultivars are at their best in full sun, surrounded by lower-growing plants such as *Sedum* 'Autumn Joy' or Goldsturm black-eyed Susan. Flower plumes emerge ruby red in late summer or fall and turn satiny cream to dazzle in the autumn sunshine. After frost, the dried foliage remains throughout the winter as a giant dried flower bouquet.
CARE: Site these grasses in plenty of sun and average soil. Irrigate until they establish. Mulch to conserve moisture. Most do fine without plant food except in the poorest soil. Soil that is too rich causes the plants to flop over. Cut grasses back in late winter before new growth starts; mixture of new and old growth is unattractive. When growing multiple cultivars, seedlings may develop due to cross-pollination. Rogue seedlings that develop to prevent them from becoming invasive.
PROPAGATION: Divide in late winter or early spring as new growth emerges.

PESTS AND DISEASES: Eulalia grass is generally free of pests.
RELATED SPECIES: Noteworthy for their refined texture and appearance are *M. s.* 'Gracillimus' (Zone 5), with graceful habit, and very late flowers; *M. s.* 'Sarabande' (Zone 5) a narrower leaved, finer-textured 'Gracillimus'; and *M. s.* 'Graziella' (Zone 5) holding its silver plumes high above upright clumps. Variegated forms include grasses with horizontal bands on green foliage. *M. s.* 'Strictus' (Zone 5) grows to an upright 8'; *M. s.* 'Hinjo' (Zone 5) grows to 6' with horizontal bands of yellow on the green foliage. Other variegations are green and white, cream, or yellow stripes along the length of the blade. *M. s.* 'Morning Light' (Zone 5) is a very upright 5' form with fine-textured foliage, white leaf margins, and late flowers; *M. s.* 'Goldfeder' (Zone 6) grows to 7' with yellow-striped foliage and plumes that open silver; *M. s.* var. *condensatus* 'Cabaret' (Zone 6) is a 9'-tall, broad-spreading clump of cream-colored foliage edged in green. It does not self-sow. *M. s.* var. *c.* 'Cosmopolitan' (Zone 6), with creamy foliage edged in green, grows to 10' tall and will tolerate light shade. Smaller forms include *M. s.* 'Aethiopien' (Zone 6) a shorter, slower-growing form that takes on bright red tones in fall; *M. s.* 'Yaku Jima' (Zone 6) which grows less than 5' tall. *M. transmorrisonensis* is a 3'-tall, fine-textured grass that blooms in summer. It is evergreen in Zone 6.

Miscanthus 'Morning Light' lives up to its name, with light airy foliage.

Cut miscanthus grasses back in late winter or very early spring.

FLAME GRASS
Miscanthus 'Purpurascens'   *mis-KAN-thus pur-pur-AH-senz*

Flame grass turns riveting red-orange in fall. Its small stature makes it ideal for limited-space gardens.

ZONES: 4–8
SIZE: 3–4'h × 2–3'w
TYPE: Warm-season, clumping perennial
FORM: Upright
TEXTURE: Coarse
GROWTH: Medium
LIGHT: Full sun
MOISTURE: Medium
SOIL: Any
FEATURES: Silver-white plumes, red-orange fall foliage
USES: Ground cover, accent
FLOWERS: ■□
FALL COLOR: ■■

SITING: Flame grass's autumn hue is spectacular when teamed with *Sedum* 'Autumn Joy.' Another redeeming quality is its size. Small scale allows it to do all of the wonderful things the big *Miscanthus* grasses do without overwhelming the smaller garden. The flowers are showy, and dazzling in the sunshine. They are earlier than those of most *Miscanthus* grasses. They bloom in midsummer, and the 4' upright foliage can take on a spectacular orange color in fall. Site the plant so the plumes can be enjoyed from inside the house.
CARE: For the best fall color, flame grass needs a sunny place in moist, fertile soil. Mulch to conserve moisture.
PROPAGATION: Divide in spring.
PESTS AND DISEASES: Flame grass is usually free of pests.
RELATED SPECIES: Flame grass is considered a hybrid beween *M. sinensis* and another unknown parent.

TALL PURPLE MOOR GRASS
Molinia caerulea ssp. *arundinacea*   *moh-LIN-ee-ah ser-OO-lee-ah uh-run-din-AY-see-uh*

Tall purple moor grass forms a kinetic sculpture with its delicate flowers on airy stems.

ZONES: 4–8
SIZE: 2–3'h × 2–3'w
TYPE: Warm-season clumping perennial
FORM: Clump
TEXTURE: Coarse
GROWTH: Slow
LIGHT: Sun to light shade
MOISTURE: Medium
SOIL: Fertile, acid
FEATURES: Delicate flowers, tall stalks
USES: Accent, border
FLOWERS: ■
FALL COLOR: ■

SITING: Tall purple moor grass merits a prominent place in the garden; the clump will remain in scale for many years. The many fine flower stalks float above the clump, swaying in the lightest breeze. It is one of the best grasses for a specimen.
CARE: Tall purple moor grass prefers morning sun and moist, fertile, acid soil. Mulch to maintain moisture. The clump remains attractive throughout the winter, but the flower stalks are too fragile to withstand snow, sleet, or hail. Cut them back when they cease to please.
PROPAGATION: Grow it from seeds or division.
PESTS AND DISEASES: No known pests affect tall purple moor grass.
RELATED SPECIES: Variegated moor grass, (*M. c.* ssp. *caerulea*), has creamy variegation. It grows only 12–18" tall. *M. c.* ssp. *a.* 'Windspiel,' has tall, delicate inflorescences. *M. c.* 'Moorhexe' holds its new purple flowers very upright; *M. c.* ssp. *a.* 'Transparent' has flowers so fine, they are almost transparent.

GULF MUHLY
Muhlenbergia capillaris   *myoo-len-BER-jee-ah kap-ih-LAHR-iss*

Gulf muhly, also known as pink muhly, brings grace to difficult sites. Clouds of magenta blooms add airiness to dry sites.

ZONES: 6–9
SIZE: 3'h × 3'w
TYPE: Warm-season clumping perennial grass
FORM: Stiff clump
TEXTURE: Fine
GROWTH: Medium
LIGHT: Sun to light shade
MOISTURE: Dry to medium
SOIL: Sandy, well drained
FEATURES: Pincushion form, magenta flowers, drought tolerant, heat tolerant
USES: Specimen, ground cover, difficult sites
FLOWERS: ■■
FALL COLOR: ■

SITING: Gulf muhly tolerates difficult sites—dry, rocky, barren soil in unremitting sun—with ease and grace. The lustrous dark green foliage forms a stiff, sculptural clump that contrasts with the delicacy and color of the flowers.
CARE: Give sun and irrigation to establish. Mature plants are drought tolerant. Cut back in late winter.
PROPAGATION: Start gulf muhly from seed or divisions in spring.
PESTS AND DISEASES: Gulf muhly is usually free of pests.
RELATED SPECIES: *M. c.* 'Lenca' (Regal Mist™) has especially fine ruby flowers.

BAMBOO MUHLY
Muhlenbergia dumosa *myoo-len-BER-jee-ah doo-MOH-sah*

Bamboo muhly is a feathery southwestern native grass adapted to dry soils.

ZONES: 7–10
SIZE: 3–6'h × 3–6'w
TYPE: Cool-season slowly rhizomatous, evergreen grass
FORM: Arching clump
TEXTURE: Feathery
GROWTH: Fast
LIGHT: Sun

MOISTURE: Dry
SOIL: Light or dry-heavy
FEATURES: Feathery foliage, heat tolerant, drought tolerant
USES: Accent, container
FLOWERS: ■

SITING: Bamboo muhly, from Arizona and Mexico, is a well-behaved substitute for bamboo that will grow in dry soil and hot-summer climates. Gardeners in hot, dry climates can pair its luxuriant light green foliage with spiky dasylirion or agave.

CARE: Site in sun in moderately moist, well-drained soil. It is drought tolerant when established.

PROPAGATION: Start bamboo muhly from seed or divisions.

PESTS AND DISEASES: Bamboo muhly is generally free of pests.

RELATED SPECIES: Seep muhly (*M. reverchonii*), a native of limestone soils in Texas and Oklahoma, is 2–2½' tall with clouds of flowers in fall.

LINDHEIMER MUHLY
Muhlenbergia lindheimeri *myoo-len-BER-jee-ah lind-HIE-mer-eye*

Lindheimer muhly tolerates calcareous (limey) soils and dry sites.

ZONES: 7–9
SIZE: 2–5'h × 3–4'w
TYPE: Cool-season clumping, semievergreen perennial grass
FORM: Stiff clump
TEXTURE: Fine
GROWTH: Medium
LIGHT: Sun
MOISTURE: Dry to medium

SOIL: Light, well drained
FEATURES: Semievergreen foliage, showy flowers
USES: Specimen, ground cover
FLOWERS: ■■
FALL COLOR: ■□

SITING: Lindheimer muhly, a native of Texas and Mexico, thrives on a sunny site. Its feathery rose-tan flowers are held upright above the clump of blue-green foliage in fall. It is a fine companion to penstemons and bush morning glory (*Ipomoea leptophylla*).

CARE: Site Lindheimer muhly in full sun and well-drained soil. It tolerates calcareous soils, heat, and drought when established.

PROPAGATION: Propagate from seed or by dividing existing plants.

PESTS AND DISEASES: No known pests affect Lindheimer muhly.

RELATED SPECIES: Mexican muhly (*M. pubescens*), with soft, hairy blue-green foliage, grows to 1' tall and produces blue flowers in early summer.

DEER GRASS
Muhlenbergia rigens *myoo-len-BER-jee-ah rih-GENZ*

Deer grass forms an impressive clump.

ZONES: 7–9
SIZE: 3'h × 3'w
TYPE: Cool season clumping, evergreen perennial grass
FORM: Clump
TEXTURE: Medium
GROWTH: Medium
LIGHT: Sun to part shade

MOISTURE: Medium to wet
SOIL: Fertile, well drained
FEATURES: Evergreen clump, attractive flowers
USES: Accent, ground cover, slope

SITING: Deer grass, a good choice for western gardens, thrives in a range of sites, from full sun to part shade and from rocky to alkaline soil. The generous clump and graceful panicles of flowers on 2–3' stems are splendid in the company of artemisia and California lilacs (*Ceanothus* spp.).

CARE: Deer grass does best in moist, well-drained, fertile soil but will tolerate a range of conditions. It will grow in hot, dry, rocky soil and in alkaline soil. It survives in dry summer climates without irrigation but will grow larger when watered in summer.

PROPAGATION: Divide deer grass in spring or sow seeds in place.

PESTS AND DISEASES: No known pests affect deer grass.

RELATED SPECIES: Purple muhly (*M. rigida*), a native of the Southwest growing 3' tall, bears purple flowers in fall.

MEXICAN FEATHER GRASS

Nassella tenuissima (Stipa tenuissima) nah-SEL-uh ten-yoo-ISS-ih-muh (STEYE-puh)

Mexican feather grass is an elegant foil for architectural plants.

ZONES: 6–8
SIZE: 18–24'h × 18–24"w
TYPE: Cool-season clumping perennial grass
FORM: Vase
TEXTURE: Very fine
GROWTH: Medium
LIGHT: Sun
MOISTURE: Dry to medium
SOIL: Well drained
FEATURES: Fine texture, graceful flowers, evergreen in mild climates
USES: Accent, ground cover, container
FLOWERS: ■
FALL COLOR: ■

SITING: Mexican feather grass has a fine texture that is an effective foil for architectural plants such as yuccas, rattlesnake masters (*Eryngium* spp.), and agaves. It thrives in sun and looks good amid rocks and boulders.

CARE: Plant in sun to light shade in well-drained soil. In cool climates it remains evergreen but will go dormant with both hot summer weather and frost. Cut back when it is no longer attractive.

PROPAGATION: Grow it from seeds.

PESTS AND DISEASES: Mexican feather grass is generally free of pests.

RELATED SPECIES: Foothill needle grass (*N. lepida*; *Stipa lepida*) is a native of coastal California that blooms in spring and goes dormant in summer; purple needle grass (*N. pulchra*; *Stipa pulchra*), another California native, blooms in spring and goes dormant in summer.

MONDO GRASS

Ophiopogon japonicus oh-fee-oh-POH-gon juh-PAHN-ih-kus

Although mondo grass looks like a grass, it belongs to the lily family.

ZONES: 7–11
SIZE: 6–10"h × 6–12"w
TYPE: Mat-forming, evergreen perennial
FORM: Upright
TEXTURE: Fast
GROWTH: Moderate
LIGHT: Part to full shade
MOISTURE: Medium
SOIL: Fertile, well drained
FEATURES: Grass-like foliage, flowers, black berries
USES: Ground cover
FLOWERS: ■□

SITING: Mondo grass, a member of the lily family, is an excellent edging plant that grows best in moist soil and morning sun. It can be used to line paths or beds or as a lawn substitute in hard-to-mow shady places where growth will be slower. Crocuses or small daffodils will grow through a ground cover of mondo grass.

CARE: Plant mondo grass in moist, fertile soil and gentle sunshine and it will quickly cover an area. Apply compost when planting. Mulch between plants to conserve moisture. Plants benefit from foliar feeding.

PROPAGATION: Divide the plant in spring.

PESTS AND DISEASES: Deer may uproot newly planted mondo grass but don't seem to eat it.

RELATED SPECIES: Black mondo grass (*O. planiscapus* 'Ebony Knight'), has a similar habit but nearly black foliage.

DWARF MONDO GRASS

Ophiopogon japonicus 'Kyoto' oh-fee-oh-POH-gon juh-PAHN-ih-kus

'Kyoto' dwarf mondo grass substitutes for lawn in shady places.

ZONES: 7–11
SIZE: 2–4"h × 4–6"w
TYPE: Mat-forming evergreen perennial
FORM: Sprawling tuft
TEXTURE: Medium
GROWTH: Fast
LIGHT: Light to full shade
MOISTURE: Medium
SOIL: Fertile
FEATURES: Deep green evergreen foliage, blue berries
USES: Ground cover, between flagstones, lawn substitute
FLOWERS: ■□

SITING: Dwarf mondo grass is superb as a lawn substitute in small, shady areas. It is also useful between stepping-stones, where it will keep down weeds. Crocuses and small daffodils will coexist with dwarf mondo grass.

CARE: For lawn substitution, plant clumps 12" apart in moist, fertile soil to develop a solid cover in three seasons.

PROPAGATION: Divide dwarf mondo grass in spring.

PESTS AND DISEASES: Deer sometimes pull out dwarf mondo grass but do not seem to eat it.

RELATED SPECIES: Lilyturf (*Liriope* spp.), also in the lily family, are large, grasslike plants that grow 12–15" tall and have lavender and white flowers.

SWITCH GRASS
Panicum virgatum *PAN-ih-kum ver-GAY-tum*

Switch grass adapts to a wide range of conditions from dry to moist soils.

ZONES: 4–9
SIZE: 3–10'h × 1–3'w
TYPE: Warm-season, clumping perennial grass
FORM: Upright
TEXTURE: Medium to coarse
GROWTH: Medium

LIGHT: Sun
MOISTURE: Dry to medium
SOIL: Any
FEATURES: Upright clump, fine flowers
USES: Ground cover, accent

SITING: Switch grass thrives in full sun. It serves as a shrublike accent with delicate flowers in late summer. It can be planted as a ground cover that is attractive in winter, when the frost-blanched foliage resembles a field of wheat.

CARE: Switch grass grows taller with more moisture and stays shorter in dry soil. Cut back in late winter or before new growth emerges in spring.
PROPAGATION: Propagate switch grass from seed or divisions.
PESTS AND DISEASES: Switch grass is generally pest free.
RELATED SPECIES: 'Cloud Nine' is an 8' upright blue-green clump with excellent autumn color; 'Shenandoah' grows to 4' tall and emerges green but takes on red coloring by summer, turning a deep ruby in fall; 'Heavy Metal' is a blue-green, extremely upright form that reaches 5' tall.

FOUNTAIN GRASS
Pennisetum alopecuroides *pen-ih-SEE-tum al-oh-pek-yer-OY-deez*

Fountain grass is the workhorse among grasses, forming an elegant clump in warm-season perennial gardens.

ZONES: 5–9
SIZE: 2–3'h × 2–3'w
TYPE: Warm-season clumping perennial grass
FORM: Clump
TEXTURE: Medium
GROWTH: Fast
LIGHT: Sun to part shade
MOISTURE: Medium

SOIL: Fertile, well drained
FEATURES: Attractive flowers, winter interest
USES: Ground cover, accent, border, container
FLOWERS: ■□
FALL COLOR: ■

SITING: Fountain grass is a grass for all situations. It is lovely massed in a meadow, where it can be interplanted with spring bulbs. Summer brings graceful foliage and white flowers. After frost strikes grasses,

this one remains attractive all winter. It is a handsome addition to a flower border, where it softens angular companions.
CARE: Grow fountain grass in sun to light shade in moist, fertile soil. Mulch to conserve moisture. Cut back in late winter before new growth emerges. Fountain grass grows poorly in dry soil or full shade.
PROPAGATION: Propagate fountain grass by divisions in spring. Seed propagated plants may become invasive.
PESTS: No known pests affect it.
RELATED SPECIES: Black fountain grass (*P. a.* 'Moudry'), boasts sensational, large, purple-black flowers. In moist soil it self-sows, but not in dry gardens.

ORIENTAL FOUNTAIN GRASS
Pennisetum orientale *pen-ih-SEE-tum or-ee-en-TAL-ee*

Oriental fountain grass has early-blooming, fuzzy flowers.

ZONES: 6–9
SIZE: 12–18"h × 12–18"w
TYPE: Warm-season clumping perennial grass
FORM: Cascading clump
TEXTURE: Medium
GROWTH: Fast
LIGHT: Sun to light shade

MOISTURE: Medium
SOIL: Well drained
FEATURES: Small size, early summer flowers
USES: Ground cover, border, accent, container
FLOWERS: ■□
FALL COLOR: ■■

SITING: Oriental fountain grass differs from fountain grass in its size and flowers. The plant is smaller and the flowers are earlier and different from those of fountain grass;

they emerge pink and then become pearly white, with a soft, cottony texture. Oriental fountain grass stays attractive from spring throughout the winter. Use in a border, in a container, or massed as a ground cover. Team it with pink-flowered verbenas or threadleaf coreopsis (*Coreopsis verticillata*).
CARE: Oriental fountain grass thrives in warm, moist soil in full sun to light shade. It requires good drainage. It sulks in shade.
PROPAGATION: Start from seed in spring.
PESTS AND DISEASES: No known pests affect Oriental fountain grass.
RELATED SPECIES: Running fountain grass (*P. incomptum*), grows 2–4' tall and spreads by runners and rhizomes. It is hardy to Zone 4.

PURPLE FOUNTAIN GRASS

Pennisetum setaceum 'Rubrum' *pen-ih-SEE-tum seh-TAY-see-um*

'Rubrum' purple fountain grass shines in borders and containers.

ZONES: 9 and 10
SIZE: 3–4'h × 3–4'w
TYPE: Warm-season clumping, tender perennial grass
FORM: Upright, arching clump
TEXTURE: Medium
GROWTH: Fast
LIGHT: Sun

MOISTURE: Any
SOIL: Well drained
FEATURES: Showy pink flowers, winter presence
USES: Container, ground cover, border, accent
FLOWERS: ■
FALL COLOR: ■

SITING: Treat purple fountain grass as an annual in Zone 8 and below. Like hardy fountain grass, it is a garden workhorse. It is especially useful adjacent to paving or pool decking where it has a softening effect. It is a superb container plant.

CARE: Purple fountain grass prefers moist, well-drained, fertile soil, and loves heat. It becomes limp in too much shade. Mulch to conserve moisture. Allow the grass to stand over the winter to enjoy the frost-blanched foliage. Even in climates where it is evergreen, cut back in late winter to enhance its looks.
PROPAGATION: Propagate purple fountain grass by division in spring.
PESTS AND DISEASES: No known pests affect purple fountain grass.
RELATED SPECIES: *P. setaceum*, hardy in Zones 9 and 10, grows 3' tall with green foliage and pink flowers; feathertop (*P. villosum*), Zones 9 and 10, grows quickly from seed to 2' tall with fat, fluffy white flowers.

RIBBON GRASS

Phalaris arundinacea var. *picta* *fuh-LAR-iss ah-run-din-AY-see-uh PIK-tuh*

Ribbon grass spreads quickly, so use caution where you plant it.

ZONES: 4–9
SIZE: 2–3'h × spreading
TYPE: Cool-season spreading perennial grass
FORM: Lax
TEXTURE: Coarse
GROWTH: Fast
LIGHT: Light shade

MOISTURE: Medium to wet
SOIL: Fertile
FEATURES: Green-and-white-variegated foliage
USES: Pondside, container, ground cover
FLOWERS: ☐
FALL COLOR: ■

SITING: Use discretion when adding ribbon grass to a border; it can spread aggressively. A better place for this attractive grass is where its growth will

be contained by paving or conditions not conducive to vigorous growth. It is stunning in a well-watered container.
CARE: Ribbon grass thrives with abundant moisture and part sun. Mulch to conserve moisture. Cut back if the foliage browns out from excessive heat or drought.
PROPAGATION: Transplant divisions to new sites in spring.
PESTS AND DISEASES: No known pests affect ribbon grass.
RELATED SPECIES: *Phalaris arundinacea* 'Feesey's Form' is similar to ribbon grass, but its white-striped foliage is tinted pink; *P. arundinacea* 'Dwarf Garters' is a shorter form, growing only about 1' high with narrower leaves.

KENTUCKY BLUEGRASS

Poa pratensis *POH-uh prah-TEN-siss*

Kentucky bluegrass is the primary lawn grass in cooler areas of North America.

ZONES: 2–7
SIZE: 12–24"h × spreading
TYPE: Cool-season sod-forming perennial grass
FORM: Tuft
TEXTURE: Fine
GROWTH: Fast

LIGHT: Sun
MOISTURE: Medium
SOIL: Fertile
FEATURES: Bright blue-green color, fine texture
USES: Lawn
FLOWERS: ☐

SITING: Kentucky bluegrass is the gold standard against which all other cool-season lawns are measured. It is a component of many lawn mixtures. It prefers full sun, but some cultivars are

Thatch builds up on the soil surface of bluegrass lawns. Dethatch when the thatch layer exceeds ¾" in depth.

KENTUCKY BLUEGRASS
continued

A power dethatcher loosens thatch.

Rake up thatch after using a dethatching machine.

A power aerator opens up the soil to air and nutrients.

tolerant of light shade. It requires regular watering to maintain its vibrant green color through dry periods.

CARE: Kentucky bluegrass grows best in full sun and rich soil with a pH above 6 and abundant moisture. It is a poor choice for extremely hot and/or dry climates where it requires constant irrigation and may become summer dormant. It is a handsome, dense turf where summers are mild and rainfall is frequent. Mow Kentucky bluegrass frequently enough so that no more than one-third of the length of the grass blades is removed at each mowing. During warmer summer months, the recommended mowing height is 2½–3"; in cooler spring and fall months 1½–2". Because Kentucky bluegrass spreads by rhizomes, it can fill in small bare patches on its own. This same growth characteristic means that Kentucky bluegrass lawns may require periodic edging to prevent rhizomes from creeping into adjacent flower beds or shrub borders. Although lawns are meant to be walked on, over time foot traffic compacts soil and limits movement of air and water into the root zone. Correct compaction by core-aerating the lawn when it is in active growth (spring or fall). Mechanical core aerators remove small plugs of soil from the sod, creating channels for nutrients and moisture to get deeper into the root zone. Compaction also leads to thatch buildup, because compacted soil lacks the oxygen needed by microorganisms that break down the thatch. Core aeration alone may correct the thatch problem. Or you may need to use a dethatcher to remove excess thatch if the thatch layer is greater than ½" thick. As a cool-season grass, Kentucky bluegrass grows most rapidly in spring and fall. Fertilizer applications should be timed

to coincide with these growth spurts, with heavier applications in fall and spring and lighter amounts in summer. Most lawn fertilizers are high in nitrogen (the first number of three on the fertilizer label).

PROPAGATION: Seed in spring or fall. Lay sod anytime the ground is not frozen.

PESTS AND DISEASES: Kentucky bluegrass is susceptible to a number of fungal diseases, including Septoria leaf spot, fusarium and Ascochyta blights, rusts and patch diseases. Where these diseases are frequent, using a mixture of disease-resistant cultivars such as 'Eclipse', 'Vantage', or 'Victa' may prevent fungal disease.

RELATED SPECIES: Annual blue grass (*P. annua*), a prolific self-sower, can be undesirable in all areas where it emerges in late summer and fall, because its flowers in spring disfigure otherwise uniformly green lawns.

Pulled soil plugs exhibit soil compression.

Fertilizer spreaders have adjustable settings to customize feeding.

A broadcast spreader allows for even coverage of fertilizer.

RAVENNA GRASS
Saccharum ravennae (Erianthus ravennae) *sah-KAR-rum ruh-VEN-ay (air-ee-AN-thus)*

Ravenna grass is a stunning giant in the fall.

ZONES: 6–10
SIZE: 4–5'h × 8'w
TYPE: Warm-season clumping perennial grass
FORM: Broad, cascading clump
TEXTURE: Coarse
GROWTH: Fast
LIGHT: Sun

MOISTURE: Medium
SOIL: Lean
FEATURES: Huge proportions, 12' tall flower stalks, blue-green foliage
USES: Specimen, screening
FLOWERS: ▨
FALL COLOR: ▨

SITING: Ravenna grass requires careful placement because it needs plenty of room to grow and to be displayed to its best advantage. Shrubs with showy autumn colors such as Virginia sweetspire *(Itea virginica)* or chokeberry *(Aronia)* are good, in-scale companions, as is prairie dock *(Silphium terebinthinaceum)*, with its huge leaves and aerial flowers.

CARE: Cut back growth in late winter. Once established, this grass is drought tolerant. Overwatering and overfertilizing result in limp, lax growth. It performs best in lean soil.

PROPAGATION: Grow from seed or divisions in spring.

PESTS AND DISEASES: No known pests are problems on ravenna grass.

RELATED SPECIES: Bent awn plume grass *(S. contortum)*, native to moist places in the United States as far west as Oklahoma, grows upright to 10' tall in flower. It is hardy to Zone 6.

LITTLE BLUESTEM
Schizachyrium scoparium *skits-uh-KEER-ee-um skoh-PAIR-ee-um*

Little bluestem thrives on lean soils. Its foliage is bluegreen to purple in summer.

ZONES: 3–10
SIZE: 2–5'h × 1–2'w
TYPE: Warm-season clumping perennial grass
FORM: Upright
TEXTURE: Fine
GROWTH: Medium
LIGHT: Sun
MOISTURE: Dry to medium

SOIL: Well drained
FEATURES: Blue-purple summer color, rusty winter color
USES: Meadow, slope, naturalizing
FALL COLOR: ▨ ■
FLOWERS: ▨

SITING: Little bluestem, once common in the prairies, is tolerant of a wide variety of conditions. It grows well in full sun in the company of wildflowers. In fall the lustrous seed heads glow in the autumn sunshine.

CARE: Little bluestem performs best in lean, well-drained soil in full sun. Mow meadows consisting of little bluestem and wildflowers once or more each year.

PROPAGATION: Start from seed or divisions in spring.

PESTS AND DISEASES: Little bluestem is generally free of pests.

RELATED SPECIES: Most cultivars of little bluestem are for forage. One meant for ornament is 'The Blues', with light gray-blue stems.

AUTUMN MOOR GRASS
Sesleria autumnalis *sess-LAIR-ee-uh aw-TUM-nal-iss*

Autumn moor grass brings a light green accent to shady places.

ZONES: 5–9
SIZE: 15–18"h × 18–24"w
TYPE: Cool-season clumping, evergreen perennial grass
FORM: Tuft
TEXTURE: Fine
GROWTH: Medium

LIGHT: Sun to light shade
MOISTURE: Moist
SOIL: Fertile
FEATURES: Chartreuse foliage
USES: Ground cover, rock garden
FLOWERS: ▨

SITING: Autumn moor grass is a good ground cover under trees and a fine accent at the edge of a woodland.

CARE: Autumn moor grass prefers moist, fertile, well-drained soil in sun or light shade. It will adjust to more shade and less water when established. Mulch to conserve moisture.

PROPAGATION: Propagate from seeds or divisions in spring or fall.

PESTS AND DISEASES: No known pests affect autumn moor grass.

RELATED SPECIES: Blue moor grass *(S. caerulea)*, grows to about 8" tall with blue foliage and is hardy in Zone 4.

INDIAN GRASS
Sorghastrum nutans *sor-GAS-trum NOO-tanz*

Indian grass produces copper flowers in the late summer meadow or garden.

ZONES: 4–9
SIZE: 5–7'h × 1–2'w
TYPE: Warm-season clumping perennial grass
FORM: Upright
TEXTURE: Medium
GROWTH: Medium
LIGHT: Sun
MOISTURE: Dry to medium

SOIL: Average, well drained
FEATURES: Showy flowers, adaptable
USES: Accent, meadow, massing, naturalizing
FLOWERS: ■ ■
FALL COLOR: ■ ■

SITING: This prairie grass adapts to mass plantings or meadows. It is also suitable for use as a specimen or accent in the sunny border. Indian grass tolerates temperature extremes from intensely cold winters to hot summers. It grows in most soils, even clay as long as it drains well.
CARE: Cut back annually in late winter. It is drought tolerant once established. Cut Indian grass flowers for use in fresh or dried floral arrangements.
PROPAGATION: The species is usually grown from seed. Plants will self-seed if seedheads are not removed. Propagate cultivars by dividing existing plants.
PESTS AND DISEASES: No known pests are found on Indian grass.
RELATED SPECIES: 'Sioux Blue' Indian grass is a robust and handsome cultivar with blue foliage.

SILVER SPIKE GRASS
Spodiopogon sibiricus *spoh-dee-oh-POH-gon seye-BEER-ib-kus*

Silver spike grass resembles bamboo.

ZONES: 4–9
SIZE: 3'h × 3-4'w
TYPE: Warm-season clumping perennial grass
FORM: Broadly upright
TEXTURE: Medium
GROWTH: Fast
LIGHT: Sun to light shade

MOISTURE: Medium
SOIL: Fertile
FEATURES: Bamboo-like foliage, attractive flowers
USES: Accent, border
FLOWERS: ■
FALL COLOR: ■

SITING: Because silver spike grass thrives in light shade and is richly textured, it looks good with broad-leaved plants such as hostas and with rhododendrons.
CARE: Grow silver spike grass in light shade and moist, fertile, well-drained soil. Mulch to conserve moisture. In too much shade, it flops. Unlike many other warm-season deciduous grasses, silver spike grass is not particularly attractive after frost. The foliage turns brown and doesn't hold up well. Cut it back as soon as it becomes unattractive.
PROPAGATION: Start from seed or divisions in spring.
PESTS AND DISEASES: No known pests are problems on silver spike grass.
RELATED SPECIES: *S. sibiricus* is the only species in this genus that is readily available commercially.

PRAIRIE DROPSEED
Sporobolus heterolepis *spor-AH-bob-lus bet-er-oh-LEP-iss*

Prairie dropseed produces sparkling, scented flowers and seeds.

ZONES: 3–9
SIZE: 2–3'h × 3'w
TYPE: Warm-season clumping perennial grass
FORM: Arching clump
TEXTURE: Fine
GROWTH: Very slow
LIGHT: Sun

MOISTURE: Dry to medium
SOIL: Well drained
FEATURES: Fragrant flowers, fine foliage, winter presence
USES: Ground cover, accent, wildlife plant
FALL COLOR: ■ ■

SITING: Prairie dropseed is stunning when massed. Flower panicles on graceful, swaying stems smell like cilantro; they appear in late summer. The autumn seed heads glisten in the sunlight, weighing down the arching stems. Team prairie dropseed with 'Fireworks' goldenrod.
CARE: Buy the biggest clumps of prairie dropseed available; it is extremely slow growing. It takes about 3 years from seed to flowering. Cut back annually in late winter. It tolerates heat and drought. In spite of its name, it doesn't self-sow freely.
PROPAGATION: Purchase mature plants grown from seed or divide well-established clumps in spring.
PESTS AND DISEASES: No known pests are problems on prairie dropseed.
RELATED SPECIES: Alkali dropseed (*S. airoides*), from the Southwest, is similar in stature and tolerates alkaline soils.

GIANT FEATHER GRASS

Stipa gigantea STY-puh jeye-gan-TAY-uh

Giant feather grass produces clouds of flowers on airy stems.

ZONES: 5–9
SIZE: 18–24"h × 2–3'
TYPE: Cool-season clumping, evergreen grass
FORM: Spiky tuft
TEXTURE: Fine
GROWTH: Medium
LIGHT: Sun

MOISTURE: Medium
SOIL: Well drained
FEATURES: Tall flower stalks, evergreen in mild climates
USES: Specimen, border
FLOWERS: ▢

SITING: Giant feather grass in bloom is spectacular and elegant. Because the flowers angle out from the clump on 6-8' stems, it needs plenty of room. Surround it with low-growing plants such as lavender (*Lavandula*), sage (*Salvia*), or junipers (*Juniperus*).

CARE: Giant feather grass grows best in cool climates such as in England or the Pacific Northwest. It requires sun, room to be appreciated, and excellent drainage.
PROPAGATION: Grow the plant from seed or divisions in spring.
PESTS AND DISEASES: Giant feather grass is generally free of pests.
RELATED SPECIES: Needle grass (*S. capillata*) grows 3' tall with delicate silvery flowers in summer.

PURPLE TOP

Tridens flavus TREYE-denz FLAY-vus

Seed heads of purple top lend a purple haze to fields and prairies.

ZONES: 5–10
SIZE: 12–18"h × 12–18"w
TYPE: Warm-season clumping perennial grass
FORM: Vase-shaped clump
TEXTURE: Coarse
GROWTH: Fast

LIGHT: Sun to light shade
MOISTURE: Medium
SOIL: Any
FEATURES: Flowers, adaptability
USES: Slope, ground cover, meadow
FLOWERS: ■
FALL COLOR: ▢

SITING: Purple top, native from New England to Texas, is the grass that creates early fall, purple haze in these regions.

CARE: Purple top grows best and fastest in full sun and moderate moisture. It tolerates moist or dry places when established. It self-sows.
PROPAGATION: Sow seeds in place, transplant self-sown seedlings, or divide existing plants in spring.
PESTS AND DISEASES: Purple top is generally free of pests.
RELATED SPECIES: Sand love grass (*Eragrostis trichoides*), is shorter but has a similar rosy cloud effect when massed in fields or meadows.

EASTERN GAMAGRASS

Tripsacum dactyloides TRIP-sih-kum dak-til-OY-deez

Eastern gamagrass provides rich foliage.

ZONES: 5–10
SIZE: 5'h × 5'w
TYPE: Warm-season clumping perennial grass
FORM: Upright, arching clump
TEXTURE: Coarse
GROWTH: Fast
LIGHT: Sun to part shade

MOISTURE: Medium to wet
SOIL: Any
FEATURES: Tropical effect, tolerates medium shade
USES: Accent, seaside
FLOWERS: ■
FALL COLOR: ■

SITING: Eastern gamagrass, native from New England to Texas, is grown for its luxuriant, cascading foliage. It is an excellent foil for perennials with bold foliage such as hostas and prairie dock.

CARE: Eastern gamagrass grows best in full sun and moist, fertile soil. It is a good plant for seaside conditions and for native installations. It will naturalize where conditions are favorable. Its sawlike leaf margins can be hazardous to gardeners who are unaware of its sharp edges.
PROPAGATION: Grow it from seed or divisions in spring.
PESTS AND DISEASES: No known pests are problems on eastern gamagrass.
RELATED SPECIES: Florida gamagrass (*T. floridana*), is less hardy (Zones 7–10) and shorter—only about 3' tall.

SEA OATS
Uniola paniculata *yoo-nee-OH-luh pan-ih-kyew-LAH-tuh*

Sea oats is a beloved feature of sea coasts with its warm brown dried seed heads.

ZONES: 7–10
SIZE: 4–6'h × spreading
TYPE: Warm-season rhizomatous perennial grass
FORM: Upright arching clump
TEXTURE: Medium
GROWTH: Medium
LIGHT: Sun

MOISTURE: Dry to medium
SOIL: Sandy, well drained
FEATURES: Attractive flowers
USES: Dune stabilizer, seaside
FLOWERS: ■
FALL COLOR: ■

SITING: A beloved feature of coastal landscapes from Virginia to Florida and along the Gulf Coast, sea oats forms dense colonies, stabilizing sand dunes. It is illegal to collect seeds or plants in most states because this grass is an endangered species. Nursery-propagated plants and seeds are difficult but not impossible to find.

CARE: Sea oats grows best in full sun and well-drained, sandy soil. It requires irrigation until established. Thereafter, it is wind, salt-spray, and heat tolerant. Plants develop showy panicles on long, arching stems in summer.

PROPAGATION: Purchase nursery-grown plants or divide existing landscape plants. Avoid seeds or plants that are not certified nursery grown.

PESTS AND DISEASES: Sea oats is generally free of pests.

RELATED SPECIES: River oats (*Chasmanthium latifolium*), a denizen of river bottoms and rich, moist soils has equally attractive flowers and seed heads.

VETIVER
Vetiveria zizanoides *vet-ih-VEHR-ee-uh zih-zan-OY-deez*

Vetiver is used in perfumery.

ZONES: 9 and 10
SIZE: 5–8'h × 3–4'w
TYPE: Warm-season clumping perennial grass
FORM: Narrow upright clump
TEXTURE: Coarse
GROWTH: Fast
LIGHT: Sun to part shade

MOISTURE: Moist
SOIL: Any
FEATURES: Upright blades have distinctive bent tips, fragrant
USES: Specimen, screen, basketry, perfumes
FALL COLOR: ■

SITING: Vetiver grows best in rich, moist soil and sun, where its upright pale green form is an excellent screen or hedge. Plants develop fluffy plumes of flowers in fall. Vetiver grows well near the sea.

CARE: Vetiver, native to moist riverbanks of Asia and Africa, may survive temperatures below freezing for a short period. Where low temperatures last longer than a few days, it is best to grow the grass in a container or dig it up and bring it into a cool greenhouse over the winter.

PROPAGATION: Grow from seed or divisions in spring.

PESTS AND DISEASES: No known pests affect vetiver.

RELATED SPECIES: No other species of *Vetiveria* is commercially available in the United States.

WILD RICE
Zizania aquatica *ziz-AY-nee-uh ah-KWAH-tih-kuh*

Wild rice produces edible seeds treasured by gourmands. It grows in standing water.

ZONES: NA
SIZE: 4–8'h × 4–8'w
TYPE: Warm-season clumping annual grass
FORM: Loose, bold clump
TEXTURE: Coarse
GROWTH: Fast
LIGHT: Sun

MOISTURE: Moist to wet
SOIL: Fertile
FEATURES: Bold foliage, showy flowers, edible seeds
USES: Water garden, wildlife planting, gourmet/edible
FLOWERS: ☐
FALL COLOR: ■

SITING: Grow wild rice as a bold accent in a garden pool or wetland area. It is native to wetlands of the eastern and central United States. Collecting enough for a meal is labor-intensive and makes wild rice a delicacy.

CARE: Wild rice grows in sun and rich, wet soil. Start seedlings indoors to plant in ponds or pools when the weather warms.

PROPAGATION: Wild rice is an annual, so it must be started from seed each year. It may self-seed on wet sites.

PESTS AND DISEASES: No insect or disease problems are serious pest of wild rice. It is a source of food for wild birds that will eat the seeds.

RELATED SPECIES: Asian wild rice (*Z. latifolia*), from the wetlands of Asia, is a perennial species hardy in Zones 7–10.

A–Z ENCYCLOPEDIA OF

FLOWER CARE

Flowering plants add beauty and delight to the landscape as the textures, colors, and fragrances intermingle. Each setting is unique and reflects the special characteristics and qualities of the people and the place.

Gloriosa Daisy, *Rudbeckia hirta* **'Toto'**

Bloody cranesbill, *Geranium sanguineum*

Cushion spurge, *Euphorbia polychroma* **(epithymoides)**

Daylily, *Hemerocallis* **'Mardi Gras Parade'**

CHAPTER **9** A–Z ENCYCLOPEDIA OF FLOWER CARE

Goldenrod,
Solidago

Grape hyacinth,
Muscari botryoides

Lupine, ***Lupinus***

Oriental poppy,
Papaver orientale

COMMON NAME INDEX FLOWERS *continued*

COMMON NAME	BOTANIC NAME	SEE PAGE
False spirea	Astilbe ×arendsii	276
False sunflower	Heliopsis helianthoides	308
Fan flower	Scaevola aemula	350
Featherleaf rodgersia	Rodgersia pinnata	345
Flossflower	Ageratum houstonianum	266
Flowering kale	Brassica oleracea	280
Flowering tobacco	Nicotiana alata	332
Foxglove	Digitalis purpurea	299
French marigold	Tagetes patula	355
Fringed bleeding heart	Dicentra eximia	297
Fuchsia	Fuchsia hybrids	301
Garden phlox	Phlox paniculata	340
Gas plant	Dictamnus albus	298
Geranium	Pelargonium ×hortorum	337
Germander	Teucrium chamaedrys	356
Giant kale	Crambe cordifolia	291
Giant onion	Allium giganteum	268
Giant taro	Alocasia macrorrhiza	268
Globe amaranth	Gomphrena globosa	305
Globe thistle	Echinops ritro	300
Gloriosa daisy	Rudbeckia hirta	346
Goatsbeard	Aruncus dioicus	273
Goldenrod	Solidago hybrids	354
Goldmoss stonecrop	Sedum acre	351
Gomphrena	Gomphrena globosa	305
Gooseneck loosestrife	Lysimachia clethroides	327
Grape hyacinth	Muscari botryoides	330
Grape-leaf anemone	Anemone vitifolia	270
Grass pink	Dianthus plumarius	297
Great white trillium	Trillium grandiflorum	359
Ground morning glory	Convolvulus sabatius	288
Hardy geranium	Geranium sanguineum	304
Heart-leaf bergenia	Bergenia cordifolia	279
Heart-leaf brunnera	Brunnera macrophylla	280
Helen's flower	Helenium autumnale	306
Heliopsis	Heliopsis helianthoides	308
Heliotrope	Heliotropium arborescens	309
Hellebore	Helleborus orientalis	309
Holly fern	Cyrtomium falcatum	293
Hollyhock	Alcea rosea	267
Hollyhock mallow	Malva alcea 'Fastigiata'	328
Hosta	Hosta hybrids	311
Houttuynia	Houttuynia cordata	313
Hyacinth	Hyacinthus orientalis	313
Hybrid bee delphinium	Delphinium elatum	295
Hybrid sage	Salvia ×superba	348
Iceland poppy	Papaver nudicaule	336
Impatiens	Impatiens walleriana	315
Jack-in-the-pulpit	Arisaema triphyllum	272

COMMON NAME	BOTANIC NAME	SEE PAGE
Japanese anemone	Anemone hupehensis	270
Japanese holly fern	Cyrtomium falcatum	293
Japanese painted fern	Athyrium nipponicum	277
Japanese spurge	Pachysandra terminalis	335
Jonquil	Narcissus jonquilla	331
Lady's mantle	Alchemilla mollis	267
Lamb's ears	Stachys byzantina	354
Lamium	Lamium maculatum	319
Lantana	Lantana camara	320
Large periwinkle	Vinca major	363
Larkspur	Consolida hybrids	287
Lavender	Lavandula angustifolia	321
Lavender cotton	Santolina chamaecyparissus	348
Leadwort	Ceratostigma plumbaginoides	285
Lemon thyme	Thymus ×citriodorus	358
Lenten rose	Helleborus orientalis	309
Lily-of-the-valley	Convallaria majalis	288
Lobelia	Lobelia cardinalis	325
Lobelia	Lobelia erinus	325
Love-in-a-mist	Nigella damascena	333
Lungwort	Pulmonaria saccharata	345
Lupine	Lupinus hybrids	326
Many-flowered sunflower	Helianthus ×multiflorus	307
Meadowsweet	Filipendula rubra	301
Mealy-cup sage	Salvia farinacea	347
Mexican heather	Cuphea hyssopifolia	293
Mexican hyssop	Agastache cana	265
Missouri primrose	Oenothera macrocarpa	333
Montbretia	Crocosmia ×crocosmiiflora	291
Morning glory	Convolvulus sabatius	288
Morning glory	Ipomoea tricolor	316
Moss phlox	Phlox subulata	341
Moss rose	Portulaca grandiflora	343
Narrow-leaf blue-eyed grass	Sisyrinchium angustifolium	352
New England aster	Aster novae-angliae	275
New Guinea impatiens	Impatiens hawkeri	315
Nicotiana	Nicotiana alata	332
Obedient plant	Physostegia virginiana	342
Orange coneflower	Rudbeckia fulgida	346
Oriental poppy	Papaver orientale	336
Ornamental pepper	Capsicum annuum	283
Ostrich fern	Matteuccia struthiopteris	328
Oswego tea	Monarda didyma	329
Oxeye	Heliopsis helianthoides	308
Ozark sundrop	Oenothera macrocarpa	333
Pansy	Viola ×wittrockiana	364
Pearly everlasting	Anaphalis margaritacea	269
Penstemon	Penstemon barbatus	338
Penstemon	Penstemon digitalis	338

COMMON NAME	BOTANIC NAME	SEE PAGE
Peony	*Paeonia officinalis*	335
Perennial salvia	*Salvia ×superba*	348
Periwinkle	*Vinca minor*	363
Perovskia	*Perovskia atriplicifolia*	339
Petunia	*Petunia ×hybrida*	340
Phlox	*Phlox paniculata*	340
Pigsqueak	*Bergenia cordifolia*	279
Pincushion flower	*Scabiosa columbaria*	350
Pink	*Dianthus chinensis*	296
Plumbago	*Ceratostigma plumbaginoides*	285
Plume poppy	*Macleaya cordata*	327
Polyanthus primrose	*Primula ×polyantha*	344
Portulaca	*Portulaca grandiflora*	343
Pot marigold	*Caladium officinalis*	281
Primrose	*Primula ×polyantha*	344
Pulmonaria	*Pulmonaria saccharata*	345
Purple coneflower	*Echinacea purpurea*	299
Purple hardy ice plant	*Delosperma cooperi*	294
Queen-of-the-prairie	*Filipendula rubra*	301
Red hot poker	*Kniphofia uvaria*	319
Rock soapwort	*Saponaria ocymoides*	349
Rodgersia	*Rodgersia pinnata*	345
Roger's flower	*Rodgersia pinnata*	345
Rose moss	*Portulaca grandiflora*	343
Rose-scented geranium	*Pelargonium graveolens*	337
Royal fern	*Osmunda regalis*	334
Russian sage	*Perovskia atriplicifolia*	339
Scabious	*Scabiosa columbaria*	350
Scaevola	*Scaevola aemula*	350
Scarlet sage	*Salvia splendens*	347
Sea pink	*Armeria maritima*	272
Sedum	*Sedum acre*	351
Sedum	*Sedum 'Autumn Joy'*	351
Shasta daisy	*Leucanthemum ×superbum*	321
Showy crocus	*Crocus speciosus*	292
Siberian bugloss	*Brunnera macrophylla*	280
Siberian iris	*Iris sibirica*	318
Siebold hosta	*Hosta sieboldiana*	312
Silver Mound artemisia	*Artemisia schmidtiana 'Silver Mound'*	273
Small Solomon's seal	*Polygonatum biflorum*	342
Smooth white penstemon	*Penstemon digitalis*	338
Snakeroot	*Cimicifuga racemosa*	286
Snapdragon	*Antirrhinum majus*	271
Sneezeweed	*Helenium autumnale*	306
Snowdrop	*Galanthus nivalis*	302
Snow-in-summer	*Cerastium tomentosum*	285
Soapwort	*Saponaria ocymoides*	349
Solomon's plume	*Smilacena racemosa*	353
Southern lupine	*Thermopsis villosa*	357

COMMON NAME	BOTANIC NAME	SEE PAGE
Southern maidenhair fern	*Adiantum capillus-veneris*	265
Spider flower	*Cleome hassleriana*	286
Spiderwort	*Tradescantia virginiana*	358
Spike gayfeather	*Liatris spicata*	322
Spike speedwell	*Veronica spicata*	362
Spotted deadnettle	*Lamium maculatum*	319
St. Johnswort	*Hypericum calycinum*	314
Strawflower	*Helichrysum bracteatum*	308
Sunflower	*Helianthus annuus*	307
Sunflower	*Helianthus ×multiflorus*	307
Sunflower heliopsis	*Heliopsis helianthoides*	308
Sweet alyssum	*Lobularia maritima*	326
Sweet flag	*Acorus calamus 'Variegatus'*	264
Sweet pea	*Lathyrus odoratus*	320
Sweet potato	*Ipomoea batatas*	316
Sweet violet	*Viola odorata*	364
Sweet william	*Dianthus barbatus*	296
Sweet woodruff	*Galium odoratum*	303
Tall cosmos	*Cosmos bipinnatus*	290
Threadleaf coreopsis	*Coreopsis verticillata*	289
Thrift	*Armeria maritima*	272
Tickseed	*Coreopsis grandiflora*	289
Toad lily	*Tricyrtis hirta*	359
Torch lily	*Kniphofia uvaria*	319
Touch-me-not	*Impatiens walleriana*	315
Tuberous begonia	*Begonia Tuberhybrida hybrids*	278
Tulip	*Tulipa hybrids*	360
Turk's cap lily	*Lillium superbum*	323
Tussock bellflower	*Campanula carpatica*	283
Verbena	*Verbena ×hybrida*	361
Veronica	*Veronica austriaca ssp. teucrium*	361
Veronica	*Veronica spicata*	362
Vinca	*Vinca major*	363
Vinca	*Vinca minor*	363
Virginia bluebell	*Mertensia virginica*	329
Wall germander	*Teucrium chamaedrys*	356
Wavy hosta	*Hosta undulata*	312
Wax begonia	*Begonia Semperflorens-Cultorum hybrids*	278
White boltonia	*Boltonia asteroides latisquama*	279
White gaura	*Gaura lindheimeri*	303
Wild blue indigo	*Baptisia australis*	277
Willow amsonia	*Amsonia tabernaemontana*	269
Woodland forget-me-not	*Myosotis sylvatica*	330
Yarrow	*Achillea 'Coronation Gold'*	264
Yellow corydalis	*Corydalis lutea*	290
Yucca	*Yucca filamentosa*	365
Zinnia	*Zinnia elegans*	365
Zonal geranium	*Pelargonium ×hortorum*	337

Russian sage, *Perovskia atriplicifolia*

Siberian iris, *Iris sibirica* 'Silver Edge'

Spike speedwell, *Veronica spicata* 'Red Fox'

Tulip, *Tulipa* 'Kees Nelis'

CHAPTER **9** A–Z ENCYCLOPEDIA OF FLOWER CARE

CORONATION GOLD YARROW

Achillea × 'Coronation Gold' *ah-KILL-ee-ah*

Coronation Gold yarrow, also known as yarrow, is a low-maintenance perennial with attractive golden-yellow flowers.

ZONES: 3–9
SIZE: 36"h × 18"w
TYPE: Perennial
FORM: Upright
TEXTURE: Medium
GROWTH: Fast
LIGHT: Full sun
MOISTURE: Medium to dry

SOIL: Fertile, well-drained
FEATURES: 3" blooms, silvery leaves
USES: Border, massing, butterflies
FLOWERS: ■
FALL COLOR: ■

SITING: Yarrow is heat tolerant and relatively drought tolerant and thrives in full sun. It prefers well-drained soil with moderate fertility and a pH of 5.5–6.6.

The 3"-diameter golden-yellow blooms with silvery foliage are good companions with 'David' garden phlox, 'The Fairy' rose, and purple coneflower.

CARE: Plant 18" apart in spring or fall. Feed with slow-release granular plant food at time of planting, or begin using water-soluble plant food 3 weeks after planting. Follow label directions for amount and frequency. Cease feeding 6–8 weeks prior to first frost date. Yarrow is drought tolerant but will perform better if it receives ample moisture during dry spells. Let the soil dry between waterings. Deadhead spent blooms to encourage reblooming.

Remove faded flowers to stimulate new blooms.

Blossoms may be cut and dried for arrangements; they hold their color best if harvested early in the bloom cycle. Apply 3" of vegetative mulch in summer and winter to reduce weed seed germination, retain soil moisture, and keep soil temperatures stable. Cut plants to the ground in late fall or leave erect for winter interest, then cut back in early spring.

PROPAGATION: In moderately fertile soil, plants may be divided every three years to maintain vigor. In rich soils, division is needed sooner to maintain vigor and control growth. Dig around the root clump and lift. Use a sharp spade to slice through the root system. The larger the portion, the larger the resulting plant during the first year. Smaller pieces may take 2–3 years to reach mature size and bloom. Reset only portions that contain both healthy roots and top shoots. Water deeply and apply 3" of vegetative mulch around, but not touching the plants.

PESTS AND DISEASES: Plants are relatively pest free.

RELATED SPECIES: Common yarrow (*A. millefolium*) is vigorous and invasive. 'Fire King', 'Cerise Queen', and 'Red Beauty' add shades of red bloom to the garden. Moonshine yarrow (*A.* × 'Moonshine') has the polite manners of 'Coronation Gold', but is slightly shorter and has a light yellow bloom.

SWEET FLAG

Acorus calamus 'Variegatus' *ah-KOR-uhs kal-AH-mus*

Sweet flag is an attractive addition to water's edge.

ZONES: 4–11
SIZE: 5'h × 24"w
TYPE: Perennial
FORM: Upright
TEXTURE: Medium
GROWTH: Fast
LIGHT: Full sun to part shade

MOISTURE: Moist to wet
SOIL: Sandy, well-drained
FEATURES: Foliage
USES: Water plant, naturalizing, container
FLOWERS: ■

SITING: Sweet flag thrives at the water's edge in full sun or partial shade. It prefers sandy loam with a pH of 5.5–7.0. It may be planted among bald cypress trees or as a companion to sweet flag iris.

CARE: Place at the edge of a pond or water feature in water up to 9" deep, or plant in moist soil that does not dry out. When placed close to a water body, do not apply fertilizers or pesticides because they may leach into the water. In gardens feed at time of planting or begin using water-soluble plant food 3 weeks after planting. Follow label directions for amount and frequency. Cease feeding 6–8 weeks prior to first frost date. Cover surface roots with mulch. Cut back brown foliage in late winter before new growth appears.

PROPAGATION: Divide rhizomes in spring or fall by separating roots using a sharp spade. Reset healthy pieces, water deeply, and apply 3" of vegetative mulch around, but not touching, the plants.

PESTS AND DISEASES: Dislodge spider mites by frequently washing the leaves.

RELATED SPECIES: Grassy-leaved sweet flag (*A. gramineus*) is a smaller, 4–18" high semievergreen for Zones 8–9. 'Ogon' has yellow and cream leaves, 'Pusillus' has dark green leaves, and 'Variegatus' has variegated white and green leaves.

1 Divide rhizomes with a sharp spade.

2 Reset healthy roots, water deeply, and apply vegetative mulch around, but not touching, plants.

SOUTHERN MAIDENHAIR FERN

Adiantum capillus-veneris ad-ee-AN-tum kab-PIL-us-VEN-er-is

Southern maidenhair fern adds grace and beauty to the landscape.

ZONES: 8–10
SIZE: 12"h × 15"w
TYPE: Perennial
FORM: Upright arching
TEXTURE: Fine
GROWTH: Medium
LIGHT: Part shade

MOISTURE: Evenly moist
SOIL: Fertile, well-drained
FEATURES: Foliage
USES: Shade border, container, woodland

SITING: Southern maidenhair fern prefers light shade, good air circulation, and protection from direct afternoon sun and strong wind. It is evergreen down to 30°F. Attractive fronds are bright green on black stalks. Plants prefer high humidity and soil rich in organic matter, with a pH of 5.5–7.0. An attractive companion to this fern is white-leaved caladium.
CARE: Plant 15" apart in spring or fall. Feed with slow-release granular plant food at time of planting, or begin using water-soluble plant food 3 weeks after planting in spring. Follow label directions for amount and frequency. Cease feeding 6–8 weeks prior to first frost date. Apply 3" of vegetative mulch in summer and winter to protect roots from summer heat and winter cold. Mulch also reduces weed seed germination, holds moisture in the soil longer, and as it decomposes, adds organic matter to the soil, which increases fertility and plant health. Water deeply whenever the soil begins to dry out 2–3" below the surface to maintain uniform moisture. Brown fronds may be caused by dry soil, lack of organic matter, low humidity, too much water, too little water, or poor air circulation. Cut back after the first hard freeze.

Water slowly and deeply to thoroughly moisten the soil.

PROPAGATION: Divide rhizomes in spring by separating roots using a sharp spade. Reset healthy pieces, water deeply, and apply 3" of vegetative mulch around, but not touching, plants. In moderately fertile soil, plants may be divided every three years to maintain vigor.
PESTS AND DISEASES: These plants are basically pest free when their cultural preferences (soil, sun, moisture) are met. If the soil is too acidic, acid rot may occur.
RELATED SPECIES: Northern maidenhair fern (*A. pedatum*), grows larger, reaching nearly 2' tall, but retains the graceful habit of the Southern maidenhair fern.

MEXICAN HYSSOP

Agastache cana ah-gub-STAK-ee KAH-nab

Fragrant foliage and summer blooms are welcome additions in the landscape.

ZONES: 5–10
SIZE: 24–36"h × 18"w
TYPE: Perennial
FORM: Upright
TEXTURE: Medium
GROWTH: Medium
LIGHT: Full sun

MOISTURE: Medium
SOIL: Fertile, well-drained
FEATURES: Flowers, foliage
USES: Border, container
FLOWERS: ■

SITING: Mexican hyssop prefers full sun and fertile, well-drained soil with a pH of 6.5–7.3. Loose spikes of deep pink to purple flowers appear in late summer and autumn. The oval blue-green leaves are fragrant. Place in odd-numbered groups in the border or informal cottage garden, or use in container plantings. Good companions include 'Taplow Blue' globe thistle, 'Fastigiata' hollyhock mallow, 'Icicle' spike speedwell, and white culver's root.
CARE: Plant 12–18" apart in spring or autumn. Feed with slow-release granular plant food in spring. Follow label directions for amount and frequency. Apply mulch to reduce weed seed germination, hold moisture in the soil, and as it decomposes, add organic matter to the soil, which increases fertility and plant health. Water deeply when the soil is dry. Deadhead spent blooms to encourage reblooming. Prune back in fall once frost withers the foliage.

PROPAGATION: Divide in spring. Dig around the root clump and lift. Use a sharp spade to slice through the root system. Reset only portions that contain healthy roots and top shoots. Water deeply and apply 3" of vegetative mulch around, but not touching, the plants.
PESTS AND DISEASES: Plants are relatively pest free when cultural requirements (sun, soil, planting depth, moisture) are met. Powdery mildew and rust may occur in dry weather.
RELATED SPECIES: Anise hyssop (*A. foeniculum*) reaches 3–5' high and bears spikes of blue flowers with violet bracts from midsummer into autumn. Anise-scented leaves are noticeably veined and whitish underneath. Plants reseed freely. rock anise hyssop (*A. rupestris*) reaches 3–4' high and bears interesting orange flowers in summer. Gray-green leaves are licorice-scented.

FLOSSFLOWER

Ageratum houstonianum a-jer-AY-tum hu-stow-nee-AY-num

Flossflower produces tight mounds of non-stop color in summer. It is also known as ageratum.

ZONES: NA
SIZE: 6–24"h × 12"w
TYPE: Annual
FORM: Rounded or clumped
TEXTURE: Medium
GROWTH: Medium
LIGHT: Full sun to part shade

MOISTURE: Medium to high
SOIL: Fertile, well-drained
FEATURES: Flowers
USES: Bedding plant, container
FLOWERS: ■ ■ □

SITING: Ageratum tolerates full sun or partial shade; it prefers soil rich in organic matter with a pH of 5.5 to 7.0. It may be massed in the sunny border or planted in the rock garden or a container. Its striking blue blooms are complemented by the white blooms and/or silver foliage of 'Silver Carpet' lamb's-ears, white-flowering petunias, 'Icicle' spike speedwell, and 'Silver White' mealycup sage.

CARE: Plant 6–12" apart in spring after the last frost. Apply slow-release granular plant food at time of planting or begin using water-soluble plant food 3 weeks after planting. Follow label directions for amount and frequency. Water deeply when

Plant ageratum 6–12" apart in staggered rows for best mass effect.

the soil feels almost dry 2–3" below the surface. Apply 2–3" of organic mulch in summer to help retain soil moisture, minimize weed seed germination, and keep foliage clean. Mulch also adds organic matter to the soil as it decomposes. Deadhead spent blossoms to encourage reblooming. Remove the entire plant after frost and keep the ground covered with mulch to preserve the topsoil.

PROPAGATION: Sow seeds at 78–82°F under lights. Keep seeds evenly moist until germination, then allow seedlings to dry slightly between waterings. After germination, reduce the temperature to 60–65°F.

PESTS AND DISEASES: Plants are relatively pest free when grown in a favorable cultural environment; however, Southern blight and crown and root rots occur. During dry weather, powdery mildew and rust may be problems; during wet, cool weather, botrytis blight may occur.

RELATED SPECIES: Cultivars are largely mound-forming, compact plants bearing small flowers held above the foliage. 'Blue Danube' is 6" tall; 'Blue Horizons' is 18" tall and produces blooms suitable for cutting.

BUGLEWEED

Ajuga reptans a-JOO-guh REP-tanz

Bugleweed, also known as ajuga, is a low-maintenance ground cover in partial shade.

ZONES: 3–9
SIZE: 6"h × 15–24"w
TYPE: Perennial
FORM: Spreading
TEXTURE: Medium
GROWTH: Medium to fast
LIGHT: Partial shade

MOISTURE: Medium
SOIL: Medium-low fertility, well-drained
FEATURES: Foliage, flowers
USES: Ground cover
FLOWERS: ■ ■

SITING: Ajuga prefers partial shade, with good protection from afternoon sun and a pH of 5.5–7.4. Plants do not tolerate salt but can withstand moderate drought. The small, glossy leaves form an attractive evergreen ground cover that gets even better when spikes of gentian blue blooms appear in late spring and early summer. It is attractive planted in the rich soil under pine trees. Siebold hosta and lady's mantle are good companions.

CARE: Plant 12–24" apart in spring or fall. Apply slow-release granular plant food at time of planting or begin using water-soluble plant food 3 weeks after planting in spring. Follow label directions for amount and frequency. Cease feeding 6–8 weeks prior to first frost date. Apply 3" of vegetative mulch in summer and winter

Shear plants after they flower to stimulate compact foliar growth and improve the plants' appearance.

to reduce weed seed, protect the shallow-rooted stolons from excessive heat in summer and cold in winter, and improve soil texture and fertility as the mulch decomposes. Provide water during establishment and prolonged drought. If ajuga is planted among tree roots, deeply water during drought. Eliminate weeds prior to planting to avoid competition.

PROPAGATION: Divide plants in spring or fall when they become crowded, or take stem cuttings during the growing season. Plantlets that form along the stolons may be lifted with roots intact and reset. To divide plants, dig around the root clump and lift. Use a sharp spade to slice through the root system. Reset only portions that contain healthy roots and top shoots. Water deeply and apply 3" of vegetative mulch around, but not touching, the plants.

PESTS AND DISEASES: Plants are relatively pest free. Southern blight, crown rot, and fungal leaf spots are sometimes found.

RELATED SPECIES: Cultivars with attractive foliage include 'Burgundy Glow', with beautiful pink, silver, and green leaves. and 'Catlin's Giant', with larger glossy, deep bronze leaves.

HOLLYHOCK

Alcea rosea al-SEE-uh ROZ-ee-uh

Hollyhock blooms produce timeless beauty and nostalgia in the landscape.

ZONES: 3–9
SIZE: 5–8'h × 2'w
TYPE: Perennial
FORM: Upright
TEXTURE: Coarse foliage
GROWTH: Fast
LIGHT: Full sun

MOISTURE: High to medium
SOIL: Fertile, well-drained
FEATURES: Flowers, foliage
USES: Back of border, specimen
FLOWERS: ■ ■ □ □ ■

SITING: Hollyhock prefers full sun and fertile, well-drained soil with a pH of 5.5–7.0. Foliage may be disfigured by disease and insect pests, so place it in the rear of the border. Plants require staking to remain erect, but a building or fence will support the plant as well. Good companions include 'The Fairy', 'Alba-Meidiland', and 'Iceberg' roses.
CARE: Plant 18–24" apart in spring or fall. Staking is usually required. Place stakes that are the same color as the stems alongside the stems and secure to the plant with green twine. Apply slow-release granular plant food at time of planting, or begin using water-soluble plant food 3 weeks after planting. Cease feeding 6–8 weeks prior to first frost date.

1 Collect hollyhock seeds before they spill to the ground.

2 Store seeds in an airtight container until ready to sow.

3 Sprinkle seeds over soilless media and lightly cover.

Deadhead spent blossoms to encourage reblooming, and remove diseased or disfigured foliage. Hollyhock is a short-lived perennial but may be treated as a biennial and cut back to 6" above the ground after blooming to extend its life span. Otherwise, cut to the ground in late fall, and remove all diseased foliage and stems from the planting area.
PROPAGATION: Sow seeds in soilless potting mix. Cover seeds lightly and provide a germination temperature of 72°F. Seeds will not produce true cultivars; the seedlings will vary.
PESTS AND DISEASES: Diseases include hollyhock rust, Southern blight, and bacterial and fungal leaf spots. Insect pests include flea beetles, Japanese beetles, aphids, and slugs.
RELATED SPECIES: 'Nigra' has single deep purplish-brown blossoms.

LADY'S MANTLE

Alchemilla mollis al-kem-ILL-uh MAH-lis

Lady's mantle is a low-maintenance perennial with superb flowers and foliage.

ZONES: 3–7
SIZE: 24"h × 24"w
TYPE: Perennial
FORM: Rounded
TEXTURE: Medium to fine
GROWTH: Medium
LIGHT: Full sun to part shade

MOISTURE: Medium
SOIL: Fertile, well-drained
FEATURES: Flowers, foliage
USES: Shade border, ground cover, container
FLOWERS: ■

SITING: Lady's mantle will thrive in full sun if the soil is fertile, but it prefers afternoon shade. It does not tolerate high humidity and prefers a pH of 5.5–7.0. Place it in the front of the border or at the edge of a container to fully enjoy the blooms and foliage. The tiny chartreuse blooms on wiry stems lace above silvery-green foliage intermittently from early summer into fall. Blooms may be used as fresh cut flowers or can be dried. Fan-shaped foliage is also a major attraction when dewdrops or water clings to it. Good companions include coral bells, astilbe, and 'The Rocket' ligularia.
CARE: Plant 18" apart in spring or fall. Apply with slow-release granular plant food at time of planting, or begin using

Plant lady's mantle 18" apart in a triangular formation for best viewing effect.

water-soluble plant food 3 weeks after planting. Follow label directions for amount and frequency. Cease feeding 6–8 weeks prior to first frost date. Water deeply during establishment and anytime rainfall is low. Allow the soil to dry between waterings. Deadhead spent blossoms to encourage reblooming. Apply 3" inches of vegetative mulch in summer and winter to retain soil moisture, reduce weed seed germination, and stabilize soil temperatures. The decomposing mulch will add beneficial organic matter to the soil. Cut plants to the ground in late fall, or leave erect for winter interest and cut back in early spring.
PROPAGATION: In moderately fertile soil, plants may be divided every 3 years. Sever the root system with a sharp spade and reset portions with healthy roots and top shoots. Water deeply and apply 3" inches of vegetative mulch around, but not touching, the plants. Newly divided plants usually take a full year before they bloom on schedule.
PESTS AND DISEASES: Fourlined plant bug occasionally feeds on the foliage of lady's mantle.

GIANT ONION
Allium giganteum *AL-ee-um jeye-GAN-tee-um*

Purple flower balls of giant onion, also known as allium, add a touch of whimsy to the landscape.

ZONES: 4–8
SIZE: 3–5'h × 2'w
TYPE: Perennial bulb
FORM: Upright
TEXTURE: Coarse foliage, fine bloom
GROWTH: Fast to medium
LIGHT: Full sun

MOISTURE: Medium
SOIL: Fertile, well-drained
FEATURES: Flowers, foliage
USES: Border, specimen
FLOWERS: ■

SITING: Giant onion requires full sun, well-drained, fertile soil with a pH of 5.5–7.0. Sandy soils are fine as long as moisture is supplied during establishment and times of low rainfall. Avoid areas with high wind. Balls of purplish-pink blooms up to 4" across are held above the foliage in early summer. Place this plant in the middle or back of the perennial border, along a fence, or against a building. Blooms attract butterflies and are suitable for cutting. Companion plants include 'The Fairy' and 'Alba Meidiland' roses, and lady's mantle.

CARE: Plant bulbs 18–24" apart in fall. Mix bonemeal into the soil at planting time, and use slow-release granular plant food in spring. If planting in sandy soils, add organic matter to increase the soil's water-holding capacity and fertility. Let foliage die back naturally. The bulbs are relatively short-lived; replace or propagate to ensure a constant presence in the landscape.

PROPAGATION: Remove bulbets from the parent plant and reset. Dig down to the bulb and gently pull off the largest of the small bulbs that are attached to it. Cover the main bulb and plant the bulblets 18–24" away from other plants. Water deeply and apply 3" of mulch.

PESTS AND DISEASES: Fungal leaf spots may occur; wet conditions cause bulb rots.

RELATED SPECIES: Drumstick chives (*A. sphaerocephalum*) is similar to but smaller than *A. giganteum*. The leaves grow up to 14" long, and the plant grows 2–3' tall when in bloom. Chives (*A. schoenoprasum*) reaches 12–24" high, produces 1" balls of edible rosy-pink flowers, and has hollow dark green leaves.

Mix bonemeal into the soil at planting time and place bulbs 18–24" apart in fall.

Mark the spot so emerging foliage is easy to spot in spring.

ELEPHANT EAR
Alocasia macrorrhiza *al-oh-KAY-zhee-uh mak-row-RYE-zuh*

Elephant ear produces dramatic, exotic foliage. It is also known as giant taro.

ZONES: 8–10
SIZE: 12'h × 6'w
TYPE: Perennial
FORM: Upright clump-forming
TEXTURE: Medium to coarse
GROWTH: Medium
LIGHT: Full sun to partial shade

MOISTURE: Medium to high
SOIL: Fertile, well-drained
FEATURES: Exotic leaves
USES: Massing, specimen, container
FLOWERS: ■

SITING: Elephant ear tolerates light shade or full sun in fertile, well-drained soil with a pH of 5.5–7.0. The exotic leaves deserve ample space and massing for best effect.

The glossy green leaves are arrow shaped at their base, with contrasting pale green veins, on stalks up to 6' long. Each leaf blade is 3–4' long. Place these dramatic plants at the base of trees in a well-lit woodland setting, in containers, or as specimens in the tropical garden.

CARE: Plant in early spring. Feed with slow-release granular plant food at time of planting, or begin using water-soluble

In cooler climates dig rhizomes in fall, cut away soft spots, and store healthy roots in a cool, dry location until spring.

plant food in spring as foliage appears. Supply water during dry times to keep the soil moist but not soggy. Allow the soil to dry slightly between waterings. Apply 3" of vegetative mulch in summer and winter to help retain soil moisture. Cut back faded foliage in fall.

PROPAGATION: Divide rhizomes in spring or summer. Dig and lift the roots, cut away healthy sections of root that contain top shoots, and reset at the same depth 3–6' from other plants. Water deeply and apply 3" of vegetative mulch.

PESTS AND DISEASES: These plants are relatively pest free. Mealybugs and scale may be occasional problems but can be managed with insecticidal soap sprays or horticultural oil. Follow the label directions for recommended frequency.

RELATED SPECIES: 'Blackie' has almost black foliage. 'Violacea' has violet-tinged foliage. Giant caladium (*A. cuprea*) grows to 3' high and wide with glossy deep green and copper-hued leaves with reddish undersides. Kris plant (*A. sanderiana*) grows to 6' tall and wide and has deep green leaves with silver margins and silver veins. Wavy leaf edges add appeal.

BLUE STAR

Amsonia tabernaemontana *am-SON-ee-uh tab-er-nay-mon-TAH-nuh*

Blue star, also known as willow amsonia, produces a multitude of periwinkle-blue blooms in late spring or early summer.

ZONES: 3–9
SIZE: 24–36"h × 18"w
TYPE: Perennial
FORM: Upright
TEXTURE: Fine to medium
GROWTH: Fast
LIGHT: Full sun to partial shade

MOISTURE: Low to high
SOIL: Fertile, well-drained, wet
FEATURES: Flowers, foliage
USES: Border, naturalizing, wetlands
FLOWERS: ■
FALL COLOR: ■

SITING: Blue Star tolerates full sun or partial shade and a wide range of soil conditions, from wet to dry. It prefers low humidity and a pH of 6.5–7.5. Tiny star-shaped periwinkle blue blooms appear in profusion during late spring, and the foliage is attractive all season long, even in autumn, when it turns from dark green to bright yellow. The blooms attract butterflies

Yellow fall foliage color is an added attraction to blue star.

and make good fresh cut flowers. Ornamental grasses make good garden companions for blue star.

CARE: Plant 18–24" apart in spring or fall. Feed with slow-release granular plant food at time of planting. or begin using water-soluble plant food 3 weeks after planting. Cease feeding 6–8 weeks prior to first frost date. This low-maintenance perennial is drought tolerant once established. All new transplants require ample and frequent moisture to grow. Cut plants to the ground in late fall, or leave erect for winter interest and cut back in early spring. Divide every 3 years or so to keep plants vigorous.

PROPAGATION: In moderately fertile soil plants may be divided every 3 years.

PESTS AND DISEASES: Plants are relatively pest free when their cultural preferences are met. Leaf spots and rust may occasionally occur.

RELATED SPECIES: Downy amsonia (*A. ciliata*) is slow growing and has threadlike leaves and panicles of blue blooms. Arkansas amsonia (*A. hubrectii*) grows to 4' wide and has panicles of sky blue blooms in late spring. Its foliage turns bright yellow in fall.

PEARLY EVERLASTING

Anaphalis margaritacea *a-NAF-uh-lis marg-uh-reet-AY-see-uh*

Silver foliage and white flowers of pearly everlasting add charm to the landscape.

ZONES: 4–8
SIZE: 24"h × 24"w
TYPE: Perennial
FORM: Upright clump forming
TEXTURE: Medium
GROWTH: Fast to medium
LIGHT: Full sun

MOISTURE: Medium to low
SOIL: Average, well-drained
FEATURES: Foliage, flowers
USES: Border, container
FLOWERS: ☐

SITING: Pearly everlasting tolerates medium fertility and drought once established. The soil must be well-drained, not soggy, with a pH range of 5.5–7.0. The silver foliage and white blooms in late summer to early fall are the chief attractions. The blooms make excellent fresh cut or dried flowers. The silver foliage softens the effects of bright-blooming plants such as red hot poker and 'Strawberrry Fields' globe amaranth. The silvery foliage and pearly blooms are also suitable for moon or white gardens. Good companions for the white garden include 'Icicle' spike speedwell and 'Silver White' mealycup sage.

CARE: Plant 18–24" apart in spring or fall in average garden soil. In fertile soil the plant may become invasive and require

Harvest flowers for drying on a dry day during prime bloom cycle, before they begin to decline.

yearly division. Apply a slow-release granular plant food at time of planting. Deadhead spent blossoms to encourage reblooming. Cut plants to the ground in late fall, or leave erect for winter interest and cut back in early spring.

PROPAGATION: In moderately fertile soil, plants may be divided every three years in fertile soil, more frequently. Sow seeds in fall or winter for flowering plants the following summer. Sow seeds in soil mix, leaving them exposed or only lightly covered. Water thoroughly and keep the mix moist but not soggy. Germination will occur in 4 to 8 days at 68–70°F (reduced to 55–58°F once plants are established). Seedlings will be ready for transplant 4–5 weeks after sowing. Take stem cuttings during the spring or summer. Remove the bottom leaves to expose nodes. Place the stems in water or soilless mix and keep moist until root growth starts.

PESTS AND DISEASES: Plants are susceptible to stem rot, rust, and Septoria leaf spot.

RELATED SPECIES: Var. *cinnamomea* is slightly smaller, with broader leaves and white or cinnamon-colored undersides.

JAPANESE ANEMONE

Anemone ×hupehensis *ah-NEHM-uh-nee byoo-peh-HEN-sis*

Pink flowers, bluegreen foliage, and seedpods of Japanese anemone add interest to the late-season landscape.

ZONES: 5–8
SIZE: 4–5'h × 2'w
TYPE: Perennial
FORM: Irregular or spreading
TEXTURE: Medium to coarse
GROWTH: Medium to fast

LIGHT: Sun to part shade
MOISTURE: High
SOIL: Fertile, well-drained, wet
FEATURES: Flowers, foliage
USES: Border
FLOWERS: ▦

SITING: Japanese anemone prefers full sun, or in hot areas partial shade. The soil should be fertile and high in organic matter

content with a pH range of 5.5–7.0. This plant performs best if sheltered from strong winds. The pale pink blooms appear in late summer and last into early fall. Blooms are semidouble, to 3½" across, with attractive prominent stamens. The appealing foliage is palmate, or lobed, with hairy undersides. Japanese anemone looks good in a border, preferably in groups or at the edge of an open woodland. Place this plant out of the reach of children, because the sap may cause skin irritation. The seedpods that remain after blooming are attractive. Good companions include climbing rose 'Zephrine Drouhin', sweet autumn clematis, and cardinal flower (*Lobelia cardinalis*).

CARE: Plant 24" apart in spring or fall. Apply slow-release granular plant food at time of planting or begin using water-soluble plant food 3 weeks after planting. Cease feeding 6–8 weeks prior to the first frost date. Water regularly; this plant does not tolerate drought. Deadhead spent blossoms to encourage reblooming. Cut plants to the ground in late fall, or leave them erect for winter interest and cut back after frost withers the foliage.

PROPAGATION: Divide every 3 years or more frequently if the plant outgrows its space. Dig around the root clump and lift. Use a sharp spade to slice through the root system. Reset only portions that contain healthy roots and top shoots. Water and mulch all pieces.

PESTS AND DISEASES: Plants are relatively pest free. Aphids are occasional visitors and may be detected if their natural predator, the ladybug, suddenly appears. Exploding aphid populations can be temporarily managed with insecticidal soap. Be sure the label on the product mentions this plant and the specific insect.

RELATED SPECIES: Grecian windflower (*A. blanda*) grows 6" tall and wide and requires light, sandy soil and full sun. The deep blue, pink, or white blooms appear in late winter and early spring and are well suited for naturalizing. Snowdrop anemone (*A. sylvestris*) spreads rapidly, grows to 12" high and wide, and has fragrant single white blooms with yellow stamens in spring. It requires fertile, moist but well-drained soil and sun or partial shade.

GRAPE-LEAF ANEMONE

Anemone vitifolia *ah-NEHM-uh-nee vit-ih-FOHL-ee-uh*

White blooms with prominent yellow stamens and robust grape-leaved foliage are late-season stars in part shade.

ZONES: 5–8
SIZE: 36"h × 18–24"w
TYPE: Perennial
FORM: Rounded or clumped
TEXTURE: Medium to coarse
GROWTH: Medium
LIGHT: Part shade

MOISTURE: High
SOIL: Sandy, fertile, well-drained
FEATURES: Flowers, foliage
USES: Border, woodland, naturalizing
FLOWERS: ☐

SITING: Grape-leaf anemone prefers full sun or in hot areas partial shade. The soil should be fertile, high in organic matter, and well-drained with a pH of 5.5–7.0. This plant prefers bright shade, with shelter from the afternoon sun. Loose umbels of white blooms 1–3" across appear in late summer and last into early autumn. The flowers close at night and on cloudy days. The robust deep green foliage resembles grape leaves. Locate this plant away from romping children because the sap may cause skin irritation. Good garden companions include 'The Rocket' ligularia, 'Federsee' astilbe, 'Straussenfeder' astilbe, and cardinal flower.

CARE: Plant 18–24" apart in spring or fall. Apply slow-release granular plant food at time of planting or begin using water-soluble plant food 3 weeks after planting. Follow label directions for amount and frequency. Cease feeding 6–8 weeks prior to first frost date. Deadhead spent blossoms to encourage reblooming. Apply 3" of vegetative mulch in summer and winter to retain soil moisture and increase organic matter content. The soil should be

moist, not soggy. When the soil feels dry or almost dry 2" below the surface, it is time to water deeply. If using an irrigation system, maintain infrequent deep waterings; avoid delivering a light sprinkle every day. Organic matter in the soil and mulch on the surface will help reduce watering frequency. Cut plants to the ground in late fall, or leave them erect for winter interest and cut back in early spring.

PROPAGATION: Divide in spring every 3 years, or more frequently if the plant outgrows its space. Dig around the root clump and lift. Use a sharp spade to slice through the root system. Reset only portions that contain healthy roots and top shoots. Water and mulch all pieces.

PESTS AND DISEASES: Nematodes (microscopic worms) are frequently a problem. Avoid cultivating around the roots; every nick or cut on the root is an easy entry point for nematodes. Caterpillars and slugs are also pests. Bt (*Bacillus thuringiensis*), a microbial insecticide, controls caterpillars.

SNAPDRAGON
Antirrhinum majus an-tih-RY-nuhm MAY-juhs

Snapdragons offer cheerful color during the cooler months of the year.

ZONES: 6–9
SIZE: 9–72"h × 6–24"w
TYPE: Perennial
FORM: Upright
TEXTURE: Medium
GROWTH: Medium
LIGHT: Full sun
MOISTURE: Dry to moist
SOIL: Fertile, well-drained
FEATURES: Flowers
USES: Bedding, container
FLOWERS: □ ▨ ■ ▨ ■

SITING: Snapdragons are fragrant, short-lived perennials that are usually grown as cool-season annuals. They extend the color palette for bedding plants into cooler temperatures in the South. Snapdragons attract butterflies and are excellent cut or dried flowers. They prefer fertile but well-drained soil with a pH of 5.5–7.0. They tolerate dry or moist soil.

CARE: Plant in spring in cooler climates or in early spring or fall in hotter areas. Apply slow-release granular plant food at the time of planting or begin using water-soluble plant food 3 weeks after planting. Water deeply whenever the soil begins to dry. Deadhead spent blossoms to

Remove faded flowers with sharp pruners to stimulate new growth and reblooming.

encourage reblooming. Remove plants after the first frost in cooler zones; leave plants in the ground in warmer climates and remove before the heat of summer.

PROPAGATION: Chill seeds for several days prior to sowing to improve germination. Sprinkle them over the soil mix and leave exposed to light. Germination should occur in 7–14 days at 70–75°F. Transplant 15–20 days after sowing, and reduce the temperature to 45–40°F.

PESTS AND DISEASES: Fungal leaf spots, aphids, beetles, spider mites, slugs, and caterpillars are all known pests of snapdragons. Bt *(Bacillus thuringiensis)* is effective against caterpillars. Spider mites and aphids can be managed by hosing them off the plants or by applying insecticidal soap or a chemical insecticide. Sprinkle diatomaceous earth or slug bait around the base of the plants to manage slugs. Beer baits are also useful for attracting slugs.

RELATED SPECIES: Tahiti Series cultivars are dwarf and rust resistant. Sonnet Series are intermediate plants that hold their color well in wet weather. 'Madame Butterfly' mixture is tall with double flowers.

COLUMBINE
Aquilegia McKana Hybrids a-kwih-LEE-juh

Columbine's foliage and flowers add a light, airy quality to the landscape.

ZONES: 3–9
SIZE: 30"h × 24"w
TYPE: Perennial
FORM: Rounded or clumped
TEXTURE: Fine
GROWTH: Medium
LIGHT: Full sun to partial shade
MOISTURE: Dry to moist
SOIL: Fertile, well-drained
FEATURES: Flowers, foliage
USES: Border, woodland
FLOWERS: ■ ▨ ■ ▨ ■

SITING: Columbine tolerates full sun or partial shade and fertile or average well-drained soil with a pH of 5.5–7.0. The plants are short lived. The blooms that appear from late spring into midsummer have spurs up to 4" long. Blooms are often two-toned and attract butterflies. Use columbine in the woodland border, for naturalizing, in the rock garden, and in containers. Good companions include hosta, lady's mantle, and Siberian bugloss.

CARE: Plant 18–24" apart in spring or fall in well-drained, fertile soil. In hotter areas provide afternoon shade. Apply slow-release plant food at the time of planting. Cease feeding 6–8 weeks prior to the first frost date. Deadhead spent blossoms to encourage reblooming. Water deeply

Deadhead faded flowers to reduce self-seeding and to prolong flowering.

whenever the soil is dry. After 2–3 years the base of this plant will become woody and both bloom and foliage will begin to decline. Replace plants when this occurs. If blooms are not harvested, plants self-seed. Cut plants to the ground in late fall after frost withers the foliage.

PROPAGATION: Fresh seed will germinate in 10–20 days at 70–75°F. Stored seed may take up to 30 days to germinate. Seeds should be exposed to light, not covered with soil, during germination. If an exact replica of the parent plant is desired, divide the plant in spring. Transplants may take a full year to exhibit full healthy form, habit, and bloom schedule.

PESTS AND DISEASES: Leaf miners disfigure the leaves with "mining" lines left by feeding insects. Apply insecticide early in the season. Remove infested leaves.

RELATED SPECIES: Biedermeier Group Hybrids reach 20" high by 12" wide. Bloom colors include white, pink, purple and blue. The foliage is an attractive blue-green. Mrs. Scott-Elliot Hybrids reach 36" high by 24" wide. Blooms occur from late spring to midsummer in a variety of shades. The foliage is medium green.

JACK-IN-THE-PULPIT

Arisaema triphyllum *uh-RISS-uh-muh try-FILL-um*

Jack-in-the-pulpit's unique purple-striped spathe (flowerlike leaf) adds wonder and delight to the woodland setting.

ZONES: 2–9
SIZE: 6–24"h × 6–12"w
TYPE: Perennial
FORM: Upright
TEXTURE: Medium
GROWTH: Slow
LIGHT: Full to partial shade

MOISTURE: High to medium
SOIL: Moist to wet
FEATURES: Foliage, spathe, fruit
USES: Woodlands, naturalizing
FLOWERS: ■■□
FALL COLOR: Red berries

SITING: Jack-in-the-pulpit is a striking native woodland plant that prefers full or partial shade. The soil should be fertile and moist but well-drained with a pH of 5.5–7.0. Cluster this plant in groups close to a woodland trail or bench to capture its subtle beauty. From spring to early summer, curious hooded spathes appear. They can be green or purple striped and 4–6" long. Large, showy clusters of red berries appear in fall and attract birds and wildlife, but are toxic when eaten by humans. Good companions include hosta, Siberian bugloss, and Bethlehem sage.

CARE: Plant 12–18" apart in spring or fall. Apply slow-release granular plant food at

Clusters of red berries appear in fall and attract wildlife.

the time of planting or begin using water-soluble plant food 3 weeks after planting. Follow label directions for amount and frequency. Cease feeding 6–8 weeks prior to the first frost date. Supply water whenever the soil begins to dry. Apply 3" of vegetative mulch in summer and winter to retain soil moisture and reduce weed seed germination. Mulch also adds beneficial organic matter to the soil as it decomposes. Jack-in-the-pulpit requires little care if sun, soil, and moisture preferences are met.

PROPAGATION: In spring, scoop away the soil to expose the tuberous root system. Gently snap or cut the offsets from the parent plant. Plant the offsets, water deeply, and apply 3" of mulch. Plants readily drop seed and self-sow easily unless foraging animals remove them.

PESTS AND DISEASES: Slugs and snails may damage foliage. Diseases include leaf blight, leaf spots, and rust. Discourage slugs and snails by sprinkling diatomaceous earth or slug bait around the plant. Good air circulation and adequate spacing will discourage disease infestations. Remove and discard diseased foliage.

SEA PINK

Armeria maritima *ar-MARE-ee-uh mare-ih-TEYE-muh*

Sea pink, also known as thrift, has mounds of pink blooms in spring and grassy foliage for the front of the border.

ZONES: 3–9
SIZE: 8"h × 12"w
TYPE: Perennial
FORM: Rounded
TEXTURE: Fine
GROWTH: Medium
LIGHT: Full sun
MOISTURE: Dry to medium

SOIL: Sandy to moderately fertile, well-drained
FEATURES: Flowers, foliage
USES: Border, rock, alpine
FLOWERS: ■

SITING: Sea pinks prefer full sun and sandy loam or moderately fertile soil with a pH of 5.5–7.0. The grasslike dark green clumps of foliage are attractive throughout the growing season. The 1" balls of deep pink blooms create a stunning show from late spring to summer and are excellent fresh cut flowers. Place at the edge of the border, in the rock garden or alpine garden, or in a container.

CARE: Plant 12" apart in spring or fall. Apply slow-release granular plant food at the time of planting or begin using water-soluble plant food 3 weeks after planting in spring. Follow label directions for amount and frequency. Cease feeding

6–8 weeks prior to the first frost date. This plant will withstand periods of drought but performs best if watered deeply during dry spells. Shear back the blossoms after blooming to stimulate rebloom. The foliage resembles clumps of grass and should be marked when not in bloom so it is not mistakenly "weeded" from the garden. Apply 3" of organic mulch in summer and winter to retain soil moisture and reduce weed seed germination. Mulch also adds beneficial organic matter to the soil as it decomposes. Cut plants to the ground in late fall.

PROPAGATION: To maintain vigor, divide every 3 years in fall or early spring. Dig around the root clump and lift. Use a sharp spade to slice through the root system. Reset only portions that contain healthy roots and top shoots, then water and mulch all the plants.

PESTS AND DISEASES: Sea pink is relatively pest free. Rust and root rot may occur if the soil is wet or heavy.

RELATED SPECIES: The cultivar 'Alba' has white blooms, 'Bloodstone' has dark red blooms, and 'Dusseldorf Pride' has rosy pink blooms.

Cut faded flowers and stalks away to stimulate reblooming.

SILVER MOUND ARTEMISIA

Artemisia schmidtiana *are-teh-MEEZ-ee-uh shmihd-tee-AY-nuh*

Mounds of soft silver foliage add interest and charm to the landscape.

ZONES: 4–8
SIZE: 12"h × 18"w
TYPE: Perennial
FORM: Rounded mound
TEXTURE: Fine
GROWTH: Slow
LIGHT: Full sun

MOISTURE: Dry to medium
SOIL: Moderately fertile, well-drained
FEATURES: Foliage, flowers
USES: Border, container
FLOWERS: ■

SITING: Silver Mound artemisia prefers full sun and well-drained, average or moderately fertile soil with a pH of 5.5–7.4. In hotter areas it will tolerate light afternoon shade. It has soft, fragrant silvery-green foliage that grows in a mound. Panicles of nonshowy yellow flowers appear in summer. Silver mound artemisia is well suited for the edge of the sunny perennial border, the rock garden, or spilling over the sides of a container. The silvery foliage is useful among bright-colored flowering plants. Companions that complement Silver Mound artemisia include Coronation Gold, Schwellenburg, and woolly yarrows.

CARE: Plant 15–18" apart in spring or fall. Apply slow-release granular plant food at the time of planting, or begin using water-soluble plant food 3 weeks after planting in spring. Cease feeding 6–8 weeks prior to the first frost date. Water deeply only when the soil is dry; this plant will not withstand constantly wet soil. Shear back heavily after bloom to restore the smooth-looking habit. If not sheared, the foliage may look untidy. Cut plants to the ground in late fall, or leave erect for winter interest and cut back in early spring.

PROPAGATION: In moderately fertile soil plants may be divided every 3 years, in spring or fall. Use a sharp spade to slice through the root system. Reset only portions that contain healthy roots and top shoots. Oftentimes the center of the plant does not produce top shoots and needs to be discarded.

PESTS AND DISEASES: Plants are relatively pest free when their cultural preferences are met.

RELATED SPECIES: 'Nana' closely resembles the species but is smaller, reaching only 3" high by 12" wide. Common wormwood (*A. absinthium*) is a woody perennial that reaches 3' high by 24" wide, and has silky silvery-gray leaves and a sprawling habit. Western mugwort (*A. ludoviciana*) has silvery-white leaves, reaches 4' high by 24" wide, and is often invasive. Western mugwort cultivars 'Silver King' and 'Silver Queen' are used in wreath making.

Shear back Silver Mound artemisia in mid-summer to retain a neat appearance.

GOATSBEARD

Aruncus dioicus *ah-RUN-kuhs dy-OH-ik-uhs*

Goatsbeard produces fernlike foliage and feathery flowers in bright shade.

ZONES: 3–7
SIZE: 6'h × 4'w
TYPE: Perennial
FORM: Upright clump-forming
TEXTURE: Fine to medium
GROWTH: Medium
LIGHT: Part shade

MOISTURE: Medium to high
SOIL: Fertile, moist, well-drained
FEATURES: Flowers, foliage
USES: Border, woodland
FLOWERS: □

SITING: Goatsbeard prefers shade in the afternoon and fertile, moist yet well-drained soil with a pH of 5.5–7.0. The panicles of white blooms appear from early to midsummer and occasionally arch with asymmetrical gracefulness. The attractive fernlike leaves can reach up to 3' long. The foliage and blooms are light and airy—you can see through this plant—so it looks best when planted in groups in the border. Good companions include Siebold hosta, Siberian bugloss, snakeroot, and 'Fanal' astilbe.

CARE: Plant 3–4' apart in spring or fall. Apply slow-release granular plant food at time of planting, or begin using water-soluble plant food 3 weeks after planting in spring. Cease feeding 6–8 weeks prior to the first frost date. If the plant is located on the bank of a natural water body, avoid chemical fertilizers; they can leach into the water. Instead, mix compost into the soil and apply 3" of vegetative mulch in summer and winter to retain soil moisture and to reduce weed seed germination. Water deeply whenever the soil begins to dry. Deadhead spent blossoms to encourage reblooming. Cut plants to the ground in late fall, or leave erect until frost damages the structure.

PROPAGATION: In moderately fertile soil divide plants in early spring or fall every 2–3 years to maintain vigor. Older rootstocks do not divide as easily because they become woody. Dig around the root clump and lift. Use a sharp spade to slice through the root system. Reset only portions that contain healthy roots and top shoots, then water and mulch. Goatsbeard seed yields good stock. Sow fresh seed (stored seeds have a greatly reduced germination rate) and lightly cover with soilless mix. Seeds germinate in 15–25 days at 70°F. Seedlings are slow growing and may take 50–70 days before they are ready for transplanting.

PESTS AND DISEASES: Plants are relatively pest free when their cultural preferences (sun, soil, moisture) are met.

RELATED SPECIES: 'Kneiffii' is slightly smaller than the species, reaching 4' high by 18" wide, with finely cut leaves and cream-colored blooms on arching stems. 'Kneiffii' must be propagated by division.

CANADIAN WILD GINGER
Asarum canadense Ah-SARE-uhm kan-uh-DEHNS

Canadian wild ginger is a superb ground cover for shade. It has heart-shaped leaves and hidden bell-shaped flowers.

ZONES: 2–8
SIZE: 6"h × 6"w
TYPE: Perennial
FORM: Spreading
TEXTURE: Medium
GROWTH: Slow
LIGHT: Full to partial shade

MOISTURE: Medium
SOIL: Fertile, moist, well-drained
FEATURES: Foliage
USES: Ground cover
FLOWERS: ■

SITING: Canadian ginger prefers shade and fertile, well-drained soil with a pH of 5.5–7.0. The main attraction of this native plant is the heart-shaped leaves. Curious bell-shaped brownish-purple flowers appear in early spring and are well hidden by the foliage. This plant is at home in the shade border or the woodland garden or under irrigated trees. Good companions include hosta, astilbe, Siberian bugloss, and Japanese painted fern.

CARE: Plant 6–12" apart in spring or fall. Apply slow-release granular plant food at time of planting, or begin using water-soluble plant food 3 weeks after planting in spring. Cease feeding 6–8 weeks prior to first frost date. Water deeply whenever the

Plant Canadian wild ginger on shady slopes to add beauty as well as stabilize the soil.

soil begins to dry out; let the soil dry slightly between waterings. Apply 3" of vegetative mulch in summer and winter to retain soil moisture and reduce weed seed germination. Plants are deciduous and will die back to the ground each winter.

PROPAGATION: Plants rarely require division. When desired, divide plants in early spring. Dig around the root clump and lift. Use a sharp spade to slice through the root system. Reset portions that contain healthy roots and top shoots, then water and mulch.

PESTS AND DISEASES: Slugs and snails are common pests. Diatomaceous earth, a powderlike substance made from fossils, or slug bait, may be sprinkled over the soil around the plant. As a soft-bodied pest slides across the powder, tiny sharp fossil points pierce the outer coat, causing dehydration. Replace diatomaceous earth frequently, especially after heavy rains.

RELATED SPECIES: European wild ginger (*A. europeum*) has darker, intensely glossy, heart-shaped leaves and reaches 3" high by 12" wide. The leaves are more striking than those of Canadian wild ginger and form an attractive ground cover.

BUTTERFLY WEED
Asclepias tuberosa Ah-SKLEEP-ee-us too-ber-OH-suh

Butterfly weed's brilliant orange blooms attract butterflies and are followed by attractive seedpods.

ZONES: 4–9
SIZE: 36"h × 12"w
TYPE: Perennial
FORM: Upright
TEXTURE: Fine to medium
GROWTH: Medium
LIGHT: Full sun

MOISTURE: Dry to moist
SOIL: Sandy loam or clay, well-drained
FEATURES: Flowers, foliage, fruit
USES: Border, naturalizing
FLOWERS: ■

SITING: Butterfly weed prefers full sun and fertile, well-drained soil but tolerates a variety of soil textures, from sandy to clayey. It prefers a pH of 5.5–7.0. This plant looks good in groups in the perennial border, in the rock garden or containers, or naturalized in sunny spots. The blooms range from orange to yellow to red from midsummer into early fall. Flowers attract butterflies. Stems exude a milky sap that may cause skin irritation. Good companions include 'Coronation Gold' yarrow, 'David' garden phlox, and 'Goldsturm' black-eyed Susan.

CARE: Plant 12" apart in spring or fall. Plants resent transplanting, so obtain container-grown stock. Apply slow-release

Spray butterfly milkweed with a strong stream of water to dislodge aphids and other pests.

granular plant food at time of planting or begin using water-soluble plant food 3 weeks after planting. Cease feeding 6–8 weeks prior to first frost date. Butterfly milkweed tolerates drought but performs better if it receives deep but infrequent waterings during dry spells. Deadhead spent flower stalks to encourage repeat blooming. Cut plants to the ground in late fall or leave erect for winter interest until frost collapses the stems. Seedpods are attractive and cling to the stems in winter. This plant is late to emerge in spring.

PROPAGATION: Sprinkle fresh seed over soil mix and either cover lightly or leave uncovered and exposed to light. Germination occurs in 21–28 days at 70–75°F. Transplant 35–55 days after sowing seed. If seed is not fresh, refrigerate moist seeds for 2 weeks, then sow seed as described above.

PESTS AND DISEASES: Caterpillars eat the foliage, but it is probably best to live with the damage, because the pests may be butterfly larvae. Aphids are also common, but attracting or introducing ladybugs can be an environmentally friendly and effective management tool.

NEW ENGLAND ASTER

Aster novae-angliae AS-stir noh-vee-ANG-lee-ee

New England aster's daisylike flowers offer late-summer and autumn interest.

ZONES: 4–8
SIZE: 5'h × 2'w
TYPE: Perennial
FORM: Upright
TEXTURE: Fine to medium
GROWTH: Medium
LIGHT: Full sun

MOISTURE: Dry to moist
SOIL: Fertile, moist
FEATURES: Flowers
USES: Border, wetlands
FLOWERS: ■ ■ ■ □

SITING: New England aster prefers full sun and fertile, moist soil with a pH of 5.5–7.0. The daisylike light violet blooms have a yellow center and appear in late summer to midautumn. The foliage is abundant; 5"-long leaves are medium green and lance-shaped. Lower leaves often drop during the summer. New England aster may require staking to remain upright and should be placed where the foliage can be supported either by stakes or other plants. This plant looks good in the back of the border, in the cottage garden, in wetland areas, or, if cut back to promote compact growth, in containers. The blooms attract butterflies and are excellent fresh cut flowers. Good garden companions include 'Snowbank' boltonia, purple-flowered Russian sage, and rosemary.

CARE: Plant New England aster 18–24" apart in spring or fall. Apply slow-release granular plant food at time of planting or begin using water-soluble plant food 3 weeks after planting in spring. Follow label directions for amount and frequency. Cease feeding 6–8 weeks prior to first frost date. If planting in a wetland, avoid fertilizers or chemical pesticides to prevent chemicals from leaching into water bodies. This plant tolerates dry soil once established but performs better in moist soils. Water deeply when the soil begins to dry out. Cut back at 6–12" and again in early to midsummer to promote compact growth. Apply 3" of vegetative mulch in summer and winter to retain soil moisture and reduce weed seed germination. Mulch also adds beneficial organic matter to the soil as it decomposes. Cut back in late fall and dispose of diseased foliage.

PROPAGATION: Divide every 2 years in spring or fall to maintain vigor and control growth. Dig around the root clump and lift. Use a sharp spade to slice through the root system. Reset portions that contain healthy roots and top shoots, then water and mulch. Discard any pieces that do not contain both healthy roots and top shoots.

PESTS AND DISEASES: Numerous insects and diseases frequent asters. Root rot is possible if the soil is too wet, and powdery mildew is likely if the soil and air are too dry. Fungal leafspot is common. Regular fungicidal treatments are needed unless the plant is at the rear of the border where the foliage is not readily visible.

Frikart's aster blooms earlier in the summer than does New England aster. 'Monch' is a popular cultivar.

RELATED SPECIES: Alpine aster (*A. alpinus*) has violet blooms with a deep yellow center in early and midsummer; the plants reach 10" high and 18" wide. They prefer moderately fertile, well-drained soil and full sun. Frikart's aster (*A. ×frikartii*) bears deep violet blooms with an orange center in late summer and early fall. It reaches 30" high and 15" wide and prefers full sun and well-drained, not wet, soil. New York aster (*A. novi-belgii*) reaches 4' high and 3' wide. Blooms are violet blue and appear from late summer into fall. The plant needs dividing every other year to maintain vigor and stem rampant growth. Cut back at 6" and again by one-half in early summer to create bushy, compact plants.

Asters that are not cut back often require staking and may appear leggy.

Cut back aster once or twice during the growing season to promote compact growth.

HYBRID ASTILBE

Astilbe ×arendsii *Ah-STIL-bee ah-REND-zee-eye*

Astilbes, also known as false spirea, are low-maintenance plants for moist sites in part or full shade.

ZONES: 4–8
SIZE: 1½–4'h × 2'w
TYPE: Perennial
FORM: Upright
TEXTURE: Medium
GROWTH: Medium
LIGHT: Partial to full shade

MOISTURE: Medium to high
SOIL: Fertile, well-drained
FEATURES: Flowers, foliage
USES: Border, woodland
FLOWERS: ■ ■ ▦ □

SITING: Astilbe prefers moist yet well-drained soil with a pH of 5.5–7.0. It prefers partial to full shade and requires shelter from the afternoon sun. It has plumes of blooms in colors ranging from purple to rose to white. The blooms attract butterflies and dry to a faded, muted color. The fernlike foliage is handsome and low maintenance. Place groups of astilbe in the shade border, the woodland garden, in wetlands, or in containers. Good companions include hosta, heuchera hybrids, and snakeroot.

CARE: Plant astilbe 18"–2' apart in spring or fall. Apply slow-release plant food, such as Miracle-Gro Shake 'n Feed All Purpose, at time of planting or begin using water-soluble plant food, such as Miracle-Gro Water Soluble All Purpose, 3 weeks after planting in spring. Follow label directions for amount and frequency. Cease feeding 6–8 weeks prior to first frost date. If planting in a wetland, avoid fertilizers and pesticides. Astilbe will not tolerate soil that dries out in summer. Water deeply whenever the soil begins to dry. Apply 3" of vegetative mulch in summer and winter to retain soil moisture and reduce weed seed germination. Mulch also adds beneficial organic matter to the soil as it decomposes. Cut back after frost collapses the foliage.

PROPAGATION: Divide in spring or fall every 3 years to maintain vigor and control growth. Dig around the rhizomes and lift. Use a sharp spade to slice through the root system. Reset portions that contain healthy roots and top shoots, then water and mulch. Discard any pieces that do not contain both healthy roots and top shoots. Cut plants to the ground in late fall or leave erect for winter interest (the dried blooms are attractive) and cut back in early spring.

PESTS AND DISEASES: Plants are relatively pest free when their cultural preferences (sun, soil, moisture) are met.

RELATED SPECIES: 'Amethyst' reaches 36" high and 24" wide and has lilac-pink blooms in early summer. 'Bressingham Beauty' is 36" high and 24" wide, with bright pink blooms in midsummer, and 'Cattleya' grows to 36" high and 36" wide, with reddish-pink blooms in midsummer. Chinese astilbe (*A. chinensis*) grows to 24" high and wide with pink blooms in late summer. *A. c.* var. *davidii* has appealing bronze-tinged leaves and bears purplish-pink blooms. It grows in sun or shade, is drought tolerant, and reaches 6" high and 24" wide. *A. c.* var. *pumila* reaches 12" high and wide and has purple flowers.

RAISED BEDS

Most annuals and perennials perform best in soil that contains organic matter and drains well. An easy way to enhance drainage and add organic matter is to create raised beds or berms. Raised beds usually have constructed sides that hold soil, while berms are free-standing beds.

■ Select the place and the plants for the bed.
■ Draw the landscape bed on paper or outline it on the ground using hoses to create the shape and landscape paint to mark the perimeter.
■ Till the area.
■ Add 6–12" of good garden soil and compost and mix thoroughly with existing soil.
■ Install the edges for raised beds. These are commonly made of timbers, blocks, or stone. Shape the berm so the top is relatively flat and the sides gently slope to the ground.
■ Set plants into place, apply 3" of vegetative mulch around, but not touching plants, and water deeply.

You can create a freestanding raised bed from cedar lumber and garden soil directly on top of existing sod.

Benefits of raised beds and berms
■ Promote water drainage.
■ Allow for importation of improved soils.
■ Raise plants higher in the landscape for better viewing.
■ Protect plants from mechanical injury.
■ Protect soil from compaction due to foot and vehicle traffic.
■ Warm soil earlier in the spring.

Showy plumes of color are held above attractive fernlike foliage.

Water astilbes deeply and let soil dry between waterings.

JAPANESE PAINTED FERN

Athyrium nipponicum *Ah-THEE-ree-uhm nip-PON-ih-kum*

Japanese painted fern's fronds are beautiful silver-gray and green with red midveins.

ZONES: 4–8
SIZE: 12"h × 12"w
TYPE: Perennial
FORM: Irregular
TEXTURE: Fine
GROWTH: Medium
LIGHT: Partial shade

MOISTURE: Medium to high
SOIL: Fertile, well-drained
FEATURES: Leaves
USES: Border, woodland, container

SITING: Japanese painted fern prefers partial shade with shelter from the afternoon sun, and fertile, well-drained soil with a pH of 5.5–7.0. The beauty of this plant is the silver-gray and green fronds with reddish midveins. It looks good in the shade border, the woodland garden, or containers. Companions include 'Mrs. Moon' Bethlehem sage, lady's mantle, heuchera hybrids, and astilbe.

CARE: Plant Japanese painted fern 12–18" apart in spring or fall in fertile soil high in organic matter. After planting, water deeply and add 3" of mulch around,

Mix organic matter thoroughly into existing soil prior to planting to increase fertility.

but not touching, the plant. Apply slow-release granular plant food at time of planting, or begin using water-soluble plant food 3 weeks after planting. Cease feeding 6–8 weeks prior to first frost date. Water deeply whenever the soil becomes dry. Cut back this deciduous fern in fall, or leave erect for late-season viewing and cut back after frost collapses the foliage.

PROPAGATION: Divide in spring or fall every 3 years. Dig around the root clump and lift. Use a sharp spade to slice through the root system. Reset portions that contain healthy roots and top shoots, then water and mulch. Discard any pieces that do not contain both healthy roots and top shoots.

PESTS AND DISEASES: Plants are relatively pest free when their cultural preferences are met. Snails and slugs may pose problems. Brown leaves can indicate too much or too little moisture, too much sunlight, or low soil fertility.

RELATED SPECIES: Lady fern (*A. felix-femina*) has light green fronds and reaches 4' high and 2' wide. Numerous choice cultivars include 'Acrocladon' (12" high and wide), 'Frizelliae' (8" high and 12" wide), and 'Verononiae' (3' high and wide).

FALSE BLUE INDIGO

Baptisia australis *bap-TEES-ee-uh aw-STRAL-is*

False blue indigo is also known as wild blue indigo or baptisia.

ZONES: 3–9
SIZE: 5'h × 2'w
TYPE: Perennial
FORM: Upright
TEXTURE: Medium to fine
GROWTH: Medium
LIGHT: Full sun to partial shade

MOISTURE: Dry to medium
SOIL: Fertile, sandy, well-drained
FEATURES: Flowers, foliage, seedpods
USES: Border, container
FLOWERS: ■

SITING: Baptisia prefers full sun and well-drained soil, preferably sandy yet fertile, with a pH of 5.5–7.0. The full-season appeal of false blue indigo starts with the deeply divided leaves, moves into the tiny deep blue blooms that cover the plant in early summer, and ends with the pealike green seedpods that eventually turn black. It is well suited for the border, the container, or the wild garden. The pods are used in flower arrangements, and the flowers are used fresh-cut or dried. Good companions include 'Goldsturm' black-eyed Susan, 'Snowbank' *Boltonia*, and purple coneflower.

Remove seedpods before seeds mature and self-sow in the landscape.

CARE: Plant 24" apart in spring or fall. Apply slow-release granular plant food at time of planting, or begin using water-soluble plant food 3 weeks after planting. Cease feeding 6–8 weeks prior to first frost date. False blue indigo tolerates drought but performs better with deep but infrequent waterings during dry spells. Apply 3" of vegetative mulch in summer and winter to retain soil moisture and reduce weed seed germination. This plant self-sows prolifically. Deadheading after bloom will thwart the proliferation but eliminate the attractive black seedpods.

PROPAGATION: Divide in fall or early spring. Dig around the root clump and lift. Use a sharp spade to slice through the root system. Because false blue indigo has a taproot, it is difficult to move, and may take several years to recover from division.

PESTS AND DISEASES: Plants are relatively pest free when their cultural preferences are met. Powdery mildew and fungal leaf spots may occur. Fungicides may be applied, or light infestations (less than 15 percent damage to foliage) can be tolerated in the landscape.

WAX BEGONIA

Begonia Semperflorens-Cultorum Hybrids *Beh-GOHN-yah sem-per-FLOR-enz-kubl-TOR-uhm*

Wax begonias are attractive, durable, and versatile in the container or landscape.

ZONES: NA
SIZE: 8–24"h × 8"w
TYPE: Annual
FORM: Rounded
TEXTURE: Medium
GROWTH: Medium
LIGHT: Full sun to part shade

MOISTURE: Medium to high
SOIL: Fertile, well-drained
FEATURES: Flowers, foliage
USES: Bedding, container
FLOWERS: ■■□

SITING: Wax begonia prefers full sun or partial shade and well-drained, fertile soil with a pH of 5.5–7.0. Tiny single or double flowers in red, pink, or white cover this plant all summer long. The stems are succulent and the green or bronze leaves have a rounded outline. The bronze-leaved plants are better adapted to full sun. This prolific bloomer is useful as a bedding plant, massed as a flowering ground cover, or in containers.

CARE: Plant 6–12" apart in spring after last frost in cooler climates. In frost-free zones, grow as a perennial. Apply slow-release granular plant food at time of planting, or begin using water-soluble plant food 3 weeks after planting. Follow label directions for amount and frequency. Water deeply whenever the soil starts to dry. Apply 3" of vegetative mulch to retain soil moisture and reduce weed seed germination. Mulch also adds beneficial organic matter to the soil as it decomposes. Plants are considered self-cleaning and do not need to be deadheaded. Remove plants before or after the first hard freeze.

PROPAGATION: Highest germination rates occur when seed is sprinkled evenly over the soil mix and temperatures are 78–80°F. Germination occurs in 14–21 days; plants are ready for transplanting 45–50 days after sowing, when the temperature can be reduced to 60°F. In frost-free areas wax begonia may be treated as a perennial and divided every spring to maintain vigor.

PESTS AND DISEASES: Wax begonia is susceptible to mealybugs, mites, thrips, powdery mildew, stem rot, and nematodes. Providing preferred cultural conditions will minimize pest infestations, though not eliminate them. Insecticidal soaps may be used to manage the insects, and fungicides may be used to manage the diseases.

1 Fill a window box with Miracle-Gro potting mix.

2 Place plants in the window box and gently firm mix around roots.

3 Apply water to thoroughly moisten the mix.

TUBEROUS BEGONIA

Begonia Tuberhybrida Hybrids *Beh-GOHN-yah too-ber-HY-brid-uh*

Tuberous begonias have lush leaves and blossoms in a variety of rich colors.

ZONES: 9–10
SIZE: 6–12"h × w
TYPE: Perennial
FORM: Rounded
TEXTURE: Medium
GROWTH: Medium
LIGHT: Partial shade
MOISTURE: Medium to high

SOIL: Fertile, well-drained
FEATURES: Flowers, foliage
USES: Bedding, container
FLOWERS: □■■ ■■□

SITING: Tuberous begonia prefers fertile, well-drained soil with a pH of 5.5–7.0 and shelter from the afternoon sun. Bright blooms up to 5" wide appear all summer long in shades of pink, red, rose, orange, or white. Stems are succulent and leaves are pointed and glossy. Tuberous begonia can be successfully used as a bedding plant, in containers, or as a houseplant.

CARE: Plant tuberous begonia 12" apart in late spring or early summer after the last frost. Apply slow-release plant food, such as Miracle-Gro Shake 'n Feed All Purpose, at time of planting or begin using water-soluble plant food, such as Miracle-Gro Water Soluble All Purpose, 3 weeks after planting. Follow label directions for amount and frequency. Water deeply whenever the soil begins to dry. Apply 3" of vegetative mulch to retain soil moisture. Plants grow from tubers that do not overwinter successfully outdoors. Lift tubers in fall, before the first hard freeze,

and let dry. Dust with fungicide and store in a cool (41–45°F), dry place. In spring replant tubers, hollow side up.

PROPAGATION: Sow seed on top of soilless potting mix exposed to light, and provide temperatures of 70–72°F for up to 30 days. Transplant 45–50 days after sowing. Begonias in the Nonstop, Clip, and Musical Series require 12-hour days from October to March to germinate. This is achieved by leaving lights on for 4 hours after sunset. After the day-length requirement is satisfied, follow regular germination procedures outlined above.

PESTS AND DISEASES: Tuberous begonia is susceptible to mealybugs, mites, thrips, powdery mildew, stem rot, and nematodes. Providing ideal cultural conditions will minimize pest infestations, though not eliminate them. Use insecticidal soaps or beneficial/predatory insects to manage the insects, and spray fungicides to manage the diseases.

HEART-LEAF BERGENIA

Bergenia cordifolia *ber-JEEN-ee-uh kord-ih-FOL-ee-uh*

Heart-leaf bergenia's evergreen leaves and rose-colored blossoms are main attractions. It is also known as pigsqueak.

ZONES: 3–8
SIZE: 24"h × 36"w
TYPE: Perennial
FORM: Rounded
TEXTURE: Medium
GROWTH: Medium
LIGHT: Partial shade to full sun
MOISTURE: Low to high

SOIL: Fertile, well-drained
FEATURES: Flowers, foliage
USES: Border, woodland
FLOWERS: ▥
FALL COLOR: ▪

SITING: Heart-leaf bergenia prefers afternoon shade and fertile, well-drained soil high in organic matter with a pH of 5.5–7.0. The heart-shaped leaves reach 12" long, and the blooms range from pale to deep pink and appear in late winter or early spring. In the border this evergreen plant offers long-season foliage color; the leaves often assume more reddish hues with cold weather. Good companions include snakeroot, European ginger, and dwarf Chinese astilbe.

CARE: Plant 24–36" apart in spring or fall. Pigsqueak tolerates poor soil but performs best in fertile, humus-rich soil. To increase organic matter in the soil, add 1–2" of composted material and till in to a depth of 12–15". After planting, water deeply and add 3" of mulch around, but not touching, the plant. Apply slow-release granular plant food at time of planting, or begin using water-soluble plant food 3 weeks after planting in spring. Follow label directions for amount and frequency. Cease feeding 6–8 weeks prior to first frost date. Water deeply whenever the soil begins to dry out, being sure to allow the soil to dry between waterings. Cut back whenever the foliage becomes leggy. Reapply mulch whenever necessary to maintain 3" in summer and winter. Mulch also adds beneficial organic matter to the soil as it decomposes. Leave erect for winter interest unless frost collapses the foliage. Heart-leaf bergenia performs best in cool weather. It dislikes the heat of summer.

PROPAGATION: Divide rhizomes in early spring or fall when clumps become crowded. Dig around the root clump and lift. Use a sharp spade to slice through the root system. Reset portions that contain healthy roots and top shoots, then water and mulch. Discard any pieces that do not contain both healthy roots and top shoots.

PESTS AND DISEASES: Plants are relatively pest free when their cultural preferences are met, although slugs and snails may feast on bergenia leaves. Brown leaves can mean too much or too little moisture, too much sun, or poor soil.

RELATED SPECIES: The cultivar 'Purpurea' has thick deep red leaves and pinkish-purple flowers. 'Perfecta' is taller than the species with rosy-red flowers and purplish leaves. 'Redstart' has red flowers in late spring, and 'Rotblum' bears red flowers and has red-tinged leaves in winter.

WHITE BOLTONIA

Boltonia asteroides latisquama 'Snowbank' *bohl-TOHN-ee-ah a-ster-OY-deez lat-is-KWA-muh*

'Snowbank' white boltonia is a low-maintenance perennial with white daisylike blooms late in the season.

ZONES: 4–9
SIZE: 5'h × 3'w
TYPE: Perennial
FORM: Upright
TEXTURE: Medium
GROWTH: Medium
LIGHT: Full sun
MOISTURE: Medium to high

SOIL: Moderately fertile, moist, well-drained
FEATURES: Flowers, foliage
USES: Border, wetlands
FLOWERS: ▢ ▪ ▥

SITING: 'Snowbank' white boltonia prefers full sun, though it tolerates light shade in the afternoon in hot climates. The soil should be moderately fertile and moist yet well-drained, with a pH of 5.5–7.0. This plant can also grow in a wetland or moist area. Clusters of tiny, daisylike white blooms appear in late summer into early fall. 'Snowbank' is a good choice because its habit is sturdy and upright, it does not need staking like other boltonias, and it is not invasive. Give this plant plenty of room in the border for mid- to late-season color and low-maintenance foliage. Flowers attract butterflies and are excellent fresh-cut. Good companions include Russian sage, bluebeard, asters, and rosemary.

CARE: Plant 36" apart in early spring or fall. Apply slow-release granular plant food at the time of planting, or begin using water-soluble plant food 3 weeks after planting in spring. Follow label directions for amount and frequency. Cease feeding 6–8 weeks prior to first frost date. Water deeply when the soil dries. Apply 3" of vegetative mulch in summer and winter to help retain soil moisture. Cut back in fall or leave erect for late-season viewing and cut back in early spring.

PROPAGATION: Divide in fall or early spring. Dig around the root clump and lift. Use a sharp spade to slice through the root system. Reset portions that contain healthy roots and top shoots, then water and mulch. Discard any pieces that do not contain both healthy roots and top shoots. Plants started from seed will not come true to type.

PESTS AND DISEASES: Plants are relatively pest free when their cultural preferences (sun, soil, moisture) are met. Moderate soil fertility helps create strong, robust foliage that is not as easily penetrated by pests. Plants grown in too-fertile soil often have more succulent leaves and are more easily invaded by pests. Powdery mildew and fungal leaf spots may occur. Fungicides may be applied, or light infestations (less than 15 percent damage to foliage) can be tolerated in the landscape.

RELATED SPECIES: 'Pink Beauty' is a cultivar with pink ray florets. Siberian boltonia (*B. incisa*) is only 2–3' tall, and bears lilac purple flowers.

FLOWERING KALE

Brassica oleracea BRASS-ik-uh oh-ler-A-see-uh

Ornamental kale adds striking color and texture to the landscape or container.

ZONES: NA
SIZE: 12–18"h × 12–18"w
TYPE: Annual
FORM: Rounded
TEXTURE: Coarse
GROWTH: Medium
LIGHT: Full sun to partial shade

MOISTURE: Medium to high
SOIL: Fertile, well-drained
FEATURES: Foliage
USES: Bedding, container

SITING: Ornamental kale prefers cool temperatures, full sun, and fertile, well-drained soil. Like cabbage and broccoli, it prefers a limed soil (pH of 5.5–7.5). The ornamental leaves are rosettes of green, pink, purple, or white. The ruffled edges on the leaves add texture to any planting. Use ornamental kale as a cool-season bedding or container plant. Companions for the container include ornamental grasses, asters, and rose-colored pansies.

CARE: Plant 12–18" apart in late summer or early spring. Apply slow-release granular plant food at time of planting. Water deeply whenever the soil is dry. Apply 3" of vegetative mulch to help retain soil moisture and keep soil temperatures from fluctuating. Remove older leaves that discolor or are damaged. When flowers appear or when temperatures near 68–70°F, remove and replace with heat-tolerant bedding plants.

PROPAGATION: Sprinkle seeds over the seed starting mix, cover lightly, and moisten. Seeds germinate in 7–14 days at 68°F. Transplant when several true leaves develop, and reduce the temperature to 55–58°F.

PESTS AND DISEASES: Pests include aphids, cabbage white butterfly, and flea beetles. Diseases problems include downy and powdery mildew.

RELATED SPECIES: Cultivars include 'Osaka' (to 12" tall, with blue-green leaves and pink or red centers), Peacock Series (red or white leaves and feathery foliage), and Sparrow Series (dwarf plants with red or white ruffled leaves).

1 Plant ornamental kale in early autumn to provide color.

2 Plant ornamental kale in containers using Miracle-Gro potting mix.

HEART-LEAF BRUNNERA

Brunnera macrophylla BRUH-ner-uh mak-ro-FY-luh

Heart-leaf brunnera, also known as Siberian bugloss, produces clouds of sky blue blossoms in spring.

ZONES: 3–7
SIZE: 18"h × 24"w
TYPE: Perennial
FORM: Rounded
TEXTURE: Medium
GROWTH: Medium
LIGHT: Full to partial shade

MOISTURE: Medium
SOIL: Moderately fertile, well-drained
FEATURES: Leaves, flowers
USES: Border, woodland
FLOWERS: ■

SITING: Light to deep shade suit heart-leaf brunnera. The soil should be moderately fertile to ensure low maintenance. The hairy, heart-shaped deep green leaves grow 2–8" long and form an attractive mound. Clusters of sky blue blooms appear in mid- to late spring and contrast beautifully with the deep green foliage. Plant brunnera in groups in a large shade border, or use singly as a specimen in a smaller space. Good companions include Bethlehem sage, Siebold hosta, astilbe, snakeroot, and Japanese painted fern.

Deadhead variegated brunnera before seeds fall to the ground to prevent nonvariegated seedlings from springing up.

CARE: Plant 24–36" apart in spring or fall. Apply slow-release granular plant food at time of planting or begin using water-soluble plant food 3 weeks after planting in spring. Cease feeding 6–8 weeks prior to first frost date. Water deeply whenever the soil begins to dry out; let the soil dry between waterings. Apply 3" of vegetative mulch in summer and winter to help retain soil moisture. The plant will lightly self-seed, but the seedlings will not be identical to the parent plant. Cut back in fall.

PROPAGATION: Divide in fall or early spring every 3 years. Dig around the root clump and lift. Use a sharp spade to slice through the root system. Reset portions that contain healthy roots and top shoots, then water and mulch. Discard any pieces that do not contain both healthy roots and top shoots.

PESTS AND DISEASES: Plants are relatively pest free when their cultural preferences (sun, soil, moisture) are met.

RELATED SPECIES: 'Dawson's White' ('Variagata') has attractive creamy white coloring along the leaf margins. 'Hadspen Cream' has narrow white leaf margins. Leaves of 'Langtree' have silver speckles.

CALADIUM
Caladium bicolor ka-LAY-dee-uhm BY-kuhl-ur

Caladium's graceful leaves and exotic colors are appealing in the shade.

ZONES: 8–11
SIZE: 24"h × 24"w
TYPE: Perennial
FORM: Irregular
TEXTURE: Medium
GROWTH: Fast
LIGHT: Full to partial shade

MOISTURE: Medium to high
SOIL: Fertile, well-drained
FEATURES: Leaves
USES: Bedding, border, container

SITING: Caladium prefers fertile, well-drained, acidic soil with a pH of 5.5–7.0, and full to part shade. The 12"-long arrowhead-shaped leaves come in pink, white, green, or red variegation. The large leaves can be damaged by excessive wind.

CARE: Plant 24" apart in late spring after the last frost. Caladium needs warm weather to grow well. Apply slow-release granular plant food at time of planting or begin using water-soluble plant food 3 weeks after planting in spring. Cease feeding 6–8 weeks prior to first frost date. Brown leaf edges may be the result of too much sun or improper watering. Lift tubers before a hard freeze and store in a cool (60–65°F), dry place during the winter.
PROPAGATION: Divide tubers in spring. Cut portions that include an "eye," or bud.

Dust with fungicide, then plant, water, and mulch.
PESTS AND DISEASES: Diseases include tuber rot, Southern blight, and bacterial and fungal leaf spots. Pests include root-knot nematodes, slugs, and snails.
RELATED SPECIES: 'Little Miss Muffet' is 12" tall and has green leaves with red veins and speckles. 'Pink Beauty' has red veins and pink-speckled margins, and 'White Queen' has white leaves with red veins and green margins. 'Florida Beauty' and "Florida Carnival' are sun tolerant.

1 Cut back the leaves before lifting the tubers for winter storage.

2 Lift tubers and brush off soil before storing them.

3 Cover tubers with dry peat moss and store in a dry, cool location until spring.

POT MARIGOLD
Calendula officinalis kuh-LEN-dyoo-luh uh-fish-ih-NAL-iss

Pot marigold produces bright yellow or orange flowers during cooler summer temperatures.

ZONES: NA
SIZE: 12–30"h × 12–18"w
TYPE: Annual
FORM: Upright
TEXTURE: Medium
GROWTH: Fast
LIGHT: Full sun

MOISTURE: Medium to high
SOIL: Moderately fertile, well-drained
FEATURES: Flowers, foliage
USES: Bedding, border, container
FLOWERS: ■ ■

SITING: Calendula prefers full sun and moderately fertile soil with a pH of 5.5–7.0. The bright orange, yellow, gold, or cream blooms provide long-season color from summer into fall. In hot climates use calendula as a cool-season annual. Place groups in the front of the border, in containers, or as bedding plants covering a large area. Pot marigold makes an excellent fresh cut flower. Container companions include 'Brilliant' and 'Autumn Joy' sedums, cockscomb, and white-flowered 'Miss Wilmott' pincushion flower.
CARE: Plant 12" apart in late spring or early summer after the last frost. Apply slow-release plant food, such as Miracle-Gro Shake 'n Feed All Purpose, at time of planting. Water deeply when the soil is dry. Deadhead the blooms to encourage reblooming. Remove the plants just prior to or after the first frost.
PROPAGATION: Sprinkle seeds over the soil mix and cover lightly. Thoroughly moisten and keep moist but not soggy. Germination will occur in 10–14 days at 70°F. After transplanting, reduce the temperature to 55°F.

PESTS AND DISEASES: Diseases include aster yellows, powdery mildew, and fungal leaf spots. Slugs feed on the foliage.
RELATED SPECIES: Cultivars include 'Art Shades' (24" tall with orange and cream flowers), 'Fiesta Giant' (dwarf that reaches 12" tall and has double flowers in light orange and yellow), 'Indian Prince' (dark orange flowers with a reddish tint), and Pacific Beauty Series (double flowers that include interesting bicolors with a mahogany-colored center).

1 Harvest flowers just as they open for use in salads.

2 Sprinkle flower petals over salad for a festive look.

CARPATHIAN HAREBELL
Campanula carpatica *kam-PAN-yew-luh kar-PAT-ih-kuh*

Carpathian harebell, also known as Carpathian bellflower or tussock bellflower, produces bell-shaped blooms.

ZONES: 2–7
SIZE: 12"h × 12–24"w
TYPE: Perennial
FORM: Mound
TEXTURE: Fine
GROWTH: Medium
LIGHT: Partial shade to full sun

MOISTURE: Medium
SOIL: Moist, well-drained
FEATURES: Flowers, foliage
USES: Border, rock garden, container
FLOWERS: ■■□

SITING: Carpathian harebell prefers full sun or partial shade and well-drained, moderately fertile soil with a pH of 5.5–7.0. The upturned, bell-shaped blooms appear in shades of blue, violet, and white during the summer. Group plants in the border or rock garden, or use in containers. Good companions include bloody cranesbill and 'Elizabeth' campanula.

CARE: Plant 12–24" apart in spring or fall. Apply slow-release granular plant food at time of planting or begin using water-soluble plant food 3 weeks after planting in spring. Water deeply when the soil is dry. Apply 3" of mulch in summer to retain soil moisture. Blooms rarely require deadheading. Cut back in late fall.

PROPAGATION: Divide every 3 years in August or September, or in early spring when the plant is dormant. Sprinkle seeds lightly over soil mix and lightly cover. Germination occurs in 14–21 days at 70°F. Transplant 20–30 days after sowing.

PESTS AND DISEASES: Plants are relatively pest free. Slugs and snails may feed on the leaves and Southern blight may be a problem on foliage.

RELATED SPECIES: Cultivars of note include 'Blue Clips' and 'White Clips', 'Bressingham White', and 'Jewel'.

1 Divide roots with a sharp spade or trowel.

2 Replant healthy roots in fertile soil, apply mulch, and water deeply.

CANNA
Canna ×generalis *KAN-uh jen-er-AL-is*

Canna has exotic foliage and vibrant-colored blooms. This is 'Black Knight'.

ZONES: 7–11
SIZE: 3–9'h × 2'w
TYPE: Perennial
FORM: Upright
TEXTURE: Coarse
GROWTH: Fast
LIGHT: Full sun
MOISTURE: Medium to high

SOIL: Fertile, moist, well-drained
FEATURES: Flowers, foliage
USES: Border, container
FLOWERS: ■■■■

SITING: Canna prefers full sun, deep, fertile soil that does not dry out or stay wet, and a pH of 5.5–7.4. The foliage is bananalike tropical. Flowers appear in terminal spikes for long-season color. Tuck canna into the back of the perennial border to soften its presence. Use daylilies 'Stella de Oro' and 'Hyperion' to edge a canna planting.

CARE: Plant canna 18–24" apart after the last frost and the soil is warm. Apply slow-release granular plant food at time of planting or begin using water-soluble plant food 3 weeks after planting. When the soil feels dry 2" below the surface, water deeply. Blooms require deadheading to maintain a good appearance. In cold climates after frost has caused the stems to turn black, remove the stems and leaves and store rhizomes in barely moist peat moss in a cool, frost-free location.

PROPAGATION: Divide stored rhizomes in spring. Cut the rhizome into sections and replant pieces that have a prominent eye, or bud.

PESTS AND DISEASES: Slugs, snails, spider mites, and caterpillars may feed on canna. Diseases include bacterial blight, rust, and fungal leaf spot.

RELATED SPECIES: 'Black Knight' bears deep red blooms. 'Wyoming' has bronze-colored leaves and orange flowers.

1 Cut back frosted foliage.

2 Dig rhizomes with a fork and shake off soil.

3 Store labelled rhizomes in a cool location.

ORNAMENTAL PEPPER

Capsicum annuum KAP-sih-kuhm AN-yew-uhm

Ornamental pepper's fruits are bright, colorful and extremely hot to the taste.

ZONES: 10 and 11
SIZE: 12–24"h × 20"w
TYPE: Annual
FORM: Upright
TEXTURE: Medium
GROWTH: Medium

LIGHT: Full sun
MOISTURE: Medium
SOIL: Fertile, moist
FEATURES: Fruit
USES: Edging, container, border
FLOWERS: ☐ ▨

SITING: Ornamental pepper is a short-lived perennial commonly grown as an annual. It prefers full sun and fertile, moist soil with ample organic matter and a pH of 5.5–7.0. The ornamental fruits appear in midsummer and last until frost. Shiny black, red, yellow, cream, or purple fruits grow 1–6" long. Tiny, star- or bell-shaped white or yellow flowers form in the leaf axils. Plant this pepper in groups for best effect. It may be used to edge a small garden or container. Select companions that have comparable bold color or act as a subtle foil and background to the peppers. Bold companions include gladiolus and dahlia. Subtle companions include rosemary, blue oat grass, and 'Gracillimus' maiden grass.

CARE: Plant 12–18" apart in spring after the last frost. Ornamental pepper performs best in fertile soil high in organic matter. To increase organic matter in the soil, add 1–2" of composted material (food and leaf waste, animal manure more than 1 year old, mushroom compost, peat moss, or bagged humus) to the planting bed and till in to a depth of 12". After planting, water deeply and add 3" of mulch around, but not touching, the plants. Apply slow-release plant food, such as Miracle-Gro Shake 'n Feed All Purpose, at time of planting or begin using water-soluble plant food, such as Miracle-Gro Water Soluble All Purpose, 3 weeks after planting in spring. Follow label directions for amount and frequency. Ornamental pepper prefers even moisture, so be sure to water deeply as soon as the soil is almost dry. Cut back the growing tips of young plants to promote branching. Remove plants after or right before the first frost. Cover the bare soil with 3" of mulch to protect the topsoil over the winter.

PROPAGATION: Sprinkle seeds over the soil mix and cover. Thoroughly moisten and keep moist, not soggy, until seeds germinate. Germination occurs in 10 days at 70°F. Transplant 21–26 days after sowing and reduce the temperature to 62°F.

PESTS AND DISEASES: Diseases include anthracnose and wilt diseases, southern blight, and fruit rot.

CUPID'S DART

Catananche caerulea kat-uh-NAN-kee sub-ROO-lee-uh

The lilac-colored flowers of Cupid's dart attract butterflies and may be used fresh or dried. It is also known as blue succory.

ZONES: 4–8
SIZE: 24–36"h × 12"w
TYPE: Perennial
FORM: Upright
TEXTURE: Medium
GROWTH: Medium
LIGHT: Full sun

MOISTURE: Medium
SOIL: Moderately fertile, well-drained
FEATURES: Flowers, foliage
USES: Border, container
FLOWERS: ▥ ▨ ☐

SITING: Cupid's dart prefers full sun and moderately fertile, well-drained soil with a pH of 5.5–7.0. Striking lilac flowers with a darker center appear from midsummer until autumn. Grasslike leaves are hairy and silvery. Flowers attract bees and butterflies and are excellent fresh cut or dried. Good companions include purple fountain grass, rosemary, and thyme.

CARE: Plant 8–12" apart in spring or fall. Apply slow-release plant food, such as Miracle-Gro Shake 'n Feed All Purpose, in spring or begin using water-soluble plant food, such as Miracle-Gro Water Soluble All Purpose, 3 weeks after planting. Follow label directions for amount and frequency. Apply 3" of vegetative mulch in summer and winter to reduce weed germination. Mulch holds moisture in the soil, and as it decomposes, add organic matter to the soil. Water deeply when the soil is dry. Deadhead spent blooms to encourage reblooming. Divide annually in spring to extend the life of these short-lived plants. Prune back in fall once frost collapses the foliage.

PROPAGATION: Divide in spring. Dig around the rhizomes and lift. Use a sharp spade to slice through the root system. Reset portions that contain healthy roots and top shoots. Discard any pieces that do not contain both healthy roots and top shoots. Water deeply and apply 3" of vegetative mulch around, but not touching, the plants.

PESTS AND DISEASES: Plants are relatively pest free when cultural requirements (sun, soil, planting depth, moisture) are met. Powdery mildew is an occasional pest.

RELATED SPECIES: 'Alba' bears white flowers, 'Bicolor' has white flowers with a deep blue center, 'Blue Giant' bears cornflower blue flowers on silvery foliage, 'Major' has deep lavender flowers, and 'Perry's White' has white blooms.

Deadhead Cupid's dart as flowers fade to stimulate rebloom throughout the summer.

COCKSCOMB
Celosia argentea sel-OH-see-uh ar-JEN-tee-uh

Cockscomb flowers add vibrant color and texture to the landscape.

ZONES: NA
SIZE: 24"h × 18"w
TYPE: Annual
FORM: Upright
TEXTURE: Medium
GROWTH: Medium
LIGHT: Full sun

MOISTURE: Medium
SOIL: Fertile, well-drained, moist
FEATURES: Flowers
USES: Bedding, container
FLOWERS: ▨ ■ ■ ▢

SITING: Cockscomb prefers full sun and fertile, well-drained soil with a pH of 5.5–7.0. Plants are technically perennials but are commonly grown as annuals. The Plumosa cultivars produce feathery flowers; Cristata cultivars bear blooms that resemble a rooster's comb, and last all summer. They are useful as bedding plants, in the border, or in containers. The orange, yellow, and red colors are perfect for the hot patio or pool area. Blooms may be dried or used as fresh cut flowers. Companions include dahlias; gladiolus, 'David' garden phlox, and goldenrod.

CARE: Plant 12–18" apart, depending on the cultivar. Apply slow-release granular plant food at time of planting, or begin using water-soluble plant food 3 weeks after planting in spring. Follow label directions for amount and frequency. Cockscomb prefers even moisture, so water deeply as soon as the soil is almost dry. Apply mulch to help retain soil moisture. Remove plants after or right before the first frost. Cover the bare soil with 3" of mulch to protect the topsoil over the winter.

PROPAGATION: Sprinkle seeds over the soil mix and cover. Thoroughly moisten and keep moist, not soggy, until seeds germinate. Germination occurs in 10 days at 75°F. Transplant 10–15 days after sowing, and reduce the temperature to 65–68°F.

1 Harvest cockscomb for drying while it is in peak bloom.

PESTS AND DISEASES: Fungal leaf spots, root and stem rots, and spider mites are occasional problems.

RELATED SPECIES: Plumosa cultivars include 'Apricot Brandy' (20" high with apricot-colored blooms), 'Fairy Fountains' (16" high, with pastel shades of pink, salmon, and yellow), Kimono Series (8" high, with large flowers of bright yellow, rose-red, cream, and salmon pink), and 'New Look' (18" high with rich red blooms and bronze-tinged foliage). Cristata cultivars include Big Chief Mix (3' high with 6"-wide yellow, pink, and red flowers), Jewel Box Mix (8" high with bright yellow, red, salmon, and pink flowers, occasionally several colors on one flower), and Kurume Series (4' high bearing a wide range of bright colors including bicolors).

2 To dry the flowers, hang them upside down in a dry location out of direct sunlight .

CORNFLOWER
Centaurea cyanus sen-TOR-ee-uh sy-AN-us

Cornflower, also known as bachelor's buttons, has blue flowers that are excellent fresh cut or dried.

ZONES: NA
SIZE: 12–30"h × 6"w
TYPE: Annual
FORM: Upright
TEXTURE: Medium
GROWTH: Fast
LIGHT: Full sun
MOISTURE: Medium

SOIL: Well-drained
FEATURES: Flowers, foliage
USES: Border, container, naturalizing
FLOWERS: ■ ▨ ▢

SITING: Cornflower prefers full sun and well-drained soil with moderate fertility and a pH of 5.5–7.5. The 1" blue blooms appear from late spring to midsummer. Plants are prolific self-seeders, so informal areas, especially cottage gardens, are ideal sites. Mass plants in the mixed border for early-season color. Cornflower blooms are excellent as fresh-cut or dried flowers. Companions include 'Strawberry Fields' globe amaranth, 'The Fairy' rose, and 'Horizon Red Halo' petunia.

CARE: Plant 6" apart in spring after the last frost. Apply slow-release plant food, such as Miracle-Gro Shake 'n Feed All Purpose, at time of planting or begin using water-soluble plant food, such as Miracle-Gro Water Soluble All Purpose, 3 weeks after planting in spring. Follow label directions for amount and frequency. Cornflower is relatively drought tolerant, so let the soil dry between waterings. Apply 3" of vegetative mulch to help retain soil moisture and as it decomposes it will add organic matter to the soil. If seedlings are not desired, deadhead blooms early on. Remove plants after or right before the first frost. Cover the bare soil with 3" of mulch to protect the topsoil over the winter.

PROPAGATION: Cornflower is easy to direct seed into the garden. Sprinkle seeds over the soil mix and lightly cover. Thoroughly moisten and keep moist, not soggy, until seeds germinate. Germination occurs in 7–14 days at 65–70°F. Transplant 20–25 days after sowing, and reduce the temperature to 50–55°F.

PESTS AND DISEASES: Downy and powdery mildew, crown rot, and rusts may occur.

RELATED SPECIES: Perennial (Zones 3–8) mountain bluet, *C. montana*, has blue flowers on plants 18–24" tall.

SNOW-IN-SUMMER
Cerastium tomentosum seh-RAS-tee-uhm toh-men-TOH-suhm

Snow-in-summer performs well in hot, dry places. Its name derives from its snowy white summer blooms.

ZONES: 3–7
SIZE: 6–8"h × 12"w
TYPE: Perennial
FORM: Spreading
TEXTURE: Medium to fine
GROWTH: Fast
LIGHT: Full sun
MOISTURE: Medium to low

SOIL: Low to moderately fertile, sandy
FEATURES: Flowers, foliage
USES: Naturalizing, ground cover, container
FLOWERS: □

SITING: Snow-in-summer prefers full sun and well-drained, sandy soil with moderate to low fertility and a pH of 5.5–7.0. This plant may be invasive, so select a location where it has room to grow, or confine it to a container. The woolly silver-gray foliage is attractive all season, and many star-shaped white flowers appear in late spring and summer. Plants are well suited for difficult hot, dry locations such as containers on pool patios, along hot walls, between stepping-stones, or as a ground cover on a steep slope.

CARE: Plant 1–2' apart in early spring or fall. Apply slow-release granular plant food at time of planting. It is relatively drought tolerant, so let the soil dry between waterings. Apply 3" of vegetative mulch to help retain soil moisture and as it decomposes it will add organic matter to the soil. To encourage a tidy appearance, cut the plants back after flowering. Cut back again in fall after frost has collapsed the foliage.

PROPAGATION: Divide the fibrous roots in spring or fall. Dig around the root clump and lift. Use a sharp spade to slice through the root system. Reset portions that contain healthy roots and top shoots, then water and mulch. Discard any pieces that do not contain both healthy roots and top shoots. Sprinkle seeds over the soil mix and leave exposed to light. Thoroughly moisten and keep moist, not soggy, until seeds germinate. Germination occurs in 7–14 days at 65°F. Transplant 15–25 days after sowing, and reduce the temperature to 50°F.

PESTS AND DISEASES: Plants are relatively pest free when their cultural preferences are met. Root rot may occur if planted in wet soil.

RELATED SPECIES: 'Silver Carpet' and 'Yo-yo' are more compact than the species. Taurus chickweed (*C. biebersteinii*) grows 6–12" tall and bears ¾" white flowers. It is hardy in Zones 3–7.

LEADWORT
Ceratostigma plumbaginoides ser-ah-toh-STIG-muh plum-ba-jih-NOY-deez

Leadwort provides attractive late-season blooms. It is also known as plumbago.

ZONES: 5–9
SIZE: 18"h × 12"w
TYPE: Perennial
FORM: Spreading
TEXTURE: Medium
GROWTH: Fast
LIGHT: Part shade to full sun
MOISTURE: Medium to low

SOIL: Moderately fertile
FEATURES: Foliage, flowers
USES: Ground cover, border, container
FLOWERS: ■
FALL COLOR: ■ ■

SITING: Leadwort prefers full sun or afternoon shade and moderately fertile, well-drained soil with a pH of 5.5–7.5. The foliage boasts red stems and bright green leaves that turn bronzy red in autumn. Pinwheellike bright blue flowers appear in late summer and last into fall. Use in containers or as a ground cover in the rock garden or shrub border.

CARE: Plant 12" apart in spring or fall. Apply slow-release granular plant food at time of planting. Leadwort is relatively drought tolerant; let the soil dry between waterings. Apply 3" of vegetative mulch to help retain soil moisture and add organic matter to the soil as it decomposes. Cut back in late fall or leave erect for late-season viewing and cut back in early spring before growth begins.

PROPAGATION: Divide in early spring. Dig around the clump and lift. Use a sharp spade to slice through the root system. Reset portions that contain healthy roots and top shoots, then water and mulch. Discard any pieces that do not contain both healthy roots and top shoots. Root softwood cuttings in spring. Remove the bottom leaves from cuttings, exposing the nodes. Each cutting should have two or three nodes exposed and one pair of leaves. Insert the cutting in moist soil mix. Nodes should be below soil level and leaves above. Keep the soil mix moist but not soggy until roots form. Ideal temperatures are 65–70°F for the soil mix and 55–60°F for the air. High humidity hastens growth.

PESTS AND DISEASES: Plants are relatively pest free when their cultural preferences are met.

Mark leadwort's location in the garden because it emerges late in spring.

SNAKEROOT
Cimicifuga racemosa *sim-ih-sih-FEW-guh ray-seh-MOH-suh*

Cimicifuga racemosa adds stately grace to the shade border. It is also known as cohosh, black cohosh, or bugbane.

ZONES: 3–8
SIZE: 4–7'h × 2'w
TYPE: Perennial
FORM: Upright
TEXTURE: Medium
GROWTH: Medium
LIGHT: Partial shade
MOISTURE: Medium to high

SOIL: Fertile, moist, well-drained
FEATURES: Flowers, foliage
USES: Border, woodland, container
FLOWERS: ☐

SITING: Snakeroot prefers afternoon shade and fertile, moist, well-drained soil with a pH of 5.5–7.0. It is a choice addition to the shade border with deep green toothed leaves and slender, curving racemes of creamy white blooms in midsummer. Place odd-numbered groups in the middle or rear of the border or use as a tall focal point in a container planting. Plants are also suited to the woodland garden. Good companions include astilbe, fingerleaf rodgersia, 'The Rocket' ligularia, and Siebold hosta.

CARE: Plant 18–24" apart in spring or fall in soil containing ample organic matter. To increase organic matter in the soil, add

Plants receiving one-sided light may lean and require staking to compensate.

1–2" of composted material and till in to a depth of 15–18". After planting, water deeply and add 3" of mulch around, but not touching, the plants. Apply slow-release granular plant food at time of planting. Water deeply whenever the soil is dry, allowing the soil to dry between waterings. Reapply mulch whenever necessary to maintain 3" in summer and winter. Mulch also adds beneficial organic matter to the soil as it decomposes. Leave plants standing in fall until they no longer look attractive, then cut back.

PROPAGATION: Snakeroot recovers slowly from division. If you decide to split clumps, divide them in spring or fall. Dig around the root clump and lift. Use a sharp spade to slice through the root system. Reset portions that contain healthy roots and top shoots, then water and mulch.

PESTS AND DISEASES: Plants are relatively pest free when their cultural preferences (sun, soil, moisture) are met.

RELATED SPECIES: Autumn snakeroot (*C. simplex* 'Brunette') has dark brown foliage with a purple tint, purple stems, and creamy white blooms with a pinkish-purple tinge.

SPIDER FLOWER
Cleome hassleriana *klee-OH-mee hass-lair-ee-AY-nuh*

Spider flowers offer a profusion of pink and purple blooms in summer.

ZONES: NA
SIZE: 5'h × 18"w
TYPE: Annual
FORM: Upright
TEXTURE: Medium
GROWTH: Fast
LIGHT: Full sun
MOISTURE: Low to medium

SOIL: Fertile, sandy, well-drained
FEATURES: Flowers, foliage
USES: Naturalizing, border, container
FLOWERS: ■ ■ ☐

SITING: Spider flower prefers full sun and fertile, sandy, well-drained soil with a pH of 5.5–7.0. This robust annual has an abundance of spidery fragrant pink, white, and purple flowers in summer. Plants self-sow freely, so place where weeding them is feasible or there is room for them to naturalize or colonize. The spines on the base of the leaf stalk warrant wearing gloves and long sleeves when working nearby. In South Carolina, spider flower is a common highway planting, testimony to its ruggedness. Plant near a white picket

Remove unwanted self-sown spider flower seedlings. They can become weedy.

fence for old-fashioned nostalgia, in the cottage garden, or in containers. Good companions include 'David' garden phlox, and 'Carefree Wonder', 'Bonica', and 'Iceberg' roses.

CARE: Plant 18" apart in spring after the last frost. Apply slow-release granular plant food at time of planting. Allow the soil to dry between waterings. Apply 3" of vegetative mulch to help retain soil moisture and as it decomposes it will add organic matter to the soil. Plants readily self-seed. Be prepared to remove volunteer seedlings the following year. Remove plants after or right before the first frost.

PROPAGATION: Sprinkle seeds over the soil mix and cover lightly. Thoroughly moisten and keep moist but not soggy until seeds germinate. Germination occurs in 10–12 days with a daytime temperature of 80°F and a nighttime temperature of 70°F. Transplant 21–25 days after sowing and reduce the temperature to 70–75°F.

PESTS AND DISEASES: Aphids are common pests. Diseases include fungal spots, rust, and powdery mildew.

RELATED SPECIES: Sparkler Series is more compact than most cultivars.

AUTUMN CROCUS
Colchicum autumnale *KOHL-chih-kuhm aw-tuhm-NAL-ee*

Clusters of autumn crocus flowers are welcome additions to the late-season landscape.

ZONES: 5–9
SIZE: 4–6"h × 4"w
TYPE: Perennial
FORM: Upright
TEXTURE: Fine to medium
GROWTH: Medium
LIGHT: Partial shade to full sun
MOISTURE: Medium to high
SOIL: Deep, fertile, well-drained
FEATURES: Flowers
USES: Naturalizing, border, container
FLOWERS: ■□

SITING: Autumn crocus prefers full sun or partial shade and deep, fertile, well-drained soil, with a pH of 5.5–7.0. It is among the earliest of the *Colchicums* to flower in fall, bearing as many as six flowers 6" high. Foliage appears after flowering. Autumn crocus looks best grown in groups among trees and shrubs, naturalized at the edge of the woodland, or placed in containers. All parts of the plant are toxic.

CARE: Plant corms 6" apart in partial shade or full sun in late summer. Apply slow-release granular plant food at time of planting. Water during dry spells. Apply 3" of vegetative mulch to help retain soil moisture and add organic matter to the soil as it decomposes. Allow leaves to die back naturally; cutting foliage prematurely weakens the corm.

PROPAGATION: Divide or separate corms while plants are dormant in summer. Small corms, called cormels, produced at the base of the parent corm, can be snapped or cut off and replanted.

PESTS AND DISEASES: Slugs are common pests on autumn crocus.

RELATED SPECIES: 'Alboplenum' has double white flowers, and 'Pleniflorum' has double pink-lilac flowers.

Healthy corms will feel firm to the touch.

Place corms, wide side down, tip up, 6" apart in a large hole.

Cover corms with soil and water deeply.

LARKSPUR
Consolida hybrids *kohn-sah-LEE-dah*

Larkspur flowers are classic additions to cottage gardens and English perennial borders.

ZONES: N/A
SIZE: 12–36"h × 6–14"w
TYPE: Annual
FORM: Upright
TEXTURE: Medium
GROWTH: Fast
LIGHT: Full sun
MOISTURE: Medium
SOIL: Fertile, well-drained
FEATURES: Flowers, foliage
USES: Border, naturalizing, container
FLOWERS: ■ ■ ■ □

SITING: Larkspur prefers full sun and fertile, well-drained soil with a pH of 5.5–7.5. Showy, delphiniumlike flowers appear in summer. The feathery bright green foliage is an added attraction. Grow in large groups and mixed colors for an old-fashioned cottage garden effect.

CARE: Plant larkspur 6–12" apart, depending on the cultivar, in late spring after frost has passed. Apply slow-release plant food, such as Miracle-Gro Shake 'n Feed All Purpose, at time of planting, or begin using water-soluble plant food, such as Miracle-Gro Water Soluble All Purpose,

Deadhead larkspur before seed pods mature to prevent self-seeding.

3 weeks after planting. Follow label directions for amount and frequency. Water deeply whenever the soil is dry. Apply 3" of vegetative mulch to help retain soil moisture and add organic matter to the soil as it decomposes. Remove plant just prior to or right after first frost.

PROPAGATION: Plants self-sow in the garden. To sow seed indoors, chill the seeds for 7 days at 35°F. Sprinkle seeds over the soil mix and cover. Thoroughly moisten and keep moist, not soggy, until seeds germinate. Germination occurs in 10–20 days at 55–65°F. Transplant 28–35 days after sowing and reduce the temperature to 50–55°F.

PESTS AND DISEASES: Slugs, snails, and powdery mildew are problems.

RELATED SPECIES: The cultivar 'Blue Bell' has sky blue flowers, 'Blue Spire' has deep blue flowers that hint of purple, 'Brilliant Rose' flowers are deep pink, 'Dazzler' flowers are scarlet, and 'Exquisite Rose' flowers are bright pink. Plants in the Imperial Series are tall, some reaching 3', with spurred double flowers in mauve, pink, blue, and white.

LILY-OF-THE-VALLEY

Convallaria majalis kahn-vuh-LAIR-ee-uh mah-JA-liss

Lily-of-the-valley produces fragrant nodding flowers in spring.

ZONES: 2–7
SIZE: 9"h × 12"w
TYPE: Perennial
FORM: Upright
TEXTURE: Medium
GROWTH: Medium
LIGHT: Full to partial shade

MOISTURE: Low to medium
SOIL: Fertile, moist
FEATURES: Flowers, foliage, fruit
USES: Ground cover, woodland
FLOWERS: □ ■

SITING: Lily-of-the-valley prefers partial or full shade and fertile, loose soil with a pH of 5.5–7.0. Lance-shaped to elliptic basal leaves are bright green and attractive all season long. Brilliant tiny, bell-shaped fragrant white blooms appear on arching stems in spring. As a ground cover, lily-of-the-valley is indispensable. It is one of the few plants that can successfully compete with tree roots. Plant in groups for best effect.

CARE: Plant 12" apart in spring or fall in humusy soil high in organic matter. To increase organic matter in the soil, add 1–2" of composted material and till in. After planting, water deeply and add 3" of mulch around, but not touching, the plants. Apply slow-release granular plant food at time of planting. Water deeply whenever the soil is dry, allowing the soil to dry between waterings. Reapply mulch whenever necessary to maintain 3" in summer and winter. Plants rarely need to be cut back in fall. If you would like to cut them back, place your lawn mower on its highest setting and mow them off.

PROPAGATION: Divide in spring or fall. Dig around the rhizomes and lift. Use a sharp spade to slice through the root system. Reset portions that contain healthy roots and top shoots, then water and mulch. Discard any pieces that do not contain both healthy root and top shoots.

PESTS AND DISEASES: Diseases that affect lily-of-the-valley include white mold, gray mold, and anthracnose. Provide good air circulation to minimized diseases.

RELATED SPECIES: 'Albostriata' has cream-striped leaves, 'Aureovariegata' has yellow-striped leaves, and var. *rosea* has pale pink flowers. No other species exists in the genus.

1 In spring or fall lift roots for dividing.

2 Separate roots so each section contains healthy top growth.

3 Reset plants in a new location.

4 Apply mulch and water deeply.

GROUND MORNING GLORY

Convolvulus sabatius kon-VULV-yew-luhs sub-BA-tee-uhs

Ground morning glory climbs along sunny slopes and banks.

ZONES: 8 and 9
SIZE: 6"h × 20"w
TYPE: Perennial
FORM: Spreading
TEXTURE: Medium
GROWTH: Fast
LIGHT: Full sun

MOISTURE: Low
SOIL: Low fertility, well-drained
FEATURES: Flowers
USES: Container, ground cover, walls
FLOWERS: ■

SITING: Ground morning glory prefers full sun and poor, well-drained soil with a pH of 5.5–7.0. It has trailing stems, evergreen leaves, and clusters of funnel-shaped lavender-blue blooms from summer to early fall. Grow in containers, along walls, or as a ground cover on a sunny bank. Shelter from wind.

CARE: Plant 12–18" apart in late spring after the last frost. Apply slow-release granular plant food at time of planting, or begin using water-soluble plant food 3 weeks after planting in spring. Follow label directions for amount and frequency. Let the soil dry between waterings. Apply 3" of vegetative mulch to help retain soil moisture and add organic matter to the soil as it decomposes. Cut plants back if more compactness is desired. Remove plants in fall after frost has collapsed the foliage in zones where it will not survive the winter.

PROPAGATION: Sow seed in spring and provide 55–65°F temperatures.

PESTS AND DISEASES: Rust may be a problem.

TICKSEED
Coreopsis grandiflora *kor-ee-OP-sis grand-ih-FLOR-uh*

Tickseed, also known as coreopsis, produces bright golden yellow summer color. Some cultivars have red centers.

ZONES: 4–9
SIZE: 18–36" × 24"w
TYPE: Perennial
FORM: Upright
TEXTURE: Medium to fine
GROWTH: Medium
LIGHT: Full sun

MOISTURE: Medium
SOIL: Fertile, well-drained
FEATURES: Flowers, foliage
USES: Border, container
FLOWERS: ■

SITING: Tickseed prefers full sun and fertile, well-drained soil with a pH of

5.5–7.0. Flowers with a deep yellow center and scalloped tips appear from late spring to late summer and are ideal for cutting. Plant in odd-numbered groups in the perennial border or place in containers. Companions include purple coneflower, 'Snowbank' white boltonia, 'David' garden phlox, and torch lily.

Deadhead flowers to stimulate reblooming.

CARE: Plant 18–24" apart in spring or fall. Apply slow-release granular plant food at time of planting. Water deeply only when the soil is dry. Apply 3" of vegetative mulch to help retain soil moisture and as it decomposes it will add organic matter to the soil. Deadhead to stimulate flowering. Cut back in fall after frost has collapsed the foliage.

PROPAGATION: Tickseed is a short-lived perennial that self-seeds. Start new plants from seed, save some of the self-sown seedlings for transplanting or divide existing plants in spring or early fall. Reset portions that contain healthy roots and top shoots, then water and mulch.

PESTS AND DISEASES: Slugs and snails are pests. Diseases include botrytis flower blight, aster yellows, and powdery and downy mildew.

RELATED SPECIES: The cultivar 'Badengold' (36" high) has golden-yellow flowers with an orange center, and 'Early Sunrise' (18" high) has semidouble yellow flowers with an orange tint near the center.

THREADLEAF COREOPSIS
Coreopsis verticillata *kor-ee-OP-sis ver-tiss-ih-LAHT-uh*

Threadleaf coreopsis is a low-maintenance long season bloomer.

ZONES: 4–9
SIZE: 24–36"h × 24"w
TYPE: Perennial
FORM: Upright
TEXTURE: Fine
GROWTH: Medium
LIGHT: Full sun

MOISTURE: Medium
SOIL: Fertile, well-drained
FEATURES: Flowers, foliage
USES: Border, container
FLOWERS: ■

SITING: Threadleaf coreopsis prefers full sun and fertile, well-drained soil with a pH of 5.5–7.0. Plants tolerate humidity and heat. The fine-textured, threadlike foliage is attractive throughout the growing season. Small yellow flowers appear in early summer and bloom through fall. Place in the front of the perennial border, or add to a mixed container planting. Good

companions include 'Coronation Gold' achillea, 'Goldsturm' black-eyed Susan, pink coreopsis; 'Stargazer' lily, and 'Stafford', 'Red Rum', 'Scarlet Orbit', and 'Red Joy' daylilies.

CARE: Plant 18" apart in spring or fall. Apply slow-release granular plant food at time of planting. Water deeply whenever

Use a sharp spade to slice through roots of threadleaf coreopsis during division.

the soil is dry; allow the soil to dry between waterings. Apply 3" of mulch and reapply whenever necessary to maintain 3" in summer and winter. Flowers are considered self-cleaning and do not need to be deadheaded. Leave plants standing in fall until frost collapses them, then cut back. Plants may be slow to appear in spring.

PROPAGATION: Divide in spring or early fall. Dig around the root clump and lift. Use a sharp spade to slice through the root system. Reset portions that contain healthy roots and top shoots.

PESTS AND DISEASES: Except for rabbits, plants are relatively pest free when their cultural preferences are met.

RELATED SPECIES: *C. verticillata* 'Zagreb' has golden-yellow flowers. 'Moonbeam', a superior cultivar, grows 18" high and wide and has threadleaf foliage and pale yellow blooms from summer through autumn. Pink coreopsis (*C. rosea*) has pink blooms on and off all summer into fall, fine texture, and a neat habit.

YELLOW CORYDALIS
Corydalis lutea *kor-IH-duh-lis LOO-tee-uh*

Yellow corydalis boasts attractive yellow tubular flowers and mounding blue-green foliage for the shade.

ZONES: 4–8
SIZE: 15"h × 12"w
TYPE: Perennial
FORM: Rounded
TEXTURE: Fine
GROWTH: Medium
LIGHT: Full sun to partial shade

MOISTURE: Medium
SOIL: Fertile, well-drained
FEATURES: Flowers, foliage
USES: Woodland, border, rock garden
FLOWERS: ▪

SITING: Yellow corydalis tolerates full sun or partial shade and prefers fertile, well-drained soil with a pH of 5.5–7.0. Fernlike leaves form mounds that are attractive throughout the growing season. Tiny, tubular yellow flowers appear from late spring into early fall. Place yellow corydalis among rocks, in the perennial border, at the edge of the woodland, or in containers. Good companions include 'Alba' fringeleaf bleeding heart, 'Moonbeam' threadleaf coreopsis, 'Rubra' Japanese blood grass, 'White Swirl' Siberian iris.

CARE: Plant 12" apart in spring or fall. Apply slow-release granular plant food at time of planting. Water deeply when the soil is dry. Plants will self-seed but will not be invasive. After frost cut back collapsed foliage.

1 Dig self-sown seedlings of yellow corydalis.

PROPAGATION: Divide in spring or early fall. Dig around the root clump and lift. Use a sharp spade to slice through the root system. Reset portions that contain healthy roots and top shoots.

PESTS AND DISEASES: Plants are relatively pest free when their cultural preferences are met. Rusts and downy mildew occasionally occur.

RELATED SPECIES: *C. flexuosa* (Zones 6–8, 12" high) has neon blue tubular blooms from late spring to summer and prefers partial shade. 'Blue Panda' (8" high) has bright blue flowers.

2 Relocate seedlings to other areas of the shade garden.

TALL COSMOS
Cosmos bipinnatus *KAHZ-mohs beye-pin-A-tuss*

A mass planting of tall cosmos creates a sea of red and pink on feathery foliage.

ZONES: NA
SIZE: 5'h × 18"w
TYPE: Annual
FORM: Upright
TEXTURE: Fine
GROWTH: Fast
LIGHT: Full sun
MOISTURE: Dry to moist

SOIL: Well-drained
FEATURES: Flowers, foliage
USES: Border, naturalizing, container
FLOWERS: ☐ ▪ ▪

SITING: Tall cosmos prefers full sun moderately fertile, well-drained soil with a pH range of 5.5–7.0. Attractive, single, 3" flowers are red, pink, or white with a yellow center; they appear in summer and attract butterflies. Foliage is feathery bright green. Plants are heat and drought tolerant. Good companions include 'The Fairy' and 'Iceberg' roses and 'David' garden phlox.

CARE: Plant 12–18" apart in late spring. Apply slow-release granular plant food at time of planting, or begin using water-soluble plant food 3 weeks after planting. Water deeply when the soil is dry. If naturalizing, water new transplants until they are actively growing. Remove plants after the first frost.

PROPAGATION: Plants self-sow in the garden. To sow seed indoors, sprinkle

Cosmos sulphureus cultivars are tall with gold or reddish-orange flowers.

seeds over the soil mix and cover. Thoroughly moisten and keep moist, not soggy, until seeds germinate. Germination occurs in 5–7 days at 70°F. Transplant 11–15 days after sowing, and reduce the temperature to 65°F.

PESTS AND DISEASES: Aphids are a common pest; powdery mildew and Rhizoctonia stem rot are known diseases.

RELATED SPECIES: 'Picotee' reaches 30" tall and has white flowers with a dark crimson margin, 'Sea Shells' grows 3' tall and has curiously rolled red, pink, or white flowers, 'Sonata Series' are 12" tall with white, red, or pink flowers, and 'Sonata White' reaches 18" tall with clear white blooms that contrast well with the feathery bright green foliage. Sulphur cosmos (*C. sulphureus*) has orange, reddish, or reddish-yellow flowers and reaches 6' tall and 18" wide. Klondike Series 'Sunny Gold' is dwarf, reaches 16" high, and has semidouble yellow flowers. Klondike Series 'Sunny Orange-Red' reaches 12" high and has reddish-orange flowers. Plants in the Ladybird Series grow 12" high and bear semidouble yellow, red, or orange flowers.

GIANT KALE

Crambe cordifolia KRAM-bee kord-ih-FOH-lee-uh

Giant kale may reach 8' high.

ZONES: 4–8
SIZE: 8'h × 5'w
TYPE: Perennial
FORM: Mound
TEXTURE: Coarse foliage, fine bloom
GROWTH: Fast
LIGHT: Full sun

MOISTURE: Medium
SOIL: Fertile, deep, well-drained
FEATURES: Foliage, flowers
USES: Accent, container
FLOWERS: ☐

SITING: Giant kale prefers full sun and deep, fertile, well-drained soil but tolerates poor soil. It prefers a pH of 5.5–7.5. Select a site that has shelter from strong winds. The plant has huge (to 15" wide) crinkled deep green leaves that die down in mid- to late summer. The plant is stately, and in full bloom is spectacular with clouds of tiny white flowers covering the top of the plant from late spring to midsummer. Place in a large space, along a stream bank, in the center of the border, or in a container. Neighboring plants should be able to cover the space left after foliage dies back in summer. Companions include 'Goldsturm' black-eyed Susan, 'Autumn Joy' sedum, Kansas gayfeather, and 'Kobold' blazing star.
CARE: Plant 3–5' apart in spring or fall. Apply slow-release granular plant food at time of planting, or begin using water-soluble plant food 3 weeks after planting in spring. Cease feeding 4–6 weeks prior to first frost date. Water deeply when the soil is dry. Apply 3" of vegetative mulch in summer and winter to help retain soil moisture and add organic matter to the soil as it decomposes.
PROPAGATION: Divide in early spring. Dig around the root clump and lift. Use a sharp spade to slice through the root system. Reset portions that contain healthy roots and top shoots, then water and mulch. Discard any pieces that do not contain both healthy roots and top shoots.
PESTS AND DISEASES: Plants are relatively pest free when their cultural preferences (sun, soil, moisture) are met.
RELATED SPECIES: Sea kale (*C. maritima*) has blue-green leaves and white flowers and grows 3' high and 2' wide.

CROCOSMIA

Crocosmia ×crocosmiiflora kroh-KOZ-mee-ah kroh-koz-mee-ih-FLO-rah

Crocosmia, also called montbretia, bears nodding yellow or orange flowers and has swordlike leaves.

ZONES: 6–9
SIZE: 2–3'h × 1'w
TYPE: Perennial
FORM: Upright
TEXTURE: Medium
GROWTH: Fast
LIGHT: Sun to partial shade

MOISTURE: Medium
SOIL: Moderately fertile, well-drained
FEATURES: Flowers, foliage
USES: Border, container
FLOWERS: ■ ■

SITING: Crocosmia tolerates full sun or partial shade and prefers moderately fertile, well-drained soil with a pH of 5.5–7.0. The nodding yellow or red-orange flowers are funnel shaped and appear along the length of the arching stems during the summer. Blooms are excellent cut flowers. Leaves are swordlike and pale green. Place odd-numbered groups in the border or in containers for best effect. Companions include 'Morning Light' maiden grass, Siberian iris, and threadleaf coreopsis.

CARE: Plant corms 3" deep and 6" apart in spring in humus-rich soil. Apply slow-release granular plant food at time of planting. Water deeply whenever the soil is dry. Apply 3" of vegetative mulch in summer and winter to help retain soil moisture and add organic matter to the soil as it decomposes. After frost, cut back foliage. In cooler locations lift corms in fall after flowering but before the first hard frost. Remove offsets (cormels), dead roots, and stems. Store firm, healthy corms and cormels in a dry, warm place (60–70°F) until spring.
PROPAGATION: Divide in spring or fall. Unearth the corm and separate offsets that form around its base. Replant healthy, firm corms 6" apart in moderately fertile, well-drained soil, then water and mulch.
PESTS AND DISEASES: Spider mites are common pests. Dislodge with a stream of water, or use a pesticide to manage troublesome infestations.
RELATED SPECIES: 'Emily McKenzie' has orange flowers; 'Golden Fleece' has yellow blooms. *C. masoniorum* is hardy in Zones 6–9 and bears red-orange flowers on plants 3' tall. Intergeneric hybrids 'Bressingham Blaze', 'Emberglow', and 'Lucifer' have outstanding red-orange blooms on plants 3' tall.

Clip faded flower stalks of crocosmia to keep the plants tidy.

SHOWY CROCUS
Crocus speciosus *KRO-kuhs spee-see-O-suhs*

Showy crocus, also known as fall crocus, is fall-blooming and durable.

ZONES: 3–8
SIZE: 4–6"h × 6"w
TYPE: Perennial
FORM: Clump
TEXTURE: Medium
GROWTH: Medium
LIGHT: Full sun
MOISTURE: Medium to low

SOIL: Moderately fertile, well-drained
FEATURES: Flowers, foliage
USES: Naturalizing, container
FLOWERS: ▣ ☐

SITING: Showy crocus prefers full sun and very well-drained, moderately fertile soil with a pH of 5.5–7.0. It is one of the earliest fall crocus to emerge. Violet-blue blooms with darker blue veins appear in fall before the leaves. The styles in the center of the flower are bright orange and contrast nicely with the flower petal color. The leaves are broad, lance shaped, and dark green. Plants are drought tolerant, low maintenance, and durable. Plant in drifts in the lawn, scatter about the base of trees and shrubs in the border, or place in mixed container plantings for late season color.

CARE: Plant corms 2–3" deep and 6" apart in spring. Apply slow-release granular plant food at time of planting. Apply 3" of vegetative mulch in summer and winter to help retain soil moisture and add organic matter to the soil as it decomposes.

PROPAGATION: Unearth the corm and separate offsets that form around its base. Replant healthy, firm corms and cormels 6" apart in moderately fertile, well-drained soil, then water and mulch.

PESTS AND DISEASE: Plants are relatively pest free when their cultural preferences are met. Squirrels and mice may feed on the corms.

RELATED SPECIES: The cultivar 'Aitchisonii' has large pale lilac flowers with darker feathered veins, 'Albus' has pure white flowers, 'Cassiope' has large pale blue blooms with a yellow throat, 'Pollux' has large light mauve flowers with a pearly-silver exterior, and 'Oxonian' has indigo blue blooms.

DUTCH CROCUS
Crocus vernus *KRO-kuhs VER-nuhs*

Dutch crocus blooms in spring.

ZONES: 3–8
SIZE: 4–6"h × 6"w
TYPE: Perennial
FORM: Clump
TEXTURE: Foliage fine, flower medium
GROWTH: Medium
LIGHT: Full sun

MOISTURE: Medium to low
SOIL: Moderately fertile, well-drained
FEATURES: Flowers, foliage
USES: Naturalizing, container
FLOWERS: ☐ ▣ ■ ▨

SITING: Dutch crocus prefers full sun and very well drained, moderately fertile soil with a pH of 5.5–7.0. Goblet-shaped purple, lavender, yellow or white blooms appear from spring to early summer. The leaves are lance-shaped and often have a silver stripe down the center. Plants are drought tolerant, low maintenance, and durable. Plant in drifts in lawns, scatter about the base of trees and shrubs in the border, or place in mixed container plantings for early-season color.

CARE: Plant corms 2–3" deep and 6" apart in autumn. Apply slow-release granular plant food at time of planting. Apply 3" of vegetative mulch in summer and winter to help retain soil moisture and add organic matter to the soil as it decomposes.

PROPAGATION: Unearth the corm and separate offsets that form around its base. Replant healthy, firm corms and cormels 6" apart in moderately fertile, well-drained soil, then water and mulch.

PESTS AND DISEASES: Plants are relatively pest free when their cultural preferences (sun, soil, moisture) are met. Squirrels and mice may feed on the corms.

RELATED SPECIES: The cultivar 'Early Perfection' has blue blooms with dark edges, 'Jeanne d'Arc' has white flowers with a dark purple base and light purple feathering, 'Kathleen Parlow' has white blooms with a purple base, 'King of the Striped' has light-and-dark-purple-striped flowers, and 'Pickwick' has white-, light-, and dark-lilac-striped flowers with a darker lilac-purple base.

1

Naturalize crocus by tossing corms on the lawn to create varied spacing.

2

Plant the corms 2–3" deep wherever they land on the lawn.

MEXICAN HEATHER
Cuphea hyssopifola *KOO-fee-uh hiss-ahp-IF-uh-luh*

Mexican heather forms small but attractive pinkish-purple blooms in the landscape.

ZONES: 8–10
SIZE: 12–24"h × 8–32"w
TYPE: Woody perennial
FORM: Upright
TEXTURE: Medium
GROWTH: Medium
LIGHT: Full sun to partial shade

MOISTURE: High
SOIL: Moderately fertile, well-drained
FEATURES: Flowers, foliage
USES: Border, container, massing
FLOWERS: ■■□

SITING: Mexican heather prefers ample and frequent moisture and plant food, full sun or partial shade, and moderately fertile, well-drained soil with a pH of 5.5–7.5. Tiny pink, pinkish purple, or white flowers appear from summer into autumn. Woody stems and tiny, pointed dark green leaves create attractive foliage. Plants may be massed in the garden, used in the front of the border in odd-numbered groupings, or placed in mixed planting containers. Companions for full sun include rosemary lavender cotton, vinca, and violet-colored pansies in autumn. Companions for part shade with complementary foliage include

Pinch back tips to encourage bushy growth.

McKana Hybrids columbine, fringeleaf bleeding heart, and wax begonia.
CARE: Plant 12–18" apart in late spring. Apply slow-release plant food, such as Miracle-Gro Shake 'n Feed All Purpose, at time of planting or begin using water-soluble plant food, such as Miracle-Gro Water Soluble All Purpose, 3 weeks after planting. Water deeply when the soil is dry. Apply 3" of vegetative mulch in summer to help retain soil moisture and add beneficial organic matter to the soil as it decomposes. Cut back tips in the growing season to encourage bushy growth. To rejuvenate, cut back woody stems in spring. In cooler climates treat as an annual and remove after the first frost.
PROPAGATION: Sow seeds at 55–60°F in early spring. Keep moist until seeds germinate, then allow soil to dry out slightly between waterings.
PESTS AND DISEASES: Whiteflies and aphids are occasional insect pests. Diseases include powdery mildew, leaf spots, and root rot.

JAPANESE HOLLY FERN
Cyrtomium falcatum *ser-TOH-mee-uhm fal-KAY-tuhm*

Japanese holly fern has shiny dark evergreen fronds.

ZONES: 6–10
SIZE: 24"h × 36"'w
TYPE: Perennial
FORM: Irregular
TEXTURE: Medium
GROWTH: Slow
LIGHT: Full to partial shade

MOISTURE: High
SOIL: Fertile, moist, well-drained
FEATURES: Leaves
USES: Border, woodland, container

SITING: Holly fern prefers full shade or partial shade with shelter from the afternoon sun and fertile, well-drained soil with a pH of 5.5–7.0. The shiny, leathery deep green fronds are evergreen and are coveted for floral arrangements. This fern does not tolerate extreme cold and benefits from shelter from direct sun and extreme wind and cold. Place in the shade border, the woodland garden, or in containers. Companions include European wild ginger, astilbe, toad lily, and false Solomon's seal.
CARE: Plant 15–18" apart in spring or fall in fertile soil high in organic matter. If in doubt take a professional soil test to determine the percentage of organic matter in the soil. To increase organic matter, add 1–2" of composted food and leaf waste, composted animal manure, mushroom compost, peat moss, or bagged humus to the planting bed and till in to a depth of 12–15". After planting, water deeply and add 3" of mulch around, but not touching, the plants. Mulch helps retain soil moisture. Apply slow-release plant food, such as Miracle-Gro Shake 'n Feed All Purpose, at time of planting or begin using water-soluble plant food, such as Miracle-Gro Water Soluble All Purpose, 3 weeks after planting in spring. Follow label directions for amount and frequency. Cease feeding 4–6 weeks prior to first frost date. Water deeply whenever the soil is dry; let the soil dry slightly between waterings. Leave this evergreen fern erect for winter viewing and cut back brown fronds in spring. In marginally hardy areas cover the crown with 3–6" of straw in winter.
PROPAGATION: Divide every 3 years in spring or fall. Dig around the rhizomes and lift. Use a sharp spade to slice through the root system. Reset portions that contain healthy roots and top shoots, then water and mulch. Discard any pieces that do not contain both healthy roots and top shoots.
PESTS AND DISEASES: Plants are relatively pest free when their cultural preferences (sun, soil, moisture) are met. Snails and slugs may pose problems. Brown leaves can indicate cold damage, too much or too little moisture, too much sun, or low soil fertility. Leaf spots occasionally plague holly fern.
RELATED SPECIES: 'Cristatum' has twisted pinnae (leaflet) tips, and 'Rochfordianum' has coarsely toothed margins.

DAHLIA
Dahlia hybrids *DAHL-yuh*

Dahlias come in a variety of sizes and a broad array of flower colors.

ZONES: 9–11
SIZE: 1–6'h × 1–3'w
TYPE: Perennial
FORM: Upright
TEXTURE: Medium
GROWTH: Medium
LIGHT: Full sun
MOISTURE: High

SOIL: Fertile, well-drained
FEATURES: Flowers, foliage
USES: Border, massing, container
FLOWERS: ▓ ▓ ▓ ▓ ▓ ▢

SITING: Dahlias prefer full sun and fertile, humus-rich, well-drained soil with a pH of 5.5–7.0. Flowers range from 2" to more than 10" across. Dahlias are considered the backbone of the late-season border, though in many parts of the country the care they require reduces their appeal. The bright-colored blooms appear from midsummer to first frost. Plant tall dahlias in groups at the back of the border. Bedding dahlias are low growing and often treated as annuals, flowering from midsummer into autumn.

They are useful in containers or in massed plantings. Dahlia blooms attract butterflies and are superb fresh cut flowers.

CARE: Plant 12–36" apart in late spring. Apply slow-release granular plant food at time of planting or begin using water-soluble plant food 3 weeks after planting. Dahlias are heavy feeders, so pay attention to soil pH and fertility. Water deeply when the soil is dry. Tall cultivars may require staking. Install stakes early in the season to avoid impaling growing tubers later on. In cool climates lift tubers when foliage has been damaged by a light frost, but before a severe frost. Dust off the soil and let dry. Store tubers in a box or breathable container in vermiculite or dry sand and place in a cool well-ventilated, frost-free place. Check periodically for fungal infection. Dispose of diseased tubers or cut away infected areas, dust again with fungicide, and replace in the container. Plant tubers outdoors in spring.

PROPAGATION: For bedding plants sprinkle seeds over the soil mix and cover. Thoroughly moisten and keep moist, not soggy, until seeds germinate. Germination occurs in 5–10 days at 60–65°F. Transplant 11–15 days after sowing and reduce the temperature to 55–60°F. Harden off and plant outdoors after all danger of frost has passed. Divide the tuberous roots in early spring after shoots have begun to grow by cutting them into sections that contain an actively growing bud or shoot. Replant pieces, then water and mulch.

PESTS AND DISEASES: Pests include aphids, stem borers, spider mites, caterpillars, plant hoppers, thrips, slugs, and snails. Diseases include powdery mildew, smut, dahlia mosaic viruses, fungal leaf spots, soft rot, crown gall, and tomato spotted wilt virus.

1 After the first light frost damages the foliage, dig the tubers for storage.

2 Remove stems from the tuberous roots and brush away soil before storing.

PURPLE HARDY ICE PLANT
Delosperma cooperi *del-oh-SPERM-uh KOOP-er-eye*

Purple hardy ice plant is a low-maintenance perennial.

ZONES: 6–10
SIZE: 4–8"h × 24"w
TYPE: Perennial
FORM: Mound
TEXTURE: Medium
GROWTH: Fast
LIGHT: Full sun
MOISTURE: Medium to low

SOIL: Moderately fertile, well-drained
FEATURES: Flowers, foliage
USES: Border, container, ground cover
FLOWERS: ▓

SITING: Purple hardy ice plant prefers full sun and moderately fertile soil with a pH of 5.5–7.0. Plants need well-drained soil. A multitude of 1–2" daisylike glossy purple flowers appear in mid- to late summer. The appealing leaves are succulent, cylindrical, and bright green. Plants are top performers in the Low-Maintenance Perennial Plant Field Trials at Clemson University's Sandhill Research and Education Center in South Carolina, testimony to their heat tolerance and pest resistance. Place in odd-numbered groups in the front of the border or in containers. Good companions include 'Moonbeam' threadleaf coreopsis, 'Red Fox' spike speedwell, and 'Blue Spruce' sedum.

CARE: Plant 18–24" apart in spring or fall. Apply slow-release granular plant food at time of planting. Cease feeding 4–6 weeks prior to first frost date. Water deeply when the soil is dry. Even though the plants are low maintenance and drought tolerant,

they perform better if watered during dry spells. Apply 3" of vegetative mulch in summer to help retain soil moisture and add organic matter to the soil as it decomposes. Cut back the foliage after frost damage.

PROPAGATION: Sow seeds at 75–80°F or take stem cuttings in spring or summer.

PESTS AND DISEASES: Plants are relatively pest free when their cultural preferences are met. Mealybugs and aphids are occasional pests.

RELATED SPECIES: Orange-yellow hardy ice plant (*D. nubigerum*) grows 2" tall and spreads. The 1" orange-yellow blooms appear in summer. Plants have attractive succulent foliage and are cold hardy in Zones 6–9.

HYBRID BEE DELPHINIUM
Delphinium elatum *del-FIHN-ee-uhm ay-LAYT-uhm*

Hybrid bee delphinium bears spikes of purple, blue, or white flowers.

ZONES: 2–7
SIZE: 5–6'h × 2–3'w
TYPE: Perennial
FORM: Upright
TEXTURE: Medium
GROWTH: Medium
LIGHT: Full sun to partial shade

MOISTURE: High
SOIL: Fertile, well-drained
FEATURES: Flowers, foliage
USES: Border
FLOWERS: ■□■

SITING: *Delphinium elatum* prefers full sun or light shade in midafternoon and fertile, well-drained soil with a pH of 5.5–7.0. This plant does not perform well in high-heat areas. Spikes of blue, lavender, purple, and white flowers appear in early and midsummer. Delphinium is a classic favorite for the cottage garden, and flowers are superb fresh cut or dried. Good companions include David Austin and 'Carefree Wonder' roses, 'David' garden phlox, baby's breath, and Claridge Druce geranium cultivars.

CARE: Plant 12–36" apart in late spring or fall. Apply slow-release granular plant food at time of planting or begin using water-soluble plant food 3 weeks after planting in spring. Delphiniums are heavy feeders, so pay attention to soil pH and fertility. Cease feeding 6–8 weeks prior to first frost date. Water deeply when the soil is dry. Tall cultivars usually require sturdy staking

Stake delphinium so the support is not visible and does not compete visually with the blooms.

or may be placed against fences or walls for support. Deadhead by cutting back spent spikes to encourage small, flowering side shoots. Cut to the ground in autumn after frost withers the foliage.

PROPAGATION: Delphinium propagation is difficult. Fresh seed (less than 6 months old) produces the best germination rates and requires no pretreatment. Store packaged seed purchased in winter in the refrigerator until ready to sow. Germination occurs in 12–18 days at 70–75°F. Divide in early spring. Dig around the root clump and lift. Use a sharp spade to slice through the root system.

PESTS AND DISEASES: Snails and slugs are common pests. Diseases include powdery mildew, bacterial leaf and fungal leaf spots, Southern blight, and root rot.

RELATED SPECIES: 'Berghimmel' reaches 6' tall and has wind-resistant stems with white blooms and a yellow bee (center), 'Jubelruf' reaches6' tall, has wind-resistant stems, and bears semidouble bright blue flowers with a white bee, and 'Rosemary Brock' reaches 5' tall and bears semidouble mauve flowers with darker sepal tips and a brown bee.

CHRYSANTHEMUM
Dendranthema ×grandiflorum *den-DRAN-theh-muh gran-dih-FLOR-uhm*

Garden chrysanthemums are a traditional sign of autumn in the landscape. They are also known as mums.

ZONES: 4–9
SIZE: 1–3'h × 12–24"w
TYPE: Perennial
FORM: Rounded
TEXTURE: Medium
GROWTH: Medium
LIGHT: Full sun
MOISTURE: High

SOIL: Fertile, well-drained
FEATURES: Flowers, foliage
USES: Border, container
FLOWERS: ■■■■ □■

SITING: Garden chrysanthemum prefers full sun and fertile, well-drained soil with a pH of 5.5–7.0. Flowers appear in late summer and autumn in shades of crimson, orange, yellow, pink, cream, and purple. It is a short-lived perennial in Zones 4 and 5 and may be grown as an annual in cool areas. Companions include 'Purpureum' fennel and 'Sky Racer' purple moor grass.

CARE: Plant 12–24" apart in spring or fall. Apply slow-release granular plant food at time of planting, or begin using water-soluble plant food 3 weeks after planting in spring. Cease feeding 6–8 weeks prior to first frost date. Water deeply whenever the soil is dry. Cut back in spring and early summer if more compactness is desired. Cut to the ground in autumn after frost withers the foliage, or leave erect for winter viewing in mild locations.

PROPAGATION: Divide every 3 years in spring to maintain vigor. Dig around the root clump and lift.

PESTS AND DISEASES: Pests include aphids, earwigs, nematodes, spider mites, fourlined plant bug and whiteflies. Viruses cause stunting, yellowing, and puckering of leaves. Other diseases include powdery mildew, crown gall, rust, and botrytis.

1 **Pinch mum tips in spring to encourage compact growth.**

2 **Cut back in fall once foliage is disfigured by frost.**

3 **Mulch with straw for added cold protection.**

SWEET WILLIAM
Dianthus barbatus *dy-AN-thubs babr-BAYT-ubs*

Sweet william is an old-fashioned favorite in the garden.

ZONES: 3–8
SIZE: 26"h × 12"w
TYPE: Biennial
FORM: Upright
TEXTURE: Medium
GROWTH: Medium
LIGHT: Full sun to partial shade

MOISTURE: Medium
SOIL: Fertile, well-drained
FEATURES: Flowers, foliage
USES: Border, container
FLOWERS: ■■□

SITING: Sweet william prefers full sun in its northern range and afternoon shade in the Deep South. Soil should be fertile but well-drained with a pH of 7.0–7.5. Clusters of pink, red, white, or various combinations and hues of these colors appear in late spring and early summer. Light to medium green leaves may be tinged with bronze. Plants are old-fashioned favorites and often appear in cottage gardens and nostalgic grandmother's gardens. The fragrant flowers are prized for cutting and for dried arrangements. Plants are suitable for early color in the border or container. Good garden companions include 'Silver Carpet' lamb's-ears, lemon thyme, pansies, and violas.

CARE: Plant 12" apart in spring or fall. Apply slow-release plant food, such as Miracle-Gro Shake 'n Feed All Purpose, at time of planting or begin using water-

Deadhead sweet william to stimulate rebloom.

soluble plant food, such as Miracle-Gro Water Soluble All Purpose, 3 weeks after planting in spring. Follow label directions for amount and frequency. Cease feeding 6–8 weeks prior to first frost date. Water deeply whenever the soil is dry. Apply 3" of vegetative mulch to help retain soil moisture and as it decomposes it will add organic matter to the soil. In the south plants can be grown as perennials if the flowers are removed before seeds form. Cut to the ground in autumn after frost withers foliage or leave erect for winter viewing in warmer locations and cut back in early spring to encourage new growth and upright habit.

PROPAGATION: Plants reseed in the landscape, which is the easiest and most reliable method of reproduction. Plants grown from seed take two seasons to bloom. Sprinkle seeds over the soil mix and cover lightly. Thoroughly moisten and keep moist, not soggy, until seeds germinate. Germination occurs in 7–10 days at 60–70°F. Transplant 13–20 days after sowing. After germination, reduce temperature to 55–59°F.

PESTS AND DISEASES: Insect pests include slugs, snails, aphids, and caterpillars. Diseases include crown rot, rust, and powdery mildew.

PINK
Dianthus chinensis *dy-AN-thubs chib-NEN-sibs*

Pink cultivars appear in a variety of patterns and attractive colors. It is also known as China pink or annual pink.

ZONES: 7–10
SIZE: 6–24"h × 6–12"w
TYPE: Annual
FORM: Mound
TEXTURE: Fine
GROWTH: Fast
LIGHT: Full sun to partial shade

MOISTURE: Medium
SOIL: Fertile, well-drained
FEATURES: Flowers, foliage
USES: Bedding, container
FLOWERS: ■■□

SITING: Pink prefers full sun in its northern range and light afternoon shade in warmer areas. Soil should be fertile and well-drained with a pH of 7.0–7.5. Fringed flowers appear all summer long in red, pink, or white, often with a purple eye. Colors may appear as patterns as well as solid. The 3"-long leaves are light to medium green. Pink is often grown as an annual, but will overwinter in Zones 7 and higher. It is an exceptional bedding plant, providing cheerful summer color. Good companions in the garden include miniature roses, sweet potato, and 'David' garden phlox.

CARE: Plant 6–12" apart in late spring after the last frost. Apply slow-release granular plant food at time of planting or begin using water-soluble plant food 3 weeks after planting. Water deeply when the soil is dry. Apply 3" of vegetative mulch to help retain soil moisture and as it decomposes it will add organic matter to the soil. Deadheading will hasten reblooming but can be tedious due to the large number of blooms on each plant. Plants will self-seed but will not become invasive. Remove plants just prior to or after the first frost.

PROPAGATION: Sprinkle seeds over the soil mix and cover lightly. Thoroughly moisten and keep moist, not soggy, until seeds germinate. Germination occurs in 7 days at 70–75°F. Transplant 18–25 days after sowing. After germination, reduce the temperature to 50–56°F.

PESTS AND DISEASES: Slugs, grasshoppers, chipmunks, squirrels, and deer are common pests. In poorly drained soils and high humidity, crown rot may be a problem.

RELATED SPECIES: Baby Doll Series cultivars have patterned red to white flowers, 'Fire Carpet' has red blooms, and 'Parfait' has weather-resistant bicolored blooms.

COTTAGE PINK
Dianthus plumarius *dy-AN-thubs ploo-MAYR-ee-ubs*

Cottage pink, also known as grass pink, is an old-fashioned favorite for the blooming cottage garden.

ZONES: 4–8
SIZE: 8–20"h × 15–24"w
TYPE: Perennial
FORM: Mound
TEXTURE: Fine
GROWTH: Slow
LIGHT: Full sun

MOISTURE: Medium
SOIL: Fertile, well-drained
FEATURES: Flowers, foliage
USES: Border, container
FLOWERS: ■□

SITING: Cottage pink prefers full sun and fertile, well-drained, alkaline soil with a pH of 7.0–7.5. Clove-scented toothed flowers appear spring through summer in rose, pink, and white. Evergreen foliage is gray-green and grasslike. Plant cottage pinks in the border, the cottage garden, and in containers. Companions include 'Bonica', 'Carefree Wonder', 'Iceberg', and 'The Fairy' roses.

CARE: Plant 12–24" apart in spring or fall. Apply slow-release granular plant food at time of planting or begin using water-soluble plant food 3 weeks after planting in spring. Cease feeding 6–8 weeks prior to first frost date. Water deeply whenever the soil is dry. Cut back immediately after flowering to look tidy. Cut to the ground in autumn after frost withers the foliage or leave evergreen foliage erect for winter viewing in milder locations.

1 Lift the entire clump to divide cottage pink. Slice through it with a sharp spade.

PROPAGATION: Divide every 2–3 years in spring to maintain vigor.

PESTS AND DISEASES: Slugs, grasshoppers, chipmunks, squirrels, and deer are common pests. Leaf spots may occur in high humidity and poor air circulation. Proper spacing and air circulation reduce susceptibility to disease.

RELATED SPECIES: 'Prairie Pink' has blue-green foliage and large, fragrant double pink flowers, 'Queen of Sheba' has single cream-colored blooms speckled with pink, and 'Raspberry Tart' has semidouble red flowers with a deep red center.

2 Separate offshoots. Relocate and replant them in the garden.

FRINGED BLEEDING HEART
Dicentra eximia *dy-SEHN-truh eks-EE-mee-uh*

Fringed bleeding heart blooms sporadically all summer.

ZONES: 3–8
SIZE: 24"h × 18"w
TYPE: Perennial
FORM: Irregular
TEXTURE: Fine
GROWTH: Medium
LIGHT: Full to partial shade

MOISTURE: Medium
SOIL: Fertile, well-drained
FEATURES: Flowers, foliage
USES: Flowers, foliage
FLOWERS: ■□

SITING: Fringed bleeding heart tolerates full shade or partial shade and prefers fertile, well-drained soil with a pH of 5.5–7.0.

Nodding stems of heart-shaped pink flowers appear in late spring and intermittently through early autumn. The red-tinted gray-green stems of deeply lobed leaflets add a graceful element to the landscape. The foliage of this low-maintenance perennial remains attractive throughout the growing season. Place in large swathes in the woodland garden, at the foot of irrigated trees and shrubs, in odd-numbered groups in the shade border, or in containers for delightful early-season color and interest. Companions that complement the gray-tinged foliage include lady's mantle, Japanese painted fern, 'Elegans' Siebold hosta, and 'Mrs. Moon' Bethlehem sage.

CARE: Plant 18" apart in spring or fall. After planting, water deeply and add 3" of mulch around, but not touching, the plants. Mulch helps retain soil moisture and as it breaks down, adds organic matter to the soil. Apply slow-release granular plant food at time of planting, or begin using water-soluble plant food 3 weeks after planting in spring. Cease feeding 6–8 weeks prior to first frost date. Water deeply whenever the soil becomes dry, letting the soil dry slightly between waterings. Cut plants to the ground in autumn after frost withers the foliage.

PROPAGATION: Plants reliably self-seed in the landscape. Divide every 3 years or when vigor declines, in spring or fall. Dig around the root clump and lift. Use a sharp spade to slice through the root system. Reset portions that contain healthy roots and top shoots, then water and mulch. Discard any pieces that do not contain both healthy roots and top shoots.

PESTS AND DISEASES: Plants are relatively pest free when their cultural preferences (sun, soil, moisture) are met. Slugs and snails are occasional pests.

RELATED SPECIES: The cultivar 'Alba' has pure white blooms and deeply divided foliage, 'Adrian Bloom' has deep carmine red flowers, and 'Bountiful' has purplish-pink flowers.

COMMON BLEEDING HEART
Dicentra spectabilis *dy-SEHN-truh spek-TAH-bih-lihs*

Common bleeding heart bears spectacular heart-shaped blooms in late spring.

ZONES: 3–9
SIZE: 4'h × 2'w
TYPE: Perennial
FORM: Irregular
TEXTURE: Fine
GROWTH: Medium
LIGHT: Full to partial shade

MOISTURE: Medium
SOIL: Fertile, well-drained
FEATURES: Flowers, foliage
USES: Woodland, border, container
FLOWERS: ■□

SITING: Common bleeding heart prefers full or partial shade and fertile, well-drained soil with a pH of 5.5–7.0. Long, arching stems of pendant pink flowers with white inner petals appear in late spring and early summer. After flowering the foliage dies back. This old-fashioned plant adds grace and delicacy to the woodland garden or the shade border. Flowers are superb additions to fresh cut arrangements. Companions include 'Elegans' Siebold hosta, heart-leaf brunnera, and 'Mrs. Moon' Bethlehem sage.

CARE: Plant 15–24" apart in spring or fall in fertile soil high in organic matter. After planting, water deeply and add 3" of mulch around, but not touching, the plant.

Interplant hosta with bleeding heart to cover space left after bleeding heart dies back in summer.

Apply slow-release granular plant food at time of planting or begin using water-soluble plant food 3 weeks after planting in spring. Water deeply whenever the soil becomes dry.

PROPAGATION: Plants lightly self-seed in the landscape. Divide every 3 years, or when vigor declines, in spring or fall. Dig around the root clump and lift. Use a sharp spade to slice through the root system. Reset portions that contain healthy roots and top shoots, then water and mulch. Discard any pieces that do not contain both healthy roots and top shoots.

PESTS AND DISEASES: Plants are relatively pest free when their cultural preferences (sun, soil, moisture) are met. Slugs and snails are occasional pests. Wet soil during the summer may contribute to disease problems.

RELATED SPECIES: The cultivar 'Alba' has pure white blooms and the same attractive foliage. Dutchman's breeches (*D. cucullaria*) bears long, arching stems of curious white flowers with a yellow tip in early spring. Deeply divided leaves are light and airy and bluish green. After flowering, the foliage dies back.

GAS PLANT
Dictamnus albus *dik-TAM-nuhs AL-bus*

Gas plant, also known as dittany, bears white flowers in early summer.

ZONES: 3–8
SIZE: 15–36"h × 24"w
TYPE: Perennial
FORM: Upright
TEXTURE: Medium
GROWTH: Slow
LIGHT: Full sun to partial shade

MOISTURE: Medium
SOIL: Moderately fertile, well-drained
FEATURES: Flowers, foliage
USES: Border
FLOWERS: □■

SITING: Gas plant prefers full sun or partial shade from the afternoon sun and well-drained, moderately fertile soil with a pH of 5.5–7.0. Flowers and unripe fruit produce a volatile oil that can be ignited in hot weather. Roots resent transplanting and disturbance. Plant in groups in the border for best effect. Companions include 'Fire King' yarrow, beardlip penstemon, smooth white penstemon, and 'Hameln' fountain grass.

CARE: Plant 18–24" apart in spring or fall. Feed with slow-release granular plant food at time of planting or begin using water-soluble plant food 3 weeks after planting in spring. Cease feeding 6–8 weeks prior to first frost date. This low-maintenance

Wear gloves when working with gas plant to protect skin from oils that may cause irritation similar to that of poison ivy.

perennial is drought tolerant once established, but new transplants require ample and frequent moisture. Prune plants to the ground in late fall or leave erect for winter interest and cut back in early spring.

PROPAGATION: All propagation techniques are difficult for gas plant. Gather seed from plants and sow immediately in a protected outdoor site. Germination should occur the following spring. Division may damage the crown of the parent plant. A sharp spade and clean cuts yield greater success. Avoid bruising, pulling, and ripping of roots. Plunge a sharp spade straight through the center of the crown to slice through the root system. Reset portions that contain healthy roots and top shoots, then water and mulch. Discard any pieces that do not contain both healthy roots and top shoots.

PESTS AND DISEASES: Plants are relatively pest free when their cultural preferences are met.

RELATED SPECIES: The cultivar 'Purpureus' has purple flowers with darker purple veins, 'Ruber' has pinkish-purple flowers, and 'Albiflorus' has white flowers with yellow veins.

FOXGLOVE

Digitalis purpurea *dihj-ih-TAH-lihs per-PER-ee-uh*

Common foxglove is a traditional English garden plant.

ZONES: 3–8
SIZE: 3–6'h × 24"w
TYPE: Biennial
FORM: Upright
TEXTURE: Medium
GROWTH: Medium
LIGHT: Full sun to partial shade

MOISTURE: Medium
SOIL: Fertile, well-drained
FEATURES: Flowers, foliage
USES: Border, woodland
FLOWERS: ■ ■ □

SITING: Foxglove prefers full sun or partial shade from the afternoon sun and fertile, well-drained soil with a pH of 5.5–7.0. Tall spikes of purple, pink, or white flowers appear in early summer. Plant in the cottage garden, the mixed perennial border, along fencerows, and in the bright woodland garden. Companions include 'Fire King' yarrow, apothecary rose, 'The Rocket' ligularia, and 'Stargazer' lily.

CARE: Plant 18" apart in spring or fall in fertile soil high in organic matter. After planting, water deeply and add 3" of mulch around, but not touching, the plants. Apply slow-release granular plant food at time of planting or begin using water-soluble plant food 3 weeks after planting in spring. Water deeply whenever the soil becomes dry. Remove flower stalks after blooms have faded or leave erect long enough for seeds to drop if

Collect foxglove seed to sow in a new area.

self-seeding is desired. If plants do not self-seed in the landscape, plan to replace every year or two with container stock.

PROPAGATION: Plants frequently self-seed in the landscape. To sow indoors sprinkle seeds over the soil mix and leave them exposed to light; do not cover. Thoroughly moisten and keep moist, not soggy, until seeds germinate. Germination occurs in 5–10 days at 60–65°F. Transplant seedlings 15–20 days after sowing. After germination, reduce temperature to 55–60°F.

PESTS AND DISEASES: Diseases include Southern blight, anthracnose, and fungal leaf spots.

RELATED SPECIES: The cultivar 'Alba' has white flowers, 'Apricot' has apricot flowers, Excelsior Hybrids come in pastel shades, and Foxy Hybrids have carmine, pink, cream, and white flowers with flecks of maroon. Yellow foxglove (*D. grandiflora*) reaches 3–4' tall and 24–36" wide and has pale yellow blooms with brown veins. Strawberry foxglove (*D. ×mertonensis*) is a perennial with strawberry pink blooms; divide every 2–3 years to maintain vigor. Strawberry foxglove plants come true from seed.

PURPLE CONEFLOWER

Echinacea purpurea *ek-in-AY-see-ah per-PER-ee-ah*

Purple coneflower is a superb low-maintenance native perennial for the summer garden.

ZONES: 3–9
SIZE: 4'h × 18"w
TYPE: Perennial
FORM: Upright
TEXTURE: Medium
GROWTH: Medium
LIGHT: Full sun
MOISTURE: Medium

SOIL: Fertile, well-drained
FEATURES: Flowers, foliage
USES: Border, container
FLOWERS: ■ □

SITING: Purple coneflower prefers full sun and fertile, well-drained soil with a pH of 5.5–7.5. Rosy-purple flowers appear from midsummer into autumn. Purple coneflower is magnificent in the full-sun border planted in groups, or placed in mixed container plantings. Flowers attract butterflies and are excellent for cutting. Good companions include 'Husker Red' smooth white penstemon, 'Purpureum' purple fountain grass, 'David' garden phlox, and 'Goldsturm' black-eyed Susan.

CARE: Plant 18" apart in early spring or fall. Apply slow-release granular plant food at time of planting or begin using water-soluble plant food 3 weeks after planting in spring. Cease feeding 6–8 weeks prior to first frost date. Water deeply when the soil dries. Remove faded flower stalks to

Butterflies are attracted to the blooms of purple coneflower.

stimulate reblooming. Prune back in fall if frost withers the foliage; in warmer areas leave erect for late-season viewing and prune back in early spring.

PROPAGATION: Divide in fall or early spring. Dig around the root clump and lift. Use a sharp spade to slice through the root system. Reset portions that contain healthy roots and top shoots.

PESTS AND DISEASES: Plants are relatively pest free. Moderate soil fertility helps create strong, robust foliage that is not as easily penetrated by pests. Powdery mildew, aster yellows, and bacterial leafspots may occur.

RELATED SPECIES: The cultivar 'Finale White' has 4" single white flowers with a greenish-brown disk, 'Magnus' has 7" deep purple flowers with a deep orange disk, 'Robert Bloom' has rich crimson-tinted mauve flowers with a deep orange-brown disk, 'The King' has large deep carmine flowers with an orange-brown disk, and 'White Swan' has honey-scented pure white flowers with an orange-brown disk. Pale purple coneflower (*E. pallida*) has light purple blooms and tolerates poor soil.

GLOBE THISTLE

Echinops ritro EK-ihn-ops REE-troh

Globe thistle bears attractive steel blue, spherical flowers.

ZONES: 3–9
SIZE: 24"h × 18"w
TYPE: Perennial
FORM: Upright
TEXTURE: Coarse
GROWTH: Fast
LIGHT: Full sun
MOISTURE: Medium to low

SOIL: Moderately fertile, well-drained
FEATURES: Flowers, foliage
USES: Border, container
FLOWERS: ■

SITING: Globe thistle prefers full sun and moderately fertile soil but tolerates well-drained sandy soils with low fertility. It prefers a pH of 6.5–7.5. It is drought tolerant and extremely low maintenance. Plant in groups in the border or in mixed container plantings. Flowers attract butterflies and are excellent for cutting and drying. Good companions include purple coneflower; 'Snowbank' white boltonia, Russian sage, gaura, and 'Kobold' blazing star.

CARE: Plant 18" apart in spring or fall. Apply slow-release granular plant food at time of planting. Cease feeding 6–8 weeks prior to first frost date. Water deeply when the soil is dry. Even though the plant is low maintenance and drought tolerant, it performs better if watered during dry spells. Plants self-seed in the landscape. If this is not desired, deadhead blooms immediately after flowering. Prune back in fall if frost withers foliage; in warmer areas, leave erect for late-season viewing, and prune back in early spring.

PROPAGATION: Divide in spring or fall.

PESTS AND DISEASES: Plants are relatively pest free when their cultural preferences are met.

RELATED SPECIES: The cultivar 'Blue Glow' has light blue flowers, 'Taplow Blue' is a strong performer with deep blue flowers, and 'Veitch's Blue' has bright blue blooms.

1 To divide globe thistle, cut back stems to 6" high.

2 Plunge a sharp spade through the root system.

3 Replant pieces that contain healthy roots and shoots.

CUSHION SPURGE

Euphorbia polychroma (epithymoides) yew-FOR-bee-uh pahl-ee-KROH-muh (ee-pith-ih-MOY-deez)

Cushion spurge, also known as euphorbia, bears yellow flowers in midspring.

ZONES: 4–9
SIZE: 15"h × 24"w
TYPE: Perennial
FORM: Rounded
TEXTURE: Medium
GROWTH: Fast
LIGHT: Full sun to partial shade
MOISTURE: Medium

SOIL: Moderately fertile, well-drained
FEATURES: Flowers, foliage
USES: Border, container
FLOWERS: ■
FALL COLOR: ■ ■

SITING: Cushion spurge prefers moderately fertile, well-drained soil with a pH of 5.5–7.0. In cooler regions plants do best in full sun; in warmer areas plants prefer afternoon shade. Chartreuse bracts surround yellow flowers in midspring. Dark green leaves turn red, maroon, or orange in autumn. Plant at the front of the border or use in container plantings. Good companions include 'Moonbeam' threadleaf coreopsis, 'Rotfuchs' spike speedwell, and 'Rosea' showy evening primrose.

Cut back cushion spurge immediately after bloom to stimulate rebloom and compact foliar growth.

CARE: Plant 18–24" apart in spring or fall. Apply slow-release granular plant food at time of planting. Cease feeding 6–8 weeks prior to first frost date. Water deeply when the soil is dry. Even though the plant is low maintenance and drought tolerant, it performs better if watered during dry spells. Plants prolifically self-seed in the landscape. If this is not desired, deadhead blooms immediately after flowering. Prune back in fall if frost withers foliage; in warmer areas, leave erect for late-season viewing, and prune back in early spring.

PROPAGATION: Divide in spring or fall. Dig around the root clump and lift. Use a sharp spade to slice through the root system. Reset portions that contain healthy roots and top shoots, then water and mulch. Discard the older woody central portion.

PESTS AND DISEASES: Plants are relatively pest free when their cultural preferences (sun, soil, moisture) are met.

RELATED SPECIES: The cultivar 'Emerald Jade' is smaller than the species and has attractive autumn hues, 'Midas' has bright yellow bracts and flowers, and 'Purpurea' has purple leaves and yellow flowers.

QUEEN-OF-THE-PRAIRIE
Filipendula rubra fihl-ih-PEN-doo-lah ROO-bruh

Queen-of-the-prairie, or meadowsweet, bears pink plumes of flowers in summer.

ZONES: 3–9
SIZE: 6–8'h × 4'w
TYPE: Perennial
FORM: Rounded
TEXTURE: Medium
GROWTH: Fast
LIGHT: Full sun
MOISTURE: Medium to high

SOIL: Moderately fertile
FEATURES: Flowers, foliage
USES: Border, wetland
FLOWERS: ■

SITING: Queen-of-the-prairie prefers full sun and moderately fertile soil with a pH of 5.5–7.0. Plants tolerate boggy conditions as well. Plumes of pink to peach flowers appear in early and midsummer. Toothed lobed leaves reach up to 8" across and are dramatic in the landscape. Plant in odd-numbered groups in a large perennial border, along the river's edge or in boggy ground. Good companions include 'Variegatus' sweet flag in wetlands, and 'Gracillimus' maiden grass and spiderwort in other sites.

CARE: Plant 3–4' apart in spring or fall. Apply slow-release granular plant food at time of planting. Follow label directions for amount and frequency. Cease feeding 6–8 weeks prior to first frost date. If planting in a wetland or on the bank of a natural water body, avoid plant foods and chemical pesticides to prevent chemicals from leaching into water bodies. Water deeply when the soil is dry. Apply 3" of vegetative mulch in summer and winter to help retain soil moisture. Prune back in fall if frost withers the foliage; in warmer areas, leave erect for late-season viewing and prune back in early spring.

PROPAGATION: Divide in fall. Dig around the root clump and lift. Use a sharp spade to slice through the root system. Reset portions that contain healthy roots and top shoots, then water and mulch. Discard any pieces that do not contain both healthy roots and top shoots.

PESTS AND DISEASES: Diseases include powdery mildew, leaf spots, and rust.

RELATED SPECIES: The cultivar 'Venusta' has deep rose flowers that lighten as they age. Queen-of-the-meadow (*F. ulmaria*) bears creamy white flowers in summer, reaches 24–36" high and 24" wide, and prefers afternoon shade. *F. ulmaria* 'Aurea' has brilliant yellow leaves in spring that lighten as the season progresses.

FUCHSIA
Fuchsia hybrids FYEW-shuh

Fuchsia hybrids are popular plants for hanging baskets.

ZONES: 8–10
SIZE: 6–36"h × 12–24"w
TYPE: Perennial
FORM: Irregular
TEXTURE: Medium
GROWTH: Medium
LIGHT: Full sun to partial shade

MOISTURE: High
SOIL: Moist, fertile, well-drained
FEATURES: Flowers, foliage
USES: Container, border
FLOWERS: ■□■■

SITING: Fuchsia hybrids prefer full sun or partial afternoon shade and moist, well-drained soil with a pH of 5.5–7.0. The flowers are usually pendant and tubular, often bicolored, and appear in early summer into autumn. They come in a variety of forms that include single, semidouble, and double. Triphylla Group fuschias have long tubes, single flowers, and leaves that are sometimes purple underneath. They are more tolerant of heat than other fuchsias. *F. procumbens* flowers are erect; foliage is mid- to light green, sometimes purplish below. Fuchsias are typically grown as annuals and are attractive in hanging baskets, in containers, or in the border. Good companions for containers include 'Sapphire' and 'Lilac Fountains' lobelia and sweet woodruff.

Remove fallen blossoms to promote sanitation.

CARE: Plant 12–18" apart in late spring after the last frost. Apply slow-release granular plant food at time of planting, or begin using water-soluble plant food 3 weeks after planting in spring. Follow label directions for amount and frequency. Apply 3" of vegetative mulch to help retain soil moisture and add organic matter to the soil as it decomposes. Shear back plant if more compactness is desired. Deadheading will stimulate reblooming but may be tedious considering the multitude of blooms. Spent blooms typically fall and should be removed to promote sanitation and reduce pest infestations. Remove plants after the first frost in cooler climates.

PROPAGATION: Sow seed at 60–75 °F in spring. Thoroughly moisten and keep moist, not soggy, until seeds germinate. Transplant outdoors after the last frost.

PESTS AND DISEASES: Insect pests include thrips, whiteflies, and aphids. Diseases include Southern blight, rusts, crown gall, and crown and root rots.

BLANKET FLOWER
Gaillardia ×grandiflora *guh-LARD-ee-uh grand-ih-FLOR-uh*

Blanket flower attracts butterflies. It blooms profusely in dry, sunny sites.

ZONES: 3–8
SIZE: 36"h × 18"w
TYPE: Perennial
FORM: Upright
TEXTURE: Medium
GROWTH: Medium
LIGHT: Full sun
MOISTURE: Medium
SOIL: Fertile, well-drained
FEATURES: Flowers, foliage
USES: Border, container
FLOWERS: ▨ ■

SITING: Blanket flower prefers full sun and fertile, well-drained soil but tolerates soil with low fertility. The preferred pH is 5.5–7.0. Daisylike flowers reach 3–5" across and are bright yellow with a red base and a mahogany central disk. Flowers appear from early summer into early autumn, attract butterflies, and are good in fresh cut arrangements. This short-lived perennial adds cheerful color to the border or container. Companions include 'Snowbank' white boltonia, rosemary, threadleaf coreopsis, and creeping zinnia.

CARE: Plant 18" apart in spring or fall. Apply slow-release granular plant food at time of planting or begin using water-soluble plant food 3 weeks after planting in spring. Cease feeding 6–8 weeks prior to first frost date. Water deeply when the soil is dry. Apply 3" of vegetative mulch in summer to help retain soil moisture. Deadhead blooms to stimulate reblooming. Cut back hard in late summer to early fall to stimulate fall bloom and new foliage growth. Do not feed at this time; new growth is susceptible to frost damage. Plants overwinter better if not cut back after frost. Trim damaged foliage in early spring.

PROPAGATION: Divide in spring or fall. Dig around the root clump and lift. Seed-grown plants will flower intermittently during the first season, with exuberance during the second. Sprinkle seeds over the soil mix and leave exposed to light; do not cover. Thoroughly moisten and keep moist, not soggy, until seeds germinate. Germination occurs in 5–15 days at 70–75°F. Transplant 30–42 days after sowing.

PESTS AND DISEASES: Insect pests include aphids, slugs, and snails. Diseases include powdery mildew, downy mildew, rust, and bacterial leaf spot.

RELATED SPECIES: The cultivar 'Baby Cole' has 3" bright red ray florets with yellow tips and a burgundy disk, 'Red Plume' has brick red flowers, 'Tokajer' has dark orange flowers, and 'Kobold' has deep red flowers with yellow tips and a red disk.

1 **Deadhead spent flowers to stimulate season-long bloom.**

2 **After deadheading, blanket flower will continue to develop new flower buds.**

COMMON SNOWDROP
Galanthus nivalis *gal-AN-thus nih-VALL-iss*

Common snowdrop appears in late winter, often in snow.

ZONES: 3–9
SIZE: 4"h × 4"w
TYPE: Perennial
FORM: Upright
TEXTURE: Fine
GROWTH: Medium
LIGHT: Partial shade
MOISTURE: High
SOIL: Moist, fertile, well-drained
FEATURES: Flowers, foliage
USES: Naturalizing, border, woodland
FLOWERS: □

SITING: Snowdrops prefer partial shade and fertile, humus-rich, moist, well-drained soil with a pH of 5.5–7.0. Blooms are pendulous, ½" long, and creamy white with a spot of green at the tip of each petal. Flowers are sweet scented and appear in late winter, often emerging through snow. Leaves are narrow and erect. Plant great swaths, hundreds of bulbs, for the best effect; a few will not catch the eye. Snowdrops add appeal to the alpine garden, rock garden, dwarf conifer garden, and woodland garden. Good companions include Christmas rose, Lenten rose, and winter aconite.

CARE: Plant bulbs 4" apart and 3" deep in autumn in well-drained soil. Apply slow-release granular plant food at time of planting. Follow label directions for amount and frequency. Snowdrops prefer even moisture and will not tolerate water-soaked soils in summer or winter. Apply 3" of vegetative mulch in summer and winter to help retain soil moisture and add organic matter to the soil as it decomposes.

PROPAGATION: Lift clumps and separate bulbs after flowering, but before the foliage dies down. Replant the bulbs at the proper spacing, water, and mulch.

PESTS AND DISEASES: Plants are vulnerable to narcissus bulb fly and botrytis.

RELATED SPECIES: The cultivar 'Flore Pleno' has double flowers and produces many offsets, 'Lady Elphinstone' has double flowers and gray-green foliage, 'Magnet' has large flowers and is a bit taller and more vigorous than the species, and 'Scharlockii' has slender flowers spotted with green on the outer petals.

SWEET WOODRUFF

Galium odoratum *GAL-ee-uhm o-der-AH-tuhm*

Sweet woodruff, also known as bedstraw, is an attractive ground cover for light shade.

ZONES: 4–8
SIZE: 18"h × 18"w
TYPE: Perennial
FORM: Spreading
TEXTURE: Fine
GROWTH: Fast
LIGHT: Partial shade
MOISTURE: Medium

SOIL: Fertile, well-drained
FEATURES: Flowers, foliage
USES: Ground cover, container, border
FLOWERS: ☐

SITING: Sweet woodruff prefers partial shade but tolerates full shade. Fertile, well-drained soil with a pH of 5.5–7.0 is ideal. Star-shaped flowers appear from late spring to midsummer. Whorls of slightly prickly deep green leaves on square stems create a handsome loose and open ground cover even when the plant is bloomless. Dried foliage smells like new-mown hay. Sweet woodruff is best at the feet of broadleaf evergreens, in the shade border, or dripping from containers. Good companions include hosta, rhododendron, and coral bells hybrids.

Sweet woodruff runners pull up easily.

CARE: Plant 12–36" apart in spring or fall. The closer the plants, the faster the ground-cover effect. Apply slow-release granular plant food at time of planting. Water deeply when the soil is dry. Even though the plants are low maintenance, they perform best if they receive ample moisture during dry spells. Excessive sun exposure and dry soil causes the foliage to yellow and prematurely die back. Plants spread by creeping rhizomes in the landscape but are easily pulled up if they are unwanted. Prune back in fall if frost wilts the foliage; in milder areas, leave erect for late-season viewing, and prune back in early spring.

PROPAGATION: Divide in spring or fall. Dig around the root clump and lift. Use a sharp spade to slice through the root system. Reset portions that contain healthy roots and top shoots then water and mulch. Discard any pieces that do not contain both healthy roots and top shoots.

PESTS AND DISEASES: Plants are relatively pest free. Occasional disease problems include powdery mildew, rust, and fungal leaf spots.

WHITE GAURA

Gaura lindheimeri *GAW-ruh lind-HEYE-mer-eye*

White gaura produces white flowers all summer long. Pink forms of gaura are also commonly available.

ZONES: 5–9
SIZE: 5'h × 3'w
TYPE: Perennial
FORM: Upright
TEXTURE: Fine
GROWTH: Medium
LIGHT: Full sun
MOISTURE: Medium

SOIL: Fertile, well-drained
FEATURES: Flowers, foliage
USES: Border, container
FLOWERS: ☐ ▦

SITING: White gaura prefers full sun and fertile, well-drained soil but tolerates drought, light afternoon shade, and humidity. The preferred pH is 6.5–7.5. Light, airy racemes of pink buds open to white flowers from late spring to early autumn. Slender stems and leaves add to the airy quality of the plant. Gaura's unique see-through effect and extensive bloom time make it a welcome addition to the perennial border. Place in odd-numbered groups in the border or container. Good companions include 'Iceberg' rose, Siberian iris, globe thistle, and 'Goldsturm' black-eyed Susan.

CARE: Plant 24–36" apart in spring or fall. Apply slow-release granular plant food at time of planting. Water deeply when the soil is dry. Even though the plants are low maintenance and drought tolerant, they perform better if watered during dry spells. Apply 3" of vegetative mulch in summer to help retain soil moisture. Flowers are considered self-cleaning and do not need to be deadheaded unless the occasional brown hue is not acceptable. Leave plants standing in fall until they wilt from frost, then prune back. Plants are short-lived, especially in cooler climates, and may need replacing every 2–3 years.

PROPAGATION: Sprinkle seeds over the soil mix and leave exposed to light; do not cover. Thoroughly moisten and keep moist, not soggy, until seeds germinate. Germination occurs in 5–12 days at 70–72°F. Transplant 20–28 days after sowing. After transplanting, reduce temperature to 50°F.

PESTS AND DISEASES: Insect pests include aphids and beetles. Disease pests include rust, leaf spots, and powdery mildew.

RELATED SPECIES: The cultivar 'Corrie's Gold' has gold-and-cream variegated leaves, and 'Crimson Butterflies' reaches 15" tall and has vibrant pink blooms and burgundy-stained foliage.

Shear back foliage in early summer to create a more compact habit.

ENDRESS'S GERANIUM
Geranium endressii jer-AY-nee-uhm ehn-DREE-see-eye

Endress's geranium blooms on and off all summer with light pink flowers.

ZONES: 5–8
SIZE: 18"h × 24"w
TYPE: Perennial
FORM: Spreading
TEXTURE: Medium
GROWTH: Fast
LIGHT: Full sun to partial shade

MOISTURE: Medium
SOIL: Moderately fertile, well-drained
FEATURES: Flowers, foliage
USES: Border, container
FLOWERS: ■

SITING: Endress's geranium prefers full sun or light shade in the afternoon and well-drained, moderately fertile soil with a pH of 5.5–7.0. Erect, trumpet-shaped light pink flowers appear in early summer to early autumn and darken as they age. Endress's geranium prefers cooler climates and stops flowering in southern midsummer heat. Plants are welcome additions to the front of the border or spilling from a mixed container planting. Good companions include 'Kobold' blazing star, lavender, and 'Bressingham White' Carpathian harebell.
CARE: Plant 18" apart in spring or fall. Apply slow-release granular plant food at time of planting or begin using water-soluble plant food 3 weeks after planting in spring. Cease feeding 6–8 weeks prior to first frost date. Water deeply whenever the soil is dry. Deadhead blooms to stimulate reblooming, The tradeoff to deadheading is the loss of the cranesbill-like fruits, which will not form unless seeds are allowed to develop. Leaves are evergreen and may be left for winter viewing unless disfigured by frost.
PROPAGATION: Divide in spring or fall every 2–3 years to maintain vigor. Dig around the root clump and lift.
PESTS AND DISEASES: Plants are relatively pest free when their cultural preferences are met. Occasional diseases include downy mildew, powdery mildew, and bacterial blight.
RELATED SPECIES: The cultivar 'Wargrave Pink' is a vigorous grower with many salmon-pink blooms in summer. 'Claridge Druce' (*G.* ×*oxonianum*) is a hybrid between *G. endressii* and *G. versicolor*. It has pink flowers with darker veins. 'Russell Prichard' (*G.* ×*riversleaianum*) is a cross of *G. endressii* and *G. traversii*.

BLOODY CRANESBILL
Geranium sanguineum jer-AY-nee-uhm san-GWIHN-ee-uhm

Bloody cranesbill blooms even in high heat. It is also known as hardy geranium.

ZONES: 4–8
SIZE: 8"h × 12"w
TYPE: Perennial
FORM: Rounded
TEXTURE: Fine
GROWTH: Medium
LIGHT: Full sun to partial shade
MOISTURE: Medium

SOIL: Moderately fertile, well-drained
FEATURES: Flowers, foliage, fruits
USES: Border, container
FLOWERS: ■
FALL COLOR: ■

SITING: Bloody cranesbill prefers full sun or light shade in the afternoon and well-drained, moderately fertile soil with a pH of 5.5–7.0. Magenta-pink flowers with darker veins and a white eye appear from early summer to early autumn. Bloody cranesbill is the best-suited perennial cranesbill for southern landscapes due to its heat tolerance. Good companions include 'Bressingham White' Carpathian harebell, 'Monroe White' lilyturf, and 'Silver Carpet' lamb's-ears.

CARE: Plant 12" apart in spring or fall. Apply slow-release granular plant food at time of planting. Water deeply when the soil is dry. Even though the plants are low maintenance and drought tolerant, they perform better if watered during dry spells. Deadhead blooms to stimulate reblooming, Leaves are evergreen in mild climates. In cool climates leaves turn crimson in autumn and may be left for winter viewing unless disfigured by frost.
PROPAGATION: Divide in spring or fall every 2–3 years to maintain vigor.
PESTS AND DISEASES: Plants are relatively pest free when their cultural preferences are met. Occasional diseases include downy mildew, powdery mildew, and bacterial blight.

RELATED SPECIES: The cultivar 'Album' has white flowers, 'Elsbeth' has pink flowers with darker veins and leaves that become vibrant red in autumn, 'Cedric Morris' has rose-magenta blooms, 'John Elsley' is prostrate with rose-pink flowers and deep green leaves, and 'Shepherd's Warning' is compact with pink blooms.

1 Cut back plants to stimulate more compact foliage.

2 Several weeks later, healthy new growth emerges.

1 Divide plants by lifting the entire plant.

2 Separate plants by pulling apart the root system.

3 Reset pieces that contain healthy roots and shoots.

GLOBE AMARANTH
Gomphrena globosa gom-FREE-nuh gluh-BOS-uh

Globe amaranth, also known as gomphrena, bears a multitude of globe-shaped flowers in summer.

ZONES: NA
SIZE: 12–24"h × 12"w
TYPE: Annual
FORM: Upright
TEXTURE: Medium
GROWTH: Fast
LIGHT: Full sun

MOISTURE: Medium
SOIL: Moderately fertile, well-drained
FEATURES: Flowers, foliage
USES: Border, container
FLOWERS: ■■□■

SITING: Globe amaranth prefers full sun and moderately fertile, well-drained soil with a pH of 5.5–7.0. Erect spikes of cloverlike flowers with vibrant pink, purple, or ivory bracts appear from summer through autumn. Opposite leaves are bright green. Plants are relatively low maintenance, even drought tolerant, and seem weather resistant. Flowers are superb fresh cut or dried. Plant in containers or in odd-numbered groups in the border. Good garden companions include 'The Fairy'

and 'Iceberg' roses, germander, and baby's breath.
CARE: Plant 12" apart in late spring after the last frost. Apply slow-release granular plant food at time of planting or begin using water-soluble plant food 3 weeks after planting in spring. Apply 3" of vegetative mulch to help retain soil moisture and add organic matter to the soil as it decomposes. Cut back plant if more compactness is desired. Deadhead to

Harvest flowers in their prime and hang them upside down in small bundles in a dry location away from direct sunlight.

stimulate rebloom. Remove plants either just before the first frost or right afterward in cooler climates.
PROPAGATION: Sprinkle seed over the soil mix and leave exposed to light or cover; either is acceptable. Thoroughly moisten and keep moist, not soggy, until seeds germinate. Germination occurs in 10–14 days at 72°F. Transplant 20–25 days after sowing. After transplanting, reduce temperature to 68°F.

PESTS AND DISEASES: Plants are relatively pest free when their cultural preferences (sun, soil, moisture) are met.
RELATED SPECIES: The cultivar 'Aurea Superba' has orange-yellow flowers with red-tinged bracts, 'Buddy' is more compact with vibrant purple flower bracts, 'Nana' has dark red flower bracts, and 'Strawberry Fields' has orange-red bracts. *G. haageana* 'Lavender Lady' has lavender flower bracts.

ANNUAL BABY'S BREATH
Gypsophila elegans jip-SOF-uh-luh EL-eh-genz

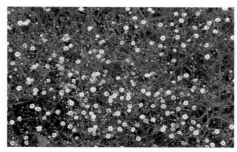

Annual baby's breath provides a light, airy quality to landscape plantings.

ZONES: NA
SIZE: 24"h × 12"w
TYPE: Annual
FORM: Rounded
TEXTURE: Fine
GROWTH: Medium
LIGHT: Full sun

MOISTURE: Medium
SOIL: Light, well-drained
FEATURES: Flowers
USES: Border, container
FLOWERS: □■

SITING: Annual baby's breath prefers full sun and light, moderately fertile, well-drained alkaline soil (pH 6.5–7.5). Tiny, starlike white or pink blooms appear on slender stalks in summer. Long-lasting flowers are ideal fresh cut or dried. Lance-shaped leaves are silvery green. Use in a mixed container planting or in airy groups in the perennial border or rose garden. Good companions include roses, purple coneflower, and globe amaranth.
CARE: Plant 12" apart in late spring after the last frost. Apply slow-release granular plant food at time of planting or begin using water-soluble plant food 3 weeks after planting in spring. Follow label directions for amount and frequency. Apply 3" of vegetative mulch to help retain soil moisture and add organic matter to the soil as it decomposes. Deadhead to stimulate rebloom. Remove plants just

before the first frost or right afterward when foliage is disfigured.
PROPAGATION: Sprinkle seeds over the soil mix and leave exposed to light or lightly cover; either is acceptable. Thoroughly moisten and keep moist, not soggy, until seeds germinate. Germination occurs in 10–15 days at 70–80°F. Transplant 21–28 days after sowing. After transplanting, reduce temperatures to 68°F.
PESTS AND DISEASES: Insect pests include slugs and snails. Diseases include crown gall, crown, and stem rot.
RELATED SPECIES: The cultivar 'Carminea' has carmine-rose flowers, 'Compacta Plena' has double light pink to white flowers, 'Covent Garden' has large white flowers, 'Red Cloud' has dark carmine pink flowers, and 'Rosea' bears soft rose pink flowers.

BABY'S BREATH

Gypsophila paniculata *jip-SOF-uh-luh pan-ik-yew-LAHT-ah*

Baby's breath lightly and artistically fills the space between other plants.

ZONES: 3–8
SIZE: 4'h × 4'w
TYPE: Perennial
FORM: Rounded
TEXTURE: Fine
GROWTH: Medium
LIGHT: Full sun

MOISTURE: Medium
SOIL: Moderately fertile, well-drained
FEATURES: Flowers
USES: Border, container
FLOWERS: □ ■

SITING: Baby's breath prefers full sun and light, moderately fertile, well-drained, alkaline soil (pH 6.5–7.5). Clouds of tiny white flowers appear in mid- to late summer, adding a delicate, airy quality to the landscape. Silvery-green leaves are 2–3" long and linear. Plant in drifts in the border or as part of a mixed container planting. Good companions include roses, lilies, daylilies, and 'Kobold' blazing star.

CARE: Plant 36" apart in spring or fall. Apply slow-release granular plant food at time of planting or begin using water-soluble plant food 3 weeks after planting in spring. Cease feeding 6–8 weeks prior to first frost date. Water deeply whenever the soil is dry. Deadhead blooms to stimulate reblooming and, if cut early, to dry for later use. Prune back in fall if frost withers the foliage; in milder areas, leave erect for late-season viewing and prune back in early spring.

Creeping baby's breath hugs the ground. This is the pink-flowered form.

PROPAGATION: Baby's breath is difficult to transplant and difficult to divide. The most common form of propagation is tissue culture, not practical for the home gardener. Cultivars do not come true from seed, and seed-grown plants are generally inferior to vegetatively propagated plants. To sow seed, sprinkle seeds over the soil mix and leave exposed to light. Germination occurs in 5–10 days at 70–80°F. Transplant 15–20 days after sowing.

PESTS AND DISEASES: Insect pests include slugs and snails. Diseases include crown gall and crown and stem rot.

RELATED SPECIES: The cultivar 'Bristol Fairy' has double clear white flowers, 'Compacta Plena' is dwarf with double white flowers, 'Double Snowflake' has an abundance of double pure white flowers, 'Flamingo' has double soft pink flowers, and 'Viette's Dwarf' is 12–16" tall with double pale pink flowers. Creeping baby's breath (*G. repens*) is an attractive ground-hugging, semievergreen perennial hardy in Zones 4–7. Plants have star-shaped white or pink blooms and bluish-green leaves.

SNEEZEWEED

Helenium autumnale *hel-EEN-ee-uhm aw-tuhm-NAH-lee*

Sneezeweed, also known as Helen's flower, has attractive daisylike flowers.

ZONES: 3–8
SIZE: 5'h × 18"w
TYPE: Perennial
FORM: Upright
TEXTURE: Medium
GROWTH: Fast
LIGHT: Full sun
MOISTURE: High, medium

SOIL: Fertile, moist, well-drained
FEATURES: Flowers, foliage
USES: Border, container, wetlands
FLOWERS: ■ ■

SITING: Common sneezeweed prefers full sun and fertile, well-drained soil with a pH of 5.5–7.0. Plants tolerate wet soils and may be planted in boggy areas. Daisylike yellow or orange flowers appear from late summer into midautumn. Plant in groups in the border, in a mixed container planting, or in a wetlands area. Companions for well-drained soil include 'Autumn Joy' sedum, Russian sage, and bluebeard. Wetlands companions include 'Variegatus' sweet flag and goatsbeard.

CARE: Plant 18" apart in spring or fall. Apply slow-release granular plant food at time of planting or begin using water-soluble plant food 3 weeks after planting in spring. Water deeply whenever the soil is dry. If planting in a wetland, avoid plant foods or chemical pesticides. Deadhead blooms to stimulate reblooming. Leave plants standing in fall until they wither from frost, then cut back.

PROPAGATION: Divide in spring or fall every 3 years to maintain vigor. Seed germination occurs in 8–12 days at 72°F. Transplant 28–35 days after sowing.

PESTS AND DISEASES: Powdery mildew and rust may occur.

RELATED SPECIES: 'Grandicephalum' has large yellow flowers, 'Peregrinum' has mahogany flowers with a yellow border, 'Rubrum' flowers are dark red, and 'Superbum' flowers are wavy and yellow.

Divide sneezeweed in spring or fall. Start by digging the entire clump.

Slice through the clump with a sharp spade and replant pieces that contain healthy roots and shoots.

ANNUAL SUNFLOWER

Helianthus annuus *heel-ee-AN-thus AN-yew-uhs*

Annual sunflower's seeds attract a variety of wildlife to the garden.

ZONES: NA
SIZE: 3–15'h × 2'w
TYPE: Annual
FORM: Upright
TEXTURE: Coarse
GROWTH: Fast
LIGHT: Full sun
MOISTURE: Medium

SOIL: Moderately fertile, moist, well-drained
FEATURES: Flowers, foliage, seed head
USES: Border, naturalizing, container
FLOWERS: ▇ ▇

SITING: Annual sunflower prefers full sun and moderately fertile, well-drained, alkaline soil (pH 6.5–7.5). Large, daisylike yellow flowers with a dark brown or mahogany central disk appear in summer. Hairy, toothed leaves are dark green and noticeable. Flowers attract butterflies and are excellent fresh cut; seeds attract birds. Staking is usually needed. Plant in groups at the back of the informal border, along a fence, or against a shed or barn.

CARE: Plant 24" apart in late spring after the last frost. Apply slow-release granular plant food at time of planting or begin using water-soluble plant food 3 weeks after planting. Water deeply whenever the soil is dry. Apply 3" of vegetative mulch in summer to help retain soil moisture. Leave seed heads for birds to feast on or cut back after blooms fade to promote tidiness. Remove plants just before the first frost or right afterward in cooler climates. Cover bare soil with 3" of vegetative mulch during the winter to protect topsoil.
PROPAGATION: Sprinkle seed over the soil mix and cover lightly. Thoroughly moisten and keep moist, not soggy, until seeds germinate. Germination occurs in 5–10 days at 68–72°F.
PESTS AND DISEASES: Diseases include downy mildew, powdery mildew, rust, and fungal leaf spots. Pests include caterpillars, beetles, weevils, and cutworms.
RELATED SPECIES: The cultivar 'Autumn Beauty' has 6" yellow-, bronze-, and red-tinted flowers, 'Music Box' has 4" flowers in shades of yellow and red with a black disk, 'Russian Giant' reaches 11' tall and has large yellow flowers, and 'Teddy Bear' reaches 3' tall, has double golden-yellow flowers, and with its short stature is ideal for growing in containers.

'Teddy Bear' sunflower produces double flowers on dwarf plants.

Stake tall sunflowers early when the root system is small. Use expandable stakes so the stake can grow as the plant grows.

MANY-FLOWERED SUNFLOWER

Helianthus ×multiflorus *heel-ee-AN-thus mull-tih-FLOR-uhs*

Many-flowered sunflower produces numerous smaller flowers in summer.

ZONES: 3–9
SIZE: 6'h × 3'w
TYPE: Perennial
FORM: Upright
TEXTURE: Coarse
GROWTH: Fast
LIGHT: Full sun
MOISTURE: Medium

SOIL: Moderately fertile, moist, well-drained
FEATURES: Flowers, foliage
USES: Border, container
FLOWERS: ▇

SITING: Many-flowered sunflower prefers full sun and moderately fertile, moist, well-drained, alkaline soil (pH 6.5–7.5). Yellow flowers with a brownish-yellow disk appear from late summer to midautumn. Lance-shaped leaves are dark green and slightly hairy. Plants perform well in the border or in large mixed container plantings. Good companions include 'Purpureum' fennel, Kansas gayfeather, and 'Summer Pastels' yarrow.
CARE: Plant 24–36" apart in spring or fall. Apply slow-release granular plant food at time of planting or begin using water-soluble plant food 3 weeks after planting in spring. Follow label directions for amount and frequency. Cease feeding 6–8 weeks prior to first frost date. Water deeply whenever the soil is dry. Apply 3" of vegetative mulch in summer to help retain soil moisture and as it decomposes it will add organic matter to the soil. Cut back when frost withers the foliage; in milder areas, leave erect for late-season viewing and cut back in early spring.
PROPAGATION: Divide in spring or fall every 3 years to maintain vigor. Dig around the root clump and lift. Use a sharp spade to slice through the root system. Reset portions that contain healthy roots and top shoots, then water and mulch. Discard any pieces that do not contain both healthy root and top shoots.
PESTS AND DISEASES: Diseases include downy mildew, powdery mildew, rust, and fungal leaf spots. Pests include caterpillars, beetles, weevils, and cutworms.
RELATED SPECIES: 'Capenoch Star' has light yellow flowers, 'Flore Pleno' has double golden flowers, 'Loddon Gold' has double vivid golden flowers, and 'Triomphe de Gand' has golden-yellow flowers.

STRAWFLOWER

Helichrysum bracteatum (Xerochrysum) *hebl-ib-KRIS-uhm brak-tee-AH-tuhm (zee-rob-KRIS-um)*

Strawflowers feel papery to the touch.

ZONES: NA
SIZE: 3–5'h × 12"w
TYPE: Annual
FORM: Upright
TEXTURE: Medium
GROWTH: Medium
LIGHT: Full sun
MOISTURE: Medium

SOIL: Moderately fertile, moist, well-drained
FEATURES: Flowers, foliage
USES: Border, container
FLOWERS: ■ ■ ■ □

SITING: Strawflower prefers full sun and moderately fertile, moist, well-drained soil with a pH of 5.5–7.0. Bright papery bracts in yellow, red, pink, and white appear from late spring into autumn. Strawflowers are simple and easy to dry if harvested early in their bloom cycle. Lance-shaped leaves are gray-green. Plant in odd-numbered, multicolored groups in the border or in containers. Good companions include 'Blackie' sweet potato, lemon thyme, and fennel.

CARE: Plant 12" apart in late spring after the last frost. Apply slow-release granular plant food at time of planting or begin using water-soluble plant food 3 weeks

Harvest strawflowers before they open for an elegant dried blossom.

after planting. Water deeply when the soil feels dry 2" below the surface. Plants are drought tolerant but look best when watered during dry spells. Apply 3" of vegetative mulch to help retain soil moisture. Remove plants just before the first frost or right afterward in cooler climates. Cover bare soil with 3" of vegetative mulch during the winter to protect the topsoil.

PROPAGATION: Sprinkle seeds over the soil mix and cover lightly. Thoroughly moisten and keep moist, not soggy, until seeds germinate. Germination occurs in 7–10 days at 70–75°F. Transplant 20–26 days after sowing. After transplanting, reduce temperature to 60–65°F.

PESTS AND DISEASES: Plants are relatively pest free when their cultural preferences are met.

RELATED SPECIES: The cultivar 'Dwarf Hot Bikini' has assorted bright-colored blooms, 'Frosted Sulphur' bears double pale yellow flowers, King Size Series bears double flowers in mixed colors, Monstrosum Series also produces double flowers in a range of colors, and 'Sky Net' bears creamy white flowers with a hint of pink.

SUNFLOWER HELIOPSIS

Heliopsis helianthoides *beel-ee-AHP-sibs beel-ee-an-THOY-deez*

Sunflower heliopsis is also known as false sunflower, heliopsis, or oxeye.

ZONES: 3–9
SIZE: 3–6'h × 24"w
TYPE: Perennial
FORM: Upright
TEXTURE: Medium
GROWTH: Medium
LIGHT: Full sun
MOISTURE: Medium

SOIL: Moderately fertile, moist, well-drained
FEATURES: Flowers, foliage
USES: Container, border
FLOWERS: ■

SITING: Sunflower heliopsis prefers full sun and moderately fertile, moist, well-drained soil with a pH of 5.5–7.0. Daisylike yellow flowers with a yellow central disk appear from midsummer to early autumn. Lance-shaped, toothed medium green leaves reach 6" long. Cultivars of this short-lived perennial have better form and habit than the species, though they may still require staking. Flowers are good for cutting. Plant in odd-numbered groups in the border or use in the center of a mixed container planting. Good companions include purple coneflower, 'Sissinghurst' verbena, and 'Vivid' obedient plant.

CARE: Plant 36" apart in spring or fall. Apply slow-release granular plant food at time of planting or begin using water-soluble plant food 3 weeks after planting in spring. Follow label directions for amount and frequency. Cease feeding 6–8 weeks prior to first frost date. Water deeply whenever the soil is dry. Apply 3" of vegetative mulch in summer to help retain soil moisture and add beneficial organic matter to the soil as it decomposes. Stake tall plants if stems flop. Deadhead blooms to stimulate reblooming. Prune back in fall if frost withers the foliage; in milder areas, leave erect for late-season viewing and prune back in early spring.

PROPAGATION: Propagate by seed, division, or cuttings. Sprinkle seeds over the soil mix and leave uncovered, exposed to light. Thoroughly moisten and keep moist, not soggy, until seeds germinate. Germination occurs in 3–10 days at 70°F. Transplant 11–20 days after sowing. Divide in spring or fall every 2–3 years to maintain vigor. Dig around the root clump and lift. Use a sharp spade to slice through the root system. Reset portions that contain healthy roots and top shoots, then water and mulch. Discard any pieces that do not contain both healthy roots and top shoots.

PESTS AND DISEASES: Aphids are a known pest; diseases include powdery mildew, aster yellows, and rust.

RELATED SPECIES: The cultivar 'Ballerina' reaches 3' tall and has single golden flowers, 'Jupiter' has single orange-yellow flowers, 'Karat' has single yellow flowers, 'Incomparablis' has double yellow-orange flowers, 'Lohfelden' has semidouble orange-golden flowers, 'Sonneschild' has double bright golden flowers, and 'Zinniflora' has double deep golden yellow flowers.

HELIOTROPE

Heliotropium arborescens *heel-ee-oh-TROP-ee-uhm ar-bor-ES-ehns*

Heliotrope has vanilla-scented flowers and leaves with a hint of purple. It is also known as cherry pie plant.

ZONES: NA
SIZE: 4'h × 12–18"w
TYPE: Annual
FORM: Upright
TEXTURE: Medium
GROWTH: Medium
LIGHT: Full sun
MOISTURE: Medium

SOIL: Fertile, moist, well-drained
FEATURES: Flowers, foliage
USES: Border, container
FLOWERS: ■ ■ □

SITING: Heliotrope prefers full sun and fertile, moist, well-drained soil with a pH of 5.5–7.0. Plants are short-lived perennials usually grown as annuals. Clusters of deep violet-blue or lavender-blue flowers, 3–4" across, appear in summer. The fragrant flowers are reminiscent of vanilla and coveted by perfumers. Deep green leaves, often with a touch of purple, have prominent veins. Plant in odd-numbered groups in the border or use freely in containers. Good companions include 'Iceberg' rose, tall cosmos, 'Summerwine', and 'Summer Pastels' yarrows.

CARE: Plant 12" apart in late spring after the last frost. Apply slow-release granular plant food at time of planting or begin using water-soluble plant food 3 weeks after planting. When the soil feels dry 2" below the surface, water deeply. Apply 3" of vegetative mulch to help retain soil moisture and as it decomposes it will add organic matter to the soil. Remove plants just before the first frost or right afterward in cooler climates. Cover bare soil with 3" of vegetative mulch during the winter to preserve the topsoil.

PROPAGATION: Sprinkle seeds over the soil mix and cover lightly. Thoroughly moisten and keep moist, not soggy, until seeds germinate. Germination occurs in 4–8 days at 70–72°F. Transplant in 14–21 days. After transplanting, reduce temperature to 62–65°F.

PESTS AND DISEASES: Plants are vulnerable to whiteflies, aphids, leaf spot, and rust.

RELATED SPECIES: The cultivar 'Alba' bears fragrant white flowers, 'Chatsworth' has fragrant purple flowers, 'Florence Nightingale' had pale mauve-tinted flowers, 'Iowa' has deep purple flowers and blue-tinted leaves, 'Lord Roberts' has light violet-blue flowers, 'Marine' reaches 18" tall and has very deep violet-blue flower clusters up to 6" across, and 'White Lady' reaches 12" tall and bears white flowers with pink-stained buds.

LENTEN ROSE

Helleborus orientalis *HELL-eh-bor-uhs or-ee-ehn-TAL-ihs*

Lenten rose bears unique flowers in midwinter. It is also known as hellebore.

ZONES: 4–9
SIZE: 18"h × 18"w
TYPE: Perennial
FORM: Upright
TEXTURE: Medium
GROWTH: Medium
LIGHT: Full to partial shade

MOISTURE: Medium
SOIL: Fertile, moist, well-drained
FEATURES: Flowers, foliage
USES: Border, woodland
FLOWERS: □ ■ ■

SITING: Lenten rose is the easiest of the hellebores to grow. It prefers full to partial shade with shelter from the afternoon sun. The soil should be fertile, moist, well-drained, and alkaline (pH 6.5–7.5). Thick stems support nodding, saucer-shaped white flowers that are sometimes stained green and pale pink. Flowers appear from midwinter into midspring. Basal leathery leaves are deep green and evergreen. Their bold texture is a pleasant addition to the landscape. Place this low-maintenance perennial in odd-numbered groups at the front of the shade perennial border, or scatter in groups throughout the irrigated woodland garden. Good companions include Japanese painted fern, 'Magnet' snowdrop, 'Mrs. Moon' lungwort, and European wild ginger.

CARE: Plant 18" apart in spring or fall. Apply slow-release granular plant food at

Trim away dead or brown leaves in late winter or early spring.

time of planting or begin using water-soluble plant food 3 weeks after planting in spring. Cease feeding 6–8 weeks prior to first frost date. Water deeply whenever the soil is dry. Apply 3" of vegetative mulch in summer and winter to help retain soil moisture. There is no need to prune back in fall because the foliage is evergreen.

PROPAGATION: Plants self-sow in the landscape. Handle and move newly emerged seedlings carefully.

PESTS AND DISEASES: Plants are relatively pest free when their cultural preferences are met. Leaf spot and black rot may appear occasionally.

RELATED SPECIES: *H. orientalis* ssp. *abchasicus* has pale green flowers stained reddish purple outside, ssp. *guttatus* has creamy white flowers spotted with maroon inside, and Millet Hybrids have larger white, pink, or red flowers. Bearsfoot hellebore (*H. foetidus*) has nodding, bell-shaped green flowers, sometimes with a purple rim, that appear from midwinter to midspring. Lobed, deep green leaves smell putrid when crushed but are handsome additions to the shaded landscape. Christmas rose (*H. niger*) has saucer-shaped white flowers, sometimes stained with pale pink and green, that appear from early winter to early spring.

DAYLILY
Hemerocallis hybrids *hehm-er-oh-KAL-iss*

Daylilies are low-maintenance perennials tolerant of most sites.

ZONES: 3–10
SIZE: 6–48"h ×
12–36"w
TYPE: Perennial
FORM: Irregular
TEXTURE: Medium
GROWTH: Medium
LIGHT: Full sun to
part shade

MOISTURE: Medium
SOIL: Fertile, moist,
well-drained
FEATURES: Flowers,
foliage
USES: Border,
container
FLOWERS: ■ ■ ■ □
■ ■

SITING: Daylilies prefer full sun and fertile, moist, well-drained soil but tolerate drought and low fertility. The preferred pH is 5.5–7.0. Daylily flowers are trumpet shaped and most last only one day. Some daylilies are repeat bloomers and will produce flowers on and off all season. Daylilies are classic low-maintenance perennials for the border. Dwarf selections are best for containers. Daylilies reign supreme when naturalized in large drifts.
CARE: Plant 12–36" apart in spring or fall. Apply slow-release granular plant food at time of planting or begin using water-soluble plant food 3 weeks after planting in spring. Cease feeding 4–6 weeks prior to first frost date. Water deeply whenever the soil is dry. Apply 3" of vegetative mulch in

Deadhead daylilies to keep the plants attractive while the additional blooms open.

summer to help retain soil moisture. Prune back if frost withers foliage; in milder areas leave erect for late-season viewing and prune back in early spring.
PROPAGATION: Divide in spring or fall every 3 years to control growth. Dig around the root clump and lift. Established clumps may be thick and dense and difficult to cut through. A sharp ax may be required. Otherwise, back-to-back garden forks can be used to pry apart the root system. Reset potions that contain healthy roots and top shoots.
PESTS AND DISEASES: Plants are relatively pest free when their cultural preferences are met. Snails and slugs are occasional problems; daylily rust is a new disease.
RELATED SPECIES: There are more than 30,000 named daylily cultivars. The cultivar 'Hyperion' reaches up to 48" tall and has fragrant rich yellow flowers midseason, 'Catherine Woodbury' reaches 2' tall and has antique-toned lavender-pink flowers, 'Eenie Weenie' reaches 10" tall and has yellow flowers with fluted edges, and 'Stella de Oro' reaches 12" tall and has reblooming bright golden yellow flowers.

CORAL BELLS
Heuchera sanguinea *HOO-ker-uh san-GWIHN-ee-uh*

Coral bells are low-maintenance perennials for sun or shade.

ZONES: 3–8
SIZE: 12–24"h ×
12"w
TYPE: Perennial
FORM: Rounded
TEXTURE: Fine
GROWTH: Medium
LIGHT: Full sun to
partial shade

MOISTURE: Medium
SOIL: Fertile, moist,
well-drained
FEATURES: Flowers,
foliage
USES: Border,
container
FLOWERS: ■ □ ■

SITING: Coral bells prefer full sun in the North and partial shade in the South. Plants prefer fertile, moist but well-drained soil with a pH of 5.5–7.0. Tubular red, white, or pink flowers appear on slender stalks in summer. Plant at the front of the shade border or add to mixed container plantings. Companions for shade include astilbes, hostas, and Japanese painted fern.
CARE: Plant 18" apart in spring or fall. After planting, water deeply and add 3" of mulch around, but not touching, the plants. Apply slow-release granular plant food at time of planting or begin using water-soluble plant food 3 weeks after planting in spring. Water deeply whenever the soil is dry. Prune back in fall if frost withers foliage; in milder areas, leave erect for late-season viewing, and prune back in early spring.
PROPAGATION: The species may be propagated by seed, but all desirable cultivars need to be vegetatively propagated. Divide in spring or fall every 3 years to maintain vigor.
PESTS AND DISEASES: Powdery mildew, rust, and leaf spots are occasional pests.

RELATED SPECIES: The cultivar 'Apple Blossom' bears pale pink flowers, 'Brandon Pink' has coral-pink flowers, 'Cherry Splash' has green and gold leaf marbling, 'Firesprite' has red flowers, 'Northern Fire' has-silver marbled leaves and bright red flowers, and 'Pearl Drops' bears arching stems of white flowers stained pink. Purple-leaf coral bells (*H. macrantha × H. americana*) is grown primarily for its colorful foliage. 'Palace Purple' has dark purple leaves. 'Chocolate Ruffles' is deep maroon, and 'Pewter Veil' is silvery.

Trim away dead leaves from heuchera in late fall or spring.

***Heuchera americana* has marbled young foliage with copper tints.**

HOSTA
Hosta hybrids *HAH-stub*

Hostas offer mounds of delightful shapes and textures for the shade.

ZONES: 3–8
SIZE: 2–48"h ×
2–48"w
TYPE: Perennial
FORM: Rounded
TEXTURE: Medium
GROWTH: Medium
LIGHT: Part to full
shade

MOISTURE: Medium
SOIL: Fertile, moist,
well-drained
FEATURES: Foliage,
flowers
USES: Border,
ground cover,
container
FLOWERS: ☐ ■ ■

SITING: Hosta prefers partial or full shade and fertile, moist but well-drained soil with a pH of 5.5–7.0. Mounds of heart-shaped, oval, or lance-shaped leaves in green, blue, yellow, and silver hues are the star attraction. Stalks of bell- or spider-shaped blue, lavender, or white flowers appear in summer. Interesting and low maintenance, hostas are elite members of the classic perennial shade border. Plant in odd-numbered groups in the border, in the woodland garden, in containers, or at the base of irrigated woody plants.

CARE: Plant 18–36" apart in spring or fall. Apply slow-release granular plant food at time of planting or begin using water soluble plant food 3 weeks after planting in spring. Follow label directions for amount and frequency. Cease feeding 6–8 weeks prior to first frost date. When the soil feels dry 2" below the surface, water deeply. Apply 3" of vegetative mulch in summer and winter to help retain soil moisture and as it decomposes it will add organic matter to the soil. Some hosta aficionados snip off developing flowers, feeling that they detract from the foliage. Cut the plant back in fall once frost withers the foliage.

PROPAGATION: Many hostas do not require division to remain vigorous and are long lived. They may be divided in spring or fall. Dig around the root clump and lift. Use a sharp spade to slice through the root system. Reset portions that contain healthy roots and top shoots, then water and mulch. Discard any pieces that do not contain both healthy roots and top shoots.

PESTS AND DISEASES: Plants are relatively pest free when their cultural preferences are met. Slugs and snails are notorious pests.
RELATED SPECIES: Fortune's hosta (*H. fortunei*) reaches 24" high and wide and has mounds of heart-shaped green to gray-green leaves. Lance leaf hosta (*H. lancifolia*) reaches 24" high and 18" wide and has pointed leaves that add drama to the edge of the border. Fragrant hosta (*H. plantaginea*) reaches 30" high and 24" wide and has large, heart-shaped yellowish-green leaves and sweetly fragrant white flowers in late summer. Thousands of other hosta varieties are available to suit most any shade gardener's preferences.

Divide hosta by lifting the entire plant from its growing bed.

Plunge a sharp spade through the crown and root system.

Select pieces with healthy roots and shoots to reset in the garden.

SIEBOLD HOSTA

Hosta sieboldiana HAH-stuh sib-bold-ee-AN-uh

Siebold hosta is a large excellent low-maintenance perennial for shade with heart-shaped blue-green or blue-gray leaves.

ZONES: 3–8
SIZE: 36"h × 4'w
TYPE: Perennial
FORM: Rounded
TEXTURE: Medium
GROWTH: Medium
LIGHT: Part to full shade

MOISTURE: Medium
SOIL: Fertile, moist, well-drained
FEATURES: Foliage
USES: Border, woodland, container
FLOWERS: ▇

SITING: Siebold hosta prefers partial to full shade and fertile, moist but well-drained soil with a pH of 5.5–7.0. Leaves reach 10–20" long and are heart-shaped or rounded and an appealing blue-green to blue-gray. In early summer bell-shaped blooms appear first as pale lavender, then fade to white. Good companions include heart-leaf brunnera, 'Deutschland' astilbe, bugbane, 'Mrs. Moon' Bethlehem sage, and European wild ginger.

CARE: Plant 36" apart in spring or fall. Apply slow-release granular fertilizer at time of planting or begin using water-

Plant Siebold hosta 36" apart in triangular formation for best effect.

soluble fertilizer 3 weeks after planting in spring. Cease fertilizing 6–8 weeks prior to first frost date. Water deeply whenever the soil is dry. Apply 3" of vegetative mulch in summer and winter to help retain soil moisture. Some hosta aficionados snip off developing flowers, feeling they detract from the foliage. Cut back in fall once frost withers the foliage.

PROPAGATION: Siebold hosta does not need dividing to maintain vigor. Should more plants be desired, division is easy. Dig around the root clump and lift. Use a sharp spade to slice through the root system. Reset portions that contain healthy roots and top shoots, then water and mulch. Discard any pieces that do not contain both healthy roots and top shoots.

PESTS AND DISEASES: Plants are relatively pest free when their cultural preferences are met. Slugs and snails are common pests. Control with traps or baits.

RELATED SPECIES: 'Aurea' has golden yellow leaves, var. *elegans* has puckered, heart-shaped bluish leaves. *H.* 'Frances Williams' has puckered, heart-shaped bluish-green leaves with an irregular golden edge.

WAVY HOSTA

Hosta undulata HAH-stuh uhn-dyew-LAH-tuh

Wavy hosta has twisted or wavy leaves with white splashes.

ZONES: 3–8
SIZE: 12–18"h × 18"w
TYPE: Perennial
FORM: Rounded
TEXTURE: Medium
GROWTH: Medium
LIGHT: Full to part shade

MOISTURE: Medium
SOIL: Fertile, moist, well-drained
FEATURES: Foliage, flowers
USES: Border, container
FLOWERS: ▇

SITING: Wavy hosta prefers partial to full shade and fertile, moist but well-drained soil with a pH of 5.5–7.0. Twisted or wavy leaves are 6" long and bright green with splashes of bright white in the center or margins. Light lilac flowers appear in midsummer. Plants withstand sun better than most hostas. Place in the border or use in shady container plantings. Good companions include goatsbeard, bugbane, sweet woodruff, lobelia Cascade Series.

CARE: Plant 36" apart in spring or fall. Apply slow-release granular plant food at time of planting or begin using water-soluble plant food 3 weeks after planting in spring. Cease feeding 6–8 weeks prior to first frost date. Water deeply whenever the soil is dry. Apply 3" of vegetative mulch in summer and winter to help retain soil moisture. Prune back in fall once frost withers the foliage.

PROPAGATION: Wavy hosta does not need dividing to maintain vigor. Should more plants be desired, division is easy.

PESTS AND DISEASES: Plants are relatively pest free when their cultural preferences are met. Slugs and snails are common pests. Control with traps or bait.

RELATED SPECIES: *H. u.* var. *albomarginata* has leaves with cream margins, and blue hosta (*H. ventricosa*) has bluegreen leaves.

1 Hosta foliage naturally turns yellow in fall.

2 Cut back hosta after frost disfigures foliage.

3 Pruned plants are ready for winter mulch.

CHAMELEON PLANT

Houttuynia cordata *boo-TOO-nee-uh kor-DAH-tuh*

Chameleon plant, also known as houttuynia, has colorful foliage and spreads rapidly.

ZONES: (5)6–11
SIZE: 6–12"h × 18"w
TYPE: Perennial
FORM: Spreading
TEXTURE: Medium
GROWTH: Fast
LIGHT: Full sun to part shade

MOISTURE: Wet
SOIL: Moderately fertile, moist
FEATURES: Foliage, flowers
USES: Ground cover, wetland, container
FLOWERS: □

SITING: Chameleon plant prefers full sun to partial shade and moist soil with a pH of 5.5–7.0. Plants have colorful foliage with splashes of blue-green, gray-green, and red. Greenish yellow flowers emerge in summer and turn white with age. Plants are invasive and should be used only where they can be managed and removed when necessary. Containers are ideal for constraining plants.

CARE: Plant 18–24" apart in spring or fall. Plants quickly spread to fill in gaps and make a solid ground cover. Chameleon plant requires constant moisture for best growth. On dry sites, the foliage will turn brown and tattered unless plants are given supplemental watering. If planting in a wetland, avoid fertilizers and chemical pesticides to prevent chemicals from leaching into water bodies. Water deeply when the soil is dry. In wetlands, apply 3" of vegetative mulch in winter to help protect roots. In containers, expect to see the roots emerge from the drainage holes.

PROPAGATION: Divide in spring. Dig around the root clump and lift. Use a sharp spade to slice through the root system. Reset portions that contain healthy roots and top shoots, then water and mulch. Discard any pieces that do not contain both healthy roots and top shoots.

PESTS AND DISEASES: Slugs and snails are common pests.

RELATED SPECIES: The cultivar 'Chameleon' is less invasive than the species and has leaves splashed with green, pale yellow, and red.

HYACINTH

Hyacinthus orientalis *hi-uh-SIHN-thus or-ee-ehn-TAL-is*

Hyacinth bulbs produce lovely fragrant bell-shaped flowers in spring.

ZONES: 4–8
SIZE: 8–12"h × 6"w
TYPE: Perennial
FORM: Upright
TEXTURE: Medium
GROWTH: Slow
LIGHT: Full sun

MOISTURE: Medium
SOIL: Moderately fertile, well-drained
FEATURES: Flowers
USES: Border, container, massing
FLOWERS: ■ ■ □ □

SITING: Hyacinth prefers full sun and moderately fertile, well-drained soil with a pH of 5.5–7.0. Bell-shaped, intensely fragrant blue, violet, pink, or white flowers appear in spring. Strap-shaped, glossy leaves are deep green. Plant in drifts in the border, mass in beds around irrigated deciduous trees, or use in container plantings. The fragrance is unmistakable and usually greatly admired.

CARE: Plant bulbs outdoors 4" deep and 4–6" apart in fall. Apply slow-release granular plant food at time of planting. Follow label directions for amount and frequency. Water deeply whenever the soil is dry. Apply 3" of organic mulch in summer and winter to help retain soil moisture and add organic matter to the soil as it decomposes.

PROPAGATION: Unearth the bulbs in summer, when dormant, and separate offsets that form around each bulb. Replant healthy, firm bulbs 4–6" apart in moderately fertile, well-drained soil, then water and mulch.

PESTS AND DISEASES: Problems include aphids, botrytis, and bulb rot. Site in well-drained soil and keep dry in summer.

1 To enjoy hyacinth blooms indoors, fill a bulb-forcing jar with water.

2 Place the bulb so that just the base is immersed in the water.

3 Maintain the water level to keep the bulb base immersed and watch the roots, shoots, and flowers grow.

AARON'S BEARD

Hypericum calycinum hi-PEER-ih-kuhm kal-ih-KYN-uhm

Aaron's beard spreads rapidly. It is also known as St. Johnswort.

ZONES: 4–9
SIZE: 24"h × 36"w
TYPE: Woody perennial
FORM: Spreading
TEXTURE: Medium
GROWTH: Fast
LIGHT: Full to part shade

MOISTURE: Medium
SOIL: Moderately fertile, moist, well-drained
FEATURES: Flowers, foliage
USES: Ground cover
FLOWERS: ■

SITING: Aaron's beard prefers partial to full shade and moderately fertile, moist, well-drained soil with a pH of 5.5–7.0. Bright yellow flowers with pronounced stamens appear from midsummer to midautumn. Evergreen leaves are dark green on top and lighter below. Plants are invasive and should be placed on banks, along fence lines, and other areas where they can ramble.

CARE: Plant 36" apart in spring or fall. Apply slow-release granular plant food at time of planting. Water deeply when the soil is dry. Apply 3" of vegetative mulch in summer and winter to help retain soil moisture and as it decomposes it will add organic matter to the soil. Cut plants back to the ground in spring to remove winter-tattered shoots and leaves. In the South plants often succumb to heat and drop their leaves in summer.

PROPAGATION: Divide in spring. Dig around the root clump and lift. Use a sharp spade to slice through the root system. Reset portions that contain healthy roots and top shoots, then water and mulch. Discard any pieces that do not contain both healthy roots and top shoots.
PESTS AND DISEASES: Problems include scale, rust, and leaf spots.
RELATED SPECIES: Some species such as tutsan (*H. androsaemum*), have become commonly used in cut flower arrangements for their ornamental seed capsules that change from greenish yellow to red and eventually black. Golden cup St. Johnswort (*H. patulum*) is an evergreen shrub that bears clusters of 2" yellow flowers in summer. 'Hidcote' and 'Sungold' are popular cultivars. *H. ×moseranum* is a hybrid of Aaron's beard and golden cup St. Johnswort. It has 3" yellow blooms.

EVERGREEN CANDYTUFT

Iberis sempervirens ih-BEER-ihs sehm-purr-VY-renz

Evergreen candytuft produces mounds of white flowers in spring.

ZONES: 3–9
SIZE: 12"h × 18"w
TYPE: Perennial
FORM: Rounded
TEXTURE: Medium
GROWTH: Medium
LIGHT: Full sun
MOISTURE: Medium

SOIL: Moderately fertile, well-drained
FEATURES: Flowers, foliage
USES: Border, container
FLOWERS: □

SITING: Evergreen candytuft prefers full sun and moderately fertile, well-drained alkaline soil (pH of 6.5–7.5). Tiny white flowers appear in late spring and early summer and cover the top of the plant. Deep green leaves, evergreen and 1" long, create appeal long after the flowers have faded. The mound-shaped habit is also pleasing. Candytuft is a low-maintenance top-performing perennial when its cultural preferences are met. Plant in odd-numbered groups at the front of the border or add to a container planting and allow it to spill over the sides. Good companions include sea pink, 'Strawberry Vanilla Latte' lily, 'Strawberry Shortcake' lily, 'Royal Wedding' Oriental poppy, 'Beauty of Livermere' Oriental poppy, germander, and 'Iceberg' rose.

CARE: Plant 18" apart in spring or fall. Apply slow-release granular plant food at time of planting. Cease feeding 6–8 weeks prior to first frost date. When the soil feels dry 2" below the surface, water deeply. Apply 3" of vegetative mulch in summer and winter to help retain soil moisture and add organic matter to the soil as it decomposes. Shear back one-third of the plant after blooming to maintain the compact, rounded habit. Plants are evergreen and do not need to be cut back in fall unless foliage is disfigured by frost.

PROPAGATION: Seed produces variable flower color and size. Cultivars are propagated by cuttings taken after flowering. Sprinkle seeds over the soil mix and leave exposed to light; do not cover. Thoroughly moisten and keep moist, not soggy, until seeds germinate. Germination occurs in 14–22 days at 60–65°F. Transplant 14–21 days after sowing. Reduce the temperature to 50°F after transplanting the seedlings.
PESTS AND DISEASES: Plants are relatively pest free when their cultural preferences are met.
RELATED SPECIES: The cultivars 'Autumn Beauty' and 'Autumn Snow' bear white flowers in spring and fall, 'Climax' has spoon-shaped leaves, 'Compacta' and 'Schneeflocke' are compact and dense, and 'Weisser Zwerg' is also compact with short, linear leaves.

Shear evergreen candytuft back after bloom is complete to stimulate compact, dense foliar growth.

NEW GUINEA IMPATIENS
Impatiens hawkeri *ihm-PAY-shenz HAW-ker-eye*

New Guinea impatiens has solid or variegated foliage and an assortment of flower colors to choose from.

ZONES: NA
SIZE: 18–36"h × 18"w
TYPE: Annual
FORM: Rounded
TEXTURE: Medium
GROWTH: Slow
LIGHT: Partial shade to full sun
MOISTURE: Medium
SOIL: Fertile, moist, well-drained
FEATURES: Flowers, foliage
USES: Border, container
FLOWERS: ■ ■ ■ ■ □

SITING: New Guinea impatiens prefers partial shade, but can be grown in full sun with adequate moisture. Provide fertile, moist, well-drained soil with a pH of 5.5–7.0. Vibrant shades of orange, salmon, rose, pink, scarlet, lavender, or white flowers appear in summer and are complemented by bronze-and-yellow variegated or solid bronze foliage. Plants are grown as annuals in most areas. New Guinea impatiens is well suited as a bedding plant, in containers, and planted in odd-numbered groups in the border. Good companions include hellebore, 'Palace Purple' heuchera, and 'Husker Red' beardtongue.

CARE: Plant 12–18" apart in late spring. Apply slow-release granular plant food at time of planting or begin using water-soluble plant food 3 weeks after planting in spring. Water deeply when the soil is dry. Apply 2–3" of organic mulch in summer to help retain soil moisture and as it decomposes it will add organic matter to the soil. Remove plants just before the first frost or right afterward.

PROPAGATION: Take cuttings in summer. Cut pieces that contain two healthy leaves and at least three nodes. Insert exposed nodes into moist soil mix, keeping leaves above the soil level. Supply bottom heat and keep the soil mix and cuttings moist, not soggy, until root and top shoot growth is evident, then transplant.

PESTS AND DISEASES: Diseases include impatiens necrotic spot virus, fungal leaf spots, and Verticillium wilt.

RELATED SPECIES: Cultivars with single flowers include 'Big Top', with white flowers, 'Showboat', with pinkish-purple flowers, and 'Star Dancer', with lavender flowers and striped leaves. Cultivars with double flowers include 'Apple Blossom', with pink flowers and 'Damask Rose', with deep red flowers.

IMPATIENS
Impatiens walleriana *ihm-PAY-shenz wall-air-ee-AN-uh*

Impatiens is often used as a bedding plant for shady spaces. It is also known as busy Lizzie or touch-me-not.

ZONES: NA
SIZE: 6–24"h × 12–24"w
TYPE: Annual
FORM: Irregular
TEXTURE: Fine
GROWTH: Medium
LIGHT: Part to full shade
MOISTURE: Medium
SOIL: Fertile, moist, well-drained
FEATURES: Flowers, foliage
USES: Bedding, container
FLOWERS: □ ■ ■ ■ ■ ■

SITING: Impatiens prefers partial shade and fertile, well-drained soil with a pH of 5.5–7.0. Orange, pink, red, purple, and white flowers appear in summer. Foliage is light to bright green and sometimes has red-stained leaves and stems. Plants are usually grown as annuals. They are well suited as bedding plants for shade, and in containers. Good container companions include heart-leaf bergenia, 'Husker Red' beardtongue, and 'Carpet of Snow' sweet alyssum.

CARE: Plant 12–24" apart in late spring. Apply slow-release granular plant food at time of planting or begin using water-soluble plant food 3 weeks after planting in spring. Water deeply when the soil is dry. Apply 3" of vegetative mulch in summer to help retain soil moisture and add organic matter to the soil as it decomposes. Remove plants either just before the first frost or right afterward.

PROPAGATION: Sprinkle seeds over the soil mix and cover lightly. Thoroughly moisten and keep moist, not soggy, until seeds germinate. Germination occurs in 10–20 days at 75–78°F. Transplant 14–21 days after sowing. Reduce the temperature to 60°F after transplanting.

PESTS AND DISEASES: Diseases include impatiens necrotic spot virus, fungal leaf spots, and verticillium wilt.

RELATED SPECIES: The cultivar 'Starbright' has a white star in the center of pink, red, violet, and orange flowers, Swirl Series has hues of pink and orange flowers rimmed with deep pink, and Super Elfin Series reaches only 10" tall and come in pastels and traditional tones.

A container of impatiens is a great way to brighten up a shady garden.

If roots are pot-bound, slice vertically through them and fan root ends out.

SWEET POTATO

Ipomoea batatas *ih-puh-MAY-ah bah-TAH-tuhs*

Ornamental sweet potato adds striking color to a container garden. 'Tricolor' has green and white leaves tinged in pink.

ZONES: 9–11
SIZE: 1'h × 5–15'w
TYPE: Perennial
FORM: Upright
TEXTURE: Coarse
GROWTH: Fast
LIGHT: Full sun
MOISTURE: Medium

SOIL: Moderately fertile, well-drained
FEATURES: Leaves, stems
USES: Container, arbor
FLOWERS: ■

SITING: Sweet potato vine prefers full sun, shelter from drying winds, and moderately fertile, well-drained soil with a pH of 5.5–7.0. Leaves are lobed, heart-shaped, or entire. Choice cultivars for the ornamental landscape include chartreuse and purplish-black leaf and stem colors. Trumpet-shaped lavender flowers appear in summer. Sweet potato vine adds texture and color to container plantings. Container companions for the chartreuse-colored vine include purple fountain grass, 'Crimson Butterflies' gaura, and 'Patty's Plum' Oriental poppy. Container companions for the purple-black vine include 'Karl Foerster' feather reed grass, gulf muhly, and 'Evelyn' beardtongue.

CARE: Plant 12–24" apart in late spring. Apply slow-release plant food, such as Miracle-Gro Shake 'n Feed All Purpose, at the time of planting or begin using water-soluble plant food, such as Miracle-Gro Water Soluble All Purpose, 3 weeks after planting in spring. Follow label directions for amount and frequency. Water deeply when the soil is dry. Apply 3" of vegetative mulch in summer to help retain soil moisture and as it decomposes it will add organic matter to the soil. Remove plants just before the first frost or right afterward. Cover bare soil with 3" of vegetative mulch during the winter to preserve the topsoil.

PROPAGATION: Take cuttings in summer. Cut pieces that contain two healthy leaves and at least three nodes. Insert exposed nodes into moist soil mix, keeping leaves above the soil level. Cover trays with plastic to increase humidity. Supply bottom heat and keep the soil mix and cuttings moist, not soggy, until root and top shoot growth is evident, then transplant.

PESTS AND DISEASES: Diseases include rust, fungal leaf spots, stem rot, and wilt.

RELATED SPECIES: The cultivar 'Blackie' has lobed purplish-black leaves. 'Black Heart' and 'Margarita' are other popular cultivars.

MORNING GLORY

Ipomoea tricolor *ih-puh-MAY-ah TRY-kuh-ler*

Morning glory blossoms are sky blue and the vines climb quickly.

ZONES: NA
SIZE: 6–12'h × 5'w
TYPE: Annual
FORM: Upright
TEXTURE: Medium
GROWTH: Fast
LIGHT: Full sun
MOISTURE: Medium

SOIL: Moderately fertile, well-drained
FEATURES: Flowers, foliage
USES: Container, arbor
FLOWERS: ■ ■ ■

SITING: Morning glory vine prefers full sun and fertile, well-drained soil with a pH of 5.5–7.0. Funnel-shaped azure blue flowers appear in summer. Heart-shaped leaves and fast-twining stems are bright medium green. Grow the vine on an arbor or a trellis or allow it to spill from a container. Good container companions include 'Bravado' purple coneflower, 'Whirling Butterflies' gaura, 'Casa Blanca' lily, and 'Carpet of Snow' alyssum.

CARE: Plant 12–24" apart in late spring where plants will receive at least 6 hours of unobstructed sunlight. Apply slow-release granular plant food at time of planting. Follow label directions for amount and frequency. (Excessive nitrogen fertilizers may result in vigorous vines but limited flowering.) Water deeply when the soil is dry. Apply 3" of vegetative mulch in summer to help retain soil moisture and as it decomposes it will add organic matter to the soil. Remove plants just before the first frost or right afterward. Cover bare soil with 3" of vegetative mulch during winter to preserve the topsoil.

PROPAGATION: Seed morning glory directly in place in the garden.

PESTS AND DISEASES: Diseases include rust, fungal leaf spots, stem rot, and wilt.

RELATED SPECIES: The cultivar 'Crimson Rambler' has red flowers with white throat, 'Heavenly Blue Improved' has sky blue flowers with a pale center, 'Flying Saucers' has marbled blue and white flowers, and 'Wedding Bells' has rosy blue flowers.

1 Soak seeds overnight before sowing to speed germination.

2 Plant seeds directly in the landscape as they resent transplanting. Chain link fencing or a trellis provide good support.

BEARDED IRIS
Iris bearded hybrids *EYE-ribs*

Bearded iris is a traditional favorite for the perennial border. It blooms in a rainbow of colors and bicolors.

ZONES: 3–9
SIZE: 6–36"h × 12–24"w
TYPE: Perennial
FORM: Upright
TEXTURE: Medium
GROWTH: Medium
LIGHT: Full sun to partial shade

MOISTURE: Medium
SOIL: Fertile, well-drained
FEATURES: Flowers, foliage
USES: Border
FLOWERS: ☐ ▦ ▦ ▦
▦ ▦ ▫

SITING: Bearded iris prefers full sun, or light afternoon shade in warmer climates, and fertile, well-drained soil with a pH of 5.5–7.0. Flower colors include shades of blue, purple, red, white, yellow, orange, and pink. Flowers have flashy standard (upright) petals, fall (drooping) petals, and beards. Beards are colored or white hairs in the center of the fall petals. Flowers appear in early spring to early summer. Shallow-rooted thick rhizomes produce fans of sword-shaped leaves. Bearded iris are classified into groups according to their size and bloom time. Groups—in ascending order of height and bloom time—include miniature dwarf bearded, standard dwarf bearded, intermediate bearded, miniature tall bearded, border bearded, and tall bearded. Plant in odd-numbered groups in the border or create an all-iris bed for the best effect. Fresh-cut flowers are spectacular and usually quite fragrant. Good companions include false indigo, delphinium, and 'Butterfly Blue' or 'Pink Mist' pincushion flower.

CARE: Plant 12–24" apart, depending on the cultivar, in fall or early spring. Plant rhizomes horizontally 1" deep, with tops exposed. Apply slow-release, low-nitrogen granular plant food at time of planting and each spring. Too much nitrogen will produce lush leaves but reduce flowering.

Louisiana iris performs well in high heat.

Add bonemeal to the soil at planting time. Water deeply when the soil is dry. Add 3" of vegetative mulch outside of the root zone; avoid placing it over the rhizomes.

PROPAGATION: Iris should be divided due to overcrowding or reduced vigor, usually every 3–4 years. Divide in mid- to late summer. Dig around the rhizomes and lift. Use a sharp spade or pruners to cut through the root system. Cut back foliage to 6". Reset portions that contain healthy roots and top shoots, then water and mulch. Discard pieces that are hollow, woody, soft, and do not contain both healthy roots and top shoots. Plants often have reduced flowering the first season after division but flower freely the second season.

PESTS AND DISEASES: Pests include iris borer, iris weevil, thrips, slugs, and snails. Diseases include rhizome rot, crown rot, and leaf spot.

RELATED SPECIES: Dwarf bearded iris (*I. pumila*) reaches 4–6" high, has gray-green leaves, and bears purple, blue, or yellow flowers in spring. Japanese iris (*I. ensata*) reaches 36" high and bears flowers with reduced standards in shades of purple and reddish purple in early summer; leaves have a pronounced midrib. Louisiana iris (*I. fulva*) reaches 18–36" high and bears nonbearded bright red to rust and occasionally yellow flowers in early summer. Louisiana iris prefers moist soil and hot summers. It may spread fast, but is suited for southern heat.

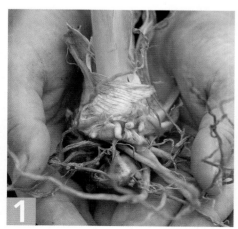

1 Divide and plant bare-root rhizomes of iris in late summer.

2 Fan the roots and cover with 1" of soil, but leave the tops of rhizomes exposed.

3 Apply a thin layer of organic mulch and water thoroughly.

SIBERIAN IRIS

Iris sibirica EYE-rihs si-BEER-ih-kuh

Siberian iris is a low-maintenance perennial with elegant blooms and grasslike foliage.

ZONES: 3–9
SIZE: 18–48"h × 24"w
TYPE: Perennial
FORM: Upright
TEXTURE: Medium
GROWTH: Fast
LIGHT: Full sun to part shade

MOISTURE: Moist
SOIL: Moderately fertile, well-drained
FEATURES: Flowers, foliage
USES: Border, container
FLOWERS: ■■□

SITING: Siberian iris prefers full sun and moderately fertile, well-drained soil with a pH of 5.5–7.0. Elegant beardless flowers, often with blue-hued petals, are held well above the foliage in early summer. Fall petals are dark-veined and marked with white or gold. Leaves are narrow and grasslike. This low-maintenance perennial is trouble-free, long-lived, and attractive throughout the growing season. Plant in odd-numbered groups in the middle or back of the perennial border, or in containers. Good companions include false indigo and 'Biokovo' cranesbill.

CARE: Plant 18–24" apart in fall or early spring. Apply slow-release granular plant food at time of planting. When the soil feels dry 2" below the surface, water deeply. Apply 3" of vegetative mulch in summer and winter to reduce weed seed germination, retain soil moisture, and keep soil temperatures stable. Trim plants to the ground in late fall after frost disfigures the foliage.

PROPAGATION: In moderately fertile soil plants may be divided every 3 years to maintain vigor. In rich soils division is needed sooner to maintain vigor and control growth. Dig around the root clump and lift. Use a sharp spade to slice through the root system. The larger the portion, the larger the resulting plant during the first year. Smaller pieces may take 2–3 years to reach mature size and bloom. Reset portions that contain healthy roots and top shoots. Discard any pieces that do not contain both healthy roots and top shoots. Water deeply and apply 3" of vegetative mulch around the plants.

PESTS AND DISEASES: Plants are relatively pest-free when cultural requirements (sun, soil, moisture, planting depth) are met.

RELATED SPECIES: *I. sibirica* 'Alba' bears white flowers, 'Ann Dasch' has dark blue flowers with yellow on the fall, 'Butter and Sugar' bears white-and-yellow flowers, 'Caesar's Brother' has deep purple flowers, 'Ego' bears brilliant blue flowers, 'Ewen' has burgundy blooms, 'Papillon' bears light blue flowers, and 'Wisley White' has white flowers with a yellow splash on the falls. Sweet iris (*I. pallida*) reaches 2–4' high and bears soft blue flowers with a yellow beard in early summer. Leaves are gray-green and sometimes evergreen. The rhizomes are powdered or dried in pea-size chunks to use as a fixative (holds scents for a long time) for potpourri. Yellow flag iris (*I. pseudacorus*) prefers moist, even wet soils. Flowers are yellow with a deeper yellow splash on each fall. Leaves are gray-green. Reticulated iris (*I. reticulata*) has a bulb instead of rhizomes, reaches 4–6" high, and produces fragrant purple-and-gold blooms in late winter or early spring. Dutch iris (*I. xiphium* hybrids) bear blue or violet or occasionally white, yellow, or mauve flowers in spring and early summer. They are hardy to Zone 5.

Siberian iris foliage is attractive throughout the growing season.

Sweet iris, with variegated foliage, is an old-fashioned but under-used iris.

Yellow flag iris performs well in moist soils or standing water.

COMMON TORCH LILY

Kniphofia uvaria nye-FO-fee-uh oo-VAR-ee-uh

Common torch lily blooms add drama to the landscape. It is also known as red hot poker.

ZONES: 5–9
SIZE: 4'h × 4'w
TYPE: Perennial
FORM: Irregular
TEXTURE: Coarse
GROWTH: Medium
LIGHT: Full sun to part shade

MOISTURE: Medium
SOIL: Fertile, moist, well-drained
FEATURES: Flowers, foliage
USES: Border, container
FLOWERS: ■ ■ ▢

SITING: Torch lily prefers full sun and fertile, moist, well-drained soil with a pH of 5.5–7.0. In warm climates provide shelter from afternoon sun. Spectacular flowers display red buds opening to orange and fading to yellow in summer. Flowers attract bees and butterflies and are excellent fresh cut. Good companions include 'Moonbeam' threadleaf coreopsis, 'Gracillimus' maiden grass, and 'Sonnenwende' evening primrose.

CARE: Plant 24–36" apart in late spring. Apply slow-release granular plant food at time of planting. When the soil feels dry 2" below the surface, water deeply. Deadhead spent blooms to encourage

Remove faded flower stalks of common torch lily to keep the plants attractive.

reblooming. Leave plants erect for winter interest, then cut back in early spring.

PROPAGATION: Divide in spring or early summer. Plants may take two seasons to recover their normal bloom cycle after division. Sprinkle seeds over the soil mix and leave exposed to light; do not cover. Thoroughly moisten and keep moist, not soggy, until seeds germinate. Germination occurs in 20–27 days at 65–75°F. Transplant 30–45 days after sowing. Reduce the temperature to 60°F after transplanting. Seed-grown plants will take three seasons to fully flower.

PESTS AND DISEASES: Plants are relatively pest free when cultural requirements (sun, soil, moisture, planting depth) are met. Wet soil often results in crown rot.

RELATED SPECIES: The cultivar 'Bressingham Comet' is dwarf-bearing and has orange flowers with red tips, 'Bressingham Torch' bears bright orange flowers intermittently throughout the summer and early autumn, 'Rosea Superba' reaches 36" high and bears rose red flowers that turn white, and 'White Fairy' reaches 3' high and bears white flowers in early summer.

SPOTTED DEADNETTLE

Lamium maculatum LAM-ee-uhm mahk-yew-LAT-uhm

Spotted deadnettle cultivars have green-and-white splashed leaves that brighten shady spaces.

ZONES: 4–8
SIZE: 8"h × 3'w
TYPE: Perennial
FORM: Spreading
TEXTURE: Medium
GROWTH: Fast
LIGHT: Full to part shade

MOISTURE: Medium
SOIL: Moderately fertile, moist, well-drained
FEATURES: Flowers, foliage
USES: Ground cover, container
FLOWERS: ■ ▢

SITING: Spotted deadnettle cultivars prefer full or partial shade and moderately fertile, evenly moist, well-drained soil with a pH of 5.5–7.0. Cultivars, rather than the invasive species, are best for landscape use. Whorls of vibrant pink flowers appear in late spring and early summer. Place at the feet of woody plants in an irrigated bed, as a ground cover for a partially shaded slope, or in a shady container planting. Good companions include 'Elegans' Siebold hosta, heart-leaf brunnera, 'Mrs. Moon' Bethlehem sage, and 'Sissinghurst White' lungwort.

In hot climates shear back lamium to promote compact growth.

CARE: Plant 12–36" apart in spring or fall. The closer the spacing the faster the ground will be covered. Apply slow-release granular plant food at time of planting or begin using water-soluble plant food 3 weeks after planting in spring. When the soil feels dry 2" below the surface, water deeply. In the South shear plants after first bloom to promote compact growth.

PROPAGATION: Divide cultivars in spring. Dig around the root clump and lift. Use a sharp spade to slice through the root system. Reset portions that contain healthy roots and top shoots.

PESTS AND DISEASES: Slugs and snails are pests. Diseases include powdery mildew, downy mildew, and leaf spots. Well-drained soil is essential. Standing water as well as prolonged dry soil may cause death of spotted deadnettle.

RELATED SPECIES: The cultivar 'Beacon Silver' has pale pink flowers and silver leaves edged in green, heat-tolerant 'White Nancy' has white flowers and silver leaves edged in green, 'Aureum' has pink flowers and gold leaves stained white, and 'Beedham's White' has white flowers and chartreuse leaves.

LANTANA

Lantana camara *lahn-TAHN-uh KAHM-er-uh*

Lantana offers vibrant nonstop summer color for hot, dry places.

ZONES: 8–10
SIZE: 3–6'h × 3–6'w
TYPE: Woody shrub
FORM: Spreading
TEXTURE: Medium
GROWTH: Fast
LIGHT: Full sun
MOISTURE: Medium to dry

SOIL: Moderately fertile, well-drained
FEATURES: Flowers, foliage
USES: Ground cover, container, border
FLOWERS: ■ ■ ■ ■ □

SITING: Lantana prefers full sun and moderately fertile, well-drained soil with a pH of 5.5–7.5. Plants are woody shrubs commonly grown as annuals; they are drought tolerant once established. Plants

and flowers are toxic, so keep them away from children. Flowers appear from late spring to late autumn in colors including shades of cream, yellow, red, orange, and pink. Fragrant foliage is wrinkled, toothed, and deep green. Stems may be slightly prickly. Flowers attract butterflies and fruits attract birds. Use as a ground cover for a sunny bank or garden bed, place in the border for bright color, or use in container plantings. Good companions include maiden grass, fountain grass, wax myrtle, and Northern bayberry.

Butterflies are attracted to the colorful blooms of lantana.

CARE: Plant 3–6' apart in late spring. Apply slow-release granular plant food at time of planting. Follow label directions for amount and frequency. Plants receiving too much nitrogen may have lush leaves but fewer flowers. When the soil becomes dry 2–3" below the surface, water deeply. Water transplants well until they are established. Apply 3" of vegetative mulch in summer and winter to help retain soil moisture and as it decomposes it will add organic matter to the soil. Prune woody growth back to the ground in late winter or early spring.

PROPAGATION: Plants often self-sow in the landscape. To sow indoors, sprinkle seeds over the soil mix and cover lightly. Keep moist, not soggy, until seeds germinate. Provide temperatures of 60–65°F until germination occurs.

PESTS AND DISEASES: Insect pests include whiteflies and spider mites. Diseases include leaf spots and rust.

RELATED SPECIES: Dwarf 'Arlequin' has deep pink and yellow flowers, 'Brazier' bears bright red flowers, 'Cream Carpet' has creamy white flowers. 'Miss Huff' and 'Mozelle' are hardy to Zone 7.

SWEET PEA

Lathyrus odoratus *LATH-ih-ruhs o-dor-AT-uhs*

Sweet peas have old-fashioned nostalgic appeal with heady fragrance.

ZONES: NA
SIZE: 10'h × 5'w
TYPE: Annual
FORM: Climber
TEXTURE: Medium
GROWTH: Fast
LIGHT: Full sun to part shade

MOISTURE: Medium
SOIL: Fertile, well-drained
FEATURES: Flowers, foliage
USES: Trellis, container, ground cover
FLOWERS: ■ ■ ▨ □

SITING: Sweet pea prefers full sun or light dappled shade and fertile, well-drained soil with a pH of 5.5–7.0. Fragrant flowers appear from summer into early autumn. Place in the woody plant border to grow

through shrubs, on an arbor or trellis for bright color, or in a container to wind through other plants. Good container companions include 'Southern Belle' hibiscus, 'Blue Bird' rose of Sharon, and 'Butterfly Blue' pincushion flower.

CARE: Plant 12–24" apart in early spring in fertile soil high in organic matter. Apply slow-release granular plant food at time of planting or begin using water-soluble plant food 3 weeks after planting in spring. Follow label directions for amount and frequency. Water deeply when the soil is

Sweet peas climb on brushwood, a trellis, an arbor or shrubby plants. Start them off by training tendrils onto the support.

dry. Apply 3" of vegetative mulch in summer to help retain soil moisture and as it decomposes it will add organic matter to the soil. Plants grown on an arbor or a trellis may need additional support. Deadhead spent blooms to encourage reblooming. Remove plants either just before the first frost or right afterward when foliage is disfigured. Cover bare soil with 3" of vegetative mulch during winter to preserve the topsoil.

PROPAGATION: To increase germination nick the seed coat with a nail file or rub with sandpaper. Then soak seeds in water for 12 hours. Sprinkle seed over the soil mix and cover. Thoroughly moisten and keep moist, not soggy. Provide temperatures of 55–60°F until seeds germinate.

PESTS AND DISEASES: Diseases include powdery mildew, Pythium root rot, and rust. Other pests include slugs and snails.

RELATED SPECIES: Spencer cultivars reach 6–8' high and produce a wide palette of solid, bicolor, picotee, and mixed colors. The Bijou Group reaches 20" high and bears flowers in shades of pink, white, red, and blue.

LAVENDER

Lavandula angustifolia lah-VAN-dyu-lah ahn-gust-ib-FOL-ee-uh

Lavender's popularity dates back to the Middle Ages.

ZONES: 5–8
SIZE: 3'h × 3'w
TYPE: Perennial
FORM: Rounded
TEXTURE: Fine
GROWTH: Slow
LIGHT: Full sun
MOISTURE: Medium

SOIL: Moderately fertile, well-drained
FEATURES: Flowers, foliage
USES: Border, container
FLOWERS: ■■□

SITING: Lavender prefers full sun and well-drained soil with a pH of 5.5–7.5. Silvery leaves contain volatile oils, which account for the classic lavender scent. The spikes of fragrant lavender flowers that appear in summer attract bees and butterflies and are excellent fresh cut or dried. Good garden companions include Culver's root, spike speedwell, lemon thyme, and gayfeather.

CARE: Plant 18–24" apart in spring. Apply slow-release granular plant food at time of planting. The soil must drain freely for lavender to thrive. Deadhead spent blooms to encourage reblooming. Shear back after first flowering to promote compact habit. Cut back in late spring once new growth is visible. To dry lavender, clip flower stalks

Snip lavender stalks while they are in the bud stage and hang upside down to dry in a shady, dry location.

before they fully open and secure in 1" or smaller-diameter bundles. Hang bundles upside down in a dry, shaded area. When they are dry, place in an airtight container until ready to use.

PROPAGATION: Plants may be layered in summer. Pin a branch to the ground so that nodes contact the soil. When roots have formed, snip the branch from the parent plant, leaving some green top growth to accompany the new root system. To increase germination rate, chill seed at 35–40°F for 4–6 weeks. Germination occurs in 14–21 days at 65–75°F. Transplant 20–35 days after sowing then reduce the temperature to 60°F.

PESTS AND DISEASES: Fusarium root rot may be a problem. Plants grown in wet soil conditions usually succumb to disease.

RELATED SPECIES: 'Hidcote' reaches 24" high, has deep purple flowers, and is more compact and tidy than the species, 'Munstead' reaches 18" high and has blue-purple flowers, and 'Nana Alba' reaches 12" high and has white flowers. 'Rosea', 'Jean Davis', and 'Lodden's Pink' have pink flowers. The cultivar 'Lavender Lady' may be grown from seed.

SHASTA DAISY

Leucanthemum ×superbum lu-KAHN-thub-mubm su-PEHR-bubm

Shasta daisy produces excellent fresh cut flowers or a long-lasting garden display.

ZONES: 4–8
SIZE: 36"h × 24"w
TYPE: Perennial
FORM: Upright
TEXTURE: Medium
GROWTH: Medium
LIGHT: Full sun to part shade

MOISTURE: Medium
SOIL: Moderately fertile, well-drained
FEATURES: Flowers, foliage
USES: Border, container
FLOWERS: □

SITING: Shasta daisy prefers full sun or light afternoon shade and moderately fertile, well-drained soil with a pH of 5.5–7.0. Plants may be short-lived in the South. White flowers with a yellow central disk appear from early summer through early autumn. Flowers are excellent for cutting. Plants are well suited for the perennial border or the container. Good companions include 'Bonica' and 'Carefree Wonder' roses, Kansas gayfeather, and 'Silver Carpet' lamb's-ears.

CARE: Plant 18–24" apart in spring or fall. Apply slow-release granular plant food at time of planting. Water deeply when the soil is dry. Apply 3" of vegetative mulch in summer and winter to reduce weed seed germination, retain soil moisture, and keep soil temperatures stable. Deadhead spent

blooms to encourage reblooming. Prune back in fall once frost withers the foliage.

PROPAGATION: Divide in spring or fall.

PESTS AND DISEASES: Diseases include crown gall, powdery mildew, leaf spots, and rust. Aphids and slugs may be troublesome.

RELATED SPECIES: 'Alaska' has single white flowers, 'Phyllis Smith' bears single white blooms with twisted petals, 'Snow Lady' has single white flowers, 'Cobham Gold' has double white flowers, and 'Wirral Pride' bears double flowers.

1 **Remove side shoots from Shasta daisy during division.**

2 **Replant pieces that contain healthy roots and vigorous shoots.**

SPIKE GAYFEATHER

Liatris spicata *LEE-ah-trihs spih-KAH-tuh*

Spike gayfeather, also known as blazing star, is a low-maintenance perennial with spectacular pinkish purple flowers.

ZONES: 3–9
SIZE: 3'h × 18"w
TYPE: Perennial
FORM: Upright
TEXTURE: Coarse
GROWTH: Medium
LIGHT: Full sun
MOISTURE: Medium

SOIL: Moderately fertile, moist, well-drained
FEATURES: Flowers, foliage
USES: Border, container, cut flower
FLOWERS: ■□

SITING: Spike gayfeather prefers full sun and moderately fertile, moist, well-drained soil with a pH of 6.5–7.5. Once established, plants are reliably low maintenance and trouble-free. Pinkish-purple flower spikes appear from mid- to late summer into early autumn. Flowers attract bees and butterflies and are excellent fresh cut or dried. Plant in the perennial border or use in mixed container plantings. Good companions include 'David' garden phlox, 'Iceberg' rose, 'Gracillimus' or 'Morning Light' maiden

Spike gayfeather cultivars other than 'Kobold' may need staking to keep them upright during bloom.

grass, Russian sage, 'Snowbank' white boltonia, and purple coneflower.
CARE: Plant 18–24" apart in spring or fall. Apply slow-release granular plant food at time of planting. Cease feeding 6–8 weeks prior to first frost date. Water deeply when the soil is dry. The cultivar 'Kobold' does not need staking; the species and other cultivars may. Deadhead spent blooms to keep plants tidy. Prune back in fall once frost withers the foliage, or leave erect in warmer zones for winter viewing.
PROPAGATION: Divide in spring or fall.
PESTS AND DISEASES: Slugs and snails are pests. Diseases include leaf spots, rust and aster yellows.
RELATED SPECIES: 'Kobold' is shorter than the species at only 24" high. 'Alba', 'Floristan', and 'Snow Queen' bear white flowers, and 'Blue Bird' has bluish flowers. Kansas gayfeather (*L. pychnostachya*) reaches 5' high; it is well adapted in the Midwest, provided soil is moderately fertile and sun is ample. If the soil is too rich, excessive nitrogen is applied, or there is too little sunlight, plants may become floppy. Staking is not normally necessary when cultural requirements are met.

BIGLEAF LIGULARIA

Ligularia dentata *lihg-yew-LAR-ee-uh dehn-TAH-tuh*

Bigleaf ligularia is a big plant for moist soil.

ZONES: 3–8
SIZE: 3–5'h × 3'w
TYPE: Perennial
FORM: Irregular
TEXTURE: Coarse
GROWTH: Medium
LIGHT: Part shade to full sun

MOISTURE: Medium to high
SOIL: Moderately fertile, moist
FEATURES: Flowers, foliage
USES: Border, wetland
FLOWERS: ■

SITING: Bigleaf ligularia prefers full sun, with light afternoon shade in warmer climates, and deep, fertile, moist soil with a pH of 5.5–7.0. Daisylike yellow-orange flowers with a brown center appear from summer into early autumn. Place this plant in an informal area where the soil is reliably moist. Good companions include 'Variagatus' sweet flag and yellow flag iris.
CARE: Plant 24–36" apart in spring or fall. Apply slow-release granular plant food at time of planting. Water deeply when the soil begins to dry. Apply 3" of vegetative mulch in summer and winter to help retain soil moisture. Deadhead spent blooms to encourage reblooming.

Ligularia often wilts in the afternoon, even when soil moisture is adequate.

If soil is dry, water deeply.

PROPAGATION: If plants are not deadheaded, they self-seed in the landscape. To reproduce desirable cultivars, divide in spring or fall.
PESTS AND DISEASES: Plants are relatively pest free when cultural requirements (sun, soil, planting depth, moisture) are met. Slugs and snails may be pests.
RELATED SPECIES: The cultivar 'Desdemona' has orange flowers and leaves that are stained burgundy underneath, 'Gregynog Gold' bears pyramidal spikes of orange flowers and has saw-edged leaves, 'Othello' bears deep orange flowers and dark purple leaves. *L. stenocephala* 'The Rocket' is the best suited ligularia for the part-shade border and for ornamental use. 'The Rocket' bears spikes of yellow flowers in early and late summer. Foliage is bold, triangular-shaped and toothed. It is not uncommon to see leaves wilting in midafternoon in Zone 5, even in moist soil in partial shade. They spring back up by early evening.

TURK'S CAP LILY

Lilium superbum *LIHL-ee-uhm su-PEHR-buhm*

Turk's cap lily bears pendulous flowers that attract butterflies.

ZONES: 3–8
SIZE: 4–10' h ×
4–6"w
TYPE: Perennial
FORM: Upright
TEXTURE: Medium
GROWTH: Medium
LIGHT: Full sun to
partial shade

MOISTURE: Medium
SOIL: Fertile, moist,
well-drained
FEATURES: Flowers
USES: Container,
woodland, border
FLOWERS: ▨ ▨ ▨ ▨
☐

SITING: Turk's cap lily prefers full sun or light afternoon shade and fertile, moist, well-drained soil with a pH of 5.5–7.0. Pendulous recurved orange flowers appear in mid- to late summer. Flowers have burgundy spots and are green-splashed near the base. Mid- to bright green leaves appear in whorls on purple-stained green stems. An abundance of flowers with recurved petals nodding well above the foliage ensures the popularity of these lilies. The flowers attract butterflies. Place in large swathes at the edge of a bright woodland, in odd-numbered groupings in the border, or in containers. Good container companions include the chartreuse-leaved sweet potato and the black-leaved 'Blackie' sweet potato, 'Moonbeam' threadleaf coreopsis, and 'Corries Gold' gaura.

CARE: Plant 6–12" apart and two to three times deeper than their diameter in spring or fall in fertile soil high in organic matter. To increase organic matter, add 1–2" of composted food and leaf waste, composted animal manure, mushroom compost, peat moss, or bagged humus to the planting bed and till in to a depth of 12–15". Add bonemeal and slow-release granular plant food at time of planting. Apply 3" of vegetative mulch in summer and winter to reduce weed seed germination, retain soil moisture, and keep soil temperatures stable. Water deeply when the soil begins to dry. Remove flowers when they fade to reduce seed set. Take as little stem as possible with cut flowers. Allow the foliage to die back naturally after blooms fade.

PROPAGATION: In spring dig down to the bulb and gently pull off the largest of the small bulbs that are attached to the main bulb. Re-cover the main bulb and plant bulblets in prepared soil 12" away from other plants. Water deeply and apply 3" of vegetative mulch.

PESTS AND DISEASES: Diseases include botrytis and viruses. Slugs and snails may feed on foliage, and deer, rabbits, and groundhogs may eat top growth.

RELATED SPECIES: Asiatic and Oriental hybrids bear scented flowers in summer. 'Casa Blanca' bears large, fragrant white

Plucking the anthers from a white lily keeps the pollen from staining the bloom.

flowers in mid- to late summer, and 'Star Gazer' has star-shaped pinkish-red flowers with dark red spots in early summer. Both add beauty to container plantings as well as the border. Aurelian hybrid lilies (*L.* ×*aurelianense*) are crosses between *L. henryi* and *L. sargentiae*. Some popular cultivars include 'Black Beauty', a deep crimson flower with recurved petals and 'Pink Perfection', with trumpet-shaped pink flowers. Martagon lily (*L. martagon*) is also known as Turk's cap lily for its nodding reddish-purple blooms borne on plants 4–6' tall.

Cut back lily foliage in fall if it has not died back naturally.

For winter protection from cold, insulate lilies with evergreen boughs.

BLUE LILYTURF

Liriope muscari *ler-EYE-oh-pee muhsk-AR-ee*

Blue lilyturf is a reliable evergreen ground cover for sun or shade.

ZONES: 6–10
SIZE: 12"h × 18"w
TYPE: Perennial
FORM: Rounded
TEXTURE: Medium
GROWTH: Medium
LIGHT: Full sun to full shade

MOISTURE: Medium to low
SOIL: Moderately fertile, well-drained
FEATURES: Flowers, foliage, berries
USES: Ground cover, container
FLOWERS: ■ ■ □

SITING: Blue lilyturf tolerates full sun, part shade, or full shade (afternoon shade is preferred in the south) and prefers moderately fertile, well-drained soil with a pH of 5.5–7.0. Protect from strong winds and wet soils in all climates. Spikes of tiny purple blooms appear from late summer through autumn. Dense clumps of narrow, arching dark green evergreen leaves are tolerant of most sun and soil situations. Deep blue berries follow blooms and last until frost. Plants are drought tolerant once established. Plants are commonly used as ground covers in tree and shrub beds, as a turf substitute, and in containers. Full-sun companions include 'Fairy Princess' and 'Krinkled White' peonies, Russian sage, bluebeard, and 'Vivid' obedient plant. Part-shade companions include 'Amethystina' toad lily, and 'Frances Williams' and 'Gold Standard' hostas.

CARE: Plant 12–18" apart in late spring. Apply slow-release granular plant food at time of planting. Cease feeding 4–6 weeks prior to first frost date. Give transplants ample water until they are established. Otherwise, water only when the soil becomes dry 2–3" below the surface. Apply 3" of vegetative mulch in summer and winter to help retain soil moisture. Deadhead spent blooms. Shear back in early spring to promote new growth. An easy way to accomplish this task is to set a lawnmower at its highest setting then mow off the tattered overwintering foliage.

PROPAGATION: Divide in spring or fall. Dig around the tubers and lift. Use a sharp spade to slice through the root system. Reset portions that contain healthy roots and top shoots, then water and mulch. Discard any pieces that do not contain both healthy roots and top shoots.

PESTS AND DISEASES: Plants are relatively pest free when cultural requirements (sun, soil, planting depth, moisture) are met. Wet soil may render plants susceptible to diseases such as anthracnose and root rot.

RELATED SPECIES: The cultivar 'Grandiflora' is taller than the species, with narrow, arching leaves and lavender flowers, 'Variagata' leaves are gold-striped, 'John Burch' leaves have a yellow-green center stripe, 'Silvery Midget' leaves are variegated white, 'Monroe White' has an abundance of white flowers, and 'Curly Twist' has curiously twisted leaves.

CREEPING LILYTURF

Liriope spicata *lehr-EYE-oh-pee spihk-AH-tuh*

Creeping lilyturf is a superb ground cover for sun or shade. It is also known as creeping liriope. Pictured is 'Silver Dragon'.

ZONES: 5–10
SIZE: 10"h × 18"w
TYPE: Perennial
FORM: Rounded
TEXTURE: Medium
GROWTH: Medium
LIGHT: Full sun, part shade, full shade

MOISTURE: Medium
SOIL: Moderately fertile, well-drained
FEATURES: Flowers, foliage, berries
USES: Groundcover, border, container
FLOWERS: ■ □

SITING: Creeping lilyturf prefers moderately fertile, well-drained soil with a pH of 5.5–7.0. It tolerates full sun, part shade, or full shade. Plants are drought tolerant once established. Spikes of tiny lavender to white flowers appear in late summer. Dark semievergreen leaves are narrow and grasslike. Deep blue berries follow blooms and persist until frost. Use as a ground cover for tree and shrub beds, as a turf replacement, in the border, and in containers. Good shade companions include 'Sunspot' heucherella, 'Silver Falls' Japanese painted fern, and 'Variegatum' Solomon's seal.

CARE: Plant 15–18" apart in spring or fall. Apply slow-release granular plant food at time of planting or begin using water-soluble plant food 3 weeks after planting in spring. Water deeply when the soil is dry. Deadhead spent blooms. Shear back in early spring to promote new growth.

PROPAGATION: Divide in spring or fall.

PESTS AND DISEASES: Plants are relatively pest free when cultural requirements are met. Anthracnose and root rot are diseases associated with wet soils. Slugs and snails may be pests.

RELATED SPECIES: The cultivar 'Alba' has white flowers, and 'Silver Dragon' has striped silver leaves, pale purple flowers, and white-green fruit.

1 Lift clumps in spring or fall for division.

2 Divide roots with a sharp spade.

3 Reset pieces that contain healthy roots and shoots.

CARDINAL FLOWER
Lobelia cardinalis *lob-BEEL-yuh kard-ihn-AHL-ihs*

Cardinal flower's red blooms attract hummingbirds.

ZONES: 3–9
SIZE: 36"h × 12"w
TYPE: Perennial
FORM: Upright
TEXTURE: Medium
GROWTH: Medium
LIGHT: Full sun to part shade

MOISTURE: Medium to high
SOIL: Fertile, moist, well-drained
FEATURES: Flowers, foliage
USES: Border, woodland, container
FLOWERS: ■ ■ □

SITING: Cardinal flower prefers full sun in northern zones and afternoon shade in the South, and deep, fertile, moist yet well-drained soil with a pH of 5.5–7.0. Red flowers appear from summer to early autumn. Bright green leaves are sometimes stained bronze. Flowers attract bees, butterflies, and hummingbirds. Good companions include red ginger lily, 'Marmorata' and 'Crow Feather' Allegheny foamflowers, 'Persian Carpet' heuchera, and 'Superba' featherleaf rodgersia.

CARE: Plant 12" apart in late spring. Apply slow-release granular plant food at time of planting. If planting in a wetland, avoid fertilizers and chemical pesticides. When the soil feels almost dry 2" below the surface, water deeply. Deadhead spent

Water plants deeply when the soil feels dry 2" below the surface.

blooms to encourage reblooming. Plants are short-lived perennials and may need to be replaced or divided every 2 years. Prune back in fall once frost withers the foliage.

PROPAGATION: Plants self-seed in the landscape. To sow indoors, sprinkle seeds over the soil mix and leave exposed to light; do not cover. Thoroughly moisten and keep moist, not soggy, until seeds germinate. Germination occurs in 8–12 days at 70°F. Transplant 25–30 days after sowing. After transplanting, reduce temperature to 60–65°F.

PESTS AND DISEASES: Rust and slugs are possible.

RELATED SPECIES: The cultivar 'Alba' bears white flowers, 'Rosea' has pink flowers, and 'Ruby Slippers' has dark red flowers.

LOBELIA
Lobelia erinus *lob-BEEL-yuh eh-RIN-uhs*

Lobelia is a fine-textured plant for bright shade.

ZONES: NA
SIZE: 4–10"h × 6–12"w
TYPE: Annual
FORM: Spreading
TEXTURE: Fine
GROWTH: Medium
LIGHT: Part shade

MOISTURE: Medium
SOIL: Fertile, well-drained
FEATURES: Flowers, foliage
USES: Border, container
FLOWERS: ■ ■ □ ■

SITING: Lobelia prefers afternoon shade and fertile, moist yet well-drained soil with a pH of 5.5–7.0. Two-lipped blue, purple, white, or pink flowers appear from summer through early autumn. Mid- to dark green leaves are sometimes stained bronze. Place in odd-numbered groups in the part-shade border, at the edge of a container, or where plants cascade over the rim of a rock wall. Good companions include 'Pictum' Japanese painted fern, heart-leaf brunnera, 'Elegans' Siebold hosta, 'Mrs. Moon' lungwort, and lady's mantle.

CARE: Plant 6–12" apart in late spring. Apply slow-release granular plant food at time of planting or begin using water-soluble plant food 3 weeks after planting in spring. Follow label directions for amount and frequency. When the soil begins to feel dry, water deeply. Maintain moist but not soggy soil. If using an irrigation system, maintain deep, infrequent waterings and avoid delivering a light sprinkle every day. Apply 2–3" of organic mulch around, but not touching, plants in summer to help retain soil moisture and as it decomposes it will add organic matter to the soil. Deadhead spent blooms to encourage reblooming. Remove plants just before the first frost or right afterward when foliage is disfigured.

PROPAGATION: Sprinkle seeds over the soil mix and leave exposed to light; do not cover. Thoroughly moisten and keep moist, not soggy, until seeds germinate. Germination occurs in 15–20 days at 70–80°F. Transplant 20–25 days after sowing. After transplanting, reduce the temperature to 60–65°F.

PESTS AND DISEASES: Rust and slugs are possible problems that may develop.

RELATED SPECIES: The cultivar 'Alba' has white flowers, 'Blue Moon' has deep blue flowers, 'Cobalt Blue' has cobalt blue blooms, 'Crystal Palace' has vibrant bright blue flowers, 'Pink Flamingo' is upright with pink flowers, and 'Sapphire' has vibrant sapphire blue flowers.

SWEET ALYSSUM
Lobularia maritima lobb-yew-LAHR-ee-uh mar-ib-TIM-uh

Sweet alyssum is a fine-textured fragrant plant for full sun locations.

ZONES: NA
SIZE: 4–12"h ×
10–12"w
TYPE: Annual
FORM: Spreading
TEXTURE: Fine
GROWTH: Fast
LIGHT: Full sun to
part shade

MOISTURE: Medium
SOIL: Moderately
fertile, well-drained
FEATURES: Flowers,
foliage
USES: Border,
ground cover,
container
FLOWERS: □ ■ ■

SITING: Sweet alyssum prefers full sun and moderately fertile, well-drained soil with a pH of 5.5–7.5. Tiny, cross-shaped, fragrant bright white, sometimes purple or pink flowers appear in summer. Leaves are slightly hairy and gray-green. Plant this dainty, cascading annual at the edge of the border or spilling from a mixed container planting. Good companions include pink coreopsis, 'Stargazer' lily, and 'Purpureum' fennel.

CARE: Plant 6–12" apart in late spring. Apply slow-release granular plant food at time of planting or begin using water-soluble plant food 3 weeks after planting in spring. Water deeply when the soil is dry. Apply vegetative mulch around, but not touching, plants in summer to help

Plant sweet alyssum as an edging plant for the flower border or in a container.

retain soil moisture. Shear back after first bloom to encourage reblooming. Remove plants just before the first frost or right afterward when foliage is disfigured.

PROPAGATION: Sprinkle seeds over the soil mix and leave exposed to light; do not cover. Thoroughly moisten and keep moist, not soggy, until seeds germinate. Germination occurs in 8–10 days at 78–80°F. After germination, reduce temperature to 50–55°F. Transplant into the garden when temperatures warm and all frost danger has passed.

PESTS AND DISEASES: Slugs, flea beetles, downy mildew, clubroot, and white blister are occasional pests.

RELATED SPECIES: Alice series cultivars are compact and bear white, pink, or purple flowers, Basket series cultivars are strong spreaders and bear rosy red, violet-blue, peach, and white flowers, 'Carpet of Snow' is low growing with white flowers, 'Navy Blue' is low and compact with deep purple flowers, 'New Purple' is low growing with purple flowers turning lighter at the margins, 'Oriental Nights' bear early-flowering rich purple blooms, and 'Wonderland Rose' bear rosy pink flowers.

LUPINE
Lupinus hybrids *lup-EYE-nubs*

Lupines are classic English perennial border plants. They require cool weather for best garden performance.

ZONES: 4–8
SIZE: 20–36"h ×
12–30"w
TYPE: Perennial
FORM: Upright
TEXTURE: Medium
GROWTH: Fast
LIGHT: Full sun to
part shade

MOISTURE: Medium
SOIL: Fertile, well-
drained
FEATURES: Flowers,
foliage
USES: Border,
container
FLOWERS: ■ ■ ■ ■
■ ■ □

SITING: Lupine prefers full sun or partial afternoon shade and fertile, well-drained soil with a pH of 5.5–6.8. Plants are short-lived perennials often grown as annuals. Cool summer temperatures are ideal. Lupine resists heat, humidity, and transplanting. Spikes of pealike blooms appear in summer. Place in groups in the border or use in container plantings. Good companions include alyssum, pink coreopsis, sweet woodruff, and 'Caesar's Brother' Siberian iris.

CARE: Plant 12–30" apart, depending on the cultivar, in late spring. Apply slow-release granular plant food at time of planting or begin using water-soluble plant food 3 weeks after planting. Cease feeding 6–8 weeks prior to first frost date if growing as a perennial. Water deeply when the soil is dry. Apply 3" of vegetative mulch in summer. Deadhead spent blooms to encourage reblooming unless self-sown seedlings are

Apply mulch to lupine to keep roots cool.

desired, then leave flowers until they drop their seeds. Trim back in fall once frost withers the foliage.

PROPAGATION: Plants lightly self-seed in the landscape. Divide in spring. Soak seed in water for 24 hours before sowing. Sprinkle seed over the soil mix and cover lightly. Germination occurs in 6–12 days at 65–75°F. Transplant 18–30 days after sowing. After transplanting, reduce temperature to 50–55°F.

PESTS AND DISEASES: Diseases include Southern blight, powdery mildew, downy mildew, rust, and stem rot.

RELATED SPECIES: Russell hybrids reach 36" high and bear spikes of flowers in red, blue, pink, white, and yellow. Gallery hybrids reach 20" high and bear spikes of blue, yellow, rose, red, and white flowers. 'Catherine of York' bears orange and yellow flowers in early and midsummer, 'Chandelier' reaches 36" high and bears spikes of yellow flowers, and 'The Chatelaine' reaches 36" high and bears pink and white flowers. Texas blue bonnet (*L. texensis*) is a stunning annual that bears bluish-purple flowers in summer.

GOOSENECK LOOSESTRIFE

Lysimachia clethroides libs-ib-MAHK-ee-ub klebtb-ROY-deez

Gooseneck loosestrife flowers attract butterflies and bees.

ZONES: 3–9
SIZE: 36"h × 24"w
TYPE: Perennial
FORM: Upright
TEXTURE: Medium
GROWTH: Fast
LIGHT: Full sun to partial shade

MOISTURE: Medium to high
SOIL: Fertile, moist, well-drained
FEATURES: Flowers, foliage
USES: Border, container
FLOWERS: □

SITING: Gooseneck loosestrife prefers full sun, or light afternoon shade in warmer climates, and fertile, well-drained, moist soil with a pH of 5.5–7.0. The rhizomes spread rapidly in moist soil. Arching white flowers resemble the profile of a goose head. Flowers attract bees and butterflies and are excellent fresh cut. Place plants in groups in the perennial border, naturalize along a stream bank, or use in container plantings. Good companions include 'Kobold' blazing star, purple coneflower, 'Goldsturm' black-eyed Susan, and 'Filagran' Russian sage.

CARE: Plant 24–36" apart in spring or fall. Apply slow-release granular plant food at time of planting. Cease feeding 4–6 weeks prior to first frost date. Maintain moist soil. When the soil begins to feel dry, water deeply. Apply 3" of vegetative mulch in summer and winter to reduce weed seed germination, retain soil moisture, and keep soil temperatures stable. Deadhead spent blooms to encourage reblooming. Prune plants back to ground level in fall once frost withers the foliage.

PROPAGATION: This plant vigorously reproduces in the landscape by spreading rhizomes. It can easily become invasive. Division will reduce plant size and restore vitality to tired plants. Divide in spring. Dig around the root clump and lift. Use a sharp spade to slice through the root system. Reset portions that contain healthy roots and top shoots, then water and mulch.

PESTS AND DISEASES: Rust and leaf spot may occasionally occur.

1 Lift the plant in the spring to divide it.

2 Tease the roots apart by hand, or slice through them with a sharp spade.

3 Reset portions that contain healthy roots and shoots.

PLUME POPPY

Macleaya cordata mahk-LAY-uh kor-DAH-tuh

Plume poppy fills large spaces in sun or bright shade.

ZONES: 4–9
SIZE: 8'h × 3'w
TYPE: Perennial
FORM: Upright
TEXTURE: Coarse
GROWTH: Fast
LIGHT: Full sun to partial shade
MOISTURE: Medium to high

SOIL: Moderately fertile, moist, well-drained
FEATURES: Foliage, flowers
USES: Border, naturalizing, container
FLOWERS: □ ▨

SITING: Plume poppy prefers full sun and moderately fertile, well-drained soil, although it tolerates moist soil and part shade. The preferred pH is 5.5–7.0. Plants spread rapidly. Large, lobed leaves are 8" across, blue-gray above, and silver beneath. Plumes of creamy white flowers appear from mid- to late summer. Plants are focal points; parade them in odd-numbered groups in the center of the border or in groups along a bank or anywhere they can spread freely. Large containers will also restrain their spread. Good container companions include flowering kale, 'Tricolor' sweet potato, and gooseneck loosestrife.

CARE: Plant 36" apart in fall or spring. Apply slow-release granular plant food at time of planting. Cease feeding 6–8 weeks prior to first frost date. Water deeply when the soil is dry. Apply 3" of vegetative mulch around, but not touching, plants in summer to help retain soil moisture. Deadhead spent blooms, or cut for use in fresh arrangements, to encourage reblooming. Prune back in fall once frost withers the foliage, or leave erect in warmer zones for winter viewing and trim back in spring.

PROPAGATION: Plume poppy reseeds readily in the landscape, sometimes becoming invasive. Transplant self-sown seedlings or divide existing clumps in spring. Dig around the root clump and lift. Use a sharp spade to slice through the root system. Reset portions that contain healthy roots and top shoots.

PESTS AND DISEASES: Plants are relatively pest free when cultural requirements (sun, soil, planting depth, moisture) are met. Slugs are occasional pests.

RELATED SPECIES: The cultivar 'Alba' bears white flowers, and 'Flamingo' has mauve-pink flowers.

HOLLYHOCK MALLOW
Malva alcea 'Fastigiata' *MAHL-vuh al-SEE-uh*

Hollyhock mallow is a low-maintenance perennial with spectacular blooms.

ZONES: 3–8
SIZE: 36"h × 24"w
TYPE: Perennial
FORM: Upright
TEXTURE: Medium
GROWTH: Medium
LIGHT: Full sun
MOISTURE: Medium

SOIL: Moderately fertile, well-drained
FEATURES: Flowers, foliage
USES: Border, container
FLOWERS: ▨

SITING: Hollyhock mallow prefers full sun and moderately fertile, well-drained soil with a pH of 5.5–7.0. Five-petaled rosy-pink flowers are produced from summer into autumn. Attractive seedpods follow the flowers. Place in the middle of the border or island bed. Good companions include 'Snowbank' white boltonia, 'Iceberg' and 'The Fairy' roses, 'Moonbeam' threadleaf coreopsis, 'Butterfly Blue' and 'Miss Willmott' pincusion flowers.

CARE: Plant 18–24" apart in spring or autumn. Apply slow-release granular plant

Cut back the spent blossoms of hollyhock mallow after it has finished blooming to promote new growth.

food at time of planting or begin using water-soluble plant food 3 weeks after planting in spring. Cease feeding 6–8 weeks prior to first frost date. Water deeply when the soil is dry. Apply 3" of vegetative mulch around, but not touching, the plants in summer to help retain soil moisture. 'Fastigiata' doesn't need staking. Deadhead spent blooms to encourage reblooming or leave some to allow for self-seeding in the landscape. Prune back in fall once frost withers the foliage.

PROPAGATION: To exactly reproduce the cultivar, propagate vegetatively, not by seed. Divide in spring or fall. Otherwise, sprinkle seeds over the soil mix and ightly cover. Thoroughly moisten and keep moist, not soggy, until seeds germinate. Germination occurs in 3–6 days at 70–75°F. Transplant 15–20 days after sowing. After transplanting, reduce temperature to 60–65°F.

PESTS AND DISEASES: Plants are relatively pest free when cultural requirements (sun, soil, planting depth, moisture) are met. Japanese beetle may be a pest in the North; in the South plants seem more susceptible to spider mites and thrips.

OSTRICH FERN
Matteuccia struthiopteris (pennsylvanica) *mah-TU-see-uh struth-ee-OHP-ter-ihs (pen-sil-VAN-ih-kuh)*

Ostrich fern is a large plant for shady sites in cooler climates.

ZONES: 3–8
SIZE: 5'h × 3'w
TYPE: Perennial
FORM: Irregular
TEXTURE: Medium
GROWTH: Medium
LIGHT: Partial shade
MOISTURE: Medium to high

SOIL: Fertile, moist, well-drained
FEATURES: Flowers, foliage
USES: Border, woodland, container

SITING: Ostrich fern prefers afternoon shade and fertile, well-drained, moist soil with a pH of 5.5–7.0. It spreads by rhizomes and may be invasive in cooler climates. Plants dislike the excessive heat and humidity of southern climates. Place groups in the middle of the shaded island bed, at the back of the border, or in the woodland garden. Good companions include 'Ursula's Red' Japanese painted fern, 'Superba' Chinese astilbe, and common bugbane.

CARE: Plant 36" apart in fall or spring in fertile soil high in organic matter. Apply slow-release granular plant food at time of planting. Apply 3" of vegetative mulch around, but not touching, the plants in summer and winter. Mulch reduces weed seed germination, holds moisture in the soil, and as it decomposes, adds organic matter to the soil. When the soil begins to feel dry 2" below the surface, water deeply. Vegetative fronds are withered by the first frost; fertile fronds last the winter. Trim plants back in spring if the fronds look ragged.

PROPAGATION: Plants will produce offspring in the landscape through spreading rhizomes. Divide in early spring. Dig around the rhizomes and lift. Use a sharp spade to slice through the root system. Reset portions that contain healthy roots and top shoots, then water and mulch. Discard any pieces that do not contain both healthy roots and top shoots.

PESTS AND DISEASES: Plants are relatively pest free when cultural requirements (sun, soil, planting depth, moisture) are met.

Dig plantlets that sprout from spreading rhizomes in early spring.

VIRGINIA BLUEBELL
Mertensia virginica *mehr-TEHN-see-uh ver-JIHN-ih-kuh*

Virginia bluebell flower buds are pink and open to bluish purple.

ZONES: 3–7
SIZE: 18"h × 8–10"w
TYPE: Perennial
FORM: Upright
TEXTURE: Medium
GROWTH: Slow
LIGHT: Part shade
MOISTURE: Medium to high

SOIL: Fertile, well-drained
FEATURES: Flowers, foliage
USES: Border, woodland, container
FLOWERS: ■■□

SITING: Virginia bluebell prefers afternoon shade and fertile, well-drained, moist soil with a pH of 5.5–7.0. Pink buds and flowers emerge in mid- to late spring and quickly turn vibrant sky blue or purple-blue. Leaves will yellow in summer and disappear by midsummer. Good companions to cover the empty space left in summer include the perennials 'Elegans' Siebold hosta and 'Superba' featherleaf

Plant shade-tolerant annuals such as impatiens among Virginia bluebells to provide color through summer.

rodgersia, and the annuals New Guinea impatiens, impatiens, and lobelia.
CARE: Plant 8–12" apart in spring in fertile soil high in organic matter. To increase organic matter, add 1–2" of compost to the planting bed and till in to a depth of 12–15". Apply slow-release granular plant food at time of planting. Apply 3" of vegetative mulch around, but not touching, the plants in summer and winter. Mulch reduces weed seed germination, holds moisture in the soil, and, as it decomposes adds organic matter to the soil. Because the plant is dormant during summer, little water is needed at that time.
PROPAGATION: Divide very early in spring before the plant blooms. Dig around the root clump and lift. Use a sharp spade to slice through the root system. Reset portions that contain healthy roots and top shoots, then water and mulch. Discard any pieces that do not contain both healthy roots and top shoots.
PESTS AND DISEASES: Slugs and snails are common pests. Diseases include rust and powdery mildew.

BEEBALM
Monarda didyma *muh-NAHR-duh DIHD-ih-muh*

Beebalm flowers attract hummingbirds and butterflies. It is also known as Oswego tea.

ZONES: 3–9
SIZE: 36"h × 24"w
TYPE: Perennial
FORM: Upright
TEXTURE: Medium
GROWTH: Medium
LIGHT: Full sun to partial shade
MOISTURE: Medium to high

SOIL: Moderately fertile, moist, well-drained
FEATURES: Flowers, foliage
USES: Border, naturalizing, container
FLOWERS: ■■■□

SITING: Beebalm tolerates full sun or light afternoon shade and needs good air circulation. It prefers moderately fertile, well-drained soil with a pH of 5.5–7.0. Whorls of scarlet red or pink flowers appear in mid- to late summer. The fragrant foliage is hairy underneath. Flowers attract hummingbirds, bees, and butterflies. Place in the border, add to container plantings, or naturalize. Good companions include daylily, sweet flag iris, and gaura.
CARE: Plant 18–24" apart in spring or autumn. Apply slow-release granular plant food at time of planting. Maintain moist soil. No staking is needed. Deadhead spent blooms to encourage reblooming. Trim back in fall once frost withers the foliage.
PROPAGATION: Divide in spring, once new growth is seen, or in autumn.

PESTS AND DISEASES: Reduce plants' susceptibility to powdery mildew by selecting mildew-resistant cultivars; selecting sites with good air circulation; keeping soil moist, not soggy or bone dry; and avoiding overcrowding.
RELATED SPECIES: Cultivars with resistance to powdery mildew include 'Aquarius', with pink flowers and bronze-stained foliage, 'Bowman', with purple flowers, 'Gardenview Scarlet', with large bright red flowers, 'Marshall's Delight', with pink flowers, and 'Violet Queen', with violet-purple flowers.

1

To divide beebalm, cut back the foliage to 3–4" above ground level.

2

Lift the entire plant and plunge a sharp spade through the roots.

3

Reset pieces with healthy roots and shoots.

GRAPE HYACINTH

Muscari botryoides muhs-KAH-ree boht-ree-OY-deez

Grape hyacinths add pink, purple, or white flower clusters to the landscape in spring.

ZONES: 3–8
SIZE: 6–8"h × 6"w
TYPE: Perennial
FORM: Irregular
TEXTURE: Medium
GROWTH: Medium
LIGHT: Full sun
MOISTURE: Medium to high

SOIL: Moderately fertile, moist, well-drained
FEATURES: Flowers, foliage
USES: Border, naturalizing, container
FLOWERS: ■□▨

SITING: Grape hyacinth prefers full sun and moderately fertile, moist yet well-drained soil with a pH of 5.5–7.0. Dense clusters of white, pink, or bright sky blue flowers appear in spring. Leaves are grasslike and medium green. Drifts of grape hyacinth in the border or rock garden, at the feet of woody shrubs, in a container, or naturalized add delightful color and texture to the spring landscape. Good companions include rosmary, evergreen candytuft, and sea pink.

Remove spent flower heads before seedpods form to reduce self-seeding in the landscape.

CARE: Plant 6" apart and 4" deep in autumn in large groups. Add bonemeal to the soil at planting time. Apply slow-release granular plant food in spring after the last frost and growth is visible or use water-soluble plant food. Follow label directions for amount and frequency. Maintain moist, not soggy, soil. If using an irrigation system, maintain deep, infrequent waterings; avoid delivering a light sprinkle every day. Apply 3" of vegetative mulch in summer and winter to help retain soil moisture and as it decomposes it will add organic matter to the soil. When applying mulch, do not let it touch plant stems.

PROPAGATION: Plants will-self sow in the landscape. Remove offsets that grow from the parent bulb and reset them in summer.

PESTS AND DISEASES: Virus diseases may occur but are not common.

WOODLAND FORGET-ME-NOT

Myosotis sylvatica meye-uh-SOHT-iss sill-VAHT-ih-kuh

Woodland forget-me-not produces sky blue blooms in partial shade.

ZONES: 3–9
SIZE: 6–12"h × 6"w
TYPE: Perennial
FORM: Upright
TEXTURE: Medium
GROWTH: Medium
LIGHT: Partial shade
MOISTURE: Medium

SOIL: Moderately fertile, moist, well-drained
FEATURES: Flowers, foliage
USES: Border, woodland, container
FLOWERS: ■▨□

SITING: Woodland forget-me-not prefers afternoon shade and moderately fertile, well-drained, moist soil with a pH of 5.5–7.0. Plants do not thrive in high heat and humidity. Bright blue flowers with a yellow eye appear from spring to early summer. Leaves are 2–3" long, hairy, pointed, and gray-green. Plants are commonly grown as biennials and may not last more than two seasons. Place in odd numbered-groups in the border, in swathes in the woodland, in containers, or scattered about the feet of irrigated woody plants. Good companions include 'Mrs. Moon' and 'Sissinghurst' lungworts, Lenten rose, and bear's foot hellebore.

CARE: Plant 10–12" apart in spring or fall. Apply slow-release granular plant food at time of planting, or begin using water-soluble plant food after the last frost and growth is visible. Follow label directions for amount and frequency. Maintain moist, not soggy, soil. When the soil begins feels dry 2" below the surface, water deeply. If using an irrigation system, maintain deep, infrequent waterings and avoid delivering a light sprinkle every day. Apply 3" of vegetative mulch in summer and winter to help retain soil moisture. When applying mulch, do not let it touch plant stems.

PROPAGATION: Plants self-sow in the landscape. To start indoors, sprinkle seeds over the soil mix and leave exposed to light; do not cover. Thoroughly moisten and keep moist, not soggy, until seeds germinate. Germination occurs in 7–14 days at 68–72°F. Transplant 15–25 days after sowing. Reduce the temperature to 55°F after transplanting. Seed-grown plants may flower lightly the first season and fully the second.

PESTS AND DISEASES: Botrytis and powdery mildew are common diseases. Slugs and snails are pests.

RELATED SPECIES: The Ball Series consists of compact 6" plants in blue, pink or white. 'Blue Bird' has bright blue flowers on plants 12" tall. Alpine forget-me-not (*M. alpestris*) is a short-lived perennial bearing blue flowers on plants 8" tall. It is hardy in Zones 4–8. Water forget-me-not (*M. scorpioides*) grows on wet sites. It is hardy in Zones 5–9.

DAFFODIL
Narcissus hybrids *nahr-SIHS-uhs*

Daffodil flowers are excellent fresh cut or dried or simply enjoyed in the landscape for their bright, cheery blooms.

ZONES: 3–8
SIZE: 5–24"h × 6–12"w
TYPE: Perennial
FORM: Upright
TEXTURE: Medium
GROWTH: Medium
LIGHT: Full sun to partial shade
MOISTURE: Medium
SOIL: Moderately fertile, well-drained
FEATURES: Flowers, foliage
USES: Border, naturalizing, container
FLOWERS: ■□

SITING: Daffodils prefer full sun or light afternoon shade and moderately fertile, well-drained soil with a pH of 5.5–7.0. Daffodils are classified into groups based on their flower form: trumpet, large cupped, small cupped, double, triandrus, cyclamineus, jonquilla, tazetta, poeticus, wild or other species, and split corona. Flowers are usually yellow or white. Daffodils may be used in groups in the border, naturalized among deciduous trees, in turf, and in container plantings. They may also be forced for indoor enjoyment.

CARE: Plant 6–12" apart in autumn, depending on the cultivar and location. Plant bulbs two to three times deeper than their diameter. Add bonemeal to the soil at planting time. Apply low-nitrogen, high-potassium plant food after flowering. Allow foliage to die back naturally so bulb can store enough energy to produce flowers the following season. Avoid braiding foliage or folding and wrapping it with rubber bands. Add 1" of vegetative mulch to daffodil planting beds. Keep soil moist during the growing season, but allow it to dry somewhat in summer to coincide with the bulbs' dormancy.

PROPAGATION: After flowering, when leaves fade, or in early autumn before new roots form, lift clumps and separate bulbs. Replant, water, and mulch.

PESTS AND DISEASES: Pests include viruses, fungal diseases, bulb scale mite, and large narcissus bulb fly.

1 Dig wide holes to hold clusters of bulbs.

2 Place the bulbs' basal plate down in hole.

JONQUIL
Narcissus jonquilla *nahr-SIHS-uhs jahn-KWIL-uh*

Jonquils bear yellow or white fragrant flowers in early spring.

ZONES: 4–8
SIZE: 6–20"h × 6–12"w
TYPE: Perennial
FORM: Upright
TEXTURE: Medium
GROWTH: Medium
LIGHT: Full sun to partial shade
MOISTURE: Medium
SOIL: Moderately fertile, well-drained
FEATURES: Flowers, foliage
USES: Border, naturalizing, container
FLOWERS: ■□

SITING: Jonquils are one classification of narcissus. Plants prefer full sun or light afternoon shade and moderately fertile, well-drained soil with a pH of 5.5–7.2. The species *jonquilla,* or jonquil, produces one to six fragrant yellow or white flowers per stem in early to midspring. Leaves are basal and somewhat cylindrical or rushlike. Flowers are excellent fresh cut and dried. Jonquils may be used in groups in the border or naturalized among deciduous trees, along lake banks, in pastures, in turf, or in container plantings. They may also be forced for indoor enjoyment.

CARE: Plant 6–12" apart in autumn, depending on the cultivar and location. Plant bulbs two to three times deeper than their diameter. Add bonemeal to the soil at planting time. Apply low-nitrogen, high-potassium plant food after flowering. Follow label directions for amount. Allow foliage to die back naturally so bulb can store enough energy to produce flowers the following season. Avoid braiding foliage or folding and wrapping it with rubber bands. Add 1" of vegetative mulch to planting beds. Keep soil moist during the growing season, but allow it to dry somewhat in summer to coincide with the bulbs' dormancy.

PROPAGATION: After flowering, when leaves fade, or in early autumn before new roots form, lift clumps and separate bulbs. Replant, water, and mulch.

PESTS AND DISEASES: Problems include viruses, fungal diseases, bulb scale mite, and large narcissus bulb fly.

RELATED SPECIES: The cultivar 'Bell Song' reaches 12" high and bears one or two nodding white flowers with a pale pink cup, 'Dainty Miss' reaches 18" high and has white flowers with a green-eyed cup, 'Intrigue' reaches 12" high and bears yellow flowers with a long, white frilly cup, 'Lintie' reaches 8" and has yellow flowers with an orange cup, 'Pink Angel' reaches 12" high and bears white flowers with a pink-edged, green-eyed, white cup, and 'Quail' reaches 15" high and has yellow flowers.

FLOWERING TOBACCO

Nicotiana alata *nihk-oh-she-AHN-uh ah-LAY-tuh*

Flowering tobacco is a popular container or flower border plant.

ZONES: NA
SIZE: 1.5–5'h × 1–2'w
TYPE: Annual
FORM: Upright
TEXTURE: Medium
GROWTH: Medium
LIGHT: Full sun to partial shade

MOISTURE: Medium
SOIL: Fertile, moist, well-drained
FEATURES: Flowers, foliage
USES: Border, bedding, container
FLOWERS: ■ ■ ■ □

SITING: Flowering tobacco prefers full sun and fertile, well-drained, moist soil with a pH of 5.5–7.0. Plants are short-lived perennials grown as annuals. Tubular red, pink, white, and green flowers are white inside and appear in summer. Flowers are fragrant and open fully during the night. Leaves are larger at the base of the plant. Place in odd-numbered groups in the border, mass as bedding plants, or use in mixed container plantings. Good companions include 'John Elsley' bloody cranesbill and 'Purpureum' fennel.

CARE: Plant 12" apart in late spring. Apply slow-release granular plant food at time of planting or begin using water-soluble plant food 3 weeks after planting. Follow label directions for amount and frequency. Water deeply when the soil is dry. Apply vegetative mulch around, but not touching, the plants in summer to help retain soil moisture and add organic matter to the soil as it decomposes. Deadhead spent blooms to encourage reblooming. Remove plants just before the first frost or right afterward when foliage is disfigured. Cover bare soil with 3" of organic mulch during winter to preserve the topsoil.

PROPAGATION: Sprinkle seeds over the soil mix and leave exposed to light; do not cover. Thoroughly moisten and keep moist, not soggy, until seeds germinate. Germination occurs in 10–15 days at 70–75°F. Transplanting may begin 20–25 days after sowing. After transplanting, reduce temperature to 60–65°F.

PESTS AND DISEASES: Diseases include mosaic virus, root rot, and downy mildew. Insect pests include aphids and spider mites. Control by spraying plants with a forceful water spray, or use an insecticide according to label directions.

RELATED SPECIES: Nicki Series cultivars reach 18" high and bear fragrant red, pink, white, and lime green flowers. Sensation Hybrids bear red, pink, and white flowers, and *N.* 'Lime Green' reaches 24" high and bears lime green flowers. *N.* ×*sanderae*, reaches 24" high and bears panicles of red (sometimes pink), white, or purple flowers. *N. sylvestris* grows to 5' tall and bears fragrant white trumpet-shaped flowers.

CUPFLOWER

Nierembergia hippomanica *neer-ehm-BERG-ee-uh hihp-oh-MAHN-ih-kuh*

Cupflower has appealing white flowers with yellow throats. This is 'Mt. Blanc'.

ZONES: 7–10
SIZE: 10"h × 10"w
TYPE: Perennial
FORM: Rounded
TEXTURE: Fine
GROWTH: Medium
LIGHT: Full sun
MOISTURE: Medium

SOIL: Moderately fertile, moist, well-drained
FEATURES: Flowers, foliage
USES: Border, container
FLOWERS: ■ □

SITING: Cupflower prefers full sun and moderately fertile, well-drained, moist soil with a pH of 5.5–7.0. Provide shelter from strong winds. Cup-shaped pale blue or white flowers with a distinctive yellow throat appear in summer. Leaves are small, narrow, and pointed. Place plants in odd-numbered groups at the front of the border, mass as bedding, or add to mixed container plantings. Good companions include gaura, 'Fastigiata' hollyhock mallow, and gulf muhly.

CARE: Plant 10" apart in late spring. Apply slow-release granular plant food at time of planting or begin using water-soluble plant food 3 weeks after planting. When the soil feels almost dry 2" below the surface, water deeply. Maintain moist, not soggy, soil. Apply 3" of vegetative mulch around, but not touching, the plants in summer to help retain soil moisture and add organic matter to the soil as it decomposes. Plants are self-cleaning, so flowers do not need to be deadheaded, but shear back lightly after flowering to encourage compact growth. Remove plants just before the first frost or right afterward when foliage is disfigured.

PROPAGATION: Sprinkle seeds over the soil mix and cover lightly. Thoroughly moisten and keep moist, not soggy, until seeds germinate. Germination occurs in 10–15 days at 70–75°F. Transplant 25–35 days after sowing. After transplanting, reduce the temperature to 60–65°F.

PESTS AND DISEASES: Diseases include tobacco mosaic virus.

RELATED SPECIES: *N. hippomanica* var. *violacea* bears violet-blue flowers, and 'Purple Robe' has purple-blue flowers.

'Purple Robe' cupflower makes a colorful addition to a sunny container garden.

LOVE-IN-A-MIST

Nigella damascena *neye-JEHL-uh dam-uh-SEE-nuh*

Love-in-a-mist is fine-textured and should be planted in groups for best effect.

ZONES: NA
SIZE: 24"h × 10"w
TYPE: Annual
FORM: Upright
TEXTURE: Fine
GROWTH: Fast
LIGHT: Full sun
MOISTURE: Medium

SOIL: Moderately fertile, well-drained
FEATURES: Flowers, foliage, seedpods
USES: Border, container
FLOWERS: ■ ■ □ ■

SITING: Love-in-a-mist prefers full sun and moderately fertile, well-drained soil with a pH of 5.5–7.5. Purplish-blue flowers lighten with age to pale blue and appear in summer. Flowers are followed by purple-and-green-striped seedpods, which are valued for use in dried arrangements. Plant in large groups; solitary plants are too slender and wispy to have a presence in the landscape. Good container companions include 'Bressingham Ruby' heart-leaf bergenia, 'Purpureum' fennel, rosemary, and lemon thyme.

Dried seedpods of love-in-a-mist are prized for flower arrangements.

CARE: Plant 6–12" apart in late spring. Apply slow-release granular plant food at time of planting. Water deeply when the soil is dry. Leave flowers to fade on plants to allow the seedpods to form. Remove plants just before the first frost or right afterward when foliage is disfigured.
PROPAGATION: Love-in-a-mist does not transplant well. Sow directly into the landscape bed after the last frost. Germination will occur in 7–14 days at 68–72°F. Germination rates may be low, so plant extra seed and thin later.
PESTS AND DISEASES: Plants are relatively pest free when cultural requirements are met.
RELATED SPECIES: Dwarf cultivars (less than 10" high) include 'Blue Midget', 'Cambridge Blue' with double blue flowers, and 'Dwarf Moody Blue' with semidouble flowers. Miss Jekyll Series reaches 18" high and bears blue, white, and pink flowers, 'Mulberry Rose' reaches 18" and has double pale pink flowers that darken with age, 'Oxford Blue' bears double large blue flowers, Persian Jewel Series bears pink, white, red, and purple flowers, and 'Red Jewel' has deep rose flowers.

OZARK SUNDROP

Oenothera macrocarpa (missouriensis) *ohn-oh-THEHR-uh mak-roh-KAR-puh (mih-zur-ee-EN-sis)*

Ozark sundrop blooms all summer long in Midwestern states. It is also known as Missouri primrose.

ZONES: 4–8
SIZE: 8"h × 24"w
TYPE: Perennial
FORM: Spreading
TEXTURE: Medium
GROWTH: Medium
LIGHT: Full sun
MOISTURE: Medium

SOIL: Moderately fertile, well-drained
FEATURES: Flowers, foliage
USES: Border, container, wall
FLOWERS: ■ ■ □

SITING: Ozark sundrop prefers full sun and moderately fertile, well-drained soil with a pH of 6.5–7.5. Plants require well-drained soil in winter as well as summer. Solitary, paper-thin bright yellow flowers appear from late spring to late summer. Plants do not perform well in southern heat. Place in groups at the front of the border, add to mixed container plantings, or allow to cascade down a wall. Good companions include 'Jackanapes' crocosmia, geum, and 'Dazzler' blanket flower.

Showy evening primrose's white or pink blooms are fragrant. It spreads quickly through the landscape.

CARE: Plant 18–24" apart in spring. Apply slow-release granular plant food at time of planting. Water deeply when the soil is dry. Apply vegetative mulch around, but not touching, the plants in summer to help retain soil moisture. Deadhead spent blooms to encourage reblooming. Trim back in fall once frost withers the foliage.
PROPAGATION: Plants may self-sow in the landscape; divide in spring. To start indoors, sprinkle seed over the soil mix and leave exposed to light; do not cover. Thoroughly moisten and keep moist, not soggy, until seeds germinate. Germination occurs in 8–16 days at 70–80°F. Transplant 20–27 days after sowing. Reduce the temperature to 55°F after transplanting.
PESTS AND DISEASES: Root rot may occur in wet soils. Powdery mildew, rust, and Septoria leaf spot are other diseases.
RELATED SPECIES: Showy evening primrose (*O. speciosa*) reaches 12" high and wide and bears fragrant white flowers that occasionally turn pink. It tolerates humidity but may be invasive in fertile, moist soil.

CINNAMON FERN

Osmunda cinnamomea *ahz-MUHND-uh sihn-uh-MOHM-ee-uh*

Cinnamon fern spores resemble cinnamon sticks nestled among its fronds.

ZONES: 3–8
SIZE: 36"h × 36"w
TYPE: Perennial
FORM: Irregular
TEXTURE: Coarse
GROWTH: Medium
LIGHT: Partial to full shade
MOISTURE: Medium to high

SOIL: Fertile, moist, well-drained
FEATURES: Foliage, fiddlehead fronds, roots
USES: Border, woodland, container
FALL COLOR: ■■

SITING: Cinnamon fern prefers full shade or heavy mid- to late-day partial shade and fertile, well-drained, moist soil with a pH of 5.5–7.0. Fertile bright green fronds appear in spring, turn cinnamon brown with spores, then decline by midsummer. Fronds turn golden yellow in fall, then brown. Plant in groups in the border, as a ground cover in the woodland, or as the focal point in a container planting. Good companions include goatsbeard, bugbane, and Siebold hosta cultivars.

CARE: Plant 36" apart in spring or fall in fertile soil high in organic matter. To increase organic matter, add 1–2" of compost to the planting bed and till in to a depth of 12–15". Apply slow-release granular plant food at time of planting.

When the soil feels dry 2" below the surface, water deeply. Apply 3" of vegetative mulch around, but not touching, the plants or rhizomes in summer and winter to help retain soil moisture and as it decomposes it will add organic matter to the soil. Prune back in fall once frost withers the foliage.

PROPAGATION: Divide in spring or fall. Dig around the rhizomes and lift. Use a sharp spade to slice through the root system. Reset portions that contain healthy roots and top shoots, then water and mulch. Discard any pieces that do not contain both healthy roots and top shoots.

PESTS AND DISEASES: Plants are relatively pest free when cultural requirements (sun, soil, planting depth, moisture) are met. Rust is an occasional problem.

A drip irrigation system efficiently delivers water to moisture-loving ferns.

ROYAL FERN

Osmunda regalis *ahz-MUHND-uh reh-GAHL-ihs*

Royal ferns are huge specimens for the shady landscape.

ZONES: 3–9
SIZE: 6'h × 6'w
TYPE: Perennial
FORM: Irregular
TEXTURE: Medium
GROWTH: Medium
LIGHT: Partial to full shade

MOISTURE: Medium to high
SOIL: Fertile, moist, well-drained
FEATURES: Foliage, roots
USES: Border, woodland, container
FALL COLOR: ■■

SITING: Royal fern prefers full to partial shade, shelter from the midday sun, and fertile, well-drained, moist soil with a pH of 5.5–7.2. Plants tolerate wet soil as well. Bright green fronds reach 3' long in spring, lengthening to 6' long in summer. Fibrous roots are visible above ground and create interest. They are used as osmunda fiber in orchid potting mix. Plant in odd-numbered groups in the large border, as a tall ground cover in the woodland or at water's edge, or as a focal point in a large container planting. Good companions include goatsbeard, 'Superba' Chinese astilbe, bugbane, and 'Francis Williams' hosta.

CARE: Plant 3–6' apart in spring or fall. Apply slow-release granular plant food at time of planting. If planting in a wetland, or near water, avoid fertilizers and chemical pesticides to prevent chemicals from leaching into water bodies. Till in organic matter to create deep, humusy, fertile soil. Apply 3" of vegetative mulch around, but not touching, the plants in summer and winter to help retain soil moisture and add organic matter to the soil as it decomposes. Maintain moist soil. If using an irrigation system, maintain deep, infrequent waterings and avoid delivering a light sprinkle every day. Prune back in fall once frost withers the foliage.

PROPAGATION: Divide in spring or fall. Dig around the rhizomes and lift. Use a sharp spade to slice through the root system. Reset portions that contain healthy roots and top shoots, then water and mulch. Discard any pieces that do not contain both healthy roots and top shoots.

PESTS AND DISEASES: Plants are relatively pest free. Rust is an occasional problem.

RELATED SPECIES: The cultivars 'Crispa' and 'Cristata' have crested tips, 'Purpurescens' has purple-stained fronds in spring, and 'Undulata' fronds have wavy edges. Interrupted fern (*O. claytoniana*) tolerates drier sites and is hardy in Zones 4–8.

JAPANESE SPURGE
Pachysandra terminalis *Pahk-ih-SAHN-druh ter-mihn-AHL-ihs*

Japanese spurge is an outstanding evergreen ground cover for shade. 'Silver Edge' is a variegated form.

ZONES: 4–8
SIZE: 8"h × 8"w
TYPE: Perennial
FORM: Spreading
TEXTURE: Medium
GROWTH: Medium
LIGHT: Partial to full shade
MOISTURE: Medium
SOIL: Moderately fertile, well-drained
FEATURES: Foliage, flowers
USES: Ground cover
FLOWERS: □
FALL COLOR: ▨

SITING: Japanese spurge prefers full or partial shade and fertile to moderately fertile, well-drained soil with a pH of 5.5–7.0. Plants have evergreen whorls of toothed, glossy dark green leaves. Spikes of tiny white flowers appear in late spring. Plants spread quickly and will coexist with tree roots. Place in prepared beds at the feet of trees, in the woody or herbaceous shade border, or in the woodland garden. Good companions in a ground cover bed include 'Pumila' Chinese astilbe, bleeding heart, and 'Elegans' Siebold hosta.

CARE: Plant 12–24" apart in late spring or fall; the closer plants are, the faster the ground will be covered. Apply slow-release granular plant food at time of planting or begin using water-soluble plant food 3 weeks after planting, especially if plants will be competing with tree or shrub roots. Water deeply when the soil is dry. Apply 3" of vegetative mulch in summer and winter to reduce weed seed germination, retain soil moisture, and keep soil temperatures stable.

PROPAGATION: Divide in spring. Dig around the rhizomes and lift. Use a sharp spade to slice through the root system. Reset portions that contain healthy roots and top shoots, then water and mulch. Discard any pieces that do not contain both healthy roots and top shoots.

PESTS AND DISEASES: Leaf spot may be a disease problem.

RELATED SPECIES: The cultivar 'Green Carpet' is compact, 'Silver Edge' has light green leaves rimmed in silver-white, and 'Variagata' has white variegated leaves and grows slowly.

PEONY
Paeonia officinalis *pay-OH-nee-uh uh-fish-ih-NAHL-ihs*

Peonies are long-lived plants with classic flowers for landscape viewing.

ZONES: 3–8
SIZE: 24–36"h × 24–36"w
TYPE: Perennial
FORM: Upright
TEXTURE: Medium
GROWTH: Medium
LIGHT: Full sun, partial shade
MOISTURE: Medium
SOIL: Fertile, moist, well-drained
FEATURES: Flowers, foliage
USES: Border
FLOWERS: ▨ ■ □

SITING: Peony prefers full sun or light afternoon shade and fertile, well-drained, moist soil with a pH of 6.5–7.2. Plants are very long lived. In the mixed border, lace groups through the middle of beds. Good companions include sea pink, gas plant, sweet woodruff, and evergreen candytuft.

CARE: Plant 24–36" apart and 2" deep in early autumn. Buds or "eyes" should be 1–2" below the soil surface and should face up. Add bonemeal and slow-release granular plant food to the soil at planting time. Select a food low in nitrogen. Apply 3" of vegetative mulch in summer. Plunge peony rings into the soil around the plant in early spring so the foliage can easily grow up through the structure; the rings will be hidden once the plant reaches full height. Maintain moist soil. Cut stems and leaves to the ground after frost disfigures the foliage. Remove peony rings and store until springtime. If disease was present, disinfect rings and pruning tools, and dispose of all trimmed foliage. Plants need at least 6 hours of unobstructed sunlight per day for the best flowering. Peonies rarely need division to maintain vigor.

PROPAGATION: To start new plants, dig around the tuber and lift. Use a sharp spade to slice through the root system. Reset portions that contain at least three healthy buds or "eyes," then water and mulch. Plants may take two seasons to resume normal bloom habits after division.

PESTS AND DISEASES: Diseases include botrytis, Verticillium wilt, ringspot virus, and stem rot. Pests include nematodes and Japanese beetles. Wet soil almost always causes disease problems.

RELATED SPECIES: Tree peony (*P. suffruticosa*) reaches up to 7' high and 3–4' wide with white, red, pink, or purple flowers. Leaves have 3–5 lobes and are light green above and blue-green below.

1 Lift peony roots in late summer to divide them.

2 Make certain each division contains three or more eyes or buds.

3 Reset healthy sections shallowly, only 1–2" deep in the soil.

Remove the plant's peony ring support at the end of the season.

Cut back the foliage to ground level after frost.

ICELAND POPPY

Papaver nudicaule *pah-PAW-vehr nood-ih-KAWL-ay*

Iceland poppy has papery flowers in delicate shades of white, salmon, orange, and yellow.

ZONES: 2–8
SIZE: 18"h × 12"w
TYPE: Perennial
FORM: Upright
TEXTURE: Medium
GROWTH: Medium
LIGHT: Full sun
MOISTURE: Medium

SOIL: Fertile, well-drained
FEATURES: Flowers, foliage
USES: Border, naturalizing, container
FLOWERS: ■□■

SITING: Iceland poppy prefers deep sun and deep, fertile, well-drained soil with a pH of 5.5–7.0. Plants are grown as short-lived perennials in cooler regions and as annuals in warmer regions. Solitary, fragrant, papery flowers in yellow, white, orange, or salmon-pink, up to 3" across, appear in spring and early summer. Leaves are blue-green and hairy. Flowers are excellent fresh cut. Good companions include 'Jackanapes' crocosmia, geum, and 'Dazzler' blanket flower.

CARE: Plant 12" apart in late spring. Apply slow-release granular plant food at time of planting. Apply 3" of vegetative mulch around, but not touching, the plant in summer and winter. Water deeply when the soil is dry.

PROPAGATION: Divide in spring. Dig around the root clump and lift. Use a sharp spade to slice through the root system. Reset portions that contain healthy roots and top shoots, then water and mulch. To start indoors, sprinkle seeds over the soil mix and leave exposed to light; do not cover. Thoroughly moisten and keep moist, not soggy, until seeds germinate. Germination occurs in 7–14 days at 65–75°F. Transplant 17–25 days after sowing. After transplanting, reduce temperature to 55°F.

PESTS AND DISEASES: Diseases include botrytis, powdery mildew, and root rot.

RELATED SPECIES: The cultivar 'Champagne Bubbles' bears flowers in pastel shades, 'Garden Gnome' has bright-colored flowers and is dwarf, 'Hamlet' bears scarlet red flowers, 'Oregon Rainbows' comes in pastel shades, and 'Pacino' is compact with yellow flowers.

ORIENTAL POPPY

Papaver orientale *pah-PAW-vehr or-ee-ehn-TAHL-ay*

Oriental poppy has papery flowers in vibrant orange-red hues to pastel pink, salmon, and white.

ZONES: 3–7
SIZE: 18–36"h × 24–36"w
TYPE: Perennial
FORM: Irregular
TEXTURE: Medium
GROWTH: Medium
LIGHT: Full sun
MOISTURE: Medium

SOIL: Fertile, well-drained
FEATURES: Flowers, foliage
USES: Border, naturalizing, container
FLOWERS: ■□■

SITING: Oriental poppy prefers full sun and deep, fertile, well-drained soil with a pH of 5.5–7.0. Protect papery flowers from strong winds. Plants prefer cool temperatures and dislike heat and humidity. Solitary, dashing red-orange flowers with black splashes in the center appear from late spring into summer. Plant in groups in the border or in containers, or naturalize in a large, prepared area. Plants become dormant in summer and die back to the ground. Companions include 'Snowbank' white boltonia, bluebeard, and Russian sage.

CARE: Plant 24" apart in autumn or spring. Apply slow-release granular plant food at time of planting in spring. Apply 3" of vegetative mulch in summer and winter to reduce weed seed germination, retain soil moisture, and keep soil temperatures stable. Water deeply when the soil is dry.

PROPAGATION: Sprinkle seeds over the soil mix and leave exposed to light; do not cover. Thoroughly moisten and keep moist, not soggy, until seeds germinate. Germination occurs in 7–14 days at 65–75°F. Transplant 17–25 days after sowing. After transplanting, reduce temperature to 55°F. Divide in mid- to late summer while dormant and before new root growth starts.

PESTS AND DISEASES: Diseases include botrytis, powdery mildew, and root rot.

RELATED SPECIES: 'Allegro' has red-orange flowers with black at the base of the petals, 'Beauty of Livermere' bears red flowers up to 8" across stained black at the base, 'Black and White' has white flowers with a reddish-black stain at the base, 'Carnival' bears crinkly red-orange flowers stained white at the base, 'Cedric Morris' has crinkly pale pink flowers stained black at the base, 'Fatima' is compact, with white flowers and pink edges and black-stained base, 'Harvest Moon' bears orange semidouble flowers, and 'May Queen' has nodding, double orange-red flowers.

1 Divide poppies after blooming when they are dormant.

2 Lift the entire plant from soil.

3 Split clump using a sharp spade.

4 Reset portions that contain healthy roots and shoots.

ROSE-SCENTED GERANIUM
Pelargonium graveolens *pell-ar-GOHN-ee-uhm grahv-ee-OH-lehns*

Rose-scented geranium's essential oils are used in perfumes.

ZONES: 9 and 10
SIZE: 18–24"h ×
12–24"w
TYPE: Perennial
FORM: Sprawling
TEXTURE: Medium
GROWTH: Medium
LIGHT: Full sun

MOISTURE: Medium
SOIL: Fertile,
well-drained
FEATURES: Flowers,
foliage
USES: Border,
container
FLOWERS: ■

SITING: Rose-scented geranium prefers full sun and fertile, well-drained soil with a pH of 5.5–7.3. Plants are commonly grown as annuals or tender perennials and moved indoors before frost. Tiny pink blooms appear in summer and complement the fragrant foliage. Good companions include fennel, lavender, and lemon thyme.

CARE: Plant 18" apart in late spring. Apply slow-release granular plant food at time of planting. Select one low in nitrogen to preserve fragrance. Water deeply when the soil is dry. Transplant into a container in late summer or early autumn to bring indoors, or treat as an annual in colder zones and remove once frost has killed the plant.

PROPAGATION: Take cuttings in summer. Cut nonwoody pieces that contain two healthy leaves and at least three nodes. Insert exposed nodes into rooting hormone, shake off the excess, and insert stems into moist soil mix, keeping leaves above the soil level. Cover with plastic to raise humidity levels. Supply bottom heat and keep moist, not soggy, until root and top shoot growth is evident, then transplant the rooted cuttings.

PESTS AND DISEASES: Insect problems include aphids and spider mites. Diseases of geranium include botrytis, black leg, and Xanthomonas blight.

RELATED SPECIES: 'Lady Plymouth' has creamy-edged leaves, compact 'Little Pet' has rose-pink flowers, and 'Mint Rose' has white-rimmed leaves and a mint scent.

Take cuttings from nonwoody stems.

Dip end tip and exposed nodes in rooting hormone.

Stick cutting in soilless growing mix.

Cover cuttings with plastic to increase humidity.

ZONAL GERANIUM
Pelargonium ×hortorum *pell-ar-GOHN-ee-uhm hor-TOR-uhm*

Zonal geranium is the classic look in summer sun.

ZONES: 9 and 10
SIZE: 5–24"h ×
6–12"w
TYPE: Perennial
FORM: Upright
TEXTURE: Medium
GROWTH: Fast
LIGHT: Full sun

MOISTURE: Medium
SOIL: Fertile,
well-drained
FEATURES: Flowers,
foliage
USES: Bedding,
container
FLOWERS: ■□■■

SITING: Zonal geranium prefers full sun and fertile, well-drained soil with a pH of 5.5–7.0. In hot climates plants may benefit from afternoon shade. Mass for bedding or use in containers. Container companions include alyssum and rosemary.

CARE: Plant 6–24" apart in late spring. Apply slow-release granular plant food at time of planting. Water deeply when the soil is dry. Deadhead spent blooms to encourage reblooming; blooms snap off easily. Dig plants in early autumn and pot up to bring indoors; or leave until disfigured by frost, then discard. Indoors, shear back foliage by one-third in winter. Plants' rootstocks may be hung in a cool spot indoors in the dark through winter, and planted back outdoors in spring. Plants may also be grown as annuals.

PROPAGATION:
Germination occurs in 7–10 days at 70–75°F. Transplant 10–15 days after sowing. After transplanting, reduce temperature to 60–65°F. Take cuttings in summer. Cut nonwoody pieces that contain two healthy leaves and at least three nodes. Insert exposed nodes into rooting hormone, shake off excess, and insert into moist soil mix, keeping leaves above soil level. Cover with plastic to raise humidity levels. Supply bottom heat and keep soil mix moist until new growth is evident, then transplant.

PESTS AND DISEASES: Insect pest problems include aphids and spider mites. Diseases of geranium include botrytis, black leg, and Xanthomonas blight.

RELATED SPECIES: Ivy geranium (*P. peltatum*) is a trailing plant well suited to container plantings or trailing over walls.

Zonal geranium's faded flowers may be snapped off by hand to stimulate reblooming.

Ivy geranium cascades nicely from containers.

BEARD TONGUE
Penstemon barbatus PEHN-stehm-uhn bar-BAY-tuhs

Beard tongue, also known as beardlip penstemon or penstemon, attracts butterflies with its tubular flowers.

ZONES: 4–9
SIZE: 18–24"h ×
12–24"w
TYPE: Perennial
FORM: Upright
TEXTURE: Medium
GROWTH: Medium
LIGHT: Full sun to
partial shade

MOISTURE: Medium
SOIL: Fertile, well-
drained
FEATURES: Flowers
USES: Border,
container
FLOWERS: ■□■■

SITING: Beard tongue prefers full sun or bright afternoon shade and fertile soil with a pH of 5.5–7.0. Plants tolerate heat and humidity. Well-drained soil in summer and winter is essential. Panicles of tubular red flowers with a yellow beard appear from late spring to early summer in the South and into early autumn in cooler regions. Flowers attract butterflies and are excellent fresh cut. Place in odd-numbered groups in the border or add freely to containers. The relative narrowness of the plant makes it ideal for container plantings. Good companions include scaevola, 'Pink Mist'

Deadhead penstemon to stimulate reblooming.

pincushion flower, and 'Burgundy Giant' purple fountain grass.
CARE: Plant 12–24" apart in spring or fall. Apply slow-release granular plant food at time of planting. Apply 3" of vegetative mulch around, but not touching, the plants in summer and winter. Water deeply when the soil is dry. Deadhead spent blooms to encourage reblooming. Older flower stalks fall and flop as they age. Plants also flop if they do not receive enough sun. Cut back in fall after frost disfigures foliage.
PROPAGATION: Sprinkle seeds over the growing medium and leave exposed to light; do not cover. Thoroughly moisten and keep moist, not soggy, until seeds germinate. Germination occurs in 7–10 days at 70°F. Transplant 25–28 days after sowing. After transplanting, reduce temperature to 55°F.
PESTS AND DISEASES: Diseases include powdery mildew, leaf spots, rust, and Southern blight.
RELATED SPECIES: 'Elfin Pink' reaches 12" high and has pink flowers, and 'Praecox Nanus Rondo' reaches 18" high and bears shades of red, purple, and pink flowers.

SMOOTH WHITE PENSTEMON
Penstemon digitalis PEHN-stehm-uhn dih-jih-TAHL-ihs

'Husker Red' foliage is semievergreen in a shade of maroon. Smooth white penstemon is also known simply as penstemon.

ZONES: 2–8
SIZE: 24–48"h ×
18"w
TYPE: Perennial
FORM: Upright
TEXTURE: Medium
GROWTH: Medium
LIGHT: Full sun to
partial shade

MOISTURE: Medium
SOIL: Fertile, well-
drained
FEATURES: Flowers,
foliage
USES: Border,
container
FLOWERS: □

SITING: Smooth white penstemon prefers full sun or bright afternoon shade and fertile soil with a pH of 5.5–7.0. Well-drained soil in summer and winter is essential. Plants tolerate high heat and humidity. Panicles of white tubular bell shaped flowers, sometimes marked with purple, appear from early to late summer. Flowers attract bees and butterflies and are excellent fresh cut. Place in groups in the border or use in containers. Good companions include 'Crimson Butterflies' gaura, 'Burgundy Giant' purple fountain grass, and 'Iceberg' rose.
CARE: Plant 18" apart in spring or autumn. Apply slow-release granular plant food at time of planting. To increase organic matter in the soil, add 1–2" of compost to the planting bed and till in to a depth of 12–15". Water deeply when the soil is dry. Apply 3" of vegetative mulch in summer and winter. Deadheading is essential to reblooming. Plants will fall and flop if they do not receive enough sun. Foliage is semievergreen, so leave plants erect for winter interest until frost disfigures foliage, then trim back.
PROPAGATION: Propagate cultivars by division or cuttings. Divide every 3 years in spring or fall to maintain vigor. Dig around the root clump and lift. Use a sharp spade to slice through the root system. Reset portions that contain healthy roots and top shoots. In summer, take cuttings from nonflowering stems. Cut pieces that contain two healthy leaves and at least three nodes. Dip exposed nodes into rooting hormone, shake off excess, and insert into moist soil mix, keeping leaves above the soil level. Sprinkle seeds over the growing medium and leave exposed to light; do not cover. Thoroughly moisten and keep moist, not soggy, until seeds germinate. Germination occurs in 7–10 days at 70°F. Transplanting may begin 25–28 days after sowing. After transplanting, reduce temperature to 55°F.
PESTS AND DISEASES: Diseases include powdery mildew, leaf spots, rust, and Southern blight.
RELATED SPECIES: The cultivar 'Husker Red' was selected as the 1996 Perennial Plant of the Year by the Perennial Plant Association. Foliage is stained maroon and flowers are tinted pink. Ornamental color may revert to green in the heat of the South. Cultivar 'Albus' bears white flowers, 'Nanus' is a dwarf form, and 'Woodville White' has white flowers.

EGYPTIAN STAR FLOWER

Pentas lanceolata   PEHN-tubs labns-ee-ob-LAT-ub

Egyptian star flower loves the heat and produces clusters of star-shaped flowers.

ZONES: 9–11
SIZE: 1–6'h × 18–36"w
TYPE: Perennial
FORM: Rounded
TEXTURE: Medium
GROWTH: Fast
LIGHT: Full sun
MOISTURE: Medium

SOIL: Fertile, well-drained
FEATURES: Flowers, foliage
USES: Border, ground cover, container
FLOWERS: ■ ■ ■ □ ■

SITING: Egyptian star flower prefers full sun and fertile, well-drained soil with a pH of 5.5–7.0. Plants are usually grown as annuals. Clusters of star-shaped flowers in bright pink, red, lavender, purple, blue, or white appear from spring to autumn. Place in groups in the border, mass as an annual ground cover, or use in containers. Good companions include 'Snowbank' white boltonia, 'Kobold' blazing star, and false indigo.

CARE: Plant 18–36" apart in late spring. Apply slow-release granular plant food at time of planting. Apply 3" of vegetative mulch in summer. Water deeply when the soil is dry. Plants withstand heavy pruning but flower production will suffer. Remove plants just before first frost or right afterward when frost disfigures the foliage.

PROPAGATION: In summer take cuttings from nonflowering stems. Cut pieces that contain at least two healthy leaves and three nodes. Dip exposed nodes into rooting hormone, shake off excess, and insert into moist growing medium, keeping leaves well above the soil level. Sprinkle seeds over the soil mix and leave exposed to light; do not cover. Germination occurs in 5–12 days at 72°F. Transplanting may begin 20–28 days after sowing. After transplanting, reduce temperature to 65°F.

PESTS AND DISEASES: Plants are relatively pest free when cultural requirements (sun, soil, planting depth, and moisture) are met.

RELATED SPECIES: The cultivar 'Avalanche' has white flowers and white-stained leaves, 'Kermesina' has bright rose flowers with a violet throat, and 'Quartiniana' has rosey-pink flowers.

RUSSIAN SAGE

Perovskia atriplicifolia   per-OV-skee-ub ab-trib-plibs-ib-FOL-ee-ub

Russian sage is a low-maintenance perennial with a long bloom cycle.

ZONES: 3–9
SIZE: 4'h × 4'w
TYPE: Perennial
FORM: Irregular
TEXTURE: Fine
GROWTH: Medium
LIGHT: Full sun
MOISTURE: Medium

SOIL: Moderately fertile, well-drained
FEATURES: Flowers, foliage
USES: Border, container
FLOWERS: ■

SITING: Russian sage prefers full sun and moderately fertile, well-drained soil with a pH of 5.5–7.3. It is heat and drought tolerant and pest resistant. Lavender flowers appear from summer into autumn. Fragrant foliage is silver-green and finely cut. Flowers attract bees and butterflies. Plant in the border, use in place of traditional woody shrubs, or use in large container plantings. Good companions in the garden include 'Kobold' blazing star, purple coneflower, and 'Snowbank' white boltonia.

CARE: Plant 24–36" apart in spring or fall. Apply with slow-release granular plant food at time of planting. Water only when the soil is dry 2–3" below the surface. Apply mulch in summer and winter. Plants are self-cleaning, so deadheading is not necessary. Plants may be rejuvenated by pruning. To rejuvenate, trim woody stems back almost to the ground once buds appear on the stems in spring. If left unpruned they become unkempt.

PROPAGATION: Plants may be layered in the landscape. Select a stem close to the ground, remove leaves to expose one or more nodes, and pin nodes directly to the soil. Cover the area with mulch. After roots form, cut the stem to separate it from the parent plant, leaving some top growth attached to new roots. New shoots that appear near the parent plant may be dug and transplanted. In spring take cuttings from new growth. Cut pieces that contain at least two healthy leaves and three nodes. Dip exposed nodes into rooting hormone, shake off excess, and insert into moist growing medium, keeping leaves well above the soil level. Supply bottom heat and keep moist, not soggy, until root and top shoot growth is evident, usually in 2–3 weeks, then transplant. To enhance humidity, cover with plastic, keeping it above the leaves.

PESTS AND DISEASES: Plants are relatively pest free when cultural requirements (sun, soil, planting depth, moisture) are met.

RELATED SPECIES: 'Blue Mist' flowers early and has light blue flowers. 'Blue Spire' bears finely cut leaves and lavender-blue flowers.

1 To layer Russian sage, pin a shoot to the ground and cover it with mulch.

2 After roots develop, dig the new plant and transplant it.

PETUNIA

Petunia ×hybrida Peh-TOO-nyuh HIH-brid-uh

Petunias produce nonstop summer color in the container or landscape.

ZONES: NA
SIZE: 6–15"h × 6–36"w
TYPE: Annual
FORM: Mounded
TEXTURE: Medium
GROWTH: Medium
LIGHT: Full sun to part shade

MOISTURE: Medium
SOIL: Moderately fertile, well-drained
FEATURES: Flowers
USES: Bedding, container
FLOWERS: ■ ■ □ ■ ■ ■ ■

SITING: Petunia prefers full sun and moderately fertile, well-drained soil with a pH of 5.5–7.0. Showy flowers appear in summer in reds, pinks, yellows, purples and white. Good container companions include alyssum, dwarf fountain grass, fan flower, and lemon thyme.

CARE: When used as bedding plants, place 12–18" apart in late spring. Feed with slow-release granular plant food at time of planting or begin using water-soluble plant food 3 weeks after planting. Follow label directions for amount and frequency. Apply mulch in summer. Water deeply when the soil is dry. Shear plants back by one-third after first flush of flowers to encourage compact growth. Remove plants just before first frost or right afterward.

Old cultivars of petunias require shearing back after first flowering to encourage bushy compact growth; newer types don't.

PROPAGATION: Sprinkle seeds over the growing medium and leave exposed to light; do not cover. Thoroughly moisten and keep moist, not soggy, until seeds germinate. Germination occurs in 10–12 days at 75–80°F. Transplant 15–20 days after sowing. Reduce the temperature to 60°F after transplanting.

PESTS AND DISEASES: Diseases include tobacco mosaic virus, impatiens necrotic spot virus, botrytis, and bacterial soft rot.

RELATED SPECIES: Wave and Easy Wave Series petunias are spreading types in a broad range of colors that begin to flower quickly and perform well all season long. Double forms are also available. Explorer Series is another spreading type, and Opera Series is a creeping type. Cascadia Series petunias have a trailing habit with medium-sized flowers. Petitunia Series has a trailing habit with numerous smaller blooms. Avalanche Series is a trailer with full-sized flowers. A petunia relative, *Calibrachoa* is a trailing plant often grown in hanging baskets. It comes in a broad array of colors. Colorburst Series, Celebration Series, and Calimor® are some popular types.

GARDEN PHLOX

Phlox paniculata FLAHKS pahn-ik-yew-LAH-tuh

Garden phlox blooms are excellent fresh cut and attract bees and butterflies.

ZONES: 3–8
SIZE: 4'h × 2–3'w
TYPE: Perennial
FORM: Upright
TEXTURE: Medium
GROWTH: Fast
LIGHT: Full sun, partial shade

MOISTURE: Medium to high
SOIL: Fertile, moist, well-drained
FEATURES: Flowers, foliage
USES: Border, container
FLOWERS: □ ■ ■ ■ ■

SITING: Garden phlox prefers full sun or light afternoon shade and fertile, well-drained, moist soil with a pH of 5.5–7.0. Good air circulation is essential to discourage powdery mildew. Clusters of white, lavender, pink, rose, and blue flowers abound from summer to early autumn. Flowers are sometimes scented, attract bees and butterflies, and are excellent fresh cut. Good companions include 'Carefree Wonder' and 'Bonica' roses, and daylily cultivars.

CARE: Plant mildew-resistant cultivars 24–36" apart in spring or fall. Apply slow-release granular plant food at time of planting. Apply 3" of vegetative mulch in summer and winter. Water deeply when the soil is dry. Deadhead spent blooms to encourage reblooming and prevent self-seeding. Cut to the ground in fall after frost disfigures the foliage.

PROPAGATION: Divide every 3 years in spring or fall to maintain plant vigor.

PESTS AND DISEASES: Powdery mildew does not need moist air to grow and prosper. It actually flourishes in dry weather. Select mildew-resistant cultivars and place plants where there is plenty of air circulation among them. Keep soil moist but not soggy. Overhead irrigation tends to spread disease, so install drip systems when possible.

RELATED SPECIES: Mildew-resistant cultivars: 'David' bears white flowers, 'Katherine' bears lavender flowers, 'Little Boy' bears two-toned mauve and white flowers, 'Blue Paradise' bears purple-blue flowers, 'Eva Cullem' has pink flowers with red centers, and 'Robert Poore' has purple flowers.

Plant in groups for best effect.

Deadhead faded flowers to stimulate reblooming.

CREEPING PHLOX

Phlox stolonifera FLAHKS stoh-luhn-IHF-er-uh

Creeping phlox is an ideal ground cover for partial shade.

ZONES: 2–8
SIZE: 6"h × 12"w
TYPE: Perennial
FORM: Spreading
TEXTURE: Medium
GROWTH: Medium
LIGHT: Partial shade
MOISTURE: Medium

SOIL: Fertile, moist, well-drained
FEATURES: Flowers, foliage
USES: Woodland, ground cover
FLOWERS: ■ ■ □

SITING: Creeping phlox prefers partial shade with protection from the afternoon sun and fertile, well-drained soil with a pH of 5.5–6.5. Lavender to purple flowers appear in spring. Leaves are dark green. Place in groups in the woodland garden or use as a ground cover among trees and shrubs. Good companions include 'Pictum' Japanese painted fern, 'Elegans' Siebold hosta, and 'Mrs. Moon' lungwort.
CARE: Plant 6–12" apart in spring or fall. Apply slow-release granular plant food at time of planting. Apply 3" of vegetative mulch in summer and winter to reduce weed seed germination, hold moisture in the soil, and as it decomposes it will add organic matter to the soil. Maintain moist, not soggy, soil. Water new transplants daily; otherwise, water deeply only when the soil feels almost dry 2" below the surface. If using an irrigation system, maintain deep, infrequent waterings and avoid delivering a light sprinkle every day. Organic matter in the soil and mulch on the soil surface help reduce watering frequency, because they help the soil retain moisture. Shear plants back after flowering to encourage compact growth.
PROPAGATION: Divide in spring or fall. Dig around the root clump and lift. Use a sharp spade to slice through the root system. Reset portions that contain healthy roots and top shoots, then water and mulch. Discard any pieces that do not contain both healthy roots and top shoots.
PESTS AND DISEASES: Spider mites and powdery mildew are problems.
RELATED SPECIES: 'Ariane' bears white flowers with a yellow center, 'Home Fires' bears pink flowers, 'Pink Ridge' has pale pink flowers, and 'Violet Vere' has violet flowers. Woodland phlox (*P. divaricata*) is a native plant hardy in Zones 4–8 bearing purple, pink or white blooms in spring.

MOSS PHLOX

Phlox subulata FLAHKS subb-yew-LAT-uh

Moss phlox brightens up the landscape in early summer.

ZONES: 2–8
SIZE: 6"h × 24"w
TYPE: Perennial
FORM: Spreading
TEXTURE: Medium
GROWTH: Fast
LIGHT: Full sun, partial shade

MOISTURE: Medium
SOIL: Fertile, well-drained
FEATURES: Flowers, foliage
USES: Ground cover
FLOWERS: ■ ■ □ ■

SITING: Moss phlox prefers full sun or dappled shade in the afternoon and fertile, well-drained soil with a pH of 5.5–7.5. Flowers appear from late spring to early summer. Evergreen foliage is bright green and hugs the ground. Lilies such as 'Ariadne', 'Casa Blanca', and 'Journey's End' grow through moss phlox foliage and bloom later in the season, making them good companions for moss phlox.
CARE: Plant 24" apart in spring. Apply slow-release granular plant food at time of planting. Maintain moist, not soggy, soil. When the soil feels almost dry 2" below the surface, water deeply. Shear back after flowering to promote compact form. Foliage is evergreen, so there is no need to trim back in autumn unless it is disfigured by frost.
PROPAGATION: Layering in the landscape is the easiest form of propagation. Select a stem close to the ground and remove leaves to expose one or more nodes; pin nodes directly to the soil and cover with mulch. After roots form, cut the stem from the parent plant, leaving some top growth attached to the new plant. Gently dig the new plant and replant, water, and mulch.
PESTS AND DISEASES: Spider mites are occasional pests.
RELATED SPECIES: The cultivar 'Apple Blossom' has lilac blooms with a purple center, 'Candy Stripe' bears white and pink flowers, 'Emerald Blue' has light blue flowers, 'Emerald Pink' has pink flowers, 'Fort Hill' has deep pink flowers, 'Red Wings' has bright red flowers with a darker center, and 'White Delight' has white flowers and light green leaves.

After bloom shear back moss phlox.

Divide moss phlox in spring or fall.

OBEDIENT PLANT

Physostegia virginiana *feye-soh-STEE-jee-uh vehr-jihn-ee-AY-nuh*

Obedient plant has moveable flowers that remain in position where they are placed.

ZONES: 3–8
SIZE: 4'h × 2'w
TYPE: Perennial
FORM: Upright
TEXTURE: Medium
GROWTH: Fast
LIGHT: Full sun to partial shade
MOISTURE: Medium

SOIL: Moderately fertile, moist, well-drained
FEATURES: Flowers, foliage
USES: Border, container
FLOWERS: ■□■

SITING: Obedient plant prefers morning sun and afternoon shade and moderately fertile, well-drained, moist soil with a pH of 5.5–7.0. If the soil is too fertile, plants may become invasive. Two-lipped purple, pink, or white flowers appear from midsummer to early autumn. Move the

flowers on the stalk and they obediently stay where placed. Plant in groups in the border or use in container plantings. Good companions for obedient plant include purple coneflower, 'Veitch's Blue' globe thistle, and hollyhock mallow.
CARE: Plant 18–24" apart in spring. Apply slow-release granular plant food at time of planting. Apply mulch in summer and

Pinch back obedient plant early in the season to promote compact, full growth.

winter. Water deeply when the soil is dry. Staking is not normally necessary when cultural requirements are met. If soil is too rich or excessive nitrogen is applied, or if there is too little sun, foliage may become floppy. Trim back in fall once frost withers the foliage.
PROPAGATION: In moderately fertile soil, plants may be divided every 3 years to control growth. In rich soils division is needed sooner to maintain vigor and control growth. Dig around the rhizomes and lift. Use a sharp spade to slice through the root system. Reset portions that contain healthy roots and top shoots. Discard any pieces that do not contain both healthy roots and top shoots. Water deeply and apply 3" of vegetative mulch around, but not touching, the plants.
PESTS AND DISEASES: Plants are relatively pest free when cultural requirements (sun, soil, planting depth, moisture) are met.
RELATED SPECIES: The cultivar 'Alba' bears white flowers, 'Bouquet Rose' has pink flowers, 'Galadriel' has pale pink flowers and is dwarf, 'Morden Beauty' has pink flowers and willowlike leaves, 'Summer Snow' has white flowers, 'Variegata' has cream-rimmed leaves, and 'Vivid' bears deep vibrant pink flowers.

SMALL SOLOMON'S SEAL

Polygonatum biflorum *puhl-ihg-ih-NAY-tum bye-FLOR-um*

Small Solomon's seal has attractive flowers, stems and leaves, and berries.

ZONES: 3–9
SIZE: 36"h × 24"w
TYPE: Perennial
FORM: Upright
TEXTURE: Medium
GROWTH: Slow
LIGHT: Partial to full shade
MOISTURE: Medium

SOIL: Fertile, moist, well-drained
FEATURES: Foliage, flowers, fruit
USES: Border, woodland, container
FLOWERS: □
FALL COLOR: ■

SITING: Small Solomon's seal prefers full to partial shade, shelter from the afternoon sun, and fertile, well-drained, moist soil

with a pH of 5.5–7.0. Small greenish-white flowers dangle from the leaf axils from late spring until midsummer. Dark black berries follow the flowers. Place in groups in the woodland garden, the shade border, or a mixed container planting. Good garden companions include 'Pictum' or 'Silver Falls' Japanese painted fern, 'Hillside Black Beauty' snakeroot, and 'Gold Standard' or 'Red October' hosta.
CARE: Plant 12–24" apart in spring or autumn in fertile soil high in organic matter. To increase organic matter, add 1–2" of compost to the planting bed and till in to a depth of 12–15". Apply slow-release granular plant food at time of planting or begin using water-soluble plant food 3 weeks after planting in spring. Cease feeding 6–8 weeks prior to first frost date. Maintain moist, not soggy, soil. When the soil feels almost dry 2" below the surface, water deeply. If using an irrigation system, maintain deep infrequent waterings and avoid delivering a light sprinkle every day. Organic matter in the soil and mulch on the soil surface help retain soil

moisture. Trim back in fall once frost withers the foliage.
PROPAGATION: Divide in spring or fall. Dig around the root clump and lift. Use a sharp spade to slice through the root system. Reset portions that contain healthy roots and top shoots. Discard any pieces that do not contain both roots and top shoots. Water deeply and apply 3" of vegetative mulch around, but not touching, the plants.
PESTS AND DISEASES: Plants are relatively pest free when cultural requirements (sun, soil, planting depth, moisture) are met.
RELATED SPECIES: Fragrant Solomon's seal (*P. odoratum*) has arching stems that reach 3' high and 2' wide. It bears pendant green-edged white flowers in late spring and early summer followed by black berries. Variegated forms are available. The cultivar 'Flore Pleno' bears double flowers, 'Gilt Edge' has gold-rimmed leaves, 'Grace Barker' bears striped creamy-white and green leaves, and 'Variegatum' has red stems early on and white-edged leaves.

CHRISTMAS FERN
Polystichum acrostichoides *pahl-ih-STIK-um ak-roh-stih-KOY-deez*

Christmas fern is a low-maintenance, hardy evergreen fern.

ZONES: 3–8
SIZE: 18"h × 36"w
TYPE: Perennial
FORM: Irregular
TEXTURE: Medium
GROWTH: Medium
LIGHT: Partial to full shade

MOISTURE: Medium
SOIL: Fertile, moist, well-drained
FEATURES: Foliage
USES: Border, woodland, container

SITING: Christmas fern prefers partial to full shade and fertile, moist, well-drained soil with a pH of 5.5–7.0. This evergreen low-maintenance fern has fronds that are narrow, lance-shaped, and deep green. Place in odd-numbered groups in the woodland garden, the shade border, or the container. Good companions include 'Frances Williams' hosta, goatsbeard, and dwarf Chinese astilbe.

CARE: Plant 24–36" apart in spring or autumn. Apply slow-release granular plant food at time of planting or begin using water-soluble plant food 3 weeks after planting in spring. Follow label directions for amount and frequency. Cease feeding 4–6 weeks prior to first frost date. Apply 3" of vegetative mulch in summer and winter to reduce weed seed germination, retain soil moisture, and keep soil temperatures stable. Water deeply when the soil is dry. Trim back damaged and dead fronds in early spring before new ones emerge.

PROPAGATION: Divide in spring. Dig around the rhizomes and lift. Use a sharp spade to slice through the root system. Reset portions that contain healthy roots and top shoots. Discard any pieces that do not contain both healthy roots and top shoots. Water deeply and apply 3" of vegetative mulch around, but not touching, the plants.

PESTS AND DISEASES: Plants are relatively pest free when their cultural requirements are met.

RELATED SPECIES: Hardy shield fern (*P. aculeatum*) is a European native hardy in Zones 3–6. It grows to 2' tall. Western sword fern (*P. munitum*) is hardy in Zones 3–8 and grows to 3'. Hedge fern (*P. setiferum*) grows 2–4' tall in Zones 6–9.

MOSS ROSE
Portulaca grandiflora *port-yoo-LAH-kuh grand-ih-FLOR-uh*

Moss rose provides nonstop color all summer long in hot, sunny, dry areas. It is also known as portulaca or rose moss.

ZONES: NA
SIZE: 6–8"h × 6–8"w
TYPE: Annual
FORM: Spreading
TEXTURE: Fine
GROWTH: Fast
LIGHT: Full sun
MOISTURE: Medium

SOIL: Moderately fertile, well-drained
FEATURES: Flowers, foliage
USES: Border, bedding, container
FLOWERS: ■□ ■ ■
■

SITING: Moss rose prefers full sun and moderately fertile, well-drained, even sandy soil with a pH of 6.5–7.5. Plants are relatively drought tolerant once established. Single and double bright rose, red, yellow, or white, sometimes striped, flowers appear in summer and open fully only in bright light. Red stems and succulent bright green leaves are additional assets. Place in odd-numbered groups in the border as a ground cover, mass as a bedding plant, or place in containers and allow stems to cascade over the sides. Good companions include heart-leaf bergenia, Russian sage, and 'Vivid' obedient plant.

CARE: Plant 6–8" apart in late spring. Apply slow-release granular plant food at time of planting. Plants that receive an abundance of water and high-nitrogen food may produce lush leaves yet few or no flowers. Provide new transplants with ample water; otherwise, water deeply only when the soil is dry 2–3" below the surface. Apply 2–3" of vegetative mulch around the plants in summer to reduce weed seed germination,

Feed moss rose regularly with Miracle-Gro plant food to promote lush growth and prolific bloom.

hold moisture in the soil, and, as it decomposes, add organic matter to the soil. Deadhead spent blooms to encourage reblooming and prevent self-seeding. Remove plants just before first frost or right afterward. Cover bare soil with 3" of vegetative mulch during winter to preserve the topsoil.

PROPAGATION: Sprinkle seeds over the growing medium and leave uncovered, exposed to light. Thoroughly moisten and keep moist, not soggy, until seeds germinate. Germination occurs in 7–10 days at 75–80°F. Transplant 35–40 days after sowing. After transplanting, reduce the temperature to 65°F.

PESTS AND DISEASES: Diseases include black stem rot and white rust.

RELATED SPECIES: 'Afternoon Delight' is dwarf with large, double flowers in pink, white, orange, and red, 'Aztec Double' bears double red and gold flowers, Cloudbeater Hybrids have double red, gold, apricot, pink, and white flowers, Sundance Hybrids are semitrailing and bear large, semidouble or double flowers, Sundial Series cultivars have double flowers that open in lower light, and 'Swanlake' bears double white flowers.

POLYANTHUS PRIMROSE

Primula ×polyantha *PRIHM-yoo-luh pah-lee-ANN-thuh*

Polyanthus primrose flowers and leaves are attractive additions to moist gardens.

ZONES: 5–8
SIZE: 6–12"h × 8–12"w
TYPE: Perennial
FORM: Rounded
TEXTURE: Medium
GROWTH: Medium
LIGHT: Full sun to partial shade
MOISTURE: Medium to high

SOIL: Moderately fertile to fertile, well-drained
FEATURES: Flowers, foliage
USES: Border, woodland, container
FLOWERS: ■ □ ■ ■ ■ ■

SITING: Polyanthus primrose prefers light shade in the afternoon and moderately fertile or fertile, well-drained soil with a pH of 5.5–7.0 Plants tolerate full sun if the soil is consistently moist (but not soggy). Bright pink, red, purple, yellow, or white flowers usually have a yellow center and appear in late spring or early summer. Rosettes of evergreen or semievergreen deep green leaves are heavily veined. Polyanthus primroses are old-fashioned favorites, comforting and nostalgic, often used in bouquets. Place in odd-numbered groups in the woodland garden, shade border, or containers. Good companions include European wild ginger, 'Pictum' Japanese painted fern, and Lenten rose.

CARE: Plant 8–12" apart in spring or autumn. Apply slow-release granular plant food at time of planting. Follow label directions for amount and frequency. Cease feeding 6–8 weeks prior to first frost date. Apply 3" of vegetative mulch in summer and winter to reduce weed seed germination, retain soil moisture, and keep soil temperatures stable. Water deeply when the soil is dry. Remove damaged or brown leaves in spring before new ones appear.

PROPAGATION: Divide in spring right after flowering or in early autumn. Dig around the root clump and lift. Use a sharp spade to slice through the root system. Reset portions that contain healthy roots and top shoots. Discard any pieces that do not contain both healthy roots and top shoots. Water deeply and apply 3" of vegetative mulch around, but not touching, the plants. To start indoors, sprinkle seeds over the growing medium and leave uncovered, exposed to light. Thoroughly moisten and keep moist, not soggy, until seeds germinate. Germination occurs in 21–28 days at 60–65°F. Transplant in 40–45 days. After transplanting, reduce temperature to 55°F. If temperatures are too warm, flower stalks may be short and hidden in the foliage.

PESTS AND DISEASES: Diseases include botrytis, root rot, rust, and leaf spots. Occasional pests include slugs, aphids, and spider mites.

RELATED SPECIES: Polyanthus primroses are complex hybrids of common cowslip (*P. veris*), English primrose (see below), and Julian primrose (*P. juliae*). All require moist soil and prefer cool temperatures.

ENGLISH PRIMROSE

Primula vulgaris *PRIHM-yoo-luh vuhl-GAR-ihs*

English primrose blooms, in bright colors, are delightful in spring.

ZONES: 4–8
SIZE: 8–10"h × 15"w
TYPE: Perennial
FORM: Rounded
TEXTURE: Medium
GROWTH: Medium
LIGHT: Partial shade
MOISTURE: Medium to high

SOIL: Fertile, moist, well-drained
FEATURES: Flowers, foliage
USES: Border, woodland, container
FLOWERS: ■ ■ □ ■ ■

SITING: English primrose prefers partial shade and fertile, well-drained soil with a pH of 5.5–7.0. Plants tolerate full sun, even southern heat, if the soil is consistently moist and deep and contains ample organic matter. Clusters of fragrant flowers appear in late spring or early summer. Cultivars are shades of white, yellow, pink, purple, and red. Rosettes of evergreen or semievergreen leaves are heavily veined and are bright glossy green. Plant in the old-fashioned cottage garden, the shade border, at the feet of shrubs, or in a container. Place in odd-numbered groups for best effect. Good companions for English primrose include peony, false indigo, and heart-leaf bergenia.

CARE: Plant 12–15" apart in spring or autumn. Apply slow-release granular plant food in spring. Follow label directions for amount and frequency. Water deeply when the soil is dry. Apply 3" of vegetative mulch in summer and winter to reduce weed seed germination, retain soil moisture, and keep soil temperatures stable. Remove damaged or brown leaves in spring before new ones emerge.

PROPAGATION: Divide right after flowering. Dig around the root clump and lift. Use a sharp spade to slice through the root system. Reset portions that contain healthy roots and top shoots. Discard any pieces that do not contain both healthy roots and top shoots. Water deeply and apply 3" of vegetative mulch around, but not touching, the plants.

PESTS AND DISEASES: Slugs and snails are common pests. Diseases include botrytis, root rot, rust, and leaf spots.

RELATED SPECIES: The cultivar 'Cottage White' has double white flowers on long stalks, 'Double Sulphur' bears double yellow flowers, 'Jack-in-the-Green' has pale yellow flowers and a green ruff, 'Marie Crousse' bears large, double violet flowers marked with white, and 'Miss Indigo' has double purple flowers rimmed in white. English primrose is one of the parents in the hybrid species polyanthus primrose (*P. ×polyantha*, see above). Other European native primroses include common cowslip (*P. veris*) and auricula primrose (*P. auricula*) with yellow or red flowers with yellow centers, for Zones 2–8. The drumstick primrose (*P. denticulata*) bears purple or white globelike heads on plants 12" tall. It is hardy in Zones 4–8. Japanese primrose (*P. japonica*) is a Candelabra type for Zones 5–7. The name derives from the whorls of flowers stacked on each flowering stem.

BETHLEHEM SAGE
Pulmonaria saccharata *pul-mohn-AR-ee-uh sahk-uh-RAH-tuh*

Bethlehem sage has violet flowers and attractive silver-splashed leaves. It is also known as lungwort or pulmonaria.

ZONES: 3–8
SIZE: 15"h × 24"w
TYPE: Perennial
FORM: Spreading
TEXTURE: Medium
GROWTH: Slow
LIGHT: Partial to full shade
MOISTURE: Medium

SOIL: Fertile, moist, well-drained
FEATURES: Flowers, foliage
USES: Border, woodland, container
FLOWERS: ■□ ■
FALL COLOR: ■

SITING: Bethlehem sage prefers partial to full shade and fertile, well-drained, moist soil with a pH of 5.5–7.0. Plants do not tolerate wet soil. Funnel-shaped flowers in shades of violet and sometimes white appear from early spring through early summer. Evergreen leaves are silver splotched and occasionally dusted in silver. Place in groups at the front of the shade border, in the woodland garden, or in containers. Good companions include 'Frances Williams' hosta, 'Elegans' Siebold hosta, heart-leaf brunnera, and fringeleaf bleeeding heart.

CARE: Plant 15–18" apart in spring or autumn. Apply slow-release granular plant

Plant Bethlehem sage in partial or full shade and provide it with adequate moisture.

food. Apply 3" of organic mulch around the plants in summer and winter. Water deeply when the soil is dry. Remove brown or damaged foliage in early spring before new growth appears. Cut it back after flowering if foliage looks tattered.

PROPAGATION: Divide after flowering or in autumn every 3 years to maintain vigor. Dig around the root clump and lift. Use a sharp spade to slice through the root system. The larger the portion, the larger the resulting plant during the first year. Smaller pieces may take 2–3 years to reach mature size and bloom. Reset portions that contain healthy roots and top shoots.

PESTS AND DISEASES: Plants are relatively pest free when cultural requirements (sun, soil, planting depth, moisture) are met. Slugs and powdery mildew are occasional problems on Bethlehem sage.

RELATED SPECIES: The cultivar 'Alba' has large white flowers and silver-splashed leaves, 'Argentea' has silver-dusted leaves, 'Janet Fisk' bears pink flowers that turn blue and has silver-spotted leaves, 'Mrs. Moon' has pink buds that open to blue flowers, and heavily silver-splashed leaves.

RODGERSIA
Rodgersia pinnata *rohd-JEHR-zee-uh pihn-AY-tuh*

Rodgersia has star-shaped flowers in mid- to late summer. It is also known as featherleaf rodgersia or Roger's flower.

ZONES: 4–7
SIZE: 4'h × 3'w
TYPE: Perennial
FORM: Rounded
TEXTURE: Coarse
GROWTH: Medium
LIGHT: Partial shade to full sun

MOISTURE: Medium
SOIL: Fertile, well-drained
FEATURES: Flowers, foliage
USES: Border, woodland, wetland
FLOWERS: ■□

SITING: Rodgersia tolerates partial shade to full sun and prefers fertile, well-drained, moist soil with a pH of 5.5–7.0. Plants in full sun require consistently moist soil; partial shade locations may have drier soils. Panicles of star-shaped pink, reddish or occasionally white flowers appear from mid- to late summer. Place in groups in the border or naturalize along the edge of a woodland. Good companions include hybrid anemone, 'The Rocket' ligularia, and royal fern.

CARE: Plant 24–36" apart in spring or autumn. Apply slow-release granular plant food. When the soil feels dry 2" below the surface, water deeply. Apply 3" of

Plants in full sun require more frequent waterings than plants in part shade.

vegetative mulch in summer and winter to reduce weed seed germination, retain soil moisture, and keep soil temperatures stable. Deadhead spent blooms to encourage reblooming. Prune back in fall once frost withers the foliage.

PROPAGATION: Divide in spring. Dig around the root clump and lift. Use a sharp spade to slice through the root system. Reset portions that contain healthy roots and top shoots. Water deeply and apply 3" of organic mulch around, but not touching, the plants.

PESTS AND DISEASES: Plants are relatively pest free when cultural requirements (sun, soil, planting depth, moisture) are met. Slugs are occasional problems.

RELATED SPECIES: The cultivar 'Alba' bears white flowers, 'Elegans' has pink-stained cream flowers, 'Rosea' bears rose flowers, 'Rubra' has deep red flowers, and 'Superba' has bronze-stained young leaves and bright pink flowers. Rodger's flower (*R. aesculifolia*) reaches 3–6' tall and bears star-shaped white or pink flowers in midsummer. Leaves grow up to 10" long and are deeply veined; leaves and stalks are red stained.

BLACK-EYED SUSAN
Rudbeckia fulgida rud-BEHK-ee-uh FUHL-jih-duh

Black-eyed Susan flowers attract butterflies and are excellent fresh cut flowers. The plant is also known as orange coneflower.

ZONES: 4–9
SIZE: 36"h × 18"w
TYPE: Perennial
FORM: Upright
TEXTURE: Medium
GROWTH: Medium
LIGHT: Full sun
MOISTURE: Medium

SOIL: Moderately fertile, well-drained
FEATURES: Flowers, foliage
USES: Border, container
FLOWERS: ■

SITING: Black-eyed Susan prefers full sun and moderately fertile, well-drained soil with a pH of 5.5–7.0. Daisylike yellow flowers with a mahogany brown disk appear from late summer through midautumn. Plants are welcome additions to the full-sun perennial border and containers. Flowers attract butterflies and bees and are excellent fresh cut. Place in groups for best effect. Good companions include 'Snowbank' white boltonia, purple coneflower, and 'Autumn Joy' sedum.

CARE: Plant 18–24" apart in spring or autumn. Apply slow-release granular plant food at time of planting. Water deeply

Remove faded flower stalks of black-eyed Susan to encourage reblooming.

when the soil is dry. If soil is too rich, or excessive nitrogen is applied, or if there is too little sun, foliage may become floppy. Staking is not normally necessary when cultural requirements are met. Apply 3" of vegetative mulch in summer and winter. Deadhead spent blooms to encourage reblooming. Prune back in fall once frost withers the foliage.

PROPAGATION: Divide in spring or autumn every 3 years to maintain vigor. Dig around the root clump and lift. Use a sharp spade to slice through the root system. Reset portions that contain healthy roots and top shoots. Discard any pieces that do not contain both healthy roots and top shoots. Water deeply and apply 3" of organic mulch around the plants.

PESTS AND DISEASES: Slugs, powdery mildew, and rust are occasional pests.

RELATED SPECIES: *R. fulgida* var. *deamii* reaches 24" high, is relatively drought tolerant, and produces many flowers over an extended time. Var. *sullivantii* 'Goldsturm' reaches 24" high, is compact, bears large golden-yellow flowers, and is low-maintenance.

GLORIOSA DAISY
Rudbeckia hirta rud-BEHK-ee-uh HER-tuh

Gloriosa daisy self-seeds well in the garden.

ZONES: 4–9
SIZE: 12–36"h × 18"w
TYPE: Perennial
FORM: Upright
TEXTURE: Medium
GROWTH: Medium
LIGHT: Full sun

MOISTURE: Medium
SOIL: Moderately fertile, well-drained
FEATURES: Flowers, foliage
USES: Border, naturalizing, container
FLOWERS: ■ ■

SITING: Gloriosa daisy prefers full sun and fertile, well-drained soil with a pH of 5.5–7.0. Plants are short-lived perennials commonly grown an annuals. Daisylike yellow flowers with a mahogany disk appear from summer to early autumn. Flowers attract butterflies and are excellent fresh cut. Plants self-seed and perform well in the sunny wildflower garden, the border, and container plantings. Good companions for gloriosa daisy include 'Snowbank' white boltonia, tall cosmos, and 'Rotfuchs' spike speedwell.

CARE: Plant 18" apart in late spring. Apply slow-release granular plant food at time of planting. Water deeply when the soil is

Transplant self-sown seedlings of gloriosa daisy to a new location where you would like the plants to grow.

dry. If soil is too rich or excessive nitrogen is applied, or if there is too little sun, foliage may become floppy. Apply 3" of vegetative mulch in summer. Deadhead spent blooms to encourage reblooming. Remove plants just before the first frost or right afterward.

PROPAGATION: Sprinkle seed over the growing medium and cover or leave uncovered. Thoroughly moisten and keep moist, not soggy, until seeds germinate. Germination occurs in 5–10 days at 70°F. Transplant 20–28 days after sowing. After transplanting, reduce temperature to 50°F.

PESTS AND DISEASES: Slugs, powdery mildew, and rust are occasional problems.

RELATED SPECIES: The cultivar 'Bambi' reaches 12" high and bears multicolored flowers of yellow, brown, and bronze, 'Goldilocks' reaches 24" high and has double and semidouble yellow-orange flowers, 'Irish Eyes' reaches 24" high and bears bright yellow flowers with a green disk, 'Marmalade' reaches 18", is compact, and has deep yellow flowers, 'Rustic Dwarfs' reach 24" high and have brownish, yellow and bicolored flowers, and 'Superba' has yellow and maroon flowers.

MEALY-CUP SAGE

Salvia farinacea *SAHL-vee-uh far-ih-NAY-see-uh*

Mealy-cup sage produces spikes of purple blossoms in summer.

ZONES: 8–10
SIZE: 18–24"h × 12"w
TYPE: Perennial
FORM: Upright
TEXTURE: Fine
GROWTH: Fast
LIGHT: Full sun

MOISTURE: Medium
SOIL: Moderately fertile, well-drained
FEATURES: Flowers, foliage
USES: Border, container
FLOWERS: ■□

SITING: Mealy-cup sage prefers full sun and moderately fertile, well-drained soil with a pH of 5.5–7.0. Plants are commonly grown as annuals. Spikes of two-lipped purple flowers appear from summer though autumn. Hairy white stems bear glossy medium green leaves. Cultivars have a tidy appearance and an abundance of blooms. Plant in odd-numbered groups in the border, mass as an annual ground cover, or place in container plantings. Good companions include gulf muhly, silver sage, and 'Silver Carpet' lamb's-ears.

CARE: Plant 6–12" apart in late spring. Apply slow-release granular plant food at time of planting, or begin using water-soluble plant food 3 weeks after planting. Follow label directions for amount and frequency. Apply 3" of vegetative mulch in summer to reduce weed seed germination, hold moisture in the soil, and as it decomposes, add organic matter to the soil. Water deeply when the soil is dry. Deadhead spent blooms to encourage reblooming. Remove plants after the first frost when foliage is disfigured. Cover bare soil with 3" of vegetative mulch during winter to preserve topsoil.

PROPAGATION: Sprinkle seeds over the growing medium and leave uncovered, exposed to light. Thoroughly moisten and keep moist, not soggy, until seeds germinate. Germination occurs in 12–15 days at 75–78°F. Transplant 14–21 days after sowing. Reduce the temperature to 60°F after transplanting.

PESTS AND DISEASES: Diseases include powdery mildew, rust, stem rot, and fungal leaf spots.

RELATED SPECIES: The cultivar 'Alba' has white flowers, 'Blue Bedder' is compact and bears deep blue flowers, 'Rhea' is compact with vibrant deep blue flowers, 'Silver' bears silvery-white flowers, 'Strata' has blue flowers with a white calyx, and 'Victoria' bears many deep blue flowers. Scarlet sage (*S. splendens*) is a perennial commonly grown as an annual and reaches 10–15" high. Plants produce spikes of tubular red flowers throughout the summer. Cultivars come in red, blue, orange, pink, mauve, and white.

Scarlet sage (*Salvia splendens*) bears blooms in red-hot colors all summer long.

Some cultivars of scarlet sage bear colorful bracts of pink, purple, or white instead of the more common red form.

PERENNIAL SALVIA

Salvia ×superba SAHL-vee-uh soo-PEHR-buh

Perennial salvia, also known as hybrid sage, produces attractive purple blooms.

ZONES: 5–9
SIZE: 24–36"h × 18–24"w
TYPE: Perennial
FORM: Upright
TEXTURE: Medium
GROWTH: Medium
LIGHT: Full sun

MOISTURE: Medium
SOIL: Moderately fertile, well-drained
FEATURES: Flowers, foliage
USES: Border, container
FLOWERS: ■

SITING: Perennial salvia prefers full sun and moderately fertile, well-drained soil with a pH of 5.5–7.0. Spikes of violet or purple flowers appear from midsummer though early autumn. Plant in groups in the border or place in container plantings. Good companions include baby's breath, gulf muhly, and 'Rotfuchs' spike speedwell.

CARE: Plant 18" apart in spring or fall. Apply slow-release granular plant food in spring. Cease feeding 6–8 weeks prior to first frost date. Apply 3" of vegetative mulch in summer and winter to reduce weed seed germination, hold moisture in the soil, and as it decomposes, add organic

Deadhead spent flowers to encourage reblooming.

matter to the soil. Water deeply when the soil is dry. Deadhead spent blooms to encourage reblooming. Shear back after flowering to encourage another flush of flowers. Prune back in fall once frost withers the foliage.

PROPAGATION: Divide in spring every 3 years to maintain vigor. Dig around the root clump and lift. Use a sharp spade to slice through the root system. Reset portions that contain healthy roots and top shoots. Discard any pieces that do not contain both healthy roots and top shoots. Water deeply and apply 3" of organic mulch around the plants.

PESTS AND DISEASES: Diseases include powdery mildew, rust, stem rot, and fungal leaf spots.

RELATED SPECIES: Common sage (*S. officinalis*) has several cultivars, hardy to Zones 7 and 8, that enhance the perennial border or container: 'Aurea' reaches 12" high and bears golden-yellow leaves, 'Berggarten' is compact, reaches 24" high, and has pebbly green leaves, 'Icterina' has variegated green-and-gold leaves, 'Purparescens' has greenish-red leaves, and 'Tricolor' has blue-green leaves stained cream and pink.

LAVENDER COTTON

Santolina chamaecyparissus san-tuh-LEE-nuh kam-uh-SIP-uh-rih-suhs

Silvery foliage and button-shaped yellow flowers are the main attractions of lavender cotton in the perennial border or container.

ZONES: 6–9
SIZE: 24"h × 36"w
TYPE: Perennial
FORM: Upright
TEXTURE: Fine
GROWTH: Medium
LIGHT: Full sun
MOISTURE: Medium

SOIL: Moderately fertile, well-drained
FEATURES: Flowers, foliage
USES: Border, container
FLOWERS: ■

SITING: Lavender cotton prefers full sun and moderately fertile, well-drained soil with a pH of 5.5–7.0. Plants are subshrubs

and develop a woody base. Buttonlike golden-yellow flowers to ½" across, appear in mid- and late summer. Silvery-green leaves are evergreen and aromatic. Place in odd-numbered groups in the border, or use in container plantings. Good companions include 'Silver Mound' artemesia, silver sage, and 'Silver Carpet' lamb's-ears.

CARE: Plant 18–24" apart in spring or autumn. Apply slow-release granular plant food. Cease feeding 6–8 weeks prior to first frost date. Apply 3" of vegetative mulch in summer to reduce weed seed germination, retain soil moisture, and keep soil temperatures stable. Deadhead spent blooms to encourage reblooming. Water deeply when the soil is dry.

PROPAGATION: Seed-grown plants flower during the second year of growth. Sprinkle seeds over the growing medium and leave uncovered, exposed to light, or cover lightly. Thoroughly moisten and keep moist, not soggy, until seeds germinate. Germination occurs in 5–10 days at 72°F. Transplant 18–25 days after sowing. After

transplanting, reduce temperature to 62°F. In summer take cuttings from new growth. Cut pieces that contain at least two or three healthy leaves and three nodes. Dip exposed nodes into rooting hormone, shake off excess, and insert into moist soil mix, keeping leaves well above the soil level. Supply bottom heat and keep moist, not soggy, until root and top shoot growth is evident, usually in 2–3 weeks, then transplant. To enhance humidity, cover with plastic and hold it above the leaves.

PESTS AND DISEASES: Plants are relatively pest free when cultural requirements (sun, soil, planting depth, moisture) are met.

RELATED SPECIES: Green lavender cotton (*S. rosmarinifolia* syn. *S. virens*) reaches 24" high and is winter hardy in Zones 6–9. Plants are heat tolerant and pest resistant. Buttonlike bright or pale yellow flowers appear atop slender stems in mid- and late summer. The finely textured foliage is fragrant. Plants are neat and attractive in and out of bloom.

CREEPING ZINNIA
Sanvitalia procumbens *san-vih-TAHL-yuh pro-KUHM-bens*

Creeping zinnia flowers well in heat, humidity, and drought.

ZONES: NA
SIZE: 8–10"h × 18"w
TYPE: Annual
FORM: Spreading
TEXTURE: Fine
GROWTH: Fast
LIGHT: Full sun
MOISTURE: Medium

SOIL: Moderately fertile, well-drained
FEATURES: Flowers, foliage
USES: Border, ground cover, container
FLOWERS: ■ ■ □

SITING: Creeping zinnia prefers full sun and moderately fertile, well-drained soil with a pH of 5.5–7.0. Plants are tough and durable, tolerating heat, drought, and humidity. Creeping stems bear zinnialike single bright yellow flowers with a dark chocolate disk in summer. Leaves are tiny, oval, and medium green. Use as a ground cover in the sunny border or allow to cascade from container plantings. Good container companions include flowering kale, 'Moonbeam' threadleaf coreopsis, and 'Purpurascens' sage.

CARE: Plant 12–18" apart in late spring. Apply slow-release granular plant food at time of planting or begin using water-soluble plant food 3 weeks after planting. Follow label directions for amount and frequency. Water deeply when the soil is dry. Apply 3" of vegetative mulch in summer to reduce weed seed germination, retain soil moisture, and keep soil cool. Deadhead spent blooms to encourage

reblooming. Remove plants just before first frost or right afterward when foliage is disfigured. Cover bare soil with 3" of vegetative mulch during winter to preserve topsoil.

PROPAGATION: Sprinkle seeds over the growing medium and cover lightly. Thoroughly moisten and keep moist, not soggy, until seeds germinate. Germination occurs in 7–10 days at 70°F. Transplant 12–15 days after sowing. Reduce the temperature to 60°F after transplanting.

PESTS AND DISEASES: Plants are relatively pest free when cultural requirements (sun, soil, planting depth, moisture) are met.

RELATED SPECIES: The cultivar 'Gold Braid' is dwarf with double gold flowers and a brown disk, 'Golden Carpet' is dwarf with orange-tinted flowers and a black disk, 'Mandarin Orange' is dwarf with vibrant orange flowers and a black disk, and 'Yellow Carpet' is dwarf with small single pale yellow flowers and a black disk.

SOAPWORT
Saponaria ocymoides *sap-oh-NAR-ee-uh os-ih-MOY-deez*

Soapwort or rock soapwort spreads fast and has pink flowers in late spring and summer.

ZONES: 3–8
SIZE: 4"h × 18"w
TYPE: Perennial
FORM: Spreading
TEXTURE: Medium
GROWTH: Fast
LIGHT: Full sun
MOISTURE: Medium

SOIL: Moderately fertile, well-drained
FEATURES: Flowers, foliage
USES: Border, groundcover container
FLOWERS: ■ □

SITING: Soapwort prefers full sun and moderately fertile, well-drained soil with a pH of 5.5–7.0. Certain cultivars have a compact, neat habit; whereas the species tends to grow with great vigor and exuberance. Plants hug the ground and produce a profusion of five-petaled bright pink flowers in late spring and summer. Leaves are bright green and hairy. Place in groups in the border to serve as a ground

cover to other perennials or use to spill over the edge of containers. Good companions include white gaura, 'Bruno' Helen's flower, and rosemary lavender cotton (*Santolina rosmarinifolia*).

CARE: Plant 12–24" apart in late spring. Apply slow-release granular plant food at time of planting. Cease feeding 6–8 weeks prior to first frost date. Soapwort plants may overwhelm their neighbors if the soil is too fertile. Apply 3" of vegetative mulch in summer and winter to reduce weed seed germination, retain soil moisture, and keep soil temperatures stable. Water deeply when the soil is dry. Shear back after first flowering to encourage compact habit. Deadhead spent blooms to encourage reblooming. Plants freely self-seed in the

landscape. Prune back in fall once frost withers the foliage.

PROPAGATION: In moderately fertile soil plants may be divided in spring or autumn every 3 years to maintain vigor. In rich soils division is needed sooner to maintain vigor and control growth.

PESTS AND DISEASES: Plants are relatively pest free when cultural requirements (sun, soil, planting depth, moisture) are met.

RELATED SPECIES: The cultivar 'Alba' bears white flowers and grows more slowly than the species, 'Bressingham' has bright pink flowers and compact growth, 'Rubra Compacta' has deep red flowers and is compact, 'Versicolor' bears rose flowers that open white.

1

Shear soapwort back after first flowering is complete to encourage rebloom.

2

Plants 2–4 weeks after being sheared exhibit attractive, compact regrowth.

SCABIOUS
Scabiosa columbaria skab-ee-O-suh kohl-uhm-BAR-ee-uh

Scabious is a low-maintenance perennial with long-season blooms. It is also known as pincushion flower or scabiosa.

ZONES: 5–8
SIZE: 24"h × 30"w
TYPE: Perennial
FORM: Rounded
TEXTURE: Fine
GROWTH: Medium
LIGHT: Full sun
MOISTURE: Medium

SOIL: Moderately fertile, well-drained
FEATURES: Flowers, foliage
USES: Border, container
FLOWERS: ■ ▨

SITING: Scabious prefers full sun and moderately fertile, well-drained soil with a pH of 6.5–7.5. Wiry stems bear solitary violet-blue flowers that resemble pincushions from summer into early autumn. Plants are heat-tolerant and pest-resistant. They bloom on and off all winter long in the South. Plant in odd-numbered groups in the border or use in container plantings. Good companions include 'Taplow Blue' globe thistle, white gaura, 'Kobold' blazing star, and 'Alba Meidiland' rose.

CARE: Plant 18–24" apart in spring or autumn. Apply slow-release granular plant food in spring. Cease feeding 6–8 weeks

Deadhead scabious to reduce self-seeding and to encourage reblooming.

prior to first frost date. Apply 3" of vegetative mulch in summer and winter to reduce weed seed germination, retain soil moisture, and keep soil temperatures stable. Water deeply when the soil is dry. Deadhead spent blooms to encourage reblooming. Plants lightly self-seed in the landscape. Prune back in fall once frost withers the foliage or leave erect in warmer zones for winter viewing and occasional flowering.

PROPAGATION: In moderately fertile soil plants may be divided in spring every 3 years to maintain vigor. Dig around the root clump and lift. Use a sharp spade to slice through the root system. Reset portions that contain healthy roots and top shoots. Discard any pieces that do not contain both healthy roots and top shoots. Water deeply and apply 3" of organic mulch around the plants.

PESTS AND DISEASES: Plants are relatively pest free when cultural requirements (sun, soil, planting depth, moisture) are met.

RELATED SPECIES: The cultivar 'Butterfly Blue' has purplish-blue flowers in midsummer, and 'Pink Mist' bears purplish-pink flowers in midsummer.

FAN FLOWER
Scaevola aemula skuh-VOL-uh AY-myoo-luh

Fan flower is a superb landscape plant for warm climates. It is also known as scaevola.

ZONES: NA
SIZE: 6–18"h × 18"w
TYPE: Annual
FORM: Spreading
TEXTURE: Fine
GROWTH: Medium
LIGHT: Full sun to partial shade

MOISTURE: Medium
SOIL: Moderately fertile, moist, well-drained
FEATURES: Flowers, foliage
USES: Border, container
FLOWERS: ■ □

SITING: Fan flower prefers full sun or light afternoon shade and moderately fertile, well-drained, moist soil with a pH of 5.5–7.0. Plants are usually grown as annuals. Purplish-blue flowers appear in summer. Leaves are evergreen and spoon shaped. Plants are excellent annual ground covers in the perennial or shrub border and add spillover charm to containers. Plant in odd-numbered groups for best effect. Companions include 'Purpureum' purple fountain grass, 'Andenken an Friedrich Hahn' beardtongue, and 'Miss Willmott' pincushion flower.

Pinch fan flower in spring to promote branching and compact habit.

CARE: Plant 12–18" apart in late spring. Apply slow-release granular plant food at time of planting. Apply vegetative mulch in summer. Water deeply when the soil is dry. Trim back new growth by one-third in late spring to encourage branching. Deadhead spent blooms to encourage reblooming. Remove plants just before first frost or right afterward when foliage is disfigured. Cover bare soil with 3" of vegetative mulch during winter to preserve topsoil.

PROPAGATION: In spring take cuttings from new growth. Cut pieces that contain at least two healthy leaves and three nodes. Dip exposed nodes into rooting hormone, shake off excess, and insert into moist growing medium, keeping leaves well above the soil level. Supply bottom heat and keep moist, not soggy, until root and top shoot growth is evident, usually in 2–3 weeks, then transplant. To enhance humidity, cover with plastic and hold it above the leaves.

PESTS AND DISEASES: Plants are relatively pest free when cultural requirements are met. Spider mites are an occasional problem during hot, dry periods.

GOLDMOSS STONECROP

Sedum acre SEE-duhm AY-kehr

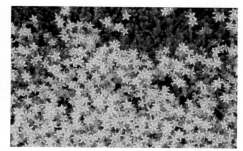

Goldmoss stonecrop, also known as sedum, is a fast-spreading ground cover with star-shaped yellow flowers.

ZONES: 3–9
SIZE: 24"h × 24"w
TYPE: Perennial
FORM: Spreading
TEXTURE: Fine
GROWTH: Fast
LIGHT: Full sun
MOISTURE: Medium to low

SOIL: Moderately fertile, well-drained
FEATURES: Flowers, foliage
USES: Border, ground cover, container
FLOWERS: ■

SITING: Goldmoss stonecrop prefers full sun and moderately fertile, well-drained soil with a pH of 6.5–7.3. Plants are invasive in fertile conditions but may be slowed slightly by providing light afternoon shade. They are also drought tolerant once established. Flat-topped clusters of tiny, star shaped yellowish-green flowers appear in summer. Use as a ground cover in the rock garden or as a spillover plant in containers. Good companions include rue, rosemary lavender cotton, and 'Autumn Joy' sedum.
CARE: Plant 18–24" apart in spring or fall. Apply slow-release granular plant food in spring. Water only when the soil is dry 2–3" below the surface.
PROPAGATION: In summer take cuttings from new growth. Cut pieces that contain at least two or three healthy leaves and

1 Take cuttings of sedum in summer.

2 Stick cuttings into growing medium.

three nodes. Plant directly in the garden where new plants are desired. Seed germination occurs in 7–14 days when daytime temperatures are 85°F and nighttime temperatures are 70°F. Transplant 20–30 days after sowing seed. After transplanting, reduce temperature to 60°F.
PESTS AND DISEASES: Plants are relatively pest free except for slugs and snails.
RELATED SPECIES: The cultivar 'Aureum' has variegated yellow leaves, 'Elegans' has silver-striped leaf tips, and 'Minor' is only 1" high. Two-row stonecrop (*S. spurium*) cultivars are popular, vigorous ground covers that reach 4" high: 'Atropurpureum' has burgundy leaves and rose-red flowers, 'Bronze Carpet' has bronze-stained leaves and pink flowers, 'Erdblut' has crimson-tipped green leaves and red flowers, 'Fuldaglut' has bronze-stained leaves and maroon flowers, 'Golden Carpet' has light green leaves and yellow flowers, 'Red Carpet' has red-stained leaves and red flowers, 'Schorbuser Blut' ('Dragon's Blood') leaves age to burgundy, and flowers are dark pink, and 'Tricolor' has cream-, green-, and pink-splashed leaves and pink flowers.

AUTUMN JOY SEDUM

Sedum × 'Autumn Joy' (*Hylotelephium* × 'Herbstfreude') SEE-duhm (high-loh-tel-EE-fee-um)

Mulch enhances 'Autumn Joy' sedum, a superb low-maintenance perennial.

ZONES: 3–10
SIZE: 24"h × 24"w
TYPE: Perennial
FORM: Upright
TEXTURE: Medium
GROWTH: Medium
LIGHT: Full sun
MOISTURE: Medium

SOIL: Moderately fertile, well-drained
FEATURES: Flowers, foliage
USES: Border, container
FLOWERS: ■

SITING: Autumn Joy sedum prefers full sun and moderately fertile, well-drained soil with a pH of 6.5–7.3. Flowers first turn pink in mid- to late summer, then rose-red, then deep brown-burgundy in late autumn. Flowers attract bees and butterflies. Good companions include purple coneflower, 'Shenandoah' switchgrass, fountain grass, and 'Color Guard' yucca.
CARE: Plant 18–24" apart in spring or fall. Apply slow-release granular plant food in spring. Apply 3" of vegetative mulch in

Autumn Joy sedum attracts butterflies late in the season when it is in bloom.

summer and winter. Water deeply when the soil is dry. In moderately fertile soil plants must be divided every 3 years to maintain form and vigor. In rich soils division is needed sooner. It is required when stems emerging in spring flop to the ground. Lack of sun also causes foliar flopping. Prune back in fall or leave erect for winter viewing.
PROPAGATION: Dig around the root clump and lift. Use a sharp spade to slice through the root system. The larger the portion, the larger the resulting plant during the first year. Smaller pieces may take 2–3 years to reach mature size and bloom. Reset portions that contain healthy roots and top shoots. Discard the center portion if it is dead. Water deeply and apply 3" of vegetative mulch around, but not touching, the plants.
PESTS AND DISEASES: Plants are relatively pest free when cultural requirements (sun, soil, planting depth, moisture) are met.
RELATED SPECIES: *S.* 'Ruby Glow' reaches 12" high and 18" wide and has red stems, bronze-stained deciduous green leaves, and ruby-red flowers from midsummer to early fall.

DUSTY MILLER

Senecio cineraria *sehn-EE-see-oh sihn-er-AR-ee-uh*

Dusty miller provides delightful silver foliage that complements pink or purple annuals and perennials.

ZONES: 8–10
SIZE: 12–24"h ×
12–24"w
TYPE: Perennial
FORM: Rounded
TEXTURE: Medium
GROWTH: Medium
LIGHT: Full sun
MOISTURE: Medium

SOIL: Moderately
fertile, well-drained
FEATURES: Flowers,
foliage
USES: Border,
ground cover,
container
FLOWERS: ■

SITING: Dusty miller prefers full sun and moderately fertile, well-drained soil with a pH of 5.5–7.0. Yellow flowers appear during the second year of growth but are rarely seen because the plants are usually grown as annuals. Place in groups among brightly colored plants; use in moon gardens, where silver and white foliage is attractive when viewed by moonlight; mass as a ground cover, or plant in containers. Good companions include cockscomb, torch lily, and 'Vivid' obedient plant.
CARE: Plant 6–12" apart in late spring. Apply slow-release granular plant food

Plant dusty miller between brightly colored annuals or perennials to soften their effect.

at time of planting. Apply 3" of vegetative mulch in summer to reduce weed seed germination, hold moisture in the soil, and as it decomposes, add organic matter to the soil. Water deeply when the soil is dry. Remove plants just before first frost or right afterward when foliage is disfigured. Cover bare soil with 3" of vegetative mulch during winter to preserve topsoil.
PROPAGATION: Sprinkle seeds over the growing medium and leave exposed to light; do not cover. Thoroughly moisten and keep moist, not soggy, until seeds germinate. Germination occurs in 10–15 days at 72°F. Transplant in 20–25 days. After transplanting, reduce the temperature to 62°F.
PESTS AND DISEASES: Rust is common.
RELATED SPECIES: The cultivar 'Alice' has deeply cut silver-white-stained foliage, 'Cirrus' has rounded bright silver leaves and is dwarf, 'New Look' has lobed pure white leaves, 'Silverdust' has lacy silver-dusted leaves, 'Silver Filigree' has gray leaves, 'Silver Queen' is compact and has silvery-white leaves, and 'White Diamond' has silvery-gray leaves.

NARROW-LEAF BLUE-EYED GRASS

Sisyrinchium angustifolium *sis-ih-RINK-ee-uhm an-gust-ih-FOHL-ee-uhm*

Narrow-leaf blue-eyed grass shows delicate blue blossoms in spring.

ZONES: 5–8
SIZE: 18–22"h ×
6–12"w
TYPE: Perennial
FORM: Upright
TEXTURE: Fine
GROWTH: Medium
LIGHT: Full sun

MOISTURE: Medium
SOIL: Moderately
fertile, well-drained
FEATURES: Flowers,
foliage
USES: Border,
container
FLOWERS: ■

SITING: Narrow-leaf blue-eyed grass prefers full sun and moderately fertile, well-drained soil with a pH of 6.5–7.3. In early spring in the South and late spring in the North, deep blue flowers with a yellow throat appear. Lance-shaped, grasslike deep green leaves are semi-evergreen. Flowers appear and disappear quickly but are considered worthy of viewing, even for a short time. Plants self-seed freely. Place in odd-numbered groups in the border or

Feed narrow-leaf blue-eyed grass with a water-soluble plant food.

rock garden, in a container, or among spring-flowering bulbs. Good companions include seapink, Johnny-jump-up, and pansy cultivars.
CARE: Plant 6–12" apart in spring or autumn. Apply slow-release granular plant food in spring or feed through the summer with a water-soluble plant food. Apply 3" of vegetative mulch in summer and winter to reduce weed seed germination, retain soil moisture, and keep soil temperatures stable. Water deeply when the soil is dry. Plants are extremely low maintenance and durable when their cultural preferences (soil, sun, planting depth, moisture) are met. Plants self-seed in the landscape.
PROPAGATION: Lift self-sown seedlings and reset in spring or autumn. Divide in spring. Dig around the clump of bulbs and lift. Use a sharp spade to slice through the root system. Reset portions that contain healthy roots and top shoots. Discard any pieces that do not contain both healthy bulbs and top shoots. Water deeply and apply 3" of vegetative mulch around, but not touching, the plants.
PESTS AND DISEASES: Plants are relatively pest free.

FALSE SOLOMON'S SEAL
Smilacena racemosa *smil-uh-SEE-nuh ray-seb-MOH-sub*

False Solomon's seal has attractive flowers, berries, and foliage. It is also known as Solomon's plume.

ZONES: 3–8
SIZE: 24–36"h × 24"w
TYPE: Perennial
FORM: Spreading
TEXTURE: Medium
GROWTH: Slow
LIGHT: Partial to full shade
MOISTURE: Medium

SOIL: Moderately fertile, moist, well-drained
FEATURES: Flowers, foliage, berries
USES: Border, woodland, container
FLOWERS: ☐
FALL COLOR: ◼

SITING: False Solomon's seal prefers partial to full shade and moderately fertile, humus-rich, moist, well-drained soil with a pH of 5.5–7.0. Panicles of fragrant creamy-white-tinged-green flowers appear in mid- and late spring. Green berries follow the flowers and turn red, sometimes splashed with purple. Berries attract wildlife. Zigzagging stems bear narrow, pointed, medium green leaves, up to 6" long, that turn an attractive yellow in autumn. Place in groups in the shade border or woodland garden, or to add arching lines to a container planting. Good companions include 'Pictum' Japanese painted fern, heart-leaf brunnera, 'Alba' bleeding heart, and Lenten rose.
CARE: Plant 12–24" apart in spring or autumn. Apply slow-release plant food, such as Miracle-Gro Shake 'n Feed All Purpose, in spring. Follow label directions for amount and frequency. Apply 3" of vegetative mulch in summer and winter to reduce weed seed germination, hold moisture in the soil, and as it decomposes, add organic matter to the soil. Water deeply when the soil is dry. Plants take a full season or two to recover after root disturbance, so move and divide only when necessary.
PROPAGATION: Divide in spring or autumn. To root in soil, dig around the rhizomes and lift. Use a sharp spade to slice through the root system. Reset portions that contain healthy roots and top shoots. Discard any pieces that do not contain both healthy roots and top shoots. Water deeply and apply 3" of vegetative mulch around, but not touching, the plants.
PESTS AND DISEASES: Plants are relatively pest free when cultural requirements (sun, soil, planting depth, moisture) are met.
RELATED SPECIES: Starflower (*S. stellata*) bears white flowers followed by black berries. It grows 8–24" tall in Zones 3–7.

COLEUS
Solenostemon scuttellaroides hybrids *soh-len-AH-steh-mun skoo-teh-labr-OY-deez*

Coleus foliage comes in many interesting color combinations.

ZONE: NA
SIZE: 6–36"h × 12–36"w
TYPE: Annual
FORM: Upright
TEXTURE: Medium
GROWTH: Fast
LIGHT: Full sun, partial shade

MOISTURE: Medium to high
SOIL: Fertile, moist, well-drained
FEATURES: Foliage
USES: Border, bedding, container
FLOWERS: ◼☐

SITING: Newer coleus cultivars prefer full sun or partial shade and fertile, well-drained, moist soil, with a pH of 5.5–7.0. Plants are evergreen perennials commonly grown as annuals. Colorful foliage thrives in bright shade. Flowers appear during summer but are considered inconsequential and are usually removed. Use as an annual ground cover for a tapestry effect or in containers. Good companions include *Bergenia cordifolia* 'Purpurea', *Heuchera micrantha* var. *diversifolia* 'Palace Purple', and *Hosta* 'Gold Standard'.
CARE: Plant 12–24" apart in late spring. Apply slow-release granular plant food at time of planting. Apply 3" of vegetative mulch in summer. When the soil feels dry 2" below the surface, water deeply. Remove plants just before first frost or right afterward when foliage is disfigured.
PROPAGATION: Seed germination occurs in 10–15 days at 72°F. Transplant 20–25 days after sowing. After transplanting, reduce temperature to 65–70°F. In summer take cuttings from new growth. Cut pieces that contain at least two to four healthy leaves and three nodes. Root cuttings in water or soil. Dip exposed nodes into rooting hormone, shake off excess, and insert into moist soil mix, keeping leaves well above the soil level.
PESTS AND DISEASES: Slugs and leaf spots are common.
RELATED SPECIES: Bellevue Hybrid Blend leaves are splashed with pink, red, ivory, and green, Dragon Series leaves are splashed with purple, black and red, rimmed with gold, Old Lace Mixed leaves are white, lilac, and salmon, with a rose center and yellow rim, and 'Striped Rainbow' leaves are heart shaped and striped red, maroon, yellow, and green.

Remove developing flower stalks to focus attention on the foliage.

Cut shoot tips for propagating new plants.

Root coleus cuttings in soilless growing mix or in water.

GOLDENROD
Solidago hybrids *sohl-ih-DAY-goh*

Beautiful goldenrod flowers appear in mid- to late summer.

ZONES: 3–9
SIZE: 36"h ×
18–24"w
TYPE: Perennial
FORM: Upright
TEXTURE: Medium
GROWTH: Fast
LIGHT: Full sun
MOISTURE: Medium
to low

SOIL: Moderately
fertile, well-drained
FEATURES: Flowers,
foliage
USES: Border,
naturalizing,
container
FLOWERS: ■

SITING: Goldenrod prefers moderately fertile, well-drained, even sandy, soil, and full sun. The preferred pH range is 5.5–7.0. Cultivars are usually well-behaved and stay within bounds. Plumelike panicles of tiny golden-yellow flowers appear in mid- and late summer. Flowers attract bees and butterflies. Plant in groups in the perennial border, naturalize along a fence, or use in mixed container plantings. Good companions include 'Snowbank' white boltonia, 'Bruno' Helen's flower, and 'Sky Racer' purple moor grass.

CARE: Plant 18–24" apart in spring or fall. Apply slow-release granular plant food in spring. Water deeply when the soil is dry. Plants self-seed; seedlings may not be as desirable as the parent plant. Prevent self-seeding by removing faded flowers before seeds fall to the ground. Prune back in fall once frost withers the foliage or leave erect in warmer zones for winter viewing.

PROPAGATION: Divide in spring or autumn, at least every 3 years, to maintain vigor and control growth. Dig around the root clump and lift.

PESTS AND DISEASES: Plants are relatively pest free when cultural requirements (sun, soil, planting depth, moisture) are met.

RELATED SPECIES: Dwarf cultivars include 'Golden Baby', 'Golden Dwarf', 'Queenie', with variegated green and gold leaves, 'Laurin', with light gold flowers, 'Golden Gate', a semi-dwarf with deep golden flowers, and 'Praecox', which flowers early. 'Crown of Rays' grows to 24" and begins blooming in mid-summer. Taller cultivars include 'Leraft', with bright yellow flowers, 'Ledsham' and 'Lemore', with paler yellow flowers, and 'Loddon Gold', with deep gold flowers. *S. sphacelata* 'Golden Fleece' tolerates considerable shade and grows to only 18" tall and tolerates dry soils well.

LAMB'S-EARS
Stachys byzantina *STAK-iss biz-uhn-TEE-nuh*

Lamb's-ears has velvety soft leaves.

ZONES: 3–8
SIZE: 18"h × 24"w
TYPE: Perennial
FORM: Spreading
TEXTURE: Medium
GROWTH: Fast
LIGHT: Full sun
MOISTURE: Medium

SOIL: Moderately
fertile, well-drained
FEATURES: Flowers,
foliage
USES: Border,
container,
ground cover
FLOWERS: ■

SITING: Lamb's-ears prefers full sun and moderately fertile, well-drained soil with a pH of 5.5–7.0. Plants are susceptible to disease in high humidity. Spikes of woolly pink flowers appear from early summer into early autumn. Soft velvety foliage is silvery green. Flowers attract butterflies and bees. Place in groups in the perennial border, use as a ground cover, or in container plantings. Good companions include 'David' garden phlox, 'The Fairy' rose, 'Freckles' violet, and Johnny-jump-up.

CARE: Plant 18–24" apart in spring or fall. Apply slow-release granular plant food in spring. Cease feeding 6–8 weeks prior to first frost date. Water deeply when the soil is dry. Groom regularly to remove brown or diseased leaves from the thick mat; cultivars rarely require foliage grooming. Deadhead spent blooms. Prune back in fall once frost withers the foliage.

PROPAGATION: Divide in spring or autumn at least every 3 years to maintain vigor and control growth. Discard any nonbearing center portions. Sprinkle seeds over the growing medium and leave exposed to light; do not cover. Thoroughly moisten and keep moist, not soggy, until seeds germinate. Germination occurs in 10–15 days at 70°F. Transplant in

20–25 days after sowing. Reduce the temperature to 60°F after transplanting. Plants grown from seed produce flowers during the second season.

PESTS AND DISEASES: Powdery mildew is the main pest. Select mildew-resistant cultivars and provide adequate air circulation and spacing.

RELATED SPECIES: *S. byzantina* 'Silver Carpet' is nonflowering, low maintenance, and tidier than the species. The cultivar 'Big Ears' has large silver-green leaves, 'Cotton Boll' has clusters of modified flowers along the stem that resemble cotton balls, 'Margery Fish' has mauve flowers, 'Primrose Heron' has yellow-green leaves, and 'Striped Phantom' has cream-striped leaves and striped flower bracts.

1 Dig the root ball of lamb's-ears to divide it.

2 Pull or cut the clump apart.

3 Reset pieces that have healthy roots and shoots.

AFRICAN MARIGOLD
Tagetes erecta tuh-JEE-teez eh-REHK-tuh

African marigolds have large flowers and may grow tall. They are also known as Aztec marigolds.

ZONES: NA
SIZE: 12–32"h × 12–18"w
TYPE: Annual
FORM: Upright
TEXTURE: Medium
GROWTH: Medium
LIGHT: Full sun
MOISTURE: Medium
SOIL: Moderately fertile, well-drained
FEATURES: Flowers, foliage
USES: Border, bedding, container
FLOWERS: ■ ■ ■ ■ □

SITING: African marigold prefers full sun and moderately fertile, well-drained soil with a pH of 5.5–7.0. Plants are relatively drought tolerant once established. Large, vibrant, double orange or yellow flowers, up to 5" across, appear from late spring through late summer. Fragrant foliage is deeply dissected and toothed. Place in groups in the border, mass as a bedding plant, or add to container plantings. Good companions include snapdragon, flowering kale, and dusty miller.

CARE: Plant 10–15" apart in late spring. Apply slow-release granular plant food at time of planting, or begin using water-soluble plant food 3 weeks after planting. Follow label directions for amount and frequency. Apply 3" of vegetative mulch in summer to reduce weed seed germination, hold moisture in the soil, and as it decomposes, add organic matter to the soil. Water deeply when the soil is dry.

Rainfall and overhead irrigation may damage heavy dense flower heads. Drip irrigation is preferred when available. Deadhead spent or damaged blooms to encourage reblooming. Remove plants by frost or after foliage is disfigured. Cover bare soil with 3" of vegetative mulch during winter to preserve topsoil.

PROPAGATION: Sprinkle seeds over the growing medium and leave exposed to light or cover lightly. Thoroughly moisten and keep moist, not soggy, until seeds germinate. Germination occurs in 7 days at 72–75°F. Transplant 10–15 days after sowing. After transplanting, reduce temperature to 65°F.

PESTS AND DISEASES: Diseases include botrytis and powdery mildew.

RELATED SPECIES: French marigold (*T. patula*) reaches 6–12" high and bears single or double flowers up to 2" across in single or multicolors including yellow, orange, and red-brown.

French marigolds are shorter and have smaller flowers than African marigolds.

1 Sprinkle seeds into a seed tray filled with Miracle-Gro soilless mix.

2 Newly emerged marigold seedlings will soon be ready to transplant.

3 Transplant marigold seedlings into cell packs or individual pots.

WALL GERMANDER
Teucrium chamaedrys TOO-kree-uhm kam-EH-drihs

Wall germander, also known as germander blooms with attractive purple flowers.

ZONES: 5–9
SIZE: 12–20"h × 18"w
TYPE: Perennial
FORM: Upright
TEXTURE: Fine
GROWTH: Medium
LIGHT: Full sun

MOISTURE: Medium
SOIL: Moderately fertile, well-drained
FEATURES: Flowers, foliage
USES: Border, knot, container
FLOWERS: ■

SITING: Wall germander prefers full sun and moderately fertile, well-drained soil with a pH of 6.5–7.5. The evergreen foliage may be sheared into a miniature hedge. Flowers attract butterflies and bees. Plants are ideal for a knot garden, in the border, or in a container. Good companions are lavender, rosemary lavender cotton (*Santolina rosmarinifolia*), creeping zinnia.

CARE: Plant 12–18" apart in spring or autumn. Apply slow-release granular plant food in spring. Cease feeding 6–8 weeks prior to first frost date. Apply 3" of vegetative mulch in summer and winter.

Germander is an excellent edging plant in a knot garden. It can be pruned and shaped to a tight form.

Water deeply when the soil is dry. Shear back low in spring to maintain a compact habit.

PROPAGATION: Divide in spring or autumn. Dig around the root clump and lift. Use a sharp spade to slice through the root system. Reset portions that contain healthy roots and top shoots. In summer take cuttings from new growth. Cut pieces that contain at least two or three healthy leaves and three nodes. Root cuttings in water or soil. To root in soil, dip exposed nodes into rooting hormone, shake off excess, and insert into moist soil mix, keeping leaves well above the soil level. Supply bottom heat and keep moist, not soggy, until root and top shoot growth is evident, usually in 2–3 weeks, then transplant. To enhance humidity, cover flat with plastic and hold it above the leaves.

PESTS AND DISEASES: Plants are relatively pest free when cultural requirements (sun, soil, planting depth, moisture) are met.

COLUMBINE MEADOW-RUE
Thalictrum aquilegifolium thuh-LIHK-trum ahk-wih-lee-jee-FOH-lee-uhm

Columbine meadow-rue is fine-textured and graceful both in and out of bloom.

ZONES: 4–9
SIZE: 36"h × 18"w
TYPE: Perennial
FORM: Upright
TEXTURE: Fine
GROWTH: Medium
LIGHT: Partial shade
MOISTURE: Medium

SOIL: Fertile, moist, well-drained
FEATURES: Flowers, foliage
USES: Border, woodland, container
FLOWERS: ■ □ ■

SITING: Columbine meadow-rue prefers partial shade and fertile, well-drained, moist soil with a pH of 5.5–7.0. Greenish-white sepals surround showy bright pink, purple, or white stamens in early summer. Blue-green foliage appears delicate and graceful. Place in odd-numbered groups in brightly shaded border, the woodland garden, or in containers. Good companions include McKana Hybrids columbine, goatsbeard, and foxglove.

CARE: Plant 18" apart in spring or autumn in fertile soil having high organic matter content. To increase organic matter, add 1–2" inches of compost to the top of the entire planting bed. Till in to a depth of 12–15". Apply slow-release granular plant food at the time of planting. Apply 3" of vegetative mulch in summer and winter to reduce weed seed germination, retain soil moisture, and keep soil temperatures stable. Water deeply when the soil feels dry 2" below the surface. Prune back in fall once frost withers the foliage.

PROPAGATION: Plants self-seed in the landscape and may be dug and transplanted. Sprinkle seeds over the growing medium and leave exposed to light; do not cover. Thoroughly moisten and keep moist, not soggy, until seeds germinate. Germination occurs in 5–10 days at 70°F. Transplant in 15–25 days after sowing. After transplanting, reduce temperature to 60°F.

PESTS AND DISEASES: Plants are relatively pest free when cultural requirements are met. Rust and powdery mildew are occasional diseases.

RELATED SPECIES: 'Atropurpureum' has dark purple stamens, 'Aurantiacum' has orange-stained stamens, 'Purpureum' has purple stamens, 'Roseum' has pink stamens, 'Thundercloud' has deep purple stamens, and 'White Cloud' has yellow-rimmed white stamens. 'Lavender Mist' (*T. rochebrunianum*) reaches 60" high and 18" wide. Loose panicles of white, sometimes lavender, flowers appear in summer.

SOUTHERN LUPINE

Thermopsis villosa *ther-MAHP-sihs vil-OH-suh*

Southern lupine is long-lived and attracts butterflies when in bloom. It is also known as Carolina lupine or false lupine.

ZONES: 3–9
SIZE: 3–5'h × 24"w
TYPE: Perennial
FORM: Upright
TEXTURE: Medium
GROWTH: Medium
LIGHT: Full sun to partial shade

MOISTURE: Medium
SOIL: Fertile, well-drained
FEATURES: Flowers, foliage
USES: Border, woodland, container
FLOWERS: ■

SITING: Southern lupine prefers full sun (part shade in warmer regions) and fertile, well-drained soil with a pH of 5.5–7.0. Racemes of pealike bright yellow flowers appear in late spring and early summer. Leaves are blue-green and divided into three leaflets, lightly hairy underneath. Plants are long-lived and resent root disturbance. Flowers attract bees and butterflies. Place in odd-numbered groups in the perennial border, cottage garden, or lightly shaded woodland garden, or in containers for early-season color. Good companions include 'Morning Light' maiden grass, Oriental poppy, and 'Aurantiacum' columbine meadow-rue.

Place a support over southern lupine in partial shade to prevent plants from toppling over.

CARE: Plant 18–24" apart in spring or fall. Apply slow-release granular plant food at time of planting. Cease feeding 6–8 weeks prior to first frost date. Apply 3" of vegetative mulch in summer and winter. Water deeply when the soil is dry. In partial shade, plants may require staking. Prune back in fall once frost withers the foliage.

PROPAGATION: Divide in spring or autumn; plants take several seasons to grow at a normal pace. Dig around the root clump and lift. Use a sharp spade to slice through the root system. Reset portions that contain healthy roots and top shoots. Discard any pieces that do not contain both healthy roots and top shoots. Water deeply and apply 3" of vegetative mulch around, but not touching, the plants. Fresh seed is essential to germination. Sow seeds in spring or early summer and maintain 50–55°F temperatures until germination occurs. Transplant seedlings directly to their landscape site as early as possible.

PESTS AND DISEASES: Powdery mildew is a problem.

BLACK-EYED SUSAN VINE

Thunbergia alata *Thuhn-BEHR-jee-uh ah-LAY-tuh*

Black-eyed Susan vine climbs on trellises or arbors up to 8' in height.

ZONES: NA
SIZE: 5–8'h × 6–12"
TYPE: Annual
FORM: Upright
TEXTURE: Medium
GROWTH: Fast
LIGHT: Full sun
MOISTURE: Medium

SOIL: Fertile, moist, well-drained
FEATURES: Flowers, foliage
USES: Trellis, container
FLOWERS: ■ ■ □

SITING: Black-eyed Susan vine prefers full sun and fertile, well-drained, moist soil with a pH of 5.5–7.0. These perennial climbing plants are usually grown as annuals. Five-petaled tubular yellow, orange, or occasionally white flowers appear from summer through autumn. The flower center is sometimes mahogany brown. Leaves are almost triangular, toothed, and medium green. Plants require support and may be used on the low trellis or arbor, in container plantings, or at the sunny base of a tree. Good container companions include 'Moonbeam' threadleaf coreopsis, 'Purpureum' purple fountain grass, and 'White Bedder' beardtongue.

CARE: Plant 12–24" apart in late spring. Apply slow-release granular plant food at time of planting. Apply 3" of vegetative mulch in summer. Maintain moist, not soggy, soil. When the soil feels almost dry 2" below the surface, water deeply. If using an irrigation system, maintain deep, infrequent waterings and avoid delivering a light sprinkle every day. Organic matter in the soil and mulch on the soil surface help reduce watering frequency. Remove plants just before first frost or right afterward when foliage is disfigured. Cover bare soil with 3" of vegetative mulch during winter to preserve topsoil.

PROPAGATION: Sprinkle seeds over the growing medium and cover lightly. Thoroughly moisten and keep moist, not soggy, until seeds germinate. Germination occurs in 6–12 days at 75°F. Transplant 15–20 days after sowing. After transplanting, reduce temperature to 60°F.

PESTS AND DISEASES: Plants are relatively pest free when cultural requirements (sun, soil, planting depth, moisture) are met.

RELATED SPECIES: The cultivar 'Alba' has white flowers, 'Aurantiaca' bears orange or yellow flowers with a dark throat, 'Bakeri' has white flowers, and Suzie Hybrids bear orange, yellow, or white flowers with a dark throat.

LEMON THYME

Thymus ×citriodorus TIME-uhs siht-ree-oh-DOR-uhs

Lemon thyme is a fragrant ground cover or container plant for full sun.

ZONES: 4–9
SIZE: 12"h × 12"w
TYPE: Perennial
FORM: Rounded
TEXTURE: Fine
GROWTH: Medium
LIGHT: Full sun
MOISTURE: Medium

SOIL: Moderately fertile, well-drained
FEATURES: Flowers, foliage
USES: Border, ground cover, container
FLOWERS: ▪

SITING: Lemon thyme prefers full sun and moderately fertile, well-drained soil with a pH of 6.5–7.5. Plants are woody subshrubs with tiny, evergreen, lemon-scented leaves. Lavender-pink flowers appear in summer. Leaves have culinary value and may be used fresh or dried. Use as a ground cover in the border or as a spillover plant in container. Summer container companions include pink coreopsis, 'Moonbeam' threadleaf coreopsis, 'Purpureum' fennel, and lavender.

CARE: Plant 6–12" apart in spring or fall. Apply slow-release granular plant food in spring at time of planting. Cease feeding 6–8 weeks prior to first frost date. Shear back hard in early spring; trim back lightly after flowering to promote compact habit. Scent is strongest when plants are grown in moderately fertile soil. For culinary use trim one-third of the leaf branch at a time. Water deeply when the soil is dry.

PROPAGATION: Plants naturally layer in the landscape. Pin a branch to the ground so that nodes connect with soil. Cover with mulch. Check periodically for root growth; when roots have formed, snip the branch from the parent plant, leaving some green top growth to accompany the new root system. In early summer, take cuttings from new growth. Cut pieces that contain at least two or three healthy leaves and three nodes. Dip exposed nodes into rooting hormone, shake off excess, and insert into moist soil mix, keeping leaves well above the soil level.

PESTS AND DISEASES: Plants are relatively pest free when cultural requirements are met.

RELATED SPECIES: 'Anderson's Gold' hugs the ground and has golden leaves, 'Archer's Gold' has bright yellow leaves, 'Argenteus' has silver leaves, 'Argenteus Variegatus' bears green leaves rimmed in silver, 'Aureus' has green leaves splashed with gold which often revert to solid green, 'Doone Valley' is prostrate with green leaves splashed with gold and stained red in winter, and 'Silver Queen' bears silver-marbled leaves.

Plant lemon thyme in a container garden to trail over the edge.

SPIDERWORT

Tradescantia virginiana trahd-ehs-KAHN-tee-uh vehr-jihn-ee-AY-nuh

Spiderwort flowers have three petals and perform best in lean soils.

ZONES: 4–9
SIZE: 18–24"h × 18–24"w
TYPE: Perennial
FORM: Spreading
TEXTURE: Medium
GROWTH: Medium
LIGHT: Full sun to partial shade

MOISTURE: Medium
SOIL: Moderately fertile, moist, well-drained
FEATURES: Flowers, foliage
USES: Border, container
FLOWERS: ▪▪▫□

SITING: Spiderwort prefers full sun or light shade during the afternoon and moderately fertile, well-drained, moist soil with a pH of 5.5–7.0. Flowers appear in shades of blue, purple, pink, or white from early summer to early autumn. Flower production is higher in full sun than in partial shade. Place in groups in the informal border, cottage garden, or bright woodland garden, or use in container plantings. Good companions include 'Ice Queen' torch lily, 'Kobold' blazing star, and 'Yankee Lady' rugose rose.

CARE: Plant 18–24" apart in spring or fall. Apply slow-release granular plant food in spring at time of planting. Plants flop or fall apart if the soil is rich and plant food is high in nitrogen. Apply 3" of vegetative mulch in spring and fall. Maintain moist soil. After the first flush of flowers, feed again and shear back plant to promote compact habit and encourage more flower production. Spiderwort is self-cleaning and does not need regular deadheading to appear attractive, though deadheading is recommended if self-sown plants are not desired in the landscape.

Cut back spiderwort after first bloom to encourage compact growth and rebloom.

PROPAGATION: Divide in spring or autumn at least every 3 years to maintain vigor. In late spring or early summer, before full bloom, take cuttings from new growth. Cut pieces that contain at least two or three healthy leaves and three nodes. Root cuttings in water or soil. Seed germination occurs in 7–14 days at 72°F. Transplant 20–30 days after sowing. Reduce the temperature to 62°F after transplanting.

PESTS AND DISEASES: Viruses are occasional problems.

RELATED SPECIES: The cultivar 'Alba' bears white flowers, 'Blue Stone' has blue flowers, 'Caerulea Plena' bears double blue flowers, 'Innocence' bears clear white flowers, 'Iris Pritchard' bears white flowers stained pale blue, 'Isis' has deep blue flowers, 'Karminglut' has red flowers, 'Osprey' bears white flowers, 'Purewell Giant' has purplish-pink flowers, 'Snowcap' bears extra large white flowers, and 'Zwanenburg Blue' has deep blue flowers.

TOAD LILY
Tricyrtis hirta Tri-SER-tuhs HER-tuh

Toad lily has exotic flowers that resemble those of an orchid.

ZONES: 5–9
SIZE: 36"h × 24"w
TYPE: Perennial
FORM: Upright
TEXTURE: Medium
GROWTH: Medium
LIGHT: Partial to full shade

MOISTURE: Medium
SOIL: Fertile, moist, well-drained
FEATURES: Flowers, foliage
USES: Border, woodland, container
FLOWERS: ☐ ▨

SITING: Toad lily prefers partial to full shade and fertile, well-drained, moist soil with a pH of 5.5–6.5. Funnel-shaped white flowers with purple specks appear in late summer. Leaves are lance shaped, pale green, and very hairy. Plants are attractive to connoisseur gardeners who collect the unusual. Place in odd-numbered groups in the shaded border or woodland garden, or use in containers. Good companions for toad lily include lady's mantle, heart-leaf brunnera, and 'Elegans' Siebold hosta, or 'Gold Standard' hosta.

CARE: Plant 12–24" apart in spring or autumn in fertile soil high in organic matter. To increase organic matter, add 1–2" of compost, peat moss, or bagged humus to the planting bed, then till in to a depth of 12–15". Apply slow-release granular plant food. Cease feeding 6–8 weeks prior to first frost date. Apply 3" of vegetative mulch in summer and winter to reduce weed seed germination, retain soil moisture, and keep soil temperatures stable. Water deeply when the soil feels dry 2" below the surface. Prune back in fall once frost withers the foliage.

PROPAGATION: Divide in early spring while plants are dormant. Plants self-seed in the landscape.

PESTS AND DISEASES: Plants are relatively pest free when cultural requirements (sun, soil, planting depth, moisture) are met. Snails and slugs may be pests.

RELATED SPECIES: 'Alba' has white flowers, 'Miyazaki' bears white flowers spotted with lilac, 'Miyazaki Gold' has leaves edged in gold, and 'White Towers' has white flowers in the leaf axils. Formosa toad lily (*T. formosana*) is hardy in Zone 4–9, and reaches 36" high and 18" wide. Attractive unusual star-shaped pinkish-purple or white flowers appear in late summer. Lightly hairy stems and glossy deep green leaves, sometimes spotted with purple, create interest. The cultivar 'Amethystina' bears amethyst blue and white flowers speckled in yellow and maroon.

Mulch toad lily to keep the surrounding soil moist and reduce weeds.

GREAT WHITE TRILLIUM
Trillium grandiflorum TRIL-ee-uhm grand-ih-FLOR-uhm

Trillium offers spectacular foliage, flowers, and berries for the shade garden. Toad trillium bears maroon flowers.

ZONES: 3–8
SIZE: 18"h × 12"w
TYPE: Perennial
FORM: Upright
TEXTURE: Medium
GROWTH: Slow
LIGHT: Partial to full shade
MOISTURE: Medium

SOIL: Fertile, moist, well-drained
FEATURES: Flowers, foliage, berries
USES: Border, woodland, ground cover
FLOWERS: ☐ ▧ ■

SITING: Great white trillium prefers partial to full shade and fertile, well-drained, moist soil with a pH of 5.5–7.0. Pure white flowers with three wavy petals and green sepals appear in midspring. Flowers often age to pink and are followed by white berries. Leaves are deep green and oval or rounded. Plants are classic woodland beauties that add grace to any shaded location that meets their cultural preferences (soil, sun, moisture, planting depth). Place plants in odd-numbered groups in the foreground of the shaded border or woodland garden, or mass as a ground cover at the feet of evergreen trees and shrubs. Woodland shade companions include 'Pictum' Japanese painted fern, kousa dogwood, and Lenten rose.

CARE: Plant 6–12" apart in spring or autumn. Apply slow-release granular plant food in spring. Apply 2–3" of organic mulch in spring and winter; as it decomposes, it adds organic matter to the soil. Maintain moist, not soggy, soil. When the soil feels almost dry 2" below the surface, water deeply. If using an irrigation system, maintain deep, infrequent waterings and avoid delivering a light sprinkle every day. Organic matter in the soil and mulch on the soil surface will help reduce watering frequency. Plants often die back to the ground by midsummer, especially if they are dry. Purchase great white trillium from a reputable nursery. Avoid digging wild plants from the woods; they are slow growing, taking 5–7 years to flower and produce seed, and do not transplant easily. Container-grown plants transplant successfully.

PROPAGATION: Let seeds self-sow in the landscape whenever possible; it may take two seasons for leaves to develop and up to 7 years for flowering and seed development. Dig plantlet in spring and reset in shaded, fertile soil; water and mulch. Divide after flowering, in early summer. Plants may take 2 years before resuming normal growth patterns.

PESTS AND DISEASES: Fungal spots, rust and smut are occasional diseases.

RELATED SPECIES: Toad trillium (*T. sessile*) reaches 12" high in late spring and bears maroon flowers above deep green leaves splashed with maroon, cream, and light green.

TULIP
Tulipa hybrids *TOO-lip-uh*

Tulips in bloom announce the arrival of springtime to the landscape.

ZONES: 3–8
SIZE: 12–30"h × 8"w
TYPE: Perennial
FORM: Upright
TEXTURE: Medium
GROWTH: Medium
LIGHT: Full sun, partial shade
MOISTURE: Medium

SOIL: Fertile, well-drained
FEATURES: Flowers, foliage
USES: Border, mass, container
FLOWERS: ■ ■ ■ □ ■ ■

SITING: Tulips prefer fertile, well-drained soil with a pH of 5.5–7.0. They prefer full sun in Zones 3–6 and partial shade in warmer zones. Most tulips are grown as annuals or short-lived perennials. Flowers appear in early, mid, or late spring, depending on species and cultivar, in cheerful crayon colors of red, yellow, pink, white, orange, and purple. Select tulips based on hardiness zone ratings; they require cold treatment to properly flower and thrive. Plants are reliably hardy in Zones 3–6. In Zones 7 and 8 plants are more sensitive and need afternoon shade. In Zones 9 and 10 plants may be grown as annuals. Tulips are classified according to their flowering characteristics. Groups include single early, double early, triumph, Darwin hybrid, single late, lily-flowered, fringed, viridiflora, parrot, Rembrandt, double late, Kaufmanniana, Fosteriana, Gregii, and miscellaneous. Place tulips in large swaths in the herbaceous border, mass as a bedding plant or ground cover, or place in containers. Annual companions to help cloak the necessary foliage dieback process include snapdragon, pot marigold, or pansy.

CARE: In autumn plant tulips 3–6" apart and two to three times deeper than their diameter. In Zones 9 and 10, precool bulbs for 8–10 weeks at 40°F before planting outdoors in early winter. Add bonemeal to the soil at planting time. Follow label directions for application amount. Apply slow-release plant food, such as Miracle-Gro Shake 'n Feed All Purpose, in spring or, if growing bulbs as perennials, begin using water-soluble plant food every week

for 3–4 weeks as flowering ends and foliage dies back. Follow label directions for application amount. Water deeply when the soil is dry. Deadheading flowers will promote perennial bulb development. Allow foliage to die back naturally so bulbs store enough energy to produce flowers the following season. Do not braid foliage or fold and wrap it with rubber bands as these practices will limit the amount of light reaching the foliage. The result will be poor bloom the following spring. Add 1" of vegetative mulch to planting beds. Keep soil moist during the growing season; allow it to dry somewhat in summer to coincide with the bulbs' dormancy.

PROPAGATION: After flowering, when leaves fade, lift clumps and separate bulbs. Replant, water, and mulch.

PESTS AND DISEASES: Root rot and bulb rot are common in soggy soils.

RELATED SPECIES: Late tulip (*T. tarda*) reaches 4–6" high and bears small, star-shaped white flowers with yellow centers in midspring. Lady tulip (*T. clusiana*) grows to 10" tall and has pink and white

Late tulip (*T. tarda*) stays small and blooms earlier than most hybrid tulips.

blooms. *T. c.* var. *chrysantha* has yellow flowers with purplish stripes. *T. praestans* produces clusters of red-orange flowers early in the season on plants 12" tall. 'Fusilier' is a common cultivar. *T. bakeri* 'Lilac Wonder' has pink to lilac blooms.

1 Dig the planting hole for tulips to a depth 2–3 times their diameter.

2 Mix bonemeal thoroughly into the soil before planting to get the phosphorus to the root zone.

3 Scatter bulbs in the hole, and space them 3–6 inches apart.

4 Cover bulbs with soil, water in, and wait for the show to begin next spring.

VERBENA

Verbena ×hybrida *ver-BEE-nuh HYE-brihd-uh*

Bedding verbena provides nonstop summer color in full sun.

ZONES: NA
SIZE: 12–18"h × 12–24"w
TYPE: Annual
FORM: Spreading or upright
TEXTURE: Medium
GROWTH: Medium
LIGHT: Full sun

MOISTURE: Medium
SOIL: Moderately fertile, well-drained
FEATURES: Flowers, foliage
USES: Border, bedding, container
FLOWERS: ■ ■ ▨ □

SITING: Bedding verbena prefers full sun and moderately fertile, well-drained soil with a pH of 5.5–7.0. Plants are usually grown as annuals. Clusters of tiny flowers in popsicle shades of red, white, pink, and purple, often with a white or yellow eye, appear from summer to early autumn. Plants may be upright or spreading, depending on cultivar. Deep to medium green leaves are hairy, rough, and toothed. Mass as bedding plants, use in odd-numbered groups in the full-sun border or use in container plantings. Good garden companions include 'Iceberg' rose, nettle-leaved mullein and *Verbena corymbosa*.
CARE: Plant 12–24" apart in late spring. Apply slow-release granular plant food at time of planting, or begin using water-soluble plant food 3 weeks after planting. Follow label directions for amount and frequency. Apply 3" of vegetative mulch in summer to reduce weed seed germination, hold moisture in the soil, and as it decomposes, add organic matter to the soil. Water deeply when the soil is dry. Deadhead spent blooms to encourage reblooming. When grown as an annual, remove plants just before first frost or right afterward when foliage is disfigured. Cover bare soil with 3" of vegetative mulch during winter to preserve topsoil.
PROPAGATION: Chill seed for 7 days before sowing. Sprinkle seeds over the growing medium and cover lightly. Thoroughly moisten and keep moist, not soggy, until seeds germinate. Germination occurs in 10–20 days at 75–80°F. Transplant 20–30 days after sowing. Reduce the temperature to 60°F after transplanting.
PESTS AND DISEASES: Diseases include powdery mildew and rust. Insect pests include aphids, spider mites, and whitefly.
RELATED SPECIES: The cultivar 'Amethyst' has small blue flowers with white eyes, 'Blue Knight' bears lilac flowers, 'Cardinal' has red flowers, 'Carousel' has purple-and-white-striped flowers, 'Imagination' has deep violet-blue flowers, and 'Peaches and Cream' has flowers in shades of peach, pink, and orange.

AUSTRIAN SPEEDWELL

Veronica austriaca ssp. *teucrium* *vuh-RAHN-ih-kuh aw-stree-AY-kuh TOO-kree-uhm*

Austrian speedwell has gentian blue flowers in early or midsummer. It is also known as veronica.

ZONES: 4–8
SIZE: 24–36"h × 24"w
TYPE: Perennial
FORM: Spreading
TEXTURE: Medium
GROWTH: Medium
LIGHT: Full sun

MOISTURE: Medium
SOIL: Moderately fertile, well-drained
FEATURES: Flowers, foliage
USES: Border, container
FLOWERS: ■ ■ ▨ □

SITING: Austrian speedwell prefers full sun (light afternoon shade in the warmer zones) and moderately fertile, well-drained soil with a pH of 5.5–7.0. Erect spikes of deep blue flowers appear in early summer in the South, midsummer in cooler zones. Place plants in groups in the border or use in containers. Companions include 'Caesar's Brother' Siberian iris, 'Silver Carpet' lamb's-ears, and 'White Icicle' spike speedwell.
CARE: Plant 18" apart in spring or fall. Apply slow-release granular plant food in spring. Water deeply when the soil is dry. Apply 3" of vegetative mulch in spring and winter. Mulch in wintertime to help keep soil temperatures from fluctuating. Soils that freeze then quickly thaw may damage root systems as they contract and expand. Sometimes plants are heaved out of the ground and perish due to physical damage, desiccation, or cold temperatures. Mulch reduces the chances of heaving. Deadhead spent blooms to encourage reblooming. Shear back hard after flowering to promote compact, attractive foliage. Prune back in fall once frost withers the foliage.
PROPAGATION: Divide in spring or fall. Dig around the root clump and lift. Use a sharp spade to slice through the root system. Reset portions that contain healthy roots and top shoots.
PESTS AND DISEASES: Diseases include powdery mildew, downy mildew, and rust. Wet soils promote root rot.
RELATED SPECIES: The cultivar 'Blue Fountain' bears bright blue flowers in summer, 'Crater Lake Blue' plants form neat mounds and bear cobalt blue flowers in early summer, 'Kapitan' has gentian blue flowers, and 'Shirley Blue' has bright blue flowers. Harebell speedwell (*V. prostrata*) is winter hardy in Zones 5–8. Plants reach 6" high. Spikelike racemes of deep blue flowers appear in early summer. The cultivar *V. prostrata* 'Alba' has white flowers, 'Heavenly Blue' bears purplish blue flowers in spring, 'Loddon Blue' has bright blue flowers, 'Mrs. Holt' bears pale pink flowers, 'Rosea' has pale pink flowers, 'Silver Queen' bears silvery-blue flowers, and 'Trehane' has violet-blue flowers and golden-tinted leaves.

Harebell speedwell is low growing and has purplish blue flowers in early summer.

SPIKE SPEEDWELL
Veronica spicata *vuh-RAHN-ih-kuh spih-KAH-tuh*

Spike speedwell's flowers appear all summer long and attract butterflies. It is also known as Veronica.

ZONES: 3–8
SIZE: 12–24"h × 18"w
TYPE: Perennial
FORM: Upright
TEXTURE: Medium
GROWTH: Medium
LIGHT: Full sun

MOISTURE: Medium
SOIL: Moderately fertile, well-drained
FEATURES: Flowers, foliage
USES: Border, container
FLOWERS: ■■□

SITING: Spike speedwell prefers full sun and moderately fertile, well-drained soil with a pH of 5.5–7.0. Erect spires of star-shaped blue flowers appear from early to late summer. Flowers attract butterflies and

bees. Place in groups in the perennial border, or use in containers. Good companions for spike speedwell include 'Shenandoah' switch grass, fountain grass, and white Culver's root.

CARE: Plant 15–18" apart in spring or autumn. Apply slow-release granular plant food in spring. Apply mulch in summer and winter. Water deeply when the soil is dry. Deadhead spent blooms to encourage reblooming. Prune back in fall once frost withers the foliage.

Cut back spike speedwell after first flush of bloom to promote compact growth and reblooming.

PROPAGATION: Reproduce cultivars through division; reproduce the species by seed or division. Divide in spring or autumn. Dig around the root clump and lift. Use a sharp spade to slice through the root system. Reset portions that contain healthy roots and top shoots. Seed germination occurs in 7–14 days at 65–75°F. Transplant 15–25 days after sowing. Reduce the temperature to 55°F after transplanting.

PESTS AND DISEASES: Plants are relatively pest free when cultural requirements (sun, soil, planting depth, moisture) are met. Root rot may occur in wet soils.

RELATED SPECIES: The cultivar 'Alba' has white flowers, 'Blue Fox' bears deep blue flowers, 'Caerula' has sky blue flowers, 'Erica' bears pink flowers, 'Heidekind' has deep red flowers and silvery-gray leaves, 'Icicle' bears white flowers, 'Minuet' reaches 10" high and has pink flowers in late spring and silvery-gray leaves, 'Rosea' bears pale pink flowers, 'Rotfuchs' ('Red Fox') is compact with deep pink flowers. *Veronica* 'Sunny Border Blue' is a low-maintenance optimum performer that reaches 18" high and 12–15" wide and bears violet-blue flowers all summer long.

CULVER'S ROOT
Veronicastrum virginicum *vuh-rahn-ih-KAST-ruhm ver-JIN-ih-kum*

Culver's root produces slender, branched flower spikes in midsummer.

ZONES: 3–8
SIZE: 6'h × 18"w
TYPE: Perennial
FORM: Upright
TEXTURE: Medium
GROWTH: Medium
LIGHT: Full sun
MOISTURE: Medium

SOIL: Moderately fertile, moist, well-drained
FEATURES: Flowers, foliage
USES: Border, container
FLOWERS: □■■

SITING: Culver's root prefers full sun and moderately fertile, well-drained, moist soil with a pH of 5.5–7.0. Slender, erect spikes of white, pink or purplish-blue flowers appear from midsummer to early autumn. Good companions for Culver's root include

'Bressingham Glow' Japanese anemone, 'Veitch's Blue' globe thistle, and 'Rotfuchs' spike speedwell.

CARE: Plant 15–18" apart in spring or fall. Apply slow-release granular plant food in

Set up supports for Culver's root to grow through. Because it is quite tall, support is often needed.

spring. Water deeply when the soil is dry. If the soil is too rich, or excessive nitrogen is applied, or if there is too little sun, foliage may become floppy. If grown in partial shade, support may be needed. Maintain moist soil. Apply 3" of vegetative mulch in summer and winter to reduce weed seed germination, hold moisture in the soil, and, as it decomposes, add organic matter to the soil. Prune back in fall once frost withers the foliage or leave erect in warmer zones for winter viewing.

PROPAGATION: Divide in spring or fall. Dig around the root clump and lift. Use a sharp spade to slice through the root system. Reset portions that contain healthy roots and top shoots. Discard any pieces that do not contain both healthy roots and top shoots. Water deeply and apply 3" of vegetative mulch around, but not touching, the plants. Plants may take up to 3 years to resume normal growth patterns.

PESTS AND DISEASES: Occasional diseases include powdery mildew, downy mildew, and leaf spots.

RELATED SPECIES: *V. virginicum* f. *album* bears white flowers. The variety *rosea* has pale pink blooms.

LARGE PERIWINKLE
Vinca major VING-kuh MAY-jur

Large periwinkle is often used in container gardens as an annual due to lack of winter hardiness in colder zones.

ZONES: 6–9
SIZE: 12–18"h × 24"w
TYPE: Perennial
FORM: Spreading
TEXTURE: Medium
GROWTH: Medium
LIGHT: Full sun to partial shade

MOISTURE: Medium to high
SOIL: Moderately fertile, well-drained
FEATURES: Flowers, foliage
USES: Ground cover, woodland, container
FLOWERS: ■□ ■
FALL COLOR: ■

SITING: Large periwinkle prefers partial shade and moderately fertile, well-drained soil with a pH of 5.5–7.3. This evergreen, woody, low-growing plant bears violet-blue flowers from midspring to autumn. It is an ideal ground cover in the bright woodland or as a spillover plant in a mixed container. Container companions include 'Bicolor' Cupid's dart, 'Sour Grapes' beardtongue, and 'Victoria' mealy-cup sage.
CARE: Plant 12–24" apart in spring or fall. Apply slow-release granular plant food

Plant large periwinkle in a pot to trail over and soften the edges of the container.

in spring. Maintain moist soil. Shear back hard in spring to keep plants tidy.
PROPAGATION: Plants naturally layer in the landscape. Pin a branch to the ground so that nodes contact the soil. Cover with mulch. Check periodically for root growth; when roots have formed, snip the branch from the parent plant, leaving some green top growth to accompany the new root system. Gently remove the new plant and reset. Divide in spring or autumn. Dig around the root clump and lift. Use a sharp spade to slice through the root system. Reset portions that contain healthy roots and top shoots. Discard any pieces that do not contain both healthy roots and top shoots. Water deeply and apply 3" of vegetative mulch around, but not touching, the plants.
PESTS AND DISEASES: Leaf spot is a common disease. Scale and leafhoppers are insect pests.
RELATED SPECIES: The cultivar 'Jason Hill' has dark green leaves and deep violet flowers, 'Maculata' bears variegated yellow-and-green leaves and pale blue flowers, 'Variegata' has yellow-white margins on dark green leaves, and white flowers.

PERIWINKLE
Vinca minor VING-kuh MYE-nur

Periwinkle is a superb evergreen ground cover for shade.

ZONES: 4–9
SIZE: 6"h × 24"w
TYPE: Perennial
FORM: Spreading
TEXTURE: Fine
GROWTH: Medium
LIGHT: Partial to full shade
MOISTURE: Medium

SOIL: Moderately fertile, well-drained
FEATURES: Flowers, foliage
USES: Ground cover, container
FLOWERS: ■■□

SITING: Periwinkle prefers partial to full shade and moderately fertile, well-drained soil with a pH of 5.5–7.0. Full sun may be tolerated in moist soil. Provide plants with shelter from strong, drying winds. Trailing stems with small, dark, evergreen leaves form an attractive ground cover. Blue flowers appear in spring and bloom lightly on and off all season long. Place at the feet of irrigated woody trees. Good companions to interplant in the ground cover for added texture and depth include 'fringed bleeding heart, 'Alba' bleeding heart, and 'Frances Williams' hosta.
CARE: Plant 12–24" apart in spring or fall. The closer the spacing, the faster the ground will be covered. Apply slow-release granular plant food in spring. Cease feeding 6–8 weeks prior to first frost date. If plants are competing with tree roots, water and feed regularly. Apply vegetative mulch in summer and winter. Water deeply when the soil is dry. Too much sun and dry soil conditions may result in yellowing or crispy brown leaves in summer.
PROPAGATION: Plants naturally layer in the landscape. Pin a branch to the ground so that nodes contact the soil. Node sites will produce roots if cultural conditions (moisture and soil) are met. Cover with mulch and check periodically for root growth; when roots have formed, snip the branch from the parent plant, leaving some green top growth to accompany the new root system. Gently remove the new plant; reset, water, and mulch. Divide in spring or autumn. Dig around the root clump and lift. Use a sharp spade to slice through the root system. Reset portions that contain healthy roots and top shoots. Discard any pieces that do not contain both healthy roots and top shoots. Water deeply and apply 3" of vegetative mulch around, but not touching, the plants.
PESTS AND DISEASES: Leaf spot is a common disease pest. Scale and leafhoppers are insect pests.
RELATED SPECIES: 'Alba Variegata' has white flowers and yellow-edged leaves, 'Argenteovariegata' bears pale blue flowers and creamy white-marked leaves, 'Atropurpurea' has burgundy flowers and deep green leaves, 'Bowle's Variety' bears large violet flowers and deep green leaves, 'Gertrude Jekyll' bears white flowers and deep green leaves, and 'Multiplex' has double burgundy flowers.

SWEET VIOLET
Viola odorata vye-OH-luh oh-duh-RAHT-uh

Sweet violet offers simple beauty to the spring and fall landscape.

ZONES: 5–8
SIZE: 4–8"h × 15"w
TYPE: Perennial
FORM: Upright
TEXTURE: Medium
GROWTH: Medium
LIGHT: Partial shade to full sun
MOISTURE: Medium

SOIL: Fertile, moist, well-drained
FEATURES: Flowers, foliage
USES: Border, woodland, container
FLOWERS: ■□

SITING: Sweet violet prefers light afternoon shade and fertile, moist, well-drained soil with a pH of 5.5–7.0. Plants tolerate full sun if the soil is consistently moist. Fragrant flowers in violet-blue and occasionally white appear in spring in cooler zones and in autumn, winter, and spring in southern zones. Bright green leaves are heart-shaped or rounded, toothed, and semievergreen. Flowers are excellent fresh cut or press dried. Good companions include bleeding heart, sweet woodruff, and Lenten rose.

CARE: Plant 8–12" apart in late spring. Apply slow-release granular plant food at time of planting. Apply vegetative mulch around, but not touching, the plants in

Press sweet violet and Johnny-jump-up blossoms in a book until dry. Place a marker in the page to find the flowers later.

summer and winter to protect roots from summer heat and winter cold. Maintain moist soil. Deadhead spent blooms to encourage reblooming. Leave flowers to fade on plant if self-seeding is desired. Prune back in fall once frost withers the foliage, or leave erect in warmer zones for winter viewing and occasional flowering.

PROPAGATION: Divide in spring or autumn. Dig around the root clump and lift. Use a sharp spade to slice through the root system. Reset portions that contain healthy roots and top shoots.

PESTS AND DISEASES: Diseases include botrytis, powdery mildew, downy mildew, rust, and root rot. Slugs and snails are occasional pests.

RELATED SPECIES: The cultivar 'Queen Charlotte' bears dark violet flowers, 'Royal Robe' has deep violet flowers, 'White Czar' bears large white flowers lightly stained purple in the center. Johnny-jump-up (*Viola tricolor*) is an old-fashioned plant with nostalgic charm. Plants are short-lived and often grown as annuals. Flowers have royal purple petals above and lavender, white, and yellow petals below. Plants self-seed freely.

PANSY
Viola ×wittrockiana vye-OH-luh wit-rahk-ee-AY-nuh

Pansy flowers perform best in the cooler weather of spring and fall.

ZONES: 5–8
SIZE: 6–10"h × 6–12"w
TYPE: Perennial
FORM: Irregular
TEXTURE: Medium
GROWTH: Medium
LIGHT: Full sun to partial shade

MOISTURE: Medium
SOIL: Fertile, moist, well-drained
FEATURES: Flowers, foliage
USES: Border, bedding, container
FLOWERS: ■□ ■ ■
■ ■ ■

SITING: Pansy prefers full sun and fertile, well-drained moist soil with a pH of 5.5–7.0. Plants are usually grown as cool-season annuals. Flowers are borne in a wide selection of colors, in solids or bicolors. Good companions include 'Purpureum' fennel, 'Tuscan Blue' rosemary, and lemon thyme.

CARE: Plant 6–12" apart in midspring or early autumn. Apply slow-release granular plant food at time of planting. Water deeply when the soil is dry. Deadhead spent blooms to encourage reblooming. When temperatures warm into the high 70s, replace with warm-season annuals.

PROPAGATION: Sprinkle seeds over the growing medium and cover lightly. Thoroughly moisten and keep moist, not soggy, until seeds germinate. Germination occurs in 7–14 days at 65–75°F. Transplant 15–25 days after sowing. After transplanting, reduce temperature to 55°F.

PESTS AND DISEASES: Diseases include powdery mildew, downy mildew, botrytis, rust, and root rot. Slugs and snails are occasional pests.

1 Replace heat-loving annuals in a container planting with pansies in the fall.

2 Add fresh Miracle-Gro planting mix to the container.

3 The finished planting will brighten autumn days.

ADAM'S NEEDLE
Yucca filamentosa YUK-ub fil-ub-men-TOH-sub

Adam's needle, also known as yucca, is spectacular in bloom.

ZONES: 5–10
SIZE: 3–6'h × 5'w
TYPE: Perennial
FORM: Rounded
TEXTURE: Coarse
GROWTH: Slow
LIGHT: Full sun
MOISTURE: Medium to low

SOIL: Moderately fertile, well-drained
FEATURES: Flowers, foliage
USES: Border, container
FLOWERS: ☐

SITING: Adam's needle prefers full sun and moderately fertile, well-drained soil with a pH of 5.5–7.3. Plants tolerate heat, humidity, and drought once established. Panicles of nodding creamy-white flowers up to 6' tall appear in mid- to late summer. Evergreen leaves are in stiff rosettes. Place in groups in the center of the sunny perennial border. Plants dislike root disturbance. Good companions include 'Bicolor' Cupid's dart, 'Sky Racer' purple moor grass, and 'Icicle' spike speedwell.
CARE: Plant 3–4' apart in spring or autumn. Apply slow-release granular plant food in

Cut back the faded flower stalk of Adam's needle after it has finished blooming.

spring. Apply 3" of vegetative mulch in summer and winter to reduce weed seed germination, hold moisture in the soil, and as it decomposes, add organic matter to the soil. Give transplants ample water; otherwise, water only when the soil is dry 2–3" below the surface. Deadhead spent blooms to encourage reblooming.
PROPAGATION: In spring remove offsets from the base of the parent plant and reset; then water and mulch.
PESTS AND DISEASES: Plants are relatively pest free when cultural requirements (sun, soil, planting depth, moisture) are met. Scale insects may be occasional pests.
RELATED SPECIES: 'Bright Edge' has gold-rimmed leaves, 'Bright Eye' leaves have bright yellow margins, 'Rosenglocken' bears pink-stained flowers, 'Schneetanne' has yellow-stained white flowers, and 'Variegata' leaves have white margins that turn pink.

BEDDING ZINNIA
Zinnia elegans ZIN-ee-uh EL-eh-gehnz

Bedding zinnia cultivars offer many bright colors to choose from.

ZONES: NA
SIZE: 12–36"h × 12"w
TYPE: Annual
FORM: Upright
TEXTURE: Medium
GROWTH: Medium
LIGHT: Full sun
MOISTURE: Medium

SOIL: Fertile, well-drained
FEATURES: Flowers, foliage
USES: Border, bedding, container
FLOWERS: ☐ ◻ ■
■ ■ ■

SITING: Bedding zinnia prefers full sun and fertile, well-drained soil with a pH of 5.5–7.0. Good air circulation is essential. The species has daisylike purple flowers; cultivars come in shades of orange, yellow, red, pink, and white in summer. Locate plants in the middle or back of the border, because the foliage may become disfigured by disease in summer. Flowers are ideal for cutting. Good garden companions include 'Moonbeam' threadleaf coreopsis, chartreuse-leaved cultivars of sweet potato, and 'Purpureum' purple fountain grass.

Narrow-leaf zinnia is a marvelous annual ground cover for full sun.

CARE: Plant 8–12" apart in late spring in well-drained soil. Spacing should promote good air circulation to reduce powdery mildew. Apply slow-release granular plant food at time of planting. Apply 3" of vegetative mulch in summer. Water deeply when the soil is dry. Deadhead spent blooms to encourage reblooming. Remove diseased foliage from plants rather than allowing leaves to fall to the ground. Remove plants after the first fall freeze.
PROPAGATION: Sprinkle seeds over the growing medium and cover. Keep moist, not soggy, until seeds germinate in 4–7 days at 70°F. Transplant 10–15 days after sowing. After transplanting, reduce temperature to 65°F. Zinnias may also be sown directly in place in the garden after frost damage has passed and soil is warm.
PESTS AND DISEASES: Diseases include powdery mildew, bacterial wilt, Southern blight, stem rots, and bacterial and fungal spots.
RELATED SPECIES: Narrow leaf zinnia (*Z. angustifolia* 'Orange Star') reaches 10" tall and is a superb annual ground cover. Tangerine flowers appear in summer. Plants are mildew resistant.

A–Z ENCYCLOPEDIA OF

TREE AND SHRUB CARE

Trees and shrubs are essential elements
in an attractive, well-designed
landscape, providing form, structure,
and seasonal interest.

Azalea, Exbury and Ghent hybrids, *Rhododendron*

Big-leaf hydrangea, *Hydrangea macrophylla*

Burning bush, *Euonymus alatus*

Flowering quince, *Chaenomeles speciosa*

Heavenly bamboo,
Nandina domestica

Japanese kerria,
Kerria japonica
'Golden Guinea'

Purple smoke tree,
Cotinus coggygria
'Purpureus'

COMMON NAME INDEX TREES AND SHRUBS *continued*

COMMON NAME	BOTANIC NAME	SEE PAGE
English walnut	Juglans regia	412
European beech	Fagus sylvatica	400
European cranberrybush	Viburnum opulus	465
European filbert	Corylus avellana	392
European hornbeam	Carpinus betulus	382
European larch	Larix decidua	416
European mountain ash	Sorbus aucuparia	456
False holly	Osmanthus heterophyllus	428
Florida anise-tree	Illicium floridanum	411
Flowering crabapple	Malus spp. and cvs.	423–424
Flowering dogwood	Cornus florida	391
Flowering quince	Chaenomeles speciosa	387
Fragrant mock orange	Philadelphus coronarius	431
Fragrant sumac	Rhus aromatica	446
Fragrant tea olive	Osmanthus heterophyllus	428
Fragrant winter hazel	Corylopsis glabrescens	392
Fragrant wintersweet	Chimonanthus praecox	389
Franklin tree	Franklinia alatamaha	402
Gardenia	Gardenia jasminoides	403
Garland flower	Daphne cneorum	396
Giant redwood	Sequoiadendron giganteum	453
Giant sequoia	Sequoiadendron giganteum	453
Ginkgo	Ginkgo biloba	403
Glossy abelia	Abelia ×grandiflora	370
Glossy buckthorn	Rhamnus frangula	443
Golden chain tree	Laburnum ×watereri	415
Golden larch	Pseudolarix amabilis	439
Golden rain tree	Koelreuteria paniculata	414
Green ash	Fraxinus pennsylvanica	402
Hackberry	Celtis occidentalis	385
Hardy catalpa	Catalpa speciosa	383
Hardy silver gum	Eucalyptus gunnii	399
Heavenly bamboo	Nandina domestica	427
Hemlock	Tsuga canadensis	463
Hinoki false cypress	Chamaecyparis obtusa	388
Holly osmanthus	Osmanthus heterophyllus	428
Hophornbeam	Ostrya virginiana	429
Hop tree	Ptelea trifoliata	440
Horsechestnut	Aesculus hippocastanum	372
Hybrid witch hazel	Hamamelis ×intermedia	405
Indian hawthorn	Raphiolepis umbellata	444
Ironwood	Ostrya virginiana	429
Japanese angelica tree	Aralia elata	374
Japanese aucuba	Aucuba japonica	376
Japanese barberry	Berberis thunbergii	377
Japanese beautyberry	Callicarpa japonica	379
Japanese camellia	Camellia japonica	381
Japanese cedar	Cryptomeria japonica	395
Japanese cryptomeria	Cryptomeria japonica	395

COMMON NAME	BOTANIC NAME	SEE PAGE
Japanese flowering cherry	Prunus serrulata	439
Japanese jewelberry	Callicarpa japonica	379
Japanese kerria	Kerria japonica	414
Japanese maple	Acer palmatum	371
Japanese pagodatree	Sophora japonica	455
Japanese pieris	Pieris japonica	433
Japanese pittosporum	Pittosporum tobira	436
Japanese privet	Ligustrum japonicum	418
Japanese red pine	Pinus densiflora	434
Japanese rose	Kerria japonica	414
Japanese skimmia	Skimmia japonica	454
Japanese snowbell	Styrax japonicus	458
Japanese spirea	Spiraea japonica	456
Japanese stewartia	Stewartia pseudocamellia	458
Japanese tree lilac	Syringa reticulata	460
Japanese umbrella pine	Sciadopitys verticillata	452
Japanese yew	Taxus cuspidata	462
Japanese zelkova	Zelkova serrata	467
Katsura tree	Cercidiphyllum japonicum	386
Kentucky coffee tree	Gymnocladus dioica	404
Korean abelialeaf	Abeliophyllum distichum	370
Larch	Larix decidua	416
Lemon bottlebrush	Callistemon citrinus	379
Leyland cypress	×Cupressocyparis leylandii	395
Lilac	Syringa vulgaris	460
Lily-of-the-valley tree	Oxydendrum arboreum	429
Linden	Tilia americana	463
Live oak	Quercus virginiana	443
London plane tree	Platanus ×acerifolia	436
Maidenhair tree	Ginkgo biloba	403
Meserve holly	Ilex ×meserveae	409
Meyer lilac	Syringa meyeri	459
Michigan holly	Ilex verticillata	410
Mimosa	Albizia julibrissin	373
Mockorange	Philadelphus coronarius	431
Monkey puzzle	Araucaria araucana	375
Mountain currant	Ribes alpinum	446
Mountain laurel	Kalmia latifolia	413
Mugo pine	Pinus mugo	434
Mulberry	Morus alba	425
Myrtle	Myrtus communis	426
New Jersey tea	Ceanothus americanus	384
Ninebark	Physocarpus opulifolius	432
Northern bayberry	Myrica pensylvanica	426
Northern catalpa	Catalpa speciosa	383
Old-fashioned weigela	Weigela florida	467
Oleander	Nerium oleander	427
Orange-eye butterfly bush	Buddleia davidii	378
Oregon fir	Pseudotsuga menziesii	440

COMMON NAME	BOTANIC NAME	SEE PAGE
Oregon grapeholly	*Mahonia aquifolium*	422
Oregon hollygrape	*Mahonia aquifolium*	422
Pacific madrone	*Arbutus menziesii*	375
Panicled golden rain tree	*Koelreuteria paniculata*	414
Paper birch	*Betula papyrifera*	377
Pearl bush	*Exochorda racemosa*	400
Peashrub	*Caragana arborescens*	381
Pea tree	*Caragana arborescens*	381
Persian ironwood	*Parrotia persica*	430
Persian parrotia	*Parrotia persica*	430
Pin oak	*Quercus palustris*	442
Pomegranate	*Punica granatum*	441
Princess tree	*Paulownia tomentosa*	430
Red ash	*Fraxinus pennsylvanica*	402
Red chokeberry	*Aronia arbutifolia*	376
Red-osier dogwood	*Cornus stolonifera*	391
Red-twig dogwood	*Cornus stolonifera*	391
Red-vein enkianthus	*Enkianthus campanulatus*	398
Redwood	*Sequoia sempervirens*	453
Rhododendron	*Rhododendron* spp.	444–445
River birch	*Betula nigra*	377
Rockspray cotoneaster	*Cotoneaster horizontalis*	394
Rocky Mountain juniper	*Juniperus scopulorum*	413
Rose cultivars	*Rosa* cvs.	447–448
Rose daphne	*Daphne cneorum*	396
Rosemary	*Rosmarinus officinalis*	449
Rose-of-Sharon	*Hibiscus syriacus*	406
Rose species	*Rosa* spp.	449
Rowan tree	*Sorbus aucuparia*	456
Royal paulownia	*Paulownia tomentosa*	430
Russian arborvitae	*Microbiota decussata*	425
Russian cypress	*Microbiota decussata*	425
Russian olive	*Elaeagnus angustifolia*	398
Sassafras	*Sassafras albidum*	452
Saucer magnolia	*Magnolia ×soulangiana*	422
Scarlet firethorn	*Pyracantha coccinea*	441
Sea buckthorn	*Hippophae rhamnoides*	407
Seven-son flower	*Heptacodium miconioides*	406
Shagbark hickory	*Carya ovata*	382
Shrub althea	*Hibiscus syriacus*	406
Shrubby plumbago	*Ceratostigma willmottianum*	386
Shrubby St. Johnswort	*Hypericum prolificum*	408
Siberian peashrub	*Caragana arborescens*	381
Silk tree	*Albizia julibrissin*	373
Silver buffaloberry	*Shepherdia argentea*	454
Slender deutzia	*Deutzia gracilis*	397
Smokebush	*Cotinus coggygria*	393
Smoke tree	*Cotinus coggygria*	393
Snowberry	*Symphoricarpos albus*	459

COMMON NAME	BOTANIC NAME	SEE PAGE
Sorrel tree	*Oxydendrum arboreum*	429
Sour gum	*Nyssa sylvatica*	428
Sourwood	*Oxydendrum arboreum*	429
Southern magnolia	*Magnolia grandiflora*	421
Spicebush	*Lindera benzoin*	418
Spreading cotoneaster	*Cotoneaster divaricatus*	393
Strawberry shrub	*Calycanthus floridus*	380
Sugar maple	*Acer saccharum*	372
Summer lilac	*Buddleia davidii*	378
Summersweet	*Clethra alnifolia*	390
Swamp candleberry	*Myrica pensylvanica*	426
Swamp holly	*Ilex verticillata*	410
Sweet box	*Sarcococca hookeriana*	451
Sweet elder	*Sambucus canadensis*	450
Sweet gum	*Liquidambar styraciflua*	419
Sweet mock orange	*Philadelphus coronarius*	431
Sweet pepper bush	*Clethra alnifolia*	390
Sweet shrub	*Calycanthus floridus*	380
Swiss mountain pine	*Pinus mugo*	434
Tamarisk	*Tamarix ramosissima*	461
Tatarian honeysuckle	*Lonicera tatarica*	420
Thornless honeylocust	*Gleditsia triacanthos inermis*	404
Tree of heaven	*Ailanthus altissima*	373
Tulip poplar	*Liriodendron tulipifera*	419
Tulip tree	*Liriodendron tulipifera*	419
Tupelo	*Nyssa sylvatica*	428
Umbrella pine	*Sciadopitys verticillata*	452
Ural false spirea	*Sorbaria sorbifolia*	455
Vanhoutte spirea	*Spiraea ×vanhouttei*	457
Varnish tree	*Koelreuteria paniculata*	414
Virgilia	*Cladrastis kentukea*	390
Virginia sweetspire	*Itea virginica*	411
Weigela	*Weigela florida*	467
Western soapberry	*Sapindus drummondii*	451
White birch	*Betula papyrifera*	377
White cedar	*Thuja occidentalis*	462
White fir	*Abies concolor*	371
White forsythia	*Abeliophyllum distichum*	370
White fringe tree	*Chionanthus virginicus*	389
White mulberry	*Morus alba*	425
White willow	*Salix alba*	450
Wild allspice	*Lindera benzoin*	418
Winged euonymus	*Euonymus alatus*	399
Winged spindle tree	*Euonymus alatus*	399
Winterberry	*Ilex verticillata*	410
Witch hazel	*Hamamelis ×intermedia*	405
Yaupon	*Ilex vomitoria*	410
Yellow locust	*Robinia pseudoacacia*	447
Yellow poplar	*Liriodendron tulipifera*	419

Serviceberry, *Amelanchier alnifolia*

Spirea, *Spiraea* 'Goldflame' and *Spiraea* 'Little Princess'

Sugar maple, *Acer saccharum*

GLOSSY ABELIA

Abelia ×grandiflora uh-BEE-lee-uh gran-dih-FLO-ruh

Trumpet-shaped flowers dangle from branches of glossy abelia, also known as arbutus.

ZONES: (5)6–9
SIZE: 3–6'h × 3–6'w
TYPE: Semievergreen shrub
FORM: Spreading, dense, rounded
TEXTURE: Medium fine
GROWTH: Medium to fast
LIGHT: Sun to part shade

MOISTURE: Even
SOIL: Acid, well drained
FEATURES: Reddish brown stems, flowers attract butterflies
USES: Massing, hedge
FLOWERS: □ ▨
FALL COLOR: ▨ ▨

SITING: Choose a site in full sun to part shade. Proper siting is necessary to avoid damage in severe winters. Plants may show iron chlorosis in high-pH soils. New growth will be less vigorous in dry soils. Glossy abelia is best for eastern and southern gardens in Zone 6 and higher. Stems may be damaged at -5°F to -10°F, but the plant won't die.

CARE: Transplant balled-and-burlapped plants in spring or container-grown anytime during the growing season.

Prune out dead wood in spring if winter dieback is a problem.

Wood can be brittle, so handle carefully. Space 3–6' apart, closer for hedge plantings. Water thoroughly after planting. Apply 2–4" of shredded bark or wood-chip mulch around plants and replenish as necessary throughout the growing season. Keep the soil evenly moist from spring until the ground freezes, watering when the top 2" of soil has dried out. Consistent watering is especially important during the first 2 years. In spring apply plant food, such as Miracle-Gro, around the base of the plant and water in well. Prune occasionally to keep the plant neat. On established plants remove one-third of the oldest shoots each year in early spring to encourage new flowering shoots. Rejuvenate old plants by cutting them back to about 6" in late winter. Plants will flower the same year after pruning. In the north prune winterkilled branches.

PROPAGATION: Take softwood stem cuttings anytime foliage is present. Sow seeds when ripe.

PESTS AND DISEASES: None are serious. Leaf spots and mildew may appear, but they are rarely more than a cosmetic problem. Aphids are sometimes a problem on soft, succulent growth.

WHITE FORSYTHIA

Abeliophyllum distichum ay-bee-lee-oh-FIL-um DIS-tih-kum

White or pink-tinged flowers of white forsythia appear in very early spring. It is also known as Korean abelialeaf.

ZONES: (4)5–8
SIZE: 3–5'h × 3–4'w
TYPE: Deciduous shrub
FORM: Rounded, arching
TEXTURE: Medium
GROWTH: Slow to fast

LIGHT: Sun to light shade
MOISTURE: Even
SOIL: Well drained
FEATURES: White flowers in early spring
USES: Early spring color
FLOWERS: □ ▨

SITING: Choose a site in full sun to light shade where you can enjoy the fragrance and early spring color. White forsythia is adaptable to many soils but prefers those that are well drained. Plant white forsythia with yellow-flowered forsythia for an extra boost in your spring show. Flower buds may be damaged at –25°F, but it won't kill the plant. In northern areas plant in a protected location to ensure flower bud hardiness.

Encourage new shoot development by cutting back to 6–12" right after flowering.

CARE: Transplant balled-and-burlapped plants in spring or container-grown plants anytime during the growing season. Space 3–4' apart. Water newly planted shrubs right after planting. Apply 2–4" of shredded bark or wood-chip mulch around plants and replenish as necessary throughout the growing season. Keep the soil evenly moist from spring until the ground freezes, watering when the top 2" of the soil has dried out. Consistent watering is especially important during the first 2 years. Shrubs benefit from a spring application of plant food, such as Miracle-Gro, sprinkled around the base of the plants and watered in well. White forsythia flowers are self-cleaning and do not require deadheading. Overgrown plants and mature shrubs benefit from renewal pruning every 3–4 years. Prune to 6–12" from the ground right after flowering to encourage new shoots. Remove a few of the oldest stems annually to improve bloom.

PROPAGATION: Root softwood stem cuttings in midsummer. Sow seeds when ripe.

PESTS AND DISEASES: None are serious.

RELATED SPECIES: 'Roseum' is a cultivar with pink flowers.

WHITE FIR

Abies concolor AY-beez CAHN-kah-lar

White fir, also known as concolor fir or Colorado fir, has dense, fine-textured, evergreen foliage.

ZONES: 4–7
SIZE: 30–50'h × 15–30'w
TYPE: Evergreen tree
FORM: Conical
TEXTURE: Medium
GROWTH: Slow to medium

LIGHT: Full to part shade
MOISTURE: Even
SOIL: Acid, well drained
FEATURES: Slow-growing evergreen
USES: Year-round color
FALL COLOR: ■

SITING: White fir makes a good accent tree in the landscape. Keep the mature size in mind when planting. Trees need good air circulation and room to grow without cramping. This evergreen is somewhat tolerant of city conditions. It grows well in rocky soil as long as it is loose.
CARE: Replace compacted soil before planting. Transplant balled-and-burlapped plants in spring or container-grown plants anytime during the growing season. Water well right after planting. Apply 2–4" of mulch around plants and replenish as necessary throughout the growing season until the trees are large enough to shade their own roots. Keep the soil evenly moist from spring until the ground freezes. Feed young trees every spring with acid plant food such as Miracle-Gro Shake 'n Feed Azalea, Camellia, Rhododendron. Plants require little or no pruning. Prune lightly to maintain the conical shape in late spring after new growth emerges.
PROPAGATION: Propagation is difficult. Seeds require moist chilling for 30 days. Take hardwood cuttings in late winter.
PESTS AND DISEASES: None serious.
RELATED SPECIES: Balsam fir *(A. balsamea)* is hardier than white fir (Zones 3–5) and grows 45–75' tall. Fraser fir *(A. fraseri)* grows 30–40' tall. It does not do well in hot, dry weather but is adapted to higher elevations of the Southeast.

Install evenly placed stakes around young trees in fall.

Attach burlap to the stakes for winter protection.

JAPANESE MAPLE

Acer palmatum AY-sir pall-MAY-tum

Some cultivars of Japanese maple are prized for their beautiful maroon, finely dissected foliage.

ZONES: 5–8
SIZE: 15–25'h × 8–25'w
TYPE: Deciduous tree
FORM: Rounded to broad rounded
TEXTURE: Medium fine
GROWTH: Slow
LIGHT: Sun to part shade

MOISTURE: Moist
SOIL: Humusy, well drained, acid
FEATURES: Sculptural, elegant form
USES: Accent groupings
FLOWER: ■■
FALL COLOR: ■■■

SITING: Japanese maple prefers morning sun and filtered shade in the afternoon. The sculptural form and striking leaf color make it an excellent accent plant. Its preference for moist soil makes it a good choice next to a water feature. Protect plants from winds and late spring frosts, which can damage the sensitive young foliage that appears early in spring. Leaf scorch can be a problem in hot, drying summer winds.
CARE: Transplant balled-and-burlapped plants in spring or container-grown plants anytime during the growing season. Water well after planting. Mulch with 2–4" of shredded bark or wood chips to retain soil moisture and keep the soil cool. Water as needed to keep the soil moist throughout the growing season, especially during the heat of summer. Japanese maple likes fertile soil and will benefit from an annual spring application of plant food, such as Miracle-Gro. Prune as needed to maintain the plant's natural outline. It can be pruned to a single-stemmed small tree or a multistemmed shrub.
PROPAGATION: Sow seeds when ripe for germination the following spring. Dried seeds require soaking for a few days followed by stratification. Take softwood cuttings in midsummer.
PESTS AND DISEASES: None serious.
RELATED SPECIES: Hedge maple *(A. campestre)* is a coarser plant with less showy fall color but a higher tolerance of poorer, drier soils. It makes a good hedge plant. Amur maple *(A. tataricum ginnala)* is not as refined as Japanese maple, but it is a good substitute in Zones 3 and 4. Tatarian maple *(A. tataricum)* is less common but is well suited to Zones 3 and 4. Fall color is variable—in shades of yellow to reddish brown—and not as showy as that of Japanese maple.

Water maples during dry periods to help prevent leaf scorch.

SUGAR MAPLE

Acer saccharum AY-sir sah-KAIR-um

ZONES: 4–8
SIZE: 60–75'h × 30–50'w
TYPE: Deciduous tree
FORM: Upright oval to rounded
TEXTURE: Medium
GROWTH: Slow
LIGHT: Sun to light shade
MOISTURE: Moderate
SOIL: Well drained, fertile, acid
FEATURES: Brilliant fall color
USES: Shade tree
FALL COLOR: ■ ■ ■

Sugar maple is noted for its outstanding fall color.

SITING: Sugar maple, a North American native, is one of the best shade trees for larger yards. It prefers well-drained, moist, fertile soil. It does not perform well in tight situations and is not a good choice for street plantings or small yards.
CARE: Transplant balled-and-burlapped plants in spring or fall. Amend the soil with peat moss, compost, or other organic matter before planting. Water well after planting. Mulch with 2–4" of shredded bark or wood chips to retain soil moisture and provide a barrier against lawn mowers and string trimmers, which can seriously damage the thin bark. Water as needed to keep the soil moist throughout the growing season, especially during the heat of summer. Leaf scorch can be a problem during dry periods, especially on young trees. Sugar maple likes fertile soil. Young trees will benefit from an annual spring application of plant food such as Miracle-Gro. Mature trees that are under stress from drought, insects, or diseases will

Wrap young trees with crepe tree wrap in winter to prevent sunscald on the trunk.

benefit from root feeding. Prune to improve shape in spring or summer to avoid bleeding sap, which occurs in late winter.
PROPAGATION: Seeds require stratification for 60–90 days.
PESTS AND DISEASES: Verticillium wilt, a soilborne disease, and pear thrips can be problems. Leaf scorch may occur on dry, windy sites. Wrap young trees in winter to protect the thin bark from sunscald.
RELATED SPECIES: Trident maple *(A. buergerianum),* growing 20–30' tall, is good in smaller spaces. Paperbark maple *(A. griseum)* grows to 25' and has very attractive peeling reddish-brown bark. Big-leaf maple *(A. macrophyllum)* is reliably hardy to Zone 6. Fall color is yellow. Norway maple *(A. platanoides)* has denser shade and yellow fall color. Red maple *(A. rubrum)* is hardier (Zone 3) and has vivid fall color and showier red flowers in spring. Silver maple *(A. saccharinum)* is hardier (Zone 3) and grows taller and faster, but the weak wood can be messy. Three-flowered maple *(A. triflorum)* is an attractive small tree, growing 20–30' with an equal spread.

HORSECHESTNUT

Aesculus hippocastanum ESS-kuh-luss hih-poh-CASS-tuh-num

Horsechestnut has spiny nuts that can be a nuisance.

ZONES: 4–7
SIZE: 50–70'h × 40–70'w
TYPE: Deciduous tree
FORM: Upright oval to rounded
TEXTURE: Medium to coarse
GROWTH: Medium
LIGHT: Sun to light shade

MOISTURE: Moderate
SOIL: Moist, well drained, acid
FEATURES: Stately, large shade tree, attractive flowers
USES: Shade
FLOWERS: ☐
FALL COLOR: ■

SITING: Horsechestnut is a large tree that needs ample room to grow. The invasive roots can break up sidewalks and patios. The heavy, dense canopy of a mature specimen makes underplanting of shrubs or flowers difficult. It needs fairly rich and moist but well-drained soil. Avoid planting it where the soil is extremely dry. The showy flowers are attractive to hummingbirds and butterflies. The spiny nuts (inedible to humans) can be messy when they fall.
CARE: Transplant balled-and-burlapped plants into moist, well-drained soil in full sun or light shade. Apply a 2–4" layer of organic mulch to help retain soil moisture.

The spiny outer covering hides a mature brown fruit.

Water as needed to keep soil moist throughout the growing season. Leaf scorch can be a problem during dry periods, especially on young trees. Feed lightly for the first few years. Prune in early spring as needed to improve shape or remove dead or diseased branches.
PROPAGATION: Seeds require stratification for 3–4 months. Sow seeds in place or transplant taprooted seedlings while they are still young.
PESTS AND DISEASES: Leaf blotch and powdery mildew are fungal problems that can defoliate trees by late summer. Clean up leaves in fall to remove overwintering sites for disease spores.
RELATED SPECIES: *A. ×carnea* has showy rose-red flowers in late spring and grows to about 40' tall. Ohio buckeye *(A. glabra)* grows to about 40' and is not as showy in flower. It is hardy to Zone 3. Bottlebrush buckeye *(A. parviflora)* is a wide-spreading, suckering shrub, growing to about 12'. The tall panicles of white flowers bloom in June and July at a time when few other shrubs are in bloom. It does not suffer from leaf blotch and powdery mildew.

TREE OF HEAVEN

Ailanthus altissima *ay-LAN-thus al-TISS-ih-muh*

Tree of heaven is a tough tree for harsh sites.

ZONES: (4)5–8
SIZE: 40–60'h ×
15–40'w
TYPE: Deciduous
tree
FORM: Open
spreading
TEXTURE: Coarse
GROWTH: Fast
LIGHT: Sun to light
shade

MOISTURE: Even
SOIL: Any
FEATURES: Fast
growing, large
leaves
USES: Specimen for
larger gardens
FLOWERS: ■ ■
FALL COLOR: ■

SITING: Plant tree of heaven where nothing
else will grow. It is adaptable to harsh city
conditions such as pollution, soot, and
grime. Greenish-white flowers appear from
mid- to late summer but are not showy.
Some trees are male; others female.

The male types have a pungent odor.
The fast-growing stems are subject to wind
damage and may create a mess on the
lawn after storms. Female plants develop
attractive red fruits in late summer. They
turn into handsome clusters of winged
red-brown seedpods that provide fall and
winter interest and are attractive in dried
arrangements. This tree tolerates full sun to

**Weedy shoots need to be removed regularly to
prevent damage to foundations and sidewalks.
Self-sown tree of heaven seedlings can be invasive.**

light shade. Soil type is not important.
Avoid planting it near foundations or
sidewalks, where the prevalent, tough
suckers can be a problem.
CARE: Plant in spring for best results.
Water well during the first season to keep
the soil evenly moist. Established trees do
not require supplemental watering. Fertile
soil leads to excessive growth and weak
stems that break during storms.
Tree of heaven usually has
some twig dieback after
every winter. Prune it out
in early spring.
PROPAGATION: Seeds may
germinate better with 60 days
of pretreatment in a moist soil
mix. Dig up suckers and
replant in spring.
PESTS AND DISEASES:
Verticillium wilt, a soilborne
fungal disease, can be a
problem but is rarely serious.
RELATED SPECIES: 'Erythrocarpa'
has dark green leaves and red
fruits. 'Pendulifolia' is a hard-to-
find cultivar that has longer
leaves that hang downward
rather than horizontally.

SILK TREE

Albizia julibrissin *awl-BIH-zee-uh joo-lih-BRISS-in*

**Silk tree, also known as mimosa, has
feathery foliage and showy flowers.**

ZONES: 6–9
SIZE: 20–35'h ×
20–40'w
TYPE: Deciduous
tree
FORM: Wide
spreading
TEXTURE: Fine
GROWTH: Medium
to fast
LIGHT: Sun to light
shade

MOISTURE: Even to
slightly dry
SOIL: Well drained
FEATURES: Fernlike
foliage, exotic
flowers
USES: Massing,
hillsides away from
residential settings
FLOWERS: ■
FALL COLOR: ■

SITING: Fernlike foliage and exotic-looking
flowers give silk tree a distinctly tropical
feel. Keep this in mind when choosing a
site. Consider it for mass plantings or on
hillsides away from residential settings,
where it can develop its natural
multitrunked form. The showy, fragrant,
fluffy pink flowers look like pincushions
and are attractive to hummingbirds and
bees. The twice-compound leaves with
many fine leaflets are light sensitive,
folding at night. The fallen leaves, flowers,
and fruits can become a litter problem, so
it is best to keep it away from sidewalks or
decks. Some of the gray-brown seedpods
persist on the tree into winter and spring,
but are not ornamental. Silk tree is
extremely adaptable to various types of
soil. It withstands drought, high-pH soil,
salinity, and wind. It tolerates light shade
but flowers best in full sun. It is best suited
to warm locations; temperatures below
−5°F for any length of time will result in
injury. This tree has become naturalized in
the southern part of the United States and
is rather invasive in edge habitats, such as

along roadsides, beside parking lots,
and bordering power lines.
CARE: Water newly established plants.
Mature plants are drought tolerant but the
leaves may take on a yellowish cast with
insufficient water. Silk tree is best left to
grow into its natural shape, without
pruning. Plants that are killed back by
disease or winterkill can be pruned to the
ground, but the resulting new growth will
not be as attractive as the original.
PROPAGATION: The seeds have a hard coat,
which can be softened by soaking in water
for several days. However self-sown
seedlings occur naturally, often becoming
weeds. Cuttings root easily in spring.
PESTS AND DISEASES: Silk tree is very
susceptible to a vascular wilt disease that
can kill plants to the ground, resulting in
an unattractive mass of suckers. Webworm
can also be highly destructive, and leaf
spot and rust can disfigure leaves.
RELATED SPECIES: 'Rosea' is smaller,
reaching two-thirds the height and spread,
and has richer pink flowers. 'Ernest Wilson'
is reputed to be cold hardier by 10°F.

APPLE SERVICEBERRY
Amelanchier ×grandiflora ah-mih-LAN-kee-er grand-ih-FLOR-uh

Apple serviceberry has delicate white flowers in early spring.

ZONES: 3–8
SIZE: 15–25'h × 20–30'w
TYPE: Deciduous tree
FORM: Rounded
TEXTURE: Medium fine
GROWTH: Medium
LIGHT: Sun to shade
MOISTURE: Even

SOIL: Well drained, acid
FEATURES: Cheery spring flowers, purple-red fruits attractive to birds
USES: Mixed border, specimen, foundation
FLOWERS: ☐
FALL COLOR: ▨ ■

SITING: Apple serviceberry can be used in windbreaks and naturalized plantings, where it will attract wildlife. Its delicate white flowers, attractive purple-red fruits, and silvery gray bark make it worthy of the mixed border. With pruning and shaping, it makes a striking specimen tree. It prefers well-drained, slightly acid, moist soil. It is shade tolerant and can be used on the north side of buildings or in the shade of larger trees. It makes a good courtyard or patio tree, because birds devour the red fruits before they fall and become messy and the strong wood is resilient in storms.

Apple serviceberry is a good small tree for landscape use.

CARE: Water as needed to keep the soil moist throughout the growing season, especially if planted in full sun. Spread 2–4" of shredded bark or wood chips to conserve soil moisture. In spring apply plant food, such as Miracle-Gro. Shrub types benefit from annual pruning out of one-third of the oldest branches. Remove lower shoots and branches to maintain a small tree. All pruning is best done in early spring.

PROPAGATION: Seeds require stratification. Propagate named selections vegetatively by removing suckers at the base of plants.

PESTS AND DISEASES: Rust and leaf spot can be cosmetic problems but do not usually affect the plant's overall health.

RELATED SPECIES: 'Autumn Brilliance' and 'Princess Diana' have abundant flowers and fruits and good fall color. Saskatoon serviceberry (*A. alnifolia*) has the highest fruit production. Downy serviceberry (*A. arborea*), one of the parents of *A. ×grandiflora*, is a common understory shrub in deciduous forests. Shadblow serviceberry (*A. canadensis*) is more erect and upright with abundant suckering branches at the base.

JAPANESE ANGELICA TREE
Aralia elata uh-RAY-lee-uh ee-LAY-tuh

Showy upright panicles of white flowers appear in late summer.

ZONES: (4)5–9
SIZE: 20–30'h × 15'w
TYPE: Deciduous tree
FORM: Upright
TEXTURE: Medium
GROWTH: Medium
LIGHT: Sun to light shade

MOISTURE: Dry to moist
SOIL: Well drained
FEATURES: Late-summer flowers, large leaves
USES: Architectural specimen
FLOWERS: ☐
FALL COLOR: ▨ ■

SITING: Japanese angelica tree has showy flowers and interesting foliage, but its tendency to sucker and its spines limit its use in formal landscapes. It is probably best used in naturalized shrub borders or at wood's edge. Large, upright panicles of white flowers are borne in the central terminal of each branch in late summer and early autumn. Flowers are followed by purplish fruits, which are quickly eaten by birds. The huge leaves are divided into many leaflets and sometimes have a bluish tint. Branches are nearly vertical and usually spiny. Japanese angelica tree

Remove suckers from the base of plants to keep them from spreading.

performs best in well-drained, moist, fertile soils but also grows in dry, rocky, or heavy soil. Give it full sun to part shade. It tolerates both acid and alkaline soils as well as city conditions. In Zone 4 it should be planted in a protected site.

CARE: Water newly established plants and maintain adequate soil moisture the first two seasons after planting. Mature plants are drought tolerant. This shrub spreads by underground stems that may need to be weeded out. Suckering greatly increases when trees are cut back to the ground.

PROPAGATION: Seeds require stratification. To propagate, dig young shoots that originate from the base, and replant them in early spring.

PESTS AND DISEASES: None serious.

RELATED SPECIES: 'Aureovariegata' is a hard-to-find cultivar with golden-variegated leaves. 'Variegata' leaves are margined and blotched with yellow-white variegation. Neither is as hardy as the species. Devils walking stick (*A spinosa*) is smaller, growing to only 10–20' and is not hardy in Zone 4. It is native to the eastern United States, where it grows as an understory plant in deciduous forests.

MONKEY PUZZLE

Araucaria araucana *ar-aw-KAY-ree-uh ar-aw-KAY-nuh*

Monkey puzzle has a loose, pyramidal shape.

ZONES: 7–10
SIZE: 50–80'h × 30–35'w
TYPE: Evergreen tree
FORM: Pyramidal
TEXTURE: Coarse
GROWTH: Slow
LIGHT: Sun to part shade
MOISTURE: Moist
SOIL: Well drained
FEATURES: Spirally arranged needles
USES: Specimen, container

SITING: This strange-looking conifer has heavy, spreading branches and ropelike branchlets closely set with sharp-pointed dark green leaves. It forms a loose, symmetrical, see-through crown, pyramidal in youth and rounded or flattish in maturity—a distinctive silhouette and an interesting skyline tree. Its large size and unique growth habit make it difficult to utilize in most garden settings, but it is an elegant specimen for large landscapes and parks. It could also be used in widely spaced groupings. Keep it away from benches and other sitting areas. It bears large, spiny, 10- to 15-pound cones that fall with a crash and the stiff branches drop regularly. The tiered branches protrude horizontally for a distance from the center of the trunk, then ascend skyward in a gentle arch. The scalelike leaves are dark green, stiff, sharp-pointed, and densely arranged on the branches, looking more reptilian than coniferous. Monkey puzzle prefers cool, moist soil, but does well in a wide range of soils as long as there is adequate drainage. It is tolerant of winds and salt spray; a group would make an excellent windbreak for a coastal landscape. It does not do well in hot, dry soils and it does not tolerate atmospheric pollution. It thrives in containers for years. It does best where the summers are cool and humid, such as the Pacific Northwest; it is a popular landscape oddity in England.

CARE: Transplant container-grown plants anytime. Give them adequate water right after planting and all season long the first 2 years. Water as necessary to keep the soil evenly moist. Mature specimens do not require supplemental water. Container plants may need water daily during hot, dry spells. Young plants will benefit from a spring application of acid plant food. Container-grown plants need regular applications of a water-soluble plant food such as Miracle-Gro.

PROPAGATION: Sow seeds or take tip cuttings from vertical shoots. Cuttings from lateral-growing shoots will develop into sprawling shrubs.

PESTS AND DISEASES: None are serious.

RELATED SPECIES: Norfolk Island pine (*A. heterophylla*) is hardy to Zone 10 or 11. It is a common landscape plant in Hawaii, and is a popular houseplant in colder climates. The juvenile leaves are narrow, ½" long, curved, and with a sharp point. Mature leaves are more triangular and densely overlapping. The tree can be held in a container for many years—outdoors in mild climates or indoors anywhere. Bunya-bunya (*A. bidwellii*) is native to Australia. It becomes a large tree (to 150'), and is hardy to Zone 9. Hoop pine or Moreton Bay pine (*A. cunninghamii*) is another large Australian native. It has reddish-brown peeling bark.

PACIFIC MADRONE

Arbutus menziesii *ar-BU-tus men-ZEE-zee-eye*

Pacific madrone has very ornamental peeling, cinnamon-red bark.

ZONES: (7)8–9
SIZE: 20–50'h × 20–50'w
TYPE: Broadleaf evergreen tree
FORM: Upright
TEXTURE: Medium
GROWTH: Slow
LIGHT: Sun to part shade
MOISTURE: Low
SOIL: Well drained
FEATURES: Multicolored peeling bark
USES: Specimen
FLOWERS: □
FALL COLOR: ■

SITING: Cinnamon red-brown bark peels away to reveal light red to terra-cotta underbark. Combine this with the shape of the trunk and you have a tree that adds interesting architecture to the landscape. Flowers are fragrant, greenish white or tinged with pink, and hang in arching panicles from spring into early summer. They are a favorite nectar source for hummingbirds. After the flowers come globe-shaped, strawberrylike orange-red fruits in autumn that persist through the winter. The leathery oval, evergreen leaves are lustrous dark green. Pacific madrone sloughs off its 2-year-old leaves when the newest ones come out in early summer. The old leaves turn brilliant red before they fall. This tree also sheds its bark regularly, so it can be messy in the garden or on the lawn. Pacific madrone is slow growing and shrublike in its first 10 years. Site it with its mature tree form in mind. It prefers light shade but can take full sun. The soil should be well drained and on the dry side. It does not tolerate excess moisture or extremely alkaline conditions. It does best when grown within its native range, which includes the Pacific Northwest into California. Defoliation may occur in severe frost conditions.

CARE: The taprooted seedlings are difficult to transplant unless very young. Greatest success comes with container-grown plants 12–18" tall. To encourage growth on this slow grower, incorporate organic matter into the planting hole and top-dress with organic matter once or twice a year. Water newly established plants regularly, and maintain adequate soil moisture the first two seasons after planting. After that, plants can tolerate somewhat dry soil conditions. Young plants respond well to annual applications of plant food, such as Miracle-Gro.

PROPAGATION: Take cuttings in early summer. It is moderately easy to grow from seed.

PESTS AND DISEASES: None serious.

RELATED SPECIES: Strawberry tree (*A. unedo*) grows to only 15–30' and is normally considered a large shrub. The abundant flowers appear from October to December and turn to strawberry-like orange berries that are edible but tasteless. The dark brown bark cracks open on larger branches and the trunk to reveal bright red inner bark. This species requires acid soil and a dry climate to grow well.

RED CHOKEBERRY

Aronia arbutifolia a-ROE-nee-uh ar-byu-tih-FOE-lee-uh

The large red berries amplify red chokeberry's fall color.

ZONES: (4)5–9
SIZE: 6–10'h × 3–5'w
TYPE: Deciduous shrub
FORM: Upright spreading
TEXTURE: Medium
GROWTH: Slow
LIGHT: Sun to part shade

MOISTURE: Even
SOIL: Well drained
FEATURES: Showy red fruits in autumn
USES: Massing, shrub border
FLOWERS: □
FALL COLOR: ■ ■

SITING: Red chokeberry is a tough, dependable shrub with multiseason interest. Plant it where you can enjoy its excellent red fall color and its profusion of red fruits. Although the pinkish-white flowers that appear in spring are not showy, they give way to ¼-inch bright red berries that persist long into winter. The fruits are ornamental enough to use in wreaths and fresh or dried floral arrangements. Red chokeberry's propensity for suckering and its tendency toward stiff, upright, leggy growth make it a good choice for massing. In the shrub border, plant it toward the back so other shrubs will hide the lower branches, which are often without leaves. Although the stems are thin, the plant withstands wind well and can be planted on exposed sites such as hillsides. It grows in sun to partial shade (best fruiting is in full sun) and tolerates a range of soil types but prefers good drainage.

CARE: Soak bare-root plants for two hours and plant as soon as possible after that in early spring. Container-grown plants are also best planted early in the season. The fibrous root system makes this shrub easy to transplant. Water newly established plants regularly and maintain adequate soil moisture the first two seasons after planting. After that plants can tolerate slightly drier soil conditions. Apply plant food, such as Miracle-Gro, every other spring. Prune out any dead or diseased stems at any time, cutting back to a live healthy bud or leaf. Avoid pruning to control height. Remove suckers. Plants self-sow but not profusely.

PROPAGATION: Divide plants in early spring with a sharp shovel. Take as many roots and as much soil as possible. Plant immediately and water well. Softwood cuttings root easily. Seeds require stratification for 3 months.

PESTS AND DISEASES: Twig and fruit blights produce a powdery gray mold over affected plant parts but are rarely serious.

RELATED SPECIES: 'Brilliantissima' is a popular cultivar with more abundant flowers and fruits and good fall color. 'Erecta' is an upright cultivar reaching 7' with a spread of about 4'. Black chokeberry (*A. melanocarpa*) grows to 3–4' in height and has less showy blackish-purple berries but equally good fall color. Its profuse suckering and more compact growth habit make it a good ground cover. It is hardier than red chokeberry.

JAPANESE AUCUBA

Aucuba japonica a-KEW-buh juh-PAHN-i-kuh

Gold variegated leaves and red berries of Japanese aucuba are ornamental.

ZONES: (6)7–10
SIZE: 6–10'h × 6–8'w
TYPE: Evergreen shrub
FORM: Rounded to rounded upright
TEXTURE: Medium
GROWTH: Slow
LIGHT: Shade
MOISTURE: Moderate

SOIL: Well drained, fertile
FEATURES: Evergreen color in shade
USES: Massed or singly on difficult sites
FLOWERS: ■
FALL COLOR: ■

SITING: This tidy evergreen is perfect for bringing greenery to dark corners of the landscape. It is tough, slow growing, tolerant of a wide range of soils, and performs well in deep shade. Interesting berrylike scarlet fruits mature in October and November and persist through the following spring. Plant Japanese aucuba under large shade trees where grass won't grow or use in foundation plantings on the north and east side of the house. It prefers well-drained, moist soil, high in organic matter. It must have shade and even tolerates deep shade. If it receives too much sun, younger leaves will blacken. A plant of each sex is required for fruit production (only females bear fruits). Foliage is damaged at temperatures below −5°F, so it's best used in southern gardens.

CARE: Transplant container-grown plants throughout the growing season. Keep the soil evenly moist, watering when the top 2" have dried out. Consistent watering during first 2 years will encourage faster growth. It responds to feeding by growing faster. Avoid excess fertilizing late in the season to reduce chances of winter dieback. Cut plants back hard to control size. In spring prune out stems suffering from winterkill.

PROPAGATION: Take stem tip cuttings almost any time of year. Seeds are difficult to germinate.

PESTS AND DISEASES: A canker can cause stem dieback. Crown rot, caused by a soilborne fungus, occurs infrequently but can be serious. Prune out infected branches; remove mulch near plants and replace with 1–2" of new, clean mulch.

RELATED SPECIES: 'Variegata' (gold dust shrub) has shiny green leaves speckled with clear yellow.

Cut out any winter-damaged branches of Japanese aucuba in spring.

JAPANESE BARBERRY
Berberis thunbergii BURR-burr-us thun-BURR-jee-eye

Japanese barberry's greatest asset is its neat, clean foliage.

ZONES: (4)5–8
SIZE: 3–6'h × 4–7'w
TYPE: Deciduous shrub
FORM: Dense rounded
TEXTURE: Medium fine
GROWTH: Moderate
LIGHT: Sun to part shade

MOISTURE: Low
SOIL: Well drained
FEATURES: Tough shrub, good foliage color
USES: Hedge, foundation, groupings
FLOWERS: ▨
FALL COLOR: ▧

SITING: Japanese barberry's profusion of thorny stems makes it an excellent choice for a barrier. Many cultivars have showy purple, gold, or variegated foliage and outstanding fall color. It adapts well to shearing and can be pruned into a formal hedge. It tolerates dry conditions but not extremely moist soil. It does best in full sun, but golden-leaved varieties need partial shade for best color. This shrub is suitable for city gardens because it is tolerant of urban conditions. It also withstands wind.

Hedge plants should be planted slightly closer than the recommended distance.

CARE: Transplant container-grown plants at any time. Maintain consistently moist soil during the first 2 years. Every spring apply plant food, such as Miracle-Gro, to produce the best foliage color. Plants are subject to winterkill in Zone 4; prune out in spring but be careful of sharp spines. This shrub can become invasive.

PROPAGATION: Seeds require stratification for at least 8 weeks. Take softwood cuttings in early summer. To propagate by layering, bend over and wound pliable stems at a point where they touch the ground. Once roots form, dig the new plants and reset them.

PESTS AND DISEASES: None serious, but bacterial leaf spot, anthracnose, root rots, verticillium wilt, mosaic virus, barberry aphid, barberry webworm, scale, and northern root-knot nematode have been reported.

RELATED SPECIES: 'Crimson Pygmy' reaches only 2' in height but spreads up to 5'. Foliage is reddish purple. Numerous other purple-leaved forms are also available. Korean barberry (*B. koreana*) has less ridged spines, making it easier to work with. It is hardy to Zone 3.

RIVER BIRCH
Betula nigra BET-yoo-luh NIGH-gruh

Peeling bark adds winter interest to river birch. It is the birch with greatest resistance to bronze birch borer.

ZONES: 3–9
SIZE: 40–70'h × 30–40'w
TYPE: Deciduous tree
FORM: Upright pyramidal
TEXTURE: Medium
GROWTH: Medium to fast
LIGHT: Sun to light shade

MOISTURE: Moist
SOIL: Well drained, acid
FEATURES: Interesting peeling bark
USES: Shade tree for large yards
FLOWERS: ▨
FALL COLOR: ▨

SITING: River birch has peeling cinnamon-brown bark. Fall color is bright or golden yellow. It is usually used as a specimen tree, although it can be short lived in the landscape. It has good resistance to bronze birch borer. To encourage a healthy, long-lived tree, keep its natural floodplain conditions in mind—cool, moist soil in lowlands. If planting in the lawn, remove all grass in a large circle under the tree and cover the soil with 2–4" of organic mulch. Avoid exposed sites with drying winds and sites with compacted soil.

CARE: Amend soil with ample organic matter before planting. Keep the soil evenly moist from spring until the ground freezes. Water lawn trees deeply to make sure available moisture reaches the tree roots. Trees that show signs of stress or insect or disease problems benefit from root feeding in spring. Remove lower branches to enhance the appearance of the coppery trunk. Do any pruning in summer to avoid sap flow from pruning wounds made during the dormant season.

PROPAGATION: Seeds require light for germination. It is difficult to propagate by cuttings.

PESTS AND DISEASES: Problems include leaf spot, dieback, and aphids, especially prevalent in stressed trees.

RELATED SPECIES: European white birch (*B. pendula*) has a graceful, pendulous growth habit, but the bark is not as showy as other species, and the tree is susceptible to bronze birch borer. Paper birch or white birch (*B. papyrifera*) has peeling chalk-white bark and is susceptible to bronze birch borer and birch leaf miner. It performs best on cool, moist shady sites.

Surround river birch with organic mulch to keep trees moist and more resistant to disease and insect problems.

BUTTERFLY BUSH

Buddleia davidii BUD-lee-uh dah-VID-ee-eye

Showy flower spikes are very attractive to butterflies. Butterfly bush is also known as summer lilac or orange-eye butterfly bush.

ZONES: 5–9
SIZE: 10–15'h × 10–15'w
TYPE: Deciduous shrub
FORM: Arching
TEXTURE: Medium
GROWTH: Fast
LIGHT: Sun
MOISTURE: Even

SOIL: Well drained, fertile
FEATURES: Fragrant, showy flowers attractive to butterflies
USES: Shrub or perennial border
FLOWERS: ■ ■ ■ □
FALL COLOR: ■

SITING: Butterfly bush brings showy, fragrant spikes of flowers to the summer garden. As its name implies, it is a must for butterfly gardens. In northern gardens it is best treated as an herbaceous perennial; it blooms from midsummer until frost. In southern gardens cut back in spring to encourage blooming. You can prune butterfly bush into a small, mop-headed tree or train it espalier style on a fence or wall. Plants are short lived without regular pruning and fertilizing. In some places butterfly bush has become invasive.

Keep plants fresh and blooming by pruning to the ground in spring.

CARE: It prefers well-drained, fertile soil high in organic matter and full sun. Keep the soil evenly moist throughout the growing season. Apply plant food, such as Miracle-Gro, each spring to encourage more flowers and a longer bloom period. Prune every year to within a few inches of the ground in early spring before growth begins. Deadheading will extend the flowering period and reduce self-sown seedlings, which can become weedy in warm climates.

PROPAGATION: Seeds germinate readily. Take cuttings in summer or winter.

PESTS AND DISEASES: Spray plants with a garden hose regularly to deter spider mites, which can be a problem in hot, dry weather.

RELATED SPECIES: 'Black Knight' has very deep violet to dark purple flowers and may be slightly hardier than other selections. 'Nanho Blue' is a slower-growing, more-compact plant with mauve-blue flowers. 'Pink Delight' has fragrant true pink flowers.

BOXWOOD

Buxus sempervirens BUK-sus sem-per-VIR-ens

Common boxwood has neat evergreen leaves that are yellowish on the underside.

ZONES: (5)6–9
SIZE: 15–20'h × 15–25'w
TYPE: Evergreen shrub
FORM: Dense rounded
TEXTURE: Medium fine
GROWTH: Slow

LIGHT: Sun to light shade
MOISTURE: Even
SOIL: Well drained, slightly alkaline
FEATURES: Evergreen leaves
USES: Hedge, topiary
FLOWERS: ■
FALL COLOR: ■

SITING: Boxwood hedges are a staple of formal gardens. Plants are slow growing, respond well to heavy pruning, and hold their foliage all the way to the ground. Flowers are barely noticeable, but have a distinctive aroma that irritates some people. Boxwood grows best in warm, moist climates without extremes of heat or cold. Plant in well-drained, moist soil amended with organic matter. It prefers slightly alkaline soil. Shade from hot summer sun the first year. Protect plants from drying winds and provide partial shade in hot climates. Avoid cultivating the soil around these shallow-rooted plants. Instead, deter weeds with an organic mulch.

Plants respond well to shearing and make good hedges.

CARE: Water throughout the growing season and until the ground freezes. Apply organic mulch to help maintain even moisture. Feed every spring with plant food, such as Miracle-Gro. Do not feed in summer; the succulent new growth is easily winterkilled. Some dieback of stem tips is common in severe winters. Remove inner dead twigs and fallen leaves in branch crotches to prevent twig canker. Avoid pruning late in season; this encourages new growth susceptible to winterkill. To avoid browning of leaves during the winter, spray foliage with an antidessicant in fall.

PROPAGATION: Take softwood cuttings in summer. Seeds may take 2 years to sprout.

PESTS AND DISEASES: None are serious. Root rot can be a problem in poorly drained soil.

RELATED SPECIES: Little-leaf boxwood (*B. microphylla*) grows to 3–5' and is slightly hardier than common boxwood. Korean boxwood (*B. microphylla* var. *koreana*) is the hardiest variety but is not as ornamental. It can be grown in Zone 4 in protected sites but suffers some tip dieback in most winters.

JAPANESE BEAUTYBERRY
Callicarpa japonica kal-ih-KAR-puh juh-PAHN-ih-kuh

Very showy, violet purple fruits develop in fall. Japanese beautyberry is also known as Japanese jewelberry.

ZONES: 5–8
SIZE: 4–6'h × 4–6'w
TYPE: Deciduous shrub
FORM: Rounded arching
TEXTURE: Medium
GROWTH: Fast
LIGHT: Sun to light shade

MOISTURE: Even
SOIL: Well drained
FEATURES: Metallic-purple fruits in autumn
USES: Grouping, shrub border, flower border
FLOWERS: ■
FALL COLOR: ■

SITING: Japanese beautyberry is most effective when planted in groups where the showy fruits make a statement. Plant in well-drained soil in full sun or light shade. The blue-green leaves take on a nearly yellow color in fall if grown in full sun. Small lilac-pink flowers appear in summer but are not showy. The real show starts in fall, when the violet to metallic-purple fruits cover the plants. Shrubs grow quickly and can become unkempt as they age. Cut them to the ground in late winter or early spring to encourage fresh, new growth. In colder areas they are best treated as herbaceous perennials.

Keep Japanese beautyberry neat by cutting it to the ground in spring.

CARE: Keep the soil evenly moist from spring until the ground freezes. Consistent watering is especially important during the first 2 years. This shrub grows best in somewhat lean soils and usually does not require additional food. Plants can look tattered with age; prune regularly to keep the plant tidy. Prune to within 4–6" of the ground every spring, especially in colder climates. If you do not prune close to the ground, remove dead limbs each spring. Flowers are produced on new wood, so the more new wood you have, the better the fruiting.

PROPAGATION: Softwood cuttings root readily. Seeds require cold, moist stratification.

PESTS AND DISEASES: None serious, but plants can suffer from leaf spots, black mold, and various stem diseases.

RELATED SPECIES: Purple beautyberry (*C. dichotoma*) is more graceful and refined, growing 3–4' tall with long, slender branches that touch the ground at their tips. The attractive foliage sets off the abundant lilac-colored fruits.

LEMON BOTTLEBRUSH
Callistemon citrinus kal-ih-STEE-mon sih-TRY-nus

Lemon bottlebrush flowers resemble brush bristles.

ZONES: (8)9–11
SIZE: 10–15'h × 10–15'w
TYPE: Evergreen shrub or tree
FORM: Rounded upright
TEXTURE: Fine
GROWTH: Medium to fast
LIGHT: Full sun

MOISTURE: Dry to moist
SOIL: Lean, acid
FEATURES: Showy red flowers in summer
USES: Specimen shrub or small tree, container
FLOWERS: ■
FALL COLOR: ■ ■

SITING: This plant is best suited to the warm climates of Southern California and Florida. Place it near a patio or deck where you can enjoy the bright red flower spikes and the hummingbirds that visit them. It also makes an attractive screen or tall, unclipped hedge. Although it is usually sold as a shrub, it can be pruned into a small tree. It can handle hot, dry conditions next to buildings or in streetside plantings. It tolerates a wide range of soil textures but prefers slightly acid soil. It is moderately salt tolerant. The flowers are followed by small, woody capsules, which last for years and are useful for dried flower arrangements.

CARE: Water young plants regularly. Apply an organic mulch to help maintain even soil moisture and get young plants off to a strong start. Once established, lemon bottlebrush is drought tolerant. Provide ample food in split applications over the growing season to maintain good flower color and dark green foliage. Branches droop as the tree grows and require pruning for clearance beneath the canopy. Remove suckers that sprout from the base of the trunk. Fruits cling to the tree, so there is no litter problem.

PROPAGATION: Seeds germinate without pretreatment and grow rapidly. Named varieties, which are usually better choices than the species, do not come true from seed. Plants can also be propagated by hardwood cuttings.

PESTS AND DISEASES: Pests which usually don't become serious include spider mites, scale, nematodes, and witches' broom. If the soil is too moist, root and crown-attacking fungus diseases can be a problem. Keep the plant on the dry side with low fertility and good air circulation. A twig gall, formed in response to a fungus, can disfigure the tree. Correct chlorosis, a systemic condition that causes new leaves to turn yellow, by treating the soil with iron sulfate or iron chelate.

RELATED SPECIES: 'Splendens' flowers heavily even as a young plant. Weeping bottlebrush (*C. viminalis*) 'Little John' is a dwarf growing 3' tall and 5' wide. 'Red Cascade' is faster growing.

CALIFORNIA INCENSE CEDAR

Calocedrus decurrens *kal-oh-SED-rus de-KERR-enz*

Evergreen leaves of California incense cedar are feathery and graceful.

ZONES: 5–8
SIZE: 30–50'h × 8–10'w
TYPE: Evergreen tree
FORM: Narrowly columnar
TEXTURE: Medium
GROWTH: Slow to medium
LIGHT: Sun to light shade

MOISTURE: Even to dry
SOIL: Well drained, fertile
FEATURES: Handsome formal shape
USES: Specimen for large areas, screening
FLOWERS: ■
FALL COLOR: ■

SITING: The narrow, upright form of this conifer is retained even as it ages. Its strictly upright form lends a formal appearance to landscapes where it is planted. It makes an excellent vertical accent as a garden specimen and can be used as a drought-tolerant screening plant or a windbreak. Use it as a backdrop for a mixed shrub planting or a large perennial bed. Unless the tree is shaded by nearby trees, the needles will remain on the lower branches even on older specimens. The bark is thin, smooth, grayish-green or scaly, and tinged with red on young stems. On older branches it takes on a yellowish-brown to red color and becomes deeply furrowed. This is an asset in the winter landscape. Leaves are an attractive green year-round and have a feathery, graceful look. This layered effect enhances the rich, soft texture of the needles. It also makes the tree more resilient to winter storm damage than arborvitaes. In warm weather the cedarlike fragrance permeates the air. This tree prefers well-drained, moist fertile soil and full sun or light shade. It adapts well to a wide range of soil types, including poor soil. Avoid planting it in smoggy or on wind-swept sites.

CARE: Plant balled-and-burlapped or container-grown specimens. Large trees are difficult to transplant, so look for smaller specimens. Water regularly during early years of establishment. Organic mulch will help maintain even soil moisture and get young plants off to a strong start. Once established, this tree is drought and heat tolerant. Young plants respond well to an annual application of plant food, such as Miracle-Gro.

PROPAGATION: Seed requires stratification for about 8 weeks but germinates readily. Cuttings are difficult to root.

PESTS AND DISEASES: Problems include heart rot, caused by a fungus, rust disease, leafy mistletoe, and incense cedar scale. None is usually serious.

RELATED SPECIES: 'Columnaris' is common in cultivation. 'Aureovariegata' is a yellow-variegated form, which can be dazzling in the right situation. 'Compacta' is a dwarf globe that matures at about 6' in height. *C. macroplepis* is a large (to 100' tall), narrow conical tree native to China. Leaves are larger and flatter than those of California incense cedar. It is hardy in Zones 5–8.

CAROLINA ALLSPICE

Calycanthus floridus *kal-ih-KAN-thus FLOR-ih-dus*

Carolina allspice is prized for its fragrant flowers. It is also known as common sweet shrub or strawberry shrub.

ZONES: (4)5–9
SIZE: 6–9'h × 6–12'w
TYPE: Deciduous shrub
FORM: Rounded
TEXTURE: Medium
GROWTH: Slow to medium
LIGHT: Light shade to sun

MOISTURE: Moderate
SOIL: Deep, moist loam
FEATURES: Fragrant, star-shaped flowers
USES: Shrub border, specimen, fragrance
FLOWERS: ■
FALL COLOR: ■

SITING: Place this shrub under a window, beside a screen door, or near an outdoor living area where you can enjoy the strawberry-like fragrance of the flowers. There is great variation in the fragrance, so smell individual plants at the nursery before purchasing. Leaves are dark green in summer and sometimes turn yellow in fall, but color is not a reliable asset from year to year. Flowers are dark reddish-brown and are up to 2" across when fully open. The greatest bloom occurs in May to July. Flowers are borne somewhat inside of the outer layer of foliage, so they are often hidden from view. They were used in years past in potpourris and to freshen the scent in dresser drawers. The leaves and fruits are aromatic when crushed. The wrinkly, balloon-shaped fruits persist into winter. This shrub can be espaliered against a wall. Plants are injured at temperatures of –15 to –20°F, but have survived temperatures of –30°F. In Zone 4 its use should be limited to protected sites. It does best in deep, moist loam. It grows in sun but gets taller in shade.

CARE: This shrub, which is usually available container-grown, is easily transplanted. Maintain consistently moist soil throughout the growing season, especially during the first 2 years of establishment. A 2–4" layer of wood chips or shredded bark will help maintain soil moisture and deter weeds. In spring apply plant food, such as Miracle-Gro. Prune after flowering to shape plants.

PROPAGATION: Sow seeds immediately after ripening, or stratify for 3 months before sowing.

PESTS AND DISEASES: None are serious.

RELATED SPECIES: 'Athens' has fragrant yellow flowers that may continue after an initial late spring flush, often into midsummer. The habit is dense and mounded (to 6' tall), with glossy leaves. 'Edith Wilder' has fragrant reddish-brown flowers. Leaves are more rounded than typical. Fall color is a reasonably good yellow. It grows larger (10' tall) than typical for the species. 'Michael Lindsey' has fragrant red-brown flowers. The habit is dense, compact, and rounded (6' to 10' tall). It has excellent shiny, dark green foliage and golden-yellow fall color. California allspice (*C. occidentalis*) is a native to the West Coast. Its red flowers are borne in summer and are less fragrant. It is hardy in Zones 6–9.

JAPANESE CAMELLIA

Camellia japonica kuh-MEEL-ee-uh juh-PAHN-i-kuh

Japanese camellia flowers and foliage have a classic beauty.

ZONES: (7)8–10
SIZE: 10–15'h × 6–10'w
TYPE: Evergreen shrub
FORM: Dense pyramidal
TEXTURE: Medium
GROWTH: Slow
LIGHT: Part shade

MOISTURE: Moderate
SOIL: Well drained, acid
FEATURES: Showy flowers in winter
USES: Specimen, mixed border
FLOWERS: □ ■ ▨
FALL COLOR: ■

SITING: Camellia's showy blooms lend it to specimen use on the lawn and for colorful accents near outdoor living areas, but it can also be used as a hedge, in mixed borders, and massed in shady gardens.

It is especially attractive and easy to grow when planted under a canopy of live oaks and pine trees, which provide broken shade. It is tolerant of urban conditions. It can be fan trained on a sheltered, shady wall. Zone 7 gardeners should limit their choices to hardy types.

CARE: Acidify soil before planting by adding peat moss or incorporating elemental sulfur or iron sulfate. Water well

Apply mulch around plants to maintain necessary soil moisture.

after planting. Camellia has a shallow root system and requires regular watering to maintain consistently moist soil throughout the growing season. A 2–4" layer of pine needles will help maintain soil moisture and acidify the soil. If the soil pH is correct and you are using an organic mulch around plants, no additional feeding should be necessary. If leaves become chlorotic, feed with an acid plant food and take steps to acidify soil. Remove dead wood in spring. Cut back after flowering to keep the plant within bounds.

PROPAGATION: Take cuttings from the current season's growth from May to September. Camellias can also be grafted, air-layered, or grown from seed.

PESTS AND DISEASES: Diseases include leaf spot, black mold on leaves and stems, leaf gall, flower blights, stem cankers, and root rots. Insect pests include tea scale and other scales, mites, mealybugs, weevils, and thrips. Prune off and destroy all infested plant parts to avoid recurrence of these problems.

RELATED SPECIES: Sasanqua camellia (*C. sasanqua*) has smaller leaves and flowers, and the growth habit is more lax, resulting in a less-formal landscape plant.

SIBERIAN PEASHRUB

Caragana arborescens kar-uh-GAY-nuh ar-bore-ESS-en

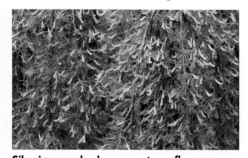

Siberian peashrub, or pea tree, flowers bright yellow among spring foliage.

ZONES: 2–7
SIZE: 15–20'h × 12–18'w
TYPE: Deciduous shrub
FORM: Erect oval
TEXTURE: Medium
GROWTH: Medium to fast

LIGHT: Sun
MOISTURE: Even to dry
SOIL: Average
FEATURES: Tough, care-free shrub
USES: Hedge, screen, windbreak
FLOWERS: ▨
FALL COLOR: ■

SITING: Peashrub is an extremely adaptable plant. It needs full sun and does poorly in shade, but it tolerates poor soil, salt,

drought, and alkalinity and is cold hardy. It can be used for an informal hedge; shearing produces denser growth. It is an ideal plant for a windbreak. Use it as a barrier plant to block traffic, noise, dust, and snow. This erect, oval shrub is often taller than it is wide, with moderate sparse branching, and can be pruned into a small tree. Bright yellow flowers appear in spring. The showier types can be used in the perennial border or as specimen plants.

CARE: Get bare-root plants in the ground as early in spring as possible. Container-grown plants are best planted in spring but can be planted throughout the growing season provided they receive adequate water. Space according to mature size; plant hedge plants a little closer. During the first month after planting, water well at least once a week. After that, water only if there is a severe drought in the first season. Saturate the soil deeply with each watering. Peashrub fixes nitrogen in the soil, so it does not require additional plant food. Prune only to control size and shape. Remove damaged, dead, or diseased stems at any time of year. To form a screen or

windbreak, let the plants grow to the desired height, then trim back to keep them from getting taller. It can be trained as a small tree. Prune after flowering if you want flowers, which appear on the previous year's growth.

PROPAGATION: Soak seeds in hot water for at least 24 hours before spring planting or sow outside in fall to germinate the following spring. Take softwood cuttings 2–4 weeks after bloom.

PESTS AND DISEASES: It is disease resistant but is plagued by a few insects. Leafhopper feeding results in yellow, stunted, disfigured new growth but is rarely serious. Spider mites show up during hot, dry periods; discourage them by regularly spraying the foliage forcefully with a hose.

RELATED SPECIES: 'Nana' is a dwarf form with contorted branches; it grows no more than 6'. 'Lorbergii' is fernlike and more graceful, with fine-textured foliage. 'Pendula' has weeping branches grafted to a standard. 'Walker' has finer foliage and a weeping growth habit.

EUROPEAN HORNBEAM

Carpinus betulus *kar-PYE-nuss BET-yoo-luss*

European hornbeam has a uniform, oval growth pattern.

ZONES: (4)5–7
SIZE: 40–60'h ×
30–40'w
TYPE: Deciduous
tree
FORM: Oval rounded
TEXTURE: Medium
fine
GROWTH: Slow to
medium

LIGHT: Sun to light
shade
MOISTURE:
Moderate
SOIL: Well drained
FEATURES: Easily
pruned small tree
USES: Specimen,
groupings, hedges
FLOWERS: ■
FALL COLOR: ■

SITING: European hornbeam is a tough, problem-free, low-maintenance ornamental tree that deserves to be used more, especially in urban settings. It is pyramidal to rounded in youth and matures to an attractive oval rounded tree. The eye-catching fluted bark is a handsome slate gray. Summer foliage is usually clean and free of disease or insect problems. It tolerates difficult conditions and is an excellent choice for screens, hedges, street plantings, and lawn groupings. It can be planted near large buildings, in malls, and in planter boxes. It grows best in moist, well-drained acid soil in full sun but tolerates light shade. The strong wood resists breaking in wind and ice. The smooth bark can be blemished by careless use of mowers and string trimmers, so surround it with a large circle of organic mulch to act as a buffer zone.

CARE: Young container-grown specimens are easy to transplant. Older, field-grown plants can be slow to recover; it may be 2 years before they start new growth. Fertilize young plants in spring to encourage growth. Sprinkle plant food, such as Miracle-Gro, around the base of the tree and water it in well. This tree withstands severe pruning and can be used as a dense hedge. Winter is the best time to prune.

PROPAGATION: Minimum seed-bearing age is between 10 and 30 years. Seeds can be sown in fall, but germination is difficult. Take cuttings in July.

PESTS AND DISEASES: None are serious. On rare occasions, trees are infected by scale insects. Prune and destroy affected plant parts. Plants in fertile soil with adequate moisture tolerate attacks better than plants that are water stressed, nutrient deficient, and overcrowded.

RELATED SPECIES: 'Fastigiata' grows in an upright form, 35–45' tall, and is a good choice for tight spots. 'Globosa' is rounded and has dense foliage. American hornbeam (*C. caroliniana*) or ironwood, is hardier (to Zone 3) and grows 15–20' tall. It has dark green foliage that turns yellow to orange and scarlet in fall. Heartleaf hornbeam (*C. cordata*) has elongated heart-shape leaves that remain green even in the autumn. It grows in a rounded form to 20–30' in Zones 5 and 6.

SHAGBARK HICKORY

Carya ovata *CARE-ee-uh oh-VAY-tuh*

Shagbark hickory has peeling bark.

ZONES: 4–8
SIZE: 60–80'h ×
35–50'w
TYPE: Deciduous
tree
FORM: Wide
spreading
TEXTURE: Medium
GROWTH: Slow to
moderate

LIGHT: Sun
MOISTURE: Even
SOIL: Well drained
FEATURES:
Exfoliating gray bark,
fall color
USES: Large shade
tree
FLOWERS: ■
FALL COLOR: ■

SITING: This large stately tree has a wide, spreading habit, exfoliating gray bark, and striking, rich golden fall color. It prefers a rich, well-drained loam but is adaptable to a wide range of soils. It readily drops nuts, leaves, and twigs, creating a hazard when mowing the lawn. The nuts, which grow up to 1½" in diameter, are edible and sweet. Squirrels love them. If you have a shagbark hickory, you will have an abundance of these furry creatures. Chips of this wood are used to flavor smoked foods.

CARE: A large taproot makes shagbark hickory difficult to transplant. Seedlings develop a deep taproot that can penetrate 2–3' the first season. Water saplings their first two seasons as needed to keep the soil evenly moist. Mature trees do not require supplemental watering. Trees grown for nut production need annual applications of plant food. Prune to maintain a central leader.

PROPAGATION: Plant seeds in fall where you want the tree to be and protect with screen mesh so the squirrels don't dig them up before they germinate. Mark the spot so you'll know if they are still there in spring.

PESTS AND DISEASES: Insects and diseases are seldom a problem on ornamental specimens, but they can inhibit nut production.

RELATED SPECIES: Pecan (*C. illinoinensis*) is the best choice for nuts. It is hardy to Zone (5)6. Shellbark hickory (*C. laciniosa*) does not grow as large as shagbark hickory and prefers a moister soil. It is hardy to Zone 5.

Fallen hickory nuts may present a litter problem in the home landscape.

BLUEBEARD
Caryopteris xclandonensis *care-ee-OP-ter-is klan-doe-NEN-sis*

Bluebeard, also known as blue mist spirea, produces showy blue flowers in late summer.

ZONES: (5)6–9
SIZE: 2–3'h × 2–4'w
TYPE: Deciduous shrub
FORM: Mounded
TEXTURE: Medium
GROWTH: Fast
LIGHT: Sun

MOISTURE: Average
SOIL: Well drained
FEATURES: Showy flowers in summer
USES: Informal hedge, shrub border, perennial borders
FLOWERS: ■

SITING: This small shrub can be used individually or massed. Showy blue flowers appear in late summer—a rare color for this time of year. The gray-green leaves provide a fine backdrop. In the colder portions of its range, bluebeard dies

back to the ground each winter. Cut-back plants are late to start growth in spring. It prefers a loose, loamy soil and full sun, but tolerates alkaline conditions often found near a foundation. Its tolerance of dry, alkaline soils makes it a good choice for xeriscape gardens. It is also suitable for rock gardens and other hot, dry sites.

Bluebeard roots easily from softwood cuttings.

CARE: Plant container-grown plants in late winter or spring. Choose a sheltered position such as near a sunny wall or a fence in colder zones. Bluebeard is fairly drought tolerant and usually does not require supplemental watering after establishment. Avoid excessive fertilization, which results in rampant growth. This plant is best treated like an herbaceous perennial and cut back in late winter, even in warmer climates where it doesn't die back, to keep it compact and increase blooms, which appear on new wood.
PROPAGATION: Take softwood cuttings in early summer. Divide in early spring and replant immediately.
PESTS AND DISEASES: None are serious.
RELATED SPECIES: 'Dark Knight' is a compact grower with silvery-gray foliage and deep purple-blue flowers. 'Ferndown' has dark blue flowers and good plant form. 'Heavenly Blue' has light blue flowers and compact growth. 'Worchester Gold' has bright yellow-green foliage, which sets off the violet-blue flowers.

NORTHERN CATALPA
Catalpa speciosa *kuh-TALL-puh spee-see-OH-suh*

Catalpa has unique, orchid-like flowers in late spring. It is also known as cigar tree or hardy catalpa.

ZONES: (4)5–8(9)
SIZE: 40–60'h × 20–40'w
TYPE: Deciduous tree
FORM: Irregular
TEXTURE: Bold
GROWTH: Medium to fast
LIGHT: Sun to part shade

MOISTURE: Even
SOIL: Deep, moist
FEATURES: Showy white flowers, interesting seedpods
USES: Large tree for difficult sites
FLOWERS: □
FALL COLOR: ■

SITING: Catalpa is often associated with old-fashioned landscapes. Plant it where

you want fast shade in an open area. It is best in naturalized settings where the flower, leaf, and seedpod litter won't be an issue. It is tolerant of various conditions but prefers deep, moist, fertile soil, and withstands wet or dry and alkaline conditions. It tolerates sun or part shade and withstands extremely hot, dry conditions. The 6–10" heart-shaped leaves are green to lime green in summer and turn brownish in fall. Leaves often fall before turning color, and raking can be a chore. Orchidlike flowers cover the tree in May or June, then fall to the ground like a

Heavy winds will bring down seedpods and broken branches.

blanket of snow. The seeds resemble bean pods; they appear in late summer and persist into winter. This tree is marginally hardy in Zone 4.
CARE: Water young trees their first 2 seasons. Mature trees do not require supplemental watering. Fertilize young plants in spring to encourage growth. The wood is brittle, and small branches break off in wind and ice, creating a litter problem. Falling seedpods contribute to the litter. For about a week in June, the lawn under the tree will be covered with a carpet of fallen flowers, but they quickly decompose.
PROPAGATION: Seeds germinate readily without pretreatment.
PESTS AND DISEASES: Leaf spots, powdery mildew, verticillium wilt, twig blight, root rot, catalpa midge, and catalpa sphinx can affect Northern catalpa but rarely cause serious problems.
RELATED SPECIES: Southern catalpa (*C. bignonioides*) has smaller leaves, and it flowers about 2 weeks later. It has a more rounded habit and only grows to 30–40' with an equal or greater spread. It is hardy in Zones 5–9.

CALIFORNIA LILAC
Ceanothus hybrids *see-uh-NOH-thuss*

California lilac is a signature shrub of California's chaparral.

ZONES: 8–10
SIZE: 1–12'h × 4–6'w
TYPE: Deciduous or evergreen shrub
FORM: Creeping to upright
TEXTURE: Medium
GROWTH: Moderate
LIGHT: Sun

MOISTURE: Low
SOIL: Sandy
FEATURES: Fragrant, showy flowers
USES: Specimen, shrub border
FLOWERS: ■ ■ □
FALL COLOR: ■

SITING: This signature shrub of California's chaparral does best in its native range. Its use is limited to the drier climate of the West Coast. Hybrids aren't hardy enough to survive in the North, and they do not tolerate the excessive rain, humidity, and wet soils found in the Southeast. This shrub is grown for its fragrance and fluffy panicles of blue, pink, or white flowers reminiscent of miniature lilac blooms. It is a must for butterfly gardens; it is a premier nectar plant for many insects, including butterflies, bees, and beneficial parasitic wasps. It is a good choice for xeriscaping.

CARE: Plant container-grown plants in spring in full sun in well-drained, rocky, or sandy soil away from sprinklers and sheltered from cold, dry winds. Give careful thought when choosing a site; it resents transplanting once established, especially the evergreen types. Most will not survive in hot, shallow, alkaline soil, though some lime is tolerable. This drought-tolerant shrub rarely requires supplemental watering once it is planted. Wet soil can lead to root rot. It is better not to prune the evergreen types, except for removing dead branches in spring. Deciduous types should have their lateral branches cut back to within 3–4" of the previous year's growth in early spring if plants become tattered. Repeated pruning will shorten a plant's life.

PROPAGATION: Propagation is moderately difficult from cuttings and seed. Take semihardwood cuttings in summer. Seeds can be sown in spring, but named varieties will not come true this way.

PESTS AND DISEASES: It is pest free, although root rot can occur if the soil is too wet or poorly drained.

RELATED SPECIES: 'Dark Star' is an evergreen with heavy clusters of honey-scented purplish-blue flowers in late spring. 'Victoria' is a vigorous, upright grower that responds well to shearing. 'Concha' is a compact evergreen with clusters of dark blue flowers opening from red buds. 'Marie Simon' is a tender, medium-size, deciduous shrub that produces panicles of pink flowers. Squaw carpet (*C. prostratus*) is a creeping evergreen that makes a thick mat up to 5' wide. In spring it is covered with bright blue flowers. New Jersey tea (*C. americanus*) grows in difficult locations. In summer branch tips bear honey-scented white flowers. It is hardy in Zones 4-9.

CEDAR OF LEBANON
Cedrus libani *SEE-druss LIB-an-eye*

Branches of cedar of Lebanon develop a wide-spreading habit.

ZONES: 5–7
SIZE: 40–60'h × 60–80'w
TYPE: Evergreen tree
FORM: Pyramidal
TEXTURE: Medium
GROWTH: Slow
LIGHT: Sun

MOISTURE: Moderate
SOIL: Well drained
FEATURES: Stately evergreen
USES: Specimen
FLOWERS: ■ ■
FALL COLOR: ■

SITING: This stately, large tree has a thick, massive trunk and wide-spreading branches. Needles are almost black-green with silver-blue stripes. They add to the impressive appearance along with the 3–5" purple-brown cones, which are held upright above the foliage. It is pyramidal when young and becomes more horizontal and flat-topped as it matures. It is a slow grower. Give it plenty of room for proper development. It prefers a pollution-free, sunny environment protected from wind. Use it as a specimen tree in large yards or parklike settings. The weeping forms make an interesting specimen and are popular in conifer gardens.

CARE: This tree is difficult to transplant. Plant container-grown or balled-and-burlapped plants in spring in deep, well-drained loam in an open, sunny, spacious location. It is intolerant of shade. Water young trees their first 2 seasons as needed to keep the soil evenly moist. Mature trees are drought tolerant and do not require supplemental watering. Fertilize young plants in spring to encourage growth. Sprinkle plant food, such as Miracle-Gro, around the base of the tree and water it in well. Stake the first year or so until it develops a strong leading shoot. Weeping forms may need support past the first year. Occasionally a competing leader must be pruned away to maintain a good form to the tree.

PROPAGATION: Grow from seed planted in fall or cold-stratified for 14 days. It seldom roots from cuttings. Cultivars are grafted.

PESTS AND DISEASES: None are serious.

RELATED SPECIES: 'Green Prince' is very slow growing. New growth is light green maturing to dark green. 'Pendula' is a slow-growing, weeping form. The variation *stenocoma* is a pyramidal form, considered the hardiest of the Lebanon cedars. 'Sargentii' is a dwarf form growing to 5' with pendulous branches. Atlas cedar (*C. atlantica*) is pyramidal when young and later flat topped with horizontal branching. It is not as hardy (Zones 6–9). 'Glauca' is a bluish form that is somewhat variable in coloration from seed. 'Glauca Pendula' is a weeping form with dark green foliage and a narrow habit. Deodar cedar (*C. deodara*) is the least hardy (Zones 7–9). It has a similar growth habit and requires similar siting and care. It suffers from top dieback, and has a useful lifespan in the landscape of only 10 to 20 years.

COMMON HACKBERRY
Celtis occidentalis SELL-tiss ahck-sih-den-TAHL-iss

Common hackberry is a tough tree for harsh sites.

ZONES: 3–9
SIZE: 40–60'h × 35–55'w
TYPE: Deciduous tree
FORM: Upright round
TEXTURE: Medium coarse
GROWTH: Medium to fast

LIGHT: Sun
MOISTURE: Moderate
SOIL: Any
FEATURES: Shade tree for difficult sites
USES: Shade, specimen, street
FLOWERS: ■
FALL COLOR: ■ ■

SITING: Hackberry is a bit coarse and rough looking, but it is a tough tree that adapts to a wide range of conditions. It prefers rich, moist soils but grows well in dry, heavy, or sandy rocky soils. It tolerates dry, windy sites, acid or alkaline conditions, and the dirt and grime of cities. It can be used as a shade tree in larger yards, but avoid planting it too close to buildings. It is among the best food and shelter trees for wildlife. Birds and mammals eat fruits, and leaves are the larval food of many butterflies. The narrow limb crotches and numerous spur branches attract many nesting birds.

Hackberry nipple gall produces wartlike growths on leaves.

CARE: Trees are somewhat slow to recover from transplanting, sometimes taking 2 years. Water young trees their first 2 seasons as needed to keep the soil evenly moist. Mature trees are drought tolerant. Young trees stressed by one of the pests listed below will benefit from root feeding in spring with an all-purpose plant food such as Miracle-Gro.
PROPAGATION: Seeds require stratification for 60–90 days. Cuttings are difficult to root.
PESTS AND DISEASES: Several problems plague hackberry but rarely cause more than cosmetic damage. Witches'-broom, caused by a mite, can totally disfigure trees with its broomlike clusters of abnormal branch growth. Infected twigs are often attacked by powdery mildew, which exacerbates the problem. Severely infected trees look bad, but they are not killed. Hackberry nipple gall is a harmless insect that attacks leaves, resulting in an abundance of wartlike growths. Various caterpillars may eat the leaves.
RELATED SPECIES: Sugar hackberry (*C. laevigata*) is similar to common hackberry, but the bark is less corky. It is hardy to Zone 5 or 6 and is resistant to witches'-broom. It is a good street tree in southern states.

BUTTONBUSH
Cephalanthus occidentalis seff-uh-LAN-thuss ahck-sih-den-TAHL-iss

Creamy white flowers have a musky scent.

ZONES: 5–11
SIZE: 3–8'h × 3–6'w
TYPE: Deciduous or evergreen shrub
FORM: Rounded
TEXTURE: Medium
GROWTH: Fast
LIGHT: Sun to light shade

MOISTURE: High
SOIL: Moist to wet
FEATURES: Long-blooming white flowers
USES: Specimen, massing in wet soils
FLOWERS: □
FALL COLOR: ■

SITING: Buttonbush requires careful siting because of its need for wet soil and its late growth in spring. It is best reserved for wet areas in naturalized situations.

To naturalize it beside a pond, plant it just at the edge so it will be inundated in spring but be out of the water in summer. Away from water in more formal situations, prune young shrubs to one trunk or two and remove dead twigs as needed in winter. Left unpruned, it becomes a loose, gangly shrub. In moist soils in a garden situation, plants can develop into small trees with smooth bark. Leaves emerge late in spring; plants look lifeless until mid-May. Leaves cluster toward the outer canopy, making this shrub ideal for underplanting with moisture-loving perennials and ground covers. The globular creamy white flowers have a musky sweet scent. The 1–1½" spheres have a tropical look and are produced throughout the summer. They are a nectar source for several butterflies. Fruits start out red and turn into a rounded mass of nutlets persisting through the winter. Birds and waterfowl eat them. Older stems take on a reddish-brown color. In colder parts of Zone 5, buttonbush dies back in severe winters and can be treated as a perennial in a mixed border. Cut it back to 6–12" every winter and it will regrow into a 3–4' rounded mound by flowering time. Flowers come from new growth, so hard pruning will not eliminate them.
CARE: Plant in moist to wet conditions in full sun. It will not survive in dry conditions. To plant this shrub in sandy soil, incorporate abundant organic matter such as peat moss, compost, or well-rotted manure before planting to improve water retention. This shrub requires moist or wet soil throughout the growing season and needs supplemental watering during dry periods. A 2–4" layer of organic mulch of wood chips or shredded bark will help conserve moisture. An annual application of plant food, such as Miracle-Gro, in spring produces the best flowers. It needs rejuvenation pruning every spring or so to maintain form and vigor.
PROPAGATION: It is moderately easy to propagate by softwood or hardwood cuttings. Seeds germinate without pretreatment.
PESTS AND DISEASES: None are serious.

SHRUBBY PLUMBAGO

Ceratostigma willmottianum ser-a-toe-STIG-muh will-mot-ee-AH-num

Showy purple flowers appear in late summer on shrubby plumbago, also known as Chinese leadwort.

ZONES: (6)7–9
SIZE: 2–4'h × 4–6'w
TYPE: Deciduous shrub
FORM: Spreading
TEXTURE: Medium
GROWTH: Moderate
LIGHT: Sun to part shade

MOISTURE: Moderate
SOIL: Well drained
FEATURES: Showy flowers
USES: Ground cover, mixed border
FLOWERS: ■
FALL COLOR: ■

SITING: This shrub is one of the jewels of autumn, with its blue flowers and yellow to red foliage. Its low habit makes it charming in both shrub and herbaceous borders. Tubular, phloxlike flowers appear in terminal clusters from July until early autumn frosts. Plants in Zone 6 may need winter protection. It prefers full sun and a light, loamy soil that is dry to moist. The best foliage and flowering occur in deep, rich soil.

CARE: Purchase container-grown plants, which are usually available in late summer. Because of the plant's growth cycle, nursery stock often looks weak and insipid in winter and early spring, but once it is planted, it grows rapidly the following spring. Shrubby plumbago is fairly drought tolerant and usually does not require supplemental watering after establishment. An annual application of plant food, such as Miracle-Gro, in spring will produce the best flowers and abundant foliage. Cut back stems hard to the ground annually in early to midspring, especially in colder climates where winter dieback may occur.

PROPAGATION: Divide plants in spring. Take softwood cuttings in midsummer. Plants can also be propagated by layering in spring. To do this, bend a low-growing branch to the ground and secure it with hardware hooks or weight it down with soil and a rock or brick. Cutting away an inch or so of bark where the branch meets the ground will encourage rooting. Once the new shrub has good root growth, cut the branch off the parent plant and pot up the new shrub.

PESTS AND DISEASES: None are serious.

RELATED SPECIES: Dwarf plumbago (*C. plumbaginoides*) is hardy into Zone 5 and grows to about a foot in height. It has neat tufts of growth covered with many flowers almost until frost. It is a wiry-stemmed ground cover that spreads rapidly by underground stems, eventually covering large areas. It is most effective in early- or midautumn when the striking deep blue flowers contrast with the reddish-bronze foliage. It grows in sun or light shade. It is semievergreen in the warmer areas but dies back in colder climates. Cut back after bloom to allow fresh, new growth each year. Plants leaf out late in spring. In coldest climates, apply winter mulch. When plants show signs of aging, remove old crowns and replant with rooted stems in spring.

KATSURA TREE

Cercidiphyllum japonicum sir-sih-dih-FYE-lum juh-PAHN-ih-kum

Katsura tree develops golden-yellow fall color.

ZONES: 5–8
SIZE: 40–60'h × 20–50'w
TYPE: Deciduous tree
FORM: Wide, spreading
TEXTURE: Medium fine
GROWTH: Medium to fast
LIGHT: Sun to part shade
MOISTURE: Moderate
SOIL: Well drained
FEATURES: Attractive foliage, dappled shade
USES: Specimen, screening
FLOWERS: ■
FALL COLOR: ■

SITING: Katsura tree is a low-maintenance tree that remains attractive in all seasons. The emerging reddish spring foliage changes to soft, heart-shaped blue-green leaves in summer, then to yellow in early fall. Young trees are pyramidal; older trees develop a graceful, stately, spreading growth habit. Single-trunk specimens are more columnar; multiple trunks result in a wide, spreading tree. Full and dense even when young, this tree is a good choice for dappled shade. Its large mature size limits its use to large yards and parks. The tree has a shallow root system; some of the roots can grow to 6" in diameter or more above the soil.

Water young katsura trees to help prevent leaf scorch.

CARE: Plant container-grown or balled-and-burlapped plants in early spring in full sun to part shade and moist, well-drained soil. Water well after planting. Provide additional moisture during periods of drought. Apply 2–4" inches of shredded bark or wood-chip mulch around plants and replenish as necessary throughout the growing season to help maintain soil moisture. Fertilize young plants in spring to encourage growth; sprinkle plant food, such as Miracle-Gro, around the base of the tree and water it in well. Prune only to shape when young; you may need to select a strong leader in a young tree.

PROPAGATION: Seeds require no pretreatment for germination. Take softwood cuttings from young trees.

PESTS AND DISEASES: None are serious. Sunscald and bark splitting may occur. Leaf scorch can be a problem during times of drought or with trees planted on dry sites.

RELATED SPECIES: 'Aureum' leaves mature to yellow after emerging purplish green. 'Pendula' is an eye-catching weeping form with blue-green leaves. 'Ruby' is a more dwarf form, reaching perhaps 30' tall, with leaves suffused with a bluish-purple hue.

EASTERN REDBUD
Cercis canadensis SIR-siss kan-uh-DEN-siss

Showy purple-pink flowers appear before leaves on Eastern redbud.

ZONES: 4–9
SIZE: 20–30'h × 25–35'w
TYPE: Deciduous tree
FORM: Spreading
TEXTURE: Medium coarse
GROWTH: Medium

LIGHT: Sun to light shade
MOISTURE: Even
SOIL: Well drained
FEATURES: Purplish flowers in spring
USES: Specimen, understory
FLOWERS: ■
FALL COLOR: ■■

SITING: This is an excellent front-yard tree to accent a shrub border or use as an understory tree near larger trees. It prefers moderately moist soils high in organic matter but will grow on drier sites once established. It prefers partial shade but will tolerate full sun and even full shade. The pink-purple flowers open in spring before the leaves appear. The attractive heart-shaped leaves can look tired and spotted by late summer but turn yellow in fall. The layered branches give trees architectural form. The zigzag branch pattern and persistent seedpods add winter interest. Plants grown in southern states are not reliably hardy in the north.

Surround trees with mulch to protect trunks from lawn mowers and string trimmers.

CARE: Plants resent being dug from fields as they get larger, so start with smaller trees. Their moderate growth rate results in a good-looking specimen in a few years. Apply a 2–4" layer of organic mulch around each plant as soon as the ground warms in spring. Replenish as necessary throughout the growing season. Keep the soil evenly moist from spring until the ground freezes in fall. Consistent watering is critical during the first 2 years and helpful throughout the plant's entire life. Feed every other spring with plant food, such as Miracle-Gro, and water in well to keep plants vigorous and better able to fend off potential canker problems. Remove any dead or diseased stems or branches immediately at any time of year.
PROPAGATION: Seeds have a hard, impermeable coat and require scarification and 5–8 weeks of cold stratification. Seeds sown in place in fall may germinate the following spring.
PESTS AND DISEASES: Canker can kill a tree. Protect the trunk and bark from damage from a lawn mower or string trimmer. Eastern redbud is also susceptible to verticillium wilt.

COMMON FLOWERING QUINCE
Chaenomeles speciosa kee-NAH-muh-leez spee-see-OH-suh

Showy red flowers stand out in early spring.

ZONES: 5–9
SIZE: 6–10'h × 6–10'w
TYPE: Deciduous shrub
FORM: Upright, spreading
TEXTURE: Medium
GROWTH: Medium
LIGHT: Sun

MOISTURE: Even to dry
SOIL: Well drained
FEATURES: Showy flowers and fruit
USES: Shrub border, specimen, hedge
FLOWERS: ■■□
FALL COLOR: ■

SITING: The showy red flowers appear in spring to early summer and sometimes rebloom lightly in fall. New growth emerges reddish-bronze and matures to a glossy dark green. The dense, tangled branches are spiny. The plant drops its leaves while green. Its use should be restricted to more difficult sites. It is tolerant of pollution and urban conditions. Fruits harvested in October can be used to make preserves.
CARE: Flowering quince is fairly drought tolerant and usually does not require supplemental watering after establishment. Leaves can turn yellow when plants are grown in highly alkaline soils. Use an acid plant food, such as Miracle-Gro Shake 'n Feed Azalea, Camellia, Rhododendron, to

Shrubs may be severely defoliated by leaf spot.

lower soil pH. Avoid overfeeding, which causes succulent growth that attracts pests. Regular renewal pruning after blooming will promote more lavish bloom. Overgrown shrubs can be cut back to 6" from the ground to renew.
PROPAGATION: Take cuttings in late summer. Layer in spring.
PESTS AND DISEASES: Leaf spot can partially defoliate plants. Clean up and destroy fallen leaves to eliminate overwintering disease sites. To control scale, prune and destroy infested parts. Spray remaining stems with horticultural oil. Control aphids by spraying regularly with a hose.
RELATED SPECIES: 'Cameo' has double peach-pink flowers and is nearly thornless. 'Jet Trail' has 1" white flowers borne on nearly thornless plants. 'Orange Delight' has bright orange flowers on low-spreading plants of about 3'. 'Scarff's Red' is an upright, nearly thornless plant with bright red flowers. 'Texas Scarlet' is an almost thornless dwarf with orange-red flowers. Japanese flowering quince (*C. japonica*) is not as ornamental and usually grows 2–3' tall.

HINOKI FALSE CYPRESS

Chamaecyparis obtusa *kam-uh-SIP-uh-riss ob-TOO-suh*

Hinoki false cypress develops an interesting foliage texture.

ZONES: 5–8
SIZE: 50–75'h × 10–20'w
TYPE: Evergreen tree
FORM: Pyramidal
TEXTURE: Medium
GROWTH: Medium
LIGHT: Sun
MOISTURE: Moderate

SOIL: Moisture retentive
FEATURES: Dark green foliage
USES: Specimen, background
FLOWERS: ■
FALL COLOR: ■

SITING: This broad, sweeping evergreen grows in a pyramidal form that remains formal throughout its life. The shredding reddish-brown bark peels off in long, narrow strips. It needs a sunny spot protected from wind and soil that is deep, loamy, moisture-retentive, and acid. Dwarf forms are valuable for rock gardens and mixed borders. Growth is best in the high humidity and abundant rainfall of the Pacific Northwest. It is often used for bonsai.

CARE: Water well after planting. Maintain consistently moist soil throughout the growing season. A 2–4" layer of wood chips or shredded bark will help maintain soil moisture and deter weeds. Feed young trees every spring with an acid plant food

Plant container-grown specimens to reduce transplant shock.

such as Miracle-Gro Shake 'n Feed Azalea, Camellia, Rhododendron. Prune to shape in late spring.

PROPAGATION: Take cuttings from new wood in fall.

PESTS AND DISEASES: Plants are subject to a fungal disease that attacks roots. Dig out and destroy diseased plants. In dry summers, spider mites can be a problem. Dislodge them with a strong spray of the garden hose.

RELATED SPECIES: Many golden, dwarf, and fern-leaved forms are available. Two of the most important for landscape use are 'Gracilis', which has slender, upright growth to 20', and 'Nana Gracilis', which has thick dark green foliage arranged on wavy branches. The habit is broad and conical, growing slowly to 6–8'. It is commonly used as a specimen or foundation planting. Lawson false cypress (*C. lawsoniana*) is a slender to broadly pyramidal tree with horizontal branches. It requires a moist soil and high humidity, making it a good choice for the Pacific Northwest. Sawara false cypress (*C. pisifera*) isn't as elegant as Hinoki false cypress in its old age. Many cultivars have been developed from this species that are better for landscape use.

DESERT WILLOW

Chilopsis linearis *kye-LOP-siss lin-ee-AIR-iss*

Fragrant, trumpet-shaped flowers in white or shades of pink form on desert willow.

ZONES: 7–9
SIZE: 10–25'h × 10–15'w
TYPE: Deciduous shrub or small tree
FORM: Floppy
TEXTURE: Fine
GROWTH: Fast
LIGHT: Sun

MOISTURE: Low
SOIL: Dry
FEATURES: Flowers
USES: Screening, background, naturalizing
FLOWERS: □ ■ ■ ▨
FALL COLOR: ■

SITING: This large deciduous shrub or small tree has long, narrow, willowlike green leaves. The trumpet-shaped, fragrant flowers in pink, white, rose, or lavender marked with purple look like those of catalpa. Blooms first appear in May and keep coming until September or frost. Prune for a handsome tree. With age it develops shaggy bark and twisting trunks. It looks dead when dormant. It drops its leaves early, then holds a heavy crop of 10"-long catalpa-like fruit through the winter, which can look messy. It grows fast (to 3' in a season) when young, then slows down. Groups can be planted in a large-scale landscape for a splash of color. It protects against soil erosion and acts as a windbreak or sunscreen. It provides nesting sites and cover for animals. Deer and birds consume the leaves, fruit, and the flowers' nectar. It is ideal for butterfly gardens and is a favorite of hummingbirds, providing nectar and shelter for nesting. It is a good choice for xeriscaping and does well in containers. The branches have been used to make thatch roofs. It prefers full sun and gravelly or sandy loam where the water table is within 30–40' of the surface. It tolerates alkaline soil, sand, clay, and seasonal flooding. In its native habitat, it grows in dry creek beds, where its long roots can access deep water. It cannot grow in wet or heavy soils.

CARE: Desert willow needs supplemental water during establishment in the first two years. Prune shrubs hard in winter to keep them neater. Cut back trees to near the ground every few years in winter to keep them dense; flowers appear on new growth. Leaf tips may freeze in winter and require cleanup pruning in spring.

PROPAGATION: Desert willow is easy to grow from seed found in the long pods.

RELATED SPECIES: 'Burgundy' has deep purplish-red flowers. 'Cameo' is pure white with a yellow-striped throat. 'Pink Star' is light pink with some purple striping. *Chilopsis* has been crossed with *Catalpa* to create ×*Chitalpa tashkentensis,* a hardier, more cold- and humidity-tolerant desert willow with wider leaves and flowers in the white to pink range. It has the same floppy tendencies as desert willow and suffers from mildew in humid climates.

FRAGRANT WINTERSWEET
Chimonanthus praecox *kye-moe-NAN-thuss PREE-kahks*

Fragrant flowers appear on bare branches in winter.

ZONES: (6)7–9
SIZE: 10–15'h × 8–12'w
TYPE: Deciduous shrub
FORM: Fountainlike
TEXTURE: Medium
GROWTH: Slow

LIGHT: Sun to part shade
MOISTURE: Even
SOIL: Well drained
FEATURES: Fragrant winter flowers
USES: Shrub border
FLOWERS: ■
FALL COLOR: ■ ■

SITING: This winter-flowering shrub is prized for its fragrant flowers, which bloom from December into February. The multistemmed, fountainlike profile becomes leggy with age. The dark green leaves change to yellow-green in fall. Fruits appear in April and May and can persist to the next winter. Wintersweet can be used in a shrub border, but it is best where its fragrance can be enjoyed. Plant it along a walkway, under a window, or in a courtyard, where the extra heat will help protect the flowers. The sweet-smelling branches can be brought indoors for use in flower arrangements. For simple forcing, cut stems about 2 weeks before they bloom outdoors; place them in a vase and mist the buds. For earlier color cut

Branches can be cut to enjoy the fragrance of wintersweet flowers indoors.

branches on a day with temperatures above freezing. Look for slightly swollen flower buds on branches with lots of buds. Make a clean cut; avoid crushing stems. Float the branches in a bathtub filled with warm water and leave them overnight. Make a fresh cut and place them in a vase with floral preservative solution.

CARE: Transplant container-grown plants into full sun or part shade. Plant at the same depth as in the container. The shrub adapts to many soils but needs good drainage. Maintain consistently moist soil throughout the growing season. A 2–4" layer of wood chips or shredded bark will help maintain soil moisture and deter weeds. An annual application of plant food, such as Miracle-Gro, in spring will produce the best flowers and abundant foliage. Prune out old canes after flowering. Prune overgrown plants to within 6–12" of the ground in late winter.

PROPAGATION: Collect seeds and sow in late May.

PESTS AND DISEASES: None are serious.

RELATED SPECIES: 'Grandiflorus' has deep yellow flowers with a red center.

WHITE FRINGE TREE
Chionanthus virginicus *kye-oh-NAN-thuss ver-JIN-ih-cuss*

The interesting flowers of white fringe tree are fragrant and showy.

ZONES: 4–9
SIZE: 12–20'h × 12–20'w
TYPE: Deciduous shrub or small tree
FORM: Spreading
TEXTURE: Medium coarse
GROWTH: Slow
LIGHT: Sun to part shade

MOISTURE: Moderate
SOIL: Deep, fertile
FEATURES: Fragrant white flowers in spring, colorful fruits in early fall
USES: Specimen, shrub border
FLOWERS: □
FALL COLOR: ■

SITING: Fringe tree is a large shrub or small tree with one or a few short trunks and a rounded crown. It has glossy dark green leaves that are late to appear in spring. Showy, sweetly fragrant white blooms appear with the foliage, cascading downward like a white beard. The fruits, which appear on female plants only, are blue-black and olivelike, held in clusters from late August through September. This is a good choice for a small specimen tree or the back of the shrub border. The flowers are attractive to a variety of insects, and fruits are highly desirable to wild turkeys and other birds. For fruits, plant several trees in a naturalized setting with the hope that at least one will be female. You can match its native habitat alongside a stream or pond. It is adaptable to a variety of light and soil conditions. It is tolerant of wind, pollution, and other urban conditions and can be planted near buildings. Consider it for a patio or courtyard garden. The white flowers look especially stunning at night when illuminated by nearby lights. Keep in mind that it becomes quite wide as it matures.

CARE: Transplant container-grown or balled-and-burlapped plants in spring into moist, well-drained soil in full sun to partial shade. Fringe tree does well in the filtered shade under large trees, but flowers are more profuse in full sun. It prefers consistent moisture throughout the growing season, especially during the first 2 years after it is planted. Feed every other spring with plant food such as Miracle-Gro. Prune out dead or diseased wood at any time. Prune right after flowering if shaping is required. Fringe tree is somewhat winter tender when young; in Zone 4 give it winter protection. Place four stakes in the ground around young plants and fasten burlap to them, leaving the bottom few inches open. Fill the enclosure with unshredded dry leaves. Remove the protection in early spring.

PROPAGATION: Sow seeds in fall. They may take 2 years to germinate. Semihardwood cuttings taken in late summer can be difficult to root.

PESTS AND DISEASES: None are serious. Powdery mildew occasionally shows up as a whitish film on the surface of the leaves. It is usually not serious enough to warrant spraying. To reduce infection, prune to open up the inside of shrub and increase the air circulation.

RELATED SPECIES: Chinese fringe tree (*C. retusus*) has smaller leaves and grows to 25' tall with a rounded, bushy form. It is reliably hardy in Zone 6.

AMERICAN YELLOWWOOD
Cladrastis kentukea (lutea) kluh-DRASS-tiss ken-TUCK-ee-uh (LOO-tee-uh)

Zigzag branches and yellow fall color add year-round interest to American yellowwood, also known as virgilia.

ZONES: 4–8
SIZE: 30–50'h × 40–55'w
TYPE: Deciduous tree
FORM: Broad rounded
TEXTURE: Medium
GROWTH: Medium
LIGHT: Sun to light shade

MOISTURE: Moderate
SOIL: Well drained
FEATURES: Flowers in spring, clean summer foliage
USES: Shade, specimen, woodland
FLOWERS: ☐
FALL COLOR: ▨

SITING: This is a refined, medium-size tree for restricted spaces. Plant it in the rear corner of the residential backyard landscape or use it as a shade tree on smaller properties. The showy, heavily fragrant white flowers are borne in hanging chains in late spring. They resemble the flowers of wisteria. Summer leaf color is bright green, almost with a tinge of blue. Fall color can be a clear yellow or sometimes a warm gold-orange. The zigzag branching pattern, seedpods, and smooth gray bark add winter interest.

Trees pruned in late winter will bleed sap.

It prefers full sun to partial shade and moist, well-drained soil. It is tolerant of acid and alkaline soils.

CARE: Transplant as a small tree in early spring. Water young trees their first two seasons as needed to keep the soil evenly moist. Mature trees are drought tolerant. Young trees grown under stressful conditions will benefit from root feeding with plant food, such as Miracle-Gro, in spring. Prune when the tree is young to eliminate weak branch forks. Without pruning, the branching structure can be weak, inviting storm damage and ultimately decay. Prune in summer to avoid excessive sap bleeding, which occurs in winter and spring. Although it does not harm trees, it is unsightly and messy. Wrap young trees in winter to protect the thin bark from sunscald.

PROPAGATION: Sow seeds in fall in place or plan on transplanting while seedlings are still young.

PESTS AND DISEASES: None are serious. Trees under stress are susceptible to verticillium wilt, a soilborne fungal disease.

RELATED SPECIES: 'Rosea' has fragrant, pink flowers.

SUMMERSWEET
Clethra alnifolia KLEE-thra all-nih-FOE-lee-uh

Fragrant spikes of summersweet, also known as sweet pepper bush, bloom in summer.

ZONES: 4–9
SIZE: 4–8'h × 4–6'w
TYPE: Deciduous shrub
FORM: Broad oval
TEXTURE: Medium
GROWTH: Slow to medium
LIGHT: Sun to part shade

MOISTURE: Moderate to wet
SOIL: Acid, well drained
FEATURES: Fragrant late-summer flowers
USES: Shrub border, shade, wet areas
FLOWERS: ☐ ▨
FALL COLOR: ▨ ■

SITING: Summersweet is a fragrant summer-flowering shrub. The white to light pink flowers appear in July and August when most flowering shrubs are taking a break. Fall color is yellow to golden brown. Showy small fruit capsules turn brown in fall and persist for a year or two, adding winter interest. This native shrub can form colonies, making it useful for screening. Site the plant near a deck, patio, or window where the fragrant flowers can be appreciated. Flowers attract butterflies and pollinating insects, and fruits attract birds. Use smaller types in the perennial border for midsummer color and fragrance. Allow summersweet to naturalize along a stream or pond, where its suckering will help control erosion. It prefers moist, acid soil with abundant organic matter worked in. Avoid hot, dry sites. It is salt tolerant. The blossoms and seed heads make interesting additions to cut and dried floral arrangements.

CARE: Plants may be slow to establish, and some twig tip dieback may occur during the first winter. It does best in light, dappled shade. Keep the soil evenly moist during the growing season. Established plants require watering during dry spells. Apply 2–4" of mildly acid mulch (shredded pine bark or pine needles) around each plant as soon as the ground warms in spring. Feed with an acid plant food such as ammonium sulfate or Miracle-Gro Shake 'n Feed Azalea, Camellia, Rhododendron around the base of each plant every spring before new growth emerges and water immediately. Feed again in mid-June. Pruning is generally not recommended during the first 3 years. For older, leggy plants, remove a few of the older branches each year over the course of 3 years. In colder zones there may be some dieback in severe winters. Prune out in spring after the plants have leafed out.

PROPAGATION: Start new plants from soft stem cuttings taken in midsummer or from seeds, which germinate readily. Dig suckers in early spring before new growth emerges and plant them immediately.

PESTS AND DISEASES: Spider mites can be severe on plants in hot, dry locations. Forcefully spray the undersides of all leaves with water to dislodge them.

RELATED SPECIES: 'Hummingbird' is a dwarf cultivar that is more compact and spreading, growing 3' by 3'. 'Ruby Spice' has intense deep rose flowers, which do not fade in the heat of summer.

FLOWERING DOGWOOD
Cornus florida *KOR-nuss FLOR-ih-duh*

Showy white bracts emerge before leaves in late spring.

ZONES: 5–9
SIZE: 12–30'h × 8–15'w
TYPE: Deciduous tree
FORM: Horizontal spreading
TEXTURE: Medium
GROWTH: Slow to medium
LIGHT: Sun to part shade

MOISTURE: Moderate
SOIL: Acid, well drained
FEATURES: Showy spring flowers, fall color
USES: Understory, specimen
FLOWERS: ☐ ▨
FALL COLOR: ▨ ▨

SITING: This is a popular small tree with season-long interest. Spring color comes from showy bracts from April to May. Leaves turn deep burgundy early in fall and showy crimson berries appear in clusters on branch tips. Robins and other birds love them. This plant is excellent as a specimen and in groupings. It prefers cool, moist, acid soil that contains organic matter. Full sun promotes the greatest flowering, but plants tolerate partial shade. It is not tolerant of stresses such as heat, drought, pollution, or road salt. Flower buds can be killed or injured by cold in Zone 5.

Help prevent leaf scorch by watering trees during drought.

CARE: This tree can be slow to reestablish following transplanting. Keep roots cool with 2–4" of organic mulch (shredded pine bark or pine needles) to avoid leaf and trunk scorch. Keep the soil evenly moist during the growing season. Dry soil can lead to leaf scorch and susceptibility to diseases. Root feeding is especially important for stressed trees. Use acidifying plant food such as Miracle-Gro Shake 'n Feed Azalea, Camellia, Rhododendron, or ammonium sulfate sprinkled around plants in spring. Prune trees after flowering only if necessary to shape.

PROPAGATION: Remove seeds from their fleshy cover and sow in fall. Take cuttings in late spring.

PESTS AND DISEASES: Anthracnose (dogwood blight) can be a serious problem. Healthy trees grown in sunny areas with good air circulation and soil moisture are rarely killed. Other problems include dogwood borer, powdery mildew, crown rot, and canker.

RELATED SPECIES: Pagoda dogwood (*C. alternifolia*) is less showy, but is a good substitute in Zones 3 and 4. It has a more horizontal branching habit. Kousa dogwood (*C. kousa*) blooms 2–3 weeks later and is resistant to many of the pests that plague flowering dogwood. Pacific dogwood (*C. nuttallii*) grows better on the West Coast.

RED-OSIER DOGWOOD
Cornus stolonifera (sericea) *KOR-nuss stoh-luhn-IHF-er-uh*

Showy white flowers and red stems add multiple interest to red-osier dogwood, also known as red-twig dogwood.

ZONES: 2–7
SIZE: 7–9'h × 10–12'w
TYPE: Deciduous shrub
FORM: Rounded spreading
TEXTURE: Medium
GROWTH: Fast
LIGHT: Sun to part shade

MOISTURE: Moderate to high
SOIL: Average to wet
FEATURES: Colorful bark, spring flowers, fall color
USES: Specimen, shrub border, hedge
FLOWERS: ☐
FALL COLOR: ▨

SITING: This tough, hardy shrub is well suited to a wide variety of situations. Colorful red to reddish-purple stems are at their peak in winter and early spring. Flat sprays of spring flowers are followed by clusters of bluish-white berries. The shrub grows rapidly with limited suckering. It is not a good choice near roads or driveways, because it does not tolerate salt well. Plants thrive in moist soils and can grow even in boggy soils. Stem color is best in full sun, but plants tolerate partial shade.

CARE: Keep the soil evenly moist from spring until the ground freezes in fall. Feed every spring with plant food, such as Miracle-Gro. Because the best bark color is on young shoots, cut out about a third of the older branches each spring to keep plants young and vigorous.

PROPAGATION: Grow from seeds sown in fall (plants often self-seed). Take cuttings in midsummer. Layering of young stems is also effective.

PESTS AND DISEASES: Leaf spot can be a problem in wet years, occurring in late summer and early fall, but is not serious enough to kill plants. Cankers causing stem dieback are usually caused by lack of water. Prune out infected stems.

RELATED SPECIES: Tatarian dogwood (*C. alba*) is prized for its neat, clean foliage. Cornelian cherry (*C. mas*) can be trained into a single-stemmed tree with early pruning. Gray dogwood (*C. racemosa*) may have good fall color.

Leaf spot disease on dogwood may detract from the plant's appearance.

Prune out older branches to encourage younger, more colorful stems.

FRAGRANT WINTER HAZEL

Corylopsis glabrescens core-ih-LOP-siss gla-BRESS-enz

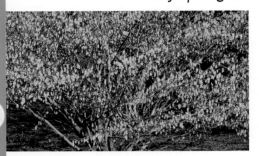

Fragrant, pale yellow flowers hang in clusters on winter hazel.

ZONES: 5–8
SIZE: 8–15'h × 8–15'w
TYPE: Deciduous shrub
FORM: Wide-spreading
TEXTURE: Medium
GROWTH: Slow to medium
LIGHT: Sun to light shade

MOISTURE: Average
SOIL: Acid, well drained
FEATURES: Early fragrant flowers
USES: Woodland, shrub border
FLOWERS: ▪
FALL COLOR: ▨

SITING: This large, dense, shrub is graced with pendulous, pale yellow flower clusters with a delicious fragrance. From a distance the shrub seems to glow a bright golden yellow. Situated in front of a dark evergreen background, this can be spectacular. The dark green summer foliage often remains on the plants until killed by a freeze. Some plants have yellow-green to gold fall color. Use fragrant winter hazel for mass plantings, in small groupings in the shrub border, or at the edge of a woodland garden. Choose a sheltered site to protect it from late spring frosts, which can kill flower buds. This is especially important in the Midwest and South, where warm periods in March can cause the buds to swell and open, only to succumb to an early April freeze. It prefers moist, acid, well-drained soil and full sun but will grow in part shade. Plants do not tolerate wet feet.

CARE: Amend soil with peat moss or leaf mold before planting. Transplant from containers in spring. Plant at the same depth as in the container. Keep the soil evenly moist during the growing season, saturating the soil deeply at each watering. Apply 2–4" of mildly acid mulch (shredded pine bark or pine needles) around each plant as soon as the ground warms in spring. Replenish mulch as needed during the growing season. Feed in spring with an acid plant food, such as Miracle-Gro Shake 'n Feed Azalea, Camellia, Rhododendron, around the base of each plant before new growth emerges and water immediately. Prune out dead or damaged wood at any time. On mature shrubs, prune after flowering to remove the oldest wood.

PROPAGATION: Seeds are difficult to germinate, requiring a warm period followed by cold. Sow them in place outside in fall. Take softwood cuttings in midsummer. Leave the cuttings undisturbed until growth begins the following spring, then transplant to a nursery bed or individual container. Shrubs can also be propagated by layering.

PESTS AND DISEASES: None are serious.

RELATED SPECIES: 'March Jewel' is dwarf with a low-spreading habit. Buttercup winter hazel (*C. pauciflora*) is smaller and daintier. It needs protection from drying winds, full sun, and high-pH soils. It is hardy in Zones 6–8. Spike winter hazel (*C. spicata*), hardy in Zones 5–8, is more wide-spreading. Mature plants are a mass of crooked, flexible branches.

EUROPEAN FILBERT

Corylus avellana CORE-ih-luss ah-vell-LAHN-uh

European filbert produces showy yellow catkins in early spring.

ZONES: 4–8
SIZE: 12–20'h × 12–20'w
TYPE: Deciduous shrub
FORM: Irregular
TEXTURE: Coarse
GROWTH: Medium to fast
LIGHT: Sun

MOISTURE: Even
SOIL: Organic, well drained, fertile
FEATURES: Nuts, spring catkins
USES: Specimen, naturalizing, wildlife
FLOWERS: ▪
FALL COLOR: ▪

SITING: This plant is best reserved for informal or naturalized settings. It is an excellent choice for wildlife plantings. The thicketlike growth provides shelter, and the nuts are a food source. The popular cultivar 'Contorta' has twisted, curling stems, leaves, and even roots, giving rise to its common name of Harry Lauder's walking stick. This form is particularly striking in winter and spring, when it is covered with dangling yellow to tan catkins that appear before the plant leafs out. It needs a protected site in Zone 4.

CARE: Get bare-root plants in the ground as soon as it can be worked in spring.

Filbert nuts are an important food source for wildlife.

Container plants can be planted all season if they are watered well, but spring is best. Plants grow well in full sun to light shade in moist, well-drained soils. They tolerate drier sites but like soil with lots of organic matter. Keep the soil evenly moist from spring until the ground freezes in fall. Feed every spring with plant food, such as Miracle-Gro, or an organic equivalent such as compost or fish emulsion. 'Contorta' is commonly sold grafted; remove suckers growing from the rootstock since the stems will not have the desired trait.

PROPAGATION: Grow from seed (nuts), if you can protect them from squirrels. Plant them outside in fall and allow to overwinter, or plant them indoors after 120 days of moist chilling. It is difficult to grow from cuttings but can be layered.

PESTS AND DISEASES: Leaf and stem blights occur but rarely cause much damage.

RELATED SPECIES: American filbert (*C. americana*) is a multistemmed, suckering shrub that produces edible nuts. Turkish filbert (*C. colurna*) is a 40–50' tree with a pyramidal crown, much more formal in habit than European filbert.

SMOKE TREE
Cotinus coggygria *koe-TINE-uss koe-GIG-ree-uh*

Showy pinkish blooms cover this plant in late spring. Smoke tree is also known as smokebush.

ZONES: 4–8
SIZE: 10–15'h × 10–15'w
TYPE: Deciduous tree or shrub
FORM: Upright spreading
TEXTURE: Medium
GROWTH: Medium
LIGHT: Sun

MOISTURE: Average to moist
SOIL: Well drained
FEATURES: Feathery pinkish plumes, foliage
USES: Shrub border, groupings
FLOWERS: ■
FALL COLOR: ■ ■ ■

SITING: This shrub or small tree is noted for its attractive, abundant flowers, which first appear in June. The hairs on the 6–8"-long panicles change color as they age, eventually becoming smoky pinkish or purplish. Leaves are medium blue-green in summer; fall color is generally fairly showy—a mix of yellow, orange, and red—but is not reliable. There are also many purple-leaved cultivars. In colder areas winter dieback is common, but the vigorous shrubs spring back the following season. This easily transplanted plant prefers full sun, is adaptable to many soils, and is tolerant of hot, dry, gravelly soils and sites. Avoid low-lying areas where soils remain soggy. A slope or hilltop is an ideal spot in colder sites, providing good drainage and protection from frost pockets.

CARE: Keep the soil evenly moist throughout the growing season. In colder climates reduce watering in fall to encourage winter dormancy. Feed every spring with plant food, such as Miracle-Gro. Cut shrubs to the ground in early spring to enhance leaf coloration, especially of the purple-leaved types, and produce a dense, multistemmed shrub with few or no flowers. In colder areas where dieback is common, wait until plants have leafed out, then remove dead stems.

1 **Prune out older branches in early spring.**

2 **Plants regrow quickly after cutting.**

PROPAGATION: Take softwood cuttings in midsummer. Seeds require scarification, soaking overnight in warm water, and stratification for 90 days.

PESTS AND DISEASES: Verticillium wilt can cause a sudden wilting of foliage. It is most common in heavy, poorly drained soils.

RELATED SPECIES: 'Nordine' and 'Royal Purple' are popular purple-leaved selections.

SPREADING COTONEASTER
Cotoneaster divaricatus *kuh-TOH-nee-as-ter di-var-ih-KAY-tus*

Cotoneaster has bright red fruits in fall.

ZONES: 4–7
SIZE: 5–6'h × 6–8'w
TYPE: Deciduous shrub
FORM: Spreading
TEXTURE: Fine
GROWTH: Medium to fast
LIGHT: Sun

MOISTURE: Even
SOIL: Well drained
FEATURES: Fall color
USES: Foundation, massing, hedges
FLOWERS: ■ □
FALL COLOR: ■ ■ ■

SITING: This shrub has glossy, dark green summer foliage and good fall color. Plant it in foundation plantings, in groups, or in mass plantings near evergreens, which set off the fall color and fruits. It makes a good hedge.

CARE: Keep the soil evenly moist from spring until the ground freezes in fall, especially during the first 2 years. Apply a 2" layer of organic mulch such as shredded bark or wood chips around each plant in late spring to retain moisture and deter weeds. Feed every other spring with plant food, such as Miracle-Gro. Sprinkle granules around the base of each plant and water well. Remove dead, damaged, or diseased wood at any time of year. Shear hedges beginning the second year.

Cotoneaster is a good plant for hedging.

A light annual shearing will promote a dense, healthy hedge.

PROPAGATION: Take softwood cuttings from new growth as it begins to harden in early summer. Seeds have a hard seed coat that should be nicked before sowing in fall.

PESTS AND DISEASES: Oystershell scale can be a serious problem, but it is rare. Prevent or control it by spraying plants with dormant horticultural oil before new growth in spring. Spider mites can appear in dry weather. Spray them off with a strong stream of water. Fire blight can rapidly kill branches and even entire plants. Prune out infected branches immediately and dispose of them off site.

RELATED SPECIES: Hedge cotoneaster (*C. lucidus*) has glossy, deep green leaves that turn red in fall. It makes a superb hedge. Space plants 18" apart for a hedge. Mature height is about 6'. Many-flowered cotoneaster (*C. multiflorus*) grows to 8–12' and spreads up to 15'. Willow-leaf cotoneaster (*C. salicifolius*) is evergreen and is hardy in Zones 6 and 7. The red fruits are showy in fall.

ROCKSPRAY COTONEASTER

Cotoneaster horizontalis kuh-TOH-nee-as-ter hor-ih-zahn-TAH-lis

Rockspray cotoneaster branches grow in a herringbone pattern.

ZONES: 5–7
SIZE: 2–3'h × 5–8'w
TYPE: Deciduous shrub
FORM: Spreading
TEXTURE: Fine
GROWTH: Slow to medium
LIGHT: Sun

MOISTURE: Moist
SOIL: Well drained
FEATURES: Foliage, fruits
USES: Ground cover, slopes, rock gardens
FLOWERS: ▪
FALL COLOR: ▪ ▪ ▪

SITING: This low-growing, flat, dense shrub has horizontally spreading branches that grow in an unusual herringbone pattern. The fine-textured foliage turns red and yellow in fall. Pink flowers in mid- to late spring are followed by showy, small coral berries that persist to late fall. Plant it where it can spill over slopes, rocks, and walls. There will be some winter damage at temperatures below −20°F. Plants are adaptable to many soils but prefer well-drained soil and sunny, airy conditions.

CARE: Transplant container-grown plants in early spring or fall. Because of their sparse root system, plants are often slow to establish. Apply 2" of organic mulch such as shredded bark to keep the soil evenly moist, especially while the shrubs are young. Keep the soil evenly moist from spring until the ground freezes in fall, especially during the first 2 years. Feed every other spring with plant food, such as Miracle-Gro. Sprinkle granules around the base of each plant and water well. Remove dead, damaged, or diseased wood at any time of year. Gardeners in Zone 5 may need to prune out some winter damage in spring after a severe winter.

PROPAGATION: Take cuttings in early summer. Sow seeds in autumn as soon as they are ripe. To propagate by layering in fall, bend over and wound pliable stems at a point where they touch the ground. In spring once roots form, dig up the new plants and replant them.

PESTS AND DISEASES: Wounds are common entry points for pests and diseases such as fire blight and borers. Be careful not to wound plants with garden tools. Fire blight can rapidly kill branches and even entire plants. Prune out infected branches immediately and dispose of them off-site. Lace bugs and spider mites can cause yellow speckling on leaves. Spray them off with a strong stream of water.

RELATED SPECIES: 'Little Gem' is a dwarf, mounded form growing to only about a foot in height. 'Variegatus' has white-edged leaves that turn pink in fall. Cranberry cotoneaster (*C. apiculatus*) grows 3' in height with a spread of 3–6' and is hardy in Zone 4. It has lovely red fall foliage and large berries that can be used for indoor arrangements. Bearberry cotoneaster (*C. dammeri*) is hardy in Zones 5–8, where it makes a good broadleaf evergreen ground cover. It is fast growing to 1–1½' in height and 6' in width. 'Streibs Findling' grows only 6" high but spreads up to 8'.

COCKSPUR HAWTHORN

Crataegus crus-galli kruh-TAY-gus krooz-GALL-eye

Cockspur hawthorn has showy fruits that persist into winter.

ZONES: 4–7
SIZE: 25'h × 30'w
TYPE: Deciduous tree
FORM: Broad
TEXTURE: Medium to fine
GROWTH: Slow to medium

LIGHT: Sun
MOISTURE: Average
SOIL: Well drained
FEATURES: Flowers, fruits
USES: Specimen, hedge
FLOWERS: □
FALL COLOR: ▪ ▪

SITING: This small, rounded tree makes a good single specimen. It can also be used in groupings, as screening or a barrier plant, or as a tall hedge. It tolerates urban conditions. It is tolerant of many soils but should be well drained. Few birds like the ornamental fruits, so they remain from late summer into winter. The 2"-long thorns can injure anyone who touches them. Variety *inermis* is a thornless type with the same features as the species.

CARE: Keep the soil evenly moist from spring until the ground freezes in fall, especially during the first 2 years. Young trees will benefit from a spring application of plant food, such as Miracle-Gro. Prune to shape in late winter or early spring. Remove dead, diseased, and rubbing branches.

PROPAGATION: Seeds require specialized treatment not recommend for homeowners.

PESTS AND DISEASES: Cedar-hawthorn rust can cover leaves in bright orange pustules. Leaf miners and aphids are minor pests. Fruit may be disfigured by cedar-quince rust if eastern red cedar trees are nearby.

RELATED SPECIES: English hawthorn (*C. laevigata*) is shrubbier and grows 15–20' in height. Washington hawthorn (*C. phaenopyrum*) has reddish-purple spring foliage that changes to a lustrous dark green. It is resistant to cedar-hawthorn rust.

Cedar-quince rust appers as spikes on fruits.

Thorns can present a problem for small children or anyone else who contacts them.

JAPANESE CEDAR

Cryptomeria japonica krip-toh-MARE-ee-uh juh-PON-ih-kuh

Japanese cedar, also known as Japanese cryptomeria, has attractive bright green summer foliage.

ZONES: (5)6–8
SIZE: 60'h × 25'w
TYPE: Evergreen tree
FORM: Pyramidal
TEXTURE: Medium
GROWTH: Medium
LIGHT: Sun to light shade
MOISTURE: High
SOIL: Rich, acid
FEATURES: Foliage
USES: Specimen
FLOWERS: ■
FALL COLOR: ■

SITING: This accommodating, handsome evergreen can be used as a specimen in the corner of a large lot. The upright, pyramidal growth habit makes it ideal for screening or as a backdrop for perennial gardens. The leaves are bright green to bluish green in summer, developing a distinct bronze to brown color during cold months, especially in windy, exposed locations. The foliage regreens in spring. The bark is an attractive reddish brown; it shreds in long strips, similar to cypress, and is quite showy. This tree is not hardy in exposed locations in Zone 6 or colder; trees will suffer from winter burn and injury. Older trees retain dead foliage and branches that can detract from their beauty. Mature specimens can reach 100' or more in height. Locate this tree in a semiprotected site near other plant groupings. It has been used as an alternative for Leyland cypress in the Southeast. It prefers a rich, deep, light, permeable acid soil with abundant moisture and an open, sunny location sheltered from high winds. It will tolerate light shade.

CARE: Keep the soil evenly moist throughout the growing season, watering when the top 2" of soil has dried out. Trees do not tolerate drought well; water during dry periods. Young trees will benefit from an annual spring application of an acid plant food such as Miracle-Gro Shake 'n Feed Azalea, Camellia, Rhododendron. Avoid excess plant food late in the season to reduce winter dieback. Remove any dead branches. In cold climates, prune out winterkill in spring.

PROPAGATION: Soak seeds in cold water for 12 hours, then put moist seeds into plastic bags and store at 34°F for 60–90 days before sowing. Cuttings taken in summer and fall will root, but slowly.

PESTS AND DISEASES: Twig blight, canker, leaf blight, and leaf spot have been seen but are not serious.

RELATED SPECIES: 'Ben Franklin' grows 30–40' and has deep green foliage and is salt tolerant. 'Sekkan-sugi' has yellow-green new foliage and grows to 15–20' tall. Compact 'Vilmoriniana' grows to about 3' tall with dense foliage that turns a mottled gold and purple color in fall. 'Winter Mint' has an open form with rich green foliage that maintains its color in winter. 'Yoshino' is a popular cultivar with blue-green summer foliage that becomes lightly bronze-green in cold weather.

LEYLAND CYPRESS

×Cupressocyparis leylandii koo-press-oh-SIP-uh-riss lay-LAN-dee-eye

Leyland cypress has a dense, pyramidal form.

ZONES: 6–10
SIZE: 65'h × 6–10'w
TYPE: Evergreen tree
FORM: Pyramidal
TEXTURE: Fine
GROWTH: Fast
LIGHT: Sun
MOISTURE: Medium to dry
SOIL: Well drained
FEATURES: Upright form, fast growth
USES: Accent, screening
FLOWERS: ■
FALL COLOR: ■

SITING: Leyland cypress easily grows 3–4' per year even in poor soils, and ultimately attains 50' or more in the West. It forms a dense oval or pyramidal outline when left unpruned, but the graceful, slightly pendulous branches will tolerate severe trimming to create a formal hedge, screen, or windbreak. The fine, feathery foliage, composed of soft, pointed leaves on flattened branchlets, is dark blue-green when mature and soft green when young. The tree holds its color well in winter. The bark is reddish brown and scaly. Leyland cypress is too big for most residential landscapes unless regularly trimmed. Although it can be sheared into a tall screen for a small lot, it should probably be saved for large-scale landscapes where it can be allowed to develop into its natural shape. Its pyramidal form makes it popular in the southern coastal areas as a cut Christmas tree. It withstands salt spray better than other conifers. It tolerates drought and a wide range of soils but not heavy, wet, or poorly drained soils. It needs full sun. It thins out in shade and grows more slowly.

CARE: It transplants readily from a container. Keep the soil evenly moist from spring until the ground freezes in fall during the first 2 years. Established trees are drought tolerant. Apply a 2" layer of organic mulch such as shredded bark or wood chips around each plant in late spring to retain moisture and deter weeds. This tree grows quickly without additional plant food, but young trees can be given a spring application of an acid plant food such as Miracle-Gro Shake 'n Feed Azalea, Camellia, Rhododendron. Prune to maintain a certain shape.

PROPAGATION: Take cuttings in summer, fall, or winter.

PESTS AND DISEASES: Bagworms are a problem; immediate removal of bags helps reduce severity. Fungal diseases can lead to cankers and dieback. Root rot may occur in wet soils.

RELATED SPECIES: 'Castlewellan Gold' has golden-yellow foliage. 'Naylor's Blue' is a pyramidal cultivar reaching 35' in height and about 15' in width. It has bluish foliage.

Remove bagworm cases as soon as you see them to prevent extensive defoliation.

ARIZONA CYPRESS
Cupressus arizonica (glabra) *koo-PRESS-us air-ih-ZON-ih-kuh (GLAY-bruh)*

Arizona cypress is a fast-growing evergreen for tough sites.

ZONES: 7–9
SIZE: 45'h × 30'w
TYPE: Evergreen tree
FORM: Pyramidal
TEXTURE: Fine
GROWTH: Medium
LIGHT: Sun

MOISTURE: Low
SOIL: Well drained
FEATURES: Tough, foliage color
USES: Screen, specimen, windbreak
FLOWERS: ▪
FALL COLOR: ▪

SITING: This rapidly growing North American native evergreen with green foliage has a silver-gray shimmer, and the branches are more open than on most junipers. The inconspicuous flowers are followed by 1" cones that persist on the tree. The peeling brown bark becomes gray with age. Arizona cypress is often used as a specimen, screen, or windbreak planting and is a common sight in western Texas and the southern High Plains where it tolerates the hot, dry conditions with ease. It prefers full sun, is drought tolerant, and likes high, dry sites. Some people think the tree smells like a skunk. Individual trees can be pyramidal or spreading in shape due to seedling variation. It has been considered for use as a Christmas tree.

CARE: Water young plants during establishment. Older plants are very drought tolerant. Young trees will grow faster if given a spring application of plant food, such as Miracle-Gro, or an organic equivalent such as fish emulsion. Remove, dead, diseased, or damaged branches.

PROPAGATION: Seeds require cold, moist stratification for 1 month. Cuttings are not easy to root.

PESTS AND DISEASES: It is subject to canker and foliar diseases, especially in humid climates.

RELATED SPECIES: 'Blue Ice' has powdery-gray-blue to icy-blue foliage. 'Carolina Sapphire' has handsome blue-gray foliage. It grows 20–25' tall. 'Limelight' has light yellow to lime green foliage. Monterey cypress (*C. macrocarpa*) is a horizontally branching, often flat-topped tree native to the Monterey peninsula in California. It grows 30–40', maturing into a picturesque specimen. It is susceptible to canker, which kills many trees, especially those grown outside their native habitat. It is salt tolerant. Italian cypress (*C. sempervirens*) is an ideal sentinel, and the strong vertical line balances horizontal architecture. It is a must for formal gardens in mild climates with its upright, narrow, columnar form. Growth is dense and thick. It can be used as a screen if planted close together. 'Glauca' has blue-green foliage. 'Swane's Golden' has bright golden-yellow new growth.

ROSE DAPHNE
Daphne cneorum *DAF-nee nee-OH-rum*

Rose daphne, also known as garland flower, has fragrant, showy flowers.

ZONES: 4–7
SIZE: 6–12"h × 2'w
TYPE: Evergreen shrub
FORM: Spreading
TEXTURE: Medium to fine
GROWTH: Slow

LIGHT: Sun
MOISTURE: Low
SOIL: Well drained
FEATURES: Flowers
USES: Foundation, mixed border
FLOWERS: ▪
FALL COLOR: ▪

SITING: Rose daphne is a tidy shrub with exquisitely scented, star-shaped flowers. It is quite demanding in its cultural requirements. It performs best in well-drained, pH neutral soil protected from hot sun and drying winds. It is primarily used as an accent plant, but it can also serve as a small-scale ground cover or be used in a rock garden. Plant it near an entrance or deck or under a window, where you can enjoy its lovely scent.

CARE: Transplant container plants in early spring or early fall. Plant high to reduce the chance of crown rot. Plants resent transplanting and are slow to establish. Water newly planted shrubs thoroughly to saturate the soil. For the next 4 weeks, water once a week, making sure the soil is thoroughly saturated. After this, water only

Protect plants from winter sun and wind with pine boughs.

if there is no rain for 2 weeks. This plant does best if kept on the dry side. It likes a cool root zone, so apply a 1" layer of organic mulch. A leafy mulch applied in early spring will supply adequate nutrients. Add some lime or hardwood ash to the soil to raise the pH if it is below 6.0. Prune established plants lightly after flowering to maintain shape. Snow cover is important for winter survival. Cover plants with pine boughs where winter sun and wind present a problem.

PROPAGATION: Seeds require cold treatment of 2–3 months. Cuttings are difficult to root. For greatest success, take cuttings after the growth flush hardens in June and July.

PESTS AND DISEASES: Few are serious. Overwatering can lead to root rot.

RELATED SPECIES: Fragrant daphne (*D. odora*) has purple-and-white flowers in February and March and grows to 4–6' in height. It is hardy in Zones 7–10. Burkwood daphne (*D. ×burkwoodii*) has extremely fragrant flowers that open white in May. It is compact and rounded and grows to about 3'. 'Carol Mackie' is a popular cultivar with blue-green foliage with a pronounced creamy margin.

DOVE TREE

Davidia involucrata   day-VID-ee-uh in-voe-loo-KRAH-tuh

Winglike white bracts surround the flowers of dove tree.

ZONES: 6–7(8)
SIZE: 30'h × 30'w
TYPE: Deciduous tree
FORM: Pyramidal
TEXTURE: Medium
GROWTH: Medium

LIGHT: Light shade to sun
MOISTURE: High
SOIL: Well drained
FEATURES: Flowers
USES: Specimen
FLOWERS: ☐
FALL COLOR: ■

SITING: This attractive tree has 1" ball-shaped clusters of flowers produced in spring, surrounded by a pair of large, petal-like, white bracts that tremble in the slightest breeze, making it look like a tree full of doves. These flowers last about 2 weeks and are followed by inedible, pear-shaped fruits about 1½" long. Dove tree begins to bloom when it is about 10 years old. It may suffer winter injury in northern gardens. The 3–6" heart-shaped bright green leaves have long stalks with white fuzz on their undersides. The bark is orange and brown and scaly, adding winter interest. Dove-tree prefers light shade but will tolerate sun if the soil is kept moist. Protect from wind. It appreciates a little shelter in its formative years, but eventually reaches a size where few other trees are large enough to shade it. Grow this tree where it has room to spread and reach its full potential.

CARE: Transplant balled-and-burlapped plants in spring into well-drained, moist soil that has been enriched with peat moss or leaf mold. Young trees are more susceptible to low temperatures than older trees. Keep the soil evenly moist throughout the growing season, watering when the top 2" of soil has dried out. Trees do not tolerate drought well; water during dry periods. Feed young plants in spring with plant food, such as Miracle-Gro. Sprinkle granules around the base of the tree and water well. Although tolerant of some pruning, dove tree cannot be successfully maintained at a reduced size. Pruning, if necessary, should be done in winter.

PROPAGATION: Sow seeds as soon as they are ripe. Plant the entire fruit for best results. If you clean away the thin fruit covering the nutlet, avoid letting the nutlet dry out; this will inhibit germination. Germination can take up to 18 months, but seedlings and saplings grow rapidly. Keep the seedlings in a cold frame until there is no danger from frost, then plant in a nursery border. Once they are 3 years of age, transplant them in their permanent positions. Take cuttings of half-ripe side shoots in late summer.

PESTS AND DISEASES: None are serious.

RELATED SPECIES: The subspecies *vilmoriniana* is the most commonly cultivated type, differing from the species in that the underside of the leaves is yellowish green or somewhat glaucous and slightly downy on the veins at first but otherwise glabrous. It is hardy in Zone 5.

SLENDER DEUTZIA

Deutzia gracilis   DOOT-see-uh gruh-SIL-iss

White flowers cover low-growing slender deutzia in spring.

ZONES: (4)5–8
SIZE: 2–4'h × 3–4'w
TYPE: Deciduous shrub
FORM: Mound
TEXTURE: Medium to fine
GROWTH: Slow to medium

LIGHT: Sun
MOISTURE: Even
SOIL: Well drained
FEATURES: Flowers
USES: Border
FLOWERS: ☐
FALL COLOR: ■

SITING: This low, mounded shrub is covered with pure white flowers for up to 2 weeks in May. Summer foliage is a nondescript green, and fall color and fruits are not interesting. Plants are twiggy, densely branched, and low growing; they require annual pruning to flower well. Growth starts early in some areas and may be damaged by late spring frosts.

CARE: Plant container-grown plants in spring into deep, moist, well-drained soil in full sun. Keep the soil evenly moist throughout the growing season, watering when the top 2" of soil has dried out. Feed young plants in spring with plant food, such as Miracle-Gro, or an organic equivalent such as fish emulsion. Sprinkle the granules around the base of each plant and water well. After flowering, thin out

Mulch plants with bark or wood chips to maintain even soil moisture.

drastically by cutting away weak and old wood and any winter dieback, but leave the young shoots; they will bear the best blooms. Older shrubs that appear unkempt may be renewal pruned in late winter. Cut back to within 6" of the ground. Flowers will be sacrificed for that year, but plants will bloom better in subsequent years.

PROPAGATION: Sow seeds in fall. Take softwood cuttings anytime during the growing season.

PESTS AND DISEASES: None are serious. Leaf spots, aphids, and leaf miner can be minor pests in some years.

RELATED SPECIES: Several cultivars are available with improved leaf color, but they are less hardy than the species. 'Aurea' has yellow leaves. 'Marmorata' has yellow-spotted leaves. 'Nikko' forms a neat, dense low mound or ground cover 2' tall and at least twice as wide. The fall foliage can be a good red. 'Variegata' is a rare form occasionally encountered in specialist nurseries. Its leaves are broadly margined with white. Lemoine deutzia (*D.* ×*lemoinei*) grows to 5–7' tall and is hardier than slender deutzia, surviving temperatures down to –30°F.

RUSSIAN OLIVE

Elaeagnus angustifolia ell-ee-AG-nus an-gus-tih-FOH-lee-uh

Russian olive is a tough plant with grayish-silver foliage.

ZONES: 2–7
SIZE: 15'h × 12'w
TYPE: Deciduous tree
FORM: Oval
TEXTURE: Medium to fine
GROWTH: Medium to fast

LIGHT: Sun
MOISTURE: Low
SOIL: Well drained
FEATURES: Foliage, salt tolerance
USES: Hedge, street, coast
FLOWERS: □
FALL COLOR: ■

SITING: Grow this tough, durable plant for its grayish-silver foliage. Use it for hedges, windbreaks, or screening or as an accent in the shrub border. Its high salt tolerance makes it a good choice in coastal areas and along highways. It performs better in dry climates than in areas with high humidity. It does best in a sunny, open exposure in light, sandy loam. The young branches can be thorny, causing a hazard for small children. The common name comes from the fruits, which appear in late summer and are eaten by birds. The small, fragrant flowers appear in spring but are difficult to see among the foliage. A native of Europe and Asia, this tree has become naturalized in parts of the United States and has been showing up on invasive

Stem canker can be a devastating disease on Russian olive.

plant lists in recent years. It does not perform well in the heat of the South.

CARE: Water newly planted trees. Once established, this tree is drought tolerant. Plants fix atmospheric nitrogen, making them amendable to poor soils. They can be pruned tightly. Landscape trees look best when they are kept vigorous with annual pruning.

PROPAGATION: Seed requires stratification for 60–90 days before they germinate. Cuttings are difficult to root.

PESTS AND DISEASES: Leaf spots, cankers, ruts, verticillium wilt, crown gall, aphids, and scale can be problems. Verticillium wilt is a soil-borne fungal disease that can kill trees. Once the soil is infected, there is no practical cure other than replanting with resistant species.

RELATED SPECIES: Shrubby silverberry (*E. commutata*) grows 6–12' high and suckers profusely to form colonies. It is hardy in Zones 4–6. Thorny elaeagnus (*E. pungens*) is hardy in Zones 6–10 and is better suited to southern gardens. It is widely used in highway plantings.

RED-VEIN ENKIANTHUS

Enkianthus campanulatus en-kee-AN-thus cam-pan-you-LAY-tus

Interesting bell-shaped flowers hang in clusters.

ZONES: 5–7
SIZE: 8–20'h × 8–10'w
TYPE: Deciduous shrub
FORM: Upright
TEXTURE: Medium
GROWTH: Slow
LIGHT: Sun to shade
MOISTURE: Moderate

SOIL: Acid
FEATURES: Flowers, fall color
USES: Foundation, shrub border, woodland
FLOWERS: □ ▨
FALL COLOR: ■ ■ ■

SITING: Red-vein enkianthus is a multistemmed, upright shrub with layered branches. The drooping, bell-shaped flowers are white with red to pink petal tips and veins. They appear from May to early June. Fall color is ornamental in combinations of red, orange, and purple. The fruit is an egg-shaped brown capsule and resembles a Dutch pipe. Red-vein enkianthus makes a good specimen plant. Site it where you can enjoy the spring flowers and fall foliage. It can also be mixed with other shrubs in a shrub border; it does especially well with rhododendrons and other acid-loving plants. It can be trained into a small tree. Flowers last a long time in arrangements. It can be grown in sheltered locations in some parts of Zone 4.

CARE: Amend the soil with peat moss or ammonium sulfate before planting to provide the necessary acid conditions. Plant container-grown shrubs in spring into moist, well-drained soil high in organic matter. This shrub does best in part shade. It needs acid, cool soil. It can be grown in dense shade but will not tolerate dry or alkaline soils. Water well during dry periods. Apply a 2–4" layer of an organic mulch such as pine needles, shredded oak leaves, or shredded pine bark to keep the soil evenly moist and to maintain soil acidity. Feed every spring with an acid plant food such as Miracle-Gro Shake 'n Feed Azalea, Camellia, Rhododendron. Prune only to remove broken or crossed branches, and do it right after flowering to avoid cutting off next year's flower buds. It blooms on the previous year's wood.

PROPAGATION: Sow seeds in early spring; however, seed-grown plants may not have the same red fall color. Take softwood cuttings in late spring. Layer in fall.

PESTS AND DISEASES: None are serious. Spider mites can be a problem in summer. To reduce the population, spray plants with a garden hose during hot, dry weather.

RELATED SPECIES: 'Albiflorus' has creamy white flowers that lack significant red markings. The plant is compact-growing with reasonably good orange-red fall color. 'Red Bells' has whitish flowers with a reddish edge. The fall color is consistently good. 'Showy Lantern' sports deep pink flowers and dense branching from the ground up. Summer foliage is dark green, and the leaves turn scarlet in fall. It is less hardy than the species. 'Variegata' has red twigs, and the green leaves have white variegations.

HARDY SILVER GUM
Eucalyptus gunnii *yoo-kuh-LIP-tuss gun-EE-eye*

Hardy silver gum thrives in dry areas of Western states.

ZONES: (7)8–10
SIZE: 60'h × 35'w
TYPE: Evergreen tree
FORM: Upright
TEXTURE: Medium
GROWTH: Fast
LIGHT: Sun

MOISTURE: Low
SOIL: Well drained
FEATURES: Leaves, bark
USES: Shade, windbreak
FLOWERS: □

SITING: Silver gum is a durable shade tree for warm, dry climates. It is one of the fastest growing and hardiest of the eucalyptus. Plant it where you want shade quickly and where the fallen leaf and stem debris won't cause a problem. Make sure the tree has room to grow to its mature size. The bark is bicolored pale green and white. Yellowish-white flowers are showy in early autumn. Eucalyptus show distinct juvenile and adult phases, particularly in leaf development. The leaves sold as dried material in florists' shops are the juvenile stage. Mature leaves are often longer and narrower. Leaves are highly aromatic when bruised. Plants will be killed back in Zone 7 and possibly Zone 8 in some winters. Use as a specimen tree, shade tree, or windbreak. Eucalyptus does not like the high humidity of the Southeast, but thrives in the drier climate of the West. It prefers full sun and well-drained soil.

Prune out winter damage in early spring.

CARE: Transplant the smallest possible trees in winter or spring. Water young trees during establishment. Older trees are drought tolerant. Trees stressed by eucalyptus longhorn beetle will benefit from root feeding and supplemental watering. Trees that experience winter damage will need pruning in spring. Avoid pruning from spring to fall to discourage eucalyptus longhorn beetle infestations. It can be cut back hard every year or so to make a multistemmed shrub.
PROPAGATION: Seeds need cold, moist stratification for 1–22 months. Cuttings are difficult to root.
PESTS AND DISEASES: Eucalyptus longhorn beetle can be a serious problem in Southern California.
RELATED SPECIES: Corkscrew gum (*E. cinerea*) is hardy in Zone 8. It grows to 50' tall with reddish bark. Blue gum (*E. globulus*) is hardy in Zone 9. The young leaves are silvery blue and mature to glossy green with a long, narrow shape. It can grow to 150' in height. It is fast growing, weak wooded, and can be seriously damaged by occasional freezes.

WINGED EUONYMUS
Euonymus alatus *you-AHN-ih-muss uh-LAY-tus*

Winged euonymus, also known as winged spindle tree or burning bush, is noted for its brilliant fall color.

ZONES: 4–8(9)
SIZE: 15–20'h × 15'w
TYPE: Deciduous shrub
FORM: Mounded
TEXTURE: Medium
GROWTH: Slow
LIGHT: Sun to shade

MOISTURE: Dry
SOIL: Well drained
FEATURES: Fall color, corky bark
USES: Specimen, shrub border, hedge
FLOWERS: □
FALL COLOR: ■

SITING: Plant this slow-growing shrub where the striking fall color can be appreciated. It can be used as a specimen, as part of a mixed shrub border, or as an informal hedge. It leafs out early in spring, and the summer foliage is clean and green. Fall color is a brilliant red. The unusual winged stems and red fruits offer winter interest. In some areas birds feed on the seeds, leading to self-seeding. Full sun is best for fall color, but plants will still have fall color in shade. It adapts to a wide range of soils but will not tolerate boggy or swamplike conditions.
CARE: Winged euonymus is easily transplanted balled-and-burlapped or from a container in spring or early fall. Water well during the first few months, then only during dry periods. Established plants are

Spray dormant oil in early spring to control oystershell scale.

drought tolerant. Feed every other spring with plant food, such as Miracle-Gro. Avoid overfertilizing. Prune out any dead, broken, or diseased branches or stems at any time of year. This shrub responds well to heavy pruning for a more dense appearance. Begin pruning hedge plants in the second year and do annual shaping after that. Prune lightly for an informal look, more severely for a tighter appearance.
PROPAGATION: Take softwood or hardwood cuttings anytime. Sow seeds in fall. Self-sown seedlings can be invasive.
PESTS AND DISEASES: Oystershell scale can be a problem, especially in warm climates. Spray plants with dormant oil in early spring before new growth emerges. Deer and rabbits like the foliage and new stems, although their feeding does not kill plants.
RELATED SPECIES: European euonymus (*E. europaeus*) is more upright, reaching 30' in height. It has attractive pink fruits that open to display an orange center in fall. Japanese euonymus (*E. japonicus*) is only reliably hardy in Zones 7–9. It is stiffer in appearance and more prone to disease and insects.

PEARL BUSH

Exochorda racemosa *ex-oh-CORE-duh ray-see-MOH-suh*

Pearl bush is covered with white flowers in spring.

ZONES: 4–8
SIZE: 10–15'h × 10–15'w
TYPE: Deciduous shrub
FORM: Irregular
TEXTURE: Medium
GROWTH: Medium

LIGHT: Sun to light shade
MOISTURE: Even
SOIL: Well drained
FEATURES: Flowers
USES: Border
FLOWERS: □
FALL COLOR: ■

SITING: This attractive shrub is easy to grow and requires minimal maintenance. It has a pleasing upright form. It is covered with large, pearl-like white buds that burst into bloom, covering the plant with bright white flowers in spring. It blooms for a fairly long time. Underplant it with yellow daffodils or red tulips for a stunning spring show. The green foliage remains clean throughout the summer but is rather nondescript, so plants are best used with other shrubs that offer summer interest. Leaves can take on a yellowish-brown color in fall, but it is not considered showy. Mature plants have peeling, birchlike bark that is attractive in late fall and winter. Plants do not self-sow. Plants in colder areas may experience some winterkill. This shrub develops its best form and bloom in full sun. It does not require protection from wind, but it needs soil that drains freely.

CARE: Transplant bare-root plants in spring as early as possible. Plant container-grown and balled-and-burlapped plants in spring or early fall. Keep the soil evenly moist from spring until the ground freezes in fall. Consistent watering is especially important during the first 2 years. Plants can withstand some dry spells once mature. Feed every spring with plant food, such as Miracle-Gro. Sprinkle granules around the base of each plant and water well. Or give plants an annual application of an organic equivalent such as fish emulsion or compost. Remove dead, diseased, or broken stems at any time of year. To control the height or shape, prune just after flowering so as not to reduce next year's bloom. Plants can become unkempt as they age and may require severe pruning and shaping to bring them back to a desirable form.

PROPAGATION: Cuttings are difficult to root. Seeds of the species can be sown outside in fall; germination is sporadic.

PESTS AND DISEASES: Plants in heavy soil may experience root rot. Amend clay soils with organic matter or Miracle-Gro Garden Soil before planting.

RELATED SPECIES: *E. ×micrantha* is a hybrid of *E. racemosa* and *E. korolkowii* that demonstrates prolific bloom. 'The Bride' grows 3–4' tall and is wider, with a somewhat weeping habit. It is less cold hardy. *E. serratifolia* 'Northern Pearl' is a more upright selection of Korean pearl bush, with larger, showier flowers in groups of eight to twelve. It is hardier than other selections, surviving temperatures down to –30°F.

EUROPEAN BEECH

Fagus sylvatica *FAY-guss sill-VAH-tih-kuh*

European beech has outstanding fall color.

ZONES: (4)5–7
SIZE: 55'h × 40'w
TYPE: Deciduous tree
FORM: Oval
TEXTURE: Medium
GROWTH: Slow to medium
LIGHT: Sun to light shade

MOISTURE: Medium to high
SOIL: Deep, rich
FEATURES: Gray bark, glossy green leaves
USES: Specimen, accent
FLOWERS: ■
FALL COLOR: ■■

SITING: European beech is a magnificent long-lived tree highly valued for its smooth gray bark and attractive glossy green leaves that turn golden bronze in fall. Leaves persist into winter. Use it as a specimen or an accent in large yards. It also makes a good hedge because it can withstand heavy pruning. The shallow root system and dense shade make it difficult to grow grass and other plants under mature trees. It is not tolerant of salt or pollution and should not be planted near streets. Grow it in protected sites in Zone 4. It prefers moist, well-drained, acid soil in full sun but will tolerate light shade and a wide range of soils. It does not like wet soils.

Install a temporary barrier to protect trees from construction damage.

CARE: Mulch around plants to protect the bark from lawn mowers and string trimmers. Water young trees when the top 2" of soil has dried out. Avoid overfeeding, which results in succulent growth that is attractive to aphids. Prune young trees in summer to establish a straight, upright trunk. The shallow, wide root system does not like compacted soils and is easily damaged by heavy construction vehicles. Protect large trees by installing temporary fencing or some other type of barrier.

PROPAGATION: Stratify seeds for 3–5 months or sow in fall. Cuttings are difficult to root.

PESTS AND DISEASES: Aphids can be a problem on young trees during hot, dry periods, but they do not do serious damage.

RELATED SPECIES: 'Asplenifolia' has fernlike foliage. 'Pendula' has weeping branches. 'Riversii' has purple foliage into summer. 'Atropunicea', also sold as 'Purpurea', has young leaves that are a deep black-red changing to purple-green as they age. American beech (*F. grandifolia*) has lighter gray bark and larger leaves and is slightly hardier.

BORDER FORSYTHIA

Forsythia ×intermedia *for-SITH-ee-uh in-ter-MEE-dee-uh*

The showy yellow flowers of forsythia signal spring's arrival.

ZONES: (4)5–8(9)
SIZE: : 8–10'h × 10–12'w
TYPE: Deciduous shrub
FORM: Arching
TEXTURE: Medium
GROWTH: Fast
LIGHT: Sun

MOISTURE: Low to medium
SOIL: Well drained
FEATURES: Flowers
USES: Specimen, border, hedge
FLOWERS: ■
FALL COLOR: ■ ■ ■

SITING: Forsythia is one of the earliest-blooming shrubs, and its cheery yellow flowers are a welcome sight in spring. An evergreen background or dark fence will set off the flowers nicely. Plant scilla, dwarf iris, and other spring bulbs under forsythia for additional color. Branches can be forced for even earlier bloom indoors. Some varieties have fall color ranging from yellow to purplish. Shrubs flower on old wood, and flower buds are not as hardy as stems, so cold-climate gardeners should plant only the hardiest types and plan on annual pruning to get good bloom. 'Northern Sun', 'Meadowlark', and 'Northern Gold' are good choices.

Flower buds are often killed back in cold winters, but stem growth may be normal.

CARE: Plant bare-root plants as early as possible in spring. Container plants can be planted throughout the growing season if given ample water. Forsythia will grow and bloom best in full sun. Keep the soil evenly moist from spring until the ground freezes.
PROPAGATION: Dig suckers in early spring and replant immediately. Take softwood cuttings from early spring to midsummer. Layer in fall.
PESTS AND DISEASES: None are serious.

Prune plants right after flowering to improve shape.

DWARF FOTHERGILLA

Fothergilla gardenii *faw-ther-GIL-luh gar-DEE-nee-ey*

Fall color of dwarf fothergilla, also known as dwarf witch-alder, is often bright orange.

ZONES: 5–8(9)
SIZE: 2–3'h × 2–3'w
TYPE: Deciduous shrub
FORM: Rounded
TEXTURE: Medium
GROWTH: Slow
LIGHT: Sun to light shade
MOISTURE: Moderate

SOIL: Acid, well drained
FEATURES: Flowers, fall color
USES: Shrub border, woodland, foundation
FLOWERS: □
FALL COLOR: ■

SITING: Dwarf fothergilla is an attractive shrub for small spaces. It is covered with fragrant white flowers in April and early May. Fall color is a brilliant yellow to orange to scarlet. Use it in foundation plantings, in mixed borders, and in masses where you can enjoy the fragrant spring flowers and fall foliage. It does especially well with rhododendrons and other acid-loving plants. It can be pruned into a small hedge. It may grow in protected sites in Zone 4. This shrub does best in part shade. It needs acid, cool soil and will not tolerate wet or alkaline soils.
CARE: Amend the soil with peat moss or ammonium sulfate before planting to

Maintain necessary soil acidity by regular use of an acid fertilizer.

provide the necessary acid conditions. Plant into moist, well-drained soil high in organic material. Water well during dry periods. Apply a 2–4" layer of organic mulch such as pine needles, shredded oak leaves, or shredded pine bark to keep the soil evenly moist and maintain soil acidity. Feed every spring with an acid plant food such as Miracle-Gro Shake 'n Feed Azalea, Camellia, Rhododendron. Occasionally thin older branches. Plants spread slowly from suckers.
PROPAGATION: Sow seeds in summer. Take cuttings in summer and leave rooted cuttings undisturbed until the following year. Layer in fall.
PESTS AND DISEASES: None are serious.
RELATED SPECIES: 'Blue Mist' leaves are an attractive blue-green, especially in light shade. The tradeoff for this unique color appears to be less cold hardiness, and fall color that is inferior to other forms. 'Mt. Airy' has dark blue-green foliage and consistent fall color and can grow to 5' in height. Large fothergilla *(F. major)* is a larger pyramidal or rounded plant growing to 9' in height. Fragrant flowers smell like honey and attract bees and butterflies.

FRANKLIN TREE

Franklinia alatamaha *frank-LIN-ee-uh al-ah-TAH-mah-ha*

Franklin tree flowers resemble camellia blossoms.

ZONES: 5–8(9)
SIZE: 18'h × 12'w
TYPE: Deciduous tree
FORM: Upright
TEXTURE: Medium
GROWTH: Medium
LIGHT: Sun to light shade

MOISTURE: High
SOIL: Acid, well drained
FEATURES: Flowers, fall color
USES: Specimen
FLOWERS: □
FALL COLOR: ■ ■ ■

SITING: This unique small tree or large shrub is not the easiest plant to grow, but its spectacular ornamental value makes it worth the effort. The most striking feature is the flowers, which appear in summer and continue until fall. The showy slightly fragrant white flowers have a yellow center and resemble single camellias. Plants are upright and spreading. The lower branches are often leafless, giving the plant an open, airy appearance. Lustrous dark green leaves in summer change to orange, red, even purple in fall. They hold onto the tree into winter. Flowers are followed by curious woody capsules that ripen over the course of the next year, so by the time the flowers open, last year's seeds have begun to shed farther down. Place it near a patio or courtyard. It can be used as a background shrub for smaller-blooming shrubs such as viburnum, spirea, and azalea. It thrives in southern New England and parts of the Midwest and mid-Atlantic but cannot be grown anywhere in its native area for long due to a root pathogen that inhabits soils in the Southeast. It does well in gardens once it is established, but it is slow to get going. In Zone 5 it needs a sheltered location and protection for the first few years; it starts slowly in spring and has trouble cycling down for winter. Established trees will suffer winterkill when temperatures drop below about –10°F, but sprouts grow back quickly below the killed part. It requires moist, acid, well-drained soil rich in organic matter. It can grow in light shade, but the best flowering and fall color is in full sun.

CARE: Franklin tree is somewhat difficult to transplant because of its sparsely fibrous root system. Move it while it is still a small container or balled-and-burlapped specimen. Provide even moisture throughout the growing season. If rainfall is insufficient, give plants an inch of water weekly. Apply a 2–4" layer of organic mulch such as pine needles, shredded pine bark, or wood chips to help maintain even moisture and acidify soil. Fertilize each spring with an acid plant food such as Miracle-Gro Shake 'n Feed Azalea, Camellia, Rhododendron.

PROPAGATION: Sow seeds as soon as the fruit has matured; avoid letting the seeds dry out. Best germination occurs after 30 days of cold stratification. Take cuttings in summer.

PESTS AND DISEASES: This tree is susceptible to phytophthora root rot. Water and fertilize infected trees to help them fight off this killing disease.

GREEN ASH

Fraxinus pennsylvanica *FRAK-sih-nus pen-sil-VAY-nih-kuh*

Green ash is a common shade tree. It is also known as red ash.

ZONES: (2)3–9
SIZE: 60'h × 40'w
TYPE: Deciduous tree
FORM: Upright
TEXTURE: Medium
GROWTH: Fast
LIGHT: Sun

MOISTURE: Moderate
SOIL: Well drained
FEATURES: Fast growth, good form
USES: Street, shade
FLOWERS: ■
FALL COLOR: ■

SITING: This tree adapts to many sites, where it offers quick shade. It grows where many other shade trees won't. Use it for framing, shade, and backyard corner plantings. It grows best in moist, well-drained soils but tolerates dry, compacted soils and street conditions. Its adaptability has led to its overuse and to many problems, which can eventually kill trees. Choose this tree only if there is no other tree suitable for your site.

CARE: Green ash transplants readily, usually balled-and-burlapped but also from containers. Water young trees until they are established. Older trees under stress will benefit from supplemental watering. Trees stressed by any of this plant's many pest problems will benefit from root feeding in spring. Leaf drop and seed litter can be heavy; seedless cultivars are available. Prune only to maintain shape.

PROPAGATION: Seeds require warm stratification for 60 days followed by 120 days at cooler temperatures.

PESTS AND DISEASES: Problems include ash borer, oystershell scale, ash flower gall, ash yellows, and ash plant bug. Many of these lead to premature leaf and flower drop, creating a mess on lawns and decks. In the past decade or so, many seemingly healthy ash trees have died rather quickly. This affliction has come to be known as ash decline and is thought to be a lethal combination of environmental stresses and insect and disease problems

RELATED SPECIES: White ash (*F. americana*) is not as hardy (Zone 4) and has the pest problems that plague green ash. Trees usually have good purple fall color.

Ash flower gall can be an unsightly problem.

CAPE JASMINE
Gardenia jasminoides (augusta) gar-DEE-nee-uh jazz-min-OYE-deez (aw-GUS-tuh)

Waxy gardenia flowers have exquisite form, and are very fragrant.

ZONES: (7)8–10
SIZE: 4–6'h × 4–6'w
TYPE: Evergreen shrub
FORM: Rounded
TEXTURE: Medium
GROWTH: Medium
LIGHT: Sun to light shade

MOISTURE: High
SOIL: Acid
FEATURES: Fragrant flowers
USES: Foundation, specimen, container
FLOWERS: □
FALL COLOR: ■

SITING: This fragrant shrub is suitable only for the warmest areas of the country. The single, semidouble, or double white flowers appear in early to midsummer and open over a long period. They have a waxy texture and become yellowish as they age. Leaves are lustrous dark green, leathery in texture, and blend into the landscape nicely after the flowers fade. They hold their green color in winter. Protect plants from hot afternoon sun and winter winds. Site plants near a patio or deck or under a window where you can enjoy the scent. It needs acid, moist, well-drained soil high in organic matter. It adapts well to container culture and makes a good greenhouse plant in colder climates. Flower buds are injured at –3°F.

CARE: Cape jasmine is easily transplanted in spring from containers. Amend the soil with peat moss and ammonium sulfate before planting. Water regularly to keep the soil evenly moist. An organic, acid mulch of pine needles or shredded pine bark will help maintain soil moisture. Feed every 3–4 weeks with an acid plant food such as Miracle-Gro Shake 'n Feed Azalea, Camellia, Rhododendron. Cut untidy plants back in early spring after flowering; pruning sooner removes flower buds. Avoid damaging plants with gardening tools. These wounds are a common entry point for diseases such as stem canker.

PROPAGATION: Take softwood cuttings in summer. Seeds can be sown after ripening but may take 2–3 years to germinate.

PESTS AND DISEASES: Common diseases include powdery mildew and canker. Insects include aphids, scale, whiteflies, thrips, mealybugs, and mites. Regular hard sprays with a garden hose will help minor infestations; plants with severe infestations should be sprayed with insecticidal soap.

RELATED SPECIES: 'Mystery' and 'Aimee' have larger flowers, up to 5" in diameter. 'Radicans' is a smaller-leaved, almost creeping version with smaller flowers. 'Radicans Variegata' is a variegated form of 'Radicans'. 'Veitchii' is a good choice for containers. 'Kleim's Hardy' is hardier than most selections, rated for Zone 7. 'Prostrata' (trailing gardenia) reaches a height of 2–3" and can spread 4–6'. This plant has an open, horizontal branching habit that makes it an attractive ground cover. It does not grow into a shrub, as does the species. White gardenia (*G. thunbergia*) is an upright shrub to 15' tall. It bears fragrant, single, tubular creamy white flowers in winter and spring. It is hardy only in Zones 10 and 11.

GINKGO
Ginkgo biloba GING-koh bye-LOH-buh

Ginkgo, also known as maidenhair tree, has brilliant yellow fall color.

ZONES: 4–8(9)
SIZE: 70'h × 35'w
TYPE: Deciduous tree
FORM: Upright
TEXTURE: Medium
GROWTH: Slow to medium

LIGHT: Sun
MOISTURE: Even
SOIL: Well drained
FEATURES: Fall color
USES: Shade, specimen
FLOWERS: ■
FALL COLOR: ▨

SITING: Ginkgo is a picturesque tree at maturity, grown for its shade, large size, and bold accent in the landscape. It has an upright columnar, sparsely branched, and open growth habit in youth, usually becoming upright oval to upright spreading with maturity. It prefers sandy, deep, moderately moist soil but grows in almost any full-sun situation. It is adaptable to poor soils, compacted soils, soils of various pH, heat, drought, winter salt spray, and air pollution. It is sometimes incorrectly planted as a street tree due to its extreme urban tolerance, but it is too big for this use. The fan-shaped leaves are medium green with a petiole that is up to 3" long; this shape and the elongated petiole cause the foliage to flutter in the slightest breeze. Fall color is usually chartreuse but may be golden yellow. A freeze will cause the leaves to drop almost overnight, even if they are still green. The fruit is a naked seed, tan to orangish in color and plumlike in shape. The fleshy covering on the seed makes the fallen fruit extremely messy and smelly. For this reason only male trees should be planted. This species may not flower (and therefore also may not fruit) until it is about 20 years old. Use ginkgo for difficult situations in large landscapes.

CARE: It transplants easily and establishes itself without difficulty. Mulch with 2–4" of shredded bark, wood chips, or compost to keep the soil evenly moist, especially while trees are young. Water young trees until they are established. Annual applications of plant food, such as Miracle-Gro, along with supplemental watering will lead to faster growth on young trees. Prune in spring to remove broken branches or to shape only if necessary.

PROPAGATION: Take cuttings of male trees in summer. Collect seeds in midfall and sow outdoors. (You will not be able to determine a tree's sex until it matures when grown from seed.)

PESTS AND DISEASES: None are serious. Leaf spotting can be seen in some years.

RELATED SPECIES: No other species exist in the genus *Ginkgo*, but numerous selections of cultivars with improved landscape characteristics have been made. 'Autumn Gold' is a male selection with a good spreading habit and bright golden fall color. 'Fastigiata' has a columnar habit. 'Laciniata' has deeply incised leaves. 'Pendula' has somewhat weeping or pendulous branches. 'Princeton Sentry' is a nearly columnar male form, slightly wider at the base. Use it architecturally for a vertical accent.

THORNLESS HONEYLOCUST

Gleditsia triacanthos var. *inermis*   gleb-DIT-see-ub try-ub-CAN-thuss ee-NER-mus

Spring color of 'Sunburst' is golden yellow.

ZONES: 4–9
SIZE: 60'h × 45'w
TYPE: Deciduous tree
FORM: Spreading
TEXTURE: Medium to fine
GROWTH: Fast

LIGHT: Sun
MOISTURE: Dry to moist
SOIL: Any
FEATURES: Foliage
USES: Shade
FLOWERS: ■
FALL COLOR: ■

SITING: Use thornless honeylocust as a shade or specimen tree. Its extremely fine-textured, filtered shade is rare in large trees. It permits shade-tolerant turfgrass and part-shade perennials to grow underneath. Fall color is normally chartreuse but is a beautiful golden-yellow in good years. Most thornless cultivars have little fruit set; some occasionally have an abundance of the twisting pods up to 18" long. They contain many hard seeds. The young bark is smooth, tan-olive to gray-olive, and rather thin. Trees prefer moist, deep soil in full sun but are adaptable to adverse conditions. Established trees tolerate heat, drought, poor soils, soils of various pH, soil compaction, flooding, and winter salt spray.
CARE: Thornless honeylocust is somewhat sensitive to being transplanted in autumn, and care should be taken to amend the soil. Water thoroughly and mulch

Protect thin trunks with hardware cloth.

adequately to enhance survival chances. Young trees should be wrapped and surrounded by mulch to protect the thin bark from damage. Water young trees until they are established. Older trees under stress will benefit from supplemental watering. Trees stressed by any of this plant's many pest problems will benefit from root feeding in spring. Fruits drop in late autumn or throughout the winter and can cause a litter problem.
PROPAGATION: Cultivars are propagated primarily by buds grafted onto seedling rootstock; the thorny species form is easily propagated by seeds.
PESTS AND DISEASES: This tree is susceptible to several cosmetic foliage problems (including leaf spot and spider mites), as well as some serious diseases (trunk, bark, and twig cankers) and insects (foliage webworms and trunk borers).
RELATED SPECIES: 'Imperial' is a compact cultivar, maturing at 30' tall by 30' wide, with dense shade. 'Sunburst' has new growth that emerges lemon yellow in spring. 'Shademaster' and 'Skyline' are other popular cultivars.

KENTUCKY COFFEE TREE

Gymnocladus dioica   jim-NO-klay-dus dye-oh-EYE-kuh

Blue-green Kentucky coffee tree leaves cast light shade.

ZONES: (3)4–8
SIZE: 65'h × 45'w
TYPE: Deciduous tree
FORM: Rounded
TEXTURE: Medium
GROWTH: Slow to medium

LIGHT: Sun
MOISTURE: Medium to high
SOIL: Deep, rich
FEATURES: Foliage
USES: Shade
FLOWERS: □
FALL COLOR: ■ ■

SITING: Kentucky coffee tree is suitable as a shade or specimen tree. It is a good replacement for the disease-prone honeylocust. Its remarkably large, compound leaves cast a light shade that permits shade-tolerant turfgrass and part-shade

Reddish-brown seedpods open to reveal dark brown seeds.

perennials to grow underneath. The leaves orient themselves parallel to the sun's rays and are an attractive dark green or blue-green. Trees are late to leaf out in spring. Fall color is inconsistent, sometimes a good yellow. Female trees produce fragrant flowers in spring followed by seeds in chunky, leathery dark reddish-brown pods. This tree prefers deep, moist, rich soil for best growth but is adaptable to many soils and is tolerant of drought, pollution, and high soil pH. It is slow to become established. The coarse branching of mature trees is picturesque in winter.
CARE: Kentucky coffee tree is difficult to transplant because of the deep taproot. Plant smaller balled-and-burlapped or container-grown specimens in early spring. Water young trees when the top 2" of soil has dried. Prune to shape young trees in late winter or early spring. Pull occasional root suckers. The large compound leaves and fruits may be a litter problem when they fall. Some people consider the persistent fruits to be ornamental in winter.
PROPAGATION: Sow seeds in place in fall. Scarification will enhance germination.
PESTS AND DISEASES: None are serious.
RELATED SPECIES: 'Espresso' is a fruitless male selection with upward-arching branches in a vaselike form. Prairie Titan® is upright spreading with good summer leaf color and interesting winter form.

CAROLINA SILVERBELL

Halesia tetraptera *hah-LEE-zee-uh teh-trup-TARE-uh*

Carolina silverbell is an attractive spring-blooming small tree for woodland's edge.

ZONES: 5–8(9)
SIZE: 35'h × 25'w
TYPE: Deciduous tree
FORM: Pyramidal
TEXTURE: Medium
GROWTH: Medium
LIGHT: Sun to light shade

MOISTURE: High
SOIL: Rich, moist
FEATURES: Flowers
USES: Specimen, woodland
FLOWERS: ☐ ■
FALL COLOR: ■ ■

SITING: Site this tree where you can enjoy the clusters of bell-shaped white flowers in late spring. Use it as a specimen near a patio, or plant it in groups to naturalize at a woodland's edge. It combines well with rhododendrons and other acid-loving plants. A background of evergreens or a dark fence will set off the flowers nicely. Fruits remain attractive in winter. It is not urban tolerant, especially to heat, drought, and poor soils, and may develop chlorotic foliage in alkaline soils. It can be used as a disease-free alternative to flowering dogwood and crabapples as an ornamental tree with white midspring flowers.

Showy clusters of white flowers in late spring dangle from branches.

CARE: Plant container-grown specimens in spring. Balled-and-burlapped trees are difficult to establish. Plant in full sun to partial shade in moist, well-drained soil that has been amended with peat moss or ammonium sulfate. Trees require an evenly moist soil throughout the growing season, right up until the ground freezes. Apply a 2–4" layer of pine needles or shredded pine bark to maintain soil moisture and soil acidity. Trees will benefit from an annual spring application of an acid plant food such as Miracle-Gro Shake 'n Feed Azalea, Camellia, Rhododendron. Prune after flowering if desired.

PROPAGATION: Seeds can take up to 2 years to germinate. Trees can also be started from sprouts from stumps.

PESTS AND DISEASES: None are serious.

RELATED SPECIES: 'Rosea' and 'Arnold's Pink' have pink flowers. 'Meehanii' is an unusual form that is more shrublike, growing to only 12' tall. The numerous white flowers are smaller than the species and the leaves are coarser and more wrinkled. 'Silver Splash' and 'Variegata' have green leaves streaked and splashed with white or yellow.

HYBRID WITCH HAZEL

Hamamelis ×intermedia *ham-a-MEAL-is in-ter-MEE-dee-uh*

Hybrid witch hazel is among the earliest blooming shrubs.

ZONES: 5–8
SIZE: 18'h × 12'w
TYPE: Deciduous shrub
FORM: Upright spreading
TEXTURE: Medium
GROWTH: Slow
LIGHT: Sun to light shade

MOISTURE: Moderate
SOIL: Acid
FEATURES: Flowers
USES: Woodland, shrub border, specimen
FLOWERS: ■ ■
FALL COLOR: ■ ■

SITING: Witch hazel blooms from late January into mid-March depending on the cultivar and location. Flower color ranges from yellow to copper. The distinct fruity fragrance is most noticeable on still, sunny days. Most plants have good fall leaf color in the yellow to orange to red range. Take advantage of these plants' shade tolerance and locate them near a wood's edge or under taller shade trees. A background of evergreens or a dark fence will set off the flowers nicely. Cut branches make good additions to indoor arrangements. Witch hazel likes fertile, moisture-retentive soil and does not like extremes of wet soil or dry sites. Plants can grow in full sun or partial shade, but flowering is best in full sun.

Root prune before planting to enhance root development.

CARE: Keep the soil evenly moist from spring until the ground freezes in fall. Apply a 2–4" layer of shredded pine bark or pine needles around each plant. Feed every spring with plant food, such as Miracle-Gro. Prune in late winter to remove dead or crossing branches or to improve the shape.

PROPAGATION: Suckers can be dug and replanted; avoid damaging the parent plant's root system. Take cuttings from late April to the end of May. Layer in late summer. Sow seeds outdoors in summer.

PESTS AND DISEASES: None are serious. Powdery mildew is sometimes seen during wet weather.

RELATED SPECIES: 'Arnold Promise' is free flowering with yellow flowers and good reddish fall color. 'Feuerzauber' has excellent coppery orange-red flowers and orange-yellow fall color. Vernal witch hazel (*H. vernalis*) is hardy into Zone 4. It suckers freely and will form a thicket in time. Common witch hazel (*H. virginiana*) blooms in fall; the flowers can be hidden by the brilliant yellow fall foliage. It is hardy to Zone 3. Chinese witch hazel (*H. mollis*) has fragrant yellow flowers.

SEVEN-SON FLOWER

Heptacodium miconioides *hep-tuh-KOH-dee-um mih-koh-nee-OYE-deez*

Fragrant white flowers appear on Seven-son flower in late summer.

ZONES: 5–8
SIZE: 20'h × 8–15'w
TYPE: Deciduous shrub
FORM: Upright
TEXTURE: Medium
GROWTH: Medium
LIGHT: Sun to light shade

MOISTURE: Medium to high
SOIL: Acid soil
FEATURES: Flowers, fruits, bark
USES: Border, specimen
FLOWERS: □
FALL COLOR: ■

SITING: The exfoliating bark of this deciduous shrub peels in thin strips to reveal a cinnamon brown color. Early autumn brings the showy, fragrant creamy white clusters of seven flowers each produced in terminal panicles. Late autumn replaces blooms with small, rounded fruits, each topped with a persistent cherry-red or purple calyx. This shrub is an excellent addition to the landscape in late summer and fall when little else is flowering. Use it as a specimen or in the shrub border. It functions best where the flowers can be observed against a dark background. It can

Keep the soil evenly moist from spring until winter arrives to prevent drought stress.

be trained as a small tree. It does best in moist, well-drained soil and full sun but will grow with partial shade.
CARE: Keep the soil evenly moist from spring until the ground freezes in fall. These shrubs are not drought tolerant and require irrigation during dry spells. Apply a 2–4" layer of organic mulch such as shredded bark, wood chips, or pine needles around each plant to retain soil moisture. Feed each spring with plant food, such as Miracle-Gro, or an organic equivalent such as fish emulsion. Sprinkle at the base of each plant and water well. Prune in late winter to remove winter-killed or crossing branches or to improve the shape. In exposed situations prune off leaves that have been tattered by wind.
PROPAGATION: Seeds require 5 months of warm temperatures followed by 3 months of cold.
PESTS AND DISEASES: No serious insect problems, but canker disease can cause dieback of branches and sometimes even death. Avoid injuring stems and keep plants well watered to avoid problems. Plants in northern areas can be injured by late freezes.

ROSE-OF-SHARON

Hibiscus syriacus *hih-BISS-kuss see-ree-AYE-kuss*

Rose-of-Sharon has showy flowers that resemble hibiscus. It is also known as shrub althea or althea.

ZONES: 5–8(9)
SIZE: 8–12'h × 6–10'w
TYPE: Deciduous shrub
FORM: Upright
TEXTURE: Medium
GROWTH: Medium

LIGHT: Sun to light shade
MOISTURE: Even
SOIL: Well drained
FEATURES: Flowers
USES: Border
FLOWERS: □ ■ ■
FALL COLOR: ■

SITING: Rose-of-Sharon is valued for large flowers produced in summer. Flower color ranges from white to red or purple. Use it in groupings, masses, and shrub borders. With aggressive regular pruning, it can

Prune back to two or three buds in late spring to get larger flowers.

be trained into a small specimen tree. Self-sown seedlings can be a problem, and this species has demonstrated an invasive tendency in the Northeast. It is best to plant one of the cultivars with low seed production.
CARE: Plant in spring or fall in deep, moist, well-drained soil in full sun. Even young, vigorous plants can be winter-killed; protect from wind and do not feed after midsummer. Keep the soil evenly moist from spring until the ground freezes in fall. These shrubs are not drought tolerant and require irrigation during dry spells.

Apply a 2–4" layer of organic mulch such as shredded bark, wood chips, or pine needles around each plant to retain soil moisture. Feed each spring with plant food, such as Miracle-Gro, or an organic equivalent such as fish emulsion. Prune plants back hard in late winter or early spring to get good flowering.
PROPAGATION: Take cuttings during summer. Layer in spring or sow from seed.
PESTS AND DISEASES: Leaf spots, blights, canker, rust, aphids, Japanese beetles, scale, and whiteflies can plague this plant. Aphids and whiteflies can be dislodged with a strong spray of a garden hose or insecticidal soap. Control Japanese beetles by knocking them into a bucket of soapy water.
RELATED SPECIES: 'Diana' is a dwarf variety with ruffled clear white flowers. 'Blue Bird' has light violet-blue flowers. 'Minerva' has a dark red eyespot and lavender petals tinged pink. Chinese hibiscus (*H. rosa-sinensis*) is reliably hardy to Zone 9 but is often grown as an annual or greenhouse plant in colder climates. The flowers are very showy in shades of white, yellow, pink, orange, and red.

SEA BUCKTHORN
Hippophae rhamnoides *HIH-puh-fay-ee ram-NOY-deez*

The grayish foliage sets off common sea buckthorn berries.

ZONES: 4–7
SIZE: 8–12'h × 10–20'w
TYPE: Deciduous shrub or tree
FORM: Spreading
TEXTURE: Medium to fine
GROWTH: Medium
LIGHT: Sun
MOISTURE: Low
SOIL: Sandy
FEATURES: Foliage, fruits
USES: Border, massing, coast
FLOWERS: □
FALL COLOR: ■

SITING: This large shrub or small tree has a spreading, rounded crown that becomes loose and open. It has silvery-green leaves that turn grayish green in fall. The yellowish flowers in spring are not showy, but the egg-shaped orange fruits that follow are striking. They are set off by the gray-green foliage and persist through the winter. Other desirable traits are this shrub's good cold hardiness as well as tolerance for dry soils and salt spray. With regular pruning, it can be trained into a single- or multitrunked small tree. The plant is dioecious, so both male and female plants must be grown to obtain fruit production. The sex of the seedlings cannot be differentiated until the plants are 3–4 years old, whereas the sex of clones is known when they are propagated by tissue culture or cuttings. This plant prefers deep, well-drained, sandy soil with ample organic matter but will grow in many soils once established. It does best at pH 6–7. It can withstand drought once established, but not wet or poorly drained soils. It can also tolerate moderate salinity.

CARE: Sea buckthorn is somewhat difficult to establish, so use care when selecting a planting site. Plant container-grown specimens in spring in full sun. Water until plants are established. After that, this plant is drought tolerant. It can fix atmospheric nitrogen, so it needs no additional fertilizer. Plants grown as small trees need regular pruning to maintain the single trunk. Remove suckers depending on the landscape situation.

PROPAGATION: Seeds require stratification for 90 days, but seedlings are often difficult to grow. Cuttings are difficult to root. Plants can be layered, and the suckers that grow around the base of plants can be dug and replanted.

PESTS AND DISEASES: None are serious.
RELATED SPECIES: 'Leikora' is a heavy-fruiting female offered by some specialty nurseries. 'Pollmix' is a male form useful as a pollinator for female clones. One 'Pollmix' can pollinate up to six female plants. 'Sprite' is a male cultivar notable for its dense, compact habit to 2–5' tall and wide. It makes an interesting silver-gray hedge, especially in seaside locations.

BIG-LEAF HYDRANGEA
Hydrangea macrophylla *bye-DRAN-juh mak-row-FILL-uh*

Showy clusters of blue flowers develop in late summer on big-leaf hydrangea.

ZONES: (5)6–9
SIZE: 3–10'h × 3–10'w
TYPE: Deciduous shrub
FORM: Rounded
TEXTURE: Medium to coarse
GROWTH: Fast
LIGHT: Sun to light shade
MOISTURE: Moderate
SOIL: Well drained
FEATURES: Flowers
USES: Specimen, border
FLOWERS: ■ ■ □
FALL COLOR: ■ ■

SITING: Large, showy blue, pink, or purple flowers appear in late summer. Plants can be rather coarse looking when they are not in flower, so plant them in the shrub border where other plants can add interest earlier in the season. They also work well as foundation plants, especially on the east or north side of buildings. Hydrangeas make good cut flowers, both fresh and dried. Plants prefer full sun and moist, rich, well-drained soil high in organic matter.

CARE: The soil pH affects the plants' uptake of aluminum, which determines whether the flowers are pink or blue. For pink flowers, apply lime to decrease soil acidity. For bluer flowers, provide extra acidity in the form of aluminum sulfate or peat moss. Mature plants can be stressed if allowed to wilt during dry periods. A 2–4" layer of organic mulch will help maintain

Panicle hydrangea is a hardier type of hydrangea that blooms on new wood.

Amend soil to adjust soil pH and determine flower color of big-leaf hydrangea.

Cut hydrangea flower heads in late summer for dried arrangements.

BIG-LEAF HYDRANGEA
continued

soil moisture. Feed once in mid-June with plant food, such as Miracle-Gro. If you want blue flowers, use an acid plant food such as Miracle-Gro Shake 'n Feed Azalea, Camellia, Rhododendron. Prune after flowering to remove flower heads; plants bloom on the previous year's growth.

PROPAGATION: Layer in summer. Take cuttings in midsummer. Sow seeds in fall; named varieties will not come true from seed.

PESTS AND DISEASES: Leaf miners can burrow into the leaves and produce brown or tan patches, but their damage is mainly cosmetic.

RELATED SPECIES: Smooth hydrangea (*H. arborescens*) is hardy in Zone 4. The large white flower clusters appear in late summer. Plants bloom on new wood, so they can be cut back to the ground in late winter and grown as a herbaceous perennial. Panicle hydrangea (*H. paniculata*) has smaller flowers but blooms earlier on new wood. It is hardy in Zone 4. Oak-leaf hydrangea (*H. quercifolia*) has large, oaklike leaves that turn rich red in fall. Flowers start out white, changing to pink then brown.

1 Smooth hydrangea blooms on new wood and can be treated as an herbaceous perennial, cutting it back to ground level.

2 Cut plants to the ground in early spring before growth begins.

3 New growth that sprouts from the cut stems will bloom later in the summer.

4 New shoots develop showy white flowers in late summer.

SHRUBBY ST. JOHNSWORT
Hypericum prolificum hye-PEAR-ih-kum pro-LIH-fih-kum

Both the flowers and fruits of shrubby St. Johnswort are ornamental.

ZONES: 4–8
SIZE: 1–4'h × 1–4'w
TYPE: Deciduous shrub
FORM: Rounded
TEXTURE: Medium to fine
GROWTH: Slow
LIGHT: Sun to light shade

MOISTURE: Low
SOIL: Well drained
FEATURES: Flowers
USES: Border, massing, rock garden
FLOWERS: ▇
FALL COLOR: ▇

SITING: Plant this dense, rounded shrub where you can enjoy the bright yellow flowers, which first appear in mid-June and continue through August. The flowers are a pollen source for bees. Place this shrub at the front of a shrub border, massed, in foundation plantings, or even in perennial beds and rock gardens. The foliage is an attractive dark bluish-green in summer. The fruit is a dried capsule that persists into winter and can be used in dried arrangements. This plant grows best in full sun and light, well-drained soil, although it tolerates dry conditions and can even grow in gravelly or rocky soils.

CARE: Transplant container-grown plants in spring or fall. Water regularly the first year until the deep roots establish themselves. Mature plants are drought tolerant. Prune in late spring after new growth hardens.

Plants self-seed, and seedlings may need to be pulled from nearby gardens.

PROPAGATION: Take cuttings in summer. Sow seeds as soon as they are ripe.

PESTS AND DISEASES: None serious. Root rot and wilt can be significant problems in hot and humid climates. Improve drainage in heavy soils by adding organic matter.

RELATED SPECIES: Golden St. Johnswort (*H. frondosum*) is a bit more refined with handsome bluish-green leaves. 'Sunburst' grows 3–4' tall and makes a lovely mass plant. This species is reliably hardy only to Zone 5. It can be evergreen in warmer climates.

1 Take cuttings in late summer.

2 Cuttings root readily in a loose soilless mix.

MESERVE HOLLY

Ilex ×*meserveae* EYE-lex me-SERV-eye-ee

Bright red berries are set off nicely by evergreen foliage.

ZONES: (4)5–8
SIZE: 8–12'h × 8–12'w
TYPE: Evergreen shrub
FORM: Rounded
TEXTURE: Medium
GROWTH: Slow
LIGHT: Sun to light shade

MOISTURE: Even
SOIL: Acid
FEATURES: Shiny leaves, fruits
USES: Specimen, foundation, massing
FLOWERS: ☐
FALL COLOR: ■

SITING: This group of hybrids is the best of the evergreen hollies for colder climates. Fruits are bright red and shiny in fall and can be quite showy. They attract robins, bluebirds, catbirds, and mockingbirds.

Plant one male plant for every three to five female plants to ensure good pollination and fruit set. The best fruiting is in full sun, but plants will grow in light shade. They prefer a moist, slightly acid, well-drained soil but are relatively adaptable. Avoid planting in south- or west-facing exposed sites, where this plant is susceptible to winter foliage burn and summer heat stress. In northern areas plant on the north or east side of the house in a sheltered location to avoid damage from winter winds and sun. It can be used as a specimen, in foundation plantings, and as a barrier hedge, where the spiny, broadleaf

Apply an antidesiccant in late fall to reduce water loss over winter.

evergreen foliage serves as a kinder and gentler alternative to thorns.
CARE: Keep the soil evenly moist from spring until the ground freezes; never allow the plants to dry out. Feed every spring with an acid plant food such as Miracle-Gro Shake 'n Feed Azalea, Camellia, Rhododendron. Avoid pruning late in the season, which would remove flower buds for the following season. Plants are prone to winter burn in cold climates; spray with an antidesiccant in fall to reduce water loss from leaves.
PROPAGATION: Propagate by rooted stem cuttings.
PESTS AND DISEASES: None are serious. Iron chlorosis may develop if the soil is too alkaline.
RELATED SPECIES: 'Blue Boy' is a male suitable for use as a pollinator. 'Blue Girl' is a 15'-tall female plant with good fruiting. 'Blue Prince' has an excellent dense, compact habit to 12' tall with shiny dark green foliage of good quality. It is an excellent pollinator and a handsome, easily pruned landscape plant. 'Blue Princess' has dark blue-green foliage. The fruit is darker red than others.

AMERICAN HOLLY

Ilex opaca EYE-lex oh-PAH-kuh

American holly is a tree-type evergreen holly that produces red berries.

ZONES: 5–9
SIZE: 45'h × 18–40'w
TYPE: Evergreen tree
FORM: Pyramidal
TEXTURE: Medium
GROWTH: Slow to medium

LIGHT: Sun to light shade
MOISTURE: Even
SOIL: Acid
FEATURES: Fruits
USES: Specimen, groupings, hedge
FLOWERS: ☐
FALL COLOR: ■

SITING: The most attractive asset of this plant is its showy red fruits. It prefers fertile, moist, loose, acid, well-drained soil in part shade or full sun. Plants grow denser in sun. Avoid planting in extremely

dry, windy, unprotected places, which can cause winter burn and summer heat stress. To ensure fruit set, plant one male for every two or three female plants.
CARE: Keep the soil evenly moist from spring until the ground freezes. Feed annually with acid plant food to keep plants green and vigorous. Lack of nitrogen can lead to yellow leaves. Prune as needed to shape in winter.
PROPAGATION: Take cuttings anytime.
PESTS AND DISEASES: Leaf miners result in brown or tan patches on the leaves. Spray

a labelled insecticide in spring as leaves form. Remove and destroy affected leaves.
RELATED SPECIES: English holly (*I. aquifolium*) has glossy, spiny leaves and is better suited to the West Coast. Chinese holly (*I. cornuta*) grows 8–10' tall and is hardy in Zones 7-9. Japanese holly (*I. crenata*) is a dense, twiggy evergreen with small, spinefree leaves and black fruits. Inkberry (*I. glabra*) has smaller, rounded leaves and small black fruits. Longstalk holly (*I. pedunculosa*) has better leaf color but is more difficult to find.

Some cultivars of American holly develop orange fruits that persist through winter.

Check the plant label to make sure you get male and female holly plants.

WINTERBERRY

Ilex verticillata EYE-lex ver-tih-sih-LAY-tah

Common winterberry, also known as coralberry, Michigan holly, or swamp holly, is a deciduous holly for colder climates.

ZONES: 3–9
SIZE: 6–10'h × 6–10'w
TYPE: Deciduous shrub
FORM: Oval
TEXTURE: Medium
GROWTH: Slow
LIGHT: Sun to light shade

MOISTURE: Medium to high
SOIL: Moist, acid
FEATURES: Fruits
USES: Border, wet sites
FLOWERS: ☐
FALL COLOR: ■

SITING: From late fall through winter, winterberry produces an outstanding display of bright red berries, which persist on the branches even after the leaves have fallen. Berries are produced only on female plants. Plant one male plant in close proximity to three to five female plants to ensure good pollination and subsequent fruit set. To add eye-catching color to a winter landscape, plant winterberry in groupings or mixed among other plants that lack winter interest. The red berries contrast nicely against background snow. The best performance is in full sun in acid, organically enriched, moist to wet soils, but it is somewhat adaptable to soils that are occasionally dry. Chlorosis and stunting occur in alkaline soils.

CARE: Female plants sited in relatively dry soils will have better berry size with irrigation during dry periods in July and August. Young plants will grow faster with annual applications of an acid plant food.

PROPAGATION: Propagate cultivars by stem cuttings taken in early summer. The species spreads by seeds or suckers. Seeds possess a dormancy, making germination tricky.

PESTS AND DISEASES: Occasional leaf spot and powdery mildew rarely cause disfiguring. Plants may develop chlorosis in high-pH soils.

RELATED SPECIES: Male plants need to be carefully matched with female plants. If little or no fruit production occurs year after year in a large landscape planting, plant an early male and a late male close by. 'Afterglow' features glossy green leaves that are smaller than typical and large orange-red berries maturing to orange. It is best pollinated with 'Jim Dandy'. 'Aurantiaca' produces orange-red fruits that fade to orange-yellow. It blooms early; pollinate with 'Jim Dandy'. 'Chrysocarpa' is a naturally occurring yellow-fruited form. 'Cacapon' is heavy fruiting, with true red fruit; the leaves are textured and dark green and glossy. Use 'Jim Dandy' as a pollinator. 'Jim Dandy' is a slow-growing, early-flowering dwarf male useful as a pollinator for early-flowering females. 'Red Sprite' is a popular dwarf female clone maturing at only 3–4' tall. Early blooms produce numerous, large red fruits that persist well into winter. Use 'Jim Dandy' to pollinate. 'Sparkleberry' reaches 12' tall and can become somewhat leggy at the base due to its upright growth habit. The main attraction is the abundant red fruits that are medium size and persist often until spring.

YAUPON

Ilex vomitoria EYE-lex vom-ih-TOH-ree-uh

Yaupon holly is a good broadleaf evergreen choice for southern landscapes.

ZONES: 7–10
SIZE: 18'h × 12'w
TYPE: Evergreen shrub
FORM: Irregular
TEXTURE: Medium to fine
GROWTH: Medium to fast
LIGHT: Sun to light shade

MOISTURE: Low to medium
SOIL: Well drained
FEATURES: Fruits, evergreen foliage
USES: Screening, hedge, foundation
FLOWERS: ☐
FALL COLOR: ■

SITING: Yaupon is among the best small-leaved evergreen hollies for southern landscapes. It is a tough, adaptable plant with dark evergreen leaves and bright red berries. Male and female flowers are borne on separate plants, so plant both male and female types if you want berries. Female flowers are followed by small bright red berries that persist through fall and winter. The bark is smooth and gray and is often mottled with yellow-green patches of lichen. Yaupon holly is commonly grown as a trimmed hedge, screen, or windbreak. Dwarf varieties are perfect for foundation plantings, and their drought and disease resistance make them ideal for low-maintenance landscapes. Use in natural plantings and whenever possible to provide food and shelter for wildlife. The berries are an important source of food for birds and other wildlife in late winter. Yaupon holly's fast growth rate and small leaves make it a perfect choice for topiary. It tolerates drought, salt, and wet soils. It grows in full sun to shade, but plants are more compact with denser foliage when grown in sun.

CARE: Easily transplanted in spring or at almost any time of year. Water new plants weekly; mature plants are drought tolerant. Prune to maintain a certain form. Plants can become weedy as birds disperse the seeds far and wide.

PROPAGATION: Propagate by seed or dig suckers. For selected varieties propagate by cuttings to preserve desirable attributes. Cuttings may be difficult to root.

PESTS AND DISEASES: Leaf miners and mites can be problems, especially on dwarf cultivars.

RELATED SPECIES: 'Nana' (dwarf yaupon holly) is a symmetrical, dense, rounded form that requires only infrequent pruning to maintain its 4–6' height and spread. Unpruned plants will eventually grow 7–10' tall and slightly wider. It is ideal as a low-growing foundation plant and as a tall ground cover for a large-scale commercial or industrial landscape. It can be sheared into a formal hedge or topiary shapes. It is often "meatballed" into a globe. The small gray-green leaves have no spines, and this cultivar of a female plant rarely produces berries. Burford Chinese holly (*I. cornuta* 'Burfordii') is a large shrub or small tree to 20' tall. It is hardy in Zones 7–9. It bears red fruits even without pollination. Japanese holly (*I. crenata*) produces black fruits on shrubs 5–10' tall in Zones 5–7.

FLORIDA ANISE-TREE

Illicium floridanum ih-LISS-ee-um flor-ih-DAY-num

Attractive red flowers and shiny foliage are assets on this shrub.

ZONES: (6)7–9
SIZE: 6–10'h × 5–8'w
TYPE: Evergreen shrub
FORM: Upright
TEXTURE: Medium
GROWTH: Medium
LIGHT: Shade

MOISTURE: Medium to high
SOIL: Well drained
FEATURES: Fragrance
USES: Border, shade
FLOWERS: ■
FALL COLOR: ■

SITING: Florida anise-tree is a broadleaf evergreen shrub or small tree. Branches droop to the ground, giving a rounded, open canopy in the shade. When crushed, leaves emit a characteristic aniselike odor, obnoxious to some but pleasant to others. The flowers are attractive but tend to be overlooked in the lush, shiny foliage. When ripe, the shiny, jewel-like seeds literally explode out of the papery star-shaped fruits. Plants prefer moist, well-drained soil high in organic matter and part to heavy shade. In full sun, leaves are light green and not as handsome as on shade-grown plants. This is a good shrub for providing a pleasing shade of green in

Add organic matter to soil before planting.

shady, moist areas in southern states. It is resistant to deer and rabbit feeding. It is perfect for natural settings but can be pruned into dense hedges or windbreaks. Cultivar selection is important in Zone 6 for best winter survival. This plant is toxic; do not ingest any part.

CARE: Plant container-grown specimens in fall. Amend the soil with generous amounts of organic matter before planting. Water during prolonged dry spells, because it has a tendency to wilt. Plants grown in full sun require a lot of additional water. An organic mulch of pine needles, shredded bark, or wood chips will help maintain soil moisture. Annual applications of organic matter will provide all the required nutrients.

PROPAGATION: Seeds germinate readily and may become weedy. Take cuttings in late summer.

PESTS AND DISEASES: None are serious. The volatile oils in the leaves and stems protect Florida anise-tree from insects and browsing mammals.

RELATED SPECIES: Yellow anise (*I. parviflorum*) has small yellow-green flowers in late spring and does not have the fragrance of Florida anise-tree, but adapts better to drier, sunnier sites.

VIRGINIA SWEETSPIRE

Itea virginica eye-TEE-ah vir-JIN-i-kuh

Bottle-brush white flowers adorn plants in early summer.

ZONES: (5)6–9
SIZE: 3–5'h × 5–8'w
TYPE: Deciduous shrub
FORM: Arching
TEXTURE: Medium
GROWTH: Medium
LIGHT: Sun to shade
MOISTURE: Medium to moist

SOIL: Moist, neutral
FEATURES: Flowers, fall color
USES: Naturalizing, woodland shrub border
FLOWERS: □
FALL COLOR: ■ ■ ▢

SITING: Virginia sweetspire is a small to medium-size, deciduous to semievergreen ornamental shrub with an upright, rounded growth habit. Fall color is crimson burgundy in full sun and a mixture of green, yellow, orange, and scarlet in partial sun to full shade. Flowers bloom from mid-June into early July; they are held upright, horizontal, or curving and are pendulous and somewhat bottlebrush-like in appearance. They are nectar sources for butterflies and other insects. Fruits are small capsules, green changing to brown, not necessarily showy but are winter persistent. This plant prefers moist, rich, slightly acid soils in partial sun to partial shade but is highly adaptable to neutral or alkaline soils and average fertility. Use it as a specimen or border, foundation or group planting. It will develop colonies and easily naturalizes. The species can be lanky and weak-stemmed, but 'Henry's Garnet' and other named selections are better suited to landscape use.

CARE: Transplant container-grown specimens in spring or fall. It requires constant soil moisture. Apply a 2–4" layer of organic mulch such as wood chips, shredded bark, or pine needles to maintain soil moisture. It grows faster with annual applications of plant food, such as Miracle-Gro. Suckers may need to be pulled if the plant is grown in landscape situations.

PROPAGATION: Take softwood cuttings in summer. Sow seed or separate and plant root suckers in spring.

PESTS AND DISEASES: None are serious.

RELATED SPECIES: The species form is rarely available, but the cultivar 'Henry's Garnet' is available. It is noted for its compact growth habit (to 3' tall by 4' wide), reddish-purple first-year twigs, and slightly zigzag basal stems that often do not branch. The showier, pendulous white inflorescences are 3–6" long. Vibrant, shiny burgundy-purple to garnet fall color develops in late October, peaks throughout November, and extends into early December. Leaves slowly drop in northern climates, but it is semievergreen in southern climates. Other available cultivars include 'Little Henry', which is more compact; 'Saturnalia', which is more heat tolerant; and 'Shirley's Compact', a dwarf form.

ENGLISH WALNUT

Juglans regia *JUG-lans REE-jee-uh*

English walnut is a medium-size tree with a spreading crown.

ZONES: (5)6–9
SIZE: 60'h × 50'w
TYPE: Deciduous tree
FORM: Spreading
TEXTURE: Medium
GROWTH: Medium to slow

LIGHT: Sun to light shade
MOISTURE: Even
SOIL: Well drained
FEATURES: Nuts
USES: Shade, specimen
FLOWERS: ■
FALL COLOR: ■ ■

SITING: This tree is commonly grown in warmer areas of the country for its edible nuts. The 1½–2" nuts are easy to shell. This tree can also be grown for its shade. There is some yellow fall color, but many trees lose their leaves while they are still green, especially in dry conditions. It prefers deep, dry, light, loamy soil and does not do well in wet or poor subsoil areas.

CARE: Transplant small plants in spring. Water newly planted trees the first 2 years until established. After that, trees are drought tolerant. Feed young trees with plant food, such as Miracle-Gro, in spring to encourage growth. Prune young trees that require shaping in summer or fall to avoid bleeding sap, which occurs in spring. Nuts can become a lawn litter problem when they fall.

Grow sensitive plants in containers under black walnuts to avoid soil contact.

PROPAGATION: Sow nuts in fall in place.
PESTS AND DISEASES: None are serious.
RELATED SPECIES: Black walnut (*J. nigra*) is a native species that is widespread in the United States; it is hardy to Zone 4. It grows 50–75' tall. It develops an extensive taproot and is difficult to transplant. The nuts are popular with people, squirrels, and wildlife. Black walnuts contain a chemical known as juglone. The greatest quantities are found in the area immediately under the walnut tree, where roots are concentrated and decaying nut hulls and leaves accumulate. It kills or inhibits the growth of many other plants. Symptoms range from stunting, yellowing, partial to total wilting, to complete death. Tomatoes and potatoes are very sensitive to juglone. Other species known to be affected include rhododendron, white pine, white birch, eggplant, pepper, lilac, cotoneaster, and privet. Plants known not be to affected by juglone include Kentucky bluegrass, forsythia, most maples, ferns, pachysandra, most viburnums, daffodils, daylilies, winged euonymus, snap beans, corn, and onions.

CHINESE JUNIPER

Juniperus chinensis *joo-NIH-per-us chih-NEN-sis*

Junipers are excellent landscape plants suitable for many situations.

ZONES: 4–9
SIZE: 50–60'h × 15–20'w
TYPE: Evergreen tree or shrub
FORM: Pyramidal to spreading
TEXTURE: Medium
GROWTH: Slow to medium

LIGHT: Sun to light shade
MOISTURE: Dry to moist
SOIL: Well drained
FEATURES: Foliage
USES: Specimen, foundation, ground cover, hedge
FLOWERS: ■
FALL COLOR: ■

SITING: Junipers come in a wide variety of shapes and sizes making them suitable for many landscape situations, including specimens, mass plantings, hedges, foundation plantings, and ground covers. They do best in full sun; foliage is sparser in shade. They prefer moist, well-drained soil but tolerate dry soils once established. Keep them away from areas near road salt, which can cause winter drying. Avoid planting them right under drip lines; falling snow can damage branches.

CARE: Water well until the plants are established; then junipers prefer to be on the dry side. Water well at the end of the growing season so plants go into winter with ample soil moisture. Feed every spring with acid plant food such as

'Saybrook Gold' has an upright pyramidal growth habit.

Prune individual branches to maintain a nonsculpted form.

Miracle-Gro Shake 'n Feed Azalea, Camellia, Rhododendron. Trim large, spreading junipers annually in early summer to keep them the right size and shape; try to maintain their natural growth habit.
PROPAGATION: Root from softwood or hardwood cuttings taken from stem tips.
PESTS AND DISEASES: Bagworms can defoliate plants. Remove and destroy all "bags" as soon as you see them. Spider mites can be a problem in hot, dry weather. Spray the foliage forcefully with water each day or use a miticide in severe cases. Juniper blight shows up during wet springs. Snip off the diseased portions.
RELATED SPECIES: Common juniper (*J. communis*) grows 5–10' in height and is hardy to Zone 2. Shore juniper (*J. conferta*) is a low ground cover especially adapted for planting on sand dunes near the seashore in Zones 6–9. Creeping juniper (*J. horizontalis*) has pendulous stems 1–2' long that turn purplish in fall. Japanese garden juniper (*J. procumbens*) grows 8–12" tall and makes a good ground cover. Savin juniper (*J. sabina*) is a 4–6' spreading shrub with especially aromatic leaves. It is hardy in Zone 3.

ROCKY MOUNTAIN JUNIPER

Juniperus scopulorum *joo-NIH-per-us skop-you-LORE-um*

Rocky Mountain juniper is a pyramidal tree-form juniper. It is also known as Colorado red cedar.

ZONES: 3–7
SIZE: 35'h × 3–15'w
TYPE: Evergreen tree
FORM: Pyramidal
TEXTURE: Medium
GROWTH: Slow
LIGHT: Sun to light shade

MOISTURE: Medium to low
SOIL: Well drained
FEATURES: Foliage
USES: Screen, hedge, background, foundation
FLOWERS: ■
FALL COLOR: ■

SITING: Rocky Mountain juniper has a rich blue and silver coloration to its leaves that is attractive in the landscape, especially in winter. Some plants have glaucous dark blue berries. It prefers well-drained soil in full sun and tolerates dry soils once established. It can be used for hedges, screening, backgrounds, and in foundation plantings on tough sites.

CARE: Water well until the plants are established, then allow to grow on the dry side. Water well at the end of the growing season so plants go into winter with ample soil moisture. Feed every spring with acid plant food such as Miracle-Gro Shake 'n Feed Azalea, Camellia, Rhododendron. Regular feeding encourages faster growth and enhances the foliage color. Trim annually in early summer to keep the

Remove the bright orange cedar-apple rust galls to reduce reinfection.

plants the right size and shape; try to maintain their natural growth habit.

PROPAGATION: Root from softwood or hardwood cuttings taken from stem tips.

PESTS AND DISEASES: Cedar-apple rust is a disease that results in galls about 1" in diameter. If left on the tree, they form strange-looking orange horns the following spring. Snip off any portion of a branch or stem with a gall on it. Bagworms can defoliate plants. Remove and destroy all "bags" as soon as you see them. Spider mites can be a problem in hot, dry weather. Spray the foliage forcefully with water each day or use a miticide in severe cases. Juniper blight shows up during wet springs. Snip off the diseased portions.

RELATED SPECIES: Single-seed juniper (*J. squamata*) is a 2'-tall shrub that forms a blue cushion of foliage. Use it in foundation plantings or in a rock garden. It does not form berries and is resistant to juniper blight. Eastern red cedar (*J. virginiana*) has sharp, needlelike foliage and peeling brownish-red bark. It is a durable, adaptable tree or large shrub but somewhat coarse; it is best used in natural landscapes.

MOUNTAIN LAUREL

Kalmia latifolia *KAL-mee-uh la-tih-FOH-lee-uh*

Showy flowers cover plants in the right conditions.

ZONES: 5–9
SIZE: 7–15'h × 7–15'w
TYPE: Evergreen shrub
FORM: Rounded
TEXTURE: Medium
GROWTH: Slow
LIGHT: Sun to light shade

MOISTURE: Moderate
SOIL: Acid
FEATURES: Flowers, shade
USES: Foundation, shrub border, wood
FLOWERS: □ ■ ■
FALL COLOR: ■

SITING: This broadleaf evergreen requires a well-aerated, acid soil similar to that preferred by rhododendrons and azaleas. Some exposure to sun is required for proper flower color development of red and pink cultivars. The showy flowers open in late spring or early summer. Breeding has produced red-budded, cinnamon-banded, pure white, and deep pink and red forms. Foliage is dark green and glossy above; in full sun it can be yellow-green. Use mountain laurel in foundation plantings, on partially shaded sites and for naturalizing. It requires cool, moist acid organic soil and partial shade to full sun. Avoid windswept sites and heavy high-pH soils. Foliar burn may occur on exposed sites. Protect from winter sun and wind in northern climates.

Remove flowers after they finish blooming.

CARE: Amend soil with peat moss, sulfur, or iron sulfate to increase soil acidity. Transplant container-grown plants in spring or fall. Supply consistent moisture if rainfall is not adequate. Mulch to help maintain soil moisture and keep the shallow roots cool. Feed every spring with an acid plant food such as Miracle-Gro Shake 'n Feed Azalea, Camellia, Rhododendron. Remove flowers after they finish blooming.

PROPAGATION: Sow seeds in early spring. Take cuttings in late summer.

PESTS AND DISEASES: Lace bugs can cause speckling on leaves. Leaf spot can be troublesome on nonresistant cultivars. Avoid damaging plants with sharp gardening tools; these wounds are common entry points for borers.

RELATED SPECIES: 'Bullseye' has white flowers with a purple band. 'Elf' is a dwarf cultivar with pink buds opening to pale pink flowers. 'Ostbo Red' has deep red buds followed by light pink flowers that deepen the longer they are open. 'Raspberry Glow' has burgundy-red buds that open to pink flowers. 'Sarah' is a compact grower with red buds that open to pinkish-red flowers.

JAPANESE KERRIA

Kerria japonica CARE-ee-uh juh-PON-ih-kuh

Bright yellow flowers appear in spring on Japanese kerria, also known as Japanese rose or kerria.

ZONES: 5–9
SIZE: 3–6'h × 6–9'w
TYPE: Deciduous shrub
FORM: Upright
TEXTURE: Fine
GROWTH: Slow to medium
LIGHT: Sun to light shade

MOISTURE: Even
SOIL: Well drained
FEATURES: Flowers, winter stems
USES: Specimen, shrub border
FLOWERS: ■
FALL COLOR: ■■

SITING: Japanese kerria is a fine-textured deciduous shrub with thin green stems. The bright yellow flowers appear in late April and May, with sporadic bloom after the primary blooming. In sun the flowers fade to a bleached color. Leaves hold late into fall, sometimes turning yellow. The shrub has distinct bright kelly green stems in winter that add to the winter landscape. Use in the shrub border or as a foundation plant. It suckers freely and can colonize areas. It does best in loamy, well-drained soil in part shade. It grows in Zone 4 in areas with good snow cover, but there will be some dieback. Reduce winter damage

Prune out dead branches to keep plants neat and in good bloom.

by planting in a protected area with well-drained soil.

CARE: Transplant balled-and-burlapped or container-grown plants in early spring. Maintain an even water supply throughout the growing season. If fertility levels are too high, plants become weedy with fewer flowers. Plants that are cut back to the ground should be fertilized with plant food, such as Miracle-Gro, or mulched with compost or rotted manure. Prune dead branches, which are inevitable. Prune to shape right after flowering; it flowers on the previous year's growth. Periodic rejuvenation by cutting plants to the ground can be beneficial.

PROPAGATION: Take cuttings in summer or fall. Divide clumps in fall.

PESTS AND DISEASES: None are serious. Leaf spot and twig blight can show up, but the damage is purely cosmetic.

RELATED SPECIES: 'Pleniflora' has ball-shaped double flowers. 'Variegata' has single flowers, and leaves deeply margined in white. 'Shannon' has larger blooms that appear earlier than the species. 'Golden Guinea' has single flowers. 'Kin Kan' stems turn yellow in winter and have thin green stripes.

GOLDEN RAIN TREE

Koelreuteria paniculata kohl-roo-TEER-ee-uh pan-ick-yoo-LAY-tuh

Golden rain tree, also known as panicled golden rain tree or varnish tree has showy yellow summer flowers.

ZONES: 5–9
SIZE: 30–40'h × 30–40'w
TYPE: Deciduous tree
FORM: Rounded
TEXTURE: Medium
GROWTH: Medium to fast

LIGHT: Sun
MOISTURE: Adaptable
SOIL: Well drained
FEATURES: Flowers
USES: Specimen
FLOWERS: ■
FALL COLOR: ■

SITING: Golden rain tree is grown for its midsummer flowers, urban tolerance, and attractive rounded growth habit. In early July, bright yellow flowers form foot-long showy clusters. They are set off nicely by the green foliage. The flowers are followed by clusters of three-sided lime-colored pods that turn brown and resemble Chinese lanterns. They persist through the winter and into the following spring. Foliage is bright green in summer, changing to yellow or golden yellow in fall but not reliably every year. This small, single-trunked or multitrunked tree quickly loses its central leaders to yield an asymmetrical or irregular growth habit in youth, becoming rounded with age. Use it as a specimen, a small shade tree near a deck or patio, a focal point, or a street tree. It performs best in full sun in moist, rich, deep, well-drained soils but is adaptable to poor soils, compacted soils, various soil pH, pollution, heat, drought, and urban stress in general. Young trees (especially those recently transplanted) may exhibit dieback or be marginally hardy in harsh winters, especially in Zone 5, but established trees are much hardier.

CARE: Plant balled-and-burlapped or container-grown plants in spring. Golden rain tree is extremely sensitive to being transplanted in autumn. If transplanting cannot be delayed until spring, amend the soil, fertilize, water thoroughly, mulch adequately, and avoid winter salt spray to enhance survival chances during the first winter. Water newly planted trees well and water as needed for 2–3 years after planting. Young trees will grow faster with a spring application of plant food, such as Miracle-Gro. Prune in winter only to shape the tree. It is weak wooded and may drop branches after a storm.

PROPAGATION: Sow seeds in fall or take root cuttings in early winter.

PESTS AND DISEASES: Trunk canker is an occasional problem.

RELATED SPECIES: 'Apiculata' has finely divided leaves. 'Fastigiata' has a narrow columnar form. 'Rose Lantern' seedpods are flushed with pink. 'September' flowers about 5 weeks later than the species and has especially large flower clusters. Bougainvillea golden rain tree (*K. bipinnata*) is similar but later blooming. It is reliably hardy in Zones 7–10.

BEAUTYBUSH
Kolkwitzia amabilis *kohl-KWIT-zee-uh uh-MAHB-uh-lis*

Beautybush has abundant showy flowers in spring.

ZONES: 5–8
SIZE: 6–10'h × 5–8'w
TYPE: Deciduous shrub
FORM: Upright arching
TEXTURE: Medium
GROWTH: Fast

LIGHT: Sun
MOISTURE: Even
SOIL: Well drained
FEATURES: Flowers
USES: Specimen, massing
FLOWERS: ■
FALL COLOR: ■ ■

SITING: This large, deciduous shrub has an upright arching habit and a multistemmed fountain shape. The showy, bell-shaped, yellow-throated pink flowers appear in May in clusters along the stems. Fruits are bristly capsules that persist into winter but aren't very ornamental. This shrub is best planted alone as a specimen to show off the flowers, even though it is showy only when it is in bloom. It can be grown in groups, but individual plants require a good deal of room for full development. The shrub tolerates pruning and may be

Beautybush can be renewal pruned. Cut stems back in early spring.

used in hedges, although much of the flowering effect and arching, branching habit is lost. It has a coarse winter appearance and can become leggy as it ages. It prefers well-drained soil and full sun.

CARE: Balled-and-burlapped plants transplant easily. Water well after planting and as needed for 2–3 years after planting. Give newly planted shrubs or shrubs that have been cut back by renewal pruning a spring application of plant food, such as Miracle-Gro. To prevent established plants from becoming leggy and bare of lower growth, annually prune to the base about a third of the old shoots. Older shrubs that have become leggy (with leaves and flowers only toward the top of the plant) can withstand renewal pruning. Simply cut all the branches to a couple of inches above the ground.

PROPAGATION: Softwood cuttings root readily in early summer. Sow seeds as soon as they are ripe.

PESTS AND DISEASES: None are serious.

RELATED SPECIES: 'Pink Cloud' is offered by specialty nurseries. It features bright pink blooms that are larger and more abundant than the species.

GOLDEN CHAIN TREE
Laburnum ×watereri *luh-BER-num wah-TER-er-eye*

Golden chain tree is named for its striking yellow flower chains.

ZONES: 5–7
SIZE: 12–15'h × 9–12'w
TYPE: Deciduous tree
FORM: Upright oval
TEXTURE: Medium to fine
GROWTH: Medium
LIGHT: Sun to light shade

MOISTURE: Moderate
SOIL: Well drained
FEATURES: Flowers
USES: Shrub border, foundation, groupings
FLOWERS: ■
FALL COLOR: ■

SITING: Golden chain tree is striking in spring when the pendulous yellow flower chains, which can be 6–10" long, hang from the branches. This small tree is dense and upright with green stems. Leaves are trifoliate, each leaflet somewhat elliptic and bright green. Fruit pods are noticeable in fall but are not very attractive. This is a short-lived tree in the East and Midwest and is not especially well-suited to the South where nighttime temperatures are too high. It prefers moist, well-drained soil; although adaptable to many situations, it prefers light shade in the hot part of the day and tolerates high-pH soils. It does not like standing water, and cold injury can be a problem. Use it in the shrub border or at corners of buildings. It is effective when planted in groups of three and five against a background of large evergreens. All parts of this tree are poisonous, but especially the fruit, causing vomiting, drowsiness, weakness, sweating, pallor, and headaches. Avoid planting it close to a sidewalk where children might pick up the fruit. Choose a spot where the olive green bark can be appreciated from indoors in winter. It can be trained over a pergola at the entrance to a garden. It can also be espaliered against a wall or fence.

CARE: Transplant balled-and-burlapped or container-grown plants in spring. Water well after planting and as needed for 2–3 years after planting. Young trees will grow faster with a spring application of plant food, such as Miracle-Gro. Prune after flowering to remove unwanted or crowded shoots. Some specimens may need pruning of basal suckers and lower branches to maintain a tree form.

PROPAGATION: Allow pods to dry on the plant; break open to collect the seeds. Sow seeds in fall; they germinate better if scarified before planting. Take leaf bud cuttings in early summer.

PESTS AND DISEASES: Leaf spot, aphids, and mealybugs can affect this plant. Twig blight can occasionally become serious. Prune out infected branches and clean up fallen leaves to reduce disease overwintering sites.

RELATED SPECIES: 'Aureum' has golden-yellow leaves. 'Involutum' has curled leaves. 'Pendulum' is a slow-growing, weeping form. 'Quercifolium' has lobed leaves. 'Vossii' has longer flower clusters and a denser habit.

CRAPE MYRTLE

Lagerstroemia indica *lah-ger-STREE-mee-uh IN-dih-kuh*

Crape myrtle has showy summer blooms.

ZONES: (6)7–9
SIZE: 15–25'h × 12–20'w
TYPE: Deciduous shrub or tree
FORM: Rounded
TEXTURE: Medium
GROWTH: Fast
LIGHT: Sun

MOISTURE: Medium to high
SOIL: Well drained
FEATURES: Flowers, bark
USES: Specimen, shrub border, hedge
FLOWERS: ☐ ■ ■ ■
FALL COLOR: ■ ■ ■

SITING: Crape myrtle makes a handsome small specimen tree with showy flowers, good fall color, and interesting bark. The curiously crinkled, showy flowers appear in terminal clusters in mid- to late summer.

The bark is smooth and gray, exfoliating to expose various-colored under-bark. The dark green summer foliage usually turns yellow orange or red in fall. Crape myrtle is best suited for southern gardens, where the climate is hot and sunny. It prefers moist, well-drained soil and full sun. At temperatures below −10°F, the plant dies back to the ground and grows as an herbaceous perennial.

CARE: Water newly planted trees as needed in their first 2–3 years. Mature specimens are somewhat drought tolerant but require watering in dry summers. Feed plants with plant food, such as Miracle-Gro, each spring. Prune in early spring, shortening the previous year's shoots by one-half to one-third of their length. Cutting off old flower heads in summer can promote a second and third round of flowering. Remove suckers to maintain the plant as a tree with distinct trunks. It reseeds prolifically.

PROPAGATION: Take cuttings in late spring to early summer.

PESTS AND DISEASES: Diseases include powdery mildew, black spot, and leaf spots. Sufficient space between plants increases air circulation and reduces powdery mildew. Plant mildew-resistant cultivars and destroy fallen foliage to reduce diseases. Insect pests include aphids, Japanese beetles, and scale. Crape myrtles are a magnet for aphids, upon whose excrement sooty mold grows. This can give the leaves a gray coating that is not harmful but is unsightly.

RELATED SPECIES: 'Catawba' has dark purple flowers and orange-red fall color and is mildew resistant. 'Centennial' was

Cut back stems in early spring to encourage better flowering.

selected for its small size and bright purple flowers. 'Natchez' has white flowers and cinnamon-brown bark. 'Watermelon Red' has vivid red flowers and golden fall color.

LARCH

Larix decidua *LARE-icks deh-SID-yew-uh*

Common larch, also known as European larch, is best reserved for large sites.

ZONES: (3)4–6(7)
SIZE: 70–75'h × 25–30'w
TYPE: Deciduous tree
FORM: Pyramidal
TEXTURE: Medium to fine
GROWTH: Medium to fast
LIGHT: Sun to light shade
MOISTURE: Medium to high
SOIL: Moist
FEATURES: Foliage
USES: Specimen, groupings
FLOWERS: ■
FALL COLOR: ■

SITING: This large, deciduous conifer is effective in large landscapes as a specimen or in groupings. Needles turn a showy golden yellow before they drop in late fall, and new spring growth is bright green. Larch prefers cool, moist conditions in full sun to light shade. It does not tolerate dry,

alkaline soils or air pollution. It is best used in areas with cool summers and cold winters. It casts light shade and can be underplanted with acid-loving wildflowers and shrubs.

CARE: Acidify soil with ammonium sulfate or peat moss before planting. Transplant when dormant (late fall or winter) into moist soil. Water young trees as needed to maintain moist soil during the growing season and into winter. Water older trees during dry periods. Apply an organic mulch of pine needles or shredded pine

Larch case-bearer can be a serious problem.

bark to help maintain soil moisture. Give young trees annual applications of acid plant food such as Miracle-Gro Shake 'n Feed Azalea, Camellia, Rhododendron. Mature trees should not require feeding unless they are seriously stressed by a pest. Prune in winter to shape if necessary. Dropped branches and cones can be a litter problem on lawns.

PROPAGATION: Sow seeds when ripe.

PESTS AND DISEASES: Larch case-bearer is a serious insect pest. It appears in spring and eats its way into needles, causing them to turn brown. Early and timely spraying of an appropriate insecticide may be needed to control severe infestations. Trees are also susceptible to cankers, leaf cast, needle rusts, larch sawfly, and gypsy moth.

RELATED SPECIES: 'Fastigiata' is a columnar form. 'Pendula' represents a group of cultivars whose branches have a distinct pendulous nature. Japanese larch (*L. kaempferi*) has bluish foliage. It is tolerant of drier soil and is more resistant to canker. Tamarack (*L. laricina*) is very hardy into Zone 1, but it is less tolerant of cultivated settings. It tolerates wet or even boggy soils.

BAY LAUREL
Laurus nobilis *LAWR-rus NOE-bill-is*

Bay laurel is an evergreen shrub with aromatic leaves.

ZONES: 8–10
SIZE: 3–10'h × 3–8'w
TYPE: Evergreen shrub
FORM: Pyramidal
TEXTURE: Medium
GROWTH: Slow
LIGHT: Light shade to sun

MOISTURE: Medium to high
SOIL: Moist
FEATURES: Leaves
USES: Woodland, specimen, hedge, container
FLOWERS: ■ ■
FALL COLOR: ■

SITING: Bay laurel is a pyramidal tree or large shrub with aromatic, evergreen leaves and shiny gray bark. It sometimes produces suckers from the base. Its leathery, thick, shiny dark green leaves can easily be pruned and clipped into hedges or topiary. Where hardy, grow bay laurel in a woodland garden or as a specimen; protect from cold winter winds. It is not fussy about soil but needs good drainage. It can be trained as a standard or allowed to grow as a spreading shrub. In cooler regions, grow it as a container plant and bring it indoors in winter. Bay leaves are used for flavoring soups, stews, pickling brines, sauces, marinades, and

Harvest bay laurel leaves for kitchen use.

poultry and fish dishes; remove the leaves before serving. Pick bay leaves early in the day and dry quickly under weight so they won't curl. Store in an airtight container.

CARE: Plant container-grown plants in spring or fall in full sun to partial shade. Water when dry. It thrives with frequent watering in rich, well-drained soil. Once plants are established, they can get by with less water. Feed landscape plants annually in spring with plant food, such as Miracle-Gro. Container plants need monthly or bimonthly applications of a water-soluble plant food such as Miracle-Gro. Bay laurel responds well to pruning and clipping at any time of year.

PROPAGATION: Seeds are slow to germinate and often rot before they do. Cuttings taken from semihard green tip shoots in summer will root in 6–9 months if they don't rot first.

PESTS AND DISEASES: None are serious.

RELATED SPECIES: 'Aurea' has yellowish young foliage. 'Angustifolia' (also called willow-leaf bay) has narrower leaves. 'Saratoga' has broader leaves and a more treelike habit. 'Undulata' has wavy leaf margins.

DROOPING LEUCOTHOE
Leucothoe fontanesiana *loo-KOH-tho-ee fon-ta-nee-zee-AN-uh*

Graceful, arching branches of drooping leucothoe give it a fountainlike appearance.

ZONES: 5–8
SIZE: 3–6'h × 3–6'w
TYPE: Evergreen shrub
FORM: Arching
TEXTURE: Medium
GROWTH: Slow to medium
LIGHT: Shade to light shade

MOISTURE: Medium to high
SOIL: Acid
FEATURES: Foliage, form
USES: Foundation, border, waterside
FLOWERS: □
FALL COLOR: ■

SITING: Drooping leucothoe is a graceful evergreen shrub with arching branches that give it a fountainlike appearance. New growth is light green with purplish tints and changes to a lustrous dark green in summer. Mature shrubs have a purplish winter coloration if grown in some sun. Flowers are white and fragrant, but are somewhat hidden by the foliage. This shrub prefers acid, moist, well-drained, organic soil. It will not withstand drought or drying winds. It prefers partial to full shade but will grow in full sun if not too dry. In warmer areas (Zones 7 and 8), it needs a cool, shady location. In colder parts of its range, drooping leucothoe is semideciduous.

CARE: Acidify the soil before planting by mixing in ammonium sulfate or peat moss. It transplants readily as a container plant in spring. Plants require consistently moist soil throughout their lives. Maintain a 2–4" layer of organic mulch such as shredded bark or wood chips to help conserve water. Give plants an annual spring application of acid plant food such as Miracle-Gro Shake 'n Feed Azalea, Camellia, Rhododendron. Annually prune oldest stems to the ground after flowering or rejuvenate old plants by cutting them back to the ground after flowering if they become overgrown.

PROPAGATION: Direct sow seeds when ripe. Take cuttings in late spring to early summer.

PESTS AND DISEASES: Leaf spot can be a problem, especially when plants are stressed by cultural conditions. On severely infected plants, leaves will drop and plants may die. To reduce chances of infection, clean up fallen leaves, prune to increase air circulation around plants, and cover soil with an organic mulch.

RELATED SPECIES: 'Nana' is a dwarf spreading form growing only 2' tall. 'Rainbow' has leaves variegated with pink, copper, and white.

Leaf spot can be a problem on plants stressed by cultural conditions.

JAPANESE PRIVET

Ligustrum japonicum lih-GUS-trum juh-PON-ih-kum

Japanese privet is a tough, low-maintenance shrub.

ZONES: 7–10
SIZE: 6–12'h × 6–8'w
TYPE: Evergreen shrub
FORM: Upright
TEXTURE: Medium
GROWTH: Medium
LIGHT: Sun to light shade

MOISTURE: Even
SOIL: Well drained
FEATURES: Foliage
USES: Hedge, screening, topiary
FLOWERS: □
FALL COLOR: ■

SITING: Japanese privet is a tough plant that requires little care and is extremely tolerant of a wide variety of soil conditions. Leaves are evergreen, opposite, and somewhat pear-shaped with a sharp terminal point. White flowers are borne on large terminal panicles and followed by dull black berries that persist most of the year and are a source of food for birds when other berries or food sources are scarce. This helps it to naturalize but unfortunately disperses the plant and makes it invasive. This versatile shrub can be used as a solid hedge for screening or allowed to become a small specimen tree. It is often used as a topiary.

CARE: It is easily transplanted from containers. It prefers sun to part shade in any soil except one that is constantly wet. Space hedge plants at least 5' apart. Water newly planted shrubs until established.

Use hedge clipper to maintain a nicely shaped hedge.

Mature plants are somewhat drought tolerant. Give young plants a spring application of plant food, such as Miracle-Gro, to encourage faster growth. Prune regularly to maintain desired shape and size; pruning can be done at any time. For flowers prune just after bloom in early summer.

PROPAGATION: Mature plants propagate themselves prolifically from seeds, which can also be planted in fall. Cuttings root readily.

PESTS AND DISEASES: In shade and when planted too close or in conditions that limit air circulation, whitefly and sooty mold can become problems. They can be controlled with a soap spray.

RELATED SPECIES: In Zones 4–7 grow Amur privet (*L. amurense*) which has less glossy foliage. California privet (*L. ovalifolium*) is a popular semievergreen hedge plant that is more heat tolerant. Common privet (*L. vulgare*) is a vigorous semievergreen with narrow leaves. Its susceptibility to pests has reduced its use. Golden vicary privet (*L. ×vicaryi*) has yellow leaves and is best used as a specimen rather than a hedge. It is hardy in Zone 5 and may survive in protected sites in Zone 4.

SPICEBUSH

Lindera benzoin lin-DER-uh BEN-zoe-in

Clusters of small yellow flowers cover branches of spicebush in early spring. It is also known as wild allspice.

ZONES: 5–9
SIZE: 6–12'h × 6–12'w
TYPE: Deciduous shrub
FORM: Rounded
TEXTURE: Medium
GROWTH: Slow to medium
LIGHT: Sun to light shade

MOISTURE: Medium to high
SOIL: Well drained
FEATURES: Flowers, fall foliage
USES: Border, naturalizing, watersides
FLOWERS: ■
FALL COLOR: ■

SITING: This large shrub is grown mainly for its bright yellow fall foliage. It grows as a multistemmed understory shrub in its native habitat. With its light green leaves, it tends to fade into the background in summer. In early spring clusters of small yellow flowers hug the branches, giving a burst of color to the spring woods before most other plants have leafed out. Flowers grow similar to those of forsythia but are not nearly as showy. The best fall color comes on plants grown in sun. It does best in moist, well-drained soils in full sun or part shade. Plants grown in shade and dry conditions are more open in form and the fall color is not as pronounced. Plants like consistently moist soil throughout the growing season. Fruits on female plants are brilliant scarlet red in autumn but are small and must be viewed from close range. Birds enjoy them so they disappear quickly. The plants are dioecious, so male plants must be nearby for fruits to set on female plants. The common name comes from the scent given off when the foliage or stems are bruised or crushed. This is a good shrub for naturalizing or for the border. It is an excellent choice for sites with moist soil and semishade, such as next to a stream or pond. It has been used in wetland reclamation projects in recent years. It can be grown on protected sites in Zone 4.

CARE: Spicebush can be difficult to transplant because of its coarsely fibrous roots system. It is somewhat slow to reestablish after planting. Have the soil well prepared beforehand. Water as needed if rainfall is insufficient. Apply a 2–4" layer of organic mulch such as wood chips or shredded bark to maintain moisture and keep soil cool.

PROPAGATION: Sow seeds in fall. Collected seed should be stratified for 30 days at warm temperatures followed by 3 months of cool temperatures. Cuttings of half-ripe shoots will root, but not easily.

PESTS AND DISEASES: None are serious.

RELATED SPECIES: 'Green Gold' is a nonfruiting form with large, ornamental yellow blooms. 'Rubra' is a nonfruiting form with deep red-brown blooms. 'Xanthocarpa' has orange-yellow fruits.

SWEET GUM
Liquidambar styraciflua *lih-kwihd-AM-bar sty-ruh-SIH-floo-uh*

Star-shaped leaves of American sweet gum develop excellent fall color.

ZONES: 5–9
SIZE: 60–75'h × 40–50'w
TYPE: Deciduous tree
FORM: Pyramidal
TEXTURE: Medium
GROWTH: Medium to fast

LIGHT: Sun to light shade
MOISTURE: Even
SOIL: Well drained
FEATURES: Fall color
USES: Shade
FLOWERS: ■
FALL COLOR: ■ ■ ■

SITING: Sweet gum is a large tree with star-shaped leaves that turn shades of purple, crimson, and orange in fall. The insignificant yellow-green flowers in spring are followed by golf-ball-size spiny fruits that drop throughout the winter and create a nuisance and a hazard in the landscape. This tree requires a large area to grow, but it makes a beautiful addition to a landscape when given ample space. It is not well suited for small city lots because of its size and messy fruits. It prefers moist, slightly acid soil and full sun to light shade. It does not tolerate air pollution and may suffer winter damage in the colder parts of Zone 5. Sweet gum is a favorite of yellow-bellied sapsuckers. Look for their parallel rows of little square holes in the bark.

Spiny fruits fall throughout the winter and can be messy.

CARE: Transplant balled-and-burlapped or container-grown plants in spring. Plants take a while to reestablish after planting. Leaves may be smaller the first season after transplanting. Make sure new transplants receive an inch of water per week the first two seasons after planting. Mature trees are drought tolerant. Give young and newly transplanted trees a spring application of acid plant food such as Miracle-Gro Shake 'n Feed Azalea, Camellia, Rhododendron. Prune in early winter only if necessary to shape young trees or to remove dead wood. The 1½" round spiny fruits drop over an extended period during fall and winter.
PROPAGATION: Sow seeds in fall. Take cuttings from semihardwood in summer.
PESTS AND DISEASES: None are serious. Iron chlorosis can be a problem in soils that are too alkaline. If this occurs, add a soil acidifier such as ammonium sulfate or peat moss.
RELATED SPECIES: 'Albomarginata' has white-edged leaves. 'Burgundy' leaves turn wine red to deep purple in fall. 'Pendula' has pendulous branches.

TULIP TREE
Liriodendron tulipifera *leer-ee-oh-DEN-dron too-lih-PIH-fur-uh*

Tulip tree flowers are very showy if you can see them high in the tree. The tree is also known as tulip poplar or yellow poplar.

ZONES: (4)5–9
SIZE: 70–100'h × 35–50'w
TYPE: Deciduous tree
FORM: Oval
TEXTURE: Medium
GROWTH: Fast
LIGHT: Sun to light shade

MOISTURE: Moderate
SOIL: Well drained
FEATURES: Flowers, fall color
USES: Shade, specimen
FLOWERS: ■ ■
FALL COLOR: ■

SITING: Tulip tree maintains a fairly narrow oval crown even as it grows older. It grows quickly at first but slows down with age. Leaves emerge folded and open up to have a nice green summer color. Fall color is gold to yellow and is more pronounced in the northern part of its range. The lightly scented, tuliplike flowers appear in midspring but are not as ornamental as other flowering trees simply because they are usually too far from view. They are large and solitary with six yellow-green petals surrounded by three green sepals and resemble a huge tulip. Flowering occurs late May and throughout June. Often trees do not flower until they reach at least 15 years of age, and even then only sparsely in the uppermost reaches of the tree. Older trees flower heavily and their lowermost branches become pendulous, allowing for better viewing of the beautiful flowers. Trees become too large for most landscape situations, but they are nice additions to large properties and parks. The soft wood reportedly is subject to storm damage.
CARE: Plant balled-and-burlapped trees in spring. Tulip tree is extremely sensitive to autumn transplanting. Extra care should be taken to amend the soil. Fertilize, water thoroughly, mulch adequately, and avoid winter salt spray to enhance survival chances during the first winter if transplanting cannot be delayed until spring. It prefers full sun in a deep, rich, moist soil. Mature trees with a fully established root system adapt to drier soils. Drought conditions in summer cause premature defoliation, especially on recently transplanted trees. Young trees should be regularly watered for at least 3 years following transplanting. Young trees will grow faster with annual applications of a plant food, such as Miracle-Gro. Prune in early winter only to shape if necessary.
PROPAGATION: Propagate by seed or from rooted cuttings.
PESTS AND DISEASES: Several relatively minor disease and insect problems affect this tree. Aphids in summer can be serious and their honeydew secretion can cause a cosmetic problem, sooty mold buildup on the leaves. Stressed trees will lose their leaves in late summer, especially in dry soil. Avoid damaging the trunk with sharp garden tools or the lawn mower, as these wounds are entry points for diseases.
RELATED SPECIES: 'Aureomarginatum' has leaves edged with yellow. 'Fastigiatum' is 50' high and spreads 10' wide.

TATARIAN HONEYSUCKLE

Lonicera tatarica *Lahn-NISS-uhr-uh tuh-TAR-ib-kuh*

Fragrant pink flowers cover plants in spring.

ZONES: 3–8
SIZE: 10–12'h × 10'w
TYPE: Deciduous shrub
FORM: Upright
TEXTURE: Medium
GROWTH: Fast
LIGHT: Sun to light shade

MOISTURE: Low to medium
SOIL: Well drained
FEATURES: Flowers
USES: Screening, hedge
FLOWERS: ■□
FALL COLOR: ■

SITING: Tatarian honeysuckle is a tough, hardy, durable shrub with fragrant blooms in shades of pink to white in spring. The foliage is bluish-green in summer. Colorful red berries appear in late June and are showy through summer if birds don't eat them. Tatarian honeysuckle is good for informal hedges and screening. It needs full sun to flower freely but is adaptable to many different soils as long as they drain freely.

CARE: Space hedge plants 24–35" apart. Keep the soil evenly moist from spring until the ground freezes in fall, especially during the first 2 years. Plants are drought tolerant once established. Feed young plants or plants stressed by insects or diseases every spring with plant food, such as Miracle-Gro. Remove dead, damaged, or diseased branches at any

Dislodge aphids from honeysuckle to prevent disfiguring witches' broom damage.

time. Prune just after flowering to shape plants. Give hedges annual light pruning to maintain dense foliage. Birds eat the berries and cause the plants to self-sow freely and become weedy and invasive.

PROPAGATION: Take softwood cuttings just as new growth begins to harden. Take hardwood cuttings in fall from the current season's growth. Sow seeds in fall.

PESTS AND DISEASES: Aphids are a major problem. Wash plants with a hard spray of water or use an insecticidal soap as soon as you notice any insects. In severe cases you may need to use a chemical insecticide. Spider mites may appear in hot, dry summers and cause foliage to turn yellow and die. Spray plants regularly with a forceful spray of water or use a miticide.

RELATED SPECIES: Winter honeysuckle (*L. fragrantissima*) has numerous small cream-colored flowers with a lemony scent and red berries. European fly honeysuckle (*L. xylosteum*) has a mounded, compact form and less-showy flowers but lovely dark blue-green foliage. It is disease and insect resistant.

CHINESE FRINGE-FLOWER

Loropetalum chinense *lor-ob-PET-ub-lum chi-NEN-seb*

Plants are named for the narrow-petaled, drooping flowers.

ZONES: 7–9
SIZE: 6–10'h × 6–10'w
TYPE: Evergreen shrub
FORM: Irregular
TEXTURE: Medium to fine
GROWTH: Fast
LIGHT: Sun to light shade

MOISTURE: Moderate
SOIL: Well drained
FEATURES: Flowers
USES: Woodland, border, screening, foundation
FLOWERS: □■
FALL COLOR: ■

SITING: Chinese fringe flower has a loose, open form and a spreading habit. Young shrubs have greater spread than height and are densely branched. The flowers have four narrow, straplike petals that droop downward. There are white- and pink-flowered forms; both bloom prolifically from late winter into spring, then continue sporadically throughout the summer. The red forms are much showier in bloom than the white. The red forms are typically darker green with burgundy, red, or copper tints depending on the selection. Chinese fringe flower's graceful, horizontally layered shape makes it a perfect foundation plant; with periodic pruning, it can be used in hedges. The red-flowered forms add contrasting color and texture in shrub borders and look good massed. Lower-growing varieties are used as large-scale ground covers. It prefers acid, moist, well-drained soil high in organic matter. It does not do well in high-pH soils or extremely dry soils. It tolerates sun or medium shade. It may be evergreen to semievergreen in Zone 7. It is hardy into the single digits once well established in the landscape.

CARE: It is easily transplanted from containers. Water new transplants when the soil surface is dry. Plants tolerate dry conditions once established. Apply an acidifying plant food if the soil pH is too high. Prune only to maintain a desired size. At the northern edge of its range, it may lose foliage and flower buds in winter and require pruning in early spring.

PROPAGATION: Take cuttings in summer. Mist regularly to enhance rooting.

PESTS AND DISEASES: None are serious.

RELATED SPECIES: 'Blush' and 'Burgundy' have pink flowers. 'Blush' has bronze-red new leaves, maturing to olive green. 'Burgundy' has red-purple new leaves; older foliage is dark reddish purple to olive green. It may exhibit an orange-red coloration in hardiness zones where it is not completely evergreen. 'Rubra' and 'Razzleberri' have red flowers and bloom earlier. 'Monraz' has clusters of fringed raspberry red flowers and burgundy-tinged new growth. Snow Dance™ is a slow-growing, compact, white-flowered form.

AMUR MAACKIA
Maackia amurensis MACK-ee-uh a-moor-EN-sis

Amur maackia is an ornamental small tree that may develop yellow fall color.

ZONES: 4–7(8)
SIZE: 20–30'h × 20–40'w
TYPE: Deciduous tree
FORM: Rounded
TEXTURE: Medium
GROWTH: Slow

LIGHT: Sun
MOISTURE: : Even
SOIL: Well drained
FEATURES: Bark
USES: Specimen, street
FLOWERS: □
FALL COLOR: ■

SITING: Amur maackia is an excellent small tree that is extremely tolerant of cold winter temperatures. In summer dense, erect, 4–8"-long racemes of off-white blooms appear. Flowers are followed by 2–3"-long flat seedpods. It has peeling shiny orange-brown bark. As the bark peels in curls, its color is amber or copper with greenish undertones. Bark that isn't exfoliating is shiny and looks varnished. Landscape specimens usually have

The peeling, orange-brown bark adds interest all year.

numerous small-diameter trunks arising from the lower trunk. Amur maackia prefers loose, well-drained soil and a sunny spot. It is a good street or container tree and is suitable for other confined soil spaces in urban areas. Its slow growth when young makes it uncommon in the nursery trade and difficult to find. It grows in protected sites in Zone 3.

CARE: Transplant balled-and-burlapped and container-grown plants in spring. Keep the soil evenly moist until the ground freezes in fall, especially during the first 2 years. Plants are drought tolerant once mature. Young plants will grow faster with plant food, such as Miracle-Gro, applied in spring. Plants fix atmospheric nitrogen and need little supplemental food. Remove dead, damaged, or diseased branches at any time. Prune in winter to shape plants.

PROPAGATION: Soak seeds in hot water overnight before sowing. Take cuttings in summer.

PESTS AND DISEASES: None are serious. Japanese beetles can feed on leaves.

RELATED SPECIES: Chinese maackia (*M. chinensis*) is not as hardy and is even more difficult to locate in the nursery trade.

SOUTHERN MAGNOLIA
Magnolia grandiflora mag-NOH-lee-uh grand-ih-FLOR-uh

Southern magnolia produces large, showy white flowers.

ZONES: (6)7–9(10)
SIZE: 60–80'h × 30–50'w
TYPE: Evergreen tree
FORM: Pyramidal
TEXTURE: Coarse
GROWTH: Slow to medium
LIGHT: Sun to part shade

MOISTURE: Moderate to high
SOIL: Rich, well drained
FEATURES: Showy flowers, evergreen leaves
USES: Specimen
FLOWERS: □
FALL COLOR: ■

SITING: This large, aristocratic tree is popular in the South. It needs ample room to develop, so it is best used as a specimen tree on large lots, planted well away from structures. It can also be massed or used for screening in parks and on large estates. It has fragrant, waxy creamy-white flowers from late spring to midsummer. They are followed by strawberry-like red fruits. The leaves are lustrous dark green above, downy below. Protect trees from winter sun and winds in the northern parts of the growing region. Plants may have flower buds damaged by late spring freezes, but this won't kill the tree. Southern magnolia has large surface roots that make ground covers or grass difficult to grow. It prefers rich, acid, well-drained soil and full sun to light shade. It thrives in consistently moist soil; however, it should drain freely and not be overly wet or boggy.

CARE: Transplant balled-and-burlapped or container-grown plants in winter or early spring. To help retain soil moisture and acidity, add lots of peat or well-rotted oak leaves to the soil at planting time. Trees may drop their leaves after transplanting, but they recover quickly. Maintain a 2–4" layer of organic mulch such as pine needles or shredded pine bark to acidify the soil and improve soil fertility. Young plants will grow faster if given an annual application of acid plant food such as Miracle-Gro Shake 'n Feed Azalea, Camellia, Rhododendron. Prune after flowering only if necessary to shape the tree. Ice and snow damage may cause twigs and small branches to fall and become a minor litter problem.

PROPAGATION: Layer in spring. Remove seeds from their covering and sow in fall. Take cuttings in mid- to late summer.

PESTS AND DISEASES: None are serious. Scales may cause yellowing of leaves. Prune out badly infested branches and spray the remaining stems with horticultural oil in spring.

RELATED SPECIES: Cucumber-tree magnolia (*M. acuminata*) is hardier, surviving temperatures as low as −25°F (protected sites in Zone 4). It is deciduous rather than evergreen; the flowers are not as showy and the fruits resemble small, unripe cucumbers. It grows well in the dappled shade of oaks.

SAUCER MAGNOLIA

Magnolia ×soulangiana mag-NOH-lee-uh soo-lan-jee-ANN-uh

Star magnolia has showy white flowers with straplike petals in spring.

ZONES: (4)5–9
SIZE: 20–30'h × 20–30'w
TYPE: Deciduous tree or shrub
FORM: Open spreading
TEXTURE: Medium coarse
GROWTH: Medium
LIGHT: Sun to light shade

MOISTURE: Moderate to high
SOIL: Acid, rich, well drained
FEATURES: Early spring flowers
USES: Specimen, groupings
FLOWERS: ☐ ▨
FALL COLOR: ▨ ▨ ▨

SITING: Saucer magnolia can be grown as a small tree or a multistemmed shrub. The roots need ample room to develop.

Flower buds are often nipped by spring frosts. Choose a protected site such as a sheltered courtyard or entryway, especially in northern zones. Plant trees where the flowers will be set off by evergreens or another dark background. It prefers acid, well-drained soil and sun to light shade.
CARE: Transplant young balled-and-burlapped or container-grown plants in early spring. Maintain a 2–4" layer of organic mulch such as pine needles or shredded pine bark to boost soil acidity and fertility. Keep the soil evenly moist from spring until the ground freezes, saturating the soil deeply with each watering. Feed every spring with acid plant

Prune magnolia right after flowering.

A dark background sets off flowers nicely.

Flower bud damaged by spring frost.

food such as Miracle-Gro Shake 'n Feed Azalea, Camellia, Rhododendron. Prune only to shape plants right after flowering in spring. Protect young plants from cold temperatures by surrounding them with a burlap screen filled with leaves. Remove the burlap in early spring just as the weather starts to warm up.
PROPAGATION: Take cuttings from new growth just as it begins to harden. Seeds require moist chilling for 4 months.
PESTS AND DISEASES: None are serious.
RELATED SPECIES: Loebner magnolia (*M. ×loebneri*) is a group of very showy hybrids that are hardier, flowering well in Zone 4 most years. Star magnolia (*M. stellata*) is one of the hardiest magnolias, surviving temperatures down to −30°F. Sweet bay magnolia (*M. virginiana*) is evergreen in warmer areas. It grows in wet and even swampy, acid soils. It is hardy in Zone 5.

OREGON GRAPEHOLLY

Mahonia aquifolium muh-HOE-nee-uh ah-kwih-FOW-lee-um

Showy yellow flowers of Oregon grapeholly turn into purplish blue berries. It is also known as Oregon hollygrape.

ZONES: 5–9
SIZE: 3–6'h × 3–5'w
TYPE: Evergreen shrub
FORM: Upright or low-spreading
TEXTURE: Medium
GROWTH: Medium
LIGHT: Sun to light shade
MOISTURE: Moderate to high

SOIL: Deep, moist, well drained, acid
FEATURES: Spring flowers, evergreen foliage
USES: Foundation, shrub border
FLOWERS: ▨
FALL COLOR: ▨

SITING: Oregon grapeholly has hollylike leaves, blue fruits, and striking yellow flowers. It grows moderately fast, spreading by its suckering root system. The reddish-bronze new growth matures into dark green leaves. The bright yellow flowers in spring are followed by clusters of grapelike blue fruits. Plants will grow in sun or shade, but should be shaded in winter to prevent the purplish leaves from browning. It prefers moist, well-drained, acid soil. Avoid hot, dry soils and desiccating winds. It grows in protected sites in Zone 4.
CARE: Amend soil with peat moss or ammonium sulfate before planting to provide acid conditions.

Maintain soil acidity by applying an acidifying plant food each spring.

Plant in spring and water well during dry periods. Apply a 2–4" layer of organic mulch. Feed every spring with acid plant food such as Miracle-Gro Shake 'n Feed Azalea, Camellia, Rhododendron. After flowering, cut a few of the oldest stems to the ground each year for more compact growth and better flowering.
PROPAGATION: Take cuttings in early winter. Sow seeds in late spring. Divide plants in fall.
PESTS AND DISEASES: This shrub is the alternate host to black stem rust; avoid it where wheat is a major commercial crop. It suffers scorch in winter in colder zones. Chlorosis is often a problem in high-pH soils.
RELATED SPECIES: 'Compactum' usually reaches only 3' tall and wide. The leaves are glossy green, bronze in winter. Other dwarf forms include 'Apollo', 'Donewell', 'Forescate', and 'Moseri'. 'King's Ransom' is an upright grower (to 5' tall) with blue-green foliage that turns bronzy purple in winter. 'Smaragd' (also known as 'Emerald') has lustrous deep green leaves that turn bronzy purple in winter.

FLOWERING CRABAPPLE

Malus species and cultivars *MAL-us*

Flowering crabapples have outstanding spring bloom.

ZONES: 4–8
SIZE: : 8–25'h ×
8–25'w
TYPE: Deciduous
tree
FORM: Rounded
upright, vase
TEXTURE: Medium
GROWTH: Slow to
medium
LIGHT: Sun

MOISTURE:
Moderate
SOIL: Well drained
loam
FEATURES: Showy
flowers and fruits
USES: Specimen,
shade
FLOWERS: ☐ ■ ■
FALL COLOR: ■ ■ ■

SITING: Flowering crabapples are popular single specimen plants, but they are also effective planted in groups of three or five of the same variety. Dwarf types can be used in the mixed border. Weeping types are best placed atop a slope or wall and are especially effective next to water. A background of evergreens will set off the red or yellow fruits which persist into winter on some varieties. They prefer well-drained, slightly acid to neutral soils that are loamy rather than sandy.

CARE: Plant crabapples as early in spring as possible. Choose a site in full sun for best flowering and to reduce the chances of disease. Plants grow best with consistent moisture during the growing season, but mature specimens are drought tolerant. Feed every spring with plant food, such as Miracle-Gro. Prune in mid- to late winter to remove dead or damaged wood and water shoots (thin stems that shoot up from the trunk or branches) and to shape trees. Many varieties develop suckers at their base that should be removed.

PROPAGATION: Most crabapples are grafted onto hardy understock. Seeds of named varieties do not come true. Sow seeds of the species in fall. Hardwood cuttings are difficult to root.

PESTS AND DISEASES: Problems include fire blight, cedar-apple rust, apple scab, canker, Japanese beetles, and scale. Plant disease-resistant cultivars. Prune trees while they are dormant to keep the center open to light and air to reduce disease problems. To reduce the possibility of rust,

plant trees at least 500' from eastern red cedar, the alternate host. Avoid over-watering trees, which can result in succulent growth attractive to insects.
RELATED SPECIES: Japanese flowering crabapple (*M. floribunda*) is one of the best species, with dark green leaves and excellent resistance to Japanese beetle.

Tea crabapple (*M. hupehensis*) is resistant to scab and Japanese beetles. Prairie crabapple (*M. ioensis*) has deep pink buds fading to light pink or white blooms. It is resistant to scab but susceptible to rust. Other cultivars vary in their flower and fruit colors, growth habit, and resistance to diseases.

Prune trees while they are dormant to reduce risk of infection from fire blight.

Cedar-apple rust is a fungal disease that attacks susceptible crabapple varieties.

FLOWERING CRABAPPLE
continued

1

Water sprouts are vigorous, upright stems that flower poorly.

2

Use a sharp pruner to remove water sprouts at their base.

3

A clean cut will quickly form a callus and heal over.

DAWN REDWOOD

Metasequoia glyptostroboides meb-tuh-seb-KWOY-yub glip-tob-strob-BOY-deez

Dawn redwood foliage is soft and feathery.

ZONES: 5–8
SIZE: 70–100'h × 25'w
TYPE: Coniferous deciduous tree
FORM: Pyramidal
TEXTURE: Fine
GROWTH: Fast
LIGHT: Sun
MOISTURE: Moderate to high
SOIL: Acid, well drained
FEATURES: Good foliage color and form
USES: Specimen, groupings
FLOWERS: ■
FALL COLOR: ■

SITING: Dawn redwood is a deciduous conifer known for its buttress-shaped trunk, attractive lacy needles, and reddish-brown bark. The trunk tapers and thickens quickly with 8 to 12 large, buttresslike root flares extending several feet up in a manner similar to some tropical trees. Butt flare can be reduced somewhat by removing the lower branches at an early age. The small, upright-spreading branches are well attached to the typically straight trunk and make for excellent climbing. Although the tree looks like an evergreen, the needles are deciduous, starting out an elegant fresh green in spring and turning a unique pinkish tan to reddish bronze before dropping in fall. The shredding and fissuring of the bark add winter interest. Lightning protection is recommended for older trees, because they usually grow taller than other trees around them. Dawn redwood is too large for most typical landscapes, although it can be used on the corner of an ample residential lot. Combine it with large shrubs or small trees for screening where there is enough space. It does best in moist or even slightly wet soils. Dry or alkaline soils will result in slower growth. It can be injured by early fall frosts. Reduce the chances of injury by locating it on a slope or in a sheltered location. It may suffer dieback in Zone 5 during severe winters. This magnificent tree has an intriguing history. It was thought extinct for more than 20 million years. Then in 1941 a single grove was discovered growing wild in central China. Today all plants are descendants of seed collected from these trees.

CARE: Transplant balled-and-burlapped or container-grown plants in spring. Keep the soil evenly moist until the ground freezes, saturating the soil deeply with each watering. Apply a 2–4" layer of organic mulch such as wood chips, pine needles, or shredded bark to maintain soil moisture. Young trees will respond to an annual application of plant food, such as Miracle-Gro. Avoid feeding after midsummer to reduce chances of injury from fall frosts. Remove broken, misshapen, or low branches. Lower branches may be removed if desired.

PROPAGATION: Sow seeds in fall or early spring. Take cuttings in late summer.

PESTS AND DISEASES: None are serious. Spider mites can show up during hot, dry conditions, especially if plants are growing on dry soils. Spray young trees with a hose to dislodge them. Japanese beetles feed on the foliage. Canker can be a problem. Avoid wounding the trunk, which is an entry point for diseases.

RELATED SPECIES: 'National' and 'Sheridan Spire' have a narrow, upright growth habit. New growth on 'Nitschke Cream' is cream colored and matures to green. 'Ogon' has golden leaves.

RUSSIAN ARBORVITAE

Microbiota decussata *meye-krow-bye-OH-tub DAY-koo-sah-tub*

Russian arborvitae makes a nice evergreen groundcover in sun or shade. It is also known as Russian cypress.

ZONES: 2–7(8)
SIZE: 1'h × 6–9'w
TYPE: Evergreen shrub
FORM: Radiating mat
TEXTURE: Fine
GROWTH: Slow
LIGHT: Sun to shade

MOISTURE: Moderate
SOIL: Well drained
FEATURES: Lacy evergreen foliage
USES: Ground cover
FLOWERS: ■
FALL COLOR: ■

SITING: Russian arborvitae is an extremely hardy evergreen shrub with foliage that changes color with the seasons. It has a radiating growth habit and is best used as a woody ground cover on flat or gently sloping ground; its root system is not strong enough to hold it in place on steep slopes or banks. The foliage starts out bright green, turns dark green by summer, then dark brown in fall and remains so throughout the winter. The leaves form sprays of foliage similar to those of arborvitae (hence the common name), with downturned ends that give it a graceful, fine-textured effect. Russian arborvitae is a good alternative in lightly shaded areas where junipers or other herbaceous evergreen ground covers will not grow. The ferny foliage looks good edging a walkway or growing over a retaining wall. The best performance is in partial sun in moist, well-drained soils, but it is adaptable to poor, dry, thin soils in wind-exposed sites. It can be grown in full sun if it has ample water. It likes cold climates and does not perform well in southern areas. Plants are slow to green up in spring. The brownish foliage should not be mistaken for dieback or winter burn.

CARE: Plant container-grown specimens in spring. Give plants plenty of room, with a minimum spacing of 48" between plants. Keep the soil consistently moist and cool until the ground freezes in fall. Russian arborvitae does not tolerate drought. Apply a 1–2" layer of shredded bark, pine needles, or wood chips around each plant as soon as the ground warms in spring, and replenish as necessary throughout the growing season. Feed every spring with plant food, such as Miracle-Gro, or an organic equivalent such as fish emulsion. Sprinkle plant food around the base of each plant before new growth starts and water well. Prune only dead or broken stems. This evergreen looks best if it is allowed to spread freely.

PROPAGATION: In early spring take hardwood cuttings from the previous season's growth.

PESTS AND DISEASES: None are serious. Plants in compacted soil can get root rot. Avoid this by properly preparing the soil beforehand. Replace heavy clay soil, or plant shrubs in a raised bed.

COMMON MULBERRY

Morus alba *MOR-us AL-buh*

Common mulberry has fleshy edible fruits. The tree is also known as white mulberry.

ZONES: 4–8(9)
SIZE: 30–50'h × 25–40'w
TYPE: Deciduous tree
FORM: Rounded
TEXTURE: Coarse
GROWTH: Fast
LIGHT: Sun to part shade

MOISTURE: Moderate
SOIL: Any
FEATURES: Tough, adaptable tree
USES: Shade, wildlife
FLOWERS: ■
FALL COLOR: ■ ■

SITING: Common mulberry is a tough tree tolerant of urban conditions, but the messy fruits make it unacceptable near sidewalks, streets, and parking areas. The fruits and the droppings from the birds that eat them stain sidewalks and driveways. It is not a suitable landscape plant except on extremely difficult sites. Fruits are fleshy edible berries. Thanks to birds, it is often seen as a shrub in fencerows, waste areas, and even along house foundations. If you

Weedy seedlings need to be removed from the landscape.

plant this tree, choose a fruitless cultivar such as 'Kingan' or 'Stribling'. Compact and weeping forms offer some landscape potential, possibly even as specimen trees. In some states the tree is banned because of its irritating pollen. Common mulberry grows in a variety of soils, including poor, dry soils. It withstands seaside conditions and a wide range of soil pH.

CARE: Mature plants are drought tolerant. Prune in winter if needed. Suckers sprout profusely and need to be pulled.

PROPAGATION: Stratify seeds for 2 months to improve germination.

PESTS AND DISEASES: None are serious. Minor insect and disease problems include powdery mildew, bacterial blight, cankers, scale, and spider mites.

RELATED SPECIES: 'Fruitless' and 'Mapleleaf' are nonfruiting male forms with deeply lobed, glossy leaves that resemble the foliage of maples. 'Laciniata' has strongly lobed, serrated leaves of finer texture. 'Nuclear Blast' leaves resemble ribbons. 'Pendula' forms a small tree to 20' tall with weeping, gnarled branches; it produces fruit. 'Urbana' is a similar fruitless cultivar. Red mulberry (*M. rubra*) is taller (40–70') and more open (40–50' wide). Autumn color is usually a fairly good yellow.

NORTHERN BAYBERRY
Myrica pensylvanica *MY-rik-uh pen-sil-VAH-ni-kuh*

Female plants produce waxy gray berries.

ZONES: (2)3–6(7)
SIZE: 5–12'h ×
5–12'w
TYPE: Deciduous or
semievergreen shrub
FORM: Rounded
upright
TEXTURE: Medium
GROWTH: Medium
LIGHT: Sun to part
shade

MOISTURE: Low to
moderate
SOIL: Infertile, sandy
FEATURES: Fragrant
foliage, waxy fruits
USES: Borders,
hedges, streetside
FLOWERS: ■
FALL COLOR: ■

SITING: Northern bayberry is a dependable
shrub for difficult situations. It grows in full
sun to partial shade and is tolerant of a
wide range of conditions, including salt
spray and wind. Taller types can be
pruned to make a hedge. Plants eventually
form large colonies that can be used for
stabilizing soil on tough sites. The foliage
contains aromatic oils that are released
when the leaves are crushed. Leaves
slowly turn bronze or tan in fall. Plants
hold onto their leaves late in fall,
sometimes even all winter. Female plants
produce clusters of hard gray berries along
the length of the previous season's twigs.
Plants are dioecious; about 20 percent of
the plants should be male to achieve good
fruit set on female plants. Birds slowly pick

**Northern bayberry, also known as
candleberry or swamp candleberry, thrives
in salty streetside locations.**

the fruits off in fall and winter. The wax
on the berries is the source of the scent for
bayberry candles.
CARE: Transplant balled-and-burlapped or
container-grown plants in spring. Soils with
a high pH should be acidified with sulfur.
Water newly planted shrubs; established
plants are drought tolerant. No plant food
is needed; plants fix atmospheric nitrogen.
Prune lightly anytime except fall to
encourage compact growth. Rejuvenate
older plants by pruning them to the
ground in spring.
PROPAGATION: Take cuttings in late spring.
Layer in fall. Soak seeds in hot water or
rub them against a rough surface to
remove the waxy coating, then sow in fall.
PESTS AND DISEASES: Leaves can become
chlorotic when plants are grown in highly
alkaline soils.
RELATED SPECIES: 'Myda' is a fruiting
female clone; 'Myriman' is a male
pollinator. 'Morton' (Silver Sprite™) is a
female fruiting clone that forms a dense,
broad-oval mound with gray-green leaves.
It grows to 5' tall. Southern wax myrtle
(*M. cerifera*) is an evergreen that grows
as a tall shrub in Zones 6–9.

MYRTLE
Myrtus communis *MUR-tus kuh-MYOON-us*

**Common myrtle is a dense, evergreen shrub
or small tree.**

ZONES: 9 and 10
SIZE: 10–15'h ×
10–12'w
TYPE: Evergreen
shrub or tree
FORM: Rounded
TEXTURE: Medium
GROWTH: Medium
LIGHT: Sun to light
shade

MOISTURE: Even
SOIL: Well drained
FEATURES: Fragrant
evergreen leaves
USES: Hedge,
massing, topiary
FLOWERS: □ ■
FALL COLOR: ■

SITING: Common myrtle is usually grown
as a dense rounded shrub, but it can be
pruned into a small tree that can grow up
to 15' tall. The leaves are aromatic. Small
pinkish buds open to small, delicate white
or rosy flowers from early spring to early
summer. They are followed by small blue-
black berries, which are somewhat hidden
by the dark green foliage. The trunk is
attractive when exposed as a small tree.
Common myrtle can be pruned to almost
any shape; it is suitable for formal and
informal hedges and topiary. Small tree
forms make good specimens near patios
and entryways. It is rated as deer resistant.
It prefers full sun to partial shade. It is

**Myrtle flowers and foliage are attractive
in the landscape or in floral arrangements.**

adaptable to a wide variety of soils but
does best in soils with average fertility and
good drainage. The flowers, leaves, and
berries are used variously in perfumery
and as a condiment. In the floral trade,
it is used as a filler green; the stiff, woody
branches make it easy to work with.
CARE: Transplant container-grown plants
in winter or spring. Water established
plants deeply about once a month. Plants
that are overwatered, watered shallowly,
or grown in poorly drained soil are prone
to chlorosis. Feed plants every other spring
with plant food, such as Miracle-Gro.
Plants used in hedges and topiary require
regular pruning to maintain their shape.
This can be done anytime.
PROPAGATION: Propagate by vegetative
cuttings or seed.
PESTS AND DISEASES: None are serious.
Spider mites and scale have been listed as
pests in Florida.
RELATED SPECIES: 'Compacta' has more
refined foliage and is recommended for
edging and low, formal hedges. It grows
slowly 2–3' tall and as wide. 'Variegata' has
small white-margined leaves and is similar
in size to 'Compacta'.

HEAVENLY BAMBOO
Nandina domestica *nan-DEE-nuh doh-MESS-tih-kuh*

Heavenly bamboo produces a striking crop of red berries in fall.

ZONES: 6–9(10)
SIZE: 6–8'h × 4–6'w
TYPE: Evergreen shrub
FORM: Upright
TEXTURE: Medium to fine
GROWTH: Medium
LIGHT: Sun to shade

MOISTURE: Moderate
SOIL: Well drained
FEATURES: Upright form, showy fruits
USES: Massing, container, hedge
FLOWERS: □
FALL COLOR: ■

SITING: Heavenly bamboo is a popular shrub in southern gardens, where it is effective in masses, as a hedge, in foundation plantings, and in containers. In cooler areas it dies back to the ground in winter. The lacy leaves start out coppery to purplish red, becoming blue-green with age. Plants grown in full sun take on a reddish tint in winter. The white flowers are borne in large clusters in midsummer; bloom is better in shade. Flowers are followed by clusters of red fruits that persist nearly all winter and stand out

Prune out older stems each spring to keep plants vigorous.

well against the foliage. Cross-fertilization improves fruiting, so plant in groups. Plants sucker slowly to form colonies. It grows best in moist, fertile soil in full sun or shade but is adaptable to a range of soils and exposure. It has become invasive in some native habitats, especially in Florida. Dwarf cultivars are often used as a low-maintenance ground cover.
CARE: Transplant container-grown plants in late winter or spring. Give newly planted specimens an inch of water a week. Mature plants are drought tolerant. Prune regularly to maintain an upright shape. Cut a few of the oldest stems to the ground each spring to encourage new growth. In northern areas, plants may suffer winterkill and require spring pruning.
PROPAGATION: Take cuttings in summer. Remove seeds from their fleshy outer covering and sow in fall. Divide suckers.
PESTS AND DISEASES: None are serious.
RELATED SPECIES: 'Alba' has white fruits. 'Compacta' is a dwarf form. 'Firepower' has bright red leaves in winter. 'Harbour Dwarf' grows into a dense, 2–3' mound with purplish winter color. 'Royal Princess' has delicate, fernlike foliage.

OLEANDER
Nerium oleander *NEAR-ee-um OH-lee-an-der*

Plants bloom in spring and sporadically throughout the summer.

ZONES: 8–10
SIZE: 6–12'h × 6–12'w
TYPE: Evergreen shrub
FORM: Broad rounded
TEXTURE: Medium fine
GROWTH: Medium to fast
LIGHT: Sun

MOISTURE: Low to moderate
SOIL: Any
FEATURES: Evergreen foliage, flowers
USES: Container, foundation, hedge, border
FLOWERS: □ ■ ■ □
FALL COLOR: ■

SITING: Oleander is used in the Deep South as a massing plant, large shrub, or small tree. It's a popular roadside plant in California and Florida. Flowers appear in terminal clusters in shades of cream, white, pink, or red in single or double forms. It blooms from spring throughout the summer. Train or prune as desired. It may suffer winter damage when temperatures fall into the low teens. Dwarf varieties are slightly more tender. All types recover quickly from frost damage. Oleander is well adapted to coastal areas and is good for seasides. Its high salt and pollution tolerance makes it suitable for use along

Oleander is a good choice for the tough conditions found along city streets.

highways and streets. It has good heat tolerance and can be grown where there is a lot of reflected light. It withstands high salt, wind, and drought. It prefers well-drained, fertile soil. All plant parts are toxic when ingested. Contact with leaves can cause dermatitis.
CARE: Give newly planted specimens an inch of water a week. Mature plants are drought tolerant. Plants will grow faster with regular applications of plant food, such as Miracle-Gro. Prune in early spring to control size and form. Pinch tips to encourage density. Pull off suckers from the base to encourage a more open habit.
PROPAGATION: Take cuttings anytime during the growing season.
PESTS AND DISEASES: Scales can turn leaves yellow. Prune out badly infested branches and spray with a dormant oil spray in late winter. Plants may get mildew in shady areas. Other minor problems include aphids, mealybugs, and nematodes.
RELATED SPECIES: 'Calypso' has single cherry-red flowers. 'Isle of Capri' has single light yellow flowers. 'Mrs. Reoding' has double salmon-pink flowers. 'Sister Agnes' has single pure white flowers.

BLACK TUPELO

Nyssa sylvatica NISS-uh sil-VAT-ih-kuh

Black tupelo foliage turns brilliant red in fall. The tree is also known as sour gum, black gum or tupelo.

ZONES: (4)5–9
SIZE: 30–50'h × 20–30'w
TYPE: Deciduous tree
FORM: Pyramidal
TEXTURE: Medium
GROWTH: Slow to medium
LIGHT: Sun

MOISTURE: Moderate to high
SOIL: Acid, well drained
FEATURES: Good summer foliage, fall color
USES: Specimen, shade
FLOWERS: ■
FALL COLOR: ■ ■ ■

SITING: Black tupelo has a pleasing outline and good summer and fall foliage color.

Leaves turn brilliant orange or scarlet in fall. The horizontal branches are somewhat pendulous. Fruits on female trees grow to about the size of navy beans, hang in small clusters, and turn dark blue in fall. They can be messy when grown near sidewalks and driveways if birds do not eat them before they drop. Black tupelo makes an excellent specimen tree. It prefers moist, well-drained, acid, deep soils in full sun or part shade, but it will

Feed trees in spring with water-soluble or granular plant food to help get them established.

grow well on drier sites. Give it a sheltered location away from winds. It does not tolerate high pH or heavily polluted areas. It may grow in the warmer parts of Zone 4 in protected locations. To grow a black tupelo for its fall foliage, choose a nursery plant in fall.

CARE: Black tupelo is somewhat difficult to transplant and establish because of its long taproot. Acidify the soil before planting by working in ammonium sulfate or peat moss. This tree requires regular watering the first 3 years or so. Mulch with a 2–4" layer of wood chips or shredded bark to help maintain soil moisture. Sprinkle plant food, such as Miracle-Gro, around plants in spring, and water well. Prune in fall as needed to shape young trees.

PROPAGATION: Sow seeds immediately when ripe in fall.

PESTS AND DISEASES: Few are serious. Cankers, leaf spots, rust, caterpillars, leaf miner, and scale can appear. Summer leaf spotting results in irregular black lesions that can be disfiguring.

HOLLY OSMANTHUS

Osmanthus heterophyllus oz-MAN-thus het-er-oh-FIL-us

'Goshiki' is a variegated form of holly osmanthus, also known as false holly or fragrant tea olive.

ZONES: (6)7–9
SIZE: 8–15'h × 8–15'w
TYPE: Evergreen shrub or tree
FORM: Upright oval
TEXTURE: Medium
GROWTH: Slow to medium
LIGHT: Sun to part shade
MOISTURE: Moderate

SOIL: Acid, well drained
FEATURES: Fragrant flowers, evergreen foliage
USES: Hedge, foundation, shrub border
FLOWERS: □
FALL COLOR: ■

SITING: This large evergreen shrub or small tree can reach 15' in height and width. Older plants grow as wide as tall and develop a vase shape with several main trunks. Juvenile leaves are spiny and oval shaped. The lustrous dark-green adult leaves have a simple margin and paler underside. A multitude of barely noticeable but extremely fragrant white blossoms appear in the axils of the leaves starting in September and continuing well into November. They perfume a large area. The nondescript black berries ripen in fall of the year following flowering, but they are seldom seen on landscape plants. Plant holly osmanthus where its lovely fragrance can be enjoyed, such as along a pathway, near windows or doors, or in outdoor sitting areas. Incorporate it into foundation plantings, at the corners of buildings, or as an accent between windows. A row of holly osmanthus makes an attractive hedge or screen. It prefers full sun to part shade and fertile, moist, well-drained, acid soil but is adapted to higher-pH soils. In areas where it is tender, grow it as a container specimen and bring indoors in winter.

CARE: It likes an even supply of soil moisture. Water well during dry periods. Apply a 2–4" layer of organic mulch such as pine needles, shredded oak leaves, or pine bark to keep the soil evenly moist and maintain soil acidity. Feed every spring with acid plant food such as Miracle-Gro Shake 'n Feed Azalea, Camellia, Rhododendron. Prune after flowering to maintain size and encourage branching.

PROPAGATION: Take cuttings in late spring or early summer.

PESTS AND DISEASES: None are serious. Scale insects may appear when growing conditions are poor.

RELATED SPECIES: 'Gulftide' is compact with shiny leaves and is hardier than the species. 'Goshiki' is a variegated form that needs some shade for best performance. Sweet olive (*O. fragrans*) grows 20–30' tall. It is not as cold hardy (Zones 7–10), but the flowers are more fragrant. Wild olive or devilwood (*O. americanus*) reaches up to 50' in height but usually grows around 10–20'. Although its native range is restricted to Zones 8 and 9, wild olive is known to be hardy in Zone 6, making it the most cold hardy of the cultivated species.

IRONWOOD
Ostrya virginiana *OSS-tree-uh ver-jin-ee-AYE-nuh*

Ironwood, also known as American hophornbeam, is a native tree with clean, disease-free foliage.

ZONES: (3)4–9
SIZE: 25–40'h × 10–18'w
TYPE: Deciduous tree
FORM: Rounded
TEXTURE: Medium fine
GROWTH: Slow
LIGHT: Sun to part shade

MOISTURE: Moderate to high
SOIL: Acid, cool, well drained
FEATURES: Pleasing shape, small size
USES: Shade, naturalizing, small yard
FLOWERS: ■
FALL COLOR: ■

SITING: Ironwood is a slow-growing, handsome, small to medium-size tree well suited to smaller city landscapes and tight spaces where most shade trees would grow too large. Its clean, disease-free, birchlike foliage provides good summer shade. The straight trunk and limbs are covered with shaggy gray bark; the wood is strong and resistant to ice and wind damage. The seeds ripen in flattened, papery pods that are strung together like

Ironwood may be planted in relatively tight spaces because it is not a large tree.

hops to form little cones and give this tree its other common name, American hophornbeam. Trees are sensitive to road salt and ocean spray. It prefers cool, moist, well-drained, slightly acid soil. It tolerates full sun or partial shade.

CARE: Transplant balled-and-burlapped or container-grown plants in early spring. Trees are slow to establish after transplanting. It likes an even supply of soil moisture. Give ample water while young and water well during dry periods. Apply a 2–4" layer of organic mulch such as pine needles, shredded oak leaves, or shredded pine bark to keep the soil evenly moist and maintain soil acidity. Regular feeding when trees are young will help plants become established. Sprinkle plant food, such as Miracle-Gro, around plants in spring, and water well. Prune in winter or early spring to remove dead or damaged branches and to shape the tree.

PROPAGATION: Sow seeds when ripe in fall. Seeds have an internal dormancy that is difficult to overcome.

PESTS AND DISEASES: Witches'-broom occurs on occasion and results in small, bunchy, twiggy growth.

SOURWOOD
Oxydendrum arboreum *awk-sih-DEN-drum ar-BORE-ee-um*

Sourwood, also known as lily-of-the-valley tree or sorrel tree, has outstanding fall color.

ZONES: 5–9
SIZE: 25–30'h × 20'w
TYPE: Deciduous tree
FORM: Pyramidal
TEXTURE: Medium
GROWTH: Slow
LIGHT: Sun to light shade

MOISTURE: Average to high
SOIL: Acid, rich, well drained
FEATURES: Fall color, summer flowers
USES: Specimen, border
FLOWERS: □
FALL COLOR: ■ ■ ■

SITING: Sourwood offers interest in all seasons. Young trees have an irregular growth habit, but as they age they develop an attractive pyramidal outline with drooping branches. Foliage turns a lustrous dark green in summer. The real show starts in fall when the leaves turn yellow, red, or purple, sometimes all on the same tree. It is one of the earliest trees to color in fall. The fragrant white flowers appear in June and early July. They grow in 4–10"-long drooping racemes that hang from the tips of the branches and give the tree a weeping softness. Bees swarm to the flowers; the result is a rich brown honey. The flowers turn into yellowish fruits that hang on the tree through the winter. Fall color is variable, so select nursery plants in fall. This tree is usually used as a specimen. Place it near a deck, patio, or terrace that can be viewed from indoors in winter. This tree also looks good at the edge of a forest or natural area. Its narrow, upright growth habit makes it good for small spaces. It prefers acid, peaty, moist, well-drained soil and full sun or partial shade. Flowering and fall color are best in full sun. It tolerates wet soils. It is not the best choice for polluted or urban areas.

CARE: Transplant balled-and-burlapped or container-grown plants in late winter or early spring. Choose a site carefully; established plants are difficult to move. This tree likes an even supply of soil moisture; water well during dry periods. Apply a 2–4" layer of organic mulch such as pine needles, shredded oak leaves, or shredded pine bark to keep the soil evenly moist and maintain soil acidity. Keep the soil rich with an annual application of acid plant food such as Miracle-Gro Shake 'n Feed Azalea, Camellia, Rhododendron. Avoid cultivating around the shallow roots.

PROPAGATION: It is somewhat difficult to propagate. Take cuttings in midsummer. They should be 2–3" long, from short side shoots with a thin heel of old wood. Bottom heat helps rooting. Sow seeds indoors in spring.

PESTS AND DISEASES: None are serious. Leaf spot and twig blight can be minor problems on sourwood.

RELATED SPECIES: 'Albomarginatum' has white leaf margins and white marbling. 'Chameleon' has an upright, conical growth habit and fall color changing from yellow, rose, and red to purple. 'Mt. Charm' has early fall color.

PERSIAN PARROTIA

Parrotia persica *par-ROH-tee-uh PURR-sih-kuh*

Interesting exfoliating bark reveals colorful under-bark on Persian parrotia, also known as Persian ironwood.

ZONES: 5–8
SIZE: 20–40'h × 15–30'w
TYPE: Deciduous tree
FORM: Rounded oval
TEXTURE: Medium
GROWTH: Medium
LIGHT: Sun

MOISTURE: Average
SOIL: Slightly acid, well drained
FEATURES: Fall color, mottled bark
USES: Specimen, street
FLOWERS: ■
FALL COLOR: ■ ■ ■

SITING: Parrotia bark exfoliates on old branches (4–8" in diameter) to reveal a gray, green, white, and brown mosaic of color. The leaves unfold reddish purple when young, maturing to a lustrous dark green through the summer, then finally putting on a brilliant fall display of various hues of vivid yellow, burnt orange, and deep, pure scarlet. The flowers appear before the leaves in spring; they have no petals, just a profusion of relatively inconspicuous deep crimson stamens. Fruits are not set in abundance and are of little consequence. This tough tree is tolerant of many landscape conditions, including drought, heat, wind, and cold. It prefers well-drained, loamy, slightly acid soil in full sun, but it will tolerate a higher pH and light shade. The best fall color is produced on specimens growing in acid soil in full sun. There may be some twig dieback in colder parts of its range. It performs best in Zones 6 and 7. It makes an excellent small lawn or street tree. It can also be used as a foundation plant near a large house. It is a striking accent plant, especially when it's older and the bark is exfoliating. It can be grown in a container or an aboveground planter. The trunk and bark character can be displayed year-round by removing lower branches and foliage.

CARE: Transplant small balled-and-burlapped or container-grown specimens in early spring. Large trees are difficult to transplant. Give newly planted specimens an inch of water a week. Mature plants are drought tolerant. Apply plant food, such as Miracle-Gro, or an organic alternative such as fish emulsion in early spring and water in well. Prune in spring. The bark is easily damaged by lawn mowers and string trimmers. To protect lawn trees, surround them with a 2–4" layer of organic mulch such as wood chips or shredded bark.

PROPAGATION: Sow seeds in fall. Take cuttings in midsummer.

PESTS AND DISEASES: None are serious. Japanese beetles can be a minor problem.

RELATED SPECIES: 'Pendula' has pendulous branches and grows 5–6' tall and 10' wide. 'Ruby Vase' is narrower than the species, growing 20' high by 10' wide; the ruby-red foliage persists into fall.

EMPRESS TREE

Paulownia tomentosa *paw-LOH-nee-uh toh-men-TOH-suh*

Fast-growing empress tree has showy purple flowers in spring. It is also known as princess tree or royal paulownia.

ZONES: (5)6–9
SIZE: 30–40'h × 30–40'w
TYPE: Deciduous tree
FORM: Rounded
TEXTURE: Coarse
GROWTH: Fast
LIGHT: Sun to part shade

MOISTURE: Moderate to high
SOIL: Well drained
FEATURES: Showy flowers, adaptable
USES: Shade, specimen
FLOWERS: ■
FALL COLOR: ■

SITING: Empress tree has a dramatic, coarse-textured appearance with its huge, heart-shaped leaves and large clusters of lavender flowers in spring. The flowers are borne in terminal panicles up to 10" long before leaf emergence. Fuzzy brown flower buds form in early autumn; they may freeze in cold weather and drop off. Leaves drop within a week following the first frost in autumn. The fruits are pointed woody capsules that turn brown as they mature in September or October and persist on the tree through the winter.

Fallen fruits, leaves, and flowers can become a maintenance issue.

Trees start bearing seed after 8–10 years and are prolific. Wind disseminates the seed capsules, which break open on the trees throughout the winter and into spring. This tree thrives in deep, moist but well-drained soil sheltered from the wind. It withstands air pollution and coastal conditions. It produces dense shade, so growing plants underneath it is difficult.

It has been grown successfully in urban areas where air pollution, poor drainage, compacted soil, and drought are common.

CARE: Water young trees as needed. Seeds germinate readily in the landscape and can become weedy. This tree is always dropping something—fruit capsules, leaves, broken branches, flowers—that can make a yard look messy.

PROPAGATION: Seeds need light for germination. Seedlings don't tolerate shade. Take lateral root cuttings of 1-year-old seedlings and propagate in place.

PESTS AND DISEASES: None are serious. Diseases include leaf spots and mildew.

AMUR CORK TREE
Phellodendron amurense *fell-oh-DEN-dron ah-mer-EN-see*

Amur cork tree has many ornamental features to offer a landscape.

ZONES: (4)5–7(8)
SIZE: 30–45'h × 30–50'w
TYPE: Deciduous tree
FORM: Broad spreading
TEXTURE: Medium
GROWTH: Medium

LIGHT: Sun
MOISTURE: Average
SOIL: Well drained
FEATURES: Picturesque form, interesting bark
USES: Shade
FLOWERS: ■
FALL COLOR: ■

SITING: Amur cork tree frequently becomes almost flat-topped with maturity, giving it a picturesque branching outline in the winter landscape. Old trees develop ridged and furrowed gray-brown bark that is soft and corklike to the touch. Leaf color is lustrous dark green in summer and yellow to yellow-gold in fall. When crushed, the foliage gives off a turpentine odor. Insignificant yellow-green flowers appear in late May to early June in 2–3½"-long panicles and are followed by small black fruits, which sometimes persist into winter if not first devoured by birds. These fruits, which appear only on female trees, give off a strong odor when crushed and create a mess on a sidewalk. To avoid this plant male trees. Amur cork tree can be used as a shade tree for large home landscapes. The shade it produces is less dense than that of other large trees, and shade-tolerant grasses and ground covers can be grown under it. It prefers full sun and moist, well-drained soils but tolerates alkaline soils, air pollution, poor drainage, compacted soil, and drought. Growth is best when the tree is not stressed by environmental conditions. Its wide-spreading root system and wide crown keep it from being used as a street tree. It can be invasive. It is hardy in the southern part of Zone 4. Growth is slow in Zone 8.

CARE: Transplant almost anytime of year. Provide young trees with an inch of water a week. Established trees are somewhat drought tolerant. Trees can naturalize and become weedy when planted next to open areas.

PROPAGATION: Sow seed anytime. Stratification of about 1 month enhances germination percentage.

PESTS AND DISEASES: None are serious.

RELATED SPECIES: 'Eye Stopper' has bright yellow fall color and is seedless. 'His Majesty', 'Macho', and 'RNI 4551' (Shademaster®) are male selections that produce no weedy seedlings or messy fruits. They can pollinate female plants. They have a spreading growth habit to 40' tall and wide with lustrous foliage.

MOCKORANGE
Philadelphus coronarius *fill-uh-DELL-fuss kor-uh-NAY-ree-us*

Mockorange, also known as sweet mock orange or fragrant mock orange, is noted for its fragrant white flowers.

ZONES: 4–8
SIZE: 10–12'h × 10–12'w
TYPE: Deciduous shrub
FORM: Rounded
TEXTURE: Coarse
GROWTH: Fast
LIGHT: Sun to light shade

MOISTURE: High to low
SOIL: Well drained
FEATURES: Fragrant, showy flowers
USES: Shrub border
FLOWERS: □
FALL COLOR: ■

SITING: Mockorange has abundant, fragrant blooms reminiscent of orange blossoms. The four-petaled white flowers have a bright yellow center and appear in spring. Smaller cultivars fit nicely into a perennial border. In colder climates mockorange suffers dieback each year. It can be cut back to live tissue in spring. To enjoy the fragrant flowers indoors, cut stems just as blooms begin to open; strip off lower leaves. Flowering is best in full sun, but plants will grow in light shade. It prefers well-drained, fertile soil but tolerates poorer, drier soils.

CARE: Although this shrub tolerates dry spells once mature, it prefers consistently moist soils throughout the growing season. Consistent moisture is especially important during the first 2 years. Feed every spring with plant food, such as Miracle-Gro. Prune regularly. Older plants can become scraggly. Prune right after flowering either by removing old wood or cutting to the ground. If you wait too long to prune, you will cut off next year's flower buds.

PROPAGATION: Take softwood cuttings from stem tips in midsummer. Take hardwood cuttings anytime during the dormant season. Layer shrubs in fall. Sow seeds of the species in fall.

PESTS AND DISEASES: Rabbits can be a problem in winter, eating stems all the way down to the snow line. Protect plants with chicken wire in late fall. Canker, leaf spot, powdery mildew, rust, aphids, leaf miner, and nematodes are minor problems on mockorange.

RELATED SPECIES: 'Aureus' has light green to gold leaves. 'Miniature Snowflake' has double flowers. 'Minnesota Snowflake' is an extra hardy hybrid with fragrant double flowers. 'Natchez' has abundant large flowers. 'Nanus' is a compact form. 'Variegatus' leaves have irregular borders of creamy white.

Prune plants right after flowering to avoid cutting off next season's flower buds.

CHINESE PHOTINIA

Photinia serratifolia *foh-TIN-ee-uh ser-at-ih-FOHL-ee-uh*

Chinese photinia is a good landscape shrub for warmer climates.

ZONES: 6–9
SIZE: 20–25'h × 12–15'w
TYPE: Evergreen shrub or tree
FORM: Irregular
TEXTURE: Coarse
GROWTH: Medium to fast
LIGHT: Sun to light shade

MOISTURE: Low to medium
SOIL: Average, well drained
FEATURES: Red-tipped evergreen leaves
USES: Hedge, screening, specimen tree
FLOWERS: □

SITING: Chinese photinia can be a large shrub or be pruned to a small tree. White flowers appear in spring in flat clusters measuring more than 7" in diameter. Although they have an unpleasant odor, they are spectacular in their profusion. The distinctive foliage is bright red when young, then reddish copper and eventually rich dark green. Young twigs are red to reddish brown. The flowers are followed by small, berrylike red fruit clusters that persist through the winter. Its dense growth allows it to serve as an effective barrier that is beautiful and functional. It tolerates shearing and can be trained into a large, formal hedge. The red-tipped foliage adds interest to a mixed shrub border. By pruning lower branches, an individual shrub can be trained into a small tree. It tolerates air pollution, poor drainage, compacted soil, and drought. It will grow in almost any soil. Dry soil will slow growth, especially on younger plants.
CARE: Keep soil moist by mulching with organic matter; water when dry. Young plants benefit from a spring application of plant food, but older plants do not require feeding. Prune lightly in summer to encourage dense growth and colorful new shoots. Prune to shape and control size in spring or summer.
PROPAGATION: Layer in spring or summer. Take cuttings anytime. Sow seeds in fall.
PESTS AND DISEASES: Leaf spot can be a serious problem. Collect fallen leaves in winter to reduce sources of the disease. Plants pruned in late summer may suffer infections on resultant new growth into the fall. Avoid frequent pruning and summer fertilization, which stimulate succulent growth. Fire blight can blacken the ends of branches. Powdery mildew may cause white spots on leaves.
RELATED SPECIES: Red tip (*P. ×fraseri*) is a hybrid of Japanese photinia (*P. glabra*), which is smaller and blooms later in the season, and Chinese photinia, which grows taller and has more leathery leaves that are bronze when young. Once widely used as a landscape plant in the southern United States, it is used less frequently now due to a leaf-spot fungus that causes gradual thinning, defoliation, and death of the plant.

NINEBARK

Physocarpus opulifolius *fye-so-KAR-pus op-yew-lih-FOH-lee-us*

This native shrub has clusters of white flowers. It is also known as common ninebark or eastern ninebark.

ZONES: 2–7
SIZE: 5–10'h × 6–10'w
TYPE: Deciduous shrub
FORM: Upright spreading
TEXTURE: Medium
GROWTH: Medium to fast
LIGHT: Sun to part shade

MOISTURE: Low to high
SOIL: Average
FEATURES: Hardiness, flowers, interesting bark
USES: Massing, border, screening
FLOWERS: □ ■
FALL COLOR: ■ ■

SITING: This tough, hardy, multistemmed shrub produces fast-growing shoots that arch out and away from the center. The flowers are grouped together in 2" heads and are followed by reddish-brown fruits. Older stems are covered with attractive shaggy bark that sloughs off in long, fibrous strips. Ninebark is a good choice in northern landscapes where many other shrubs won't survive. It makes an effective hedge, screen, or windbreak. It is good in naturalized settings, where it gives cover to wildlife. It grows best in full sun and can withstand windy sites.
CARE: Young plants should be kept well watered, but mature shrubs prefer soil that is on the dry side. Feed every spring with

Cut plants to the ground in late winter to keep them looking nice.

plant food, such as Miracle-Gro. Prune out any dead, damaged, or diseased branches at any time. Prune to control form and size immediately after flowering. Begin light pruning of hedges the first year after planting. As plants become more vigorous, prune more heavily. Cut overgrown shrubs all the way back to the ground in early spring to renew.
PROPAGATION: Take softwood cuttings from new growth just as it begins to harden. Take hardwood cuttings anytime during the dormant season. Seeds germinate readily without pretreatment; however, named varieties do not come true from seed.
PESTS AND DISEASES: None are serious. Powdery mildew may show up on hedge plants. Snip out the infected areas and dispose of the foliage.
RELATED SPECIES: Var. *intermedius* grows smaller and denser, to 4' tall. 'Nanus' is even smaller—to 2' tall and wide. 'Dart's Gold' has yellow foliage and grows to 5' tall and wide with bright leaf color. 'Nugget' has golden-yellow foliage and a denser habit; it reaches 6' tall and wide. 'Monlo' (Diabolo®) is a popular cultivar with leaves that emerge deep purple.

COLORADO SPRUCE

Picea pungens PEYE-see-uh PUN-jenz

Colorado spruce has bluish needles.

ZONES: 3–7(8)
SIZE: 30–60'h × 10–20'w
TYPE: Evergreen tree
FORM: Pyramidal
TEXTURE: Medium to coarse
GROWTH: Slow to medium
LIGHT: Sun

MOISTURE: Moderate to high
SOIL: Rich, well drained
FEATURES: Evergreen foliage
USES: Specimen, groupings
FLOWERS: ■
FALL COLOR: ■ ■

SITING: This popular evergreen grows too large for most city lots, but it makes a striking specimen where it can grow to its full width without crowding. There are many compact and dwarf forms available.

It prefers cool climates and moist, humus-rich, well-drained soil and full sun. It is intolerant of heat, drought, and air pollution.
CARE: Keep the soil evenly moist from spring until the ground freezes. Feed every spring with acid plant food. Light tip pruning in early summer just as new growth begins to harden off will help maintain the distinct pyramidal shape. Avoid removing lower branches.
PROPAGATION: Take hardwood cuttings in midwinter. Sow seeds of the species when ripe. Graft onto seedling rootstocks.

Closely spaced plants are likely to develop cytospora canker.

Prune trees lightly in spring to shape.

PESTS AND DISEASES: Sawflies can leave bare spots on trees. In hot, dry weather, spider mites can be a problem. Spruce gall aphids can cause distorted tip growth. Cankers, which appear as oozing wounds on trees and branches, can be fatal. Prevent cankers by giving trees ample spacing and proper growing conditions. Needle cast shows up as purplish discoloration of needles, affecting older branches first. Control of both of these diseases is difficult, and severely infected trees usually die.

RELATED SPECIES: Norway spruce (*P. abies*) is faster growing and commonly used as a windbreak or screen. Leaf color is dark green. White spruce (*P. glauca*) has ash-gray needles, is more adaptable to harsh growing conditions, and is less subject to the insect and disease problems.

JAPANESE PIERIS

Pieris japonica pee-AIR-us juh-PAHN-ih-kuh

Clusters of dangling white flowers adorn Japanese pieris.

ZONES: 5–9
SIZE: 9–12'h × 6–8'w
TYPE: Evergreen shrub
FORM: Upright
TEXTURE: Medium
GROWTH: Slow
LIGHT: Sun to light shade
MOISTURE: Average to high

SOIL: Acid, humusy, rich, well drained
FEATURES: Showy flowers, good foliage color
USES: Specimen, shrub border, foundation
FLOWERS: □
FALL COLOR: ■

SITING: Japanese pieris has dark green leaves that are often bronze or reddish

when young. The fragrant white flowers in pendulous clusters appear in early spring. Flowers are sometimes injured by frosts. It prefers rich, acid, well-drained soil and full sun or light shade; some shade is necessary in southern areas. Shelter from wind in any climate. It does not tolerate wet soils. It does well in a semishady shrub border or as an informal hedge. It is often grown in the woodland garden. It makes a good specimen shrub for the light shade under large oaks or pines. Combine Japanese pieris with other acid-loving broadleaf evergreens such as rhododendrons and hollies. Plants grown in colder zones may die back after severe winters. It is deer resistant.
CARE: Maintain a 2–4" layer of organic mulch. The soil should drain freely and not be overly wet or boggy. Young plants grow faster if given an annual application of acid plant food such as Miracle-Gro Shake 'n Feed Azalea, Camellia, Rhododendron. It blooms on the previous season's growth, so avoid pruning in winter. If the fruits are allowed to develop, there may be fewer flowers the following

year, so cut off spent flowers right away and it will produce more flowers the next year. Prune foliage that becomes desiccated in winter.
PROPAGATION: Take cuttings in summer. Layer in spring or summer. Sow seeds in fall or early spring.
PESTS AND DISEASES: Lace bugs suck sap and cause yellow leaves. To control, spray leaves, especially the undersides, with insecticidal soap. Plants grown in heavy soils may get root rot. Leaf spots, dieback, scale, spider mites, and nematodes can also be problems.
RELATED SPECIES: 'Dorothy Wycoff' is a compact grower with deep red buds that open to pink. 'Mountain Fire' has exceptional orange-red new growth and large white flowers. 'Red Mill' is hardier. 'Valley Valentine' bears long-lasting deep pink flowers. 'Variegata' has white-edged leaves. 'White Cascade' has pure white flowers. Mountain pieris (*P. floribunda*) is more cold tolerant (to Zone 5) and grows 2–6' tall and wide. It is resistant to lace bug and is tolerant of higher-pH soils.

JAPANESE RED PINE

Pinus densiflora PEYE-nus den-sih-FLOH-ra

Japanese red pine has an interesting irregular growth habit.

ZONES: (5)6–7
SIZE: 40–60'h × 40–60'w
TYPE: Evergreen tree
FORM: Irregular
TEXTURE: Medium
GROWTH: Slow to medium
LIGHT: Sun

MOISTURE: Average
SOIL: Slightly acid, well drained
FEATURES: Orange-red bark, picturesque form
USES: Specimen, bonsai
FLOWERS: ■
FALL COLOR: ■

SITING: Japanese red pine has an irregular, crooked growth habit and frequently leans as it grows older. The showy orangish to orangish-red bark peels off in thin scales.

It prefers well-drained, slightly acid soil and full sun. It is not salt tolerant.
CARE: Pines are best transplanted balled and burlapped. Keep the soil evenly moist from spring until the ground freezes in fall. Mature plants are drought tolerant. Feed every spring with acid plant food such as Miracle-Gro Shake 'n Feed Azalea, Camellia, Rhododendron. Prune the new growth just as candles begin to harden off in late spring or early summer; pinch back by about one-third.
PROPAGATION: Seeds require no stratification and germinate readily.
PESTS AND DISEASES: Pine shoot moth bores into the tips of new shoots, killing

them. Snip off infected tips and destroy them. Sawfly larvae nibble on needles, causing bare patches. Pick off the yellow worms by hand, or spray trees with an insecticide. Pine needle scale causes needles to turn yellow and eventually die; spray trees with a dormant oil spray in early spring.
RELATED SPECIES: Lacebark pine (*P. bungeana*) is hardy in Zone 5. It has attractive peeling bark. Limber pine (*P. flexilis*) is tolerant of tough conditions and grows in Zone 4. Austrian pine (*P. nigra*) is hardy to Zone 3 and has a more pyramidal growth habit. It makes a good windbreak or screen.

Prune pines by pinching back the new growth before needles elongate.

Always allow at least one-half of the candle to remain.

DWARF MOUNTAIN PINE

Pinus mugo PEYE-nus MYOO-goh

Swiss mountain pine, also known as mugo pine, can become a large shrub.

ZONES: 3–7(8)
SIZE: 15–20'h x 20–25'w
TYPE: Evergreen shrub
FORM: Broad, bushy
TEXTURE: Medium
GROWTH: Medium
LIGHT: Sun to part shade

MOISTURE: Average
SOIL: Well drained
FEATURES: Orange-red bark, picturesque form
USES: Specimen, foundation
FLOWERS: ■
FALL COLOR: ■

SITING: Dwarf mountain pine has bright green, rigid needles in bunches of two. The needles may take on a yellowish cast in winter, especially at their tips. Mature

specimens can have a variable shape, ranging from prostrate to pyramidal. Keep the mature size of this shrub in mind when choosing a site. It starts out as a little "button," but grows into a large plant that often outgrows its site. Use it in groups or mass plantings, in foundation plantings, or as a border. It can also be used as a specimen with regular pruning. It is one of the few pines that is tolerant of some shade. It can be used in planters or raised containers.
CARE: Mugo pines are available balled and burlapped and container grown. They are easy to transplant in spring or fall. They prefer well-drained conditions in full sun. They are not salt tolerant. Keep soil evenly moist from spring until the soil freezes in fall. Mature plants are drought tolerant. Feed every spring with an acid plant food such as Miracle-Gro Shake 'n Feed Azalea, Camellia, Rhododendron. Prune annually in spring by removing two-thirds of each young, expanding candle. Choose dwarf varieties if you want a plant less than 15' tall and wide.
PROPAGATION: Seeds require no stratification and germinate readily.

PESTS AND DISEASES: Scale can cause needles to turn yellow and eventually die. Kill scale eggs by spraying trees with a dormant oil spray in early spring.
RELATED SPECIES: Many selections of mugo pine are available, ranging from true dwarfs to large shrubs, but they are often mixed up in the nursery trade. 'Compacta' grows to 3' tall and 4' wide. Var. *mugo* is a mounded form with a tufted appearance that grows 8' tall and 10' wide. The variety *pumilio* is a variable prostrate form. 'Amber Gold' is a mounding selection that is compact and slow growing. The needles turn orange-yellow in the cold months, fading to green again in spring. 'Mops' is a popular dwarf form (to 3' tall) that remains very tight and small without pruning. 'Slowmound', another popular true dwarf selection (to 3' tall), forms a dark green, dense mound and won't outgrow its planting space. 'Tannenbaum' is a larger grower, forming a nicely pyramidal shape with dense habit and deep green needles. It grows 10' tall with a spread of 6'. 'Teeny' is perhaps the smallest form available, exhibiting very short needles and short growth to form a compact 10" bun.

EASTERN WHITE PINE

Pinus strobus *PEYE-nus STROH-bus*

Eastern white pine has soft needles.

ZONES: 3–7(8)
SIZE: 50–80'h × 20–40'w
TYPE: Evergreen tree
FORM: Pyramidal
TEXTURE: Medium fine
GROWTH: Fast
LIGHT: Sun

MOISTURE: Low to high
SOIL: Fertile, well drained
FEATURES: Soft foliage
USES: Specimen, screening, windbreak
FLOWERS: ■
FALL COLOR: ■

SITING: This large, fast-growing tree is best reserved for rural landscapes or large estates. It makes a magnificent specimen where allowed to grow to its full height and width. Smaller species are better choices for city landscapes. Pines prefer well-drained, slightly acid soil and full sun. They are not salt tolerant. Keep them away from roadways, where salt will cause the needles to brown.

CARE: Keep soil evenly moist from spring until the ground freezes in fall. Mature plants are drought tolerant. Leave fallen needles to form a natural acid mulch around the tree. Feed every spring with acid plant food such as Miracle-Gro Shake 'n Feed Azalea, Camellia, Rhododendron. Prune only if needed to shape trees. Prune new growth just as it begins to harden off in late spring or early summer; cut back by about one-half to one-third.

Get rid of nearby currants and gooseberries to reduce rust.

Road salt damage results in browned needles.

PROPAGATION: Seeds should be stratified for 60 days or more. It is difficult to root from cuttings.

PESTS AND DISEASES: White pine is susceptible to white pine blister rust, which shows up as a powdery red rust on the bark. Avoid planting pines near the alternate hosts, currants and gooseberries. White pine weevil kills terminal shoots, causing trees to become bushy and unsightly. The same insect pests listed under Japanese red pine (page 434) can infect this group of pines.

RELATED SPECIES: Ponderosa pine (*P. ponderosa*) is better suited to western states, where it is used in shelter belts. Red or Norway pine (*P. resinosa*) is a good choice for cold climates. It is hardy in Zone 2. Scotch pine (*P. sylvestris*) is hardy and wind resistant and has a more irregular but picturesque growth habit. Loblolly pine (*P. taeda*) is hardy in Zones 6–9 and is more resistant to the insects and diseases that plague other pines. It is a good choice for southern gardens.

CHINESE PISTACHIO

Pistacia chinensis *pis-TAH-shee-uh cheye-NEN-sis*

Chinese pistachio, also known as Chinese pistache, is a good choice for southern landscapes.

ZONES: 6–9
SIZE: 30–35'h × 25–35'w
TYPE: Deciduous tree
FORM: Rounded oval
TEXTURE: Medium
GROWTH: Medium
LIGHT: Sun

MOISTURE: Low to high
SOIL: Well drained
FEATURES: Bark, adaptable to tough conditions, fall color
USES: Street, shade
FLOWERS: ■
FALL COLOR: ■ ■ ■

SITING: Chinese pistache is a tough, adaptable, trouble-free tree that is a good choice for city conditions in the South. The leaves hold late into fall, turning brilliant yellow, orange, and orange-red. Its desirable fall color makes it an outstanding specimen, shade, or street tree. The oval rounded canopy and open branching habit create light shade, so it can be interplanted with shade-loving shrubs. Lower branches often droop toward the ground with time, forming a spreading crown. The attractive peeling bark becomes scaly and develops shallow furrows with age. Scales flake off to expose salmon-colored inner bark. The inconspicuous flowers are borne in panicles in spring. Female trees develop small, spherical red clusters of peppercorn-like seeds that turn blue when they ripen in fall. They are attractive to birds. Fruits are reasonably showy but not a reason to grow the tree. The best growth is in moist, well-drained soils and full sun, but it is adaptable to a wide range of conditions, including poor, dry soils, poor drainage, compacted soil, drought, heat, and air pollution. It is a good sidewalk tree and can withstand the harsh conditions in cut-out sidewalk areas. Young trees are asymmetrical and a bit awkward looking unless properly pruned in the nursery. This gawky young stage is one reason this tree has not been widely planted. It grows best in Zones 7–9, where its makes a good substitute for the North's sugar maple, with its desirable fall color.

CARE: Transplant balled-and-burlapped or container-grown specimens. Young trees require an inch of water a week for the first year or two after planting. Mature specimens are drought tolerant but should receive one or two deep irrigations per month in the hottest season. It needs pruning, and possibly staking, in youth to form a straight trunk and a good crown. If birds do not eat fruits, seed drop on female trees can be messy.

PROPAGATION: Collect seeds from the bluest fruits. Clean pulp from seeds and sow in moist soil mix at about 40°F.

PESTS AND DISEASES: None are serious.

JAPANESE PITTOSPORUM
Pittosporum tobira *pit-oh-SPOH-rum toh-BEER-ruh*

Japanese pittosporum is only suitable for the warmest areas of the country.

ZONES: (8)9 and 10
SIZE: 10–12'h × 15–20'w
TYPE: Evergreen shrub or tree
FORM: Broad spreading
TEXTURE: Medium
GROWTH: Slow
LIGHT: Sun to shade
MOISTURE: Low to high

SOIL: Well drained
FEATURES: Fragrant flowers, leathery leaves
USES: Hedge, massing, foundation, screening, container
FLOWERS: □
FALL COLOR: ■

SITING: Japanese pittosporum is a popular southern shrub, especially in Florida. It is dense and compact, making it a popular choice for screens and informal hedges. It can be closely sheared to create formal hedges and topiary. By selectively trimming and removing the lower limbs, it can be grown as a small tree. Plants grown in full sun are more compact. Flowers are five petaled and creamy white with a strong orange-blossom scent; they appear in spring. It prefers full sun to

Young plants will require regular pruning, especially in hedges.

partial shade but tolerates deep shade. It adapts to sandy and clay soils as long as they are well drained, and it tolerates acid to alkaline soils. It thrives in sandy soils and hot, dry locations. Its drought and salt tolerance make it a good choice for seasides. It grows best in Zones 9 and 10.
CARE: Transplant from containers at any time. Water young specimens as needed until they are established. Mature shrubs are drought tolerant. Young shrubs benefit from a spring application of plant food, such as Miracle-Gro. Rapid growth when young makes this a fairly high-maintenance shrub, requiring frequent pruning, but growth slows with age as the plant reaches about 10' tall.
PROPAGATION: Woody cuttings root easily at any time.
PESTS AND DISEASES: None are serious. Leaf-spot disease, stem canker, and mealybugs can show up in some years. Aphids and scale congregate along the midrib on the underside of leaves.
RELATED SPECIES: 'Variegatum' has white and gray-green foliage and grows about 5' tall. 'Wheeler's Dwarf' grows to about 2' tall; 'Nana' is about 3' tall.

LONDON PLANE TREE
Platanus ×acerifolia *PLAH-tuh-nuss ay-sir-ih-FOH-lee-uh*

Interesting exfoliating bark is showy year-round.

ZONES: (5)6–8
SIZE: 70–100'h × 65–80'w
TYPE: Deciduous tree
FORM: Pyramidal to open
TEXTURE: Medium coarse
GROWTH: Medium
LIGHT: Sun to light shade

MOISTURE: Medium to high
SOIL: Fertile, well drained
FEATURES: Handsome bark
USES: Street, specimen, shade
FLOWERS: ■
FALL COLOR: ■ ■

SITING: London plane tree develops a massive trunk and heavy branches. Its bark exfoliates in large flakes, creating layers of green, tan, and yellowish white. Autumn color is a poor yellow-brown. Ball-shaped fruits persist into winter. Dropped leaves, twigs, and fruits can be a litter problem. The tree can be used as a shade or specimen tree, but with caution because of its large size and its pest and litter problems. It prefers deep, rich, moist, well-drained soils but will grow in almost anything, including high-pH soils. The best growth is in full sun, but it tolerates part

Canker stain can be a serious problem on London plane tree.

shade. It tolerates air pollution and other harsh conditions of cities.
CARE: Young plants grow best with consistent moisture; mature specimens are drought tolerant. Feed young trees or diseased trees in spring with plant food, such as Miracle-Gro. Prune in winter if needed to shape. Trees withstand heavy pruning and can be pleached to form allées. Wrap young trees in winter to prevent frost cracking on the trunk.
PROPAGATION: Seeds require cold treatment for 3 months. Take hardwood cuttings in winter.
PESTS AND DISEASES: Canker stain can kill large trees. Avoid damaging the bark with sharp gardening tools and power equipment. Anthracnose (a leaf-spot disease) and powdery mildew can be problems on some trees. Clean up dropped leaves and twigs to remove overwintering sites for disease spores. Plant disease resistant cultivars.
RELATED SPECIES: 'Bloodgood', 'Liberty', and 'Yarwood' have good resistance to anthracnose and powdery mildew. Sycamore (*P. occidentalis*) is hardier, into the southern part of Zone 4.

CHINESE PODOCARPUS

Podocarpus macrophyllus poh-doh-KAR-pus mak-roh-FILL-us

Chinese podocarpus makes a good screen in mild climates.

ZONES: 8–10
SIZE: 20–40'h ×
10–15'w
TYPE: Evergreen
tree or shrub
FORM: Upright to
oval
TEXTURE: Medium
fine
GROWTH: Slow
LIGHT: Sun to
part shade

MOISTURE: Low to
medium
SOIL: Fertile, well
drained
FEATURES: Graceful
evergreen foliage
USES: Hedge,
specimen, container
FLOWERS: ■
FALL COLOR: ■

SITING: This striking evergreen tree or large shrub has a graceful, Asian look. It is popular as a dense screen or hedge. It can reach 40' in height when not sheared. If space permits, leave the lower limbs on the tree for an almost sprucelike appearance. It has limber branches that can be easily trained as an espalier specimen on a wall or fence. On female trees, the inconspicuous flowers are followed by fleshy, small purple fruits that are very good to eat and attract birds. It prefers well-drained, fertile soils and full sun or light shade. It does not tolerate wet feet. The soil can be neutral, slightly acid, or slightly alkaline. It is tolerant of salt spray and is often used next to light-colored buildings in coastal areas. Keep its mature size in mind if planting it near buildings or sidewalks. It can be grown as a greenhouse plant in a large tub in northern climates.

CARE: Transplant from containers at almost any time of year. Plants grown in highly alkaline soils may show iron chlorosis. Young plants grow best with consistent moisture during the growing season; mature specimens are drought tolerant. Apply a 2–4" layer of organic mulch such as wood chips, shredded oak leaves, or pine bark to keep the soil evenly moist. In spring feed young trees or stressed trees with plant food, such as Miracle-Gro, or an organic equivalent such as fish emulsion. Container-grown plants need regular applications of water-soluble plant food such as Miracle-Gro. It can be pruned to shape at any time.

PROPAGATION: Seeds require 2 years to germinate. Hardwood cuttings root easily in late summer and fall.

PESTS AND DISEASES: Root rot can be a problem if plants are grown in heavy soil; amend with a mixture of sand and peat moss to loosen soil and improve drainage. Scale shows up occasionally but is usually not serious.

RELATED SPECIES: 'Maki' is a shrubby form that grows slowly to 10' tall. 'Brodie' and 'Spreading' are spreading types with a ground-cover habit. 'Variegatus' has variegated creamy white to white foliage.

EASTERN COTTONWOOD

Populus deltoides POP-yew-lus del-TOY-deez

Eastern cottonwood, also known as cottonwood, has good fall color.

ZONES: 3–9
SIZE: 75–100'h ×
50–75'w
TYPE: Deciduous
tree
FORM: Broad vase
TEXTURE: Medium
coarse
GROWTH: Fast
LIGHT: Sun

MOISTURE: Low to
high
SOIL: Deep, well
drained
FEATURES: Tolerant
of difficult sites
USES: Screening,
massing
FLOWERS: ■
FALL COLOR: ■

SITING: This large tree is weak wooded. It is best used where you need a screen quickly. It is short lived and disease prone, so you should also plant a slower-growing, longer-lived tree or erect a fence with it to maintain screening. This is a messy tree, dropping leaves, flowers, fruits, twigs, and branches in high winds. Keep the spreading roots away from sidewalks, buildings, and septic systems. It prefers moist sites along water but tolerates dry soil. It also tolerates saline conditions and air pollutants.

CARE: Transplant in spring or fall. Water young trees as needed. Prune in summer to avoid bleeding, which occurs at other times. Stray seedlings will appear in open areas.

Suckers need to be removed regularly on landscape plants.

Canker is a serious problem on Lombardy poplar.

PROPAGATION: Take cuttings in late summer or winter. Sow seeds in summer.

PESTS AND DISEASES: Several cankers severely damage trunks and stems, causing trees to become disfigured or die. Leaf diseases, including leaf spots, rust, and powdery mildew, disfigure leaves and often lead to premature defoliation. Insect pests include aphids, borers, scale, and willow leaf beetle.

RELATED SPECIES: Lombardy poplar (*P. nigra* 'Italica') is a popular cultivar with a narrow, columnar growth habit and short, ascending branches all along the trunk. It is often used for quick screening and windbreaks. It is susceptible to cytospora canker, which can kill younger trees and severely disfigure older trees. Quaking aspen (*P. tremuloides*) has quaking leaves that add sound and animation to a landscape. It is hardier (Zone 2) and grows best in cooler climates. The foliage turns brilliant yellow in fall.

BUSH CINQUEFOIL

Potentilla fruticosa poh-ten-TILL-uh froo-tih-KOH-suh

Bush cinquefoil is a long-blooming shrub for tough sites.

ZONES: 2–6(7)
SIZE: 1–4'h × 2–4'w
TYPE: Deciduous shrub
FORM: Low rounded
TEXTURE: Fine
GROWTH: Slow
LIGHT: Sun
MOISTURE: Low to medium

SOIL: Fertile, well drained
FEATURES: Showy summer flowers
USES: Shrub border, foundation, hedge
FLOWERS: □ ▨ ▨ ▨
FALL COLOR: ▨

SITING: This low-growing, tough plant has an extremely long bloom period—from late June until the first frost. Flowers come in shades of white, yellow, and gold, which hold up well in summer heat, and orange, pink, and red, which require cooler summer temperatures to hold their color. Plants are salt tolerant, so this is a good shrub to plant along sidewalks and roadways. It can also be used in rock gardens, in the front of a shrub border, or mixed in perennial borders. It can be used as a large-scale ground cover on

Dislodge aphids with a strong spray from a garden hose.

slopes. It thrives in hot, open sites with full sun and can tolerate wind and salt.
CARE: This plant needs good drainage. Amend compacted soils with organic matter or plant in a raised bed. Keep the soil evenly moist from spring until the ground freezes in fall, especially during the first 2 years. A 1–2" layer of organic mulch will help maintain even moisture. Feed every spring with plant food, such as Miracle-Gro. Prune annually as older stems produce fewer flowers. Cut all stems back by one-third or remove a few of the oldest stems at ground level in late winter or early spring.
PROPAGATION: Take cuttings in summer. Sow seeds in fall.
PESTS AND DISEASES: Spider mites can be a problem in hot, dry weather, causing foliage to become yellowish and speckled. Spray plants forcefully with a hose to deter them.
RELATED SPECIES: 'Coronation Triumph' is a vigorous form with soft green foliage and bright yellow flowers. 'Abbotswood' and 'Mount Everest' have large white flowers. 'Pink Beauty' has deep pink flowers. 'Tangerine' has orange flowers when grown in light shade in cooler areas.

CAROLINA CHERRY LAUREL

Prunus caroliniana PROO-nus kair-oh-lin-ee-ANN-uh

Carolina cherry laurel has fragrant flowers in early spring.

ZONES: 7–10
SIZE: 20–30'h × 15–25'w
TYPE: Evergreen shrub or small tree
FORM: Pyramidal oval
TEXTURE: Medium
GROWTH: Fast
LIGHT: Sun to part shade

MOISTURE: Low to medium
SOIL: Well drained
FEATURES: Adaptable to tough sites
USES: Screening, hedge
FLOWERS: □
FALL COLOR: ▨

SITING: This versatile evergreen is usually kept at shrub stature by pruning, but it is attractive when maintained as a small tree by removing suckers and limbs. Avoid planting it close to buildings; it tends to overgrow its boundaries. Fragrant white flowers appear in late winter and early spring and are followed by blue-black fruits that are a favorite food of birds. Birds eat fruits and deposit seeds all over the landscape, and stray seedlings can appear everywhere. Flower and fruit litter can be a problem if planted near sidewalks or driveways. It adapts to many types of soil but prefers moist, well-drained soil. It becomes chlorotic in alkaline soils. It is subject to ice, snow, and wind damage. It grows in urban areas where air pollution, poor drainage, compacted soil, or drought are common. A southern favorite for trimmed hedges and screens, it can be used for topiary and specimen trees as well.
CARE: Keep the soil evenly moist from spring until the ground freezes in fall, especially during the first 2 years. A 1–2" layer of organic mulch such as wood chips or shredded bark will help maintain even moisture. Feed every spring with plant food, such as Miracle-Gro, or an organic equivalent such as fish emulsion. It withstands heavy pruning, which is best done after flowering.
PROPAGATION: Sow seeds in fall for germination the following spring. Take hardwood cuttings in winter.
PESTS AND DISEASES: None are serious. Minor problems include leaf spot and damage from chewing insects. Shot hole is a disease that causes small, circular lesions on the leaves of infected plants. Tissue from the lesions is shed by the plant, leaving numerous holes in infected leaves that are sometimes confused with insect feeding damage.
RELATED SPECIES: 'Bright 'N Tight'™ (also sold as 'Compacta') is a compact, tightly branched form with smaller leaves; it grows better in most landscape situations. English laurel (*P. laurocerasus*) is hardy in Zones 6–8 and usually grows 10–18' tall. It makes a good hedge plant in the South and in California. It forms upright clusters of white flowers, which become showy black berries in fall if they haven't been pruned off in hedges.

JAPANESE FLOWERING CHERRY

Prunus serrulata PROO-nus sair-yew-LAH-tuh

Clusters of pink flowers cover Japanese flowering cherry trees in early spring.

ZONES: 5–8
SIZE: 25–30'h × 20–25'w
TYPE: Deciduous tree
FORM: Vase-shaped to rounded
TEXTURE: Medium
GROWTH: Fast
LIGHT: Sun

MOISTURE: Medium to high
SOIL: Well drained, fertile
FEATURES: Showy spring flowers, reddish new foliage
USES: Specimen, massing
FLOWERS: ☐ ■
FALL COLOR: ■ ■

SITING: The new foliage is often reddish tinged and eventually changes to dark green. Fall color is bronze to reddish.

Clustered single or double white or pink flowers appear in spring, usually before the foliage. It does not like poorly drained soil but tolerates windy locations. Plants tend to be short lived.

CARE: Uniform moisture throughout the growing season results in better bloom. Avoid overfeeding, which can stimulate succulent growth that is susceptible to insects and diseases. Prune minimally just after flowering to shape or control size.
PROPAGATION: Sow seeds in fall. Take cuttings in summer or fall.

Prune out black knot about 4 inches below the infection.

PESTS AND DISEASES: Black knot, a fungal disease, appears as a swollen portion of the stem tissue that matures into a black knot on the stem. Cut out about 4" below the knot and destroy the upper portion of the stem.
RELATED SPECIES: Myrobalan plum (*P. cerasifera*) is a small tree or shrub with starlike flowers. The dark purple fruits are edible. Purple-leaf sand cherry (*P. ×cistena*) is a deciduous shrub that grows 7–10' tall. The foliage is reddish purple throughout the summer. It is hardy to Zone 4, but stems often die back in winter. Amur chokecherry (*P. maackii*) is a 35' tree with a pleasing upright form and showy tan to coppery-brown bark. It has many clusters of tiny flowers in spring and fruits in fall. It is hardy to Zone 3. Sargent cherry (*P. sargentii*) is covered with clouds of pink flowers in spring. This small tree (to 30') grows best in Zones 5 and 6. Higan cherry (*P. subhirtella*) is a bushy plant with small, fine-textured leaves. Common chokecherry (*P. virginiana*) often grows as large thickets of irregular small trees. The fruits are a favorite of birds. It is less susceptible to black knot and is hardy in Zone 2.

GOLDEN LARCH

Pseudolarix amabilis soo-doh-LAIR-iks uh-MAHB-uh-lis

This open, spreading tree becomes pyramidal with age.

ZONES: (5)6–7
SIZE: 30–50'h × 20–40'w
TYPE: Deciduous coniferous tree
FORM: Pyramidal, wide spreading
TEXTURE: Medium
GROWTH: Slow

LIGHT: Sun to light shade
MOISTURE: Moderate
SOIL: Light, acid, well drained
FEATURES: Graceful horizontal branches
USES: Specimen
FLOWERS: ■
FALL COLOR: ■

SITING: Golden larch is one of the few narrow-leaved trees that are also deciduous. It gets its common name from the soft foliage that turns golden yellow

in autumn. It has open, broadly spreading branches that become more horizontal as it ages. Leaves are needles arranged both spirally on twigs and in clusters on short lateral spurs. The needles are 1½–2½" long. They start out emerald green in spring, turning bluish green in summer. The needles are much longer and softer than on larch, which it is often compared to. Fall color is a showy ochre yellow, perhaps better than on Japanese larch but shorter lived. The needles often fall within 1–2 weeks of turning. Mature cones are 2–3" long and 1½–2½" wide. They start out green to purple-green during the summer, then turn golden brown in fall. The cones add ornamental interest, but they are often born in the upper reaches of the tree and are difficult to see. The bark is reddish brown on younger trees, grayish brown on older trees, with some ridges and furrowing. It does best in a light, moist, acid, deep, well-drained soil. It can tolerate light shade and heavier soils, but it does not tolerate high pH soils. It should be protected from high winds. It is somewhat resistant to air pollutants. It is a beautiful specimen tree in large areas. It can be

used in city parks, golf courses, campuses, and large estates. It grows slowly enough that it could be integrated into the small landscape.

CARE: Plant balled-and-burlapped plants in spring or fall. Amend the soil with peat moss or ammonium sulfate before planting to provide acid conditions. Keep the soil evenly moist from spring until the ground freezes in fall. Surround young trees with a 2–4" layer of acid organic mulch such as pine needles or shredded pine bark. Mature plants are drought tolerant. Fallen needles form a natural acid mulch around large trees. Feed young trees every spring with acid plant food such as Miracle-Gro Shake 'n Feed Azalea, Camellia, Rhododendron or cottonseed meal, which is organic. Prune only to remove dead wood.

PROPAGATION: It is difficult to find fertile seeds. Trees grown in groves produce viable seed more readily. Propagation by cuttings is virtually impossible.

PESTS AND DISEASES: None are serious.
RELATED SPECIES: 'Annesleyana' is a bushy, dwarf form with short, horizontal, pendulous branches.

DOUGLAS FIR

Pseudotsuga menziesii soo-doh-TSOO-guh men-ZEE-see-eye

Douglas fir, also known as Oregon fir, has a nice pyramidal form.

ZONES: (3)4–6
SIZE: 40–80'h × 12–20'w
TYPE: Evergreen tree
FORM: Pyramidal
TEXTURE: Medium
GROWTH: Medium
LIGHT: Sun
MOISTURE: Medium to high
SOIL: Acid, well drained
FEATURES: Handsome evergreen
USES: Specimen, groupings, massing
FLOWERS: ■■
FALL COLOR: ■

SITING: Douglas fir is an upright, stately evergreen conifer with dark green to blue-green needles and small, feathery, pendulous cones. Many birds and mammals feed on the cones. It makes an attractive specimen tree but can also be used for screening or massing. Give plants plenty of room to develop their full pyramidal shape. It prefers slightly acid, moist, well-drained soils and full sun. It does not do well in dry, poor soils and windy sites. It grows best in the humid, cooler areas of the Pacific Northwest. Keep it away from hot pavement.

CARE: Amend heavy soils with organic matter before planting. Keep the soil

Improve heavy clay soil by adding organic matter before planting.

evenly moist from spring until the ground freezes in fall. Surround young trees with a 2–4" layer of acid organic mulch, such as pine needles or shredded pine bark. Mature plants are more drought tolerant. Feed young trees every spring with acid plant food such as Miracle-Gro Shake 'n Feed Azalea, Camellia, Rhododendron. Prune only to remove dead or winter-killed branches.

PROPAGATION: Seeds germinate easily without pretreatment. Cuttings are difficult to root.

PESTS AND DISEASES: Possible problems include cankers, leaf casts, leaf and twig blight, needle blight, witches'-broom, aphids, bark beetles, scale, and gypsy moths. None are serious enough to make this tree unsuitable for landscape use.

RELATED SPECIES: Subspecies *glauca* is stockier, slower growing, and more cold hardy; it is best for northern locations. 'Fastigiata' has a columnar growth habit and is useful as an accent specimen.

HOP TREE

Ptelea trifoliata TEE-lee-uh try-foh-lee-AH-tuh

Hop tree is a good choice for naturalizing on tough sites.

ZONES: 4–9
SIZE: 15–20'h × 15–20'w
TYPE: Deciduous shrub or tree
FORM: Rounded
TEXTURE: Medium
GROWTH: Slow to medium
LIGHT: Sun to shade
MOISTURE: Medium to high
SOIL: Well drained
FEATURES: Fruits, foliage
USES: Shrub border
FLOWERS: ■
FALL COLOR: ■

SITING: Hop tree is a small tree or large shrub with a dense, rounded crown that forms a broad canopy over a slender gray trunk. As a small tree, it has low branches. The trifoliate, 4–6"-long leaves are shiny and dark green on top and pale and hairy below, turning yellow in fall. Selected plants have good fall color. Inconspicuous greenish-white flowers with a delicious orange blossom-like perfume appear in terminal clusters in June. The fruit is a compressed, broadly winged samara that turns brown at maturity. It is conspicuous and ornamental from late summer through fall, sometimes persisting into winter. These flattened tan "wafers" are often consumed by wildlife. In the past this bitter fruit was used as a substitute for hops in brewing beer. Fruits and bark contain a bitter substance and the stems are pungent when bruised. The dark gray bark has warty protrusions, and young plants have reddish-brown stems. It grows best in well-drained soils but is adaptable to various soils. It will grow in sun or shade. In its native habitat, it grows in moist woodlands as an understory plant. It is a good choice for naturalizing, massing, or grouping. It tends to sucker. It is grown in small quantities by a small number of nurseries, so it may be difficult to locate.

CARE: Transplant bare-root or container-grown plants in early spring. Keep the soil evenly moist from spring until the ground freezes in fall. A 2–4" layer of organic mulch such as wood chips, pine needles, or shredded pine bark will help maintain moisture. Young shrubs benefit from a spring application of plant food, such as Miracle-Gro. Prune in late winter to remove dead or crossing branches or to improve the shape. Avoid overpruning shrubs; keep them more natural looking. Remove suckers if they spread too far.

PROPAGATION: Seeds require a 3–4 month cold period. Take cuttings in June and July.

PESTS AND DISEASES: None are serious. Various leaf spots and a rust disease may show up some years.

RELATED SPECIES: Subspecies *polyadenia* grows lower, into a shrub. It fruits heavily. 'Aurea' is a yellow-leaved form with bright gold young leaves that fade to light yellow-green by midsummer. 'Glauca' has blue-green foliage.

POMEGRANATE

Punica granatum PUE-nih-kuh grah-NAY-tum

Pomegranate fruits are edible as well as ornamental.

ZONES: (7)8–10
SIZE: 12–20'h ×
10–18'w
TYPE: Deciduous or
evergreen shrub or
tree
FORM: Rounded
TEXTURE: Medium
GROWTH: Medium
LIGHT: Sun to part
shade

MOISTURE: Medium
to high
SOIL: Well drained
FEATURES: Flowers,
fruits
USES: Border,
groupings, container
FLOWERS: ■ ■ □ ▨
FALL COLOR: ▨ ■

SITING: Pomegranate is a small tree or
large shrub, usually multistemmed.

The foliage is shiny and dark green, and the stems are somewhat thorny. Originally grown for its edible fruit, it is also known for the red-orange flowers that appear for several months in spring and early summer. If you are interested in fruit production, avoid the miniature or double-flowered varieties; they produce few or small fruits. The leathery skinned, attractive red or yellow fruits are 2–5" in diameter and appear from midsummer to late fall. The juicy pulp is the edible portion of the fruit. It may be sucked from the fruit or made into a cooling drink by the addition of sugar and water. Pomegranate is useful for screening or large hedges. It prefers a sunny location and deep soil. It thrives in acid or alkaline soils and tolerates heavy clay as long as there is sufficient drainage. Even though it is hardy in Zone 7, it rarely produces fruit and may die back to the ground. Dwarf pomegranate blooms when about 1' tall, making it excellent for containers.

CARE: Once flowering has begun in late summer, water the plant several times a week to enhance fruiting. Fruit often splits after rainy spells following extended dryness, so maintain even moisture. Mature specimens withstand drought well. Feed with water-soluble plant food once a month. If unpruned, pomegranate develops into a tree 15–20' in height, but it is easily kept to a bush of 6–12'. Birds enjoy the pomegranate fruits; the seeds are not digested, so seedlings appear in the proximity of a fruit-producing tree.

PROPAGATION: Seeds usually produce inferior plants. Take softwood cuttings in summer or hardwood cuttings in December and bury them in sand or soil, leaving just the top two buds visible. Layering and grafting are also used.

PESTS AND DISEASES: None are serious.

RELATED SPECIES: Dwarf pomegranate 'Nana' reaches 3–4' in containers. Single orange-red flowers appear from late summer into fall and are followed by 2" red fruits. 'Chico' is a dwarf with double orange-red flowers; it is almost everblooming but sets no fruit. 'Wonderful' is the most common fruiting variety; red blossoms in April are followed by 4" fruits, ripening in fall.

SCARLET FIRETHORN

Pyracantha coccinea pye-ruh-KAN-thuh kok-SIN-ee-uh

Showy orange-red fruits persist into winter.

ZONES: 6–9
SIZE: 6–18'h × 6–18'w
TYPE: Evergreen or
deciduous shrub
FORM: Open
spreading
TEXTURE: Medium
GROWTH: Medium
to fast
LIGHT: Sun to light
shade

MOISTURE: Medium
to high
SOIL: Deep, organic,
well drained
FEATURES: Showy
fruits and flowers
USES: Specimen,
foundation, espalier,
hedge
FLOWERS: □
FALL COLOR: ■

SITING: Scarlet firethorn is an evergreen
with stiff, thorny branches and an open
habit. The leaves are dark green in
summer, remaining green in mild climates

but turning brownish in winter in harsher areas. White flowers appear in spring on last year's growth. They are showy because of their numbers. The berrylike, round ¼" fruits are orange-red, ripening in September and persisting into winter. Scarlet firethorn is often used as an informal hedge or a barrier plant. It adapts well to espalier on walls and fences. It prefers deep, moist, humus-rich, well-drained soil. Plants do well where the soil

Scarlet firethorn adapts well to espalier along a wall.

is dry in summer. Full sun produces the best fruiting, but plants will grow in part shade. It adapts to a wide range of soil pH. Cold temperatures can damage leaves; some cultivars are hardier than others. It can be grown in containers.

CARE: Give young plants 1" of water a week until they are established. Keep older plants on the dry side. Young shrubs benefit from a spring application of plant food, such as Miracle-Gro. Considerable pruning done any time is necessary to keep it in bounds. Wear heavy gloves to protect hands from the spines.

PROPAGATION: Seed should be stratified for 90 days at 41°F. Softwood cuttings root readily under mist.

PESTS AND DISEASES: Fire blight can be a serious problem. Avoid overfertilization, which can promote succulent growth that is subject to fire blight. Plant disease-resistant cultivars. Scab turns fruits a dark sooty color. Other problems include twig blight, leaf blight, root rot, aphids, lace bugs, and scale.

RELATED SPECIES: 'Aurea' has yellow fruit. 'Lalandei' is somewhat hardier. 'Mohave' has upright growth and is resistant to scab and fire blight.

BRADFORD CALLERY PEAR

Pyrus calleryana 'Bradford' *PYE-russ kah-lair-ee-AY-nuh*

White blooms cover Bradford callery pear in spring.

ZONES: 5–8(9)
SIZE: 30–50'h × 20–35'w
TYPE: Deciduous tree
FORM: Pyramidal
TEXTURE: Medium
GROWTH: Fast
LIGHT: Sun

MOISTURE: Medium to high
SOIL: Well drained
FEATURES: Showy flowers, good form, fall color
USES: Specimen
FLOWERS: □
FALL COLOR: ■ ■

SITING: 'Bradford', the original selection of Callery pear, is one of the most common and recognizable ornamental trees in the American landscape. This early-flowering tree is popular for its dense branching and broadly pyramidal habit. However it forms tight branch crotch angles, which are points of weakness. Unless pruned, the tree will eventually split under its own weight. It blooms profusely in late winter to early spring. The small red-brown fruits attract birds but are not ornamentally significant. Leaves are glossy dark green and turn gold-orange or red-mahogany in late autumn. Leaves tend to hold late, and freezes may occur before color fully develops. It is tolerant of dry, hot sites and city conditions. It is usually used as a specimen tree or street tree.

CARE: Transplant container-grown or balled-and-burlapped specimens in late winter while they are still dormant. Give young trees an inch of water a week. Established trees are somewhat drought tolerant. Feed every spring with plant food, such as Miracle-Gro, or an organic equivalent such as fish emulsion. Prune young trees while dormant, in late winter or early spring, to reduce or eliminate limb breakage.

PROPAGATION: Cultivars don't come true from seed. Propagate callery pear from softwood cuttings.

PESTS AND DISEASES: None are serious. Although it is usually resistant to fire blight, this disease can affect the tree.

RELATED SPECIES: 'Aristocrat' limbs have a wider branching angle, which makes the tree less likely to split. It reaches 35' tall with a slightly narrower spread. It may be more susceptible to fire blight than 'Bradford'. 'Autumn Blaze' is considered the hardiest cultivar. Fall foliage is a reliable red-purple, but the plant is prone to fire blight and bears some thorns. 'Capital' is narrow and upright, growing to 35' tall and 10' wide. It is susceptible to fire blight. 'Glen's Form' has an upright, pyramidal habit and is longer lived and perhaps hardier than 'Bradford'. It shows good fire blight resistance and attractive red-purple fall color. 'Jaczam' (Jack™) and 'Jilzam' (Jill™) have a dwarf habit, dense growth, and a mature size less than half that of standard forms (to 20' tall and wide). Ussurian pear *(P. ussuriensis)* is the hardiest pear, surviving in parts of Zone 3.

PIN OAK

Quercus palustris *KWER-kuss pah-LUSS-tris*

Pin oak is a majestic tree for large sites.

ZONES: 4–8
SIZE: 60–70'h × 25–40'w
TYPE: Deciduous tree
FORM: Pyramidal
TEXTURE: Medium
GROWTH: Slow to medium
LIGHT: Sun

MOISTURE: Moderate to high
SOIL: Moist, rich, acid, well drained
FEATURES: Fall color, good shade
USES: Shade, specimen, street
FLOWERS: ■
FALL COLOR: ■

SITING: Pin oak has deeply lobed, sharp-pointed, glossy green leaves that turn russet, bronze, or red in fall. It is one of the best oaks for street tree use. It prefers moist, rich, acid, well-drained soil but will tolerate wet soils. Oaks are sensitive to soil compaction, so care should be taken when heavy construction equipment is used around their roots. Acorn litter can be messy.

CARE: This oak is easier to transplant than others because of its shallow, fibrous root system. Iron chlorosis is a problem if the soil pH is too high. Acidify the soil before planting and as soon as you see leaves starting to yellow. Water young trees as needed to keep the soil moist throughout the growing season. Feed young trees with acid plant food. Prune in winter only as needed. Avoid pruning in summer, when oak wilt can be transmitted by beetles attracted to pruning wounds.

PROPAGATION: Sow seeds in place in fall.

PESTS AND DISEASES: Oak wilt, which can be fatal, attacks the water-conducting system, causing upper parts of the tree to die back. It is spread by beetles and root grafts. Nonserious problems include galls, scale, anthracnose, and lace bug.

RELATED SPECIES: White oak *(Q. alba)* has deeply cut, rounded leaves, is slower growing, and is difficult to transplant because of its taproot. It is less susceptible to oak wilt. Swamp white oak *(Q. bicolor)* has rounded leaves and grows best in acid, heavy soils that retain moisture most of the growing season. Northern pin oak *(Q. ellipsoidalis)* is a northern version of pin oak that is less susceptible to iron chlorosis. Bur oak *(Q. macrocarpa)* is hardy in Zone 3. It has rounded leaves that turn yellow-brown in fall. Chinkapin oak *(Q. muehlenbergii)* usually grows to about 45'. Red oak *(Q. rubra)* is round topped and has pointed, lobed, shiny dark green leaves. It is faster growing than most oaks but is susceptible to oak wilt.

Trenching helps stop the spread of oak wilt through root grafts.

Apply a soil acidifier to prevent iron chlorosis.

LIVE OAK
Quercus virginiana *KWER-kuss vir-jin-ee-AYE-nuh*

Live oak is a stately, wide-spreading tree for southern gardens.

ZONES: (7)8–10
SIZE: 40–80'h × 60–100'w
TYPE: Evergreen or deciduous tree
FORM: Wide spreading
TEXTURE: Medium
GROWTH: Medium
LIGHT: Sun

MOISTURE: Medium to high
SOIL: Any
FEATURES: Magnificent form
USES: Shade, street, specimen
FLOWERS: ■
FALL COLOR: ■

SITING: Live oak is a noble tree with large, spreading, horizontal branches. The leathery dark green leaves are evergreen and drop in spring instead of fall except in the northern part of its range. The bark is dark red-brown to gray and deeply furrowed, eventually becoming almost black and blocky. The flowers, typical of oaks, are catkins that hang down 2–3". They appear in early spring and dust the countryside with yellow pollen. Brownish-black acorns about an inch long mature in autumn of the same year on the current season's twigs. The sweet acorns are a favorite food of birds, squirrels, and deer. Live oaks are often festooned with Spanish moss, resurrection fern, and other epiphytes, giving them a mystical quality. Trees tolerate auto exhaust and are popular choices for street trees, often forming stately "canopy roads" in southern cities. It is not a tree for small properties, but it is suitable for parks, golf courses, universities, and mansions. Young trees often have an unkempt look because they lack a strong central leader, but trees eventually take shape nicely. It is pH-adaptable and tolerant of drought and poor soils, although it does not tolerate poorly drained soils or extremely well-drained, deep sand. It is tolerant of compacted soils and salt spray. Trees grown on drier sites usually don't get as large.

CARE: Transplant small nursery trees that have a strong central leader. Water young trees as needed to keep the soil evenly moist throughout the growing season. Mature trees are drought tolerant. Young trees grow faster with an annual application of plant food, such as Miracle-Gro. Pruning to shape should begin when the tree is young. Remove limbs that have a narrow crotch angle. Thin the canopy of larger trees every 3–5 years so wind can move freely through the branches, reducing limb breakage. Thin the large, heavy tufts of growth on the ends of the branches. These limbs often break during storms because of the great weight that causes them to sway back and forth.

PROPAGATION: Sow seeds in place when they are ripe.

PESTS AND DISEASES: Problems include gall insects, root rot (in coastal areas), oak wilt, and bacterial leaf spot.

GLOSSY BUCKTHORN
Rhamnus frangula *RAM-nus FRAN-gyew-luh*

Glossy buckthorn has become an invasive weed in most areas of the country.

ZONES: 3–7
SIZE: 10–12'h × 8–12'w
TYPE: Deciduous shrub or tree
FORM: Upright spreading
TEXTURE: Medium
GROWTH: Medium to fast
LIGHT: Sun to shade

MOISTURE: Low to high
SOIL: Average, well drained
FEATURES: Clean foliage, black fruits
USES: Hedge, screening
FLOWERS: ■
FALL COLOR: ▨

SITING: Glossy buckthorn was once used extensively as a hedge plant because of its upright growth, disease-free green foliage, fast growth rate, and ability to withstand pruning. It is no longer recommended, because it spreads readily by seed and has become invasive in many areas.

CARE: It prefers well-drained soil; compacted soil will reduce the overall size. It transplants easily. It adapts to sun or shade. Water young plants as needed to maintain an even supply of moisture throughout the growing season. Mature plants can survive dry periods. A spring application of plant food, such as

Remove entire seedlings or apply a herbicide to cut stumps of established plants to prevent resprouting.

Miracle-Gro, encourages faster growth in young plants. Prune hedge plants in early spring. Pruning after flowering will cut back on fruit set and reduce seed distribution. Seedlings can easily become weeds in gardens and other unmowed areas of the landscape. They can be pulled when they are young, but older, woodier specimens require digging or the use of an herbicide applied to a cut trunk.

PROPAGATION: Buckthorn is easily propagated by seed. Take softwood cuttings in early summer.

PESTS AND DISEASES: This tough plant is basically problem free. Hedge plants may suffer dieback from a canker or wilt, and leaf spots, rust, and aphids may mar the summer foliage.

RELATED SPECIES: 'Asplenifolia' has narrow foliage with a wavy margin. It grows to 12' tall and 10' wide and has an overall ferny texture. 'Columnaris' (tall-hedge glossy buckthorn) is offered as hedging by discount merchants. It has a narrow, upright habit and may be sheared. Common buckthorn (*R. catharticus*) was used extensively for hedges in the past but is no longer recommended because of its invasive tendencies.

INDIAN HAWTHORN

Rhaphiolepis umbellata *rah-fee-oh-LEP-is um-bel-LAH-tuh*

Showy white flowers appear in late spring.

ZONES: 8–10
SIZE: 4–6'h × 4–6'w
TYPE: Evergreen shrub or tree
FORM: Mounded
TEXTURE: Medium
GROWTH: Slow
LIGHT: Sun to part shade
MOISTURE: Low to moderate

SOIL: Well drained
FEATURES: Spring flowers, evergreen foliage
USES: Massing, informal hedge, container
FLOWERS: □ ■
FALL COLOR: ■

SITING: This dense, mounded shrub can be pruned into a small tree. The evergreen leaves often take on a purplish tinge that holds through the winter. Slightly fragrant white flowers are attractive in late spring. Purple-black fruits appear in early fall and persist through the winter, but they may be hard to see against the dark foliage. Use Indian hawthorn as a low background plant, for massing, for an informal hedge, or as a large-scale ground cover. It tolerates restricted root space and will grow well in containers and aboveground planters. It prefers moist, well-drained soils with a pH of 6–7 and sun, but it will tolerate drought and part shade. It is salt tolerant and therefore a good choice for coastal areas. It is a favorite food of browsing deer. Leaves show cold injury at 0°F.

CARE: Water young plants as needed to maintain an even supply of moisture throughout the growing season. Use an organic mulch of wood chips or shredded bark to help keep disease spores from splashing up on foliage. A spring application of plant food, such as Miracle-Gro, or an organic equivalent encourages faster growth in young plants. Prune as needed to shape in winter.

PROPAGATION: Collect seeds in February, remove pulp, and plant. Propagate with semihardwood and hardwood cuttings.

PESTS AND DISEASES: Leaf spot can be a major problem, especially on plants grown in part shade where moisture remains on leaves. Some shrubs may be completely defoliated by the end of summer. Reduce disease problems by cleaning up and disposing of fallen leaves. Indian hawthorn is also susceptible to fire blight. Prune in winter to reduce chance of infection.

RELATED SPECIES: Most cultivars are either *R. indica* or *R. umbellata* hybrids and may be listed with *R. indica*. 'Clara' has new foliage that emerges red. 'Enchantress' is more compact, with rose-pink flowers in large panicles. 'Minor' has smaller leaves and grows 3–4' tall. 'Spring Rapture' has abundant rose-red flowers. 'White Enchantress' is low growing with single white flowers. Indian hawthorn (*R. indica*) is a smaller version with thinner, narrower leaves. It is slightly less hardy.

RHODODENDRON

Rhododendron spp. *roh-doh-DEN-dron*

There are many beautiful rhododendron hybrids available. This one is called 'Markeeta's Prize'.

ZONES: 4–10
SIZE: 1–20'h × 1–20'w
TYPE: Evergreen or deciduous shrub
FORM: Upright to spreading
TEXTURE: Medium to coarse
GROWTH: Slow
LIGHT: Shade to sun

MOISTURE: Medium to high
SOIL: Acid, well drained
FEATURES: Showy spring flowers
USES: Shrub border, groupings, massing
FLOWERS: □ ■ ■ ■ ■ ■
FALL COLOR: ■ ■

SITING: Rhododendrons and azaleas are noted for their gorgeous and abundant spring bloom. Bloom time can be long in a cool, humid spring. Summer foliage is not particularly attractive on deciduous azaleas, but evergreen types have attractive green leaves. These plants are in the genus *Rhododendron* but are generally separated into rhododendrons or azaleas based on their leaf and flower type. In general, azaleas are deciduous and rhododendrons are evergreen. Rhododendron flowers resemble bells; azalea blossoms are more funnel shaped. They both make excellent specimen plants and are good for massing on larger sites. Evergreen types can be used in foundation plantings. In cold climates deciduous types grow well in full sun or partial shade. Evergreen types need partial shade. In the South both types need shade. They need well-drained, acid soil. Acidify the soil before planting. Do not plant them in poorly drained soil, near salt spray, in high-pH soil, or on exposed sites with winter sun and wind.

CARE: Transplant container-grown or balled-and-burlapped plants in spring. Plants show iron chlorosis (yellow leaves)

Korean rhododendron is a good choice for landscape use.

'Roseum Elegans' is a Catawba hybrid with showy pink flowers.

RHODODENDRON
continued

if the soil is too alkaline. Mulch with pine needles, shredded pine bark, or compost to keep the shallow roots cool and moist and the soil acid. Feed the plants every spring with acid-based fertilizer such as Miracle-Gro Shake 'n Feed Azalea, Camellia, Rhododendron. Maintain an even supply of moisture throughout the growing season. Prune after flowering if necessary.

PROPAGATION: Take hardwood cuttings in midsummer. Layer in summer right after flowering. Sow seeds of the species indoors in winter.

PESTS AND DISEASES: Root rot is a problem in poorly drained soils. Powdery mildew can be a problem in humid weather. Canker and leafspot are common diseases. Lacebugs, Japanese beetle and spider mites attack rhododendrons. Good cultural practices will reduce the chance of disease and insect problems.

RELATED SPECIES: Carolina rhododendron (*R. carolinianum*) is an evergreen hardy in Zones 5–8; it grows 3–6' in height. Flowers range from pure white to rose to lilac-rose and appear in mid- to late spring. Catawba rhododendron (*R. catawbiense*) is an evergreen reliably hardy in Zones 5–8 but can be grown in protected sites in Zone 4. It grows 6–10' in height and has good evergreen foliage. Flowers are lilac-purple with green or yellow-brown markings inside and appear in mid- to late spring. Korean rhododendron (*R. mucronulatum*) is reliably hardy in Zones 5–8 but can be grown in protected sites in Zone 4. It grows 4–8' tall. The rosy-purple flowers are among the first of the species

Rhododendrons require acid soil to do well. Apply peat moss, sulfur, or ammonium sulfate to the soil regularly and feed with an acidifying plant food such as Miracle-Gro Azalea, Camellia, Rhododendron plant food.

rhododendrons to appear in spring. P.J.M hybrids are among the hardiest rhododendrons—to Zone 4. They have lavender-pink flowers. There are many hybrid groups of azaleas. Gable hybrids are small-leaved evergreens hardy in

Zones 6–8. Their flowers are generally red to purple. Ghent azaleas are deciduous with single or double flowers. The Lights Series are the hardiest azaleas, all surviving in Zone 4 and some in Zone 3. Colors range from lemon yellow to lilac.

Pinch new growth to promote branching.

Remove spent flower clusters to keep plants neat.

Water plants during dry periods to help reduce leaf scorch and winter injury.

FRAGRANT SUMAC

Rhus aromatica ROOS air-oh-MAT-ih-kuh

Fragrant sumac is known for its colorful red or yellow fall foliage.

ZONES: 3–9
SIZE: 2–6'h × 6–10'w
TYPE: Deciduous shrub
FORM: Low spreading
TEXTURE: Medium
GROWTH: Slow to medium
LIGHT: Sun to part shade

MOISTURE: Low to medium
SOIL: Acid, well drained
FEATURES: Fall color, toughness
USES: Ground cover, erosion control
FLOWERS: ▪
FALL COLOR: ▪▪

SITING: Fragrant sumac forms a dense mound of branches covered with three-lobed, slightly glossy leaves. Fuzzy, berrylike red fruits form at the tips of some of the branches of plants grown in full sun. They often persist into winter. Fall color varies from red to yellow. It tolerates full sun to partial shade. The soil should be slightly acid for best growth. It grows well in poor soil. Because of its suckering root system and tolerance of poor soils, it is highly valued as a plant for slopes, rough terrain, ground covers, and informal hedges. It is generally planted in groups.

Sumacs are good for holding the slope on steep hillsides.

CARE: Plant bare-root or container-grown plants in early spring. Keep the soil evenly moist from spring until the ground freezes in fall, especially during the first 2 years. Apply a 1–2" layer of organic mulch, such as shredded bark or wood chips, around each plant. If fall color is poor, it may be an indication that the soil is too fertile. If a plant gets out of control, shear it back in midwinter to ground level. Remove suckers in spring if they are encroaching into areas where they are not wanted.
PROPAGATION: Dig up suckers in early spring and replant immediately. Layer in summer. Seeds should be nicked before sowing in a moist, soilless potting mix.
PESTS AND DISEASES: None are serious.
RELATED SPECIES: 'Gro-low' stays at 2' or less in height and spreads up to 8' wide. It is a superb ground cover that is drought tolerant when mature. Staghorn sumac (*R. typhina*) can be shrubby or be pruned into a small tree. It has dense, velvety hairs on its stems. Foliage is medium green and turns orange, red, or yellow in fall. Female plants bear showy, upright clusters of red fruits that turn crimson in fall and persist through the winter.

ALPINE CURRANT

Ribes alpinum RYE-beez al-PEYE-num

Alpine currant, also known as mountain currant, is a hardy shrub suitable for hedging or as a mass planting.

ZONES: 2–7
SIZE: 3–6'h × 3–6'w
TYPE: Deciduous shrub
FORM: Dense rounded
TEXTURE: Medium fine
GROWTH: Medium
LIGHT: Sun to part shade

MOISTURE: Medium
SOIL: Rich, well drained
FEATURES: Easy to grow, adaptable
USES: Hedge, massing
FLOWERS: ▪
FALL COLOR: ▪

SITING: Alpine currant has a dense, twiggy, rounded growth habit and a fibrous root system that readily spreads. Stems grow quickly and multiply each year, making it a popular hedge plant. If properly pruned and cared for, plants will form a dense green barrier that will live for years. It leafs out early in spring. The leaves are deep bright green in summer, turning a poor yellow in fall. Flowers are not particularly showy. Female plants develop scarlet berries in summer, but most landscape plants are male. It tolerates most soil types and full sun or shade. It does well in alkaline soils.
CARE: Keep the soil evenly moist from spring until the ground freezes in fall, especially during the first 2 years. Apply 2–4" of mulch around each plant in late spring to retain moisture and deter weeds. Feed every spring with plant food, such as Miracle-Gro, or an organic equivalent. Prune to shape plants from early spring to midsummer. Avoid pruning in late summer and fall; it can stimulate late growth that is prone to frost damage. Pruning out older stems on a regular basis encourages the growth of new stems from the base. Trim hedge plants back lightly in the second year. Keep the top of the hedge narrower than the bottom so that light can reach the lower portions of the plant and promote leaf growth.
PROPAGATION: Take softwood cuttings in early summer. Sow seeds in fall, or give 3 months cold stratification and sow them in spring.
PESTS AND DISEASES: Alpine currant is occasionally bothered by aphids. Spraying plants daily with a garden hose can dislodge minor infestations. If they become serious, spray with an insecticidal soap or insecticide. Leaf spot may indicate that the soil is too heavy or poorly drained. If spotting is a problem on one or two branches, snip them off at their base. Anthracnose can cause serious problems in wet years, showing up as dark, water-soaked spots on leaves. If severe, plants may become defoliated. There is no practical control. If the disease appears 2–3 years in a row, cut plants back severely and start over, or replace them.
RELATED SPECIES: Clove currant (*R. odoratum*) is not as hardy, but is more resistant to foliar diseases. It has fragrant yellow flowers in spring.

BLACK LOCUST
Robinia pseudoacacia *roh-BIN-ee-uh soo-doh-uh-KAY-see-uh*

Clusters of fragrant white flowers appear in spring on black locust. The tree is also known as yellow locust.

ZONES: 4–8(9)
SIZE: 30–50'h × 20–35'w
TYPE: Deciduous tree
FORM: Open upright
TEXTURE: Coarse
GROWTH: Fast
LIGHT: Sun to part shade

MOISTURE: Low to high
SOIL: Slightly alkaline, well drained
FEATURES: Toughness, fragrant flowers
USES: Difficult sites
FLOWERS: □
FALL COLOR: ▪▪

SITING: Black locust grows in tough conditions where most other shade trees won't. It is a good choice for poor, sandy soils and for reclamation projects. It grows in almost any soil except those that are permanently wet. The showy white flowers hang in long, pendulous clusters in early summer and are fragrant and attractive to

Prune plants in late summer or fall to prevent sap flow.

bees. The thorns that form along the branches can be hazardous.

CARE: Transplant in late winter or early spring. It fixes atmospheric nitrogen, so it doesn't need supplemental feeding. Prune in late summer or fall to avoid bleeding sap, which appears if pruned in spring. Trees often produce numerous suckers at their base that may need to be pruned out.

PROPAGATION: The tough seed coat should be scarified or soaked in hot water before sowing. Suckers can be dug and replanted in early spring.

PESTS AND DISEASES: Locust borer can riddle through trees quickly and kill them. Healthy, vigorously growing trees are more resistant to borer damage. Other problems include canker, leaf spots, powdery mildew, leaf minor, and scale.

RELATED SPECIES: 'Frisia' has golden-yellow leaves. 'Burgundy' has deep pink flowers. 'Semperflorens' blooms intermittently all summer.

ROSE
Rosa hybrids and cultivars *ROH-zuh*

Hybrid tea rose 'Anne Harkness' develops pale apricot yellow blooms.

ZONES: 3–10
SIZE: 1–20'h × 1–18'w
TYPE: Deciduous shrub
FORM: Upright to spreading to vining
TEXTURE: Medium
GROWTH: Fast
LIGHT: Sun
MOISTURE: Medium

SOIL: Fertile, well drained
FEATURES: Showy, often fragrant flowers
USES: Specimen, border, container, cutting
FLOWERS: □▪▪ ▪▪▪
FALL COLOR: ▪

SITING: Hybrid roses are prized for their elegant flowers and delightful fragrance. Choose a site where you can enjoy the

'Brass Band' is an apricot blend floribunda rose.

'Crimson Bouquet' is a dark red grandiflora rose.

'Vanity' is a deep pink hybrid musk rose.

Regular spraying with a fungicide will help prevent black spot.

Prune hybrid tea roses in early spring.

ROSE
continued

showy flowers, which appear most of the summer and often into fall. Depending on the type, roses can be used for informal hedges, for covering trellises or arbors, for edging gardens, as specimen plants, or in gardens devoted just to roses. In colder climates most roses need some type of winter protection, which is often unattractive or requires space in the garden. Keep this in mind when siting the plants. They prefer slightly acid soil that has been generously amended with compost. All roses require full sun for the best flowering.

CARE: Plant bare-root roses in spring, and container-grown roses in spring or fall. Hybrid teas, floribundas, and grandifloras require regular watering throughout the growing season. They also need regular feeding from spring through midsummer to ensure many blooms. Prune hybrid teas, floribundas, miniatures, and grandifloras in early spring and climbers and shrub roses after flowering. So-called climbing types often attach themselves to their supports by their thorns but still need to be fastened or tied. Most are reliably hardy only into Zone 5. In Zones 3 and 4 they require elaborate winter protection to ensure survival. Where winters are not as severe, this can consist of mounding soil around the base and piling leaves around the plants. In extremely cold areas, a more reliable method of winter protection involves bending over the canes, laying them in a trench, and covering them with soil and/or straw or leaves.

1 Protect tender roses for winter by mounding soil around the base.

2 Surround plants with a ring of leaves held by a collar.

3 Pile several inches of soil on top of the leaves.

PROPAGATION: Take softwood cuttings in summer, hardwood cuttings in winter. Layer in spring or fall.

PESTS AND DISEASES: Problems include black spot, powdery mildew, cankers, aphids, beetles, borers, rose slugs, thrips, and spider mites. To help reduce the chances of diseases, choose a site with full sun and good air circulation, and plant disease-resistant selections. Avoid wetting foliage when watering to reduce the incidence of black spot on leaves. You may have to spray with regular applications of a combination insecticide-fungicide. If aphids or spider mites attack, spray with insecticidal soap. Knock Japanese beetles into a bucket of soapy water. Shrub roses are more resistant to most diseases.

RELATED SPECIES: Hybrid teas produce large flowers borne singly on long stems. Grandifloras have flowers similar to hybrid teas but they are often clustered. Floribundas bear clusters of smaller flowers on shorter stems and have a more bushy growth habit. They have better disease resistance than hybrid teas and tend to be slightly hardier. Climbers have long, flexible canes that can be tied to an arbor, wall, fence, and trellis. Without some type of support, they form tall, arching shrubs or sprawling mounds. Miniatures are replicas of hybrid teas but with smaller leaves, canes, and flowers. They are good for containers and low hedges. Shrub roses include the classic roses, which have a bushy, spreading habit and are cold hardy, robust, and floriferous. Modern shrub roses blend the lush form, color, and scent of old garden roses with the repeat bloom of hybrid roses. They are compact, bushy shrubs hardy in Zone 4 and some in Zone 3.

1 The Minnesota tip method is a good way to protect tender roses in Zone 4 and colder.

2 Gently pry plants from their upright position and lay them down in a trench.

3 Cover the roses with soil or bags of leaves and leave in place until spring.

SPECIES ROSES
Rosa spp. *ROH-zuh*

Species roses are usually tougher and more adaptable than their hybrid cousins.

ZONES: 3–7(8)
SIZE: 4–6'h × 4–6'w
TYPE: Deciduous shrub
FORM: Upright
TEXTURE: Medium
GROWTH: Fast
LIGHT: Sun
MOISTURE: Medium

SOIL: Well drained
FEATURES: Fragrant flowers, adaptability
USES: Mixed border, specimen, difficult sites
FLOWERS: □ ■ ■
FALL COLOR: ■ ■

SITING: Species roses are upright to low-spreading, stiff-caned shrubs armored with many thorns or bristles. They bear fragrant, five-petaled flowers for 2–4 weeks in early summer. The single white or pink flowers have a fringed ring of bright yellow anthers in the center. They set good quantities of red rose hips, which add winter interest and provide food for birds. They are hardier, more adaptable, and more disease and insect resistant than hybrid roses. Most tolerate saline conditions and drought, making them good for banks, street plantings, and other difficult sites. They grow best in slightly acid soil that has been generously amended with compost, but they tolerate a wide range of soil conditions. They require full sun to grow and flower best.
CARE: Plant container-grown specimens in spring or fall. Provide new transplants with a regular supply of water throughout the growing season; plants are drought tolerant once established. An application of plant food, such as Miracle-Gro, in spring helps increase vigor and blooming. Prune after flowering as needed to shape the plant.
PROPAGATION: Remove seeds from the fleshy covering and sow in spring or fall. Take softwood cuttings in summer, hardwood cuttings in winter. Layer in spring or fall.
PESTS AND DISEASES: These roses can be afflicted with the same problems as hybrid roses but usually not to the same extent.
RELATED SPECIES: Red-leaf rose (*R. glauca*) is usually grown more for its foliage. In full sun it has a purplish cast; in less sun it appears grayish red. Flowers are rose pink and attractive but short lived. Rugosa rose (*R. rugosa*) has red, pink, or white flowers and crinkly foliage that turns an attractive orange color in fall. It is tolerant of seaside and city conditions and less subject to insects and diseases than most roses. It is hardy in Zones 3–10.

ROSEMARY
Rosmarinus officinalis *robz-mair-EYE-nus oh-fish-ih-NAL-is*

Although prized for its aromatic leaves, rosemary also has showy purple flowers.

ZONES: (6)7–9
SIZE: 2–4'h × 3–5'w
TYPE: Evergreen shrub
FORM: Irregular
TEXTURE: Medium
GROWTH: Fast
LIGHT: Sun
MOISTURE: Low to medium

SOIL: Well drained
FEATURES: Edible, fragrant leaves; attractive flowers
USES: Kitchen herb, hedge, container
FLOWERS: ■
FALL COLOR: ■

SITING: Although usually thought of as a kitchen herb, rosemary makes an attractive and adaptable garden shrub as well. This Mediterranean native has a bushy, irregular growth habit that makes it a good addition to any landscape. It can be easily pruned into formal shapes or left to grow naturally to help dress down a formal garden. The needlelike foliage is gray-green and contrasts nicely with other dark green shrubs when it is used in the shrub border or foundation plantings. The leaves emit an unmistakable aromatic odor when bruised. The pale to dark blue flowers are borne in leaf axils from fall to spring. Their color makes it hard to see them in the foliage at times, especially in hot weather when the flowers tend to fade. Rosemary flourishes on the West Coast, where the climate is hot and dry. It is tolerant of heat, sun, infertile soil, and drought, but it can't take wet feet. Make sure the soil is well drained before planting. It needs full sun. It is easily sheared to make a hedge, and it can be used in the dry shrub border, in rock gardens, and in xeriscapes. It is salt tolerant and deer resistant. In colder climates it can be grown in containers and overwintered in a sunny window or under lights.
CARE: Plant container-grown plants anytime during the growing season. Water well for the first few weeks after planting. Avoid overwatering and overfeeding. Harvest leaves for cooking at any time. Plants that need shaping, such as hedge plants, can be pruned from spring through midsummer.
PROPAGATION: Take cuttings almost any time of year. Use a well-drained soil mix.
PESTS AND DISEASES: None are serious.
RELATED SPECIES: 'Arp' may grow in Zone 6. 'Collingwood Ingram' and 'Tuscan Blue' have bright blue flowers and an erect growth habit. 'Lockwood de Forest' has good blue flowers and a prostrate growth habit. 'Prostratus' makes a good ground cover because of its ability to spread 4–8'. 'Roseus' has pink flowers.

Harvest rosemary leaves anytime for kitchen use.

WHITE WILLOW

Salix alba SAY-liks AL-buh

Consider using white willow on wet soils.

ZONES: 2–8
SIZE: 75–100'h × 50–100'w
TYPE: Deciduous tree
FORM: Rounded, weeping
TEXTURE: Fine
GROWTH: Fast
LIGHT: Sun

MOISTURE: Medium to high
SOIL: Moisture retentive
FEATURES: Graceful stems
USES: Specimen, moist or wet sites
FLOWERS: ■
FALL COLOR: ■

SITING: White willow is a good choice for wet places where few other large trees will grow. It is one of the first trees to leaf out in spring and one of the last to hold its leaves in fall, when they turn a bronzy yellow. Ice and wind break the weak wood and create almost constant litter under trees. The spreading, suckering root system can damage sewer and septic lines. It is at its best when planted so the branches can hang over ponds. It is a short-lived tree that requires a good deal of maintenance. It is not recommended for

Willow branches litter yards after a windstorm.

small lawns or for street plantings. It grows best in moist soil or when planted next to a water feature.

CARE: Apply a 2–4" layer of organic mulch such as shredded bark or wood chips to help conserve moisture. Avoid injuring with garden tools and power equipment, which can provide entry points for diseases and insects. Prune in summer or fall, if needed, to avoid bleeding sap in spring.

PROPAGATION: Sow seeds in place. Take softwood or hardwood cuttings at any time of year.

PESTS AND DISEASES: Problems include cankers, aphids, powdery mildew, rusts, twig and leaf blights, anthracnose, and willow leaf beetle.

RELATED SPECIES: Golden weeping willow 'Tristis' is the most common and perhaps hardiest cultivar. The stringy, pendulous branchlets are a bright straw yellow that is prominent in winter. Pussy willow (*S. caprea*) is an erect tree growing to 15–25'. Its large male catkins appear in March and early April. It is hardy in Zone 4. Corkscrew willow (*S. matsudana*) 'Tortuosa' has contorted branches. It is reliably hardy in Zone 5.

AMERICAN ELDER

Sambucus canadensis sam-BYOO-kus kan-uh-DEN-sis

American elder has dense, flat-topped clusters of flowers. It is also known as elderberry, sweet elder, or elder.

ZONES: 3(4)–9
SIZE: 5–12'h × 5–12'w
TYPE: Deciduous shrub or tree
FORM: Broad, rounded
TEXTURE: Medium
GROWTH: Fast
LIGHT: Sun to part shade

MOISTURE: Medium to high
SOIL: Well drained
FEATURES: Attractive foliage, flowers, and fruits
USES: Naturalizing, screening, edible fruits
FLOWERS: □
FALL COLOR: ■ ■

SITING: This large shrub or small tree has multiple stems that are spreading or arching and a trunk that is usually short. Flowers are borne in dense, flat-topped clusters, up to 8" across in June and July. The flowers are followed by purple-black fruits in late summer. The fruits are used to make elderberry jam and are favorites of birds. American elder does best in moist soils but tolerates dry soils; it does well in acid or alkaline soils. It is difficult to utilize in most home landscapes because of the unkempt growth habit. It suckers profusely and must be pruned regularly to keep it looking neat.

Plants produce many suckers at their base.

CARE: American elder is drought tolerant once established, but plants will bloom and fruit better if given ample water and a spring feeding. Prune back hard in spring to keep it in bounds. If you are growing it for the fruit, plant at least two different cultivars for cross-pollination.

PROPAGATION: Suckers can be dug and planted in spring. Seeds require stratification in moist sand for 2 months. Softwood cuttings root easily.

PESTS AND DISEASES: None are serious.

RELATED SPECIES: 'Acutiloba' ('Laciniata') is a more demure form with deeply incised leaflets. It does not fruit as well as the species. 'Adams' and 'York' have larger, more numerous fruits. 'Aurea' has golden leaves that hold their color. It reaches 10' tall and wide but can be pruned harshly every spring to force fresh foliage. 'Variegata' has narrow leaflets outlined in creamy white-yellow. It appreciates some protection from direct sun. Common elder (*S. nigra*) grows to more than 20' tall. Flowers are borne in flat-topped cymes in June. 'Black Beauty' has superb dark purple foliage and contrasting pink flowers that have a sweet lemon fragrance.

WESTERN SOAPBERRY

Sapindus drummondii *sab-PIN-dus drum-MON-dee-eye*

Western soapberry is a good choice for arid conditions of the Southwest.

ZONES: 6–9
SIZE: 25–30'h × 25–30'w
TYPE: Deciduous tree
FORM: Oval to rounded
TEXTURE: Medium
GROWTH: Medium
LIGHT: Sun

MOISTURE: Low to medium
SOIL: Well drained
FEATURES: Tolerance of dry sites; fall color
USES: Shade, specimen
FLOWERS: □
FALL COLOR: ▣ ▪

SITING: Western soapberry is a single-stemmed, low-branched tree with a vase-shaped to rounded broad crown. The crown is usually open, showing the trunk and some major limbs, but this varies from tree to tree. The glossy medium green leaves have a downy underside; they turn deep yellow-gold in fall. The small yellowish-white springtime blooms appear in 6–10" terminal panicles and are followed by translucent, grapelike yellow-orange fruits that persist through the fall, eventually ripening to black. The low-branching habit, furrowed red-brown to gray-brown bark covering the strong, broad trunk, and clusters of translucent berries provide winter interest when the branches are bare. This trouble-free plant is adaptable to a wide variety of soils but they must be well drained. It is an excellent choice for dry soil areas in the South and Southwest. It is tolerant of high pH soils, so it grows well where many other trees do not. It flowers best in full sun but will tolerate light shade. The crown is much denser in full sun. It is extremely tolerant of pollution and other urban situations. The close-grained wood makes it a strong tree that is wind resistant. The fruits can be messy when they fall. Keep this tree away from sidewalks, driveways, decks, and patios. It may grow in protected sites in Zone 5. Native Americans made soap from the fruit, which will lather when rubbed with water between your hands. The fruits and seeds are poisonous.

CARE: Transplant container-grown or balled-and-burlapped plants in spring or fall. Loosen heavy soils before planting by adding sand and organic matter. It needs only minimal irrigation. Seedlings can appear throughout the landscape and become weedy.

PROPAGATION: Seeds are difficult to germinate; they require scarification in sulfuric acid and 3 months of cold stratification. Cuttings taken in May and June root in about 6 weeks.

PESTS AND DISEASES: None are serious.

RELATED SPECIES: 'Narrow Leaf' is a hard-to-find cultivar with narrower leaves. Chinese soapberry (*S. mukorossi*) is a somewhat brittle evergreen tree to 45' tall. It is hardy to Zone 9. Jaboncillo or false dogwood (*S. saponaria*) is native to tropical America. It grows to 30' and produces 10" panicles of white blooms that later develop ¾-inch orange-brown berries.

SWEET BOX

Sarcococca hookeriana *sar-koh-KOK-uh hook-er-ee-AYE-nuh*

Small but fragrant white flowers appear in spring and sometimes again in fall.

ZONES: (5)6–8
SIZE: 4–6'h × 4–6'w
TYPE: Evergreen shrub
FORM: Dense mounded
TEXTURE: Medium fine
GROWTH: Slow to medium

LIGHT: Part shade to shade
MOISTURE: Medium
SOIL: Acid, humusy, well drained
FEATURES: Handsome foliage, fragrant flowers
USES: Ground cover
FLOWERS: □
FALL COLOR: ▪

SITING: Sweet box is a dense evergreen shrub with a mounded outline. It spreads by rhizomes to form a colony but is not aggressive and seldom gets out of bounds. The leaves are a lustrous dark green; they turn lighter in color when plants are grown in high-pH soils or on sites with more sun. The small flowers are off-white and fragrant. They usually open in March or April, but they occasionally show up in fall too. They are difficult to see in the dense foliage, but their scent reveals their presence. Site sweet box where its fragrance can be appreciated when in bloom. Fruits are rare; they are small, shiny black drupes that persist into winter. They are not particularly showy because of the masking foliage. It prefers loose, acid, moist, well-drained soil high in organic matter. Sweet box tolerates higher-pH soils but does not grow as well and the foliage will not be as attractive. It prefers shade to partial shade and will become off-color if grown in full sun. Use sweet box for massing and as an evergreen ground cover where some height is required. It is useful in groups as a filler or as a background plant. It is an excellent low foundation plant and can be used in the shady perennial garden.

CARE: Transplant from containers. Give young plants supplemental water as needed to establish strong root systems. Mature plants are drought tolerant.

PROPAGATION: Collect fruits when ripe, remove pulp, and sow seeds in well-drained soil mix. Cuttings can be taken year-round.

PESTS AND DISEASES: None are serious.

RELATED SPECIES: Var. *digyna* is more compact, growing 2–3' tall and wide. It produces black fruits. 'Purple Stem' has purple-tinted young stems. Var. *humilis* is hardier than the species, surviving temperatures down to −3°F. It is smaller in all its parts and has black fruits. It is usually more readily available than the species. *S. confusa* is a 3–5' tall evergreen shrub that produces highly fragrant white flowers in early spring, followed by ¼-inch blue-black fruits. It is hardy in Zones 6–9. Fragrant sarcocca (*S. ruscifolia*) is 3' tall and bears white flowers followed by red fruits. It grows in Zones 7–9. Thicket-forming *S. saligna* grows 3' tall with a 6' spread. Its flowers are unscented, and they develop into ½-inch purple fruits. It is hardy in Zones 9 and 10.

SASSAFRAS
Sassafras albidum   SASS-a-frass al-BEYE-dum

Common sassafras has outstanding fall color.

ZONES: (4)5–9
SIZE: 30–60'h × 25–40'w
TYPE: Deciduous tree
FORM: Pyramidal
TEXTURE: Medium
GROWTH: Medium to fast
LIGHT: Sun to light shade

MOISTURE: Moderate to high
SOIL: Acid, well drained
FEATURES: Interesting leaves, fall color
USES: Shade, naturalizing
FLOWERS: ■
FALL COLOR: ■ ■

SITING: This tree is pyramidal when young but later develops a rounded canopy made up of many short, horizontal branches that give the tree an interesting layered effect. The 5" leaves are fragrant when crushed. They are transformed into shades of orange to pink to yellow to red in autumn. Leaves on mature trees are normally unlobed, but those of young trees are variable and often have one or two lobes, giving them a mitten shape. The twigs and roots are aromatic when bruised. Trees are either male or female and have lovely clusters of yellow flowers in early spring. Birds quickly devour the purple fruits borne on bright red stems. You need both male and female trees to get fruits. The showy fall colors are especially prominent when sassafras is planted as a specimen or in a mixed shrubbery border with a background of dark evergreens. It prefers acid, well-drained soils and full sun or light shade. It develops iron chlorosis in high-pH soils. The tree suckers and will form thickets in an undisturbed area. When grown in a regularly mown lawn, the suckers will not become a problem. It is good for massing and naturalizing in large areas, where it can separate landscapes and natural areas. In early spring the tender roots can be peeled and brewed to make sassafras tea or root beer. Deer, turkey, bear, and many birds eat the fruits in early fall, and the foliage is the primary larval host for the spicebush swallowtail butterfly. Sassafras may grow in protected locations of Zone 4.

CARE: Sassafras is difficult to transplant because of its taproot. Plant young balled-and-burlapped trees in early spring. Acidify the soil before planting by working in peat moss or ammonium sulfate. Give young trees acid plant food each spring to help them overcome transplant shock. Prune trees in winter as needed to shape. Remove unwanted suckers at any time.

PROPAGATION: Seeds have a strong dormancy, which can be overcome with moist stratification at 41°F for 4 months. Take root cuttings in winter.

PESTS AND DISEASES: None are serious. Possible problems include cankers, leaf spots, mildew, wilt, root rot, Japanese beetles, borers, scale, and bagworms.

RELATED SPECIES: *S. albidum* is the only readily available species of the genus.

JAPANESE UMBRELLA PINE
Sciadopitys verticillata   seye-ah-DOP-ih-tis ver-tih-sih-LAY-tuh

Japanese umbrella pine maintains a dense, compact growth habit.

ZONES: 5–7
SIZE: 20–30'h × 15–20'w
TYPE: Evergreen tree
FORM: Broadly pyramidal
TEXTURE: Medium coarse
GROWTH: Slow
LIGHT: Sun

MOISTURE: Medium
SOIL: Rich, acid, well drained
FEATURES: Interesting shape
USES: Specimen, rock garden, foundation
FLOWERS: ■
FALL COLOR: ■

SITING: This small to medium-size tree is planted for its unusual texture and growth habit. On young plants the dense, compact branches are held straight out from the single, straight trunk, but they become more open and pendulous with age, and the tree takes on a more pyramidal shape overall. The effect is much like the ribs on an umbrella. The distinctive long bright green needles are produced in whorls. There are two kinds of leaves. Large linear leaves are in terminal whorls of 20 to 30 and grow 2–5" long and are somewhat flattened. Smaller, scalelike leaves are distributed around the shoot below each whorl of needles. The reddish-brown bark exfoliates in shreds or strips but is generally hidden by the dense foliage. The tree grows best in rich, moist, acid soils. Avoid difficult sites with sweeping winter winds. Full sun is best, but late-afternoon sun is advantageous. Umbrella pine is used primarily as a specimen or an accent plant. Choose a site carefully; this long-lived tree is an investment in the future. Its tight growth habit makes it useful in narrow spots and foundation plantings. It can also be used in rock gardens, in conifer gardens, or as a patio or entry tree. This slow-growing tree may be difficult to find and expensive to purchase.

CARE: Transplant balled-and-burlapped or container-grown specimens in spring or fall. Give young trees an inch of water each week. Feed with acid plant food such as Miracle-Gro Shake 'n Feed Azalea, Camellia, Rhododendron every spring.

PROPAGATION: Umbrella pine is difficult to propagate. Seeds require warm stratification for 100 days or cold for 90 days. Dormant season cuttings can be taken, but rooting is slow.

PESTS AND DISEASES: None are serious. Windburn can occur on exposed sites in colder zones. The dense foliage makes Japanese umbrella pine somewhat susceptible to snow and ice damage.

RELATED SPECIES: 'Aurea', 'Ossorio Gold', and 'Ann Haddow' have golden-yellow needles. 'Jim Cross' grows slowly and densely to 10' tall. 'Joe Kozey' maintains a columnar habit with healthy green needles. 'Pendula' has weeping branches. 'Variegata' has green-and-yellow variegated needles. 'Wintergreen' features a narrow, conical habit and bright green foliage that does not discolor in winter. It grows slowly and often looks so pristine that one could mistake it for plastic.

GIANT SEQUOIA
Sequoiadendron giganteum *seh-KWOY-uh-den-dron jye-GAN-tee-um*

Giant redwood is one of the largest trees on earth. It is also known as big tree.

ZONES: 6–8
SIZE: 60–300'h × 25–23'w
TYPE: Evergreen tree
FORM: Pyramidal
TEXTURE: Medium
GROWTH: Medium
LIGHT: Sun to part shade

MOISTURE: Medium
SOIL: Well drained
FEATURES: Majestic form and size
USES: Specimen, windbreak
FLOWERS: ▧
FALL COLOR: ■

SITING: This majestic, columnar evergreen is dense and pyramidal to oval shaped in youth. Old trees lose their lower branches and become more flat topped with age. In cultivation, giant sequoia usually grows no more than 60–100' tall and retains its lower branches. In its native habitat of the Pacific Northwest, it can grow to 300' tall. Its rich reddish-brown buttressed trunk stands out in any landscape. The deeply fissured rusty red bark of mature trees is thick, protecting it from all but the most intense fires. The bright gray-green leaves are scalelike, sharp-pointed, ½" long, overlapping one another, and completely covering the twigs. The egg-shaped cones are 1½–3" long and remain on the tree for up to 20 years. Unlike the related California redwood, giant redwood does not sprout from the roots. Giant redwood makes a magnificent specimen tree if you have the space. It prefers moderately fertile, deep, well-drained soil. Seedlings and young saplings do best in partial shade. It can tolerate slightly alkaline soils and is slightly drought tolerant once established. It likes a cool, humid climate, yet does much better in the eastern United States than California redwood. Protect it from cold winter winds. It makes an excellent specimen tree or it can be grouped in a buffer strip. Trees planted 20' apart serve as an excellent windbreak.

"General Sherman" is a giant redwood growing in Sequoia National Park in California that is said to be the largest living thing on earth. It is 275' tall, and its crown is 107' in diameter.

CARE: Transplant container-grown specimens into soil that retains some moisture through the summer in a spot that receives at least 3–4 hours of sun per day. Trees grow rapidly for the first few centuries, then slow down as they surpass 150' in height. The average precipitation in the natural range of giant sequoia is 45–60" per year, mostly from snow. Water young specimens deeply and often until they are fully established.

PROPAGATION: Giant redwood is fairly easy to grow from seed. Take cuttings in winter.

PESTS AND DISEASES: None are serious.

RELATED SPECIES: 'Pendulum' has a crooked trunk with outer branches that droop. 'Pygmaeum' has a shrubby, dwarf habit, growing only 2' high and 9' wide. 'Les Barres' and 'Glauca' have bluish foliage. 'Hazel Smith' is a strong-growing upright tree with bluish needles and greater hardiness. 'Barabits Requiem' has a weeping form.

COAST REDWOOD
Sequoia sempervirens *seh-KWOY-yuh sem-per-VYE-rens*

Coast redwood, also known as redwood does best in the humid conditions of the Pacific Northwest.

ZONES: 7–9
SIZE: 40–300'h × 15–30'w
TYPE: Evergreen tree
FORM: Pyramidal
TEXTURE: Medium
GROWTH: Fast to slow
LIGHT: Sun

MOISTURE: Medium to high
SOIL: Acid, deep, well drained
FEATURES: Majestic form and size
USES: Specimen
FLOWERS: ■
FALL COLOR: ■

SITING: Coast redwoods grow 3–5' per year in the right conditions and are remarkably pest free. The largest trees have a straight, slightly tapered trunk that is heavily buttressed at the base. The trunk may rise for more than 100 feet before the first horizontal, slightly drooping, branches mark the bottom of a rounded crown. Younger trees are narrowly pyramidal and have branches all along the trunk. The bark is reddish brown, thick, and soft with longitudinal fissures. Redwoods have two kinds of leaves: Those on tip and flowering shoots are scalelike and overlapping; those on other branches are linear. The egg-shaped purplish-brown cones are about an inch long and mature in one season yet persist on the tree after the seeds are released. Plant redwood where it has ample room to grow and spread. It requires moist, acid, deep, well-drained soils in areas of high atmospheric moisture. It tolerates only slight alkalinity and does not tolerate drought. It is tolerant of flooding, making its best growth along stream banks and floodplains. It prefers the coastal regions of Northern California and extreme southwestern Oregon, thriving in the summer fog and humid atmosphere. It does not grow as well or as large in eastern parts of the country. In areas outside California and the Northwest, it is probably best used occasionally as a novelty specimen.

CARE: Plant container-grown trees in spring or fall. Seedlings need irrigation or constant rain to survive, but after they become established they can grow with little care. Mulch with a 2–4" layer of organic mulch such as wood chips, pine needles, or shredded bark to help maintain even moisture. Feed young trees in spring with acid plant food such as Miracle-Gro Shake 'n Feed Azalea, Camellia, Rhododendron. Young seedlings should be staked and pruned to make sure a strong leader develops. Tall, mature specimens should be pruned only by a professional.

PROPAGATION: Sow seeds in place or start in pots indoors. Take cuttings from young branches.

PESTS AND DISEASES: None are serious.

RELATED SPECIES: 'Prostrata' is a dwarf form that stays small with pruning. 'Adpressa' has broad, scalelike leaves that lie flat on the stem and are creamy white when young; 'Nana Pendula' has drooping branches. 'Simpson's Silver' has silvery-blue leaves; 'Filoli' has blue foliage.

SILVER BUFFALOBERRY

Shepherdia argentea she-PER-dee-ah are-JEN-tee-ah

Silver buffaloberry is a coarse shrub with gray-green leaves.

ZONES: 2–6
SIZE: 6–18'h × 14–18'w
TYPE: Deciduous shrub
FORM: Rounded
TEXTURE: Medium
GROWTH: Slow to medium
LIGHT: Sun

MOISTURE: Low to medium
SOIL: Poor, well drained
FEATURES: Grows in tough sites
USES: Wildlife plantings, shrub border
FLOWERS: ■
FALL COLOR: ■

SITING: Silver buffaloberry is a loosely branched, thorny shrub. It has silver to gray-green foliage from summer and into fall. Its silver stems and red to yellow fruit make it attractive in its dormant state. Plants are dioecious (male and female flowers on separate plants). Flowers are small and yellowish brown, appearing in spring but not particularly showy. Fruits on female trees are red berries ⅛–¼" long and covered with silvery scales. They appear in summer. The fruit is sour tasting when raw but becomes sweeter after a frost. It is used for jams and jellies. The fruits are also a favorite food of birds, so you'll need to protect fruits if you want to harvest them yourself. Silver buffaloberry is native throughout much of North America. It is a tough shrub that grows well in dry or moist conditions, poor soil, high winds, saline soils, and extremes of heat or cold. It likes full sun but will tolerate light shade. It also tolerates standing water. In the landscape it can be used in xeriscape beds or as a screen. The shrub suckers, so it will form a colony. The foliage offers pleasing contrast in the shrub border, but the suckers will need to be controlled to prevent it from overtaking nearby plants. Silver buffaloberry is good for attracting birds and for use in a butterfly garden. It's a good substitute for the more aggressive Russian olive, which has been banned in some states.

CARE: Transplant container-grown plants in spring. This plant does well in poor soil because it can fix nitrogen. Young plants may need supplemental water, but mature plants are drought tolerant. Shear plants in spring. Prune out unwanted suckers at any time.

PROPAGATION: Plant seeds outdoors in fall after giving them an acid scarification treatment. Take cuttings in summer.

PESTS AND DISEASES: None are serious. In regions with high humidity, it may get leaf spot.

RELATED SPECIES: 'Sakakawea' has desirable fruits. 'Goldeye' and 'Xanthocarpa' are yellow-fruited forms. Russet buffaloberry (*S. canadensis*) stays smaller, growing 6–8' tall. It is less ornamental and has limited landscape value, but it can be planted in poor soils and used for erosion control.

JAPANESE SKIMMIA

Skimmia japonica SKIM-ee-uh juh-PAHN-ih-kuh

Japanese skimmia prefers shade.

ZONES: (6)7–8(9)
SIZE: 3–4'h × 3–4'w
TYPE: Evergreen shrub
FORM: Mounded
TEXTURE: Medium
GROWTH: Slow
LIGHT: Shade to part shade
MOISTURE: Medium to high

SOIL: Acid, humusy, well drained
FEATURES: Evergreen foliage, fragrant flowers
USES: Foundation, container, shrub border
FLOWERS: □
FALL COLOR: ■

SITING: Japanese skimmia is one of the most attractive and reliable of all early-spring-flowering shrubs. The leaves are glossy dark green above and yellow-green below and aromatic when bruised. Japanese skimmia is an understory shrub of woodlands. It flowers before the tree canopy closes over in early spring. Flowers can smother a bush with sweetly scented heads of off-white blossoms. Flowers on male plants are larger and more fragrant than on female plants. Fruits are usually red but sometimes white. Both male and female plants are needed to get fruits. One male plant per six female plants will give good fruit set. Japanese skimmia prefers moist, acid soil high in organic matter. It grows in part shade to shade but not full sun, which will bleach the foliage. Plants need winter protection in Zone 6. The entire plant is poisonous.

CARE: Water plants during dry periods. Use acid mulch such as pine needles or shredded pine bark to help maintain even moisture. Feed each spring with acid plant food such as Miracle-Gro Shake 'n Feed Azalea, Camellia, Rhododendron. Prune right after flowering.

PROPAGATION: Sow seeds as soon as they are ripe. Remove pulp before sowing. Take cuttings from new growth in summer to fall. Layering is another possibility.

PESTS AND DISEASES: Spider mites can disfigure foliage and give plants a sunburned look. A daily spray with the garden hose will help dislodge minor infestations. Severely affected plants may require insecticidal soap or a miticide.

RELATED SPECIES: 'Rubella' is a male cultivar with large, red-budded flower heads that open to powerfully scented flowers. *S. j. reevesiana* is similar, but lower growing, self-fertile, with dull crimson fruit.

Colorful red berries of Japanese skimmia persist on the plant through the winter.

JAPANESE PAGODATREE
Sophora japonica *soh-FOR-uh juh-PAHN-ih-kuh*

Pealike white flowers hang from Japanese pagodatree in late summer. It is also known as Chinese scholartree.

ZONES: 5–7
SIZE: 50–75'h × 40–60'w
TYPE: Deciduous tree
FORM: Rounded
TEXTURE: Medium fine
GROWTH: Medium to fast

LIGHT: Sun
MOISTURE: Medium
SOIL: Well drained
FEATURES: Summer flowers, light shade
USES: Shade, specimen, street
FLOWERS: ☐
FALL COLOR: ■

SITING: Japanese pagodatree is an upright to spreading, well-branched tree. The showy creamy-white flowers are produced in mid- to late summer and are slightly fragrant. Most trees do not bloom until they are at least 10 years old, but 'Regent' blooms earlier. The fruit is a 3–8" green pod with a constriction between each seed, giving the appearance of a string of beads. Fruits turn yellow and eventually brown and persist into winter. The bark on the trunk is furrowed into rounded, interlacing ridges. The young green twigs turn dark gray with age. Trees are weak wooded; there may be twigs and small branches to clean up after a windstorm. Japanese pagodatree has a rapid growth rate so it quickly contributes to the landscape. It prefers a sunny, open location and moist, fertile, well-drained soil. It grows in urban areas where air pollution, poor drainage, compacted soil, and drought are common. It makes a good lawn tree; turf grows well beneath it due to its light shade. Winter dieback and twig kill can be severe in Zone 5, especially on trees with a trunk diameter of less than 1½". Fallen flowers can stain sidewalks, and fruit pods can be a litter problem.

CARE: Transplant young balled-and-burlapped plants in spring or fall. Water young trees as needed. Feed in spring with plant food, such as Miracle-Gro, or an organic equivalent. Prune as needed in fall. Young trees may need training to develop a strong central leader.

PROPAGATION: Soak seeds overnight before sowing in place or take softwood cuttings. Most named varieties are grafted.

PESTS AND DISEASES: Young trees are especially susceptible to twig blight, powdery mildew, and leafhoppers, which can result in witches'-broom growth. Trees can be killed by a canker that is made worse by cold injury.

RELATED SPECIES: 'Princeton Upright' has a more upright growth habit. 'Pendula' is a weeping form useful as an accent plant; it grows 15–25' tall. Its smooth green stems are showy during the winter, but it rarely flowers. 'Regent' has good symmetry and rapid growth when young. It blooms at an early age. It is resistant to leafhoppers, twig dieback, and stem canker.

URAL FALSE SPIREA
Sorbaria sorbifolia *sor-BARE-ee-uh sor-bi-FOE-lee-ah*

Ural false spirea is good for erosion control on slopes.

ZONES: 2–7
SIZE: 5–10'h × 5–10'w
TYPE: Deciduous shrub
FORM: Erect to spreading
TEXTURE: Medium to coarse
GROWTH: Fast

LIGHT: Sun to part shade
MOISTURE: Medium
SOIL: Well drained
FEATURES: Showy flowers, delicate foliage
USES: Erosion control, massing
FLOWERS: ☐
FALL COLOR: ■

SITING: Ural false spirea is a fast-growing, spreading, suckering shrub that produces clusters of white flowers that look like a giant white astilbe. It blooms in midsummer with large terminal panicles. The pearl-budded white flowers contrast nicely with the tropical-looking pinnate foliage. It is one of the first shrubs to leaf out in spring, and the leaves have a purplish tinge when young, turning dark green in summer. Somewhat showy dried brown flower heads remain into winter. It prefers moist, well-drained, organic soil and full sun to partial shade, but it will adapt to a wide range of conditions. Plants do not grow as vigorously or as tall in dry soils. Ural false spirea's suckering habit should be taken into consideration when siting. Use it for massing or grouping in a large shrub border. It can be planted on slopes for erosion control. Keep it away from foundations and sidewalks. If it is growing next to a lawn area, install a barrier to keep it from creeping into the grass.

CARE: Transplant at almost any time of year. Water young plants as needed. Prune annually in winter or early spring to maintain shape and size. Remove unwanted suckers regularly to keep them under control. Cut this shrub almost to the ground to force a younger appearance.

PROPAGATION: Root softwood or hardwood cuttings. Dig suckers and replant in spring. Sow seeds as soon as they are ripe.

PESTS AND DISEASES: None are serious.

RELATED SPECIES: Kashmir false spirea (*S. aitchisonii*) is slightly larger overall. Tree false spirea (*S. arborea*) is larger (to 15') with a more spreading growth habit and flower panicles up to 15" long. Both species are less hardy, only to Zone 5.

Plants sucker profusely and may need regular grooming.

EUROPEAN MOUNTAIN ASH

Sorbus aucuparia SOR-buss aw-kyoo-PAIR-ee-uh

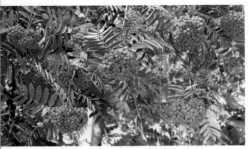

Showy orange berries of European mountain ash stand out in late summer. It is also known as rowan tree.

ZONES: 3–7
SIZE: 20–40'h × 15–30'w
TYPE: Deciduous tree
FORM: Pyramidal to oval
TEXTURE: Medium fine
GROWTH: Medium

LIGHT: Sun to part shade
MOISTURE: Medium
SOIL: Well drained
FEATURES: Showy flowers and fruits
USES: Specimen, shade, courtyard
FLOWERS: □
FALL COLOR: ■■■

SITING: European mountain ash grows best in cooler climates with ample moisture. It prefers moist, slightly acid, well-drained soils and full sun. It is short lived in alkaline or dry soils. Place it where you can enjoy the light shade, spring flowers, and especially the bright orange fruits that appear in late summer.

CARE: Water young trees on a regular basis; irrigate trees of any age during dry periods. Young trees will benefit from an application of plant food, such as Miracle-Gro, in spring. Mulch young trees, especially those growing in a lawn, to protect them from lawn mower damage and to keep the soil evenly moist. Wrap young trees in winter to prevent sunscald. Prune only as needed to shape while the

Prune out fire blight, cutting back into healthy wood.

tree is dormant to reduce the chance of spreading fire blight.

PROPAGATION: Seeds require cold moist stratification for 2–4 months. Cuttings are difficult to root. Cultivars are budded or grafted.

PESTS AND DISEASES: Fire blight can kill infected trees. Avoid overfeeding, which can stimulate young, succulent growth that is more susceptible to this disease. Prune out infected branches, sterilizing pruning tools in a bleach solution between each cut, and dispose of the prunings off site. Borers often attack stressed or diseased trees. Less-serious problems include canker, leaf rusts, scab, aphids, sawfly, and scales. Rabbits may eat the tender bark in winter if trees are not protected.

RELATED SPECIES: 'Edulis' bears large fruit, often used for preserves. 'Fastigiata' is an upright, columnar form. 'Pendula' is a weeping form. 'Xanthocarpa' has yellow-orange fruits. Korean mountain ash (*S. alnifolia*) is larger, to 50' tall, has better fall color (red-orange to golden brown), and is less susceptible to borers. Fire blight is still a major problem, however. The tree is hardy to Zone 4.

JAPANESE SPIREA

Spiraea japonica spy-REE-uh juh-PAHN-ih-kuh

'Goldflame' spirea is a popular blooming landscape shrub.

ZONES: 4–8
SIZE: 4–5'h × 4–5'w
TYPE: Deciduous shrub
FORM: Low, spreading
TEXTURE: Medium
GROWTH: Fast
LIGHT: Sun

MOISTURE: Medium
SOIL: Well drained
FEATURES: Showy flowers
USES: Groupings, shrub border
FLOWERS: ■□
FALL COLOR: ■

SITING: Japanese spirea is grown for its showy pink to rose-red flowers and attractive summer foliage. Flowers appear in clusters from late spring to early summer. Leaves may be light to deep green, lime green, bronze, yellow, and even reddish. It is usually best planted in groups, and it can be used in informal hedges. It prefers well-drained soil; plants do not do well in boggy or constantly wet conditions. Plants grown in overly alkaline soils may develop chlorosis. It prefers full sun but tolerates partial shade; flowering and foliage color are poorer in shade. Japanese spirea has become invasive in some areas.

Prune pink-flowered spirea after flowering to shape the shrub or to improve its appearance. As a bonus it may rebloom.

CARE: Keep the soil evenly moist from spring until the ground freezes in fall. Feed every spring with plant food, such as Miracle-Gro. Avoid overfeeding, which promotes succulent growth attractive to aphids. Prune out dead, diseased, or broken branches at any time. Prune to shape right after flowering.

PROPAGATION: Plant seeds outdoors in fall. Plants are easily propagated by layering and softwood or hardwood cuttings.

PESTS AND DISEASES: Aphids may appear on soft, new growth at the tips of stems. Leaf spot diseases may mar the foliage, especially toward late summer, but they are usually only a cosmetic problem. Rabbits and deer may browse on plants.

RELATED SPECIES: Bumald spirea (*S. j.* 'Bumalda') has white to deep pink flowers. It is usually less than 3' in height but may reach 4–5'. It is hardier, to Zone 3. It may develop iron chlorosis if the soil pH is too high. The popular cultivar 'Anthony Waterer' is a 3–4'-tall plant with showy carmine-pink flowers that bloom for most of the summer. 'Goldflame' has bright golden-yellow leaves that turn green in summer and red in fall.

VANHOUTTE SPIREA

Spiraea ×vanhouttei spy-REE-uh van-HOOT-ee-eye

Old-fashioned Vanhoutte spirea is covered with white flowers in spring. It is also known as bridalwreath.

ZONES: 3–8(9)
SIZE: 6–8'h × 10–12'w
TYPE: Deciduous shrub
FORM: Arching
TEXTURE: Medium to fine
GROWTH: Fast
LIGHT: Sun

MOISTURE: Medium
SOIL: Well drained
FEATURES: Showy flowers
USES: Groupings, shrub border, foundation
FLOWERS: □
FALL COLOR: ■

SITING: This popular, time-tested shrub is tough and adaptable. It is showy when in bloom in mid- to late spring. The small white flowers appear in 1–2" clusters at the branch tips and almost cover the plant. Foliage is dull bluish green in summer and occasionally reddish in fall. It prefers well-drained soil; plants do not do well in boggy or constantly wet conditions. Plants grown in overly alkaline soils may develop chlorosis. Plants prefer full sun but tolerate partial shade; flowering and foliage color are poorer in shade. Vanhoutte spirea can be used as a specimen or in groups. It is a good candidate for the mixed shrub border or for foundation plantings. It brings an old-fashioned charm to any landscape.
CARE: Plant bare-root plants in early spring; plant container plants in spring or late summer. Keep the soil evenly moist from spring until the ground freezes in fall. Feed every spring with plant food, such as Miracle-Gro, or an organic equivalent. Avoid overfeeding, which promotes succulent growth attractive to aphids. Mature plants can tolerate drought but prefer consistently moist soil. Prune out dead, diseased, or broken branches at any time. Prune to shape right after flowering. Remove a few of the older stems each spring to stimulate new growth and better flowering.
PROPAGATION: Plant seeds outdoors in fall to accomplish natural stratificaiton. Named varieties do not come true from seed.

Plants are easily propagated by layering and softwood or hardwood cuttings.
PESTS AND DISEASES: Aphids may appear on soft, new growth at the tips of stems. Wash off with a hard stream of water once a day for several days, or use insecticidal soap. Leaf spot diseases may mar the foliage, especially toward late summer, but they are usually only a cosmetic problem. Rabbits and deer may browse on plants, especially in winter.
RELATED SPECIES: The young foliage of 'Pink Ice' is splashed with pink and white. It may revert and the leaves usually mature to a uniform green by summer. 'Renaissance' exhibits greater resistance to foliar disease. 'Snow White' grows compactly to 5' and appears less prone to foliar disease. The dead blooms are self-cleaning and the foliage is larger and healthy green. Snow-mound nippon spirea (*S. nipponica*) grows 3' tall and is covered with white flowers in mid- to late spring. The summer foliage is dark green. Prune plants immediately after flowering. Thunberg spirea (*S. thunbergii*) is the earliest spirea to bloom. It has white flowers and good fall color.

CUT-LEAF STEPHANANDRA

Stephanandra incisa stef-uh-NAN-druh in-SYE-zuh

Cut-leaf stephanandra spreads rapidly to form a dense ground cover.

ZONES: 4–7
SIZE: 4–7'h × 4–7'w
TYPE: Deciduous shrub
FORM: Wide, spreading
TEXTURE: Medium to fine
GROWTH: Fast
LIGHT: Sun to part shade

MOISTURE: Medium to high
SOIL: Acid, well drained
FEATURES: Handsome foliage
USES: Ground cover, massing, hedge
FLOWERS: □
FALL COLOR: ■ ■

SITING: Cut-leaf stephanandra is a dense, compact shrub that spreads readily by suckering. It has a graceful growth habit with wide-spreading, arching, slender branches. The leaves are lobed and have a reddish-bronze tinge when unfolding, later turning bright green. They take on red-orange to red-purple tints in fall but are not particularly showy. Flowers are small and inconspicuous in late spring. It prefers moist, acid, well-drained soil that has been supplemented with peat moss or leaf mold, although it is tolerant of most soils. Give it full sun or light shade. Cut-leaf stephanandra is outstanding for massing or as a ground cover. It is a good choice where you need a fine-textured, low, informal hedge that requires little pruning. It will root where it touches moist soils, but it is easily pulled up if it spreads too far.
CARE: Transplant container-grown plants in spring. Plants may suffer branch dieback in exposed, windswept areas; prune back to live wood in spring. Cut-leaf stephanandra develops iron chlorosis in high-pH soils. Feed each spring with an acid plant food such as Miracle-Gro Shake 'n Feed Azalea, Camellia, Rhododendron. Mulch with pine needles or shredded pine bark to maintain soil moisture and acidity.
PROPAGATION: Take cuttings at any time of year. Seeds require a warm-cold period and are difficult to work with.
PESTS AND DISEASES: None are serious.
RELATED SPECIES: 'Crispa' is the most widely available form. It differs from the species with its dissected, crinkly foliage and low-spreading, ground cover habit. The thin, dense stems spread over the ground in a tangle to 3' tall and much wider. The plant becomes slightly mounded in the middle but prostrate at the edges. It may be used as a ground cover, foundation shrub, or draped over a wall or raised bed. Tanaka stephanandra (*S. tanakae*) is a thicket-forming shrub that grows 6–10' tall and wide. It bears yellow-green flowers in summer, and develops yellow to orange fall foliage. It is hardy in Zones 5–8.

JAPANESE STEWARTIA

Stewartia pseudocamellia stew-AR-tee-uh soo-doh-kuh-MEEL-ee-uh

Japanese stewartia has attractive, white summer flowers.

ZONES: 5–7(8)
SIZE: 30–40'h × 25–30'w
TYPE: Deciduous tree
FORM: Pyramidal to oval
TEXTURE: Medium
GROWTH: Slow
LIGHT: Sun to part shade

MOISTURE: Medium to high
SOIL: Acid, humusy, well drained
FEATURES: Showy flowers, interesting bark
USES: Specimen, shrub border
FLOWERS: □
FALL COLOR: ■ ■

SITING: Japanese stewartia is an all-season performer, starting in winter with the silky brown buds and distinctly zigzag stems.

The smooth, muscled bark is spectacular, peeling off and exposing a camouflage pattern of orange, green, and gray. In summer it's a gem of a flowering tree with its camellia-like white blossoms opening from large, pearl-like buds. Each of the 2–2½" flowers has five white petals surrounded by an attractive cluster of bright orange anthers. Although the individual flowers do not last long, they develop over 3–4 weeks. Most other trees have finished flowering by the time these flowers emerge. The oval, thick apple green leaves put on an autumn display of reddish-purple hue before falling. The tree could be grown for its fall color alone. It prefers acid soil, amended with leaf mold or peat moss. It grows best where soils are on the moist side but not excessively wet or dry during all the seasons. It dislikes intense heat and drought and prefers light shade during the heat of the day. It is an excellent, small- to medium-size tree often multitrunked or branching low. It makes a good patio tree or could accent an entryway or be grown as a canopy tree over a sidewalk. A row of these trees spaced 15' apart on either side of a

sidewalk makes an outstanding covered walkway. It could be planted as a slow-growing street tree beneath power lines due to its small stature. Use it in shrub borders or in lawns. Wherever you plant it, make sure it can be viewed all year.
CARE: This tree is somewhat difficult to transplant and establish and should be moved while still young in early spring. Routinely apply bark mulch over the root system. Water during dry periods in summer, especially the first 3 years after planting.
PROPAGATION: Take 3–4" cuttings with a heel of older wood in spring or early summer. Bottom heat encourages rooting. Sow seeds in fall; they may take up to 2 years to germinate.
PESTS AND DISEASES: None are serious.
RELATED SPECIES: 'Ballet' has a more spreading habit and larger flowers, to almost 4" wide. 'Cascade' is a semiweeping form with gently drooping branches and growing tips. It grows slowly. 'Milk and Honey' bears profuse quantities of larger blooms and has brighter bark color. 'Pink Form' has whitish-pink flowers that open from pinkish buds.

JAPANESE SNOWBELL

Styrax japonicus STYE-raks juh-PAHN-ih-kus

Place Japanese snowbell where you can enjoy the showy flowers.

ZONES: 5–8
SIZE: 20–30'h × 20–30'w
TYPE: Deciduous tree
FORM: Horizontal
TEXTURE: Medium fine
GROWTH: Medium
LIGHT: Sun to light shade

MOISTURE: Medium to high
SOIL: Acid, humusy, well drained
FEATURES: Spring flowers, attractive branching pattern
USES: Specimen, shade, courtyard
FLOWERS: □ ■
FALL COLOR: ■ ■

SITING: This small tree brings a graceful touch to any landscape with its strong horizontal appearance. Leaves change to

a yellowish or reddish color in fall and hold onto the tree late. Pendulous white flowers bloom in late spring and continue into early summer. They are slightly fragrant and easy to see because they hang below the foliage. They are followed by somewhat attractive fruits that persist into fall. The handsome gray-brown bark is smooth with some orangish-brown areas that add winter interest. Use Japanese snowbell as a specimen tree in a courtyard or in an entryway. The branches will droop nicely over a patio or deck. It prefers moist, humusy, well-drained, acid soil. Plants can grow in full sun to light shade. They do not grow well in dry or alkaline

Acidify soil before planting by working in peat moss.

soil. It tolerates city conditions but should be sheltered from strong winds.
CARE: Acidify the soil before planting by working in ammonium sulfate or peat moss. Transplant container-grown or balled-and-burlapped specimens in early spring. Water as needed throughout the growing season to keep the soil evenly moist. Mulch with pine needles or shredded pine bark to retain moisture and maintain soil acidity. Feed in spring with acid plant food such as Miracle-Gro Shake 'n Feed Azalea, Camellia, Rhododendron. Prune plants lightly each winter to retain their desired shape.
PROPAGATION: Take softwood cuttings in summer. Sow seeds in summer; they may take 2 years to germinate.
PESTS AND DISEASES: Borers can be a minor problem.
RELATED SPECIES: 'Angyo Dwarf' grows 8–10' tall. 'Emerald Pagoda' has larger leaves and flowers and better heat tolerance. 'Pendula' and 'Carillon' are weeping forms. 'Pink Chimes' has pink flowers. Fragrant snowbell (*S. obassia*), hardy in Zone 6, is upright with large clusters of fragrant flowers.

SNOWBERRY

Symphoricarpos albus *sim-for-ih-KAR-pus AL-bus*

Common snowberry's greatest asset is its decorative whitish fruits.

ZONES: 3–7
SIZE: 3–6'h × 3–6'w
TYPE: Deciduous shrub
FORM: Rounded
TEXTURE: Medium
GROWTH: Fast
LIGHT: Sun to shade

MOISTURE: Low to medium
SOIL: Well drained
FEATURES: Showy fruits, adaptability
USES: Naturalizing, shade
FLOWERS: ☐
FALL COLOR: ■

SITING: This native, hardy shrub tolerates deep shade. It has bluish-green leaves but no significant fall color. Flowers are small and pinkish and appear in late summer. Berrylike white fruits ½" in diameter appear from September into November and persist into winter. Plants sucker freely and soon form a thicket, making them good for covering slopes and other tough-to-mow sites. The thickets provide excellent cover for wildlife, and the berries provide food for birds. Hummingbirds are attracted to the flowers. Fruiting stems make attractive additions to autumn cut-flower bouquets. Common snowberry grows in almost any light and in any soil. Foliage is denser and the flowering heavier in full sun to partial shade. It prefers consistently moist soil throughout the season but will survive in moderately dry conditions.

CARE: Give young plants a spring application of plant food, such as Miracle-Gro, or an organic equivalent. Sprinkle the granules around the base of each plant and water in well. Cut out entire stems or portions of stems in early spring to control the overall size and shape.

PROPAGATION: Take softwood cuttings in summer. Seeds have a hard coat; nick and soak them overnight in warm water before planting. They require a warm period followed by a cool period; germination takes several months.

PESTS AND DISEASES: Diseases include anthracnose, blights, and powdery mildew. These diseases cause spotting on the fruits and leaves, discolored foliage, and occasionally rotting of the fruits. If plants are severely affected for two seasons in a row, spray with a preventative fungicide in spring. Aphids sometimes attack new growth. Spray them off with a strong stream of water or use insecticidal soap. Prevent scale infections by spraying plants with dormant oil spray in late fall and early spring.

RELATED SPECIES: Indian currant coralberry (*S. orbiculatus*) is lower growing and wider spreading. The smaller berries are dark rose to purplish red. Chenault coralberry (*S. ×chenaultii*) is low spreading and arching. The fruits range in color from white to rosy pink. It is hardy to Zone 4.

MEYER LILAC

Syringa meyeri *sir-RING-uh MY-er-eye*

Meyer lilac is covered with fragrant flowers in May.

ZONES: 3–7
SIZE: 4–8'h × 6–10'w
TYPE: Deciduous shrub
FORM: Rounded
TEXTURE: Medium fine
GROWTH: Slow
LIGHT: Sun

MOISTURE: Medium
SOIL: Well drained
FEATURES: Showy fragrant flowers
USES: Shrub border, foundation
FLOWERS: ■ ■
FALL COLOR: ■

SITING: Meyer lilac is one of the easiest lilacs to grow. It starts to flower when plants are only about a foot tall. The violet-purple flowers are packed in 4"-long panicles that cover the plant in May. Their fragrance is different from that of common lilac. New leaves have a purplish margin turning dark green in summer. This lilac grows best in full sun and in soil with good drainage. It prefers fertile loam rich in organic matter, but it tolerates most soils. Plant it in the shrub border with an evergreen background to set off the early flowers. In colder climates, flower buds may be injured by a late freeze. Plants may sucker lightly or not at all. Meyer lilac does better in the South than most lilacs.

CARE: This plant prefers consistent moisture throughout the growing season, but once mature it can withstand drought. Feed every spring with plant food, such as Miracle-Gro. Faded flowers turn into unsightly seed heads; remove right after blooming is finished. Prune to shape right after flowering.

PROPAGATION: Plants do not come true from seed; cuttings are difficult to root.

PESTS AND DISEASES: Lilacs are susceptible to several insect and disease problems, but most are not serious enough to kill plants. Problems include scale, stem borers, and powdery mildew, although Meyer lilac is not as susceptible to powdery mildew as other lilacs are.

RELATED SPECIES: 'Palabin' is a popular cultivar with a more compact form, growing to only 4–5' tall. The flowers are lighter in color, with more of a pinkish tinge. Miss Kim lilac (*S. patula* 'Miss Kim') has a more upright growth habit. It blooms later, with blue-lavender flowers. Leaves may take on a burgundy color in fall. It is resistant to powdery mildew. Persian lilac (*S. ×persica*) has a more arching growth habit. Flowers are pale lilac.

1 After bloom is completed, faded flowers detract from attractive foliage.

2 Remove spent flowers to keep plants neat and to encourage bloom.

JAPANESE TREE LILAC
Syringa reticulata *sir-RING-uh reh-tik-yoo-LAH-tuh*

Japanese tree lilac is a good small tree for cold climates.

ZONES: 3–7
SIZE: 20–30'h × 15–25'w
TYPE: Deciduous tree
FORM: Oval to rounded
TEXTURE: Medium
GROWTH: Medium
LIGHT: Sun

MOISTURE: Medium
SOIL: Well drained
FEATURES: Showy, fragrant flowers, interesting bark
USES: Specimen, street
FLOWERS: □
FALL COLOR: ■

SITING: Japanese tree lilac is an upright, spreading, usually multistemmed small tree. It blooms much later than common lilac. In early summer it is covered with large clusters of cream-colored flowers. The flowers have a pleasant, honeylike scent less intense than that of common lilac. The tree also has attractive deep green leaves and dark brown to reddish-brown bark. It prefers full sun (at least 6 hours a day) and soil with good drainage. Plants grow and flower best in fertile loam rich in organic matter, but they tolerate most soils. It makes an excellent specimen, entry, or street tree. The dried seed heads make interesting additions to dried arrangements.

CARE: Plant balled-and-burlapped and container-grown plants in early spring.

Use long-pole pruners to remove browned flower heads.

It prefers consistent moisture throughout the growing season, but once mature it can withstand drought. Feed every spring with plant food, such as Miracle-Gro, or an organic equivalent. Prune to shape right after flowering. Removing the flower heads right after blooming will help the plant produce more blooms the next year. Remove suckers at the base of the plant at any time.

PROPAGATION: Sow ripe seeds in moist peat moss and keep at room temperature for 90 days. Follow this with cold temperatures for at least 120 days. Cuttings are challenging for the home gardener.

PESTS AND DISEASES: Japanese tree lilac is not as susceptible to the insects and diseases that plague most lilacs. It is resistant to powdery mildew.

RELATED SPECIES: 'Ivory Silk' flowers at a young age and is sturdy and compact. Peking lilac *(S. pekinensis)* is another late-blooming lilac, although not as late as Japanese tree lilac. It is an upright, spreading tree of 15–20' and produces clusters of small cream-colored flowers with a mild honey scent. It is reliably hardy in Zone 4.

LILAC
Syringa vulgaris *sir-RING-uh vul-GAR-is*

Common lilac is an old-fashioned favorite for its fragrance flowers.

ZONES: 3–7
SIZE: 8–15'h × 6–12'w
TYPE: Deciduous shrub
FORM: Upright irregular
TEXTURE: Medium to coarse
GROWTH: Medium

LIGHT: Sun
MOISTURE: Medium
SOIL: Well drained
FEATURES: Showy, fragrant flowers
USES: Shrub border, hedge
FLOWERS: □ ■ □
FALL COLOR: ■

SITING: Common lilac is an old-fashioned shrub that grows well in colder climates. It prefers full sun and well-drained soil. Plants grow and flower best in fertile loam rich in organic matter, but they tolerate most soils. The fragrant lilac-colored flowers are the only ornamental part of this plant, so it is best used in the shrub border where other plants can offer summer and fall interest. The flowers are often used for cutting.

CARE: Lilacs prefer consistent moisture throughout the growing season, but once mature they can withstand drought. Feed every spring with plant food, such as Miracle-Gro. Remove flower heads right after blooming to prevent seed formation, which reduces flowering the next year.

1 Thin out older branches in early spring.

2 Improved air circulation reduces powdery mildew.

Remove a few of the oldest stems all the way to the ground each year to keep plants from becoming overgrown.

PROPAGATION: Plant seeds in moist peat moss and moist-chill for 90 days followed by warm temperatures for 60 days. Some plants produce suckers that can be dug in early spring and replanted.

PESTS AND DISEASES: Lilacs are susceptible to several insect and disease problems, but most are not serious enough to kill plants. Reduce chances of powdery mildew by planting in full sun and thinning out some branches each year to increase air circulation. Plants rarely die from powdery mildew, and the timing of spraying a fungicide is difficult so spraying is not recommended as a control measure.

RELATED SPECIES: Preston lilac *(S. ×prestoniae)* hybrids bloom later, and the scent is not as sweet. Flower clusters tend to hang or nod. Plants are resistant to powdery mildew; they sucker lightly or not at all. Early flowering lilac *(S. ×hyacinthiflora)* has a more formal growth habit. The green summer foliage often turns reddish purple in fall. Plants do not sucker.

TAMARISK

Tamarix ramosissima *TAM-a-riks ram-oh-SIS-ih-muh*

Plumes of feathery, pink flowers cover plants in summer.

ZONES: (3)4–8
SIZE: 10–15'h ×
8–10'w
TYPE: Deciduous
shrub
FORM: Loose, open
TEXTURE: Fine
GROWTH: Fast
LIGHT: Sun

MOISTURE: Low to
medium
SOIL: Well drained
FEATURES: Showy
flowers and foliage
USES: Shrub border,
coast
FLOWERS: ■
FALL COLOR: ■

SITING: Tamarisk is a graceful, open, thicket-forming shrub. It has fine-textured, juniper-like foliage, arching branchlets, pale gray-green leaves, and plumes of feathery pink flowers in summer. Fruits are dry capsules that split open when ripe to release abundant seeds. Use tamarisk in borders and naturalized areas. It does best in slightly acid, sandy loam in full sun, but it has a wide range of soil tolerance, including poor soils of low fertility. It is good for sunny areas with poor or alkaline soils. It may be used as a windbreak or an informal hedge in remote areas of the landscape where its scraggly winter appearance will not be a problem. It can be effective on dry slopes for erosion control and it is valued in seashore areas because of its salt tolerance. It has

Rejuvenate overgrown plants by cutting them to the ground.

naturalized in many areas of the West, Southwest, and Great Plains. In these warm-winter climates, it has become a noxious weed. It accumulates salt in its tissues, which is later released into the soil, making it unsuitable for many native species. It colonizes stream banks along rivers and streams, dropping seed into the water for distribution and further colonization downstream.
CARE: Water newly planted shrubs their first 2 years; mature shrubs are drought tolerant. Feed only if plants are under stress. This rapid grower blooms on new wood, so annual pruning will induce good flowering. Prune within several inches of the ground in late winter.
PROPAGATION: Fresh seeds self-sow and germinate readily.
PESTS AND DISEASES: Cankers, powdery mildew, root rot, and scale can be minor problems on tamarisk.
RELATED SPECIES: 'Pink Cascade' has dark pink flowers and is more vigorous. 'Rosea' has rosy-pink flowers that occur later. It is more hardy than the species. 'Rubra', 'Cheyenne Red', and 'Summer Glow' flowers are darker pink than the species.

BALD CYPRESS

Taxodium distichum *Tax-oh-dee-um DISS-tih-kum*

The fall color of common bald cypress is an attractive coppery brown.

ZONES: 5–10
SIZE: 50–70'h ×
20–30'w
TYPE: Deciduous
tree
FORM: Pyramidal
TEXTURE: Medium
fine
GROWTH: Medium
LIGHT: Sun

MOISTURE: High
SOIL: Moisture
retentive
FEATURES:
Tolerance of wet
sites
USES: Waterside,
shade
FLOWERS: ■
FALL COLOR: ■

SITING: Common bald cypress thrives in standing water. It does this by sending up "knees," outgrowths of the roots that form in shallow water and rise above the high water mark. Young trees have a pyramidal form with a rounded top. Leaves have a soft, fresh green texture, giving them a fernlike look. It loses its leaves in winter and grows a new crop of needles each spring. Needles turn a striking coppery brown before dropping. Conspicuous catkins are attractive in late winter. The peeling reddish-brown bark adds interest to the buttressed trunk. Grow bald cypress in large areas where it can develop properly. The knees will pop up several feet from the trunk, so plant it away from mown lawns. It prefers heavy soil or soil rich in organic mater. It will grow away

Maintain soil acidity by applying an acid plant food in spring.

from water if the soil is reasonably moist. Trees do not develop as many knees in drier soils. Once established, plants are almost carefree.
CARE: Acidify the soil before planting by working in ammonium sulfate or peat moss. Transplant young balled-and-burlapped plants in fall or spring. Young seedlings must have constant access to surface water until they sink their roots below the water table. Trees may show iron chlorosis in alkaline soils. Maintain soil acidity by feeding each spring with acid plant food such as Miracle-Gro Shake 'n Feed Azalea, Camellia, Rhododendron.
PROPAGATION: Take cuttings in early summer. Sow seeds in fall; they must have constant moisture to germinate.
PESTS AND DISEASES: None are serious. It may occasionally be attacked by spider mites, cypress moth, twig blight, or wood decay.
RELATED SPECIES: 'Pendens' is a pyramidal form with horizontal branches drooping at the tips. 'Shawnee Brave' has a narrow pyramidal habit. Pond cypress (*T. ascendens*) is a smaller, narrower tree. It has flattened needles that hang in branchlets like giant club moss.

JAPANESE YEW

Taxus cuspidata TAKS-us kus-pi-DAH-tuh

Japanese yew is available in many forms.

ZONES: 4–7
SIZE: 10–40'h ×
10–40'w
TYPE: Evergreen
shrub
FORM: Irregular to
upright
TEXTURE: Medium
GROWTH: Slow
LIGHT: Sun to shade

MOISTURE: Medium
SOIL: Well drained
FEATURES: Year-
round color
USES: Hedge,
foundation,
groupings
FLOWERS: ■
FALL COLOR: ■

SITING: This versatile evergreen is slow
growing and has few pest problems,
making it a popular choice for landscaping.
The deep green foliage is attractive

year-round. Its ability to withstand severe
pruning makes it ideal for formal hedges
and topiary. It withstands urban conditions
and is a popular foundation plant in city
gardens. It requires fertile soil, sufficient
moisture, and excellent drainage. In soggy
or wet soil, the foliage turns yellow and
plants may die. It grows equally well in
sun or shade but dislikes windy sites,
especially in colder areas. It grows well
in the Midwest and Northeast, but dislikes
extreme cold or heat. Foliage and fruits

**Winter burn can be a problem. Prune out
affected branches in spring.**

are poisonous, so warn children not to
put them in their mouths.
CARE: Transplant balled-and-burlapped
or container-grown plants in spring or fall.
Needles may turn brown or yellow in
winter due to drying winds. Help reduce
winter burn by keeping the soil evenly
moist until the ground freezes. Feed each
spring with plant food, such as Miracle-
Gro, or an organic equivalent. Yews can
be pruned winter through midsummer.
Although these plants sprout new growth
from fairly old wood, it is better to prune
regularly rather than drastically cutting
back overgrown plants.
PROPAGATION: Take cuttings from late
summer through winter.
PESTS AND DISEASES: None are serious.
Scale is a potential threat and deer are
attracted to the foliage.
RELATED SPECIES: 'Capitata' is a good
choice for hedges. English yew (*T. baccata*)
is an upright plant growing 30–60' tall. It is
reliably hardy in Zone 5. Anglo-Japanese
yew (*T. ×media*) is a group of hybrid
cultivars with good foliage color and form;
they are hardy in Zone 5.

AMERICAN ARBORVITAE

Thuja occidentalis THEW-yuh ok-sih-den-TAL-is

**American arborvitae, also known as Eastern
arborvitae or white cedar, is a good choice
for cold climates.**

ZONES: 3–7
SIZE: 40–60'h ×
10–15'w
TYPE: Evergreen
shrub
FORM: Broad
pyramidal
TEXTURE: Medium
fine
GROWTH: Slow to
medium

LIGHT: Sun
MOISTURE: Medium
to high
SOIL: Humusy, well
drained
FEATURES: Year-
round color
USES: Specimen,
hedge, screening
FLOWERS: ■
FALL COLOR: ■

SITING: American arborvitae is widely used,
especially in colder climates where good

green color is prized throughout the year.
The fragrant foliage consists of many short,
scalelike leaves carried in soft, flat sprays.
Eastern arborvitae is used for screening,
hedges, foundation plantings, and as
accents. Plants can get sun scorch when
planted in areas with bright afternoon
winter sun and wind. It grows well in full
sun but tolerates part shade. It thrives in
a wide range of soils as long as they drain
freely. Avoid planting under a roofline
where falling snow can break branches.

**Spray plants with a strong stream of water
to dislodge spider mites.**

CARE: Mulch to keep the soil evenly moist.
Water deeply in fall to help prevent winter
burn. Feed each spring with plant food,
such as Miracle-Gro. Prune in spring just
after new growth has emerged. Prune
formal hedges again later in the season,
but avoid pruning in fall.
PROPAGATION: Sow seeds in fall or spring.
Take cuttings in late summer.
PESTS AND DISEASES: Problems include
bagworm, leaf miner, spider mites, and
deer browsing. Cut bagworm cocoons from
trees as soon as you see them. Spray
plants with a garden hose to dislodge
spider mites. If deer are a problem in your
area, protect plants with fencing or spray
them frequently with repellent.
RELATED SPECIES: 'Techny' grows only
10–15' tall, making it a good choice for
hedging. It has excellent deep green
foliage color and resists winter burning.
'Little Gem' is a good globe form, growing
to about 3' in height and width. 'Sunkist'
has golden-yellow foliage when grown in
full sun. Western arborvitae (*T. plicata*) is a
tree form growing 50–70' tall. It is hardy in
Zones 5–8.

AMERICAN LINDEN
Tilia americana *TILL-ee-uh uh-mer-ih-KAY-nuh*

American linden is a hardy native tree for large landscapes. Basswood is another common name for it.

ZONES: 3–8
SIZE: 60–80'h × 40–60'w
TYPE: Deciduous tree
FORM: Pyramidal to rounded
TEXTURE: Coarse
GROWTH: Medium
LIGHT: Sun to part shade

MOISTURE: Medium
SOIL: Fertile, well drained
FEATURES: Fragrant flowers, attractive shape, healthy foliage
USES: Shade, street, lawn
FLOWERS: ▢▢
FALL COLOR: ◼◻

SITING: American linden is a stately, well-formed tree with a clean, straight trunk.

The heart-shaped leaves fade to pale green or yellow before dropping in autumn. American linden has distinctive straplike bracts that support clusters of sweetly fragrant (but not very showy) flowers. The flowers are pollinated by bees, which make a delicious honey from their harvests. The small, round gray fruit persists until midwinter. The bark is light brown and smooth, becoming darker and deeply furrowed on older trees. American linden is a fine shade and street tree, although it is not used as much as European and Asian linden, which are smaller and more tolerant of urban conditions. This is a large tree, well suited for large estates. It does best in deep, moist, fertile soils but will grow in drier, heavier soils. It tolerates full sun to partial shade. It casts dense shade, so growing grass under it is difficult. It needs adequate root space.

CARE: American linden transplants easily. Young trees need ample water in the first 3–5 years after planting. Mature trees can take short dry spells but benefit from deep watering in dry summers. Organic mulch helps maintain even moisture. Prune trees as needed to shape in winter when you can see the outline. Prune out root sprouts from the base of the tree at any time.
PROPAGATION: Seeds are difficult to germinate, requiring acid scarification and cold stratification.
PESTS AND DISEASES: Problems include Japanese beetles, spider mites, aphids, borers, leaf miners, and scale.
RELATED SPECIES: 'Redmond' is a popular street and lawn tree due to its uniform pyramidal habit. 'Continental Appeal' has a wide, dense crown supported by narrow, ascending branches. The leaves have attractive silvery undersides, and the tree tolerates poor environmental conditions. 'Wandell' (Legend™) is a handsome pyramidal selection with symmetrical branching and a strong leader. Little-leaf linden (*T. cordata*) grows best in Zones 4–7. 'Greenspire' is a vigorous grower that develops a narrow, oval crown with a straight trunk. Silver linden (*T. tomentosa*) tolerates heat and drought better than other lindens and is less prone to insect damage. The leaves are silvery green underneath and often have good yellow fall color.

CANADIAN HEMLOCK
Tsuga canadensis *SOO-guh kan-a-DEN-sis*

Canadian hemlock, also known as Eastern hemlock, is tolerant of partial shade.

ZONES: (3)4–7
SIZE: 40–70'h × 25–35'w
TYPE: Evergreen tree
FORM: Pyramidal
TEXTURE: Fine
GROWTH: Medium
LIGHT: Sun to part shade
MOISTURE: Medium to high

SOIL: Acid, deep, well drained
FEATURES: Shade tolerance, fine-textured evergreen foliage
USES: Specimen, screen, grouping
FLOWERS: ◼
FALL COLOR: ◼

SITING: Canadian hemlock is a long-lived, graceful evergreen. The deep green needles hold their color well all year. Use it as a specimen, hedge, or screening plant. It is one of the few evergreens that can tolerate shade, but it is sensitive to heat, drought, wind, salt spray, air pollution, and poor drainage. The best site is partially shaded with cool, moist, well-drained, acid soil. It can be grown in full sun as long as it has good drainage, a soil high in organic matter, and no strong, drying winds. It tolerates winter cold but can be damaged by unseasonable frosts. Sun scorch can occur when temperatures reach 95°F, killing the ends of branches.

1 **Woolly adelgid damage can be a serious problem.**

2 **Surround trees with mulch to prevent moisture stress.**

CARE: Purchase trees from local sources for greatest success. Transplant balled-and-burlapped plants in early spring or fall. Water young trees as needed and established trees during drought. Apply organic mulch to keep the soil evenly moist and protect against lawn mowers and sharp gardening tools; injured plants are more susceptible to pests. Young trees benefit from a spring application of acid plant food. Prune in late spring.
PROPAGATION: Sow seeds in fall. Take cuttings in late summer.
PESTS AND DISEASES: Woolly adelgid is a serious pest, especially on the East Coast. Control with horticultural oil sprays, systemic pesticides, or natural predators. Other problems include leaf blight, cankers, rust, borers, leaf miners, mites, and scale.
RELATED SPECIES: Carolina hemlock (*T. caroliniana*) has smaller, whorled needles that give it a denser look.

AMERICAN ELM

Ulmus americana *UL-mus uh-mer-i-KAY-nuh*

Once common, American elm has been decimated by Dutch elm disease.

ZONES: 3–9
SIZE: 60–80'h × 40–60'w
TYPE: Deciduous tree
FORM: Vase shaped
TEXTURE: Medium
GROWTH: Medium to fast

LIGHT: Sun
MOISTURE: Medium
SOIL: Well drained
FEATURES: Vase-shaped silhouette
USES: Shade, street
FLOWERS: ■
FALL COLOR: ■

SITING: Where American elm trees have been spared the devastation of Dutch elm disease, they can still be seen arching gracefully over streets. They are a favorite because of their urban tolerance, fast growth, and vase-shaped silhouette; trees need regular care, and the possibility of Dutch elm disease is always there. Breeders are working on resistant cultivars. American elm prefers rich, moist soils but grows well under a variety of conditions.

CARE: Vigorous trees are less susceptible to pests, so keep trees mulched and water during dry periods. Prune in fall to avoid spreading diseases. Seedlings can become weedy. The shallow, flaring roots may lift adjacent sidewalks and driveways.

PROPAGATION: Sow seeds in fall. Take cuttings in early June.

Dutch elm disease symptoms include wilted yellow leaves.

Paint fresh wounds in summer to help avoid infection.

PESTS AND DISEASES: Dutch elm disease is a fungus spread by elm bark beetles and through root grafts. Trees infected by feeding beetles show wilting, curling, and yellowing of leaves on one or more branches in the upper portion of the tree. Large trees may survive and show progressively more symptoms for one or more years. Other problems include leaf miners, stem cankers, bacterial wet wood, and elm yellows.

RELATED SPECIES: Smooth-leaved elm (*U. carpinifolia*) is more pyramidal and is hardy in Zones 5–7. It has some resistance to Dutch elm disease. Chinese or lacebark elm (*U. parvifolia*) is a round-topped tree with mottled bark and red-bronze fall color. It is hardy in Zones 5–9 and is resistant to Dutch elm disease. Siberian elm (*U. pumila*) is a fast-growing, weedy tree with little ornamental value. It is hardy in Zones 4–9.

BURKWOOD VIBURNUM

Viburnum xburkwoodii *vye-BUR-num berk-WOOD-ee-eye*

Burkwood has fragrant pink-white flowers in midspring.

ZONES: 5–8
SIZE: 8–10'h × 6–8'w
TYPE: Deciduous shrub
FORM: Upright, straggly
TEXTURE: Medium
GROWTH: Slow to medium

LIGHT: Sun to part shade
MOISTURE: Medium
SOIL: Slightly acid, well drained
FEATURES: Fragrant flowers
USES: Shrub border
FLOWERS: □ ■
FALL COLOR: ■ ■

SITING: Plant this shrub, a cross between *V. carlesii* and *V. utile,* for its spicy aromatic fragrance and semievergreen leaves. Flowers occur in 2–3"-wide balls. They are pink in bud; they turn white as they open fully in spring and last about 2 weeks. The flowers are widely spaced on the plant, so they provide only a moderately effective show. The fruit is an elliptical drupe that turns from green to red to black as it matures. Fruits are sparsely produced from July through August and are not showy. The glossy dark green leaves feel rough to the touch on the upper surface, but below they are brown and softly woolly. Burkwood viburnum holds its green leaves late. In most years, some leaves remain all winter, although they will have turned to purple or brown. Sometimes they turn slightly reddish in fall. It is an excellent plant for a shrub border. It is an especially good choice for the Midwest and southern United States because of its heat and cold tolerance. It thrives in a moist, well-drained site with slightly acid soil, although it tolerates neutral soils. It needs sun for optimal flowering. It is also tolerant of urban conditions such as air pollution.

CARE: Transplant as a balled-and-burlapped shrub. Keep the soil evenly moist throughout the growing season, especially the first 2–3 years after planting. Feed every spring with plant food, such as Miracle-Gro, or an organic equivalent. Prune right after flowering.

PROPAGATION: It is difficult to grow from seed. Take cuttings in early summer.

PESTS AND DISEASES: None are serious. Occasional problems may include bacterial leaf spot, powdery mildew, crown gall, rusts, aphids, and thrips. These can usually be prevented if the shrub is placed in a well-drained site. Nematodes may be a problem in the South.

RELATED SPECIES: 'Chenault' is a more compact form producing slightly earlier and more profuse flowers 'Mohawk' has dark red flower buds that open to white petals with red blotches. It has a compact growth habit. The foliage is resistant to leaf spots and mildew. Leaves turn brilliant orange-red in fall. Korean spice viburnum (*V. carlesii*) has spicy-sweet pinkish-white flowers in spring on a rounded, dense shrub 4–8' tall, hardy in Zones 5–7.

ARROWWOOD VIBURNUM
Viburnum dentatum vye-BUR-num den-TAY-tum

Arrowwood viburnum is hardy and adaptable to harsh conditions.

ZONES: 3–8
SIZE: 6–15'h ×
6–15'w
TYPE: Deciduous
shrub
FORM: Rounded
TEXTURE: Medium
GROWTH: Medium
LIGHT: Sun to part
shade

MOISTURE: Medium
SOIL: Well drained
FEATURES: Shade
tolerance, showy
flowers, clean foliage
USES: Shrub border,
shade garden,
screening
FLOWERS: ☐
FALL COLOR: ▣ ■

SITING: Arrowwood viburnum is a large, multistemmed shrub with showy creamy-white flowers in spring and attractive fall color. The common name comes from the straight, thin, upright stems. New leaves have a folded, accordion-like appearance. Leaves turn yellow, red, or reddish purple before falling. Blue-hued fruits appear in September to October. The color differs in brightness from plant to plant, affecting the showiness. It prefers moist, well-drained soil and sun but can tolerate moderate amounts of shade. It makes a good hedge or screen and works well massed in a

Prune suckers in spring to keep plants in bounds.

shrub border. It attracts wildlife, especially birds, which eat the fruits. Because it suckers and spreads, it is best suited to a contained space or naturalized situations.
CARE: Arrowwood viburnum is easily transplanted. Plants may suffer in drought conditions. Keep the soil evenly moist throughout the growing season, especially the first 2–3 years after planting. Feed every spring with plant food, such as Miracle-Gro. Prune right after flowering. Prune suckers to keep plants from getting out of bounds.
PROPAGATION: Take stem tip cuttings in early summer.
PESTS AND DISEASES: None are serious.
RELATED SPECIES: Linden viburnum (*V. dilitatum*) produces copious amounts of red fruit. It is hardy in Zones 4–7. Wayfaringtree viburnum (*V. lantana*) is more upright. The leathery, glossy, wrinkled leaves are dark green. Fruits change from green to cream to red to blue to black and persist into winter. Birds readily spread seedlings. Lantanaphyllum (*V. ×rhytidophylloides*) has large, leathery, semievergreen leaves and is hardy in Zones 5–8.

EUROPEAN CRANBERRYBUSH
Viburnum opulus vie-BUR-num OH-pyoo-lus

Showy red fruits hang in clusters in late summer on European cranberrybush.

ZONES: 3–8
SIZE: 8–15'h ×
10–15'w
TYPE: Deciduous
shrub
FORM: Upright
spreading
TEXTURE: Medium
GROWTH: Medium

LIGHT: Sun to part
shade
MOISTURE: Medium
SOIL: Well drained
FEATURES: Showy
flowers and fruits
USES: Specimen,
shrub border
FLOWERS: ☐
FALL COLOR: ■

SITING: This adaptable shrub has incised medium green leaves that resemble those of maple. Fall color is often green when the leaves fall, but it may have tinges of purple or red. White flowers appear in late May and early June. Fruits change to bright cherry red in late August. They are persistent and attractive throughout the autumn, then shrivel and fade in winter and remain into the following spring. It thrives in a moist, well-drained site with slightly acid soil, although it tolerates neutral soils. It needs sun for optimal flowering. Use European cranberrybush as a formal or an informal hedge, in a shrub border, in an entranceway, for foundation plantings, or as a specimen.

Keep plants vigorous by pruning out a few large canes each spring.

CARE: Transplant balled-and-burlapped or container-grown plants in spring or fall. Keep the soil evenly moist, especially the first 2–3 years after planting. Feed every spring with plant food, such as Miracle-Gro. Remove a few older stems each year to keep plants neat.
PROPAGATION: Take softwood cuttings from stem tips in midsummer.
PESTS AND DISEASES: Aphids cause mottled, distorted foliage. Keep them in check by spraying regularly with a strong blast of the hose or using insecticidal soap. Borers and/or blight can cause individual stems to die back all the way to the ground as the shrub reaches maturity.
RELATED SPECIES: 'Compactum' is the standard red-fruiting cultivar. It is more compact (to 8' tall by 8' wide), densely flowering, and densely fruited. American cranberrybush (*V. trilobum*) has smoother edged leaves. It is hardier, to Zone 2, and more resistant to aphids. Sargent viburnum (*V. sargentii*) has a more rounded form. The lace cap flowers have purplish anthers. Large clusters of bright red fruits persist through the winter. It is more resistant to aphids.

BLACK HAW VIBURNUM

Viburnum prunifolium vye-BUR-num proo-nih-FOH-lee-um

Black haw viburnum is a good choice for wildlife plantings.

ZONES: 3–9
SIZE: 12–15'h × 8–12'w
TYPE: Deciduous tree or shrub
FORM: Rounded
TEXTURE: Medium
GROWTH: Slow to medium
LIGHT: Sun to part shade

MOISTURE: Medium to low
SOIL: Well drained
FEATURES: Attractive flowers, small size
USES: Specimen tree, massing, border
FLOWERS: □
FALL COLOR: ■

SITING: Black haw viburnum is noted for its spring flowers, autumn fruits, fall color, and dense twigginess, which makes it ideal as a wildlife haven, a nonthorny barrier hedge, or a naturalized group planting.

Fall color is variable, including green, burgundy, red, orange, yellow, and purple. The creamy-white flowers bloom in early May. Fruits are a mixture of green, yellow, and red-pink, changing to blue-black or blue-pink at maturity, and are attractive to wildlife. It prefers moist, well-drained soils of average fertility, but is adaptable to poor soils, compacted soils, soils of various pH, permanently moist soils, and dry soils. It prefers full sun, and tolerates moderate shade, heat, drought, and pollution.
CARE: Keep the soil evenly moist throughout the growing season, especially the first 2–3 years after planting. Feed every spring with plant food, such as Miracle-Gro, or an organic equivalent. Remove a few older stems each year to keep plants from becoming overgrown and unkempt.
PROPAGATION: Take stem tip cuttings in early summer.
PESTS AND DISEASES: None are serious.
RELATED SPECIES: Nannyberry viburnum (*V. lentago*) is a large, upright shrub also available as a single-stemmed tree. It is subject to powdery mildew, which does not kill plants. Siebold viburnum (*V. sieboldii*) is hardy in Zones 4–8. It is usually grown as a large, multitrunked shrub or small tree, reaching about 20' high and 10–12' wide, creating an upright silhouette with short, firm branches.

1 **Black haw viburnum may be planted as a bare-root plant in early spring.**

2 **Backfill around the root system with existing soil**

3 **Water in thoroughly to remove air pockets.**

CHASTE TREE

Vitex agnus-castus VYE-teks AG-nuss-KAS-tus

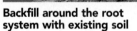

Lavender blooms of chaste tree attract butterflies and bees.

ZONES: 7–9
SIZE: 15–20'h × 10–15'w
TYPE: Deciduous tree or shrub
FORM: Rounded
TEXTURE: Medium
GROWTH: Medium
LIGHT: Sun

MOISTURE: Low
SOIL: Well drained
FEATURES: Showy summer flowers, drought tolerance
USES: Specimen, shrub border, massing
FLOWERS: ■ ■ □ □

SITING: Chaste tree can be grown as a large, deciduous, multistemmed shrub

or a small tree. The trunk is gray and knotty and somewhat ornamental. The strongly aromatic, sage-scented grayish leaves palmate, shaped like a hand. Its showy, fragrant, upwardly pointing panicles of lavender blooms attract butterflies and bees in summer. Round, fleshy green fruits follow the flowers, turning brown and persisting through winter. Chaste tree seems impervious to excessive heat if given sufficient water and provides a dramatic flowering during the time when many other plants are suffering drought stress or have gone into summer dormancy. In some regions this species has become naturalized and is considered weedy. It is good as a specimen plant and for the border and massing. In warm climates it forms a large shrub or small tree; where winters are cold, it dies back to the ground. It prefers full sun and well-drained, loamy soil. It is salt tolerant and can be used in seaside plantings.
CARE: Roots are few and coarse; avoid exposing them to sun and wind during transplanting. Water young plants as

needed; established plants are drought tolerant. Train young plants into a tree form if desired. Regularly remove suckers on small trees. It may winterkill in colder areas. Prune shrubs to the ground each spring to grow as an herbaceous perennial, with flowers blooming on new growth. In warmer climates remove the entire top and any dead wood in early spring for best flowering. Removing spent flowers may help plants rebloom later in summer.
PROPAGATION: Softwood cuttings taken in early summer root easily.
PESTS AND DISEASES: None are serious.
RELATED SPECIES: 'Serrata' has serrated leaflets. 'Alba' and 'Silver Spire' have white flowers. 'Colonial Blue' has good blue flower color. 'Rosea' has pink flowers. 'Latifolia' is more vigorous and hardier than the species. Chaste tree (*V. negundo*) is hardier and has highly dissected leaves shaped like cut-leaf Japanese maple. It is smaller (10–15' tall), shrubbier, and more open and vase shaped.

WEIGELA

Weigela florida *wye-JEE-luh FLOR-ih-duh*

Hummingbirds flock to showy weigela flowers. The shrub is also known as old-fashioned weigela.

ZONES: 4–8
SIZE: 6–9'h × 9–12'w
TYPE: Deciduous shrub
FORM: Spreading, scraggly
TEXTURE: Medium
GROWTH: Medium
LIGHT: Sun to light shade
MOISTURE: Medium

SOIL: Humusy, well drained
FEATURES: Showy flowers, foliage
USES: Specimen, shrub border, mixed border, foundation
FLOWERS: ☐ ▨ ▮ ▮
FALL COLOR: ▮

SITING: Weigela has funnel-shaped rosy-pink flowers that cover the plant for a long time in late spring. They are attractive to hummingbirds and bees. Plants may bloom intermittently throughout the summer. When not in bloom, weigela can be coarse, especially in winter. It prefers cool, deep, moist, humus-rich, well-drained soil and full sun to light shade. Flowering is best in full sun. Site it in shrub borders or in mixed foundation plantings. Smaller types can be included in mixed borders.

Prune shrubs after flowering to improve shape and appearance.

CARE: Transplant bare-root or container-grown plants in spring. Keep the soil evenly moist during the growing season. Reduce watering by mid-September to help plants go into winter dormancy and reduce the risk of winter dieback. Feed every spring with plant food, such as Miracle-Gro. In early spring, snip off dead portions of stems. Prune plants severely after flowering to shape them. Old canes produce few flowers; cut out one-third of the older stems each year to encourage new growth from the base and keep plants at a manageable size.
PROPAGATION: Take softwood cuttings of weigela in summer.
PESTS AND DISEASES: None are serious. Occasionally aphids attack new growth.
RELATED SPECIES: 'Red Prince' has crimson-red flowers. 'Wine and Roses' has rose flowers and reddish-purple foliage. 'White Knight' has white flowers tinged with pink, and light green foliage. 'Eva Supreme' is dwarf with deep red flowers. 'Variegata' leaves are edged with pale yellow. 'Polka' is hardy to Zone 3. It is covered in late spring by deep pink blooms.

JAPANESE ZELKOVA

Zelkova serrata *zel-KOH-vuh sare-AH-tuh*

Leaf shape and plant form are similar to American elm.

ZONES: 5–8
SIZE: 50–80'h × 40–60'w
TYPE: Deciduous tree
FORM: Vase shaped
TEXTURE: Medium fine
GROWTH: Medium

LIGHT: Sun to light shade
MOISTURE: Medium
SOIL: Well drained
FEATURES: Pleasing shape, good foliage
USES: Shade, lawn, street
FLOWERS: ▮
FALL COLOR: ▨ ▮

SITING: Japanese zelkova is a large-size tree with a graceful vase shape that is compared to the American elm. Fall color varies from yellow-orange to red or reddish purple. Young trees have smooth gray bark, but as they mature it becomes scaly and exfoliates to expose showy inner orange-brown bark. The tree prefers well-drained, moist, deep, fertile soil and full sun. It is tolerant of drought, wind, and pollution once established. Its ease of transplanting and tolerance of urban conditions make it a good replacement tree for American elm along city streets. It is a good shade tree for medium to large yards. The leaves are easy to rake in fall. Choose a site where it will have room to develop its wide crown. In northern areas, plant in a protected site to avoid frost damage.

Fall color of zelkova ranges from yellow to reddish purple.

CARE: Water young trees as needed to keep the soil evenly moist. Young trees benefit from a spring application of plant food, such as Miracle-Gro, and an organic mulch. Prune young trees only as needed to shape by thinning out crowded branches. Young trees are subject to frost injury in colder climates; prune out any affected parts in spring.
PROPAGATION: Sow seeds in fall. Take cuttings in summer.
PESTS AND DISEASES: None are serious. It is susceptible to some of the same problems as elms, but to a lesser degree. It shows fairly good resistance to Dutch elm disease and bacterial canker, but it is not immune. It also has good resistance to elm leaf beetle and Japanese beetle.
RELATED SPECIES: 'Autumn Glow' has deep purple fall color. 'Green Vase' is strongly vase shaped and vigorous, with good fall color. 'Green Veil' is more upright and narrow. 'Halka' is a rapid grower with a somewhat loose and open growth habit and yellowish fall color. 'Village Green' is a rapid grower with a smooth, straight trunk and rusty red fall color. 'Illinois Hardy' is considered more reliably cold hardy than other cultivars.

A–Z ENCYCLOPEDIA OF
VEGETABLE, FRUIT, AND HERB CARE

Grow your own vegetables, fruits, and herbs for a flavorful gardening experience. With proper care of your kitchen garden and home orchard you'll reap a bounty of fresh produce.

COMMON NAME	BOTANIC NAME	SEE PAGE
Alligator pear	*Persea americana*	537
Almond	*Prunus dulcis*	546
American grape	*Vitis labrusca*	566–567
American persimmon	*Diospyros virginiana*	512
American plum	*Prunus americana*	549
Apple	*Malus* spp.	526–530
Apple mint	*Mentha suaveolens*	531
Apricot	*Prunus armeniaca*	543
Artichoke	*Cynara scolymus*	510
Arugula	*Eruca sativa*	513
Asparagus	*Asparagus officinalis*	483
Asparagus bean	*Vigna unguiculata* ssp. *sesquipedalis*	565
Aubergine	*Solanum melongena*	559
Avocado	*Persea americana*	537
Banana	*Musa acuminata,* *Musa* ×*paradisiaca*	532
Basil	*Ocimum basilicum*	533
Bean	*Phaseolus* spp.	538–539
Beet	*Beta vulgaris*	484
Belgian endive	*Cichorium endivia*	496
Bell pepper	*Capsicum annuum*	491-493
Blackberry	*Rubus* spp.	556–557
Black currant	*Ribes nigrum*	555
Black-eyed pea	*Vigna unguiculata*	565
Black raspberry	*Rubus occidentalis*	556–557
Blueberry	*Vaccinium* spp.	562–563
Bok choy	*Brassica rapa* Chinensis group	489
Borecole	*Brassica oleracea* Acephala group	486
Boysenberry	*Rubus* spp.	556–557
Broad bean	*Vicia faba*	564
Broadleaf cress	*Lepidium sativum*	521
Broccoli	*Brassica oleracea* Italica group	488
Brussels sprouts	*Brassica oleracea* Gemmifera group	487
Burnet	*Sanguisorba minor*	558
Burnet bloodwort	*Sanguisorba minor*	558
Bush bean	*Phaseolus vulgaris*	538–539
Cabbage	*Brassica oleracea* Capitata group	487
Cantaloupe	*Cucumis melo melo*	503
Caper	*Capparis spinosa*	490
Carrot	*Daucus carota sativus*	511
Cauliflower	*Brassica oleracea* Botrytis group	486
Celeriac	*Apium graveolens* var. *rapaceum*	480
Celery	*Apium graveolens*	479
Celery mustard	*Brassica rapa* Pekinensis group	489

COMMON NAME	BOTANIC NAME	SEE PAGE
Celery root	*Apium graveolens* var. *rapaceum*	480
Cherimoya	*Annona cherimola*	478
Cherry	*Prunus* spp.	544–545
Chervil	*Anthriscus cereifolium*	479
Chestnut	*Castanea* spp.	495
Chili pepper	*Capsicum annuum*	491-493
Chinese cabbage	*Brassica rapa* Pekinensis group	489
Chinese gooseberry	*Actinidia deliciosa*	473
Chinese spinach	*Amaranthus tricolor*	476
Chives	*Allium schoenoprasum*	475
Chocolate mint	*Mentha* ×*piperata* 'Chocolate'	531
Cilantro	*Coriandrum sativum*	502
Citron	*Citrus medica*	499
Collards	*Brassica oleracea* Acephala group	485
Common guava	*Psidium guajava*	552
Concord grape	*Vitis labrusca*	566–567
Coriander	*Coriandrum sativum*	502
Corn salad	*Valerianella locusta*	564
Corsican mint	*Mentha requienii*	531
Cowpea	*Vigna unguiculata*	565
Crabapple	*Malus* spp.	526-530
Cranberry	*Vaccinium macrocarpon*	563
Crenshaw melon	*Cucumis melo melo*	503
Cucumber	*Cucumis sativus*	505
Curly cress	*Lepidium sativum*	521
Curly-leaved parsley	*Petroselinum crispum*	537
Currant	*Ribes* spp.	555
Date palm	*Phoenix dactylifera*	541
Dewberry	*Rubus* spp.	556–557
Dill	*Anethum graveolens*	478
Eggplant	*Solanum melongena*	559
Endive	*Cichorium endivia*	496
English pea	*Pisum sativum*	542
Escarole	*Cichorium endivia*	496
European plum	*Prunus* ×*domestica*	548–549
Fava bean	*Vicia faba*	564
Feijoa	*Feijoa sellowiana*	513
Field mint	*Mentha arvensis*	531
Fig	*Ficus carica*	514
Filbert	*Corylus* spp.	502
Flat-leaved parsley	*Petroselinum crispum*	537
Florence fennel	*Foeniculum vulgare azoricum*	514
Fox grape	*Vitis labrusca*	566–567
French tarragon	*Artemisia dracunculus sativa*	481
Frisée	*Cichorium endivia*	496
Garden cress	*Lepidium sativum*	521

'Gala' apple, *Malus sylvestrus* ×*domestica*

Asparagus, *Asparagus officinalis*

'Blue Lake' bush bean, *Phaseolus vulgaris*

'Purple Cape' cauliflower, *Brassica oleracea* Botrytis group

CHAPTER **11** A–Z ENCYCLOPEDIA OF VEGETABLE, FRUIT, AND HERB CARE

Grape, Vitis vinifera

Red 'Mars' and yellow 'Candy' onions, Allium cepa

Heirloom peppers, Capsicum annuum

Potatoes, Solanum tuberosum

COMMON NAME INDEX VEGETABLES, FRUITS & HERBS *continued*

Radish, *Raphanus sativus*

'Painted Lady' scarlet runner bean, *Phaseolus coccineus*

Tomatoes, *Lycopersicon esculentum*

'Delicata' winter squash, *Cucurbita* spp.

Nothing compares with the satisfaction of growing your own food. Fresh fruits and vegetables carried from garden to kitchen taste better and have more nutritional value than those shipped long distances. But homegrown produce has an intrinsically healthy value just as tangible as its flavors: Your own work in the garden has made it possible.

You're the one who studies the catalogs each winter and chooses plant varieties that will thrive in your climate and growing space. You survey your plot and design a planting scheme to take advantage of sun, site, and water availability. You build the beds and prepare the soil, hoeing weeds, raking rocks and digging in compost and manure. You sow seeds and plant seedlings you've started indoors or selected from your favorite source. You water and feed the growing plants, weeding between the rows and pinching back the herbs, training a vine up a fence and pruning suckers from a tree. You may even lose a bit of sleep researching the best ways to keep insects and infections from undermining your efforts.

But when harvest time comes—when you savor the first sweet strawberry right off the vine, slice into a warm, juicy tomato, make the extra zucchinis into pickles for winter, or take a basket of just-ripe peaches to a friend—you know that what you have grown is the best it can be. The care you give your garden and the plants growing in it results in healthy, delicious food and an easily sustainable source of more to come. What could possibly be more nourishing?

OKRA

Abelmoschus esculentus ab-bel-MOS-kus es-kyoo-LEN-tus

Pick red okra pods at 2–4" long. Okra is also known as gumbo or ladies' fingers.

ZONES: NA
SIZE: 2–8'h × 1–1½'w
TYPE: Tropical annual
GROWTH: Fast

LIGHT: Full sun
MOISTURE: Average
FEATURES: Hibiscus-type flowers, edible seedpods

SITING: Direct-seed ½" deep after danger of frost is past and soil temperature is at least 60°F. Seeds will germinate in 1–2 weeks. Or plant transplants 1–2' apart in rows 2' apart in fertile, loamy, neutral or slightly alkaline soil after the ground has been above 60°F for at least 2 weeks. Use black plastic to warm the soil in cooler zones. Okra does best if the soil dries between waterings; it can tolerate short periods of drought but will not thrive in wet conditions. Transplants are sun sensitive; keep the roots moist until the plants are established.

CARE: Okra is a member of the mallow family, related to hibiscus and hollyhock. Its large pale yellow flowers attract pollinating insects. Broad leaves shade the soil below, so mulch may not be needed. Low-growing, shade-tolerant herbs such as summer savory can be planted between the rows. Use starter solution, such as Miracle-Gro Liquid Quick Start Plant Food, to prevent transplant shock. Use water-soluble plant food, such as Miracle-Gro Water Soluble All Purpose every 2–4 weeks when plants are in flower. Wear gloves when handling varieties with spiny hairs, which can irritate skin.

PROPAGATION: Soak seeds overnight to speed germination. Or start plants indoors 6–8 weeks before the last frost date; thin seedlings to one per pot by snipping weak ones instead of pulling them out, to avoid disturbing the roots.

HARVEST: Pods mature about 60 days after flowering. They can quickly become tough, so harvest frequently from the plant when 3–5" long. Store unwashed pods in the refrigerator for use within a few days; pressure-can or blanch and freeze pods for longer storage. Store away from fruits and vegetables that give off ethylene gas. The pods are high in calcium and fiber and can be boiled, fried, sautéed, dried, pickled, or added to soups, stews, and gumbos. Pods release a mucilaginous compound; to minimize it cook pods whole with the caps still attached. The sticky substance is a thickening agent that may be desired in some dishes. Mature pods add interest to dried flower arrangements. Okra is related to cotton; its long stem fibers can be used to make paper and rope. Oil extracted from the seeds is commonly used for cooking in Mediterranean countries. Dry and grind the ripe seeds for a caffeine-free coffee substitute.

PESTS AND DISEASES: Okra is susceptible to root knot nematode and fusarium wilt, and to southern blight in hot, humid zones. Blights and wilt are best controlled through crop rotation. Green stinkbugs, Japanese beetles, and leaf miners may feed on the leaves but generally are not a serious problem. Severely curled pods and pods with warty bumps indicate earlier feeding by stinkbugs or leaf-footed bugs. Damage to leaves does not affect harvest.

RECOMMENDED CULTIVARS: 'Clemson Spineless' grows well north and south. 'Red Velvet' has wine-red pods and stems. Early-yielding 'Cajun Delight' is good in northern gardens. Dwarf 'Baby Bubba' works well in containers and small spaces.

Cook pods whole to minimize the sticky substance they release.

Gently pull the pods away from the stem and clip free with sharp scissors.

KIWIFRUIT
Actinidia deliciosa ak-tih-NID-ee-uh deh-lih-see-OH-suh

Taste one fruit to test for ripeness before picking others. Kiwifruit is also known as Chinese gooseberry.

ZONES: 8–11
SIZE: 9–12'h × 18–30'w
TYPE: Woody perennial vine
GROWTH: Fast

LIGHT: Full sun to part shade
MOISTURE: High
FEATURES: Attractive ornamental plant, edible fruits

SITING: Kiwis do best in deep, well-drained loam that is mildly acid and low in sodium. Plants are susceptible to damage from frost and wind, so locate them in a protected area. Space plants 15–20' apart, leaving room to erect a trellis. Water deeply and often when vines are in bloom or fruit, less often in dormancy.

CARE: Kiwifruit vines are fast growing but take 8 years to fruit. Work slow-release plant food into the soil around young vines. Older vines are heavy feeders; use water-soluble plant food every 2 weeks during the growing season. Train the vines up strong posts. Pinch off suckers, but wait to prune until after the male vines have flowered and females have set fruit. Prune again when the plants are dormant.

PROPAGATION: Grow from hardwood cuttings ½" in diameter with several nodes.

Feed often at the base of vines and pinch off any suckers.

Vines are male or female; use one male per one to eight females. Choose cultivars with the same chilling requirements so they flower at the same time.

HARVEST: The fruit takes about 5 months after achieving full size to develop the desired taste and texture. Test for maturity by picking one and allowing it to soften at room temperature for a few days before eating it. If it tastes sweet, pick all the fruits and keep them refrigerated. Fruits can stay on the vine as long as there is no threat of frost.

PESTS AND DISEASES: Treat leaf-rolling caterpillars with Bt. Treat scale with neem oil. Careful preparation and proper watering of a well-drained planting site is the best way to avoid root rot and other stress-related diseases.

RECOMMENDED CULTIVARS: 'Hayward' is the most common kiwi in North America and is easy to grow except in areas with very warm winters. *A. arguta* has smaller red or green fruits the size of large grapes; the skin is edible. *A. kolomikta* has very small fruit but is an especially cold-hardy species. *A. chinensis* 'Zespri™ Gold' has bright yellow flesh sweeter than 'Hayward'.

MUSHROOM
Agaricus bisporus uh-GAIR-ih-kuhs by-SPOR-us

Mushrooms grow in little or no light.

ZONES: NA
SIZE: ½–8"h × ¼–8"w
TYPE: Fungi
GROWTH: Rapid to average

LIGHT: Low to none
MOISTURE: High
FEATURES: Edible stems

SITING: Plant button mushroom spawn in trays filled with a manure-based soil mix of compost mixed with straw. Plug shiitake (*Lentinus edodes*) spores into specially prepared hardwood logs, usually oak. The growing area must be 55–70°F with high humidity, even moisture, good air circulation, and little or no light.

CARE: Mushrooms require decaying organic matter to grow. Some species develop quickly and are easy to cultivate; others require considerable attention over a period of months. All require constant high humidity (80–85 percent) and misting. When flushes (groups of mature heads) stop appearing, compost the exhausted soil mix and logs.

PROPAGATION: Grow from spores, called spawn, available from commercial growers.

Cut or twist mature mushroom stems close to the growing surface.

HARVEST: Pinheads develop into flushes every week or two until the nutrients in the soil mix are exhausted. The first flush of button mushrooms occurs 30–60 days from spawning; shiitakes take 6–9 months; oyster mushrooms (*Pleurotus*) take 3 weeks. Pick mushrooms by cutting or twisting the stems near the medium surface, then cut the stem stumps below the surface to prevent disease. Common white and brown button mushrooms are eaten raw in salads and can be dried, pickled, sautéed, grilled, fried, or added to soups and stews. Large brown *cremini* (portobello) mushrooms are often used as meat substitutes. Shiitake, enoki, oyster, chanterelle, and other exotic types add an earthy, nutty flavor to dishes.

PESTS AND DISEASES: Slugs love mushrooms, so elevate and enclose outdoor growing areas. Cleanliness and moisture control prevent problems caused by competing molds. Properly prepared compost eliminates insect larvae.

RECOMMENDED SPECIES: *Volvariella volvacea* (straw mushroom) and *Morchella esculenta* (morel, which requires sunlight) are additional edible types of mushrooms.

ONION

Allium cepa AL-lee-um SEE-puh

Harvest green shallots when the bulbs begin to swell.

ZONES: NA
SIZE: 4–8"h × ¼–5"w
TYPE: Herbaceous perennial usually grown as annual

GROWTH: Average
LIGHT: Full sun
MOISTURE: High
FEATURES: Edible bulbs and stems

SITING: Plant in well-drained soil rich in organic matter. The soil should be consistently moist but never waterlogged.
CARE: Cultivate onions for their immature green stems, called scallions; for their immature bulbs, called green onions; or for their mature, storable bulbs. Shallots are grown for use as dried bulbs and have a more delicate flavor than onions. A month before the first frost-free date, direct-sow seed ½" deep in rows 12–18" apart, thinning throughout the season. In early spring in northern zones and in autumn in warmer climates, plant bulbs or transplants 4–6" apart in rows 1' apart (or 6" apart for shallots in raised beds), with the pointed end just showing above ground. Weed frequently to reduce competition for nutrients. Remove seed heads. Mulch lightly to prevent sunscald. Use water-soluble plant food twice a month during the growing season. Shallots can be left in the ground from year to year but grow and taste better if lifted and stored each fall.
PROPAGATION: Onions grown from seed need 90 to 120 days to mature, so plant sets or transplants in northern zones.

'White Lisbon' scallions are grown and harvested as immature green onions.

Shallots are grown from individual bulbs or sets available commercially.
HARVEST: Dig or pull scallions and green shallots when the tops are 4–8" tall and green onions when the tops are 6–8" tall and bulbs have begun to swell. To use as dried bulbs, wait until the green tops have withered and browned, then stop watering. Lift shallots after a week; let onions cure in the ground for 2 weeks before digging. Store for 1 week in a dry, shady spot. When they are completely dry, remove any remaining stalks and trim the roots, then hang the bulbs in mesh onion bags in a cool (35–55°F), dry location.
PESTS AND DISEASES: Onions are susceptible to thrips, maggots, and soilborne diseases, all best avoided by crop rotation. Shallots are susceptible to pink rot, particularly in the South; treat garden soil with fungicide.
RECOMMENDED CULTIVARS: Choose onions based on their day-length requirements. Bermuda and Spanish onions do best in warm climates; 'White Lisbon' (often harvested for green onions) and 'Yellow Globe' grow well in cooler areas. *A. fistulosum* (Japanese bunching onion) is the common commercial green onion. 'Yellow Multiplier' and 'French Red' shallots thrive in all zones and keep well.

LEEK

Allium porrum AL-lee-um POR-rum

Mound soil on leek stalks to blanch the lower part of the stems.

ZONES: NA
SIZE: 8–18"h × ½–2"w
TYPE: Biennial grown as annual

GROWTH: Average
LIGHT: Full sun
MOISTURE: High
FEATURES: Edible shanks, frost tolerant

SITING: Plant in well-drained soil rich in organic matter. In clay soil areas, plant bulbs in a raised bed amended with humus. The soil should be consistently moist but not waterlogged.
CARE: Leeks mature in 70–150 days but grow rapidly in cool weather. To increase the amount of white shank on the stalk, blanch the stems by mounding soil around them, or plant the leeks in the bottom of trenches, gradually filling in with soil as the stems grow. Weed around plants frequently to discourage competition. Use water-soluble plant food, such as Miracle-Gro Water Soluble All Purpose, twice a month. In cool zones, dig plants and store in a cool location before the first frost date, or leave them in the garden under heavy mulch and harvest as needed. Dig any remaining leeks in spring.
PROPAGATION: Seed germinates best in soil temperatures from 70–75°F but can be sown a month before the last frost date. Seedlings started indoors can be transplanted around the last frost date and anytime up to a month before the first frost.

HARVEST: Dig or pull leeks any time after the shanks are ½" or more in diameter. Leeks are famous in potato-leek soup (vichyssoise) but can be eaten raw in salads and baked, broiled, or sautéed like root crops.
PESTS AND DISEASES: None are significant.
RECOMMENDED CULTIVARS: 'American Flag' and 'Giant Musselburgh' are good choices.

Leeks can be left in the garden all winter and harvested as needed. Mulch them well for protection.

GARLIC
Allium sativum *AL-lee-um sub-TEE-vum*

Save some garlic cloves to start next year's crop. Store the rest in a cool, dry location.

ZONES: NA
SIZE: 8–24"h × 1–4"w
TYPE: Herbaceous perennial usually grown as an annual

GROWTH: Average
LIGHT: Full sun
MOISTURE: Average
FEATURES: Edible bulb

SITING: Plant the cloves pointed end up in well-drained, fertile, friable loam. Plant 2–3" deep and 6" apart in midautumn or early spring in northern zones and in late autumn or early winter in the South.
CARE: Garlic needs regular moisture but will rot in soil that stays wet all the time. Keep weeds removed and cut off flower heads to encourage bulb production. Use water-soluble plant food, such as Miracle-Gro Water Soluble All Purpose, once a week until summer. Mulch well around plants to retain moisture.
PROPAGATION: Grow from individual cloves split from a bulb.
HARVEST: Hard-neck garlics produce a coiled seed stalk in summer and white, red, or purple-striped bulbs with large cloves. Soft-neck garlics are tan, white, or purple-tinged and do not produce seed stalks. Mature bulbs are ready to dry in 90–110 days. Push the tops over to the ground and stop watering when about half the lower leaves begin to wither and turn brown. Let the bulbs cure for a week in the garden, then lift them and hang them for a week in a dry, shady location with good air circulation. Trim off any leaf stalks and cut the roots close to the base of each bulb. Store the bulbs in mesh bags in a cool (35–55°F), dry location. Save the largest cloves for planting next season—they'll produce the largest bulbs.
PESTS AND DISEASES: Avoid soilborne diseases and insects by crop rotation and clean planting practices. Pink rot and mildew can be problems in warm, humid climates; treat garden soil with fungicide.
RECOMMENDED CULTIVARS: 'German Porcelain' is a popular hard-neck garlic with white-wrapped cloves. 'Killarney Red' is a hard-neck with large pink-skinned cloves. Soft-neck 'Silverskin' types are well suited to cooler climates and store well. 'Red Toch' is a large Russian soft-neck type that grows well in warm climates. Elephant garlic (*A. scorodoprasum*) is more closely related to leeks but produces huge, garlic-type bulbs with a mild flavor.

1 To plant garlic, separate the cloves.

2 Plant the pointed ends up.

3 Mulch with straw over winter.

Harvest and hang bulbs to dry.

CHIVES
Allium schoenoprasum *AL-lee-um skee-noh-PRAY-zum*

Fragrant chive flowers are attractive edible garnishes. The tubular stems can be used to flavor foods as well.

ZONES: 3–10
SIZE: 8–12"h × 8–12"w
TYPE: Herbaceous perennial
GROWTH: Fast

LIGHT: Full sun to part shade
MOISTURE: Average
FEATURES: Edible leaves and flowers

SITING: Plant in average, well-drained soil in beds or pots. Chives are evergreen in warm climates but die back to the ground in cooler zones in winter.
CARE: Chives are somewhat drought tolerant and don't require plant food or much attention besides regular cutting. They eventually become overcrowded, so dig and divide clumps every few years and plant the divisions in new locations.
PROPAGATION: Grow from seed in early spring or by division in spring or fall.

Harvest a few stems as needed from container-grown plants.

HARVEST: These tiny onions are grown for their hollow leaf stems, not their bulbs. Chives are ready to cut in 75–85 days when grown from seed. Snip chives as needed by cutting through them just above the ground with scissors or a sharp knife. Chives can be dried but retain their color and flavor better when frozen. Snip a few leaves in salads, sauces, and quiches; add to baked potatoes and egg dishes at the end of cooking to preserve the garlicky flavor. The small, fragrant pinkish-purple flowers are also edible and can be used as a garnish.
PESTS AND DISEASES: Chives are seldom bothered by pests and may even repel Japanese beetles.
RECOMMENDED CULTIVARS: 'Forescate' has rose-red flowers. 'Ruby Gem' has gray-green foliage and red flowers. Chinese or garlic chives (*A. tuberosum*) grow taller than common chives and have flat leaves and white flowers. They can be invasive.

VEGETABLE AMARANTH

Amaranthus tricolor am-uh-RAN-thus TRY-kuh-lor

Chinese spinach or tampala tolerates hot weather. It is also known as pigweed.

ZONES: NA
SIZE: 1–3'h × 1'w
TYPE: Annual
GROWTH: Fast
LIGHT: Full sun
MOISTURE: Average
FEATURES: Edible leaves

SITING: Broadcast seed in loose, fertile, well-drained soil and cover with a fine layer of sifted soil or compost. Amaranth is adaptable but grows best in consistently moist soil. It is an excellent substitute for spinach and lettuces that bolt in hot summers. Because it is quick to mature, it can also be grown in temperate zones in midsummer.

CARE: Thin seedlings to 6" apart in rows 12" apart. Keep young plants watered well and feed them two or three times a month with high-nitrogen, water-soluble plant food. Pinch off terminal buds to promote branching. Keep the soil evenly moist around the roots and pull any weeds. Mulch during periods of prolonged drought. Cut the entire plant at ground level before the first frost.

PROPAGATION: Grow from seed.

HARVEST: Unlike ornamental and grain amaranths, vegetable amaranth—also called Chinese spinach, tampala, and pigweed—is grown for its edible leaves, which are high in vitamins A and C and rich in minerals. Amaranth is commonly used in Asian, African, and West Indian cuisines. Young leaves and thinnings are used raw in salads; older leaves are steamed like spinach or added to soups and stews. Leaves are ready to pick in about 50 days when grown from seed. Pinch out new leaf rosettes and cut individual leaves at least once a week to encourage plants to produce new leaves. Freeze some leaves for winter use.

PESTS AND DISEASES: Chewing insects, such as Japanese and cucumber beetles, may damage the leaves. Use floating row covers to discourage them.

RECOMMENDED CULTIVARS: 'Green Leaf' is the most common; 'Calaloo' has purple-veined dark green leaves; 'Garnet Red' has ruby leaves; 'White Leaf' is a dwarf type with light green leaves and tender stems.

PINEAPPLE

Ananas comosus uh-NAN-us koh-MOH-sus

Locate the spiny-leaved plants away from people and pets.

ZONES: 9–11
SIZE: 3–5'h × 4–5'w
TYPE: Herbaceous perennial
GROWTH: Slow
LIGHT: Full sun
MOISTURE: High
FEATURES: Attractive plant, edible fruits

SITING: Plant crowns or offsets 4–6" deep and 12–18" apart in acid, well-drained sandy loam. The leaves are sometimes spiny, so locate plants away from the outside edges of garden plots.

CARE: Water and weed often, especially while plants are becoming established. Use Miracle-Gro Fruit & Citrus Fertilizer Spikes between rows, and side dress plants with compost or seaweed once a month before fruiting. Mulch to discourage weeds.

PROPAGATION: Grow from offsets or crowns. Cross-pollination is required.

HARVEST: Growing pineapple is a slow and often high-maintenance process with a tremendous reward. Plants bloom after a year or so, in knobs of reddish flower clusters over a period of 2–3 weeks. Each flower produces one fruitlet; the fruitlets eventually merge into a single fruit, the pineapple. Mature pineapples give off a strong fragrance. Test for ripeness by pulling on leaves near the crown; they will be loose on mature fruit. Cut the stalk with a sharp knife a couple of inches below the fruit. Store the fruit whole until ready to eat or cook it. Pineapples are sweetest near the base, so the day before using one, cut off the top and turn the fruit upside down in a shallow bowl in the refrigerator to let the juice filter down through the whole fruit. Add fresh pineapple to salads and desserts or use it in jams, preserves, syrups, and juices.

PESTS AND DISEASES: Mealybugs, scales, and mites are the most common pests. Remove them by washing the leaves in a mild soap solution and rinsing well. Hot sun will usually kill nematodes. Treat rots with a fungicide labeled for pineapple.

RECOMMENDED CULTIVARS: 'Smooth Cayenne' is among the most common types, with sweet, highly acidic bright yellow flesh that keeps well. 'Red Spanish' has pale yellow to white flesh and is best eaten fresh.

Leaves near the crown will be loose on mature pineapples.

IMPROVING SOIL WITH COVER CROPS

Does your garden need more compost than you can manufacture in one season? Consider cultivating "green manure" cover crops as a way to improve soil texture and fertility while the garden rests during the winter. If you are a four-season gardener, think about dividing your plot into two or more sections, so you can grow cover crops in one or more of them while the others produce food crops.

Grow fall-seeded legumes where winters are warm.

Winter rye and buckwheat are good cover crops in northern zones.

GREEN GOLD

Growing cover crops and tilling them in as "green manure" (not yet decomposed) adds organic matter and nutrients to the soil. The crops themselves keep the soil aerated and protected from erosion, and also help discourage weed growth. Cover crops grown between rows of fruit trees help to prevent soil erosion and protect the tree roots. Some cover crops produce flowers that attract honeybees, which benefit the whole garden.

WHAT TO PLANT

Choose cover crops based on where you live and the type of soil you want to improve. Cereal grains such as winter rye and buckwheat are commonly grown as cover crops in northern zones, as are annual ryegrass and legumes such as soybeans. In warmer climates, fall-seeded legumes such as hairy vetch and bigflower vetch, crimson clover, and alfalfa are popular choices; rye and oats are good nonlegume choices. Legumes are the preferred choice for soil enrichment. Bacteria in nodules that form on the roots of legumes convert nitrogen in the atmosphere into nitrogen in the soil, where it remains available to the crops you plant after you till in the cover crop. To speed up the nitrogen-fixing process, dust your cover crop seeds with rhizobium, a bacterial inoculant. For smaller gardens where growing space is limited, quick-growing rye, hull-less oats, millet, or wheat may be a better choice than legumes. Oilseed radish, a type of mustard, grows quickly in cool weather and is a good choice for use in compacted soil or dry conditions. In northern climates you can plant a nonlegume cover crop in autumn when the harvest is over, and it will have time to sprout and grow before dying in winter. Till it under in early spring; wait a few weeks to be sure it has all decomposed, and then begin planting your vegetable crops. In warm-winter areas, sow cover crops in summer and till them under in fall a few weeks before planting. For an appealing late-season cover crop that attracts beneficial insects, grow sunflowers (*Helianthus annuus*) every third or fourth year. For help in deciding which cover crop will work best in your garden, contact the county extension agent in your area.

WHEN TO TILL

You can turn under a cover crop anytime, but to be considered "green manure" it needs to be tilled when it is still green—usually just as the buds are about to open, when the crop is about a foot tall. If you're on vacation when the buds blossom and the plants get big and tough, don't despair. You can till under the entire mature crop, but you'll need to add real manure to the plot to help with decomposition. In the South you may be able to plant again in the same year. If you need to till under a mature crop but also need to plant again soon, just cut the crop low with a regular lawn mower and compost the clippings, then till the rest under. You can plant again in a few weeks.

1 Clear the plot of vegetation.

2 Broadcast quick-growing rye seed.

3 Rake it into the soil and then water.

DILL
Anethum graveolens   uh-NEE-thum grub-VEE-oh-lenz

Dill tolerates cool temperatures and is not bothered by pests.

ZONES: NA
SIZE: 12–36"h × 6–24"w
TYPE: Annual
GROWTH: Very fast

LIGHT: Full sun
MOISTURE: Average
FEATURES: Edible leaves and seeds

SITING: Broadcast seed in nutrient-rich, moist, well-drained soil and cover with a fine layer of sifted compost. Dill grows well interplanted with almost anything but other carrot family members. It is tolerant of cool weather; it is often the last herb standing in a late-autumn garden.

CARE: Thin plants when they are large enough to use in the kitchen. Sow seed once a month for a continuous supply of ferny new growth. Hand-weed around young plants. Remove buds and flowers to encourage foliage and prevent self-sowing, or let some plants flower and go to seed for new crops. Feed monthly with high-nitrogen, water-soluble plant food. Dill is adaptable but does best in consistently moist soil.

PROPAGATION: Grow from seed. Established plants will self-sow.

HARVEST: Dill is ready for leaf harvest 30–55 days after seeding. It goes to seed in 75–100 days. Snip leaves as needed or pull whole stems for thinning. To save seeds, cut 4" below the flower heads when the seeds are turning brown, and hang the heads upside down inside paper bags to catch the seeds as they ripen. Leaves can be air-dried or frozen for long-term storage. Fresh leaves add flavor and visual interest in salads, sauces, soups, breads, pesto, potato salad, and egg dishes. Use the dried seeds in pickling brine.

PESTS AND DISEASES: Dill is sometimes attacked by parsleyworm. Hand pick them to control.

RECOMMENDED CULTIVARS: 'Bouquet' is the most commonly grown. 'Fernleaf' is a dwarf blue-green variety with high leaf yield, excellent for kitchen gardens or containers. 'Superdukat' is high in essential oils and thus has intense flavor.

Interplant dill with anything but carrots.

Harvest the ripened brown seeds of dill for cooking or planting.

CHERIMOYA
Annona cherimola   uh-NOH-nuh chair-ih-MOH-la

Eat cherimoyas fresh off the tree but avoid the toxic seeds.

ZONES: 10 and 11
SIZE: 15–25'h × 15–25'w
TYPE: Subtropical briefly deciduous tree or shrub

GROWTH: Slow
LIGHT: Full sun
MOISTURE: Average
FEATURES: Edible fruits

SITING: Plant young trees 25–30' apart in 2'-wide pits enriched with compost. Cherimoya grows best in medium soil of moderate fertility kept consistently moist except during dormancy.

CARE: Seeds may take up to 2 months to germinate. Use plant food, such as Miracle-Gro Fruit & Citrus Fertilizer Spikes, twice a year on young trees during the first and second years. In the third year switch to 10-15-15 fruit tree spikes. Prune lower branches during dormancy to improve tree form and allow sunlight to penetrate the canopy. Irrigate two or three times a month except when the trees are dormant. Sweetly fragrant flowers bloom from late winter through early summer. Hand-pollinate by gathering pollen from blossoms in the male stage, storing it for 36 hours in a plastic bag, then applying it when the blossoms are in the female stage.

PROPAGATION: Grow from seed, air layering, or by grafting.

HARVEST: Trees grown from seed will fruit in 3–4 years. Fruits on most cultivars ripen from October to May. Ripe fruits look a bit like upside-down artichokes; they are heavy, pale green to yellow, and firm but may give just a little. Fruit deteriorates rapidly off the tree, so use it immediately or freeze it to eat like ice cream later. Cut the fruit in half and scoop out the flesh with a spoon. The seeded pulp (the seeds are toxic) can be used in salads, beverages, and sherbets. Because it is almost always consumed fresh off the tree, cherimoya makes a perfect choice for the home garden in areas where winter temperatures do not dip below freezing but do fall below 45°F for a few weeks.

PESTS AND DISEASES: Few problems affect cherimoya. Knock off mealybugs with a sharp stream from a garden hose.

RECOMMENDED CULTIVARS: 'Bays' is a favorite for superior flavor. 'Chaffey' bears well even without hand pollination. 'Booth' is more cold tolerant than most other types. 'Ott' ships better than some other types. *A. cherimola* ×*squamosa* (atemoya), a hybrid of cherimoya and custard apple (*A. reticulata*), is even sweeter tasting.

CHERVIL
Anthriscus cereifolium *an-THRIS-kus ser-ee-ih-FOH-lee-um*

Chervil needs full sun to germinate but light shade for best flavor.

ZONES: NA
SIZE: About 20"h × 8"w
TYPE: Annual
GROWTH: Very fast

LIGHT: Part shade
MOISTURE: Average
FEATURES: Edible leaves

SITING: Chervil does not transplant well, so broadcast seed directly into the garden several times throughout the spring and summer for a continuous supply. The seeds need sunlight to germinate, but plants grow best in light shade. Interplant it among taller crops to provide the shade it needs. Keep the soil continuously moist.
CARE: Thin seedlings for kitchen use. Pinch out flower stalks to promote foliage growth. Mulch around plants to keep roots cool and moist. Overwinter in a cold frame or grow in a pot indoors for year-round use.

Pinch out the flower stalks to promote growth of new leafy stems.

PROPAGATION: Grow from seed.
HARVEST: Plants are ready for kitchen use in 30–40 days. Snip bits of chervil from the outside edges of a plant as needed and use immediately. The leaves lose their flavor rapidly and should not be cooked. A relative of carrots and parsley, chervil is an essential ingredient, along with parsley, thyme, chives, and tarragon, in the French fines herbes. It is rich in vitamin C, beta-carotene, iron, and magnesium. Chervil's faintly aniselike flavor is excellent paired with salmon, asparagus, eggs, cream soups, cottage cheese, butter, mayonnaise, carrots, peas, or potatoes.
PESTS AND DISEASES: Chervil has no significant pest problems. Its essential oil may repel slugs and aphids.
RECOMMENDED CULTIVARS: Chervil comes in flat and curly-leaf types. Some growers think that curly chervil has a slightly bitter taste. 'Brussels Winter' is larger and slower to bolt than standard varieties.

CELERY
Apium graveolens *AY-pee-um grah-VEE-oh-lenz*

Keep the soil consistently moist to avoid black heart of celery.

ZONES: NA
SIZE: 2'h × 1'w
TYPE: Biennial grown as an annual
GROWTH: Slow

LIGHT: Full sun to part shade
MOISTURE: High
FEATURES: Edible leaf stalks (petioles) and leaves

SITING: Plant in muck or in deep, fertile, well-drained soil that holds moisture well. Direct-sow in Zones 8–10; sow indoors in Zones 4–7 and transplant when the soil temperature is above 55°F.
CARE: Sow seeds for transplanting in individual pots, just a few seeds to each pot. Thin seedlings several times until there is just one plant per pot. Transplant outdoors after the last frost date, 1' apart in rows 2' apart, using water-soluble transplant-starter solution. Thin direct-sown seedlings to the same spacing. Side dress with compost and seaweed or bone meal for added calcium every few weeks. Add mulch around the plants as often as needed to retain moisture. Irrigate frequently; too little moisture or dry weather will cause the stalks to crack and be underdeveloped, which invites disease. Use a water-soluble plant food, such as Miracle-Gro All Purpose, twice a month. Wrap cardboard, brown paper bags, newspapers, or drainage tiles around Pascal-type celery stalks, leaving the top few inches of leaf exposed, to blanch them. Cover plants if frost is possible.
PROPAGATION: Grow from seed.

Blanch tall cultivars with a drainage tile or another method of sun protection.

HARVEST: Stalks are ready to eat 3–5 months from transplanting. Cut the entire plant at ground level with a sharp knife when stalks are about 1' tall. Use the outermost stalks for cooking only (not eating raw), or compost them, especially if they have insect damage. Chill the cut plant quickly to preserve its crispness. Store at 32°F in high humidity, such as in the refrigerator crisper drawer.
PESTS AND DISEASES: Slugs, aphids, leafhoppers, and caterpillars are attracted to celery. Use slug traps and floating row covers; knock insects off with a strong stream of water from the garden hose every few days or spray plants with insecticidal soap or neem. Treat blights and leaf spot with fungicide labeled for celery. If rot develops, destroy infected plants and rotate crops elsewhere for at least 4 years. Black heart, the most common malady, is caused by uneven soil moisture.
RECOMMENDED CULTIVARS: Pascal (green) cultivars are most popular in the United States. 'Ventura' and 'Comet' are tall cultivars ready to harvest in 90 to 100 days. Yellow cultivars are more common in Europe. Try 'Golden Self-Blanching', which matures in about 100 days.

CELERIAC

Apium graveolens var. *rapaceum* AY-pee-um grub-VEE-o-lenz rub-PAY-see-um

Celeriac needs a long, cool growing season. It is also known as German celery, celery root, or turnip-rooted celery.

ZONES: NA
SIZE: 1'h × 1'w
TYPE: Herbaceous perennial grown as an annual

GROWTH: Average
LIGHT: Full sun to part shade
MOISTURE: High
FEATURES: Edible roots

SITING: Direct-sow in Zones 8–11; sow indoors in Zones 4–7 and transplant when the soil temperature is above 55°F. Transplant or thin seedlings 4–6" apart in rows 18–24" apart in fertile, well-drained soil that holds moisture well.

CARE: Like celery, celeriac needs a long, cool growing season. Irrigate frequently and mulch to keep roots cool. Use a balanced water-soluble plant food twice a month. After harvesting, compost the stalks, which are usually too bitter to eat.
PROPAGATION: Grow from seed.

Use a garden fork to dig celeriac when roots are large enough.

HARVEST: Celeriac is easier to grow than celery but adds the same flavor and crunch to foods. Dig roots when they reach several inches in diameter, about 100–150 days from sowing. Dig any remaining roots; store for the winter at 32°F in buckets or boxes filled with moist soil or sand. Celeriac stores well for up to 4 months. It can also be frozen but is suitable only for cooking once thawed. Peel and dice the thick, tuberous roots into salads or use cooked just like carrots or potatoes.
PESTS AND DISEASES: Use bait or traps if slugs are a problem. Carrot rust flies are best controlled through crop rotation, although drenching the soil with parasitic nematodes may control damage for the current season. Control leaf spot with clean cultural practices and crop rotation.
RECOMMENDED CULTIVARS: 'Diamant' and 'Giant Prague' are vigorous growers.

PEANUT

Arachis hypogaea AR-uh-kis hy-poh-JEE-uh

Ripe peanut seeds fill the pods, which are light-colored inside. Peanut is also known as groundnut.

ZONES: NA
SIZE: 1–2'h × 1–3'w
TYPE: Annual
GROWTH: Average

LIGHT: Full sun
MOISTURE: Average
FEATURES: Edible seeds (nuts)

SITING: Plant 2" deep and 4" apart in rows 20" apart, or in hills a bit closer together, in deep, highly fertile, loose, well-drained soil. Add gypsum if the soil is low in calcium. Rotate peanuts to a new location each year.
CARE: Mix slow-release plant food, such as Miracle-Gro Shake 'n Feed All Purpose, into the soil before planting. In summer peanuts send up short stems, each bearing a yellow pea-type flower. The mature

heads form "pegs" that gradually bend over and plant themselves into the soil to form new nuts. Mulch lightly around plants to maintain soil moisture and control weeds. Keep the soil consistently moist until a week before harvest. Discard any moldy peanuts.
PROPAGATION: Direct-sow raw, shelled seed with the skins intact as early as possible in spring, or start indoors in northern climates a month before the last

Once peanut flowers are pollinated, they produce "pegs" that burrow into the soil.

frost date. Use seed inoculated with rhizobium if the site has not been previously planted with legumes.
HARVEST: Each plant produces 25 to 50 peanuts 90–120 days from sowing. Dig or pull peanuts when the kernels fill the pods and the pod interiors are still light in color. Dry the pods outside in full sun or indoors in a warm, ventilated area for 4–7 days before separating the pods from the plants and storing them. The nuts, which are actually seeds, are high in protein, unsaturated oil, and vitamins E and B. Peanuts can be eaten raw or roasted, salted or not; ground into peanut butter; chopped into desserts and baked goods; or processed for cooking oil. Remove the skins by blanching the nuts in boiling water. Roast in a single layer in a 325°F oven for 20 minutes.
PESTS AND DISEASES: Hungry animals sometimes dig up peanuts. Rot is caused by overly wet or heavy soil. Healthy plants and timely irrigation are the best defenses against insect pests. To control leaf spot, avoid wetting the foliage.
RECOMMENDED CULTIVARS: Virginia types, such as 'Virginia Jumbo', are the best choice for boiling or roasting. 'Early Spanish' is good in northern climates.

HORSERADISH

Armoracia rusticana *arm-or-AY-see-a rus-tih-KAY-na*

Isolate horseradish to prevent it from spreading too far.

ZONES: 3–9
SIZE: 1–4'h × 1–2'w
TYPE: Herbaceous perennial; can be grown as an annual
GROWTH: Slow
LIGHT: Full sun to shade
MOISTURE: Average
FEATURES: Edible roots

SITING: Although horseradish thrives in cool climates, it is not fussy about location and grows so vigorously that it can become invasive if left unattended. Choose a spot where the soil can be prepared a foot deep or more. A raised or otherwise isolated bed helps to keep horseradish from spreading too far. It is grown for its roots but has large dark green leaves that provide vertical interest at the back of an herb bed. It is highly adaptable but does best in soil that can be kept consistently moist.

CARE: Plant root cuttings 3" deep and 12" apart. Thin overcrowded plants in autumn by harvesting. If the roots seem small and underdeveloped, add potassium to the soil, working it in as deeply as possible. To encourage large taproots, remove a few inches of topsoil in midsummer and trim the fine lateral roots off the main root, then replace the soil.

Cut away the lateral roots to promote growth of the long taproot.

PROPAGATION: Start from lateral root cuttings from near the top of the taproot.

HARVEST: Cuttings planted in spring will be mature roots in 180–240 days but have the best flavor if left in the ground until after a few frosts have sweetened them. Loosen the soil with a pitchfork and pull up the roots by hand, using those that are 6–12" long and replanting the smaller ones. Save some cuttings for next year's crop, or simply leave the plants in the ground and mulch them for winter protection. Store unwashed harvested roots in plastic bags in the refrigerator as you would carrots. Horseradish root is ground and used as a condiment with meat. The flesh smells and tastes quite sharp—often too piquant for some palates. Grate washed and peeled roots with a ginger grater or in a food processor and serve fresh, or mix with a small amount of vinegar and store in the refrigerator for up to 6 months.

PESTS AND DISEASES: None are serious.

RECOMMENDED CULTIVARS: 'Bohemian' is popular because of its hardiness and high-quality roots. A distant relative used in Asian foods, wasabe (*Wasabia japonica*), is grown in streams in mild climates for its highly aromatic, spicy rhizomes.

FRENCH TARRAGON

Artemisia dracunculus sativa *ar-tih-MIZ-ee-uh druh-KUN-kyoo-lus suh-TY-vuh*

Tarragon's lance-shaped leaves are ornamental as well as edible.

ZONES: 3–9
SIZE: 12–24"h × 12–18"w
TYPE: Herbaceous perennial often grown as an annual
GROWTH: Fast
LIGHT: Full sun to part shade
MOISTURE: Average
FEATURES: Edible leaves

SITING: Plant cuttings 18–24" apart in fertile, well-drained soil in a location with good air circulation. Allow the soil to dry between waterings. Tarragon can be grown indoors or outside in containers.

CARE: An attractive ornamental, tarragon has glossy, lance-shaped leaves on slender stems. Remove flowers to encourage foliage growth. Plants will grow vigorously if cut regularly. Cut them back in fall and

Cut back the plants and pinch out the flowers to promote new growth.

mulch for winter protection or take cuttings in late summer for overwintering indoors in containers. Divide plants in spring or take cuttings in spring or late summer.

PROPAGATION: Grow from rooted cuttings or divisions. Plants rarely produce seed and must be replaced every few years.

HARVEST: French tarragon's anise-flavored leaves are used to season a wide variety of salads, soups, and fish and poultry dishes—and are the key to a perfect béarnaise sauce. Snip leaves as needed from the tops of stems. Add leaves just before hot foods are served to enjoy the most flavor. Store in vinegar or freeze. Essential oil of tarragon is used commercially in mustards, vinegars, and other foods, as well as in some cosmetic products.

PESTS AND DISEASES: None are serious.

RECOMMENDED CULTIVARS: Although Russian tarragon (*A. dracunculoides*) can be sown from seed and is hardier than French cultivars, it does not have the flavor desired for culinary uses. Mexican mint marigold (*Tagetes lucida*) has similar flavor but is more heat tolerant than tarragon.

PAWPAW

Asimina triloba ah-sih-MY-nuh try-LOH-buh

The sweet fruit of pawpaw can be eaten fresh, but the seeds are toxic. It is also known as Michigan banana.

ZONES: 5–8
SIZE: 10–20'h × 6–10'w
TYPE: Deciduous tree
GROWTH: Slow

LIGHT: Part sun to shade
MOISTURE: Average
FEATURES: Attractive ornamental tree, edible fruits

SITING: Pawpaw is a small, shade-tolerant ornamental tree native to North America. Mature trees will flower in sun or shade. Although not as well known as other indigenous fruit, pawpaw is easy to grow. Basically unchanged from trees grown hundreds of years ago, they are often found growing wild in hardwood understories or along the shady, protected edges of old-growth forests. They grow well in urban settings, providing tropical-tasting fruit in climates where true tropicals do not grow, and have unusual and attractive foliage and flowers. The open branches droop. Exotic dark red to purple blossoms hang upside down among the long dark green leaves in early spring. Choose a shady, fertile, well-drained location protected from wind, where the soil can be prepared deeply. Plant seeds 1' apart and 1" deep; thin seedlings to the healthiest specimens. Or plant young trees 8' apart. Keep consistently moist but not wet or waterlogged.

CARE: Protect transplants and young seedlings from the sun until they are 3 years old. Provide water-soluble plant food, such as Miracle-Gro Water Soluble All Purpose, until roots are established, then feed with fruit tree spikes, such as Miracle-Gro Fruit & Citrus Fertilizer Spikes. Flower stigmas ripen before the pollen, and the trees often bloom before flies and bees are active, so hand pollinate with a small brush or swab to ensure fruit formation. Prune out dead or damaged limbs and remove suckers.

PROPAGATION: Grow from seed or by grafting or budding, although transplanting can be difficult. Seedlings are not identical to the parents. Because of pawpaw's long taproot, container-grown trees have the best survival rate. Almost all types are self-incompatible, so plant more than one cultivar for successful pollination. Grafted trees may bear fruit in as few as 3 years.

HARVEST: Trees fruit in 5–8 years when grown from seed. Pawpaw fruit ripens approximately 180 days after flowering—in late summer to early autumn, depending on cultivar and zone. Ripe fruit is noticeably fragrant and comes off easily by hand or by shaking the tree gently (don't stand under it!). Check the ground beneath trees for ripe fruit that has already fallen. Ripe skin is medium to dark green, often mottled with dark brown or purple streaks like a banana; it becomes darker if stored after picking. The large, heavy, distinctive butter yellow fruits are extremely high in vitamin C, potassium, iron, calcium, and magnesium. They taste like banana and caramel with a hint of citrus or berry and have a custardlike texture and large, dark seeds. Eat fresh out of hand or in ice cream, or process the pulp for use in pies and other baked goods (it can be used in place of persimmon pulp). Pawpaw seeds are toxic; neither seeds nor skin should be consumed. Pawpaws can be stored for a week in the refrigerator. Store seeds in a plastic bag on an open shelf in the refrigerator for planting in spring; they should not freeze or dry out.

PESTS AND DISEASES: Pawpaws have few significant pests. Natural compounds in the leaves, bark, and tissue have insecticidal properties. Peduncle borers (moth caterpillars) may cause the flowers to drop before fruit sets. Be careful when removing caterpillars; the larvae of zebra swallowtails also like pawpaws, so sharing may be in order. Raccoons and squirrels eat the fruit as it ripens.

RECOMMENDED CULTIVARS: 'Davis' has large, fragrant fruit and refrigerates well. 'Duckworth', a shrub form, and 'White', a white-fleshed variety, can be grown in the Deep South. 'Susquehanna' is less fragile than older cultivars but just as sweet.

Trees bloom early and so may need assistance with pollination.

Pawpaws will flower and set fruit in sun or part shade.

The large, heavy fruits will fall to the ground when completely ripe.

ASPARAGUS
Asparagus officinalis uh-SPAIR-uh-gus ob-FISH-ih-nal-is

Let some spears grow into ferns to produce energy for next year's crop.

ZONES: 4–9
SIZE: 7–10"h ×
12–24"w
TYPE: Herbaceous
perennial
GROWTH: Slow

LIGHT: Full to part
sun
MOISTURE: High
FEATURES: Edible
stems (spears)

SITING: Choose a level, well-drained location with light, friable, fertile soil where asparagus has not been grown previously and where supplemental irrigation can be provided. Plan on future space needs because mature crowns may grow up to 24" wide and unharvested spears grow into ferns more than 6' tall. Although the plants take time to establish, they may produce spears for up to 20 years. Transplant seedlings at 90 days in mounds 3" tall in the middle of furrows 6" deep and 4' apart. Or plant crowns with the buds up 12" apart in furrows 4' apart and 6" deep and covered with 2" of soil, gradually filling in the furrows as the spears grow.

CARE: Amend the soil annually with well-composted horse or cow manure. Asparagus prefers a soil pH slightly greater than 7.0; have a soil sample analyzed to be sure. If the test shows low availability of phosphorus or potassium, use appropriate plant food to correct that, being careful not to add much nitrogen. Water frequently until the plants are well established; watering during hot summer weather and post-harvest drought for maximum fern production. Control weeds in the first year with a hand cultivator or hoe. In subsequent years, lightly till large beds as soon as the soil dries out in spring but before spears emerge. To avoid damage to spears underground, control weeds by shallow hoeing, or use an asparagus herbicide labeled for the specific weed to be eradicated. After 4–6 weeks of harvesting, allow spears to grow into ferns, which produce food for next year's crop. Let them remain standing for as long as any green shows, even through the winter. Check them routinely for signs of pests or

disease, which will reduce the following year's yield.

PROPAGATION: Transplanting year-old dormant roots (crowns) saves a year in production time. Choose male hybrids to avoid unwanted seedlings.

HARVEST: Begin harvesting when spears are at least 5" tall, ½" in diameter, and have closed tips. Pick for just 2 weeks during the first harvest season, increasing to 4 weeks the second season and 6 weeks in years thereafter or for as long as the spear size is normal. Break or cut spears off at or near ground level. Cool spears immediately to preserve their nutritional content and crisp texture. Store the spears for several days in the refrigerator upright in a jar holding an inch of water, or wrapped in moist paper toweling inside a plastic bag in the crisper drawer.

1 Use a spade or shovel to dig trenches 6" deep and 4' apart.

2 Plant crowns 12" apart in the trenches with the buds pointed up.

3 Lightly cover the crowns with soil. Fill in the trenches as the spears grow.

4 Begin harvesting spears when they are about ½" in diameter.

PESTS AND DISEASES: Soilborne pathogens cause fusarium stem and crown rot and fusarium wilt and root rot. Disinfect seeds and roots with fungicide before planting and plant in an area where asparagus has not been grown for at least 8 years. Control asparagus rust with fungicide; begin regular applications at the first sign of infection. Asparagus beetles and aphids are the most damaging pests; control them with specifically labeled insecticides. Follow label instructions carefully so that beneficial bees are not harmed.

RECOMMENDED CULTIVARS: 'Washington' varieties are still the most popular although all-male hybrids such as 'Greenwich', 'Jersey Knight', and 'Jersey Giant' may have greater disease resistance and higher yields. In mild winter regions such as California grow 'UC157'.

BEET

Beta vulgaris BAY-tuh vul-GAIR-is

Leave an inch of foliage on beets to be cooked to prevent color bleeding. Beets are also known as red beets.

ZONES: NA
SIZE: 2–12"h ×
2–12"w
TYPE: Annual
GROWTH: Fast

LIGHT: Full sun to part shade
MOISTURE: Average
FEATURES: Edible roots and leaves

SITING: Beets grow best in loose, fertile, slightly alkaline soil cleared of rocks and amended with well-rotted compost. Plant seeds ½" deep and 1" apart in rows 12" apart. Keep the soil uniformly moist.
CARE: Gradually thin beets to 4" apart for best root development, eating the thinnings as greens. Mulch the plants to keep them cool and moist, and weed around them carefully by hand. In cool climates sow beet seed at 3-week intervals for an all-season supply. In warmer zones, plant seeds in late summer and early autumn.
PROPAGATION: Grow from seed.
HARVEST: Beets are often the first and last vegetables harvested from the garden, providing both tender greens for salads and crisp roots for cooking, pickling, and canning. Dig or pull small globe varieties when the roots are 1" in diameter; dig large and cylindrical types when they reach 2",

Thin young beets and use the thinnings as fresh salad greens.

about 45–55 days from seeding. Leave an inch of foliage on roots to prevent bleeding of the strong colors, which permanently stain porous cookware and serving dishes. Harvest beets for greens at any time, but smaller leaves up to 4" have better flavor. Store unwashed beets as you would carrots, at 32–40°F in high humidity. Leave fall crops in the ground until needed or until the soil begins to freeze.
PESTS AND DISEASES: Leaf miners may overwinter in the soil. Aphids, flea beetles, and other insects may do minor damage to the leaves or roots. Use floating row covers to protect seedbeds from egg-laying adults. Control leaf spot with fungicide. Sugar-beet cyst nematodes may be a problem in cool climates and are best controlled through crop rotation.
RECOMMENDED CULTIVARS: 'Red Ace' is highly adaptable to a variety of soil and weather conditions. 'Big Top' has the largest, most prolific greens. 'Golden' has yellow flesh. 'Forono' has long, smooth deep purple roots that are prized for canning. 'Chioggia' is an heirloom variety with pink and white rings. 'Lutz Green Leaf' provides a winter crop of greens.

SWISS CHARD

Beta vulgaris cicla BAY-tuh vul-GAIR-is SIH-kluh

Cut chard back in late summer for a new flush of leaves in autumn.

ZONES: NA
SIZE: 6–20"h ×
10–30"w
TYPE: Annual
GROWTH: Fast

LIGHT: Full sun to part shade
MOISTURE: Average
FEATURES: Edible leaves and stalks

SITING: Plant seeds ½" deep and 1" apart in rich, slightly alkaline soil.
CARE: Plants tolerate summer heat and light frost. Keep the soil constantly moist until seedlings are established, then mulch with straw to keep roots cool and moist. Thin young plants to 2" apart, using the thinnings in salads. Use balanced water-soluble plant food twice a month. Cut plants back in late summer to rejuvenate them for fall production.
PROPAGATION: Grow from seed soaked overnight to speed germination.
HARVEST: Begin harvesting when leaves are about 5" tall. Break off only one or two outer leaves from each plant, leaving the inner leaves to develop. Eat young leaves raw in salads and cook mature ones like spinach or other greens. Mature ribs (stalks) are often used as a cooked vegetable in Asian cuisine.

PESTS AND DISEASES: Aphids and leaf miners sometimes bother chard. Remove and destroy affected leaves. Pick off corn borer larvae by hand. Young leaves may show evidence of flea beetle feeding; dust with rotenone. Use bait or traps for slugs and snails. Choose varieties resistant to downy mildew.
RECOMMENDED CULTIVARS: 'Fordhook Giant' is a dependable, hardy dark green chard with white ribs. 'Rhubarb' has red ribs. 'Bright Lights' and 'Rainbow' ribs are vivid reds and yellows.

Harvest a few outer leaves and petioles (stalks) as needed.

Some cultivars have ribs in bright colors. This is 'Bright Lights'.

RUTABAGA

Brassica napus BRASS-ih-kuh NAP-us

Rutabaga, also known as Swede, tastes sweeter if harvested after a few frosts.

ZONES: NA
SIZE: 12–18"h × 8–12"w
TYPE: Biennial grown as annual
GROWTH: Average

LIGHT: Full sun to part shade
MOISTURE: Average
FEATURES: Edible roots

SITING: Plant seeds ½" deep and 2" apart in rows 18" apart in deep, fertile, loose, well-drained soil enriched with humus and cleared of stones and other debris. Amend the soil if it is low in potassium, but do not add nitrogen. Keep the soil consistently moist; choose a planting location where you can provide supplemental irrigation during hot or dry periods.

CARE: Gradually thin seedlings to 8" apart; pull weeds by hand. Mulch rows to keep roots cool and moist. Overwinter autumn-grown roots in the ground under heavy mulch.

PROPAGATION: Grow from seed planted 4–6 weeks before the last frost in spring

Mulch rutabagas to keep them cool in summer and protected in winter.

and 90 days before the first autumn frost date.

HARVEST: Easy to grow, rutabagas are larger and hardier than turnips but the leaves are bitter. The roots have a slightly sweet, nutty flavor between turnip and cabbage. Dig rutabagas about 90 days after seeding, or anytime after they are 3–5" in diameter. Pull only what you need and leave the rest in the ground. Autumn-grown rutabagas taste sweeter if harvested after a few frosts. Cook rutabagas as you would turnips or potatoes—steamed and mashed, baked as a side dish, or diced and added to soups and stews. Small roots can be eaten raw in salads or served as crudités. Store harvested rutabagas like other root crops, in cool but not freezing temperatures and high humidity.

PESTS AND DISEASES: Knock aphids off with a strong stream from the garden hose. Dust with rotenone to combat flea beetles if they are present in significant numbers. Control clubroot through clean gardening practices and crop rotation.

RECOMMENDED CULTIVARS: 'American Purple Top' and 'Laurentian' are dependable and sweet.

COLLARDS

Brassica oleracea Acephala group BRASS-ih-kuh oh-leh-RAY-see-uh ay-SEF-uh-luh

Collards are adapted to most climates but grow best in cool weather.

ZONES: NA
SIZE: 24–36"h × 18–36"w
TYPE: Biennial grown as an annual
GROWTH: Average

LIGHT: Full sun to light shade
MOISTURE: Average
FEATURES: Edible leaves

SITING: Plant seeds ½" deep and 1" apart, or transplant 3" seedlings 6" apart in rows 24–36" apart, 30 days before the last frost date in the spring and 90 days before the first autumn frost date, in well-drained sandy soil or loam amended with organic matter. Collards tolerate periods of drought but do best in consistently moist soil.

CARE: Although collards are typically associated with southern cooking, they are adaptable to a wide range of climates and taste best when they mature during cool weather. They are more heat tolerant than other cole crops and slower to bolt. Thin seedlings to 8" apart when they are 4" tall. Side dress with well-rotted manure or compost, hand-weed carefully, and mulch well during warm weather. Use water-soluble plant food, such as Miracle-Gro Water Soluble All Purpose, every 2 weeks. Mulch to overwinter.

Leave the topmost bud on the plant to encourage new leaf growth.

PROPAGATION: Grow from direct-sown seed or from transplants started indoors.

HARVEST: Leaves will be ready to pick 70–85 days after seeding. Pick leaves from the top of the plants. The topmost bud is a delicacy, but leave it if you want the plant to produce more leaves. Or cut the entire plant at the ground. Collards can be stored for several weeks in the crisper drawer of the refrigerator. The curly blue-green leaves are high in vitamins C and A and rich in potassium and calcium. Steam or braise them and season like cabbage.

PESTS AND DISEASES: Knock off aphids with a strong stream from the garden hose. Remove cabbage worms and loopers by hand, or use Bt for serious infestations. Handpick harlequin bugs or control with pyrethrum. Control clubroot through clean gardening practices and crop rotation.

RECOMMENDED CULTIVARS: 'Georgia Southern' is the most common variety and is well known for tolerance of heat and poor soil. 'Champion' and 'Flash' are fast, vigorous, cold-tolerant choices. The heirloom variety 'Green Glaze' is pest resistant.

KALE

Brassica oleracea Acephala group *BRASS-ih-kuh oh-leh-RAY-see-uh ay-SEF-uh-luh*

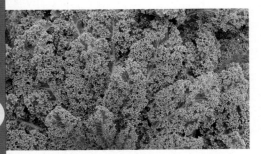

'Dwarf Blue' is a tightly curled Scotch kale, sometimes called borecole.

ZONES: NA
SIZE: 12–18"h × 12–36"w
TYPE: Biennial grown as an annual
GROWTH: Average

LIGHT: Full sun to light shade
MOISTURE: Average
FEATURES: Edible, sometimes ornamental, leaves

SITING: Plant seeds ½" deep and 1" apart, or transplant 3" seedlings 6" apart, in rows 24–36" apart, 30 days before the last frost date in spring and 70 days before the first autumn frost date, in well-drained, fertile loam amended with organic matter. Keep the soil consistently moist.

CARE: Kale is a nonheading cross between cabbage and greens. Scotch kale is the type most often grown for commercial sale. It has tightly curled grayish-green leaves. The leaves of Siberian kale are smoother but have frilly edges. Ornamental kales are also edible but not as tasty. All varieties taste best when planted so they mature during cool weather. Gradually thin seedlings to 1' apart. When plants are about 4" tall, side dress with slow-release plant food and mulch well to conserve moisture and control weeds.

Kale's flavor is improved by frost.

PROPAGATION: Grow from direct-sown seed or transplants started indoors.
HARVEST: Leaves are ready to pick 55–75 days from seeding. Pick the large basal leaves, or cut the entire plant at ground level. The central rosette is the most delicious part of the plant, but leave it growing if you want the plant to produce more leaves. Tender young leaves harvested in cool weather are delicious in salads. More mature leaves are used like cabbage.
PESTS AND DISEASES: Knock off aphids with a strong stream from the garden hose. Remove cabbage worms and loopers by hand or use Bt for serious infestations. Handpick harlequin bugs or control with pyrethrum. Kale is somewhat resistant to clubroot.
RECOMMENDED CULTIVARS: 'Winterbor' (green) and 'Redbor' (purple) are frilly types used for garnishes. 'White Peacock' and 'Red Peacock' have finely cut edges; young leaves are good in salads. Blue Siberian types grow well in warm climates; 'Dwarf Blue Curled' is a good choice for harvesting even in snow.

CAULIFLOWER

Brassica oleracea Botrytis group *BRASS-ih-kuh oh-leh-RAY-see-uh boh-TRY-tis*

The leaves of self-blanching cauliflower curl up to protect the heads from sun.

ZONES: NA
SIZE: 8–12"h × 18–36"w
TYPE: Annual
GROWTH: Average

LIGHT: Full sun to light shade
MOISTURE: Average
FEATURES: Edible heads

SITING: Sow seed 90 days before the first frost date ½" deep and 24" apart in rows 3' apart in rich, well-drained soil. Or transplant seedlings that have at least three true leaves.
CARE: Thin seedlings when they are about 1" tall. Mulch and water regularly to keep the soil cool and moist. Weed carefully by hand, taking care not to damage the leaves, which can lead to buttoning (underdeveloped heads). To protect standard white-head varieties from sunscald, blanch by pulling the longest leaves up and over the head and holding them in place with twine or strips of soft nylon. Begin blanching as soon as you can see the head; make sure it's dry before you wrap it with leaves. Purple and green heads do not need to be blanched.
PROPAGATION: Grow from transplants for spring crops and from seed or transplants for fall crops.

Purple-head types need extra space.

Tie the longest leaves together over the heads to blanch them.

HARVEST: Cut the heads below the inner leaves when the heads are 6–8" in diameter. Heads past their peak will show curds that have begun to separate. To store whole heads for 2–3 weeks, cut them below the outer leaves and wrap those leaves around the heads. Uncooked cauliflower is more nutritious and has a stronger flavor than cooked. Purple- and green-headed types are the most nutritious.
PESTS AND DISEASES: Knock off aphids with a strong stream from the garden hose. Remove cabbage worms and loopers by hand or use Bt for serious infestations. Handpick harlequin bugs or control with pyrethrum. Control clubroot through clean gardening practices and crop rotation.
RECOMMENDED CULTIVARS: 'Early Snowball' matures quickly on small plants that fit well in a garden with limited space. 'Snow Crown' is a standard white type that matures before the weather turns hot. Purple-headed types need a lot of space but are heat and cold tolerant and freeze well. 'Chartreuse' is a tasty bright green head that's a good choice for southern climates or for fall crops in the North.

CABBAGE

Brassica oleracea Capitata group   *BRASS-ih-kuh oh-leh-RAY-see-uh kap-ih-TAY-ta*

Keep the soil consistently moist to keep cabbage heads from cracking.

ZONES: NA
SIZE: 6–12"h × 10–30"w
TYPE: Biennial grown as annual
GROWTH: Average

LIGHT: Full sun to light shade
MOISTURE: Average
FEATURES: Edible leaves

SITING: Plant in deep, well-drained loam. Sow seeds ½" deep and 1" apart, or plant 4" seedlings in rows 18–24" apart. Cabbage is a good vegetable to interplant with earlier crops in small gardens.

CARE: Maintain consistent soil moisture to prevent the heads from cracking. Water from the sides to avoid wetting any part of the plants and weed carefully to avoid damaging the roots. Use mulch to conserve moisture and discourage weeds. Use water-soluble plant food twice a month until harvest. Some types may resprout new, smaller heads after the first harvest.

PROPAGATION: Grow from seeds sown indoors and transplanted 3–5 weeks after the last frost date for spring crops; direct sow for summer and fall crops.

HARVEST: Cut heads with a sharp knife at ground level when they are tight and firm and 4–10" in diameter. Discard outer leaves and inspect heads for insects before storing. Cracked heads indicate cabbages past their peak. Flavor is best right after harvest, but cabbage stores well in cool, humid conditions for several months. Green cabbage has smooth leaves and compact heads; Savoy types have flat or semiflat heads of curly leaves. Some midseason cultivars have red leaves.

PESTS AND DISEASES: Use a cutworm collar around seedlings. Knock off aphids with a strong stream from the garden hose. Remove cabbage worms and loopers by hand or use Bt. Control harlequin bugs and flea beetles with labelled insecticides. Dust plant bases with diatomaceous earth to prevent cabbage maggots. Control clubroot and black rot through clean cultivation and crop rotation. Choose varieties with resistance to yellows.

RECOMMENDED CULTIVARS: Early types include 'Farao' (green), 'Red Express', and 'Gonzales' (a green, dwarf variety good for small gardens). Midseason types include 'Tendersweet' (green) and 'Regal Red'. Savoy types, 'Drumhead', or 'Red Perfection' grow well late in the season.

Savoy types have crinkly leaves.

Mulch with straw to conserve moisture.

Water heads from the sides.

Test for firmness before harvesting.

BRUSSELS SPROUTS

Brassica oleracea Gemmifera group   *BRASS-ih-kuh oh-leh-RAY-see-uh jem-MIF-er-uh*

A space-efficient plant for small gardens, each tall stalk bears dozens of heads.

ZONES: NA
SIZE: 12–36"h × 8–18"w
TYPE: Biennial grown as annual
GROWTH: Average

LIGHT: Full sun to light shade
MOISTURE: Average
FEATURES: Edible heads (sprouts)

SITING: Plant seeds ½" deep and 2" apart in an outdoor seedbed about 90 days before the first frost date; transplant 5" seedlings into deep, friable soil rich with added compost or composted manure. Choose a location where you can water during high heat or drought.

CARE: Each stalk may bear 50 to 100 sprouts at the points where the leaves join the stalk. Brussels sprouts are a good cool-weather crop for small gardens, where they can be interplanted with lettuces or other quick-maturing crops. Use plant food such as Miracle-Gro Liquid Quick Start, and shade seedlings from direct sun until they are established. Use a cutworm collar around seedlings. Water frequently during dry or hot spells. Mulch well to conserve moisture and prevent weeds. Weed carefully to avoid damaging shallow roots. Use water-soluble plant food, such as Miracle-Gro Water Soluble All Purpose, twice a month while sprouts are developing. Stake stems to prevent wind damage. Break off yellowing leaves as sprouts grow.

PROPAGATION: Grow from seeds or transplants. In cold climates seeds can be started indoors 125–135 days before the first frost date.

HARVEST: Begin cutting sprouts from the bottom of the stalks when they are ¾–1½" in diameter. Frost improves their flavor.

PESTS AND DISEASES: The same pests that affect cabbage attack Brussels sprouts.

RECOMMENDED CULTIVARS: 'Long Island Improved' and 'Catskill' (a dwarf variety) are heat sensitive and best grown as fall crops. 'Jade Cross' and 'Oliver' mature in 90 days and are more heat tolerant than other types.

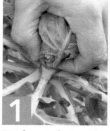

1 Pinch out the growing tip when bottom sprouts are ½" wide.

2 Begin cutting the bottom sprouts when they are ¾" or larger.

KOHLRABI

Brassica oleracea Gongylodes group *BRASS-ih-kuh oh-leh-RAY-see-uh gon-gy-LOH-deez*

Kohlrabi's rounded stems taste similar to turnips but milder.

ZONES: NA
SIZE: : 9–12"h ×
9–12"w
TYPE: Biennial
grown as annual
GROWTH: Fast

LIGHT: Full sun to
light shade
MOISTURE: Average
FEATURES: Edible
stems ("bulbs")

SITING: Kohlrabi thrives in any medium-textured, nutrient-rich soil that is free of rocks and holds moisture well. Sow seeds ¼" deep and 1" apart in rows 18" apart (10" in raised beds). Space transplants 10" apart.

CARE: Thin seedlings to 10" apart. Mulch to conserve soil moisture and prevent weeds. Water during hot or dry periods. Weed by hand to avoid disturbing the roots. Use a soluble plant food twice a month.
PROPAGATION: Grow from seed. Direct-sow 4–6 weeks before the last frost date, or transplant 4 weeks before to 2 weeks

Slice off the bulb at the base when the stem is 2–3" in diameter.

after the last frost date. Sow again about 10 weeks before the first autumn frost date for a fall harvest.
HARVEST: Kohlrabi is a fast-growing cabbage family member with stems that swell into rounded bulb shapes just above the soil. The flavor is similar to turnip but milder. Slice through the stems below the bulbs when they are at least 1½" but no more than 3" in diameter, approximately 50–70 days from seeding. Remove the leaves and store the bulbs up to 3 weeks in a root cellar or the refrigerator crisper drawer. Peel and eat kohlrabi raw in salads or with dips or cooked like turnips. Dice, blanch, and freeze pieces for later use.
PESTS AND DISEASES Remove cabbage worms by hand or use Bt for serious infestations. Handpick harlequin bugs or control with pyrethrum or other labelled insecticide. Dust with rotenone or spray with an appropriate insecticide to control flea beetles. Control clubroot through clean cultivation and crop rotation.
RECOMMENDED CULTIVARS: 'Grand Duke' matures quickly. 'Early Purple Vienna' is a good choice for late-season crops.

BROCCOLI

Brassica oleracea Italica group *BRASS-ih-kuh oh-leh-RAY-see-uh ih-TAL-ih-kuh*

Broccoli thrives with consistent moisture in cool weather.

ZONES: NA
SIZE: About 2'h ×
2'w
TYPE: Biennial
grown as annual
GROWTH: Fast

LIGHT: Full sun to
part shade
MOISTURE: Average
FEATURES: Edible
heads (florets)

SITING: Broccoli needs rich soil with plenty of nitrogen and calcium. Work in several inches of well-rotted manure or compost before planting. Plant three seeds together ½" deep every 18" in rows 36" apart, thinning 1" seedlings to the most vigorous one in each group. Or transplant seedlings in the same row spacing.
CARE: Broccoli grows quickly and vigorously in cool weather; in cool climates

with a long growing season, two plantings are possible. Sprouting plants produce side shoots after the main heads are harvested. Use a collar around seedlings to discourage cutworms. Maintain consistent moisture to prevent slowed growth. Buttons indicate lack of water or plant food or both. Weed carefully to avoid damaging the roots. Use mulch to conserve moisture and discourage weeds. Use balanced water-soluble plant food twice a month until harvest.
PROPAGATION: Grow from seed when the soil is 40°F or above, or from transplants when the soil reaches 60°F.

Side shoots may grow larger after the main head is harvested.

HARVEST: Cut heads with a sharp knife when they are tight and firm, about 55–85 days after seeding. Heads with buds beginning to separate into yellow flowers indicate broccoli past its peak, although it is still edible. Discard any outer leaves and inspect the heads for insects before storing. Flavor is best right after harvest, but broccoli stores well in cool, humid conditions for a week or more.
PESTS AND DISEASES: Knock off aphids with a strong stream from the garden hose. Remove cabbage worms and loopers by hand or use Bt for serious infestations. Handpick harlequin bugs or spray with an appropriate insecticide to control them. Dust plant bases with diatomaceous earth to control cabbage maggots. Control clubroot through clean gardening practices and crop rotation.
RECOMMENDED CULTIVARS: 'Green Comet' and 'Spartan Early' have dark green heads 7" across. 'Gypsy' and 'Arcadia' mature early and are disease resistant. 'DeCicco' and all other varieties produce side shoots for an extended period after the main harvest. Broccoli raab (*B. rapa ruvo*) is a related species grown for its turniplike greens and immature flower buds; try 'Super Rapini'.

BOK CHOY

Brassica rapa Chinensis group *BRASS-ih-kuh RAY-puh chi-NEN-sis*

Bok choy, or pak choi, forms an upright bunch similar to chard. It is also known as celery mustard.

ZONES: NA
SIZE: 9–20"h × 6–9"w
TYPE: Annual
GROWTH: Fast to average

LIGHT: Full sun to part shade
MOISTURE: Average
FEATURES: Edible leaves

SITING: Chinese cabbage (*B. r.* Pekinensis group) and bok choy are highly adaptable to all soils but will grow largest in fertile loam amended with several inches of well-rotted compost or manure. Grow from seed direct-sown ½" deep and 2" apart in rows 18–24" apart. Thin seedlings or space transplants 10–18" apart. Keep the soil continuously moist.

CARE: Chinese cabbage forms heads of crinkly leaves; bok choy forms loose bunches of thick-ribbed leaves similar to chard. They are grown similarly to most cole crops. Protect seedlings from sunscald and cold temperatures. Mulch around plants to conserve soil moisture and deter weeds. Water during dry periods. Water from underneath or to the sides of plants rather than from above, which can invite disease problems. Use water soluble plant food twice a month.

PROPAGATION: Grow from seed started indoors 4–6 weeks before the last frost

Some Chinese cabbages form elongated, rounded heads. This is 'Kasumi'.

date. Direct-seed fall crops about 90 days before the first frost date.

HARVEST: Plants are ready to harvest in 21–75 days, depending on type. Pull out whole plants as needed when they have reached mature size, or pick outer leaves and leave the plant to produce new ones for later harvest. Chinese cabbage and bok choy are easier to digest than standard cabbage but just as nutritious. Both species can be eaten raw in salads or steamed, stir-fried, or added to soups. Store plants for up to a month in a refrigerator crisper drawer.

PESTS AND DISEASES: Use a cutworm collar around seedlings. Knock off aphids with a strong stream from the garden hose. Remove cabbage worms and loopers by hand or use Bt for serious infestations. Handpick harlequin bugs or control with pyrethrum. Dust with rotenone to control flea beetles.

RECOMMENDED CULTIVARS: 'Joi Choi' bok choy is tolerant of heat and cold and is slow to bolt. 'Greenwich' Chinese cabbage is large and disease resistant. 'Minuet', a smaller Chinese cabbage that is also disease-resistant, is a good choice for small gardens.

TURNIP

Brassica rapa Rapifera group *BRASS-ih-kuh RAY-puh ray-pih-FAIR-uh*

Use the young tops as greens but leave some to feed the roots.

ZONES: NA
SIZE: 6–12"h × 4–6"w
TYPE: Biennial grown as annual
GROWTH: Fast to average

LIGHT: Full sun to part shade
MOISTURE: Average
FEATURES: Edible leaves and roots

SITING: Sow seeds in groups of three about ½" deep and 2" apart in rows 12" apart in rich, friable soil 4–6 weeks before the last frost date in spring and 70 days before the

first autumn frost date. Keep the soil consistently moist.

CARE: Thin seedlings (and enjoy them in salads) when the first true leaves appear and again if any plants touch one another until they are 6" apart. Cut (rather than pull) the seedlings to avoid damaging the roots of those that remain. Mulch to conserve soil moisture and deter weeds. Water during dry periods.

PROPAGATION: Grow from seed.

Dig turnip roots in cool weather while they are still tender.

HARVEST: Like beets, turnips are an important early crop, bearing greens and edible roots. The roots are nutritious and the greens are extremely high in vitamins and minerals. Pick or cut leaves as needed about 40–80 days after seeding. Dig roots while they are young and tender, no more than 3" in diameter. If the weather turns hot, dig the whole crop and store the turnips unwashed in the refrigerator crisper drawer for up to several weeks, or slice, blanch, and freeze them for cooking later. Cook the spicy leaves like greens or use them raw in salads; leave some if you want to harvest roots later.

PESTS AND DISEASES: Most cultivars are disease resistant. Pick off harlequin bugs and cabbage worms by hand, or use Bt for serious infestations. Remove and destroy leaves infested with leaf miners and use floating row covers to discourage them.

RECOMMENDED CULTIVARS: Grow 'Just Right' for greens. For early-season turnips, grow fast-maturing 'Tokyo' cultivars. For fall crops, plant 'Purple-Top White Globe' or 'Aberdeen', a yellow variety.

CAPER

Capparis spinosa *kap-PAR-is spin-OH-sub*

Caper blooms are fragrant but the immature buds are a delicacy.

ZONES: (8) 9–11
SIZE: 3'–5'h ×
5'–10'w
TYPE: Deciduous
perennial shrub
GROWTH: Slow
LIGHT: Full sun

MOISTURE: Low
FEATURES:
Ornamental plant,
edible immature
flower buds and
berries

SITING: Capers thrive in dry, rocky, poor soils and along sandy shorelines where temperatures do not fall below 20°F. Choose a location where you can water transplants easily.

CARE: Capers are the immature flower buds of a spiny shrub. The flowers are fragrant and attractive, resembling cleome. Space plants 10' apart and mulch heavily to conserve soil moisture. (Remove the mulch as soon as the plants are well rooted.) Keep transplants moist until they are established; cover them with clear plastic and provide shade from direct sun so they don't wilt. Use balanced water-soluble plant food during the first 3 years. Avoid pruning plants until the third year, then cut them to the ground late in the year.

Collect the buds by hand when they are swollen but not yet open.

PROPAGATION: Caper is slow to germinate from presoaked seed; it is best established from stem cuttings taken in late winter or early spring.

HARVEST: The caper bush buds in the fourth year in U.S. coastal zones and lives 20–30 years. Pick flower buds early in the morning just before they are about to flower. They should be about ⅛–¼" in diameter. Soak the buds in a brine solution for 30 days, then pickle them in salted vinegar and store in glass jars for up to 6 months. Pickling brings out their peppery flavor, which comes from a type of mustard oil contained in the plant tissues. The smallest buds are considered the most desirable.

PESTS AND DISEASES: Viruses may be introduced when cuttings are taken or plants are grafted. Clean cultural practices help to avoid such problems. Pick off weevils and cabbage worms by hand or treat serious infestations with Bt or labeled insecticide. Water plants from underneath to avoid mold and botrytis.

RECOMMENDED CULTIVARS: 'Josephine' and 'Nocellana' are bred to be spineless. Spineless types may be more pest-resistant.

MARVELOUS MULCH

Mulch can be the key to survival for many garden plants. During the growing season, mulch around plants to help conserve moisture in the soil and discourage weeds from growing. Mulch keeps the soil cool so that temperature spikes won't dry out tender roots, and it reduces the amount of moisture lost to evaporation through the soil surface.

PLAYING IT COOL

Perennial plants such as strawberries need mulch during winter. Although a covering of mulch provides some protection from harsh winter conditions, another goal of using it in winter is to prevent dormant plants from beginning growth too early. Temperature spikes can cause the soil to thaw and heave shallow-rooted plants out of the ground.

TIMING AND QUANTITY

Timing and quantity are important factors when applying mulch. In autumn or winter wait until air temperatures have been below 32°F for 2 weeks and plants are completely dormant before covering them with 4–8" of mulch. Remove the mulch in early spring so that the sun can warm the soil around the plants. When temperatures climb in summer, replace the mulch around the plants to keep the soil cool and moist. Most garden plants benefit from mulch during the growing season. Even vegetables and herbs growing in partly shaded conditions need protection from soil moisture evaporation caused by wind. Unlike in winter, just a couple of inches of mulch are enough. Too much mulch can provide safe haven for pests to hide and encourage disease development by trapping too much moisture around plants.

WHAT TO USE

Black plastic mulch is an effective barrier against weeds and helps to warm the soil in spring, but it may cause the soil to become too warm in summer. Cover the plastic with straw or shredded bark to keep the soil cool. Reflective silver mulch repels aphids and is used primarily with winter squash and potato crops. Red plastic mulch may benefit squashes and melons. Clear plastic and fabric barriers let sunlight through and encourage weeds to grow. More effective mulch materials include straw, shredded pine bark, or pine needles, grass, or small stones. Compost left on the surface around plants as a mulch may encourage weed growth. Organic mulches may cause a slight nitrogen deficiency in the soil as they decompose, but you can easily remedy that with regular applications of a balanced plant food.

PEPPER

Capsicum annuum KAP-sih-kum AN-yoo-um

Green bell peppers grow sweeter when ripened to red on the plant.

ZONES: NA
SIZE: 6–30"h ×
6–24"w
TYPE: Annual
GROWTH: Average

LIGHT: Full sun
MOISTURE: Average
FEATURES: Edible fruits; some plants are ornamental

SITING: Pepper seeds require a high soil temperature to germinate, so in all but the hottest climates start them indoors 40–60 days before transplanting time. Choose a location where the temperature is 70–75°F in the daytime and no lower than 60°F at night. When the soil temperature is consistently 60°F or more, set transplants 12–24" apart in rows 24–36" apart in well-drained loam

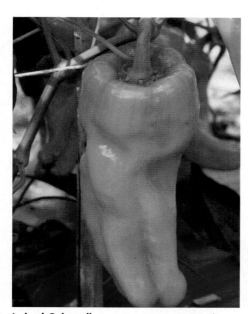

Lobed Cubanelle sweet peppers come in a variety of colors and are good fresh, fried, stuffed, or roasted.

amended with rotted manure or compost. If the soil is low in magnesium, dig in a dusting of Epsom salts. Plant sweet and hot varieties as far apart as possible in the garden to avoid cross-pollination. (In small gardens, expect sweet peppers to have a mildly tangy flavor from cross-pollination.)

Medium-hot Hungarian wax peppers can be used at any stage of maturity.

CARE: Use starter solution, such as Miracle-Gro Liquid Quick Start, to prevent transplant shock. Keep the soil weed free and consistently and thoroughly moist. Use a soaker hose if necessary during periods of drought or high heat. Feed with Miracle-Gro Water Soluble All Purpose Plant Food twice a month while plants are in flower. Peppers usually don't need staking, but large cultivars planted where they are exposed to strong winds will benefit from tomato cages. Prolonged temperatures below 60°F or above 90°F cause blossom drop, so be prepared to protect plants from such extremes with row covers, cloches, or a cold frame to

Mildly hot poblanos, also called ancho peppers, ripen from green to red.

'Jimmy Nardello' is a sweet nonbell cultivar good in salads and stir-fries.

conserve warmth in cool weather, and shade cloth or other sun blocker and mulch when it's hot. Lush plants with no peppers can also be a sign of excess nitrogen or low humidity. Caution: Wear rubber gloves when handling or harvesting hot peppers and keep your hands away from your face.
PROPAGATION: Grow from seeds or transplants.
HARVEST: Pick sweet peppers at any color. Pick hot peppers anytime for fresh use, but leave them on the plants until fully ripe if you want to dry them. Pick often so the plants continue to produce new fruits. Use garden scissors to cut the

Habaneros come in a rainbow of hues but all are blistering hot.

PEPPER
continued

Capsaicin, a compound suppressed in sweet peppers, is the source of heat in hot varieties but does not cause ulcers.

stems and avoid damaging the plants. Peppers are high in fiber, beta-carotene, and vitamins C and A. Red bell peppers contain more vitamin C than an orange. Although people with a preexisting gastrointestinal disorder may find peppers hard to digest, hot peppers do not cause ulcers. The heat comes from capsaicin, a naturally occurring compound that is suppressed in sweet peppers by a recessive gene. Use sweet peppers raw in salads, on sandwiches, and as crudités. Roast, grill, or stir-fry hot peppers and add them judiciously to any dish that calls for a little zing. Poke small holes into a few small hot peppers and drop them into a bottle of olive or other vegetable oil. Within days you'll have a zesty cooking oil worthy of any Asian cuisine. Store unwashed fresh peppers in the refrigerator for up to a week. To dry hot peppers, string them together by running needle and thread through the tops near the caps and hang them in a cool, dry location with good air circulation. Store dried ground peppers in a tightly sealed glass jar in a cool location away from sunlight. Peppers freeze well and do not need to be blanched first. Just wash and dry them

well, slice or chop, and place in thin layers in plastic freezer bags.

PESTS AND DISEASES: Knock off aphids with a strong spray from the garden hose; use a mild soap solution for heavy infestations. Handpick and destroy any beetles and caterpillars. If whole peppers rot, check for pepper maggots or corn earworms and destroy the entire plant

Mulch plants to conserve moisture and control weeds.

if it is infested. Discourage tarnished plant bugs through clean cultivation practices. Choose cultivars with resistance to viruses. Avoid bacterial problems through clean cultivation and crop rotation. Control blossom-end rot by providing consistent moisture throughout the growing season.

RECOMMENDED CULTIVARS:

SWEET PEPPERS: 'California Wonder' and 'Whopper Improved' are among the most popular green bell peppers because of high yields over a long period and virus resistance (70–80 days to maturity, based on the time transplants are set out). 'Labrador' bell ripens to a bright yellow (60–80 days). 'Ariane' is a large orange bell resistant to mosaic virus (60–75 days). 'Big Early' produces enormous bells up to 8" long and 4" in diameter that can be picked green or left to ripen to red (65–75 days). 'Ace' red bells are smaller but more prolific and resistant to blossom drop. 'Lipstick' is an early, short, lobeless, tapering bell that ripens to an extremely sweet red (55–75 days). 'Blushing Beauty' bells start out ivory and blush from yellow to light orange-red to deep scarlet, never showing any green. The plant is resistant to bacterial leaf spots and many viruses (65–75 days). 'Tequila' bells start out purple and fade to red as they mature (65–75 days). 'Hershey' bells mature from green to chocolate-brown (70–80 days). For a sweet pepper that is ornamental as well as tasty, try 'Roumainian Rainbow'. The fruits turn from ivory to orange to red; plants often have peppers in all stages of coloration simultaneously (60–70 days).

SWEET NONBELL PEPPERS: 'Banana Supreme' is an 8" early banana pepper that ripens to red (60–75 days). For frying peppers that are also good in salads, try

Water with a soaker hose during drought or high heat.

PEPPER
continued

'Cubanelle' (yellow-green) or 'Corno di Toro', available in red or yellow varieties (65–70 days). 'Giant Marconi', an early, hardy, highly disease-resistant grilling pepper, is sweetest when left to turn red on the vine. 'Cherry Pick' is a 1½" round cherry pepper that can be pickled green or red (65–75 days). 'Pimento L' bears 4"-long heart-shaped fruit that can be eaten fresh or processed as traditional pimientos (90–100 days). 'Sweet Cayenne' (up to 12") and 'Jimmy Nardello' (6–8") look like long, hot cayenne peppers *(C. frutenscens)* but actually are among the sweetest nonbell peppers available (75–85 days). For container growing, try 'Sweet Pickle', an edible ornamental plant that holds its 2" yellow, orange, red, and purple peppers upright on compact plants (75 days). 'Chilly Chili' peppers look like little cayennes but are not hot. The compact, colorful, and extremely heat-tolerant plants are perfect for patio containers (70–80 days).

HOT PEPPERS: 'Robustini' is a mildly hot pepperoncini good for salads or for pickling (62 days). 'Paprika Supreme' has 6–8" tapered, sweet red fruits with just a hint of warmth. Remove the ribs to eliminate the heat. Use fresh, or dry

Always wear rubber gloves when handling hot peppers to avoid transferring the heat-bearing capsaicin to your skin.

Cut the peppers off with scissors or pruning shears to avoid tearing the stems.

them for grinding into paprika powder (55–80 days). 'Hungarian Hot Wax' has 5–6" fruits that ripen from pale yellow to bright red and are good for frying and pickling (55–85 days). 'Big Chili' is a mildly hot 8–10" Anaheim cultivar good fresh or cooked (75–85 days). 'Cherry Bomb' is a small, medium-hot, high-yielding round

cherry pepper that ripens from green to red (65–85 days). Use 'Ancho 101' in chile rellenos recipes (75–85 days). It is a prolific producer over a long season. 'Jaloro' is an unusual yellow jalapeno that ripens to orange and then red, and is especially virus resistant (70 days). 'Mucho Nacho' is a traditional green-to-red jalapeno that is larger and hotter than the standard varieties (70–80 days). 'Serrano' is a hot chile good for salsa or salads, if you dare (75–85 days). 'Serranno del Sol' is a hybrid with longer fruits that mature earlier (65 days).

EXTREMELY HOT PEPPERS: 'Super Cayenne II' is prolific and especially disease resistant, with 5–6" peppers (70 days). 'Habanero' *(C. chinense)* is a small but extremely hot pepper that ripens from green to orange. Remove the ribs and seeds to reduce the heat (75–100 days). For high yields try its relatives 'Congo Trinidad' (red), 'Jamaican Hot' (yellow and red), or 'Yellow Mushroom', also available in a red cultivar (75–95 days). 'Jamaican Hot Chocolate' is a reddish-brown habanero-type pepper with a smoky flavor (85 days). 'Scotch Bonnet' is similar to habanero but grows well only in long-season areas (120 days). 'Tabasco' *(C. frutescens)* is a small chile that packs the punch its namesake sauce made famous (80 days). 'Thai Hot' holds its peppers up above the leaves and thus makes an attractive ornamental, but keep it away from children (90 days). Beware the tiny 'Chiltepin', a blistering hybrid of the bird pepper plants that grow wild in the southeastern United States (90–100 days).

Congo peppers are hot at any stage of development.

PAPAYA

Carica papaya KAIR-ih-kuh puh-PY-uh

Hand-pollinate papaya flowers to ensure high fruit yields. It is also known as pawpaw and Hawaiian papaya.

ZONES: 10 and 11
SIZE: Up to 30'h × 6'w
TYPE: Perennial grown as a tree

GROWTH: Fast
LIGHT: Full sun
MOISTURE: Average
FEATURES: Edible fruits

SITING: Plant 8–10' apart in light, well-drained soil not overly rich in organic matter. Although papaya needs consistent moisture, it does not tolerate even brief periods of standing water. Provide a windbreak if planting in an open area.
CARE: One male plant can pollinate up to 25 females. Cover unopened female flowers with paper bags; after blossoms open use a small brush to dust pollen onto pistils. Bagging bisexual flowers in the same way helps to guarantee self-pollination. Water plants at least once a week during dry weather. Use plant food, such as Miracle-Gro Water Soluble All Purpose, according to label directions. Plants produce well for 3–4 years before weakening. Start a few new plants each year to replace those you must retire and plant them in a different location. Remove and compost any plant debris to avoid soilborne diseases.

PROPAGATION: Grow papaya from seed. Germination takes 3–5 weeks; washing the seeds in water to remove the gelatinous membrane before planting saves a week or two of germination time.

Save germination time by washing the seeds before planting.

HARVEST: Spring transplants are ready for harvest by November. Each plant produces two to four fruits per week. Cut the short stalks with a clean knife. Fruits will ripen off the tree but are not as sweet as those picked ripe. Gardeners who are allergic to papain or latex should not touch any part of the papaya plant.
PESTS AND DISEASES: Use sulfur to combat powdery mildew and fungicides for ring spot, black spot, blights, anthracnose, and other diseases. Control mosaic virus with clean cultural practices and pesticides labeled for green citrus aphids. Spray whiteflies with insecticidal soap. Spray *Btk* on webworm larvae; knock caterpillars into a bucket of soapy water to kill them. Remove and destroy any branches infested with scales, then wipe off any scales on the trunk with an insecticidal soap solution.
RECOMMENDED CULTIVARS: 'Solo' cultivars bear the small, hermaphroditic papayas often sold commercially. 'Blue Solo' is a low-growing hybrid that does well in Florida. 'Solo Sunrise' has larger than average red-fleshed fruits that keep well. 'Red Thai' has sweet reddish-orange flesh.

PECAN

Carya illinoinensis KAR-ee-uh ill-ih-NO-een-en-sis

Shake or knock ripe nuts from the tree onto the ground for easy gathering.

ZONES: 5–9
SIZE: 60–150'h × 60–100'w
TYPE: Deciduous tree

GROWTH: Slow
LIGHT: Full sun
MOISTURE: High
FEATURES: Edible seeds (nuts)

SITING: Plant bare-root trees in deep, well-drained, acid soil in an elevated area to avoid frost damage. Pecans do not tolerate salinity.
CARE: Use a balanced plant food once in early spring at a rate of 1 pound per year of age for immature trees and 4 pounds per inch of trunk diameter just below the scaffold branches for bearing trees. Water newly planted trees thoroughly and maintain consistent moisture. Water mature trees during dry spells. Train each tree to a central leader with lateral branches spaced 8–18" apart.
PROPAGATION: Grow pecans from grafted rootstock. Plant at least two different varieties to ensure cross pollination.
HARVEST: Trees start to bear 5–8 years after planting but have a productive life of at least 50 years. Nuts ripen from late summer to autumn; gather by knocking them from the tree with a long pole or mechanical

Choose cultivars resistant to pecan scab disease and bred for your climate.

shaker onto a sheet spread below. Dry the nuts in burlap bags hung in a warm, dry area with good air circulation. Freeze nutmeats for best long-term storage.
PESTS AND DISEASES: Pecan scab disease can be a problem in high heat and humidity. Use a fungicide labeled for pecans early in the season on susceptible cultivars. Use insecticides labeled for yellow and black pecan aphids. Twig girdlers, pecan weevils, and stink bugs attack nuts late in the season. Gather and destroy infested nuts and fallen twigs, and remove other vegetative debris from the area that can harbor insects. Deer eat young shoots and rub their antlers on the bark; squirrels and birds eat the nuts.
RECOMMENDED CULTIVARS: Eastern varieties, such as 'Desirable', have large nuts and are resistant to pecan scab disease; western cultivars, such as 'Wichita', have medium-size nuts and are susceptible to pecan scab, so they are suitable only for desert and dry southwestern areas. Both can be pollinated with 'Western Schley' or 'Cheyenne'. 'Kanza' and 'Pawnee' are disease-resistant cultivars developed for Zones 6 and 7.

WHITE SAPOTE

Casimiroa edulis *kah-see-mi-ROH-uh ED-yoo-lis*

Grafted white sapotes can be grown in containers if pruned regularly.

ZONES: 9 and 10
SIZE: 15–50'h ×
15–50'w
TYPE: Evergreen
tree
GROWTH: Slow
LIGHT: Full sun
MOISTURE: Average
FEATURES: Edible
fruits

SITING: White sapote grows anywhere where oranges grow successfully. Plant in any well-drained soil away from patios or other areas where visiting bees, flies, and ants would be a nuisance and where fallen twigs and fruit make a mess.

CARE: White sapote is drought tolerant but does best with regular deep watering to discourage surface roots that ruin lawns or break through pavement. Established trees tolerate wet roots and some frost, to 25°F. Feed with plant food such as Miracle-Gro Water Soluble All Purpose. Pinch out the terminal bud to encourage branching, then prune for compact growth.

PROPAGATION: Grow from grafted rootstock; seedlings produce inferior fruit.

HARVEST: Grafted trees bear fruit in 3–4 years. The apple-size fruit ripens 6–9 months after flowers bloom, from midsummer to February depending on the

Locate the tree away from areas where fallen fruit will make a mess.

cultivar and locale. Tree-ripened fruit has the best flavor but is likely to fall first; the fruit bruises easily, and the flesh beneath bruises turns bitter. Handle fruits gently and as little as possible. Clip mature fruits with short stems attached; the stems will fall off when the fruit is ready to eat. Store ripe fruits in the refrigerator for up to 2 weeks. The flesh is creamy white to yellow and tastes like custard. Avoid eating the peel and seeds. Eat fresh fruit out of hand or in salads, or mash and freeze the pulp to use in ice cream or baked goods.

PESTS AND DISEASES: Temperature extremes cause temporary defoliation, and harsh winds can cause fruit drop. Control weeds and use traps against snails. Discourage fruit flies by keeping fallen fruit and other vegetative debris collected and destroyed. Prune and destroy branches infested with black scale. Spray mealybugs with insecticidal soap. Control aphids with a sharp spray from the garden hose; use insecticidal soap for heavy infestations. Birds eat the fruit; be prepared to share.

RECOMMENDED CULTIVARS: 'Louise', 'Suebelle', and 'Michele' are nearly everbearing small to medium-size trees.

CHESTNUT

Castanea spp. *kas-TAY-nee-uh*

Squirrels avoid the spiny pods only until the pods split and release the nuts.

ZONES: 4–9
SIZE: 40–100'h ×
40–100'w
TYPE: Deciduous
tree
GROWTH: Fast
LIGHT: Full sun
MOISTURE: Average
FEATURES: Edible
seeds (nuts)

SITING: Plant 20–40' apart in deep, acid, fertile, well-drained soil.

CARE: Chestnuts bear on new wood, so pruning isn't necessary for good fruit set. Train young trees to a central leader. Water in hot or dry periods, especially in late summer when the pods are filling out. Mulch to keep the soil moist, but keep it away from the trunks. Use a balanced plant food once a year, in spring, at a rate of 1 pound per year of tree age or per inch of trunk diameter.

PROPAGATION: Grow from grafted cultivars. Chestnuts are self-infertile, so plant more than one type to ensure pollination.

HARVEST: Chestnuts begin bearing 3–6 years after planting. The spiny pods split open in early autumn, releasing one to three nuts. Gather the nuts daily and dry them in the sun for a few days to bring out their sweetness. Store them in a cool, dry location.

Dry harvested nuts in the sun to bring out their natural sweetness.

PESTS AND DISEASES: Chestnut weevils lay their eggs in ripening nuts; larvae emerge from fallen nuts and burrow into the ground. Control adult weevils with insecticides labeled for chestnuts. Chinese cultivars are susceptible to blight, especially in eastern regions; prune out infected branches or replace trees with resistant types. The spiny pods are squirrelproof until they split open; harvest daily to avoid loss. Use a tree shelter to protect the trunk from deer, but remove it in autumn to allow the tree to harden off.

RECOMMENDED CULTIVARS: 'Revival' is a Chinese chestnut (*C. mollissima*) that grows well in the South and is hardy to 15°F. 'Grimo' cultivars of 'Layeroka' (*C. sativa* ×*mollissima*) are crosses between European and Chinese chestnuts resulting in large, blight-resistant, early-bearing trees hardy to –25°F. 'American Hybrid' (*C. dentata* ×*mollissima*) is a cross of American and Chinese types resulting in an upright growth habit and blight resistance. It is hardy to Zone 4. For small spaces, try 'Chinquapin' (*C. pumila*), a dwarf grown as a shrub 6–10' tall. It is hardy to –30°F.

ENDIVE

Cichorium endivia *sih-KOR-ee-um en-DY-vee-uh*

Curly-leaf endive cultivars are also called frisée or Belgian endive. Light frost improves the flavor.

ZONES: NA
SIZE: 3–9"h × 6–18"w
TYPE: Herbaceous annual
GROWTH: Average
LIGHT: Full sun to part shade
MOISTURE: Average
FEATURES: Edible leaves

SITING: Sow seeds 4 weeks before the last frost date, and again in mid- to late summer for a fall crop, ¼" deep in rows 12–18" apart, in well-drained soil to which rotted compost has been added.
CARE: Thin seedlings to 8" apart when they are about 3" tall and then to 18" apart as you begin harvesting (use thinnings in salads). Use water soluble plant food, such as Miracle-Gro Water Soluble All Purpose, once a month, watering to the sides of each row and not on the endive leaves themselves. Remove any flower stalks as soon as they appear. Water frequently

Broad-leaf endive, or escarole, forms a loose bunch.

during periods of high heat or drought; both will cause endive to bolt and taste bitter. To prevent bitterness in warm weather, blanch the leaves: Pull the outer leaves together over the smaller, inner leaves (hearts) and hold them loosely in place with string or a rubber band. An easier method is to invert empty pots over the heads to block out the light for 2 weeks before harvest, being sure to cover the drainage hole with a rock or wood chip.
HARVEST: Leaves are ready to harvest in 65–100 days. Pick outer leaves as needed, or wait until a head is fully developed and cut it at the base. Store unwashed leaves and heads for up to 1 week in the refrigerator. Plants can be mulched and protected in a cold frame for winter harvest. Light frost improves the flavor.
PESTS AND DISEASES: Use bait or traps for snails and slugs. Handpick caterpillars.
RECOMMENDED CULTIVARS: 'Green Curled Ruffec' is a curly-leaved type sometimes called frisée. 'Batavian Full-Heart' is a broad-leaved escarole that almost forms a head at maturity.

GARDENING IN RAISED BEDS

You don't need much space to grow a productive vegetable garden if you raise your planting beds 6–12" above ground level. If you amend the soil so that roots can grow deeply, vegetables and herbs can be interplanted intensively—even touching one another at maturity. Design your bed so you can work in or harvest it from either side.

Raised beds offer benefits in addition to space saving. Drainage and aeration are improved in raised beds. Raised beds dry out and warm up earlier, so you can plant sooner.

Another advantage to raised beds is that weeding is less of a chore. Unlike ground-level garden plots open to invasion by competing grasses and weeds, raised beds are relatively protected. Any weeds introduced by birds or breezes are easily removed without the need to walk over large planted beds, which causes soil compaction.

CREATING NEW BEDS

Choose a sunny location with room to create walking paths. Leave space for one wide path large enough to accommodate a garden cart or wheelbarrow. Use a spade to dig a trench along the width of one side of the plot and move the soil to the opposite side of the plot. Spread 2–4" of well-rotted compost or manure along the bottom of the trench. Then

Raised beds increase drainage and aeration as well as soil temperature.

dig a second trench next to the first, turning the dug layer of soil into the first trench. Repeat until you have an empty trench at the opposite side; fill it with the soil you moved from the first trench. Because you have loosened and aerated a layer of soil and added a layer of organic matter, the bed will be raised above the surrounding ground level. Now install structured sides to the plot, using landscape timbers, concrete blocks, bricks, stones, or other decorative supports. Use additional topsoil, compost, or blended product such as Miracle-Gro Enriched Garden Soil, or manure to fill in low spots.

If the soil in your planned plot is severely compacted or heavy in clay, consider double-digging to a depth of 2'. Follow the trenching and turning method above, but after removing the top layer of soil in a trench, dig down an additional spade depth the length of the trench. Then dig the next trench and move that soil over to the first one, and so on.

WATERMELON
Citrullus lanatus sih-TRULL-us luh-NAY-tus

Choose cultivars resistant to fusarium wilt and anthracnose.

ZONES: NA
SIZE: 1'h × 6'w
TYPE: Annual vine
LIGHT: Full sun

MOISTURE: High
FEATURES: Edible fruits

SITING: Watermelons require a lot of space in a sunny location with highly fertile, slightly acid, well-drained soil. Amend clay soil with organic matter. Tender vines do best in a site protected from strong winds. Direct-sow seed in southern climates after the last frost date in soil hilled 3" deep and 12" in diameter, six seeds to a hill, with hills at least 6' apart. In the North, start seeds in peat pots indoors 3 weeks before the last frost date, then transplant them into the garden with the pot tops level with the soil at least 2 weeks after the last frost date.

CARE: Thin direct-sown seedlings to a few plants per hill after the first set of true leaves appears, then thin again to one or two vines when they are 12–24" long. Remove weeds by hand to avoid damaging the fragile vines. Watermelons are heavy feeders; use plant food, such as Miracle-Gro Water Soluble All Purpose, throughout the growing season and add potassium or phosphorus if a soil sample analysis indicates the need for it. Mulch only during the hottest part of summer to avoid lowering the soil temperature. Place squares of cardboard under ripening fruits to protect them from rot and insects. Some types can be trained up a fence or trellis, but fruits must be supported. Make slings from bird netting or mesh bags and tie to the support. When nights grow cool in northern areas, pinch out the tips of the vines and remove new flowers as they appear to encourage existing fruits to ripen.

PROPAGATION: Grow from seed or transplants. Seedless varieties require pollination by another cultivar planted nearby. Saved seed usually does not breed true.

HARVEST: Depending on the variety, melons ripen 70–90 days after planting. They don't ripen off the vine, but you can tell when they are ready to pick. The green stem and tendrils near the top of the melon will dry out and turn brown when the melon is ripe. The underside of some cultivars turns from white to yellow when the fruit is ripe. Some gardeners rap melons with their knuckles to listen for a telltale hollow "thunk" of ripeness. Watermelon tastes best chilled. Enjoy it as is or blend it into smoothies and fruit juices. Toss chunks or slices in lemon juice and freeze for later use. The rind can be pickled and pressure canned.

PESTS AND DISEASES: Discourage cucumber beetles and aphids with floating row covers (but remove the fabric when the flowers bloom). Wash off aphids with a mild soap solution. Red dots on the underside of leaves are squash bugs. Scrape them off; spray rotenone late in the day if the infestation is heavy. Watermelons

are susceptible to fusarium wilt and mildews. Ask your county extension agent which diseases affect watermelons in your area and choose cultivars resistant to those problems. Watermelon fruit blotch is a common bacterial rot in hot, humid climates. Cultivars with a lighter green rind may be more susceptible. Purchase only inspected seeds or transplants, use clean cultural practices, avoiding wetting the leaves and handling wet plants, and rotate crops to avoid infection.

RECOMMENDED CULTIVARS: 'Crimson Sweet' is a round light green melon with dark green stripes and mild dark red flesh. Fruits reach 25 pounds even in northern areas; plants are resistant to fusarium wilt and anthracnose. 'Fiesta', 'Regency', and 'Sangria' are traditional striped dark green melons, 20–25 pounds, resistant to fusarium wilt. 'Orangeglo' has extrasweet flesh with a tropical flavor and is resistant to pests and wilt. For small gardens, grow 'Sugar Bush', 'Sugar Baby', or yellow-fleshed 'Yellow Doll'—all compact vines with smaller melons that fit in the refrigerator. Another small cultivar, 'Golden Midget', turns yellow when ripe but has sweet brilliant pink flesh. It weighs just a few pounds but ripens in 70 days. For a state fair competitor, try 'Mountain Hoosier', which develops melons up to 80 pounds in 85 days. Seedless varieties take the longest to ripen and thus do best in southern climates and drier conditions. They are not truly seedless but contain less conspicuous, edible pips. 'Tri-X-313' and 'SummerSweet' produce melons 15–20 pounds in 90 days. Germination of seedless types is most successful indoors.

The stem-end tendrils of a ripe melon are brown and dry.

Small-fruited watermelons grow on compact vines.

GRAPEFRUIT, LEMON, LIME, ORANGE

Citrus spp. *SIH-trus*

Limes *(C. aurantiifolia)* thrive in hot, humid areas in soil that drains well.

ZONES: 8–11
SIZE: 10–40'h ×
10–40'w
TYPE: Evergreen
shrub or tree

GROWTH: Slow
LIGHT: Full sun
MOISTURE: Average
FEATURES: Edible
fruits

SITING: Grow in deep, well-drained, acid silty soil in a sunny area protected from strong winds and located where you can water easily in dry weather. In hot climates

Pummelo *(C. maxima)* is grapefruit's tropical ancestor but not as sweet.

choose a site protected from midday sun. In cooler zones choose early-maturing varieties and plant in the warmest microclimate possible. All citrus plants do best in light soils, but sour orange rootstock will grow in heavier soils. Add sulfur if necessary to increase acidity or lime to increase alkalinity. Space most citrus plants 25' apart in both directions. Mandarins and limes can be planted as close as 15'.

CARE: Successful growth requires a long growing season with temperatures between 65 and 90°F. Lemons, limes, and oranges need the most heat; grapefruits and mandarins are the most cold tolerant, but mandarins suffer the most frost damage. Most trees need no pruning the first several

years. Painting a commercial sprout inhibitor on the trunks of young trees is preferable to using protective wraps, which can encourage insects and diseases. Prune dead and damaged wood and any branch that interferes with the growth of scaffold limbs from mature trees. Remove extremely low limbs to provide better access for irrigation and air circulation and to prevent brown rot of low-hanging fruit. Hedge pruning may be necessary on tightly spaced trees to maintain a manageable shape for harvesting, but it will reduce yields. Top pruning controls tree size and encourages fruit growth but may not be necessary in home gardens with just a few specimens. Remove sprouts flush with the trunk and prune any suckers from the rootstock before the thorns harden. Pull weeds manually or by light tilling; citrus is highly sensitive to herbicides. Feed several times a year from late autumn to midspring, increasing the amount of plant food as trees mature. Monitor nitrogen carefully; it increases yield but also increases the likelihood of scab. Use foliar sprays to add needed minerals such as copper, zinc, manganese, and boron so that excess salts do not accumulate in the soil. Moisture stress harms the fruit; water during dry

Citron *(C. medica)* is typically grown for its rind, used in candy and cooking.

'Improved Meyer' lemon has good disease-resistance and few thorns.

periods but do not allow the trees to stand in water. Excessive moisture promotes the fungus that causes scab.

PROPAGATION: Grow from seed, bud grafting, air layering, or cuttings, depending on the variety. Plants grown from root cuttings may fruit several years earlier than budded trees.

HARVEST: Lemons and limes are ready to pick 5–9 months after flowering; oranges and grapefruits need 8–12 months. Some varieties, such as 'Valencia' oranges, hold well on the tree for up to several months; others need to be picked regularly to encourage the next crop. Fruits are easily damaged, so handpick dry fruit whenever possible, wearing gloves to protect against contact dermatitis from the peel oils. Move harvested fruits out of the sun as quickly as possible to prevent stylar-end rot. Store in cool but not cold temperatures and very high humidity, or cure for long-term storage. Use lemons and limes as garnishes, for juice, and to remove stains. Flavor baked goods with Key limes. Eat oranges and mandarins fresh out of hand or cut the sections into salads. Halve and sweeten grapefruits and pummelos to eat fresh for breakfast or broiled and served as an appetizer at dinner. Drink citrus juice fresh or use it as a flavoring in sauces, desserts, and beverages. Make marmalade from sour oranges. Make candied peel from citrus rinds.

PESTS AND DISEASES: Citrus plants are sensitive to a variety of environmental problems, the most serious of which are wind and water damage. Proper

GRAPEFRUIT, LEMON, LIME, ORANGE

continued

siting and consistent but not too much moisture are key to their survival. They are susceptible to leaf miners, aphids, scales, and other pests as well as to a host of diseases, including viruses, rots, molds, spots, and anthracnose. Cultivars sold for use in your geographic area are bred and grafted to reduce the likelihood of pest infestation or infection. Ask your extension agent or a nursery owner for spraying guidelines specific to the plants you choose and follow directions carefully when using pesticides.

RECOMMENDED CULTIVARS: Citrus plants propagated by bud grafting to a specific

Grapefruit is among the largest and most cold-hardy of the citrus trees.

rootstock are the most reliable. They begin fruiting sooner and have increased resistance to cold, wind, pests, and diseases. Choose plants according to rootstock selected for its compatibility with your particular soil type.

CITRON: *C. medica* is a small, spiny, evergreen shrub or tree 8–15' tall. Its flowers are fragrant and its leaves smell like lemon. The rough, bumpy rind is lemon yellow when ripe; the pulp is not juicy and has many seeds. It will not tolerate temperature extremes and is highly sensitive to heat, drought, and frost but adaptable to many soils. It is often bud grafted onto lemon, grapefruit, or orange to improve adaptability. 'Etrog' is the most commonly grown cultivar but only the rind is used in candy and marmalades. It begins to bear in 3 years and lives as long as 25 years.

GRAPEFRUIT: This popular citrus fruit is not related to grapes. *C. ×paradisi* is a cross of sweet orange with pummelo (*C. maxima*), a grapefruit ancestor, and is larger and somewhat more cold hardy than other citrus plants. The thorny, evergreen trees can grow 30–35' feet tall or more and often have trunks several feet in diameter, so they should be spaced

Tangerine is a type of mandarin orange with a thin, loose peel.

farther apart than other citrus trees. The 3½–5"-diameter fruits have few or no seeds and tart, juicy pale yellow, pink, or red pulp. Most types stay on the tree for several months, although red-fleshed fruits fade as the season progresses and late harvests reduce the next year's crop. High soil salinity reduces yields, and excess nitrogen causes malformed fruits. Use nutritional sprays to add copper and zinc as needed. Grapefruit attracts fruitflies and is susceptible to anthracnose, root rots, leaf spots, and molds. Choose cultivars bred for resistance to citrus canker and viruses. 'Redblush' and 'Ray Ruby' are popular red-fleshed grapefruits. Common white-fleshed types are 'Marsh' or 'Duncan'.

LEMON: True lemon (*C. limon*) bears fragrant flowers and sharp thorns on trees 10–20' tall. Most types have seeds and

some have variegated flowers and fruits. Lemon is more sensitive to cold than orange; sudden temperature drops below 30°F will kill flowers and fruit; below 25°F can damage the wood. The most flavorful fruits are grown in coastal areas too cool for oranges and grapefruit. 'Eureka' is an early-bearing, almost thornless, disease-resistant cultivar suitable for hot, dry climates. Meyer lemon (*C. meyeri*) is a cross with mandarin orange (*C. reticulata*) and thus better suited to coastal areas and container growing. 'Improved Meyer' is resistant to citrus viruses and is less thorny. Rough lemon (*C. ponderosa*) is a cross of lemon and citron (*C. medica*). It is more sensitive to cold than true lemons but produces large fruit on compact trees. If the soil is alkaline, choose a cultivar grafted onto sour orange stock or alemow (×*C. macrophylla*), a hybrid of lemon and pummelo. Use labeled pesticide sprays for infestations of mites and scales. A copper fungicide will control red algae in summer. *C. meyeri* and *C. ponderosa* are small, shrubby cultivars good for container growing. If you keep container citrus plants outdoors in summer, move them to a somewhat shady spot for a couple of weeks before bringing them indoors, to help them acclimate to lower light.

LIME: *C. aurantiifolia* grows well in hot climates that are also humid, although it is more drought tolerant and also more sensitive to cold than lemon. It will not

Japanese Satsuma mandarin cultivars are more cold-hardy than others.

GRAPEFRUIT, LEMON, LIME, ORANGE

continued

All citrus trees require a long growing season with warm temperatures.

thrive in heavy soils but can be grown in porous lava or other gravelly soils. If soil nitrogen is too low, mulch with cured seaweed or plant leguminous cover crops between rows. Mexican or Key limes are small, often shrubby evergreen trees 6–13' tall with aromatic leaves and sharp spines. The flowers are not fragrant. Seedlings fruit in 3–6 years. Although the trees are everbearing, the best harvests are in late spring and late autumn. Resist the urge to pick fruits until they have ripened from dark green to light greenish yellow and are slightly soft to the touch. Tahitian or Persian limes are larger and hardier than Mexican limes and also usually seedless and free of thorns. The trees grow to 20' tall in sandy soil or even in crushed limestone. They are sensitive to excess water, so in low-lying areas plant them in raised beds. Hand-harvest the fruits from spring through fall, with best yields during the summer months. For containers grow dwarf 'Thornless Key Lime', which is less productive but tasty and thorn free. Kaffir

Round or common oranges, like 'Valencia', are grown for juicing.

'Minneola' is a cold-tolerant hybrid of tangerine and grapefruit.

lime (*C. hystrix*) is grown for its aromatic leaves, which are popular in Asian cuisine.

MANDARIN: A catchall name for oranges with a thin, loose peel, mandarin includes traditional Willowleaf or Chinese cultivars, such as 'Ledar' and 'Changsha'; tangerines, such as 'Clementine', which has a weeping habit, and 'Murcott Honey', prized for its extrasweet fruit; Japanese Satsuma cultivars, such as the extremely cold-hardy 'Kara'; as well as light-skinned hybrids, such as the large-fruited 'Ugli', a cross of mandarin orange and grapefruit that has few or no seeds and better flavor than some grapefruits. *C. reticulata* Blanco trees are evergreen and often smaller than other oranges. Although mandarins are more cold hardy and drought tolerant than some other citrus species, the fruits are easily damaged by frost. Tangelo (*C. ×tangelo*) is a cross of tangerine and grapefruit. The cultivars 'Minneola' and 'Orlando' are more cold tolerant than grapefruit. Tangelo fruits are the size of oranges or larger and extremely easy to peel. Tangors are the result of crossing mandarin and sweet orange (*C. reticulata* with *C. sinensis*). 'Temple' is a popular cultivar and often used as a pollinator for other citrus trees. For container growing, try everbearing calamondin (×*Citrofortunella microcarpa*), a cross between mandarin

orange and kumquat (*Fortunella*), often called miniature orange. It is compact and bears fragrant flowers and small but sweet, juicy fruit. Mandarin or Rangpur lime (*C. ×limonia*), sometimes also called miniature orange, is not a true lime but a cross of lemon and mandarin orange suitable for indoor growing. It has fragrant flowers and no thorns. The edible fruit has dark orange pulp that smells somewhat like lime and is sour but makes good marmalade.

ORANGE: Sour or bitter orange was the original species introduced to Native Americans and early settlers in Florida. Although its oil has value and its pulp and rind can be used in marmalade, *C. aurantium* is too sour to be eaten fresh. It is highly susceptible to tristeza and other citrus viruses as well as to fungal problems. It can tolerate light frosts for short periods and is adaptable to most soil conditions, including clay, so it is used principally as a rootstock for sweeter citrus species. Bergamot orange (*C. bergamia*), such as 'Bouquet', is cultivated for its oil, which flavors Earl Grey tea. Sweet orange (*C. sinensis*) is divided into a number of subtypes. Round or sweet oranges are often grown for juicing. 'Hamlin' and

Choose dwarf shrub cultivars to grow citrus fruits in small gardens.

GRAPEFRUIT, LEMON, LIME, ORANGE
continued

'Valencia' are popular cultivars. Navel oranges get their name from a small, secondary fruit at the stylar end of the main fruit. Early to ripen and easy to peel, navel oranges are large and seedless. 'Washington' cultivars are the most popular. Blood oranges, such as 'Moro', have a high concentration of red pigments in the peel and pulp. Coloration varies with climate. Low-acid oranges such as 'Succari' and 'Lima' are available; the juice is sweet but not as flavorful as that of acidic cultivars. Trifoliate oranges (*C. trifoliata* syn. *Poncirus trifoliata*) are small, shrubby deciduous plants that have naturalized in the southeastern United States. The small, bumpy fruits are too sour to eat, but the plant is often used as a dwarfing rootstock for other citrus plants because of its cold hardiness. A citrange is a *trifoliata* × *sinensis* hybrid developed for resistance to root rot, nematodes, and tristeza virus. It is hardy to Zone 8.

PUMMELO: Also called shaddock, *C. maxima* is a tropical ancestor of grapefruit. It typically grows 16–50' tall but can be pruned for use as a dwarf type. The tree bears thorns as well as fragrant flowers, and the large, round to pear-shaped fruits have pale yellow to pink or red pulp that is not as sweet as that of grapefruit—sometimes even bitter in cool climates. 'Chandler' is a good cultivar for warm zones. 'Hirado' is more cold hardy. Aging the fruits up to 3 months increases juice and flavor. Young trees are sun sensitive, and root rot can be a problem at any stage of maturity. Control common and brown aphids to prevent the spread of tristeza virus. Eliminate scale, which can cause sooty mold.

Mulch to conserve soil moisture and control weeds.

RECOMMENDED CITRUS VARIETIES FOR HOME GARDENS

CA = CALIFORNIA; DS = DESERTS; FL = FLORIDA; GC = GULF COAST; HI = HAWAII; TX = TEXAS

NAVEL ORANGE

'Cara Cara' and 'Washington' (CA, DS, FL, GC, HI, TX); 'Everhard' (TX)

SWEET ORANGE

'Diller' (FL, GC); 'Hamlin' (DS, FL, GC, HI, TX); 'Marrs' (DS, FL, GC, HI, TX); 'Parson Brown' (DS, FL, GC, HI, TX); 'Pineapple' (DS, FL, GC, HI, TX); 'Shamouti' (DS, CA); 'Trovita' (DS, CA); 'Valencia' (CA, DS, FL, GC, HI, TX)

BLOOD ORANGE

'Moro' (CA, DS, FL, GC, HI, TX); 'Sanguinelli' (CA, DS, FL, GC); 'Tarocco' (CA, DS)

SOUR ORANGE

'Chinotto' and 'Seville' (CA, DS, FL, GC, HI, TX)

MANDARIN ORANGE (AND TANGERINE)

'Ambersweet' (CA, FL, GC); Calamondin (CA, DS, FL, GC, HI, TX); 'Changsha' (GC, TX); Clementine (CA, DS, FL, GC, HI, TX); 'Dancy' (DS, FL, GC, HI, TX); 'Encore' (DS, FL, GC); 'Fairchild' (DS, CA, GC); 'Honey' (DS, FL, GC, HI); 'Kara' (CA); 'Kinnow' (CA, DS); 'Page' (DS, FL, GC, HI); 'Pixie' (CA); Satsuma (CA, FL, GC); 'Wilking' (HI)

LEMON

'Eureka' (CA, DS); 'Improved Meyer' (CA, DS, FL, GC, HI, TX); 'Lisbon' (CA, DS); 'Ponderosa' (DS, FL, GC);

LIME

'Bearss', 'Mexican', and 'Rangpur' (CA, DS, FL, GC, HI, TX); 'Nitta' (HI)

GRAPEFRUIT

'Duncan' (FL, GC); 'Flame' (FL, GC); 'Marsh' (CA, DS, FL, GC, TX); 'Melogold' (CA, DS); 'Oroblanco' (CA, DS); 'Redblush' (CA, DS, FL, GC, HI, TX)

PUMMELO

'Chandler' (CA, DS, FL, GC, HI, TX)

TANGELO

'Minneola' and 'Orlando' (CA, DS, FL, GC, HI, TX)

TANGOR

'Temple' (FL, HI, TX); 'Murcott' (CA, FL)

CORIANDER, CILANTRO
Coriandrum sativum *kor-ee-AN-drum sa-TY-vum*

Cilantro thrives in hot weather but may also survive winter in a cold frame.

ZONES: NA
SIZE: 5–24"h × 4–10"w
TYPE: Herbaceous hardy annual
GROWTH: Fast

LIGHT: Full sun to part shade
MOISTURE: Average
FEATURES: Edible leaves (cilantro), seeds (coriander), and roots

SITING: Direct-sow seeds after the last frost date in average, well-drained, slightly acid soil in a location where plants can remain; they have a deep taproot and are not tolerant of transplanting. Cilantro can be interplanted with peas, beans, peppers, and tomatoes.

CARE: Keep seeds and seedlings evenly moist. Gradually thin seedlings to about 1' apart. Water during dry weather. Plants tend to bolt in hot, dry conditions, so make successive plantings 2–4 weeks apart to maintain a steady crop all summer long. Plant again in autumn for spring harvest in warm climates. Plants can often be overwintered in a cold frame in northern gardens and will grow well indoors sown directly into deep pots.
PROPAGATION: Grow from seed.

Cut stems as needed or harvest whole plants to thin crowded plants.

HARVEST: Thin out whole plants as needed, or begin picking leaves from the lower part of the plant when several stems have developed. The lower leaves, called cilantro or Chinese parsley, look similar to Italian flat parsley and have more of the desired spicy flavor than the upper foliage, which resembles dill. The flowers are tiny white or lavender umbels and are edible; however, their presence indicates that the plant is past its flavor peak. Add leaves to cooked foods just before serving; heat dissipates the flavor. The leaves can be dried for later use, but the flavor is much milder. Leaves are best used fresh and can be stored for up to 2 weeks in the refrigerator. Cut the heads when the seedpods begin to turn brown. Hang the heads upside down in paper bags to catch the seeds. Use some whole or ground as coriander, a common ingredient in many Oriental and Middle Eastern cuisines. Save some seeds for the next planting.
PESTS AND DISEASES: No significant problems affect cilantro.
RECOMMENDED CULTIVARS: 'Santo' is among the most popular cultivars for fresh leaves because it is slow to bolt.

HAZELNUT
Corylus spp. *KOR-ih-lus*

Hazelnuts, or filberts, have tough shells that must be cracked open.

ZONES: 2–9
SIZE: 8–15'h × 10–20'w
TYPE: Deciduous shrub or small tree
GROWTH: Slow

LIGHT: Full sun to part shade
MOISTURE: Average
FEATURES: Edible seeds (nuts)

SITING: Filberts do best in deep, fertile, slightly acid, sandy loam. Plant them 10–20' apart to allow for air circulation. They tolerate some shade but produce more nuts in full sun.
CARE: Most types require cross-pollination by another cultivar for successful fruiting. Prune minimally to remove dead or

damaged wood and to maintain shape for best harvest. Prune severely every fourth or fifth year to restore plant vigor. Yield will be reduced that year but much improved in following years. Water in periods of drought or in particularly dry climates.
PROPAGATION: Hazelnuts grow best from layering; also from seed, or sprouts from root suckers.
HARVEST: Most filberts start to bear at 4 years and are productive for many decades. The nuts are ready for harvest from August to October; pick them as soon

In order to thwart squirrels, pick the nuts as soon as you can twist open their papery coverings.

as you can easily twist open the papery covering. Let the nuts dry in the sun for several days. The husk is thin but tough and must be cracked to get to the nutmeat inside. The white nutmeats are covered with a thin, papery reddish-brown covering similar to that on peanuts. Store the dried nuts in airtight packaging in cool but not freezing temperatures for up to a year.
PESTS AND DISEASES: European filberts are susceptible to eastern filbert blight, which is caused by a fungus. American types are less susceptible but can serve as the host. All types are susceptible to filbert bacterial blight, which is spread by water splash and contaminated tools. Prune and remove infected wood immediately and water and feed affected trees to maintain vigor. Use malathion or insecticidal soap to control aphids, whiteflies, weevils, and galls. Use netting if necessary to protect nuts and catkins from birds and squirrels.
RECOMMENDED CULTIVARS: Plant 'Bixby' and 'Potomac' hybrids together for cross-pollination. 'Winkler', an American hazelnut hybrid (*C. americana*), is self-fruitful. Hazelberts (*C. americana* ×*avellana*) work well as shrubs.

MELON

Cucumis melo melo kew-KEW-mis MEE-lo

Pick crenshaw and other "winter" melons when the smooth skin turns pale.

ZONES: NA
SIZE: 1'h × 10–20'w
TYPE: Annual vine
GROWTH: Average

LIGHT: Full sun
MOISTURE: High
FEATURES: Edible fruits

SITING: Plant seeds or seedlings in full sun in light, fertile, well-drained, slightly acid soil rich in organic matter. Soil temperature should be at least 60°F for transplants and 70°F for seeds to germinate. Choose a location protected from strong winds and large enough to accommodate the long vines, which grow to 10' or more. Direct-sow seeds in hills 4–6' apart, six seeds per hill, 1–2 weeks after the last frost date, or start indoors in peat pots 1 month before the last frost date and transplant 1' apart in rows 3' apart 2 weeks after the last frost date. Melons cross-pollinate easily. Crossed seed will be fertile, so keep varieties separated in the garden if you want saved seeds to be true to type.

CARE: Thin out hilled seedlings to two or three plants per hill. Water thoroughly and consistently, especially while the plants are in flower and developing fruits. Water in dry climates or during periods of drought, to provide at least 1" of water per week; ripening fruits need less water. Be sure leaves that wilt in the hot midday sun have enough moisture to recover at night. Black plastic mulch helps to increase the soil

Muskmelons, often called cantaloupes, give off a strong aroma when ripe.

temperature and conserve moisture. You can use organic mulch around plants to conserve moisture, but apply it after the soil temperature reaches 70°F. Weed by hand until the foliage is large enough to shade out new weeds. Feed at planting time, again when fruits start to set, and about 2 weeks after fruit-set with a low-nitrogen fruit plant food high in phosphorus, potassium, magnesium, and boron. Support trellised melons in slings made from strong netting or mesh fabric. Protect ripening melons from damp ground, especially overnight, by placing them on inverted pots, boards, or pieces of cardboard. If fruits are still ripening when nighttime temperatures begin to decrease in autumn, place melons on cardboard covered with aluminum foil or other reflective material to concentrate daytime heat and encourage quick maturation. Melons grow best when air temperatures average 70°F. Cool or cloudy weather and too much moisture during fruit development lessen flavor.

PROPAGATION: Grow from seed.

HARVEST: Depending on the variety, melons ripen from mid- to late summer or early autumn, about 35–55 days after pollination. Muskmelons (often called

Honeydews picked a bit too early can be ripened at room temperature.

MELON
continued

cantaloupes) and true cantaloupes give off a distinct odor when ripe. The skin color of ripe muskmelons becomes lighter under the netting, changing from green to tan or yellow. If a melon of mature size can be easily separated from the vine, it is ripe. Harvest carefully to prevent damaging the vines. The winter melons—honeydews, casabas, and crenshaws, which grow best in warm, dry zones—are ready to cut from the vine when their smooth green skin turns pale and the blossom ends are slightly soft. If they are picked a few days early, simply store them at room temperature until they are fully ripe. Store muskmelons and cantaloupes for up to a week in the warmest part of the refrigerator. Winter melons will keep for up to a month in the coldest (but not freezing) part of the refrigerator. All melons are best eaten fresh in slices or in cubes or balls in salads. They can also be made into juice, preserves, and pickles. Slices with

the rind removed can be kept in the freezer for up to 1 year.

PESTS AND DISEASES: Striped and spotted cucumber beetles are the most significant pests; they spread bacterial wilt. See additional information about them on this page. Aphids carry cucumber mosaic virus; knock them off with water from the hose, or dust the plants with rotenone if the infestation is severe. Most varieties are resistant to squash bugs, but pick off and destroy any you see. Choose varieties resistant to fusarium wilt, anthracnose, black rot, gummy stem blight, and powdery mildew. Apply labeled fungicides if necessary to control these problems, and remove and destroy any plants that become infected. Crop rotation also helps to control disease.

RECOMMENDED CULTIVARS: Determine the number of suitable growing days in your area and choose cultivars developed for that particular climate. 'Ambrosia' is a

medium-size muskmelon with a small seed cavity and sweet, juicy flesh. It's mildew resistant and a good choice in average and warm climates. 'Passport' is an early-maturing green-fleshed variety. In short-season zones, try 'Sweet 'n Early', with bright salmon flesh. 'Burpee's Early Hybrid' crenshaw is a large yellow-green melon with pink flesh. Southern-zone gardeners will appreciate the enormous 'Morning Dew' melon, which grows up to 12 pounds. In northern zones try 'Honey Pearl', a medium-size pale gold honeydew with almost white flesh. 'Casaba Golden Beauty' has spicy-sweet almost white flesh. For true European cantaloupes, which have rough or warty skin without netting, grow 'Charentais', an early, small melon, or 'Savor', a small grayish-green melon with sweet orange flesh. Both are resistant to fusarium wilt and powdery mildew.

Provide early season warmth with plastic tunnels.

Handpick and destroy cucumber beetles.

Reflective material under the fruit hastens ripening.

Ripe muskmelons separate easily from the vine.

CUCUMBER BEETLES

Cucumber beetles are ¼"-long winged insects with black stripes or spots on their backs. Adults feed on many vegetables but primarily on cucumber and melon flowers, leaves, and fruit, and larvae eat the roots. As adults feed, they may transmit an incurable bacterial wilt from one plant to another, affecting nonresistant melons and cucumbers. The bacteria survive in

the digestive tract of beetles that have overwintered in the ground. Bacterial wilt causes vines to wither and die within a week or two. Protect young plants with sealed row covers or cones. Examine flowering and fruiting plants regularly; pick off and destroy any beetles you see. Treat heavily infested plants weekly with rotenone dust. Flying insects, including honeybees, pollinate cucumbers

and melons, and cucumber beetles have natural predators, such as wasps, so use an insecticide only if an infestation is severe. Insecticides may kill all insects, including the beneficial ones. Cucurbits are prone to pesticide injury, so be sure to use a product specifically labeled for cucumbers or melons and follow the instructions carefully to avoid injury.

CUCUMBER
Cucumis sativus *kew-KEW-mis sa-TY-vus*

Pick cucumbers frequently to encourage more fruits.

ZONES: NA
SIZE: 12–72"h × 12–18"w
TYPE: Annual bush or vine
FORM: Fast
LIGHT: Full sun
MOISTURE: High
FEATURES: Edible fruits

SITING: Choose a warm, sunny location with humus-enriched soil that drains well. Direct-sow seed when soil and air temperatures reach at least 60°F, planting 1½" deep and 2' apart in rows 2–3' apart (those to be trellised can be as close as 10" apart), or in hills of five to seven seeds. In short-season areas, start seeds indoors 4 weeks before the last frost date and transplant after the last frost date. Use black plastic to warm the soil in short-season climates to prevent transplant shock. In warm climates two or three successive plantings may be possible. Cucumbers can be interplanted with cole crops, corn, peas, beans, radishes, carrots, tomatoes, and herbs.

CARE: Thin hilled plants to three per hill. Hand-weed carefully around these shallow-rooted plants to reduce competition for moisture and nutrients. Use row covers to protect young plants from pests and cold. Remove covers when vines begin to bloom, but check plants daily for signs of infestation. Train vining types onto trellises or other supports. The soil should be continuously moist. Plants should receive ½" of water per week or more during periods of high heat. Fruits from plants allowed to dry out will taste bitter. Spread organic mulch when seedlings are several weeks old.

PROPAGATION: Grow from seed.

HARVEST: Cucumbers grow quickly and are ready to pick 50–70 days after planting. Harvest when they are about 8–12" long for slicing varieties and as small as 2" for pickling types. Larger fruits will have more and harder seeds. Picking frequently also encourages more production. Snip the stems with garden scissors. Small-fruited types will produce almost all at once. Be sure to pick every day to prevent fruits from becoming too large. Eat all varieties fresh in salads and soups or use them for pickling. Fresh cucumbers can be stored in the refrigerator for up to 2 weeks. Cucumber soup can be frozen for up to a year.

PESTS AND DISEASES: Cucumbers are susceptible to a wide variety of problems, but new hybrids have been developed for disease resistance. Choose cultivars that have been bred specifically for your climate. Avoid pesticides to prevent killing beneficial pollinators. Striped and spotted cucumber beetles are the most significant pests; they spread bacterial wilt. See additional information about them on page 504. Aphids carry cucumber mosaic virus; knock them off with water from the hose or dust the plants with rotenone if the infestation is severe. Most varieties are resistant to squash bugs, but pick off and destroy any you see. Choose varieties resistant to fusarium wilt, anthracnose, black rot, gummy stem blight, and powdery mildew. Apply labeled fungicides if necessary to control these problems, and remove and destroy any plants that become infected. Crop rotation also helps to control disease. Bitterness often develops in fruits that are stressed. Water to avoid moisture stress and select bitter-free cultivars.

RECOMMENDED CULTIVARS: 'Little Leaf' pickling cucumber sets fruit without pollination and will climb up supports without tying. It yields well even during dry spells. In short-season areas try 'Northern Pickling', which produces fruit in 45–50 days. 'Marketmore' and 'General Lee' cultivars are among the most popular slicing types, producing 8–9" fruits in 55–60 days. 'Diva' is an awarding-winning seedless type that cucumber beetles don't seem to like. In cool climates try seedless 'Socrates'. Extralong burpless 'Suyo Long' and 'Tasty Jade' must be trellised to support the 12–15" fruits. Try 'Spacemaster' or 'Salad Bush' compact bush types in small gardens or patio containers.

Plant bush varieties in hilled-up soil, 5–7 seeds per hill.

Thin the seedlings to 3 per hill and remove any weeds.

Train vining cucumbers onto a fence or trellis for support.

Long-fruited cultivars have room to develop when grown on a trellis.

PUMPKIN, SUMMER & WINTER SQUASH

Cucurbita spp. *kew-KUR-bih-tuh*

Large winter squashes (*C. maxima*) often win giant pumpkin contests.

ZONES: NA
SIZE: 2'h × 10'w
TYPE: Annual bush or vine
GROWTH: Fast to average

LIGHT: Full sun
MOISTURE: High
FEATURES: Edible fruits

SITING: Choose the sunniest and largest site so plants can spread unimpeded. The soil should be slightly acid, drain easily, and be amended with lots of well-composted manure. Direct-sow seed when soil and air temperatures reach at least 70°F. Plant bush types 1½" deep and 4' apart in rows 4' apart, or in hills of five to seven seeds. Plant vining squashes 2' apart in rows 4' apart, and large pumpkins 4' apart in rows 8' apart. In short-season areas start seeds indoors 4 weeks before the last frost date and transplant after the last frost date. Use black plastic to warm the soil in short-season climates to prevent transplant shock. Interplant rows with corn or herbs.

CARE: Squash and pumpkins have high moisture and nutrient requirements. Feed twice a month with water-soluble plant food for vegetables. Maintain consistently moist but not waterlogged soil. Moisture-stressed plants are more susceptible to pests and diseases and have lower yields.

Hand-weed carefully to avoid disturbing the tender vines. If fruit set is poor, hand-pollinate flowers with a small brush or swab to ensure fruiting. Handle plants and fruits only when they are dry to avoid injuring them or spreading pathogens. Because winter squash and pumpkins rest

Jack-o'-lanterns are typically carved from hard-shelled orange winter squashes.

on the ground a long time while they mature, slip a piece of cardboard or another barrier underneath each fruit to prevent rot. In short-season areas or late in the growing season anywhere, remove blooms that appear after there are fruits maturing elsewhere on the vines. Pinching out those flowers and even the tips of the vines encourages the plant to direct its energy into the existing fruits. Trellis winter squash to save space; suspend fruits in strong netting or mesh bags securely tied to the supports. Or let vines run out of the garden and onto a patio or lawn if there is space. If frost is predicted, pick any ripe fruits and cover the others with mulch or blankets overnight.

PROPAGATION: Grow from seed.

HARVEST: Summer squash taste best when picked small—zucchinis, crooknecks, and straightnecks at about 6" long and scallops

Pinch out small fruits to promote the growth of larger ones.

Slip a barrier between fruit and ground to prevent rot.

PUMPKIN, SUMMER & WINTER SQUASH
continued

Cushaw is grown for its flesh and seeds.

Some cucurbit cultivars have been bred for resistance to squash bugs, a major pest.

Leave any harvested ones that you do not intend to eat immediately in a warm, humid location for several weeks to cure. Wipe off any dirt or moisture before storing them.

PESTS AND DISEASES: Squash bugs are the most

at about 3" across. Pick some every day when plants are at the height of production. Use a clean, sharp knife to cut the stems about an inch above the fruits. Eat them uncooked—sliced, chopped, or grated into salads or as crudités. Use medium-sized fruits in stir-fries or steamed as a side dish. Store them for up to 2 weeks in the refrigerator. Slices can be blanched, towel-dried, and frozen for up to 6 months for later cooking uses. The bigger summer squashes are allowed to grow, the tougher their flesh and seeds will be. Any fruits that escape detection and grow to enormous size can still be used. Remove the seeds and grate the flesh for use in baked goods, soups, and stews; or cut the

fruits in half lengthwise, hollow out the halves, and fill them with stuffing as a main dish. Summer squash blossoms are also edible; try them lightly sautéed as an appetizer. Try to pick mostly male blossoms (with slender flower stalks) for cooking and leave the female blooms to produce fruit. Leave winter squash and pumpkins on the plants until they are mature; they will not ripen further once picked and do not taste good immature. Use a clean, sharp knife to cut the stems a few inches above the fruits. Carry the fruits carefully from underneath to prevent any nicks or bruises, which interfere with long-term storage. All winter types but acorn squash need to be cured before storing.

significant pests. Winter squashes are especially susceptible. Choose cultivars that have been bred for resistance. Adult squash bugs are difficult to eradicate, so apply neem extract or carbaryl pesticide when you first see the nymphs. Avoid pesticides if possible to prevent killing beneficial pollinators. Squash bugs like to hide, so place a piece of cardboard beneath plants. Destroy bugs that gather on the underside of it and remove and destroy any infested vegetation. Buttercup and cushaw squashes can be decimated by squash vine borers. Crop rotation can help control them. Remove and destroy any dead vines to interrupt the borers' life cycle. Cucumber beetles are also

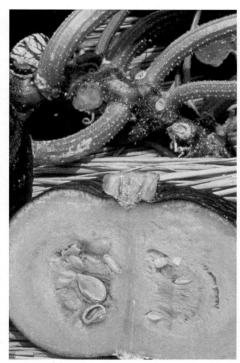
Buttercup types are winter squashes related to hubbards.

The dry flesh of butternut squash, *C. moschata*, stores well.

Hubbard squashes, *C. maxima*, come in many colors, including blue.

PUMPKIN, SUMMER & WINTER SQUASH

continued

Acorn-type squashes have hard shells and yellow-orange flesh.

troublesome pests; they spread bacterial wilt. See additional information about them on page 504. Aphids carry mosaic virus; knock them off with a stream of water from the hose, or dust the plants with rotenone if the infestation is severe. Choose varieties resistant to fusarium wilt, anthracnose, rots, leaf spots, gummy stem blight, and powdery mildew. Apply labeled fungicides if necessary to control these problems and remove and destroy any plants that become infected. Crop rotation also helps to control the spread of soilborne disease.

RECOMMENDED CULTIVARS: Squashes, pumpkins, and gourds belong to the cucurbit family but are not always called by their accurate names. The so-called summer squashes *(C. pepo),* including bush-type summer crooknecks, straightnecks, pattypans, pumpkins and vining gourds, can cross with one another. If you grow pumpkins and summer squash in your garden, don't save the seeds. 'Black Beauty' is an early, prolific, tender zucchini. 'Yellow Crookneck' is an easy-to-grow heirloom favorite. 'Golden Scallopini Bush' is a productive pattypan squash that can be eaten fresh or stored like a winter squash for later use. 'Sunburst Scallop' is a good pattypan for small gardens. 'Cornell's Bush Delicata' is an early-maturing, disease-resistant green-and-cream-striped squash with flesh similar to that of sweet potato. Only the flesh is eaten, like a winter squash, and the plant is open pollinated, so you can save the seed. Spaghetti squash is another *C. pepo* type eaten like a winter squash. Spaghetti squashes are so-called because the cooked flesh can be raked out in slender ribbons with the tines of a fork and served as a pasta substitute. To save space in the garden, try 'Tivoli', a bush-type cultivar. In warm climates try chayote squash,

Acorn squash cultivars grow on sprawling vines or compact bushes.

or mirliton *(Sechium edule),* which grows on a perennial vine. The small, pear-shaped fruits are white to light green, smooth or wrinkled, and prickly but contain only one seed, like an avocado. Cook them as you would summer squash.

Bottle gourd *(Lagenaria siceraria)* is a cucurbit with night-blooming white flowers. The tan or brown skin hardens into a tough shell as the fruits mature. They can be eaten like summer squash if picked when they are less than 6" long. They can tolerate a light frost but take much longer to cure than other gourds. Yellow-flowered cucurbita gourds have colorful hard shells and are popular in autumn centerpieces. Grow them as you would winter squash, but soak the hard

Pumpkins, gourds, and squashes all belong to the same family.

Use black plastic mulch to warm the soil before planting.

PUMPKIN, SUMMER & WINTER SQUASH
continued

Summer squashes *(C. pepo),* such as this yellow zucchini, are the immature fruits of true pumpkins.

seeds overnight before planting to hasten germination. Because they are lighter weight than other squashes, they are ideal for growing on a fence or trellis. Leave them on the vines to ripen, but pick them before any possibility of frost. Then wipe them clean and let them dry in a warm room with good air circulation, which can take from a week to several months depending on the size of the gourd. Gardeners can grow *Luffa acutangula,* a cucurbit vine with fruits somewhat similar to okra. The small, immature fruits can be cooked as a vegetable but are more often left on the vine to full maturity, when they are brown and dry. The large fruits are then soaked in water until the peel can be removed and the seeds emptied through a cut in one end. What remains is a scratchy sponge substitute perfect for use in the shower or bathtub.

True squashes are called winter squashes and include the very large orange-skinned cultivars grown for pumpkin contests. 'Big Max' *(C. maxima)* and 'Atlantic Giant' are known for their size, but their stems are soft and they do not make good jack-o'-lanterns. 'Rouge Vif d'Estampes' is a flattened, heavily creased, deep red-orange type sometimes sold as 'Cinderella' pumpkin. For small spaces, try 'Small Sugar', which grows to only 8 pounds. Other *C. maxima* types include hubbards, which come in a variety of colors, such as 'Red Kuri' and 'True Green Improved'. For a distinctive two-tiered, colorful squash, try 'Turk's Turban'. For acorn squashes, try *C. pepo* 'Table

Zucchini flowers are a culinary delicacy served sautéed or deep-fried.

Harvest crooknecks when they are no more than 7" long for best flavor.

Queen' (vine) and 'Table King' (bush). *C. moschata* 'Puritan' and 'Zenith' are good butternuts. 'Sweet Mama' is a tasty buttercup. 'Blue Banana' and 'Jumbo Pink Banana' have dry, sweet flesh.

Southern gardeners grow 'Green Striped Crookneck Cushaw' *(C. mixta)* for its tasty pumpkin seeds, but the pale creamy yellow-orange flesh is perfect in soups and baked goods. 'Tricolor Cushaw' is attractively streaked with white, green, and orange. 'Japanese Pie' or 'Chinese Alphabet' is a black fruit with white flesh.

Pick pattypans at about 3".

Hand-pollinate blossoms for high yields.

Keep fruits picked to promote new ones.

LEMONGRASS
Cymbopogon citratus sim-boh-POH-gon sy-TRAY-tus

Grow lemongrass as an annual in northern climates where it is not hardy.

ZONES: 9–11
SIZE: 3–6'h × 5–8'w
TYPE: Herbaceous perennial
GROWTH: Average
LIGHT: Full sun
MOISTURE: Average
FEATURES: Edible leaves, essential oil

SITING: Plant 4' apart each direction in full sun, in sandy or other well-draining, fertile, slightly acid soil. Cut back the tops of transplants to about 4" to encourage root growth.

CARE: Maintain plants at the desired size by frequent pruning and harvesting. Divide plants at 4–8 years to restore their vigor. Water in dry climates and periods of drought. Protect plants from frost. Those in Zone 9 may go dormant during the winter; water them occasionally if there has been no rain. Grow lemongrass as an annual in Zones 5–8. Dig a clump to bring indoors for winter use and for a supply of new outdoor plants next spring. Cut a potted plant back to 8" to encourage growth of the bulbous ends and maintain the plant at a manageable size indoors.

PROPAGATION: Grow from root or plant divisions or from side shoots.

Snip leaves near the base or dig whole stalks to use the bulbous ends.

HARVEST: Cut leaves at the base anytime, or dig up a whole section to use the entire stalk. Steep the leaves for an herbal tea or add to soups and stocks as you would bay leaves. The tender white bulbous ends are chopped and used in Asian cuisine and baked goods. The chopped pieces can be frozen for up to a year. Hang leaves upside down in a dark room to dry them for later use. Citral, commercially extracted from the plant's essential oil, is used in perfumes and cosmetics and to flavor soft drinks.

PESTS AND DISEASES: The plant's volatile oils are a natural pesticide that repels insects; they also have natural antimicrobial and antifungal properties.

RECOMMENDED CULTIVARS: East Indian lemongrass (*C. flexuosus*) matures faster and has a higher content of citral. West Indian lemongrass is the type most commonly grown for culinary use. The stalks are more numerous, and the bulbous ends are larger. Citronella (*C. nardus*) is a close relative of lemongrass and the source of citronella oil, used as an insect repellent. Citronella is not edible but can be grown as an ornamental in the garden.

ARTICHOKE
Cynara scolymus SIN-uh-ruh SKOLL-ih-mus

Artichokes, also known as globe artichokes, can be grown as annuals or perennials.

ZONES: 8–10
SIZE: 3–5' h × 4–6'w
TYPE: Herbaceous tender perennial
GROWTH: Average
LIGHT: Full sun
MOISTURE: High
FEATURES: Edible leaf base and flower buds

SITING: After the last frost date, direct-sow with seed that has been soaked for 48 hours and held at 35–40°F for 4 weeks in loose (not shredded) sphagnum moss. Better results are likely with transplants held at 40°F for 2–4 weeks. Artichokes grow best in humid areas where they can receive the required amount of time at temperatures below 50°F. They prefer a deep, fertile, well-drained location. Where grown as perennials, space the plants 3–4' apart in rows 6–10' apart. For use as annuals, space 2–3' apart in rows 3–4' apart.

CARE: Keep seedlings and transplants consistently moist until they are established. Use water-soluble plant food just before planting and again 6–8 weeks later. Feed perennials in subsequent years when they bud in spring. Hot, dry weather may cause the buds to open prematurely. Mulch heavily with compost in summer to maintain soil moisture and with straw to

Harvest immature flower buds when they are 3–4" in diameter.

overwinter plants in Zones 8 and 9. Plants become less productive after the fifth or sixth year; replace with new plants grown from suckers.

PROPAGATION: To obtain suckers for transplanting, cut off shoots from around the base of the parent plant when they are 8–10" long, making sure each has a piece of root attached. Plant the suckers 4" deep at the spacing recommended above.

HARVEST: Cut the edible flower buds when they are still immature and about 3–4" in diameter. After harvesting, prune the entire plant back by one-third to encourage a new crop of buds for fall harvest.

PESTS AND DISEASES: Obtain clean planting stock to avoid transmission of crown and bud decay diseases. Curly dwarf virus causes stunted growth. Botrytis, a fungal disease, can be a problem if humidity and moisture are too high. Choose cultivars developed for resistance to these diseases.

RECOMMENDED CULTIVARS: 'Green Globe Improved' grows best from crown divisions and is the best choice for perennial plants. 'Imperial Star' can be grown from seed and is both heat and cold tolerant.

CARROT
Daucus carota sativus *DAW-kus ka-RO-tuh sa-TY-vus*

Miniature carrots grow well in containers and in gardens with heavy soil.

Cultivars come in a wide variety of shapes, sizes, and colors.

Thinning young carrots gives others a chance to grow larger.

ZONES: NA
SIZE: 6–12"h ×
6–12"w
TYPE: Biennial
grown as annual
GROWTH: Fast to
average

LIGHT: Full sun to
part shade
MOISTURE: High
FEATURES: Edible
taproots and leaves

SITING: Choose a sunny location with loose, fertile, sandy loam that has been worked deeply and raked free of any rocks. Direct-sow carrot seeds in rows 12" apart 2–4 weeks before the last frost date, or in late summer and autumn for winter and spring crops in warm climates. Wet the soil before planting to help keep the tiny seeds from blowing away. Scatter unpelletized seed along a row and cover with ¼" of fine soil. Sow pellets ½" apart and ½" deep. Water again gently with a mist to keep from disturbing the seeds. Rows can be interplanted with lettuces, beans, peas, tomatoes, and peppers. Carrots grow well in raised beds; small cultivars can be grown in containers.
CARE: Keep seeds evenly moist to ensure germination, which can take up to 3 weeks, especially if seeds are pelletized for uniform sowing. If the soil dries between waterings, cover the rows with a layer of burlap to help retain moisture until the seeds germinate; water right through the burlap. Thin seedlings to about 3" apart; plant more seeds if necessary to fill in gaps in rows. Weed carefully by hand between rows to remove competition for moisture and nutrients. After the roots are well established, hoe lightly. Use straw or other organic mulch between rows to retain moisture and minimize weeds, but keep it off the leafy tops.
PROPAGATION: Grow from seed.
HARVEST: Begin pulling carrots as soon as they are at full color. This is also a good way to thin rows to give the remaining carrots a chance to grow larger. In northern zones, wait until after the ground has begun to freeze before digging the rest of the carrots; the cold will increase their

sweet flavor. Carrots can also be overwintered in the ground. Cut off the green tops to about an inch and mulch the plants heavily. In extremely cold-winter areas, use a coldframe as well as mulch. Carrots are low in calories and a good source of Vitamin A. Although they are delicious as crudités and chopped, sliced, or grated raw into salads and slaws, they are actually more nutritious cooked, which makes their calcium available. They can be steamed, grilled, baked, stir-fried, and microwaved or cooked in soups, stews, and stocks. Try them boiled and mashed like potatoes. Many herbs and spices, including dill, chervil, fennel, mint, cumin, and ginger, enhance their flavor. Chop the leafy green tops into soups, casseroles, and stews. When keeping carrots in the refrigerator, cut off the green tops to prevent moisture loss and store in a plastic bag.
PESTS AND DISEASES: None are significant in home gardens.
RECOMMENDED CULTIVARS: For small gardens, containers, or where soil cannot be worked deeply, try 'Kinko',

a 4" minicarrot ready to harvest in 50–55 days, or 'Round Romeo', a petite, smooth-skinned, ball-shaped cultivar about 1–1½" in diameter. It's a good choice for children learning how to garden, and is ready to harvest in 55–60 days. Easy-to-grow, short, early carrots ready in 65–70 days include 'Danvers Half Long', 'Scarlet Nantes', and 'Chantenay' cultivars. 'Oxheart' is a good choice for growing in heavy soil; carrots are 4–5" long and wide and can weigh up to a pound apiece. Sweet 'Napoli' is recommended for fall sowing; 'Ithaca' can be sown summer or fall and is good for juicing or storage. Both grow to about 7" long. For traditional long carrots that are good fresh or stored, grow 'Tendersweet', 'Sugarsnax', or 'Bolero', all ready to harvest in 70–80 days. If your garden soil is deep and loose, try 'Japanese Imperial Long', which holds the world's record for the longest carrot. It will grow to at least a foot long in 90–100 days. 'Yellowstone' is another extra long variety and is bright canary yellow. 'BetaSweet' has maroon skin and an orange interior which makes attractive sticks and slices.

1 To overwinter carrots in the ground, first cut off the green tops.

2 Mulch the carrots with a thick layer of straw for protection over winter.

PERSIMMON

Diospyros spp. *dye-AH-spih-rohs*

Asian cultivars have larger fruits than American types but are less hardy.

ZONES: 5–9
SIZE: 15–60'h × 10–20'w
TYPE: Deciduous tree
GROWTH: Average

LIGHT: Full sun to part shade
MOISTURE: Average
FEATURES: Edible fruits, valuable hardwood

SITING: Persimmons adapt to any fertile soil as long as it drains well. Space trees 20' apart. Choose cultivars according to your climate. Japanese persimmon (*Diospyros kaki*) is hardy to about 10°F but produces larger fruit than American cultivars, which are hardy to –25°F.

CARE: Young trees need consistent moisture to develop properly. Water mature trees in dry climates. Thinning fruit is unnecessary and impractical for large trees but can help to reduce cleanup around smaller trees. Remove any weak or willowy branches in late winter. Prop up fruit-laden branches to prevent breaking. Some types may bear fruit only in alternate years.

PROPAGATION: Graft Oriental cultivars onto American persimmon (*D. virginiana*) rootstock for enhanced cold tolerance.

Thinning isn't necessary but branches heavy with fruit may need supporting.

Propagate American cultivars from bud grafts or root cuttings. Both male and female trees are required for pollination.

HARVEST: Trees begin to bear fruit at 3–6 years in autumn and may be fruitful for many decades. The flesh is bitter and astringent until fully ripe. Frost does not improve or harm the flavor. Eat ripe Japanese persimmons out of hand or cut in half and eat with a spoon, with or without lemon juice or sugar. The fruit tastes best chilled. Add the flesh to salads, ice cream, yogurt, or make it into jams. The puréed pulp is used in baked goods and can be frozen for up to 2 years. Freeze whole ripe fruits or dry for long-term storage.

PESTS AND DISEASES: Persimmons in the home garden are relatively insect free, although birds and raccoons eat the fruit. Keep debris from trees raked and composted to avoid pest infestations.

RECOMMENDED CULTIVARS: 'Early Golden', 'John Rick', and 'Meader' are reliable American cultivars. Japanese types include astringent 'Maru' types and 'Eureka', which become nonastringent when ripe, and nonastringent types 'Fuyu' and 'Great Wall'. 'Gailey' is often planted as a cross-pollinator.

LOQUAT

Eriobotrya japonica *eh-ree-oh-boh-TRY-uh juh-POH-nih-kuh*

Cover ripening fruits with a bag to prevent sunburn and moth infestation. Loquat is also known as Japanese medlar.

ZONES: 8–10
SIZE: 15–30'h × 15–30'w
TYPE: Evergreen tree or shrub
GROWTH: Slow

LIGHT: Full sun to part shade
MOISTURE: High
FEATURES: Fragrant flowers, edible fruits

SITING: Loquats are adaptable to all moderately fertile soils that drain well. Plant them in spring 20–30' apart.
CARE: Apply soluble plant food three times during active growth or use slow-release fruit tree spikes. Mulch with composted manure. Water when flower buds swell

and again several times during harvest season. Thin flowers and fruits to increase the size of remaining fruit. Enclose fruit clusters in paper bags to prevent sunburn (purple staining) in hot climates. Prune after harvest to prevent alternate-year bearing. Weed around young trees by hand and around mature trees with light hoeing.
PROPAGATION: Bud-grafted trees produce fruit most quickly, in 3–5 years.
HARVEST: Loquats typically bloom in fall and fruit in spring. The fruits mature about 90 days after flowering. The best indication of ripeness is full color. Use a clean, sharp

Loquat can be trained as an espalier to save space in the garden and take advantage of extra warmth from the wall.

knife or clippers to cut the fruits; leave their stalks attached to avoid tearing the skin. Store at room temperature for up to 10 days or refrigerate for up to 2 weeks.
PESTS AND DISEASES: Caribbean fruit fly is a problem in Florida; keep the area underneath and around the tree cleared of fallen fruit. Fire blight (Southeast) and pear blight (West) bacteria may infect trees. Remove and destroy any affected branches at least 6" below the visible infection using loppers sterilized between cuts with bleach or rubbing alcohol. Pick off and destroy any caterpillars. Codling moth may be a problem in California; scrape the cocoons off the bark in late winter and spray with dormant oil. Tie the developing fruits in paper bags to prevent moths from laying eggs on them. Spray dormant oil in winter to combat aphids and scales. Cover trees with netting to protect fruit from birds.
RECOMMENDED CULTIVARS: In the southeast, try 'Tanaka', which is partially self-fertile and more cold hardy than average. 'Advance' is a late-fruiting, blight-resistant natural dwarf about 5' tall, often used as a pollinator for other cultivars. In California, 'Golden Red' is popular.

ARUGULA

Eruca sativa eh-ROO-kuh sa-TY-vuh

Arugula, or roquette, is a spicy green often found in mesclun mixes.

ZONES: NA
SIZE: 3–6"h × 3–6"w
TYPE: Annual
GROWTH: Fast

LIGHT: Full sun to part shade
MOISTURE: Average
FEATURES: Edible leaves

SITING: Choose a sunny or partly sunny location with rich, well-drained soil. Direct-sow seed ¼" deep and 1" apart in rows 8–12" apart, or broadcast seed and cover with ¼" of fine soil 4 weeks before the last frost date or in late summer for a fall crop. Sow small amounts once a month for continuous harvest and to replace plants that have bolted during hot weather.

CARE: Thin seedlings to 8" apart when they are 3–4" tall. Protect plants with shade cloth in intense summer sun. Water during dry periods. Sidedress rows with compost or well-rotted manure. Arugula tolerates a light frost but does best if protected under plastic tents or cold frames.

HARVEST: Plants that reach maturity while temperatures are cool have the best flavor. Begin harvesting from the center of the plants 3–6 weeks after sowing, or pull whole plants to thin rows. The youngest leaves have the best sweet-spicy flavor. Use them in salads, on sandwiches, in pesto and salsa, and added to soups and stews just before serving. Store unwashed leaves in plastic bags for up to 2 weeks.

PROPAGATION: Grow arugula from seed.

PESTS AND DISEASES: Use row covers to protect seedlings from beetles that chew on the leaves.

RECOMMENDED CULTIVARS: 'Astro' and 'Runway' are two early, vigorous forms.

1 **Grow arugula in a cold frame for harvest throughout the winter.**

2 **Pick the center leaves or pull whole plants as needed.**

PINEAPPLE GUAVA

Feijoa sellowiana fay-YO-uh sell-oh-ee-AY-nuh

Pineapple guavas have attractive blossoms that develop into fruits that drop to the ground when ripe.

ZONES: 8–11
SIZE: 8–15'h × 8–15'w
TYPE: Evergreen shrub or small tree

GROWTH: Slow
LIGHT: Part shade
MOISTURE: Average
FEATURES: Edible flowers and fruits

SITING: Choose a partially shaded site where the tender fruits will be protected from hot midday sun. *Feijoa* does best in rich organic acid loam that is well drained. Plant large cultivars 15–20' apart.

CARE: *Feijoa* grows well in subtropical climates with low humidity. The flavor of the fruit is improved by cool weather. Some cultivars are more heat tolerant, but all types need watering during extremely hot or dry weather to develop fruit and prevent internal decay. The root system is shallow, so weed by hand or hoe carefully. Use a low-nitrogen fruit plant food at flowering. Prune lightly after harvest to encourage new growth; fruit sets on young wood. Thinning helps air circulate and makes harvesting easier. Remove low-hanging limbs to keep fruit at least 12" off the ground. In mild-winter areas protect from spring frosts.

Plant feijoa where the tree will be shaded from midday sun.

HARVEST: Shrubs propagated by air layering or grafting will fruit the second year, plants grown from seed in the third to fifth year. Fruits drop to the ground when ripe. Almost-mature fruits can be picked and allowed to finish ripening at room temperature but will decay after only a few days. Keep unbruised fruits for up to a week in cool storage.

PROPAGATION: Best grown by air layering or grafting, or from seed.

PESTS AND DISEASES: Scale may cause sooty mold. Use dormant oil in winter if infestations are heavy. Fruit flies are attracted to the strong aroma of ripening fruit. Keep the ground beneath and around the tree cleared of dropped flowers, fruits, and other debris. High humidity may cause fungal infections. Treat with a fungicide labeled for the specific problem.

RECOMMENDED CULTIVARS: If you have room for just one feijoa, plant 'Edenvale Improved Coolidge', a self-fertile cultivar. In warmer climates try 'Pineapple Gem', which matures earlier. It is self-fruitful but bears more heavily if cross-pollinated. In large gardens grow an 'Apollo' and a 'Gemini' together for fruit all season.

FIG

Ficus carica FY-kus KARE-ee-kuh

Wear gloves to handle unripe figs, which exude gummy latex.

ZONES: 7–9
SIZE: 10–30'h × 10–30'w
TYPE: Deciduous tree
GROWTH: Medium
LIGHT: Full sun
MOISTURE: Average
FEATURES: Edible fruits

SITING: Choose a sunny location with well-drained soil. Figs grown for drying do best in sandy soil. Space trees 10–25' apart depending on the cultivar and the soil type. In climates where temperatures fall below 20°F, grow figs in 10- to 15-gallon half barrels or other large containers so you can move them indoors in winter.

CARE: One-year-old cuttings will fruit within a year of transplanting. Shade young trees from hot midday sun. Apply low-nitrogen plant food twice a year to in-ground trees or use slow-release fruit spikes for trees in containers. Water during hot or dry weather to prevent premature fruit drop, but do not allow trees to stand in water. Stop watering after harvest. Prune heavily in fall or winter when trees are dormant to remove buds of the early-season (breba) crop and increase the main crop. Trees are fruitful for up to 15 years.

Insect pollinators enter the open end of the developing flower to pollinate it.

PROPAGATION: Figs are best propagated by cuttings of mature wood. Use rooting hormone and plant cuttings within 24 hours. They may also be started by air layering or seed.

HARVEST: Unripe fruits are gummy with latex which can irritate skin. Wear gloves when working with them. Most cultivars bear two crops each year, with the early (breba) crop producing acid fruits inferior to those of the main crop that follows. Ripe fruits soften and turn downward.

PESTS AND DISEASES: Protect fig trees from root-knot nematodes with a thick layer of mulch, or use a labeled nematicide for serious infestations. Prolonged high humidity or drought may invite scale insects. Scrape them off the bark. Pick off and destroy leaves infected with rust and follow clean cultivation practices.

RECOMMENDED CULTIVARS: 'Celeste' produces one heavy crop of short duration, and rarely produces a breba crop. It is more tolerant of cold than heat. 'Brown Turkey' has a small, early breba crop and a large main crop in midsummer. 'Black Mission' and 'Kadota' cultivars are preferred for dried or candied figs.

FLORENCE FENNEL

Foeniculum vulgare azoricum feh-NIK-yoo-lum vul-GARE-ee az-OR-ik-um

Grow Florence fennel as you would celery, with plenty of plant food.

ZONES: NA
SIZE: 2'h × 1'w
TYPE: Annual
GROWTH: Average
LIGHT: Full sun
MOISTURE: Medium
FEATURES: Edible leaves and bulbs (swollen leaf bases)

SITING: Florence fennel is adaptable to any soil but does best in neutral soil prepared as you would for celery—deep, loose, and heavily amended with organic matter. Direct-sow seed in warm climates ½" deep and 4" apart in rows 18" apart, or start seed indoors 3 weeks before the last frost date and transplant after that date. Like its

relative the carrot, fennel grows well in raised beds.

CARE: Florence fennel grows like celery but forms a broad, bulblike structure where the leaf bases swell at ground level. To provide ample room for the bulbs to grow, thin seedlings to 8" apart. Fennel is frost sensitive and has a tendency to bolt in hot midsummer weather. Water during dry periods to help prevent bolting. Like celery, fennel is a heavy feeder. Use a balanced soluble plant food or sidedress with manure tea every 2 weeks. Mulch

Dig the whole plant when the bulb of the swollen stem is 3" in diameter.

between rows to conserve moisture, keep the soil cool, and combat weeds. When the bulbs reach about 2" in diameter, blanch them by mounding soil or mulch around the entire plant, leaving just the feathery top uncovered.

PROPAGATION: Grow from seed.

HARVEST: The leaves are ready to harvest when they are about 18" tall. Bulbs are fully formed (about 3" in diameter) in 80–100 days. Dig the whole plants at that size and store in the refrigerator until needed; it becomes tough and stringy if left in the ground. Cut off the roots and the tops of the tallest leaves. Pull apart the bulb sections.

PESTS AND DISEASES: No significant problems affect Florence fennel.

RECOMMENDED CULTIVARS: 'Zefa Fino' has a large bulb and is slow to bolt. In northern zones, try 'Orion', which matures in 75–80 days. The perennial herb common fennel (*F. vulgare dulce*) does not form a swollen base and is grown instead for its feathery, anise-flavored foliage and seeds, which are used to flavor cheese, sausage, eggs, cabbage, sauerkraut, liqueurs, and breads.

KUMQUAT
Fortunella margarita *for-tyew-NEL-la mar-guh-REE-tuh*

Many kumquat cultivars are sweet enough to eat straight from the tree.

ZONES: 8–10
SIZE: 6–15'h × 6–15'w
TYPE: Evergreen shrub or small tree

GROWTH: Slow
LIGHT: Full sun
MOISTURE: Average
FEATURES: Fragrant flowers, edible fruits

SITING: Grow in deep, well-drained, acid silty soil in a sunny area protected from strong winds and located where you can water in dry weather. In hot climates, choose a site protected from midday sun. Plant kumquats 8–12' apart, or 5' apart for use as hedges. Some kumquats are thorny, so locate them well back from paths.

CARE: Like citrus, *Fortunella* species need consistently moist soil but should not be held in standing water. On mature trees, prune dead and damaged wood and any branch that interferes with the growth of scaffold limbs. Hedge pruning may be necessary on tightly spaced trees to maintain a manageable shape for harvesting. Pull weeds manually or till lightly. Feed several times a year from late autumn to midspring, increasing the amount of plant food as trees mature. Use foliar sprays to add needed micronutrients.

Plant a kumquat in a container for the deck or patio.

HARVEST: Kumquats are ripe when they are fully colored. Eat unpeeled. Eat 'Nagami' and 'Meiwa' fresh out of hand; 'Marumi' is less sweet and better used for preserving. To store fruits, let them cure for a few days to lose some of their moisture, then dry them or can them in syrup.

PESTS AND DISEASES: Container plants are susceptible to mealybugs. Wash them off with a sharp stream from the hose or spray with insecticidal soap. Kumquats are attacked by common citrus pests, and in unfavorable conditions may be infected by rots, spots, gummosis, and anthracnose.

RECOMMENDED CULTIVARS: *F. margarita* 'Nagami' bears oval yellow-skinned fruit and grows to 15'. It is the most common kumquat, bearing the sweetest fruit in hot summers but also tolerant of light frost. *F. japonica* 'Marumi' bears round orange-skinned fruit and is a better choice for northern zones. *F. japonica* 'Meiwa' is a dwarf but has large, sweet fruits, the best choice for eating fresh. It grows well in containers. Try limequat 'Eustis' or 'Tavares', and orangequat 'Nippon'. All three are well suited to containers.

GARDENING IN CONTAINERS

I f you live in a short-season, cool zone or don't have room for an in-ground garden, you can still grow your own nutritious vegetables and fruits in containers on a patio or balcony. Many vegetable plants are well suited for container growing, including small carrots, bush tomatoes, peppers, bush beans, herbs and salad greens, and bush cucumbers. Dwarf lemon, lime, calamondin, fig, or kumquat trees can be grown in containers indoors in winter and moved outside during the summer. Even strawberries can thrive in pots right outside your back door.

Choose broad containers made of nontoxic materials—window boxes, plastic tubs, gallon buckets, lined whiskey half barrels—because they retain more soil moisture than narrow ones. Pots 6–10" in diameter are the right size for herbs, green onions, lettuces, and other small crops. Containers holding 5 to 15 gallons or more are best for larger plants and small trees. Grow two or three pepper plants in a whiskey half barrel or interplant a tomato with some herbs.

Make sure all containers have drainage holes in the bottom. Cover them with fine-mesh screen or a few shards of broken clay pots; gravel or rocks do not improve drainage, and they make the container heavier. Instead of garden soil, which might be contaminated, use a high-quality potting soil labeled for food crops such as Miracle-Gro Enriched Potting Mix, and mix in some well-rotted compost. Position bare-root plants on enough tamped-down potting mixture so the crown of the plant is slightly below the rim of the container when the roots are touching the soil. Fill in around the plants with more potting mix and water thoroughly, adding more mix to about an inch below the pot rim. For nursery-grown fruits, remove the commercial container and loosen the roots with your fingers or a garden fork. Use a clean knife or scissors to cut away any long roots that have circled the pot. Set the plant in your own container at the same depth as it was in the nursery pot, fill with potting mix to about an inch below the rim, and water thoroughly.

Soil dries out more quickly in containers than in the garden. Water frequently—sometimes every day in hot weather and whenever the soil just beneath the surface is dry—until you see water run out the bottom of the container. Feed twice as often with half as much plant food as you would use for in-ground plants, because container plants are limited to whatever nutrients are in the pots and some may wash out with watering. Container plants are not as cold tolerant as those in the ground, so provide protection or move them indoors at temperatures below 40°F.

STRAWBERRY

Fragaria spp. *fra-GARE-ee-uh*

Choose strawberry cultivars bred for successful growing in your region.

ZONES: 3–10
SIZE: 6"h × 18"w
TYPE: Herbaceous perennial

GROWTH: Average
LIGHT: Full sun
MOISTURE: High
FEATURES: Edible berries

SITING: Choose a warm, sunny, elevated location for adequate surface drainage, preferably in well-drained loam or sandy loam. In areas with heavy soil, plant strawberries in raised beds at least 6" deep. Amend all soils with well-rotted compost or manure. Space plants 18–24" apart in rows 2–4' apart depending on the size of the strawberry bed and how much access you need for maintenance and harvest. Day-neutral types (those that bear fruit regardless of daylength) can be planted closer together. Position plant crowns at the soil surface, then spread out the roots and firm soil over them. Another method is to scoop out a shallow pocket of soil for each plant, make a small mound of soil in

the center with the top of the mound level with the bed level, and place the plant on top of the mound so the roots drape out and over the mound and into the pocket. Cover the roots with soil and water thoroughly after planting. Strawberries can also be planted in containers, such as strawberry pots, which makes maintenance and pest control much easier.

CARE: Keep nursery-bought plants moist and cool until you are able to plant them. If possible, grow a green manure crop such as oats in the location you want strawberries the year before building a bed, especially if your bed is located where sod has grown previously. Till the cover crop under in autumn and begin a program of weed control. Keep the beds free of weeds for maximum yield. Herbicides usually aren't necessary for most home gardens, which can be weeded by hand or with a hoe or tiller.

Begin pinching flowers off of spring-planted strawberries as soon as they develop to encourage plant growth and early formation of runners for new plants. If the bed becomes a solid mat of plants, cut or till 8" open areas between the rows. For everbearing and day-neutral types, pinch off flowers until July 1, then allow the plants to bloom and fruit. In beds with limited space, follow the spaced-row system. Position the runners to develop rows 18–24" wide. When rows are as densely planted as you want them, cut off new runners as they develop. If not kept

in check, runners quickly overtake the bed, forming dense mats that drain energy from everbearing plants, which reduces fruiting. If your growing area is large enough, you can train runners for rows of new plants each year and turn under the oldest rows, a practice that helps to maintain high yields. Day-neutral strawberries put out few runners, so they can be planted anytime and closer together, up to 12" apart in each direction. Remove any runners that do form. In a few years the plants will have multiple crowns and begin to have lower yields. Then you can let runners develop to replace the older plants.

Apply a balanced water-soluble plant food as buds develop; dry plant food particles caught on plants can burn them. Carefully follow label instructions for the product you choose in order to apply the correct rate for the size of your bed. You can also use well-rotted manure around first-year, spring-planted strawberries. Renovate your strawberry bed as soon after harvest as possible to control pests and diseases. Mow or cut the leaves close to the ground but without cutting into the crowns. Till or cut back the edges of the rows to about 12" wide. Continue weeding and apply a broadleaf herbicide, if necessary, after harvest and again when the plants are dormant. Apply a balanced water-soluble plant food to help bud formation for next season. Keep weeding until the plants are dormant and the

Rake off mulch in early spring so the ground warms up quickly and drains well.

Berries are ripe when they attain full color, regardless of size.

STRAWBERRY
continued

1 Renovate beds after harvest by mowing the leaves close to the ground.

2 Then till between rows to trim plants and control weeds.

3 Apply a broadleaf herbicide and balanced plant food, then mulch well.

ground has begun to freeze, then mulch for winter with clean straw. Remove the mulch in early spring so the ground can warm up and drain well. Install row covers to discourage pests. Protect plants from late-spring frosts with mulch and row covers.

PROPAGATION: Grow from runners.

HARVEST: Begin harvesting most types of strawberries the year after planting—about 14 months from planting in northern zones and 9 months in the South. Highest yields will come from the youngest plants. Berries will be ready to pick about a month after the plants bloom. Day-neutral plants will be ready to harvest about 90 days after planting. Berries are ripe when they attain full color for their cultivar, regardless of size. Ripe berries left on the plants will quickly become overripe and start to decay, which attracts pests, so take all the ripe berries each time you pick. Pick berries as often as every other day. Pinch the stems between your thumbnail and forefinger, leaving the leaf cap and short stem attached. Store unwashed berries in the refrigerator for up to a week. Enjoy fresh berries out of hand; sliced, sugared, and served with milk or cream; in salads and on breakfast cereal; and as the essential ingredient in strawberry shortcake. Use them in pies and other baked goods; for juice, jam, jelly, and marmalade; and added to ice cream, yogurt, and smoothies. Freeze strawberries for up to a year for use in cooked recipes.

PESTS AND DISEASES: Purchase new plants guaranteed to be disease free rather than taking runners from a friend's yard that might be contaminated with insects or viruses. Strawberries are particularly susceptible to botrytis fruit rot (gray mold), leaf spot, and leaf scorch. All can be controlled with fungicides, clean cultivation practices, and attention to soil drainage.

To control gray mold, apply fungicide every 10 days for as long as the weather is wet after the plants bloom. Strawberries are also susceptible to red stele root rot and verticillium wilt. Plants infected with red stele have roots with a rotted-looking red core. Avoid root rot by purchasing resistant cultivars and plants guaranteed to be disease free. If plants become infested, till them under after harvest and do not plant strawberries again in that location or anywhere that Solanaceae crops (tomatoes, peppers, potatoes, and eggplant) or other berries, melons, or roses have been planted. To avoid wilt, purchase resistant plants and use row covers to keep temperatures around the plants too high for fungi to survive. Root weevils may be a problem in some areas. Remove and destroy damaged plants after harvest and rotate the next crop of strawberries to another area. Clean cultural practices discourage sap beetles, which are attracted to damaged and decaying fruit. Regularly remove overripe or rotting fruit and any vegetative debris from the bed and compost it. Use row covers to discourage tarnished plant bugs. Aphids and spider mites can be washed off by hard rains or watering. If you must use a pesticide, do not apply when plants are blooming or fruiting. Use bait or traps for snails and slugs. Cover plants with tunnels made from chicken wire to keep rabbits, birds, chipmunks, and raccoons from eating the fruit.

RECOMMENDED CULTIVARS: Strawberries are cultivated to succeed in specific climates and conditions. Select cultivars bred for your locale. *F. ×ananassa* includes June-bearing, everbearing, and day-neutral strawberries. Everbearing strawberries do not actually fruit all season, especially in hot climates. They produce heavily in spring, sporadically or not at all

during the summer, then again in late summer or early autumn, although generally not as prolifically as in spring. Pinch flowers off of spring-planted everbearers until July 1. Early spring-bearing cultivars include 'Earliglow', which has good flavor but modest yields; 'Northeaster', a heavier producer with a slightly grape aftertaste; and 'Avalon', a vigorous producer of large dark red berries. In northern zones, try the Canadian strain of 'Mohawk', which is resistant to red stele. In Southern California, 'Sequoia' may bear as early as December, and 'Douglas' produces large berries in early spring. For midseason berries, grow 'L'Amour' or 'Mesabi', best for eating fresh. 'Northwest' is a late midseason berry in the Pacific Northwest, good fresh or preserved. 'Shasta' is a fairly vigorous cultivar for California growing. For late-season berries, 'Clancy', 'Winona', 'Sparkle', 'Delite', and 'Marlate' are all good choices. Try 'Ozark Beauty' in northern zones. With plastic mulch and row covers, 'Quinault' can be grown as an annual in Alaska. Day-neutral strawberries flower and fruit anytime temperatures are between 40 and 80°F. You can allow them to fruit in the planting year. 'Tribute' and 'Tristar' are the most commonly grown cultivars. Their fruits are smaller and less prolific than other cultivars, but they are disease resistant and provide crops when other strawberries are not producing. 'Seascape' is a popular cultivar in California and can be grown elsewhere as an annual. Alpine strawberry (*F. vesca*)—a small-fruited berry much like wild strawberry—is a day-neutral type. Most alpine varieties are propagated from seed and often grown as ornamental plants. 'Improved Rugen' is hardy and produces no runners. It fruits heavily even in late summer, tolerates some shade, and grows well in containers.

SOYBEAN
Glycine max   *GLY-seen max*

Like other legumes, soybeans are cultivated for use fresh and dried.

ZONES: NA
SIZE: 12–24"h ×
12–24"w
TYPE: Annual
GROWTH: Average

LIGHT: Full sun
MOISTURE: Average
FEATURES: Edible
seeds (beans)

SITING: Soybeans are adaptable to many soil types but do not tolerate standing water. They do best in neutral to slightly acid, well-drained, warm soil. Use black plastic to warm the soil for a few weeks in advance of planting in short-season areas. Direct-sow seeds that have been soaked overnight and inoculated with bacteria to fix nitrogen in the roots. Plant them 1½" deep in moist soils and 2" deep in dry soils in hot climates, 2" apart in rows 24–30" apart. In raised beds they can be planted 12" apart in both directions.

CARE: Soybeans are cultivated much like other legumes. Thin 3" seedlings to 4" apart and mulch to conserve soil moisture. Keep the soil consistently moist until pods have set. Weed by hand or lightly with a hoe, but avoid working among plants when they are wet to prevent injury and the spread of disease. Too much nitrogen interferes with production of pods and seeds. Protect from frost damage.

Soak seeds overnight and inoculate them with rhizobial bacteria.

PROPAGATION: Grow from seed.
HARVEST: For use as fresh beans, pick the pods as you would pick shelling peas—when they are filled out and still green. Steam them for a few minutes to make hulling easier. To store soybeans dried, wait to harvest them until the pods are dry but not split open. Dried soybeans are cooked like navy beans or processed into soymilk, flour, miso paste, or the meat substitutes tofu and tempeh. Dried soybeans can be stored in airtight containers for many years.

PESTS AND DISEASES: Bacterial blight is common in prolonged cool, rainy weather and can be made worse if too much nitrogen is present in the soil. Remove and destroy any infected plants. Japanese beetles will visit soybeans. Handpick the beetles if they are numerous. Cutworms, white grubs, grasshoppers, and other legume-loving pests may cause some plant damage, but infestations in the home garden are usually not severe.

RECOMMENDED CULTIVARS: 'Vinton', 'Envy', and 'Butterby' grow well in all areas. Field soybeans are not suitable as a vegetable.

JERUSALEM ARTICHOKE
Helianthus tuberosus   *hee-lee-AN-thus too-bur-OH-sus*

Jerusalem artichokes, also known as sunchokes, are sunflower relatives, not artichokes and not from Jerusalem.

ZONES: 4–10
SIZE: 2–8'h × 1–4'w
TYPE: Herbaceous
perennial
GROWTH: Average
but invasive

LIGHT: Sun to part
shade
MOISTURE: Average
FEATURES: Edible
tubers, attractive
flowers

SITING: Plant Jerusalem artichoke outside the vegetable garden in a permanent area where you can control its spread or allow it to grow freely. Although it is not fussy about location, loose, well-drained, acid soil gives it the best start. Plant entire tubers or pieces that each contain an "eye." Plant them 4" deep and 18" apart in a single row at the back of a bed or along a fence 2–4 weeks before the last frost date, or as soon as the soil can be worked. In southern zones plant tubers in fall for a spring crop. Mature plants benefit from a windbreak.

CARE: Keep the soil consistently moist until plants are established and remove weeds by hand. Tubers sprout 1–3 weeks after planting. Each tuber sends up multiple stalks, which will eventually crowd out most weeds. Cut off the flower heads the first year to help keep energy in the tubers.

Harvest the edible tubers in autumn after the soil is cold.

Mulch plants in summer to conserve soil moisture or for protection during severe winters.

PROPAGATION: Grow by division.
HARVEST: Jerusalem artichoke is not from Jerusalem and is not an artichoke but a type of sunflower grown for its edible tubers, which can be sliced raw into salads, steamed or sautéed as a vegetable, or cooked like potatoes. You can harvest tubers anytime after the soil has cooled in late autumn. In northern zones wait until the foliage has turned brown and the ground has begun to freeze before digging the tubers. The cold improves their sweet, nutty taste. Dig the whole plant with a garden fork; tubers that remain in the soil will become next year's plants. Dig only what you will use within a few days; tubers stored in the refrigerator are not as tasty as those freshly dug. Brush off the dirt and clean the tubers thoroughly under cold water with a scrubbing brush. Peeling is unnecessary.

PESTS AND DISEASES: None significant.
RECOMMENDED CULTIVARS: 'Stampede' and 'Mammoth French White' are vigorous producers in all climates.

SWEET POTATO

Ipomoea batatas *ip-oh-MEE-uh bah-TAH-tas*

Sweet potatoes, often confused with yams, can be grown as annuals.

ZONES: NA
SIZE: 12–30"h × 12–24"w
TYPE: Perennial herbaceous bush or vine usually grown as an annual

GROWTH: Average
LIGHT: Full sun to part shade
MOISTURE: Average
FEATURES: Edible tuberous roots

SITING: Moderately deep, friable, slightly acid, sandy loam is best. Plant sweet potato slips 3–4 weeks after the last frost date 12–18" apart in rows 48" apart for vining plants and 30" apart for bush types. Water with 4-12-4 starter solution to prevent transplant shock.

CARE: Cutting the vines while they are growing will cause the roots to sprout. Keep the soil consistently moist for proper growth and to avoid root cracks. If soil is poor, sidedress plants once with a low-nitrogen plant food. Sweet potatoes are drought tolerant for short periods. Avoid planting them in the same place more than once every 3 or 4 years to prevent soilborne diseases.

PROPAGATION: Grow from rooted slips.

HARVEST: Dig carefully, loosening the soil with a garden fork to avoid injuring the roots. Cure sweet potatoes for 2–3 weeks in a warm, humid area. Store cured roots wrapped in newspaper in a dry location at 55–60°F. Do not store in the ground or the refrigerator; they are injured by chilling.

PESTS AND DISEASES: Diseases are more common in soil that is not acid enough. Purchase certified disease-free slips for planting. Use row covers to protect young plants from flea beetles and cutworms. Overwatering may attract root weevils.

RECOMMENDED CULTIVARS: 'Centennial' is a popular cultivar that is susceptible to rots. 'Allgold' has moist salmon-colored flesh and is resistant to stem rot. Choose bush types, such as 'Vardaman' and 'Porto Rico', for small gardens and containers.

Harvest sweet potato when the vines are frosted.

Cut away the damaged foliage tops first.

Then dig the tubers with a garden fork.

WALNUT

Juglans spp. *JUG-lanz*

Plant walnut trees away from other crops whose growth they might inhibit.

ZONES: 4–9
SIZE: 60–100'h × 60–100'w
TYPE: Deciduous tree
GROWTH: Average

LIGHT: Full sun
MOISTURE: Average
FEATURES: Edible nuts (seeds), oil from fruit flesh, hardwood

SITING: Choose a sunny site with deep, fertile, well-drained, slightly alkaline soil. *Juglans* species secrete juglone in their tissues, which inhibits the growth of many other plants. Black walnut (*J. nigra*) and butternut (*J. cineria*) are particularly toxic to roses, potatoes, tomatoes, eggplant, and peppers, as well as pine and apple trees.

CARE: Keep the soil consistently moist until the trees are established, and for mature trees during dry spells. Prune the limbs to a central leader with lateral branches at least 18" apart. Examine trees regularly for signs of pests and diseases and treat problems immediately. Use foliar sprays to add needed minerals such as copper, zinc, manganese, and boron.

PROPAGATION: Named cultivars are bud-grafted to a rootstock.

HARVEST: Black walnuts drop while still in the husk, which is difficult to remove. Cut the husks off with a sharp knife or crush them underfoot—but wear gloves and stay off of pavement, because the husks stain everything they touch. After hulling, rinse nuts with a garden hose and spread on shallow trays two or three nuts deep. Place the trays in a cool, dry, well-ventilated area out of direct sun for 2 weeks to cure the nuts. Store fresh nutmeats in a glass jar or plastic bag for up to 6 months in the refrigerator, or up to 1 year in the freezer.

PESTS AND DISEASES: Walnut is prone to many blights and fungi, especially when stressed by improper culture and high heat. Choose cultivars that are disease resistant and bred for your climate. Walnut anthracnose defoliates trees in summer and blackens the nut kernels. Darker than usual husks may be a sign of insect damage. Aphids, scales, worms, caterpillars, flies, fall webworms, curculios, maggots, and twig girdlers can all be problems.

RECOMMENDED CULTIVARS: Some English or Persian walnuts (*J. regia*) are not self-fertile and thus need cross pollination. Self-fruitful 'Buccaneer' and 'Broadview' form large nuts. 'Rita' is a smaller self-fertile cultivar good for ornamental use. 'Carpathian' is extremely cold tolerant.

Drive over the tough husks to crush them open.

Wear gloves to avoid the dark pigment in husks.

LETTUCE

Lactuca sativa lak-TOO-kuh suh-TY-vuh

Grow heat-tolerant bibb lettuce for spring and autumn harvests.

Serve early-season butterhead lettuce whole as an individual salad.

Iceberg and other crisphead lettuces require a long, cool growing season.

ZONES: NA
SIZE: 2–10"h × 2–8"w
TYPE: Annual
GROWTH: Fast

LIGHT: Sun to part shade
MOISTURE: High
FEATURES: Edible leaves

Sow romaine in a cold frame for fresh lettuce until winter.

Interplant leaf lettuces among taller crops that provide shade.

SITING: Start head lettuce indoors 6 weeks before the last frost date and transplant outdoors 3 weeks before it. Direct-sow other lettuces in early spring or fall. Choose a site with loose, fertile, slightly acid, sandy loam amended with well-rotted manure or compost and raked free of any dirt clods and rocks. Sow in wide rows or broadcast and cover with ¼" of fine soil.

CARE: Thin seedlings to 4–8" apart, or 12" apart for head lettuces, in rows 18" apart. Pull weeds by hand or hoe lightly to avoid disturbing the shallow roots. Keep the soil consistently moist but not waterlogged. Mulch the rows with organic matter to keep the soil cool and moist. Make successive plantings for prolonged harvest. Seedlings will tolerate a light frost.

PROPAGATION: Grow from seed.

HARVEST: Leaf lettuce is the fastest-growing type and can be picked when the leaves are as small as 2". Take leaves from the outside of the plants so new leaves will continue to form. When leaves are 4-6", pull the entire plant before it becomes tough and bitter. Pick outside leaves of butterhead and romaine or cut the entire head about an inch above the soil surface. A new head may grow. Pick head lettuce when the center is firm.

PESTS AND DISEASES: Purchase seeds or plants from seeds pretreated with fungicide to prevent damping off and downy mildew. Thin plants to the appropriate spacing to help prevent botrytis. Plants grown in raised beds are less susceptible to root rots and leaf drop. Handpick beetles and caterpillars; use row covers to protect seedlings from infestations. Wash away aphids with a strong stream from the hose.

RECOMMENDED CULTIVARS: Head lettuces need a long growing period in cool weather. They are the most difficult type to grow at home. 'Ithaca' is a heat-tolerant cultivar slow to bolt. 'Sierra' is an iceberg type that grows best in cool coastal areas. 'Rouge de Grenoblouse' is a loose crisphead type that matures quickly and is bolt resistant. For early-season butterhead lettuce, try 'Boston' or 'Four Seasons'. 'Buttercrunch' and 'Summer Bibb' are heat-tolerant types for late spring and autumn. 'Bronze Mignonette' has frilly red-edged leaves and does well in hot climates. 'Tom Thumb' is a fast-maturing miniature bibb lettuce 3–5" tall. It interplants well and each plant can be served whole as an individual salad. Plant 'Winter Marvel' or 'North Pole' in autumn; they will overwinter with protection in mild climates. The looseleaf lettuces 'Salad Bowl', 'Oakleaf', and 'Red Deer Tongue' are heat tolerant but do best planted in the shade of taller crops, such as tomatoes. 'Black Seeded Simpson' is a good choice for early-season lettuce. 'Red Sails' has crinkly leaves with burgundy edges and is slow to bolt. Romaine types grow best in cool weather. 'Little Gem' is a 5–7" cultivar good for small gardens. Plant hardy 'Paris Island Cos' and red-tinged 'Rouge d'Hiver' in fall and protect them in a cold frame for lettuce until winter.

Snip individual leaves as needed for salads and sandwiches.

Pull entire plants by hand to avoid disturbing nearby plants' shallow roots.

GARDEN CRESS

Lepidium sativum lep-ih-DEE-um suh-TY-vum

Peppery garden cress is related to mustard greens. It is also known as peppergrass, curly cress, or broadleaf cress.

ZONES: NA
SIZE: 3–12"h × 6"w
TYPE: Annual
GROWTH: Fast

LIGHT: Full sun to part shade
MOISTURE: High
FEATURES: Edible leaves and stems

SITING: Direct-sow anytime indoors in pots and keep in a bright location. Or broadcast in the garden, in a windowbox, or in a container in spring and autumn, and cover with a ¼" layer of fine soil. A small area—no more than 1–2' square—provides a lot of leaves. Garden cress does best in fertile, well-drained soil or potting mix to which well-rotted compost has been added. Interplant it with carrots, radishes, and lettuces.

CARE: Thin seedlings to 6" apart when they are 3" tall; use the thinnings in salads. Hand-weed to avoid disturbing shallow roots. Keep the soil continuously moist. Garden cress will bolt under moisture and heat stress. Leaves become bitter above 85°F. In hot climates protect from midday sun.
PROPAGATION: Grow from seed.
HARVEST: Seedlings are ready to thin in as little as 2 weeks. Cut or pull entire clumps when they are no more than 6" tall (about 2–4 weeks after seeding) for the best flavor and texture. Snip them into salads and use as garnishes. Garden cress is related to mustard; the leaves have a peppery aroma and taste. Cut plants will regrow, but make

Protect curly cress from hot midday sun for best foliage and flavor.

successive plantings of new seed for a continuous supply until frost.
PESTS AND DISEASES: Garden cress has no significant problems. Use row covers if insects bother young plants.
RECOMMENDED CULTIVARS: Like parsley, garden cress comes in flat and curly types. 'Cressida' and 'Persian' have flat leaves and are sometimes marketed as peppercress, although they are not of that species (*L. virginicum*). 'Wrinkled Crinkled' is a bolt-resistant curly type that looks like parsley. 'Presto' is a small, ruffled cultivar bred to taste like watercress. Although watercress (*Nasturium officinale*) is grown and used in much the same way as garden cress, it is not related. Plant it at the edge of a pond or stream where it can get some shade and the constant moisture it requires to thrive, or grow it in containers that you can set inside pans of water. Snip leaves or pull whole plants for use in salads, sandwiches, and soups. Another fast-growing plant with peppery leaves good in salads is nasturtium (*Tropaeolum majus*), sometimes called Indian cress. It is usually grown for its colorful flowers, which are also edible. Unlike garden cress and watercress, nasturtium grows best in poor soil and full sun.

LOVAGE

Levisticum officinale leh-VIS-tih-kum off-fih-sih-NAH-lay

Use lovage's tender leaves and stems in place of celery.

ZONES: 3–7
SIZE: 2–4'h × 2–4'w
TYPE: Herbaceous perennial
GROWTH: Average

LIGHT: Full sun to part shade
MOISTURE: High
FEATURES: Edible seeds, leaves, and stalks; essential oil

SITING: Direct-sow seed after the last frost date in deep, fertile, consistently moist soil, or start indoors or in cold frames 4 weeks before the last frost date. Transplant seedlings when they are 3–6" tall to

4' apart or use just a few plants as ornamentals at the back of perennial flower beds.
CARE: Keep the soil consistently moist and water during high heat or periods of drought. Remove flowers as they appear to stimulate growth of leaf stalks, or let some flowers develop so you can collect the dried seed. Lovage will self-sow if flowers

Use the leaves as an herb or harvest whole stalks for use as a vegetable.

go to seed. To collect seed, cut the seedheads with an inch of stalk attached and hang them upside down in bunches in paper bags to catch the seeds. Mulch lovage for overwintering in cold climates.
PROPAGATION: Grow from seed or by division in spring.
HARVEST: Lovage is ready to use about 90 days after sowing. Pick the tender leaves and stalks anytime during the growing season and use fresh in salads. Blanch the leaf stalks as a vegetable side dish, or chop the stems and use in cooking as you would celery. The leaves can be dried or frozen for use within 1 year. The dried seeds are used in pickles.
PESTS AND DISEASES: Lovage contains a highly aromatic essential oil that naturally repels insects. Maintain adequate space between plants to help avoid blights. If any stems rot or leaves turn yellow or reddish, pull and destroy the whole plant and sow seed in a new location.
RECOMMENDED CULTIVARS: Lovage is marketed under its common name.

LYCHEE

Litchi chinensis LEE-chee chi-NEN-sis

Lychees are ripe when they reach their full cultivar color of red, pink, or amber. Litchi is a variant spelling of this plant.

ZONES: 9–11
SIZE: 30–100'h × 30–100'w
TYPE: Evergreen tree
GROWTH: Slow

LIGHT: Full sun
MOISTURE: High to average
FEATURES: Edible fruits

SITING: Lychee grows best where summers are hot and wet and winters are cool and dry without frost. It is adaptable to a wide range of soils, including clay and alkaline ones, and can tolerate brief flooding but not salinity. It does best in deep alluvial loam with high acidity. Space trees at least 40' apart and 40' away from other trees and structures that might shade them.

CARE: Protect young trees from wind and high heat. Prune them to a central leader and remove any low and acute-angle branches. Add plant food to the planting hole and feed once a year until the tree is large enough to bear fruit, then feed only immediately after harvest. Bearing trees need less phosphorus than developing trees. Lychees require insects for good pollination, primarily honeybees, so avoid using pesticides. Water during hot months. Heavy rain or fog and hot, dry winds during flowering can cause blossom drop and splitting of fruit. Shaded portions of a tree will not bear fruit. Too much nitrogen causes fruits to crack.

PROPAGATION: Grow it by air layering.

HARVEST: Air-layered trees fruit 2–5 years after planting and will bear for many decades. Fruits mature 4–5 months after flowering. Harvest every few days over a period of a few weeks. Yields vary with environmental conditions, cultivar, tree age, cultural practices, and availability of pollinators. Fruits are ripe when they reach the full cultivar color. The aromatic oval fruits are red, pink, or amber and look like strawberries hanging in clusters. The swelling of maturing fruit causes the warty bumps on the skin to flatten out somewhat. Clip clusters with some stem and leaves attached; pulling fruit will break the skin. Use a pruning pole to clip clusters overhead.

Fresh flesh is white, grayish white, or pinkish white and juicy. The seed comes out easily and is not edible. Lychee dries naturally; the skin turns brown and brittle and the flesh turns dark brown and wrinkly. The dried flesh is dark and rich, similar to a large raisin. Eat lychees fresh out of hand or peeled and pitted and added to salads, baked goods, and sherbet. Store fresh fruits in a cool, dry location with good air circulation to prevent rotting. They hold their color and quality for just a few days. Refrigerate them for up to 2 weeks, or freeze them whole after peeling and seeding. Thaw frozen lychees in tepid water and eat immediately before they discolor. To dry lychees, hang them up or layer them in mesh trays and store in a cool, dry area. To hasten the process, use a drying oven or a regular oven at low temperature. Dried lychees can be stored in tightly sealed containers at room temperature for up to a year.

PESTS AND DISEASES: Lychees are susceptible to algal leaf spot, leaf blight, dieback, and mushroom root rot. Avoid planting them where oak trees once grew. Birds, bats, and bees can damage ripe fruits. Raccoons and rodents are attracted to the aroma of ripe fruit. Use netting if necessary to protect the fruit from invaders. Grasshoppers, katydids, and crickets may eat the foliage. Other damaging insects include stinkbugs, borers, aphids, scale, and twig-pruners.

RECOMMENDED CULTIVARS: Some lychees leak juice when the skin is broken. Those that don't are most desirable and are referred to as "dry and clean." 'Brewster', 'Peerless', and 'Bengal' withstand light frosts and are good choices in Florida. They fruit midseason. In Hawaii 'Kaimana', 'Kwai Mi', and 'Groff' are popular cultivars that fruit in August and September. 'Groff' and 'Kwai Mi' (or 'Mauritius') are also popular in California, along with 'Amboina', which ripens in spring.

TOMATO

Lycopersicon esculentum ly-ko-PER-si-con es-kew-LEN-tum

Plant early season cultivars for harvest while other types are still growing.

ZONES: NA
SIZE: 8–72"h × 8–36"w
TYPE: Annual
GROWTH: Average

LIGHT: Full sun
MOISTURE: High
FEATURES: Edible fruit

SITING: Tomatoes are adaptable to many soil types but grow best in deep, highly fertile, well-drained, slightly acid, loamy soil. Work the soil thoroughly before planting, amending it with well-rotted compost or manure. Although tomato seed can be sown directly into the garden, most home gardeners purchase transplants for a head start on the growing season. Seed can be started indoors in greenhouse conditions 6–10 weeks before the planting date. Plant seedlings in a sunny location after the last frost date. Plant 1½–2' apart for small bush tomatoes and 3–4' apart for larger types if not staked. Add a handful of well-rotted compost to each hole as you plant. Water thoroughly and use a starter plant food. In cool zones warm the soil with black plastic before setting out plants.

CARE: In hot climates new transplants may need to be shaded until they are established. Protect them from strong or cold winds. Add stakes or cages at planting time to avoid injuring roots later. Training indeterminate plants up stakes or growing them inside stiff wire cages elevates the foliage for better air circulation and holds the fruits off the ground. Also, caged tomatoes tend to be more productive. Make sure that openings in cages are large enough to reach through for harvest and that stakes are at least 8' tall, 1" in diameter, and of sturdy wood or metal. Sink each stake at least 1' deep and about 4" away from the plant. Begin tying the stem to the stake when the terminal end is tall enough to droop over toward the ground. Use strips of soft cloth or garden

TOMATO
continued

Midseason tomatoes are great for slicing fresh or cooking.

Yellow tomatoes are higher in sugar than red ones but don't keep as well.

1 Add a handful of well-rotted compost to each hole as you plant.

2 Plant leggy transplants deeply in a trench. New roots will form on the stem.

3 Stakes and cages promote air circulation and keep fruits off the ground.

twine to tie the stems in figure-eight loops so that they are not in contact with the stakes. Check staked indeterminate plants regularly for suckers—side branches that form in the joints where leaves join the stems—and pinch them out just beyond the first two leaves that develop. Do not prune determinate tomatoes. Tomatoes need plenty of water to develop juicy fruits and maintain resistance to disease. Use organic mulch around plants to control weeds and conserve soil moisture, especially during midsummer. Feed with a water-soluble tomato plant food such as Miracle-Gro Water Soluble Tomato Plant Food, according to package directions. Feed plants grown in containers with

tomato plant food according to package directions or use a potting mix with plant food already in the mix.

PROPAGATION: Grow from seed.

HARVEST: Begin picking tomatoes when they have reached full cultivar size and color. Tomatoes will continue ripening off the plant and even in the dark. The pigments that give fruits their distinctive color do not develop well in high temperatures, so tomatoes harvested during midsummer may have more yellow coloration than in cooler weather. Pick any fruits remaining on the vine when the first autumn frost is predicted. Green tomatoes can be fried or pickled. Those that have even a hint of yellow may continue to ripen if held in a dark, warm location (about 65°F) in single layers between sheets of newspaper. Check them once a week or so for ripe fruits, and remove any tomatoes that are decayed or show no signs of ripening. Another method is to pull up whole plants and hang them upside down in a cool area, where fruits can continue to ripen on the vine. Once

picked, ripe fruits can be stored for up to another 2 weeks at 55°F. They also can be stored in the refrigerator but will not taste as good as those stored at cool room temperature. Tomatoes are high in vitamins A, C, and K. They also contain lycopene, a powerful antioxidant. Enjoy fresh tomatoes right off the vine, in salads, on sandwiches, and cooked in soups, stews, and casseroles. Use them fresh or cooked in salsas and slow-cooked into tomato sauce and catsup. Many cooks immerse tomatoes in almost-boiling water for 30–60 seconds, depending on fruit skin thickness, to remove the peel. Use only firm, fully ripe tomatoes for canning. Low-acid tomatoes, which are actually higher in sugar than they are lower in acid, are safe to can as long as they are ripe.

PESTS AND DISEASES: Tomatoes are susceptible to a wide variety of diseases and physiological disorders caused by environmental stress. Choose cultivars bred for resistance to disease and tolerance of problems common to your geographical area. Among the most common diseases

1 Blossom end rot, a common problem, is a symptom of calcium deficiency.

2 Keeping the soil consistently moist helps to prevent blossom end rot.

3 Add mulch over the soaker hose to conserve soil moisture.

Keep ripe tomatoes picked to encourage more fruits to develop.

TOMATO
continued

are anthracnose, early blight, Septoria leaf spot, tobacco mosaic virus, fusarium wilt, and verticillium wilt. Typical physiological problems include blossom-end rot, caused by moisture extremes; blossom drop, caused by temperature extremes; skin cracking, caused by hot, rainy periods following dry spells; sunscald, caused by overexposure to the sun on one side of the fruit; and catfacing, a puckering and scarring at the blossom end of fruit caused by cool weather or herbicides. Excessive nitrogen, extreme temperatures, dry soil, or too much shade causes poor fruit set. Too much soil moisture can cause blotchy ripening. Puffiness—a condition where the inside of the fruit cavity does not fully develop—can be the result of hot or cold temperature extremes at pollination, too much nitrogen, not enough sun, or too much moisture.

Use cardboard collars around tomato transplants to discourage cutworms. Hand-pick and destroy Japanese beetles and hornworms. Control fruitworms and stinkbugs with a labeled insecticide.

RECOMMENDED CULTIVARS: Determinate tomatoes grow to a genetically predetermined, compact height, then produce clusters of flowers at the growing tip. The plants set fruit along the stem within 2–3 weeks and the fruits ripen almost simultaneously. Tomatoes labeled "semideterminate," "strong determinate," or "vigorous determinate" produce a heavy crop, as do regular determinates, but then can be pruned back for a light second crop in late summer to early autumn. Many paste and early-season tomatoes are determinate. Although many paste tomatoes are good eaten fresh, they are most often used for cooking because of the lower moisture content in the fruit. Indeterminate tomatoes continue to grow throughout the season because the terminal end of the stem produces leaves instead of flowers. New flowers appear continuously along the side shoots and bloom as long as growing conditions are favorable. For a steady supply of tomatoes all season, plant some indeterminate types. To have ripe tomatoes in the shortest amount of time, choose early-season varieties. Late-season cultivars include the types that grow to immense size, but many of those are susceptible to skin cracking. For ornamental value, choose small-fruited types, which can be grown in hanging baskets or patio pots, or grow some of the many varieties bred for unusual colors. Select disease-resistant cultivars developed for your area.

Big beefsteak tomatoes ripen late in the season but are worth the wait.

Choose disease-resistant cultivars developed for use in your region.

DETERMINATE TOMATOES

SMALL FRUITED: 'Tumbler' is a hybrid developed for hanging baskets (50 days). 'Gold Nugget' is an early yellow cherry tomato (55 days). 'Tiny Tim' is a compact plant suitable for flowerpots (60 days). 'Patio' is a popular dwarf hybrid for small gardens or containers (70 days). 'Micro-Tom' produces miniature fruit on plants 5–8" tall (75 days).

EARLY SEASON: New hybrids of 'Bush Early Girl' are small and disease resistant and bear big, flavorful fruit in 55 days. 'Orange Blossom' bears large, mild-flavored orange-yellow tomatoes (60 days). In areas where summer nights are cool, try 'Oregon Spring Bush' (60 days). 'Silvery Fir Tree', a Russian heirloom tomato, does well in overcast coastal areas (60 days). 'Matina' produces small to medium-size fruits in 60 days, but they taste as rich as late-season beefsteak tomatoes. 'Taxi' is a compact grower with sweet bright yellow fruit. It is cold tolerant and adaptable to all soil types (65 days).

MIDSEASON: 'Celebrity' is a disease-resistant midseason cultivar with 7–8-ounce fruits. It does best in areas with consistent moisture (72 days). In the South grow 'Heatwave', which yields best when daytime temperatures are above 90°F (70 days), or 'BHN-444', a high-yielding hybrid with resistance to spotted wilt virus (75 days). 'Sun Chaser' and 'Sunmaster' are flavorful, disease-resistant varieties that also perform well in high heat (75 days). 'Homesweet' and 'Rutgers' are widely adaptable, disease-resistant cultivars

(75 days). 'Shady Lady' is popular in hot climates because its ample foliage protects the fruit from sunscald (75 days). 'Burbank' is an heirloom slicing tomato on a compact plant that needs no support (75 days).

LATE SEASON: 'Bradley' is a favorite canning tomato in southern zones (80 days). 'Ace 55' produces high yields of medium-size tomatoes (80 days). 'Super Bush' bears large, meaty fruit all season but is only 3' tall and wide and requires no stakes or cages (85 days). 'Long-Keeper' lives up to its name, producing long clusters of medium-size light orange-red tomatoes that keep for several months if stored properly after picking (85 days).

PASTE: 'Roma' (75 days) and 'LaRoma' (60 days) have rich, meaty, almost seedless fruits on compact, disease-resistant vines. Use them for cooking. In northern climates try 'Bellstar' (3–4 ounces), developed in Canada or 'Oregon' (6–8 ounces); both are cold-tolerant cultivars bearing full-flavored fruits good fresh or in sauce (60–65 days). 'Ropreco' is ideal for canning and sauces (70–75 days). 'Windowbox' is good for container growing. Its small fruits are good fresh or cooked (70 days). 'Health Kick' is a 4' plant that bears medium-size plum-type tomatoes containing 50 percent more of the antioxidant lycopene than other tomatoes (75 days). 'Jersey Devil' has long, tapered bright red fruits shaped like peppers (80 days).

TOMATO
continued

INDETERMINATE TOMATOES

SMALL FRUITED: 'Grape' is a sweet, early, disease-resistant and heat-tolerant cultivar (55 days). 'Sunsugar' has sugary-sweet bright orange fruit (60 days). 'Sugar Snack' is a cherry-size hybrid that produces high yields all season (65 days). 'Sweet Million' is an improved version of 'Sweet 100', with the same flavor but better resistance to disease (65 days). 'Jolly' is a prolific bearer of extra sweet fruits whose tips are pointed like peaches (70 days). 'Isis Candy' has sweet, cherry-type yellow-gold fruits streaked with red (70 days). 'Red Pear' is less commonly grown than 'Yellow Pear' but is equally good in salads or right off the vine (80 days). 'Ceylon' is a 2" tomato that looks like a miniature beefsteak variety and has a rich, almost spicy flavor (80 days).

EARLY SEASON: 'Early Girl' is a popular early slicing tomato that adapts well to almost any climate and is disease-resistant (55 days). 'Early Cascade' bears clusters of fruits not much larger than cherry types. It provides a steady supply all season (55 days). 'Lime Green Salad' is a small plant with 3–5-ounce tangy chartreuse fruit that add interest to salads. It grows well in containers (60 days). 'Tigerella', sometimes called 'Mr. Stripey', bears big yields of small red tomatoes with clearly defined yellow-orange stripes that look good in salads (60 days). 'Fireworks' and 'Siletz' are the largest red slicing tomatoes available early in the season (60 days). 'Moskvich' produces medium-size fruits that taste as rich as late-season tomatoes (60 days). In warm climates try 'Jetsetter' and 'Miracle Sweet' hybrids, which are vigorous producers and highly resistant to disease (65 days).

MIDSEASON: 'Champion' was bred specifically as a slicing tomato. It is disease resistant and bears high yields of fruits larger than 'Early Girl' and earlier than 'Better Boy' (70 days). 'Sioux' is an heirloom variety of average size but exceptional flavor; it yields reliably even in hot weather (70 days). 'Giant Valentine' has heart-shaped fruits that look like a cross between a paste tomato and an oxheart type. They stay sweet and juicy even in mediocre growing conditions (75 days). 'Pink Ping Pong' is a prolific bearer of fruits that match its name, but they are juicy and flavorful (75 days). 'Big Boy' and 'Big Girl' hybrids are longtime favorites because of their large, meaty fruits produced all season (75 days).

'Big Beef' hybrid is disease resistant and keeps producing large tomatoes even at the end of the season (75 days). 'Cabernet' is a tall, vigorous greenhouse tomato that produces flavorful fruit outdoors too (75 days). 'Ugly' is the popular commercial beefsteak tomato recently made available to home gardeners (75 days). 'Paul Robeson' is a richly flavored deep maroon heirloom black tomato (75 days). 'Green Zebra' has unusual and attractive mottled fruit that is ripe when the skin gets a yellow blush. The light green flesh is tangy (75 days).

LATE SEASON: 'Moneymaker' is a medium-size greenhouse variety that does best in extremely humid areas (75–80 days). 'Brandywine' and 'German Johnson' hybrids are heirloom beefsteak varieties with very large dark pink fruit often weighing a pound or more apiece. Both come in curly- and potato-leaf (flat-leaf) types. They do best in temperate zones; potato-leaf plants may slow production during extremely hot weather (75–90 days). 'Beefmaster' is popular for its flavorful fruits that weigh up to 2 pounds apiece (80 days). 'Costoluto Genovese' is a deeply ribbed Italian heirloom tomato that does well in hot weather (80 days). 'Supersonic' does well in temperate areas and requires stakes or other supports for its substantial vines and 8–12-ounce fruits

(80 days). 'Pink Ponderosa' (80 days) is a longtime favorite beefsteak type with fruits up to 2 pounds apiece. To prevent sunscald grow plants in wire cages rather than staking them to poles and pruning out side shoots. 'Mortgage Lifter' is not quite as big but is pink and meaty and has few seeds (85 days). 'Purple Calabash' is a medium-size black tomato with a flattened, deeply ribbed shape, nearly true purple color, and a winey taste (80–90 days). 'Hawaiian Pineapple' is a yellow-orange beefsteak tomato with a distinctly pineapple flavor when ripe (90–95 days). 'Martian Giant' produces sweet scarlet-red fruits that weigh up to a pound apiece (90–100 days). 'Big Rainbow' has huge golden-orange fruits streaked with red (90–100 days).

PASTE: 'Super Marzano' is an improved hybrid of 'San Marzano.' Plants are tall with 5"-long fruits (70 days). 'Sausage' produces long, curved, meaty tomatoes good for cooking (75–80 days). 'Italian Red Pear' has 6-ounce pear-shape tomatoes with thin skin and sweet flavor, good for eating fresh or cooked (80 days). 'San Marzano' is an heirloom plant with heavy yields of small, flavorful tomatoes (80–90 days). 'Amish Paste' produces sweet, oblong, oxheart-type heirloom tomatoes (85 days).

TOMATO DISEASE-RESISTANCE ABBREVIATIONS

Seed packets and seedling tags are often marked with one or more of the following abbreviations, indicating that the cultivar has been bred for specific resistance to one or more viruses, bacteria, fungi, or physiological problems. Combinations of V, F, and N are the most important to look for, but choose cultivars bred for resistance to problems common to your geographic area.

ASC = alternaria stem canker
BC = bacterial canker
BSK = bacterial speck
BST = bacterial spot
BW = bacterial wilt
C1, C2, etc. = leaf mold
CMV = cucumber mosaic virus
CR = corky root
EB = early blight
F1, F2, etc. = fusarium wilt races
FCRR = fusarium crown and
      root rot

LB = late blight
N = root-knot nematode
PM = powdery mildew
PVY = potato virus Y
Si = silvering
St = gray leaf spot
TEV = tobacco etch virus
ToMV = tobacco mosaic virus
ToMoV = tobacco mottle virus
TW, TSWV = spotted wilt virus
TYLC = tomato yellow leaf curl
V = verticillium wilt

MACADAMIA

Macadamia integrifolia mak-uh-DAY-mee-uh in-teg-rih-FOH-lee-uh

Choose macadamia trees hybridized for best flavor and yields.

ZONES: 9–11
SIZE: 15–40'h ×
20–30'w
TYPE: Woody
evergreen tree
GROWTH: Slow

LIGHT: Full sun to
part shade
MOISTURE: High
FEATURES: Edible
seeds (nuts)

SITING: Macadamias are suitable for tropical and subtropical climates only. Choose a sunny area where the brittle trees will be protected from wind. Space them at least 30' apart. Macadamias are adaptable to a wide range of soils, but the location must be well drained and not saline.

CARE: Consistent moisture is crucial, particularly from time of nut set to harvest. Young trees need more water than mature ones, and all need watering in heat and drought. Long periods of high heat reduce yields. Leach the soil annually in areas with low rainfall. Macadamias are not hardy; trees are killed below 25°F, flowers below 30°F, and young trees even by light frost. Where bees are not active,

macadamias may need cross-pollination by hand. Different types grow naturally into different mature shapes but can be pruned to maintain a rounded form. Train all types to a central leader, because macadamias tend to produce multiple trunks that split.

PROPAGATION: Macadamia is best grown from grafts, or from air layering or cuttings.

HARVEST: Grafted trees bear within 2–8 years and continue producing for 8–10 years before yields levels off. Mature nuts fall to the ground. Collect them on a tarp spread under the tree. Use a long pole to knock down mature nuts that are out of reach. Shaking the tree can bring down immature nuts and cause brittle limbs to break. Remove the husks and cure the nuts by spreading them in single layers on trays kept in a dry location out of direct sun for 2–3 weeks. Finish drying them in the oven at 100–110°F for about 12 hours. Check them frequently to make sure they aren't

Collect fallen nuts from the ground. Dry them in a shady location for several weeks.

cooking, and stir them to distribute the heat evenly. Crack dried nuts with a nutcracker. Roast whole or halved nuts for 45–50 minutes in a shallow pan, stirring frequently, just until they start to turn light golden brown. Salt the nuts if desired and allow them to cool completely, then store them in airtight containers at cool room temperatures, or double-wrap and store in the freezer.

PESTS AND DISEASES: Macadamias are naturally resistant to avocado root rot and are sometimes planted to replace avocados damaged by fungus. They are susceptible to anthracnose in humid climates. Thrips, mites, and scales may be a problem, but avoid using pesticides that can kill bees, which are needed for pollination.

RECOMMENDED CULTIVARS: *M. integrifolia* is a tropical species with creamy-white flowers in early summer, high yields, and good heat tolerance. 'Keauhou' is popular in Hawaii because it is resistant to anthracnose. 'Keaau' is wind resistant and yields even more highly. *M. tetraphylla* is a subtropical species with large racemes of pink flowers and rough-shelled nuts. It flowers August through October, often simultaneously with fruiting, and produces one main crop. The nut quality is more variable and the yields are not as high, but the taste is sweeter. 'Cate' is a popular cultivar in California, ripening in October and November. Hybrids of the two species such as 'Vista' and 'Beaumont' combine the best qualities and are the most reliable choices for home gardens.

APPLE, CRABAPPLE

Malus **spp.** *MAY-lus*

'Gala' is a sweet, midseason apple popular in many zones.

ZONES: 3–10
SIZE: 6–40'h ×
2–40'w
TYPE: Deciduous
tree

GROWTH: Average
LIGHT: High
MOISTURE: Average
FEATURES: Fragrant
flowers, edible fruits

SITING: Choose a sunny, protected site with deep, fertile, slightly acid soil that drains well and is not in a low-lying area where frost may collect. A gentle slope (no more than 20 degrees) provides the best drainage. Apple trees are intolerant of salinity. Plant in early spring in northern climates and anytime the trees are dormant in warm zones. Use two or more cultivars that bloom at the same time to ensure cross-pollination and a variety of fruits, or choose a self-pollinating cultivar if you have room for just one tree. Planting holes should be wide and deep enough that the roots are not crowded or bent. Plant so the graft is at least 2" above the soil to prevent the wood above the graft from rooting. Space trees as far apart as they will be tall when mature, or as close as 6' for

hedgerows. Spur-type cultivars can be planted closer together. Make a trench in a ring around the edge of each hole as a reservoir for water.

CARE: Use no plant food at planting. Cut back young trees by about one-third to just above a bud. Cut back any branches by up to one-third to a bud that faces out. Remove any buds growing between branches or in crotches. Hand-weed an area 4–6' around the trunk. Use mulch to control weeds and conserve moisture in a circle as wide as the drip line, but keep it away from the trunks of trees. Use nutritional foliar sprays to correct mineral deficiencies. In dry conditions water newly planted trees until they are well established. Water mature trees according to your soil type—as often as once a week

APPLE, CRABAPPLE

continued

Trees with multiple grafts make it possible to harvest a variety of apples from one tree.

in areas with sandy soil—and make sure the entire area beneath the canopy is moist to a depth of 18". Most apple cultivars are hardy, but flowers and fruitlets are damaged below 30°F, so protect trees from late frosts. Train young trees to a modified central leader and thin the branches to 1–2' apart. Train early-bearing trees while they are young. Thin fruit on full-size apple cultivars by hand to one per spur. Prune moderately each year during the dormant season. Prune for wide crotch angles, which are stronger and less prone to breaking. Feed mature trees with low-nitrogen fruit tree spikes. Remove water sprouts in summer to maintain an open canopy that sun can penetrate. Dwarf trees have a shallow root system, so they must be staked, often permanently, or espaliered against a wall or other support.

PROPAGATION: Grow by grafting. Dwarf and semidwarf types are most often grafted or budded onto East Malling or Malling-Merton rootstocks; standard-size varieties are grafted to young apple seedlings.

HARVEST: Expect to wait 3–5 years for your first full harvest. Fruits ripen 70–180 days from bloom, depending on the cultivar.

Rake up dropped fruit, leaves, and other debris to prevent apple scab and reduce pests such as apple maggot.

Pick apples by hand to avoid bruising them. A ripe apple separates easily from the fruiting spur and has firm flesh. A soft apple is overripe but can still be used in cooking. Late-season varieties are the best for long-term storage at cool room temperatures. Some types, such as Cox, McIntosh, and Jonathan, decay if stored in the refrigerator.

PESTS AND DISEASES: Early-ripening cultivars are the most susceptible to apple maggot. Plant late-season trees, especially in warm climates, and regularly pick up dropped fruit from the ground around the tree. Use insecticidal soap or dormant oil spray in late winter before bud swell to control codling moths, plum curculios, scale, leaf rollers, mites, and aphids. Use a delayed dormant spray when bud tips are ¼" long. Removing water sprouts reduces aphids. Use pesticide sprays only when the petals fall but not while the trees are in bloom to avoid killing pollinating bees and honeybees. Rake up and destroy leaves and other debris, especially during summer fruit drop, to control apple scab and pests. Avoid apple scab by choosing resistant cultivars and planting where air circulation is good. Use sulfur spray as directed on infected trees. Bitter rot and botryosphaeria canker are fungal diseases that cause stem and twig cankers, which should be pruned out and destroyed. Tart cultivars such as 'Granny Smith' tend to resist rots better than soft, sweet-fleshed types such as 'Red Delicious'. Corking is caused by insufficient calcium. Overpruning results in succulent growth that is susceptible to fire blight, a bacterial disease that occurs most often in warm, humid climates. Fly speck and sooty blotch may appear on fruits in summer during hot, humid periods but can usually be removed with scrubbing. Eastern red cedar (*Juniperus virginiana*) is a host of cedar-apple rust, a fungal disease that can cause defoliation and poor fruit quality. If there are red cedar trees on or adjacent to your property, be sure to choose apple cultivars labeled for resistance to cedar-apple rust. In cool, humid climates choose cultivars resistant to powdery mildew, a fungus that causes a bumpy brown netting on developing fruits. Use hardware cloth or plastic guards around the lower part of tree trunks to prevent rabbits and mice from eating the bark.

RECOMMENDED CULTIVARS: Apple (*Malus sylvestris* ×*domestica*) is the most widely adapted of all temperate-zone fruit trees. However, many cultivars have chilling requirements that must be met for fruits to develop properly.

Failure to thin fruitlets to one per spur on full-size cultivars results in undersize apples.

Low-chill varieties, suitable for Florida, California, and Arizona, need only 100–400 hours below 45°F. Try 'Anna', similar to 'Red Delicious', for a crop in June, but plant another early bloomer to ensure pollination. 'Dorsett Golden' is an early-season cultivar and self-fruitful. 'Tropic Sweet' is lighter red than 'Anna' but sweeter. Fruits can

Branches heavily laden with fruits may need to be propped up to avoid breaking.

be stored in the refrigerator for up to 2 months.

Moderate-chill varieties need about 400–700 hours below 45°F. 'Macoun' is a deep red McIntosh-type apple resistant to fire blight and hardy to Zone 4. 'Granny Smith' bears tart green apples in late October to early November that store well. The tree thrives in hot climates with long summers and is a good pollenizer.

High-chill varieties need at least 700–1,600 hours below 45°F. Such trees are hardy and do not thrive in hot climates. 'Liberty' is highly disease resistant and bears medium to large reddish-gold fruits in early October that are good fresh or cooked and store well. It is interfruitful with 'Royal Empire', a popular cider apple.

APPLE, CRABAPPLE
continued

Almost all apple cultivars require other apple cultivars for pollination. Some cultivars—such as 'Jonagold', 'Mutsu' ('Crispin'), 'Spigold', 'Winesap', 'Gravenstein', and sports of 'Stayman'—are poor pollenizers. They can be pollinated by other cultivars but cannot be used to pollinate others. If you have room for only one apple tree, choose a cultivar that is self-fruitful. 'Priscilla' is a disease-resistant bright red over yellow apple with an unusual spicy flavor, and it stores well. 'Prima' is yellow with a bright red blush and a rich flavor. Ready for harvest in early September, it keeps a month or more at cool temperatures. 'Dorsett Golden', an early-season cultivar similar to 'Golden Delicious' in appearance and flavor, needs only 100 hours of chilling. 'Gordon' is another low-chill cultivar popular in warm climates, where it bears from August through October. It has red stripes over green skin and tastes good fresh or cooked.

Many of the most well-known apple cultivars have been made better through hybridization. Look for improved strains of these old favorites and be sure to check pollination requirements. 'Calville Blanc d'Hiver' apples (800–1,000 hours of chilling; mid-October) have pale yellow to white skin when ripe but are often harvested green and allowed to mature in storage. They are excellent for cooking and cider. 'Cortland' (800–1,000 hours; mid-September) develops many small branches, so it requires more pruning than other types but is hardy to Zone 3. 'Esopus Spitzenberg' (800 hours; late September to early October) is prized for its crisp flesh and rich flavor. 'Delicious' and 'Golden Delicious' (700 hours; October) have a tendency to develop weak crotches. Thin excess fruitlets or fruits will not develop characteristic colors. 'Jonathan' (700–800 hours; early October) is self-fruitful but susceptible to fire blight. 'Lodi' (800–1,000 hours; August) is similar to 'Yellow Transparent' but keeps better. McIntosh (900 hours; early September) bears early and produces best in cool climates. It is partially self-fruitful. New strains have improved color, flavor, and disease resistance. 'Melrose' (800–1,000 hours; mid- to late October) is a cross of 'Jonathan' and 'Delicious' and is partially self-fruitful. Its extra large fruits make fruit thinning a

'Granny Smith' is more resistant to rots than many red apples and thrives in hot weather.

requirement, and regular pruning is necessary to keep them from being shaded so much that their red color doesn't develop. Similarly, 'Rome Beauty' (1,000 hours; November) must be thinned and pruned for best harvest. A good choice for cool climates because it blooms late, it is excellent for cooking.

'Zestar' (August) is an excellent all-purpose white-fleshed red apple that is hardy to Zone 3. 'Crispin', also called 'Mutsu' (600 hours; mid- to late September), is an extremely sweet yellow-green apple that is good fresh or in pies. It does best in Zones 5–9. 'Fuji' (600 hours; mid-September) is a good pollenizer with large, sometimes russeted fruits that store for up to 6 months. It's a popular cultivar in California. 'Sun Fuji' bears fruits with an orange-pink blush over yellow skin that ripen in October (Zones 5–8). 'Gala' (600 hours; September) is a sweet midseason apple popular in many zones. Thinning is difficult because the tree blooms over a long period. The fruits are small and sometimes pale red. 'Galaxy Gala' and 'Scarlet Gala' have been bred for better color. 'Gala' Mitchell and Buckeye strains (early September) are hardy to Zone 3. All are best consumed within a month or two.

'Gravenstein' strains (700 hours) are good fresh or cooked and bear early in the season, but they require pollinizers. 'Braeburn' (700 hours; October to November) is a self-fruitful tree that bears late. Its fruits are green blushed with red and have a better flavor than 'Granny Smith'. 'Empire' (800 hours; September) is a self-fruitful cultivar good for hot summer climates; it is a reliable pollinizer. 'Jonagold' (700-800 hours) is a compact tree with juicy, sweet, all-purpose red fruits that

ripen in early October. 'Honeycrisp' (800–1,000 hours; September) has sweet, juicy red over gold fruits best eaten fresh. 'Stayman Winesap' (800 hours; October) is a favorite red baking and cider apple in Zones 5–8 that keeps well. 'Idared' (800–1,000 hours) is hardy to Zone 4, blooms early, and ripens in late October. The bright red fruit has aromatic white flesh that is excellent in desserts. 'Goldrush' is a disease-resistant tart yellow apple that ripens in late October. It keeps well, and the flavor sweetens in storage.

Columnar apples such as 'Scarlet Sentinel', 'Golden Sentinel', and 'Northpole' are hybrids that grow as single-trunked, branchless trees that produce full-size apples along the length of the trunk. They are easy to maintain at 8' or less in containers, suitable for deck or patio gardening. They require about 800 chilling hours and bear in September. Plant one of each to ensure pollination if other apple trees are not present in the landscape.

Red-fleshed apples are prized for their ornamental value; their blooms are abundant and colorful like those of pink- and red-flowering crabapples. Their full-size fruits can be almost oblong and colored rose over greenish yellow to entirely dark red. The flesh is pink to dark red and has an intense sweet-tart flavor. 'Hidden Rose' bears medium to large greenish-yellow apples flushed with a hint of red in early October. The flesh is dark pink. 'Scarlet Surprise' bears dark red fruit with deep purple-red flesh in mid- to late August. Even the leaves and bark of the tree have a red cast. It requires about 800 chilling hours and needs a pollenizer.

Columnar apples are single-trunked upright hybrids that bear full-size apples.

SPRAYING FRUIT TREES

Fruit trees offer ornamental beauty as well as delicious harvests year after year if they are carefully managed. Obtaining picture-perfect fruit in a home garden requires special attention to pruning, fruit thinning, and controlling pests and diseases. Careful planning begins with the correct choice of cultivar for your climate and site. There are so many varieties of fruit trees available that you can look for cultivars bred for resistance to the diseases common in your growing area. Check with your local extension agent to find out which types are best.

Few fruit trees perform reliably year after year without the use of pesticides. You can help to prevent pests and diseases by keeping the ground around your trees free of dropped fruit and vegetative debris. For guaranteed pest-free harvests, however, you will need to learn how and when to spray your trees.

For home-garden spraying of just a few trees, a conventional pump sprayer may be sufficient, although a motorized sprayer is easier on your hands. Wear long pants, a long-sleeved shirt, protective eyewear, and rubber gloves while mixing and spraying chemicals. Read and follow the label instructions completely, measure carefully, and do not exceed the recommended application. Keep children and pets away from the area until the spray has dried. Mix only what you need for one application; a small amount of excess can be sprayed onto the trees. No amount should ever be stored.

Apply dormant oil before buds swell, when the tree is dormant and the temperature is above 40°F, to smother insects that have overwintered on the tree. Dormant oil or horticultural oil applied a little later, when green leaves on apples and pears are ¼" to ½" long, may be even more effective. Bordeaux mixture can also be applied at this stage. Pesticides to control mites, aphids, leaf miners, scale, and psylla should also be used at this green-tip stage but should not be applied at the same time as or directly after the oils.

Spray insecticides when buds are fully formed and showing color but aren't open. Fungicides for control of scab, rust, and powdery mildew are also applied at this stage and again on open blossoms. Avoid spraying insecticides when flowers are in bloom to avoid killing pollinators such as honeybees. Spray insecticides and fungicides again to apples, pears, and cherries when nearly all of the flower petals have fallen—a good time to prevent plum curculio, leaf rollers, stinkbugs, and other pests as well as diseases encouraged by hot, humid weather. (Wait for 10 days after petal fall on other fruit trees before spraying to control rots.) Use either or both again at 10-day intervals until fruit sets. Fall-fruiting trees can be sprayed again with insecticidal soap or pesticide at 14-day intervals throughout the summer as long as the temperature is not above 90°F.

1 Follow label directions carefully to measure the correct amount for one application only.

2 Fill the sprayer with the correct amount of water for the amount of pesticide added to the sprayer.

3 A conventional pump sprayer is sufficient for home-garden treatment of just a small few trees.

4 Adjust the nozzle for accurate spraying and to avoid drift onto nontarget areas.

5 Spray fall-fruiting trees with pesticide through summer but stop applications at the appropiate time.

APPLE, CRABAPPLE

continued

Crabapples are *Malus* species with highly ornamental flowers and small, sour fruits less than 2" in diameter. Like larger-fruited species, they grow slowly and do best in consistently moist, slightly acid soil. Because they flower profusely, crabapples are often interplanted with standard apples to ensure pollination. Most have moderate chill requirements. White-flowering varieties are the most disease resistant and the best pollenizers. Crabapples grown for their fruit include Siberian crabapple (*M. baccata*) which grows best in Zones 2–7. 'Jackii' is the most popular. *M. sargentii* cultivars such as 'Sargent' and 'Tina' are dwarf types and the most disease resistant of all crabapples. *M. × zumi* var. *calocarpa* 'Golden Hornet' is a self-fertile white-flowered tree with golden-yellow fruit, but it is not entirely disease resistant. Unlike standard apples that need regular pruning and thinning, prune crabapples only to control their size

and shape and to encourage growth. Prune just after the petals fall.

To grow crabapples as ornamentals for pollenizing standard apples, choose cultivars guaranteed to bloom annually and hold their fruit through winter and are resistant to apple scab and fire blight. Those with larger fruit, such as 'Transcendent' or 'Whitney', which is sweet enough to be eaten fresh, are easier to pick for culinary use but may drop some fruit in summer and autumn. Harvest or rake up fallen fruit to discourage pests and prevent disease.

'Holiday Gold' is a good pollenizer that holds its yellow fruit until spring and is resistant to scab. 'Adirondack' is a tall, upright type with persistent red fruits. 'Jewelberry' is an excellent choice for small spaces. 'Professor Sprenger' is among the taller crabapple cultivars and has orange-red fruits. 'Ormiston Roy' is also tall and has yellow fruits with an orange blush. 'Sargent' and 'Tina' are short, wide-

Large-fruited crabapples are easier to pick than small types but may drop more fruit.

spreading shrub-type cultivars with persistent red fruits. 'Evereste' and 'Winter Gem' ('Glen Mills') are highly disease-resistant trees that produce abundant crops of showy red fruits.

MANGO

Mangifera indica man-JIF-er-a IN-di-ka

Protect mangoes from sunburn in hot climates and water trees weekly.

ZONES: 9–11
SIZE: 30–100'h × 50–100'w
TYPE: Nearly evergreen tree
GROWTH: Fast

LIGHT: Full sun to part shade
MOISTURE: High
FEATURES: Edible fruits

SITING: Plant at the top of a slope for the best drainage and good air circulation, but provide a windbreak or stake young trees. In desert locations plant mangoes in the shade to prevent sunburn of fruits. In cooler zones plant them on the south side of the house for maximum sun and warmth. Mangoes grow well in almost any moderately acid soil but not in heavy clay or other wet soils.

CARE: Mangoes thrive only in frost-free zones. Night temperatures above 55°F are required for pollination. Water trees weekly in warm weather to keep the soil consistently moist until fruit is harvested. In the desert, trees may need daily watering until harvest. Hard water can cause fruit flesh to be stringy. Mangoes are sensitive to chemical plant foods but need regular applications of nitrogen and iron. Work fish emulsion or composted manure into the soil around the trees every 2 weeks until July. Wear gloves while working with mango trees; the leaves and fruit skins contain a toxic sap that can cause a painful dermatitis. Prune trees in late winter or early spring to control size and shape. To avoid alternate-year bearing, remove some flower clusters in years when blooms are too abundant. Thinning the fruit also helps to encourage annual bearing.

PROPAGATION: Grow by grafting or from nursery-grown trees.

HARVEST: Fruits mature 100–180 days after the flowers bloom. They are oval or kidney shape. Ripe fruit skin is pale green or yellow blushed with red and is soft to the touch. Tree-ripened fruits have the best flavor. Pick fruit from late-bearing trees if temperatures fall; ripen indoors with the

stem ends down in trays covered with a damp cloth to prevent shrinkage. Keep at cool room temperatures not below 50°F. Ripe fruits can be refrigerated for up to 3 weeks.

PESTS AND DISEASES: Anthracnose is often a problem in wet, humid weather. Choose cultivars with resistance or use copper spray or fungicide. Too much nitrogen causes shriveling at the fruit apex, called "soft nose." Control fruit flies and sand weevils by keeping dropped fruit and vegetative debris around the trees picked up and destroyed. Use dormant oil or insecticidal soap to control scale, mealybugs, and mites.

RECOMMENDED CULTIVARS: In Hawaii 'Pairi' is popular for greenhouse and home-garden growing but is not as reliable an annual producer as 'Gouveia'. In Florida try 'Kiett', which is mildew resistant, or fiberless 'Kent'. 'Edward' grows well in all interior locations. 'Earlygold' is an anthracnose-resistant, very early bearer for coastal areas. All mangoes are self-fertile, so you can plant just one tree if space is limited. 'Brooks' is a late-bearing, anthracnose-resistant, somewhat dwarf cultivar suitable for outdoor container growing.

MINT
Mentha spp. *MEN-thuh*

Common spearmint is best known for its aromatic oil used in mints and gum.

ZONES: 4–10
SIZE: 1–4'h × 1–4'w
TYPE: Herbaceous perennial
GROWTH: Fast

LIGHT: Full sun to part shade
MOISTURE: Moderate
FEATURES: Edible leaves

SITING: Choose a sunny location with rich, well-drained, slightly acid soil or muck. Plant rooted stem cuttings or runners 3" deep and 2' apart in fall or spring. Space cultivars far apart to avoid cross-pollination. Plants in northern areas get the right amount of sun for best mint oil production.

CARE: Remove flowers as they appear and pinch back the stems to encourage bushier growth. Keep the area around mint free of weeds and grass, which reduce yields. Mint can be mowed and will quickly come back. Set boards 12" deep in the soil around the plants to slow the spread of runners. Or grow mint in a container to control its growth. To overwinter indoors cut the plant back to 6" and leave it outside through autumn for proper chilling.

Pineapple mint is as popular for its variegated foliage as it is for its distinctive fruity fragrance.

PROPAGATION: Grow mint from stem cuttings or divisions.

HARVEST: Mint oil is stored in glands on the undersides of leaves and is at its peak in mid-June to late September. Pinch out the topmost leaves as needed all season. Cut the leaves and the flower tops when plants start to flower; hang them upside down to dry in small bundles, or spread them loosely in a shallow tray. When the stems are brittle, remove the leaves and flowers and store in airtight containers. Add fresh leaves to brewed tea while

it is still hot, or snip leaves into fruit salad, ice cream and sherbet, and any dish containing peas. Mix with yogurt and diced cucumber for a refreshing salad dressing. Chop or process just before serving; leaves turn dark quickly. Mint is also made into sauce and jelly as an accompaniment to lamb and game meats. It is a key flavoring ingredient in many Asian, Mediterranean, and Middle Eastern dishes. Fresh leaves can be frozen to retain their bright color. Use dried leaves in tea.

PESTS AND DISEASES: Most are not significant in home gardens. Knock off mites and aphids with a spray from the garden hose, being careful to spray the undersides of leaves. Choose cultivars with improved resistance to verticillium wilt and mint rust. Avoid using pesticides when plants are in bloom; the flowers attract beneficial bees and flies that pollinate many plants and trees.

RECOMMENDED CULTIVARS: Common spearmint (*M. spicata*) and peppermint (*M. piperita*) are best known for their aromatic oils, used to flavor beverages, candies, and medicines. Others rich in menthol include field mint (*M. arvensis*), Japanese mint (*M. arvensis* var. *piperascens*), horsemint (*M. longifolia*), orange mint (*M. ×piperita* 'Citrata'), and water mint (*M. aquatica*).

Austrian and Vietnamese mints (*M. ×gracilis*), curly mint (*M. spicata* 'Crispa'), Moroccan mint (*M. spicata* 'Moroccan'), 'Bowles' (*M. ×villosa alopecuroides*), red raripila mint (*M. ×smithiana*), and 'Kentucky Colonel' (*M. ×cordifolia*) are all used in cuisine. 'Kentucky Colonel' is often used in mint juleps.

Flavored mints are prized for their distinctive fragrance and often variegated foliage. Among the most popular are apple mint (*M. suaveolens*), pineapple mint (*M. s.* 'Variegata'), ginger mint (*M. ×gracilis* 'Variegata'), and chocolate mint (*M. ×piperita* 'Chocolate').

Some mints form low-growing mats that make excellent ground covers. Corsican mint (*M. requienii*) has tiny leaves on plants only an inch or so tall but releases a strong menthol fragrance when touched and is not invasive. It should be treated as an annual in northern zones. Pennyroyal (*M. pulegium*) grows to 18" tall and spreads rapidly, like most mints. Its oil has long been used as an insect repellent, but pennyroyal is not edible.

1 Root stem cuttings in peat pots and transplant them in spring or fall in full sun to part shade.

2 Pinch out the topmost leaves to encourage bushier plants, and enjoy the trimmings in tea or food.

BANANA

Musa acuminata and *M. xparadisiaca*   *MEW-sa a-kew-mi-NA-ta, M. pair-uh-dee-zee-AH-kuh*

Bananas and plantains are heavy feeders that require lots of plant food.

ZONES: 9–11
SIZE: 5–25'h ×
5–25'w
TYPE: Herbaceous
perennial

GROWTH: Average
LIGHT: Full sun
MOISTURE: High
FEATURES: Edible
fruits

SITING: Choose a warm, sunny, protected location with deep, moist, rich, slightly acid soil that drains well. Bananas do not tolerate standing water or salinity and will not thrive in sand or heavy soil. Plant suckers or large chunks of corm in holes 3' wide and 2' deep amended with well-rotted compost. Space plants as far apart as they will be tall at maturity.

CARE: Bananas and plantains are heavy feeders, so maintain soil nutrients with fruit tree plant food spikes and monthly applications of compost or manure mulch in a wide circle under the plant but not touching it. Soil that is too acid or infertile will decrease yields. Mulch is also necessary to conserve soil moisture and control weeds. Keep the soil moist but not waterlogged. In dry climates water deeply a few times a year to leach the soil of excess mineral salts. *Musa* has shallow roots but huge leaves up to 9' long and 2' wide that make the plants top-heavy, so protect them from wind. Strong breezes may also shred leaves, which interferes with plant metabolism. Nearly all types stop growing in temperatures below 55°F. Plants die back to the ground in freezing temperatures, but the underground rhizomes survive to 25°F. Wrap young trees in blankets if frost is predicted. Grow dwarf plants indoors in full sun where air circulates well and temperatures are consistently above 65°F.

Cut off all but one stalk (actually a pseudostem made up of clustered leaf stalks) per plant and keep new suckers pruned off at ground level. When the main stalk is 6–8 months old, allow one new sucker to develop for the following season. Prop up the fruiting stalk when it begins to bend over from the weight of developing fruit. Use a sturdy forked pole or two stakes fastened together to form an X to hold the bunch. If there are more than six clusters of fruits ("hands") on a bunch, remove the terminal male bud several inches below the last hand to encourage fuller fruits. After harvest cut the current season's fruiting branch back to the ground.

PROPAGATION: Grow from suckers, pieces of budded corm, or nursery transplants.

HARVEST: Plants are mature 1–3 years from planting, depending on the method of propagation, and bear fruits 10–24 months from planting. Cut clusters of plump fruits that are still green with a clean, sharp knife and hang them to ripen in a dry, shady area or indoors at warm room temperatures for 1–2 weeks. Individual fruits ("fingers") left on the plant will split open as they ripen and the fruit will decay rapidly. Banana fruits, which technically are berries, are highly perishable when ripe but can be peeled, cut into chunks, and frozen in plastic bags for later use in cooking. They also can be dried but should not be refrigerated. Bananas are preferred for eating out of hand and in desserts; the more nutritious plantains are used primarily in cooking because their flavor is milder. Ripe raw bananas are used in fruit salads, on sandwiches, and in beverages, desserts, and baked goods. Unripe bananas can be boiled, fried, or grilled in their skins. Green or ripe plantains are most often peeled, sliced, fried in oil, and sweetened as an accompaniment to a main dish. They can also be cooked, mashed, and incorporated in a sweet or savory casserole.

PESTS AND DISEASES: Few pest problems develop in home gardens. Control nematodes and weevils if they are present.

RECOMMENDED CULTIVARS: Choose plants bred for your climate. 'Gros Michel' is a popular but somewhat disease-prone tall cultivar in Hawaii. 'Lady Finger', a tall plant with small sweet fruits, grows well in Florida and Hawaii. 'Bluggoe' and 'Ice Cream' are often grown for use as cooking bananas. 'Silk' is a medium-size plant with abundant apple-scented fruits that keep well. For deck or patio growing, try 'Dwarf Cavendish', a hardy, wind-resistant clone that bears full-size fruits on plants only 5–8' tall. It grows well in containers and indoors in greenhouse conditions. Several *Musa* species provide ornamental appeal as well as tasty fruit. 'Red' (also called 'Red Fig', 'Red Cuban', and other names) is a tender, large plant that takes 18 months to mature but bears purple-red fingers that become orange-yellow and aromatic as they ripen. 'Orinoco' is a medium-size plant popular in California that produces sparsely; the fruit flesh is salmon pink. It is best used like a plantain, in cooking. 'Macho' is a popular plantain in Florida. 'Common Dwarf' and 'Maricongo', a tall plant, are widely grown.

1 Spread well-rotted compost or manure in a wide circle under the tree once a month for high yields.

2 Mulch helps to hold moisture in the soil and controls weeds. Keep the soil wet but not waterlogged.

BASIL

Ocimum basilicum   OS-i-mum ba-SIL-i-kum

Basil is easy to grow in any size garden and can be harvested all season.

ZONES: NA
SIZE: 1–3'h × 1–3'w
TYPE: Annual
GROWTH: Fast
LIGHT: Full sun
MOISTURE: Average
FEATURES: Edible leaves and flowers

SITING: Choose a sunny location with rich, moist, friable, slightly acid soil that drains well. Plant seeds or seedlings in the garden 12–36" apart after the last frost date. Basil is highly adaptable and grows well almost anywhere, including raised beds and containers. It does well when interplanted with tomatoes.

CARE: Basil is very tender; growth slows in cool weather and leaves may wither and discolor if nighttime temperatures are consistently below 45°F. Keep plants inside cloches or cold frames in cool zones or anytime frost is predicted. Pinch out the tops of newly planted tall seedlings to about 6" to promote root growth. Cut or pinch off flowers as they appear to encourage bushier growth. Keep the soil around plants consistently moist and weed free. Side dress plants with well-rotted compost and use mulch to conserve soil moisture.

PROPAGATION: Grow basil from seed.

HARVEST: Begin harvesting basil as soon as there are at least four sets of true leaves. Pinch out the topmost set of leaves and any flowers as needed for use in salads, tomato-based recipes, and pesto, a paste made of basil, garlic, nuts, and oil and used on pasta, pizza, and bread. Snip large leaves or add small whole ones into cooked dishes just before serving to preserve basil's spicy anise flavor. Substitute basil leaves for lettuce on sandwiches for a tangy treat. Store unwashed basil as you would lettuce, but only for a day or two; basil begins to decay as soon as it is picked. Preserve fresh leaves and flowers in vinegar and olive oil to prevent oxidation. Basil can be processed with oil and stored in the freezer for up to 2 years or in the refrigerator for up to 3 months. If you use only part of what you have stored, cover any unused portion with more oil. Basil can be dried but is not as flavorful and colorful as when it is preserved with oil. At the end of the growing season in temperate climates, pull up the plants by their roots and harvest any remaining leaves before the first frost date. In hot zones basil can be cut back to 6" above ground and regrown several times in one year before the final harvest.

PESTS AND DISEASES: Many insects are attracted to basil, but no pesticide is safe for use on edible herbs. Discourage pests by keeping mulch from touching the plants, and remove and destroy any leaves that look unhealthy. Spray off aphids and mites with a garden hose. Basil is susceptible to fusarium wilt in hot, humid weather; look for cultivars bred for resistance and plant them in soil that drains well. Remove and destroy infected plants, including the roots and surrounding soil.

RECOMMENDED CULTIVARS: There are dozens of basil types with variations in leaf size, coloration, fragrance, and growth habit. 'Aroma 2', with 2" leaves, and 'Nefar', with 4" leaves, are two traditional Genovese-type basils that make excellent pesto. 'Italian Large Leaf' has a slightly sweeter taste than 'Genovese', which smells a bit like cloves. Both have 4" leaves on plants 2–3' tall. 'Genovese Compact Improved' has small leaves on an 18" plant suitable for container growing. 'Napoletano' has large, frilly light green leaves that look good in salads and on sandwiches. 'Fino Verde' bears flavorful 1" leaves on compact plants only 18" tall. 'Spicy Bush' forms dense mounds of 1" leaves on plants up to 12" tall. 'Greek' is the smallest basil of all. Its ¼" to ½" leaves on plants 6–9" tall make it a perfect choice for container growing. 'Red Rubin' has eye-catching foliage. The bronze-purple Italian-type leaves grow to 4" long on compact 2' plants. The frilly leaves of 'Purple Ruffles' are almost brown by comparison but taste and smell strongly of cloves and licorice. The plant is compact and grows well in containers. 'Osmin Purple' has a sweet, almost fruity aroma. The 2" leaves are glossy and slightly ruffled; the flowers are lavender. The plants are sometimes variegated green and purple. 'Magical Michael' has medium-long red-veined green leaves and burgundy flowers with a sweet, fruity taste. 'Sweet Thai' basil has reddish-purple stems and flowers and spicy 2" leaves. 'Thai Magic' has larger, milder-tasting leaves and bright magenta flowers that give it extra appeal as an ornamental. 'Holy Basil' (*O. tenuiflorum*), typically grown only as an ornamental, has slender purple and green leaves and purple flowers. 'Mexican Spice' has distinctive reddish-brown stems and flowers in addition to its unmistakable aroma and flavor of cinnamon. The dark green leaves are small and glossy. 'Sweet Dani' is a tall plant with large olive-green leaves that taste and smell of lemon. 'Mrs. Burns' Lemon' (*O. basilicum citriodora*) is an old Mexican variety with a sweet lemony flavor. 'Lime' basil (*O. americanum*) adds a strong lime flavor and aroma to Thai or Mexican cuisine and is also good chopped and added to sherbet.

Red- or purple-leaved cultivars have a strong anise or clove flavor and are as ornamental as they are tasty.

Harvest basil early and often, pinching out the topmost leaves and any flowers to encourage new growth.

Thai and cinnamon basils have reddish-brown stems and flowers and a spicy aroma and flavor.

OLIVE

Olea europaea ob-LAY-ub yur-OH-pee-ub

Pick green olives for curing when they reach full cultivar size.

ZONES: 8–11
SIZE: 15–35'h × 15–35'w
TYPE: Evergreen tree or shrub
GROWTH: Slow

LIGHT: Full sun
MOISTURE: Low
FEATURES: Fragrant flowers, edible fruits (olives)

SITING: Plant olive trees in full sun in well-drained, alkaline soil with as much space between them as possible and away from sidewalks or patios where fallen fruit will leave stains. Choose a site where breezes can help to pollinate the flowers. Olive trees will not thrive in waterlogged soil or high humidity but are tolerant of high pH and salinity.

CARE: Water olive trees deeply once a month in dry climates. Feed with tree spikes until fruit set. Thinning the crop as soon as possible after fruit set to 2 or 3 per foot will increase the size of remaining fruits. Pruning at least annually is necessary to control height and ensure annual bearing. Olives bear on the previous year's growth and never on the same wood twice, so current fruiting wood can be removed after harvest. Prune suckers and low branches to achieve a single trunk, or enourage the attractive gnarled appearance of multiple trunks by staking suckers at the desired angles. Because they can withstand severe pruning, olive trees can be maintained at small size in containers or pruned to espaliers for use in limited spaces. Protect trees from spring frosts that will kill the blossoms. Green fruit is damaged below 30°F, ripe fruit below 25°F.

PROPAGATION: Grow from cuttings or plant grafted trees.

HARVEST: Trees begin to bear about 4 years after planting and are long lived—up to hundreds of years. Fruits mature in 6–8 months. Pick olives to be cured while green when they have reached full cultivar size. Harvest olives for other uses anytime thereafter, keeping in mind that the riper the olives, the more easily they are bruised in handling. Cure the fruits in processing marinades to remove the tannins which cause bitterness, then pack them in oil for long-term storage.

PESTS AND DISEASES: Peacock spot, a fungal disease, may occur in wet years. Olive knot, a bacterial disease, spreads during prolonged rainy spells. Clean tools after every use and sterilize them between pruning cuts to avoid spreading disease. Use commercially available traps to kill olive fruit flies and keep the ground around the trees cleared of fallen fruits and vegetative matter, which will also help to prevent verticillium wilt. Avoid chemical sprays; their odors are retained in olive flesh.

RECOMMENDED CULTIVARS: Most olives require at least 200–300 chilling hours (about 2 weeks below 45°F) to set fruit properly. Choose a self-pollinating type if you have room for just one tree. 'Ascolano' is a hardy, disease-resistant tree with light-colored olives ready in late September or early October. 'Manzanillo' and 'Barouni' are shorter, spreading trees. 'Mission' grows quite tall but bears small black olives with high oil content in late October or early November. It is susceptible to peacock spot but resistant to olive knot and quite hardy. The large blue-black fruits pickled and sold commercially as "black olives" come from the tender 'Sevillano' tree. The tiny reddish-black Picholine olives sold in specialty markets are typically salt-brine cured.

SWEET MARJORAM

Origanum majorana or-IG-ab-num mah-jor-RAY-nuh

Marjoram can be used in place of oregano but is sweeter and milder.

ZONES: 8–11
SIZE: 12–18"h × 12–18"w
TYPE: Perennial grown as an annual
GROWTH: Average

LIGHT: Full sun to part shade
MOISTURE: Average
FEATURES: Edible leaves and flowers

SITING: Choose a sunny or mostly sunny, well-drained location. Marjoram is adaptable but does best in light, fertile, slightly alkaline soil. Plant divisions in spring 12" apart after all danger of frost has passed.

CARE: Sweet marjoram is the most tender of the *Origanum* species but can be grown as an annual. It is well suited to container growing and looks especially attractive in hanging baskets. Cut the trailing stems frequently to encourage bushier growth. Protect from midday sun in hot climates. Marjoram dries out quickly, so keep the soil consistently moist but not waterlogged. Dig and divide plants every few years when they become woody. Overwinter in mild climates by covering plants with mulch, or dig and divide plants in autumn and pot some for use indoors.

HARVEST: The leaves have a sweeter, milder flavor and aroma than those of oregano. Marjoram can be used in place of oregano, but because of its sweetness can also be used in soups, herb butter, and egg dishes as well as to flavor spinach, beans, and other vegetables. Try it in addition to or in place of sage in poultry stuffing and pork sausage. Snip leaves fresh into salads or cooked dishes just before serving. Hang the stems upside down to dry in a cool, dark location with good air circulation. Pull the leaves from the stems when they are completely dry, crumble them, and store in airtight jars. Dried marjoram retains its flavor better than dried oregano.

PROPAGATION: Grow by division or from stem cuttings. It is slow to start from seed.

PESTS AND DISEASES: None are significant in home gardens.

RECOMMENDED CULTIVARS: 'Sweet Max' is a tall, upright marjoram with yellow-green leaves. 'Erfo' has pale grayish-green leaves that have a balsamlike fragrance. Hardy marjoram, sometimes sold as Italian oregano (*O.* ×*majoricum*), is a cold-tolerant hybrid of wild oregano and sweet marjoram that is both pungent and sweet. Pot marjoram (*O. onites*) is not as flavorful and is typically grown as an ornamental.

GREEK OREGANO

Origanum vulgare hirtum *or-IG-ab-num vul-GARE-ay HEER-tum*

Oregano is a cold-hardy perennial with fragrant, spicy leaves.

ZONES: 5–11
SIZE: 12–24"h × 24–40"w
TYPE: Semiwoody perennial

GROWTH: Average
LIGHT: Full sun
MOISTURE: Average
FEATURES: Edible leaves and flowers

SITING: Choose a sunny location with well-drained soil. Oregano is adaptable but does best in light, fertile, slightly alkaline soil. The more sun it receives, the more pungent the flavor of the leaves. Space plants 24" apart.

CARE: Oregano's purple or pink flowers attract bees and butterflies, but the leaves are best picked just before the buds open. Divide plants every few years when they become woody. To obtain two large harvests, cut the whole plant back to 3" just before it flowers, then again in late summer. Water only during periods of drought to avoid root rot.

HARVEST: Cut succulent stems as needed, and snip fresh leaves into salads or cooked dishes just before serving. Oregano has a particular affinity with members of the Solanaceae family—potatoes, tomatoes, eggplants, and peppers—and is a key ingredient in many Mediterranean poultry and lamb dishes. Hang stems upside down to dry in a cool, dark location with good air circulation. Pull the leaves from the stems when they are completely dry, crumble them, and store in airtight jars. Fresh leaves can also be frozen for later use.

PROPAGATION: Grow by division or from stem cuttings; growth is slow from seed.

Clip or pinch off oregano above the woody stems.

Tie the stems into small bunches and hang them upside down to dry.

When they are dry, strip the leaves from the stems for storing.

PESTS AND DISEASES: None are significant.

RECOMMENDED CULTIVARS: 'Aureum', sometimes sold as creeping golden marjoram, has yellow-green leaves. 'Aureum Crispum' has curly golden leaves and pink flowers. Try 'Compactum' for a low-growing aromatic and edible ground cover that rarely blooms. 'Thumbles Variety' forms low, small mounds of gold and green variegated foliage. 'Kaliteri' has spicy silver-gray leaves. 'White Anniversary' is a tender cultivar with variegated green and white foliage. Italian oregano (*O. ×majoricum*) is a hybrid of wild oregano and sweet marjoram that is both pungent and sweet but also hardy.

PASSIONFRUIT

Passiflora edulis *pass-i-FLOR-a ed-YEW-lis*

Carpenter bees help to carry passionfruit's heavy pollen. The plant is also known as purple granadilla.

ZONES: 10 and 11
SIZE: To 50'h
TYPE: Woody evergreen perennial vine
GROWTH: Fast

LIGHT: Full sun
MOISTURE: High
FEATURES: Showy, fragrant flowers; edible fruits

SITING: Choose a sunny location protected from strong winds. Passionfruit does best in neutral-pH sandy loam enriched with organic matter well in advance of planting. The plants are highly susceptible to root and crown rots, so good drainage is essential. Plant them 4'–8' apart and next to a fence, trellis, or tree for support.

CARE: Prune lightly after the last harvest to control excess growth. The purple passionfruit tolerates more pruning than the yellow. Purple types flower twice a year, in spring and fall. Yellow types flower just once, in spring or fall, depending on location. Passionfruit pollen is large and heavy; only bees are sturdy enough to carry it from flower to flower. In the absence of bees, pollinate the flowers by hand using a small brush or swab. To cross yellow and purple vines, use the purple as the receptacle plant. For best results with cross-pollination in home gardens, plant two vines of different parentage. Keep the soil continuously moist for best fruiting. Use a soluble, high-potassium plant food at a rate of 3 pounds per plant four times a year. Too much nitrogen causes brown rot and fruit drop. Hand-weed to protect the shallow roots from damage. Protect plants when frost is predicted.

HARVEST: Passionfruit vines begin to bear 1–3 years from planting. Fruits turn from green to deep purple or yellow in 70–80 days, then fall to the ground. Pick them when they have achieved full cultivar color or gather from the ground each day; they are highly perishable. Ripen yellow passionfruits at room temperature in plastic bags to retain humidity. Store unwashed fruits in plastic bags in the warmest part of the refrigerator for up to 1 week.

PROPAGATION: Grow from cuttings, grafts, or seeds, or by air layering.

PESTS AND DISEASES: Choose hybrids of purple and yellow types to avoid woodiness, a viral disease transmitted by aphids, as well as fungal infections and nematode infestations. Keep fruit and other vegetative matter picked up from the ground around the vines. Avoid insecticide sprays, which kill bees. Remove, destroy, and replace diseased plants.

RECOMMENDED CULTIVARS: Yellow passionfruit (*P. edulis flavicarpa*) is fungus and nematode resistant, so it is widely used as a rootstock. The fruit of the purple vines is juicier and less acidic. 'Brazilian Golden' bears large yellow fruits that are slightly tart. 'Kahuna' has very large purple fruits with sweet flesh. 'Red Rover' is a cross of 'Kahuna' and 'Brazilian Golden'.

PARSNIP
Pastinaca sativa pah-stih-NAH-kuh suh-TY-vuh

Parsnips can be overwintered in the garden and dug as needed.

ZONES: NA
SIZE: 6–12"h ×
6–12"w
TYPE: Biennial
grown as annual
GROWTH: Average

LIGHT: Full sun to
part shade
MOISTURE: Average
FEATURES: Edible
taproots

SITING: Direct-sow parsnip seed in rows ½" deep and 12–18" apart in deep, loose, rich, slightly acid soil in spring or early summer. Make sure the soil is free of rocks and clumps of dirt.
CARE: Keep the seeds consistently moist. Germination is slow, especially in cold soil. If the soil dries too much between waterings, cover the rows with a layer of burlap to help retain moisture until the seeds germinate. Thin the seedlings to 12" apart. Water only in times of drought and use a soluble high-potassium plant food once a month. Plant more seeds if necessary to fill in gaps in rows. Weed carefully by hand between rows to remove competition for moisture and nutrients. After the roots are well established, you can hoe lightly. Use mulch between rows to retain moisture and deter weeds.
HARVEST: Dig spring-planted parsnips beginning in late September. Wipe free of dirt and store unwashed like carrots in the refrigerator for up to 2 months. Their flavor is improved by a few frosts, so you can store them in the ground under mulch and harvest as needed throughout the winter.
PROPAGATION: Grow from seed.
PESTS AND DISEASES: Crop rotation helps to control blights and molds. Use floating row covers to protect young plants from leafhoppers and keep the soil free of all weeds.
RECOMMENDED CULTIVARS: 'Hollow Crown', also called 'Long Guernsey Smooth', is the old-time standard and a reliable yielder. 'Harris Model' holds its white color after harvest. 'Gladiator' is a sweet hybrid with excellent disease resistance. 'White Gem' grows in all soil types. 'Javelin' has been bred for canker resistance. Try 'Premium', a short-rooted variety, if you garden in a short-season zone or have heavy soil. 'Cobham Improved' is a good choice for overwintering in the ground.

Organic mulch conserves moisture in summer and protects plants in winter.

COOL CROPS FOR
WINTER HARVEST

Just because you live in a northern climate doesn't mean you have to limit your growing season to the months between the last and first frosts. With a little planning, you can extend your harvest of home-grown vegetables and herbs to every month of the year.

Some crops benefit from cold weather; their flavor improves after a few fall frosts. Leeks, garlic, parsley, cilantro, carrots, parsnips, parsley, rutabagas, some types of cabbage, beets, and turnips can be left in the ground under mulch all winter in raised beds or in climates where the ground temperature stays above 30°F. As long as hardy vegetables are protected from wind and cold, you can harvest them directly from the garden.

Salad greens are the most reliable winter producers. Arugula, chard, claytonia, mâche, mizuna, sorrel, and spinach can all be sown in late summer through autumn for harvest through the winter. Endive, escarole, sugarloaf chicory, and radicchio also thrive in cold weather; even when their outer leaves are mushy from ice, the tender hearts are still delectable. Kale requires frost to develop its best flavor and easily remains green throughout the winter in a cold frame.

Simple cold frames—bottomless, slanted boxes topped with glass or heavy, clear plastic—provide the windbreak and solar heating required to overwinter hardy crops and serve double duty for germinating spring-sown seeds. Most home garden models are quickly assembled from leftover or recycled lumber and wooden storm windows. You can even fashion a makeshift one from straw bales and a sheet of plastic. For more permanent use, you may want to build a frame of insulated wood, concrete blocks, or bricks, with custom-fitted window lids that keep the soil and air temperatures inside above freezing.

Position cold frames facing south or southwest in a protected area of the garden that will receive full sun during the winter. Choose a location you'll be able to reach easily even when there is snow on the ground. Make sure the soil beneath the cold frames drains well so that vegetables don't rot. Sow seeds inside the frames, or in the open garden and add the frames later, when the temperatures begin to drop.

To determine when to sow seed for winter-harvest crops, add about 3 weeks to the number of days from seeding or transplanting outdoors to harvest, indicated on the seed package (add 4 weeks north of Zone 5). That sum equals the number of days to count back from the first frost date in your area to determine the best time to plant. If the weather is still hot when you sow seeds, be sure to keep the soil moist and weed free, and protect young seedlings from midday sun.

AVOCADO

Persea americana PER-see-uh uh-mer-ih-KAY-nuh

Space avocado trees far enough apart that they do not touch at maturity. Avocado is also known as alligator pear.

ZONES: 9–11
SIZE: 8–60'h × 6–40'w
TYPE: Briefly deciduous tree
GROWTH: Fast
LIGHT: Full sun
MOISTURE: Average
FEATURES: Edible fruits

SITING: Choose a protected, sunny location with deep, rich, friable soil. Avocado is adaptable to all slightly acid soils and will even grow in alkaline soil in Florida and Hawaii. The site must have excellent drainage. Space trees so that they will not touch at maturity. Plant any time of year except in the high heat of midsummer.

CARE: Use a transplant starter solution at the time of planting, then a balanced plant food every 2 months except when the tree blooms and fruits. Hand-weed and water frequently until the roots are established. Use foliar sprays to correct mineral deficiencies. Prune to control size. Water only in times of drought. Maintain a wide circle of organic mulch under the tree canopy but not touching the trunk. Protect trees from frost.

HARVEST: Grafted trees usually bear the third year after planting. Avocados will not ripen on the tree but should be picked when they have reached full cultivar size. Fully mature fruits may drop but can be bruised or split open as a result. Because the trees bloom over a long period, fruits will not mature all at once. Skins will darken or lose their glossy sheen when mature. Pick the largest, fullest ones first, using clippers to cut the stems. Fruits will ripen at room temperature in 5–10 days. Hasten ripening by placing an avocado in a paper bag with an apple or a banana. To preserve half a fruit for later use, leave the seed in, moisten the exposed flesh with citrus juice, and wrap tightly in plastic wrap. Store whole ripe avocados in the refrigerator for up to 1 week.

PROPAGATION: Grow by grafting.

PESTS AND DISEASES: Choose cultivars bred for resistance to problems in your locale. Avoid using insecticides, which also kill the insects necessary for pollination. Use fungicides to prevent rots in humid areas.

RECOMMENDED CULTIVARS: Guatemalan and Mexican types grow best in California and tolerate some cold. 'Edranol' is a disease-resistant tree with sweet, nutty fruits borne over a long period. Mexican trees bloom in winter and are ready to harvest the following summer or fall. 'Hass' is the standard Mexican avocado popular in California but is being replaced by hybrids that are more pest resistant, such as 'Lamb Hass' and 'Sir Prize'. West Indian varieties thrive in the high humidity and salinity of Florida and Hawaii and are less hardy, but they bloom in spring and the fruits ripen in the same year. The fruits of 'Russell', a West Indian type recommended for home gardens, ripen in late summer. 'Hall' is a Guatemalan × West Indian hybrid that bears heavily in late fall. It is hardy but susceptible to scab.

PARSLEY

Petroselinum crispum peh-troh-seh-LY-num KRIS-pum

'Moss Curled' is the most popular type of parsley in home gardens. It is also known as curly-leaved parsley.

ZONES: 3–10
SIZE: 8–24"h × 8–24"w
TYPE: Biennial grown as annual
GROWTH: Fast
LIGHT: Full sun to part shade
MOISTURE: Average
FEATURES: Edible leaves and stems

SITING: Sow seeds or plant transplants in early spring. The location should have rich, moist, friable, well-drained, acid to neutral soil. Space transplants and seedlings 12–18" apart in each direction.

CARE: Parsley seed is slow to germinate. Warm the seedbed with black plastic or use a cold frame to concentrate heat. Keep the soil evenly moist and weed free. Use a balanced soluble vegetable plant food on mature plants once a month. Use mulch around curly parsley to keep soil particles from gathering in the leaf crevices.

HARVEST: Harvest parsley and encourage new growth by cutting outer stems at least 1" above the soil as needed. The whole plant can be cut before winter or mulched for overwintering in the garden. Plants kept in an insulated cold frame continue to produce new stems until the following spring. Collect the seeds for a new crop or allow the old plants to self-sow. Leaves and stems can be refrigerated for up to 1 month or frozen for up to 1 year. To dry parsley, hang the stems upside down or spread them in a single layer on screens in a cool, shady, well-ventilated location.

PROPAGATION: Grow parsley from seed.

PESTS AND DISEASES: Avoid using insecticides, because parsley attracts swallowtail butterflies. Knock off aphids with a strong spray from the garden hose. Carrot weevils may overwinter on parsley or nearby carrot tops. Parsley is susceptible to bacterial spot and Septoria leaf spot. Both overwinter in crop debris and can be spread by wind, rain, or dirty tools. Parsley is also susceptible to aster yellows, a viral disease spread by leafhoppers. Protect young plants with floating row covers and keep the area around them weed free. Remove and destroy any infected plants.

RECOMMENDED CULTIVARS: 'Moss Curled' is the most popular curly-leaf parsley. 'Giant of Naples' is a flat-leaf Italian parsley.

Some cooks prefer the sweeter flavor of flat-leaf parsley.

Cover plants with floating row covers to discourage pests.

Parsley is easy to grow in pots and hanging baskets.

BEAN

Phaseolus spp. *fa-ZEE-o-lus*

Scarlet runner beans have ornamental value as well as edible seeds.

ZONES: NA
SIZE: 8–72"h × 6–24"w
TYPE: Annual
GROWTH: Fast
LIGHT: Full sun
MOISTURE: High
FEATURES: Edible seeds and immature pods

SITING: Choose a sunny location where legumes have not been grown in the last 3 years. Beans are highly adaptable but do best in rich, well-drained, friable, slightly acid to neutral soil. Plant seeds after all danger of frost has passed. In northern zones warm the soil with black plastic for rapid germination, or plant seedlings started indoors several weeks before the last frost date. Dust dampened seeds with rhizobial inoculant before planting to fix nitrogen in the soil for the crop that follows the beans. Plant all *Phaseolus* seeds except limas 1" deep in heavy soils or 1½" in light soils. Space seeds 2" apart in rows 24" apart. Plant limas later than other beans, when the soil reaches 65°F, and ½–1" deep. Plant pole beans 2" deep, four to six seeds per hill or 6" apart in rows 36" apart against a fence or trellis. Beans do well interplanted with corn, sweet potatoes, and tomatoes.

CARE: Beans do best where daytime temperatures are 70–80°F and may drop their blossoms above 85°F. They are also sensitive to frost. Temperatures below 35°F kill the flowers and pods. Create a tripod of three poles 6–8' tall for each hill of pole beans to climb. Cut off the terminal end of each vine when it gets to the top of the tripod to encourage branching. Tie string 5" above the ground between two short stakes on either side of each row of bush beans to hold the plants off the soil. Bean plants are tender and easily damaged by garden tools, so weed by hand if possible. Keep the soil consistently moist, but water only in the morning so the plants dry quickly, which reduces the potential for disease. Extremes in soil moisture result in malformed pods. To avoid injury to the plants and the spread of fungal spores, work around and harvest beans only when

they are not wet. Beans supply their own nitrogen but benefit from a monthly application of soluble plant food high in phosphorus and potassium.
PROPAGATION: Grow beans from seed.
HARVEST: Pinch or cut the pods off carefully to avoid uprooting the plant if it is still producing. Pick fresh beans at least every few days for optimum tenderness. Harvest dry beans when the pods are fully mature and have changed color. Dry pods may shatter and eject the beans, so put a sheet down between rows, or hold a pan underneath the plants as you pick. If you live in an area of high humidity, pull the plants when the pods have changed color and hang them upside down to dry in a well-ventilated area protected from rain. Immature pods of snap and pole beans are ready to harvest 6–9 weeks from planting. Eat them fresh—whole or cut, raw, steamed, boiled, or stir-fried—and blanch some for freezer storage or pressure canning. The pods of some shelling beans also can be eaten when immature. Horticultural beans are ready for shelling 8–10 weeks from planting. Use them uncooked or steamed in salads or added to soups and stews. Beans grown for their dried seeds are ready for harvest 12–15 weeks from planting. They are presoaked and slow cooked in soups, stews, and casseroles. Store fresh beans in a plastic bag for up to a week in the refrigerator. Dried beans can be stored in an airtight container in a cool, dry location.
PESTS AND DISEASES: Choose cultivars bred for resistance to bacteria and viruses and pretreated with fungicide for prevention of blights, rots, rusts, and anthracnose. Practice crop rotation to avoid diseases that persist in the soil. All beans are visited by a host of damaging insects, including aphids, thrips, beetles, weevils, mites, stinkbugs, and tarnished plant bugs. The Mexican bean beetle is the main pest in home gardens; it lays its eggs on the underside of bean leaves. Handpick and destroy eggs and larvae, or use neem oil for heavy infestations. Ask your local extension agent which other pests are most common in your locale and how to deter them. Avoid using insecticides on beans. Bean flowers attract beneficial ladybugs and predatory wasps and are pollinated by bumblebees.
RECOMMENDED CULTIVARS: Tepary bean (*P. acutifolius*) is a drought-tolerant species grown for its dried seeds. It grows well in desert climates. 'Blue Speckled' produces plump beans in 60–90 days. Scarlet runner bean (*P. coccineus*), a climbing type, is

often grown only for its ornamental value, but the mature pods bear tasty shelling beans. 'Scarlet Emperor' has vivid red flowers that attract hummingbirds and bears long, stringless pods with large black- and purple-mottled white beans in 90–95 days. Lima bean (*P. lunatus*) typically thrives in areas with long, hot summers, but 'Fordhook' cultivars do well even in northern climates if the soil drains well. Green limas are ready to shell in 85 days or can be harvested at 95–100 days for dried butter beans.

Most of the beans that home gardeners grow are *P. vulgaris* determinate cultivars. For early fresh snap green beans, grow bush types that produce abundantly in 50–55 days. 'Tenderlake' is a good choice for home gardens. The pods are sweet and the plants are heat resistant. 'Xera' has attractive dark green pods with white seeds that are slow to develop. It was bred for exceptional heat tolerance but is adapted to most climates and is disease resistant. 'Indy Gold' is a wax-type bush bean that bears short, green-tipped vivid yellow pods with white seeds. 'Provider' can be eaten as a fresh green bean, or the seeds can be dried for soup beans. It is virus resistant.

'Fordhook' cultivars grow well in northern climates where other lima bean varieties do not.

'Normandie' is a French haricot-type, disease-resistant bean with pencil-thin pods that are excellent eaten fresh, steamed, stir-fried, or dilled. 'Dragon Tongue' has flat pale yellow pods with purple streaks that disappear when cooked. 'Royalty Purple' beans also turn green when cooked. Snap beans are still sometimes called string beans, but all contemporary cultivars are actually stringless. For a continuous fresh harvest of determinate beans, sow

BEAN
continued

Most home gardeners grow *P. vulgaris* snap beans like 'Provider' or 'Tenderlake', which are stringless.

new seed every 2–3 weeks throughout the summer.

Most fresh snap pole beans are ready for harvest in 60–65 days but are indeterminate and continue to produce over several months. 'Black Seeded Blue Lake' is a vigorous producer of stringless pods that are good fresh, frozen, or canned. 'Cascade Giant' bears abundant stringless dark green pods mottled with purple. It is tolerant of drought and damp weather and is good for canning. 'Kentucky Wonder' is an old favorite variety with green pods and tan seeds. 'Romano' has wide, fat, stringless, tender pods with an excellent flavor cooked or canned. 'Triofono' purple pods turn green when cooked. 'Fortex' pods grow to 11" long but are tender at all lengths and

a good choice for home gardens. 'Northeaster' pods are large, flat, stringless, tender, and sweet.

Horticultural types bear large beans that are ready for fresh shelling in 75–80 days. 'Tongue of Fire' has red-streaked ivory pods and beans that can be eaten as snap beans when young or shelled fresh. 'Flagrano' has straight green pods with easy-to-shell light green seeds that can also be dried. 'Cannellini' is an old favorite half-runner type with long white pods and large, nutty-flavored white beans that are good in minestrone. It also can be shelled fresh when the pods are yellow-green.

Dried bush beans come in a wide variety of sizes and colorations, including pea or navy, field or pinto, great northern, black, butter (lima), and marrow types. They are ready to harvest in 90–105 days, which means they do best in long-season areas where the autumn is dry. 'Vermont Cranberry' has attractive red- and pink-mottled pods and beans that also can be shelled green at 75 days. 'Topaz Pinto' is a short, compact plant adapted to northern climates and easy to shell by hand. It is excellent for frijoles. 'Midnight Black Turtle Soup' is a tall upright plant

that bears small beans good for soups and canning. 'Yellow Eye' is a marrow type that becomes creamy when cooked. It makes tasty baked beans. 'Jacob's Cattle' is a good choice for short-season northern areas. Its kidney-shaped white beans with dark red splotches are excellent in soups

Unlike bush beans, pole beans are indeterminate and continue to produce throughout the season.

and casseroles and can be shelled for fresh use at 85–90 days. 'Red Hawk' produces dark red kidney beans on erect, disease-resistant bushes. They are good for canning.

Not all beans belong to the genus *Phaseolus*. For information on soybeans, see page 518. For information on fava beans, see page 564. For information on adzuki beans, asparagus beans (or yard-long beans), cowpeas (or blackeyed peas), and mung beans, see page 565. Chickpeas (*Cicer arietinum*), also called garbanzo beans, are neither beans nor peas but legumes called pulses. They require a long, dry, cool growing season of 100 days or more and do best in the coastal Southwest. The small pods bear just two seeds each so are not efficient producers for small home gardens. 'Baron' seeds are the traditional light golden-brown color. 'Black Kabouli' is a vigorous producer of small, dark seeds.

Provide support for bush bean pods by tying string to short stakes on either side of each row.

Pick snap beans every few days while they are still tender. Pinch or cut off the pods to avoid uprooting the plants.

SOIL TESTING

Healthy soil is one of the keys to growing edible crops. A simple and inexpensive test of your garden soil will help you make decisions about plant food and other amendments.

A basic soil test measures pH (the degree of acidity or alkalinity in the soil), the presence of phosphorus and potassium, and organic matter (a measure of nitrogen availability). Soil pH affects the availability of nutrients for uptake. A neutral pH is 7. Above 7 soil is alkaline; below 7 it is acid. Most edible plants grow best in slightly acid soil—a pH of about 6–7. Asparagus and onions grow well in alkaline soils with a pH up to 8, whereas potatoes and radishes thrive in acid soil, as low as 4.5. If the soil pH is not appropriate for the crop grown, nutrients in the soil won't be available to the plants.

Lime reduces acidity (raises pH); sulfur increases it (lowers pH). Testing the soil before applying either one helps to determine which type and how much of either application is needed, if any. Some soils may be deficient in phosphorus or potassium, which are necessary for plants to bloom and fruit. Additional tests are available to assess the need for any mineral amendments needed for optimum gardening.

A soil test every 3–5 years is usually often enough for most home gardens. If you routinely plant a crop not typically grown in your geographic area, you may want to have the soil tested annually. If a problem arises during the growing season that points to soil fertility as the cause, have the soil tested immediately. Otherwise, take the soil sample in autumn so you have time to incorporate any needed amendments before the next spring planting season.

Use a soil probe created just for sampling, or a clean, sharp knife or trowel, to take samples from the soil. Allow wet soil to dry, then break up any lumps. Remove any surface debris, then dig to a depth of 6–8". Taking samples from more than one area of the garden will help you decide where to locate specific crops and can provide helpful comparisons when diagnosing plant health problems. Draw a diagram of your garden and label the areas where you took the

Testing garden soil measures its acidity or alkalinity and helps to determine which nutrients need adjustment, if any. Using clean tools, place each sample in a separate, labeled container to send to a soil testing laboratory.

1

Home soil test kits are less precise than the results from commercial laboratories, but they can provide rough estimates of needs.

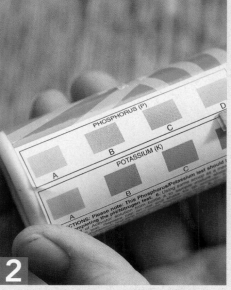

2

You will need to interpret the results on your own if using a home soil test kit.

samples with letters or numbers. Place each sample in a separate clean, dry box or plastic container with a corresponding number or letter label.

If you are testing the soil before you have planted the garden, take several samples from various locations and mix them together to get an analysis representative of the area as a whole. In planted gardens take samples from between plants to avoid any plant foods and mulches added between rows.

Contact your local extension agent for a list of laboratories that provide soil testing in your area. The laboratory you choose will provide instructions on how to package your samples for mailing or delivery, as well as information on how to interpret the results.

DATE PALM
Phoenix dactylifera *FEE-nix dak-tee-LIH-fer-uh*

Plant at least two date palm trees for the best yields.

ZONES: 8-10
SIZE: 50–100'h × 20–30'w
TYPE: Evergreen tree
GROWTH: Slow

LIGHT: Full sun
MOISTURE: High
FEATURES: Edible drupes (dates), seeds, and terminal buds

SITING: In North America, date palm grows only in Arizona, California, Hawaii, and Mexico where days and nights are hot and the air is dry. It tolerates moderate salinity and does best in areas where the water table is high. Choose a site where fruit that drops will not create a maintenance problem. Plant the offshoots 25–30' apart.

CARE: Water newly planted offshoots frequently, and use mulch around the base to conserve moisture and reduce weeds. Protect young trees from cold weather with commercial wraps or old palm fronds wrapped around the trunks. Most date palms are dioecious—some trees are male and some are female—but just one male tree can produce enough pollen for up to fifty female trees. Hand pollination guarantees the best results. The easiest method is to collect pollen from staminate (male) flowers on a sheet of white paper or in a white paper cup, then dip tiny wads of cotton in the pollen and insert them into the female flowers. Remove fronds in late summer as they turn brown, and cut off any sharp thorns at the leaf bases to make pollination and harvest less difficult.

PROPAGATION: Grow from offshoots of a mature female tree or nursery transplant.

HARVEST: Date palm begins to bear 3–5 years after planting, and may bear for 100 years. The fruits mature from green when unripe to reddish brown when fully ripe. Each tree produces five to twelve bunches, and each bunch may contain many hundreds of fruits, but they ripen at different times. Harvest the dates once a week as they become ready. Pick soft and semidry cultivars when they reach their preripe yellow, pink, or red color, then dry them in the sun to increase their sugar content and retard spoilage. Dry dates can be left on the tree to cure. Store them in plastic or glass in the refrigerator for up to a year, or freeze them for up to several years. Date seeds—one per fruit—can be roasted whole and eaten like nuts. Also, try the peeled and sliced terminal buds of branches, called hearts of palm, in vegetable salads and on pizza.

PESTS AND DISEASES: A wide variety of insects and animals are attracted to the fruits. Use labeled insecticides if necessary to control heavy infestations, and netting or paper bags to protect fruit clusters from animals.

RECOMMENDED CULTIVARS: 'Deglet Noor' is famous for its rich flavor and semidry texture. 'Medjool' is the best-known soft date in the United States. It is more tolerant of humidity than most cultivars. 'Thoory' is a dry date with large, firm, fruits that mature late in the season.

TOMATILLO
Physalis ixocarpa *FY-sah-lis ix-oh-KAR-pa*

Tomatillo fruits develop inside green or purple papery husks. It is also known as husk tomato.

ZONES: NA
SIZE: 2–6'h × 2–6'w
TYPE: Herbaceous annual
GROWTH: Average

LIGHT: Full sun
MOISTURE: Moderate
FEATURES: Edible fruits (berries)

SITING: Choose a sunny location with rich, well-drained, slightly acid loam. Start seeds indoors and transplant outside when all danger of frost has passed in spring.

CARE: Tomatillos are grown just like tomatoes (see page 522) and will sprawl across the ground if not staked or caged. Unlike tomatoes, however, tomatillo fruits develop inside green and purple calyces. Keep the soil around the plants moist but not waterlogged, and remove all weeds. Feed with a soluble tomato plant food twice a month.

PROPAGATION: Grow from seed.

HARVEST: Tomatillos begin to bear 60–80 days after transplanting and produce fruits for about 6 weeks. Ripe fruits are bright green, yellow, purple, or reddish, and the husks are light brown but not shriveled or dry. Unripe fruits have a slightly sticky surface. Tomatillos fall before

Grow tomatillos just like tomatoes, starting the seed indoors 6–10 weeks before the last frost date in spring.

they are ripe; collect them daily and allow the husks to finish drying for 1–3 weeks. Store individual unhusked fruits in a cool, dry location or pull the entire plant if frost is predicted and hang it upside down in a protected area until needed. Remove the husks and wash the fruits when they are fully ripe. You can store tomatillos in their husks in the refrigerator for up to 2 weeks.

PESTS AND DISEASES: Plant tomatillos where other Solanaceae crops have not been grown previously to avoid diseases that persist in the soil. Use cardboard collars around tomatillo transplants to discourage cutworms. Handpick and destroy Japanese beetles and hornworms.

RECOMMENDED CULTIVARS: 'Verde Puebla' plants grow 6–8' tall; stake or cage to hold the 1½" pale yellow-green fruits off the ground. They are ready to harvest in 75 days. 'Rendidora' cultivars have smaller but firmer lime-green fruits ready in 60–75 days. 'Cisneros' produces large green fruits in just 75 days. *P. philadelphica* 'Purple De Milpa' bears 2" fruits with a sharp, sweet flavor; they're good fresh or cooked. It bears later in the season, at about 90 days.

PEA

Pisum sativum *PY-sum sub-TY-vum*

Traditional shelling cultivars are called green peas, English peas, or garden peas.

ZONES: NA
SIZE: 1–6'h × 6–12"w
TYPE: Annual
GROWTH: Fast

LIGHT: Full sun to part shade
MOISTURE: High
FEATURES: Edible pods and seeds

SITING: Plant peas in early spring in a location where they can be protected from midday sun if temperatures are over 80°F. Choose a sunny area of the garden where legumes have not been grown in the last 3 years. Peas are highly adaptable but do best in rich, well-drained, friable, slightly acid to neutral loam. They do well interplanted with corn, tomatoes, garlic, onions, and lettuce. Dust dampened seeds with rhizobial inoculant before planting to fix nitrogen in the soil for the crop that follows the peas. Plant the seeds 1" deep and 2" apart in rows 8–12" apart. In hot climates or areas with dry soil, try the trench-planting method for establishing peas. Dig a furrow about 2" wide and 4" deep across the front of whatever supports you will use. Lightly water the trench, then plant the seeds as above and cover them with 2" of soil. The trench serves as a catch for water as the seedlings grow. Gradually fill it in with more soil as they get taller.

CARE: Peas are cool-weather crops but plants can be damaged by a late frost. They tolerate brief periods of temperatures to 25°F, but prolonged exposure will interfere with later development. Flowers drop and vines wither in temperatures over 80°F. All but the most dwarf pea plants require stakes, trellises, or other supports for the vines to climb. Keep the soil consistently moist and weed by hand to avoid disturbing tender vines and roots. Work around and harvest from vines only when they are not wet to avoid spreading disease. Keep mature peas picked regularly for best flavor and to promote the development of other pods.

PROPAGATION: Grow from seed.

HARVEST: English or shelling peas are ready to pick when the pods are fully rounded. The seeds are shelled from the pods and used raw in salads, steamed as a vegetable, or cooked in soups and stews. Store unshelled peas for up to 3 days and shelled peas for up to 7 days in the refrigerator. Shelled peas can be blanched and kept in the freezer for up to 1 year. Leave some pods to dry on the vine if you want to keep seed for next year's crop. Harvest snow peas when the pods are still flat and the seeds inside are small and undeveloped. Use them raw in salads or as crudités for dipping, or add to stir-fries for a crunchy texture. Pick snap varieties when the pods are plump and the seeds are fully developed. The pods of snap peas are edible and, like snow peas, are a fun addition to a platter of raw dipping vegetables. They are most often served steamed or sautéed with butter and herbs but also make a delicious pea soup. Store snow and snap peas in the refrigerator for up to 1 week or blanched and frozen for up to 1 year.

PESTS AND DISEASES: Peas may be susceptible to leaf spot or scab, blights and rots, fusarium wilt, powdery mildew, botrytis and other molds, damping-off, and mosaic virus. Choose cultivars bred for resistance to bacteria and fungi common in your area, and rotate legume crops each year to avoid diseases that persist in the soil. Beneficial insects control most aphids and thrips, but you can knock these pests off mature plants with a stream of water from the garden hose, or use insecticidal soap or neem oil spray if infestations are severe. Use floating row covers on young plants to discourage weevils. Tiny holes in pea pods may indicate an infestation by pea moths. Pick and destroy any yellowing pods and destroy all the plant debris after harvest.

RECOMMENDED CULTIVARS: Green peas, also called English peas, are cultivars grown for shelling. 'Dakota' is a very early variety ready to harvest in 50–55 days. The vines are short enough to be grown without supports. 'Caseload' is an extra sweet shelling pea ready in 55–60 days and slow to become starchy. 'Maestro' and 'Eclipse' are good choices for hot southern zones. They are disease resistant and ready in 60–65 days. 'Alderman', sometimes called 'Tall Telephone', grows to 5' or more tall and bears long pods, each with eight to ten extremely sweet peas in 75 days. 'Alaska' is a short-season variety ready in just 55 days and is best canned. 'Oregon Trail' (55–70 days) is a prolific producer of small pods with sweet peas, delicious raw or cooked. 'Little Marvel' (60–65 days) and 'Wando' (65–70 days) are popular home-garden cultivars because of their heat tolerance. Use them fresh, frozen, or canned.

P. sativum var. *macrocarpon* varieties are grown for their edible pods, called snow peas, which may require stringing. 'Oregon Giant' is a disease-resistant variety that produces sweet, large pods in 60–70 days and throughout the summer. 'Sugar Pod 2' is a better choice for cool zones, bearing in 60–70 days. Other edible-pod varieties, called snap peas, are harvested after the seeds have filled out. 'Sugar Ann' is the earliest variety, ready to harvest in 50–55 days. 'Sugar Snap' produces plump, succulent pods in 60–70 days in both cool and hot weather. Remove the strings on the pods before eating or cooking them. 'Sugar Pop' and 'Sugar Daddy' are stringless varieties. 'Super Sugar Snap' is resistant to powdery mildew.

Direct-sow seed in early spring; peas do not transplant well.

All but the most dwarf plants require some type of support.

Harvest snow peas while the pods are still flat. Remove any strings.

Let the edible pods of snap peas fill out before harvesting them.

STONE FRUIT

Trees in the genus *Prunus* bear the most commonly grown stone fruits in North America—plums, apricots, cherries, almonds, peaches, and nectarines. Stone fruits have in common a single hard seed called a pit or stone that is surrounded by juicy flesh. Most *Prunus* species are not native to North America and therefore require more effort to cultivate successfully in home gardens than apples or pears. Most types are susceptible to winter injury, although cherries and plums are generally the hardiest of the genus. All are attractive to pests and susceptible to diseases, and all must have systematic pruning to provide the highest yields. Although their abundant, fragrant flowers alone are reason enough to include *Prunus* trees in the landscape, the extra effort to promote healthy fruits reaps delicious rewards.

APRICOT
Prunus armeniaca PROO-nus ar-men-ee-AY-kuh

Apricot is susceptible to late spring frost damage because it blooms early.

ZONES: 5-9
SIZE: 6–30'h × 6–30'w
TYPE: Deciduous tree
GROWTH: Slow
LIGHT: Full sun
MOISTURE: Moderate
FEATURES: Fragrant, showy flowers; edible fruits

SITING: Choose a protected, sunny site with deep, loose, well-drained, slightly acid soil. Plant the tree in a north-facing position if late spring frosts occur in your locale. Space standard varieties 25' apart, semidwarfs 15' apart, and dwarfs 6' apart. Use no plant food at planting.
CARE: Prune the new tree to a central leader with three or four scaffold branches at staggered intervals around the trunk (see pages 550–551). In the following year prune the scaffold branches back to form secondary branches. Rub or cut off any sprouts coming from the trunk. Cut the leader back even with the top scaffold branch when the tree has reached the desired height. Because apricot is an early bloomer, it is susceptible to late spring frost damage, which results in no fruiting. If possible cover trees if frost is predicted. Apricot does not tolerate drought. Keep the soil consistently moist but never waterlogged. Provide weekly deep watering during warm weather. Use tree plant food spikes if trees do not grow 1–2' each year. Prune lightly once a year after flowering to remove old fruiting spurs and control tree height. After normal fruit drop, thin to the healthiest fruit on each spur and leave 3" between fruits. Thin the branches of shrubby cultivars to allow sunlight to penetrate the interior of trees.
PROPAGATION: Grow from cuttings or by grafting.
HARVEST: European apricots begin producing at 4–5 years, Asian varieties as early as 3 years. Both may live 15–30 years or more, depending on care. Older varieties may drop ripe fruit, but newer hybrids need to be picked ripe from the tree. The velvety-skinned fruits look like miniature peaches and are ready to harvest when all green coloration is gone and the flesh is just starting to soften, usually in early July to mid-August. Pull off the fruit by twisting it up and away from the spur. Pick a few apricots from different parts of the tree and test them for full flavor before harvesting any others. Store ripe fruits in the refrigerator for up to 2 weeks.
PESTS AND DISEASES: Apricots are susceptible to the same problems as peaches. Prune out diseased and damaged wood immediately, and keep the ground around trees cleaned of dropped fruit and other vegetative matter that harbors pests and encourages disease. Most diseases can be avoided by choosing resistant cultivars and practicing clean cultural habits to keep

Thinning fruits to 3" apart allows them to develop to full size.

pests away. If necessary, spray dormant oil during winter to control serious infestations of peachtree borer; spray *Btk* at bloom time and during the summer to control the caterpillars. Cultivate the soil around the tree shallowly to destroy pupae. Avoid using insecticides while trees are in flower to protect pollinators. Use a fungicide spray at 10–14-day intervals until petal drop and again in autumn after leaf fall to prevent brown rot, twig blight, green fruit rot, and other infections. Use dormant oil in winter to control scale, mites, and borers. Use netting to protect trees from birds, and trunk wraps in winter to prevent rodent damage.
RECOMMENDED CULTIVARS: Choose apricots grafted to rootstocks that do well in your locale and cultivars bred for disease resistance. Their chilling hour requirements vary from 300 to 1,000. Popular European varieties include 'Stark Sweetheart', which has edible pits, 'Aprigold', 'Autumn Royal', 'Earligold', 'Wenatchee', and 'Puget Gold'. 'Blenheim' is a good choice for eating fresh or for drying and canning. Asian and hybrid types include 'Brookcot', 'Moongold', and 'Sunrise'. Manchurian apricot (*P. mandshurica*) is similar to Oriental bush cherry but grows to 25' tall and is not a reliable annual producer. Plant two for the best yield of 1" yellow-orange fruits. It is hardy to Zone 4. Japanese apricot (*P. mume*) is the small-fruited cultivar used to make plum sauce in Asian cuisines. It has showy red, white, or pink flowers, grows to 30' tall, and is hardy to Zone 6. Asian apricots are hardier than European varieties but may not fruit in climates where winter temperatures vary, such as in Zones 5 and 6. (Try 'Scout' in those zones.) Consistently cold or warm winters are required for fruiting. European apricots thrive where peaches grow, typically in Zones 8 and 9. Hybrids of apricots and plums called apriums, pluots, and plumcots combine the best features of each species.

CHERRY
Prunus **spp.** *PROO-nus*

'Lambert' is a hardy sweet cherry and a good pollenizer for other types.

ZONES: 3-8
SIZE: 8–80'h × 6–50'w
TYPE: Deciduous tree
GROWTH: Slow

LIGHT: Full sun
MOISTURE: Average
FEATURES: Fragrant, showy flowers; edible fruits

SITING: Choose a sunny location at the top of a slope in deep, fertile, moist, well-drained, slightly acid soil. Plant the tree in a north-facing position if late spring frosts occur in your locale. Bush-type cherries can tolerate heavier and alkaline soils. Dig the hole to the same depth as the roots and somewhat wider than their mass when spread out. The bud union should be several inches above the soil. Firm the soil around the roots by hand to make sure there are no air pockets and water well. Space standard varieties 25–50' apart, semidwarfs 15–25' apart, and dwarfs 8–12' apart. Use no plant food at planting.
CARE: Train sour cherries to an open or vase shape (see pages 550–551). Train sweet cherries to a central leader. After planting, cut off all the side branches but leave the leader. In late winter or early spring of the second year, choose a branch about 3' from the ground for the top scaffold branch, then select a few more at staggered intervals around the tree and not right above one another. Prune out all other branches, trim back the scaffolds to even their lengths, then cut back the leader to a point above the topmost scaffold where you want another one to form. In the following years, prune lightly but continue to develop new scaffold branches and remove any branches that compete. Branches become unfruitful after 3–5 years; prune them out. Feed mature trees with low-nitrogen fruit tree spikes, and water in dry weather, especially when the fruits are ripening. Remove water sprouts in summer to maintain an open canopy that sun can penetrate. Cut off suckers at ground level as soon as they appear.

Hand-weed an area 4–6' around the trunk. Use mulch to control weeds and conserve moisture in a circle as wide as the drip line, but keep it away from the trunks of trees. Use nutritional foliar sprays to correct mineral deficiencies. In dry conditions, water newly planted trees daily until they are well established.

Sour cherries are more tolerant of cold and heat and bloom later than sweet types, but protect both from frost damage. Either one may be killed below −20°F. Keep competing shrubs and trees pruned; too much shade makes even sweet cherries tart and less flavorful.

Sweet cherries (*P. avium*) are either crisp or soft fleshed. Crisp types are more desirable for cooking but tend to split as they ripen and become susceptible to brown rot. Sweet cherry trees can grow quite tall and are therefore more difficult to protect from birds. Put netting around the parts you can reach and let the birds have the cherries at the top, which is hard to harvest anyway. When training scaffolds, choose only wide-angled branches, which are less prone to breaking. Increase the angle of desirable young branches by weighting them down or using a wedge against the trunk.
PROPAGATION: Grow by bud grafting.
HARVEST: Sour cherries begin to bear 3–4 years from planting. Fruits ripen about 60 days after bloom, from late May to mid-June. Sweet cherries begin producing heavy yields in their fifth year and bear fruit in July. Store ripe cherries for up to a week in the refrigerator. Also called pie cherries, sour cherries are used for cooking only, because they are usually too tart to eat fresh from the tree. A few cultivars will become sweet if left on the tree until completely ripe.

PESTS AND DISEASES: Humidity and heat encourage fusarium wilt, rots, and molds. Clean cultural practices are essential to the health of cherry trees. Remove and destroy diseased fruit, leaves, twigs, and branches. Choose cultivars bred for your weather and soil conditions and with resistance to pests and diseases common in your locale. Varieties susceptible to brown rot are best grown in dry climates. Plum curculio, brown rot, fruit flies, leaf spot, and bacterial canker are common problems of cherry trees. See page 529 for information on spraying trees to prevent or control infection and infestation. Cover trees with netting to protect the fruit from birds. Use trunk wraps in winter to protect trees from gnawing rodents.

RECOMMENDED CULTIVARS: Sour cherries (*P. cerasus*) are self-fruitful and need about 1,000 chilling hours below 45°F. They are subdivided into two types: Morellos have dark skin, red flesh, and acidic juice; amarelles have red skin, yellow flesh, and clear juice and are more disease tolerant.

Sweet cherries thrive in warm climates but most are not self-fruitful. Plant compatible pollenizers nearby to ensure a good crop.

CHERRY
continued

Self-fruitful amarelle types are tart cherries good for cooking. They are also known as pie cherries. This is 'Montmorency'.

Cover the parts of cherry trees that you can reach with netting to protect the fruits from birds and squirrels.

Choose varieties grown on dwarf rootstock to keep them to 10'. 'Montmorency' is a tart amarelle cherry that blooms late and ripens over a long season. For small gardens try 'Northstar', which has similar fruit on a genetic dwarf tree. 'Meteor' is a semidwarf amarelle tree that bears abundantly late in the season. 'Early Richmond' is an old-fashioned morello with small, acidic fruits. 'English Morello' is a large, hardy, late-bearing shrub with dark, acidic fruits that freeze well.

Acerola or Barbados cherry *(Malpighia glabra)* is a distantly related shrub or small tree 5–20' tall with pink or red flowers and juicy bright red fruits resembling cherries. Acerola blooms throughout the summer and bears several crops of fruit beginning the third or fourth year from planting. The fruits are too tart to be eaten raw but make excellent sweetened juice and preserves that can be frozen for later use. Duke cherries *(P. ×gondovinii)* are hybrids of sweet and sour cherries. 'Royal Duke' is a hardy and productive cultivar. The flavorful fruits are dark red with light, soft flesh. Because sweet cherries need 600–700 chilling hours, they grow well in mild climates—typically anywhere where peaches thrive. Most need a compatible

pollenizer; ask your local extension agent or nursery grower which ones will work best together in your garden. 'Stark Gold' is a universal pollinator and hardy to Zone 4. 'Bing' is a well-known crisp-fleshed variety good for eating fresh but is susceptible to disease. 'Lambert' is hardier and more vigorous and can be used as a pollenizer. It has dark purple-red skin and pale flesh and is good for canning.

'Windsor' is another firm-fleshed dark red cultivar that is good fresh or processed and has disease resistance. 'Royal Ann' (also called 'Napoleon') is a large midseason yellow cherry blushed with red. Its sweet, firm flesh is good fresh or cooked. Choose 'Rainier' if you need an earlier tree with the same characteristics. Try self-fruitful 'Stella' or 'Starkrimson' which is both self-fruitful and a good pollinator, if your growing space is limited; or 'Black Tartarian', an early, soft-fleshed

cultivar, if you have room for two or more trees in a home garden.

Nanking cherries *(P. tomentosa)* are extremely cold-hardy shrubs with tart fruits good for canning or wine making. Oriental bush cherry *(P. japonica)* fruits in 2–3 years from seed, grows to 8', and is hardy to Zone 4. Other bush-type cherries that thrive in northern climates are pin cherry *(P. pensylvanica)* and chokecherry *(P. virginiana)*. Astringent, orange-fruited chokecherry *(P. virginiana flava)* is a shade-tolerant native wild cherry adaptable to most soils. It grows 25–40' tall. All parts of the chokecherry except the ripe fruits are toxic. Western sand cherry *(P. besseyi)* cultivars 'Hanson', 'Amber', and 'Black Beauty' are hardy to Zone 3, and 'Brooks' grows in Alaska. They are cold and drought tolerant and rarely bothered by pests or disease.

ALMOND
Prunus dulcis *PROO-nus DULL-sis*

Almond is the only *Prunus* tree grown solely for its edible seeds.

ZONES: 8-10
SIZE: 10–30'h × 8–25' w
TYPE: Deciduous tree
GROWTH: Slow

LIGHT: Full sun
MOISTURE: Average
FEATURES: Lightly fragrant, showy flowers; edible seeds (nuts)

SITING: Almond does best where summers are long, warm, and dry. Choose a sunny, elevated location with deep, fertile, well-drained, slightly acid soil. A shallow site is acceptable if irrigation means are available. Keep the tree roots damp while you prepare the site. The hole should be deep enough for the roots to be spread out without being bent or crowded. The bud union of a grafted tree should be several inches above the soil line. Fill the soil in by hand, packing it around the roots for maximum contact. Water to eliminate air pockets, then add more soil. Use no plant food at planting.

CARE: Of all the *Prunus* trees, only almond is cultivated solely for its seeds. It is the first in its genus to bloom in spring. A dormant tree will survive a temperature dip into the teens, but protect a blooming tree from frost. Almond is deep rooted and thus drought tolerant, but prolonged temperatures over 80°F can cause bud failure the following season. Prune almond to an open shape or a modified leader shape and remove excess new branches (see pages 550–551). Unlike other *Prunus* trees cultivated for the flesh of their fruits, almond does not need to be thinned. Spread mulch around the tree to the drip line to keep the roots cool, but don't let it touch the trunk. Use a foliar zinc spray if soil analysis indicates the need.

PROPAGATION: Grow by grafting or from seed.

HARVEST: Trees begin fruiting in 3–4 years and can produce for 50 years or more. Fruits develop on shoot spurs, which are productive for up to 5 years and then should be pruned out. Pick when fruits split open, 180–240 days from flowering. Spread a sheet or tarp beneath the tree and shake to loosen the fruits. Ripe fruits left on the tree attract pests. Hull the ripe fruits and spread the shells in single layers in trays in a dry, shady area with good air circulation. Almonds are ready to eat when the shells are brown and completely dry and the nuts are crunchy. Eat them raw or roasted, or use in baked goods and almond butter and as a topping for casseroles and desserts. Store dried nuts in plastic or glass at room temperature for up to 1 year and in the freezer for many years. Freezing nuts for 2 weeks kills any weevils or worms that may be present.

PESTS AND DISEASES: Avoid insecticides if possible to protect bees and other beneficial insects that pollinate fruit trees. Keep the area around the tree cleaned of dropped fruits and other vegetative matter than can harbor pests and diseases. Use a fungicide spray at 10–14-day intervals until petal drop and again in autumn after leaf fall to prevent brown rot, twig blight, green fruit rot, and other fungal infections. For more information on spraying fruit trees, see page 529. Use dormant oil in winter to control scale, mites, and borers. Use netting to protect trees from birds, and trunk wraps in winter to prevent rodent damage.

RECOMMENDED CULTIVARS: Almonds are subdivided into bitter and sweet types and hard- and soft-shelled varieties. Most are self-sterile and require pollinators. They need only 250–500 chilling hours below 45°F. Sweet soft-shelled almonds are the type most often grown in home gardens in the United States. 'Cavaliera' is a very early cultivar suitable for areas with warm weather year-round. 'Nonpareil' is the most commonly grown midseason variety. It blooms in February and fruits in late August or early September. Use 'All-in-One', a self-fruitful semidwarf cultivar, as a pollenizer. 'Ferragnes' fruits in mid-September, 'Marcona' in late September, and 'Texas' in early October. 'Garden Prince' is a midseason self-fruitful genetic dwarf good for container growing.

Almonds are ready to harvest when the fruits split open. Shake the nuts from the tree onto a sheet spread below.

PEACH
Prunus persica *PROO-nus PER-sih-kuh*

Peach trees require long, hot summers and mild winters.

ZONES: 5–8
SIZE: 6–20'h × 6–20'w
TYPE: Deciduous tree
GROWTH: Slow
LIGHT: Full sun
MOISTURE: Moderate
FEATURES: Edible fruits

SITING: Peaches and nectarines are the least hardy of the *Prunus* trees and the most demanding to grow, so plant them in a sunny, protected location. Plant in spring on the north side of your property if late spring frosts are a problem in your area; otherwise, a south-facing slope is the best site. In hot southern climates plant peaches and nectarines in autumn. They are shallow rooted, so they do best in rich, moist, well-drained, slightly acid soil. Choose 1-year-old trees about 4' tall and at least ½" in diameter grown on rootstock suitable for your climate. Container-grown trees can be planted at any time of year; plant bare-root trees in spring in areas with cold winters or in fall in areas with mild winters. Soak both in a weak solution of transplant starter for several hours before planting. Space them as far apart as they will be tall when mature. Prune out any dead or damaged wood, and cut away any roots that encircle the root ball. Remove any wires and ties from the trunk and roots, and make room for stakes if they are needed. The holes should be large enough to accommodate the roots without crowding or bending them. The graft union should be several inches above the soil surface. The top layer of soil should be light and friable so the crown will dry quickly to prevent disease. Make a shallow trench around the tree 8–12" from the trunk to catch water.

CARE: Train trees to an open center as you would sour cherries (see pages 550–551). Keep the soil consistently moist but not waterlogged. High humidity increases the likelihood of brown rot. Spread several inches of well-rotted manure or mulch around the tree but away from the trunk to avoid pest and fungal damage and control

weeds. Remove any sprouts and suckers. A healthy tree grows 12–24" a year; if yours does not, have the soil tested to determine its nutrient needs. Unnecessary feeding encourages new succulent growth, which is susceptible to frost damage and insect infestation. Trees bear on 1-year-old wood only, so prune out old wood each year while trees are dormant and dry. Thin fruits to 6" apart after normal fruit drop. Prop up sagging fruit-laden limbs to keep them from breaking.

PROPAGATION: Grow by grafting.

HARVEST: Peach and nectarine trees bear in 2 or 3 years. Fruits ripen in midsummer to midautumn, depending on cultivar and zone. Pick them when all green coloration is gone. Ripe fruits easily come off the tree with a slight upward twist, but handle them gently because they bruise easily. Store ripe fruit in the refrigerator for a few days. Pressure-can fruits for long-term storage. Sliced fruits bathed in lemon juice to retard discoloration can be stored in the freezer for up to 6 months.

PESTS AND DISEASES: Prune out sick and damaged wood immediately, and keep the ground around trees cleaned of dropped fruit and other matter that harbors pests and encourages disease. Most diseases can be avoided by choosing resistant cultivars and practicing clean cultural habits to keep pests away. If necessary, spray dormant oil during the winter to control serious infestations of peachtree borer, scale, and mites; spray *Btk* at bloom time and during the summer to control the caterpillars. Cultivate the soil around the tree shallowly to destroy pupae. Avoid using insecticides while trees are in flower to protect beneficial bees and other pollinators. Nectarines are more susceptible than peaches to plum curculio and brown rot, possibly because of their smooth skin. Use a fungicide spray at 10–14-day intervals until petal drop and again in autumn after leaf fall to prevent peachleaf

curl, brown rot, twig blight, green fruit rot, and other infections. For more information on spraying fruit trees, see page 529. Use netting to protect fruis from birds, and trunk wraps in winter to prevent rodent damage.

RECOMMENDED CULTIVARS: Peaches and nectarines differ by just one gene. Peach has the gene for fuzzy skin and nectarine does not. Most are self-pollinating and live only 10–15 years. Fruits are ready to harvest 2–3 years from planting. The flesh of most types is yellow but some are white. Peaches are further subdivided as freestone or clingstone. The pits are easy to remove in freestones but are still attached to the flesh in clingstone varieties. They bloom very early so are susceptible to frost. Choose cultivars with chilling hours appropriate for your area and bred for resistance to pests and diseases in your climate. Nectarine 'Garden Beauty' is a natural dwarf growing 4–6'. 'Durbin' is an early, disease-resistant variety good for southern gardens. 'Sunglo' bears large, juicy freestone fruits. 'RedGold' is a heavy-bearing, disease-resistant yellow freestone nectarine with bright red skin.

'Harbinger' is a very early, small yellow clingstone peach. Other early varieties include 'Early Redhaven', a peach that freezes well; 'Garnet Beauty', a yellow semifreestone type; and 'Florida King', a low-chill variety good for the South. Midseason varieties include 'Cresthaven', a yellow freestone resistant to browning; 'Polly', a semidwarf, self-fertile, white variety hardy to Zone 4; and 'Reliance', the most cold-hardy peach. 'Compact Redhaven' and 'Compact Elberta' are genetic dwarf peaches. Late varieties include 'Elberta', a large yellow freestone good fresh and canned; 'Belle of Georgia', an old-fashioned white-fleshed freestone cultivar; and 'Yakima Hale', a self-fruitful, large, flavorful yellow freestone. They ripen in late August.

Nectarines are peaches without the gene for fuzzy skin.

Thin peaches and nectarines to 6" apart to give them room to develop fully.

Prevent peachleaf curl, rots, and blights with fungicide applications.

PLUM
Prunus spp. *PROO-nus*

European plum cultivars bloom late but also fruit late in the season.

ZONES: 2–9
SIZE: 8–25'h ×
10–20'w
TYPE: Deciduous
tree
GROWTH: Slow

LIGHT: Full sun
MOISTURE: High
FEATURES: Showy,
fragrant flowers;
edible drupes

SITING: Choose a sunny, protected location with deep, rich, fertile loam. Plant plums on the north side of your property if late spring frosts are a problem in your area; otherwise, a south-facing slope is the best site. Plant 1-year-old dormant stock in spring in cold winter climates and in autumn in mild climates. Prune back to 3–4' tall and plant the tree at the same depth it grew in the nursery. Space standard-size trees 20' apart, semidwarf trees 15' apart, and dwarf trees and shrubs 8–10' apart. Spread a layer of well-rotted compost or manure around the tree and cover that with a couple inches of mulch to the drip line, but keep both away from the trunk.

CARE: Because European plums have deep roots, they can tolerate heavy soils. Japanese trees have shallower roots and can't tolerate waterlogged soil but are drought resistant. European plums should grow 12" a year, and Asian plums should grow up to 20". If not, have soil samples analyzed to determine the nutrient deficiencies before adding any needed amendments. Overfeeding encourages new succulent growth which is susceptible to pests and diseases. Train European plums to a central leader and Japanese plums and all shrub types to an open center (see pages 550–551). Prune after flowering to remove dead or diseased wood only. Fruits develop on long-lived spurs. European fruits develop toward the interior of the tree, so thinning branches promotes ripening. American plums are shrubby and need thinning to make harvest easier. Thin the fruits by hand after normal fruit drop, leaving only the best plum on each spur and 4–6" between fruits. Red cultivars need more thinning than blue ones, and

heavily fruiting branches may need to be propped up.

PROPAGATION: Grow by grafting.

HARVEST: Blue plums bear 4–5 years from planting and red ones 3–4 years. Most trees are productive for 10–15 years. Plums are ready to harvest when they come off in your hand with a gentle twist. Unripe fruit won't come off the spur without tugging. Sample a few from different parts of the tree before making a significant harvest. Japanese plums can be picked before they are completely ripe; they will continue to ripen off the tree. American plums are ready to harvest when they are soft. European plums must ripen on the tree but should be picked before they are mushy. Ripe plums left on the tree will rot. Store all types of ripe plums for up to 2 weeks in the refrigerator. European plums can be sundried whole for use as prunes. All sweet-fleshed varieties are excellent eaten out of hand or sliced in fresh fruit salads, and can be used for cooking and canning. Tart cultivars are good in jams, jellies, preserves, baked goods, and wine.

PESTS AND DISEASES: Plums are susceptible to black knot, a fungus that produces hard black bumps on twigs and branches. Prune out infected areas in winter by cutting the

wood well below the knots and destroying the cuttings. Sterilize your pruning tools between cuts. Use a labeled fungicide to prevent brown rot. Prune out sick and damaged wood immediately, and keep the ground around trees cleaned of dropped fruit and other vegetative matter that harbors pests and encourages disease. Most diseases can be avoided by choosing resistant cultivars and practicing clean cultural habits to keep pests away. Spray dormant oil in winter to control aphids, scale, and borers. Use insecticides to control heavy infestations of plum curculio, but avoid spraying when trees are in bloom to protect bees and other beneficial pollinators. See page 529 for more information on spraying fruit trees. Use netting to protect fruits from birds, and trunk wraps in winter to prevent rodent damage.

RECOMMENDED CULTIVARS: Choose a self-fruitful tree if you have room for just one. To grow those that need pollenizers, be sure to choose cultivars whose bloom times overlap and at least one that bears annually. Select European (*P. ×domestica*) varieties for late-season freestone plums to dry as prunes. They are hardier than Japanese types and bloom later in spring

Use sterilized pruning tools to cut out twigs and branches infected with black knot, a fungus common in plum trees.

PLUM
continued

American plums are cold-hardy and tolerant of heat and drought but aren't as sweet as other species.

so are safe for zones where late spring frosts may occur. However, they fruit late in September and into October and thus may be damaged by an early autumn frost. Their freestone pits make them easy to process for canning. European prune plums include 'Bluefree', with large blue-skinned freestone fruits; 'Damson' (derived from *P. institia*), a small, self-pollinating tree with tart blue plums good for cooking; 'French Prune', a small, self-pollinating tree with very sweet, small red to purple fruits; 'Sugar', a large purple-red plum that's also good right off the tree; and 'Stanley', a vigorous annual producer of medium-size purple-blue fruits with sweet yellow flesh, excellent fresh, dried, or canned. Gage plums are light green and sweet. Most are self-fruitful but will yield more heavily with a pollenizer nearby. 'Reine Claude' ripens in mid- to late summer. It can be planted in all zones because it has a low chill requirement and is cold hardy.

Japanese plums (*P. salicina*) are shorter, spreading, early-blooming trees with sweet clingstone fruits. They have low chill requirements and not all are hardy. 'Catalina' is a self-fruitful pollinator good for home gardens with room for just one tree. 'Early Golden' and 'Abundance' (midseason) are yellow-fleshed types that tend to bear biennially. 'Omaha' is a hardy, late-season cultivar with sweet, juicy red-and-yellow-speckled fruits. 'Santa Rosa' is a hardy, midseason tree with fragrant, flavorful dark red plums with yellow flesh. 'Superior' is a Japanese × American hybrid with large, tasty red plums that can be peeled like peaches. It is hardy but needs a pollenizer such as 'Toka'. The hybrid cherry-plum is a cross of Japanese plum and western sand cherry (*P. besseyi*). The result is improved flavor in fruits from short-lived, self-sterile, frost-intolerant shrubs. Crosses of plums and apricots are discussed on page 543.

American varieties (*P. americana*) include 'Newport', 'Fairlane', and 'Manet'. All are cold hardy and tolerate heat and drought. The fruit ripens in August but is only of fair quality. Chickasaw plum (*P. angustifolia*) is faster growing than other American types, easy to prune to a central leader, and reaches 12–25' tall. The tart 1" bright red fruits ripen in September, but the tree bears biennially. Canada plum (*P. nigra*) is a native tree hardy to Zone 2. It grows to 10' and bears 1" oval red fruits that are good in preserves. Sloe plum (*P. spinosa*) is a dwarf shrub growing to 4' high and wide. It covers itself with small blue fruits that are bitter when fresh but excellent in jams and jellies and for flavoring gin.

Beach plum (*P. maritima*) grows to 6' in sandy soil and tolerates salinity. It can be used as a hedge or grown in a container. The ½–1" fruits come in black, blue, red, or yellow. 'Grant' is blue and has the largest fruits at 1". 'Red' has red skin and sweet yellow flesh. *P. maritima* ×*americana* hybrids include 'Flava', with sweet yellow-skinned fruits, and 'Dunbars', with bright red freestone fruits. They make delicious preserves.

SPACE-SAVING TIP

Gardeners with limited space can obtain a variety of fruits by planting trees with multiple cultivar grafts. A single plum tree, for example, can be grafted to produce both red and yellow fruits of different cultivars. Or a branch from a suitable pollenizer can be grafted to a cultivar that's not self-fertile. Just be sure to choose cultivars of similar vigor, bloom time, and disease susceptibility, and tag any individual grafts so they aren't accidentally pruned out.

Choose a self-fruitful small shrub or dwarf tree cultivar to grow plums in a patio container.

PRUNING AND TRAINING FRUIT TREES

Pruning and training your fruit trees are the most effective means of keeping them healthy and productive for many years. By creating a strong structure to support the weight of the crops and keeping all parts of the trees open to sunlight, you are helping to prevent damage from wind, pests, and diseases, promoting the development of high yields, and making it easy to harvest when the time comes.

Apples, pears, cherries, and plums produce their best fruit on 2–3-year-old wood. Almonds and apricots add new fruiting spurs each year but need the oldest ones removed. Peaches and nectarines bear their fruit on last year's growth. Pruning each year encourages productive fruiting wood. Unpruned trees quickly lose their productivity and become more susceptible to health problems.

PRUNING METHODS

Prune mature trees in late winter to early spring in cold-winter climates and when trees are dormant in warm-winter climates (between leaf fall and the start of new bud swell).

There are two basic types of pruning cuts: heading back and thinning. Thinning cuts remove wood to stop growth and are made at the base of a branch or sucker so that no buds are left to sprout. Begin by using loppers and a long-handled pruning saw to remove any dead or damaged wood. Make all cuts at an angle and close to nodes where new shoots will grow. The stubs left at the cuts should be no more than ¼" long to prevent decay and a possible point of entry for disease. Next remove any branches that grow toward the trunk or point downward toward the soil. Then remove any branches that cross over one another. To further reduce the density of the tree canopy, use hand

1 Make thinning cuts to remove buds and stop excess growth.

2 Cut at an angle and leave no more than ¼" of stub to prevent decay.

1 Make heading cuts to stimulate new branches. Remove the terminal buds of young saplings to encourage growth.

2 Cutting off the terminal bud at the end of the branch will encourage growth at the vegetative lateral buds below.

pruners to snip thin twigs. Cut or rub off water sprouts and remove any suckers.

Heading cuts shorten branches to stimulate new growth. Fruit trees vary in the amount and type of heading cuts needed. Young trees—sometimes whips with no branches—are often cut back at the time of planting to remove the terminal bud. The bud at the end of any branch is a terminal bud. Cutting off a terminal bud stimulates the growth of branches to either side. Lateral buds are those spaced along the length of a branch, sometimes in clusters or pairs. Cutting off a branch just above a lateral bud will direct new growth in the direction the bud is pointing. Make pruning cuts to buds on the outside of branches so that new growth will be directed away from the center of the tree.

TRAINING METHODS

Fruit trees should be trained to one of three forms—vase or open, central leader, or modified central leader—beginning when they are planted. Training creates a structure appropriate for optimum health and productivity. Left untrained, fruit trees become overgrown with weak, twiggy branches and small, sometimes diseased fruit.

The vase or open training method shapes the tree to a short trunk about 3' tall from which rise three or four main limbs, each of which has secondary branches. This method is commonly used for peach and nectarine trees and some apples, pears, and cherries.

Central leader training shapes the tree into one straight trunk with whorls of branches around it spaced 6–10" apart vertically. This creates a pyramid or Christmas-tree shape that is strong but difficult to maintain or harvest if the tree is tall. Dwarf apple trees are often trained to this shape.

A tree trained to a modified central leader combines the strength of a central trunk with the open habit of a vase-shaped tree. The main trunk is allowed to grow as a central leader but the top of the tree is cut back each year to force the growth of lower branches. This method is used for some apple and pear trees.

Training individual branches while trees are young helps to avoid breakage and disease later on. Ideally branches should be balanced around the trunk at an angle to it of about 45–60 degrees. Branches that grow parallel to the ground or slightly upward will be the strongest and most fruitful. If a young branch is in a desirable scaffold position but has a narrower angle, use a wedge of wood between it and the trunk to spread the angle as the branch grows, or tie a bag of sand to the outside end of the branch to weigh it down as it grows. Remove the wedge or weight when the branch holds the angle on its own.

After mature trees begin to bear big crops, thinning of large-fruited cultivars, such as apples and peaches, is necessary to achieve maximum production of top-quality, full-size fruits. Trees naturally drop some fruit in summer but not enough to prevent overcrowding in healthy trees. The best time to thin fruit is just after a tree's natural fruit drop, typically a few weeks after bloom. Start by removing any underdeveloped, infested, and disease-injured fruits. Then remove all but one healthy fruit where there are several in a cluster. Finally, thin the remaining fruits so they are spaced 6" apart. If you are skeptical about the value of thinning, leave one branch unthinned and compare the size and quality of its fruit to those on thinned branches at harvest.

Fruit trees can also be grown as hedges or espaliers, which save space but require routine training and pruning. Espalier training directs the growth of a tree or shrub flat against a wall, trellis, or other support. Dwarf apples and pears are best suited to the rigors of espalier training because they bear on old wood. Peaches, nectarines, guavas, apricots, and plums are better sculpted as hedges, where old, nonfruiting wood can be removed without ruining the design.

Cut to buds or branches on the outside of the stem so that new branches grow away from the tree's interior.

Prune scaffold branches as if they were young trees, heading back or removing any that overtake the leader.

Prune out broken or narrow-angled branches. Those that grow at a slightly upward angle are the strongest.

Prune out suckers and water sprouts at the base of the branches so that no buds are left to sprout.

COMMON GUAVA
Psidium guajava SID-ee-um gwah-HAH-vuh

Most guavas are self-fruitful, but yields are improved with pollenizers. Common guava is also known as tropical guava.

ZONES: 9–11
SIZE: 6–40'h ×
8–25'w
TYPE: Evergreen tree
or shrub
GROWTH: Fast

LIGHT: Full sun
MOISTURE:
Moderate
FEATURES: Edible
fruits

SITING: Choose a sunny, protected location with soil that drains well. Plant guavas on a north-facing exposure if late spring frosts are a problem; otherwise, a south-facing slope is best. Space strawberry guavas (*P. littorale* var. *longipes*) 10–15' apart. Small cultivars can be grown in containers.

CARE: Guava grows best where daytime temperatures are 70–85°F. It is susceptible to frost and not tolerant of extreme heat. Water in times of drought. Most are self-fruitful but will yield more heavily when a pollenizer is planted nearby. Guavas fruit on new growth, so prune them only to shape the trees and remove suckers. Feed common guavas with balanced plant food monthly during the first year after planting and every other month thereafter. Feed strawberry guavas half that often. Use foliar sprays if soil sample analysis indicates nutritional deficiencies. Rejuvenate old trees by severe pruning.

PROPAGATION: Grow common guavas by grafting; grow strawberry guava from seed or cuttings.

HARVEST: Guavas fruit 2–4 years from planting and are productive for at least 15 years. The fruits mature 90–150 days after flowering. Leave them on the tree to ripen, but protect them from birds, bats, and fruit flies. Ripe fruits can be shaken from the tree and caught in nets, but they bruise easily. Almost-ripe yellow-green guavas can be clipped from the tree and will ripen at room temperature within

1 week. Ripe fruits covered with plastic wrap will keep in the refrigerator for up to 2 weeks. Store ripe guavas away from other fruits and vegetables that release ethylene.

PESTS AND DISEASES: Mites, thrips, aphids, fruit worms, sucking bugs, and fruit flies may cause problems. Damaged fruits are subject to rots. Avoid using insecticides when the trees are in bloom to protect pollinators. Use dormant oil spray in winter to control infestations, and keep the ground around trees clean of dropped fruit and vegetative matter that harbors pests and diseases. Control algal spots and anthracnose with labeled fungicides. Use netting and noisemakers to discourage birds and bats.

RECOMMENDED CULTIVARS: 'Ruby' bears red-fleshed fruits in fall and early winter in Florida and Hawaii. 'Ka Hua Kula' is a pink-fleshed dessert-type that grows well in humid climates. 'Detwiler' produces greenish-yellow fruits with sweet yellow to pink flesh. It grows well in California. Strawberry guavas bear 1–1½" red-skinned fruits with white flesh or yellow fruits.

POMEGRANATE
Punica granatum poo-NEYE-kuh gra-NAY-tum

Pomegranates must ripen on the tree but clip them off before they crack open.

ZONES: 8–11
SIZE: 10–30'h ×
10–30'w
TYPE: Evergreen or
deciduous tree or
shrub
GROWTH: Slow

LIGHT: Full sun
MOISTURE:
Moderate
FEATURES: Showy
flowers, edible
fruits

SITING: Choose a sunny, warm location with moist, well-drained soil. Plants may produce lower yields and fruit quality in sandy and clay soils but are tolerant of alkalinity. Plant 10–20' apart.

CARE: Pomegranate does best in areas with cool winters and hot, dry summers. It is

drought tolerant but yields best if the soil is consistently moist. Water young plants until they are established and mature trees with ripening fruit. Provide balanced plant food once in spring the first 2 years only. Apply a mulch each year, but keep it from touching the trunks. Plants can be pruned to a few trunks or trained as fountain-shaped shrubs for ornamental value. For multiple trunks, select five or six suckers to develop, then prune out all the others. Fruits form on the tips of the current year's

Train pomegranate to multiple trunks to increase its ornamental value.

growth, so prune young trees and shrubs to encourage new shoots on all sides. After the third year, prune out only dead wood and suckers.

PROPAGATION: Grow from hardwood cuttings.

HARVEST: Fruits ripen 180–220 days after flowering, from late July through September. Fruits ready for harvest make a slight metallic or cracking sound when tapped. The fruits must be ripened on the tree, but clip them off before they become overripe and crack. Their flavor improves in storage. Fruits can be kept for 6 months in cool but not freezing temperatures and high humidity.

PESTS AND DISEASES: Spray plants with a forceful water spray periodically to prevent spider mites. Spray flowers twice 30 days apart to control pomegranate fruit borers. Excessive moisture causes heart rot. Cover ripening fruit with netting or bags to protect fruit from birds.

RECOMMENDED CULTIVARS: 'Wonderful' bears large dark purple-red fruit with juicy deep red flesh. 'Granada' is darker red and sweeter than 'Wonderful' and ripens a month earlier. Both have semihard seeds. 'Sweet' is greenish with a red blush when ripe but much sweeter than other cultivars. 'Utah Sweet' has pink skin and pulp and soft seeds. Cultivars with soft seeds are often described as seedless. For container growing, try 'Nana', a dwarf pomegranate that grows to 3' tall and wide.

PEAR
Pyrus communis PY-rus kom-MEW-nis

Select a self-fruitful pear cultivar if you have room for just one tree.

ZONES: 3–8
SIZE: 8–25'h × 8–25'w
TYPE: Deciduous tree

GROWTH: Slow
LIGHT: Full sun
MOISTURE: Average
FEATURES: Edible fruits

SITING: Choose a sunny, well-drained location. Plant in a north-facing location to delay blooming in areas with variable spring weather. Pears are deep rooted and can grow in any soil but do best in rich, heavy loam. Plant a 1-year-old whip at the same depth it grew in the nursery, then cut back the top to about 3'. Space standard cultivars 16–20' apart, dwarfs 10–12'. Plant pears while they are dormant in frost-free areas or in spring in cold-winter zones.

CARE: Pears are related to apples but more difficult to grow. Standard varieties require 800–1,110 chilling hours below 45°F; Asian pears require 400–900 hours. They are all hardy, but the flowers can be killed by a late spring frost. Most pears require cross-pollination, so plant at least two or three. Keep the soil consistently moist; lack of moisture causes fruits to drop. In areas with hot summers, shade developing fruits from sunscald and provide supplemental irrigation. Use plant food only if a soil sample analysis indicates the need; excess nitrogen encourages fire blight. After normal fruit drop, thin the remaining fruits for best size. Train standard trees to a central leader. In the dormant season head back any side branches that compete with the central leader. Dwarf cultivars can be grown as hedges or espaliered. For more information on training and pruning fruit trees, see pages 550–551.

PROPAGATION: Grow by grafting.

HARVEST: Standard pear trees begin to bear fruit in 5–6 years, dwarf trees in 3–4. The fruits—roughly the size of an elongated apple—ripen in August through September. Pick pears by hand 1–2 weeks before they are completely ripe. Lift the fruit up with a twisting motion rather than pulling on it. Allow pears to ripen at room temperature, or store them in a cool, dark place and bring them out to ripen as needed. To hasten ripening place several pears together in a sealed plastic container. Unripe pears can be refrigerated for months and brought out to ripen about a week before needed. Eat them fresh out of hand, sliced into salads and baked goods, or processed for jelly, chutney, and wine.

PESTS AND DISEASES: Prune and destroy branches infected with fire blight, a bacterial disease for which there is no cure. Pear psylla can be controlled with a precisely timed dormant oil spray in late winter or early spring; ask your local

Harvest pears a week or two before they are completely ripe and store them in cool darkness until needed.

Pears bruise and tear easily, so pick them by hand with an upward twisting motion instead of pulling down.

Remove and destroy any branches infected with fire blight, an incurable bacterial disease common in older pear cultivars.

extension agent for help determining when treatment will be most effective. Use insecticide sprays only after the petals have fallen to avoid killing pollinating honeybees. For additional information on spraying fruit trees, see page 529. Remove water sprouts to reduce aphid populations. Rake up and destroy dropped fruits and vegetative debris to control pear scab and pests. Use hardware cloth or plastic guards around the lower part of tree trunks to prevent rabbits and mice from eating the bark.

RECOMMENDED CULTIVARS: Most well-known pears including 'Aurora', 'Bartlett', 'Bosc', and 'Comice' are highly susceptible to disease. Choose newer hybrids and cultivars resistant to fire blight and pear scab. Be sure to select self-fruitful types if you have room for just one tree. Otherwise, choose trees that are compatible pollenizers. 'Duchess' is self-fruitful and late bearing, a good pollinator for other trees, and grows well in northern zones. 'Moonglow' thrives in all pear-growing regions and is early, blight resistant, and good fresh or canned. Late-season 'Seckel' bears small, very sweet yellow-brown pears that are good fresh or canned. The tree is hardy, resistant to fire blight, sometimes self-fruitful, and does well everywhere but the deepest south. It's a good choice for home gardens. 'Mericourt' grows well in southern zones and is good fresh or canned. 'Anjou' (sometimes 'D'anjou') does well in the cool climates of the Pacific Northwest and Great Lakes regions but not in hot-summer areas. The large fruits are green with a pink blush and have good flavor and texture fresh or cooked.

Asian pears (*P. serotina*) bear true pears that look like yellow apples. They have crisp, smooth flesh ready to eat when picked, and keep in the refrigerator for up to 6 months without becoming mushy. They grow best in cool-winter areas along the West Coast. Prune them like standard pears or train them as an espalier. Asian pears are self-fruitful but do best with pollenizers planted nearby. 'Shinseiki', an early-maturing flat yellow pear, and '20th Century', a flat green pear, may need to be cross-pollinated with a European cultivar for good fruit set annually in cooler climates.

Quince (*Cydonia oblonga*) rootstocks are used for dwarfing standard pears. Fruits of quince are good only when cooked in jelly and preserves.

RADISH
Raphanus sativus *RAF-an-us sub-TY-vus*

'D'Avignon' is a tapered French cultivar ready for harvest in just a few weeks.

ZONES: NA
SIZE: 2–6"h x 2–6"w
TYPE: Annual
GROWTH: Fast

LIGHT: Full sun to part shade
MOISTURE: High
FEATURES: Edible roots

SITING: The planting area should be weed free because emerging seedlings are difficult to distinguish and easily out-competed. Plant seeds ½" deep and 1" apart in rows 8–12" apart. Interplant with slower-developing crops such as carrots, beans, and cucumbers. Radish is a cool-weather crop; plant 3–4 weeks before the last spring frost and 6 weeks before the first fall frost in northern climates. Plant seeds in early autumn in southern zones.

CARE: Plant small amounts of seed every few weeks so you can pick and eat radishes at their peak. Thin the seedlings to 2" apart when they are 1" tall. Pull weeds by hand and keep the soil consistently moist.

PROPAGATION: Grow from seed.

HARVEST: Radishes are ready to pull up in 20–30 days. Those left in the ground too long crack or become pithy. Trim off the tops and roots and scrub off the dirt under running water. Radishes keep well in the refrigerator for up to 1 month. Daikon radishes are often grated and pickled for long-term storage.

Plant Daikon radishes in midsummer for autumn harvest.

PESTS AND DISEASES: Choose cultivars labeled for disease resistance. Control clubroot through clean gardening practices and crop rotation in well-drained soil. Pick off harlequin bugs and cabbageworms by hand or use *Bt* for serious infestations. Remove and destroy leaves infested with leaf miners and use floating row covers to discourage them and cabbage maggot flies. Knock aphids off with a strong stream from a garden hose. Interplant radishes with taller crops that will provide shade to discourage flea beetles.

RECOMMENDED CULTIVARS: 'D'Avignon' is a 3–4" tapered, cylindrical French red radish with a white tip. It is ready in only 21 days. 'Cherry Belle' and 'Comet' are among the earliest globe radishes, ready in 20–25 days. Round bright red 'Sora' can be planted at any time of year and is ready in 25–30 days. 'White Icicle' has 4–5" slender roots ready in 25–30 days. 'Crunchy Royale' is a sweet, round red radish ready in 30 days. 'Shunkyo Semi-Long' has 4–5"-long cylindrical pink roots with white flesh, ready in 35 days. It can be sown anytime and is slow to bolt. 'Miyashige' is a traditional daikon radish for late planting only. The long, cylindrical white roots are banded in green at the top and are ready in 50 days.

RHUBARB
Rheum xcultorum *ROOM kul-TOR-um*

Cool temperatures promote the best color in red-stalked rhubarb cultivars. Rhubarb is also known as pie plant.

ZONES: 2–8
SIZE: 1–3'h x 2–4'w
TYPE: Herbaceous perennial
GROWTH: Average

LIGHT: Full sun
MOISTURE: Average
FEATURES: Edible petioles (stalks)

SITING: Choose a permanent location in a sunny space. Rhubarb needs deep, rich, well-drained soil. Plant the crowns 2" deep and 6' apart each way. Add no plant food to the holes. Set the roots so that the central bud is 2" below the soil surface.

CARE: Cool weather promotes the best red color in rhubarb. When daytime temperatures climb above 80°F, add 2" of organic mulch around the plants to keep the roots cool. Keep the ground around plants free of weeds and debris where pests can hide. Cut off flower stems as they appear. Use a sharp spade to divide and replant rhubarb every 6–8 years or when stalks have become thin. Divide plants in early spring or in fall if you mulch plants with straw or manure after a few frosts. Divide the crown so that each new piece has some buds and as many roots as possible. Plant the new pieces immediately. Side-dress plants with well-rotted compost or manure after the last harvest and feed with balanced plant food.

Divide rhubarb in spring or fall every 6–8 years.

Divide the crown so that each piece has stems and roots.

PROPAGATION: Grow by crown division.

HARVEST: Allow plants to grow and develop without cutting stalks the first year after planting. Begin harvesting in the second season when stalks are 8–15" tall. Take just a few stalks each week for 2 weeks. In the third season cut one-third to one-half of the thickest stalks each week for up to 4 weeks. In subsequent years harvest up to two-thirds of the stalks each week for 8–10 weeks. Cut or twist the stalks from the crown, then cut off the toxic leaf blades and compost them. Store the unwashed stalks in a plastic bag in the refrigerator for up to 2 weeks, or blanch and freeze chopped stalks for up to 1 year.

PESTS AND DISEASES: Purchase certified disease-free plants to avoid crown rot. Vigorous plants will not be bothered by most pests, but handpick and destroy curculio beetles, caterpillars, and Japanese beetles. Plant rhubarb in well-drained soil or raised beds to prevent verticillium wilt.

RECOMMENDED CULTIVARS: 'MacDonald' is a good choice for heavy soils. 'Valentine' needs less sweetening than most other cultivars. 'Canada Red' keeps its color even when cooked. 'Victoria' has green stalks.

CURRANT, GOOSEBERRY

Ribes spp. *RY-beez*

American gooseberry cultivars such as 'Poorman' are disease-resistant.

ZONES: 2–9
SIZE: 3–6'h x 2–5'w
TYPE: Woody deciduous shrub
GROWTH: Slow
LIGHT: Part shade
MOISTURE: Average
FEATURES: Edible berries

SITING: Gooseberries and currants grow best in cool, humid regions that provide some winter chilling hours. Currants are hardy farther north than gooseberries. Both are adapted to a variety of conditions but thrive in rich, moist, well-drained, slightly acid loam that has been heavily amended with organic matter and cleared of all perennial weeds. The plants do not tolerate drought or standing water. Because they flower early, a sunny, northern exposure helps to delay blooming long enough to avoid frost damage and also provides shade for the berries from hot midday sun in summer. Plant vigorous, well-rooted 1-year-old plants in spring 4–5' apart in each direction. Spread the roots out carefully and make sure they do not touch any fresh manure or plant food, which could burn them. Set container-grown plants in the soil at the same level they were growing in the nursery. Plant bare-root stock so that the lowest branch is just above the soil surface, and cut the tops back to about 6" above ground level. *Note: Ribes is an alternate host of white pine blister rust; black currant is banned in many states. Plant all varieties at least 1,000 feet from white pine trees.*
CARE: Gooseberries and currants are shrubby, but in limited space they can be trained to a trellis. Prune them while they are dormant to improve air circulation and encourage new growth. Remove branches older than 3 years. Plants should have equal numbers of new, 1-year-old, and 2-year-old canes. Because they are partially self-sterile, multiple plants will result in higher yields. Thin developing fruits to increase the size of the remaining fruits. Use drip irrigation if necessary to keep the soil moist until the berries are harvested. If growing conditions are less than optimal

or if plants are located near competing trees and shrubs, feed them once a year with ¼–⅓ pound of balanced plant food per plant, in early spring before they break dormancy or in autumn after all the berries have been harvested.
PROPAGATION: Grow from hardwood cuttings or by layering.
HARVEST: Gooseberries and currants grow in long clusters on the shrubs. They ripen in late summer over a period of 4–6 weeks. Pick them before they are fully ripe for best use in cooking. Let them ripen on the plant for up to several weeks for fresh use. They sunburn easily, so keep freshly harvested ones in a shady spot while you pick. Wear gloves to pick gooseberries; most cultivars have thorns. Healthy plants may be productive for up to 20 years. Currants and gooseberries are most often used in pies, jams, and jellies but also make good sweet wine.
PESTS AND DISEASES: Plants are less susceptible to powdery mildew in full sun but more susceptible to fungal infections in prolonged wet weather. Spray fungicide according to label directions if needed. Prune out and destroy diseased or damaged wood, watching for signs of cane borers. Spray with insecticide to control heavy infestations of fruit fly maggots, but avoid spraying while plants are in bloom to protect beneficial pollinating insects. Remove and destroy plants infected with gall mites. Pick off any worms. Hard rain will wash off most aphids, or use a spray from the garden hose. Cover plants with netting to protect ripening fruits from birds.

Choose only currant cultivars that are immune to white pine blister rust.

RECOMMENDED CULTIVARS: Purchase certified disease-free stock. Gooseberries are divided into two groups. American gooseberry cultivars (*R. hirtellum*) have the best disease resistance. 'Red Jacket' is a nearly thornless variety. 'Poorman' is a good choice for home gardens because it is less thorny than other cultivars and its red berries are good fresh. European types (*R. uva-crispa*) are more susceptible to disease but have larger, sweeter fruit than American gooseberries. 'Fredonia' is a good late cultivar. 'Hinnomaki Yellow' is a mildew-resistant plant with pale yellow-green berries. Black currant (*R. nigrum*) is banned in many states; check with your local natural resources department before planting it. 'Consort' and 'Crusader' are

Pick slightly unripe berries for cooking or let them ripen on the bush to eat fresh.

rust-immune black cultivars acceptable for planting in some states. Red and white varieties are less likely to be hosts of white pine blister rust. Red currants (*R. silvestre*) are more flavorful for cooking. 'Red Lake' is a disease-resistant, late-ripening cultivar that is easy to pick. 'Wilder' is a vigorous midseason variety with large berries on long, compact clusters. Because white currants have lower acidity they are better for eating fresh. 'White Imperial' bears large pale yellow berries of excellent quality. 'Gloire des Sablons' (*R. rubrum*) is a pink cultivar with an upright habit. Jostaberry (*R. nidigrolaria*) is a fast-growing hybrid of black currant and gooseberry with reddish-black fruits. Buffalo currant (*R. aureum*) is more closely related to gooseberry and has a broader, weeping habit. It is cold hardy but has low chilling hour requirements and tolerates alkaline soils. It grows well in Southern California.

ROSEMARY

Rosmarinus officinalis ros-muh-RY-nus off-iss-ih-NAY-lis

Rosemary cultivars may have spreading or upright growth habits.

ZONES: (6)7–10
SIZE: 1–3'h x 1–3'w
TYPE: Woody
evergreen perennial
GROWTH: Slow

LIGHT: Full sun
MOISTURE: Average
FEATURES: Edible
leaves and flowers

SITING: Plant it in a sunny, protected location that drains well. Rosemary is a member of the mint family and grows well in average, neutral-pH garden soil as well as containers indoors and out. It thrives in raised beds and is drought tolerant.

CARE: Plan to grow rosemary as an annual in Zones 4–6. In short-summer areas plant it in pots for easy relocation if frost is predicted. Regular harvest of a few stems throughout the season encourages bushier growth. In warm-winter areas protect rosemary from harsh winds that may dry it out.

PROPAGATION: Grow from cuttings or by layering.

HARVEST: Cut a few succulent stems above woody growth as needed throughout the growing season. Strip the resinous leaves from the stems and chop or grind them for use with meats; in recipes that include potatoes, tomatoes, eggplant, or peppers;

Grow rosemary indoors in winter for fresh leaves year-round.

and in soups, stews, and marinades. Insert a few stems into bottles of vinegar or olive oil to flavor them. Use the tiny flowers in salads or as a garnish. Tie harvested stems in small bunches and hang them upside down in a cool, airy space to dry. In northern climates pull the plants up before the first frost and hang them by their roots to dry. Pull the dried leaves from the stems and store in an airtight container for up to 2 years. Pulverize them before adding them to foods; the whole leaves can be chewy. Rosemary also can be frozen for long-term storage but loses its rich color.

PESTS AND DISEASES: None are significant.

RECOMMENDED CULTIVARS: Varieties with an upright growth habit include 'Madalene Hill' and 'Arp', which are hardy to Zone 6. 'Arp' has gray-green foliage and blue flowers. 'Madalene Hill' has dark green leaves and pale blue flowers. In the Midwest try 'Athens Blue Spires', a cultivar that may be hardy to Zone 6. 'Blue Boy' is a compact dwarf variety that grows well in containers. 'Majorca' has an intermediate habit—upright but spreading with some trailing stems. 'Rexford' is a warm-climate cultivar with especially good flavor.

BLACKBERRY, RASPBERRY

Rubus spp. ROO-bus

Raspberries can be identified by their hollow cores.

ZONES: 4–9
SIZE: To 6'h x 3'w
TYPE: Woody
perennial shrub
GROWTH: Average

LIGHT: Full sun
MOISTURE: Average
FEATURES: Edible
berries

SITING: Brambles grow best in areas with long, mild springs and cool summer nights. They thrive in all but the most acid soils as long as the drainage is good. They need good air circulation to ward off disease. Avoid planting them in areas where tomatoes, potatoes, eggplants, and peppers have recently grown, because the site may harbor verticillium wilt. Select a site away from patios, decks, and recreational use areas where bees and dropped fruit can interfere. Plant rooted cuttings 4–6' apart in moist soil in early spring, 1 month before the last frost date. Set commercially grown canes at the same depth they were grown in the nursery.

CARE: Cane berries sprout new biennial canes each year. Blackberries become invasive if not pruned regularly. Because brambles bloom late in spring, frost is not a problem. Blackberries are drought tolerant; raspberries are not, but regular irrigation results in better yields for both. Blackberries are more tolerant of hot summer weather than raspberries, but mulch both species well to conserve soil moisture, control weeds, and increase yields. Prune off unwanted blackberry canes underground. Prune out any stubs that do not sprout in spring to avoid anthracnose. Fruit is borne only on 1-year-old blackberry canes. Top new canes to 6" to promote branching; prune out 1-year-old canes immediately after they finish fruiting. Prune trailing types to 6–10" in

Pick ripe raspberries in the morning after the dew has dried but while the plants are still cool.

Prune out the current season's fruiting canes immediately after harvesting the summer crop of raspberries.

BLACKBERRY, RASPBERRY
continued

Pinch out the new cane tips of purple and black raspberry cultivars in summer to promote branching.

winter after the first growing season and train them onto trellises. Thereafter prune them like erect types. Prune everbearing raspberries twice each season. In spring remove old canes as well as any damaged, diseased, or dead canes. Then pinch out the tips of canes where the fall crop was borne. The new summer crop fruits on the lower buds of the canes where the previous fall crop developed. Immediately after harvesting the summer crop, remove those canes entirely. Prune red and yellow one-crop raspberries by removing fruiting canes after harvest but do not pinch back new cane tips. Pinch out the tips of black and purple varieties to about 3' in summer to promote branching. Remove fruiting canes immediately after harvest.

PROPAGATION: Grow from root or stem cuttings, new suckers, or tip layering.

HARVEST: Pick in the morning when fruits and plants are dry and cool. Watch out for bees before you reach in. Carry the berries in shallow trays, because they are easily crushed. They also are highly perishable, so keep picked berries in the shade and move them to a cool location as soon as possible. Blackberries fruit the first year following planting. The fruit's green receptacle separates from the plant when the fruit is picked. The core should be small and soft. Raspberries bear a small crop the second year after planting and a full crop the third year, and remain productive for 5–8 years. The receptacle separates from the fruit when picked, leaving raspberry its definitive empty core.

PESTS AND DISEASES: Purchase certified disease-free stock. Uproot and destroy virus-infected plants so that aphids don't transmit the disease to healthy plants. Black raspberries are the most susceptible of the brambles to viruses. If spider mites are a problem in hot, dry weather, dislodge them with the garden hose. Wilted tips are a sign of borers; cut out and destroy the canes. Avoid using insecticides that might harm beneficial insects.

RECOMMENDED CULTIVARS: Most cane berries are self-fruitful. Blackberries require 200–800 chilling hours below 45°F. Blackberries are divided into two types, erect or trailing. The erect type grows to 6' tall. 'Brainerd' is a semihardy, drought-resistant cultivar with large black berries. 'Darrow' is a hardy, erect black-fruited cultivar that grows well in northern climates. Thornless cultivars are available but tend to be less hardy. Thorny cultivars of 'Brazos' grow best in southern climates. The trailing blackberry vine spreads to 15' and is grown mainly on the West Coast. 'Cascade' is an early variety that grows well in Pacific coastal regions. It has soft dark red berries. Boysenberry is a trailing hybrid of 'Youngberry' and blackberry that grows well in mild-winter climates. 'Dewberry' (*R. ursinus, R. canadensis*) is sometimes smaller than standard blackberries. Its flavor varies, but it grows well in southeastern and mid-Atlantic states, even in rocky soil. Prune back the entire plant after harvest to reduce the possibility of disease and to give plants time to regrow in warm regions. Youngberry is a tender, trailing cross of dewberry and loganberry with fruits that look like elongated blackberries but are red and taste like sweetened loganberries. Marionberry is a trailing, vigorous plant with mercifully few canes and does well in mild regions. Loganberry may be a cross between raspberry and dewberry. It is a late, trailing type that bears firm, blackberry-type fruits with a tart raspberry flavor. It is not hardy in the eastern United States, where 'Lucretia' grows better. Raspberries require 800–1,600 chilling hours below 45°F. They are divided by fruit colors—red, purple, yellow, and black—and by fruiting frequency—summer bearing (single crop) or everbearing (two crops). 'Heritage' is everbearing and has medium-size red fruits. 'Autumn Bliss' is everbearing and has high yields of large red berries. 'Fallgold' is a sweet yellow raspberry good for northern climates. Try 'Goldie' in warmer zones. 'Hilton' is the largest of the

Black raspberries are native to North America and therefore cold hardy.

'Thornfree' blackberry produces tasty fruit in mid-summer. Since its canes have no thorns, harvest is less difficult.

one-crop red raspberries (*R. idaeus*). It grows well in cold-winter areas. 'Willamette' is a midseason red berry popular in the Pacific Northwest. 'Latham' is a midseason, disease-resistant red berry commonly grown in the eastern United States. 'Pocahontas' is a hardy red raspberry bred for use in the South. 'Prelude' is an early, very hardy red berry. Black raspberries (*R. occidentalis*) are native to North America and the least tolerant of mild-winter climates. 'Cumberland' is a midseason black raspberry with large, firm fruits. 'Allen', 'Blackhawk', and 'Jewel' are popular cultivars in the Pacific Northwest. 'Bristol' grows well in the Southeast and Midwest. 'Brandywine' is an exceptionally vigorous purple raspberry. 'Royalty' has extra large purple fruits that are good fresh, frozen, or canned, and the plant is immune to raspberry aphids.

Propagate blackberry canes by tip layering.

Bend a cane over and bury it in the soil, then mulch.

When the tip is rooted, clip it from the mother plant.

Dig the rooted tip to relocate it to a new planting site.

GARDEN SAGE
Salvia officinalis SAL-vee-uh off-iss-ih-NAY-lis

Sage's pebbly-textured leaves are as ornamental as they are fragrant.

ZONES: 4–10
SIZE: 1 ½–2'h x 2–3' w
TYPE: Woody perennial shrub

GROWTH: Average
LIGHT: Full sun to part shade
MOISTURE: Average
FEATURES: Edible leaves

SITING: Sage is adaptable to most soils but does best in rich loam that drains well. Plant it in spring where soils are heavy and in autumn elsewhere. Sage is not drought tolerant and will not thrive in standing water or saturated soils.
CARE: Trim sage to shape it after it has finished blooming, but leave the woody stems to resprout new growth. Dig plants in late autumn and pot them in containers to overwinter indoors in cold climates. Plant vigor diminishes after 4–6 years; replace old plants with new ones.
PROPAGATION: Grow from cuttings or division, or by layering.
HARVEST: Sage's pebbly-textured leaves can be cut the first year after planting. About 6–8" of succulent growth above the woody stems can be harvested two or three times before the plants bloom in summer. Take cuttings in the morning after the dew has dried; leaves cut in the heat of the day have reduced flavor. Rinse off any dust or dirt in cold water and shake off the

Plant rooted cuttings in rich soil that drains well. Replace plants every 4–6 years as vigor diminishes.

excess. Tie cuttings together in small bunches and hang upside down or spread out on screens in a dark, airy space to dry. Crumble the dried leaves off the stems and store in airtight jars up to 3 years. The fresh leaves are good snipped into egg and cheese dishes. The dried leaves are added to poultry stuffing and ground into a dry-rub powder for meats.
PESTS AND DISEASES: None are significant.
RECOMMENDED CULTIVARS: 'Icterina' is variegated green and gold. 'Tricolor' leaves are variegated green, cream, and purple. 'Extrakta' has smooth green leaves and is exceptionally flavorful. 'Dwarf White' is a good choice for small gardens and container growing. Its silver-white foliage and white flowers are aromatic, and the plant grows only to 12". Clary sage (*S. sclarea*) is a biennial to 5' tall that is grown for its essential oil. It can be invasive; some states ban its growth. Pineapple sage (*S. elegans*) has scarlet flowers that attract hummingbirds. It is a half-hardy perennial grown as an annual, but the leaves are edible and have a fruity aroma. Mediterranean sage (*S. fruticosa*) is sold for culinary use. White sage (*S. apiana*) is dried and bundled as "smudge sticks," a type of incense.

SALAD BURNET
Sanguisorba minor san-gwih-SOR-buh MY-nor

Salad burnet, also called pimpernel and burnet bloodwort, is cold hardy.

ZONES: 4-9
SIZE: 1–2' h x 1'w
TYPE: Herbaceous evergreen perennial
GROWTH: Fast

LIGHT: Full sun to part shade
MOISTURE: Average
FEATURES: Edible leaves

SITING: Choose a permanent location at one side of the garden or in a nearby perennial bed or border. Start seed indoors 4–6 weeks before the last frost date or direct-sow in spring in warm climates. Salad burnet is adaptable to most soils and grows well in large containers. It will thrive interplanted with peas or lettuce.
CARE: Use mulch around plants to conserve moisture and reduce weeds. Salad burnet may reseed itself; if so, develop new seedlings each year for the most vigorous plants. Prune off flower

Grow salad burnet if there is no room for cucumbers in the garden. The leaves have a similar flavor.

heads to encourage leaf growth. The plants are extremely cold hardy, but mulch them well for overwintering north of Zone 4.
PROPAGATION: Grow from seed.
HARVEST: Begin cutting salad burnet about 70 days from seeding or 30 days after setting established plants in the garden. The leaves are high in vitamin C and have a mild cucumber flavor. Use fresh leaves only; they lose their color and flavor when dried or frozen. Because salad burnet tastes like cucumber, the leaves are perfect in salads, vinegars, butters, and tomato juice. A few blooming stems make an attractive aromatic and edible plate garnish.
PESTS AND DISEASES: No significant disease problems affect salad burnet. Beneficial insects control most pests.
RECOMMENDED CULTIVARS: Salad burnet is a good herb to grow in small gardens without room for cucumbers. It is sold under its common name and also as pimpernel, burnet bloodwort, and great burnet. It also may be labeled with the alternate name, *Poterium sanguisorba*.

SAVORY

Satureja spp. *sat-yew-REE-yuh*

Annual summer savory has a sweet flavor that goes well with beans.

ZONES: 2–11
SIZE: 3–18"h x 2–24"w
TYPE: Herbaceous annual or semievergreen perennial
GROWTH: Average
LIGHT: Full sun
MOISTURE: Average
FEATURES: Edible leaves

SITING: Savory is adaptable to most soils. Direct-sow summer savory after the last frost date in spring in northern climates or anytime during the growing season in mild-winter zones. It does not transplant easily. Plant the seeds ½" deep and 1" apart. Interplant with beans, beets, eggplant, or cucumbers. Start winter savory seed indoors 4–6 weeks before the last frost date or plant rooted cuttings after the soil warms.

CARE: Keep the soil consistently moist but not waterlogged. Hand-weed around young plants. Trim annual savory regularly to encourage new growth. Prune perennial savory to a miniature hedge.

PROPAGATION: Grow either type from seed; grow the perennial from cuttings.

HARVEST: Summer savory is ready to harvest in 60–70 days from sowing seeds.

Perennial winter savory has a stronger piney scent and taste.

Winter savory can be trimmed the first time 50 days after planting cuttings or 75-100 days after planting seed. Cut stems from either plant for drying when flowers begin to form. Spread them on screens or tie them in small bunches and hang upside down in a dark, airy space. When the leaves are completely dry, strip them from the stems, making sure to remove any woody parts. Store the leaves in airtight containers for up to 2 years.

PESTS AND DISEASES: None are significant. Savory's essential oil repels some insects.

RECOMMENDED CULTIVARS: Summer savory *(S. hortensis)* is a sweet-flavored, upright annual with tiny white or pink flowers. 'Aromata' is a peppery cultivar bred for high leaf yields. Winter savory *(S. montana)* is a semievergreen spreading perennial with trailing stems and petite purple flowers. Its pine scent and flavor are stronger than summer savory's. 'Nana' is an extremely cold-hardy dwarf variety only 3" tall that spreads to 2'. African savory *(S. biflora)* has a spicy lemon aroma and flavor that blends well in sweet or savory dishes, but it is a tropical plant suitable only for Zones 9–11.

EGGPLANT

Solanum melongena *so-LAY-num mel-on-GEE-nuh*

Eggplant thrives in heat and humidity and needs lots of plant food. It is also sometimes called aubergine.

ZONES: NA
SIZE: 1–3"h x 1–2"w
TYPE: Annual
GROWTH: Average
LIGHT: Full sun
MOISTURE: Moderate
FEATURES: Edible fruits

SITING: Direct-sow eggplant in hot climates. In northern zones, start seeds indoors 8 weeks before the last frost date and transplant at least 2 weeks after the last frost. Use black plastic to warm the soil before planting in cool climates. Eggplant does best in rich, slightly acid, well-draining soil with compost added.

CARE: Eggplant thrives in high heat and humidity. Grow eggplant under tunnels, cloches, or row covers in cool climates to increase the temperature around the plants. Plants will not set fruit where nighttime temperatures are consistently below 65°F. Eggplant is a heavy feeder. Side-dress plants with well-rotted compost or manure and feed once a month with soluble plant food. Keep the area free of weeds, and mulch around the plants in hot weather to conserve soil moisture.

PROPAGATION: Grow eggplant from seed or transplants.

HARVEST: Cut fruits from the plant when they reach full cultivar color and are firm and glossy, about 60–90 days from transplanting.

PESTS AND DISEASES: Pick off and destroy any beetles, worms, and caterpillars. Shake or knock Colorado potato beetles off plants and onto a sheet early in the morning, then destroy them. Protect young plants from flea beetles with floating row covers. Choose virus-resistant cultivars. Use fungicide to prevent anthracnose. Follow clean cultural practices to avoid blights.

RECOMMENDED CULTIVARS: 'Ichiban' bears elongated purple fruits in 65 days. 'Neon' bears medium-size bright pinkish-purple fruits. 'Black' is a dark purple cultivar with 4–6" fruits ready in 70–75 days. 'Rosa Bianca' is an almost round Italian white eggplant blushed with purple. 'Black Beauty' is a plump heirloom variety with large fruits ready for harvest in 80–85 days.

Eggplant is ready to harvest when firm and glossy.

Clip ripe fruits regularly to promote new ones.

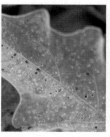

Use row covers to protect plants from flea beetles.

POTATO

Solanum tuberosum *so-LAY-num too-ber-OH-sum*

Potatoes come in a variety of shapes, sizes, and colors.

ZONES: NA
SIZE: 1 ½'h x 1 ½'w
TYPE: Annual
GROWTH: Average

LIGHT: Full sun to part shade
MOISTURE: Average
FEATURES: Edible tubers

SITING: Choose a sunny location with well-drained, acid soil amended with lots of organic matter but where no lime has been added previously. If possible, grow an autumn green manure crop where potatoes will grow and turn it under before planting in spring. In small gardens grow potatoes in their own raised bed. Potatoes grow best planted in cool climates 2–4 weeks before the last frost date. Use commercial seed tubers; grocery store potatoes are usually treated to inhibit sprouting. Cut whole seed potatoes into pieces, each with one or two eyes and some fleshy tuber attached. Dry the pieces overnight before planting them to help protect them from rot. Plant the pieces eyes up in trenches dug 4" deep in heavy soil and 6" deep in light soil. Space them 12-15" apart in rows 20-24" apart, depending on the mature size of the cultivar, and cover with 2–4" of soil. Presprouted seed potatoes will lead to faster development of the tubers.

CARE: Keep the soil consistently moist but not waterlogged until the plants emerge. Thereafter water in periods of high heat or when rainfall is inadequate. Tubers develop best when the daytime air temperature is 60–65°F and nighttime temperatures are about 10 degrees cooler, but there are cultivars available for warm climates. Potatoes are heavy feeders; provide plant food higher in phosphorus and potassium than in nitrogen, which reduces plant vigor and can lead to disease. Begin hilling soil around the bottoms of the stems when the plants are 6–8" tall and repeat frequently as they grow taller. Hilling builds up the area where the tubers will develop. When the plants reach full height, add mulch on top of the hills to conserve moisture and hold weeds down. Cover any tubers that poke through the surface with more soil. Tubers exposed to the sun turn green and develop a mild toxin. Work around and harvest potatoes when the plants and soil are dry.

PROPAGATION: Grow from seed "eyes" or pieces of sprouting tubers.

HARVEST: Potatoes are a universal culinary ingredient good boiled, baked, fried, mashed, roasted, and scalloped, added to soups and stews and meat hash, and dried and ground into flour. New potatoes are delicious cooked with spring peas. Early varieties are best suited for use as new potatoes, which can be harvested as soon as they reach usable size. Check them about a week after the plants flower to see if they are ready. Carefully loosen the soil with a digging fork and reach in by hand to pull those you want away from the parent plant. Continue harvesting until the plant tops have died back, then pull up the entire plants with a garden fork to get those that remain. You can leave potatoes to cure in the ground for up to a few weeks after the tops die if you garden in a warm, dry climate. Pest- or disease-damaged tubers are still edible once the bad spots are removed but won't store well. Potatoes that have frozen in the ground are inedible. Brush any loose dirt off harvested potatoes and cure them unwashed in a dark, humid spot at 65–70°F for about 2 weeks. Then move them to a cool, dark, humid garage, shed, or cellar for storage at 40–45°F for up to 9 months. Potatoes bruise easily; handle them gently.

PESTS AND DISEASES: Keeping the soil pH acidic helps to prevent scab disease. Use a fungicide to prevent anthracnose. Follow clean cultural practices to avoid blights; destroy vegetative debris where pests may overwinter. Rotate crops each year. Choose virus-resistant cultivars. Pick off and destroy any beetles, worms, and caterpillars. Shake or knock Colorado potato beetles off plants and onto a sheet early in the morning, then destroy them. Use Bt or a neem-based insecticide if infestations are severe. Control leafhoppers with insecticidal soap. Use floating row covers to protect young plants from flea beetles. Interplant potatoes with taller crops that provide some shade, which flea beetles do not tolerate. If gophers are a problem, catch them in traps.

RECOMMENDED CULTIVARS: Early-maturing varieties ready to harvest in 55–75 days include 'Adora', 'Charlotte', and 'Yukon Gold', all yellow fleshed. 'Shepody' is a blocky white-skinned potato good for French fries. 'Red Pontiac' is a highly adaptable, easy-to-grow red potato. 'Purple Peruvian' is a medium to large fingerling potato with purple skin and flesh. Fingerling 'Red Thumb' has red skin and red flesh. Midseason varieties mature in 80–90 days. 'Bellisle' is a Canadian white cultivar good for mashed potatoes. 'Ida Rose' is an Idaho potato with rose-red skin and white flesh. 'Island Sunshine' is a yellow-skinned potato with yellow flesh. It's resistant to late blight. 'Kennebec' is the well-known Maine potato with tan skin and white flesh. It's an especially good baking potato and stores well. 'Pink Wink' is a floury-textured Irish potato with pink eyes. 'Red Gold' has red skin and yellow flesh. It sprouts in storage. 'Saginaw Gold' is a virus-resistant yellow potato that keeps well until midspring. 'Sieglinde' is an old German heirloom yellow potato popular for its thin skin and good flavor. 'Viking Red' is a fast-growing, heat-resistant red-skinned variety. 'Anna Cheeka' is an Ozette fingerling potato with pale gold skin and creamy yellow flesh best cooked only lightly to bring out its nutty flavor. Late-maturing potatoes are ready to harvest in 90 days or more. 'Butte' is a russet variety resistant to scab and late blight. 'German Butterball' is an award-winning yellow cultivar. Try 'Nooksack', a russet baker, in coastal regions. 'Russian Banana' is an easy-to-grow fingerling potato with excellent disease resistance. For sweet potatoes, see page 519.

1 Cut seed potatoes into pieces that each have eyes.

2 Dry them overnight and then plant them eyes-up in trenches.

3 Loosen soil with a digging fork to harvest potatoes.

4 Brush off loose dirt and cure them in a cool, dark spot.

SPINACH

Spinacea oleracea *spin-ACH-ee-uh oh-ler-AY-see-uh*

Semi-savoyed spinach cultivars are bred for cultivation in warm weather.

ZONES: NA
SIZE: 3–8"h x 2–8"w
TYPE: Annual
GROWTH: Fast

LIGHT: Full sun to part shade
MOISTURE: Average
FEATURES: Edible leaves

SITING: Soak spinach seed overnight and sow it directly into fertile, moist, well-drained soil. Broadcast the seed in a patch, or plant it ¼" deep and 1" apart in rows 12" apart. Spinach seed will germinate at soil temperatures as low as 35°F, so begin planting 4–6 weeks before the last spring frost date in northern climates.

CARE: Thin plants to 6" apart when they reach 3" tall. Keep the soil consistently moist and mulch to keep the roots cool. Water in the morning so that plants have time to dry and keep them thinned for good air circulation to avoid rust. Make successive sowings of spinach every few weeks to extend the harvest until late spring. In warmer weather plant cultivars slow to bolt. You can grow spinach year-round in mild-winter climates and even through the winter in a cold frame in all but the coldest northern zones.

PROPAGATION: Grow from seed.

HARVEST: Leaves are large enough to harvest in 35–50 days.

PESTS AND DISEASES: Cover young plants with floating row covers to protect them from leaf miners and flea beetles. Aphids can be knocked off by a strong spray from the garden hose. Handpick and destroy caterpillars. Choose cultivars that are resistant to downy mildew and mosaic virus to avoid those diseases.

RECOMMENDED CULTIVARS: Smooth-leaf spinaches such as 'Olympia' grow best in cool weather. Semi-savoyed cultivars such as 'Tyee', 'Space', and 'Melody' are slow to bolt. Savoyed types such as 'Winter Bloomsdale' are deeply crinkled and grow best in autumn and winter. 'Nordic' is a smooth-leaf type that thrives in cold weather. Heat- and drought-tolerant spinach substitutes include Malabar spinach (*Basella alba* 'Rubra'), a tropical perennial usually grown as an annual in the United States, and New Zealand spinach (*Tetragonia expansa*) an annual slow to germinate but extremely heat-tolerant.

Grow spinach in a cold frame to extend the harvest season through winter.

THYME

Thymus vulgaris *TY-mus vul-GARE-is*

Creeping thyme forms a low ground cover that is ornamental as well as flavorful.

ZONES: 4–9
SIZE: 3–12"h x spreading
TYPE: Herbaceous perennial

GROWTH: Average
LIGHT: Full sun to part shade
MOISTURE: Average
FEATURES: Edible leaves

SITING: Plant divisions in spring in average, well-drained soil. Space plants 8–12" apart, or interplant with Solanaceae family crops—tomatoes, potatoes, eggplant, and peppers. Thyme can also be grown in containers indoors or out.

CARE: Water when needed to maintain soil moisture, but do not overwater. Clear weeds by hand. Shear off the tiny flowers after plants finish blooming to keep energy concentrated in the leaves. Plants may lose vigor and need replacing in a few years.

PROPAGATION: Grow by division or from cuttings or layering.

HARVEST: Strip the leaves from the stems and use in salads, soups, stews, stuffings, vinegars, and vegetables. Thyme blends well with almost any beef, pork, poultry, or seafood dish and adds a sophisticated flavor to cheese and egg dishes. Harvest

Thyme thrives interplanted with peppers, potatoes, tomatoes, and eggplants.

handfuls of the stems and tie small bundles together. Hang them upside down in a cool, airy room to dry. When the leaves are completely dry, crumble them off the stems and store in airtight glass jars for up to 2 years.

PESTS AND DISEASES: None are significant. Roots may rot if plants are overwatered.

RECOMMENDED CULTIVARS: Thymes labeled French or English are intended for cooking, but many of the creeping *T. serpyllum* and *T. pulegioides* ground-cover cultivars can do double duty in the kitchen. Of the common varieties, 'German Winter' is an especially hardy thyme good for cold-winter climates. Grow 'Summer Thyme' as an annual above Zone 6. It is smaller than average with a spicier flavor. Try 'Orange Balsam Thyme' straight from the plant on fish and vegetable dishes. It is hardy to Zone 5. 'Hi Ho Silver' is a green and white variegated cultivar, hardy to Zone 4. 'Italian Oregano Thyme' tastes like the name implies and is hardy to Zone 5. 'Lemon' and 'Lime' thymes (*T. ×citriodorus*) have a citrusy fragrance but the flavor is lost in cooking. They are hardy to Zone 4.

BLUEBERRY

Vaccinium spp. *vak-SIN-ee-um*

Tasty blue fruits and colorful red fall foliage make blueberries outstanding additions to the landscape.

ZONES: 3–9
SIZE: 1 ½–7'h x 2–10'w
TYPE: Woody perennial shrub

GROWTH: Slow
LIGHT: Full sun
MOISTURE: Moderate
FEATURES: Edible berries

SITING: Choose a sunny, breezy location in well-drained, sandy, acid loam with a pH of 4.5–5.5. Have the soil tested before planting to determine pH and what amendments are needed. If possible, grow a green manure cover crop on the site and till it under before planting blueberries. Plant them in spring in northern zones and in late fall in the South, in holes spaced 6' apart for highbush plants, 2' apart for lowbush, and 3–4' for dwarf or hedge highbush varieties. No plant food should be added to the holes. Keep the plants continuously moist before planting them. Carefully spread the roots out and firm the soil around them, then water well. Set bare-root stock at the same depth it was grown in the nursery, then cut the plants back by half to remove buds.

CARE: Because blueberry roots lack root hairs, they are sensitive to changes in soil moisture. Keep the plants consistently moist. They need 1–2" of good-quality water low in mineral salts each week. Harvested fruits retain their stems if drought stressed. Spread mulch 6–8" deep and 2–4' wide along the row. Feed plants each year at flowering with acidic compost or plant food for acid-loving plants. Excessive nitrogen causes low yields. Blueberries fruit on 1-year-old wood. Pinch off developing fruits until plants are 3–4 years old, to encourage the bush to grow. Blueberries tend to overbear, which wears out the plants in just a few years if left unchecked. Prune them with loppers when they are fully dormant in late winter.

Flower buds will be visible on 1-year-old wood. Heavy pruning results in earlier ripening, which may be especially desirable in the South, and also yields larger berries. Renewal-prune annually to remove old canes. In the first 2 years of growth, remove weak, diseased, or damaged canes only. In subsequent years remove weak, diseased, or damaged canes along with some of the oldest canes. Remove excess young canes to encourage the growth of others, and prune to reduce the density of the branches at the tops of plants. Careful selection of canes to prune helps to balance the fruit load on the plant in the next season. Each mature plant should have 15–25 canes of varying ages. Canes decline in productivity after 5–6 years.

PROPAGATION: Grow from rooted cuttings.

HARVEST: Blueberries are ready to pick 2–4 months after flowering, from July to September. Hold a container in one hand and use your other hand to gently loosen berries from the cluster so they drop into the container. Ripening berries turn from green to pinkish red to blue, but not all blue ones are fully ripe. Blueberries are extremely perishable. Store them unwashed in the refrigerator for up to 1 week. Enjoy them fresh out of hand or on cereals and in fruit salads, or cooked in baked goods, jams, and preserves. They also make delicious sweet wine. Rinse and dry berries and freeze them in single layers in plastic for long-term storage. Blueberries can also be dried and stored in airtight containers for up to 3 years.

PESTS AND DISEASES: Choose cultivars bred for resistance to viruses. Use labeled fungicides according to directions to control phomopsis canker, root rot, mummyberry, and twig blight. Japanese beetles may bother blueberries in the home garden. Keep the ground clean of dropped fruit and vegetative debris to discourage fruit flies and maggots.

Use insecticidal sprays if needed to control them and fruit worms, curculios, leafhoppers, scale, and borers, but avoid spraying when plants are in bloom to protect beneficial insect pollinators such as bumblebees and southeastern blueberry bees. Use reflective tape or balloons, noisemakers, or netting that covers the plants all the way to the ground to protect ripening fruits from birds.

RECOMMENDED CULTIVARS: The most commonly grown blueberry is the highbush (*V. corymbosum*). It is native to the eastern United States and grows to 8' where soil is highly acid and drains well. Highbush is a hardy blueberry species, requiring 650–850 chilling hours and 160 frost-free days. The buds are hardy to –20°F, the stems to –30°F, and the flowers to 25–30°F. 'Earliblue', 'Bluetta', and 'Duke' are early cultivars. 'Spartan' is a good choice for regions with late spring frosts; it blooms late but ripens early. Late-ripening cultivars include 'Blueray', a large-fruited variety good for hot climates, and 'Berkeley', which grows well in light soils. 'Olympia' has good flavor and freezes well. 'Coville' is resistant to phomopsis canker. 'Lateblue' and 'Elliott' are medium-size berries good for eating fresh. 'Sierra' is an interspecific hybrid of *V. constablaei*, *V. darrowi*, *V. corymbosum*, and *V. ashei*, that requires 1,000 chilling hours. Rabbit-eye blueberry (*V. ashei*) is a highbush species native to the southeastern United States that can reach 20' tall. It needs only 250 chilling hours, tolerates heat and dry weather, and is hardy to Zone 7. It ripens later than northern highbush types, and the fruits are not as sweet off the vine but are good for baking. Because it is partially or completely self-sterile, rabbit-eye blueberry requires pollenizers. The fruits are sometimes shiny; frequent harvests promote their ripening. 'Climax' is an early cultivar with good flavor. 'Premier' is a large, early- to midseason cultivar with

Choose cultivars resistant to canker.

Test the soil before planting to determine pH and what amendments are needed.

Plant bare-root stock at the same depth it was grown in the nursery.

BLUEBERRY
continued

Highbush blueberry is a hardy and common species, with cultivars available for a variety of regions.

Rabbit-eye is a highbush blueberry for southern climates. The berries are tart and good for baking.

superior flavor. 'Centurion' is adapted to heavy soils; it blooms late and ripens late. It is a good dessert fruit. Southern highbush cultivars include crosses of

V. australe and *V. corymbosum* with *V. darrowi* as well as crosses of highbush and lowbush called half-high blueberries, bred to create southern-type fruits on

plants that are hardy to −20°F. They are self-sterile and require pollenizers. 'Sapphire', 'Sharpblue', and 'Gulf Coast' are popular in Florida. 'Northland' and 'St. Cloud' are early cultivars; 'Northblue' is midseason; and 'Northcountry' is good for northern zones. It has the naturally sweet flavor of its lowbush ancestor. Lowbush blueberry (*V. angustifolium*) is the native species that thrives in the northeastern United States. *V. myrtilloides* is the lowbush species of eastern Canada. The wild plants are managed with sprays and pruning for best yields. Multiple plants are necessary for successful pollination. They are hardy to −20°F and need 1,000 chilling hours below 45°F. The branches spread like a ground cover to 2'. Huckleberry (*V. ovatum* and others) is a related evergreen plant with small, edible blue berries. It grows best in cool, dry climates. Lingonberry (*V. vitis-idaea*), also called cowberry, is a creeping evergreen hardy to Zone 2 that bears small, sour, cranberry-like fruits. Bilberry (*V. myrtillus*) is a deciduous shrub that thrives in the Pacific Northwest. Its aromatic purple berries are used in jam, jelly, and wine.

CRANBERRY
Vaccinium macrocarpon vak-SIN-ee-um mak-roh-KAR-pon

Cranberries thrive in the acidic soil of swamps, bogs, and shorelines.

ZONES: 3-8
SIZE: 1'h x 4'-6'w
TYPE: Woody evergreen perennial shrub
GROWTH: Slow

LIGHT: Full sun to part shade
MOISTURE: High
FEATURES: Edible berries

SITING: Cranberry grows best in cool climates, planted in weed-free acid soil in the standing water of swamps and bogs or along wet shorelines. Plant 6–8"-long cuttings 18" apart in peat or sandy acid loam where the top 6" of soil can be kept constantly moist year-round to prevent wind desiccation in freezing temperatures.

CARE: Cranberry is not truly hardy and is susceptible to fungal diseases in warm climates. Because the roots have no root hairs, the plants won't tolerate drought. Cranberry plants self-pollinate but yield bigger crops if pollinated by bumblebees. Keep the planting area weed free. Pruning is required only to reduce the density of upright branches on vigorous plants.
PROPAGATION: Grow from rooted cuttings.
HARVEST: Use a berry scoop to pick the shiny berries in mid- to late autumn when they turn red. Rinse them thoroughly and discard any that are shriveled or damaged. Cranberries are too tart to eat raw, but the sweetened fruits are used in juice cocktail, baked goods, stuffings, relishes, gelatin salads, citrus fruit salads, chutneys, marinades, and condiments for meat, poultry, and fish. Fresh unwashed berries keep in the refrigerator for up to 3 weeks but can be frozen for long-term storage or dried to use like raisins. Cranberries are traditionally strung together in strands to use as holiday decorations in December.
PESTS AND DISEASES: Cranberries are largely untroubled in the home garden. Keep the dropped fruit and vegetative

debris where pests can hide picked up and destroyed. Use insecticidal sprays if needed to control serious insect infestations, but avoid spraying when plants are in bloom to protect beneficial pollinators. Pick off and destroy Japanese beetles. Pests in commercial plantings are controlled with periodic flooding; try that at home only if your plants are located in a suitable low-lying spot where you can add sand to cover the roots afterward. Flooding in winter also protects plants from cold injury. Use reflective tape or balloons, noisemakers, or netting to protect ripening fruits from birds.
RECOMMENDED CULTIVARS: Cranberry is native to North America, where it thrives in swampy areas primarily in the northeastern United States, upper Midwest, and Pacific Northwest. They are closely related to blueberries and huckleberries. 'HyRed', 'Franklin', and 'Beaver' are early cultivars; 'Ben Lear', 'Crowley', 'Stevens', and 'Bergman' are all midseason varieties; and 'Pilgrim' is late. Highbush cranberry (*Viburnum* spp.) is unrelated. It bears small, tart, cranberry-like fruits used in jam, syrup, and wine.

CORN SALAD

Valerianella locusta *vuh-lair-ee-uh-NEL-luh loh-KOO-stuh*

Mâche, also called corn salad or lamb's lettuce, is the smallest mesclun-mix leaf.

ZONES: NA
SIZE: 2–4"h x 4–8"w
TYPE: Annual
GROWTH: Fast
LIGHT: Full sun to part shade
MOISTURE: Average
FEATURES: Edible leaves

SITING: Mâche is often included in mesclun salad seed mixes but is easier to manage by itself because of its small size. Sow anytime in early spring or autumn. Broadcast seed in a small, moist patch of rich soil at least 1' square that has been cleared of all weeds, or in clearly marked rows 6" apart so that seedlings will be distinguishable from weeds. Mâche, also called lamb's lettuce because sheep graze on it in Europe, looks much like a broadleaf weed and can get lost among true weeds in the garden. Cover the seeds with ¼" of fine soil and gently water.

CARE: Begin thinning plants when the rosettes of leaves are large enough to grasp—about 3". Use the thinnings in salads. Make successive plantings every 3 weeks for a continuous supply. Water as necessary to maintain soil moisture. Mâche is a cold-weather plant hardy to 5°F and easy to grow throughout the winter. Even in northern zones you can grow it in a cold frame or in the open garden with just some straw mulch. Cold weather enhances the flavor. It tastes good even if it has been frozen.

PROPAGATION: Grow from seed.

HARVEST: Mâche is ready to harvest about 50 days from planting. Pinch off leaf clusters or pull entire plants when they are 3–4" tall. When the plants send up flower stalks in hot weather, harvest the whole crop and sow new seed if daytime temperatures are still below 80°F. The spoon-shaped leaves add a mildly nutty flavor to salads and sandwiches. They can also be steamed or boiled and prepared like cole-crop greens or added to soups and stews a few minutes before serving. Store the unwashed leaves in the crisper drawer of the refrigerator for up to 2 weeks. Rinse leaves well before eating to remove any sand or dirt.

PESTS AND DISEASES: None are significant.

RECOMMENDED CULTIVARS: 'Jade' holds its elongated dark blue-green leaves upright and is resistant to mildew and yellows. 'Vit' also has an upright habit and a mild, minty flavor. 'Broad Leaved' is heat tolerant and a good choice for temperate climates. 'Gross Graine' is a slightly larger plant popular in Europe. 'Verte D'Etampes' has crinkly leaves like savoy cabbage.

FAVA BEAN

Vicia faba *VEE-see-uh FAY-buh*

Grow fava beans, also known as broad beans or horse beans, on a trellis to support the long vines and pods.

ZONES: NA
SIZE: 12–72"h x 6–24"w
TYPE: Annual
GROWTH: Fast
LIGHT: Full sun
MOISTURE: High
FEATURES: Edible seeds

SITING: Choose a sunny location where legumes have not been grown in the last 3 years. Dust dampened seeds with rhizobial inoculant before planting to fix nitrogen in the soil. *Vicia* is adaptable and more tolerant of acidity than other beans but does best in rich loam. Sow seed 4–8 weeks before the last frost date, 2–4" deep and 6" apart in rows 18–24" apart. Fava bean also can be grown as a winter annual in subtropical zones that have no frost.

CARE: Fava beans do best in areas with a long, cool growing season. The long, vining plants require staking or trellising to support the developing pods. Beans prefer daytime temperatures of 70–80°F and may drop their blossoms above 85°F. They are also sensitive to frost. Temperatures below 35°F kill the flowers and pods. Bean plants are tender and easily damaged by garden tools, so weed by hand if possible. Keep the soil consistently moist, but water only in the morning so the plants dry quickly, which reduces the potential for disease. Extremes in soil moisture result in malformed pods. To avoid injury to the plants and the spread of fungal spores, work around and harvest beans only when they are not wet. Beans supply their own nitrogen but benefit from a monthly application of soluble plant food high in phosphorus and potassium.

PROPAGATION: Grow from seed.

HARVEST: The beans mature 90–200 days after planting. Pull up the plants when the lower pods are full and dry and the upper ones are developed but still green. Use a sheet under the plants to catch any seeds that fall when dry pods shatter. The seeds can be canned when fully developed but not dry. Pinch the beans from their protective coatings before use.

PESTS AND DISEASES: Choose cultivars bred for resistance to blights, rust, and anthracnose and pretreated with fungicide. Practice crop rotation to avoid diseases that live in the soil. All beans are attacked by a host of damaging insects, including aphids, thrips, beetles, weevils, mites, stinkbugs, and tarnished plant bugs. The Mexican bean beetle is the main pest in home gardens; it lays its eggs on the underside of bean leaves. Handpick and destroy eggs and larvae, or use neem oil for heavy infestations. Ask your local extension agent which other pests are most common in your locale and how to deter them. Avoid using insecticides when the plant is in bloom; fava bean flowers attract beneficial ladybugs and predatory wasps and are pollinated by bumblebees.

RECOMMENDED CULTIVARS: Windsor cultivars, also called broad beans, horse beans, or English beans, have short pods containing four large seeds each. 'Aprovecho' is ready for harvest in 75–85 days or 140–180 days if planted in fall. Longpod or tick types contain up to eight smaller seeds. 'Banner' is a cold-tolerant variety good for overwintering in areas with mild winters. It is ready for harvest in 80–90 days, or 200–240 days if fall planted.

COWPEA
Vigna unguiculata *VIG-nuh un-gwih-kew-LAH-tuh*

Cowpea, also known as black-eyed pea or Southern pea, is actually a type of bean grown for green shelling or dried use.

ZONES: NA
SIZE: 8–36"h x 6–24"w
TYPE: Annual
GROWTH: Average

LIGHT: Full sun
MOISTURE: Average
FEATURES: Edible seeds

SITING: Choose a sunny location where legumes have not been grown in the last 3 years. Dust dampened seeds with rhizobial inoculant before planting to fix nitrogen in the soil for the crop that follows the cowpeas. Plant cowpeas 1–1½" deep and 2–4" apart in rows 12–24" apart in well-drained, acid, sandy loam when the soil temperature is at least 65°F. Seeds may rot in cool, wet soils. Strongly determinate bush types can be planted closer together than indeterminate vines.

CARE: Cowpea has a long taproot and is more drought resistant than common beans. It is a warm-season crop that does best in humidity but is also adapted to dry conditions. Keep the soil consistently moist from planting through bloom and control weeds. Remove and destroy any plants showing signs of infection or infestation.

PROPAGATION: Grow from seed.

HARVEST: Cowpea can be used at any stage of development but is most often used as a green-mature bean in western cooking, ready for harvest 70–90 days after planting. Store the shelled seeds in the warmest part of the refrigerator and use them within a few days.

PESTS AND DISEASES: Choose cultivars bred for resistance to bacteria and viruses and pretreated with fungicide for prevention of blights, rots, rusts, and anthracnose. Practice crop rotation to avoid diseases that live in the soil. All beans are visited by a host of damaging insects, including cowpea curculio, aphids, thrips, beetles, mites, stinkbugs, and tarnished plant bugs. The Mexican bean beetle is the main pest in home gardens; it lays its eggs on the underside of bean leaves. Handpick and destroy eggs and larvae or use neem oil for heavy infestations. Ask your local extension agent which pests are most common in your locale and how to deter them. Avoid using insecticides when the plant is in bloom; cowpea flowers attract beneficial insects.

RECOMMENDED CULTIVARS: There are vining, semivining, and bush types; all grow well in humid climates, but bush types do best in northern climates. Seed coats may be speckled or have a distinctive spot or "eye." Pods are 6–10" long and can be green, yellow, or purple as the seeds reach green maturity but turn tan or brown when dry. 'Whippoorwill' is a climbing type grown for its dried seeds. 'California Blackeye' is good for green-mature cooking. Adzuki bean (*V. angularis*), bears small, oval dark red beans used to make sweet bean paste, a popular ingredient in Asian cuisines. Another related species, mung bean (*V. radiata*), is grown primarily for bean sprouts.

ASPARAGUS BEAN
Vigna unguiculata ssp. *sesquipedalis* *VIG-nuh un-gwih-kew-LAH-tuh seh-skwih-peh-DAY-lis*

Asparagus or yard-long beans will grow to 3' but aren't tender at that length.

ZONES: NA
SIZE: 6–12'h x 1½–2½'w
TYPE: Annual
GROWTH: Average

LIGHT: Full sun
MOISTURE: Moderate
FEATURES: Edible seeds and immature pods

SITING: Choose a sunny location where legumes have not been grown in the last 3 years. Dust dampened seeds with rhizobial inoculant before planting. Plant seeds 1–2" deep and 12" apart in rows 3–4' apart after all danger of frost has passed and the soil temperature is at least 65°F.

CARE: Plants require support on poles or trellises. Train the vines on their supports; if needed attach them loosely with figure-eight loops of soft twine. To encourage fruiting pinch out the terminal ends of vines when they reach the top of the supports. Consistent soil moisture keeps the pods from turning tough and fibrous. Yard-long beans thrive in high heat and do not tolerate frost or cool temperatures.

PROPAGATION: Grow from seed.

HARVEST: The pods are ready to harvest when they are 10–12" long but before the

Yard-long beans are related to cowpeas but grown for the immature pods, which are eaten like snap beans.

seeds have filled out, about 7–10 days from flowering. Pick pods every few days for maximum tenderness. Yard-long beans will live up to their name if allowed to mature, but at 3' long the pods are too tough to eat and the beans should be shelled out and used like cowpeas. Keep freshly harvested pods moist and cool to prevent rusty-looking patches from developing. Store them in the refrigerator for up to 1 week.

PESTS AND DISEASES: Plants will outgrow thrip infestations, but black bean aphids and Mexican bean beetles may require treatment with a labeled insecticide. Avoid using insecticides when the plants are in bloom to protect beneficial insects that pollinate the flowers. Choose cultivars bred for resistance to bacteria and viruses and pretreated with fungicide to prevent blights, rots, rusts, and anthracnose.

RECOMMENDED CULTIVARS: 'Liana' vines grow vigorously to 12' if not pinched back. 'Orient Extra Long' thrives in the heat and humidity of tropical zones. 'Red Stripe' is a good choice for home gardens and will tolerate cool temperatures. The seeds have red and white stripes.

GRAPE

Vitis spp. *VY-tis*

American grapes, also called fox or Concord grapes, must be sprayed.

ZONES: 4–10
SIZE: 4–10'h x 6–12'w
TYPE: Woody perennial vine

GROWTH: Fast
LIGHT: Full sun
MOISTURE: Moderate
FEATURES: Edible berries

SITING: Choose a south- or east-facing slope in an area with good air circulation to prevent mildew and rot. Grapes adapt to all soils but do best in deep, well-drained, light, slightly acid to neutral soil. Table grapes grow best in areas with long, hot, dry summers and mild winters. Wine and muscadine grapes thrive in humid temperate climates, but muscadines need a longer growing season and milder winter than Concord grapes. In late winter or early spring, dig the holes 1' in diameter, leaving adequate room to place a stake, post, or trellis before the roots are positioned. Position the lowest bud on the trunk even with the soil line. Tamp soil lightly over the roots and flood the hole with water, repeating until the soil settles at ground level.

CARE: Test the soil every 3–5 years. Highly fertile soil detracts from the flavor of wine grapes. Irrigation also may be harmful and even illegal for wine grapes but is beneficial for table and raisin grapes. Spread mulch around the base of the vines for protection in cold-winter areas. In extremely cold winter zones, untie the vines and bend them to the ground, then cover them with soil or straw. Provide

windbreaks in exposed areas. Rake back the mulch in spring, add new well-rotted compost or manure, and replenish the mulch.

To train a grapevine to a wire trellis, begin the winter after planting. Prune off all shoots but the strongest cane to train as the trunk. Tie it loosely to an upright support pole. When the trunk grows as tall as the first wire (3' above ground) in the next season, prune out all but two branches to form two main lateral arms, and tie those in either direction along the wire. Each year cut fruiting growth back to three nodes. When the main trunk reaches the height of the second wire (5½' above ground), select another pair of strong canes to train as arms like the first ones, then cut off the top of the trunk above the wire. In each following spring prune out all other canes coming off the trunk and suckers growing from the base.

Spurs and canes grow from the permanent trunk and arms (called cordons) trained to the trellis. Grapes fruit on lateral shoots from the current season's woody growth. All grapes should be pruned each year as close to the arms as possible to produce the best fruit. Without pruning, the grapes grow increasingly far from the main trunk on the ends of long canes. Wine grapes and muscadines are cane- or spur-pruned after the first three growing seasons; American grapes and 'Thompson Seedless' are cane-pruned only. To spur-train grapes, cut all side branches on lateral arms to two buds in winter. Two new shoots will grow on each remaining spur, and each of those will yield one to three fruit bunches. The spurs should be spaced 6" apart. Keep some one-bud renewal spurs to develop for next year's fruiting wood.

Cane pruning leaves two whole canes from the previous season and two additional canes near the head of the trunk, cut back to buds. Gather fruiting canes upward and tie them together toward the tip. Let growth from the

renewal buds trail. The Kniffen two-arm system leaves canes only on the top wire; the four-arm and six-arm systems leave canes at two or three levels. Use the four-arm and six-arm systems only where vigorous top growth on the higher wire will not shade out the canes on the bottom one. Growing grapes on an arbor is a good way to use vertical space in a small garden for ornamental as well as edible purposes. To grow vines on an arbor, train and tie one strong cane up a post as a trunk and prune out the side canes. When the trunk reaches the top of the arbor in the second or third season, select a single cane from it to develop as a cordon across the top of the framework. Then begin pruning to train two-bud spurs across the top. Head back all the vines in late winter to a few buds per cane. (Prune muscadines in early winter to reduce bleeding.) For very large arbors, grow vines up opposite posts and train canes to cross one another over the framework. Vigorous vines overproduce; thinning fruit bunches helps the remaining grapes to become sweet.

PROPAGATION: Grow by grafting, rooted cuttings, or layering.

HARVEST: Vines bear the second or third year after planting. American and table grapes are ready when they have reached full cultivar size and color, in about 150–165 days. Leave raisin grapes on the vines to ripen completely before picking. The best time to pick wine grapes depends on the type of wine to be made. Both the Brix (sugar) level and the pH are determining factors. Concord juice grapes are ready to harvest when the Brix level is about 15°. Use a digital wine refractometer to measure the Brix level. Muscadine grapes are ready for harvest in about 200 days. Clip grape clusters from the vines with sharp scissors and handle them as little as possible to avoid damage. Picking bunches with grapes of varying degrees of ripeness is desirable for making jelly and jam. Pick grapes for fresh eating and juice two or three times over a period

Prune out all but two branches to form the lateral cordons (arms).

Tie grapevines loosely to a trellis or other strong support. Untie in winter to mulch.

Healthy vines bear too many bunches. Thin some out to make the remaining fruits sweeter.

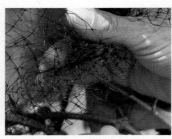

Cover ripening grapes with netting to protect them from hungry birds.

GRAPE
continued

of several weeks as the grapes ripen. Store them in the refrigerator for up to 2 weeks.

PESTS AND DISEASES: Many grape diseases can be prevented with good air circulation and clean cultural practices. Black rot overwinters on infected vines, leaves, and unpicked grapes. Keep vines pruned and trellised so that air circulates well. Choose cultivars resistant to botrytis bunch rot, downy mildew, and powdery mildew. Remove and destroy infected plants immediately. Copper and sulfur fungicides are effective controls but may damage the vines. Choose cultivars resistant to gall phylloxera and pretreated for crown gall. Pick and destroy grape berry moth cocoons and infested grapes and leaves. Spray labeled insecticide for heavy infestations of whiteflies and leafhoppers. Use sticky bands around trunks to control ants. Scrape off loose bark to expose mealybugs. Pick and destroy Japanese beetles. Keep old wood pruned out to control scale. Use netting, reflective tape, or balloons to discourage birds, or enclose whole bunches of ripening grapes in paper bags.

RECOMMENDED CULTIVARS: Most grapes are self-fruitful and self-pollinating. If you have pruned and maintained healthy plants in a sunny location but the fruits never sweeten, replant with another type. Ask your local extension agent which grapes are better suited to your area.

American grapes (*V. labrusca*), also called fox grapes or Concord grapes after the main cultivar, grow well in all but the hottest climates and are adaptable to many soils. The fruits are slipskin type—a tough skin that separates easily from the pulpy flesh. American grapes are susceptible to disease and require spraying to obtain high yields of good-quality berries. 'Catawba' is a hardy red grape but more susceptible to fungal diseases than 'Concord'. 'Niagara' is not as cold hardy as 'Concord' and ripens earlier. The low-acid white grapes are eaten fresh or used in wine and juice. 'Delaware' is an early-ripening red grape. It does not thrive in heavy soils. Hybrids of American and riverbank grapes (*V. labrusca* × *V. riparia*) are especially cold hardy.

Muscadines (*V. rotundifolia*) are the best choice for gardens in the Deep South. They are not as hardy as other grapes but are highly disease resistant. 'Southland' is a large purple grape that grows well in the Gulf Coast states. 'Yuga' has sweet reddish-bronze fruits of excellent quality that ripen late. 'Scuppernong' is an old cultivar with fruits good for eating fresh or wine.

Hybrids of American and riverbank grapes are cold-hardy.

To grow common or European grapes (*V. vinifera*) for wine, choose certified virus-free planting stock grafted to American grape rootstock. Most varieties are hardy to Zone 7 but few are grown outside of California. 'Chardonnay' is the most commonly grown white wine grape in the eastern United States. It is cold hardy but susceptible to botrytis bunch rot. 'Riesling' and 'Cabernet Franc' are more cold hardy but also susceptible. 'Pinot Blanc', the white-fruited form of 'Pinot Noir', has more resistance, as does 'Pinot Gris', although they are not as cold hardy. They grow well in the Pacific Northwest. 'Cabernet Sauvignon' is among the most cold-hardy and disease-resistant red wine grapes but ripens late. 'Pinot Noir' is fairly cold hardy and ripens early but is susceptible to bunch rot. 'Merlot' needs a long season to fully develop and tends to produce heavy canopies that shade the fruit and encourage bunch rot. 'Zinfandel' grapes are the most adaptable and can be used for white or red wine.

French-American hybrid grapes are grown primarily for making wine but also are good eaten fresh. 'Chambourcin', a late-ripening medium blue grape, needs a long growing season in a mild-winter climate. 'St. Croix' is a comparable grape that is very hardy and disease resistant. 'Maréchal Foch' and 'Léon Millot' are early, hardy, small black grapes that grow well in the Midwest. 'Cayuga White' is a popular dessert grape in the eastern United States.

Muscadine grapes grow well in the Deep South and are disease resistant.

'Ravat' is an early, hardy, disease-resistant vine with pink to red grapes used in white wines. 'Villard Blanc' requires a long growing season but produces good dessert grapes when fully ripe. 'Seyval' is commonly grown in dry climates east of the Rockies. 'LaCrosse' was derived from 'Seyval' but is earlier and more cold hardy.

Table grape clusters must be thinned to produce large grapes free from rot and insect damage. 'Kay Gray' is perhaps the hardiest seeded grape available (to Zone 3). 'Buffalo' has medium blue grapes with a fruity flavor but is susceptible to powdery mildew. 'Edelweiss' is a very cold hardy American white grape. 'Golden Muscat' has large amber fruits that ripen late. 'Price' is an early-ripening, small to medium Concord-type grape. 'Sheridan' is a hardy, late-ripening Concord. Hardy 'Steuben' is a good choice for home gardens. Its spicy-sweet blue-black fruits grow in long clusters that are attractive on an arbor. 'Yates' is a hardy, late-ripening, sweet red grape. 'Thompson Seedless' grows well only in hot climates. The mild-flavored green berries are excellent fresh or dried as raisins. 'Himrod' is a cross of

European or common grapes are usually not cold hardy or disease resistant.

'Thompson Seedless' and labrusca grapes that is moderately hardy and produces large bunches of honey-flavored pale green fruits that are good fresh or as raisins. 'Canadice' is a hardy red grape derived from 'Himrod'. It grows best in dry climates. 'Einset' is an early, hardy red grape with strawberry flavor. 'Interlaken' is similar, but the smaller amber fruits ripen earlier. 'Glenora' is a hardy, disease-resistant, seedless variety recommended for home gardens. The large dark blue grapes have a spicy flavor that's good fresh or in Riesling wine. 'Mars' is a cold-hardy and disease-resistant seedless blue grape used in pies and preserves. 'Saturn' has red fruits and grows best in hot climates. 'Reliance' is a very cold hardy red grape.

SWEET CORN

Zea mays *ZEE-uh MAYZ*

Plant bicolor corn in small gardens to get the best of both yellow and white types.

ZONES: NA
SIZE: 3–8'h x 1–3'w
TYPE: Annual
GROWTH: Average
LIGHT: Full sun
MOISTURE: High
FEATURES: Edible seeds (kernels)

SITING: Corn needs warm soil to germinate. It will grow in any well-drained, deeply dug soil but does best in rich, loose, slightly acid soil and especially well where legumes have grown previously. Direct-sow about 2 weeks after the last frost date ½" deep in moist soils or 1–1½" deep in dry soils. Use fresh seed each year; its quality declines quickly. Space the seeds 8–12" apart, using the closest spacing for early cultivars and in small gardens. Because corn is pollinated by the wind, plant the seeds in blocks of three or more in each direction instead of in rows. Planting in blocks also protects shallow-rooted corn from toppling over in high winds. Don't reseed where some seeds in a block fail to germinate. The taller plants will shade the younger ones and they won't all be ready for pollination at the same time.

CARE: Choose cultivars carefully for home gardening. Yellow and white varieties will easily cross-pollinate and turn white corn yellow; this does not affect the taste. In a small garden, plant all yellow, all white, or all bicolor cultivars. Remove weeds by hand or hoe shallowly to avoid damaging roots. Water during periods of drought, especially when ears are developing. To hand-pollinate, place pollen from tassels into an envelope, then sprinkle the pollen on the silks. Corn is a heavy feeder. Side dress plants with 33-0-0 plant food at the equivalent of 3 pounds per 100 foot row when they are 12–18" tall.

Sugar-enhanced (se and se+) varieties are more tender and sweeter than standard corn. Super-sweet (sh2) varieties are much sweeter and more tender than standard and sugar-enhanced varieties and have special cultural requirements. They will cross-pollinate with standard (su) and sugar-enhanced types, which results in starchy kernels in all plants. To avoid this problem in a small garden, plant cultivars that do not form silks at the same time. Supersweet varieties need very warm soil—at least 60°F—and more moisture than standard types in order to germinate. To preserve the high sugar content, cool the ears immediately after picking and store them in the refrigerator.

PROPAGATION: Grow from seed.

HARVEST: Pick sweet corn ears in the milk stage—when kernels are fully formed but not mature, about 20 days after the first silks appear. The silks will be starting to dry and turn brown, and the ears will feel full and firm. Carefully peel back the husk on an ear to see if it is ready. The kernels should be plump and squirt a milky juice when punctured. Most types remain in the milk stage for less than a week, so pick frequently. Immature kernels will have watery juice; overmature ones will be tough and doughy. Use a sharp, downward, twisting motion to break the shank (stem) below the ear without tearing the shank from the stalk. Eat or process the corn as soon as possible. Even in the sweetest cultivars, the sugar in corn turns to starch—especially in warm summer weather. Store ears in their husks in the refrigerator if you can't use them immediately. Pull off the silks and roast unhusked ears on a grill or in an open pit for 10–15 minutes, turning them a bit every few minutes. The silks will come off when you remove the husks. Or remove the husks and silks and cook the corn wrapped in aluminum foil. To prepare corn for eating fresh on the cob, first remove the husks and gently scrub away the silks under cool water. Cut away any discolored or wormy areas. Drop into boiling water for just 3 or 4 minutes or steam ears for 8 minutes. Enjoy as-is or with melted butter or lemon juice. Ears blanched in boiling water can be cooled and frozen whole or the kernels stripped and frozen or pressure-canned. Dried kernels can be ground into cornmeal, hominy (grits), and flour.

Leave popcorn and ornamental corn to dry on the stalks until the first frost in dry climates. In areas with rainy weather, cut the stalks when the corn is mature and hang them to dry in a well-ventilated area protected from rain and animals. Remove the husks when they are dry and cure the cobs in the sun or in the oven at the lowest setting. Store the dried cobs whole or strip the kernels off. Keep both in airtight containers in cool storage.

PESTS AND DISEASES: Choose cultivars resistant to leaf blight, smut, and bacterial wilt. Use floating row covers on young plants to prevent infection by flea beetles, which cause bacterial wilt. Use seed pretreated with fungicide to control seed rot and seedling blight. Control earworm on early and midseason varieties with regular applications of labeled insecticide spray. Use fencing around the garden to keep out deer and raccoons.

RECOMMENDED CULTIVARS: Sweet corn is most often grown in home gardens for eating fresh on the cob or for freezing and canning. Hybrids of 'Seneca' are popular in

1 Collect pollen from corn tassels into a cup or an envelope.

2 Sprinkle the pollen from the tassels onto the corn silks.

3 Carefully peel back the husk to check for ripeness for picking.

4 Mature ears are plump and squirt a milky juice when punctured.

Control earworms with regular applications of labeled pesticide spray.

SWEET CORN
continued

Grow popcorn in large, long-season gardens for fun and food. This is a collection of heirloom types.

northern zones. The 7–8" yellow, white, or bicolor ears grow on stalks up to 6' tall and are ready to harvest in 60–65 days. 'Kandy' cultivars grow well in warmer climates and are available in early, midseason, and late varieties. Try 'Golden Midget' in small gardens, where its 3' stalks and 4" ears take up little room and are ready in 60 days. 'Fleet' bears bicolor ears on 5' plants in 65 days. 'Northern Xtra

Sweet' yields 8–9" yellow ears on 5' plants in 70 days. It germinates well in cool soil.

The larger ears of midseason cultivars may be worth waiting for another couple of weeks if space permits the 6–7' stalks. 'True Platinum' produces only two long white ears per stalk, but the dark burgundy husks add ornamental value in the garden. 'Butter and Sugar', a bicolor type, and 'Merit', a traditional yellow corn with good disease resistance, and 'Silver King', a white type, are good choices ready in 75–85 days. 'Double Standard' is an open-pollinated bicolor sweet corn with 7" ears on 5' stalks ready in 75 days.

'Silver Queen' has long been a favorite late-season white corn. The 8" ears are ready to harvest in 95 days. 'Golden Bantam' is an open-pollinated yellow heirloom variety known for its sweetness. The slender ears are ready in 80 days and should be cooked within a few hours of harvest to retain the best flavor. 'Stowell's Evergreen' is an heirloom variety that gets

its name from white kernels that stay in the milk stage a long time. The 8–9" ears grown on 8' stalks and are ready in 100 days.

Some cultivars can be enjoyed fresh in the milk stage or dried for cornmeal. 'Mandan Red Flour' has 4–5' stalks with 6 ears of pale yellow kernels that mature to deep red when dry. It is ready in 80–85 days. 'Oaxacan Green Dent' has 5–6' stalks with 6" ears of emerald green, dented kernels. It thrives in cool climates and is ready in 70–75 days.

Where space and climate permit, popcorn is a fun and often ornamental food crop. 'Ruby Red' and 'Shaman's Blue' have 8–9" ears of colorful kernels that are ornamental as well as tasty when popped. They are ready in 110–115 days. 'Robust' is a high-yielding yellow variety with tender kernels ready in 100–115 days. The hulls of 'Japanese Hulless' almost disappear when popped and the flavor is nutty and sweet. Three to six 4" ears grow on 4–5' plants ready in 95–105 days. Try 'Tom Thumb' where space is limited. Larger cultivars bear more tender corn, but the 3–4" ears of this miniature variety grow on stalks 3–4' tall and are ready in just 85 days.

GINGER
Zingiber officinale ZIN-jib-ber off-fib-sib-NAY-lay

Grow ginger as an annual in northern zones and overwinter it indoors.

ZONES: 8–11
SIZE: 2–4'h x 2–4'w
TYPE: Herbaceous perennial
GROWTH: Average
LIGHT: Full sun to part shade
MOISTURE: Average
FEATURES: Edible rhizomes

SITING: Plant ginger in rich, well-drained, slightly acid soil that has been deeply worked to be loose and free of rocks or organic debris.
CARE: Keep the soil consistently moist. Ginger goes dormant in winter in tropical climates, although the stems may remain

green. Grow it as an annual in cold-winter climates, and pot one or more rhizome pieces after harvest for overwintering indoors. Keep the plants in a sunny window and water just enough to keep the soil moist but not wet. Replant the rhizomes outdoors in spring after the last frost date. Lay the pieces horizontally 1–1½" deep. Each piece should have two or more growth nodes.
PROPAGATION: Grow by division.
HARVEST: Dig the rhizomes in autumn. They should be firm and feel heavy. Wrinkled rhizomes are old or dry and will taste bitter. Cut away the stalks and fibrous roots. Peel and grate or slice ginger into salads, stir-fries, curries, marinades, and baked goods. It combines particularly well with chicken and fish; sweet potatoes, carrots, winter squash, pumpkin, carrots, lemons, peaches, and apricots. Diced dried ginger is sugared and served as a sweet with tea. Ground dried ginger is used as a cooking condiment. Pickled ginger is a popular condiment in Japanese cuisine. Store fresh, unpeeled ginger wrapped in

damp paper towels in a plastic bag in the crisper drawer of the refrigerator for up to 3 weeks. To keep it longer, peel it, break it into pieces, and store the pieces in the refrigerator covered with sherry or vodka in a glass jar.
PESTS AND DISEASES: Bacterial soft rot and Pythium fungus may develop in waterlogged soil. Rotate ginger to new locations in the garden to avoid root-knot nematodes. Protect new shoots from cutworms with cardboard or aluminum collars pressed an inch into the soil. Keep the ground around plants cleaned of decaying vegetative matter, which might encourage fusarium rhizome rot.
RECOMMENDED CULTIVARS: In addition to common ginger, there are several related plants cultivated for similar culinary use. Thai ginger or galangal (*Alpinia galanga*) is a tropical perennial herb grown for its flowers and young shoots as well as its underground stems. Japanese woodland ginger (*Zingiber mioga*) is grown for its edible shoots and flowers, which taste like bergamot.

CHAPTER 12 PLANTS FOR LANDSCAPE USE

**Butterfly weed,
*Asclepias tuberosa***

**Crape myrtle,
*Lagerstroemia
indica***

**Persian lilac,
*Syringa persica***

BOTANICAL NAME	COMMON NAME	ZONES
LIGHT AND MOISTURE CONDITIONS		
Sunny, tolerant of short drought periods		
Abies ×concolor	White fir	4–7
Acer buergerianum	Trident maple	5–8
Acer platanoides	Norway maple	3–7
Acer tataricum ginnala	Amur maple	2–7
Achillea filipendula	Threadleaf yarrow	3–9
Aesculus glabra	Ohio buckeye	4–7
Amelanchier ×grandiflora	Apple serviceberry	3–8
Artemisia ludoviciana 'Silver King'	Silver King artemisia	4–9
Asclepias tuberosa	Butterfly weed	4–9
Baccharis pilularis	Dwarf coyote bush	7–10
Berberis koreana	Korean barberry	3–7
Berberis thunbergii	Japanese barberry	(4)5–8
Bougainvillea glabra	Bougainvillea	10–11
Callicarpa dichotoma	Purple beautyberry	5–8
Callistemon viminalis	Weeping bottlebrush	8–10
Caryopteris ×clandonensis	Bluebeard	(5)6–9
Ceanothus americanus	New Jersey tea	4–9
Cedrus deodara	Deodar cedar	7–9
Cercis canadensis	Eastern redbud	4–9
Chamaecyparis pisifera 'Boulevard'	Sawara false cypress	5–8
Coreopsis lanceolata	Lanceleaf coreopsis	4–9
Cornus mas	Cornelian cherry	4–7
Cornus stolonifera	Red-osier dogwood	2–7
Corylus colurna	Turkish filbert	4–8
Cotinus coggygria	Smoke tree	4–8
Cotoneaster apiculatus	Cranberry cotoneaster	4–7
Cotoneaster horizontalis	Rockspray cotoneaster	5–7
Crataegus phaenopyrum	Washington hawthorn	5–8
Crataegus viridis 'Winter King'	Winter King hawthorn	4–7
Cupressus sempervirens	Italian cypress	8–10
Echinacea purpurea	Purple coneflower	3–9
Euonymus alatus	Winged euonymus	4–8(9)
Forsythia ×intermedia	Forsythia	(4)5–8(9)
Fraxinus americana	White ash	4–9
Fraxinus pennsylvanica	Green ash	(2)3–8(9)
Gaillardia ×grandiflora	Blanket flower	3–8
Ginkgo biloba	Ginkgo	4–8(9)
Gleditsia triacanthos var. inermis	Thornless honeylocust	4–9
Hemerocallis cultivars	Daylily	3–10
Hypericum kalmianum	Kalm's St. Johnswort	4–7
Iberis sempervirens	Evergreen candytuft	3–9
Ilex cornuta	Chinese holly	7–9
Iris hybrids	Bearded iris	3–9
Juniperus chinensis	Chinese juniper	4–9
Juniperus horizontalis	Creeping juniper	4–9
Juniperus procumbens	Japanese garden juniper	4–8
Juniperus sabina	Savin juniper	3–7

BOTANICAL NAME	COMMON NAME	ZONES
Juniperus virginiana 'Canaertii'	Canaert eastern red cedar	3–9
Kerria japonica	Kerria	5–9
Koelreuteria paniculata	Golden rain tree	5–9
Kolkwitzia amabilis	Beautybush	5–8
Lagerstroemia indica	Crape myrtle	(5)6–10
Lantana montevidensis	Trailing lantana	9–10
Larix decidua	European larch	(3)4–6(7)
Magnolia stellata	Star magnolia	4–8
Malus spp.	Flowering crabapple	4–8
Myrica pensylvanica	Northern bayberry	(2)3–6(7)
Oenothera fruticosa	Sundrops	4–8
Paeonia cvs.	Peony cultivars	3–8
Papaver orientale	Oriental poppy	3–7
Phellodendron amurense	Amur corktree	(4)5–7(8)
Phlox subulata	Creeping phlox	2–8
Physocarpus opulifolius	Ninebark	2–7
Picea abies	Norway spruce	2–6
Picea glauca	White spruce	2–6
Picea pungens var. glauca	Colorado blue spruce	3–7
Pinus mugo	Mugo pine	3–7(8)
Pinus strobus	Eastern white pine	3–7(8)
Pistacia chinensis	Chinese pistachio	6–9
Potentilla fruticosa	Bush cinquefoil	2–6(7)
Prunus tomentosa	Nanking cherry	3–6
Pseudotsuga menziesii	Douglas fir	(3)4–6
Pyracantha coccinea	Scarlet firethorn	6–9
Pyrus calleryana 'Bradford'	Bradford callery pear	5–8(9)
Quercus robur	English oak	5–8
Quercus rubra	Northern red oak	3–7
Rhus aromatica	Fragrant sumac	3–9
Rhus typhina	Staghorn sumac	4–8
Rosa rugosa	Rugosa rose	3–7
Schinus molle	Pepper tree	9–10
Sedum spectabile	Showy stonecrop	3–10
Spiraea japonica 'Anthony Waterer'	Anthony Waterer spirea	3–8
Spiraea japonica 'Bumalda'	Bumald spirea	4–7
Syringa meyeri 'Palibin'	Dwarf Meyer lilac	3–7
Syringa vulgaris	Common lilac	3–7
Taxus ×media	Anglo-Japanese yew	5–7
Thuja orientalis	Oriental arborvitae	6–9
Tilia cordata	Littleleaf linden	4–7
Veronica spicata	Spike speedwell	4–8
Viburnum carlesii	Korean spice viburnum	5–7
Viburnum opulus 'Compactum'	Compact European cranberrybush	4–7
Viburnum trilobum	American cranberrybush viburnum	2–7
Weigela florida	Weigela	4–8
Wisteria sinensis	Chinese wisteria	5–9

BOTANICAL NAME	COMMON NAME	ZONES
Sunny, moist but without standing water		
Acer griseum	Paperbark maple	4–8
Acer palmatum	Japanese maple	5–8
Acer rubrum	Red maple	3–9
Acer saccharum	Sugar maple	4–8
Alnus glutinosa	European black alder	4–7
Aralia elata	Japanese angelica tree	(4)5–9
Araucaria araucana	Monkey-puzzle tree	7–10
Aronia arbutifolia	Red chokeberry	(4)5–9
Betula nigra	River birch	4–9
Buxus sempervirens	Common boxwood	(5)6–9
Carya illinoinensis	Pecan	5–9
Cercidiphyllum japonicum	Katsura tree	5–8
Chionanthus virginicus	Fringe tree	4–9
Cladrastis kentuckea	American yellowwood	4–8
Clematis cvs.	Clematis cultivars	3–8
Clethra alnifolia	Summersweet	4–9
Cornus alternifolia	Pagoda dogwood	3–7
Cornus kousa	Kousa dogwood	5–8
Corylus americana	American hazelnut	4–8
Dendranthema ×grandiflorum	Chrysanthemum	4–9
Deutzia gracilis	Slender deutzia	(4)5–8
Dictamnus albus	Gas plant	3–8
Digitalis purpurea	Foxglove	3–8
Eremurus spp.	Foxtail lily	5–8
Euonymus atropurpurea	Eastern wahoo	4–9
Fagus sylvatica	European beech	(4)5–7
Fothergilla gardenii	Dwarf fothergilla	5–8(9)
Geranium sanguineum	Bloody cranesbill	4–8
Gymnocladus dioica	Kentucky coffee tree	(3)4–8
Halesia tetraptera	Carolina silverbell	5–8(9)
Hamamelis virginiana	Common witch hazel	3–8
Hydrangea paniculata	Panicle hydrangea	4–8
Hydrangea petiolaris	Climbing hydrangea	5–8
Ilex decidua	Possum haw	5–9
Ilex verticillata	Winterberry	3–9
Itea virginica	Virginia sweetspire	(5)6–9
Jasminum polyanthum	Pink Chinese jasmine	9–10
Kniphofia uvaria	Red hot poker	5–9
Larix kaempferi	Japanese larch	4–7
Leucanthemum ×superbum	Shasta daisy	4–8
Liatris spicata	Spike gayfeather	3–9
Liquidambar styraciflua	American sweet gum	5–9
Liriodendron tulipifera	Tulip tree	(4)5–9
Magnolia grandiflora	Southern magnolia	(6)7–9(10)
Metasequoia glyptostroboides	Dawn redwood	5–8
Monarda didyma	Bee balm, Oswego tea	3–9
Nyssa sylvatica	Black gum, tupelo	(4)5–9
Perovskia atriplicifolia	Perovskia, Russian sage	3–9
Philadelphus coronarius	Mockorange	4–8
Phlox paniculata	Garden phlox	3–8
Pinus flexilis	Limber pine	4–7

BOTANICAL NAME	COMMON NAME	ZONES
Quercus bicolor	Swamp white oak	4–8
Quercus phellos	Willow oak	5–9
Scabiosa caucasica	Pincushion flower	3–8
Taxodium distichum	Bald cypress	5–10
Thuja occidentalis	Eastern arborvitae	3–7
Thuja plicata	Western arborvitae	5–8
Tsuga canadensis	Canadian hemlock	(3)4–7
Viburnum dentatum	Arrowwood viburnum	3–8
Suitable for constantly wet to nearly bog conditions		
Alocasia cvs.	Elephant's ear	8–10
Chelone lyonii	Pink turtlehead	8–10
Eupatorium purpureum	Joe-Pye weed	4–8
Gunnera manicata	Gunnera, Giant rhubarb	8–10
Iris ensata	Japanese iris	4–9
Iris sibirica	Siberian iris	4–9
Isolepis cernua	Fiber optic plant	8–10
Ligularia dentata	Bigleaf ligularia	3–8
Lobelia cardinalis	Cardinal flower	3–9
Lysimachia nummularia	Moneywort	3–8
Lysimachia punctata	Yellow loosestrife	4–8
Magnolia virginiana	Sweet bay magnolia	5–9
Malva moschata	Musk mallow	3–8
Matteuccia struthiopteris	Ostrich fern	3–8
Myosotis scorpioides	Forget-me–not	3–8
Metasequoia glyptostroboides	Dawn redwood	5–8
Osmunda regalis	Royal fern	3–9
Primula japonica	Japanese primrose	5–7
Rodgersia pinnata	Rodgersia	4–7
Salix babylonica	Weeping willow	5–9
Smilacina racemosa	False Solomon's seal	4–9
Tradescantia virginiana	Spiderwort	4–9
Zantedeschia aethiopica	Calla lily	9–10
Suitable for standing water or shallow ponds		
Acorus gramineus	Japanese sweet flag	8–9
Aponogeton distachyos	Cape pond weed	9–10
Arundo donax	Giant reed	7–10
Caltha palustrus	Marsh marigold	4–7
Carex elata 'Bowles' Golden'	Bowles' Golden sedge	5–9
Colocasia esculenta	Taro	10–11
Cyperus profiler	Dwarf papyrus	9–10
Iris ensata	Japanese iris	4–9
Iris pseudacorus	Yellow flag	5–9
Iris versicolor	Blue flag iris	6–9
Juncus effusus	Soft rush	6–9
Nelumbo nucifera	Sacred lotus	8–10
Nymphaea cvs.	Tropical water lily cultivars	10–11
Nymphaea odorata	Fragrant water lily	3–8
Oenanthe javanica	Japanese watercress	10
Osmunda regalis	Royal fern	3–9
Pistia stratiotes	Water lettuce	10
Taxodium distichum	Bald cypress	5–10
Zantedeschia aethiopica	Calla lily	9–10

Japanese maple, *Acer palmatum* 'Ichigyoji'

Foxglove, *Digitalis purpurea* 'Excelsior' strain

Beebalm, *Monarda didyma* 'Panorama'

Cardinal flower, *Lobelia cardinalis*

Yellow flag iris, *Iris pseudacorus*

Camellia, *Camellia japonica* 'Apple Blossom'

Bigleaf hydrangea, *Hydrangea macrophylla*

Astilbe, *Astilbe ×arendsii* 'Hyacinth'

Spotted deadnettle, *Lamium maculatum*

Fortune's hosta, *Hosta fortunei* 'Albomarginata'

BOTANICAL NAME	COMMON NAME	ZONES
Light to medium shade		
Abelia ×grandiflora	Glossy abelia	(5)6–9
Acer palmatum	Japanese maple	5–8
Acer pensylvanicum	Striped maple	3–6
Aconitum carmichaelii	Monkshood	3–7
Adiantum pedatum	Maidenhair fern	4–8
Ajuga reptans	Ajuga, Bugleweed	3–9
Amelanchier arborea	Downy serviceberry	4–9
Ampelopsis brevipedunculata	Porcelain berry	4–8
Anchusa azurea	Italian alkanet	3–8
Anemone ×hupehensis	Japanese anemone	5–8
Astilbe ×arendsii	Astilbe	4–8
Bergenia crassifolia	Leather bergenia	3–8
Camellia japonica	Japanese camellia	(7)8–10
Camellia sasanqua	Sasanqua camellia	7–10
Celastrus scandens	American bittersweet	3–8
Ceratostigma plumbaginoides	Leadwort, Plumbago	5–9
Cercis canadensis	Eastern redbud	4–9
Chamaecyparis obtusa	Hinoki false cypress	5–8
Chionanthus virginicus	White fringe tree	4–9
Clethra alnifolia	Summersweet	4–9
Convallaria majalis	Lily-of-the-valley	2–7
Cornus florida	Flowering dogwood	5–9
Daphne odora	Winter daphne	7–10
Digitalis purpurea	Common foxglove	3–8
Doronicum orientale	Leopard's bane	4–7
Fatsia japonica	Japanese fatsia	8–10
Fothergilla major	Large fothergilla	5–8(9)
Fuchsia magellanica	Magellan fuchsia	7–10
Hamamelis mollis	Chinese witch hazel	5–8
Heuchera sanguinea	Coral bells	3–8
Hibiscus moscheutos	Common rose mallow	5–8
Hydrangea macrophylla	Big leaf hydrangea	(5)6–9
Hydrangea quercifolia	Oakleaf hydrangea	5–9
Hypericum ×cyanthifolium	Gold cup St. Johnswort	5–7
Ilex crenata	Japanese holly	6–8
Ilex ×meserveae cvs.	Meserve holly	(4)5–8
Laurus nobilis	Bay laurel	8–10
Leucothoe fontanesiana	Drooping leucothoe	5–8
Ligustrum japonicum	Japanese privet	7–10
Ligustrum obtusifolium	Border privet	4–7
Lindera benzoin	Spicebush	5–9
Liriope spicata	Lilyturf	5–10
Lobelia siphilitica	Great blue lobelia	4–8
Lonicera sempervirens	Trumpet honeysuckle	3–9
Mahonia repens	Creeping mahonia	5–9
Monarda didyma	Bee balm	3–9
Nandina domestica	Heavenly bamboo	6–9(10)
Ophiopogon japonicus	Mondo grass	7–11
Philodendron spp.	Philodendron	10–11
Phlox stolonifera	Creeping phlox	2–8
Photinia serrulata	Chinese photinia	6–9
Pieris japonica	Japanese pieris	5–9

BOTANICAL NAME	COMMON NAME	ZONES
Platycodon grandiflorus	Balloon flower	3–8
Podocarpus macrophyllus var. maki	Chinese podocarpus	8–10
Prunus caroliniana	Carolina cherry laurel	7–10
Rhamnus frangula	Glossy buckthorn	3–7
Rhododendron catawbiense	Catawba rhododendron	5–8
Rudbeckia laciniata	Cutleaf coneflower	3–9
Sabal minor	Dwarf palmetto	9–10
Saxifraga stolonifera	Strawberry geranium	6–9
Skimmia japonica	Japanese skimmia	(6)7–8(9)
Taxus ×media cvs.	Anglo-Japanese yew	5–7
Thalictrum aquilegifolium	Meadow rue	4–9
Trachelospermum jasminoides	Star jasmine	8–10
Tricyrtis hirta	Toad lily	5–9
Vaccinium corymbosum	Highbush blueberry	3–7
Xanthorhiza simplicissima	Yellowroot	3–9
Zenobia pulverulenta	Dusty zenobia	5–9
Medium to heavy shade		
Aesculus parviflora	Bottlebrush buckeye	4–9
Alchemilla mollis	Lady's mantle	3–7
Aquilegia ×hybrida	Columbine hybrids	3–9
Arum italicum	Italian arum	6–9
Aruncus dioicus	Goatsbeard	3–7
Asarum europaeum	European wild ginger	4–7
Aspidistra elatior	Cast-iron plant	8–11
Aucuba japonica	Japanese aucuba	(6)7–10
Begonia grandis evansiana	Hardy begonia	6–9
Cyrtomium falcatum	Japanese holly fern	6–10
Dicentra eximia	Fringed bleeding heart	3–8
Dicentra spectabilis	Common bleeding heart	3–9
Epimedium ×rubrum	Red barrenwort	4–8
Geranium sylvaticum	Woodland cranesbill	5–8
Hedera helix	English ivy	5–10
Helleborus orientalis	Lenten rose	4–9
Heuchera micrantha	Small-flowered alum root	4–8
Hosta species and cultivars	Hosta	3–8
Lamium galeobdolon	Yellow archangel	4–9
Lamium maculatum	Lamium, spotted deadnettle	4–8
Lysimachia nummularia	Moneywort	3–8
Mertensia virginica	Virginia bluebells	3–7
Pachysandra terminalis	Japanese spurge	4–8
Phlox divaricata	Woodland phlox	3–9
Pittosporum tobira	Japanese pittosporum	(8)9–10
Polygonatum biflorum	Small Solomon's seal	3–9
Pulmonaria angustifolia	Blue lungwort	3–8
Pulmonaria saccharata	Bethlehem sage	3–8
Rhodotypos scandens	Jetbead	4–8
Sanguinaria canadensis	Bloodroot	3–9
Smilacina racemosa	False Solomon's seal	4–9
Tellima grandiflora	Fringe cup	4–7
Tiarella cordifolia	Alleghany foam flower	3–8
Vinca major	Vinca, large periwinkle	6–9
Vinca minor	Common periwinkle	4–9
Viola cornuta	Viola	5–9

BOTANICAL NAME	COMMON NAME	ZONES
SOIL SITES AND PROBLEMS		
Tolerant of heavy clay soils		
Acer campestre	Hedge maple	5–8
Acer platanoides	Norway maple	3–7
Alnus glutinosa	European black alder	3–7
Asclepias tuberosa	Butterfly weed	4–9
Betula nigra	River birch	4–9
Caragana arborescens	Siberian peashrub	2–7
Celtis occidentalis	Hackberry	3–9
Cornus stolonifera	Red-osier dogwood	2–7
Elaeagnus angustifolia	Russian olive	2–7
Euonymus alatus	Winged euonymus	4–8(9)
Forsythia ×intermedia	Forsythia	(4)5–8(9)
Gleditsia triacanthos var. inermis	Thornless honeylocust	4–9
Juniperus chinensis	Chinese juniper	4–9
Koelreuteria paniculata	Golden rain tree	5–9
Larix decidua	European larch	(3)4–6(7)
Leucanthemum vulgare	Ox-eye daisy	4–9
Lonicera spp.	Honeysuckle	2–9
Malus spp.	Flowering crabapple	4–8
Myrica pensylvanica	Northern bayberry	(2)3–6(7)
Paeonia cvs.	Peony	3–8
Physostegia virginiana	Obedient plant	3–8
Picea abies	Norway spruce	2–7
Pinus strobus	Eastern white pine	3–7(8)
Potentilla fruticosa	Bush cinquefoil	2–6(7)
Pyrus calleryana cvs.	Callery pear cultivars	5–8(9)
Quercus macrocarpa	Bur oak	3–8
Quercus palustris	Pin oak	4–8
Salix alba	White willow	2–8
Syringa vulgaris	Common lilac	3–7
Thuja occidentalis	Eastern arborvitae	3–7
Tilia cordata	Littleleaf linden	4–7
Viburnum spp.	Viburnum	2–8
Tolerant of sandy soils		
Acer campestre	Hedge maple	5–8
Berberis thunbergii	Japanese barberry	(4)5–8
Buddleia davidii	Butterfly bush	5–9
Chaenomeles speciosa	Flowering quince	5–9
Elaeagnus angustifolia	Russian olive	2–7
Ilex opaca	American holly	5–9
Juniperus chinensis	Chinese juniper	4–9
Juniperus conferta	Shore juniper	6–9
Juniperus horizontalis	Creeping juniper	3–9
Kerria japonica	Kerria	5–9
Lantana montevidensis	Trailing lantana	9–11
Ligustrum amurense	Amur privet	4–7
Myrica pensylvanica	Northern bayberry	(2)3–6(7)
Picea glauca	White spruce	2–6
Pinus thunbergii	Japanese black pine	5–8
Pistacia chinensis	Chinese pistachio	6–9
Pittosporum tobira	Japanese pittosporum	(8)9–10
Platanus ×acerifolia	London plane tree	(5)6–8

BOTANICAL NAME	COMMON NAME	ZONES
Punica granatum	Pomegranate	(7)8–10
Rhus aromatica	Fragrant sumac	3–9
Santolina chamaecyparissus	Lavender cotton	6–9
Spiraea japonica	Japanese spirea	4–8
Adapted to acid soils		
Arctostaphylos spp.	Manzanita	8–10
Calluna vulgaris	Scotch heather	5–7
Camellia japonica	Camellia	(7)8–10
Coreopsis verticillata	Threadleaf coreopsis	4–9
Cytisus scoparius	Scotch broom	5–8
Erica carnea	Winter heath	5–7
Halesia carolina	Carolina silverbell	5–9
Ilex spp.	Holly	3–9
Kalmia latifolia	Mountain laurel	5–9
Leptospermum laevigatum	Australian tea tree	9–10
Lupinus cvs.	Lupine cultivars	4–8
Oxydendrum arboreum	Sourwood	5–9
Picea spp.	Spruce	2–8
Pieris japonica	Japanese pieris	5–9
Pinus wallichiana	Himalayan pine	5–7
Populus tremuloides	Quaking aspen	1–6
Pseudotsuga menziesii	Douglas fir	(3)4–6
Quercus palustris	Pin oak	4–8
Rhododendron	Azalea	4–10
Sapium sebiferum	Chinese tallow tree	8–9
Tsuga canadensis	Canadian hemlock	(3)4–7
Tolerant of alkaline soils		
Aesculus parviflora	Bottlebrush buckeye	4–8
Alnus rugosa	Speckled alder	3–6
Asimina triloba	Pawpaw	5–8
Berberis julianae	Wintergreen barberry	5–8
Callistemon citrinus	Lemon bottlebrush	(8)9–11
Caragana arborescens	Siberian peashrub	2–7
Carpinus caroliniana	American hornbeam	3–9
Catalpa bignonioides	Southern catalpa	5–9
Celtis laevigata	Sugarberry	5–9
Celtis occidentalis	Hackberry	3–9
Cladrastis kentuckea	American yellowwood	4–8
Cornus mas	Cornelian cherry	4–8
Deutzia spp.	Deutzia	(4)5–8
Elaeagnus angustifolia	Russian olive	2–7
Filipendula rubra	Queen-of-the-prairie	3–9
Forsythia ×intermedia	Forsythia	(4)5–8(9)
Juniperus chinensis	Chinese juniper	4–9
Koelreuteria paniculata	Golden rain tree	5–9
Platanus occidentalis	American sycamore	4–9
Pyracantha coccinea	Scarlet firethorn	6–9
Rhus aromatica	Fragrant sumac	3–9
Robinia pseudoacacia	Black locust	4–8(9)
Sassafras albidum	Sassafras	(4)5–9
Syringa persica	Persian lilac	3–7
Ziziphus jujuba	Chinese jujube	6–9

Border forsythia, *Forsythia* ×*intermedia*

Flowering crabapple, *Malus* spp.

Rhododendron, *Rhododendron* 'Hydon Mist'

Chinese juniper, *Juniperus chinensis* 'Hetzii Columnaris'

Rose-of-Sharon, *Hibiscus syriacus*

Lady's mantle, *Alchemilla mollis*

Pinks, *Dianthus plumarius*

Johnny-jump-up, *Viola tricolor*

Caladium, *Caladium bicolor* 'Rose Bud'

BOTANICAL NAME	COMMON NAME	ZONES
Tolerant of soil salts, salt spray, as in seaside garden		
Araucaria heterophylla	Norfolk Island pine	10–11
Arbutus unedo	Strawberry tree	7–9
Armeria maritima	Sea thrift	3–9
Baccharis halimifolia	Groundsel bush	5–9
Bougainvillea glabra	Bougainvillea	9–10
Callistemon viminalis	Weeping bottlebrush	8–10
Caragana arborescens	Siberian peashrub	2–7
Carissa macrocarpa	Natal plum	10–11
Chamaerops humilis	Fan palm	9–10
Cordyline australis	Cabbage tree	9–10
Cortaderia selloana	Pampas grass	8–10
Elaeagnus angustifolia	Russian olive	2–7
Hibiscus syriacus	Rose of Sharon	5–8(9)
Lampranthus spectabilis	Trailing ice plant	9–10
Leptospermum scoparium	New Zealand tea tree	9–10
Ligustrum japonicum	Japanese privet	7–10
Nerium oleander	Oleander	8–10
Pinus halepensis	Aleppo pine	8–10
Pinus thunbergii	Japanese black pine	5–8
Populus alba	White poplar	3–10
Pyracantha coccinea	Scarlet firethorn	6–9
Quercus virginiana	Southern live oak	(7)8–10
Robinia pseudoacacia	Black locust	4–8(9)
Rosmarinus officinalis	Rosemary	(6)7–9
Tamarix ramosissima	Tamarisk	3(4)–8
Ziziphus jujuba	Chinese jujube	6–9
TEMPERATURE		
Cool climate plants—decline in hot weather		
Abies balsamea	Balsam fir	2–5
Abies procera	Noble fir	5–7
Acer platanoides	Norway maple	3–7
Aconitum carmichaelii	Monkshood	3–7
Aesculus hippocastanum	Horsechestnut	4–7
Alchemilla mollis	Lady's mantle	3–7
Alnus glutinosa	European black alder	3–7
Bellis perennis	English daisy	4–6
Calendula officinalis	Pot marigold	NA
Calluna vulgaris	Scotch heather	4–6
Caragana arborescens	Siberian peashrub	2–7
Convallaria majalis	Lily-of-the-valley	2–7
Delphinium ×elatum	Hybrid bee delphinium	2–7
Dianthus plumarius	Pinks	4–9
Doronicum orientale	Leopard's bane	4–7
Elaeagnus angustifolia	Russian olive	2–7
Erica carnea	Winter heath	5–7
Eupatorium purpureum	Joe-Pye weed	4–7
Fagus sylvatica	European beech	(4)5–7
Laburnum ×watereri	Golden chain tree	6–7
Larix kaempferi	Japanese larch	4–6
Lathyrus odoratus	Sweet pea	NA
Lupinus hybrids	Lupine	4–8
Myrica pensylvanica	Northern bayberry	(2)3–6(7)

BOTANICAL NAME	COMMON NAME	ZONES
Papaver nudicaule	Iceland poppy	2–8
Papaver orientale	Oriental poppy	3–7
Pinus wallichiana	Himalayan pine	5–7
Populus tremuloides	Quaking aspen	1–6
Primula japonica	Japanese primrose	5–7
Saponaria ocymoides	Soapwort	3–8
Saxifraga ×arendsii	Rockfoil	5–7
Trollius ×cultorum	Globeflower	3–6
Viola tricolor	Johnny-jump-up	4–7
Viola ×wittrockiana	Pansy	5–8
Hot weather plants—not frost tolerant		
Abelmoschus moschatus	Musk mallow	9–11
Abutilon ×hybridum	Flowering maple	8–10
Acalypha wilkesiana	Copperleaf	10–11
Agapanthus africanus	Lily-of-the-Nile	10–11
Allamanda cathartica	Golden trumpet	10–11
Alocasia macrorrhiza	Elephant's ear	8–10
Anthurium andraeanum	Anthurium, flamingo flower	10–11
Bougainvillea glabra	Bougainvillea	10–11
Brugmansia suaveolens	Angel's trumpet	10–11
Brugmansia versicolor	Apricot moonflower	9–11
Caladium bicolor	Caladium	8–11
Catharanthus roseus	Vinca	10–11
Colocasia esculenta	Taro	10–11
Cyathea australis	Australian tree fern	9–10
Datura metel	Horn of plenty	9–11
Ensete ventricosum 'Maurellii'	Red Abyssinian banana	10–11
Euphorbia pulcherrima	Poinsettia	10–11
Hedychium coronarium	White ginger	9–11
Heliconia spp.	Lobster claw	10–11
Hibiscus rosa-sinensis	Chinese hibiscus	10–11
Hippeastrum cvs.	Amaryllis	10–11
Hylocereus undatus	Dragon fruit, stawberry pear	10–11
Ipomoea alba	Moonflower vine	8–10
Ipomoea quamoclit	Cypress vine	8–10
Ipomoea tricolor	Morning glory	NA
Ipomoea tuberosa	Wood rose	10–11
Ixora coccinea	Jungle flame	10–11
Justicia carnea	Brazilian plume flower	10–11
Lagerstroemia indica	Crape myrtle	(5)6–10
Mandevilla ×amabilis	Mandevilla	10–11
Murraya paniculata	Orange jessamine	10–11
Musa spp.	Ornamental banana	10–11
Nerium oleander	Oleander	8–10
Pachystachys lutea	Lollipop plant	10–11
Pandorea jasminoides	Bower vine	10–11
Plumbago auriculata	Cape leadwort	9–11
Plumeria rubra	Frangipani	10–11
Stigmaphyllon ciliatum	Golden vine	10–11
Strelitzia reginae	Bird of paradise	9–11
Thunbergia grandiflora	Bengal clock vine	10–11
Xanthosoma violaceum	Blue tannia	10–11
Zantedeschia cvs.	Calla lily	9–11

BOTANICAL NAME	COMMON NAME	ZONES
PLANTS SENSITIVE TO WALNUT TOXICITY		
Asparagus officinalis	Asparagus	4–9
Betula pendula	European white birch	2–6
Brassica oleracea capitata	Cabbage	NA
Capsicum annuum	Pepper	NA
Colchicum autumnale	Autumn crocus	5–9
Cotoneaster spp.	Cotoneaster	4–7
Ligustrum vulgare	Common privet	4–7
Lycopersicon esculentum	Tomato	NA
Magnolia ×soulangiana	Saucer magnolia	4–9
Malus spp.	Flowering crabapple	4–8
Malus sylvestris var. *domestica*	Apple	3–10
Paeonia officinalis	Peony	3–8
Picea abies	Norway spruce	2–7
Pinus resinosa	Red pine	2–6
Pinus strobus	Eastern white pine	3–7(8)
Pinus sylvestris	Scotch pine	2–8
Potentilla fruticosa	Bush cinquefoil	2–6(7)
Rhododendron spp.	Rhododendron, Azalea	4–10
Rubus laciniatus	Blackberry	4–9
Solanum tuberosum	Potato	NA
Syringa vulgaris	Common lilac	3–7
Tilia americana	American linden	3–8
PLANTS SOMEWHAT RESISTANT TO DEER		
Ajuga reptans	Bugleweed	3–9
Astilbe ×arendsii	Astilbe	4–8
Berberis spp.	Barberry	3–8
Buddleia davidii	Butterfly bush	5–9
Buxus spp.	Boxwood	(5)6–9
Clematis terniflora	Sweet autumn clematis	5–8
Clethra alnifolia	Summersweet	4–9
Cornus florida	Flowering dogwood	5–9
Cotinus coggygria	Smoke tree	4–8
Cytissus scoparius	Scotch broom	5–8
Delphinium spp.	Delphinium	2–7
Deutzia gracilis	Slender deutzia	(4)5–8
Digitalis purpurea	Foxglove	3–8
Elaeagnus angustifolia	Russian olive	2–7
Epimedium spp.	Barrenwort	5–8
Fagus sylvatica	European beech	(4)5–7
Forsythia ×intermedia	Forsythia	(4)5–8(9)
Fraxinus spp.	Green Ash, white ash	(2)3–9
Gardenia spp.	Gardenia	(7)8–10
Ginkgo biloba	Ginkgo	4–8(9)
Helleborus orientalis	Lenten rose	4–9
Ilex vomitoria	Yaupon	7–10
Jasminum spp.	Jasmine	8–10
Juniperus spp.	Juniper	2–9
Kerria japonica	Japanese kerria	5–9
Lamium maculatum	Spotted deadnettle	4–8
Larix spp.	Larch	(3)4–6(7)
Leucanthemum vulgare	Ox-eye daisy	3–8
Leucothoe fontanesiana	Drooping leucothoe	5–8
Lobelia cardinalis	Cardinal flower	3–9

BOTANICAL NAME	COMMON NAME	ZONES
Lonicera sempervirens	Trumpet honeysuckle	4–9
Lupinus hybrids	Lupine	4–8
Mahonia aquifolium	Oregon grapeholly	5–9
Metasequoia glyptostroboides	Dawn redwood	5–8
Nandina domestica	Heavenly bamboo	6–9(10)
Narcissus spp.	Narcissus, daffodil	3–8
Nerium oleander	Oleander	8–10
Perovskia atriplicifolia	Russian sage	3–9
Picea spp.	White, Norway, Colorado spruces	2–7
Pieris japonica	Japanese pieris	5–9
Pulmonaria cvs.	Lungwort	3–8
Rhododendron catawbiense	Catawba rhododendron	5–8
Salvia ×superba	Sage	4–9
Taxodium distichum	Bald cypress	5–10
Thuja occidentalis	American arborvitae	3–7
Veronica spicata	Speedwell	3–8
Viburnum spp.	Viburnum	2–8
Vinca minor	Periwinkle	4–9
PLANTS FAVORED BY DEER		
Abies spp.	Fir	2–7
Acer platanoides	Norway maple	3–7
Amelanchier arborea	Downy serviceberry	4–9
Capsicum annuum	Pepper	NA
Cercis canadensis	Eastern redbud	4–9
Clematis ×jackmanii	Jackman clematis	3–8
Cornus mas	Cornelian cherry	4–8
Cornus stolonifera	Red-osier dogwood	2–7
Cucumis spp.	Cucumber, muskmelon	NA
Cucurbita spp.	Pumpkin, squash	NA
Dendranthema ×grandiflorum	Chrysanthemum	4–9
Euonymus japonicus	Japanese euonymus	7–9
Hedera helix	English Ivy	4–9
Hemerocallis hybrids	Daylily	3–10
Heuchera sanguinea	Coral bells	3–8
Hosta hybrids	Hosta	3–8
Hydrangea spp.	Hydrangea	3–9
Lilium cvs.	Lily	3–8
Lycopersicon esculentum	Tomato	NA
Malus sylvestris var. *domestica*	Apple	3–10
Phlox paniculata	Garden phlox	3–8
Pisum sativum	Garden pea, English pea	NA
Prunus spp.	Cherry, plum	2–9
Rhododendron spp.	Azalea	4–10
Rosa cvs.	Rose	3–10
Rubus spp.	Blackberry, raspberry	4–9
Salix alba	White willow	2–8
Sedum spectabile	Showy stonecrop	3–10
Symphorocarpos spp.	Coralberry, snowberry	3–7
Taxus ×media	Anglo-Japanese yew	5–7
Tradescantia ×virginiana	Spiderwort	4–9
Tulipa hybrids	Tulip	3–8
Viola spp.	Violet	4–9

Pepper, *Capsicum annuum* 'Gypsy'

Saucer magnolia, *Magnolia soulangiana*

Ginkgo, *Ginkgo biloba*

Cucumber, *Cucumis sativus* 'Burpless Bush'

Sweet corn, *Zea mays* 'Sugar Dots'

Bonica shrub rose,
***Rosa* 'Bonica'**

**Tulip, *Tulipa*
'Keiserskroon'**

**Black locust,
*Robinia
pseudoacacia*
'Frisia'**

**Austrian pine,
Pinus nigra
'Hornibrookiana'**

BOTANICAL NAME	COMMON NAME	ZONES
PLANTS SOMEWHAT RESISTANT TO RABBITS		
Allium spp.	Onion, chive, garlic	3–10
Artemisia ludoviciana albula	White sage	4–9
Buddleia davidii	Butterfly bush	5–9
Capsicum annuum	Pepper	NA
Cucurbita spp.	Gourd, pumpkin, squash	NA
Euonymus fortunei	Wintercreeper euonymus	4–8
Forsythia ×intermedia	Forsythia	(4)5–8(9)
Fraxinus americana	White ash	4–9
Ilex opaca	American holly	5–9
Juniperus spp.	Juniper	3–9
Lamium maculatum	Spotted deadnettle	3–8
Lycopersicon esculentum	Tomato	NA
Picea spp.	Spruce	2–8
Pinus spp.	Pine	3–8
Solanum tuberosum	Potato	NA
Thymus serphyllum	Wild thyme	4–9
PLANTS FAVORED BY RABBITS		
Acer spp.	Maple	2–9
Berberis thunbergii	Japanese barberry	(4)5–8
Beta vulgaris	Beet	NA
Brassica oleracea capitata	Cabbage	NA
Carpinus caroliniana	American hornbeam	3–9
Cladrastis kentuckea	American yellowwood	4–8
Cornus spp.	Dogwood	2–9
Daucus carota sativa	Carrot	NA
Gleditsia triacanthos var. inermis	Thornless honeylocust	4–9
Malus sylvestris var. domestica	Apple	3–10
Phaseolus vulgaris	Green bean, string bean	NA
Pisum sativum	Garden pea, English pea	NA
Quercus spp.	Oak	3–9(10)
Rhus typhina	Staghorn sumac	4–8
Rosa spp.	Rose	3–10
Rubus spp.	Blackberry, red raspberry	4–9
Salix babylonica	Babylon weeping willow	5–8
Sorbus aucuparia	European mountain ash	3–7
Tilia americana	American linden	3–8
Tulipa hybrids	Tulip	3–8
PLANTS RESISTANT TO GYPSY MOTH		
Abies balsamea	Balsam fir	2–5
Catalpa spp.	Catalpa	(4)5–8(9)
Cornus florida	Flowering dogwood	5–9
Cornus racemosa	Gray dogwood	4–8
Fraxinus spp.	Green ash, white ash	(2)3–9
Ilex spp.	Holly	3–9
Juglans nigra	Black walnut	4–9
Juniperus virginiana	Eastern red cedar	2–9
Liriodendron tulipifera	Tulip tree	(4)5–9
Platanus ×acerifolia	London plane tree	5(6)–8
Platanus occidentalis	American sycamore	4–9
Pseudolarix amabilis	Golden larch	(5)6–7
Robinia pseudoacacia	Black locust	4–8(9)

BOTANICAL NAME	COMMON NAME	ZONES
PLANTS FAVORED BY GYPSY MOTH		
Acer spp.	Maple	2–9
Alnus glutinosa	European black alder	3–7
Carya spp.	Hickory, pecan	4–9
Crataegus spp.	Hawthorn	4–8
Malus spp.	Apple, flowering crabapple	4–8
Nyssa sylvatica	Black gum, black tupelo	(4)5–9
Picea spp.	Spruce	2–8
Pinus spp.	Pine	3–8
Populus spp.	Cottonwood, poplar	1–9
Pseudotsuga menziesii	Douglas fir	(3)4–6
Quercus spp.	Oak	3–9(10)
Salix spp.	Willow	2–8
Sassafras albidum	Sassafras	(4)5–9
Thuja occidentalis	American arborvitae	3–7
Tilia spp.	Linden	2–8
Tsuga canadensis	Canadian hemlock	(3)4–7
Ulmus spp.	American elm, Siberian elm	2–9
PLANTS RESISTANT TO JAPANESE BEETLE		
Cornus spp.	Dogwood	2–9
Forsythia ×intermedia	Forsythia	(4)5–8(9)
Ginkgo biloba	Ginkgo	4–8(9)
Ilex opaca	American holly	5–9
Syringa spp.	Lilac	3–7
Tamarix ramosissima	Tamarisk	(3)4–8
Tilia tomentosa	Silver linden	4–7
PLANTS FAVORED BY JAPANESE BEETLE ADULTS		
Acer spp.	Japanese maple, Norway maple	2–8
Aesculus hippocastanum	Horsechestnut	4–7
Alcea rosea	Hollyhock	3–9
Ampelopsis brevipedunculata	Porcelain berry	4–8
Astilbe ×arendsii	Astilbe	4–8
Chaenomeles speciosa	Flowering quince	5–9
Hibiscus syriacus	Rose of Sharon	5–8(9)
Lagerstroemia indica	Crape myrtle	(5)6–10
Ligustrum ovalifolium	California privet	5–8
Malus spp.	Apple, flowering crabapple	4–8
Myrica pensylvanica	Northern bayberry	(2)3–6(7)
Parthenocissus quinquefolia	Virginia creeper	3–9
Petunia ×hybrida	Petunia	NA
Platanus occidentalis	American sycamore	4–9
Polygonum aubertii	Silver lace vine	4–7
Prunus spp.	Flowering cherry, peach	3–9
Rhododendron cvs.	Azalea	4–10
Rosa spp.	Rose	3–10
Rubus idaeus	Raspberry	3–7
Salix discolor	Pussy willow	4–8
Tagetes spp.	Marigold	NA
Tilia spp.	Linden	2–8
Ulmus spp.	Elm	2–9
Vaccinium spp.	Blueberry	3–9
Viburnum spp.	Viburnum	2–8
Vitis spp.	Grape	4–10

PLANTS FOR LANDSCAPE USE BASED ON SIZE AND SPECIAL INTEREST

BOTANICAL NAME	COMMON NAME	ZONES
TREES BY SIZE		
Small trees—to 25 feet		
Acer buergerianum	Trident maple	5–8
Acer griseum	Paperbark maple	4–8
Acer palmatum	Japanese maple	5–8
Acer tataricum	Tatarian maple	3–7
Acer tataricum ginnala	Amur maple	2–8
Amelanchier arborea	Downy serviceberry	4–9
Cercis canadensis	Eastern redbud	4–9
Chionanthus virginicus	White fringe tree	4–9
Cornus florida	Flowering dogwood	5–9
Cornus kousa	Kousa dogwood	5–8
Crataegus phaenopyrum	Washington hawthorn	5–8
Eriobotrya japonica	Loquat	8–10
Franklinia alatamaha	Franklin tree	5–8(9)
Hamamelis virginiana	Witch hazel	3–8
Ilex decidua	Possumhaw	5–9
Laburnum ×watereri	Golden chain tree	6–7
Lagerstroemia indica	Crape myrtle	(5)6–10
Malus spp.	Flowering crabapple	4–8
Prunus serrulata	Japanese flowering cherry	5–8
Stewartia pseudocamellia	Japanese stewartia	5–7(8)
Styrax japonicus	Japanese snowbell	5–8
Viburnum prunifolium	Black haw viburnum	3–9
Medium trees—25 to 50 feet		
Abies concolor	White fir	4–7
Acer campestre	Hedge maple	5–8
Acer rubrum	Red maple	3–9
Aesculus glabra	Ohio buckeye	4–7
Alnus glutinosa	European black alder	3–7
Betula pendula	European white birch	2–6
Calocedrus decurrens	Incense cedar	5–8
Carpinus caroliniana	American hornbeam	3–9
Cephalotaxus harringtonia	Japanese plum yew	6–9
Chamaecyparis lawsoniana	Lawson false cypress	5–7
Cladrastis kentuckea	American yellowwood	4–8
Cryptomeria japonica	Japanese cedar	(5)6–8
Cupressus arizonica	Arizona cypress	7–9
Halesia tetraptera	Carolina silverbell	5–8(9)
Hovenia dulcis	Japanese raisin tree	5–7
Ilex aquifolium	English holly	7–9
Ilex opaca	American holly	5–9
Juniperus virginiana	Eastern red cedar	2–9
Koelreuteria paniculata	Golden raintree	5–9
Magnolia virginiana	Sweet bay magnolia	5–9
Nyssa sylvatica	Black gum, black tupelo	(4)5–9
Oxydendrum arboreum	Sourwood	5–9
Phellodendron amurense	Amur cork tree	(4)5–7(8)
Picea pungens	Colorado spruce	3–7(8)

BOTANICAL NAME	COMMON NAME	ZONE
Pinus thunbergii	Japanese black pine	5–8
Pistacia chinensis	Chinese pistachio	6–9
Prunus subhirtella	Higan cherry	4–8
Pyrus calleryana cvs.	Callery pear	5–8(9)
Quercus acutissima	Sawtooth oak	6–9
Quercus robur	English oak	5–8
Robinia pseudoacacia	Black locust	4–8(9)
Sassafras albidum	Sassafras	(4)5–9
Sorbus aucuparia	European mountain ash	3–7
Syringa reticulata	Japanese tree lilac	3–7
Thuja occidentalis	American arborvitae	3–7
Ulmus parvifolia	Chinese elm, lacebark elm	5–9
Large Trees—over 50 feet		
Abies balsamea	Balsam fir	2–5
Abies procera	Noble fir	5–6
Acer saccharum	Sugar maple	4–8
Aesculus hippocastanum	Horsechestnut	4–7
Araucaria heterophylla	Norfolk Island pine	10–11
Betula nigra	River birch	4–9
Catalpa speciosa	Northern catalpa	(4)5–8(9)
Cedrus deodara	Deodar cedar	7–9
Cercidiphyllum japonicum	Katsura tree	5–8
Fagus sylvatica	European beech	(4)5–7
Fraxinus americana	White ash	4–9
Fraxinus pennsylvanica	Green ash	(2)3–9
Ginkgo biloba	Ginkgo	4–8(9)
Gleditsia triacanthos inermis	Thornless honeylocust	4–9
Gymnocladus dioica	Kentucky coffee tree	(3)4–8
Larix decidua	European larch	(3)4–6(7)
Liquidambar styraciflua	Sweetgum	5–9
Liriodendron tulipifera	Tulip tree	(4)5–9
Magnolia grandiflora	Southern magnolia	(6)7–9(10)
Metasequoia glyptostroboides	Dawn redwood	5–8
Picea abies	Norway spruce	2–7
Pinus strobus	Eastern white pine	3–7(8)
Pinus sylvestris	Scotch pine	2–8
Platanus ×acerifolia	London plane tree	(5)6–8
Platanus occidentalis	American sycamore	4–9
Pseudotsuga menziesii	Douglas fir	(3)4–6
Quercus alba	White oak	3–9
Quercus palustris	Pin oak	4–8
Quercus rubra	Red oak	4–8
Quercus virginiana	Live oak	(7)8–10
Taxodium distichum	Bald cypress	5–10
Tilia americana	American linden	3–8
Tilia cordata	Littleleaf linden	4–7
Tsuga canadensis	Canadian hemlock	(3)4–7
Zelkova serrata	Japanese zelkova	5–8

Redbud, *Cercis canadensis*

Japanese snowbell, *Styrax japonicus* 'Issai'

Hinoki false cypress, *Chaemacyparis obtusa* 'Koskii'

White pine, *Pinus strobus*

Little-leaf linden, *Tilia cordata*

Birdsnest spruce, *Picea abies* 'Nidiformis'

Sourwood, *Oxydendrum arboreum*

American holly, *Ilex opaca* f. *xanthocarpa*

Red maple, *Acer rubrum*

BOTANICAL NAME	COMMON NAME	ZONES
TREES WITH SEASONAL INTEREST		
Evergreen foliage		
Abies spp.	Balsam fir, noble fir, white fir	3–7
Araucaria heterophylla	Norfolk Island pine	10–11
Calocedrus decurrens	Incense cedar	5–8
Cedrus spp.	Atlas cedar, deodar cedar	5–9
Cephalotaxus harringtonia	Japanese plum yew	6–9
Chamaecyparis spp.	False cypress	5–8
Cinnamomum camphora	Camphor tree	9–10
Cryptomeria japonica	Japanese cedar	(5)6–8
Cunninghamia lanceolata	China fir	7–9
Cupressus arizonica	Arizona cypress	7–9
Eriobotrya japonica	Loquat	8–10
Ilex spp.	Holly	5–9
Juniperus virginiana	Eastern red cedar	2–9
Leptospermum laevigatum	Australian tea tree	9–10
Magnolia spp.	Magnolia	(4)5–9(10)
Picea spp.	Colorado spruce, Norway spruce	2–9
Pinus spp.	Pine	2–8
Pseudotsuga menziesii	Douglas fir	(3)4–6
Quercus spp.	Live oak, holly oak	8–10
Sciadopitys verticillata	Umbrella pine	5–7
Sequoia sempervirens	Coast redwood	7–9
Sequoiadendron giganteum	Giant sequoia	6–8
Thuja spp.	Arborvitae	2–8
Tsuga canadensis	Canadian hemlock	(3)4–7
Ornamental flowers		
Acacia pruinosa	Bronze acacia	10–11
Aesculus spp.	Buckeye, horsechestnut	4–7
Albizia julibrissin	Mimosa, silk tree	6–9
Amelanchier arborea	Downy serviceberry	4–9
Catalpa speciosa	Northern catalpa	(4)5–8(9)
Cercis canadensis	Eastern redbud	4–9
Chionanthus virginicus	White fringe tree	4–9
Cladrastis kentuckea	American yellowwood	4–8
Cornus florida	Flowering dogwood	5–9
Cornus kousa	Kousa dogwood	5–8
Crataegus phaenopyrum	Washington hawthorn	5–8
Franklinia alatamaha	Franklin tree	5–8(9)
Halesia tetraptera	Carolina silverbell	5–8(9)
Hamamelis virginiana	Witch hazel	3–8
Hydrangea paniculata	Panicle hydrangea	4–8
Jacaranda mimosifolia	Jacaranda	10–11
Koelreuteria paniculata	Golden rain tree	5–9
Laburnum ×*watereri*	Golden chain tree	6–7
Lagerstroemia indica	Crape myrtle	(5)6–10
Liriodendron tulipifera	Tulip tree	(4)5–9
Magnolia spp.	Magnolia	(4)5–9(10)
Malus spp.	Flowering crabapple	4–8
Oxydendrum arboreum	Sourwood	5–9
Paulownia tomentosa	Royal paulownia,	(5)6–9
Prunus spp.	Flowering cherry	3–8

BOTANICAL NAME	COMMON NAME	ZONES
Pyrus calleryana	Callery pear	5–8(9)
Robinia pseudoacacia	Black locust	4–8(9)
Salix caprea	Pussy willow	4–8
Stewartia pseudocamellia	Japanese stewartia	5–7(8)
Styrax japonicus	Japanese snowbell	5–8
Syringa reticulata	Japanese tree lilac	3–7
Ornamental fruit		
Arbutus unedo	Strawberry tree	7–9
Celtis laevigata	Sugarberry	5–9
Crataegus phaenopyrum	Washington hawthorn	5–8
Ilex spp.	Holly	3–9
Malus spp.	Flowering crabapple	4–8
Ostrya virginiana	American hophornbeam	(3)4–9
Sorbus aucuparia	European mountain ash	3–7
Viburnum prunifolium	Black haw viburnum	3–9
TREES WITH OUTSTANDING FALL FOLIAGE COLOR		
Yellow		
Acer spp.	Norway maple, striped maple	2–7
Betula pendula	European white birch	2–6
Cercis canadensis	Eastern redbud	4–9
Chionanthus virginicus	White fringe tree	4–9
Cladrastis kentuckea	American yellowwood	4–8
Fagus sylvatica	European beech	(4)5–7
Ginkgo biloba	Ginkgo	4–8(9)
Hamamelis virginiana	Witch hazel	3–8
Koelreuteria paniculata	Golden rain tree	5–9
Liriodendron tulipifera	Tulip tree	(4)5–9
Populus spp.	Quaking aspen, white poplar	1–9
Reddish Purple		
Cornus kousa	Kousa dogwood	5–8
Fraxinus americana	White ash	4–9
Juniperus virginiana	Eastern red cedar	2–9
Quercus alba	White oak	3–9
Stewartia pseudocamellia	Japanese stewartia	5–7(8)
Orange to Red		
Acer spp.	Red maple, sugar maple	2–9
Amelanchier arborea	Downy serviceberry	4–9
Carpinus caroliniana	American hornbeam	3–9
Cercidiphyllum japonicum	Katsura tree	5–8
Liquidambar styraciflua	American sweetgum	5–9
Sassafras albidum	Sassafras	(4)5–9
Sorbus aucuparia	European mountain ash	3–7
Red		
Acer spp.	Amur maple, Japanese maple	2–8
Cornus florida	Flowering dogwood	5–9
Crataegus phaenopyrum	Washington hawthorn	5–8
Franklinia alatamaha	Franklin tree	5–8(9)
Nyssa sylvatica	Black gum, black tupelo	(4)5–9
Oxydendrum arboreum	Sourwood	5–9
Quercus palustris	Pin oak	4–8
Quercus rubra	Red oak	4–8
Viburnum prunifolium	Black haw viburnum	3–9

BOTANICAL NAME	COMMON NAME	ZONES
SHRUBS BY SIZE		
Low shrubs—up to 3 feet		
Buxus microphylla	Littleleaf boxwood	5–9
Caryopteris ×clandonensis	Blue mist spirea, Bluebeard	(4)5–9
Ceanothus americanus	New Jersey tea	4–9
Chaenomeles japonica	Japanese flowering quince	4–8
Cotoneaster apiculatus	Cranberry cotoneaster	4–7
Cotoneaster horizontalis	Rockspray cotoneaster	5–7
Daphne cneorum	Rose daphne	4–7
Deutzia gracilis	Slender deutzia	(4)5–8
Forsythia viridissima 'Bronxensis'	Dwarf forsythia	5–8
Fothergilla gardenii	Dwarf fothergilla	5–8(9)
Genista tinctoria	Dyer's greenwood	3–6
Hypericum spp.	St. Johnswort	4–9
Iberis sempervirens	Candytuft	3–9
Juniperus spp.	Juniper	3–9
Potentilla fruticosa	Bush cinquefoil	2–6(7)
Spirea japonica 'Bumalda'	Bumald spirea	3–8
Medium shrubs—3 to 6 feet		
Abelia ×grandiflora	Glossy abelia	(5)6–9
Abeliophyllum distichum	White forsythia	(4)5–8
Berberis spp.	Mentor barberry, Japanese barberry	4–8
Callicarpa dichotoma	Chinese beautyberry	5–8
Clethra alnifolia	Summersweet	4–9
Cotoneaster divaricatus	Spreading cotoneaster	4–7
Cytisus scoparius	Scotch broom	5–8
Daphne odora	Winter daphne	7–9
Gardenia jasminoides	Gardenia	(7)8–10
Hydrangea spp.	Hydrangea	3–9
Hypericum prolificum	Shrubby St. Johnswort	4–8
Ilex spp.	Inkberry, Japanese holly	4–9
Itea virginica	Virginia sweetspire	(5)6–9
Jasminum nudiflorum	Winter jasmine	6–10
Leucothoe fontanesiana	Drooping leucothoe	5–8
Mahonia aquifolium	Oregon grapeholly	5–9
Pieris japonica	Japanese pieris	5–9
Rhus aromatica	Fragrant sumac	3–9
Spiraea japonica	Japanese spirea	4–8
Symphoricarpos albus	Snowberry	3–7
Taxus ×media	Anglo-Japanese yew	5–7
Viburnum davidii	David viburnum	8–9
Large shrubs—over 6 feet		
Aesculus parviflora	Bottlebrush buckeye	4–8
Buddleia davidii	Butterfly bush	5–9
Buxus sempervirens	Boxwood	(5)6–9
Calycanthus floridus	Carolina allspice	(4)5–9
Camellia japonica	Japanese camellia	(7)8–10
Camellia sasanqua	Sasanqua camellia	7–10
Caragana arborescens	Siberian peashrub	2–7
Cephalanthus occidentalis	Buttonbush	5–11
Chaenomeles speciosa	Flowering quince	5–9
Choisya ternata	Mexican orange	7–9

BOTANICAL NAME	COMMON NAME	ZONES
Cornus mas	Cornelian cherry dogwood	4–8
Cornus stolonifera	Red-osier dogwood	2–7
Corylus americana	American filbert	4–8
Cotinus coggygria	Smoke tree	4–8
Enkianthus campanulatus	Redvein enkianthus	5–7
Euonymus alatus	Winged euonymus	4–8(9)
Euonymus kiautschovicus	Spreading euonymus	5–8
Exochorda racemosa	Pearlbush	4–8
Fatsia japonica	Japanese fatsia	8–10
Forsythia ×intermedia	Forsythia	(4)5–8(9)
Fothergilla major	Large fothergilla	5–8(9)
Hibiscus syriacus	Rose-of-Sharon	5–8(9)
Ilex cornuta	Chinese holly	6–9
Ilex ×meserveae	Blue holly	(4)5–8
Ilex verticillata	Winterberry	3–9
Jasminum officinale	Jasmine	8–10
Juniperus chinensis	Chinese juniper	4–8
Kerria japonica	Kerria	5–9
Kolkwitzia amabilis	Beautybush	5–8
Leptospermum scoparium	New Zealand tea tree	9–10
Lespedeza thunbergii	Thunberg bush clover	5–8
Ligustrum amurense	Amur privet	4–7
Ligustrum japonicum	Japanese privet	7–10
Lindera benzoin	Spicebush	5–9
Lonicera tatarica	Tatarian honeysuckle	3–8
Magnolia ×soulangiana	Saucer magnolia	(4)5–9
Magnolia stellata	Star magnolia	4–8
Myrica pensylvanica	Northern bayberry	(2)3–6(7)
Nandina domestica	Nandina, heavenly bamboo	6–9(10)
Nerium oleander	Oleander	8–10
Osmanthus heterophyllus	Holly osmanthus	(6)7–9
Philadelphus coronarius	Mockorange	4–8
Photinia serratifolia	Chinese photinia	6–9
Pittosporum tobira	Japanese pittosporum	(8)9–10
Podocarpus macrophyllus	Yew pine	8–10
Prunus ×cistena	Purpleleaf sand cherry	4–8
Prunus laurocerasus	Cherry laurel	6–8
Pyracantha coccinea	Scarlet firethorn	6–9
Rhododendron spp.	Rhododendron , azalea	4–10
Rhus typhina	Staghorn sumac	4–8
Rosa spp.	Rose	3–10
Sambucus canadensis	American elder	(3)4–9
Sorbaria sorbifolia	Ural false spirea	2–7
Spiraea ×vanhouttei	Vanhoutte spirea	3–8(9)
Syringa villosa	Late lilac	2–7
Syringa vulgaris	Common lilac	3–7
Vaccinium corymbosum	Highbush blueberry	4–7
Viburnum opulus	European cranberrybush	3–8
Viburnum plicatum tomentosum	Double file viburnum	5–8
Viburnum ×rhytidophylloides	Leatherleaf viburnum	5–8
Viburnum trilobum	American cranberrybush viburnum	2–7
Weigela florida	Weigela	4–8

Rockspray cotoneaster, *Cotoneaster horizontalis*

Glossy abelia, *Abelia ×grandiflora*

Sasanqua camellia, *Camellia sasanqua* 'Single Red'

Large fothergilla, *Fothergilla major*

Spice bush, *Lindera benzoin*

Rose daphne, *Daphne cneorum* **'Ruby Glow'**

Japanese garden juniper, *Juniperus procumbens*

Rhododendron, *Rhododendron* **'Dopey'**

Weigela, *Weigela florida* **'Variegata'**

Vinca, *Vinca major* **'Maculata'**

BOTANICAL NAME	COMMON NAME	ZONES
SHRUBS WITH SEASONAL INTEREST		
Evergreen foliage		
Low shrubs – up to 3 feet		
Buxus microphylla	Littleleaf boxwood	5–9
Daphne cneorum	Rose daphne	4–7
Hypericum ×cyanthiflorum	Gold cup St. Johnswort	5–7
Juniperus procumbens	Japanese garden juniper	4–9
Medium shrubs – 3 to 6 feet		
Abelia ×grandiflora	Glossy abelia	(5)6–9
Daphne odora	Winter daphne	7–10
Gardenia jasminoides	Gardenia	(7)8–10
Ilex crenata	Japanese holly	6–8
Leucothoe fontanesiana	Drooping leucothoe	5–8
Mahonia aquifolium	Oregon grapeholly	5–9
Pieris japonica	Japanese pieris	5–9
Taxus ×media	Anglo-Japanese yew	5–7
Viburnum davidii	David viburnum	8–9
Large Shrubs – over 6 feet		
Buxus sempervirens	Boxwood	(5)6–9
Camellia spp.	Camellia	7–10
Fatsia japonica	Japanese fatsia	8–10
Ilex spp.	Holly	3–9
Juniperus chinensis	Chinese juniper	4–9
Ligustrum japonicum	Japanese privet	7–10
Nerium oleander	Oleander	8–10
Osmanthus heterophyllus	Holly osmanthus	(6)7–9
Pittosporum tobira	Japanese pittosporum	(8)9–10
Podocarpus macrophyllus	Yew pine	8–10
Prunus laurocerasus	Cherry laurel	6–8
Rhododendron spp.	Rhododendron, azalea	4–10
Viburnum ×rhytidophylloides	Leatherleaf viburnum	5–8
COLORFUL FLOWERS AND/OR FRUIT		
Flowers		
Buddleia davidii	Butterfly bush	5–9
Camellia japonica	Camellia	(7)8–10
Caryopteris ×clandonensis	Bluebeard	(4)5–9
Chaenomeles japonica	Japanese flowering quince	4–8
Forsythia ×intermedia	Forsythia	(4)5–8(9)
Hydrangea spp.	Hydrangea	3–9
Kerria japonica	Kerria	5–9
Kolkwitzia amabilis	Beautybush	5–8
Magnolia spp.	Magnolia	(4)5–9(10)
Nerium oleander	Oleander	8–10
Philadelphus coronarius	Mockorange	4–8
Potentilla fruticosa	Bush cinquefoil	2–6(7)
Rhododendron spp.	Rhododendron, azalea	4–10
Rosa spp.	Rose	3–10
Spiraea spp.	Spirea	3–8

BOTANICAL NAME	COMMON NAME	ZONES
Syringa vulgaris	Common lilac	3–7
Viburnum spp.	Viburnum	2–8
Weigela florida	Weigela	4–8
Fruit		
Callicarpa dichotoma	Chinese beautyberry	5–8
Cotoneaster spp.	Cotoneaster	4–7
Ilex spp.	Holly	3–9
Mahonia aquifolium	Oregon grapeholly	5–9
Myrica pensylvanica	Northern bayberry	(2)3–6(7)
Nandina domestica	Nandina, heavenly bamboo	6–9(10)
Pyracantha coccinea	Scarlet firethorn	6–9
Viburnum spp.	Viburnum	2–8
COLORFUL FOLIAGE (MAINLY FALL COLOR)		
Aronia arbutifolia	Red chokeberry	(4)5–9
Berberis thunbergii	Japanese barberry	(4)5–8
Cornus stolonifera	Red-osier dogwood	2–7
Cotinus coggygria	Smoke tree	4–8
Euonymus alatus	Winged euonymus	4–8(9)
Fothergilla major	Large fothergilla	5–8(9)
Hydrangea quercifolia	Oakleaf hydrangea	5–9
Itea virginica	Virginia sweetspire	(5)6–9
Leucothoe fontanesiana	Drooping leucothoe	5–8
Nandina domestica	Nandina, heavenly bamboo	6–9(10)
Photinia serrulata	Chinese photinia	6–9
Prunus ×cistena	Purpleleaf sand cherry	3–8
Rhus aromatica	Fragrant sumac	3–9
Rhus typhina	Staghorn sumac	4–8
Rosa rugosa	Rugosa rose	3–10
Vaccinium corymbosum	Highbush blueberry	3–7
GROUNDCOVERS		
Evergreen		
Arctostaphylos uva-ursi	Bearberry	3–6
Asarum europaeum	European wild ginger	4–7
Cotoneaster dammeri	Bearberry cotoneaster	5–8
Epimedium grandiflorum	Longspur barrenwort	5–8
Euonymus fortunei	Wintercreeper euonymus	5–9
Hedera helix	English ivy	5–9
Juniperus spp.	Juniper	3–9
Lamiastrum galeobdolon	Yellow archangel	4–9
Liriope spp.	Blue lily-turf, creeping lilyturf	5–9
Pachysandra terminalis	Japanese spurge	4–8
Paxistima canbyi	Cliff green	4–7
Rosmarinus officinalis 'Prostratus'	Trailing rosemary	7–9
Sarcococca hookerana humilis	Dwarf sweet box	(5)6–8
Sedum acre	Stonecrop	3–9
Thymus praecox	Creeping thyme	4–8
Vinca major	Large periwinkle	6–9
Vinca minor	Vinca, periwinkle	4–9
Waldsteinia fragarioides	Barren strawberry	4–8

BOTANICAL NAME	COMMON NAME	ZONES
ANNUALS (A), BIENNIALS (B), AND TENDER PERENNIALS (P) FOR FLOWER BORDERS		
Low—for edging or front border (to 1 foot)		
Ageratum houstonianum	Ageratum	A
Anagallis arvensis	Scarlet pimpernel	A/B
Begonia Semperflorens-cultorum hyb.	Wax begonia	A
Bellis perennis	English daisy	P
Brassica oleracea	Flowering kale, flowering cabbage	B
Browallia speciosa	Browallia	A
Eschscholzia californica	California poppy	A
Convolvulus tricolor	Dwarf morning glory	A
Felicia bergeriana	Kingfisher daisy	A
Fragaria vesca 'Semperflorens'	Alpine strawberry	P
Gazania rigens	Gazania	A
Lobelia erinus	Edging lobelia	A
Lobularia maritima	Sweet alyssum	A
Malcomia maritima	Virginia stock	A
Mimulus ×hybridus	Monkey flower	A
Myosotis sylvatica	Woodland forget-me-not	B/P
Nierembergia hippomanica	Cupflower	A
Phacelia campanularia	California bluebell	A
Phlox drummondii	Annual phlox	A
Portulaca grandiflora	Moss rose	A
Primula ×polyantha	Polyanthus primrose	P
Reseda odorata	Mignonette	A
Sanvitalia procumbens	Creeping zinnia	A
Scaevola aemula	Fan flower	A
Tagetes tenuifolia	Signet marigold	A
Torenia fournieri	Wishbone flower	A
Verbena ×hybrida	Verbena	A
Viola ×wittrockiana	Pansy	A
Zinnia angustifolia	Narrowleaf zinnia	A
Medium—for middle border (to 3 or 4 feet)		
Antirrhinum majus	Snapdragon	A
Arctotis ×hybrida	African daisy	A
Calendula officinalis	Pot marigold	A
Callistephus chinensis	China aster	A
Campanula medium	Canterbury bells	B
Catananche caerulea	Cupid's dart	P
Catharanthus roseus	Vinca	A
Celosia argentea	Cockscomb	A
Centaurea cyanus	Cornflower	A
Consolida ambigua	Larkspur	A
Cosmos sulphureus	Yellow cosmos	A
Cuphea ignea	Firecracker plant	P
Cynoglossum amabile	Chinese forget-me-not	B
Dianthus barbatus	Sweet William	B/P
Dimorphotheca sinuata	Cape marigold	A
Emilia coccinea	Tassel flower	A
Erysimum cheiri	Wallflower	B/P
Euphorbia cyathophora	Painted leaf, fire on the mountain	A
Euphorbia marginata	Snow-on-the-mountain	A
Eustoma grandiflorum	Prairie gentian	A

BOTANICAL NAME	COMMON NAME	ZONES
Felicia amelloides	Blue daisy	P
Gaillardia pulchella	Blanket flower	A
Gerbera jamesonii	Barberton daisy	P
Gomphrena globosa	Globe amaranth	A
Gypsophila elegans	Annual baby's breath	A
Helichrysum bracteatum	Strawflower	A
Impatiens balsamina	Garden balsam	A
Impatiens walleriana	Impatiens	A
Lantana camara	Lantana	P
Limonium sinuatum	Statice	P
Lunaria annua	Honesty	B
Machaeranthera tanacetifolia	Tahoka daisy, tansy aster	A
Matthiola incana	Stock	B
Mirabilis jalapa	Four-o-clock	P
Moluccella laevis	Bells of Ireland	A
Nicotiana ×sanderae	Flowering tobacco	A
Nigella damascena	Love-in-a-mist	A
Osteospermum	Daisy bush	A
Papaver rhoeas	Shirley poppy	A
Pelargonium ×hortorum	Geranium, zonal geranium	P
Petunia ×hybrida	Petunia	A
Salpiglossis sinuata	Painted tongue	A
Salvia splendens	Scarlet sage	A
Scabiosa atropurpurea	Pincushion flower	A
Schizanthus pinnatus	Butterfly flower	A
Senecio cineraria	Dusty miller	A
Solenostemon scutellarioides	Coleus, painted nettle	A
Tagetes erecta	African marigold	A
Tagetes patula	French marigold	A
Trachymene coerulea	Blue laceflower	A
Tropaeolum majus	Nasturtium	A
Xeranthemum annuum	Immortelle, everlasting	A
Zinnia elegans	Zinnia	A
Tall—for back border (over 3 feet)		
Alcea rosea	Hollyhock	B/P
Amaranthus caudatus	Love-lies-bleeding	A
Amaranthus tricolor	Joseph's coat	A
Centaurea americana	American star thistle	A
Cleome hassleriana	Spider flower	A
Cosmos bipinnatus	Cosmos	A
Cynara cardunculus	Cardoon	P
Dahlia spp.	Dahlia	P
Datura metel	Horn of plenty	A
Digitalis purpurea	Foxglove	B/P
Helianthus annuus	Sunflower	A
Kochia scoparia	Mexican fireweed	A
Lavatera arborea	Tree mallow	B
Nicotiana alata	Jasmine tobacco	A
Oenothera biennis	Evening primrose	B
Ricinus communis	Castor bean	A
Thunbergia alata	Black-eyed Susan vine	A
Tithonia rotundifolia	Mexican sunflower	A

Sweet alyssum, *Lobularia maritima*

Pot marigold, *Calendula officinalis*

Gomphrena, *Gomphrena globosa* 'Gnome Pink'

Cosmos, *Cosmos bipinnatus* 'Sonata Mixed'

Sunflower, *Helianthus annuus* 'Cutting Gold' and 'Autumn Beauty'

CHAPTER **12** PLANTS FOR LANDSCAPE USE

Sea thrift, *Armeria maritima*

Globe thistle, *Echinops ritro*

Goatsbeard, *Aruncus dioicus*

New England aster, *Aster novae-angliae* **'Alma Potschke'**

False sunflower, *Heliopsis helianthoides* **'Goldgreenheart'**

BOTANICAL NAME	COMMON NAME	ZONES
HARDY PERENNIALS FOR FLOWER BORDERS		
Low—for front border (to 1 ½ feet)		
Achillea ptarmica 'The Pearl'	Sneezewort	4–9
Alchemilla mollis	Lady's mantle	3–7
Aquilegia spp.	Columbine	3–9
Armeria maritima	Sea thrift	3–9
Artemisia schmidtiana	Silver mound artemisia	4–8
Aster alpinus	Alpine aster	3–7
Bergenia cordifolia	Heart-leaf bergenia	3–8
Brunnera macrophylla	Heart-leaf brunnera	3–7
Campanula carpatica	Carpathian bellflower	2–7
Campanula rotundifolia	Harebell, bluebell	3–7
Coreopsis verticillata	Threadleaf coreopsis	4–9
Dendranthema ×grandiflorum	Chrysanthemum	4–9
Dianthus spp.	Pinks	4–8
Euphorbia polychroma	Cushion spurge	4–9
Geranium sanguineum	Bloody cranesbill	4–8
Helianthemum nummularium	Sun rose	5–7
Helleborus orientalis	Lenten rose	4–9
Heuchera sanguinea	Coral bells	3–8
×Heucherella tiarelloides	Foamy bells	3–8
Linum perenne	Perennial flax	5–9
Mertensia virginica	Virginia bluebells	3–7
Nepeta ×faassenii	Catmint	3–8
Oenothera macrocarpa	Ozark sundrops	4–8
Primula auricula	Auricula primrose	2–8
Primula ×polyantha	Polyanthus primrose	4–8
Pulmonaria saccharata	Bethlehem sage	3–8
Santolina chamaecyparissus	Lavender cotton	6–9
Scabiosa caucasica	Pincushion flower	4–7
Stachys byzantina	Lamb's-ears	3–8
Tiarella cordifolia	Alleghany foam flower	3–8
Verbena canadensis	Rose vervain	4–9
Medium—for middle border (to 4 feet)		
Acanthus mollis	Bear's breeches	7–10
Achillea filipendulina	Fern-leaf yarrow	3–9
Aconitum carmichaelii	Azure monkshood	3–7
Amsonia tabernaemontana	Blue star	3–9
Anemone ×hybrida	Hybrid anemone	5–8
Asclepias tuberosa	Butterfly weed	4–9
Aster ×frikartii	Frikart's aster	5–8
Astilbe ×arendsii	Astilbe	4–8
Baptisia australis	Blue false indigo	3–9
Chelone glabra	Pink turtlehead	3–8
Coreopsis lanceolata	Tickseed	4–9
Delphinium ×belladonna	Belladonna delphinium	2–7
Dendranthema ×grandiflorum	Chrysanthemum	4–9
Dicentra spectabilis	Bleeding heart	3–9
Dictamnus albus	Gas plant	3–8
Echinacea purpurea	Purple coneflower	3–9
Echinops ritro	Globe thistle	3–9
Gaillardia ×grandiflora	Blanket flower	3–8

BOTANICAL NAME	COMMON NAME	ZONES
Gaura lindheimeri	White gaura	6–8
Geum hybridum	Geum hybrid cultivars	4–7
Gypsophila paniculata	Baby's breath	3–8
Helenium autumnale	Helen's flower	3–8
Hemerocallis	Daylily	3–10
Hosta	Hosta	3–8
Hylotelephium telephium	Live-forever	3–10
Iris bearded hybrids	Bearded iris	3–9
Iris sibirica	Siberian iris	4–9
Leucanthemum ×superbum	Shasta daisy	4–8
Liatris spicata	Spike gayfeather	3–9
Ligularia dentata	Bigleaf ligularia	3–8
Lobelia cardinalis	Cardinal flower	3–9
Lupinus hybrids	Lupine	4–8
Lychnis chalcedonica	Maltese cross	3–9
Monarda didyma	Bee balm, Oswego tea	3–9
Oenothera fruticosa	Sundrops	4–8
Paeonia spp.	Peony	3–8
Papaver orientale	Oriental poppy	3–7
Penstemon barbatus	Beardlip penstemon	4–9
Phlox paniculata	Garden phlox	3–8
Physostegia virginiana	Obedient plant	3–8
Platycodon grandiflorus	Balloon flower	3–8
Polemonium caeruleum	Jacob's ladder	2–7
Rodgersia pinnata	Featherleaf rodgersia	4–7
Rudbeckia nitida	Shining coneflower	4–10
Salvia spp.	Salvia	4–9
Stokesia laevis	Stoke's aster	5–9
Thalictrum aquilegifolium	Columbine meadow-rue	4–9
Tradescantia virginiana	Spiderwort	4–9
Tricyrtis hirta	Toad lily	5–9
Trollius europaeus	Globeflower	4–6
Verbena bonariensis	Verbena	7–9
Veronica spp.	Speedwell	3–8
Tall—for back border (over 4 feet)		
Aconitum ×cammarum	Monkshood cultivars	3–7
Aruncus dioicus	Goatsbeard	3–7
Aster novae-angliae	New England aster	4–8
Aster novi-belgii	New York aster	3–8
Boltonia asteroides latisquama	White boltonia	4–9
Cimicifuga racemosa	Snakeroot	3–8
Delphinium	Hybrid delphinium	2–7
Eremurus ×isabellinus	Foxtail lily	5–9
Eryngium giganteum	Miss Wilmott's Ghost	4–8
Eupatorium purpureum	Joe-Pye weed	4–9
Filipendula rubra	Queen-of-the-prairie	3–9
Helianthus ×multiflorus	Many-flowered sunflower	3–9
Heliopsis helianthoides	False sunflower	3–9
Kniphofia uvaria	Red hot poker	5–9
Lilium spp.	Lily	3–8
Macleaya cordata	Plume poppy	4–9
Perovskia atriplicifolia	Russian sage	3–9

BOTANICAL NAME	COMMON NAME	ZONES
PLANTS GROWING FROM BULBS		
Late winter or spring flowering		
Anemone blanda	Greek anemone	5–8
Calochortus spp.	Mariposa lily	6–9
Camassia leichtlinii	Leichtlin quamash	3–7
Chionodoxa luciliae	Glory-of-the-snow	4–8
Convallaria majalis	Lily-of-the-valley	2–7
Crocus spp.	Spring crocus	3–8
Eranthis hyemalis	Winter aconite	5–8
Erythronium americanum	American trout lily	3–7
Fritillaria imperialis	Crown imperial	4–8
Fritillaria meleagris	Checkered lily	4–7
Galanthus nivalis	Snowdrop	3–9
Hyacinthus orientalis	Hyacinth	4–8
Ipheion uniflorum	Spring starflower	6–9
Iris reticulata	Netted iris	4–8
Leucojum aestivum	Summer snowflake	4–8
Muscari botryoides	Grape hyacinth	3–8
Narcissus spp.	Narcissus, daffodil	3–8
Ornithogalum nutans	Nodding star-of-Bethlehem	6–8
Puschkinia scilloides	Striped squill	3–8
Ranunculus asiaticus	Persian buttercup	8–10
Scilla siberica	Siberian squill	3–8
Triteleia grandiflora	Tritelia	5–8
Tulipa spp.	Tulip	3–8
Summer or fall flowering		
Agapanthus africanus	Lily-of-the-Nile, agapanthus	9–10
Allium giganteum	Giant allium	4–8
Alocasia macrorrhiza	Elephant's ear	8–10
Alstroemeria	Peruvian lily	7–10
Amaryllis belladonna	Belladonna lily	8–10
Begonia Tuberhybrida	Tuberous begonia	9–10
Caladium bicolor	Caladium	8–11
Canna ×*generalis*	Canna	7–11
Colchicum autumnale	Fall crocus	5–9
Colocasia esculenta	Elephant's ear	10–11
Crinum bulbispermum	Milk-and-wine lily	8–10
Crocosmia spp.	Crocosmia, montbretia	6–9
Crocus speciosus	Showy crocus	3–8
Dahlia hybrids	Dahlia	9–11
Eremurus ×*isabellinus*	Foxtail Lily	5–9
Freesia hybrids	Freesia	9–10
Galtonia candicans	Summer hyacinth	5–9
Gladiolus spp.	Garden gladiolus	9–10
Gloriosa superba	Gloriosa lily	9–11
Hippeastrum spp.	Amaryllis	9–11
Hymenocallis narcissiflora	Peruvian daffodil	9–10
Lilium spp.	Lily	3–8
Lycoris radiata	Spider lily	6–10
Lycoris squamigera	Resurrection lily	4–9
Oxalis spp.	Wood sorrel	7–10
Polianthes tuberosa	Tuberose	9–11
Sprekelia formosissima	St. James lily	9–11

BOTANICAL NAME	COMMON NAME	ZONES
Sternbergia lutea	Lily-of-the-field	7–10
Tigridia pavonia	Tiger flower	7–10
Zantedeschia spp.	Calla lily	9–11
Zephranthes candida	La Plata lily	9–10
PLANTS FOR SPECIAL USES		
Rock gardens		
Achillea tomentosa	Woolly yarrow	3–8
Alyssum montanum	Basket of gold	6–8
Aquilegia spp.	Columbine	3–9
Arabis caucasica	Wall rockcress	4–8
Armeria maritima	Sea thrift	3–9
Asarum spp.	Wild ginger	2–8
Aster alpinus	Alpine aster	3–9
Aubrieta ×*cultorum*	Aubretia	6–8
Aurinia saxatalis	Basket-of-gold	3–7
Bergenia cordifolia	Heart-leaf bergenia	3–8
Brunnera macrophylla	Heart-leaf brunnera	3–7
Campanula spp.	Bellflower	2–7
Cerastium tomentosum	Snow-in-summer	3–7
Ceratostigma plumbaginoides	Leadwort	5–9
Cymbalaria muralis	Kenilworth ivy, pennywort	3–8
Dianthus deltoides	Maiden pink	3–8
Dianthus gratianopolitanus	Cheddar pink	3–8
Dicentra eximia	Fringed bleeding heart	3–8
Dodecatheon meadia	Shooting star	3–8
Geranium sanguineum	Bloody cranesbill	4–8
Gypsophila repens	Creeping baby's breath	4–7
Helianthemum nummularium	Sun rose	5–9
Hepatica nobilis	Liverleaf	5–8
Heuchera ×*brizoides*	Hybrid coral bells	4–8
Houstonia caerulea	Bluets	6–8
Iberis sempervirens	Evergreen candytuft	3–9
Iris spp.	Crested iris, dwarf iris	3–9
Lavandula angustifolia	Lavender, English lavender	5–8
Mertensia virginica	Virginia bluebell	3–7
Minuartia verna	Sandwort	3–6
Mitella diphylla	Bishop's cap	3–7
Myosotis scorpioides	Forget-me-not	3–9
Oenothera macrocarpa	Ozark sundrops	4–8
Petrorhagia saxifraga	Tunic flower	6–8
Phlox subulata	Creeping phlox	2–8
Primula spp.	Primrose	4–9
Pulmonaria saccharata	Bethlehem sage	3–8
Rosa chinensis 'Minima'	Miniature rose	6–9
Sanguinaria canadensis	Bloodroot	3–7
Saponaria ocymoides	Soapwort	3–8
Saxifraga stolonifera	Strawberry geranium	5–9
Sedum spp.	Sedum	3–10
Sempervivum spp.	Hen and chicks, house leek	4–10
Thymus serpyllum	Wild thyme	4–9
Veronica prostrata	Prostrate speedwell	4–8
Viola cornuta	Viola	5–9

Lily-of-the-valley,
Convallaria majalis

Giant flowering
onion, *Allium
giganteum*

Autumn crocus,
*Colchicum
autumnale*

Dahlia, *Dahlia*
'Kidd's Climax'

Creeping phlox,
Phlox subulata

Virginia bluebell,
Mertensia virginica

False blue indigo,
Baptisia australis

Bachelor's buttons,
Centaurea cyanus

Helen's flower,
Helenium autumnale
'Red Gold Hybrid'

Gayfeather, ***Liatris***
ligulistylus

BOTANICAL NAME	COMMON NAME	ZONES
Woodland wildflowers		
Anemonella thalictroides	Rue-anemone	4–8
Aquilegia canadensis	Canadian columbine	3–8
Arisaema triphyllum	Jack-in-the-pulpit, Indian turnip	2–9
Campanula americana	Tall bellflower	4–8
Cardamine laciniata	Toothwort	6–8
Claytonia virginica	Spring beauty	4–8
Cornus canadensis	Bunchberry	2–5
Delphinium tricorne	Dwarf larkspur	4–7
Dicentra cucullaria	Dutchman's breeches	4–7
Epigaea repens	Trailing arbutus	2–5
Erythronium americanum	American trout lily	3–6
Gaultheria procumbens	Wintergreen	4–7
Geranium maculatum	Wild geranium	4–8
Hepatica americana	Hepatica	4–8
Lobelia silphilitica	Great blue lobelia	4–8
Mertensia virginica	Virginia bluebell	3–7
Phlox divaricata	Woodland phlox	4–8
Podophyllum peltatum	May apple	4–8
Polemonium reptans	Greek valerian	4–7
Polygonatum biflorum	Small Solomon's seal	3–9
Sanguinaria canadensis	Bloodroot	4–8
Silene virginica	Fire pink	5–8
Smilacina racemosa	False Solomon's seal	4–9
Stylophorum diphyllum	Celandine poppy	6–8
Tiarella cordifolia	Allegheny foam flower	3–8
Trillium spp.	Trillium	3–8
Uvularia sessilifolia	Bellwort	4–8
Viola spp.	Violet, viola	3–9
Meadow and prairie wildflowers		
Achillea millefolium	Yarrow	2–9
Asclepias tuberosa	Butterfly weed	4–9
Baptisia australis	Blue false indigo	3–9
Callirhoe involucrata	Purple poppy mallow	4–9
Castilleja coccinea	Indian paintbrush	4–8
Centaurea cyanus	Cornflower	6–8
Coreopsis lanceolata	Tickseed	4–9
Echinacea purpurea	Purple coneflower	3–9
Gaillardia aristata	Blanket flower	8–9
Helenium autumnale	Helen's flower	3–8
Helianthus occidentalis	Western sunflower	4–9
Lavatera assurgentiflora	Rose malva	9–10
Leucanthemum vulgare	Ox-eye daisy	3–9
Liatris spicata	Gayfeather	3–9
Linum perenne	Perennnial flax	4–9
Lupinus texensis	Texas bluebonnet	7–8
Monarda spp.	Bee balm, bergamot	3–9
Oenothera spp.	Evening primrose	4–8
Penstemon spp.	Beard tongue	4–9
Physostegia virginiana	Obedient plant	3–8
Ratibida columnifera	Mexican hat	4–9
Rudbeckia fulgida	Black-eyed Susan	4–9

BOTANICAL NAME	COMMON NAME	ZONES
Salvia azurea	Blue sage	4–8
Saponaria officinalis	Soapwort	3–8
Silphium lacinatum	Compass plant	4–8
Solidago hybrids	Goldenrod	3–9
Tradescantia virginiana	Spiderwort	4–9
Verbena canadensis	Rose vervain	4–9
Ornamental grasses		
Arundo donax	Giant reed	7–10
Briza media	Quaking grass	4–10
Calamagrostis ×acutiflora	Feather reed grass	4–9
Chasmanthium latifolium	Northern sea oats	5–9
Cortaderia selloana	Pampas grass	8–10
Deschampsia caespitosa	Hairgrass	4–9
Eragrostis curvula	Weeping love grass	7–10
Erianthus ravennae	Ravenna grass	6–9
Festuca glauca	Blue fescue	4–8
Hakonechloa macra	Hakone grass	4–8
Helictotrichon sempervirens	Blue oat grass	4–9
Leymus arenarius	Lyme grass	5–9
Miscanthus sinensis	Maiden grass	4–9
Molinia caerulea	Purple moor grass	5–9
Panicum virgatum	Switch grass	4–9
Pennisetum alopecuroides	Fountain grass	5–9
Pennisetum setaceum 'Rubrum'	Purple fountain grass	9–10
Phalaris arundinacea 'Picta'	Ribbon grass	4–9
Sesleria autumnalis	Autumn moor grass	5–9
Sorghastrum nutans	Indian grass	4–9
Spodiopogon sibiricus	Silver spike grass	4–9
Sporobolus heterolepsis	Prairie dropseed	3–9
Stipa gigantea	Giant feather grass	6–9
PERENNIAL VINES		
Climb by twining or with tendrils		
Actinidia kolomikta	Hardy variegated kiwi	4–9
Aristolochia macrophylla	Dutchman's pipe	5–10
Campsis radicans	Trumpet vine	4–9
Celastrus scandens	American bittersweet	3–8
Clematis spp.	Clematis	4–8
Cobaea scandens	Cup-and-saucer vine	9–10
Gelsemium sempervirens	Carolina jessamine	7–9
Jasminum officinale	Jasmine	7–10
Lonicera sempervirens	Trumpet honeysuckle	4–9
Mandevilla laxa	Chilean jasmine	9–10
Passiflora spp.	Passion flower	8–11
Plumbago auriculata	Cape leadwort	9–10
Polygonum aubertii	Silver lace vine	5–9
Trachelospermum jasminoides	Star jasmine	9–10
Wisteria spp.	Wisteria	5–8
Cling by rootlets or tendrils with disks		
Euonymus fortunei 'Vegetus'	Wintercreeper euonymus	6–9
Ficus pumila	Creeping fig	9–10
Hedera helix	English ivy	5–9
Hydrangea petiolaris	Climbing hydrangea	5–8
Parthenocissus tricuspidata	Boston ivy	4–9

BOTANICAL NAME	COMMON NAME	ZONES
FOR SPECIAL LANDSCAPE NEEDS		
Tolerant of frequent shearing		
Abelia ×grandiflora	Glossy abelia	(5)6–9
Abies concolor	White fir	4–7
Acer spp.	Amur maple, hedge maple	2–8
Berberis spp.	Japanese barberry, Mentor barberry	4–8
Buxus sempervirens	Boxwood	(5)6–9
Caragana arborescens	Siberian peashrub	2–7
Carpinus betulus	European hornbeam	(4)5–7
Chaenomeles japonica	Japanese flowering quince	4–8
Chamaecyparis pisifera	Sawara false cypress	5–8
Cornus mas	Cornelian cherry	4–8
Cotoneaster lucidus	Hedge cotoneaster	3–7
Elaeagnus angustifolia	Russian olive	2–7
Euonymus japonicus	Japanese euonymus	7–9
Ilex spp.	Chinese holly, English holly	7–9
Juniperus chinensis	Chinese juniper	4–9
Ligustrum spp.	Privet	4–10
Myrtis communis	Myrtle	9–10
Nerium oleander	Oleander	8–10
Osmanthus heterophyllus	Holly osmanthus	(6)7–9
Picea glauca	White spruce	2–6
Pittosporum tobira	Japanese pittosporum	(8)9–10
Prunus laurocerasus	English laurel	6–8
Pyracantha coccinea	Scarlet firethorn	6–9
Quercus ilex	Holly oak	9–10
Ribes alpinum	Alpine currant	2–7
Syringa meyeri	Meyer lilac	3–7
Taxus ×media	Anglo-Japanese yew	5–7
Thuja spp.	Arborvitae	2–8
Tsuga canadensis	Canadian hemlock	(3)4–7
Viburnum dentatum	Arrowwood viburnum	3–8
Suitable for screening		
Shrubs		
Acer campestre	Hedge maple	5–8
Berberis thunbergii	Japanese barberry	(4)5–8
Cornus mas	Cornelian cherry	4–8
Forsythia ×intermedia	Forsythia	(4)5–8(9)
Hamamelis vernalis	Vernal witch hazel	5–8
Hippophae rhamnoides	Sea buckthorn	4–7
Ilex spp.	Chinese holly, Japanese holly	7–9
Juniperus chinensis	Chinese juniper	4–9
Ligustrum spp.	Privet	4–10
Myrica pensylvanica	Bayberry	(2)3–6(7)
Nerium oleander	Oleander	8–10
Philadelphus coronarius	Mockorange	4–8
Physocarpus opulifolius	Ninebark	2–7
Rosa rugosa	Rugosa rose	3–10
Spiraea ×vanhouttei	Vanhoutte spirea	3–8(9)
Syringa reticulata	Japanese tree lilac	3–7
Syringa vulgaris	Common lilac	3–7
Taxus ×media 'Hicksii'	Hicks Anglo-Japanese yew	5–7

BOTANICAL NAME	COMMON NAME	ZONES
Viburnum lentago	Sheepberry	2–8
Viburnum trilobum	American cranberrybush viburnum	2–7
Trees		
Acer tataricum ginnala	Amur maple	2–8
Juniperus virginiana	Eastern red cedar	2–9
Maclura pomifera	Osage orange	5–9
Picea spp.	Colorado spruce, Norway spruce	2–8
Pinus strobus	Eastern white pine	3–7(8)
Sassafras albidum	Sassafras	(4)5–9
Sophora japonica	Japanese pagoda tree	5–7
Thuja occidentalis	American arborvitae	3–7
Tilia cordata	Littleleaf linden	4–7
Tsuga canadensis	Canadian hemlock	(3)4–7
Viburnum prunifolium	Black haw viburnum	3–9
Useful in windbreaks; wind-tolerant plants		
Acer campestre	Hedge maple	5–8
Amelanchier alnifolia	Saskatoon serviceberry	2–5
Arctostaphylos manzanita	Manzanita	8–10
Calocedrus decurrens	Incense cedar	5–8
Caragana arborescens	Siberian peashrub	2–7
Celtis occidentalis	Hackberry	3–9
×Cupressocyparis leylandii	Leyland cypress	6–10
Elaeagnus angustifolia	Russian olive	2–7
Fraxinus pennsylvanica	Green ash	(2)3–9
Gleditsia triacanthos inermis	Thornless honeylocust	4–9
Juglans nigra	Black walnut	4–9
Juniperus scopulorum	Rocky Mountain juniper	3–7
Juniperus virginiana	Eastern red cedar	3–9
Laurus nobilis	Sweet bay	8–10
Lonicera tatarica	Tatarian honeysuckle	3–8
Maclura pomifera	Osage orange	5–9
Nerium oleander	Oleander	8–10
Picea spp.	Norway spruce, white spruce	2–8
Pinus ponderosa	Ponderosa pine	3–6
Populus deltoides	Eastern cottonwood	3–9
Pseudotsuga menziesii	Douglas fir	(3)4–6
Quercus spp.	Shingle oak, bur oak, willow oak	3–9
Salix alba	White willow	2–8
Sequoia sempervirens	Coast redwood	7–9
Syringa vulgaris	Common lilac	3–7
Thuja occidentalis	American arborvitae	3–7
Plants with some fire resistance		
Achillea tomentosa	Woolly yarrow	3–7
Atriplex semibaccata	Australian saltbush	9–10
Baccharis pilularis	Dwarf coyote bush	8–10
Cistus ladanifer	Gum rockrose	9–10
Eriodictyon trichocalyx	Yerba santa	9–10
Hedera helix	English ivy	4–9
Helianthemum nummularium	Rock rose	5–7
Lotus berthelotti	Parrot's beak	9–10
Mesembryanthemum guerichianum	Ice plant	A/B
Rosmarinus officinalis 'Prostratus'	Trailing rosemary	7–9
Santolina rosmarinifolia	Green lavender cotton	7–9

English laurel, *Prunus laurocerasus* 'Zabeliana'

Common lilac, *Syringa vulgaris*

Vanhoutte's spirea, *Spiraea ×vanhouttei*

Catawba rhododendron, *Rhododendron catawbiense*

Sassafras, *Sassafras albidum*

Santolina, *Santolina chaemacyparissus*

Bethlehem sage, *Pulmonaria saccharata* 'Roy Davidson'

Hyacinth, *Hyacinthus orientalis*

Sweet pea, *Lathyrus odoratus*

BOTANICAL NAME	COMMON NAME	ZONES
PLANTS WITH ADDED ATTRACTIONS		
Fragrant foliage		
Abies balsamea	Balsam fir	2–5
Allium schoenoprasum	Chives	3–10
Buxus sempervirens	Boxwood	(5)6–9
Calocedrus decurrens	California incense cedar	5–8
Cinnamomum camphora	Camphor tree	9–10
Eucalyptus spp.	Eucalyptus	(7)8–10
Juniperus spp.	Juniper	3–9
Lantana camara	Lantana	8–10
Laurus nobilis	Laurel, sweet bay	8–10
Lavandula angustifolia	English lavender	5–8
Melianthus major	Honey bush	10–11
Mentha ssp.	Mint	4–10
Origanum vulgare	Oregano	5–11
Pelargonium spp.	Scented geraniums	9–10
Picea pungens	Colorado spruce	3–7(8)
Pinus spp.	Pine	3–8
Rosmarinus officinalis	Rosemary	(6)7–9
Salvia officinalis	Garden sage	5–10
Santolina chamaecyparissus	Lavender cotton	6–9
Thymus serpyllum	Wild thyme	4–9
Fragrant flowers		
Acacia farnesiana	Sweet acacia	9–10
Bouvardia longiflora	Sweet bouvardia	9–10
Brugmansia versicolor	Angel's trumpet	9–10
Buddleia davidii	Butterfly bush	5–9
Citrus spp.	Citrus	8–11
Clematis ternifolia	Sweet autumn clematis	5–8
Clethra alnifolia	Summersweet	4–9
Convallaria majalis	Lily-of-the-valley	2–7
Daphne spp.	Daphne	4–9
Dianthus gratianapolitanus	Cheddar pink	3–9
Freesia cvs.	Freesia	9–10
Gardenia jasminoides	Gardenia	(7)8–10
Hedychium coronarium	White ginger	10–11
Heliotropium arborescens	Heliotrope	NA
Hosta plantaginea	August lily	3–9
Hyacinthus orientalis	Hyacinth	4–8
Iris bearded hybrids	Bearded iris	3–9
Jasminum officinale	Jasmine	8–10
Lilium spp.	Lily	3–8
Magnolia virginiana	Sweet bay magnolia	5–9
Murraya paniculata	Orange jessamine	10–11
Osmanthus heterophyllus	Holly osmanthus	(6)7–9
Paeonia	Peony	3–8
Philadelphus coronarius	Mockorange	4–8
Phlox paniculata	Garden phlox	3–8
Plumeria rubra	Frangipani	10–11
Polianthes tuberosa	Tuberose	9–11
Ribes odoratum	Clove currant	4–7
Robinia pseudoacacia	Black locust	4–8(9)
Rosa spp.	Rose	3–10

BOTANICAL NAME	COMMON NAME	ZONES
Sarcococca hookeriana	Himalayan sweet box	(5)6–8
Syringa vulgaris	Lilac	3–7
Trachelospermum jasminoides	Star jasmine	8–9
Viburnum ×burkwoodii	Burkwood viburnum	4–8
Viburnum ×carlcephalum	Fragrant viburnum	5–8
Viburnum carlesii	Korean spice viburnum	4–7
Viola odorata	Sweet violet	5–9
Wisteria floribunda	Japanese wisteria	5–9
COLORFUL SUMMER FOLIAGE		
Red foliage		
Acer palmatum 'Bloodgood'	Bloodgood Japanese maple	5–8
Acer platanoides 'Crimson King'	Crimson King maple	3–7
Berberis thunbergii 'Atropurpurea'	Red-leaf Japanese barberry	(4)5–8
Iresine herbstii 'Brilliantissima'	Bloodleaf	9–11
Purple foliage		
Cercis canadensis 'Forest Pansy'	Forest Pansy redbud	5–8
Cotinus coggygria 'Royal Purple'	Purple-leaf smoke bush	4–8
Fagus sylvatica purpurea	Copper beech	5–6
Heuchera micrantha 'Palace Purple'	Palace purple alumroot	4–8
Prunus cerasifera 'Thundercloud'	Thundercloud cherry plum	5–8
Strobilanthes dyerianus	Persian shield	10–11
Blue-green foliage		
Cedrus libani atlantica 'Glauca'	Blue atlas cedar	5–9
Eucalyptus cinerea	Silver dollar	9–10
Festuca glauca	Blue fescue	4–8
Hosta sieboldiana var. *elegans*	Giant blue hosta	3–8
Juniperus horizontalis 'Blue Chip'	Creeping juniper	3–7
Picea pungens var. *glauca*	Blue spruce	3–7(8)
Gray, gray-green foliage		
Achillea tomentosa	Woolly yarrow	3–8
Artemisia ludoviciana albula	Silver King artemisia	4–9
Cerastium tomentosum	Snow-in-summer	3–7
Elaeagnus angustifolia	Russian olive	2–7
Eucalyptus macrocarpa	Mottlecah	10–11
Helichrysum petiolare	Licorice plant	9–11
Lavandula angustifolia	Lavender	5–8
Olea europaea	Olive	9–10
Populus alba	White poplar	3–8
Senecio cineraria	Dusty miller	8–10
Tilia tomentosa	Silver linden	4–7
Vitex agnus-castus	Chaste tree	7–9
Yellow, yellow-green foliage		
Gleditsia triacanthos 'Sunburst'	Sunburst honeylocust	4–8
×Heucherella 'Sunspot'	Foamy bells	4–8
Hosta fortunei aurea	Gold-leaf hosta	3–8
Humulus lupulus 'Aureus'	Golden hops	4–9
Juniperus chinensis 'Saybrook Gold'	Saybrook Gold juniper	4–9
Ligustrum ×vicaryi	Vicary golden privet	5–8
Lonicera japonica 'Aureoreticulata'	Golden honeysuckle	4–9
Philadelphus coronarius 'Aureus'	Golden mockorange	4–8
Platycladus orientalis 'Aurea Nana'	Golden oriental arborvitae	6–8
Thuja occidentalis 'Rheingold'	Rheingold arborvitae	4–8

BOTANICAL NAME	COMMON NAME	ZONES
PLANTS TO ATTRACT BIRDS		
Amelanchier canadensis	Shadblow serviceberry	3–8
Aronia arbutifolia	Red chokeberry	(4)5–9
Celastrus scandens	American bittersweet	3–8
Celtis occidentalis	Hackberry	3–9
Cephalanthus occidentalis	Buttonbush	5–11
Cornus alternifolia	Pagoda dogwood	3–7
Cornus mas	Cornelian cherry	4–8
Cornus stolonifera	Red-osier dogwood	2–8
Crataegus phaenopyrum	Washington hawthorn	5–8
Ilex decidua	Possumhaw	5–9
Ilex opaca	American holly	5–9
Ilex verticillata	Winterberry	4–9
Juniperus virginiana	Eastern red cedar	2–9
Larix decidua	European larch	(3)4–6(7)
Lonicera spp.	Honeysuckle	3–8
Malus spp.	Flowering crabapple	4–8
Morus rubra	Red mulberry	4–8(9)
Myrica cerifera	Wax myrtle	6–9
Nyssa sylvatica	Tupelo, black gum	(4)5–9
Parthenocissus tricuspidata	Boston ivy	4–8
Prunus spp.	Cherry, plum	3–9
Rhus typhina	Staghorn sumac	4–8
Sambucus canadensis	American elder	(3)4–9
Sorbus aucuparia	European mountain ash	3–7
Symphoricarpos orbiculatus	Coralberry	2–7
Tsuga canadensis	Canadian hemlock	(3)4–7
Viburnum prunifolium	Black haw viburnum	3–9
Viburnum trilobum	American cranberrybush viburnum	2–7
PLANTS TO ATTRACT BUTTERFLIES		
For nectar		
Achillea filipendulina	Fernleaf yarrow	3–9
Asclepias tuberosa	Butterfly weed	4–9
Aster spp.	Aster	4–8
Bouvardia longiflora	Bouvardia	9–10
Buddleia davidii	Butterfly bush	5–9
Citrus spp.	Orange, lemon, lime	8–11
Clethra alnifolia	Summersweet	4–9
Coreopsis lanceolata	Tickseed	4–9
Cosmos bipinnatus	Cosmos	A
Delphinium spp.	Hybrid delphinium	2–7
Echinacea purpurea	Purple coneflower	3–9
Eupatorium purpureum	Joe-Pye weed	4–9
Heliotropium arborescens	Heliotrope	10–11
Hylotelephium spectabile	Showy sedum	4–9
Lantana camara	Lantana	8–10
Liatris spicata	Spike gayfeather	3–9
Lobularia maritima	Sweet alyssum	A
Pentas lanceolata	Egyptian star flower	9–11
Phlox paniculata	Garden phlox	3–8
Rhododendron spp.	Azalea	4–10
Rudbeckia laciniata	Cutleaf coneflower	3–9
Tagetes patula	French marigold	A

BOTANICAL NAME	COMMON NAME	ZONES
For larval food		
Achillea millefolium	Yarrow	3–9
Asclepias syriaca	Milkweed	3–8
Chelone lyonii	Pink turtlehead	3–8
Citrus spp.	Orange, lemon, lime	9–10
Helianthus ×multiflorus	Many-flowered sunflower	3–9
Lindera benzoin	Spice bush	5–9
Liriodendron tulipifera	Tulip tree	(4)5–9
Malus spp.	Flowering crabapple	4–8
Malva alcea	Hollyhock mallow	3–8
Passiflora spp.	Passion flower	7–10
Prunus serotina	Black cherry	3–9
Rosa spp.	Rose	3–10
Salix spp.	Willow	2–8
Trifolium spp.	Clover	4–9
Ulmus spp.	Elm	2–9
Viola spp.	Violet	4–9
ANNUALS AND PERENNIALS FOR CUT FLOWERS		
Achillea filipendulina	Fernleaf yarrow	3–9
Alstromeria hybrids	Peruvian lily	9–11
Anemone ×hybrida	Anemone	5–8
Antirrhinum majus	Snapdragon	6–9
Aster novae-angliae	New England aster	4–8
Callistephus chinensis	China aster	A
Centaurea cyanus	Cornflower	A
Consolida orientalis	Larkspur	A
Coreopsis lanceolata	Tickseed	4–9
Cosmos bipinnatus	Cosmos	A
Dahlia hybrids	Dahlia	9–11
Delphinium elatum	Hybrid delphinium	2–7
Dendranthema ×grandiflorum	Chrysanthemum	4–9
Echinacea purpurea	Purple coneflower	3–9
Eustoma grandiflorum	Lisianthus	9–10
Freesia spp.	Freesia	9–10
Gerbera jamesonii	Barberton daisy	8–10
Gladiolus spp.	Gladiolus	9–10
Gomphrena globosa	Globe amaranth	A
Gypsophila paniculata	Baby's breath	3–8
Helichrysum bracteatum	Strawflower	A
Iris spp.	Iris	3–9
Lathyrus odoratus	Sweet pea	A
Liatris spicata	Spike gayfeather	3–9
Lillium spp.	Lily	3–10
Narcissus spp.	Narcissus, daffodil, jonquil	3–8
Paeonia officinalis	Peony	3–8
Phlox paniculata	Garden phlox	3–8
Polianthes tuberosa	Tuberose	9–11
Rudbeckia hirta	Black-eyed Susan	A
Tagetes erecta	African marigold	A
Tithonia rotundifolia	Mexican sunflower	A
Tulipa hybrids	Tulip	3–8
Zantedeschia cvs.	Calla lily	9–11
Zinnia elegans	Zinnia	A

Red-osier dogwood, *Cornus stolonifera*

American cranberrybush, *Viburnum trilobum*

Lantana, *Lantana camara* 'Samantha'

Snapdragon, *Antirrhinum majus* 'Bells Mix'

Baby's breath, *Gypsophila paniculata*

Love-in-a-mist,
Nigella damascena

Moss rose,
***Portulaca grandiflora* 'Sundial'**

Scarlet sage, ***Salvia splendens* 'Feverfunke'**

French marigold,
***Tagetes patula* 'Seven Star Red'**

Coleus,
***Solenostemon scutellarioides* 'Wizard Mix'**

BOTANICAL NAME	COMMON NAME	ZONES
PLANTS OF EASY CULTURE		
Annuals that self-sow		
Ageratum houstonianum	Ageratum	A
Browallia speciosa	Browallia	A
Celosia argentea	Cockscomb	A
Centaurea cyanus	Cornflower	A
Clarkia amoena	Godetia	A
Cleome hassleriana	Spider flower	A
Consolida orientalis	Larkspur	A
Cosmos bipinnatus	Cosmos	A
Eschscholzia californica	California poppy	A
Euphorbia marginata	Snow-on-the-mountain	A
Gaillardia pulchella	Blanket flower	A
Helianthus annuus	Sunflower	A
Ipomoea purpurea	Morning glory	A
Linum grandiflorum	Flowering flax	A
Lobularia maritima	Sweet alyssum	A
Lunaria annua	Honesty	A
Lychnis coronaria	Rose campion	A
Mirabilis jalapa	Four-o-clock	A
Moluccella laevis	Bells of Ireland	A
Myosotis sylvatica	Forget-me-not	A
Nicotiana alata	Flowering tobacco	A
Nierembergia hippomanica	Cupflower	A
Nigella damascena	Love-in-a-mist	A
Papaver rhoeas	Shirley poppy	A
Papaver somniferum	Peony-flowered poppy	A
Petunia integrifolia	Violet-flowered petunia	A
Portulaca grandiflora	Moss rose	A
Tagetes patula	French marigold	A
Annuals that can be sown directly into the garden		
Amaranthus spp.	Joseph's coat, love-lies-bleeding	A
Centaurea cyanus	Cornflower	A
Clarkia amoena	Godetia	A
Consolida orientalis	Larkspur	A
Coreopsis tinctoria	Calliopsis	A
Eschscholzia californica	California poppy	A
Euphorbia marginata	Snow-on-the-mountain	A
Gilia capitata	Gilia, Queen Anne's thimble	A
Gypsophila elegans	Annual baby's breath	A
Helianthus annuus	Sunflower	A
Hunnemannia fumariifolia	Golden cup, Mexican tulip poppy	A
Iberis umbellata	Globe candytuft	A
Impatiens balsamina	Garden balsam	A
Ipomoea quamoclit	Cypress vine	A
Ipomoea tricolor	Morning glory	A
Lathyrus odorata	Sweet pea	A
Lavatera arborea	Tree mallow	A
Mirabilis jalapa	Four-o-clock	A
Nemophila menziesii	Baby-blue-eyes	A
Nigella damascena	Love-in-a-mist	A
Papaver rhoeas	Shirley poppy	A

BOTANICAL NAME	COMMON NAME	ZONES
Phaseolus coccineus	Scarlet runner bean	A
Phlox drummondii	Annual phlox	A
Portulaca grandiflora	Moss rose	A
Ricinus communis	Castor bean	A
Tropaeolum majus	Nasturtium	A
Easy to propagate from cuttings		
Begonia spp.	Wax begonia, Rex begonia	A
Codiaeum variegatum	Croton	10–11
Dendranthema ×*grandiflorum*	Chrysanthemum	4–9
Dianthus caryophyllus	Carnation	8–10
Dieffenbachia spp.	Dieffenbachia, Dumb cane	10–11
Dracaena spp.	Dracaena	9–11
Epiphyllum spp.	Orchid cactus	9–11
Euonymus spp.	Euonymus	4–9
Ficus spp.	Rubber plant, weeping fig	10–11
Forsythia spp.	Forsythia	(4)5–8(9)
Hedera helix	English ivy	5–9
Heliotropium arborescens	Heliotrope	10–11
Impatiens spp.	Impatiens	10–11
Iresine herbstii	Bloodleaf	9–10
Lantana camara	Lantana	8–10
Lonicera spp.	Honeysuckle	3–9
Nerium oleander	Oleander	8–10
Pelargonium spp.	Geranium	9–10
Peperomia spp.	Peperomia	10–11
Petunia ×*hybrida*	Petunia	8–10
Philodendron	Philodendron (climbing types)	10–11
Saintpaulia ionantha	African violet	10–11
Salix spp.	Willow	2–8
Salvia spp.	Sage	4–10
Sinningia speciosa	Gloxinia	10–11
Solenostemon scutellarioides	Coleus, painted nettle	10
Tropaeolum majus	Nasturtium	9–10
Verbena ×*hybrida*	Verbena	9–10
Rapidly spreading perennial plants		
Achillea millefolium	Yarrow	3–9
Adenophora confusa	Ladybells	3–8
Artemisia ludoviciana albula	Silver King sage	4–9
Campanula glomerata	Clustered bellflower	3–8
Campanula latifolia	Great bellflower	3–7
Duchesnea indica	Mock strawberry	5–9
Houttuynia cordata 'Chameleon'	Chameleon plant	(5)6–11
Lamium galeobdolon	Yellow archangel	4–9
Lysimachia clethroides	Gooseneck loosestrife	3–9
Lysimachia nummularia	Moneywort	3–8
Lythrum salicaria	Purple loosestrife	3–9
Macleaya cordata	Plume poppy	4–9
Oenothera biennis	Evening primrose	B
Physalis alkekengi	Chinese lantern	3–9
Polygonum japonicum	Japanese knotweed	3–7
Ranunculus repens	Creeping buttercup	4–8
Saponaria officinalis	Soapwort	2–8

BOTANICAL NAME	COMMON NAME	ZONES
OUTSTANDING HOUSEPLANTS		
Tolerant of low light		
Aglaonema commutatum	Chinese evergreen	NA
Aspidistra elatior	Cast-iron plant	NA
Aucuba japonica	Japanese aucuba	NA
Chamaedorea elegans	Parlor palm	NA
Chlorophytum comosum	Spider plant	NA
Cissus antarctica	Kangaroo vine	NA
Cissus rhombifolia	Grape ivy	NA
Cyrtomium falcatum	Japanese holly fern	NA
Dieffenbachia maculata	Spotted dumb cane	NA
Dracaena fragrans 'Massangeana'	Corn plant	NA
Dracaena reflexa	Pleomele, song of India	NA
Epipremnum aureum	Golden pothos	NA
Philodendron scandens	Heart-leaf philodendron	NA
Podocarpus macrophyllus	Yew pine	NA
Pteris cretica	Table fern	NA
Sansevieria trifasciata	Snake plant	NA
Spathiphyllum wallisii	Peace lily	NA
Syngonium podophyllum	Arrowhead vine	NA
Best in medium light		
Adiantum pedatum	Maidenhair fern	NA
Aechmea fasciata	Vase plant	NA
Aeschynanthus radicans	Lipstick plant	NA
Aloe vera	Medicine plant	NA
Anthurium scherzerianum	Flamingo flower	NA
Aphelandra squarrosa	Zebra plant	NA
Araucaria heterophylla	Norfolk Island pine	NA
Ardisia crispa	Coralberry	NA
Asparagus densiflorus	Asparagus fern	NA
Asparagus setaceus	Plumosa fern	NA
Asplenium nidus	Bird's nest fern	NA
Begonia coccinea	Angel wing begonia	NA
Begonia Rex-cultorum hybrids	Rex begonia	NA
Calathea majestica	Calathea	NA
Cryptanthus bivittatus	Earth star	NA
Cycas revoluta	Sago palm	NA
Davallia fejeensis	Rabbit's foot fern	NA
Episcia cvs.	Episcia, flame violet	NA
Ficus benjamina	Weeping fig	NA
Ficus elastica	Rubber tree	NA
Howea forsteriana	Kentia palm	NA
Kalanchoe blossfeldiana	Kalanchoe	NA
Lilium longiflorum	Easter lily	NA
Maranta leuconeura	Prayer plant	NA
Nephrolepis exaltata	Boston fern, sword fern	NA
Pandanus veitchii	Screw pine	NA
Pedilanthus tithymaloides	Devil's backbone, ribbon cactus	NA
Peperomia caperata	Emerald ripple peperomia	NA
Peperomia obtusifolia	Baby rubber plant	NA
Phalaenopsis cvs.	Moth orchid	NA
Philodendron bipinnatifidum	Tree philodendron	NA
Phoenix roebelinii	Dwarf date palm	NA

BOTANICAL NAME	COMMON NAME	ZONES
Pilea cadierei	Aluminum plant	NA
Plectranthus australis	Swedish ivy	NA
Saintpaulia ionantha	African violet	NA
Schefflera actinophylla	Umbrella tree	NA
Schefflera arboricola	Schefflera	NA
Schefflera elegantissima	False aralia	NA
Schlumbergera ×*buckleyi*	Christmas cactus	NA
Schlumbergera truncata	Thanksgiving cactus	NA
Sinningia speciosa	Gloxinia	NA
Soleirolia soleirollii	Baby's tears	NA
Solenostemon scutellarioides	Coleus, painted nettle	NA
Tolmiea menziesii	Piggyback plant	NA
Tradescantia spathacea	Boat lily	NA
Tradescantia zebrina	Wandering Jew	NA
Vriesia splendens	Flaming sword	NA
Need bright light		
Abutilon ×*hybridum*	Flowering maple, Chinese lantern	NA
Acalypha hispida	Chenille plant	NA
Beaucarnea recurvata	Ponytail palm	NA
Bougainvillea glabra	Bougainvillea	NA
×*Citrofortunella microcarpa*	Calamondin orange	NA
Citrus meyeri	Meyer lemon	NA
Clerodendrum thomsoniae	Glorybower	NA
Codiaeum variegatum	Croton	NA
Cordyline terminalis	Hawaiian ti plant	NA
Crassula ovata	Jade plant	NA
Crossandra infundibuliformis	Crossandra, firecracker flower	NA
Cyclamen periscum	Cyclamen	NA
Dendranthema ×*grandiflorum*	Chrysanthemum	NA
Dracaena surculosa	Gold dust dracaena	NA
Euphorbia milii	Crown-of-thorns	NA
Euphorbia pulcherrima	Poinsettia	NA
Freesia hybrids	Freesia	NA
Gardenia augusta	Gardenia	NA
Gynura aurantiaca	Purple passion	NA
Hibiscus rosa-sinensis	Rose mallow	NA
Hippeastrum spp.	Amaryllis	NA
Hoya carnosa	Wax plant	NA
Hydrangea macrophylla	Hydrangea	NA
Hypoestes phyllostachya	Polka-dot plant, freckle-face	NA
Iresine herbstii	Bloodleaf	NA
Justicia brandegeana	Shrimp plant	NA
Kalanchoe tomentosa	Panda plant	NA
Mammillaria spp.	Snowball cactus	NA
Musa acuminata	Banana	NA
Oxalis spp.	Oxalis	NA
Passiflora coccinea	Red passion flower	NA
Pelargonium graveolens	Rose-scented geranium	NA
Pelargonium ×*hortorum*	Geranium, zonal geranium	NA
Plumeria rubra	Frangipani	NA
Polyscias scutellaria	Balfour aralia	NA
Strelitzia reginae	Bird-of-paradise	NA

Grape ivy, *Cissus rhombifolia*

Parlor palm, *Chamaedorea elegans*

Aluminum plant, *Pilea cadeiri*

Calamondin orange, ×*Citrofortunella microcarpa*

Glorybower, *Clerodendrum thomsoniae*

USDA PLANT HARDINESS ZONE MAP

This map of climate zones helps you select plants for your garden that will survive a typical winter in your region. The United States Department of Agriculture (USDA) developed the map, basing the zones on the lowest recorded temperatures across North America. Zone 1 is the coldest area and Zone 11 is the warmest area.

Plants are classified by the coldest temperature and zone they can endure. For example, plants hardy to Zone 6 survive where winter temperatures drop to –10°F. Those hardy to Zone 8 die long before it's that cold. These plants may grow in colder regions but must be replaced each year. Plants rated for a range of hardiness zones can usually survive winter in the coldest region as well as tolerate the summer heat of the warmest one.

To find your hardiness zone, note the approximate location of your community on the map, then match the color band marking that area to the key.

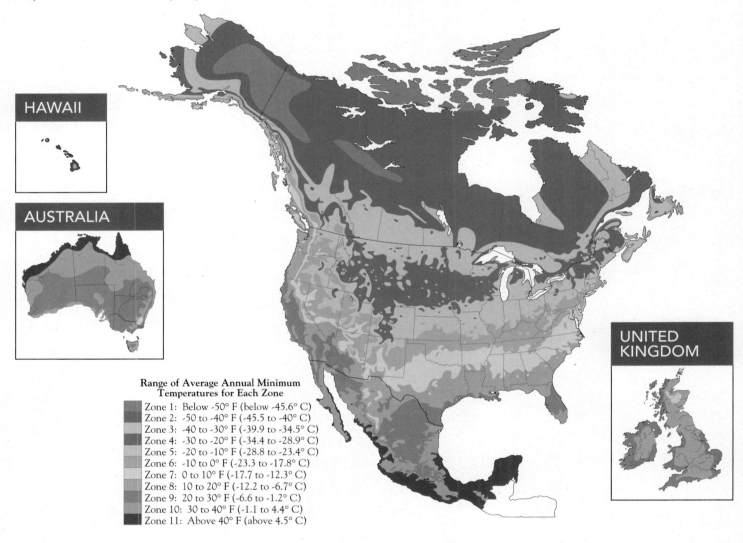

HAWAII

AUSTRALIA

UNITED KINGDOM

Range of Average Annual Minimum Temperatures for Each Zone

Zone 1: Below -50° F (below -45.6° C)
Zone 2: -50 to -40° F (-45.5 to -40° C)
Zone 3: -40 to -30° F (-39.9 to -34.5° C)
Zone 4: -30 to -20° F (-34.4 to -28.9° C)
Zone 5: -20 to -10° F (-28.8 to -23.4° C)
Zone 6: -10 to 0° F (-23.3 to -17.8° C)
Zone 7: 0 to 10° F (-17.7 to -12.3° C)
Zone 8: 10 to 20° F (-12.2 to -6.7° C)
Zone 9: 20 to 30° F (-6.6 to -1.2° C)
Zone 10: 30 to 40° F (-1.1 to 4.4° C)
Zone 11: Above 40° F (above 4.5° C)

METRIC CONVERSIONS

U.S. Units to Metric Equivalents			Metric Units to U.S. Equivalents		
To Convert From	Multiply By	To Get	To Convert From	Multiply By	To Get
Inches	25.4	Millimeters	Millimeters	0.0394	Inches
Inches	2.54	Centimeters	Centimeters	0.3937	Inches
Feet	30.48	Centimeters	Centimeters	0.0328	Feet
Feet	0.3048	Meters	Meters	3.2808	Feet
Yards	0.9144	Meters	Meters	1.0936	Yards

To convert from degrees Fahrenheit (F) to degrees Celsius (C), first subtract 32, then multiply by ⅝.

To convert from degrees Celsius to degrees Fahrenheit, multiply by ⅗, then add 32.

These maps indicate the average dates for the first and last frosts across North America. Many factors influence the accuracy of these dates. For example, at the bottom of a north-facing hill, spring comes later and fall earlier than on the top of the hill. Your local cooperative extension service can provide a more precise date for your location.

Light frosts occur when the temperature falls below 33°F. Light frost rarely poses a threat to cool-season annuals, such as pansies and ornamental cabbage, which grow quite well in cold weather in spring and fall.

Warm-season annuals are more variable. Some quickly succumb to light frost, whereas others, such as petunias, survive until a hard frost (around 28°F) knocks them down. However, it's best to wait until after the last frost in spring to set out warm-season annuals in the garden, and to rely on cool-season annuals to provide fall bloom.

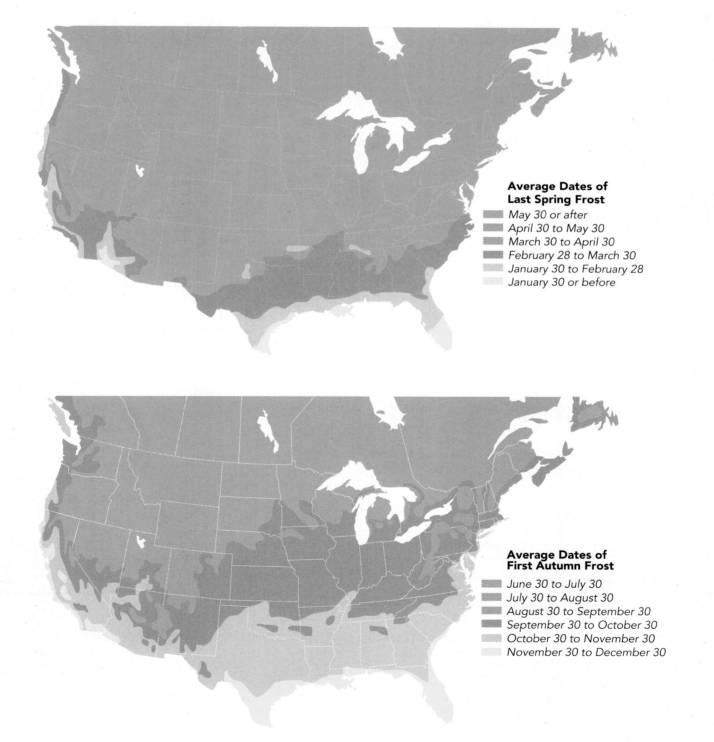

**Average Dates of
Last Spring Frost**

May 30 or after
April 30 to May 30
March 30 to April 30
February 28 to March 30
January 30 to February 28
January 30 or before

**Average Dates of
First Autumn Frost**

June 30 to July 30
July 30 to August 30
August 30 to September 30
September 30 to October 30
October 30 to November 30
November 30 to December 30

RESOURCES FOR PLANTS AND SUPPLIES

HOUSEPLANTS

Alannah's Greenhouses
Box 1342
Grand Forks, BC V0H 1H0
Canada
250/442-2552
www.alannahs.com
African violets, gesneriads, specialty geraniums, and assorted flowering tropical houseplants

Davidson-Wilson Greenhouses
3147 E. Ladoga Rd.
Crawfordsville, IN 47933
877/723-6834
Houseplants; specialty geraniums

Glasshouse Works
Church St., P.O. Box 97
Stewart, OH 45778
740/662-2142
Orders: 800/837-2142
www.glasshouseworks.com
Tropical and rare plants

Harborcrest Gardens
1581-H Hillside Ave., Suite 230
Victoria, BC V8T 2C1 Canada
250/642-7309
www.harborcrestgardens.com
Tropical plants and African violets

Hobbs Farm & Greenery
979 Barnestown Rd.
Hope, ME 04847
207/763-4746
www.hobbsfarm.com
Houseplants; ivies

Kartuz Greenhouses,
Sunset Island Exotics
1408 Sunset Dr.
Vista, CA 92085
760/941-3613
www.kartuz.com
Gesneriads, begonias, flowering tropicals, subtropicals, vines

Lauray of Salisbury
432 Undermountain Rd., Rte. 41
Salisbury, CT 06068
860/435-2263
www.lauray.com
Cacti, succulents, orchids, begonias

Logee's Greenhouses
141 North St.
Danielson, CT 06239
888/330-8038
www.logees.com
Tropicals and subtropicals

Lyndon Lyon Greenhouses
P.O. Box 249
14 Mutchler St.
Dolgeville, NY 13329
315/429-8291
www.lyndonlyon.com
African violets and orchids

McKinney's Glasshouse
P.O. Box 782282
Wichita, KS 67278
316/686-9438
Gesneriads, rare and exotic tropicals, supplies

Northridge Gardens
9821 White Oak Ave.
Northridge, CA 91325
818/349-9798
Succulents, hard-to-find items

Oak Hill Gardens
P.O. Box 25
37W 550 Binnie Rd.
Dundee, IL 60118
847/428-8500
www.oakhillgardens.com
Specialty plants, orchids, and supplies

Packer Nursery
P.O. Box 4056
Kailua-Kona, HI 96745
888/345-5566
www.alohapalms.com
Palms and tropicals

P. & J. Greenhouses
20265 82nd Ave.
Langley, BC V2Y 2A9 Canada
604/888-3274
Geraniums and fuchsias

Rainbow Gardens Nursery & Bookshop
1444 E. Taylor St.
Vista, CA 92084
760/758-4290
www.rainbowgardensbookshop.com
Plants and books

Stokes Tropicals
4806 W. Old Spanish Trail
Jeanerette, LA 70544
337/365-6998
Orders: 800/624-9706

Sunrise Nursery
13105 Canyon View
Leander, TX 78641
512/267-0023
Succulents, cacti

Tiki Nursery
P.O. Box 187
Fairview, NC 28730
828/628-2212
Gesneriads (African violets)

SUPPLIES

Eco Enterprises
1240 N.E. 175th St., Suite B
Shoreline, WA 98155
800/426-6937
www.ecogrow.com
Growing supplies, lighting

Charley's Greenhouse & Garden
17979 State Route 536
Mount Vernon, WA 98273
800/322-4707
www.charleysgreenhouse.com
Growing supplies, greenhouses, lighting

www.miracle-gro.com

For more information on how to garden successfully, go to www.miracle-gro.com where you'll find:

- **Miracle-Gro Garden Helpline: 800/645-8166**
- **Email Reminder Service:** Free gardening tips and reminders sent to you via e-mail.
- **Miracle-Gro Product Consumer Guide:** The latest information on all Miracle-Gro products, including plant foods, soil mixes, plants, and exciting new product lines from Miracle-Gro.
- **Garden Problem Solver:** Link into a comprehensive library of diagnostic tools and solutions for insect, disease, and weed problems.
- **Streaming How-to Videos:** Click into a library of more than 50 quick gardening and lawn care video clips.

Gardener's Supply Co.
128 Intervale Rd.
Burlington, VT 05401
800/955-3370
www.gardeners.com
Seed-starting supplies, organic
fertilizers and pest controls,
hand tools, and watering systems

Hydro-Farm
755 Southpoint Blvd.
Petaluma, CA 94954
707/765-9990
www.hydrofarm.com
High-intensity lighting and
indoor growing supplies

Indoor Gardening Supplies
P.O. Box 527
Dexter, MI 48130
800/823-5740
www.indoorgardensupplies.com
Growing supplies

The Scotts Company
800/225-2883
www.scotts.com
www.ortho.com
www.miracle-gro.com
Fertilizers, mulches, and pest controls

Windowbox.com
3821 S. Santa Fe Ave.
Vernon, CA 90058
888/427-3362
323/277-1137
www.windowbox.com
Container gardening supplies

FLOWERS

Bluestone Perennials, Inc.
7211 Middle Ridge Road
Madison, OH 44057-3096
800/852-5243
www.bluestoneperennials.com
Perennials and shrubs

Cooley's Gardens
P.O. Box 126-PE
Silverton, OR 97381
503/873-5463
800/225-5391
www.cooleysgardens.com
Bearded irises

High Country Gardens
2902 Rufina Street
Santa Fe, NM 87507-2929
800/925-9387
www.highcountrygardens.com
Drought-tolerant plants

Jackson & Perkins
1 Rose Lane
Medford, OR 97501
800/292-4769
www.jacksonandperkins.com
Perennials, roses, and Dutch bulbs

Klehm's Song Sparrow Perennial Farm
13101 E. Rye Road
Avalon, WI 53505
800/553-3715
www.songsparrow.com
Peonies, daylilies, hostas, and
newer perennials

Northstar Nurseries, Inc.
13450 Willandale Road
Rogers, MN 55374-9585
763/428-7601
Daylilies

Paradise Garden
474 Clotts Road
Columbus, OH 43230
614/893-0896
www.paradisegarden.com
Daylilies, hostas, irises, peonies, roses,
grasses, perennials, and herbs

Spring Hill Nurseries
110 West Elm Street
Tipp City, OH 45371-1699
812/537-2177
www.springhillnursery.com
Perennials, roses, trees, and shrubs

Van Bourgondien
245 Route 109
P.O. Box 1000-MGA
Babylon, NY 11702-9004
800/622-9997
www.dutchbulbs.com
Perennials and bulbs

Wayside Gardens
1 Garden Lane
Hodges, SC 29695-0001
800/845-1124
www.waysidegardens.com
Perennials, bulbs, shrubs, trees,
and gardening aids

White Flower Farm
P.O. Box 50
Litchfield, CT 06759-0050
800/503-9624
www.whiteflowerfarm.com
Perennials, annuals, bulbs, and seeds

SEEDS

Ed Hume Seeds
P.O. Box 73160
Puyallup, WA 98373
Fax: 253/435-5144
Flower and herb seeds

McKenzie Seed Co.
30 Ninth Street
Brandon, MB R7A 6E1 Canada
204/571-7500
Flower and vegetable seeds and
perennial plants; (Canada only)

Park Seed
P.O. Box 31, Hwy 254
Greenwood, SC 29648
800/845-3369
www.parkseed.com
Flower seeds and plants

Seeds of Change
P.O. Box 15700
Santa Fe, NM 87506
888/762-7333
www.seedsofchange.com
Organic seeds, bulbs, and plants

Select Seeds Company
180 Stickney Hill Rd.
Union, CT 06076-4617
860/684-9310
www.selectseeds.com
Heirloom flower seeds and plants

Stokes Seeds
P.O. Box 548
Buffalo, NY 14240-0548
800/396-9238
www.stokeseeds.com
Flowers, herbs, and vegetables

Thompson & Morgan Seedsmen, Inc.
P.O. Box 1308
Jackson, NJ 08527-0308
800/274-7333
www.thompson-morgan.com
Flower and vegetable seeds

TREES AND SHRUBS

Arborvillage
P.O. Box 227
Holt, MO 64048
816/264-3911
e-mail: arborvillage@aol.com

Bovee's Nursery
1737 SW Coronado
Portland, OR 97219
800/435-9250
www.bovees.com

Camellia Forest Nursery
9701 Carrie Rd.
Chapel Hill, NC 27516
919/968-0504
www.camforest.com

Carroll Gardens
444 E. Main St.
Westminster, MD 21157
800/638-6334
www.carrollgardens.com

Eastern Plant Specialties
Box 226
Georgetown, NE 04548
732/382-2508
www.easternplant.com

Forestfarm
990 Tetherow Rd.
Williams, OR 97544
541/846-7269
www.forestfarm.com

Gossler Farms Nursery
1200 Weaver Rd.
Springfield, OR 97478
541/746-3922

Greer Gardens
1280 Goodpasture Island Rd.
Eugene, OR 97401
800/548-0111
www.greergardens.com

Heirloom Roses
24062 NE Riverside Dr.
St. Paul, OR 97137
503/538-1576
www.heirloomroses.com

Jackson & Perkins
1 Rose Lane
Medford, OR 97501
800/854-6200
www.jacksonandperkins.com

Louisiana Nursery
5853 Highway 182
Opelousas, LA 70570
337/948-3696
www.Durionursery.com

Mellinger's
2310 W. South Range Rd.
North Lima, OH 44452-9731
800/321-7444
www.mellingers.com

Plants of the Southwest
3905 Agua Fria Rd.
Santa Fe, NM 87507
505/438-8888
Catalog: $3.50
www.plantsofthesouthwest.com

Richard Owen Nursery
2300 E. Lincoln St.
Bloomington, IL 61701
309/663-9551
www.excitinggardens.com

Roses of Yesterday & Today
803 Brown's Valley Rd.
Watsonville, CA 95076
831/728-1901
www.rosesofyesterday.com

Roslyn Nursery
211 Burr's Lane
Dix Hills, NY 11746
631/643-9347
www.roslynnursery.com

Siskiyou Rare Plant Nursery
2825 Cummings Rd.
Medford, OR 97501
541/772-6846

Wayside Gardens
1 Garden Lane
Hodges, SC 29695
800/845-1124
www.waysidegardens.com

White Flower Farm
P.O. Box 50
Litchfield, CT 06759-0050
800/503-9624
www.whiteflowerfarm.com

Woodlanders Inc.
1128 Colleton Ave.
Aiken, SC 29801
803/648-7522
www.woodlanders.net

Yucca Do Nursery
P.O. Box 907
Hempstead, TX 77445
979/826-4580
www.yuccado.com

VEGETABLES AND HERBS

Abundant Life Seed Foundation
P.O. Box 772
Port Townsend, WA 98368
360/385-5660
www.abundantlifeseed.org

Bountiful Gardens
18001 Shafer Ranch Rd.
Willits, CA 95490-9626
707/459-6410
www.bountifulgardens.org

Comstock, Ferre & Co.
263 Main St.
Wethersfield, CT 06109
800/733-3773
www.comstockferre.com

D. Landreth Seed Co.
P.O. Box 6398
Baltimore, MD 21230
800/654-2407
www.landrethseeds.com
Catalog: $2.00

DeGiorgi Seeds & Goods
6011 N St.
Omaha, NE 68117
800/858-2580

Earl May Seed & Nursery
Shenandoah, IA 51603
800/831-4193
www.earlmay.com

Evergreen Y.H. Enterprises
P.O. Box 17538
Anaheim, CA 92817
714/637-5769
www.evergreenseeds.com

Ferry-Morse Seed Co.
P.O. Box 1620
Fulton, KY 42041
800/283-6400
www.ferry-morse.com

Harris Seeds
P.O. Box 24966
Rochester, NY 14692-0966
800/514-4441
www.harisseeds.com

High Altitude Seeds
4150B Black Oak Dr.
Hailey, ID 83333
208/788-4363
www.seedstrust.com
Catalog: $3.00

Irish Eyes—Garden City Seeds
P.O. Box 307
Thorp, WA 98946
509/964-7000
www.irish-eyes.com

J.L. Hudson, Seedsman
Star Route 2, Box 337
La Honda, CA 94020
www.jlhudsonseeds.net

Johnny's Selected Seeds
184 Foss Hill Rd.
Albion, ME 04910-9731
207/437-4301
www.johnnyseeds.com

J.W. Jung Seed Co.
335 S. High St.
Randolph, WI 53957-0001
800/297-3123
www.jungseed.com

Native Seeds/SEARCH
526 N. 4th Ave.
Tucson, AZ 85705-8450
520/622-5561
www.nativeseeds.org

Nichols Garden Nursery
1190 N. Pacific Hwy.
Albany, OR 97321-4598
541/928-9280
www.nicholsgardennursery.com

Ornamental Edibles
3272 Fleur de Lis Ct.
San Jose, CA 95132
408/929-7333
www.ornamentaledibles.com

Otis S. Twilley Seed Co., Inc.
121 Gary Rd.
Hodges, SC 29653
800/622-7333
www.twilleyseed.com

Park Seed Co.
1 Parkton Ave.
Greenwood, SC 29649
800/213-0076
www.parkseed.com

Pinetree Garden Seeds
P.O. Box 300
New Gloucester, ME 04260
207/926-3400
www.superseeds.com

Redwood City Seed Co.
P.O. Box 361
Redwood City, CA 94064
650/325-7333
www.ecoseeds.com

Renee's Garden
888/880-7228
www.reneesgarden.com

R.H. Shumway's
P.O. Box 1
Graniteville, SC 29829-0001
803/663-9771
www.rhshumway.com

Sand Mountain Herbs
321 County Road 18
Fyffe, AL 35971
256/528-2861
www.sandmountainherbs.com

Sandy Mush Herb Nursery
Rt. 2, Surrett Cove Rd.
Leicester, NC
704/683-2014
www.brwm.org/sandymushherbs
Catalog: $4.00

Seeds Blum
Idaho City Stage
Boise, ID 83706
208/343-2202
Catalog: $3.00

Seeds of Change
P.O. Box 15700
Santa Fe, NM 87506
888/762-7333
www.seedsofchange.com

Seeds West Garden Seeds
317 14th St. NW
Albuquerque, NM 87104
505/843-9713
www.seedswestgardenseeds.com
Catalog: $2.00

Stokes Seeds Inc.
P.O. Box 548
Buffalo, NY 14240-0548
800/396-9238
www.stokeseeds.com

Territorial Seed Co.
P.O. Box 157
Cottage Grove, OR 97424
541/942-9547
www.territorial-seed.com

The Cooks' Garden
P.O. Box 5010
Hodges, SC 29653-5010
800/457-9703
www.cooksgarden.com

The Pepper Gal
P.O. Box 23006
Ft. Lauderdale, FL 33307
954/537-5540
www.peppergal.com

Thompson & Morgan, Inc.
P.O. Box 1308
Jackson, NY 08527-0308
800/274-7333
www.thompson-morgan.com

Tomato Growers Supply Co.
P.O. Box 2237
Ft. Myers, FL 33902
888/478-7333
www.tomatogrowers.com

Vesey's Seeds Ltd.
P.O. Box 9000
Calais, ME 04619-6102
800/363-7333
www.veseys.com

Vermont Bean Seed Co.
Garden Lane
Fair Haven, VT 05743
803/663-0217
www.vermontbean.com

W. Atlee Burpee & Co.
300 Park Ave.
Warminster, PA 18991
800/888-1447
www.burpee.com

FRUITS

Adams County Nursery, Inc.
26 Nursery Rd.
P.O. Box 108
Aspers, PA 17304
717/677-8105
www.acnursery.com

Ames' Orchard and Nursery
18292 Wildlife Rd.
Fayetteville, AR 72701
501/443-0282

Ahrens Strawberry Nursery
RR1
Huntingburg, IN 47642
812/683-3055

W. F. Allen, Co.
Box 1577
Salisbury, MD 21801

Brittingham Plant Farms
P.O. Box 2538
Salisbury, MD 21801
301/749-5153

Columbia Basin Nursery
P.O. Box 458
Quincy, WA 98848
800/333-8589
www.cbnllc.com

Edible Landscaping
P.O. Box 77
Afton, VA 22920
804/361-9134
www.eat-it.com

Garden of Delights
14560 SW 14th St.
Davie, FL 33325-4217
800/741-3103
www.gardenofdelights.com

Greenmantle Nursery
3010 Ettersburg Rd.
Garberville, CA 95542
707/986-7504

Hartmann's Plantation Inc.
P.O. Box E
Grand Junction, MI 49056
616/253-4281
www.hartmannsplantcompany.com

Indiana Berry & Plant Co.
5218 West 500
South Huntingburg, IN 47542-9724
800/295-2226
berryinfo@inberry.com
www.inberry.com

Just Fruits Nursery
30 St. Frances St.
Crawfordville, FL 32327
850/926-5644

Kelly Nurseries
P.O. Box 800
Dansville, NY 14437
800/325-4180
www.kellynurseries.com

Lawson's Nursery
2730 Yellow Creek Rd.
Ball Ground, GA 30107
770/893-2141

Miller Nurseries
5060 W. Lake Rd.
Canandaigua, NY 14424-8904
800/836-9630
www.millernurseries.com

New York State Fruit Testing
Cooperative Association, Inc.
P.O. Box 462
Geneva, NY 14456
315/787-2205

Nourse Farms Inc.
41 River Rd.
South Deerfield, MA 01373
413/665-2658
www.noursefarms.com

One Green World
P.O. Box 1080
Molalla, OR 97038
503/651-3005
www.onegreenworld.com

Oregon Exotics Rare Fruit Nursery
1065 Messinger Rd.
Grants Pass, OR 97527
541/846-7678
www.exoticfruit.com

Paradise Nursery
6385 Blackwater Rd.
Virginia Beach, VA 23457-1040
757/421-0201
www.paradisenursery.com

Raintree Nursery
391 Butts Rd.
Morton, WA 98356
360/496-6400
www.raintreenursery.com

Southmeadow Fruit Gardens
P.O. Box 211
Baroda, MI 49101
269/422-2411
www.southmeadowfruitgardens.com

Spring Hill Nurseries
110 W. Elm St.
Tipp City, OH 45371
513/354-1509
www.springhillnursery.com

Stark Brothers Nurseries & Orchards
P.O. Box 10
Louisiana, MO 63353
800/325-4180
www.starkbros.com

The Banana Tree, Inc.
715 Northampton St.
Easton, PA 18042
610/253-9589
www.banana-tree.com

Van Well Nursery
2821 Grant Rd.
Wenatchee, WA 98807
800/572-1553
www.vanwell.net

INDEX

*Note: Page references in bold type refer to Encyclopedia entries. Page references in italic type refer to additional photographs, illustrations, and information in captions. Plants are listed under their common names.

Miracle-Gro *Encyclopedia of Plant Care*

Editor: Denny Schrock

Contributing Writers: Janna Beckerman, Kate Jerome, Elsa Kramer, Carole Ottesen, John Pohly, Ray Rothenberger, Curtis Smith, Lynn Steiner, Ellen Strother, Jon Traunfeld

Contributing Technical Reviewer: Ashton Ritchie

Photo Researcher: Harijs Priekulis

Copy Chief: Terri Fredrickson

Publishing Operations Manager: Karen Schirm

Edit and Design Production Coordinator: Mary Lee Gavin

Editorial and Design Assistants: Kathleen Stevens, Kairee Windsor

Marketing Product Managers: Aparna Pande, Isaac Petersen, Gina Rickert, Stephen Rogers, Brent Wiersma, Tyler Woods

Book Production Managers: Pam Kvitne, Marjorie J. Schenkelberg, Rick von Holdt, Mark Weaver

Photographers: Marty Baldwin, Scott Little, Blaine Moats, Dean Schoeppner, Jay Wilde

Contributing Production Designer and Stylists: Karen Weir Jimerson, Brad Ruppert, Sundie Ruppert

Contributing Copy Editors: Barbara Feller-Roth, Fran Gardner

Contributing Technical Proofreaders: Deb Brown, B. Rosie Lerner, Mary H. Meyer, Bob Polomski, Ann Marie VanDer Zanden, Douglas F. Welsh

Contributing Proofreaders: Mary Duerson, Terri Krueger, Courtenay Wolfe

Contributing Map Illustrator: Jana Fothergill

Contributing Prop/Photo Stylist: Susan Strelecki

Indexer: Ellen Davenport

Additional Editorial Contributions from
  Art Rep Services

Director: Chip Nadeau

Illustrator: Dave Brandon

Additional Editorial Contributions from
  Shelton Design Studios

Director: Ernie Shelton

Meredith® Books

Executive Director, Editorial: Gregory H. Kayko

Executive Director, Design: Matt Strelecki

Executive Editor/Group Manager: Benjamin W. Allen

Senior Associate Design Director: Tom Wegner

Publisher and Editor in Chief: James D. Blume

Editorial Director: Linda Raglan Cunningham

Executive Director, Marketing: Jeffrey B. Myers

Executive Director, New Business Development: Todd M. Davis

Executive Director, Sales: Ken Zagor

Director, Operations: George A. Susral

Director, Production: Douglas M. Johnston

Business Director: Jim Leonard

Vice President and General Manager: Douglas J. Guendel

Meredith Publishing Group

President: Jack Griffin

Senior Vice President: Bob Mate

Meredith Corporation

Chairman and Chief Executive Officer: William T. Kerr

President and Chief Operating Officer: Stephen M. Lacy

In Memoriam: E.T. Meredith III (1933-2003)

Thanks to

Ames True Temper, Inc., Janet Anderson, Kathryn Anderson, Staci Bailey, Black & Decker, Dennis Blake, Walt Blake, Will Bruere, Charley's Greenhouse & Garden, Dixon Industries, Inc., Callie Dunbar, Fiskars, Khanh Hamilton, Harvey's Greenhouse, C.D. Henry, Holub's Greenhouse, Wes Hunsberger, Hydrofarm, Iowa Arboretum, Rosemary Kautzky, A.M. Leonard, Inc., Cathy Long, L.R. Nelson Corporation, Mary Irene Swartz, The Toro Company

All of us at Meredith® Books are dedicated to providing you with the information and ideas you need to enhance your home and garden. We welcome your comments and suggestions about this book. Write to us at:

Meredith Gardening Books
1716 Locust St.
Des Moines, IA 50309–3023

If you would like to purchase any of our gardening, home improvement, cooking, crafts, or home decorating and design books, check wherever quality books are sold. Or visit us at: meredithbooks.com

If you would like more information on other Miracle-Gro products, call 888-295-6902 or visit us at: www.miraclegro.com

Note to the Readers: Due to differing conditions, tools, and individual skills, Meredith Corporation assumes no responsibility for any damages, injuries suffered, or losses incurred as a result of following the information published in this book. Before beginning any project, review the instructions carefully, and if any doubts or questions remain, consult local experts or authorities. Because codes and regulations vary greatly, you always should check with authorities to ensure that your project complies with all applicable local codes and regulations. Always read and observe all of the safety precautions provided by manufacturers of any tools, equipment, or supplies, and follow all accepted safety procedures.

Photographers

(Photographers credited may retain copyright ©
to the listed photographs.)

L = Left, R = Right, C = Center, B = Bottom, T = Top

William D. Adams: 26B, 58B, 107TR, 107BL, 107BR, 117TL, 480B, 482BL, 482BC, 494B, 501T, 547BC, 563TR, 567B; **Liz Ball/Positive Images:** 388B, 431T, 512TR, 585C, 587T; **Black & Decker:** 82TL; **Margaret Brezden/Photographers Direct:** 548B; **Brussel's Bonsai Nursery:** 74; **Patricia Bruno/Positive Images:** 15BR, 291T, 316BL, 337BR, 347BL, 583B; **Gay Bumgarner/Positive Images:** 409BL; **Karen Bussolini/Positive Images:** 191BL, 237B, 249BL, 333BL; **Rex A. Butcher/Positive Images:** 480BL, 584C; **Les Campbell/Positive Images:** 443T; **Rob Cardillo:** 506BR; **David Cavagnaro:** 29T, 29BL, 111BL, 117B, 124, 126BC, 127TC, 139BL, 144BL, 148T, 155T, 176T, 198BL, 201T, 221T, 224BL, 227T, 230BL, 236C, 238T, 240B, 241C, 245B, 250T, 256C, 257B, 259T, 261B, 263T, 266T, 266BL, 267T, 271BL, 272TR, 273T, 274T, 274BL, 277BL, 278B, 279B, 280T, 283BL, 285T, 287BL, 288T, 296T, 299T, 299BL, 300BL, 302T, 305T, 306T, 307T, 308T, 314BL, 318T, 320BL, 322BL, 325T, 328T, 328BL, 329BL, 333T, 338T, 338B, 341BL, 343BL, 346T, 348T, 351T, 352BL, 353BL, 354T, 355C, 360TR, 361BL, 363B, 365T, 365B, 368T, 369C, 373B, 381BL, 382T, 389B, 392T, 399BL, 404T, 408TCR, 415T, 423T, 432T, 433T, 433B, 441BL, 442BL, 443BL, 444BL, 447CLC, 449T, 455BL, 460T, 461T, 462BL, 464T, 465T, 466B, 468, 470BC, 471TC, 472T, 474BL, 474B, 475BL, 476T, 477TL, 477TR, 478T, 479T, 480T, 480TR, 481BL, 483T, 486T, 486TR, 486BC, 487BL, 489TR, 489BL, 490T, 491TL, 491TR, 491BC, 491BR, 492T, 493B, 496TR, 498TR, 499T, 502T, 502BL, 503B, 505T, 506T, 506TR, 507BC, 507BR, 508TL, 509BL, 510B, 511TC, 512T, 514T, 515TR, 518B, 519T, 520TL, 520TC, 520TR, 520CL, 522B, 524TL, 524TR, 531TL, 533BL, 536T, 537BLC, 539TL, 539TR, 542T, 554TR, 554BL, 557TR, 557CR, 558T, 558BL, 559TR, 559BL, 560T, 561T, 562T, 564T, 565T, 565BL, 566T, 568T, 569T, 571B, 572TC, 573TC, 574TC, 574C, 575C, 576TC, 577T, 577B, 581T, 583BC, 584B, 586BC, 589BC; **Walter Chandoha:** 561TR; **Craftsman:** 82BR; **Richard Day/Daybreak Imagery:** 351B; **Alan & Linda Detrick:** 133BL, 153BL; **Michael Dirr:** 384T, 387B, 399T, 407T, 417B, 418B, 421TR, 438B, 446B, 451T; **Wally Eberhart/Positive Images:** 470TC, 471BC, 471B, 474TR, 484T, 485T, 488T, 497T, 500TL, 511TL, 516T, 518T, 533T; **Beat Ernst/Antje Kohrs Waxman:** 495TR; **Derek Fell:** 14T, 17TR, 28TL, 30L, 62L, 78BL, 202T, 244C, 246B, 436T, 436TR, 473B, 478B, 482T, 482BR, 490TR, 494BL, 495T, 498B, 512B, 514TR, 521TR, 526C, 527TL, 530B, 538B, 544T, 546T, 547BL, 552T, 553T, 563B; **John Glover:** 34B, 73TR, 73CL, 73C, 111TL, 117TC, 134T, 163TC, 163TR, 191B, 193BL, 198B, 200TR, 228T, 229BL, 230T, 247T, 247C, 247B, 248B, 258T, 261T, 262T, 263TC, 275T, 278T, 280BL, 281BL, 284B, 286BL, 295T, 295BL, 298T, 302B, 303BL, 306BL, 307TC, 307B, 312BL, 313CL, 315BL, 326BL, 329T, 333TR, 336CL, 339BL, 345T, 347T, 347BR, 352T, 353T, 355T, 359T, 359B, 361B, 364BL, 367BC, 369B, 370BL, 374B, 375T, 379B, 386T, 387BL, 389T, 393T, 393BL, 394T, 400BL, 403T, 407CL, 413BL, 421B, 422T, 422BL, 424B, 426B, 447CL, 454B, 457T, 459BL, 460BL, 461BL, 467T, 469T, 469TC, 470T, 475T, 481T, 530T, 531TR, 537T, 538T, 541T, 548T, 554T, 555T, 559T, 563TL, 570B, 571TC, 572C, 572BC, 573T, 573BC, 574B, 575TC, 576T, 579TC, 579C, 580C, 581BC, 582T, 582TC, 582C, 583TC, 583C, 584TC, 586T, 586B, 587B, 588T, 588C, 588BC; **John Glover/Positive Images:** 133T, 198T, 219TR, 366, 367T, 405BL, 450T, 528T, 580B; **Harry Haralambou/Positive Images:** 158BL, 388T; **Jerry Harpur:** 147T, 165T; **Jessie M. Harris:** 256B, 258B, 259B, 567T; **Kim Hawks:** 258C; **Meredith Hebden/Positive Images:** 346BL; **Margaret Hensel/Positive Images:** 298BL, 351BL; **Jean Higgins/Unicorn Stock Photos:** 382B; **Neil Holmes/Garden Picture Library:** 535B; **Saxon Holt:** 391T; **Horticultural Photography:** 547T; **Jerry Howard/Positive Images:** 59B, 73TL, 197B, 262TC, 289T, 323T, 473BL, 518BL; **Russell Illig/Positive Images:** 408BL, 543B, 578B; **Irene Jeruss/Positive Images:** 140TC, 149BL, 184BL, 190BL, 410T, 442T, 589T, 589B; **Bill Johnson:** 138BC, 305B, **Dency Kane:** 565B, **Glenda Kapsalis/Photographers Direct:** 15T, **Rosemary Kautzky:** 122BL, 129CR, 135BL, 135B, 136TR, 138BL, 138BR, 140BC, 140TR, 141BL, 143T, 144BR, 152B, 153BR, 154TL, 154TR, 155TR, 159TR, 160TR, 162TR, 163BC, 163BR, 167BL, 167B, 170T, 171BL, 171CR, 171BR, 173T, 173TR, 174T, 174TR, 175TR, 175B, 176BL, 176B, 177TR, 178T, 179BL, 180B, 181BL, 182T, 182TR, 183T, 183TR, 185B, 186BL, 186B, 189TC, 189B, 190T, 195T, 195TR, 195BL, 197BL, 200BL, 200BCL, 200BCR, 200BR, 205TR, 208BL, 208B, 209T, 209BL,

210B, 212B, 213B, 215B, 216T, 217BL, 217B, 218TR, 219TR, 223TL, 223TR, 225TR, 225B, 226B, 231T, 232BL, 232B, 233BL, 242B, 250B, 257C, 297B, 304LC, 310BR, 316T, 318BL, 331B, 332BL, 364T, 370TR, 370B, 399TR, 400T, 405TR, 410B, 413B, 416T, 416BL, 418T, 420B, 430B, 432BL, 435B, 443BR, 446T, 463T, 547BR, 569B; **Andrew Lawson:** 165TC; **Scott Leonhart/Positive Images:** 404B, 476BL; **Lee Lockwood/Positive Images:** 173BL, 263B, 485BL; **David Liebman:** 320TR; **Ivan Massar/Positive Images:** 545TL, **Mayer/LeScanff/Garden Picture Library:** 495B, 499B; **Elvin McDonald:** 79CR; **Jacob Mosser III/Positive Images:** 262BC; **Thomas N. Munoz/Photographers Direct:** 148BL; **Carole Ottesen:** 237T, 238C, 238B, 239C, 241T, 241B, 242C, 244B, 245T, 249T, 251T, 251B, 252B, 256T; **Jerry Pavia:** 109L, 117TR, 126TC, 127T, 137B, 141BR, 147BL, 149BR, 151BL, 160TL, 161T, 166T, 170B, 171T, 174BL, 175BL, 177T, 189T, 200T, 202BL, 203T, 208T, 211T, 213BL, 214B, 225T, 236T, 239B, 240T, 240C, 242T, 243C, 243B, 249BC, 250C, 251C, 252C, 253B, 254C, 257T, 259C, 261TC, 262B, 264T, 264BL, 265T, 267BL, 268BL, 269BL, 270T, 271T, 272T, 273B, 276BL, 279T, 283T, 285BL, 286T, 288B, 290B, 293T, 293B, 296B, 297T, 301T, 301BL, 304T, 306TR, 310T, 313T, 318BR, 319BL, 320T, 321BL, 324T, 324BL, 326T, 327B, 330B, 332T, 333B, 335T, 337T, 337BL, 343T, 344B, 345BL, 348B, 349T, 350T, 350BL, 356B, 357T, 358T, 360TL, 362BL, 365BL, 370T, 372BL, 374BL, 375B, 379T, 380T, 381T, 385B, 391BL, 394BL, 395T, 395BL, 397BL, 402T, 404BL, 405T, 406BL, 407BL, 409T, 411B, 412BL, 413T, 414T, 414B, 415B, 417T, 425T, 426BL, 427T, 427BL, 428B, 429B, 431BL, 434T, 436BL, 437BL, 438T, 439T, 444T, 452T, 452B, 453T, 453B, 454T, 456BL, 457B, 459T, 462T, 463BL, 464B, 466T, 470B, 474T, 488BL, 491BL, 494T, 496T, 497BL, 498TL, 498BL, 499CL, 500BL, 500BR, 507TL, 509TR, 510T, 512BL, 513B, 521BL, 526T, 534B, 535T, 549T, 552BL, 552B, 555BL, 564B, 571T, 571C, 572B, 574BC, 576BC, 576B, 577TC, 577C, 577BC, 578T, 578BC, 579BC, 580T, 580BC, 581TC, 581C, 582BC, 585TC, 585BC, 587TC; **Rhoda Peacher:** 528B, 544B, 558B; **Pam Peirce/Susan A. Roth & Co.:** 500TR, 513BL; **Ben Phillips/Positive Images:** 254T, 526B; **Photostudio Visions/Darwin Plants:** 119T; **Sergio Piumatti:** 19TR; **Helen Placanica/Photographers Direct:** 148B; **Diane A. Pratt/Positive Images:** 294B, 330T, 469B, 541BL; **Jay W. Pscheidt/Oregon State University:** 439T; **Ram Cordua Dixon:** 83L; **Ann Reilly/Positive Images:** 236B, 253T, 367TC, 396BL, 425BL, 465BL, 507BL, 514BL, 570C, 580TC; **Howard Rice/ Garden Picture Library:** 402BL; **Kenneth Rice:** 129TL; **Susan A. Roth:** 147TR, 156T, 269TR, 374TR, 385T, 390B, 419T, 429T, 439B, 455T, 463BC, 467BL, 467B, 476B, 546B, 579B; **Scotts Training Institute:** 50TC, 50TR, 50BR, 119BR, 123TR, 151B, 157BR, 173B, 395B, 398TR, 402B, 413TR, 436B, 464TC, 507TR, 562BL; **Richard Shiell:** 369T; **J. S. Sira/Garden Picture Library/Alamy:** 389TR; **Pam Spaulding/Positive Images:** 260, 268T, 269T, 303T, 311T, 340T, 341T, 358BL, 397T, 409BC, 428T, 447CR, 449BL, 582B, 584T; **Albert Squillace/Positive Images:** 261BC, 317T, 362T; **Friedrich Strauss/Garden Picture Library:** 521T; **Michael S. Thompson:** 11BL, 15BC, 24, 29, 31TL, 35B, 37BR, 65BL, 65BR, 68T, 73CR, 73B, 78TL, 87, 112T, 114B, 126T, 136T, 136B, 137BL, 140T, 144TC, 149T, 149TR, 149BC, 153BC, 156BL, 157BC, 161B, 163T, 163BL, 175T, 183BL, 185BL, 188T, 188B, 193T, 194B, 197T, 201BL, 205T, 208TR, 211BL, 215BL, 216B, 218BR, 220T, 223BL, 226T, 226BL, 228TC, 232T, 237C, 239T, 243T, 244T, 245C, 246T, 246C, 248T, 248C, 252T, 263BC, 270B, 272BL, 275TC, 276T, 277T, 281T, 284T, 287T, 289BL, 291BL, 292T, 292BL, 308T, 309T, 309BL, 312T, 314T, 315T, 317C, 318BC, 322T, 325B, 327T, 334T, 334B, 335CL, 336T, 339T, 340BL, 342T, 342B, 344T, 349BL, 354BL, 356T, 356TR, 357B, 361T, 363T, 367B, 368C, 368B, 371BL, 372T, 372B, 376T, 376BL, 376BR, 380B, 381TR, 382BL, 383BL, 384B, 386BL, 387T, 390T, 392BL, 392B, 394BR, 396T, 398T, 398B, 401T, 401BL, 403B, 406T, 411T, 412T, 412BC, 417BL, 419B, 420T, 426T, 427TR, 427B, 430T, 430BL, 434B, 437T, 440T, 440B, 441T, 444BC, 444BR, 447T, 447CRC, 450BL, 451B, 454BL, 456T, 458T, 458BL, 469BC, 471T, 473BC, 479BL, 479BR, 486BL, 487T, 487TCL, 491TC, 495BL, 497BR, 502B, 503T, 503TR, 505BR, 508TR, 509TL, 509C, 510T, 513T, 515T, 519BL, 523TL, 523CL, 532T, 534T, 536T, 543T, 556T, 561BL, 567CR, 570T, 571BC, 572T, 573B, 574T, 575T, 575BC, 575B, 578TC, 579T, 581B, 583T, 584BC, 585T, 585B, 586TC, 587C, 587BC, 588TC, 588B, 589TC, 589C; **The Toro Company:** 82TR; **Ann Truelove/Unicorn Stock Photos:** 269B; **Martien Vinesteijn Photography/Positive Images:** 310BL, 319T, 331T, 522T; **Rick Wetherbee:** 300T; **Lee Anne White/Positive Images:** 193B, 421T

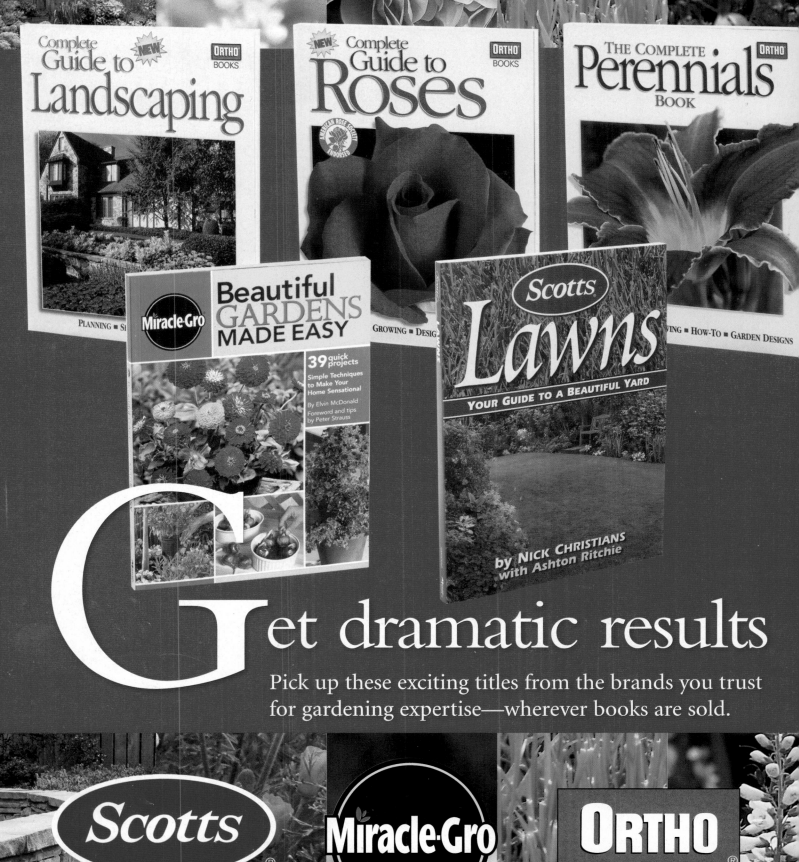
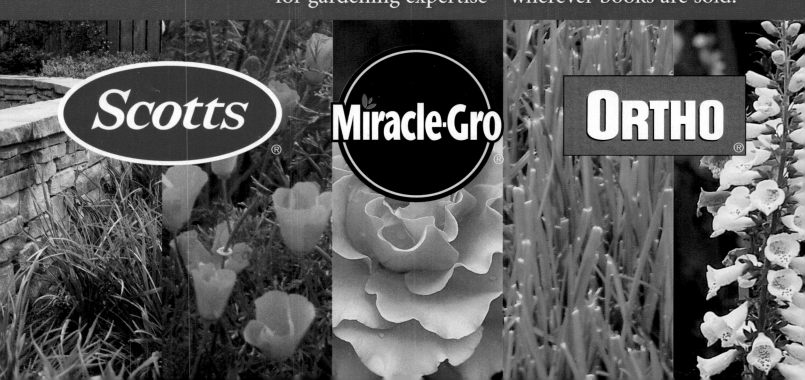